SONG FINDER

Recent Titles in the Music Reference Collection

The American Wind Symphony Commissioning Project: A Descriptive Catalog of
Published Editions, 1957–1991
Jeffrey H. Renshaw

Piano Music by Black Women Composers: A Catalog of Solo and Ensemble Works
Helen Walker-Hill

The Choral Music of Latin America: A Guide to Compositions and Research
Suzanne Spicer Tiemstra

Keyboard Music of Black Composers: A Bibliography
Aaron Horne, compiler

Salsa and Related Genres: A Bibliographical Guide
Rafael Figueroa, compiler

A Conductor's Repertory of Chamber Music: Compositions for Nine to Fifteen Solo
Instruments
William Scott, compiler

Opera Mediagraphy: Video Recordings and Motion Pictures
Sharon G. Almquist, compiler

American Fuging-Tunes, 1770–1820
Karl Kroeger, compiler

Classical Singers of the Opera and Recital Stages: A Bibliography of Biographical
Materials
Robert H. Cowden

Rock Stars/Pop Stars: A Comprehensive Bibliography, 1955–1994
Brady J. Leyser, compiler

The Johnny Cash Record Catalog
John L. Smith, compiler

Thesaurus of Abstract Musical Properties: A Theoretical and Compositional Resource
Jeffrey Johnson

SONG FINDER

A Title Index to 32,000
Popular Songs in Collections,
1854–1992

Compiled by
Gary Lynn Ferguson

Under the auspices of
the State Library of Louisiana

Music Reference Collection, *Number 46*

GREENWOOD PRESS
Westport, Connecticut • London

Library of Congress Cataloging-in-Publication Data

Ferguson, Gary Lynn.
    Song finder : a title index to 32,000 popular songs in
collections, 1854–1992 / compiled by Gary Lynn Ferguson.
       p.   cm.—(Music reference collection, ISSN 0736–7740 ; no.
46)
    Compiled from collections held by the State Library of Louisiana.
    Includes bibliographical references (p.   ).
    ISBN 0–313–29470–4
    1. Songs—19th century—Indexes. 2. Songs—20th century—Indexes.
3. State Library of Louisiana—Catalogs. I. Series.
ML128.S3F47   1995
016.78242—dc20   95–9936

British Library Cataloguing in Publication Data is available.

Library of Congress Catalog Card Number: 95–9936
ISBN: 0–313–29470–4
ISSN: 0736–7740

First published in 1995

Greenwood Press, 88 Post Road West, Westport, CT 06881
An imprint of Greenwood Publishing Group, Inc.

Printed in the United States of America

The paper used in this book complies with the
Permanent Paper Standard issued by the National
Information Standards Organization (Z39.48–1984).

10 9 8 7 6 5 4 3 2 1

To my parents,
Donald Ray and Elizabeth Sewell Ferguson,
with love and gratitude

CONTENTS

PREFACE

Song Finder is an index to 621 song books in the collection of the State Library of Louisiana. The song books date from as early as 1854 (a reprint) to 1992, and their contents cover the musical spectrum from lieder to Cajun folk songs. Over 75% of these books have never been indexed, and 85% are not included in any index currently in print.

Access is by song title, only. This allows for a very compact index to a large number of songs. As approximately one-third of the 32,000 songs included do not appear in any standard index, Song Finder adds significantly to the body of songs that can be retrieved through indexes.

Arrangement and Format of Entries

Song Finder is divided into two parts. The first part is a list of the song books that have been indexed, and it is arranged in alphabetical order by the letter symbols that represent each title. Entries provide sufficient bibliographical information to identify the books, and OCLC numbers are given to facilitate interlibrary loan.

The second part of the book is the alphabetical list of song titles. Below each title are the letter symbols of the collections in which the song appears. Each symbol is followed by letters (w or m or w,m) to indicate whether the book provides words only, music only, or both words and music for the song. After that, if applicable, is a foreign language designation enclosed in parentheses. For example, (Italian only) means that lyrics are given only in Italian, while (Italian) indicates that lyrics are given in both Italian and English.

Sample Entry

> Calm As the Night
> FSY-W,M (German) SL-W,M

This song is found in the two books represented by the symbols FSY and SL. Each book contains both the words and music of the song. The version in FSY has lyrics in German as well as English, while the version in SL is in English only. Look up the symbols in the list of song books to find the author, title, place of publication, publisher, date, and OCLC number of each book.

Filing and Cross References

Following standard library practice, initial articles (a, an, the) are ignored for filing purposes and have been deleted unless needed to distinguish between otherwise identical titles ("Shenandoah" and "Shenandoah, The"). When an article must be used, it appears as the last word in the title. Initial articles in a foreign language, however, do serve as the primary filing element. This is done for the benefit of users who do not know the foreign language and who will expect to find "La Paloma" filed under "La." A cross reference from the first substantive word in the title to the article will assist the user who does know the language ("Paloma" see "La Paloma").

Song titles are written as they appear in the song books. This causes problems when the same song appears under different titles or variant spellings. To help the user find all the available versions of a song, cross references have been added to link alternate titles (**America see also My Country 'Tis of Thee**) and variant or dialectal spellings (**Other Side of Jordan see also Odder Side of Jordan**).

Users looking for advertising jingles or theme songs from movies and television programs will find cross references from the name of the company, the movie, or the television show to the correct song title. (**Buick Automobile Jingle see Wouldn't You Really Rather Have a Buick; Godfather Love Theme see Speak Softly Love**). Note, however, that no cross reference is added for a jingle when the company name is the first word in the title of the song. ("Ford, It's the Going Thing").

Cross references are also used to compensate for nonstandard spellings which make some songs hard to find in the index. (**Mares Eat Oats see Mairzy Doats; Nothing for Christmas see Nuttin' for Christmas; Ricky Don't Lose That Number see Rikki Don't Lose That Number**).

Users should note that, as in the foregoing examples, all cross references appear in boldface to distinguish them from other entries.

Identical Titles

Another kind of problem is caused by different songs that have the same title. In these cases, the composer's name, additional words from the song, the first line, or other identifying information is added in parentheses, as in these examples:

Consolation (Mendelssohn)
Consolation (Watts)

Country Boy (at Heart)
Country Boy (Who Rolled the Rock Away)
Country Boy (You Got Your Feet in L.A.)

Dolores
Dolores (Love Theme from Pirates)

Origin, Scope, and Comparison with Other Indexes

Song Finder began as a working tool for Reference staff at the State Library of Louisiana. The intent was to index all the song books in the collection that were not covered by existing indexes. When work began on Song Finder in 1978, there were few readily available song indexes. Minnie Sears's pioneering Song Index (1926, 1934 supplement) had to wait nearly forty years for a successor, Robert Leigh's self-published Index to Song Books (1964). Both were general song indexes. The first of the specialized indexes, Cushing's Children's Song Index (1936), had been joined three decades later by Diehl's Hymns and Tunes-- An Index and de Charms's and Breed's Songs in Collections: An Index, which focused on art songs and operatic arias. There was nothing more until Patricia Havlice issued the first volume of the Popular Song Index in 1975.

Like the indexes compiled by Sears and Leigh, Song Finder was intended to be broad in scope and to encompass a wide variety of musical genres and styles. Users will find indexed here a large number of collections of theater songs, folk songs, children's songs, and religious music, as well as folios of rock, country, and pop music "standards." Also well represented are African-American music, movie and television theme songs, seasonal music, patriotic songs, military music, and songs of foreign lands. Not only does Song Finder provide a stand-alone index to this broad range of songs, but it also serves to supplement and update the coverage of such earlier, more narrowly focused indexes as: Index to Children's Songs (1979); Folk Song Index (1981); Find That Tune (1984, 1988 supplement), which covers rock and related pop music; and Wedding Music (1992). Song Finder also complements the coverage of indexes of broader scope such as the Popular Song Index (last supplement 1989) and Where's That Tune (1990), which indexes the abbreviated versions of songs found in musicians' fake books. By including older, out-of-print works, Song Finder also supplements the coverage of MUSI*KEY, a bimonthly guide for music retailers to the contents of currently available song folios and sheet music.

Song indexes differ not only in scope of coverage but also in the number of access points that are provided. Beginning with Sears's Song Index in 1926, some indexes have provided access by first line and composer/lyricist in addition to song title.

Popular Song Index expanded the first line index to include the first line of the chorus as well. Other access points that have been used occasionally are performer (Find That Tune), instrument (Wedding Music), subject (Index to Children's Songs) and country of origin (Songs in Collections: An Index).

Works that take a minimalist approach and limit access to title only are Robert Leigh's Index to Song Books, Florence Brunnings's Folk Song Index, and now, Song Finder. The limitations of this approach are offset by the opportunity it affords to index more songs in fewer pages, and by the addition of useful details on each printing of a song. By distinguishing instrumental and lyrics only versions from "complete" songs, and by noting lyrics in a foreign language and the availability of an English translation, Song Finder should help users to find a version of a song that is suitable to their needs.

ACKNOWLEDGMENTS

Song Finder was begun in 1978 as a project of the Reference and Bibliography Section of the State Library of Louisiana. In its gradual evolution from index card file to computer file to printed book, several present and former staff members have played key roles. The compiler offers heartfelt thanks to the following:

Margaret Schroth, Head of Reference, for the idea;

Claire McCoy, former reference librarian, for designing and implementing the index and serving as first editor;

Anna (Bobby) Ferguson for adding features that significantly improved Song Finder, and for indexing a large number of books while serving as second editor;

Eordonna D'Andrea for supervising the conversion of the index to computerized form, overseeing the production of camera-ready copy, coping with countless computer glitches, and providing indispensable assistance at every stage of the project;

Jean Holmes, Shannon Lowrey, and Mona Morris for painstakingly keyboarding the bulk of the index and assisting with proofreading;

Basanti Baksi, Nora Jenkins, and Roblyn Schwehm, my colleagues in the reference section, for enabling me to devote time to the index;

and Blanche Cretini, Coordinator of User Services, for encouragement to publish the index and for frequent, therapeutic applications of the whip.

PUBLISHED SONG INDEXES: A BIBLIOGRAPHY

Below is a list of general and specialized song indexes that have been published in the United States since the first one, Sears's Song Index, appeared in 1926. The brief annotations make it possible to compare the indexes on the basis of size (number of song books and individual songs indexed), access points (title, first line, composer, etc.), and types of songs covered.

Brunnings, Florence E. Folk Song Index: A Comprehensive Guide to the Florence E. Brunnings Collection. New York: Garland, 1981.
> An index to 49,400 songs found in 832 collections (plus 283 issues of magazines and 695 records). Access is by title only.

Cushing, Helen Grant. Children's Song Index: An Index to More Than 22,000 Songs in 189 Collections Comprising 222 Volumes. New York: H.W. Wilson, 1936. Reprint, St. Clair Shores, MI: Scholarly Press, 1976.
> An index with entries for title, first line, composer, author, and subject in one alphabetical sequence.

De Charms, Desiree, and Paul F. Breed. Songs in Collections: An Index. Detroit, MI: Information Service Incorporated, 1966.
> An index to 9,493 songs from 411 collections published between 1940 and 1957. Emphasis on art songs and operatic arias with some coverage of folk songs, Christmas carols, sacred songs, and community songs. Songs can be found by title, first line, composer, author, and for folk songs, country of origin.

Denning, Leslie. Sheet Music Magazine... The First Fifteen Years: A Standard Piano Edition Index. Belton, MO: Pot O' Gold Publications, 1993.
> Indexes 1,400 songs by title, composer, lyricist, publication date, instrument, and musical style. Pop and folk songs predominate, though some classical works are included.

Diehl, Katharine Smith. Hymns and Tunes-- An Index. New York: Scarecrow Press, 1966.
> Indexes 12,000 hymns from 78 hymnals by first line, author, composer, tune name, and melody. The hymnals chosen were used by Catholic, Jewish, and Protestant congregations and published between 1876 and 1966.

Gargan, William and Sue Sharma. Find That Tune: An Index to Rock, Folk-Rock, Disco, & Soul in Collections. New York: Neal-Schuman Publishers, 1984.
------. 2d ed. New York: Neal-Schuman Publishers, 1988.
> The second edition indexes a different set of song books than the first. The two volumes together index 8,000 songs from 405 collections by title,

first line, composer/lyricist, and
performer.

Goodfellow, William D. Wedding Music: An
   Index to Collections. Metuchen, NJ:
   Scarecrow Press, 1992.
      Indexes 3,400 vocal and instrumental
   songs in 191 collections by title, first
   line, composer, and instrument.

Goodfellow, William D. Where's That Tune:
   An Index to Songs in Fakebooks.
   Metuchen, NJ: Scarecrow Press, 1990.
      Indexes 13,500 songs from 64
   fakebooks by title and composer.
   Fakebooks provide club musicians with
   shortened versions of songs, usually
   consisting of the melody line, chord
   symbols, and lyrics. Fakebooks often
   print two songs to the page.

Havlice, Patricia Pate. Popular Song Index.
   Metuchen, NJ: Scarecrow Press, 1975.
------. First Supplement. Metuchen, NJ:
   Scarecrow Press, 1978.
------. Second Supplement. Metuchen, NJ:
   Scarecrow Press, 1984.
------. Third Supplement. Metuchen, NJ:
   Scarecrow Press, 1989.
      The four volumes together index
   35,000 songs from 710 collections by
   title, first line of song and chorus,
   composer, and lyricist. The first
   volume indexes song books published
   between 1940 and 1972, and the
   supplements primarily cover
   subsequent years. The songs indexed
   are folk songs, pop tunes, spirituals,
   hymns, blues, children's songs, and
   sea chanteys.

Leigh, Robert. Index to Song Books: A Title
   Index to Over 11,000 Copies of Almost
   6,800 Songs in 111 Song Books Published
   between 1933 and 1962. Stockton, CA:
   Robert Leigh, 1964. Reprint, New York:
   Da Capo Press, 1973.
      A self-published, title only index to a
   variety of songs of all kinds.

Peterson, Carolyn Sue and Ann D. Fenton.
   Index to Children's Songs: A Title, First

Line, and Subject Index. New York: H.W.
   Wilson, 1979.
      An index to 5,000 songs from 298
   collections by title, first line, and
   subject.

Rogal, Samuel J. Guide to the Hymns and
   Tunes of American Methodism. Westport,
   CT: Greenwood Press, 1986.
      Indexes 4,000 hymns found in 6
   hymnals published between 1878 and
   1964. Hymns can be located by
   author, composer, first line, and tune
   name.

Rucker, Randy and Linda Rucker. MUSI*KEY:
   "The Reference Guide of Note." Bimonthly.
   2 vols. Tucson, AZ: MUSI*KEY, 1985-.
      A massive index to song folios and
   sheet music currently in print. The
   main volume of each bimonthly issue
   indexes some 34,000 songs from
   6,400 collections by title only. A
   supplementary volume gives the table
   of contents of each song book and lists
   folios designed for specific instruments
   or devoted to the works of individual
   composers or performers. Intended as
   a guide for the music retailer to pop,
   folk, and gospel collections and their
   contents.

Sears, Minnie Earl. Song Index: An Index to
   More Than 12000 Songs in 177 Song
   Collections Comprising 262 Volumes. New
   York: H.W. Wilson, 1926.
------. Song Index Supplement: An Index to
   More Than 7000 Songs in 104 Song
   Collections Comprising 124 Volumes. New
   York: H. W. Wilson, 1934. Reprint (2
   vols. in 1), N.p.: Shoe String Press, 1966.
      The two volumes together index
   19,000 songs from 281 collections by
   title, first line, composer, and author.
   A general song index, the first of its
   kind to be published for library use.

Studwell, William E. Christmas Carols: A
   Reference Guide. New York: Garland,
   1985.
      Indexes 789 carols (1,300 including
   variant titles) found in 147 collections.
   The carols are indexed by title,
   composer/lyricist, and place of origin.

SONG FINDER

SONG BOOKS INDEXED

A Rodgers, Richard. Allegro: A Musical Play. New York: A.A. Williamson Music, c1948. OCLC # 19234639.

AA Niles, John Jacob. The Anglo-American Ballad Study Book, Containing Eight Ballads in Current Tradition in the U.S.A. New York: Schirmer, c1945. OCLC # 5198296.

AAF Krehbiel, Henry Edward. Afro-American Folksongs: A Study in Racial and National Music. 4th ed. New York: Schirmer, 1914. OCLC # 536250.

AAP All-American Patriotic Song Book. Ojai, CA: Creative Concepts Publishing Corp., c1986. OCLC # 17536295.

AF Wallrich, William. Air Force Airs: Songs and Ballads of the United States Air Force. New York: Duell, Sloan, and Pearce, c1957. OCLC # 4738994.

AFB Silverman, Jerry. The Art of the Folk-Blues Guitar: An Instruction Manual. New York: Oak Publications, 1964. OCLC # 7862964.

AFP Greenway, John. American Folksongs of Protest. New York: A.S. Barnes, 1960 (c1953). OCLC # 410899.

AFS Seegar, Ruth Crawford. Animal Folk Songs for Children: Traditional American Songs. Garden City, NY: Doubleday, c1948. OCLC # 246142.

AG America's Gospel Top Forty: Southern Gospel's Best. Winona, MN: Hal Leonard Pub. Corp., 1986? OCLC # 15023573.

AH Lloyd, Ruth. The American Heritage Songbook: 120 Great Songs from Our Nation's Past. New York: American Heritage, c1969. OCLC # 2321462.

AHO Christ-Janer, Albert, et al.. American Hymns Old and New. New York: Columbia University, c1980. OCLC # 7203431.

AL Foner, Philip S. American Labor Songs of the Nineteenth Century. Urbana, IL: University of Illinois Press, c1975. OCLC # 1085697.

Am Guthrie, Woody. American Folksong: Woody Guthrie. New York: Oak Publications, c1961. OCLC # 1167206.

AME A.M.E. Hymnal: With Responsive Scripture Readings Adopted in Conformity with the Doctrines and Usages of the African Methodist Episcopal Church. N.p.: A.M.E. Sunday School Union, 1954. OCLC # 1281979.

AmH Wier, Albert Ernest. American Home Music Album. New York: Appleton, c1915. OCLC # 2570797.

AmS Sandburg, Carl. American Songbag. New York: Harcourt Brace, and Co., c1927. OCLC # 5354945.

AN White, Newman Ivey. American Negro Folk-Songs. Cambridge, MA: Harvard University Press, c1928. OCLC # 411447.

ANS Neeser, Robert Wilden. American Naval Songs and Ballads. New Haven, CT: Yale University Press, c1938. OCLC # 2947300.

AO Taylor, Russ. All-Organ Biggest Pop Hits and Great Standards: Words, Chords, Music. New York: Big 3 Music Corp., 1973. OCLC # 28837945.

Ap Strouse, Charles. Applause: A Musical Comedy. New York: E.H. Morris, c1970. OCLC # 780901.

AS Breach, William. Art-Song Argosy: A Collection

for Use in Class Voice Instruction. New York: G.
Schirmer, c1937. OCLC # 9427417, 6184206.

ASB
1-6
Beattie, John Walter. American Singer. Books
1-6. New York: American Book Co., c1944-1947.
OCLC # 989402.

AST
Coleman, Satis Narrona. Another Singing Time:
Songs for Nursery and School. New York: Reynal
& Hitchcock, c1937. OCLC # 1349932.

AT
The American Treasury of Popular Movie Songs:
100 Nostalgic Hits. New York: C. Hansen, c1976.
OCLC # 3923645.

ATC1
All Time Country Hits: Words, Music, Guitar
Chords. Vol. 1. Los Angeles, CA: West Coast
Publications, 1968. OCLC # 12434054.

ATC2
All Time Country Hits: Words, Music, Guitar
Chords. Vol. 2. Los Angeles, CA: West Coast
Publications, 1968. OCLC # 12434054.

ATM
Hausman, Ruth L. Australia: Traditional Music
in Its History. North Quincy, MA: Christopher
Publishing House, c1975. OCLC # 3255476.

ATS
Luther, Frank. Americans and Their Songs. New
York: Harper, c1942. OCLC # 931882.

AWB
Eggleston, George Cary. American War Ballads and
Lyrics: A Collection of the Songs and Ballads of
the Colonial Wars, the Revolution, the War of
1812-15, the War with Mexico, and the Civil War.
Vol. 1. New York: Granger Book Co., 1978
(1889). OCLC # 4372722.

AWS
The Award Winning Songs of the Country Music
Association. 2d ed. Winona, MN: Hal Leonard
Pub. Corp., c1988. OCLC # 18659705.

B
Handy, William C. Blues: An Anthology. Revised by
Jerry Silverman. New York: Macmillan, c1972.
OCLC # 356307.

Ba
Strickland, Lily. Bayou Songs. New York: J.
Fischer, c1921. OCLC # 13152934.

BaB
Monroe, Mina. Bayou Ballads: 12 Folk Songs
from Louisiana. New York: G. Schirmer, c1921.
OCLC # 16936848.

BB
Pollard, Michael. Ballads and Broadsides. New
York: Pergamon Press, c1969. OCLC # 2551.

BBB
The Best Big Band Songs Ever: Piano, Vocal,
Guitar. Winona, MN: Hal Leonard Publishing
Corp., 1987? OCLC # 16926380.

BBe
The Beatles Best. Winona, MN: Hal Leonard
Pub. Corp., c1987. OCLC # 18767428.

BBF
Commins, Dorothy Berliner. The Big Book of
Favorite Songs for Children. New York: Grosset
& Dunlap, c1951. OCLC # 1581725.

BC1
The Bicentennial Collection of American Music.
Vol. 1, 1698-1800. Carol Stream, IL: Hope Pub.
Co., c1974. OCLC # 1170761.

BCC
Cross, Christopher. The Best of Christopher
Cross. New York: Warner Bros. Publications,
c1984. OCLC # 12019579.

BCh
Best of Christmas: Complete Words and Music:
80 Great Songs for the Holiday Season. Miami
Beach, FL: Hansen House, c1980? OCLC #
8014298.

BCS
The Best Christmas Songs Ever: Piano/Vocal/
Guitar. Winona, MN: H. Leonard, 1986. OCLC
16697360.

BCT
Miles, John Jacob. Ballads, Carols, and Tragic
Legends from the Southern Appalachian
Mountains. New York: Schirmer, c1937. OCLC
772102.

BDF
Bacharach, Burt F. The Bacharach and David Fun
Way Choral Book. New York: Charles Hansen,
1971. OCLC # 1547455.

BDP
Parton, Dolly. The Best of Dolly Parton
Songbook. Hialeah, FL: Columbia Pictures
Publications, 1977. OCLC # 3742263.

BDW
McIlhenny, Edward Avery. Befo' de War
Spirituals: Words and Melodies. Boston, MA:
Christopher Publishing House, c1933. OCLC #
2709146.

Be1
Lennon, John. Beatlemania. Vol.1, 1963-1966.
New York: Warner Bros. Publications, 196?.
OCLC # 6114892.

Be2
Lennon, John. Beatlemania. Vol. 2, 1967-1970.
New York: Warner Bros. Publications, 197?
OCLC # 6114892.

BeB
Gearhart, Livingston. Belles and Beaus: 3- or 4-
Part Songs for Teen-age Choral Groups.
Delaware Water Gap, PA: Shawnee Press,
c1957. OCLC # 10084956.

BeL
Best Loved Standards. Milwaukee, WI: Hal
Leonard, 1989. OCLC # 22942178.

BF
Silverman, Jerry. Beginning the Folk Guitar: An
Instruction Manual. New York: Oak
Publications, 1964. OCLC # 2498544.

BH
Frey, Hugo. Bill Hardey's Songs of the Gay
Nineties and Other Old Favorites. New York:
Robbins Music Corporation, c1942. OCLC #
2462622.

BHB
Big Hits in Big Notes for Easy Guitar. Marietta,
GA: Hansen Publications, 1967. OCLC #
12434086.

BHO
The Biggest Hits of 1987-88: Voice, Piano,
Guitar. Secaucus, NJ: Warner Bros.
Publications, c1988. OCLC # 18109551.

BJ
The Best of Jethro Tull, Volumes I and II.
Hollywood, CA: Almo Publications, c1978.
OCLC # 4961797.

BI
Handy, William Christopher. Blues: An

Anthology. New York: A. & C. Boni, c1926. OCLC # 2503302.

BIS   Cyporyn, Dennis. The Bluegrass Songbook. New York: Macmillan, c1972. OCLC # 988572.

BM   Nye, Robert E. Basic Music for Classroom Teachers: An Activities Approach to Music Fundamentals. New York: Prentice-Hall, c1954. OCLC # 5156313.

BMC   Slind, Lloyd H. Bringing Music to Children: Music Methods for the Elementary School Teacher. New York: Harper and Row, c1964. OCLC # 611479.

BMM   Thomas, Jeannette Bell. Ballad Makin' in the Mountains of Kentucky. New York: H. Holt, c1939. OCLC # 819209.

BNG   Bradley, Richard. Bradley's New Giant Piano Book: Pops, Movie Themes, T.V. Themes, Inspirational Songs, T.V. Commercials. Updated ed. (5 books in 1). New York: Bradley Publications, c1987. OCLC # 18157187.

Bo   Boy Scouts of America. Boy Scout Songbook: Ballads of the Trail, Many Chorded for Guitar. North Brunswick, NJ: Boy Scouts of America, c1970. OCLC # 10632285.

BOA   Jarreau, Al. The Best of Al Jarreau: Piano, Vocal, Guitar. New York: MCA Music Publishing, 1990. OCLC # 22604081.

Boo   Taylor, Mary Catherine. The Book of Rounds. New York: E.P. Dutton, 1977. OCLC # 2951653.

BP   Romberg, Sigmund. The Blue Paradise: A Viennese Operetta. New York: G. Schirmer, c1915. OCLC # 12029374.

BPM   Benedict, Helen Dymond. Belair Plantation Melodies. New Orleans, LA: Benedict, c1924. OCLC # 5506398.

BR   The Best of Rock Time: From the Beatles to the Osmonds. New York: Charles Hansen Educational Music and Books, 1973. OCLC # 12374901.

BRB   Green, William H. Baton Rouge Blues. Baton Rouge, LA: Scalawag Press, c1969. OCLC # 12497127.

BS   Coward, Noel. Bitter Sweet: An Operetta in Three Acts. New York: Harms, c1929. OCLC # 3315409.

BSB   Spaeth, Sigmund Gottfried. Barber Shop Ballads and How to Sing Them. New York: Prentice-Hall, 1940. OCLC # 1574928.

BSC   Belden, Henry Marvin. Ballads and Songs Collected by the Missouri Folklore Society. 2d ed. Columbia, MO: University of Missouri, c1955. OCLC # 2703482.

BSG   Bock, Fred. The Best of Sacred Music: Strum a Song Guitar Edition. New York: C. Hansen, 1970?

OCLC # 9265780.

BSo   Wernick, Peter. Bluegrass Songbook. New York: Oak Publications, c1976. OCLC # 2870835.

BSP   Bock, Fred. The Best of Sacred Music: Piano/Vocal Edition. New York: C. Hansen, c1972. OCLC # 2025420.

BT   Wells, Evelyn Kendrick. The Ballad Tree: A Study of British and American Ballads, Their Folklore, Verse, and Music, Together with Sixty Traditional Ballads and Their Tunes. New York: Ronald Press Company, c1950. OCLC # 398418.

BV   Molzer, Felix. In a Bohemian Village. Boston, MA: Ginn, 1960. OCLC # 11898074.

C   Kander, John. Cabaret: The New Musical. New York: New York Times Music Corp., c1968. OCLC # 1232881.

CA   Thiel, Mildred. Chorus and Assembly: Choruses Arranged for Mixed Voices. Chicago, IL: Hall and McCreary, 1946. OCLC # 3477606.

CaF   Petitjean, Irene M. "Cajun" Folk Songs of Southwest Louisiana. New York: Columbia University Thesis, 1930. OCLC # 10884978.

CC   Van Loon, Hendrik Willem. Christmas Carols, Illustrated and Done into Simple Music. New York: Simon & Schuster, 1937. OCLC # 1304149.

CCH   Dann, Hollis. Christmas Carols and Hymns for School and Choir. New York: American Book Co., c1910. OCLC # 863880.

CCM   Carols of Christmas from Many Lands. Minneapolis, MN: Augsburg Pub. Co., c1958. OCLC # 1353161.

CCS   Cowboy Copas Song and Picture Folio. New York: Hill and Range Songs, 1967. OCLC # 12442394.

CDM   Canciones de Mi Isla = Songs of My Island. New York: A.R.T.S., c1975. OCLC # 2405153.

CE   Gilmore, Jeanne. Chantez Encore: South Louisiana French Folk Songs. Lafayette, LA: Acadiana Music, 1977. OCLC # 4686531.

CEM   Climb Ev'ry Mountain: The Inspirational Song-book: A Collection of Favorite Inspirational and Religious Songs Arranged for Piano, Organ and Guitar. New York: Chappell/Intersong, 197? OCLC # 15648494.

CF   Kern, Jerome. The Cat and the Fiddle: A Musical Love Story. New York: T.B. Harms Co., c1932. OCLC # 522518.

CFB   1987-1988 Chartbuster Fake Book. Winona, MN: H. Leonard Pub. Corp., 1989? OCLC # 19828692.

CFS   Gibbon, John Murray. Canadian Folk Songs (Old and New). New York: E.P. Dutton, c1927. OCLC # 7929828.

Ch   Chansons. Paris: Editions Bias, c1959. OCLC # 7530513.

CI   Christmas Is a Time: For All Organs. New York: Hansen, c1962. OCLC # 12029422.

CJ   Denver, John. Classic John Denver. Port Chester, NY: Cherry Lane Music Co., c1988. OCLC # 18944631.

CL   Hamlisch, Marvin. A Chorus Line: Vocal Selections. New York: E.H. Morris, c1975. OCLC # 3596703.

CLaL   Gilmore, Jeanne Leblanc. Chantez, La Louisiane! Louisiana French Folk Songs. Lafayette, LA: Acadiana Music, 1970. OCLC # 4743788.

CM   Clark, Mary Margaret. Classical Melodies for Children to Sing: A Collection of Songs Taken from the Music of Great Composers. New York: Paulist Press, c1976. OCLC # 2706195.

CMF   Wagoner, Porter. Porter Wagoner: Country Music Favorites. New York: Hill and Range Songs, 1957. OCLC # 6623279.

CMG   Okun, Milton. The New York Times Country Music's Greatest Songs. New York: Times Books, 1978. OCLC # 4584537.

CMV   Kander, John. Chicago: A Musical Vaudeville: Vocal Selections. Chappell, c1975. OCLC # 6906185.

Co   Sondheim, Stephen. Company: A Musical Comedy. New York: C. Hansen, c1971. OCLC # 4362031.

CoF   Winston, Carol. The Cobbler of Fairyland: A Juvenile Operetta in Three Acts. Minneapolis, MN: T.S. Denison, c1936. OCLC # 6608098.

CoH   Country Hits. Milwaukee, WI: Hal Leonard, 1989. OCLC # 22942213.

CoS   Collegiate Song Book: Eastern Section. Chicago, IL: Cole Pub. Co., c1929. OCLC # 8394231.

CS   Cavalcade of Song Hits. New York: Leo Feist, c1947. OCLC # 3392878.

CSB   Gearhart, Livingston. A Christmas Singing Bee: Two-Part Songs for Treble Voices. Delaware Water Gap, PA: Shawnee Press, c1962. OCLC # 2478382.

CSD   Wehrmann, Henry. Creole Songs of the Deep South. New Orleans, LA: Philip Werlein, c1946. OCLC # 5963684.

CSF   Zell, Armada. Christmas Song Favorites (Words Only). Louisville, KY: American Printing House for the Blind, 1976. OCLC # 5791124.

CSG   Johnston, Peter F. Children's Singing Games. London: Bayley & Ferguson, c1968. OCLC # 11130349.

CSo   Newton, Ernest Richard. Community Song Book... with Words, Tonic Sol-Fa and Piano Accompaniments. Complete ed. London: Keith Prowse Music Pub., 1967? OCLC # 1702569.

CSp   The Country Spotlight: Guitar, Vocal, Piano for Hits Recorded by Johnny Cash, Buck Owens, Eddy Arnold and Roger Miller. Los Angeles, CA: West Coast Publications, 1969. OCLC # 12496553.

CSS   Boy Scouts of America. Cub Scout Songbook. North Brunswick, NJ: The Scouts, c1969. OCLC # 2845619.

CUP   Conniston, Ruth Muzzy. Chantons Un Peu: A Collection of French Songs. Garden City, NY: Doubleday, Doran, & Co, c1929. OCLC # 1155641.

D   Ritchie, Jean. The Dulcimer Book. New York: Oak Publications, 1963. OCLC # 823239.

DB   Grant, Micki. Don't Bother Me, I Can't Cope: Vocal Selections. New York: Fiddleback Music Pub. Corp., c1973. OCLC # 20472196.

DBC   The Definitive Broadway Collection: The Most Comprehensive Collection of Broadway Music Ever Compiled into One Volume. Winona, MN: Hal Leonard, c1988. OCLC # 18595484.

DBL   Titon, Jeff Todd. Downhome Blues Lyrics: An Anthology from the Post-World War II Era. Boston, MA: Twayne Publishers, c1981. OCLC # 7283493.

DC   Coates, Dan. The Dan Coates Family Songbook: 102 Songs to Play and Sing. Secaucus, NJ: Warner Bros. Publications, c1988. OCLC # 19926146.

DD   Thomas, Jeannette Bell. Devil's Ditties, Being Stories of the Kentucky Mountain People with the Songs They Sing. Chicago, IL: W.W. Hatfield, c1931. OCLC # 276520.

DDH   Disco Dance Hits: 20 Super Discotheque Smashes. New York: Big 3 Music Corp., 1976. OCLC # 3450368.

DE   Nathan, Hans. Dan Emmett and the Rise of Early Negro Minstrelsy. Norman, OK: University of Oklahoma Press, c1962. OCLC # 165397.

DJ   The Definitive Jazz Collection: Piano-Vocal-Guitar. Winona, MN: Hal Leonard, c1988. OCLC # 20288307.

DP   Disco Pop: 45 Smash Hits. New York: Chappell Music, 1976? OCLC # 3718867.

DPE   Deluxe Peaceful Easy Feeling Songbook: Voice/Piano/Guitar. Rev. ed. Secaucus, NJ: Warner Bros. Publications, c1988. OCLC #

20558612.

DR Styne, Jule. Do-Re-Mi. New York: Chappell, c1961. OCLC # 1984484.

DRR The Definitive Rock 'n Roll Collection (1955-1966). Milwaukee, WI: H. Leonard Pub. Corp., 1989. OCLC # 21182246.

DS Romberg, Sigmund. The Desert Song: A Musical Play in Two Acts. New York: Samuel French, c1932. OCLC # 597008.

E Herbert, Victor. Eileen: A Romantic Comic Opera in Three Acts. New York: M. Witmark, c1917. OCLC # 13625953.

EA Vinson, Lee. The Early American Songbook: Based on the Alan Landsburg Television Series, The American Idea. Englewood Cliffs, NJ: Prentice-Hall, 1974. OCLC # 1141330.

EAG2 Lane, John. Easy Arrangements for the Guitar with Big Notes, Large Diagrams and Strokes. No. 2. New York: Robbins Music Corp., 195?. OCLC # 2104760.

EC Encyclopedia of Country Music: Voice/Piano/Guitar. Rev. ed. Secaucus, NJ: Warner Bros. Publications, 1987? OCLC # 18269194.

EFS Everybody's Favorite Songs of the Gay Nineties. New York: Amsco Music Publishing Co., 1943. OCLC # 12442321.

EL English Love Songs. London: Stainer and Bell, c1980. OCLC # 7164761.

ELO Electric Light Orchestra Anthology. Los Angeles, CA: United Artists Music, 1978? OCLC # 8663443.

EP Elvis Presley: His Best, Volume One. Ojai, CA: Creative Concepts Publishing Corp., 1987? OCLC# 21236346.

ER Parker, Alice Stuart. An Easter Rejoicing. Boston, MA: Schirmer, c1972. OCLC # 939023.

ERM Encyclopedia of Rock Music: 50's & 60's. Secaucus, NJ: Warner Bros. Publications, c1988. OCLC # 19866995.

ESB Dare, George Stanley. Everybody's Song Book. New York: A.B. Barnes, c1938. OCLC # 1593664.

ESU Jackson, George S. Early Songs of Uncle Sam. Boston, MA: B. Humphries, c1933. OCLC # 971740.

ETB Franklin-Pike, Eleanor. The Easiest Tune Book of Negro Spirituals and American Plantation Songs. London: E. Ashdown, c1966. OCLC # 12433421.

EY 80 Years of Popular Music: Stage & Screen: Vocal/Piano/Guitar. Secaucus, NJ: Warner Bros. Publications, c1988. OCLC # 19416528.

F1 Britten, Benjamin. Folksong Arrangements. Vol. 1, British Isles: Medium Voice. London: Boosey & Hawkes Ltd., c1943. OCLC # 9676507.

F2 Britten, Benjamin. Folksong Arrangements. Vol. 2, France: Medium Voice. London: Boosey & Hawkes Ltd., 1943. OCLC # 9676507.

F3 Britten, Benjamin. Folksong Arrangements. Vol. 3, British Isles: Medium Voice. London: Boosey & Hawkes Ltd, c1943. OCLC # 9676507.

Fa Schmidt, Harvey. The Fantasticks. New York: Chappell, c1963. OCLC # 1291948.

FAW Folk and Western Songs. Miami Beach, FL: Hansen House, c1983. OCLC # 14362404.

FBI Regier, Don. Folksongs of the British Isles: For 2 Part General Music or Teen Age Chorus. Park Ridge, IL: Kjos Music Co., c1965. OCLC # 12433222.

FC Tinsley, Jim Bob. For a Cowboy Has to Sing. Orlando, FL: University of Central Florida Press, c1991. OCLC # 22494690.

FD Ch'en, Chin-Hsin Yao. The Flower Drum and Other Chinese Songs. New York: John Day Co., c1943. OCLC # 978307.

FF Salisbury, Helen Wright. Finger Fun: Songs and Rhythms for the Very Young. Los Angeles, CA: Cowman, c1955. OCLC # 1410155.

FG1 Silverman, Jerry. The Folksinger's Guitar Guide. Vol. 1, An Instruction Manual. New York: Oak Publications, 1962. OCLC # 17603334.

FG2 Silverman, Jerry. The Folksinger's Guitar Guide. Vol. 2, An Advanced Instruction Manual. New York: Oak Publications, c1964. OCLC # 6779370.

FGM Silverman, Jerry. Folk Guitar Method. New York: Grosset & Dunlap, 1974. OCLC # 992107.

FH Bonsall, Elizabeth Hubbard. Famous Hymns with Stories and Pictures. 2d ed. Philadelphia, PA: Union Press, 1927. OCLC # 3107592.

FHR Foster, Stephen Collins. Foster Hall Reproductions: Songs, Compositions, and Arrangements. Indianapolis, IN: J.K. Lilly, 1933. OCLC # 2908193.

Fi Friml, Charles Rudolf. The Firefly: A Comedy Opera in Three Acts. 2d ed. New York: G. Schirmer, c1912. OCLC # 9380304.

Fif Schaum, John W. Fifty Songs--Fifty States: A Song for Every State in the U.S.A. Milwaukee, WI: Schaum Pubs., c1971. OCLC # 3649631.

FiS Fifty-Two Sacred Songs You Like to Sing. New York: G. Schirmer, c1939. OCLC # 4418229.

FM Favorite Melodies. Miami Beach, FL: Hansen House, c1975. OCLC # 14362353.

FMT Hudson, Arthur Palmer. _Folksongs of Mississippi and Their Background_. Chapel Hill, NC: University of North Carolina Press, c1936. OCLC # 926199.

FN White, Clarence Cameron. _Forty Negro Spirituals_. Philadelphia, PA: Theodore Presser Co., c1927. OCLC # 1807957.

Fo Sondheim, Stephen. _Follies_. New York: C. Hansen, c1974. OCLC # 1295013.

FOC _51 Country Standards_. Milwaukee, WI: H. Leonard Pub. Corp., c1988. OCLC # 22441515.

FoM Hudson, Arthur Palmer. _Folk Tunes from Mississippi_. 2d ed. New York: Da Capo Press, c1977 (1937). OCLC # 3356607.

FoR Sears, Jerry. _Folk Rock: Top Recorded Hits_. New York: M. Witmark, 1965? OCLC # 11392472.

FoS Ades, Hawley. _The Folk-Singers_. Delaware Water Gap, PA: Shawnee Press, c1964. OCLC # 6619196.

FP Miller, Mary. _Finger Play: Songs for Little Fingers_. New York: Schirmer, c1955. OCLC # 3492378.

FPG Silverman, Jerry. _The Flat-Picker's Guitar Guide: An Advanced Instruction Manual and Song Book_. New York: Oak Publications, 1966. OCLC # 1477574.

FPS Simon, William L. _Reader's Digest Festival of Popular Songs_. Pleasantville, NY: Reader's Digest Association, c1977. OCLC # 3252096.

FR Lane, Burton. _Finian's Rainbow_. Vocal score. London: Chappell, c1947. OCLC # 1260404.

FrF Fender, Freddy. _Freddy Fender: Voice, Piano and Guitar with Spanish Lyrics_. New York: Big 3 Music Corp., 1976. OCLC # 6578553.

FRH _50 Rare Hits of the 50's: Complete Original Sheet Music Editions_. Ojai, CA: Creative Concepts Pub. Corp., 1989? OCLC # 20874918.

FrS Sinatra, Frank. _Frank Sinatra Songbook_. Secaucus, NJ: Warner Bros. Publications, c1989. OCLC # 19866873.

FS _Carl Anderson's 46 Sacred Songs: The Best of Sacred Music_. New York: Charles Hansen, c1971. OCLC # 17988855.

FSA1 Armitage, Marie Teresa. _Folk Songs and Art Songs for Intermediate Grades_. Book I. Boston, MA: C.C. Birchard & Co., c1924. OCLC # 1349847.

FSA2 Armitage, Marie Teresa. _Folk Songs and Art Songs for Intermediate Grades_. Book II. Boston MA: C.C. Birchard & Company, c1924. OCLC # 1349847.

FSB 1-3 Weissman, Dick. _Playing the Five String Banjo_. Vols. 1-3. 4th ed. New York: Big 3 Music Corp., 1974-1979. OCLC # 1430623.

FSD Rinehart, Carroll. _Folk Songs with Descants: 2 Part Songs, Melody and Descant_. Park Ridge, IL: Kjos Music Co., c1964. OCLC # 4061409.

FSE Lloyd, Albert Lancaster. _Folk Song in England_. New York: International Publishers, c1967. OCLC # 429559.

FSF Scott, Barbara. _Folk Songs of France: 25 Traditional French Songs with Guitar Chords, in Both French and English_. New York: Oak Pubs., c1966. OCLC # 1282330.

FSN Fremont, Robert A. _Favorite Songs of the Nineties: Complete Original Sheet Music for 89 Songs_. New York: Dover Publications, 1973. OCLC # 690068.

FSO Berry, Cecelia Ray. _Folk Songs of Old Vincennes_. Chicago, IL: H.T. Fitzsimons Company, c1946. OCLC # 10490865.

FSS Vincent, Charles John. _Fifty Shakspere Songs_. Boston, MA: Oliver Ditson, c1906. OCLC # 2862337.

FSSC Joyner, Charles W. _Folk Song in South Carolina_. Columbia, SC: University of South Carolina Press, c1971. OCLC # 194632.

FSt Taussig, Harry A. _Folk Style Autoharp: An Instruction Method for Playing the Autoharp and Accompanying Folk Songs_. New York: Oak Publications, 1967. OCLC # 1082991.

FSTS Geller, James Jacob. _Famous Songs and Their Stories_. New York: Macaulay Company, c1931. OCLC # 1891619.

FSU Combs, Josiah Henry. _Folk-Songs of the Southern United States_. Austin, TX: University of Texas Press, c1967. OCLC # 954021.

FSY _Fifty-Six Songs You Like to Sing_. New York: G. Schirmer, 1937. OCLC # 657872.

FT Herbert, Victor. _The Fortune Teller: A Comic Opera_. New York: M. Witmark, c1898. OCLC # 1996864.

FU Bay, Melbourne Earl. _Mel Bay's Fun with the Ukulele_. Kirkwood, MO: Mel Bay Publications, 1961. OCLC # 6451613.

FuB Bay, Melbourne Earl. _Mel Bay's Fun with the Banjo: Five String or Plectrum_. Pacific, MO: M. Bay Publications, c1962. OCLC # 8088467.

FVV _Folk Visions & Voices: Traditional Music and Song in North Georgia_. Athens, GA: University of Georgia Press, c1983. OCLC # 10133334.

FW Silber, Irwin. _Folksinger's Wordbook_. New York: Oak Publications, 1973. OCLC # 741135.

FWS Ades, Hawley. _Fred Waring Songbook, for_

Singing Everywhere. Delaware Water Gap, PA: Shawnee Press, 1962. OCLC # 1075930.

G Schwartz, Stephen. Godspell: Vocal Selections. New York: Valando Music, 1971. OCLC # 2958601.

GA White, John I. Git Along, Little Dogies: Songs and Songmakers of the American West. Urbana, IL: University of Illinois Press, c1975. OCLC # 1255042.

GAR The Golden Age of Rock & Roll: Featuring the Classics of Leiber and Stoller. Secaucus, NJ: Warner Bros. Publications, c1987. OCLC # 17464361.

GB Andrews, Edward Deming. The Gift to Be Simple: Songs, Dances, and Rituals of the American Shakers. New York: Dover, 1967. OCLC # 796055.

GBC The Galliard Book of Carols. London: Stainer and Bell, c1980. OCLC # 7164545.

GC Towner, Earl. Glee and Chorus Book for Male Voices. New York: Silver Burdett, c1922. OCLC # 8211164.

GCM 35 Years of Great Country Music: Voice, Piano, Guitar. Secaucus, NJ: Warner Bros. Publications, 1991? OCLC # 24777142.

GeS Gearhart, Livingston. Gentlemen Songsters: Two-, Three-, and Four-Part Songs for Male Voices. Delaware Water Gap, PA: Shawnee Press, c1959. OCLC # 1077677.

GG 1-5 Silverman, Jerry. Jerry Silverman's Graded Guitar Method. Vols. 1-5. New York: Robbins Music, c1970. OCLC # 4558801.

GH Sankey, Ira David. Gospel Hymns Nos. 1 to 6 Complete. New York: DaCapo Press, c1972 (1895). OCLC # 581828.

GI Palmer, Edgar A. G.I. Songs. New York: Sheridan House, c1944. OCLC# 8989052.

GiS Sullivan, Arthur Seymour. Gilbert & Sullivan Operettas, Adapted for Half-Hour Performance. Boston, MA: Plays, c1976. OCLC # 2670774.

GM Wilson, Harry Robert. Growing with Music: Kindergarten Book. Englewood Cliffs, NJ: Prentice Hall, c1966. OCLC # 3898972.

GMD Ellington, Duke. The Great Music of Duke Ellington. Melville, NY: Belwin Mills, c1973. OCLC # 813961.

GO Posselt, Eric. Give Out! Songs of, by and for the Men in Service. New York: Arrowhead Press, 1943. OCLC # 1044445.

GOB Gershwin, George. Gershwin on Broadway: From 1919-1933. Secaucus, NJ: Warner Bros. Publications, c1987. OCLC # 17203490.

GOI7 Brimhall, John. The Golden Organ Instructor. Vol 7, Deluxe All Organ Album Easy Pop Big Note. New York: Charles Hansen, c1972. OCLC # 715621.

GP Glorious Praise: Great Songwriters and Songs. Winona, MN: H. Leonard Pub. Corp., c1988. OCLC # 19059422.

Gr Grease (Motion Picture). Songs from the Robert Stigwood/Allen Carr Motion Picture "Grease" for Paramount Pictures. New York: Warner Bros. Publications, c1978. OCLC # 6597337.

GrG Dorsey, Thomas Andrew. Great Gospel Songs of Thomas A. Dorsey: Piano, Vocal, Guitar. Winona, MN: H. Leonard Pub. Corp., c1988. OCLC # 20544002.

GrH Paskas, Andy. Great Hits: Complete with Words, Music, Chords, and Instruction. New York: Big 3 Music Corp., 1974. OCLC # 12497625.

GrM Orr, James L. Grange Melodies. New York: Arno Press, 1975 (c1891). OCLC # 3966500.

GrS Okun, Milton. The New York Times Great Songs of the Seventies. New York: Times Books, c1978. OCLC # 25708144.

GS1 Morgan, Joe Miller. Gospel Sing: Piano, Voice, Guitar. Vol. 1. Nashville, TN: Peaceful Valley Music, c1976. OCLC # 6588090.

GSF Great Songs of the '40s: Voice, Piano, Guitar. New York: Big 3 Music Corporation, 1977? OCLC # 6568070.

GSM Great Songs of Madison Avenue. New York: Quadrangle, c1976. OCLC # 2702556.

GSN1 The Greatest Songs of 1890-1920: Piano, Vocal, Chords. Miami, FL: CPP/Belwin, c1990. OCLC # 22989490.

GSN2 The Greatest Songs of 1920-1940: Piano, Vocal, Chords. Miami, FL: CPP/Belwin, c1990. OCLC # 22989485.

GSN3 The Greatest Songs of 1940-1960: Piano, Vocal, Chords. Miami, FL: CPP/Belwin, c1990. OCLC # 22989489.

GSN4 The Greatest Songs of 1960-1975: Piano, Vocal, Chords. Miami, FL: CPP/Belwin, c1990. OCLC # 22989488.

GSN5 The Greatest Songs of 1975-1990: Piano, Vocal, Chords. Miami, FL: CPP/Belwin, c1990. OCLC # 22989487.

GSO Great Songs of the '30s. New York: Big 3 Music Corp., 1976? OCLC # 5429813.

GST Great Songs of the '20s: Voice, Piano, Guitar. New York: Big 3 Music Corporation, c1976. OCLC # 5429819.

GTV Lane, John. Great TV Themes. Vocal and

piano edition, with chords. New York: Robbins Music Corp., 1966. OCLC # 2460352.

Gu   Noad, Frederick M. The Guitar Songbook. London: Collier-Macmillan,1969. OCLC # 1360365.

GuC   Timmerman, Maurine. Guitar in the Classroom. Dubuque, IA: W.C. Brown Co., 1971. OCLC # 172575.

GUM1   Krone, Beatrice Perham. Growing Up with
GUM2   Music. Complete edition. Chicago, IL: Neil A. Kjos, c1937-8. OCLC # 6566267.

GV   MacDermot, Galt. Two Gentlemen of Verona. Vocal score. New York: Chappell, c1973. OCLC # 982765.

H   MacDermot, Galt. Hair: The American Tribal Love-Rock Musical. New York: Pocket Books, 1969 (c1966). OCLC # 626531.

HA   Hear America Singing. Nashville, TN: Ideals Publishing, c1992. OCLC # 28165111.

HAS   Loesser, Arthur. Humor in American Song. New York: Howell, Soskin, c1942. OCLC # 939007.

HB   Ohrlin, Glenn. The Hell-Bound Train: A Cowboy Songbook. Urbana, IL: University of Illinois Press, c1973. OCLC # 880942.

HC1   The Heritage Collection of the Best Loved Songs of the American Stage. Vol. 1. New York: Chappell Music Co., c1976? OCLC #12706692.

HC2   The Heritage collection of the Best Loved Songs of the American Stage. Vol. 2. New York: Chappell Music Co., c1976? OCLC # 12706692.

HCY   Allen, David B. How to Create Your Own Sing Out. 2d ed. Los Angeles, CA: Pace Publications, c1966. OCLC # 12433178.

HD   Bacharach, Burt. Hal David Songbook. Milwaukee, WI: Hal Leonard, c1990. OCLC # 23445649.

HF   Kennedy, Pamela. Hymns of Faith and Inspiration. Nashville, TN: Ideals, c1990. OCLC # 22304384.

HFH   Hooray for Hollywood! Deluxe edition. Secaucus, NJ: Warner Bros. Publications, c1988. OCLC # 18499957.

HHa   Homeland Harmony: New Songs, Great Songs, Timeless Songs. Nashville, TN: Homeland Pub., c1988. OCLC # 19258671.

HJ   Friml, Charles Rudolf. High Jinks: A Musical Farce in Three Acts. New York: G. Schirmer, c1914. OCLC # 2059273.

HLS1   Home Library Series. Vol. 1, 71 Songs, 1890-1920. New York: Big 3 Music Corporation, c1976. OCLC # 5120515.

HLS2   Home Library Series. Vol. 2, 72 Songs, 1920-1940. New York: Big 3 Music Corporation, c1976. OCLC # 5120515.

HLS3   Home Library Series. Vol. 3, 70 Songs, 1940-1960. New York: Big 3 Music Corporation, c1976. OCLC # 5120515.

HLS5   Home Library Series. Vol. 5, 69 Songs, Movie Music. New York: Big 3 Music Corporation, c1976. OCLC # 5120515.

HLS7   Home Library Series. Vol. 7, 77 Songs, Inspirational Music. New York: Big 3 Music Corporation, c1976. OCLC # 5120515.

HLS8   Home Library Series. Vol. 8, 57 Songs from Broadway. New York: Big 3 Music Corporation, c1976. OCLC # 5120515.

HLS9   Home Library Series. Vol. 9, 63 Songs, Best in Country Music. New York: Big 3 Music Corporation, c1976. OCLC # 5120515.

HOH   Fife, Austin E. Heaven on Horseback: Revivalist Songs and Verse in the Cowboy Idiom. Logan, UT: Utah State University Press, c1970. OCLC # 134636.

HR   Chipman, Bruce L. Hardening Rock: An Organic Anthology of the Adolescence of Rock 'n Roll. Boston, MA: Little, Brown, c1972. OCLC # 303916.

HRB1   History of Rhythm and Blues. Vol. 1, The Roots, 1947-52. New York: Progressive Music Pub. Co., c1969. OCLC # 7682277.

HRB2   History of Rhythm and Blues. Vol. 2, The Golden Years, 1953-55. New York: Progressive Music Pub. Co., c1969. OCLC # 7682277.

HRB3   History of Rhythm and Blues. Vol. 3, Rock and Roll, 1956-57. New York: Progressive Music Pub. Co., c1969. OCLC # 7682277.

HRB4   History of Rhythm and Blues. Vol. 4, The Big Beat, 1958-1960. New York: Progressive Music Pub. Co., c1969. OCLC # 7682277.

HS   Dallin, Leon. Heritage Songster: 320 Folk and Familiar Songs. Words, Music, Legends, Chord Symbols: Guitar, Ukulele, Banjo, Autoharp, Piano. Dubuque, IA: W.C. Brown Company Publishers, 1970 (c1966). OCLC # 2612555.

HSA   Nelson, Esther L. Holiday Singing and Dancing Games. New York: Sterling Publishing Co., c1980. OCLC # 7101247.

HSD   Heart Songs Dear to the American People, Contributed in Their Search for Treasured Favorite Songs. Boston, MA: J.M. Chapple, c1937. OCLC # 4250661.

HSe   Hits of the Seventies & Eighties: Organ, Piano, Guitar and Chord Organ: Easy-to-Read Big Note-Name. New York: Shattinger-International Music Corp., 1980? OCLC # 8676058.

HSi   Hits of the Sixties: Organ, Piano, Guitar and

Chord Organ: Easy-to-Read Big Note-Name. New York: Shattinger-International Music Corp., c1976. OCLC # 6925655.

HSS   Simeone, Harry. Have Songs-Will Sing: Three Part Songs for Teen-Age Choral Groups. Delaware Water Gap, PA: Shawnee Press, c1962. OCLC # 1448336.

HST   Simeone, Harry. Have Songs--Will Sing, for Three-Part Treble Voices. Delaware Water Gap, PA: Shawnee Press, c1963. OCLC # 5748972.

HW   Williams, Hank. Hank Williams' Favorite Songs. Nashville, TN: Fred Rose Music, c1953. OCLC # 5470764.

HWS   Tinsley, Jim Bob. He Was Singin' This Song: A Collection of Forty-Eight Traditional Songs of the American Cowboy. Orlando, FL: University Presses of Florida, 1981. OCLC # 8293958.

Hy   The Hymnbook. Atlanta, GA: Presbyterian Church in the United States; The United Presbyterian Church in the U.S.A.; Reformed Church in America, 1955. OCLC # 11633125.

I   Schmidt, Harvey. I Do! I Do!. New York: Portfolio Music/Chappell, c1968. OCLC # 255728.

ID   Molzer, Felix. In a Dutch Village: A Music Drama in One Act. Boston, MA: Ginn, c1960. OCLC # 11898098.

IF   Nettl, Bruno. An Introduction to Folk Music in the United States. Rev. ed. Detroit, MI: Wayne State University Press, 1962. OCLC # 299683.

IFM   MacColl, Ewan. I'm a Freeborn Man, and Other Original Radio Ballads and Songs of British Workingmen, Gypsies, Prizefighters, Teenagers, and Contemporary Songs of Struggle and Conscience. New York: Oak Publications, 1968? OCLC # 1472012.

IH   McCall, Harlo E. Instrumental Hymn Favorites. Vol. 2, B-flat Book. New York: R.D. Row Music Co., c1963. OCLC # 12129401.

IHA   Arnett, Hazel. I Hear America Singing: Great Folk Songs from the Revolution to Rock. New York: Praeger, c1975. OCLC # 18843572.

IL   Richman, Gloria. Ivy League Song Book: 180 Songs: Ivy League College Songs, Drinking Songs, Folk Songs, Christmas Songs, Other College Songs. Greenville, DE: Rolor, c1958. OCLC # 3075559.

ILF   I Love the '50s: Voice, Piano, Guitar. New York: Big 3 Music Co., 196? OCLC # 6925735.

ILS   I Love the '60s: Voice, Piano, Guitar. New York: Big 3 Music Co., 197?. OCLC # 6925792.

ILT   Stern, Dick. It's Love...That's All. New York: Columbia House, c1978. OCLC # 9383399.

IN   Molzer, Felix. In a Norwegian Village: A Music Drama in Three Acts. Boston, MA: Ginn, c1960. OCLC # 11898809.

IPH   Instant Play Harmonica: A Complete Instruction Book. Miami Beach, FL: Hansen House, c1980. OCLC # 9977677.

IS   Graeme, Joy. The Irish Songbook. New York: Macmillan, c1969. OCLC # 33446.

ITP   Roberts, Leonard. In the Pine: Selected Kentucky Folksongs. Pikeville, KY: Pikeville College Press, 1978. OCLC # 4758466.

J   Raim, Walter. The Josh White Song Book. Chicago, IL: Quadrangle Books, c1963. OCLC # 938978.

JBF   John Brimhall's 46 Sacred Songs: The Best of Sacred Music. Miami Beach, FL: Hansen House, 197? OCLC # 9782627.

JC   Croce, Jim. Jim Croce, His Life and Music. New York: Blendingwell Music, 1974. OCLC # 1720467.

JD   Davis, James Houston. Jimmie Davis Folio of Favorite Songs. New York: Jimmie Davis Music Corp., c1948. OCLC # 11002343.

JF   Dowdey, Landon Gerald. Journey to Freedom: A Casebook with Music. Chicago, IL: Swallow Press, c1969. OCLC # 45180.

JOC   The Joy of Christmas: A Selection of Carols. New York: Oxford University Press, 1978. OCLC # 4377460.

JP   Hamlisch, Marvin. Joseph Papp Presents A Chorus Line. New York: E.H. Morris, c1977. OCLC # 6202046.

JS   Idelsohn, Abraham Zebi. Jewish Song Book for Synagogue, School, and Home. Cincinnati, OH: Idelsohn, c1928. OCLC # 5083268.

JW   Liebert, Billy. America, Why I Love Her. New York: Simon and Schuster, c1977. OCLC # 3456561.

K   Friml, Charles Rudolf. Katinka, the Musical Play. New York: G. Schirmer, c1916. OCLC # 1329887.

KH   Weill, Kurt. Knickerbocker Holiday: A Musical Comedy. New York: Crawford, c1951. OCLC # 6081981.

Ki   Wright, Robert Craig. Kismet: A Musical Arabian Night. New York: Frank Music Corp., 1955. OCLC # 8821049.

KS   Bradford, Margaret. Keep Singing, Keep Humming: A Collection of Play and Story Songs. New York: W.R. Scott, c1946. OCLC # 1468356.

L   Hammerstein, Oscar. Lyrics. New York: Simon

& Schuster, 1949. OCLC # 760628.

LA   The Latin-American Song Book: A Varied and
      Comprehensive Collection of Latin-American
      Songs. Boston, MA: Ginn, c1942. OCLC #
      6025593.

LaS   The Latin Song Book: Chord Organ. Miami
      Beach, FL: Hansen House, 1982? OCLC #
      14362452.

LC   Cater, Harry. Living Country Blues. Detroit, MI:
      Folklore Associates, 1969. OCLC # 52101.

LD   Weill, Kurt. Lady in the Dark: A Musical Play.
      New York: Chappell, c1941. OCLC # 1524302.

Le   Ledbetter, Huddie. The Leadbelly Songbook:
      The Ballads, Blues, and Folksongs of Huddie
      Ledbetter. New York: Oak Publications, c1962.
      OCLC # 588741.

LH   Clarke, Nicholas. Left Handed Guitar. New
      York: The Bold Strummer, 1974. OCLC #
      2049426.

LJ   Rodgers, James Charles. The Legendary Jimmie
      Rodgers Memorial Folio. Vol 1. New York: Peer
      International, c1967. OCLC # 5392284.

LL   Loewe, Frederick. The Lerner & Loewe Song
      Book. New York: Simon & Schuster, c1962.
      OCLC # 1140783.

LM   Let Me Entertain You Songbook: Over 100
      Popular Songs. New York: Hansen House,
      c1974. OCLC # 1454851.

LMR   Dykema, Peter William. Let Music Ring!
      Boston, MA: C.C. Birchard, c1949. OCLC
      # 2588977.

LMS   Besoyan, Rick. Little Mary Sunshine: A New
      Musical. New York: New York Times Music
      Corp., c1965. OCLC # 4366102.

LN   Sondheim, Stephen. A Little Night Music: A
      New Musical Comedy. New York: Dodd, Mead,
      c1974. OCLC # 983325.

Lo   Kershaw, Doug. Lou'siana Man: The Doug
      Kershaw Songbook. New York: Macmillan,
      c1971. OCLC # 926190.

LOM   Lean on Me and the Best in Inspirational Pop.
      Secaucus, NJ: Warner Bros., c1990. OCLC #
      25352708.

LoS   National Congress of Parents and Teachers.
      Louisiana Branch. Louisiana Sings. Delaware,
      OH: Cooperative Recreation Service, c1957.
      OCLC # 12497191.

LS   Weill, Kurt. Lost in the Stars: A Musical
      Tragedy. New York: Chappell, c1950.
      OCLC # 9893592.

LSB   Lady Sings the Blues: Vocal Selections: The
      Songs of Billie Holiday from the Motion Picture

Soundtrack. Los Angeles, CA: West Coast
Pubs., c1973. OCLC # 7799661.

LSO   Gershwin, Ira. Lyrics on Several Occasions: A
      Selection of Stage and Screen Lyrics. New
      York: Knopf, c1959. OCLC # 538209.

LSR   Cohen, Norm. Long Steel Rail: The Railroad in
      American Folksong. Urbana, IL: University of
      Illinois Press, c1981. OCLC # 6277736.

LT   Forcucci, Samuel L. Let There Be Music: A Basic
      Text for General Music Classes. Boston, MA:
      Allyn & Bacon, c1969. OCLC # 4887100.

LTL   Cooper, Grosvenor. Learning to Listen: A
      Handbook for Music. Chicago,IL: University of
      Chicago Press, c1957. OCLC # 910191.

LW   Silverman, Jerry. The Liberated Woman's
      Songbook. New York: Macmillan, c1971.
      OCLC # 294793.

LWT   Abramson, Frank. Lawrence Welk TV Song
      Favorites. Santa Monica, CA: Vogue Music,
      c1963. OCLC # 12029132.

M   Herbert, Victor. Mlle. Modiste: A Comic Opera.
      New York: M. Witmark, c1905. OCLC #
      1963942.

MA   Kern, Jerome. Music in the Air: A Musical
      Adventure in Two Acts. New York: T.B.
      Harms Co., 1933. OCLC # 1334364.

MAB1 Master Accompaniment Books for "Memories
      Sing Along Song Books." Vol 1. Minneapolis,
      MN: LeAnn Pub. Co., c1977. OCLC #
      12433285.

MaG   Westervelt, Marie. Mardi Gras. Bryn Mawr, PA:
      Oliver Ditson, c1952. OCLC # 12497272.

MAR   Ginglend, David R. Music Activities for Retarded
      Children: A Handbook for Teachers and
      Parents. New York: Abingdon Press, c1965.
      OCLC # 594364.

MAS   Wilson, Harry Robert. Music Americans Sing.
      New York: Silver Burdett, c1948. OCLC #
      1349580.

MBS   Strickland, Lily Teresa. Mo' Bayou Songs. New
      York: J. Fischer, c1925. OCLC # 5467149.

MC   Musical Christmas with Peter Duchin: A Festival
      of Holiday Songs in New Arrangements for
      Piano and Guitar. New York: Holt, Rinehart, &
      Winston, c1976. OCLC # 253360.

MCG   Nelson, David. Mammoth Collection of the
      Greatest Hits of the 60's and 70's: Words,
      Chords, Music. New York: Big 3 Music Corp.,
      1974? OCLC # 6609182.

Me   Kennedy, Robert Emmet. Mellows: A Chronicle
      of Unknown Singers. New York: A. and C.
      Boni, c1925. OCLC # 6608765.

MES1   Nye, Robert Evans. _Music in the Elementary_
        School. Englewood Cliffs, NJ: Prentice-Hall,
        c1957. OCLC # 398153.

MES2   Nye, Robert Evans. _Music in the Elementary_
        School. 2nd ed. Englewood Cliffs, NJ: Prentice-
        Hall, c1964. OCLC # 390486.

MF   _The Most Fantastic Fakebook in the World._
        Secaucus, NJ: Warner Bros., c1992. OCLC #
        28539289.

MG   Bergethon, Bjornar. _Musical Growth in the_
        Elementary School. New York: Holt, Rinehart &
        Winston, c1963. OCLC # 619058.

MGT   Sullivan, Sir Arthur Seymour. _Martyn Green's_
        Treasury of Gilbert and Sullivan. New York:
        Simon & Schuster, c1961. OCLC #
        4009569.

MH   McConathy, Osbourne. _The Music Hour in the_
        Kindergarten and First Grade. New York: Silver
        Burdett, c1938. OCLC # 7958785.

MHB   McConathy, Osbourne. _Music Highways and_
        Byways. New York: Silver Burdett Co., c1936.
        OCLC # 1039031.

ML   Porter, Cole. _Music and Lyrics by Cole Porter: A_
        Treasury of Cole Porter. New York: Chappell,
        c1972. OCLC # 846171.

MLM   Leigh, Mitch. _Man of La Mancha: A Musical_
        Play. New York: S. Fox, c1967. OCLC #
        3699722.

MLS   Legrand, Michel. _The Michel Legrand Songbook._
        Winona, MN: Hal Leonard, c1988. OCLC #
        18280772.

MM   Ades, Hawley. _Music, Men: Four-Part Men's_
        Chorus. Delaware Water Gap, PA: Shawnee
        Press, c1963. OCLC # 1061155.

MML   McConathy, Osbourne. _Music of Many Lands_
        and Peoples. New York: Silver Burdett, c1932.
        OCLC # 1592227.

MMM   Rossi, Nick. _Musical Masterpieces for Men's_
        Voices. New York: MCA Music, c1966. OCLC #
        5748950.

MMW   Rossi, Nick. _Musical Masterpieces for Women's_
        Voices. New York: MCA Music, c1967. OCLC #
        1088113.

MMY   Rossi, Nick. _Musical Masterpieces for Young_
        Voices. New York: MCA Music, c1970. OCLC #
        1838622.

Mo   Brimhall, John. _The Morris 747 Fake Book._
        N.p.: E.H. Morris, c1970. OCLC # 7900462.

MoA   _1988 Movie Award Songs._ Miami, FL: Columbia
        Pictures Publications, c1988. OCLC # 18347658.

MoM   Kennedy, Robert Emmet. _More Mellows._ New York:
        Dodd, Mead & Company, c1931. OCLC #
        1471369.

MP   _Mon Premier Livre de Chansons._ Paris: Librairie
        Larousse, 1973 (c1962). OCLC # 3637874.

MPM   Romberg, Sigmund. _Maytime: A Play with_
        Music in Four Acts. New York: G. Schirmer,
        c1946. OCLC # 2975363.

MPP   Lawrence, Vera Brodsky. _Music for Patriots,_
        Politicians and Presidents: Harmonies and
        Discords of the First Hundred Years. New
        York: Macmillan, c1975. OCLC # 1602329.

MR   Remick Music Corp. _More Remick Hits through_
        the Years: Words and Music Complete, Chord
        Symbols Included. New York: Remick, c1954.
        OCLC # 11562563.

MS   Schwartz, Stephen. _The Magic Show: Vocal_
        Selections from the Hit Show. Melville, NY:
        Belwin Mills, c1975. OCLC # 3101446.

MSA1   _Memories Sing Along Song Book._ Vol. 1.
        Minneapolis, MN: LeAnn Pub. Co., c1977.
        OCLC # 5794654.

MSB   Ashton, John. _Modern Street Ballads._ New York:
        B. Blom, c1968. OCLC # 452339.

MSH   Niles, John Jacob. _More Songs of the Hill Folk:_
        Ten Ballads and Tragic Legends from Kentucky,
        Virginia, Tennessee, North Carolina, and
        Georgia. New York: Schirmer, c1936. OCLC #
        2116009.

MSS   Martens, Frederick Herman. _Mexican and Spanish_
        Songs. New and enlarged ed. New York:
        Ditson, c1928. OCLC # 8760915.

MU   McConathy, Osbourne. _Music, the Universal_
        Language. New York: Silver Burdett Co.,
        c1941. OCLC # 401500.

MuM   Pitts, Lilla Belle. _Music Makers._ Boston, MA:
        Ginn, c1967. OCLC # 5167462.

My   Jessye, Eve A. _My Spirituals._ New York:
        Robbins Engel, c1927. OCLC # 2340923.

N   _Nashville Number 1 Country Songs._ New York:
        Your Music Store, 1973. OCLC # 7403435.

NA   _New Anthology of American Song: 25 Songs by_
        Native American Composers. New York: G.
        Schirmer, c1942. OCLC # 17709489.

NaM   Herbert, Victor. _Naughty Marietta: A Comic_
        Opera. New York: M. Witmark, c1910. OCLC
        # 1003268.

NAS   Oberndorfer, Marx E. _The New American_
        Songbook: A Century of Progress in American
        Song. Chicago, IL: Hall & McCreary, c1933.
        OCLC # 4219016.

NB   McKuen, Rod. _New Ballads._ Los Angeles, CA:
        Stanyan Books, 1970. OCLC # 89465.

NCB The New Complete Book of Wedding Music: Original Sheet Music Editions in Four Categories: All-Time Favorites, Standard Wedding Songs, Classical Wedding Songs, Popular Wedding Songs. Piano/vocal. Miami Beach, FL: Hansen House, 198? OCLC # 9106875.

Ne Romberg, Sigmund. The New Moon: A Musical Romance. New York: Harms, c1928. OCLC # 1342500.

NeA Sandburg, Carl. New American Songbag. New York: Broadcast Music, c1950. OCLC # 3962359.

NeF Lomax, John Avery. Negro Folk Songs As Sung by Lead Belly, "King of the Twelve-String Guitar Players of the World," Long-Time Convict in the Penitentiaries of Texas and Louisiana. New York: Macmillan Company, 1936. OCLC # 665363.

NF Talley, Thomas Washington. Negro Folk Rhymes, Wise and Otherwise. Port Washington, NY: Kennikat Press, 1968 (c1922). OCLC # 270210.

NFS Burlin, Natalie Curtis. Negro Folk-Songs. New York: G. Schirmer, c1918. OCLC # 3569948.

NH Odum, Howard Washington. The Negro and His Songs: A Study of Typical Negro Songs in the South. Hatboro, PA: Folklore Associates, Inc., 1964 (c1925). OCLC # 890704.

NI The New Illustrated Disney Songbook. New York: Abrams, c1986. OCLC # 17231662.

NK Cole, Nat King. Nat "King" Cole. Ojai, CA: Creative Concepts, 1989. OCLC # 21681180.

NM Brimhall John. The New Morris 555 Fake Song Book of Show Music. Glen Rock, NJ: E.H. Morris, c1966. OCLC # 7907658.

NMH Haggard, Merle. The New Merle Haggard Anthology: Piano, Vocal, Guitar. Milwaukee, WI: H. Leonard Pub. Corp., c1991. OCLC # 23593110.

NN2 Youmans, Vincent. No, No, Nanette! New York: Harms, c1925. OCLC # 2364557.

NN7 Youmans, Vincent. No, No, Nanette! New York: Warner Bros. Music, c1971. OCLC # 3365555.

NO Gillock, William L. New Orleans Jazz Styles. Cincinnati, OH: Willis Music Co., c1965. OCLC # 3603008.

NoS The Novelty Songbook. Winona, MN: H. Leonard Pub. Corp., c1982. OCLC # 9436258.

NSS Fisher, Miles Mark. Negro Slave Songs in the United States. New York: Russell & Russell, 1968 (c1953). OCLC # 436335.

NYT Gershwin, George. The New York Times Gershwin Years in Song. New York: Quadrangle, 1973. OCLC # 792186.

O Bart, Lionel. Oliver!: A New Musical. New York: TRO Hollis Music Inc., c1960. OCLC # 1067775.

OA1 Copland, Aaron. Old American Songs, Newly Arranged. Vol. 1. New York: Boosey & Hawkes, 1950. OCLC # 187267.

OA2 Copland, Aaron. Old American Songs, Newly Arranged. Vol. 2. New York: Boosey & Hawkes, 1954. OCLC # 187267.

OAP 100 All-Time Popular Hits. Selected by the editors of Sheet Music Magazine. Katonah, NY: Ekay Music, c1990. OCLC # 22933411.

OB Dearmer, Percy. The Oxford Book of Carols. London: Oxford University Press, c1964. OCLC # 597739.

OBN 101 Big Note Piano Pieces. Cincinnati, OH: Willis Music Co., c1978. OCLC # 6671009.

OE Bailey, Catherine. Old English Carols for Christmas. Cambridge, MA: Washburn & Thomas, c1929. OCLC # 1665869.

OFS 120+ Folk Song Favorites. Miami, FL: CPP/Belwin, c1990. OCLC # 24705882.

OG Herbert, Victor. The Only Girl: A Musical Farcical Comedy. New York: M. Witmark, c1914. OCLC # 1964029.

OGC1 100 Great Country and Western Songs. Vol. 1. New York: Hill and Range Songs, 1962. OCLC # 12442417.

OGC2 100 Great Country and Western Songs. Vol. 2. New York: Hill and Range Songs, 1962. OCLC # 12442417.

OGR Our God Reigns: The Praise and Worship Collection. Winona, MN: Hal Leonard Pub. Corp., 1987? OCLC # 15724716.

OH Bantock, Sir Granville. One Hundred Songs of England. New York: Oliver Ditson, c1914. OCLC # 6507289.

OHB 100 Best Songs of the 20's and 30's. New York: Harmony Books, 1973. OCLC # 781890.

OHF Mercer, Johnny. Our Huckleberry Friend: The Life, Times and Lyrics of Johnny Mercer. Secaucus, NJ: Lyle Stuart, c1982. OCLC # 8627220.

OHG Dichter, Harry. One Hundred Great American Songs in Facsimile. Philadelphia, PA: Musical Americana, 1956. OCLC # 7432656.

OHN Nelson, David. 190 Children's Songs. New York: Robbins Music Corp., 1967. OCLC # 3462108.

OHO Cohen, Mike. 101 Plus 5 Folk Songs for Camp. New York: Oak Publications, c1966. OCLC # 2867173.

OHT   Schmidt, Harvey. _110 in the Shade._
        Piano/vocal score. New York: Chappell,
        c1964. OCLC # 2171257.

OM   Osbeck, Kenneth W. _101 More Hymn Stories._
        Grand Rapids, MI: Kregel Publications, c1985.
        OCLC # 11533394.

On   Brimhall, John. _100 Greatest Hits of the 70's,
        Including a Special Tribute to George Gershwin._
        New York: C. Hansen, 1973. OCLC # 1099599.

OnT1   _100 Top Pop Songs._ Vol. 1. Miami Beach, FL:
        C. Hansen, 1968? OCLC # 6112515.

OnT6   _100 Top Pop Songs._ Vol. 6. Miami Beach, FL:
        C. Hansen, 1968? OCLC # 6112515.

OP1   Hermanns, Al. _Organ-izing Popular Music._
        Book 1. New York: Robbins Music Corp.,
        1969. OCLC # 4679713.

OP2   Hermanns, Al. _Organ-izing Popular Music._
        Book 2. New York: Robbins Music Corp.,
        1969. OCLC # 4679713.

OPS   _101 Popular Songs for Accordion: With Guitar
        Chords._ Miami Beach, FL: Hansen House, 198?
        OCLC # 12845472.

OS   Braille and Sight Saving School, Jacksonville, IL.
        125 Songs for Group Singing. Louisville, KY:
        American Printing House for the Blind, c1960.
        OCLC # 3092333.

OT   Gershwin, Ira. _Of Thee I Sing._ New York:
        Warner Bros. Publications, c1932. OCLC #
        4335596.

OTJ   _1000 Jumbo: The Children's Song Book: With
        the Complete Songs of Mother Goose and Other
        Delights._ New York: C. Hansen Distributors,
        c1975. OCLC # 2390498.

OTO   _1001 Show Tunes and Movie Themes._ Miami
        Beach, FL: Hansen, c1975. OCLC # 4078405.

OU   Gearhart, Livingston. _Once upon a Song:
        Three- and Four-Part Songs for Treble Voices._
        Delaware Water Gap, PA: Shawnee Press, c1961.
        OCLC # 2804032.

Oz1   Randolph, Vance. _Ozark Folksongs._ Vol. 1,
        British Ballads and Songs. Rev. ed. Columbia,
        MO: University of Missouri Press, c1980 (1946).
        OCLC # 6442634.

Oz2   Randolph, Vance. _Ozark Folksongs._ Vol. 2,
        Songs of the South and West. Rev. ed. Columbia,
        MO: University of Missouri Press, c1980 (1946).
        OCLC # 6442634.

Oz3   Randolph, Vance. _Ozark Folksongs._ Vol. 3,
        Humorous and Play-Party Songs. Rev. ed.
        Columbia, MO: University of Missouri Press,
        c1980 (1946). OCLC # 6442634.

Oz4   Randolph, Vance. _Ozark Folksongs._ Vol. 4,
        Religious Songs and Other Items. Rev. ed.

Columbia, MO: University of Missouri Press,
c1980 (1946). OCLC # 6442634.

P   Geld, Gary. _Purlie: Vocal Selections._ New York:
        Mourbar Music Corp., c1970. OCLC #
        2041974.

PAJ   Peaslee, Richard. _The Persecution and
        Assassination of Jean-Paul Marat._ Vocal score.
        New York: Highgate Press, c1966. OCLC #
        2304936.

PaS   Beckman, Frederick. _Partner Songs: A Collection
        of Well-Known Melodies._ Boston, MA: Ginn,
        c1958. OCLC # 1275497.

PB   _Play by Chords: It's the Easiest._ New York:
        Hansen Music Co., c1963. OCLC # 10132538.

PF   Hague, Albert Martin. _Plain and Fancy: A Musical
        Comedy._ New York: Random House, 1955.
        OCLC # 413732.

PL   Blondie (Musical Group). _Parallel Lines._
        Hollywood, CA: Almo Publications, c1979.
        OCLC # 6114360.

PIS   Pitcher, Gladys. _Playtime in Song: Folk Songs in
        Simple Dance and Play Patterns._ New York: M.
        Witmark, c1960. OCLC # 10555648.

PM   Croce, Jim. _Photographs and Memories: His
        Greatest Hits._ New York: Blendingwell Music,
        c1974. OCLC # 3044673.

PMC   McCartney, Paul. _Paul McCartney, Composer/
        Artist._ New York: MPL Communications,
        c1981. OCLC # 8070099.

PO   Silverman, Jerry. _The Panic Is On and 62 Other
        Songs--Outrageous, Irreverent, Subversive, and
        Far-Out._ New York: Oak Publications, c1966.
        OCLC # 1352544.

PoG   Okun, Milton. _Pocket Guitar._ Greenwich, CT:
        Cherry Lane Music Co., c1980. OCLC #
        7403969.

PoS   Jackson, Richard. _Popular Songs of Nineteenth
        Century America: Complete Original Sheet
        Music for 64 Songs._ New York: Dover
        Publications, 1976. OCLC # 2327053.

POT   Silverman, Jerry. _Play Old-Time Country Fiddle._
        Radnor, PA: Chilton Book Co., 1975. OCLC #
        3048219.

PS   Simon, Paul. _Paul Simon._ New York: Charing
        Cross Music, c1972. OCLC # 8130261.

PSD   Johns, Altona Trent. _Play Songs of the Deep
        South._ Washington, DC: Associated Publishers,
        c1944. OCLC # 931936.

PSN   Silber, Irwin. _Reprints from the People's Songs
        Bulletin, 1946-1949._ New York: Oak
        Publications, c1961. OCLC # 2936178.

PT   _Polka Time!_ New revision. Winona, MN: Hal

Leonard Pub. Corp., c1988. OCLC # 19009568.

R   Woldin, Judd. Raisin. New York: Blackwood
        Music & Raisin Music, c1974. OCLC # 3423826.

RB   Spinner, Stephanie. Rock Is Beautiful: An
        Anthology of American Lyrics, 1953-1968. New
        York: Dell Pub. Co., c1970. OCLC # 3494915.

RBO   Paxton, Tom. Ramblin' Boy and Other Songs.
        New York: Oak Publications, c1965. OCLC #
        6610488.

RC   Remick Music Corp. Remick Collection of Old
        Popular Standard Favorites. New York: Remick,
        c1959. OCLC # 12432900.

RDF   Simon, William L. Reader's Digest Family
        Songbook of Faith and Joy: 129 All-Time
        Inspirational Favorites. Pleasantville, NY:
        Reader's Digest Association, 1991 (c1975).
        OCLC # 1831239.

RDT   Simon, William L. Reader's Digest Treasury of
        Best Loved Songs: 114 All-Time Family Favorites.
        Pleasantville, NY: Reader's Digest Association,
        c1972. OCLC # 794866.

Re   Wellman, Manly Wade. The Rebel Songster:
        Songs the Confederates Sang. Charlotte, NC:
        Heritage House, c1959. OCLC # 926439.

ReG   Gershwin, George. Rediscovered Gershwin:
        Piano/Vocal. Secaucus, NJ: Warner Bros.
        Publications, c1991. OCLC # 24228179.

RF   Dett, Robert Nathaniel. Religious Folk-Songs of
        the Negro As Sung at Hampton Institute.
        Hampton, VA: Hampton Institute Press, 1927.
        OCLC # 1867958.

RJ   Roto, Nino. Romeo & Juliet Souvenir Music
        Album. Miami Beach, FL: Charles Hansen,
        1968. OCLC # 14362680.

RM   Friml, Charles Rudolf. Rose-Marie: A Musical
        Play. New York: Harms, c1925. OCLC #
        3056979.

Ro   Bock, Jerry. The Rothschilds: Vocal Selections.
        New York: New York Times Music Corp., c1970.
        OCLC # 4885904.

RoE   Romantic Encounters. New York: Ekay Music,
        c1989. OCLC # 20647370.

RoS   Rolling Stones. Rolling Stones Complete.
        London: Omnibus Press, c1981. OCLC #
        9079474.

RS   Simeone, Harry. Rise and Shine: Two-Part
        Songs. Delaware Water Gap, PA: Shawnee
        Press, c1960. OCLC # 10127952.

RSC   Pressman, Aron. Russian Songs for Colleges,
        As Sung at Middlebury College Russian Summer
        School. New York: Pitman, c1956. OCLC #
        7295501.

RSL   Nocera, Sona D. Reaching the Special Learner
        through Music. Morristown, NJ: Silver Burdett
        Co., c1979. OCLC # 5212372.

RSW   Regier, Don. Rails, Sails, and Wagon Trails: For
        2 Part General Music or Teen Age Chorus. Park
        Ridge, IL: Neil A. Kjos Music Co., c1963.
        OCLC
        # 5469658.

RT4   Remember These: Movie Songs of the 40's.
        New York: Big 3 Music Corp., 1971? OCLC #
        3472171.

RT5   Remember These: Movie Songs of the 50's. New
        York: Big 3 Music Corp., 1966? OCLC #
        3472186.

RT6   Remember These: Movie Songs of the 60's. New
        York: Big 3 Music Corp., 1969? OCLC #
        3472274.

RTH   Logan, William Augustus. Road to Heaven:
        Twenty-Eight Negro Spirituals. University, AL:
        University of Alabama Press, 1955. OCLC #
        983046.

RuS   Silverman, Jerry. Russian Songs: Forty
        Contemporary and Traditional Songs in
        Russian and English. New York: Oak
        Publications, c1966. OCLC # 1282336.

RV   Damsker, Matt. Rock Voices: The Best Lyrics of
        an Era. New York: St. Martin's Press, c1980.
        OCLC # 6533095.

RW   Wolfe, Richard. Richard Wolfe's Legit
        Professional Fake Book: More Than 1010
        Songs. New York: Big 3 Music Corporation,
        1978? OCLC # 5088698.

RY   Rock, Yesterday and Today. New York: Big 3
        Music Corp., 1974? OCLC # 6587278.

RYT   Rock, Yesterday and Today: Guitar. New York:
        Big 3 Music Corp., 1975. OCLC # 12496587.

SA   Colcord, Joanna Carver. Songs of American
        Sailormen. New York: Oak Publications, 1964.
        OCLC # 1573303.

SAC   Superior Arrangements for the Christmas Season:
        For All Organs. Miami Beach, FL: Hansen,
        c1963. OCLC # 8204737.

SAm   Scott, Thomas Jefferson. Sing of America: Folk
        Tunes. New York: Crowell, c1947. OCLC #
        931929.

SAR   Rabson, Carolyn. Songbook of the American
        Revolution. Peaks Island, ME: NEO Press,
        c1974. OCLC # 1022830.

SaS   White, Alice Margaret Geddes. The Saucy Sailor
        and Other Dramatized Ballads. New York: E.P.
        Dutton, 1940. OCLC # 2928135.

SB   Kern, Jerome. Show Boat. New York: T.B.
        Harms Co., c1927. OCLC # 949439.

SBA   Moore, Frank. _Songs and Ballads of the_
American Revolution. Port Washington, NY:
Kennikat Press, 1964 (c1855). OCLC # 998370.

SBB   Brander, Michael. _Scottish and Border Battles_
and Ballads. New York: C.N. Potter, 1976. OCLC
1991146.

SBF   Choate, Robert A. _Sound, Beat, and Feeling._
New York: American Book Co., c1972. OCLC #
824470.

SBJ   _Sing and Be Joyful: Chapel Songbook._
Washington, D.C: The Chaplain, U.S. Marine
Corps, 1975? OCLC # 2214357.

SBS   Schiff, Ronny S. _The Sherman Brothers_
Songbook. Milwaukee, WI: Hal Leonard Pub.
Corp., c1991. OCLC # 25106723.

SC   Coleman. Cy. _Vocal Selections from Sweet_
Charity. New York: Notable Music Co., c1969.
OCLC # 2946365.

SCa   Scarborough, Dorothy. _A Song Catcher in_
Southern Mountains: American Folk Songs of
British Ancestry. New York: Columbia University
Press, c1937. OCLC # 1333752.

SCL   Association for Childhood Education
International. _Songs Children Like: Folk Songs_
from Many Lands. Washington, DC: The
Association, c1958. OCLC # 3265601.

SCo   Harwell, Richard Barksdale. _Songs of the_
Confederacy. New York: Broadcast Music,
c1951. OCLC # 7507544.

SCS   Illinois Braille and Sight-Saving School,
Jacksonville, IL. _Selected Christmas Songs._
Louisville, KY: American Printing House for the
Blind, 1960. OCLC # 3954229.

SD   Dubsky, Dora. _Sing and Dance: Original_
Children's Songs and Dances for Home and
School. New York: Stephen Daye Press, c1955.
OCLC # 1670419.

SE   Wright, Robert L. _Swedish Emigrant Ballads._
Lincoln, NE: University of Nebraska Press, 1965.
OCLC # 330307.

SeS   Hopekirk, Helen. _Seventy Scottish Songs._ New
York: Dover, c1992 (1905). OCLC # 25051348.

SF   Davis, James Houston. _Song Folio._ New York:
Peer International Corp., c1942. OCLC #
12497512.

SFB   Simeone, Harry. _Songfest: For the Beginning_
Four-Part Chorus. Delaware Water Gap, PA:
Shawnee Press, c1956. OCLC # 2804086.

SFF   Carawan, Guy. _Sing for Freedom: The Story of_
the Civil Rights Movement through Its Songs.
Bethlehem, PA: Sing Out Corp., c1990. OCLC
22812178.

SFM   Berger, Melvin. _The Story of Folk Music._ New

York: S.G. Phillips, c1976. OCLC # 2284093.

SG   Thomas, Jeannette Bell. _The Singin' Gatherin':_
Tunes from the Southern Appalachians. New
York: Silver Burdett, c1939. OCLC # 268126.

SGT   Elder, Jacob D. _Song Games from Trinidad and_
Tobago. N.p.: American Folklore Society, 1965
(c1962). OCLC # 477222.

Sh   Geld, Gary. _Shenandoah._ Vocal score. New
York: E.H. Morris, c1977. OCLC # 3250729.

SHP   _Songs and Hymns for Primary Children._
Philadelphia, PA: Westminster Press, c1963.
OCLC # 927667.

SHS   Walker, William. _The Southern Harmony_
Songbook. New York: Hastings House, c1939
(1854). OCLC # 1485660.

SI   Silber, Irwin. _Songs of Independence._
Harrisburg, PA: Stackpole Books, c1973.
OCLC # 765599.

SiB   Gearhart, Livingston. _A Singing Bee: Two-Part_
Songs for Treble Voices. Delaware Water Gap,
PA: Shawnee Press, c1956. OCLC # 2478430.

SiM   Kjelson, Lee. _The Singer's Manual of Choral_
Music Literature. Melville, NY: Belwin Mills
Pub. Corp., c1973. OCLC # 1910387.

Sin   Glass, Paul. _Singing Soldiers: The Spirit of the_
Sixties: A History of the Civil War in Song.
New York: Grosset & Dunlap, 1968 (c1964).
OCLC # 512144.

SiP   Bantock, Sir Granville. _Sixty Patriotic Songs of All_
Nations. New York: C.H. Ditson & Co., c1913.
OCLC # 1727573.

SiR   Pitts, Lilla Belle. _Singing and Rhyming._ Boston,
MA: Ginn, c1950. OCLC # 1186543.

SiS   Heaps, Willard Allison. _The Singing Sixties: The_
Spirit of Civil War Days Drawn from the Music
of the Times. Norman, OK: University of
Oklahoma Press, 1960. OCLC # 1021189.

SJ   Thalman, Norman. _Songs of Joy through the_
Church Year. Philadelphia, PA: Fortress Press,
c1963. OCLC # 2354535.

SL   Armitage, Marie Teresa. _Senior Laurel Songs for_
High Schools. Boston, MA: Birchard, c1926.
OCLC # 400848.

SLB   Marrone, Sandy. _The St. Louis Blues and Other_
Song Hits of 1914. New York: Dover, c1990.
OCLC # 20755683.

SLS   _Songs of Louisiana State University._ Baton
Rouge, LA: Louisiana State University Student
Council, c1949. OCLC # 5590806.

SM   Rodgers, Richard. _The Sound of Music: A_
Musical Play. New York: Random House,
c1960. OCLC # 411455.

SMa   Surette, Thomas Whitney. <u>Songs from Many Lands</u>. Boston, MA: Houghton Mifflin, c1937. OCLC # 1368127.

SMW   Adler, Kurt Herbert. <u>Songs of Many Wars: From the Sixteenth to the Twentieth Century</u>. New York: Howell, Soskin, 1943. OCLC # 686641.

SMY   Tobitt, Janet Evelyn. <u>Sing Me Your Song, O!</u> New York: Janet E. Tobitt, c1941. OCLC # 2587026.

SN   Wright, Robert Craig. <u>Song of Norway: An Operetta</u>. New York: Chappell, c1951. OCLC # 4587159.

SNS   Tinsley, Vallie. <u>Some Negro Songs Heard on the Hills of North Louisiana</u>. Thesis. Baton Rouge, LA: Louisiana State University, 1928. OCLC # 10887202.

SNZ   Freedman, Sam. <u>Songs of New Zealand: Maori Music, a Complete Collection of Maori Favorites</u>. Wellington, NZ: Seven Seas, c1964. OCLC # 1356628.

SoC   Thorp, Nathan Howard. <u>Songs of the Cowboys</u>. New York: C.N. Potter, 1966. OCLC # 711616.

SoF   Davison, Archibald Thompson. <u>Songs of Freedom</u>. Boston, MA: Houghton Mifflin, 1942. OCLC # 1599538.

SoH   <u>Soul Hits of the 70's: Piano, Vocal, Guitar</u>. Milwaukee, WI: Hal Leonard, c1992. OCLC # 26566098.

SoM   Ward-Steinman, David. <u>The Song of Moses</u>. Vocal score. San Diego, CA: San Diego State College Press, c1968. OCLC # 613143.

SOO   Pitts, Lilla Belle. <u>Singing on Our Way</u>. Boston, MA: Ginn, c1949. OCLC # 5164512.

SoP   Shumate, Aura Medford. <u>Songs for the Pre-School Age, for Use in the Sunday School, Home and Kindergarten</u>. Nashville, TN: Broadman Press, c1947. OCLC # 12433331.

SOT   Rhys-Herbert, William. <u>Sylvia: A Pastoral Operetta in Two Acts</u>. New York: J. Fischer, c1906. OCLC # 4871453.

SOW1   <u>Songs of Worship: A Collection of Sacred Songs for the Church Soloist</u>. Vol 1. Bryn Mawr, PA: Presser Co., c1949. OCLC # 12432930.

SOW2   <u>Songs of Worship: A Collection of Sacred Songs for the Church Soloist</u>. Vol. 2. Bryn Mawr, PA: Presser Co., c1949. OCLC # 12432930.

SP   Rodgers, Richard. <u>South Pacific: A Musical Play</u>. New York: Williamson Music, c1949. OCLC # 655816.

SpS   <u>Spiritual Songs: Carl Andersen's Play by Numbers Chord Organ Book</u>. Miami Beach, FL: Hansen House, c1976. OCLC # 12748516.

SR   Bradley, S.A.J. <u>Sixty Ribald Songs from Pills to Purge Melancholy</u>. New York: Praeger, c1967. OCLC # 1351494.

SRE 1   <u>Songs Recorded by Elvis Presley: Voice, Piano, Guitar</u>. Vol. 1. New York: Big 3 Music Corp., 1968. OCLC # 3044395.

SRE 2   <u>Songs Recorded by Elvis Presley: Voice, Piano, Guitar</u>. Vol 2. New York: Big 3 Music Corp., 1968. OCLC # 3044395.

SRS   Aidman, Charles. <u>Spoon River Song Album</u>. New York: Warner Brothers Publications, 1964? OCLC # 8225373.

SS   <u>Sacred Songs You Enjoy: All Portable Chord Organs Starting With Treble Key C</u>. Boston, MA: Boston Music Co., c1960. OCLC # 12129501.

SSA   Weill, Kurt. <u>Street Scene: An American Opera</u>. New York: Chappell, c1948. OCLC # 245588.

SSB   Chambers, Herbert Arthur. <u>A Shakespeare Song Book</u>. London: Blandford Press, c1957. OCLC # 1671799.

SSe   Bruderhof Communities. <u>Sing through the Seasons: Ninety-Nine Songs for Children</u>. Rifton, NY: Plough Publishing House, c1972. OCLC # 873425.

SSF   Foster, Stephen Collins. <u>Songs of Stephen Foster</u>. Prepared for schools and general use. Pittsburgh, PA: University of Pittsburgh Press, 1953 (c1938). OCLC # 4377122.

SSFo   Foster, Stephen Collins. <u>The Songs of Stephen Foster</u>. Edited by Albert E. Wier. New York: Harcourt, Brace and Co., 1935. OCLC # 1700009.

SSN   Sourire, Sister. <u>The Songs of the Singing Nun</u>. New York: General Music Co., c1963. OCLC # 8401350.

SSo   Niles, John Jacob. <u>Singing Soldiers</u>. Detroit, MI: Singing Tree Press, 1968 (c1927). OCLC # 2928643.

SSP   Kines, Tom. <u>Songs from Shakespeare's Plays, and Popular Songs of Shakespeare's Times</u>. New York: Oak Publications, c1964. OCLC # 899670.

SSS   Brand, Oscar. <u>Songs of 76: A Folksinger's History of the Revolution</u>. New York: M. Evans, c1972. OCLC # 740722.

ST   Friml, Charles Rudolf. <u>Some Time: A Musical Romance in Two Acts</u>. New York: G. Schirmer, c1946. OCLC # 4202837.

Sta   Lee, Marshall. <u>Stardust: Music for Great Song Hits of the 1920's-50's</u>. New York: H.N. Abrams, c1990. OCLC # 21039479.

STP   <u>Songs to Play and Sing for Portable Chord</u>

Organs. New York: Fox Pub. Co., c1959. OCLC # 12433044.

STR   Songs to Remember. New York: Hansen House, c1976. OCLC # 10119202.

STS   Coleman, Satis Narrona. Singing Time: Songs for Nursery and School. New York: John Day, c1929. OCLC # 8276060.

STW   Sweet Adelines, Inc. Singing on Top of the World: 18 Arrangements in Barbershop Style for Women's Voices. New York: Robbins Music Corporation, c1968. OCLC # 3464663.

Su   Kern, Jerome. Sunny: A Musical Comedy in Two Acts. New York: Harms, 1934. OCLC # 6384743.

SUH   Block, Leon. Sing unto Him: For Guitar. New York: Valley, c1963. OCLC # 12029512.

SuS   Kristofferson, Kris. Sunlight and Shadows. New York: Chappell, 1972. OCLC # 7799186.

Sw   Herbert, Victor. Sweethearts: A Comic Opera in Two Acts. New York: Schirmer, c1941. OCLC # 774012.

SWF   Fowke, Edith Fulton. Songs of Work and Freedom. Chicago, IL: Roosevelt University, c1960. OCLC # 1805721.

SwS   Lennon, John. John Lennon and Paul McCartney's Sweet Sixteen. Miami Beach, FL: Hansen Publications, 1969. OCLC # 12442325.

SY   Jordan, Philip Dillon. Songs of Yesterday: A Song Anthology of American Life. Garden City, NY: Doubleday, Doran, c1941. OCLC # 1013255.

SYB   Benton, Gene. Sure As You're Born: A Musical Revue. New York: Williamson Music, c1967. OCLC # 21240816.

T   Whitcomb, Ian. Tin Pan Alley: A Pictorial History (1919-1939) with Complete Words and Music of Forty Songs. New York: Paddington Press, 1975. OCLC # 1119487.

TB   Poling, Daniel Alfred. A Treasury of Best-Loved Hymns with Their Stories. New York: Pickwick Press, c1942. OCLC # 1477922.

TBF   Cox, John Harrington. Traditional Ballads and Folk-Songs Mainly from West Virginia. N.p.: American Folklore Society, c1964. OCLC # 641947.

TF   Birchard, Clarence C. Twice 55 Community Songs: The Green Book. Evanston, IL: Summy-Birchard Pub. Co., c1930. OCLC # 8249666.

TFC   Orbison, Roy. 24 Classic Hits. Miami, FL: Columbia Pictures Publications, c1988. OCLC # 19255061.

TG   Rodgers, Richard. The Theatre Guild Presents

Carousel, a Musical Play. New York: Williamson Music Corp., c1945. OCLC # 655476.

TGO   Rodgers, Richard. The Theatre Guild Presents Oklahoma!, a Musical Play. New York: Williamson Music Corp., c1943. OCLC # 9563818.

TH   Kwalwasser, Jacob. Two Hundred Songs for Junior and Senior High School. Atlanta, GA: Smith, Hammond, c1929. OCLC # 9428012.

THN   Lane, John. Top Hits of 1967 and Great Standards. New York: Robbins Music Corp., c1967. OCLC # 8622490.

TI1   This Is the Ultimate Fake Book. Vol. 1, It Contains Over 1200 Songs for Piano, Organ, Guitar, and All "C" Instruments. Winona, MN: Hal Leonard, 1981. OCLC # 13736741.

TI2   This Is the Ultimate Fake Book. Vol. 2, It Contains Over 800 Songs for Piano, Vocal, Guitar, Electronic Keyboards, and All "C" Instruments. Winona, MN: Hal Leonard Pub. Corp., 1985. OCLC # 13736741.

TM   Hansen, Susan. This Is My Wedding Day: The Deluxe Book of Wedding Music. New York: C. Hansen, c1970. OCLC # 5974506.

TMA   Ford, Ira W. Traditional Music of America. New York: E.P. Dutton, c1940. OCLC # 1262274.

TO   The Weavers. Travelin' On with the Weavers. New York: Harper & Row, 1966. OCLC # 1387764.

TOC 82   The Top 100 Country of 1982. Hialeah, FL: Columbia Pictures Publications, 1982. OCLC # 11146532.

TOC 83   The Top 100 Country of 1983. Hialeah, FL: Columbia Pictures Publications, 1983. OCLC # 10854101.

TOF   Manilow, Barry. This One's for You. New York: Kamakazi Music Corp., 1976. OCLC # 3397817.

TOH   The Top 100 Country of 1980. Hialeah, FL: Columbia Pictures Publications, 1980. OCLC # 7510736.

TOM   The Top 100 Movie Themes. Hialeah, FL: Columbia Pictures Publications, 1982. OCLC # 9583215.

ToO 76   The Top 100 of 1976. Hialeah, FL: Columbia Pictures Publications, 1976. OCLC # 3349780.

ToO 79   The Top 100 of 1979. Hialeah, FL: Columbia Pictures Publications, 1979. OCLC # 6741116.

ToS   Torch Songs: A Collection of Sultry Jazz and Big Band Standards. Milwaukee, WI: H. Leonard Pub. Corp., 1991. OCLC # 24146352.

TP   Hamlisch, Marvin. They're Playing Our Song: Vocal Selections. New York: Chappell, c1979. OCLC # 7548099.

Tr   Traditional Gospel. Winona, MN: Hal Leonard, c1986. OCLC # 19081999.

TRR   Top Rock 'n' Roll Hits of the 60's: Piano, Vocal, Guitar/Billboard. Milwaukee, WI: Hal Leonard Pub. Corp., c1992. OCLC # 25363822.

TS   Hart, Dorothy. Thou Swell, Thou Witty: The Life and Lyrics of Lorenz Hart. New York: Harper & Row, c1976. OCLC # 2090827.

TT   McKuen, Rod. Twenty-Three Rod McKuen Songs. New York: Stanyan Music Co., c1968. OCLC # 8982019.

TTH   Top 200 of 1986-87 Fake Book for All Keyboards: 200 Great Songs. Miami, FL: Columbia Pictures Publications, 1986. OCLC # 18269132.

TV   Olsen, David C. 1983/1984 T.V. Songbook. Hialeah, FL: Columbia Pictures Publications, c1983. OCLC # 10556406.

TVT   TV Theme Book: A Musical History of Television, 1948 to Present. Secaucus, NJ: Warner Bros. Publications, 1985. OCLC # 13292893.

TW   Their Words Are Music: The Great Theatre Lyricists and Their Lyrics. New York: Crown, c1975. OCLC # 1583978.

TWD   Those Were the Days: Pop, Rock, Folk, Broadway, Jazz Hits. Ft. Lauderdale, FL: TRO Songways Service, 1990? OCLC # 23450911.

TWS   Campbell, Colin and Murphy, Allan. Things We Said Today: The Complete Lyrics and a Concordance to the Beatles' Songs, 1962-1970. Ann Arbor, MI: Pierian Press, c1980. OCLC # 7036049.

U   Ulverscroft Large Print Song Book. Revised and enlarged edition. Leicestershire, Eng.: F.A. Thorpe, c1974. OCLC # 4352892.

UBF   The Ultimate Broadway Fake Book: Over 625 Songs from Over 195 Shows: For Piano, Vocal, Guitar, Electronic Keyboards and All "C" Instruments. Winona, MN: Hal Leonard Pub. Corp., 198?. OCLC # 19334761.

UF   Botsford, Florence Hudson. The Universal Folk Songster for Home, School, and Community. New York: G. Schirmer, c1937. OCLC # 173435.

UFB   This Is the Ultimate Fake Book: It Contains Over 1200 Songs. N.p.: Hal Leonard, c1981. OCLC # 8073471.

V   Styne, Jule. Vocal Selections from Lorelei. New York: Consolidated Music, c1974. OCLC # 3389584.

VA   Wolfe, Irving. Voices of America. Chicago, IL: Follett, c1963. OCLC # 1087597.

VB   The Very Best of Contemporary Christian Words and Music: A Collection of Over 375 Songs for Piano, Vocal, Guitar, Organ, and All "C" Instruments. Winona, MN: Hal Leonard Pub. Corp., 1986? OCLC # 15306157.

VK   Friml, Charles Rudolf. The Vagabond King: A Musical Play. New York: Famous Music Corp., c1930. OCLC # 9186103.

VP   Mulcahy, Michael. The Voice of the People: Songs and History of Ireland. Dublin: O'Brien Press, 1982. OCLC # 9539178.

VS   Dane, Barbara. The Vietnam Songbook: More Than 100 Songs from the American and International Protest Movements and Fighting Songs of the Vietnamese People. New York: Guardian, 1969. OCLC # 409078.

VSA   Strouse, Charles. Vocal Selections from Applause. New York: Strada Music, c1970. OCLC # 6588038.

W   Coleman, Cy. Wildcat: A Musical Comedy. New York: Morley Music Co., c1964. OCLC # 2364473.

WA   The Who Anthology. Winona, MN: Hal Leonard Pub., 1981. OCLC # 8364703.

WD   Sherman, Richard M. Walt Disney's Mary Poppins: The Complete Musical Score. New York: Hansen, c1964. OCLC # 6557885.

WDS   Donaldson, Walter. The Walter Donaldson Songbook. Winona, MN: Hal Leonard Publishing Corp., c1988. OCLC # 20504773.

WF   The World's Funniest Songbook. Katonah, NY: Ekay Music, c1990. OCLC # 22871298.

WG   The World's Greatest Piano Book. Greenwich, CT: Cherry Lane Music Co., c1979. OCLC # 6226664.

WGB/O   World's Greatest Book of Wedding Songs. All organ. Miami Beach, FL: Hansen House, 1982. OCLC # 10192094.

WGB/P   World's Greatest Book of Wedding Songs. Piano/ vocal. Miami Beach, FL: Hansen House, 1980. OCLC # 7647653.

Wi   Smalls, Charlie. The Wiz: The New Musical Version of the Wonderful Wizard of Oz. Los Angeles, CA: Fox Fanfare Music, c1975. OCLC # 1850663.

WiS7   Wier, Albert Ernest. The Scribner Music Library. Vol. VII, Songs from the Operas; Sacred Music; Vocal and Piano. New York: Scribner, 1955. OCLC # 998554.

WiS8   Wier, Albert Ernest. The Scribner Music Library. Vol. VIII, Favorite Songs of Every Character,

Vocal. New York: Scribner, 1955. OCLC # 998554.

WiS9   Wier, Albert Ernest. The Scribner Music Library. Vol. IX, Supplementary Compositions, Piano and Vocal. New York: Scribner, 1955. OCLC # 998554.

WN   Jackson, George Pullen. White and Negro Spirituals. New York: J.J. Augustin, c1944. OCLC # 403638.

WNF   Fowler, Lane Nelson. Willie Nelson Family Album. Amarillo, TX: H.M. Poirot Company, 1980. OCLC # 6890678.

WO   Arlen, Harold. The Wizard of Oz: Vocal Selections. Los Angeles, CA: United Artists, c1968. OCLC # 6181097.

WS   Siegmeister, Elie. Work and Sing: A Collection of the Songs That Built America. New York: W.R. Scott, c1944. OCLC # 1707225.

WSB   The Weavers. The Weavers' Song Book. New York: Harper, 1960. OCLC # 16690787.

WU   Siegmeister, Elie. 'Way Up on Old Smoky: Songs of Mountain Folk, Cowboy Music, Play Party Tunes, Work Songs, Spirituals, Blues, Campus Melodies, Love Songs, Ballads.

Chosen and arranged for girls' and women's voices. Boston, MA: Ginn, c1950. OCLC # 4038164.

WW   Alloy, Evelyn. Working Women's Music: The Songs and Struggles of Women in the Cotton Mills, Textile Plants, and Needle Trades. Somerville, MA: New England Free Press, c1976. OCLC # 4446939.

Y   Simeone, Harry. Youth Sings at Christmas: Two- and Three-Part Songs for Teen Age Choral Groups. Delaware Water Gap, PA: Shawnee Press, c1960. OCLC # 12433134.

YC   Bozyan, H. Frank. The Yale Carol Book. New Haven, CT: Yale University Press, c1944. OCLC # 1358576.

YG   Gesner, Clark. You're a Good Man, Charlie Brown: A Musical Entertainment. Mamaroneck, NY: Jeremy Music, c1972. OCLC # 14004682.

YL   Friml, Charles Rudolf. You're in Love: A Musical Play in Two Acts. New York: Schirmer, c1917. OCLC # 8533731.

YS   Simeone, Harry. Youth Sings: Two- and Three-Part Songs for Teen-Age Choral Groups. Delaware Water Gap, PA: Shawnee Press, c1954. OCLC # 4359510.

SONG TITLES

A

AAF Ground Crew Song
GO-W

A & P Grocery Store Jingle see Big Red Team

ABC
NF-W

ABC Monday Night Baseball Theme No. 3 see Slugger Theme

ABC Tumble Down D
MH-W,M

ABC's of Love
ILF-W,M MF-W,M

A.R.U.
AL-W AFP-W

A.S.T.P.
GI-W

A Atocha Va Una Nina
LA-W,M (Spanish)

A Banda
BHB-M LaS-M

A Cada Instante Te Miro
LA-W,M (Spanish)

A Cantar A Una Nina
LA-W,M (Spanish)

A-Caroling We Go
BCh-W,M

A Dieu Seul Soit Honneur
Boo-W,M (French Only)

A Ce Village Ou Je Restais
CaF-W (French Only)

A-Gardening We Will Go
CSS-W

A-Goin' Shout
AFP-W

A-Hunting We Will Go
BBF-W,M CSG-W,M CSo-W,M
HS-W,M OTJ-W,M TH-W,M

A-Hunting We Will Go see also O A-Hunting We Will Go

A Is for Apple Pie
Oz4-W

A La Bien Aimee
AmH-M

A La Claire Fontaine
CFS-W,M (French) Ch-W (French Only) CUP-W,M (French Only)
FW-W (French) MP-W,M

(French Only) OTJ-W,M (French Only)

A La Lac Arthur
CaF-W (French Only)

A La Maison
CaF-W (French Only)

A La Peche Des Moules
FSF-W (French)

A La Puerto Del Cielo
HS-W,M (Spanish)

A La Volette
MP-W,M (French Only) TO-W,M

A Los Arboles Altos
ESB-W,M (Spanish Only)

A Media Luz
LaS-M

A Paris
CE-W,M (French)

A Paris Y A-t-eine Fille
CaF-W (French Only)

A Piao
LA-W,M (Spanish)

A Pombinha Voou
LA-W,M (Spanish)

A-Ridin' Old Paint
GuC-W,M

A-Rockin' All Night
MAS-W,M

A-Roving
CSo-W,M FW-W HS-W,M IL-W,M
LH-W,M OTJ-W,M RSW-W,M
SA-W,M SL-W,M

A Solis Ortus Cardine
GUM2-W,M (Latin)

A-Tisket, A-Tasket
GG1-W,M GM-W GSO-W,M
RW-W,M

A-Tisket, A-Tasket see also Green and Yellow Basket and I-Tisket, I-Tasket

A to Z
LC-W

A Veces Tu, A Veces Yo
TI1-W,M (Spanish Only) YFB-W,M (Spanish Only)

A You're Adorable
MF-W,M

Aba Daba Honeymoon
GSN1-W,M HLS1-W,M RW-W,M
SLB-W,M STW-W,M

Abalone
GeS-W,M NeA-W,M

Abalone Song
ATS-W,M

Abdallah Kansas
CoS-W,M

Abdul Abulbul Amir
ATS-W HAS-W,M

Abdul the Bulbul Ameer
FW-W GI-W GO-W,M OTJ-W,M

Abdullah Bulbul Amir
BF-W,M, FGM-W,M

Abe Lincoln
ATS-W

Abe of Illinois
LMR-W,M

Abe-iad
Sin-W,M SY-W,M

Abelachao
JF-W,M (Spanish)

Abends
AS-W,M (German)

Abide in Me, O Lord
AME-W,M

Abide in Me, O Lord, and I in Thee
AHO-W,M

Abide Not in the Realm of Dreams
AHO-W,M

Abide with Me
AME-W,M AmH-W,M ASB6-W,M
BNG-W,M Bo-W,M CEM-W,M
CSo-W,M DC-W,M ESB-W,M
FH-W,M FM-W,M FWS-W,M
GH-W,M HF-W,M HLS7-W,M
HSD-W,M IH-M JBF-W,M
MAB1-W MF-W,M MSA1-W,M
NAS-W,M PoG-W,M RDF-W,M
RW-W,M SFB-W,M SL-W,M
TB-W,M TF-W,M TH-W,M U-W
WiS7-W,M

Abide with Me, Fast Falls the Eventide
Hy-W,M

Abiding Love

BSG-W,M BSP-W,M JBF-W,M
Abie's White Mule
  BMM-W
Abilene
  FG2-W,M FW-W
Abolition Show
  FHR-W,M
Abolitionist Hymn
  SWF-W,M
Abortive Van Buren Convention
  MPP-W
About a Quarter to Nine
  HFH-W,M MF-W,M T-W,M
About Savannah
  SBA-W
About the Emigration
  SE-W (Swedish)
Above It All
  OGR-W,M
Above the Clouds
  ELO-W,M
Above the Storm
  VB-W,M
Above the World the Winter Stars
  SHP-W,M
Abraham
  WiS9-W,M
Abraham Lincoln
  MH-W,M
Abraham, Martin and John
  AAP-W,M OTJ-W,M TI1-W,M
  UFB-W,M
Abraham the Great and General
  Grant His Mate
  SiS-W
Abraham's Daughter
  Sin-W,M SiS-W,M
Abraham's Draft
  SiS-W
Abram Brown
  SA-W,M
Abrazame
  TI1-W,M (Spanish Only)
  UFB-W,M (Spanish Only)
Absence Makes the Heart Grow
  Fonder
  BH-W,M EFS-W,M
Absence of Malice (Theme)
  TOM-M
Absent-Minded Serenade
  SL-W,M
Absolutely Right
  MCG-W,M
Abundantly Able to Save
  GH-W,M
Acadian Boatman's Song
  AAF-W,M (French Only)
Acapoulco Polka
  TI1-W,M UFB-W,M
Ac-cent-tchu-ate the Positive
  Mo-W,M NM-W,M OTJ-W,M
  OTO-W TI2-W,M
Accentuate the Positive
  OHF-W
Accept Our Praise
  TH-W,M
Acceptable Tribute
  GrM-W,M
According to My Lord's Command
  MoM-W
According to Thy Gracious Word
  AME-W,M Hy-W,M OM-W,M
Ace in the Hole
  HC1-W,M OAP-W,M TI1-W,M
  UBF-W,M
Ach! Du Lieber Augustin
  FW-W (German Only) HS-W,M

(German) OTJ-W,M (German
  Only)
Ach Ja
  HS-W,M
Ach Kinder Wollt Ihr Lieben
  AHO-W,M (German)
Ach Synku
  IF-W,M (Czech)
Acid Queen
  WA-W,M
Acordei De Madrugada
  LA-W,M (Spanish)
Acquisition of Louisiana
  MPP-W,M OHG-W,M
Acres of Clams
  FG2-W,M FW-W OTJ-W,M
  SWF-W,M
Acres of Diamonds
  HLS7-W,M
Across the Alley from the Alamo
  TI1-W,M UFB-W,M
Across the Border
  ELO-W,M
Across the Field
  Mo-W,M TI2-W,M
Across the Fields
  OHO-W,M
Across the Hall
  Oz3-W,M
Across the Sea
  GOB-W,M GSF-W,M
Across the Universe
  BBe-W,M Be2-W,M TWS-W
Across the Western Ocean
  FW-W RW-W,M SA-W,M
Across the Wide Missouri
  see Shenandoah
Act Naturally
  CMG-W,M
Act One
  TW-W
Adam
  RS-W,M
Adam and Eve
  ATS-W ESU-W FSO-W,M (French)
Adam Catched Eve
  Boo-W,M
Adam Et Eve
  FSO-W,M (French)
Adam in de Garden Pinnin' Leaves
  BDW-W,M
Adam in the Garden Pinning
  Leaves
  FW-W
Adam Lay Ybounden
  OB-W,M
Adams and Liberty
  AH-W,M BC1-W,M ESU-W
  MPP-W,M OHG-W,M SAR-W,M
Adam's Fall
  SI-W
Adam's Fall see also Trip to
  Cambridge
Addams Family
  MF-W,M
Addie's at It Again
  Mo-W,M NM-W,M OTO-W
Addir Hu
  JS-W,M (Hebrew)
Address for All
  SHS-W,M
Address of the Women to the
  Southern Troops
  SiS-W
Address to the Journeymen
  Cordwainers L.B. of Philadelphia
  AL-W

Ad-dressing of Cats
  UBF-W,M
Adelaide's Lament
  TW-W UBF-W,M
Adelita
  ATS-W,M FW-W (Spanish)
  LaS-W,M (Spanish Only)
Adeste Fideles
  DC-W,M ESB-W,M (Latin) FW-W
  GBC-W,M (Latin) GC-W,M
  HS-W,M (Latin) IL-W,M JOC-W,M
  LTL-W,M (Latin) MAS-W,M (Latin)
  OPS-W PoG-W,M PoS-W,M
  (Latin Only) SHP-W,M TI1-W,M
Adeste Fideles see also Come All
  Ye Faithful and O Come All Ye
  Faithful
Adieu
  BSC-W
Adieu Dundee
  SeS-W,M
Adieu La Fleur De Ma Jeunesse
  CaF-W (French Only)
Adieu Sweet Amarillis
  Boo-W,M MU-W,M
Adieu 'Tis Love's Last Greeting
  HSD-W,M
Adieu to Cold Weather
  BSC-W
Adieu to Dark Weather
  Oz4-W,M
Adieu to Dear Cambria
  SoF-W,M
Adieu to the Star-Spangled Banner
  for Ever
  SiS-W
Adios
  TOM-W,M (Spanish Only)
Adios, Au Revoir, Auf Wiedersehn
  TI1-W,M
Adios Muchachos
  LaS-M MF-M TI1-M UFB-M
Adios Te Digo
  MHB-W,M (Spanish)
Adir Hu
  SBJ-W,M (Hebrew)
Adiuva Nos Deus
  Boo-W,M (Latin Only)
Admiral Walks His Quarterdeck
  GO-W
Adon Olom
  Bo-W,M (Hebrew Only) JS-W,M
  (Hebrew) SBJ-W,M (Hebrew
  Only)
Adonai
  VB-W,M
Adonoy, Adonoy
  JS-W,M (Hebrew Only)
Adonoy, Moh Odom
  JS-W,M (Hebrew Only)
Adoramus Te (Gasparini)
  SiM-W,M (Latin)
Adoramus Te (Lasso)
  MMW-W,M (Latin)
Adoration
  JS-W,M (Hebrew)
Adresse Aux Maries see Une
  Adresse Aux Maries
Adulterations
  ESU-W
Advent Candles
  GBC-W,M
Adventure
  DR-W,M MML-W,M
Adventures in Paradise (Theme)
  GTV-W,M
Advice

ASB5-W,M
Aeroplane
  MH-W,M SiR-W,M
Aeroplane Song
  BMM-W
**Aesthete on Clark Street see
  Esthete on Clark Street**
Aeterna California
  Fif-W,M
Afar Yet Near
  FSA1-W,M
Affair at Newport
  SSS-W,M
Affair of Honor
  SBA-W
Affair of State
  IFM-W
Affair to Remember
  GG4-W,M HLS5-W,M RT5-W,M
  RW-W,M
Affection
  TTH-W,M
Affluent Society
  Mo-W,M NM-W,M OTO-W
Afloat on the Ocean
  ANS-W
Afrikaan Beat
  MF-M
Afskeds-Sang Till Svenska
  Emigranter
  SE-W (Swedish)
After
  GH-W,M OM-W,M
After All (Love Theme from
  Chances Are)
  BOA-W,M GSN5-W,M
After Calvary
  BSG-W,M BSP-W,M
After Five
  GOI7-M
After Hours
  TOH-W,M
After I Say I'm Sorry
  HLS2-W,M WDS-W,M
**After I Say I'm Sorry see also
  What Can I Say After I Say I'm
  Sorry**
After Midnight
  ERM-W,M MF-W,M
After Much Debate Internal
  GiS-W,M
After Sunset
  FSA2-W,M
After the Ball
  AF-W ATS-W FSN-W,M
  FSTS-W,M FWS-W,M GSN1-W,M
  HLS1-W,M MF-W,M OS-W
  OTJ-W,M RW-W,M SB-W,M
  TI1-W,M U-W UFB-W,M
  WiS9-W,M
After the Ball Is Over
  FW-W
After the Battle
  SiS-W
After the Commonweal March Is
  Over
  AL-W
After the Fox
  RW-W,M
After the Gold Rush
  DPE-W,M MF-W,M
After the Great Depression
  TOC83-W,M
After the Lights Go Down Low
  TI1-W,M UFB-W,M
After the Long Strike
  AL-W

After the Love Has Gone
  SoH-W,M ToO79-W,M
After the Lovin'
  GSN5-W,M ToO76-W,M
After the Rain
  FSA1-W,M MLS-W,M
After the Roundup
  GA-W
After the Storm
  FSA2-W,M
After the War
  SiS-W
After the War Is Over
  Oz4-W
After the Weekend
  IFM-W
After 'While
  NH-W
After You
  TOC83-W,M ToS-W,M
After You've Gone
  DJ-W,M Mo-W,M NM-W,M
  On-W,M TI2-W,M UBF-W,M
Afterglow
  FSA2-W,M
Aftermash
  TVT-M
Afternoon
  GrS-W,M
Afternoon Delight
  PoG-W,M WG-W,M
Afterwards
  AmH-W,M HSD-W,M
Afton Water
  SeS-W,M
Again
  GG3-W,M GSF-W,M HLS3-W,M
  RW-W,M
Again As Evening's Shadow Falls
  AHO-W,M Hy-W,M
Again Returns the Day of Holy
  Rest
  AME-W,M
Against All Odds
  MoA-W,M
Against the Storm
  SMW-W,M (Czech)
Against the Wind
  MF-W,M
Age
  JC-W,M
Age of Gold
  OHG-W,M
Age of India Rubber
  ESU-W
Age of Not Believing
  SBS-W,M
Ageless Dancer
  VB-W,M
Agincourt Song
  SSp-W
Agnus Dei (Bizet)
  FiS-W,M (Latin) TM-M WGB/O-M
  WiS9-W,M (Latin)
Agrarian Ball
  AL-W
Agreement, The
  Boo-W,M
Agricultural Song
  ESU-W
Ah Ca Ira
  SiP-W,M (French) SMW-W,M
  (French)
Ah! Camminare
  Mo-W,M NM-W,M OTO-W
Ah, Dearest Jesus, Holy Child
  Hy-W,M MC-W,M SHP-W,M

Ah, Grand Dieu, Que Je Suis-t-a
  Mon Aise
  CaF-W (French Only)
Ah, Holy Jesus
  SJ-W,M
Ah, Holy Jesus, How Hast Thou
  Offended
  Hy-W,M
Ah! How Sweet It Is to Love
  EL-W,M
Ah, How the Moon Is Shining
  SMY-W,M
Ah! I Have Sighed to Rest Me
  AmH-W,M HSD-W,M WiS7-W,M
Ah, It Will Go! see Ah Ca Ira
Ah, La Grand Dieu, Que Je Suis A
  Mon Aise
  CaF-W (French Only)
Ah, Leave Me Not Alone
  SL-W,M
Ah, Leave Me Not to Pine
  MGT-W,M
Ah! Lovely Appearance of Death
  AHO-W,M
Ah, Lovely Meadows
  MHB-W,M (Czech)
**Ah, Lovely Meadows see also
  Lovely Meadows**
Ah Marie
  FWS-W,M
Ah! May the Red Rose Live Alway
  FHR-W,M SSFo-W,M
Ah Me! What Perils
  Boo-W,M
Ah, Melanie
  CSD-W,M (French)
Ah! Mon Beau Chateau
  CE-W,M (French)
Ah Mon Fils
  FHR-W,M
Ah, My Heart
  GH-W,M
Ah, Paris!
  Fo-W,M OTO-W UBF-W,M
Ah, Poor Bird
  FW-W OHO-W,M OTJ-W,M
Ah! Qui Me Passera Le Bois?
  CFS-W,M (French)
Ah Roop Doop Doop
  Oz3-W
Ah! Si Mon Moine Voulait Danser
  CFS-W,M (French) FW-W (French
  Only)
Ah! So Pure
  AmH-W,M HSD-W,M MF-W,M
  OBN-W,M WiS7-W,M
Ah, Suzette, Chere
  BaB-W,M (French)
Ah! Sweet Mystery of Life
  MF-W,M
**Ah, the Apple Trees see When the
  World Was Young**
Ah! the Sighs That Come fro' My
  Heart
  OH-W,M
Ah! the Sighs That Come fro' the
  Heart
  SSP-W
Ah, the Songs of Cherubini
  Boo-W,M
Ah! Tis a Dream
  TF-W,M
Ah, Whither Should I Go
  AME-W,M
Ah Who Will Guide Me thro' the
  Wood?
  CFS-W,M (French)

Ah, Yes!
PIS-W,M
Aida (Excerpts)
LMR-W,M
Aida (Grand March)
OBN-M
Aida Triumphal March
CA-W,M
Ailie Bain o' the Glen
SeS-W,M
Aimables Catin
CaF-W (French Only)
Aimee McPherson
FW-W
Aimez Les Yeux Noirs
CaF-W (French Only)
Ain' Goin' Down to de Well No
Mo'
NeF-W
Ain' Gonna Grieve My Lord
WU-W,M
Ain't A-Gonna Do
Am-W
Ain't Dat a Shame
BH-W,M EFS-W,M
**Ain't Dat a Shame see also Ain't
That a Shame**
Ain't Dat Good News
BDW-W,M
Ain't Goin' Er Tarry Here
BDW-W,M
Ain't Going to Rain No More
Oz3-W,M
Ain't Gonna Grieve My Lord No
More
AN-W FW-W IL-W,M
Ain't Gonna Let Nobody Turn Me
Around
FW-W JF-W,M
Ain't Gonna Let Nobody Turn Me
Round
SFF-W,M
Ain't Gonna Study War No More
IL-W,M
**Ain't Gonna Study War No More
see also Going to Study War No
More, I Ain't Goin' to (Gwine)
Study War No More, and Study
War No More**
Ain't Gonna Work Tomorrow
BSo-W,M
Ain't Got Long to Stay Heah
My-W,M
Ain't Got No
H-W,M
Ain't Got No Home in This World
Anymore
AFP-W
Ain't I Glad I Got Out de
Wilderness
PoS-W,M
Ain't It a Bloody Shame
AF-W
Ain't It a Shame
FW-W Le-W,M PSN-W,M
Ain't It Amazing Grace
N-W,M
Ain't It Awful, the Heat
SSA-W,M
Ain't It Hard to Be a Nigger
NH-W
Ain't Misbehavin'
BeL-W,M DJ-W,M GSN2-W,M
TI1-W,M TTH-W,M UBF-W,M
UFB-W,M
Ain't No More Cane on This Brazos
FW-W

Ain't No Mountain High Enough
THN-W,M
Ain't No Stoppin' Us Now
ToO79-W,M
Ain't No Trick (It Takes Magic)
TOC83-W,M
Ain't No Woman (Like the One I
Got)
SoH-W,M
Ain't Nothing Like the Real Thing
ToO76-W,M
Ain't She Sweet
MF-W,M OHB-W,M U-W
Ain't That a Shame
ILF-W,M RW-W,M
**Ain't That a Shame see also Ain't
Dat a Shame**
Ain't That Beautiful Singing
CEM-W,M
**Ain't That Good News see Ain't
Dat Good News**
Ain't That Just Like a Woman
OnT6-W,M
Ain't We Got Fun
MF-W,M MR-W,M OHB-W,M
T-W,M
Ain't You Glad
Le-W,M
Air
H-W,M
Air Corps Lament
AF-W
Air Corps Roar
GO-W,M
Air Force 801
AF-W
Air France Makes It Easy to Get
There
GSM-W,M
Air Mail Special
TI1-M UFB-M
Air-Minded Executive
OHF-W
Air of May
LMR-W,M
Air Voyage
FSA2-W,M
Airman's Lament
AF-W
Airman's Song
AF-W ASB6-W,M
Airplane
ASB2-W,M MH-W,M
Airplane Song
THN-W,M
Airplanes
GUM1-W,M
Airport Love Theme (Winds of
Chance)
TI2-W,M
Aja Lejber Man
IF-W,M (Czech)
**Ajax Cleanser Jingle see Use Ajax
the Foaming Cleanser**
Al Di La
MF-W,M
Al Pasar La Barca
LA W,M (Spanish)
Al Pasar Por Sevilla
LA-W,M (Spanish)
Ala En El Rancho Grande
FC-W,M (Spanish)
Alabam'
ASB5-W,M CCS-W,M
Alabama
Fif-W,M SHS-W,M
Alabama, The

SA-W,M Sin-W,M SiS-W,M
SY-W,M
Alabama and the Kearsarge
Sin-W,M SiS-W
Alabama Bound
FW-W Le-W,M RW-W,M SFM-W
**Alabama Bound see also Alabamy
Bound**
Alabama Jubilee
MF-W,M TI2-W,M
Alabama Lullaby
CS-W,M
Alabama Rain
JC-W,M
Alabama Way
NF-W
Alabamy Bound
MF-W,M TI1-W,M UFB-W,M
**Alabamy Bound see also Alabama
Bound**
Alabamy Home
GMD-W,M
Aladdin
HR-W
Aladdin and the Lamp
FSA1-W,M
Alaiyo
R-W,M
Alalimon
LA-W,M (Spanish)
Alamo
OHG-W,M
Alas and Did My Savior Bleed
AME-W,M
Alas and Did My Saviour Bleed
Hy-W,M
Alas, the Time Is Past
BS-W,M
Alas, What Hourly Dangers Rise
AME-W,M
Alaska Hahves' Moon
NeA-W,M
Alaskans (Gold Fever Theme)
TVT-W,M
Alaska's Flag
Fif-W,M VA-W,M
Alberta
FW-W LC-W
Albion
SHS-W,M
Albumblatt
RW-M
Albumblatt see also Fur Elise
Aldermanic Board
TW-W
Aldonza
MLM-W,M
Ale House see Girl Died for Love
Alessandro the Wise
LSO-W
Alexander's Ragtime Band
GSN1-W,M HFH-W,M MF-W,M
OAP-W,M U-W
Alfie
AT-WM GOI7-W,M HD-W,M
LM-W,M OTO-W RDT-W,M TOM-
W,M
Algo Mas
TI1-W,M (Spanish Only) UFB-
W,M (Spanish Only)
Algonquins from Harlem
KH-W,M
**Alice (Theme) see There's a New
Girl in Town**
Alice B
AmS-W,M
Alice Blue Gown

HLS1-W,M HLS8-W,M OPI-W,M
RDT-W,M RW-W,M T-W,M
Alice in Wonderland
OTJ-W,M
Alice Was Her Name
VS-W,M
Alice Where Art Thou?
AmH-W,M HSD-W,M SL-W,M
WiS8-W,M
Alka Seltzer Theme
BNG-W,M
Alknomook
EA-W,M
All
TI2-W,M
All Aboard
KS-W,M
All Aboard for Blandet Bay
LWT-W,M
All Aboard for Louisiana
JD-W,M
All about You
RoS-W,M
All Alone
LWT-W,M
All American Boy
RB-W
All American Girl
STW-W,M
All and Some
OB-W,M
All around Our World Today
SHP-W,M
All around the Christmas Tree
BCh-W,M
All around the Jailhouse
AFP-W
All around the Maypole
ASB2-W,M
All around the World
RB-W
All at Once
TTH-W,M
All At Once You Love Her
HC1-W,M OTJ-W,M OTO-W
TI1-W,M UBF-W,M UFB-W,M
All Beautiful the March of Days
Hy-W,M
All Bells in Paradise
OB-W,M
All Blues
MF-M
All Bow Down
TBF-W
All By Myself
TI2-W,M
All Choked Up
Mo-W,M OTO-W
All Creatures of Our God and King
HS-W,M Hy-W,M SHP-W,M SJ-
W,M VA-W,M
**All Creatures of Our God and King
see also Alleluia (All Creatures of
Our God and King)**
All Cried Out
TTH-W,M
All Day and All of the Night
DRR-W,M
All Day Long
FHR-W,M
All Day on the Prairie
AS-W,M
All Day System
AL-W
All Dem Mount Zion Member
NSS-W
All down the Line

RoS-W,M
All er Nothin'
TGO-W,M UBF-W,M
All er Ma Sins Are Taken Away
BDW-W,M
**All er Ma Sins Are Taken Away
see also All My Sins Been Taken
Away**
All for Baby
FF-W
All for Me
GH-W,M
All for the Best
G-W,M OTO-W UBF-W,M
All for the Cause
AL-W,M
All for the Love of Sunshine
HLS9-W,M
All Glory Be to God on High
SJ-W,M
All Glory, Laud, and Honor
AME-W,M HS-W,M Hy-W,M IH-M
MM-W,M OM-W,M SHP-W,M
SJ-W,M
All God's Children
BSG-W,M BSP-W,M FS-W,M
**All God's Children see also Goin'
to Shout All over God's Heav'n,
Heab'n, and Heaven (I Got a
Robe)**
All God's Children Got Shoes
FW-W
All God's Chillun Got Wings
WiS7-W,M
All Good Gifts
G-W,M On-W,M OTO-W
UBF-W,M
All Good Times Are Past and Gone
Oz4-W,M
All Hail the Political Honeymoon
KH-W,M
All Hail the Power
GH-W,M U-W
All Hail the Power of Jesus' Name
AH-W,M AME-W,M Bo-W
CEM-W,M HF-W,M Hy-W,M IH-M
TB-W,M
All Hail the Pow'r of Jesus Name
BNG-W,M WiS7-W,M
All Hail to Massachusetts
Fif-W,M
All Hail to the Days That Merit
More Praise
YC-W,M
All Hail to the Reign of Peace
SiS-W
All Hail to the Stars and Stripes
SiS-W
All Hail to Ulysses
SiS-W
All Hallow's Eve
GBC-W,M
All I Ask of You
UBF-W,M
All I Can Do
BDF-W,M
All I Care About
CMV-W,M
All I Do Is Dream of You
GG3-W,M HLS5-W,M OPI-W,M
RW-W,M
All I Ever Need Is You
HLS9-W,M MCG-W,M RW-W,M
RYT-W,M
All I Have to Do Is Dream
FOC-W,M MF-W,M OPS-W,M
TI1-W,M UFB-W,M

All I Need
NB-W
All I Need Is the Girl
UBF-W,M
All I Needed to Say
VB-W,M
All I Really Want to Do
FoR-W,M
All I Touch
Mo-W,M NM-W,M OTO-W
All I Want for Christmas Is My
Two Front Teeth
BCh-W,M DC-W,M MF-W,M
All in a Fairy Ring
Boo-W,M
All in a Garden Green
SSP-W
All in a Night's Work
OTO-W
All in All
CEM-W,M
All in Love Is Fair
ToO76-W,M
All in My Mind
RY-W,M RYT-W,M
**All in the Family Theme see Those
Were the Days**
All in the Morning
OB-W,M
All In to Service
Boo-W,M
All In to Service the Bells Toll
Boo-W,M
All Ireland Championship
VP-W
All Is Quiet
HSD-W,M
All Is Well
SHS-W,M SL-W,M WN-W,M
All I've Got to Do
TWS-W
All Jolly Fellows Who Follow the
Plough
BB-W
All Kinds of Giants
Mo-W,M
All Kinds of People
OTJ-W,M
All-Knowing God, 'Tis Thine to
Know
AHO-W,M
All Mixed Up
JF-W,M
All My Children
TVT-W,M
All My Ex's Live in Texas
AWS-W,M
All My Heart This Night Rejoices
Hy-W,M SJ-W,M
All My Life
OnT6-W,M TOC83-W,M VB-W,M
All My Love
MF-W,M
All My Loving
BBe-W,M Be1-W,M PMC-W,M
SwS-W,M TWS-W WG-W,M
All My Rowdy Friends
TOC83-W,M
All My Sins Been Taken Away
AN-W NH-W
**All My Sins Been Taken Away see
also All er Ma Sins Are Taken
Away**
All My Tomorrows
FrS-W,M MF-W,M
All My Trials
FG2-W,M FW-W TI1-W,M

UFB-W,M
All Nature's Works His Praise
  Declare
  ESB-W,M Hy-W,M
All Night All Day
  HS-W,M PaS-W,M RS-W,M
All Night Long
  FGM-W,M FW-W TO-W,M
  TOC82-W,M
All ober Dis Worl
  BDW-W,M
All of Me
  DJ-W,M LSB-W,M RoE-W,M
  TI1-W,M UFB-W,M
All of Me Is Mine
  TT-W,M
All of My Life
  DR-W,M
All of You
  HC1-W,M LM-W,M ML-W,M
  TI1-W,M UBF-W,M UFB-W,M
All on Account of a Bold Lover
  Gay
  BSC-W
All or Nothing see All er Nothin'
All or Nothing at All
  FrS-W,M TI2-W,M
All Over Again
  OGC2-W,M
All over Arkansas
  Oz3-W
All over the World
  VB-W,M
**All over This World see All ober
  Dis Worl**
All People That on Earth
  GH-W,M
All People That on Earth Do Dwell
  AME-W,M ESB-W,M Hy-W,M
  SHP-W,M
All Praise to God on High
  MML-W,M
All Praise to Thee
  AHO-W,M
All Praise to Thee, My God, This
  Night
  Hy-W,M SHP-W,M SJ-W,M
All Pull Together
  FSA1-W,M
All Quiet along the Potomac
  Re-W,N SiS-W
All Quiet along the Potomac
  Tonight
  AH-W,M MPP-W PoS-W,M
  SCo-W,M Sin-W,M
All Right
  BCC-W,M
All Rise
  VB-W,M
All round My Hat
  MSB-W
All Shook Up
  DRR-W,M ILF-W,M RW-W,M
  RY-W,M RYT-W,M TI1-W,M
  TOC83-W,M UFB-W,M
All Sold Out
  RoS-W,M
All Soul's Day (Allerseelen)
  FSY-W,M (German) WiS9-W,M
All That I Am
  AHO-W,M SRE2-W,M
All That Love Went to Waste
  HLS5-W,M
All the Birds Sing
  SSe-W,M
All the Dearly Beloved
  I-W,M

All the Ducks
  GM-W
All the Good Times Are Past and
  Gone
  BSo-W,M
All the King's Horses
  VS-W,M
All the Live Long Day
  OTO-W
All the Madmen
  RV-W
All the Past We Leave Behind
  AHO-W,M
All the Pretty Little Horses
  FoS-W,M FSSC-W,M FW-W
  LMR-W,M MG-W,M OTJ-W,M
  PSN-W,M SCL-W,M
All the Things You Are
  BeL-W,M DJ-W,M L-W RDT-W,M
  RW-W,M TI1-W,M UFB-W,M
All the Time
  TOF-W,M
All the Way
  EY-W,M FrS-W,M HFH-W,M
  MF-W,M RoE-W,M VS-W,M
All the Way Home
  OTO-W
All the Way My Saviour Leads Me
  AME-W,M FW-W GH-W,M
  Hy-W,M
All the World Shall Come to Serve
  Thee
  SBJ-W,M
All the World Wakens
  LMR-W,M
**All Them Mount Zion Members see
  All Dem Mount Zion Member**
All Things Are Possible
  VB-W,M
All Things Are Thine, No Gift Have
  We
  Hy-W,M
All Things Bright and Beautiful
  Hy-W,M OTJ-W,M RW-W,M
  SHP-W,M
All Things Come of Thee, O Lord
  AME-W,M Hy-W,M
All This and Heaven Too
  MF-W,M
All thro' the Night
  FSA2-W,M
All through the Day
  HC2-W,M
All through the Night
  ASB4-W,M BCh-W,M BM-W
  BMC-M CSo-W,M ESB-W,M
  FSD-W,M FW-W FWS-W,M
  GC-W,M Gu-W,M GuC-W,M
  HS-W,M IL-W,M LT-W,M
  LTL-W,M MF-W,M MML-W,M
  NAS-W,M OAP-W,M OS-W,M
  OTJ-W,M RW-W,M SL-W,M SMa-
  W,M TH-W,M U-W WiS8-W,M
All to Astonish the Browns
  MSB-W
All to Christ I Owe
  GH-W,M
All to Jesus I Surrender
  AME-W,M
All Together Now
  BBe-W,M BE2-W,M TWS-W
All Tomorrow's Parties
  RB-W
All We Do
  GI-W,M GO-W
All We Here or the Agreement
  Boo-W,M

All Who Sing
  Boo-W,M
All Ye Dwellers of the Earth
  JS-W,M
All Ye That Fear God's Holy Name
  Hy-W,M
All Ye That Weep
  SL-W,M
All You Need Is a Quarter
  DR-W,M
All You Need Is Love
  BBe-W,M BE2-W,M RDF-W,M
  TWS-W
Alla En El Rancho Grande
  LA-W,M (Spanish) TI2-W,M
  (Spanish)
Alla Trinita Beata
  MU-W,M (Italian)
Alla Turca
  RW-M
Alla Turca see also Turkish March
Allah
  FSA2-W,M SL-W,M
Allah's Holiday
  K-W,M
Allea Alleo
  UF-W,M
Allee Allee O
  GM-W
Allegheny Moon
  HLS3-W,M TI1-W,M UFB-W,M
Allegretto from Symphony No. 3
  (Brahms)
  RW-M
Allegretto from Symphony No. 7
  (Beethoven)
  RW-M
Allegro
  A-W,M L-W
Allelu
  BSG-W,M BSP-W,M
Alleluia
  SBF-W,M SSN-W,M (French)
Alleluia (All Creatures of Our God
  and King)
  MG-W,M
**Alleluia (All Creatures of Our God
  and King) see also All Creatures
  of Our God and King**
Alleluia (Alleluia! Praise His Holy
  Name!)
  SL-W,M
Alleluia (Come All Ye People,
  Come and Sing)
  UF-W,M
Alleluia (From All That Dwell below
  the Skies)
  ASB6-W,M
**Alleluia (From All That Dwell below
  the Skies) see also From All That
  Dwell below the Skies**
Alleluia (Mozart)
  Boo-W,M
Alleluia (Round)
  LMR-W,M
Alleluia, Christ Is Coming
  VB-W,M
Alleluia, Christ Is Risen Today
  AHO-W,M
Alleluia, Song of Sweetness
  SJ-W,M
Allelujah Bound
  LoS-W,M
Alleluya
  OTJ-W,M
Allerseelen (All Souls' Day)
  FSY-W,M (German) WiS9-W,M

Alley Cat
 RW-M
Alley Cat Song
 OBN-W,M OnT1-W,M OPS-W,M
 TI1-W,M UFB-W,M
Alley Special
 DBL-W
Alley Oop
 NoS-W,M
Allez-Vous-En, Go Away
 HC2-W,M ML-W,M TI1-W,M
 UBF-W,M
Allons Cher Camarade A L'Armee
 CaF-W (French Only)
Allons A La Promenade
 CaF-W (French Only)
Allons A Lafayette
 CaF-W (French Only)
Alls Right with the World
 MM-W,M
Alls Well
 SiS-W
Allt Under Himmelens Faste
 AS-W,M (Swedish)
Ally, Ally Oxen Free
 OTJ-W,M
Alma Mater
 MML-W,M Mo-W,M OTO-W
Alma Mater (L.S.U.)
 SLS-W,M
Almighty Father, Hear Our Prayer
 AME-W,M Hy-W,M
Almighty Father, Strong to Save
 Hy-W,M RDF-W,M
Almighty God in Being Was
 AHO-W,M
Almighty God, Thy Constant Care
 AHO-W,M
Almighty Lord, with One Accord
 AHO-W,M
Almighty Sovereign of the Skies
 AHO-W,M
Almighty Spake and Gabriel Sped
 AHO-W,M
Almost
 Mo-W,M NM-W,M OTO-W
 UBF-W,M
Almost Dead Blues
 LC-W
Almost Done
 TO-W,M
**Almost Done Suffering see Most
 Done Suffering**
Almost Done Traveling
 WN-W,M
**Almost Done Traveling see also
 Most Done Trabelling**
Almost Gone
 ToO79-W,M
Almost Grown
 HR-W
Almost in Your Arms
 OTO-W
Almost Like Being in Love
 HC1-W,M HLS8-W,M HSS-W,M
 HST-W,M LL-W,M OnT1-W,M
 OU-W,M RW-W,M STP-W,M
Almost Over
 WN-W,M
Almost Paradise (Love Theme from
 Footloose)
 GSN5-W,M
Almost Persuaded
 AHO-W,M AME-W,M ATC2-W,M
 GH-W,M HLS9-W,M Hy-W,M
 TI1-W,M UFB-W,M
Aloha Oe (Farewell to Thee)

ATS-W CSo-W,M (Hawaiian)
 FSY-W,M (Hawaiian) GuC-W,M
 HLS1-W,M HS-W,M (Hawaiian)
 NAS-W,M RW-W,M TI1-W,M
 WiS8-W,M
Alone
 BHO-W,M GSO-W,M MF-W,M
Alone Again (Naturally)
 GrS-W,M
Alone and Forsaken
 HW-W,M
Alone and Motherless
 FVV-W,M
Alone at Last
 GAR-W,M
Alone at the Drive-In Movie
 Gr-W,M Mo-W,M OTO-W
Alone Together
 MF-W,M TW-W
Alone Too Long
 Mo-W,M NM-W,M OTO-W
 UBF-W,M
Along Came Jones
 WF-W,M
Along Comes Mary
 RB-W
Along the Banks
 AHO-W,M
Along the Navajo Trail
 FC-W,M
Along the Picket Line
 SiS-W
Along the River of Time
 GH-W,M
Along the Santa Fe Trail
 FC-W,M MF-W,M
Alonza
 MLM-W,M
Alouette
 Bo-W,M (French Only) CE-W,M
 (French) CSo-W,M (French Only)
 CSS-W (French Only) CUP-W,M
 (French Only) FSO-W,M (French)
 FW-W (French Only) HS-W,M
 (French Only) IL-W,M (French
 Only) LoS-W,M (French Only)
 MAS-W,M (French) MF-W,M
 (French Only) MML-W,M (French)
 NAS-W,M (French Only)
 OFS-W,M (French Only) OS-W
 (French Only) OTJ-W,M (French
 Only) RW-W,M (French Only)
 SMY-W,M (French Only)
 STR-W,M (French Only) TF-W,M
 (French only) TI1-W,M (French
 Only) UFB-W,M (French Only)
 VA-W,M (French Only)
Alouette, Gentille Alouette
 Ch-W (French Only)
Alphabet
 ASB4-W,M GM-W
Alphabet for Little Masters and
 Misses
 SBA-W
Alphabet Song
 OTJ-W,M Oz4-W,M
Alphonse and Gaston
 MF-M
Alright, Okay, You Win
 BBB-W,M TI2-W,M
**Als Die Alte Mutter see Songs My
 Mother Taught Me**
Als Ik Des Herren Werk
 AHO-W,M (Dutch)
Also Sprach Zarathustra
 EP-M On-M
Although Our Dark Career

SL-W,M
Altoona Freight Wreck
 LSR-W,M
Always
 GSN5-W,M
Always and Forever
 GSN5-W,M
Always Do As People Say You
 Should
 FT-W,M
Always Happy
 ESU-W
Always on My Mind
 BNG-W,M DC-W,M EC-W,M
 GCM-W,M MF-W,M TOC82-W,M
 TOC83-W,M TOH-W,M
Always Something There to
 Remind Me
 HD-W,M RW-W,M TI1-W,M
 UFB-W,M
Always Take Mother's Advice
 EFS-W,M
Always True to You in My Fashion
 TI1-W,M TW-W UBF-W,M
 UFB-W,M
Always Wanting You
 NMH-W,M
Am I a Soldier of the Cross?
 AME-W,M Hy-W,M OM-W,M
Am I Blue?
 HFH-W,M MF-W,M OHB-W,M
Am I in Love
 MF-W,M OTO-W
Am I My Brother's Keeper
 ESU-W
Am I the Queen or Am I Not
 CoF-W,M
Am Schonsten Sommerabend
 War's
 EL-W,M (German)
Am Yisroel Chay
 JS-W,M (Hebrew Only)
Amalfi Bay
 ASB4-W,M
Amanda
 TI2-W,M
Amapola
 TI2-W,M
Amarillo by Morning
 EC-E,M
Amaryllis
 AmH-M MAR-M RW-M
Amazing Grace
 AH-W,M BNG-W,M BSG-W,M
 BSo-W,M BSP-W,M CEM-W,M
 DC-W,M FS-W,M FW-W HF-W,M
 HLS7-W,M IF-W,M JBF-W,M
 MF-W,M OAP-W,M OBN-W,M
 On-W,M OPS-W,M OTJ-W,M
 PoG-W,M RDF-W,M RDT-W,M
 RW-W,M TI1-W,M TO-W,M
 UFB-W,M
Amazing Grace! How Sweet the
 Sound
 AME-W,M GH-W,M Hy-W,M
Amazing Love
 JF-W,M
Amazing Sight! the Savior Stands
 AHO-W,M
Amber Tresses Tied in Blue
 Oz4-W
Ambition
 DR-W,M
Ambos A Dos
 CDM-W,M (Spanish)
Ambrosia
 OTO-W

Amelia
RV-W
Amelia Earhart's Last Flight
LW-W,M
Amen
Hy-W,M RDF-W,M RW-W,M
TI1-W,M UFB-W,M
Amen, Amen
GI-W
America
AAP-W,M AH-W,M AME-W,M
AmH-W,M ASB2-W,M ASB3-W,M
BM-W Bo-W CSS-W EA-W,M
ESB-W,M FM-W,M FWS-W,M
HA-W,M HS-W,M HSD-W,M
LMR-W,M LoS-W,M MAS-W,M
MES1-W,M MF-W,M MH-W,M
MML-W,M MU-W,M NAS-W,M
OHG-W,M OS-W OTJ-W,M
PoS-W,M RW-W,M SBF-W,M
SBJ-W SI-W,M SiR-W,M
SL-W,M SMa-W,M SMW-W,M
SoF-W,M SOO-W,M TF-W
TH-W,M TI1-W,M TTH-W,M
UF-W UFB-W,M VA-W,M
WiS8-W,M
**America see also My Country 'Tis
of Thee**
America (Billings)
BC1-W,M
America--1895
AL-W
America (Friends, Hear about the
Battle Wild)
SE-W (Swedish)
America (My Soul, Repeat His
Praise)
SHS-W,M
America (Parody)
AL-W
America (Paul Simon)
RV-W
America and France
MPP-W
America Commerce and Freedom
EA-W,M OHG-W,M
America for Me
FSA2-W,M
America Forever
ANS-W
America I Love You
AAP-W,M
America Is
TTH-W,M
America Is My Home
RB-W
America Letter
SE-W,M (Swedish)
America My Home
ASB3-W,M
America My Land
GC-W,M
America Our Heritage
AAP-W,M MM-W,M SiB-W,M
YS-W,M
America Song
SE-W,M (Swedish)
America the Anchor and Hope
ESU-W
America the Beautiful
AAP-W,M AH-W,M ASB3-W,M
ATS-W BM-W Bo-W,M CSS-W
DC-W,M ESB-W,M FSA1-W,M
FW-W FWS-W,M HA-W,M HF-
W,M HS-W,M JF-W,M LMR-W,M
LoS-W,M LT-W,M MAB1-W,M
MAS-W,M MF-W,M MHB-W,M

MML-W,M MSA1-W MuM-W,M
NAS-W,M OM-W,M OS-W
OTJ-W,M OU-W,M PoG-W,M
RDF-W,M RW-W,M SiR-W,M
SL-W,M SoF-W,M SOO-W,M
STR-W,MTB-W,MTF-W TH-W,M
TI1-W,M UF-W, UFB-W M
VA-W,M WiS9-W,M
**America the Beautiful see also O
Beautiful for Spacious Skies**
American Bases
VS-W,M
American Beauty Rose
Fi-W,M HD-W,M
American Boy Grows Up
JW-W,M
American Captive's Emancipation
MPP-W,M
American Constitution Frigate's
Engagement with the British
Frigate Guerriere
ANS-W
American Cradle Song
AmH-W,M
American Dream
PoG-W,M
American Folk Trilogy
AAP-W,M
American Freedmen
SiS-W
American Freedom
MPP-W
American Frigate
SSS-W,M
**American Gigolo Theme see Call
Me**
American Heart of Oak
EA-W,M
American Hearts of Oak
SBA-W
American Hero
EA-W,M SI-W,M
American History
ESU-W
American Hymn
ESB-W,M HSD-W,M TH-W,M
WiS9-W,M YS-W,M
American in Paris
MF-M NYT-M
American Is a Very Lucky Man
BeB-W,M RS-W,M
American Jubilee
SiS-W
American Liberty
MPP-W
American Patrol
MF-M OTJ-M RW-M TI1-M UFB-M
American Pie
GrH-W,M GRS-W,M GSN4-W,M
RV-W
American Prayer
CA-W,M
American Road
LMR-W,M
American Rule Britannia
SI-W,M
American Star
ESU-W
American Taxation
SBA-W Si-W SSS-W,M
American Trilogy
EP-W,M
American Tune
GrS-W
American Vicar of Bray
SAR-W,M SI-W,M
American Way

ASB4-W,M
Americas Shake Hands
ASB6-W,M
Amerika
SE-W (Swedish)
Amerikabrev
SE-W,M (Swedish)
Amerikavisan
SE-W,M (Swedish)
Amherst
SHS-W,M
Amici
ESB-W,M
Amid the New Mown Hay
FSA1-W,M
Amid the Trials Which I Meet
AME-W,M
Amity
SHS-W,M
Among Assembled Men of Might
AME-W,M
Among My Souvenirs
BBB-W,M BeL-W,M TI1-W,M
UFB-W,M
Among the First to Know
Mo-W,M
**Amongst Other Folks see 'Mongst
Other Folks**
Amor Llamo see El Amor Llamo
**Amore, Scusami see My Love,
Forgive Me**
Amos Amas
ESU-W HAS-W,M
Amos Kendall's Lament
OHG-W,M
Amour Sans Soucis
EL-W,M
Amsterdam
FSA1-W,M SoF-W,M
Amy's Theme
TI2-M
An' Am I Born to Die
WN-W,M
**An' Am I Born to Die see also And
Am I Born to Die**
An' I Cry
My-W,M
An Poc Ar Buile
IS-W,M (Gaelic Only)
Ana Bekorenu
SiP-W,M (Hebrew)
Anach Cuain
VP-W (Gaelic Only)
Anacreontic Song
BC1-W,M EA-W,M MPP-W,M
Analization
HAS-W,M
Anastasia
GG4-W,M HLS3-W,M
Anatevka
OTO-W UBF-W,M
Anchor Line
NF-W
Anchored
ESB-W,M
Anchors Aweigh
AAP-W,M GSN1-W,M HA-W,M
HLS1-W,M OS-W RW-W,M
Ancient Fish of the Sea
TW-W
Ancient Nursery Ballad
AL-W
Ancient of Days, Who Sittest
Throned in Glory
AHO-W,M AME-W,M Hy-W,M
Ancient Prophecy
AWB-W

Ancient Sailor
MMY-W,M
Ancient Wisdom
FSA1-W,M
"...And..."
JP-W,M
And All That Jazz
CMV-W,M UBF-W,M
And Am I Born to Die
AME-W
And Am I Born to Die see also An'
Am I Born to Die
And Are We Yet Alive
AME-W,M
And Are Ye Sure the News Is True
NSS-W
And Can I Yet Delay
AME-W,M
And Canst Thou, Sinner, Slight
AHO-W,M
And God Shall Wipe Away All
Tears
FiS-W,M
And Have the Bright Immensities
AHO-W,M
And Her Tears Flowed Like Wine
MF-W,M
And I Cry see An' I Cry
And I Looked at You a Long Time
NB-W
And I Love Her
BBe-W,M BeL-W,M FPS-W,M
SwS-W,M PMC-W,M TWS-W
And I Love You So
GrH-W,M GSN4-W,M RW-W,M
And I Was Beautiful
Mo-W,M OTO-W
And I Would Flee Away
CFS-W,M (French)
And I'll Sing Hallelujah
NSS-W
And I'll Thank God Almost Over
NSS-W
And It Stoned Me
RV-W
And Justice for All Theme see
There's Something Funny Going
On
And Let Me the Canakin Clink
FSS-W,M SSP-W
And Let Our Bodies Part
AME-W,M
And Let This Feeble Body Fail
AME-W,M
And Love Was Born
L-W
And Must I Be to Judgment
Brought
AME-W,M
And Must I Part with All I Have
AME-W,M
And Must This Body Die
AME-W,M
And Now Tomorrow
OTO-W
And Roses and Roses
OnT6-W,M
And See'st Thou My Cow
Boo-W,M
And So Goodbye
NA-W,M
And the Angels Sing
DC-W,M MF-W,M OHF-W
And the Beat Goes On
PoG-W,M
And the Cock Begins to Crow
AHO-W,M

And the Glory of the Lord
LMR-W,M
And the Golden Hair Was Hanging
down Her Back
EFS-W,M
And the Lord Spoke
SoM-W,M
And Then Some
TOC82-W,M
And There Arose
SoM-W,M
And They Called It Dixieland
MR-W,M
And This Is My Beloved
DBC-W,M HC2-W,M ILT-W,M
Ki-W,M
And Tonight
NB-W
And Truly It Is a Most Glorious
Thing
AHO-W,M
And Wasn't That a Tidy One
ESU-W
And We Hunted and We Hunted
AFS-W,M
And We Were Lovers
RT6-W,M THN-W,M
And When I Die
BSB-W,M
And When the Leaves
BSB-W,M
And Who, Pray, Is Martin Van
Buren
ESU-W
And Will He Not Come Again
SSP-W
And Will the Judge Descend
AME-W,M
And Will the Mighty God
AME-W,M
And You Know It's Right
VB-W,M
And Your Bird Can Sing
TWS-W
Andante Cantabile
RW-M TI1-M TM-M UFB-M
WGB/O-M
Andante Religioso
WiS7-M
Andantino
WGB/P-M WiS7-M
Andersonville Prison
Oz2-W
Andiamo
Mo-W,M
Andreas Hofer
SMW-W,M (German)
Andrew Bardeen
Oz1-W,M
Andrew Bartin
FSSC-W
Andrew Jackson's Raid
BSC-W
Andrew Rose
SA-W,M
Andy Bardan
BSC-W
Andy Griffith Show Theme see
Fishin' Hole
Andy Williams Show Theme see
May Each Day
Ane Et Le Loup see L'Ane Et Le
Loup
Anema E Core
TI2-W,M
Angel
CFB-W,M MF-W,M SRE1-W,M

TH-W,M
Angel Baby
MF-W,M
Angel Band
BSo-W,M MAR-W,M MG-W,M
NH-W OHO-W,M RSL-W,M
Angel Dun Change-er Ma Name
BDW-W,M
Angel Dun Change-er Ma Name
see also Angels Done Changed
My Name
Angel Eyes
DJ-W,M NK-W,M RoE-W,M
TI1-W,M TI2-W,M ToO79-W,M
ToS-W,M UFB-W,M
Angel Gabriel
GBC-W,M GUM2-W,M OB-W,M
Angel of Death
Oz4-W,M
Angel of Music
UBF-W,M
Angel of Peace
ESB-W,M
Angel of Peace, Thou Hast
Wandered Too Long
AHO-W,M
Angel Voices
MML-W,M
Angel Voices Ever Singing
Hy-W,M TH-W,M
Angela (Theme from Taxi)
TV-M
Angelic Songs Are Swelling
HSD-W,M
Angelica
Mo-W,M NM-W,M OTO-W
Angelina
Mo-W,M NM-W,M OTO-W
Angelina Baker
AH-W,M FHR-W,M LMR-W,M
SSF-W,M SSFo-W,M
Angels
VB-W,M
Angels and Shepherds
CA-W,M FSA2-W,M
Angels Are Singing unto Me
FHR-W,M
Angels Done Changed My Name
Me-W,M
Angels Done Changed My Name
see also Angel Dun Change-er Ma
Name
Angels Ever Bright and Fair
HSD-W,M
Angels from Heaven
RW-W,M
Angels from the Realms
OB-W,M
Angels from the Realms of Glory
AME-W,M BCh-W,M BCS-W,M
CCH-W,M CI-W,M CSF-W GBC-
W,M Hy-W,M MC-W,M MF-W,M
OPS-W,M RW-W,M SAC-W,M
Y-W,M YC-W,M
Angels Holy
OB-W,M
Angels Hovering Round
WN-W,M
Angels Keep Watching over Me
GrG-W,M
Angels Meet Me at the Crossroads
MM-W,M
Angel's Message
ASB4-W,M
Angel's Serenade
AmH-M WiS7-M
Angels Sung a Carol

AHO-W,M
Angel's Waitin' at de Tomb
MoM-W,M
Angels Watching over Me
MAR-W,M
Angels We Have Heard on High
BCh-W,M BCS-W,M BMC-W,M
CCM-W,M CI-W,M CSF-W
FWS-W,M FW-W HS-W,M
Hy-W,M IL-W,M MAS-W,M
MC-W,M MF-W,M OAP-W,M
OPS-W,M RW-W,M SJ-W,M
TF-W,M YC-W,M YS-W,M
Angels Will Guide Me
HHa-W,M
Angelus, The
UF-W,M
Angelus, The (Asa Hunt)
SL-W,M
Angelus, The (Jules Massenet)
FSA1-W,M WiS7-M
Angelus, The (Victor Herbert)
Sw-W,M
Angelus Ad Virginem
OB-W,M (Latin Only)
Angie
RoS-W,M
Angie Mimey
FoM-W,M
Angry
BBB-W,M Mo-W,M NM-W,M
On-W,M TI2-W,M
Animal Attire
NF-W
Animal Crackers
MH-W,M
Animal Crackers in My Soup
OTJ-W,M
Animal Fair
ATS-W,M Bo-W,M CSS-W
HAS-W,M MAS-W,M NF-W
OTJ-W,M
Animal Friends
ASB2-W,M
Animal Persecutors
NF-W
Animal Song
AFS-W,M BMC-W,M SD-W,M
Animal Talk
MES1-W,M MES2-W,M
Animals Go to Sleep
STS-W,M
Animals Wake Up
STS-W,M
Animals Went in Two by Two
CSo-W,M
Anitra's Dance
AmH-M RW-M
Anna
TI1-W,M UFB-W,M
Anna Fell
ESU-W
Anna Lee
Oz4-W,M
Anna Maria
ASB6-W,M
Annabel Lee
RW-M
Annabelle
TI1-W,M UFB-W,M
Annapolis
BC1-W,M
Annapolis Memories
Mo-W,M
Anna's Rosy Cheeks
MHB-W,M
Anne's Theme

DC-M
Annie
TI2-W,M
Annie Doesn't Live Here Anymore
OnT6-W,M
Annie Girl
FMT-W
Annie Laurie
AmH-W,M CSo-W,M ESB-W,M
FM-W,M FW-W FWS-W,M Gu-
W,M HS-W,M HSD-W,M IL-W,M
NAS-W,M OS-W OTJ-W,M
RW-W,M SeS-W,M SL-W TF-W
TH-W,M U-W WiS8-W,M
Annie Lisle
HSD-W,M
Annie My Own Love
FHR-W,M SSFo-W,M
Annie of the Veil
BSC-W
Annie's Song
CJ-W,M GrS-W,M PoG-W,M
WG-W,M
Anniversary
FSA1-W,M
Anniversary Song (Oh! How We
Danced on the Night We Were
Wed)
HLS5-W,M ILT-W,M MF-W,M
RDT-W,M RT4-W,M TI1-W,M
UFB-W,M
Anniversary Song (We Hail Today,
the Patron's Day)
GrM-W,M
Anniversary Waltz
HLS3-W,M NM-W,M RW-W,M
TI1-W,M UFB-W,M
Ann's Teeth
MH-W,M
Anons Au Bal Calinda
LC-W (French)
Another Autumn
LL-W,M
Another Brick in the Wall
UFB-W,M
Another Day
HHa-W,M PMC-W,M
Another Day, Another Town
JC-W,M
Another Day in Paradise
MF-W,M
Another Day's Journey
SFF-W,M
Another Girl
TWS-W
Another Glorious Victory
ANS-W
Another Goodbye
WG-W,M
Another Happy Birthday
SHP-W,M
Another Heartache
TTH-W,M
Another Heaven Song
HHa-W,M
Another Human Being of the
Opposite Sex
Mo-W,M NM-W,M
Another Hundred People
Co-W,M OTO-W TW-W UBF-W,M
Another Man Done Gone
FW-W NeA-W,M
Another Op'nin', Another Show
DBC-W,M TI1-W,M UBF-W,M
UFB-W,M
Another Prophecy
SBA-W

Another Rainy Day in New York
City
ToO76-W,M
Another Saturday Night
ToO76-W,M
Another Sleepless Night
TI2-W,M
Another Soldier Gone
AME-W,M
Another Somebody Done
Somebody Wrong Song
CMG-W,M FOC-W,M TI2-W,M
Another Song about Paris
RoE-W,M WF-W,M
Another Suitcase in Another Hall
UBF-W,M
Another Time, Another Place
OTO-W
Another Tricky Day
WA-W,M
Another Yankee Doodle
SiS-W
Answer
ASB6-W,M
Answer Me, My Love
NK-W,M TI1-W,M UFB-W,M
Answer to My Maryland
SiS-W
Answer to Nobody's Darling but
Mine
SF-W,M
Answer to the Gypsy's Warning
Oz4-W
Answer to Tom's Jolly Nose
Boo-W,M
Answer to Twenty-One Years
Oz2-W
Ante-Bellum Chanted Prayer
AN-W
Ante-Bellum Courtship Inquiry
NF-W
Ante-Bellum Marriage Proposal
NF-W
Anthem of the Ilgwu
SWF-W,M
Anthony Wayne
SSS-W,M
Anti-Hitler Song
SMW-W,M
Anti-Monopoly War Song
AL-W,M
**Anticalomel see Go Call the
Doctor--Be Quick**
Anticipation
RoE-W,M
Antioch
GH-W,M SHS-W,M
Antioch Church House Choir
AG-W,M
Antoinette
OG-W,M
Ants Go Marching
RSL-W,M
Anvil Chorus
GC-W,M LMR-W,M RW-M
Any Day Now
CoH-W,M FOC-W,M MF-W,M
Any Kind of Man
ST-W,M
Any Old Iron
U-W
Any Old Place with You
TS-W
Any Old Time
LJ-W,M
Any Old Time of the Day
HD-W,M

Any Place I Hang My Hat Is Home
HC2-W,M LM-W,M OHF-W
UBF-W,M
Any Place Where I Make Money
T-W,M
Any Rags?
EFS-W,M
Any Time
FOC-W,M GrH-W,M HLS3-W,M
OGC2-W,M RW-W,M TI1-W,M
UFB-W,M
Any Time At All
TWS-W
Any Time's the Time for Prayer
SHP-W,M
Any Way You Want It
ILS-W,M
Any Way You Want Me
SRE2-W,M
Anybody Else's Heart but Mine
TOC83-W,M
Anyone Can Move a Mountain
RDF-W,M TI1-W,M UFB-W,M
Anyone Can Whistle
UBF-W,M
Anyone Who Had a Heart
GAR-W,M HD-W,M MF-W,M
Anyone Would Love You
UBF-W,M
Anyplace Is Paradise
SRE1-W,M
Anything
Oz3-W
Anything Goes
DC-W,M EY-W,M MF-W,M
OHB-W,M
Anytime, Anyplace, Anywhere
HRB1-W,M
Anytime at All
BBe-W,M
Anywhere I Wander
RW-W,M TI2-W,M
Anywhere the Heart Goes
MF-W,M TVT-W,M
Apache
TI1-M UFB-M
Apartment (Theme)
TI2-W,M
Apparitions
MM-W,M
Appeal to Loyalists
SAR-W,M
Appeal to Workingmen
AL-W
Applause
Ap-W,M HC1-W,M HLS8-W,M
LM-W,M Mo-W,M OTO-W
RW-W,M VSA-W,M
Applause, Applause!
LSO-W
Apple Blossom Time
U-W
Apple Honey
TI2-M
Apple Tree (Big Apple Tree)
STS-W,M
Apple Tree (The Leaf Buds of April
Showed Green thro' the Brown)
FSA2-W,M
Apple Tree (Listen Closely, Let Me
Fill You In)
TI2-W,M
Apples
ASB1-W,M
Apples and Bananas
TI1-M UFB-M
Apples and Roses

FSA1-W,M
Apprentice Boy
Oz1-W
Approach, My Soul, the Mercy
Seat
Hy-W,M
Approach of the Storm
FSA2-W,M
Approach of Winter
ASB5-W,M TH-W,M
April (April, Dear April, Your
Blossoms Are Sweet)
ASB1-W,M
April (The April Rain Is Falling from
Stormy Clouds on High)
ASB6-W,M
April (April, Twining a Garland of
Flowers)
FSA2-W,M
April (Fair April, the Maiden,
Comes Down from the Sky)
ASB4-W,M
April (Now April Has Come)
OB-W,M
April Fools
HD-W,M MF-W,M
April in Fairbanks
TW-W
April in Paris
EY-W,M (French) FrS-W,M
(French) MF-W,M OHB-W,M
April in Portugal
LM-W,M TI1-W,M UFB-W,M
April Is in My Mistress' Face
MU-W,M
April Love
GG3-W,M GSN3-W,M HLS5-W,M
RT5-W,M RW-W,M THN-W,M
April Rain
ASB5-W,M MH-W,M
April Showers
DBC-W,M MF-W,M TI2-W,M
April Smiles
AmH-M
April Wakes
SL-W,M
April's Here Again
ESB-W,M
Ap's
AF-W
Aqua Velva Man
GSM-W,M
Aqualung
BJ-W,M
Aquarela Do Brasil see Brazil
Aquarius
H-W,M HLS8-W,M ILS-W,M
MCG-W,M RW-W,M RY-W,M
RYT-W,M
Aquellos Ojos Verdes (Green Eyes)
FPS-W,M (Spanish) TOM-W,M
(Spanish Only)
Ar Fol Lol Lol O
IS-W,M
Arab Dance (from the Nutcracker
Suite)
MF-M
Aragonaise
AmH-M LaS-M
Arapaho Indian Peyote Song
IF-W,M (Arapaho Only)
Arapaho Indian Thunderbird Song
IF-M
Arbor Day
MH-W,M
Arbor Day Tree
MH-W,M

Archangel see Arkangel
Archie O'Cawfield
SBB-W
Are My Ears on Straight
BCh-W,M
Are the Good Times Really Over
for Good
NMH-W,M
Are Ye Able, Said the Master
AME-W,M
Are You Careful
NF-W
Are You Coming Home
GH-W,M
Are You from Dixie ('Cause I'm
from Dixie Too)
MF-W,M
Are You Havin' Any Fun
HC1-W,M RW-W,M
Are You Having Any Fun
TI1-W,M UBF-W,M UFB-W,M
Are You Hung Up
RB-W
Are You Lonesome Tonight?
EP-W,M FOC-W,M ILS-W,M
RW-W,M TI1-W,M TWD-W,M
UFB-W,M
Are You Ready
BDW-W,M
Are You Really Mine
MF-W,M
Are You Sleeping?
ASB4-W,M BM-W BMC-W,M
Bo-W,M CSS-W ESB-W,M
HS-W,M (French) MG-W,M
(French) PIS-W,M SMa-W,M
SOO-W,M
**Are You Sleeping see also Brother
John and Frere Jacques**
Are You Sleeping?--Three Blind
Mice
Boo-W,M
Aren't You Billy Fisher
OTO-W
Aren't You Glad You're You
LMR-W,M TI1-W,M UFB-W,M
Aren't You Glad You've Got
Religion
HLS7-W,M
Aren't You Kind of Glad We Did
LSO-W
Argentine Fire Brigade
Mo-W,M NM-W,M
Ariel
HSD-W,M
Ariel's Song
SL-W,M
Arioso
WGB/O-M
Arise
JF-W,M
Arise and See the Glorious Sun
AHO-W,M
Arise and Shine
GH-W,M
Arise! Arise!
SCa-W
Arise, Gird on Thy Strength
GrM-W,M
Arise, My Soul
HSD-W,M
Arise, My Soul, and Stretch Thy
Wings
DD-W,M
Arise, My Soul, Arise
GH-W,M
Arise My Soul! with Rapture Rise!

AHO-W,M
Arise, O Glorious Zion
  AHO-W,M
Arise O Lord
  FiS-W,M
Arise, O Lord, Our God, Arise
  Hy-W,M
Arise, Shine
  VB-W,M
Arise, Ye Garvey Nation
  AFP-W
Arise, Ye Saints of Latter Days
  AHO-W,M
Arise! Ye Sons of Labor!
  AL-W
Aristocracy of Democracy
  ESU-W
Aristocrats' Election Song
  AL-W
Arizona
  Fif-W,M
Arizona Home
  GA-W,M
Ark
  NF-W
Arkangel
  BDW-W,M
Arkansas
  Fif-W,M Oz3-W
Arkansas Boys
  Oz3-W,M
Arkansas Traveler
  AmH-M ASB6-W,M BSC-W
  FSB3-M FVV-W,M FW-W HAS-
  W,M OHG-W,M OHO-W,M
  OTJ-W,M Oz3-W,M PoS-W,M
  RS-W,M SFM-W STR-M
Arkansas Traveller
  POT-W,M
Arkansaw Traveler
  ATS-W,M TBF-M TF-W,M
Arlington
  SHS-W,M
**Arm & Hammer Baking Soda Jingle
  see Don't Think the Future**
Arm, Arm, Ye Brave
  FiS-W,M
Arm of the Lord, Awake, Awake
  Hy-W,M
Armadillo
  ASB5-W,M
Armistice Day
  PS-W,M
Armoraider's Song
  GO-W,M
Armored Cruiser Squadron
  GO-W,M
**Armour Hot Dog Theme see Dogs
  Kids Love to Bite**
Arms of Love
  OGR-W,M VB-W,M
Armstrong at Fayal
  ANS-W
Army Bean
  Sin-W,M SiS-W
Army Blue
  ATS-W,M
Army Blues
  LC-W
Army Bugs
  Sin-W,M SiS-W
Army Chair Corps Song
  AF-W GI-W
Army Flying Corps
  GO-W
Army Goes Rolling Along
  VA-W,M

Army Life
  Le-W,M
**Army Life see also Gee but I
  Wanna Go Home, I Don't Want
  No More Army, and I Don't Want
  No More of Army Life**
Army Mule, the Navy Goat
  GO-W
Army of Labor
  AL-W
Army of New Amsterdam
  KH-W,M
Army of the Lord
  VB-W,M WN-W,M
Army's Appeal to Mothers
  VS-W,M
Arnold Is As Brave a Man
  SSS-W,M
Aroha
  SNZ-W,M (Maori)
Around... see also Round...
Around and Around
  HR-W
Around Her Neck She Wore a
  Yellow Ribbon
  IHA-W,M
**Around Her Neck She Wore a
  Yellow Ribbon see also Round
  Her Neck She Wears (Wore) a
  Yellow Ribbon**
Around the Campfire Bright
  Bo-W,M
Around the Corner
  FW-W
Around the World
  FPS-W,M OTJ-W,M OTO-W
  RW-W,M
Around the World in Eighty Days
  TW-W
Arre Buey
  LA-W,M (Spanish)
Arrivederci Roma
  GrH-W,M HLS3-W,M RDT-W,M
  RT5-W,M RW-W,M TI1-W,M
Arrow through Me
  PMC-W,M TI2-W,M
Arroyo Claro
  LA-W,M (Spanish)
Arroz Con Leche
  CDM-W,M (Spanish) LA-W,M
  (Spanish)
Ars Longa, Vita Brevis
  Boo-W,M (Latin Only)
Art Thou the Christ
  FiS-W,M
Art Thou Weary
  GH-W,M OM-W,M
Art Thou Weary, Art Thou Languid
  Hy-W,M
Art Thou with Me
  MMM-W,M
**Arthur Godfrey and His Friends
  Theme see Seems Like Old Times**
Arthur Murray Taught Me Dancing
  in a Hurry
  OHF-W OTO-W
Arthur's Theme (Best That You
  Can Do)
  BCC-W,M BNG-W,M DC-W,M
  EY-W,M HFH-W,M MF-W,M
  RoE-W,M
Artificial Flowers
  UBF-W,M
Artistry in Rhythm
  GSF-W,M
Artist's Life
  MF-M TI1-M UFB-M

Artist's Life Waltz
  RW-M
Artza Alinu
  RW-W,M (Hebrew Only) TI1-W,M
  (Hebrew Only) UFB-W,M (Hebrew
  Only)
As Candles Glow
  CCM-W,M
As down a Lone Valley
  AHO-W,M
As Far As I'm Concerned
  OGC1-W,M
As Flows the Rapid River
  AHO-W,M
As Gentle Dews Distill
  AHO-W,M
As I Love My Own
  NB-W
As I Me Walked
  Boo-W,M
As I Put Off from Shore
  MML-W,M
As I Reminisce
  SNZ-W,M (Maori)
As I Roved Out
  IS-W,M
As I Sail Home to Galveston
  LMR-W,M
As I Sailed Out One Friday Night
  Oz1-W,M
As I Sat on a Sunny Bank
  MC-W,M
As I Walked Forth
  OH-W,M
As I Walked Out
  SCa-W,M
As I Walked Out One May Morning
  SCa-W
As I Walked Out One Morning in
  Spring
  FVV-W,M
As I Was Walkin' down Wexford
  Street
  AmS-W,M
As I Went by the Way
  Boo-W,M
As I Went Down in de Valley to
  Pray
  NSS-W
As I Went Down to David's Town
  AHO-W,M
As I Went over Tawny Marsh
  Boo-W,M
As I Went to Shiloh
  NF-W
As Jenny One Morning
  Boo-W,M
As Joseph Was A-Walking
  BCh-W,M MC-W,M
As Lately We Watched
  CSF-W Y-W,M
As Long As He Needs Me
  DBC-W,M HC2-W,M HLS8-W,M
  ILT-W,M MF-W,M O-W,M
  TI1-W,M UBF-W,M UFB-W,M
As Long As I Have You
  RW-W,M SRE2-W,M
As Long As I Live
  MF-W,M Mo-W,M NM-W,M
As Long As the World Goes Round
  TW-W
As Long As There's an Apple Tree
  OTJ-W,M
As Long As We Got Each Other
  (Theme from Growing Pains)
  BNG-W,M DC-W,M MF-W,M
As On through the Seasons We

Sail
ML-W,M

As Once I Loved You
UBF-W,M

As Pants the Hart
GH-W,M

As Pants the Hart for Cooling
Streams
Hy-W,M

As Rhyming's the Rage
ESU-W

As Shadows Cast by Cloud and
Sun
AHO-W,M

As Simple As That
Mo-W,M NM-W,M OTO-W

As Spring the Winter Doth
Succeed
AHO-W,M

As Tears Go By
MF-W,M RoS-W,M TI1-W,M
TWD-W,M UFB-W,M

As the Backs Go Tearing By
IL-W,M

As the Moments
Boo-W,M

As the Sun Doth Daily Rise
ESB-W,M Hy-W,M

As There Be Three Blewe Beans
Boo-W,M

As through the Town
Boo-W,M

As Time Goes By
BNG-W,M DC-W,M EY-W,M
HFH-W,M MF-W,M RoE-W,M

As Tranquil Streams
AHO-W,M

As We Go Forth to Labor
GrM-W,M

As We Make It
GrM-W,M

As We Sail to Heaven's Shore
GP-W,M

As Welcome As the Flowers in
May
Oz4-W

As with Gladness Men of Old
AME-W,M CCH-W,M CI-W,M
Hy-W,M SJ-W,M

As You Were--So You Remain
RSC-W,M (Russian Only)

Ase's Death
RW-M

Ash Grove
BM-W BMC-W,M FBI-W,M
F1-W,M FSD-W,M Gu-W,M
Gu-W,MHS-W,M (Welsh)
MML-W,M NAS-W,M OTJ-W,M
SL-W,M TF-W,M U-W

Ashland Tragedy
BMM-W,M

Asi Eres Tu
LA-W,M (Spanish)

Ask Any Mermaid
BNG-W,M GSM-W,M

Ask Me Again
MF-W,M ReG-W,M

Ask Me Why
TWS-W

Ask Me Why I Do Not Sing
Boo-W,M

Ask Ye What Great Thing I Know
GH-W,M Hy-W,M

Ask Yourself Why
MLS-W,M

Asking for You
DR-W,M

Asleep at the Switch
LSR-W,M Oz4-W

Asleep in Jesus, Blessed Sleep
AME-W,M

Asleep in the Deep
FAW-W,M FSN-W,M FSTS-W,M
OFS-W,M OTJ-W,M

Asleep in the Light
VB-W,M

Aspiration (If I Wus de President)
NF-W

Aspiration (Out of the Dark the
Circling Sphere)
MHB-W,M

Aspirations
FSA2-W,M

Assassination of Governor William
Goebel
BMM-W

**Assassination of J. B. Marcum see
J. B. Marcum**

Assassin's Vision
SiS-W

Assembly
ASB6-W,M

Assignation
Boo-W,M

Assis Dans La Fenetre De Ma
Chambre
CaF-W (French Only)

Association Song
AL-W

Asteroid Light
FW-W

Astutus Constabularius
SR-W (Latin Only)

At a Georgia Camp Meeting
BH-W,M EFS-W,M FSTS-W,M
OFS-W,M OTJ-W,M

At a Time Like This
TW-W

At Barnum's Show
Oz3-W

At Beneficial (Doot Doot) You're
Good for More
TI1-W,M UFB-W,M

At Calvary
OM-W,M

At Christmastime
SN-W,M TI1-W,M UFB-W,M

At Close of Day
LMR-W,M

At Dawning
TM-M WGB/O-M

At Easter Time
SiR-W,M

At Eight in the Morning
SiS-W

At Even Ere the Sun Was Set
AME-W,M GH-W,M

At Even When the Sun Was Set
Hy-W,M

At Evening
MML-W,M SL-W,M

At Half Past Seven
ReG-W,M

At Home in a Spot
Mo-W,M

At Home Our Friends Are Dying
SiS-W

At Last
GG4-W,M GSF-W,M HLS3-W,M
RT4-W,M RW-W,M

At Length the Busy Day Is Done
AHO-W,M

At Length There Dawns the
Glorious Day

AHO-W,M

At Long Last Love
FrS-W,M ML-W,M OTO-W
UBF-W,M

At Market
ASB1-W,M

At My Front Door
TI1-W,M UFB-W,M

At My Side
MF-W,M

At My Window
Am-W,M

At Pierrot's Door
MG-W,M (French) MML-W,M
(French) NAS-W,M

**At Pierrot's Door see also Au Clair
De La Lune and By the Light of
the Moon**

At Seventeen
GrS-W,M RW-W,M

At Stony Brook (on the Road to
Munich)
MA-W,M

At Summer Morn
Boo-W,M

At Sundown
GG4-W,M GSN2-W,M GST-W,M
HLS2-W,M RT4-W,M RW-W,M
WDS-W,M

At Tamhran Dochais
VP-W (Gaelic Only)

At Tea
MH-W,M

At the Bakery
ASB2-W,M

At the Ballet
CL-W,M JP-W,M UBF-W,M

At the Blacksmith
RSC-W,M (Russian Only)

At the Circus
MH-W,M

**At the Clear Running Fountain see
A La Claire Fontaine**

At the Close of the Evening
Boo-W,M

At the Codfish Ball
OTJ-W,M

At the Cross
AME-W,M GH-W,M

At the Door of Mercy Sighing
AHO-W,M

**At the End of the Rainbow see
End, The (At the End of the
Rainbow)**

At the Fair
SCL-W,M

At the Feet of Jesus
GH-W,M

At the Foot of the Cross
CEM-W,M

At the Foot of Yonders Mountain
FGM-W,M MHB-W,M

At the Forge
FSA1-W,M

At the Gate of Heaven
HS-W,M (Spanish) MG-W,M
OU-W,M VA-W,M (Spanish)

At the Gym
FSA1-W,M

At the Hop
DRR-W,M ERM-W,M PoG-W,M
TI2-W,M

At the Jazz Band Ball
HLS1-W,M

At the Moving Picture Ball
T-W,M

At the Name of Jesus

Hy-W,M
At the Rink While Skating
  OHG-W,M
At the River
  OA2-W,M
At the Roxy Music Hall
  TS-W
At the Seaside
  MH-W,M
At the Sign of the Barber
  UF-W,M
At the Spinning Wheel
  FSA2-W,M SL-W,M
At the Zoo
  MH-W,M
At What Age
  TW-W
At Work beside His Father's Bench
  SHP-W,M
Athens
  OB-W,M
Atlanta Blues
  B-W,M Bl-W,M
Atlanta Burned Again Last Night
  TOC83-W,M
Atlanta's Ours and Fairly Won
  SiS-W
Attache
  SY-W,M
Attend My People
  Boo-W,M
Attention! see Tenshun!
Attoh Echod
  JS-W,M (Hebrew Only)
Attoh Horesoh
  JS-W,M (Hebrew Only)
Attractions of Philadelphia
  ESU-W
Au Bois Mesdames
  FSO-W,M (French)
Au Clair De La Lune
  BM-W BMC-W,M (French Only)
  Ch-W (French Only) CUP-W,M
  (French Only) FW-W (French)
  LTL-W,M (French Only) MP-W,M
  (French Only) OTJ-W,M (French
  Only)
**Au Clair De La Lune see also At
  Pierrot's Door and By the Light of
  the Moon**
Au Clair De La Lune Mon Ami
  Pierrot
  FSO-W,M (French)
Au Illonois
  CaF-W (French Only)
Au Na'c'itoches
  CaF-W (French Only)
Au Privave
  TI1-M UFB-M
Aubade
  LMR-W,M
Auf Ihr Christen
  AHO-W,M (German)
Auf Wiedersehen
  BP-W,M U-W
Auf Wiedersehen, My Dear
  MF-W,M
Auld Lang Syne
  AmH-W,M ASB4-W,M BCS-W,M
  BeB-W,M BH-W,M BMC-W,M
  Bo-W CSo-W,M ESB-W,M FW-W
  FWS-W,M HS-W,M HSD-W,M
  IL-W,M IPH-W,M LMR-W,M
  MAB1-W,M MAS-W,M MF-W,M
  MSA1-W NAS-W,M OAP-W,M
  OP2-M OS-W OTJ-W,M PoG-W,M
  RW-W,M SeS-W,M SiP-W,M

SL-W TH-W,M TI1-W,M U-W
  UFB-W,M VA-W,M WiS8-W,M
Auld Robin Gray
  HSD-W,M SeS-W,M
**Auld Wife beyond the Fire see Old
  Wife**
Aunt Clara
  NeA-W,M
Aunt Dinah Drunk
  NF-W
Aunt Dinah's Quilting Party
  ATS-W FW-W IL-W,M LMR-W,M
Aunt Hagar's Children
  B-M Bl-M
Aunt Hagar's Children Blues
  B-W,M
Aunt Harriet Beecha Stowe
  MPP-W SY-W,M
Aunt Jemima
  NF-W
Aunt Jemima (Jingle)
  GSM-W,M
Aunt Jemima's Plaster
  TBF-W,M
Aunt Molly's Appeal
  AFP-W
Aunt Molly's Bible Song
  AFP-W
Aunt Rhody
  BF-W,M FW-W MES2-W,M
  OTJ-W,M Oz2-W WSB-W,M
**Aunt Rhody see also Go Tell Aunt
  Rhodie (Rhody)**
Aunt Sal's Song
  BT-W,M
Aupres De Ma Blonde
  FSF-W (French) FW-W (French
  Only) IL-W,M (French Only)
  OTJ-W,M (French Only)
Aura Lee
  ATS-W BSB-W,M FSA1-W,M
  FWS-W,M GeS-W,M Gu-W,M
  HS-W,M HSD-W,M IL-W,M
  LMR-W,M OFS-W,M OTJ-W,M
  PoS-W,M Sin-W,M WU-W,M
Aurora's Christening
  FSA1-W,M
Aurore Pradere
  AAF-W,M (French) CSD-W,M
  (French)
Australian Christmas Carol
  ATM-W,M
Austrian Hymn
  AmH-W,M (German) MG-W,M
  (German)
**Austrian Hymn see also Gott
  Erhalte Franz Den Kaiser**
Auto
  ASB1-W,M MH-W,M
Auto Horns
  ASB1-W,M
Autograph
  PoG-W,M
Autolycus' Song
  FSS-W,M
Automan
  TVT-M
Automatic Love
  RB-W
Automation
  IHA-W,M SWF-W,M
Autumn (Cold through the
  Meadow Autumn Winds Are
  Blowing)
  ASB5-W,M
Autumn (Gently the Trees Are
  Swaying)

ASB1-W,M
Autumn (Sumac Leaves Are
  Turning Red)
  ASB4-W,M
Autumn (The Trees Are All
  Wonderful Yellow and Red)
  SOO-W,M
Autumn and Winter Winds
  MH-W,M
Autumn Chorus
  ASB3-W,M
Autumn Comes
  ASB4-W,M
Autumn Fires
  MH-W,M
Autumn Hiking Song
  SSe-W,M
Autumn Holiday
  ASB6-W,M
Autumn in New York
  FrS-W,M HC1-W,M MF-W,M
  OHB-W,M
Autumn Is Here
  ASB3-W,M
Autumn Leaves
  ASB2-W,M GOI7-W,M MH-W,M
  Mo-W,M OBN-W,M OHF-W
  OnT1-W,M PB-W,M RDT-W,M
  SOO-W,M TI2-W,M
Autumn Leaves Falling
  SiR-W,M
Autumn Leaves Have Fallen Down
  OTJ-W,M
Autumn Nocturne
  MF-W,M
Autumn of My Life
  HLS9-W,M RW-W,M
Autumn Roundelay
  SSe-W,M
Autumn Scene
  SL-W,M
Autumn Serenade
  GG5-W,M HLS3-W,M
Autumn Song
  MHB-W,M SSe-W,M
Autumn Twilight
  MML-W,M
Autumn Wind
  ASB3-W,M
Autumn's Ballad
  HFH-M
**Auxville Love see Love Has
  Brought Me to Despair**
Av Horahameem
  SBJ-W,M Hebrew Only)
Avalon
  MF-W,M MR-W,M OHB-W,M
Ave Maria (Arcadelt)
  LMR-W,M (Latin) MuM-W,M
  (Latin)
Ave Maria (Bach/Gounod)
  AmH-W,M SL-W,M (Latin) TI1-M
  TM-M UFB-M WiS7-W,M (Latin)
Ave Maria (Gabrieli)
  OU-W,M (Latin Only)
Ave Maria (Mascagni)
  AmH-W,M WiS7-W,M
Ave Maria (Mozart)
  Boo-W,M (Latin Only)
Ave Maria (Schubert)
  AmH-M FiS-W,M (German, Latin)
  FSY-W,M (German, Latin)
  MF-W,M NCB-W,M (Latin Only)
  OTJ-W,M (Latin Only) RW-W,M
  TI1-W,M TM-M UFB-W,M
  WGB/O-M WiS7-M WiS9-W,M
Ave Maris Stella

RJ-W,M
Ave Verum
TF-W,M
Ave Verum see also Voice of Praise
Average Boy
Oz4-W
Average Rein
HB-W,M
Avondale Mine Disaster
AL-W
Awake
AL-W FSA2-W,M
Awake and Sing the Song
AME-W,M GH-W,M
Awake! Awake!
SCa-W,M
Awake! Awake! Awake! Awake!
Boo-W,M
Awake! Be Free!
AL-W
Awake, Glad Soul! Awake! Awake!
AME-W,M
Awake, My Soul
FH-W,M GB-W,M GH-W,M
Awake, My Soul, and Meet the Day
AME-W,M
Awake, My Soul, and with the Sun
AME-W,M ESB-W,M Hy-W,M
Awake My Soul, Betimes Awake
AHO-W,M
Awake, My Soul! in Grateful Songs
AHO-W,M
Awake, My Soul, in Joyful Lays
AME-W,M
Awake, My Soul, Stretch Every Nerve
GH-W,M Hy-W,M
Awake My Soul Stretch Ev'ry Nerve
AME-W,M
Awake, Sweet Love
MU-W,M OH-W,M
Awake, Sweet Love, Thou Art Return'd
EL-W,M
Awake the Harp
SiM-W,M
Awake! the Torpor of This Dream
AL-W
Awake to Arms in Texas
SiS-W
Awake, You Lazy Sleepers
VA-W,M (German)
Awakening
FSA1-W,M
Away Down East
SY-W,M
Away Down Souf
SSFo-W,M
Away Down South
FHR-W,M
Away Down South There Is Rebellion
SiS-W
Away for Rio
CA-W,M MML-W,M VA-W,M
Away Goes Cuffee
SiS-W
Away High Up in the Mogliones
HOH-W,M
Away in a Manger
AHO-W,M AME-W,M BCh-W,M
BCS-W,M CC-W,M CCM-W,M
CEM-W,M CI-W,M CSF-W
FH-W,M FW-W FWS-W,M

GBC-W,M HS-W,M JOC-W,M
MC-W,M MF-W,M OAP-W,M
OPS-W,M PoG-W,M RW-W,M
SCS-W SHP-W,M SiB-W,M
SJ-W,M SOO-W,M U-W YC-W,M
Away in a Manger see also Cradle Hymn (Martin Luther)
Away in a Manger, No Crib for His Bed
Hy-W,M
Away over Jordan
WN-W,M
Away over Yonder
JF-W,M
Away with Rum
FW-W
Away with the Traitor Tyler
MPP-W
Aweigh, Santy Ano
TO-W,M
Awful Harbingers
NF-W
Axel and Hilda
SE-W,M (Swedish)
Axel Och Hilda
SE-W,M (Swedish)
Axis
SBF-W,M
Ay, Ay, Ay
HS-W,M (Spanish) LaS-W,M
(Spanish) LMR-W,M
Ay, This Land Her Sons and Daughters
SiP-W,M (Norwegian)
Ay, Zamba!
LA-W,M (Spanish)
Aye, Aye, Aye-Aye
OTJ-W,M
Aye, Drink a Little Longer
ESU-W
Aye Wakin', O
SeS-W,M
Ayleeyohu Hanovee
SBJ-W,M (Hebrew Only)
Aylesbury
SHS-W,M
Ayl Odon
SBJ-W,M (Hebrew Only)
Ayn Kaylohaynu
SBJ-W,M (Hebrew Only)
Ayn Komoho
SBJ-W,M (Hebrew Only)
Aytz Hayeem Hee
SBJ-W,M (Hebrew Only)
Az Yashir Moshe
SiP-W,M (Hebrew)
Azinon
SHS-W,M
Azure
GMD-W,M
Azzie's Song
SNS-W

B

B C Gave Me K P in a Hurry
GO-W
Baa, Baa, Black Sheep
AmH-W,M BBF-W,M GM-W
HS-W,M KF-W,M MH-W,M NF-W
OTJ-W,M RW-W,M SMa-W,M
Baba O'Riley
WA-W,M
Babbitt and the Bromide
GOB-W,M LSO-W NYT-W,M
Babe Is Born

CEM-W,M OB-W,M
Babe Lies in the Cradle
MC-W,M
Babe of Bethlehem
SHS-W,M
Babel's Streams
SHS-W,M
Babes in Arms
TI1-W,M UFB-W,M
Babes in the Wood
BB-W BSC-W FMT-W MSB-W
TBF-W
Babes in the Woods
ITP-W,M Oz1-W,M
Baby (You've Got What It Takes)
FRH-W,M LWT-W,M TI1-W,M
UFB-W,M
Baby, Baby
J-W,M
Baby, Baby, Baby
OTO-W
Baby Be Mine
Mo-W,M NM-W,M
Baby Birds
MH-W,M
Baby Buds
MH-W,M
Baby Bumble Bee
GM-W
Baby Bunting
HSD-W,M
Baby Bye Bye
EC-W,M
Baby Doll
MH-W,M ST-W,M
Baby, Don't Get Hooked on Me
MF-W,M
Baby, Don't You Want to Go
LC-W
Baby, Dream Your Dream
MF-W,M TW-W
Baby Elephant Walk
AT-W,M GOI7-M OnT6-M
OTJ-W,M OTO-W TOM-M
Baby Face
MF-W,M MR-W,M OHB-W,M
TI2-W,M
Baby Fir Trees
GM-W
Baby, I Don't Care
GAR-W,M MF-W,M SRE1-W,M
Baby I Lied
TI2-W,M
Baby, I Love Your Way
GrS-W,M RW-W,M
Baby, I'm A-Want You
MF-W,M TOH-W,M
Baby I'm Burning
ToO79-W,M
Baby in a Guinea Blue Gown
NeA-W,M
Baby, It's Cold Outside
TI2-W,M UBF-W,M
Baby Just like You
PoG-W,M
Baby Leaves
MH-W,M
Baby, Let Me Bring My Clothes Back Home
NH-W
Baby, Let the Deal Go Down
NH-W
Baby Let's Play House
EP-W,M
Baby Love
TTH-W,M
Baby Mine

FW-W HSD-W,M NH-W NI-W,M
Baby, Please Don't Go
 FW-W LC-W
Baby Sleep Shadows Creep
 SiS-W
Baby Talk
 TW-W
Baby, Talk to Me
 Mo-W,M NM-W,M OTO-W
Baby Wants Cherries
 NF-W
Baby, We're Really in Love
 HW-W,M
Baby, What Have I Done?
 NH-W
Baby, Won't You Please Come Home
 TI2-W,M ToS-W,M
Baby, You Sho Lookin' Warm
 NH-W
Baby, You're a Rich Man
 BBe-W,M Be2-W,M TWS-W
Baby You're Something
 TOH-W,M
Babylon
 BT-W,M
Babylon Is Fallen
 AFP-W WN-W,M
Babylon Is Falling
 Oz2-W,M
Babylonian Captivity
 SHS-W,M
Babylon's Fallen
 SiS-W
Babylon's Fallin'
 RF-W,M
Baby's Bath
 FF-W
Baby's Birthday
 MH-W,M
Baby's Got Her Blue Jeans On
 AWS-W,M
Baby's in Black
 BBe-W,M Be1-W,M TWS-W
Baby's in Memphis
 NH-W
Baby's Lullaby
 MH-W,M
Baby's Song
 ASB1-W,M
Baby's Way
 MH-W,M
Babysitter's Song see Vigndig A Fremd Kind
Baccalaureate Hymn
 SL-W,M
Bachelor Bold and Young
 FMT-W
Bachelor's Blues
 LC-W
Bachelor's Fare
 ESU-W
Bachelor's Hall
 D-W,M Oz3-W
Bachelor's Lament
 SY-W,M
Bachelor's Song
 SG-W,M
Bachelor's Walk
 VP-W,M
Bacio see Il Bacio
Back Again
 GM-W
Back Again at Michigan
 CoS-W,M
Back Bay Polka
 LSO-W NYT-W,M OTO-W

Back Home Again
 CJ-W,M CMG-W,M LC-W
 PoG-W,M WG-W,M
Back Home Again in Indiana see Indiana (Back Home Again in Indiana)
Back in the High Life Again
 BHO-W,M MF-W,M
Back in the Saddle Again
 Bo-W,M FC-W,M HLS9-W,M
 RW-W,M
Back in the U.S.A.
 TI1-W,M UFB-W,M
Back in the U.S.S.R.
 BBe-W,M Be2-W,M TWS-W
Back in Your Own Backyard
 HSS-W,M TI1-W,M UFB-W,M
Back of My Auntie's House
 CFS-W,M (French)
Back of the Loaf Is the Snowy Flour
 SHP-W,M
Back Street Affair
 OGC2-W,M
Back Street Girl
 RoS-W,M
Back to Arizona
 GA-W
Backlash Blues
 VS-W,M
Backside of Albany
 ATS-W
Backstage Babble
 Ap-W,M Mo-W,M OTO-W
 VSA-W,M
Backstreets
 RV-W
Backward, Turn Backward (Parody)
 HB-W,M
Backwater Blues
 AFB-W,M FW-W LC-W,M Le-W,M
Bacon on the Rind
 HAS-W,M
Bad
 BHO-W,M
Bad Ale Can Drag a Man Down
 BMM-W
Bad, Bad Leroy Brown
 GrH-W,M GrS-W,M JC-W,M
 PM-W,M RW-W,M RY-W,M
 RYT-W,M
Bad Boy (Boys Will Be Boys, Bad Boy, Bad Boy)
 TTH-W,M
Bad Boy (I Used to be a Bad Boy)
 DBL-W
Bad Brahma Bull
 HWS-W,M
Bad Companions
 Oz2-W
Bad Company
 OFS-W,M
Bad Features
 NF-W
Bad Girls
 ToO79-W,M
Bad Girl's Lament
 SoC-W
Bad in Ev'ry Man
 TS-W
Bad Lan' Stone
 NH-W
Bad Lee Brown
 Oz2-W,M
Bad Life Blues
 DBL-W
Bad Lover Blues

DBL-W
Bad Luck an' Trouble
 LC-W
Bad Moon Rising
 BR-W,M
Bad to Me
 ILS-W,M RY-W,M
Bad Tom Smith
 FSU-W
Bad Woman Blues
 DBL-W
Badge My Soldier Wore
 SiS-W
Badinage
 ASB1-M
Baduma Paddler's Song
 IF-W,M (French Only)
Baganda Song
 IF-W,M
Bagatelle
 ASB1-M
Baggage Coach Ahead
 Oz4-W
Bagpiper
 ASB5-W,M
Bagpipers
 ASB6-W,M
Bahama Mama
 LaS-W,M
Baiao see Delicado
Baieolle
 CaF-W (French Only)
Bailiff's Daughter of Islington
 BSC-W,M CSo-W,M ESB-W,M
 FMT-W FW-W OH-W,M SaS-W,M
Bainbridge's Victory
 ANS-W
Baissez Dung
 SGT-W,M
Bajour
 Mo-W,M NM-W,M OTO-W
Bake a Cake
 SOO-W,M
Baker Man
 ASB3-W,M
Baker Shop Boogie
 DBL-W
Baker Street
 TI2-W,M
Baker's Shop
 MH-W,M
Baking Apples
 STS-W,M
Bal Chez Boule
 CFS-W,M (French)
Bald-Headed End of the Broom
 Oz3-W,M
Bald Knobber Song
 Oz2-W,M
Balham Vicar
 PO-W,M
Bali Ha'i
 BeL-W,M HC1-W,M L-W
 OTJ-W,M OTO-W RW-W,M
 SP-W,M TI1-W,M UBF-W,M
Ball of Fire
 MF-W,M
Ballad
 BMC-M SBA-W
Ballad for Americans (Opening Theme)
 GG2-W,M
Ballad for Bill Moore
 SFF-W,M
Ballad for Un-American Blues
 PSN-W,M
Ballad of a Victor

Ballad of Accounting
IFM-W

Ballad of Aimee McPherson
LW-W,M PO-W,M

Ballad of All the Trades
SR-W,M

Ballad of Baby Face McGinty
LSO-W

Ballad of Barney Graham
AFP-W,M

Ballad of Ben Hall's Gang
ATM-W,M

Ballad of Big Ed
OTJ-W,M

Ballad of Billy the Bull Rider
HB-W,M

Ballad of Bloody Thursday
AFP-W SoC-W

Ballad of Bunker Hill
SI-W,M

Ballad of Cat Ballou
HFH-W,M

Ballad of Davy Crockett
NI-W,M On-W,M OTJ-W,M
OTO-W RW-W,M

Ballad of Gilligan's Isle
GTV-W,M

Ballad of Harriet Tubman
AFP-W LW-W,M

Ballad of Henry Ford
AFP-W

Ballad of Herbert Lee
SFF-W,M

Ballad of Ho Chi Minh
FW-W IFM-W VS-W,M

Ballad of Ira Hayes
IHA-W,M

Ballad of Jane McCrea
SSS-W,M

Ballad of Jed Clampett
BSo-W,M

Ballad of John and Yoko
BBe-W,M Be2-W,M TWS-W

Ballad of John Catchins
AFP-W

Ballad of Little Fauss and Big
Halsey
OTO-W

Ballad of MacTavish Mackee
MuM-W,M

Ballad of Nathan Hale
AWB-W

Ballad of Ole' Betsy
RB-W

Ballad of Ralph Nader
WF-W

Ballad of Richard Campos
VS-W,M

Ballad of Sam Hall
FW-W

**Ballad of Sam Hall see also Sam
Hall**

Ballad of Sergeant Champe
SSS-W,M

**Ballad of Sergeant Champe see
also Sergeant Champe**

Ballad of Sharpeville
IFM-W

Ballad of Sherman Wu
SoC-W

Ballad of Springhill
FW-W

Ballad of Sweeney Todd
UBF-W,M

Ballad of Talmadge
AFP-W

Ballad of the American War
SI-W,M

Ballad of the Blue Bell Jail
AFP-W WW-W,M

Ballad of the Boll Weevil
FW-W HAS-W,M

**Ballad of the Boll Weevil see also
Ballit of de Boll Weevil and Boll
Weevil**

Ballad of the Chicago Steel
Massacre
AFP-W

Ballad of the Fort Hood Three
VS-W,M

Ballad of the Non-Vietnamese
VS-W,M

Ballad of the Robbers
KH-W,M

Ballad of the Sad Young Men
UBF-W,M

Ballad of the Shop Girl
AL-W

Ballad of the Student Sit-Ins
SFF-W,M

Ballad of the Tea Party
ESU-W

Ballad of the Unknown Stuntman
TVT-W,M

Ballad of Thomas Appletree
BT-W,M

Ballad of Trenton
SBA-W,M SSS-W,M

Ballad of Voight's Camp
AFP-W

Ballad of Waterhole #3
BHB-W,M OnT6-W,M

Ballad of William White
VS-W,M

Ballad of Woodsy Owl
OTJ-W,M

Ballerina
MF-W,M NK-W,M TI1-W,M
UFB-W,M

Ballerma
SHS-W,M

Ballet Music
ReG-M

Ballet of Barbara Allan
SCa-W

**Ballet of Barbara Allan see also
Barbara Allen**

Ballet of the Unhatched Chicks
(Moussorgsky)
GM-M

Ballin' the Jack
BBB-W,M BeL-W,M GSN1-W,M
NoS-W,M OAP-W,M TI2-W,M

Ballinamona
VP-W,M

Ballit of de Boll Weevil
NeF-W

**Ballit of de Boll Weevil see also
Ballad of the Boll Weevil**

Balloon Man
ASB3-W,M MH-W,M

Balloons (Balloon! Balloon! Come
Buy Your Balloon!)
SOO-W,M

Balloons (Floating High, Floating
By)
ASB2-W,M

Ballot
AL-W

Ballroom Dancing
TI2-W,M

Ballstown
SHS-W,M

Ballymurphy
FW-W

Balm in Gilead
FW-W MuM-W,M WN-W,M

Balm of Gilead
ATS-W,M

Balmy Afternoon in May
LA-W,M (Spanish)

Balooloo My Lammie
SeS-W,M

Baltimore Oriole
MF-W,M

Balulalow
OB-W,M

Balzamina
UF-W,M

Bambocheur see Un Bambocheur

Bamboo Briars
BSC-W

**Bamboo Cage see Smellin' of
Vanilla**

Banana Boat Song
FAW-W,M LaS-W,M OBN-W,M
OFS-W,M TI2-W,M

Banbury Ale
Boo-W,M

Band
ASB2-W,M ASB4-W,M MAR-W,M

Band ob Gideon
RF-W,M

Band of Children
OB-W,M

Band of Gold
SoH-W,M TI1-W,M UFB-W,M

Band on the Run
GrS-W,M On-W,M PMC-W,M
TI2-W,M

Band Played On
ATS-W BeB-W,M BH-W,M
EFS-W,M FSN-W,M FSTS-W,M
FW-W GSN1-W,M HLS1-W,M
IL-W,M MAS-W,M MF-W,M
OAP-W,M OBN-W,M OS-W
PoG-W,M RW-W,M TI1-W,M
UFB-W,M

Bandit Ball
TOC83-W,M

Bandstand Boogie
TI2-W,M

Bandura
UF-W,M

Bang Bang
JD-W,M

Bang! Bang! Bang!
AL-W

Bangidero
SA-W,M

Bangum and the Boar
BSC-W

**Bangum and the Boar see also Old
(Ole) Bangum**

Banished Defender
VP-W,M

Banishment
BSC-W

Banjo Blues
Bl-W,M

Banjo Picking
NF-W

Banjo Song
L-W Oz2-W,M TH-W,M

Bank Melodies No. 1
AL-W

Bank Melodies No. 2
AL-W

Banks of Brandywine
ESU-W

Banks of Claudie
FMT-W FoM-W,M
Banks of Claudy
BSC-W SCa-W,M
Banks of Cloddy
Oz1-W,M
Banks of Dundee
BSC-W
Banks of Marble
FW-W TO-W,M
Banks of Newfoundland
SA-W,M
Banks of Ohio
ESU-W
Banks of Sacramento
AmS-W,M
**Banks of Sacramento see also
Banks of the Sacramento and On
the Banks of the Sacramento**
Banks of Schuylkill
ESU-W
**Banks of Schuylkill see also Banks
of the Schuylkill**
Banks of the Condamine
ATM-W,M
Banks of the Dee
EA-W,M SAR-W SBA-W SI-W
SSS-W,M UF-W,M
Banks of the Dee (Parody)
SI-W,M
Banks of the Little Eau Pleine
AH-W,M
Banks of the Nile
Oz1-W,M
Banks of the Ohio
BF-W,M BIS-W,M BSo-W,M
FGM-W,M FSt-W,M FW-W
RW-W,M
Banks of the Old Raritan
ESB-W,M
Banks of the Roses
FW-W
Banks of the Sacramento
ATS-W,M
**Banks of the Sacramento see also
Banks of Sacramento and On the
Banks of the Sacramento**
Banks of the Schuylkill
Oz4-W,M
**Banks of the Schuylkill see also
Banks of the Schuylkill**
Banks of the Verigo
OHO-W,M
Banks They Are Rosy
IFM-W
Banner of the Cross
GH-W,M
Banner of the Sea
ANS-W SiS-W
Banner of the Stars
AWB-W SiS-W
Banquets, Parties, and Balls
AF-W
Banshee
VP-W
Baptizin'
BDW-W,M
Baptizing Hymn
AAF-W,M WN-W,M
Bar-Z of a Sunday Night
HOH-W,M
Barbara Allen
AH-W,M ATS-W,M BSC-W
BT-W,M CSo-W,M DD-W,M
FoM-W,M FSSC-W,M FVV-W,M
FW-W Gu-W,M GuC-W,M
HS-W,M HSD-W,M IL-W,M

ILS-W,M ITP-W,M NAS-W,M
OH-W,M OHO-W,M Oz1-W,M
SCa-W,M SFM-W SoF-W,M
**Barbara Allen see also variant titles
below, from Barbara Ellen to
Barbry Ellen**
Barbara Ann
DRR-W,M ERM-W,M GAR-W,M
ILS-W,M MF-W,M
Barbara Ellen
BSC-W DD-W,M SCa-W
Barbara Frietchie
OHG-W,M
Barbara Polka
PT-M
Barbare Allen
SCa-W
Barbary Allen
RW-W,M SCa-W,M
Barbary Ellen
MSH-W,M SG-W,M
Barber
GM-W MH-W,M
Barber, Spare Those Hairs
HAS-W,M
Barberie Allen
SCa-W
Barbery Allen
FMT-W SCa-W,M
Barbra Allen
AmS-W,M OTJ-W,M
Barbra Ellen
SAm-W,M
Barbrey Allen
ITP-W,M
Barbro Buck
Oz2-W
Barbry Allen
ASB6-W,M J-W,M Oz1-W
Barbry Ellen
D-W,M MSH-W,M SCa-W
SG-W,M
Barcarolle (Lovely Night)
FSY-W,M (French) OTJ-W,M
RW-M
**Barcarolle (Lovely Night) see also
Lovely Night (Offenbach)**
Barcarolle (Sail on, Poor Barque,
Sail On)
TH-W,M
Barcelona
Co-W,M TW-W
Bard of Armagh
FW-W IS-W,M
Bardomshemmet
SE-W,M (Swedish)
**Bare Essence Theme see In Finding
You I Found Love**
Bare Necessities
NI-W,M OTJ-W,M
Barefoot Boy with Boots On
Oz3-W
Barefoot in the Park
OTO-W
Barefooted Dancer
SMa-W,M
Bargain
WA-W,M
Bark Canoe
SL-W,M TF-W,M
Bark for Barksdale
TI1-M UFB-M
Barley Mow
OH-W,M
Barn Burning
PF-W,M
Barn Dance

LMR-W,M
Barnacle Bill the Pilot
AF-W
Barnacle Bill the Sailor
OFS-W,M
Barney Buntline
OTJ-W,M TH-W,M
Barney Google
MF-W,M OHB-W,M WF-W,M
Barney Graham
PSN-W,M
Barney McCoy
Oz4-W,M TMA-M,W
Barney's Invitation
ANS-W
Barnyard
DD-W,M SOO-W,M
Barnyard Song
FoS-W,M FSA2-W,M HAS-W,M
HS-W,M TF-W,M
Barnyards of Delgaty
FW-W
Baron (Theme)
GTV-M
Baron of Brackley
BT-W,M
Barrel of Pork
MSB-W
Barrymore Tithe Victory
VP-W,M
Barter
LMR-W,M
Baruch Hashem Adonai
OGR-W,M VB-W,M
Baseball Game
YG-W,M
Basement Blues
B-W,M
Basie's Back in Town
MF-M
Basin Street Blues
B-W,M BBB-W,M Mo-W,M
NM-W,M On-W,M TI2-W,M
Basket House
ASB2-W,M
Basket Makers
FSA1-W,M
Basket-Maker's Child
Oz4-W,M
Bastard Child
LC-W
Bastard King of England
FW-W GO-W,M PO-W,M
Bat! Bat!
NF-W
Bath
BR-W,M
Batman (Theme)
GTV-W,M
Battle between the Chesapeake
and Shannon
ANS-W
Battle Cry of Freedom
AH-W,M AmH-W,M ATS-W
FW-W HA-W,M HSD-W,M
MPP-W,M NAS-W,OTJ-W,M
PoS-W,M Sin-W,M SiS-W TH-W
TMA-W,M WiS8-W,M
Battle Cry of Freedom (Southern
Version)
Sin-W,M
Battle Hymn
LoS-W,M
Battle Hymn of Freedom
AL-W
Battle Hymn of the Hussites
SMW-W,M

Beach Boy Blues
  SRE1-W,M
Beacon
  FSA2-W,M
Beale Street Blues
  B-W,M
Beam of the Morning
  ESU-W
Beams of Heaven
  AME-W,M
Beams of Heaven As I Go
  AME-W,M
Bean Bag
  OnT6-M
Beans and Hardtack
  GI-W
Beans, Bacon and Gravy
  AFP-W,M FW-W IHA-W,M
  SWF-W,M
Beans for Breakfast
  GO-W
Bear Came, The
  ASB2-W,M
Bear Dance
  FSA2-W,M
Bear de Burden
  FN-W,M
Bear the Cross Ye Sons of Men
  AME-W,M
Bear Them Home Tenderly
  SiS-W
Bear This Gently to My Mother
  SiS-W
Bear Went over the Mountain
  FSA1-W,M
Bear Yo' Burden
  NH-W
Bearers of the Law
  JS-W,M
Bears
  OTJ-W,M
Bears' Lullaby
  ASB4-W,M
Beast of Burden
  RoS-W,M
Beat Goes On
  MF-W,M RB-W
Beat It
  MF-W,M
Beat Me Daddy, Eight to the Bar
  TI2-W,M
Beat Out Dat Rhythm on a Drum
  L-W
Beat the System
  VB-W,M
Beau Soir (Evening Fair)
  FSY-W,M (French)
Beauregard
  Sin-W,M
Beauregard Manassas Quickstep
  SCo-W,M
Beautiful
  Mo-W,M NM-W,M OTO-W
Beautiful, Beautiful Brown Eyes
  IL-W,M
**Beautiful, Beautiful Brown Eyes
  see also Beautiful Brown Eyes**
Beautiful, Beautiful World
  UBF-W,M
Beautiful Bells
  HSD-W,M
Beautiful Bill
  Oz3-W,M
Beautiful Brown Eyes
  FW-W MAB1-W,M MSA1-W,M
  OFS-W,M OTJ-W,M RW-W,M
Beautiful Brown Eyes see also

Beautiful, Beautiful Brown Eyes
Beautiful Child of Song
  FHR-W,M SSF-W,M
Beautiful City
  DC-W,M HFH-W,M JF-W,M
Beautiful Day
  MES1-W,M MES2-W,M
Beautiful Dead
  GrM-W,M
Beautiful Dreamer
  ATS-W,M FHR-W,M FW-W
  HSD-W,M IL-W,M LoS-W,M
  MAB1-W,M MSA1-W OAP-W,M
  OFS-W,M OS-W PoG-W,M
  RW-W,M SSF-W,M SSFo-W,M
  U-W WiS8-W,M
Beautiful Francesca
  FSO-W,M (French)
Beautiful Friendship
  TI1-W,M UFB-W,M
Beautiful Girls
  Fo-W,M OTO-W
**Beautiful Girls see also Prologue
  (Beautiful Girls)**
**Beautiful Girls Walk a Little Slower
  see This Is All I Ask**
Beautiful Golden Somewhere
  GrM-W
Beautiful Grange
  GrM-W,M
Beautiful Gypsy
  ReG-W,M
Beautiful Heaven
  HS-W,M (Spanish)
**Beautiful Heaven see also Cielito
  Lindo**
Beautiful Isle of Somewhere
  AME-W,M BSG-W,M BSP-W,M
  FS-W,M FSN-W,M HLS7-W,M
  JBF-W,M OAP-W,M RDF-W,M
Beautiful Isle of the Sea
  ATS-W HSD-W,M
Beautiful Land
  GH-W,M
Beautiful Land Called Home
  SS-W
Beautiful Life
  BSo-W,M
Beautiful Light o'er the Sea
  BSC-W
Beautiful Love
  OnT6-W,M
Beautiful Morning
  WN-W,M
Beautiful Music to Love By
  Mo-W,M
Beautiful Nebraska
  FiF-W,M
Beautiful Night
  ST-W,M
Beautiful Noise
  TI2-W,M
Beautiful Ohio
  Fif-W,M HLS1-W,M MF-W,M
  RDT-W,M TI1-W,M UFB-W,M
Beautiful River
  PoS-W,M
Beautiful Savior
  CSF-W SCS-W
Beautiful Saviour
  SJ-W,M
Beautiful Ship from Toyland
  Fi-W,M
Beautiful Shore
  FHR-W,M
Beautiful Star in Heaven So Bright
  HSD-W,M

Beautiful Sunday
  GrH-W,M
Beautiful, Wonderful Sights to See
  SHP-W,M
Beautiful Yuletide
  CCM-W,M
Beauty
  FSA1-W,M
Beauty around Us
  OU-W,M RS-W,M
Beauty, Beauty Bride
  Oz1-W,M
**Beauty in Love's Garden see La
  Belle Est Au Jardin D'Amour**
Beauty Queen
  SYB-W,M
Beauty School Dropout
  Gr-W,M Mo-W,M OTO-W TW-W
  UBF-W,M
Beauty's Eyes
  AmH-W,M WiS8-W,M
Beaver Cap
  BSC-W Oz3-W,M
**Bebe Et Le Gaimbleur see La Bebe
  Et Le Gaimbleur**
Because (Lennon/McCartney)
  BBe-W,M Be2-W,M OnT1-W,M
  TWS-W
Because (Teschemacher/
  d'Hardelot)
  FS-W,M FSN-W,M (French)
  GSN1-W,M HLS1-W,M JBF-W,M
  MAB1-W,M MSA1-W OAP-W,M
  RW-W,M TI1-W,M TM-W,M
  UFB-W,M WGB/O-W,M
  WGB/P-W,M
Because All Men Are Brothers
  JF-W,M RDF-W,M
Because, Because
  GOB-W,M OT-W,M
Because God Loves All People
  SHP-W,M
Because He Joined the Grange
  GrM-W,M
Because He Lives
  OM-W,M
Because He Was Only a Tramp
  LSR-W,M
Because I Knew Not When My Life
  Was Good
  Hy-W,M
Because My Baby Don't Mean
  Maybe Now
  WDS-W,M
Because of Thy Great Bounty
  FiS-W,M
Because of Who You Are
  VB-W,M
Because of You
  PB-W,M
Because She Ain't Built That Way
  TMA-W,M
Because They're Young
  TI1-W,M UFB-W,M
Because You're Mine
  GG5-W,M HLS5-W,M RT5-W,M
  RW-W,M
Because You're You
  HSD-W,M
Becky at the Loom
  Oz4-W
Becky Dean
  NeF-W
Bed Bug
  NF-W
Bed of Primroses
  DD-W,M

Bed Time (When the Day Is Done)
MH-W,M
Bedelia
FSN-W,M RC-W,M
Bedouin Love Song
GC-W,M
Bedroom
TOH-W,M
Bedroom Ballad
TOH-W,M
Bedroom Window
BSC-W
Beds
MH-W,M
Bedtime (Hurry to Bed It's Getting
Late)
SOO-W,M
Bedtime (When the Sun, a Ball of
Red)
ASB2-W,M
Bee, The (Buzz, Buzz, Buzz, Busy
Little Bee)
ASB5-W,M
Bee, The (Into the Blossom Goes
the Bee)
MH-W,M
Bee, The (Yesterday I Met a Bee)
MHB-W,M
Bee and the Ant
ASB2-W,M
Bee-Baw-Babbity
CSG-W,M
Beehive State
RB-W
Been by de Watah
BPM-W,M
Been Down into the South
SFF-W,M
Been in Jail
Am-W
Been in the Pen So Long
FG2-W,M FW-W
Been in the Storm So Long
FSSC-W,M
**Been in the Storm So Long see
also I Been in the Storm So Long**
Been Out West, Headed East
LC-W
Been Wash in de Blood ob de
Lamb
BDW-W,M
Beep Beep
ERM-W,M GAR-W,M ILF-W,M
MF-W,M
Beer Barrel Polka
HLS2-W,M MF-W,M PT-W,M
MF-W,M RDT-W,M TI1-W,M
**Beer Barrel Polka see also Roll Out
the Barrel**
Beer, Beer, Beer
AF-W
Beer Call Chant
AF-W
Bees and Frogs
SOO-W,M
Before Dawn
UF-W,M
Before I Gaze at You Again
LL-W,M OTO-W
Before I Kiss the World Goodbye
TW-W
Before I Met You
BIS-W,M BSo-W,M
Before I'd Be a Slave
AL-W WN-W,M
Before Jehovah's Awful Throne
AME-W,M Hy-W,M WiS7-W,M

Before School
MH-W,M
Before the Day Draws near Its
Ending
Hy-W,M
Before the Next Teardrop Falls
CMG-W,M FrF-W,M (Spanish)
HLS9-W,M MF-W,M RW-W,M
Before the Parade Passes By
Mo-W,M NM-W,M OTO-W
TI2-W,M UBF-W,M
Before the Sun Was Risen
SoF-W,M
Before They Make Me Run
RoS-W,M
Before We Play
MAR-W,M
Before You Make a Promise
Boo-W,M
Beg, Borrow and Steal
OnT6-W,M
Beggar Man
PIS-W,M
Beggarman
IS-W,M
Beggarman's Song
VP-W,M
Beggar's Petition
MPP-W,M
Begging Dance
FSA2-W,M
Begging to You
FrF-W,M
Begin, My Tongue, Some Heavenly
Theme
Hy-W,M
Begin the Beguine
BNG-W,M DBC-W,M DC-W,M
HC1-W,M MF-W,M ML-W,M
Beginner's Luck
LSO-W OTO-W SRE2-W,M
Beginning to Grow
MH-W,M
Begone, Dull Care
OH-W,M SMY-W,M TF-W,M
TH-W,M
Begone, Pernicious Tea
SSS-W,M
Begone, Unbelief
WN-W,M
Behind Blue Eyes
WA-W,M
Behind Closed Doors
EC-W,M GCM-W,M MF-W,M
Behold a Host
SJ-W,M
Behold, a Stranger's at the Door
AME-W,M
Behold a Tender Newborn Babe
CSB-W,M
Behold, It Is the Spring-Tide of the
Year
SBJ-W,M
Behold the Amazing Gift of Love
Hy-W,M
Behold the Lamb
HHa-W,M VB-W,M
Behold the Lamb of God
SHS-W,M
Behold the Lone Star
MPP-W
Behold the Lord High Executioner
GiS-W,M MG-W,M OTJ-W,M
SL-W,M
Behold the Savior of Mankind
AME-W,M RW-W,M
Behold, the Shade of Night Is Now

Receding
AHO-W,M
Behold What Wondrous Grace
AME-W,M
Behold with Joy
AHO-W,M
Behy Eviction
VP-W,M
Bei Der Wiege
AS-W,M (German)
Bei Mir Bist Du Schon
MF-W,M OHB-W,M
Bein' Green
FPS-W,M
Being Alive
Co-W,M OTO-W TW-W UBF-W,M
Being for the Benefit of Mr. Kite
Be2-W,M TWS-W
Bekehrte see Die Bekehrte
Bel' Layotte
CSD-W,M (French)
**Belgian National Hymn see La
Brabanconne**
Believe
OTO-W UBF-W,M
Believe in Yourself
MF-W,M
Believe Me Dearest Susan
SA-W,M
Believe Me If All Those Endearing
Young Charms
AmH-W,M ESB-W,M FW-W
Gu-W,M HSD-W,M IL-W,M
MF-W,M NAS-W,M OAP-W,M
OS-W RW-W,M TH-W,M
WiS8-W,M
Believer, O Shall I Die
NSS-W
Believers
VB-W,M
Believing for the Best in You
VB-W,M
Bell Bottom Blues
HD-W,M
Bell Bottom Trousers
FW-W OFS-W,M OTJ-W,M
TI1-W,M UFB-W,M
Bell Buoy
FSA2-W,M MML-W,M
Bell Buoy's Song
KS-W,M
Bell Canon
OTJ-W,M
Bell Carol
OB-W,M
Bell Doth Toll
Boo-W,M EFS-W,M SOO-W,M
Bell Dun Ring
BDW-W,M
Bell of Creation
GBC-W,M
Bell Round
BMC-M
Bell Song
GUM1-W,M MuM-W,M
Bell Trio
LMR-W,M
Bella
LW-W,M PO-W,M
Bella Ciao
FW-W (Italian)
Bella Notte
NI-W,M OTJ-W,M
**Belle Au Bois Dormant see La Belle
Au Bois Dormant**
Belle Bayou
MBS-W,M

Belle Bergere see Eine Belle Bergere
Belle Brandon
Oz4-W
Belle Creole
CaF-W (French Only)
Belle J'ai V'nu Pou' Vous Dire
CaF-W (French Only)
Belle Mahone
HSD-W,M
Belle Missouri
SiS-W
Belle of the Ball
Sta-W,M
Belle S'en Va Au Jardin D'Amour see La Belle S'en Va Au Jardin D'Amour
Belle Starr
Am-W
Belles Filles see Les Belles Filles
Bellman's Song
OB-W,M
Bells
ASB1-W,M ASB5-W,M GM-W
SOO-W,M
Bells Are Ringing
U-W UBF-W,M
Bells of Aberdovey
SL-W,M UF-W,M
Bells of Canterbury see Paper of Pins
Bells of Rhymney
TI1-W,M UFB-W,M
Bells of St. Mary's
BCh-W,M IL-W,M OTJ-W,M
RT4-W,M TI1-W,M UFB-W,M
Bells of St. Paul's
GBC-W,M
Bells of Shandon
VP-W,M
Bells of Washington
Mo-W,M
Belly Up to the Bar, Boys
TI2-W,M
Beloved Emblem
SoF-W,M
Beloved One
SNZ-W,M (Maori)
Below the Gallows Tree
TO-W,M
Belt-Line Girl
SMW-W,M
Ben
TOM-W,M
Ben Backstay
ANS-W
Ben Bolt
AmH-W,M EFS-W,M FW-W OTJ-W,M PoS-W,M WiS8-W,M
Ben Casey (Theme)
Mo-M
Ben Dewberry's Final Run
LSR-W,M
Ben Franklin, Esq.
IL-W,M
Ben Johnson's Carol
OB-W,M
Bend a Little My Way
RW-W,M
Bend Down, Sister
Mo-W,M NM-W,M OTO-W
Bendemeer's Stream
BF-W,M FW-W HS-W,M LoS-W,M
MML-W TH-W,M VA-W,M
Bendigo Champion of England
MSB-W
Beneath... see also 'Neath...

Beneath a Bridge in Sicily
AF-W GI-W,M
Beneath a Weeping Willow's Shade
EA-W,M NAS-W,M
Beneath in the Dust
Boo-W,M
Beneath My Little Window
FSF-W (French)
Beneath Our Flag see 'Neath Our Flag
Beneath the Belgian Watertank
GO-W
Beneath the Cross of Jesus
AME-W,M Hy-W,M
Beneath the Eastern Moon
ReG-W,M
Beneath the Elms see 'Neath the Elms
Beneath the Southern Moon see 'Neath the Southern Moon
Beneath This Window see 'Neath This Window
Beneath Thy Wings
JS-W,M (Hebrew)
Benedic, Domine, Nobis His
Boo-W,M (Latin Only)
Benediction
YS-W,M
Beneficial Finance Theme see At Beneficial (Doot Doot) You're Good for More
Benevento
SHS-W,M
Benjy Havens
Oz2-W,M
Bennie and the Jets
TI2-W,M
Benny Haven's O
SiS-W
Benny Havens Oh
ATS-W
Benton County, Arkansas
Oz3-W,M
Berceuse (Lullaby from Jocelyn)
AmH-W,M FSY-W,M (French)
MML-W,M (French) TF-W,M
WiS7-W,M
Berceuse Bearnaise
CUP-W,M (French Only)
Berelin Barlengot
CaF-W (French Only)
Berg Op Zoom
SMW-W,M (Dutch)
Bergen Op Zoom
SiP-W,M (Dutch)
Berger, Berger
CaF-W (French Only)
Berkeley Woman
CMG-W,M
Berkshire Tragedy
OH-W,M SCa-W
Berlin Wall
SFF-W,M
Bernie's Tune
DJ-M TI1-W,M UFB-W,M
Berosh Hashonoh
JS-W,M (Hebrew Only)
Besame Mucho
TOM-W,M (Spanish Only)
Beseda
MHB-W,M (Czech)
Beside a Babbling Brook
MF-W,M WDS-W,M
Beside a Belgian 'Staminet
AF-W
Beside a Korean Waterfall

AF-W
Beside a New Guinea Waterfall
AF-W
Bess You Is My Woman
LM-W,M On-W,M OTO-W
UBF-W,M
Bess You Is My Woman Now
NYT-W,M
Bessie Bell and Mary Gray
SCa-W
Best Bedroom in Town
TOC82-W,M
Best Days
DBL-W
Best Disco in Town
ToO76-W,M
Best Is Yet to Come
MF-W,M Mo-W,M NM-W,M
TI2-W,M
Best Little Whorehouse in Texas Theme see I Will Always Love You
Best Minute of the Day
BNG-W,M
Best Night of My Life
Ap-W,M Mo-W,M OTO-W
VSA-W,M
Best of Buddies
RSL-W,M
Best of Everything
GOB-W,M
Best of Friends
NI-W,M TI2-W,M
Best of Me
TTH-W,M
Best of My Love
DPE-W,M MF-W,M
Best of Times
DBC-W,M TI2-W,M UBF-W,M
Best Old Feller in the World
Oz3-W,M
Best That You Can Do see Arthur's Theme
Best Thing of All
TW-W
Best Thing That Ever Happened to Me
SoH-W,M
Best Thing We Can Do
ESU-W
Best Thing You've Ever Done
Mo-W,M
Best Things in Life Are Free
BeL-W,M DBC-W,M HC1-W,M
MF-W,M RDF-W,M TI1-W,M
UBF-W,M UFB-W,M
Best Years of His Life
LD-W,M
Bethany
FMT-W
Bethel
AWB-W
Bethlehem
CCH-W,M OB-W,M (French)
Bethlehem Morning
OGR-W,M
Beth'lem Night
ASB6-W,M
Betsey Brown
Oz3-W,M
Betsy
FVV-W,M
Betsy Baker
ESU-W Oz1-W,M
Betsy from Pike
ASB6-W,M BSC-W
Betsy from Pike see also Sweet

Betsy from Pike

Betsy Is a Beauty Fair
  Oz1-W,M

Betsy Monger
  SNS-W

Better Days Are Coming
  FHR-W,M

Better Days to Come
  GrM-W,M

Better Homes and Gardens
  TI1-W,M UFB-W,M

Better Love Next Time
  ToO79-W,M

Better Times Are Coming
  FHR-W,M SiS-W

Better Walk Steady
  MoM-W,M

Betty and Dupree
  FW-W

Betty, Betty, Where Are You
  SOT-W,M

Betty Lou Got a New Pair of Shoes
  FRH-W,M

Betty Martin
  ASB1-W,M

Between 18th and 19th on
  Chestnut Street
  TI2-W,M

Between the Devil and the Deep
  Blue Sea
  MF-W,M TI2-W,M

Between You and Me
  ML-W,M

Betwixt Dick and Tom see 'Twixt
  Dick and Tom

Beulah Land
  FW-W

Beverly Hillbillies Theme see Ballad
  of Jed Clampett

Beware, Brother, Beware
  OnT6-W,M

Beware! Dearest Comrades
  Boo-W,M

Beware: Here Come Friends
  VS-W,M

Beware of a Cowboy Who Wears a
  White Hat
  SoC-W

Beware, Oh Beware
  Oz3-W,M

Beware Oh Take Care
  FW-W OHO-W,M

Bewitched
  DBC-W,M HC2-W,M HLS8-W,M
  MF-W,M OTO-W RW-W,M
  ToS-W,M TI1-W,M TVT-W,M
  UBF-W,M UFB-W,M

Bewitched, Bothered and
  Bewildered
  TS-W TW-W

Beyond My Wildest Dreams
  UBF-W,M

Beyond That Road
  Fa-W,M

Beyond the Blue Horizon
  AT-W,M MM-W,M OnT1-W,M
  OTO-W

Beyond the Reef
  TI2-W,M

Beyond the Sea
  TI1-W,M TI2-W,M UFB-W,M

Beyond the Sunset
  BSG-W,M BSP-W,M CCS-W,M
  CEM-W,M HHa-W,M OM-W,M
  RDF-W,M

Beyond Tomorrow
  AT-W,M

Bibbidi Bobbidi Boo
  NI-W,M On-W,M OTJ-W,M
  OTO-W

Bible Song
  SoP-W,M

Bible Tells How Sky and Sea
  SHP-W,M

Bible Tells Me So
  AT-W,M BSG-W,M BSP-W,M
  IPH-W,M OTJ-W,M RDF-W,M

Bible Tells of God's Great Love
  SHP-W,M

Bible Tells of God's Great Plan
  SHP-W,M

Bible That Mother Gave to Me
  HLS7-W,M

Bicera, The
  BSC-W

Bicycle Built for Two
  EFS-W,M FM-W,M FW-W
  LoS-W,M MAS-W,M OTJ-W,M
  RW-M TI1-W,M UFB-W,M

Bicycle Built for Two see also
  Daisy Bell and Daisy Daisy

Bid Me Discourse
  FSS-W,M OH-W,M

Bid Me to Live
  OH-W,M

Biddle, Let the Bank Alone
  AL-W

Bidin' My Time
  BNG-W,M GOB-W,M LSO-W,M
  MF-W,M NYT-W,M OHB-W,M
  TW-W

Big Ball in Boston
  BSo-W,M

Big Bass Drum
  GM-W

Big Beat
  OTO-W RW-W,M UBF-W,M

Big Bells
  AST-W,M

Big Bells Ringing
  SiR-W,M

Big Black Hearse
  AF-W

Big Bomber Blues
  AF-W

Big Boots
  SRE1-W,M

Big Boss Man
  DBL-W FrF-W,M RB-W TI1-W,M
  UFB-W,M

Big Brass Band from Brazil
  Mo-W,M NM-W,M OTO-W

Big Broadcast of 1938 Theme see
  Thanks for the Memory

Big Brother
  TS-W

Big Chief Wotapotami
  SiB-W,M

Big City
  NMH-W,M

Big Corral
  ATS-W GA-W,M HWS-W,M
  WS-W,M

Big Country
  OTO-W

Big D
  TI2-W,M TW-W UBF-W,M

Big Daddy
  MF-W,M

Big Drum
  MH-W,M

Big Fat Boss and the Workers
  AFP-W

Big Fish

NH-W

Big Fish, Little Fish
  P-W,M

Big Girls Don't Cry
  DRR-W,M ILS-W,M TI2-W,M

Big Hunk of Love
  SRE2-W,M TI1-W,M UFB-W,M

Big Meeting Tonight
  Mo-W,M NM-W,M OTO-W

Big Mole
  LS-W,M

Big Mountain's Song
  FSA2-W,M

Big Movie Show in the Sky
  OHF-W

Big Noise from Winnetka
  MF-W,M

Big Ranch Boss
  HOH-W

Big Red Team
  GSM-W,M IL-W,M

Big Rock Candy Mountain
  AFP-W FoS-W,M FW-W IHA-W,M
  PSN-W,M RW-W,M SiB-W,M

Big Sheep
  AFS-W

Big Ship Sailing
  FW-W

Big Spender
  MF-W,M RW-W,M SC-W,M
  TW-W

Big Sunflower
  ATS-W,M LMR-W,M

Big Tall Indian
  STS-W,M

Big Time
  OTO-W

Big Town Playboy
  DBL-W

Big Wheel
  JC-W,M

Bilbao Song
  OHF-W

Bile Them Cabbage Down
  BF-W,M BIS-W,M FW-W
  OHO-W,M POT-W,M

Bill
  HLS8-W,M SB-W,M TI1-W,M
  UFB-W,M

Bill Bailey
  FPG-W,M FW-W IPH-W,M
  OnT1-W,M OPS-W,M OTJ-W,M
  PO-W,M PoG-W,M

Bill Bailey, Won't You Please Come
  Home?
  EFS-W,M FSN-W,M FSTS-W,M
  GG2-W,M GSN1-W,M HLS1-W,M
  MAB1-W,M MF-W,M MSA1-W
  OAP-W,M RW-W,M TI1-W,M
  UFB-W,M

Bill Groggin's Goat
  FW-W OHO-W,M OTJ-W,M

Bill Mason
  LSR-W,M

Bill McCandless' Ride
  FGM-W,M

Bill Safford
  SoC-W

Bill Sticker
  MSB-W

Bill the Bullocky
  ATM-W,M

Bill Vanero
  Oz2-W,M

Bill Vanero see also Billy Venero

Billboard
  HAS-W,M

Billboard March
TI1-M UFB-M

Billie Boy
TH-W,M

Billie Boy see also Billy Boy

Billie Jean
MF-W,M

Billie Ma Hone
SCa-W

Billy
OTO-W

Billy (I Always Dream of Billy)
TI2-W,M

Billy and Me
FSA2-W,M

Billy Barlow
BF-W,M BSC-W,M FGM-W,M
FW-W

Billy Barlow in Australia
ATM-W,M

Billy Boy
ATS-W,M BM-W BSC-W
EFS-W,M FMT-W FSA2-W,M
HS-W,M IL-W,M IPH-W,M
ITP-W,M NAS-W,M OFS-W,M
OS-W,M OTJ-W,M Oz1-W,M
POT-W,M SAm-W,M SCa-W,M
SFM-W TF-W,M U-W

Billy Boy see also Billie Boy

Billy Don't Be a Hero
TI2-W,M

Billy Grimes
BSC-W

Billy in de Lowlands
NeF-W

Billy in the Lowland
DD-W,M

Billy Magee Magaw
FW-W

Billy Malone
SCa-W,M

Billy Paterson
DE-W,M

Billy Pitt and the Union
VP-W

Billy Pringle
OTJ-W,M

Billy Richardson's Last Ride
LSR-W,M

Billy Riley O
SA-W,M

**Billy Rose's Diamond Horseshoe
Theme see More I See You**

Billy the Kid
Am-W,M FW-W HWS-W,M
RW-W,M

Billy Venero
HB-W,M HWS-W,M

Billy Venero see also Bill Vanero

Billy's New Skates
AST-W,M

Biloxi
RV-W

Bim Bam Boom
RW-M

Bimbombey
MF-W,M

Bimini Bay
T-W,M

**Bind' Auf Dein Haar see My
Mother Bids Me Bind My Hair**

Bingo
CSG-W,M CSS-W FW-W
HAS-W,M HS-W,M OTJ-W,M
RSL-W,M

Biquette
MP-W,M (French Only)

Birch and Green Holly
Boo-W,M

Birch Tree
ASB4-W,M FSA1-W,M
FSA2-W,M

Bird, The (Billings)
BC1-W,M

Bird, The (Jerry Reed)
TOC83-W,M

Bird, The (Swedish Folk Song)
SMa-W,M

Bird and Flower
ASB4-W,M

Bird Came
SiR-W,M

Bird Dog
MF-W,M TI1-W,M UFB-W,M

Bird Dreams
ASB4-W,M

Bird in a Cage
MES1-W,M MES2-W,M

Bird in a Gilded Cage
FSN-W,M FW-W HLS1-W,M
LWT-W,M OBN-W,M RW-W,M
TI1-W,M UFB-W,M

Bird in the Cage
BSC-W

Bird Magic
Fa-W,M

Bird Nest
GM-W

Bird of Heaven
GBC-W,M

Bird of Passage
LS-W,M

Bird of the Wilderness
NA-W,M

Bird on Nellie's Hat
FSN-W,M

Bird Song
AH-W,M FSA1-W,M HAS-W,M

Birdie
ASB3-W,M

Birdie Darling
BSC-W

Birdie's Aria
TW-W

Birdland
DJ-W,M

Birdland Blues
MF-M

Birds (The Bluebird Has a Coat of
Blue)
MH-W,M

Birds (A Cuckoo Flew Under the
Wintry Sky)
ASB5-W,M

Birds (From Out of a Wood Did a
Cuckoo Fly)
JOC-W,M OB-W,M

Birds and the Bees
DRR-W,M TRR-W,M

Birds' Chorus
ASB2-W,M

Birds' Courting Song
ASB5-W,M VA-W,M

Birds in the Night
HSD-W,M

Birds' Lullaby
OTJ-W,M

Birds of a Feather
OTO-W

Birds' Skyway
ASB3-W,M

Birds' Song
RS-W,M

Birds That Homeward Fly

MMY-W,M

Birkas Hachodesh
JS-W,M (Hebrew)

Birmingham Blues
ELO-W,M

Birmingham Breakdown
GMD-W,M

Birmingham Sunday
JF-W,M SFF-W,M

Birth of a Band
MF-M

Birth of La Conga
PSN-W,M

Birth of the Blues
DBC-W,M FrS-W,M HC2-W,M
MF-W,M OHB-W,M TW-W

Birth, Parentage, and Education of
Dennis Bulgruddery
ESU-W

Birthday
BBe-W,M TWS-W

Birthday Greeting
SoP-W,M

Birthday March
SoP-W,M

Birthday of a King
BCh-W,M CA-W,M CCH-W,M
CI-W,M HS-W,M VA-W,M

Birthday Song
ASB1-W,M GM-W MAR-W,M
MH-W,M SiR-W,M STS-W,M
TI1-M UFB-M

Birthdays Are Such Jolly Times
SOO-W,M

Biscuit Bakin' Woman
LC-W

Biscuits Mis' Flanagan Made
Oz3-W,M

Bit-O-Honey
GSM-W,M

Bit o' the Brogue
RW-W,M

Bitch
RoS-W,M

Bitter Lovers' Quarrel
NF-W

Bitter Was the Night
GBC-W,M JF-W,M

Bitter Withy
BT-W,M

Bittersweet
MF-W,M

Bivouac of the Dead
AWB-W

Black
OTO-W UBF-W,M

**Black and Blue see What Did I Do
to Be So Black and Blue**

Black and White
AAP-W,M GOI7-W,M IFM-W
On-W,M OPS-W,M OTJ-W,M

Black Ball Line
SA-W,M

Black Betty
Le-W,M

Black Bill's Wonderment
GB-W,M

Black Birds see also Blackbirds

Black Birds (Two Little Black Birds
Sitting on a Hill)
FF-W

Black Brigade
DE-W,M SiS-W

Black, Brown and White Blues
FPG-W,M

Black Bull
SoC-W

Black Butterfly
GMD-W,M
Black Cat Blues
LC-W
Black Cat Bone
LC-W
Black Cavalry
IS-W,M
Black Coffee
ToS-W,M
Black Denim Trousers and
Motorcycle Boots
RB-W
Black-Eyed Mary
Oz4-W,M
Black-Eyed Peas for Luck
NF-W
Black-Eyed Susan
J-W,M OH-W,M Oz3-W,M
SG-W,M
Black-Eyed Susie
FoS-W,M FSB2-W,M FW-W
POT-W,M RS-W,M
Black Girl
J-W,M Le-W,M
Black Horse Troop
OTJ-W,M
Black Is the Color
FoS-W,M FW-W IL-W,M
OAP-W,M SBF-W,M
Black Is the Color of My True
Love's Hair
LT-W,M MM-W,M MSH-W,M
OFS-W,M
Black Jack Daley
BSC-W
Black Jack Davey
ITP-W,M
Black Jack David
FMT-W FoM-W,M FSt-W,M
Black Jack Davy
BSC-W SCa-W,M
Black Label Beer Jingle see Hey,
Mable, Black Label
Black Limousine
RoS-W,M
Black Magic Woman
TI1-W,M UFB-W,M
Black Man Blues
DBL-W
Black Moonlight
OTO-W
Black Mountain Rag
POT-M
Black Mustache
FSU-W
Black National Anthem see Lift
Every Voice and Sing
Black Night Fallin'
LC-W
Black Nose
KS-W,M
Black Sheep, Black Sheep
AFS-W,M
Black Sheep Lullaby
Oz2-W,M
Black Snake Blues
LC-W
Black Snake, Where Are You
Hidin'?
PSD-W,M
Black Them Boots
Oz3-W,M
Black Thief
MH-W,M
Black Troops of Florian Geyer
SMW-W,M (German)

Blackbeard Was a Pirate Bold
OBN-W,M
Blackberry Woman
Me-W,M
Blackbird
BBe-W,M Be2-W,M JF-W,M
Oz1-W,M TWS-W
Blackbird of Sweet Avondale
VP-W,M
Blackbirds see also Black Birds
Blackbirds
AF-W
Blackbirds (One, Two, Three,
Blackbirds Three)
ASB1-W,M
Blackfoot Indian Song
IF-W,M
Blackfoot Rangers
BSC-W
Blackleg Miner
BB-W
Blacklisted
AL-W
Blacksmith
ASB5-W,M FSA1-W,M HS-W,M
TH-W,M
Blacksmith Courted Me
EL-W,M
Blacksmith's Song
TH-W,M
Blackwater Side
IS-W,M
Blah, Blah, Blah
LSO-W NYT-W,M ReG-W,M
Blake's Cradle Song
OB-W,M
Blame It on My Youth
TI1-W,M UFB-W,M
Blame It on the Bossa Nova
MF-W,M
Blanche Alpen
HSD-W,M
Blanche's Song
SNS-W TW-W
Blanket on the Ground
HLS9-W,M
Blantyre Explosion
SWF-W,M
Bleking
MAR-W,M
Bless Each Home
LoS-W,M
Bless 'Em All
OTJ-W,M OnT6-W,M U-W
Bles' My Soul an' Gone
My-W,M
Bless My Swanee River Home
WDS-W,M
Bless, O My Soul, the Living God
Hy-W,M
Bless Our Cub Scouts
CSS-W
Bless the Beasts and Children
HFH-W,M
Bless the Lord, O My Soul
AME-W,M
Bless Them All see Bless 'Em All
Bless Them That Curse You
Boo-W,M
Bless This House
RDF-W,M U-W
Bless Thou the Gifts Our Hands
Have Brought
Hy-W,M
Bless You Darlin' Mother
OTJ-W,M
Bless You Lord

OGR-W,M
Blessed Am Dem Dat Spects
Nuttin
DE-W,M
Blessed Are the Believers
TI2-W,M
Blessed Are the Peacemakers
SL-W,M
Blessed Assurance
AME-W,M BSG-W,M BSP-W,M
HF-W,M IH-M JBF-W,M RDF-W,M
Blessed Assurance, Jesus Is Mine
AHO-W,M CEM-W,M Hy-W,M
Blessed Be That Maid Marie
GBC-W,M
Blessed Be the Lord God of Israel
Hy-W,M
Blessed Comforter Divine
AHO-W,M
Blessed Hope
NH-W
Blessed Is Everyone
AHO-W,M
Blessed Jesus
HLS7-W,M
Blessed Jesus at Thy Word
SHP-W,M
Bless'd Land of Love and Liberty
SY-W,M
Blessed Messiah
VB-W,M
Blessed Redeemer
BSG-W,M BSP-W,M JBF-W,M
OM-W,M
Blessed Saviour, Thee I Love
WiS7-W,M
Blessed Sunshine
AME-W,M
Blessing
OGR-W,M VA-W,M VB-W,M
Blessing and Honor and Glory and
Power
Hy-W,M
Blessing in Disguise
TI2-W,M
Blessing on Brandy and Beer
IHA-W,M
Blessings
NF-W
Blessings for Kindling of the
Chanukah Lights
JS-W,M (Hebrew Only)
Blest Are the Pure in Heart
Hy-W,M
Blest Be the Dear Uniting Love
AME-W,M
Blest Be the Tie
IH-M
Blest Be the Tie That Binds
AME-W,M CEM-W,M GH-W,M
HF-W,M Hy-W,M NAS-W,M
RDF-W,M RW-W,M WiS7-W,M
Blest Be the Wondrous Grace
AHO-W,M
Blest, Blest Is He
Boo-W,M
Blest Is the Man Whose Tender
Breast
AHO-W,M
Bli-Blip
GMD-W,M
Blin' Man
FN-W,M
Blin' Man see also Blind Man
Blind and Helpless Child
ITP-W,M
Blind Boy

OTJ-W,M
Blind Child
Oz4-W,M
Blind Child's Prayer
TBF-W,M
Blind Fiddler
BSC-W FW-W
Blind Lemon
NeF-W
Blind Man
JF-W,M LA-W,M (Spanish)
Blind Man see also Blin' Man
Blind Man Blues
B-W,M Bl-W,M
Blind Man Stood by the Way and
Cried
NH-W
Blind Man Stood on de Road and
Cried
Me-W,M
Blind Man's Lament
BMM-W,M
Blind Minstrel
FSA1-W,M
Blind Soldier's Lament
SiS-W
Blindfold Play Chant
NF-W
Bling! Blang!
PSN-W,M
Blissful Dreams Come Stealing o'er
Me
WGB/O-W,M
Blizzard of Lies
WF-W,M
Blob
OTJ-W,M
Blood Done Sign My Name
NH-W
Blood on the Saddle
FW-W HWS-W,M PO-W,M
RW-W,M
Blood Red Roses
FW-W
Bloody Breathitt
BMM-W
Bloody Dagger
SCa-W
Bloody Mary
SP-W,M UBF-W,M
Bloody Thursday
SoC-W
Bloomer's Complaint
MPP-W
Blooming Youth Lies Buried
Boo-W,M
Blossom Fell
NK-W,M
Blossom Time
FSA2-W,M
Blossoms
MH-W,M
Blow Away the Morning Dew
FW-W LW-W,M
Blow, Blow, Thou Winter Wind
FSS-W,M OH-W,M SSB-W,M
Blow, Boys, Blow
HSD-W,M OTJ-W,M SA-W,M
TMA-W,M
Blow, Bugle, Blow
BM-W
Blow Gab'l
RTH-W
Blow, Gable, Blow
NH-W
Blow, Gabriel
FN-W,M

Blow, Gabriel, Blow
MF-W,M
Blow High, Blow Low
L-W OH-W,M TG-W,M
Blow on the Sea Shell
LA-W,M (Spanish)
Blow the Candle Out
FSU-W
Blow the Candles Out
FW-W
Blow the Man Down
ATM-W,M ATS-W,M Bo-W,M
CSo-W,M ESB-W,M FW-W
GUM1-W,M HS-W,M HSD-W,M
IHA-W,M IL-W,M MAS-W,M
MM-W,M MML-W,M NAS-W,M
OFS-W,M OTJ-W,M RW-W,M
SA-W,M SFM-W STR-W,M
TMA-W,M
Blow the Trumpets! Bang the
Brasses
OTJ-W,M
Blow the Wind Southerly
HS-W,M OTJ-W,M RSW-W,M
Blow Wind, Blow, and Go Mill, Go
SSe-W,M
Blow Winds
GOI7-W,M
Blow Ye Winds
ASB4-W,M BMC-W,M FoS-W,M
HS-W,M IS-W,M SA-W,M
Blow Ye Winds in the Morning
FGM-W,M FW-W SWF-W,M
Blow Ye Winds of Morning
OTJ-W,M
Blow Ye Winds Westerly
FW-W
Blow Yo' Whistle, Freight Train
LSR-W,M
Blow Your Trumpet, Gabriel
ETB-W,M FSSC-W,M NSS-W
Blue
AN-W
Blue (and Broken Hearted)
TI2-W,M
Blue Aegean
SoF-W,M
Blue Alsatian Mountains
AmH-W,M HSD-W,M NAS-W,M
Blue and Sentimental
MF-W,M TI1-W,M UFB-W,M
Blue and the Gray
SiS-W
Blue Angel
TFC-W,M
Blue Autumn
RW-W,M
Blue Bayou
MF-W,M TFC-W,M
Blue Bell
BH-W,M
Blue Bell Bull
HB-W,M
Blue Bells
OU-W,M
Blue Bells of Scotland
AmH-W,M ASB5-W,M CSo-W,M
FSA1-W,M FW-W Gu-W,M
HSD-W,M OFS-W,M OS-W
OTJ-W,M SeS-W,M TF-W,M
TH-W,M WiS8-W,M
Blue Bird of Happiness
RDF-W,M TI1-W,M UFB-W,M
Blue Blue Blue
GOB-W,M NYT-W,M
Blue Bonnets
SMW-W,M

Blue Cat
GOI7-M OnT6-M
Blue Champagne
BBB-W,M TI2-W,M
Blue Cheese
SSe-W,M
Blue Christmas
BCS-W,M TI1-W,M UFB-W,M
Blue Danube
ASB5-W,M CA-W,M
Blue Danube Waltz
ASB1-M MF-M RW-M
Blue Dawn
OTO-W
Blue Duck
ASB6-W,M
Blue-Eyed Boy
BSC-W
Blue-Eyed Ellen
TBF-W
Blue Eyes Don't Make an Angel
TOC82-W,M
Blue Flame
Mo-W,M NM-W,M
Blue Flower
SL-W,M
Blue Flowers
ASB5-W,M
Blue Gardenia
MF-W,M NK-W,M
Blue, Green, Grey, and Gone
MLS-W,M
Blue Guitar
CMF-W,M RW-W,M
Blue Gummed Blues
B-W,M
Blue Hawaii
AT-W,M GSN2-W,M LM-W,M
OTO-W RDT-W,M TOM-W,M
Blue Heaven
SoF-W,M
Blue in Green
MF-W,M
Blue Jay
GM-W
Blue Jay Way
TWS-W
Blue Jungle
NMH-W,M
Blue Juniata
ATS-W,M FMT-W FSA1-W,M
HSD-W,M LMR-W,M NAS-W,M
Blue Light Boogie
OnT6-W,M
Blue Monday
HR-W ILF-W,M RB-W
Blue Moon
GG3-W,M Gr-W,M GSN2-W,M
GSO-W,M HLS2-W,M RDT-W,M
RT4-W,M RW-W,M T-W,M
THN-W,M TS-W
Blue Moon of Kentucky
TOH-W,M
Blue on Blue
AT-W,M HD-W,M LM-W,M
Blue Prairie
OGC2-W,M
Blue Prelude
TI2-W,M
Blue Rendezvous
TOC82-W,M
Blue Ridge Mountain Blues
BSo-W,M
Blue Rondo A La Turk
BOA-W,M
Blue Room
HC1-W,M MF-W,M TS-W TW-W

Blue Roses
  MoA-M
Blue Shadows on the Trail
  FC-W,M NI-W,M
Blue Skirt Waltz
  TI2-W,M
Blue Star
  LM-W,M TI1-W,M UFB-W,M
Blue-Stone Mountain
  Oz2-W,M
Blue Suede Shoes
  DRR-W,M FOC-W,M GrH-W,M
  HLS9-W,M ILF-W,M RW-W,M
  SRE1-W,M TI1-W,M UFB-W,M
Blue Sunday
  OnT6-M
Blue Tail Fly
  DE-W,M FU-W,M FuB-W,M FW-W
  GuC-W,M HS-W,M IL-W,M
  IPH-W,M MAS-W,M MES2-W,M
  OFS-W,M OS-W OTJ-W,M
  PoS-W,M SAm-W,M TI2-W,M
  WU-W,M
**Blue Tail Fly see also Jim Crack
  Corn, Jimmie Crack Corn, and
  Jimmy Crack Corn**
Blue Tango
  RDT-W,M
Blue Turning Grey over You
  Mo-W,M NM-W,M
Blue Turns to Grey
  RoS-W,M
Blue Velvet
  DRR-W,M LWT-W,M TI1-W,M
  UFB-W,M
Blue Velvet Band
  Oz4-W
Blue Yodel
  LJ-W,M
Blueberry Hill
  DP-W,M DRR-W,M FPS-W,M ILF-
  W,M LM-W,M TI1-W,M UFB-W,M
Bluebird
  ASB1-W,M GM-W PMC-W,M
  TI2-W,M
Bluebird Bluebird
  MG-W,M SiR-W,M SOO-W,M
Bluebird, Bluebird Fly through My
  Window
  FW-W
Bluebird Island
  OGC1-W,M
**Bluebird of Happiness see Blue Bird
  of Happiness**
Bluebirds Are Singing for Me
  BSo-W,M
Bluebirds over the Mountain
  FRH-W,M
Bluebonnets of Texas
  VA-W,M
Bluegrass Express
  BSo-W,M
Blues
  TW-W
Blues Ain't Nothin'
  WU-W,M
Blues Are Brewin'
  Mo-W,M NM-W,M OTO-W
Blues Bittersweet
  MF-M
Blues for Daddy-O
  MF-W,M
Blues in Hoss' Flat
  MF-M
Blues in My Heart
  OGC1-W,M
Blues in the Night

AF-W FrS-W,M HFH-W,M
MF-W,M OHF-W
Blues I've Got
  B-W,M BI-W,M
Blues Serenade
  TI2-W,M
Bluesette
  DJ-W,M TI2-W,M
Bluet
  FSA1-W,M
Blumenlied see Flower Song
Blythe, Blythe and Merry Was She
  SeS-W,M
Bo Diddley
  ILF-W,M TI1-W,M UFB-W,M
Bo Weevil
  RW-W,M
Boarding-House
  Oz3-W,M
Boar's Head Carol
  GUM2-W,M MM-W,M OB-W,M
  OE-W,M TF-W,M
Boat, a Boat!
  Boo-W,M MML-W,M
Boat, a Boat to Cross the Ferry
  HS-W,M
Boat Maiden
  ASB6-W,M
Boatin' up Sandy
  SG-W,M
Boating Song
  MH-W,M
Boatman
  LA-W,M (Spanish)
Boatman Dance
  FGM-W,M POT-W,M
Boatman's Dance
  ATS-W,M DE-W,M FW-W
Boatmen Dance
  FSB2-W,M
Boatmen's Dance
  HSD-W,M OA1-W,M
Boatmen's Song
  WS-W,M
Boats Sail on the Rivers
  MH-W,M
Boatsman's Song
  OTJ-W,M
Boatswain's Mate's Poetry
  ANS-W
Bob Logic's Description of the
  New Brighton Diligence for Inside
  Passengers Only
  MSB-W
**Bob Newhart Show Theme see
  Home to Emily**
Bob Sims see Logan County Jail
Bob White
  MF-W,M OHF-W
Bob White's Song
  NF-W SNS-W
Bobbie Sue
  EC-W,M GCM-W,M MF-W,M
  TOC82-W,M
Bobbie's Blues
  LC-W
Bobbin' Around
  SY-W,M
Bobby Baby
  Co-W,M
Bobby Campbell
  FW-W
Bobby Shafto
  FSA2-W,M FW-W HS-W,M
  MH-W,M SiR-W,M TF-W,M
Bobby Shaftoe
  OTJ-W,M SMa-W,M

Bobolink
  MH-W,M
Bobree Allin
  FSSC-W
Bobree Allin see also Barbara Allen
Bob's Song
  GUM1-W,M SNS-W
Bodeguero see El Bodeguero
Body and Soul
  DJ-W,M MF-W,M OHB-W,M
  RoE-W,M TW-W
Boer National Song
  AmH-W,M
Bog in the Valley-O
  OHO-W,M
Boggy (Boggus) Creek
  SoC-W
Bohemian Carol
  SMY-W,M
Bohunkus
  HSD-W,M
**Boil Them Cabbage Down see Bile
  Them Cabbage Down**
Bois Epais
  MU-W,M (French)
Bold an' Free
  Oz3-W,M
Bold Daniels
  SA-W
Bold Fenian Men
  FW-W
Bold Fisherman
  OHO-W,M WS-W,M
Bold Irish Yankey Benicia Boy
  MSB-W
Bold Jack Donahue
  ATM-W,M BT-W,M FW-W
**Bold Pedlar and Robin Hood see
  Robin Hood and the Pedlar**
Bold Poacher
  MSB-W
Bold Princess Royal
  BB-W
Bold Ranger
  Oz1-W,M
Bold Soldier
  FW-W,M
Bold Soldier Boy
  FSA1-W,M HSD-W,M
Bold Tenant Farmer
  IS-W,M
Bold Volunteer
  SSS-W,M
Bold William Taylor
  MSB-W
Bold Wolfe
  BB-W
Boldly with Mettle
  Boo-W,M
Boll Weevil
  FSB2-W,M FSB3-W,M HS-W,M
  IHA-W,M J-W,M Le-W,M
  MAS-W,M MF-W,M OTJ-W,M
  RS-W,M RW-W,M SWF-W,M
  WS-W,M WSB-W,M
**Boll Weevil see also Ballad of the
  Boll Weevil**
Boll Weevil an' the Bale Weevil
  LC-W
Boll Weevil Blues
  ATS-W,M LC-W,M
Boll Weevil Song
  AmS-W,M
Bombardment of Bristol
  SI-W,M
Bombed Last Night
  GI-W,M GO-W,M

Bombo Lao
  OU-W,M (Bantu Only)
Bon Ton
  PSD-W,M
Bon Vivant
  OHF-W SN-W,M
Bon Voyage Monsieur Dumollet
  OTJ-W,M (French Only)
Bonanox
  Boo-W,M (German Only)
Bones
  RSL-W,M
Boney
  SA-W,M
Boney Is Down
  VP-W
Boney Was a Warrior
  FW-W
Bonfire
  SiR-W,M
Bonfire Carol
  GBC-W,M
**Bongo, Bongo, Bongo see
Civilization**
Bonjour, Mes Amis
  CE-W,M (French)
Bonne Nuit, Merci
  BS-W,M
Bonnie
  HSD-W,M
**Bonnie Banks o' Loch Lomon' see
Loch Lomond**
Bonnie Barbara Allen
  Oz1-W
Bonnie Black Bess
  Oz2-W,M
Bonnie Blue Eyes
  RW-W,M
Bonnie Blue Flag
  AAP-W,M AH-W,M ATS-W,M
  AWB-W BSC-W HSD-W,M
  MPP-W OHG-W,M Oz2-W,M
  PoS-W,M Re-W,M SCo-W,M
  Sin-W,M SiS-W TMA-W,M
Bonnie Blue Flag with the Stripes
  and Stars
  Sin-W,M
Bonnie Doon
  ASB6-W,M ESB-W,M FSA2-W,M
  TF-W,M
**Bonnie Doon see also Ye Banks
and Braes (o' Bonnie Doon)**
Bonnie Dundee
  HSD-W,M SBB-W
Bonnie Earl of Murray
  FW-W
Bonnie Eloise
  ATS-W,M FoS-W,M OTJ-W,M
  WiS8-W,M
**Bonnie Eloise see also Bonny
Eloise**
Bonnie Flag with the Stripes and
  Stars
  SiS-W
Bonnie George Campbell
  ASB5-W,M BMM-W,M
Bonnie House o' Airlie
  SBB-W
Bonnie James Campbell
  FSU-W
Bonnie Johnnie Campbell
  FSU-W
Bonniest Lass
  PO-W,M
Bonny Barbara Allan
  AA-W,M
Bonny Barbara Allen

FMT-W
Bonny Black Bess
  HB-W,M
Bonny Earl o' Moray
  F1-W,M
Bonny Earl of Moray
  Gu-W,M
Bonny Earl of Murray
  SBB-W
Bonny Eloise
  FW-W HSD-W,M MML-W,M
  NeA-W,M
**Bonny Eloise see also Bonnie
Eloise**
Bonny Grey
  MSB-W
Bonny John Seton
  SBB-W
Bonny Lass o' Fyvie
  BSC-W
Bonny Ship the Diamond
  BB-W FW-W
Bonny Wee Window
  Oz1-W
Bonsoir Madame La Lune
  SSN-W,M (French)
Bonsoir, Mes Amis
  SBF-W (French)
Bonsoir Mes Bon Gens
  CaF-W (French Only)
Bonsoir Mes Gens
  CaF-W (French Only)
Bony Moronie
  ERM-W,M GAR-W,M
Boo
  SOO-W,M
Boo Hoo
  BBB-W,M MF-W,M OPS-W,M
  TI2-W,M
Boodle-am
  B-W,M
Boogie
  LC-W
Boogie Down
  BOA-W,M
Boogie Fever
  SoH-W,M ToO76-W,M
Boogie Man
  OTJ-W,M
Boogie Wonderland
  SoH-W,M ToO79-W,M
Boogie Woogie
  TI2-M
Boogie Woogie Bugle Boy
  BBB-W,M BeL-W,M TI2-W,M
Boogie Woogie Dancin' Shoes
  WG-W,M
Boogie Woogie Flying Cloud
  OGC2-W,M
Boogie Woogie on St. Louis Blues
  B-M
Book of Books, Our People's
  Strength
  Hy-W,M
Book of Love
  DRR-W,M GAR-W,M ILF-W,M
  TI1-W,M UFB-W,M
Book Report
  YG-W,M
Book-Worm's Lament
  SoC-W
Books of the Bible
  Oz4-W
Boola Boo
  YL-W,M
Boola Boola
  IL-W,M

Boola Song
  ESB-W,M
Boom! Boom! Gee It's Great to Be
  Scouting
  Bo-W,M
Boom Fa-De-Ral-La
  VA-W,M
Boomerang
  TTH-W,M
Boomtown Bill
  Am-W
Boone (Theme) see Rock with Me
Boot Maker's Great Strike
  AL-W
Boot, Saddle, to Horse and Away
  GC-W,M
Boothbay Whale
  FW-W OHO-W,M
Boots and Saddle
  OTJ-W,M
Boot's Song
  GO-W
Bop
  AWS-W,M
Boplicity
  MF-M
Border Affair
  GA-W,M
Border Ballad
  SoC-W
Border Lord
  SuS-W,M
Border Trail
  OHO-W,M
Border Trail--Winter Version
  OHO-W,M
Borechu
  JS-W,M (Hebrew Only)
Borhu
  SBJ-W,M (Hebrew Only)
Borinquena
  LaS-M
Born Again
  VB-W,M
Born Free
  BHB-W,M BNG-W,M DC-W,M
  HFH-W,M MF-W,M OnT1-W,M
  TOM-W,M
Born in Hard Luck
  FSSC-W,M
Born in Zion
  VB-W,M
Born Is He
  SMa-W,M
Born Is Jesus, the Infant King
  SHP-W,M
**Born Is Jesus, the Infant King see
also He Is Born, the Divine Christ
Child**
Born to Be Alive
  ToO79-W,M
Born to Be Blue
  TI2-W,M
Born to Be Wild
  TRR-W,M
Born to Be with You
  Mo-W,M NM-W,M
Born to Fly
  VB-W,M
Born to Hand Jive
  Gr-W,M Mo-W,M OTO-W
Born to Run
  GrS-W,M TOC82-W,M
Born Today Is the Child Divine
  CSB-W,M JOC-W,M
Born Too Late
  FRH-W,M

Borneo
WDS-W,M
Borsalino (Theme)
OTO-W
**Bosco Chocolate Flavored Syrup
Jingle see I Love Bosco**
Borrow Love and Go
Le-W,M
Boruch Habboh
JS-W,M (Hebrew Only)
Boruch Ovos
JS-W,M (Hebrew Only)
Boruch Shehecheyonu
JS-W,M (Hebrew Only)
Boruch Yotzer
JS-W,M (Hebrew Only)
Bosom Buddies
AF-W Mo-W,M NM-W,M OTO-W
Bossa Brasilia
GO17-M
Bossa Nova Baby
MF-W,M SRE1-W,M
Bossa Nova U.S.A.
LaS-M
Bossin' Blues
LC-W
Boston
SA-W,M
Boston Beguine
TW-W
Boston Burglar
FW-W SCa-W,M TBF-W,M
Boston Come All Ye
LMR-W,M SA-W,M VA-W,M
Boston Frigate's Engagement
ANS-W
Boston Massacre
SAR-W,M SSS-W,M
Boston Post Office
ESU-W
Boston Tea Tax Song
PSN-W,M SI-W,M
Botany Bay
ATM-W,M FW-W MSB-W
OTJ-W,M Oz1-W,M
Both Sides Now
ERM-W,M OnT1-W,M
Bothwell Bridge
SBB-W
Bottle Let Me Down
NMH-W,M
Bottle O!
SA-W,M
Bottle of Wine
RBO-W,M
Bottle Up an' Go
LC-W
Bottle Up and Go
FW-W
Bought a Rooster
TMA-W,M
Bought Me a Cat
SHP-W,M
Boulavogue
IS-W,M
Boule's Hop
CFS-W,M (French)
Boulevard of Broken Dreams
MF-W,M
Boum Badiboum
CFS-W,M (French)
Boum-ba-di-boum
FSO-W,M (French)
Boun' fer Canaan Lan'
BDW-W,M
Bounce Around
ASB1-W,M

Bouncing Ball
ASB2-W,M
Bound for Amerikee
DD-W,M
Bound for Canaan
SHS-W,M
Bound for Glory
GG1-W,M OHO-W,M
Bound for the Promised Land
WN-W,M
**Bound for the Promised Land see
also I am (I'm) Bound for the
Promised Land**
Bound to Go
AH-W,M
Bound to Ride
BIS-W,M BSo-W,M
Bound upon th' Accursed Tree
AME-W,M
Boundless Love
HHa-W,M
Bounty Jumper's Lament
SiS-W
Bounty of Jehovah Praise
AHO-W,M
Bouquet of Roses
HLS3-W,M HLS9-W,M
OGC1-W,M RDT-W,M RW-W,M
TI1-W,M UFB-W,M
Bourbon Street Beat
TVT-W,M
Bouree
BJ-W,M
Bouree (Bach)
RW-M
Bourgeois Blues
AFP-W Le-W,M SFF-W,M
Bow and Balance
FGM-W,M
Bow Belinda
HS-W,M LMR-W,M MES1-W,M
Bow Down, Mountain
AHO-W,M
Bow Down, O Belinda
OTJ-W,M
Bow-Legged Ike
SoC-W
Bow Low, Elder
MoM-W,M
Bow Wow
FSA1-W,M
Bow Wow Wow
MH-W,M
Bower of Prayer
SHS-W,M
Bowery, The
ATS-W BH-W,M EFS-W,M
FGM-W,M FSN-W,M FSTS-W,M
IL-W,M OBN-W,M RW-W,M
Bowery Lass
ESU-W
Bowl of Green Peas
Oz3-W
Bowld Sojer Boy
FSA1-W,M HSD-W,M
Bowling Green
FGM-W,M FW-W
Bowling Song
Mo-W,M NM-W,M
Box #10
JC-W,M
Box of Rain
RV-W
Boxing Day in 1847
MSB-W
Boy and Goat
ASB5-W,M

Boy and the Billy Goats Three
ASB1-W,M
Boy Blue
ELO-W,M
Boy for Sale
O-W,M
Boy from New York City
ERM-W,M GAR-W,M HR-W
MF-W,M
Boy Gets Around
TOC83-W,M
Boy He Had an Auger
LMR-W,M
Boy in Blue
Oz4-W
Boy Like Me, a Girl Like You
SRE2-W,M
Boy Like You
SSA-W,M
Boy Meets Horn
GMD-W,M
Boy Named Sue
CMG-W,M
Boy Next Door
GG5-W,M GSF-W,M GSN3-W,M
HLS5-W,M RT4-W,M RW-W,M
Boy Scouts' Marching Song
MML-W,M
Boy Scouts of America
Bo-W,M
Boy Scout's Prayer
Bo-W,M
Boy Thoughts
Mo-W,M NM-W,M OTJ-W,M
OTO-W
Boy Wanted
GOB-W,M
Boy! What Love Has Done to Me!
GOB-W,M LSO-W
Boycott Armour
AL-W
Boycott Them
AL-W
Boys and Girls Like You and Me
UBF-W,M
Boys Are Marching Home
SiS-W
Boys Around Here
Oz3-W
Boy's Best Friend Is His Mother
EFS-W,M
Boys from Company A
GI-W
Boys in Blue
ITP-W,M Oz4-W,M
Boys in Blue Will See It Through
ATS-W,M
Boys in the Bowery Pit
ESU-W
Boys Keep Your Powder Dry
OTJ-W,M SCo-W,M Sin-W,M
SiS-W
Boys of Cold Water
ESU-W
Boys of Virginia
Oz4-W
Boys Remember the Maine
OHG-W,M
Boys Will Soon Be Home
SiS-W
Boys with the Auburn Hair
SiS-W
Boys Won't Do to Trust
Oz3-W
Boze Cos Polske (Lord for Poland)
MML-W,M (Polish) SiP-W,M
(Polish)

Bozrah
SHS-W,M
Brabanconne see La Brabanconne
Bracken's World Theme see
 Worlds
Brady
NH-W
Brag and Boast
NF-W
Brahms' Lullaby
RDF-W,M RW-M SiB-W,M TI1-M
UFB-M YS-W,M
Brahms' Lullaby see also Lullaby
 (Brahms)
Braid the Raven Hair
MGT-W,M
Brakeman's Blues
LJ-W,M
Branch of the Sweet and Early
 Rose
MHB-W,M
Brand New Heartache
TI1-W,M UFB-W,M
Brand New Key
GrS-W,M
Brand New Morning
TI1-W,M UFB-W,M
Brand New Shoes
BSo-W,M
Brand New Socialist Way
WW-W,M
Brand New Start
VB-W,M
Branded (Theme)
GTV-W,M
Branded Man
NMH-W,M
Brands
SoC-W
Brandy (You're a Fine Girl)
DP-W,M TI1-W,M UFB-W,M
Brandy in Me Tea
LaS-W,M
Brandy Leave Me Alone
FW-W
Brass Band
BMC-W,M
Brass-Mounted Army
Oz2-W,M
Brave Boys Are They
SiS-W
Brave Bull Fighter
SoF-W,M
Brave Fireman
Oz4-W
Brave Irish Lady
BSC-W
Brave Lieutenant
ITP-W,M
Brave Lord Willoughby
BB-W
Brave Nelson
MSB-W
Brave Old Oak
ESB-W,M
Brave Paulding and the Spy
SBA-W SI-W,M
Brave Soldier
GB-W,M SCa-W,M
Brave Songs
CA-W,M
Brave Wolfe
EA-W,M ESU-W FSU-W Oz4-W,M
SI-W,M
Braving the Wilds All Unexplored
AHO-W,M
Brazil (Aquarela Do Brasil)

DP-W,M TOM-W,M
Brazos River
Oz2-W,M TO-W,M
Bread and Cheese and Watercress
SOT-W,M
Bread and Cherries
MH-W,M
Bread and Gravy
OTJ-W,M
Bread and Roses
LW-W,M SWF-W,M WW-W,M
Bread of the World in Mercy
 Broken
Hy-W,M
Bread upon the Water
VB-W,M
Break at Jerry's Rock
ITP-W,M
Break Bread Together
JF-W,M
Break, Break, Break
HSD-W,M
Break Down the Walls
TTH-W,M
Break Forth, O Beauteous
 Heavenly Light
MML-W,M SL-W,M
Break Forth, O Beauteous Light
TF-W,M
Break of Day
MES1-W,M MES2-W,M
Break Right
AF-W
Break the News Gently
Oz4-W
Break the News to Morgan
AL-W
Break the News to Mother
FSN-W,M OTJ-W,M
Break Thou the Bread of Life
AHO-W,M AME-W,M FH-W,M
Hy-W,M SJ-W,M
Breakdown
SuS-W,M
Breakers
SL-W,M
Breakfast
BSB-W,M
Breakfast at Tiffany's Theme see
 Moon River
Breakin' Away
BOA-W,M
Breakin' Up Is Breakin' My Heart
TFC-W,M
Breaking Point
Mo-W,M NM-W,M
Breaking Up Is Hard to Do
DC-W,M HR-W MF-W,M
RoE-W,M ToO76-W,M TRR-W,M
Breaking Waves Dashed High
ESB-W,M
Breath of a Rose
NA-W,M
Breathe It Softly to My Loved Ones
SiS-W
Breathe on Me, Breath of God
AME-W,M Hy-W,M
Breathless
OGC1-W,M
Breeze (El Cefiro)
LaS-W,M (Spanish) MSS-W,M
(Spanish)
Breeze and I
RDT-W,M TI2-W,M
Breeze Kissed Your Hair
CF-W,M
Breezes

GI-W
Breezes Are Blowing
RSL-W,M
Breezin' Along with the Breeze
MF-W,M NK-W,M
Breezy's Song
MLS-W,M
Brennan on the Moor
BSC-W BT-W,M FGM-W,M FW-W
OFS-W,M Oz2-W
Brennan on the Moor see also
 Young Brinnon on the Moor
Brer Rabbit
NH-W
Brian o' Lyn
BT-W,M
Brian o' Lyn see also Bryan O'Lynn
Brian's Song
BNG-M DC-M MF-M
Brian's Song see also Hands of
 Time
Bricks in My Pillow
AFB-W,M
Bridal Chorus (Lohengrin)
HSD-W,M MF-M NCB-M TF-W,M
TM-M WGB/O-M WGB/P-M
Bridal March (Lohengrin)
PoG-M RW-M TI1-M UFB-M
WiS7-M
Bride
ESU-W K-W,M
Bride of American Town
VS-W,M
Bridegroom
ESU-W
Bride's Farewell
ESU-W
Bridge at Remagen
RW-M
Bridge of Avignon
ASB4-W,M HS-W,M (French)
Bridge of Avignon see also On the
 Bridge of Avignon and Sur Le
 Pont D'Avignon
Bridge over Troubled Water
CEM-W,M GSN4-W,M On-W,M
Bridges at Toko-Ri
OTO-W
Bridget Donahue
Oz4-W TMA-M,W
Bridle Up a Rat
NF-W
Brief Life Is Here Our Portion
Hy-W,M
Brigadoon
LL-W,M RW-W,M
Brigadoon (Medley of Songs)
OU-W,M
Briggs Breakdown
DE-W,M
Brigham Young
FW-W
Bright and Glorious Is the Sky
SJ-W,M
Bright Angels on the Water
NSS-W
Bright College Years
IL-W,M
Bright Hills of Glory
FHR-W,M
Bright Shines the Moon
FPG-M
Bright Sparkles in de Churchyard
RF-W,M
Bright Visions
GrM-W,M
Brighten the Corner Where You

Are
HLS7-W,M RDF-W,M RW-W,M

Brighten Up the Dark
TW-W

Brightest and Best
U-W WiS7-W,M Y-W,M

Brightest and Best of the Sons of
the Morning
Hy-W,M YC-W,M

Brightly Beams Our Father's Mercy
AME-W,M

Brightly Dawns Our Wedding Day
MGT-W,M

Brightly Gleam
ESB-W,M

Brilliant Naval Victory
ANS-W MPP-W

Brilliant Naval Victory on Lake
Champlain
ANS-W

Brilliant Victory
ANS-W

Brilliant Victory Obtained by
Commodore Decatur
ANS-W

Brinca La Tablita
CDM-W,M (Spanish)

Bring a Little Water, Sylvie
FGM-W,M

**Bring a Little Water, Sylvie see
also Bring Me a Little Water,
Sylvie**

Bring a Pail of Water
ID-W,M

Bring a Torch, Jeanette, Isabella
BeB-W,M CSF-W HS-W,M
(French) LTL-W,M MML-W,M
(French) YC-W,M

**Bring a Torch, Jeanette, Isabella
see also Un Flambeau, Jeannette,
Isabelle**

Bring Back My Kitchen to Me
GI-W

Bring 'Em Home
FW-W

**Bring Good Things to Life see
General Electric Company Theme**

Bring Him Home
UBF-W,M

Bring It on Home
TOH-W,M

Bring It on Home to Me
ATC1-W,M

Bring Me a Little Water, Sylvie
FW-W Le-W,M

**Bring Me a Little Water, Sylvie see
also Bring a Little Water, Sylvie
and Bring Me Li'l Water, Silvy**

Bring Me Back from Vietnam
VS-W,M

Bring Me Li'l Water, Silvy
NeF-W

**Bring Me Li'l Water, Silvy see also
Bring Me a Little Water, Sylvie**

Bring Me On My Supper, Boys
NeA-W,M

Bring Me Out of the Desert
AG-W,M

Bring Me Sunshine
U-W

Bring My Brother Back to Me
FHR-W,M SiS-W

Bring on Your Hot Corn
NF-W

Bring the Bat
SOO-W,M

Bring the Tea Tray

Boo-W,M

Bring the Wagon Home
TF-W,M

Bring the Wagon Home, John
BSB-W,M SL-W,M

Bring Them In
AME-W,M

Bring Thy Treasures
Boo-W,M

Bring Your Sweet Self Back to Me
OGC2-W,M

Bringing in That New Jerusalem
FSSC-W,M

Bringing in the Boar's Head
MML-W,M

Bringing in the Sheaves
AH-W,M AME-W,M FH-W,M
FW-W IH-M JBF-W,M OBN-W,M
OTJ-W,M RDF-W,M RW-W,M

Bringing Mary Home
BSo-W,M

Bringing Up Baby
GSM-W,M

Brisk Young Bachelor
LW-W,M

Brisk Young Farmer
DD-W,M Oz1-W,M

Bristol Stomp
DRR-W,M TRR-W,M

British Grenadiers
CSo-W,M FBI-W,M FW-W
HSD-W,M MPP-W,M OFS-W,M
OH-W,M OTJ-W,M SI-W SiP-W,M
SMW-W,M

British Light Infantry
SAR-W,M SBA-W SI-W,M

Broad Is the Road
AHO-W,M

Broad Is the Road That Leads to
Death
AME-W,M

Broadway Baby
Fo-W,M OTO-W TI2-W,M
UBF-W,M

Broadway Melody
GG5-W,M HLS5-W,M RW-W,M

Broadway Opera and Bowery
Crawl
ATS-W,M

Broadway Sights
SY-W,M

Broke My Mother's Rule
LC-W

Broken Arrow
RV-W

Broken Bridges
CSG-W,M

Broken Engagement
BSC-W Oz4-W,M

Broken Heart
Oz4-W,M

Broken Heart, My God, My King
AME-W,M

Broken Hearted (Here Am I)
TI1-W,M UFB-W,M

Broken Hearted Gardener
MSB-W

Broken Hearted Me
TI1-W,M UFB-W,M

Broken Hearted Melody
FRH-W,M HD-W,M TI2-W,M

Broken Home
Oz4-W,M

Broken Rose
HHa-W,M

Broken Shovel
LMR-W,M

Broken Troth
SMY-W,M

Broken Vessel
BSG-W,M BSP-W,M

Broken Vow
Oz4-W

Bronco
TVT-W,M

Bronco Buster
ATS-W,M HB-W SoC-W,M

Brook
MH-W,M

Brook Music
FSA2-W,M

Brooklet
ASB5-W,M ASB6-W,M SMY-W,M

Brooklyn Fire
Oz4-W

Brooklyn Roads
TI2-W,M

Brooklyn Trollilee
AL-W,M

Brooklyn's Gift to the Army
GI-W,M

Broom
MH-W,M SOO-W,M

Broom Dance
ASB3-W,M

Broom, Green Broom
OTJ-W,M SR-W,M

Broomfield Hill
FSU-W

Brother and the Fallen Dragoon
SiS-W

Brother Ben and Sister Sal
NF-W

Brother, Can You Spare a Dime
FPS-W,M MF-W,M OHB-W,M
TW-W

Brother, Come and Dance with Me
OTJ-W,M TH-W,M

Brother Eden's Got a Coon
AN-W

**Brother George see Brudder
George**

Brother Green
BSC-W Oz2-W,M

**Brother Guide Me Home see
Brudder Guide Me Home**

Brother, Hast Thou Wandered Far
AHO-W,M

Brother James
ESB-W,M

Brother James' Air
ASB5-W,M

Brother John
HS-W,M (French) SWF-W,M

**Brother John see also Are You
Sleeping and Frere Jacques**

Brother Jonathan's Lament for
Sister Caroline
AWB-W

Brother Love's Travelling Salvation
Show
BR-W,M TI2-W,M

**Brother Moses see Brudder Moses
Brother Mosey see Brudder Mosey**

Brother Soldiers All Hail
MPP-W,M OHG-W,M

Brother Sun, Sister Moon
AT-W,M OTO-W

Brother, Tell Me of the Battle
HSD-W,M Sin-W,M SiS-W

Brother, Though from Yonder Sky
AHO-W,M

Brother When Will You Come
Back?

SiS-W
Brother, You Oughtta Been There
  FVV-W,M
Brother, You'd Better Be A-Prayin'
  NH-W
Brotherhood
  SL-W,M
Brotherhood of Man
  TI2-W,M UBF-W,M
Brotherly Love
  TOC82-W,M
Brotherly Shove
  MF-M
Brother's Fainting at the Door
  SiS-W
Brothers, Let Us Dance
  SiR-W,M
Brown Alma Mater
  IL-W,M
Brown Cheering Song
  IL-W,M
Brown-Eyed Girl
  Oz4-W
Brown Eyes
  BIS-W,M FPG-W,M
Brown Gal in da Ring
  SGT-W,M
Brown Girl
  BSC-W FMT-W FoM-W,M
  Oz1-W,M SCa-W,M
Brown Jug
  Oz3-W,M
Brown Skin Gal in the Calico Gown
  GMD-W,M
Brown Sugar
  RoS-W,M
Brownie Eyes
  MF-W,M
Brownies
  MH-W,M
Brownies and Witches
  ASB1-W,M
Brown's Ferry Blues
  FPG-W,M FW-W,M
Brownskin Woman
  LC-W
Bruce
  WF-W,M
Bruce's Address
  HSD-W,M SHS-W,M
Brudder George Is A-Gwine to
  Glory
  NSS-W
Brudder Guide Me Home an' I Am
  Glad
  NSS-W
Brudder Moses Gone to de
  Promised Land
  NSS-W
Brudder Mosey
  NSS-W
Brush Creek Wreck
  BSC-W
Brush Up Your Shakespeare
  TI2-W,M TW-W UBF-W,M
Brush Your Teeth with Colgate
  GSM-W,M
Bryan O'Lynn
  ITP-W,M Oz3-W,M
Bryan O'Lynn see also Brian o' Lyn
Brylcreem, a Little Dab'll Do Ya
  GSM-W,M
Bubble
  HJ-W,M
Bubble Pipe Dream
  ASB4-W,M
Bubbles

Mo-W,M
Bubbles in My Beer
  OGC2-W,M
Bubbles in the Wine
  AT-W,M WGB/P-W,M
Bubbling and Splashing
  Boo-W,M
Bublichki
  OTJ-M
Buchenwald Alarm
  RuS-W,M (Russian)
Buck and Berry
  NF-W
Buck Passing
  GI-W
Buck Up
  YL-W,M
Buckeye Battle Cry
  Mo-W,M TI2-W,M
Buckeye Jim
  FW-W RW-W,M
Buckeye Song
  MPP-W
Buck-Eyed Rabbit! Whoopee!
  NF-W
Bucking Bronco
  FW-W Oz2-W,M SoC-W,M
Buckle Down, Winsocki
  TI1-W,M TW-W UBF-W,M
  UFB-W,M
Buckleys Sleighing Song
  SY-W,M
Buck's Private Confession Publicly
  Revealed
  MPP-W
Buckskin Joe
  SoC-W
Buckskin Sam
  OHG-W,M
Bud and Bloom
  GrM-W,M
Bud on Bach
  MF-M
Buddy
  WNF-W,M
Buddy Holly Story Theme see
  Great Pretender
Buddy, Won't You Roll down the
  Line
  AL-W FGM-W,M
Budget
  NF-W
Budweiser Beer Jingle see Here
  Comes the King, When You Say
  Budweiser, You've Said It All and
  Where There's Life, There's Bud
Budweiser Theme Song see
  Thracian Horse Music
Buena Vista
  ATS-W,M AWB-W BSC-W
Buenos Aires
  UBF-W,M
Buffalo Boy
  FW-W GuC-W,M OHO-W,M
Buffalo Gals
  ASB5-W,M BF-W,M BM-W
  FSB1-W,M FU-W,M FuB-W,M
  FW-W HS-W,M HSD-W,M
  IHA-W,M IL-W,M IPH-W,M
  LT-W,M MAS-W,M MF-W,M
  MG-W,M OFS-W,M OS-W
  OTJ-W,M Oz3-W,M PaS-W,M
  POT-W,M SBF-W,M SoC-W
  WiS9-W,M
Buffalo Hunt
  SoC-W
Buffalo Range

SoC-W
Buffalo Skinners
  FW-W PSN-W,M SoC-W,M
  SWF-W,M
Buffalo Song
  SoC-W
Bugaboo see Foggy Dew
Bugle
  GB-W,M
Bugle Call Blues
  LC-W
Bugle Call Rag
  BBB-W,M TI2-W,M
Bugle Note
  BMC-W,M
Bugle Song
  ESB-W,M
Bugler
  SiS-W
Bugs Bunny Show Theme see This
  Is It!
Buick Automobile Jingle see
  Wouldn't You Really Rather Have
  a Buick
Build a Cave
  DBL-W
Builders
  OB-W,M
Building a Nation
  HCY-W,M
Building an Airplane
  AST-W,M
Building Blocks
  GM-W
Building the Canoe
  FSA1-W,M
Built on a Rock
  SJ-W,M
Built on the Rock the Church Doth
  Stand
  Hy-W,M
Bull Connor's Jail
  SFF-W,M
Bull Dog
  ESB-W,M HAS-W,M HSD-W,M
  NAS-W,M
Bull Dog see also Bulldog on the
  Bank
Bull Frog Put On the Soldier
  Clothes
  NF-W
Bull upon the Battrey-Jigs
  DE-W,M
Bulldog
  GC-W,M
Bulldog see also Bulldog on the
  Bank
Bulldog and the Bullfrog
  OHO-W,M OTJ-W,M
Bulldog and the Bullfrog see also
  Bulldog on the Bank
Bulldog Blues
  LC-W
Bulldog on the Bank
  FW-W TMA-W,M WU-W,M
Bulldog on the Bank see also
  Bull Dog, Bulldog, and Bulldog
  and the Bullfrog
Bullocky-O
  ATM-W,M
Bully of the Town
  FSt-M POT-W,M
Bully Song
  BH-W,M OTJ-W,M
Bullyin' Jack-a-Diamonds
  SFF-W,M
Bumble Bee Tuna Jingle see Yum,

Yum, Bumble Bee
Bum's Rush
MF-M
Bunches of Grapes
SL-W,M
Bungalow Bill
JF-W,M
Bungle in the Jungle
BJ-W,M
Bungle Rye
IS-W,M
Bunker Hill
GeS-W,M HSD-W,M OTJ-W,M
SAR-W,M SSS-W,M
Bunker's Hill
MPP-W
Bunny
MH-W,M
Bunny Hop
OTJ-W,M
Bunny Rabbit
FF-W,M
Buoy Bells for Trenton
AFP-W
Buoy, Buoy
SiR-W,M
Burdens Are Lifted at Calvary
OM-W,M
Burgoyne's Defeat
SSS-W,M
Burgoyne's Disgrace
SI-W
Burgoyne's Overthrow at Saratoga
SBA-W
Burgoyne's Proclamation
SBA-W
Burgundian Carol
GUM2-W,M WSB-W,M
Buried beneath the Yielding Wave
AME-W,M
Burke's Confession
BB-W
Burlesque Band
CSG-W,M
Burlington Bertie
U-W
Burn, Baby, Burn
JF-W,M SFF-W,M
Burnin' Hell
DBL-W
Burning Heart
HFH-W,M TTH-W,M
Burning Like a Flame
BHO-W,M
Burning of Charleston
SBA-W
Burning of the Bayou Sara
BSC-W
Burrowing Yankees
SBA-W SI-W,M SSS-W,M
Bury Me beneath the Willow
BSo-W,M FG1-W,M FGM-W,M
FoS-W,M FSt-W,M FW-W
OFS-W,M Oz4-W,M RW-W,M
WSB-W,M
Bury Me in the Morning, Mother
FHR-W,M
Bury Me Not on the Lone Prairie
BMC-W,M FW-W HS-W,M
**Bury Me Not on the Lone Prairie
see also O Bury Me Not (on the
Lone Prairie)**
Bury the Brave Where They Fall
SiS-W
Bus
SiR-W,M SOO-W,M
Buses Are A-Comin', Oh Yes

SFF-W,M
Bushel and a Peck
DBC-W,M TI2-W,M TW-W
UBF-W,M
Busted
HR-W RB-W TI2-W,M
TOC82-W,M
Busted Cowboy's Christmas
GA-W
Buster Brown Shoes
GSM-W,M
Buster Goes A-Courtin'
SoC-W
Bustopher Jones, the Cat about
Town
UBF-W,M
Busy Bee
ASB3-W,M
Busy Children
GM-W
Busy Cobbler
MH-W,M
Busy, Curious, Thirsty Fly
Boo-W,M
Busy Farmer
GUM1-W,M
Busy Postman
MH-W,M
Busybody
OGC1-W,M
But Alive
Ap-W,M Mo-W,M OTO-W
VSA-W,M
But Beautiful
ILT-W,M RoE-W,M TI1-W,M
UFB-W,M
But He Ain't Comin' Here t' Die No
Mo'
RF-W,M
But I Do
TI1-W,M UFB-W,M
But in the Morning, No
ML-W,M
But My Sweets
UF-W,M
But Not for Me
DC-W,M DJ-W,M GOB-W,M
LSO-W MF-W,M NYT-W,M
OHB-W,M RoE-W,M
But This I Pray, Oh Lord,
Remember Me
HLS7-W,M
But You Know I Love You
TI1-W,M TWD-W,M UFB-W,M
Butcher Boy
BSC-W FGM-W,M IS-W,M
ITP-W,M Oz1-W,M SCa-W,M
Butcher's Boy
ATS-W,M BSC-W FMT-W FW-W
RW-W,M SCa-W,M
Butler War Song
CoS-W,M
Butter Milk Man
Me-W,M
Butterbean Pickers' Song
Me-W,M
Butterflies Are Free
PoG-W,M
Butterfly
SiR-W,M
Butterfly (Pretty Liddle Butterfly,
Yaller As de Gold)
NF-W
Butterfly (Where Are You Going?)
SOO-W,M
Butterfly (You Fickle Creature)
LA-W,M (Spanish)

Butterfly, The (The Butterfly on
Fairy Wing)
ASB2-W,M
Butterfly, The (Calixa Lavallee)
AmH-M
Butterfly, The (Herne/Schumann)
MML-W,M
Butterfly and Honeybee
MH-W,M
Buttermilk Hill
FW-W TO-W,M
Button Up Your Overcoat
DBC-W,M FPS-W,M HC2-W,M
LM-W,M MF-W,M OTJ-W,M
OTO-W TI1-W,M UBF-W,M
UFB-W,M
Button Willow Tree
HB-W,M
Button, You Must Wander
RSL-W,M
Buttons and Bows
AT-W,M HC2-W,M LM-W,M
MAB1-W,M MSA1-W OBN-W,M
OnT1-W,M OTJ-W,M OTO-W
TOM-W,M
Buvant De La Commerce
CaF-W (French Only)
Buxom Lassies
MHB-W,M (Swedish)
Buy
MH-W,M
Buy a Broom
AmH-W,M HSD-W,M SY-W,M
TMA-W,M
Buy a Charter Oak
Oz3-W,M
Buy a Penny Ginger
SGT-W,M
Buy a Pretty Pony
AFS-W,M
Buy Me a China Doll
Oz3-W,M
Buy My Dainty Fine Beans
Boo-W,M
Buy My Primroses
Boo-W,M
Buy My Tortillas
MHB-W,M
Buzz, Buzz, Buzz
SiR-W,M
Buzz, Buzz, Quoth the Blue Fly
Boo-W,M
Buzz Me
OnT6-W,M
Buzzardaree
AFP-W
By a Bank As I Lay
OH-W,M
By a Waterfall
MF-W,M
By All Whom Thou Hast Made
Hy-W,M
By an' By (I'm Gwine ter Lay
Down My Heavy Load)
WiS7-W,M
By and By (Hooker/Gershwin)
ReG-W,M
By and By (I'm Goin' to Lay Down
This Heavy Load)
FN-W,M RF-W,M
By and By (Star Shines Down on
Number One)
AH-W,M FW-W OHO-W,M
**By and By (Star Shines Down on
Number One) see also Bye'm Bye**
By and By I'm Goin' to See Them
NH-W

By Babel's Streams
AHO-W,M
By My Side
G-W,M On-W,M OTO-W
UBF-W,M
By My Spirit
VB-W,M
By Myself
HC1-W,M OTO-W TI1-W,M
TW-W UBF-W,M UFB-W,M
By Peaceful Hearth
SL-W,M
By Shady Woods
Boo-W,M
By Strauss
NYT-W,M LSO-W OTO-W
TI1-W,M UBF-W,M UFB-W,M
By the Banks of Red River
SiS-WB
By the Beautiful Sea
MF-W,M SLB-W,M TI1-W,M
UFB-W,M
By the Blazing Council Fire
Bo-W
By the Cradle
AS-W,M (German)
By the Fireside
ASB6-W,M
By the Light of the Moon
ASB4-W,M (French) BMC-W,M
(French)
**By the Light of the Moon see also
At Pierrot's Door and Au Claire
De La Lune**
By the Light of the Silvery Moon
GSN1-W,M MF-W,M OAP-W,M
RC-W,M RoE-W,M TI2-W,M U-W
By the Old Oak
RuS-W,M (Russian)
By the Sad Sea Waves
HSD-W,M
By the Seashore
RuS-W,M (Russian)
By the Stream So Pure and Clear
SeS-W,M
By the Time I Get to Phoenix
FOC-W,M GrH-W,M RB-W
RYT-W,M RW-W,M TI2-W,M
By the Waters of Minnetonka
SLB-W,M
By Vows of Love Together Bound
AHO-W,M
By Yon Bonnie Banks
SeS-W,M
**By Yon Bonnie Banks see also
Loch Lomond**
**By Yonder Flowing Fountain see A
La Claire Fontaine**
Bye, Baby Bunting
OTJ-W,M
Bye Baby Bye
TO-W,M
Bye Bye Baby
DP-W,M V-W,M
Bye Bye Barbara
OTO-W
Bye Bye Birdie
Mo-W,M NM-W,M OTO-W
TI2-W,M
Bye Bye Blackbird
BBB-W,M MF-W,M MR-W,M
OHB-W,M TW-W
Bye Bye Blues
HSS-W,M HST-W,M TI1-W,M
UFB-W,M
Bye Bye Love
DRR-W,M FRH-W,M HLS9-W,M

MF-W,M RW-W,M TI1-W,M
UFB-W,M
Bye Bye Rock-a-Bye
SOO-W,M
Bye Yum Pum Pum
OnT1-W,M
Bye'm Bye
AH-W,M HS-W,M MG-W,M
NeA-W,M
**Bye'm Bye see also By and By
(Star Shines Down on Number
One)**

C

C-A-T Is a Cat
GM-W
C & O Wreck
FSU-W
C. C. Rider
EP-W,M HRB3-W,M LC-W NeF-W
OFS-W,M OTJ-W,M RYT-W,M
TI1-W,M UFB-W,M
C-H-R-I-S-T-M-A-S
BCS-W,M OGC2-W,M TI1-W,M
UFB-W,M
C.I.O.
BMM-W
C-O-F-F-E-E
Boo-W,M
Ca, C'est L'Amour
HC2-W,M ML-W,M OTO-W TI1-
W,M UFB-W,M
Cab, Cab, Cab
MSB-W
Cabaletta
AmH-M
Cabaret
C-W,M DBC-W,M FPS-W,M
HC1-W,M LM-W,M On-W,M
OTO-W TI2-W,M UBF-W,M
Cabbage Patch Dreams
SBS-W,M
Cabin Creek Flood
BMM-W
Cabin in the Hills
BMM-W
Cabin in the Sky
HLS5-W,M HLS8-W,M RT4-W,M
RW-W,M
Cabin in the Wood
RSL-W,M
Cache Cache
WA-W,M
Cactus Flower
SSN-W,M (French)
Cade's County (Theme)
TVT-M
Cadet
LA-W,M (Spanish)
Cadet Rousselle
Ch-W (French Only) CUP-W,M
(French Only) MP-W,M (French
Only) OTJ-W,M (French Only)
Cae Cae
RW-M
Cagaran Gaolach
SeS-W,M
**Cage Aux Folles see La Cage Aux
Folles**
Cagney & Lacey Theme
TV-W
Caisson Song
HS-W,M MAS-W,M MES2-W,M
OTJ-W,M
Caissons Go Rolling Along

AAP-W,M GO-W HA-W,M
OP2-W,M RW-W,M WiS9-W,M
Caissons Song
FWS-W,M SiB-W,M UFB-W,M
**Caissons Song see also Field
Artillery Song**
Cajun Joe (the Bully of the Bayou)
Lo-W,M
Calcutta
MF-W,M OBN-W,M OPS-W,M
PB-W,M
Caldonia
BBB-W,M OnT1-W,M TI2-W,M
Caledonia
SoC-W
Calen O Custore Me
OTJ-W,M
Calendar Girl
GAR-W,M MF-W,M TRR-W,M
Calendar Song
OTJ-W,M
Calf of Gold
MMM-W,M
California
AmS-W,M ATS-W U-W
California (Movie Theme)
TOM-W,M
California Blues
LC-W LJ-W,M
California Boy
BSC-W
California Dreamin'
DRR-W,M MCG-W,M RB-W RV-W
RW-W,M RYT-W,M TI2-W,M
California Girls
RB-W
California Here I Come
MF-W,M OHB-W,M TI1-W,M
UFB-W,M
California Joe
ITP-W,M
California or the Feast of Gold
OHG-W,M
California Pioneers
OHG-W,M SY-W,M
California Prison Song
AFP-W
California Rose
OTO-W
California Stage
SoC-W
California Sun
MF-W,M
California Trail
SoC-W
Californy
MAS-W
Calino Custurame
SSP-W
Caliph's News
Ki-W,M
Call
SL-W,M
Call 'Em Names, Jeff
Sin-W,M SiS-W
Call for Philip Morris
GSM-W,M
Call for the Reck'ning
Boo-W
Call for the Best
Boo-W,M
Call Girl
TW-W
Call Home
TTH-W,M
Call Jehovah Thy Salvation
ESB-W,M Hy-W,M

Call John the Boatman
 MuM-W,M
Call Me
 HSe-W,M LWT-W,M TI2-W,M
 TOM-W,M TTH-W,M
Call Me Darling
 HLS2-W,M
Call Me Gone
 AG-W,M
Call Me Home
 OTJ-W,M
Call Me Irresponsible
 AT-W,M FrS-W,M GOI7-W,M
 HSi-W,M LM-W,M OnT1-W,M
 OTO-W RDT-W,M
Call Me Pet Names
 HSD-W,M
Call Me Thine Own
 AmH-W,M
Call Me Uncle
 Fi-W,M
Call of Erin
 VP-W
Call of Life
 BS-W,M
Call of Quantrell
 BSC-W
Call of the Canyon
 FC-W,M
Call of the Far-Away Hills
 OTO-W
Call of the North
 ASB6-W,M
Call of the Sea
 NN2-W,M NN7-W,M
Call of the Wild
 Mo-W,M
Call Them In
 GH-W,M
**Call Them Names, Jeff see Call
 'Em Names, Jeff**
Call to Arms
 AL-W
Call to Work or Play
 MH-W,M
Calla Lily Lady
 GV-W,M
Called from Above, I Rise
 AME-W,M
Callers
 MH-W,M
Caller's Song
 ASB4-W,M
Calling
 ASB1-W,M
Calling America
 TTH-W,M
Calling Me Back Home
 VA-W,M
Calling Now
 GH-W,M
Calling to Thee
 GH-W,M
Calling Your Name
 BSo-W,M
Calliope Song
 CSS-W
Calm As the Night
 FSY-W,M (German) SL-W,M
**Calm As the Night see also Still As
 the Night**
Calm He Rests
 Boo-W,M
Calm on the Listening Ear of Night
 AHO-W,M CCH-W,M
Calomel
 BSC-W FMT-W

Calton Weaver
 FW-W
Calvary (Every Time I Think about
 Jesus)
 AHO-W,M FN-W,M
Calvary (On Calvary's Brow My
 Saviour Died)
 GH-W,M
Calvary (The Pilgrims Throng thro'
 the City Gates)
 AmH-W,M FiS-W,M WiS7-W,M
Calvary's Love
 GP-W,M VB-W,M
Calypso
 GrS-W,M PoG-W,M WG-W,M
Calypso Joe
 Mo-W,M NM-W,M
Cam' Ye by Atholl
 SeS-W,M
Cambrian Colliery Disaster
 IFM-W
Cambric Shirt
 BSC-W FW-W Oz1-W,M
Cambridge Short Tune
 BC1-W,M
**Came Ye by Atholl see Cam' Ye by
 Atholl**
Camel
 ASB5-W,M OU-W,M
Camelot
 DBC-W,M LL-W,M OTO-W
 TI1-W,M TW-W UBF-W,M
 UFB-W,M
Camino De Valencia
 LA-W,M (Spanish)
Camp Douglas by the Lake
 SiS-W
Camp Fire Song
 SiS-W
Camp Menu Song
 Bo-W,M
Camp Song
 SL-W,M
Campaign of 1856
 BSC-W
Campaign Song
 AL-W
Campaign Song for Abraham
 Lincoln
 SiS-W
Campana Sobre Campana
 LaS-W,M (Spanish Only)
Campanas Vespertinas
 SBF-W,M (Spanish)
**Campanile Serenade see Sweet
 Dreams**
Campanitas De Cristal
 CDM-W,M (Spanish)
**Campbell Soup Jingle see MMM,
 MMM, Good**
Campbells Are Comin'
 FBI-W,M FW-W NAS-W,M
 SeS-W,M SMW-W,M
Campbells Are Coming
 AmH-W,M FG2-M HSD-W,M
 OTJ-W,M TMA-W,M
Campfire
 TH-W,M
Campfire Has Gone Out
 SoC-W
Campfire Medley
 Bo-W
**Campfire Song see Camp Fire
 Song**
Camping
 FSA2-W,M
Camporee or Jamboree Hymn

Bo-W,M
Camptown Races
 AH-W,M ATS-W BMC-W,M
 CSo-W,M FHR-W,M FW-W
 GG1-W,M GuC-W,M HAS-W,M
 HS-W,M HSD-W,M IL-W,M
 IPH-W,M LMR-W,M MAB1-W,M
 MAS-W,M MHB-W,M MSA1-W
 OAP-W,M OFS-W,M OS-W
 OTJ-W,M PoS-W,M POT-W,M
 RW-W,M SoF-W,M SSF-W,M
 SSFo-W,M U-W WiS8-W,M
Can Anyone Explain
 MF-W,M
Can Can
 OTJ-M OTO-W PaS-W,M
 TI1-W,M UFB-W,M
Can I Come Home from Canada?
 SiS-W
Can I Forget You?
 L-W
Can I Leave Off Wearin' My
 Shoes?
 Mo-W,M NM-W,M OTO-W
Can I Sleep in Your Barn Tonight?
 ATS-W Oz4-W,M
**Can I Sleep in Your Barn Tonight?
 see also May I Sleep in Your Barn
 Tonight Mister?**
Can It Be Possible?
 Mo-W,M NM-W,M OTO-W
Can It Be Right?
 GH-W,M
Can It Be Right for Me to Go
 AME-W,M
Can the Circle Be Unbroken?
 FW-W CMG-W,M Oz4-W,M
**Can the Circle Be Unbroken? see
 also Will the Circle Be Unbroken?**
Can the Soldier Forget?
 SiS-W
Can This Be Love
 MF-W,M OHB-W,M
Can You Cook
 ASB5-W,M
Can You Do It
 ToO76-W,M
Can You Feel the Beat
 TTH-W,M
Can You Hear the Music
 RoS-W,M
Can You Play?
 ASB4-W,M
Can You Reach My Friend
 VB-W,M
Can You Read My Mind
 BNG-W,M DC-W,M DPE-W,M
 EY-W,M HFH-W,M MF-W,M
 RoE-W,M
Can You Sew Cushions?
 OTJ-W,M
**Can You Sew Cushions? see also
 O Can Ye Sew Cushions?**
Can You Show Me How the
 Farmer?
 MH-W,M
Canaanland Is Just in Sight
 AG-W,M HHa-W,M
Canada
 DD-W,M
Canada-I-O
 ESU-W FW-W SoC-W
Canaday-I-O
 SWF-W,M
Canadian Boat Song
 CSo-W,M NAS-W,M OTJ-W,M
Canadian Capers

MF-W,M TI2-W,M
Canadian National Song see Maple Leaf Forever
Canadian Sunset
LWT-W,M TI1-W,M UFB-W,M
Canadien Errant see Un Canadien Errant
Canady-I-O
IF-W,M
Canal Street Boogie
MaG-W,M
Canards see Les Canards
Canary
STS-W,M
Cancion De Cuna
ASB3-W,M (Spanish)
Candida
MCG-W,M RYT-W,M TI2-W,M
Candle
ASB2-W,M
Candle Complains
GM-W
Candle in the Wind
CFB-W,M
Candle on the Water
NI-W,M
Candlemas Eve
GBC-W,M OB-W,M
Candles of Hannukah
RSL-W,M
Candy
BBB-W,M NK-W,M TI1-W,M
UFB-W,M
Candy Kisses
HLS9-W,M OGC2-W,M TI1-W,M
UFB-W,M
Candy Kitchen
DBL-W
Candy Man
IPH-W,M On-W,M OPS-W,M
OTJ-W,M RW-W,M TFC-W,M
Candy Man Blues
FW-W
Candy Shop
MH-W,M
Cane Chopping Song
LC-W
Cane Field Song
Me-W,M
Cannibal King
Bo-W,M IL-W,M
Cannibal Maid
GO-W,M
Cannily, Cannily
FW-W
Cannonball Blues
LSR-W,M
Canoe
STS-W,M
Canoe Poi
SNZ-W,M (Maori)
Canoe Round
RSL-W,M
Canoe Song
HS-W,M MG-W,M OHO-W,M
VA-W,M
Canoeing
SL-W,M
Canon
SHS-W,M
Canon (Tallis)
BMC-W,M MAS-W,M SCL-W,M
Canon (Tallis) see also Tallis' Canon
Canon in D (Pachelbel)
WGB/O-M
Canon in D Major (Pachelbel)

BNG-M
Canon in Four Parts (Slind)
BMC-M
Can't Be Yo' Turtle Any Mo'
NH-W
Can't Buy Me Love
BBe-W,M Be1-W,M TRR-W,M
TWS-W
Can't Fight This Feeling Anymore
RoE-W,M
Can't Get It Out of My Head
ELO-W,M
Can't Get Used to Losing You
TI1-W,M UFB-W,M
Can't Give You Anything
DDH-W,M
Can't Help Falling in Love
ILS-W,M RW-W,M SRE1-W,M
TI1-W,M UFB-W,M
Can't Help Lovin' Dat Man
L-W RDT-W,M SB-W,M TI1-W,M
ToS-W,M UFB-W,M
Can't Reach You
WA-W,M
Can't Smile without You
TI2-W,M
Can't Stan' de Fier
NSS-W
Can't Stand the Fire
NSS-W
Can't Stop My Heart from Lovin' You
FOC-W,M
Can't Stop My Heart from Loving You
AWS-W,M
Can't Wait Another Minute
TTH-W,M
Can't We Be Friends
MF-W,M OHB-W,M RoE-W,M
Can't We Fall in Love
WDS-W,M
Can't We Talk It Over
MF-W,M MR-W,M
Can't We Try
CFB-W,M
Can't Yo' Heah Me Callin', Caroline
MF-W,M SLB-W,M
Can't You Dance the Polka?
BF-W,M FGM-W,M FW-W
SA-W,M
Can't You Hear America Calling
HCY-W,M
Can't You Hear Me Knocking
RoS-W,M
Can't You Just See Yourself
Mo-W,M NM-W,M OTO-W
UBF-W,M
Can't You Line 'Em
Le-W,M
Can't You See It?
Mo-W,M NM-W,M OTO-W TW-W
Can't You See That She's Mine
Mo-W,M
Cantandole Al Mar
TI1-W,M (Spanish Only)
Cantate Domino
Boo-W,M (Latin Only)
Canterbury Tune
BC1-W,M
Cantiamo Compagni
Boo-W,M (Italian Only)
Canticle
SMY-W,M
Cantina Band
HFH-M TOM-M

Cantique De Noel
CCH-W,M FiS-W,M (French)
IL-W,M
Canuck's Lament
HB-W
Canzonet
FSA2-W,M
Canzonetta
AmH-M
Cape Ann
FW-W
Cape Cod Chantey
ASB5-W,M BeB-W,M HAS-W,M
HS-W,M
Cape Cod Girls
FW-W OTJ-W,M
Capital and Labor
AL-W
Capital Ship
FBI-W,M FW-W HAS-W,M IL-W,M
LMR-W,M OTJ-W,M
Capitalistic Boss
PSN-W,M
Capitan see El Capitan
Capotin see El Capotin
Capped Teeth and Caesar Salad
UBF-W,M
Capriccio Espagnol Theme (Rimsky-Korsakov)
LTL-M
Capricious and Fickle
TW-W
Capstone
BSC-W
Captain Andy's Entrance and Bally Hoo
SB-W,M
Captain Carey U.S.A. Theme see Mona Lisa
Captain Coon
NF-W
Captain Hook's Waltz
Mo-W,M NM-W,M OTJ-W,M
OTO-W
Captain Hornblower Theme
HFH-M
Captain Hull's Victory
ANS-W
Captain Jinks
ATS-W BH-W,M BMC-W,M FW-W
GI-W,M HS-W,M HSD-W,M
MAS-W,M OBN-W,M OTJ-W,M
Oz3-W,M POT-W,M TMA-W,M
VA-W,M
Captain Jinks of the Horse Marines
HAS-W,M HSA-W,M
Captain Jones's Invitation
ANS-W
Captain Kidd (Oh, I Was Once a Pirate)
FSA2-W,M SL-W,M
Captain Kidd (Oh, My Name Is Captain Kidd)
BB-W FW-W SA-W,M
Captain Kidd (Through All the World Below)
SHS-W,M
Captain of Her Heart
TTH-W,M
Captain of the Pinafore
LMR-W,M
Captain Wedderburn's Courtship
BT-W,M SCa-W
Captain with His Whiskers
Oz2-W,M Re-W,M SiS-W
Captive Knight
ESB-W,M

Capture of Burgoyne
EA-W,M
Capture of Little York
ANS-W
Capture of Major Andre
SSS-W,M
Capture of the Essex
ANS-W
Car Trouble
HR-W
Car Trouble Blues
LC-W
Car Wash
SoH-W,M
Cara Mamma, Io Sono Malata
LW-W,M (Italian)
Cara Mia
DRR-W,M GSN3-W,M HLS3-W,M
ILS-W,M MF-W,M RW-W,M
TI2-W,M TRR-W,M
Caravan (Duke Ellington)
GMD-W,M TI2-W,M
Caravan (Tramp, Tramp, Heavy Go
the Camels)
FSA2-W,M
Card Song
OHO-W,M
Cardinal
ASB3-W,M ASB6-W,M VS-W,M
Cardinal and Robin
ASB5-W,M
Care in Bread-Making
NF-W
Career
OTO-W
Careers
ASB5-W,M
Careful Man
JC-W,M
Carefully on Tiptoe Stealing
GiS-W,M MGT-W,M
Carefully Taught
SP-W,M
Careless
TI1-W,M UFB-W,M
Careless Hands
Mo-W,M NM-W,M
Careless Jackie
ASB2-W,M
Careless Kisses
OGC2-W,M
Careless Love
AFB-W,M AmS-W,M B-W,M
BF-W,M BI-W,M FAW-W,M
FMT-W FoM-W,M FSB1-W,M
FW-W IL-W,M LC-W LH-W,M
MF-W,M NeF-W OFS-W,M
OTJ-W,M Oz4-W,M PoG-W,M
RW-W,M SAm-W,M TI1-W,M
UFB-W,M
Careless Shepherd
BMC-W,M
Careless Whisper
TI2-W,M
Carem Carmela
SL-W,M
Carillon
CA-W,M
Carioca
HLS5-W,M TI1-W,M
Caris Viron
SoC-W
Carkies' Rally
SiS-W
Carl Johan
SiP-W,M (Swedish)
Carling Black Label Beer Jingle see

Hey, Mable, Black Label
Carlson's Raiders
GI-W
Carmagnole see La Carmagnole
Carman's Whistle
OH-W,M SSP-W
Carme
WiS8-W,M
Carmela
LaS-W,M (Spanish Only)
MML-W,M (Spanish) MSS-W,M
(Spanish)
Carmelina
SL-W,M
Carmen Bellicosum
AWB-W
Carmena
TF-W,M
Carnal and the Crane, The
GBC-W,M OB-W,M
Carnations (Clavelitos)
MSS-W,M (Spanish)
Carnival of Venice (Come Out!
Come Out! Come Hurry!)
PaS-W,M
Carnival of Venice (Julius
Benedict)
RW-M TI1-M UFB-M
Carnival of Venice, The (The
Carnival of Venice Began One
Saturday)
OTJ-W,M
Carnsville see Christian, The
Caro Mio Ben
FSY-W,M (Italian) SL-W,M
(Italian)
Caro Mio Ben see also Dear One,
Believe and Dearest Believe
Caro Nome
RW-M
Carol
MHB-W,M (French)
Carol, Carol, Christians
WiS7-W,M
Carol for Christingle
GBC-W,M
Carol for Christmas Day
CCH-W,M
Carol for Christmas Eve
CCH-W,M
Carol for Easter Saturday
GBC-W,M
Carol for New Year's Day
GBC-W,M
Carol for the Sunday after
Christmas
GBC-W,M
Carol of Beauty
OB-W,M
Carol of Saint Staffan
GBC-W,M
Carol of Service
OB-W,M
Carol of the Advent
OB-W,M
Carol of the Bells
BCh-W,M OAP-W,M OTJ-W,M
Carol of the Birds
ATM-W,M BMC-W,M SL-W,M
Carol of the Flowers
CCH-W,M GBC-W,M
Carol of the Kingdom
OB-W,M
Carol of the Mouse
GBC-W,M
Carol of the Shepherds
MML-W,M

Carol of the Star
HSS-W,M HST-W,M
Carol of the Universe
GBC-W,M
Carol of the Wind
CSB-W,M
Caroleen
CSD-W,M (French)
Carolina
SiS-W
Carolina Dreams
TOC83-W,M
Carolina in My Mind
RV-W
Carolina in the Morning
MF-W,M MR-W,M OHB-W,M
T-W,M WDS-W,M
Carolina in the Pines
EC-W,M
Carolina Moon
RW-W,M TI1-W,M TI2-W,M
UFB-W,M
Carolina Rolling Stone
Sta-W,M
Carolina's Sons
SiS-W
Caroline
A-W,M (Spanish) AAF-W,M
(French Only) CE-W,M (French
Only) CSD-W,M (French)
NAS-W,M
Caroline of Edinborough Town
Oz1-W,M
Caroline of Edinburgh Town
FMT-W
Caroling, Caroling
TI1-W,M UFB-W,M
Caroling We Go
BCh-W,M
Carolyn
NMH-W,M
Carousel see Carrousel
Carousel Waltz
TG-W,M
Carpenter
ASB5-W,M
Carpenters
MH-W,M
Carpenters' Song
MH-W,M
Carpet-Bagger
MPP-W
Carpet Man
TI2-W,M
Carrie
BHO-W,M
Carrie Anne
TI2-W,M
Carried by the Angels
GH-W,M
Carrier Dove
FSA1-W,M HSD-W,M SL-W,M
Carrier Pigeon
ASB2-W,M SOO-W,M
Carrier Pigeons
KS-W,M
Carrillon
FSA2-W,M
Carrion Crow
BSC-W
Carrot Song
GUM1-W,M
Carrousel
HS-W,M
Carrousel Waltz see Carousel
Waltz
Carry It On

SFF-W,M
Carry Me Back to Old Virginny
 AAP-W,M ATS-W BH-W,M
 BSB-W,M EFS-W,M Fif-W,M
 FM-M FSY-W,M HSD-W,M
 MAS-W,M MF-W,M OFS-W,M1
 PoS-W,M RW-W,M SL-W
 TMA-W,M WiS9-W,M
Carry Me Back to Ole Virginny
 AmH-W,M
Carry Me Back to the Lone Prairie
 FC-W,M
Carry That Weight
 BBe-W,M Be2-W,M TWS-W
Carry the Big Fresh Flavor
 TI1-W,M UFB-W,M
Cars Go Up and Down
 SOO-W,M
Carta Del Rey Ha Venido
 LA-W,M (Spanish)
Carve 'Im to de Heart
 NH-W
Carwash see Car Wash
Casa Loma Stomp
 Mo-M
Casanova O'Reilly
 GI-W,M
Cascade
 FSA2-W,M
Case of You
 RV-W
Casey Jones
 AF-W FMT-W FSTS-W,M FW-W
 HAS-W,M LSR-W,M NH-W
 SWF-W,M TI1-W,M UFB-W,M
Casey Jones, the Union Scab
 AFP-W
Casey Junior
 NI-W,M
Casey Would Waltz with a
 Strawberry Blonde see Band
 Played On
Casey's Last Ride
 SuS-W,M
Cash in Hand
 ANS-W
Casino Boogie
 RoS-W,M
Casino Royale
 BDF-W,M
Casper the Friendly Ghost
 LM-W,M
Cassidy
 RV-W
Cassville Prisoner
 Oz2-W,M
Cast Thy Bread upon the Waters
 AHO-W,M GH-W,M
Cast Thy Burden
 ESB-W,M
Cast Thy Burden upon the Lord
 LMR-W,M
Cast Your Fate to the Wind
 OnT1-M OPS-M
Castanet Song from Carmen
 RW-M
Castanets Are Sounding
 HSD-W,M
Castaways
 TW-W
Casting All Your Care
 GH-W,M
Castle Island Song
 SBA-W SAR-W,M
Castle on a Cloud
 UBF-W,M
Castle Steps She Climbs

FSF-W (French)
Castles in the Air
 FSA2-W,M
C-A-T Is a Cat
 GM-W
Cat and Bird
 ASB1-W,M
Cat and the Catboat
 SL-W
Cat and the Dog
 MH-W,M
Cat Came Back
 FSN-W,M FW-W OHO-W,M
 OTJ-W,M Oz3-W,M WF-W,M
Cat Came Fiddling
 SiR-W,M
Cat Is in the Snow
 SOO-W,M
Cat Song
 OTJ-W,M
Catch a Cricket
 GSM-W,M
Catch a Falling Star
 MF-W,M
Catch a Pebble
 MLS-W,M
Catch Me If You Can
 SiR-W,M
Catch Me If You Can
 (Hughes,Rice/Weill)
 SSA-W,M
Catch Me I'm Falling
 CFB-W,M
Catch That Is Merry
 Boo-W,M
Catch Us If You Can
 ILS-W,M MF-W,M
Caterina
 OPS-W,M
Caterpillar
 MH-W,M
Caterpillars
 SSe-W,M
Cathedrals
 OTJ-W,M (French Only)
Catholic Rent
 VP-W
Cats and Dogs
 SOO-W,M
Catskill Festival
 PSN-W,M
Cattle Call
 FC-W,M
Cattle Island Song
 EA-W,M
Caucus
 AL-W
Caught by the Witch Play
 NF-W
Caught Up in the Rapture
 DPE-W,M
Caution
 FSA1-W,M
Cavalier Song
 FSA2-W,M
Cavaliers of Dixie
 SiS-W
Cavalry of the Steppes
 SMW-W,M (Russian)
Cavalry of the Steppes see also
 Meadowland (Red Army Song)
Cavatina
 DPE-M FSA2-M HFH-M MF-M
 TOM-M
Cease Sorrows Now
 OH-W,M
Cecilia

FSO-W,M (French)
Cecilia (Does Your Mother Know
 You're Out)
 HSS-W,M TI1-W,M TI2-W,M
 UFB-W,M
Cefiro see El Cefiro
Celebrate
 VB-W,M
Celebrate His Good Life
 VB-W,M
Celebrate the Lord
 VB-W,M
Celebrated Waltzes
 RW-M
Celebration (Celebrate Good
 Times, Come On!)
 MF-W,M
Celebration (Jones/Schmidt)
 Fa-W,M
Celebration (We're Gonna Have a
 Great Celebration)
 VB-W,M
Celebrons Sans Cesse
 Boo-W,M (French Only)
Celery Song
 GUM1-W,M
Celeste Aida
 AmH-W,M RW-M
Celeste Aida see also Heav'nly
 Aida
Celia the Fair
 EL-W,M
Cement Mixer
 WF-W,M
Cemetery Blue
 AN-W
Centennial Hymn
 MPP-W,M
Centennial Meditation of Columbia
 MPP-W
Centennial Wail
 AL-W
Centipede and the Frog
 OTJ-W
Certain Smile
 HLS5-W,M RT5-W,M RW-W,M
Certainly, Lord
 SFF-W,M
C'est Benir Ton Nom
 Boo-W,M (French Only)
C'est Eine Jeune Fille
 CaF-W,M (French Only)
C'est L'aviron
 LA-W,M (Spanish)
C'est L'aviron Qui Nous Mene En
 Hout
 CFS-W,M
C'est La Belle Francoise
 FSO-W,M (French)
C'est La Poulette Grise
 FSO-W,M (French)
C'est Le Vent Frivolant
 OTJ-W,M (French Only)
C'est Magnifique
 HC2-W,M ML-W,M OTO-W
 TI1-W,M UBF-W,M UFB-W,M
C'est Moi
 OTO-W
C'est Pas La Bague
 CE-W,M (French Only)
C'est Si Bon
 TI2-W,M
C'est Un Rempart Que Notre Dieu
 CUP-W,M (French Only)
Cet A'bre
 CaF-W (French Only)
Cette Larme

CaF-W (French Only)
Cha Cha Cubana
GO17-M
Chain Store Daisy
TW-W
Chained to a Memory
OGC1-W,M
Chains of Love
HRB1-W,M
Chair at Tremblant
OHO-W,M
Chair Song
Mo-W,M NM-W,M
Chairs to Mend
Boo-W,M GuC-W,M SSP-W
TF-W,M
Challenge to Youth
MHB-W,M
Chamaritta
FSA1-W,M
Champagne Charlie
HAS-W,M PoS-W,M
Champagne Time
LWT-W,M TI1-M UFB-M
Champagne Waltz
AT-W,M LM-W,M WGB/P-W,M
Champion
VB-W,M
Champion of Love
HHa-W,M
Champion of the Battle
VB-W,M
Chances Are
MF-W,M TI2-W,M
**Chances Are (Love Theme) see
After All**
Chandler's Wife
FW-W
Chang Fu Ch'u Tang Ping
(Husband Goes to War)
FD-W,M (Chinese)
Change Is Gonna Come
RB-W
Change Me Lord
HHa-W,M
Changes
WDS-W,M
Changing Partners
OnT1-W,M RW-W,M TI2-W,M
Channing Way
TT-W,M
Chanson D'Amour
BeL-W,M (French) TI1-W,M
(French)
**Chanson D'Eine Vielle Fille see La
Chanson D'Eine Vielle Fille**
Chanson De L'Annee Du Coup
BSC-W
Chanson De Mai
CUP-W,M (French Only)
**Chanson Des Metamorphoses see
La Chanson Des Metamorphoses**
**Chant Du Depart see Le Chant Du
Depart**
Chant Sans Paroles
AmH-M
Chantez, Chantez
TI1-W,M
Chantez Les Bas (Sing 'Em Low)
B-W,M
Chanticleer
FSA1-W,M OB-W,M
Chantilly Lace
DRR-W,M
Chantons, Bergers, Noel, Noel
CCH-W,M
Chanukah Song

TI1-M
**Chanukah Song see also Hannukah
Song and Hanuka Song**
Chanuke, O Chanuke
FW-W (Yiddish)
**Chanuke, O Chanuke see also
Hanukkah O Hanukkah**
Chaparral Song
Bo-W,M
Chapel of Love
DRR-W,M ERM-W,M GAR-W,M
TI1-W,M UFB-W,M
Chapter of Good Things
ESU-W
Charade
OHF-W PoG-W,M WG-W,M
Charbonnier Mon Ami
FSF-W (French)
Charcoal Man
Me-W,M
Charge by the Ford
AWB-W
**Charge the Can Cheerily see Naval
Song: Charge the Can Cheerily**
Charge to Keep I Have
AME-W,M Hy-W,M OM-W,M
Chariots of Fire
BNG-M DC-M DPE-M EY-M
HFH-M MF-M
Charles Guiteau
ATS-W,M BSC-W FMT-W FW-W
Oz2-W,M
Charles J. Guiteau
FSU-W
Charles John, Our Brave King
AmH-W,M (Swedish)
Charles Stewart Parnell's Grand
Triumphant Procession
VP-W
Charleston
HC1-W,M MF-W,M OHB-W,M
Charleston Gals
NSS-W
Charleston Is Ours
SiS-W
Charleston Song
SSS-W,M
Charlestown
SHS-W,M
Charlestown Land Shark
AFP-W
Charley Brooks
Oz4-W,M
Charley My Boy
TI1-W,M UFB-W,M
Charley over the Water
OTJ-W,M
**Charley over the Water see also
Charlie over the Water**
Charley Ross
Oz4-W,M
Charlie Brown
HRB4-W,M ILF-W,M RB-W
TI1-W,M UFB-W,M
Charlie Condemned
SG-W,M
Charlie Is My Darling
FBI-W,M FW-W OFS-W,M
OTJ-W,M SL-W,M U-W
**Charlie Is My Darling see also Oh,
Charlie Is My Darling**
Charlie Knapp
MHB-M
Charlie Knows How to Beat That
Drum
RSL-W,M
Charlie Mopps

PO-W,M
Charlie over the Water
RSL-W,M
**Charlie over the Water see also
Charley over the Water**
Charlie Quantrell, Oh
HB-W,M
Charlie's Place
OTO-W UBF-W,M
Charlotte Town
OTJ-W,M
Charlotte's Web
SBS-W,M TI2-W,M
Charm
FSA2-W,M
Charmaine
EAG2-W,M GG5-W,M GST-W,M
HLS5-W,M RW-W,M T-W,M
TI2-W,M
Charmer
DP-W,M
Charming Betsey
Oz3-W,M
Charming Young Widow I Met in
the Train
Oz3-W,M
Charmin's Lament
MS-W,M
Charms Are Fairest When They're
Hidden
K-W,M
Charollet
BSC-W
Charro see El Charro
Chartists Are Coming
MSB-W
Chase
ToO79-W,M
Chase, The
Su-W,M
Chase of the O. L. C. Steer
SoC-W
Chase the Squirrel
Oz3-W,M
Chasin' That Neon Rainbow
GCM-W,M
Chatsworth Wreck
BSC-W Oz4-W,M
Chattanooga Choo Choo
CS-W,M GG2-W,M GSF-W,M
GSN3-W,M HLS3-W,M RT4-W,M
RW-W,M
Chatter with the Angels
Oz2-W,M
Chattering Squaw
TF-W,M
Cheatin' on Me
MF-W,M
Check It Out
BHO-W,M
Chee Lai
FW-W (Chinese) SMW-W,M
**Cheech and Chong's Nice Dreams
Theme see Nice Dreams**
Cheer, Boys, Cheer
FSA1-W,M
Cheer Illini
CoS-W
Cheer the Weary Traveller
BI-W,M
Cheer Up
CoF-W,M
Cheer Up Brave Boys
SiS-W
Cheerful
SHS-W,M
Cheerful Day Is Dawning

Boo-W,M
Cheerful Little Earful
 MF-W,M OHB-W,M
Cheerily the Huntsman
 TF-W,M
Cheering Song
 LMR-W,M
Cheerio
 SiR-W,M SL-W,M
**Cheerios Cereal Jingle see Pow,
 Pow, Powerful**
Cheer'ly Man
 SA-W,M
Cheers
 HB-W
**Cheers Theme see Where
 Everybody Knows Your Name**
Cheery Fact
 FSA1-W,M
Chega De Saudade
 TI1-W,M UFB-W,M
Chelsea Morning
 DPE-W,M ERM-W,M
Cher Mo L'Aime Toi
 CSD-W,M (French)
Cher Petit Papa
 CLaL-W,M (French)
Cherchez La Femme
 ToO76-W,M
Chere Amie
 CaF-W (French Only)
Cherish
 DPE-W,M ERM-W,M LOM-W,M
 MCG-W,M MF-W,M RYT-W,M
Cherokee
 MF-W,M TI1-W,M UFB-W,M
Cherokee Indian Harvest Song
 SG-W,M
Cherries Are Ripe
 SiR-W,M
Cherries Ripe
 MH-W,M
Cherry Bloom
 MHB-W,M (Japanese) SL-W,M
Cherry Bomb
 BHO-W,M
Cherry, Cherry
 BR-W,M On-W,M TI2-W,M
Cherry Pie
 FRH-W,M
Cherry Pies Ought to Be You
 TW-W UBF-W,M
Cherry Pink and Apple Blossom
 White
 OTO-W TI1-W,M UFB-W,M
Cherry Point
 MF-M
Cherry Ripe
 FSA2-W,M OH-W,M OTJ-W,M
Cherry Tree
 MH-W,M
Cherry Tree Carol
 ASB6-W,M BMM-W,M BT-W,M
 CEM-W,M CSB-W,M FW-W
 ITP-W,M OB-W,M OPS-W,M Oz1-
 W,M PSN-W RW-W,M Y-W,M
Chers Yeux Noirs
 CaF-W (French Only)
Cherubic Hymn
 LMR-W,M
Chesapeake and Shannon
 ANS-W
Cheshire Man
 OH-W,M
Chessboard of Vietnam
 VS-W,M
Chester

AH-W,M ATS-W,M EA-W,M
 MPP-W,M NAS-W,M OTJ-W,M
 SAR-W,M SBF-W,M SI-W,M
 TO-W,M
**Chester see also Let Tyrants Shake
 Their Iron Rod**
**Chesterfield Cigarettes Jingle see
 Chesterfield, Twenty-One Great
 Tobaccos and Sound Off for
 Chesterfield**
Chesterfield, Twenty-One Great
 Tobaccos
 GSM-W,M
Chestnuts Roasting on an Open
 Fire
 BCh-W,M OTJ-W,M
**Chestnuts Roasting on an Open
 Fire see also Christmas Song
 (Chestnuts Roasting on an Open
 Fire)**
Chevaliers De La Table Ronde
 FSF-W (French) FW-W (French)
**Chevrolet Automobile Jingle see
 See the U.S.A. in Your Chevrolet**
Chevy Chase
 OH-W,M
**Chevy Chase see also Hunting of
 the Cheviot**
Chewing Gum
 FW-W
Cheyenne
 FC-W,M TVT-W,M
Chez Mon Pere
 CaF-W (French Only)
Chi-Baba Chi-Baba
 MF-W,M TI1-W,M
Chi Chi
 HJ-W,M
Chiapanecas
 CA-W,M MAR-W,M SFB-W,M
 TI1-M VA-W,M
Chicago
 PB-W,M
Chicago Blues
 DBL-W
Chicago Bound
 LC-W
Chicago Gouge
 B-W,M BI-W,M
Chicchirichi
 SiR-W,M SOO-W,M
Chick-a-Boom
 MF-W,M
Chicka Hanka
 NFS-W,M RSL-W,M UF-W,M
Chickama, Chickama, Craney
 Crow
 PSD-W,M SiR-W,M
Chickee Chickee Ma Craney Crow
 Oz3-W
Chicken
 GM-W
Chicken Butcher
 SSo-W,M
Chicken in the Bread Tray
 NF-W SNS-W
Chicken Never Roost Too High for
 Me
 AFP-W
**Chicken of the Sea Theme see Ask
 Any Mermaid**
Chicken Pie
 NF-W
Chicken Reel
 AmS-M OTJ-M POT-M
Chicken Run Fast
 Oz2-W

Chicken Talk
 ASB2-W,M
Chickens and Ducks
 ASB1-W,M
Chickery Chick
 NoS-W,M TI1-W,M UFB-W,M
**Chiclets Chewing Gum Jingle see I
 Like Chiclets**
Chico and the Man
 TVT-W,M
Chico the Chihuahua
 GM-W
Chicora
 SiS-W
Chief Aderholt
 AFP-W,M
Chigger
 GI-W
Child and the Sparrow
 MH-W,M
Child and the Star
 ASB1-W,M
Child Has Been Born
 CCM-W,M
Child Is Born in Bethlehem
 RW-W,M
Child of a King
 GH-W,M
Child of Clay
 BHB-W,M
Child of God
 FW-W
Child of Sin and Sorrow
 GH-W,M
Child of the King
 AME-W,M
Child of the Moon
 RoS-W,M
Child This Day
 JOC-W,M OB-W,M
Child This Day Is Born
 GUM2-W,M
Childhood Home
 SE-W,M (Swedish)
Children Are Crying and Calling
 Your Name
 BSo-W,M
Children at Play (Kabalevsky)
 GM-M
Children, Go Where I Send Thee
 FW-W TO-W,M
Children, Good-By
 MH-W,M
Children of the Heavenly Father
 SJ-W,M
Children of the Heavenly King
 AME-W,M Hy-W,M SiR-W,M
Children Playing (Moussorgsky)
 GM-M
Children, We All Shall Be Free
 RF-W,M
Children, You'll Be Called On
 SpS-W,M
Children's Hosanna
 WiS7-W,M
Children's Marching Song
 HLS3-W,M
Children's Polka
 MAR-W,M
Children's Prayer
 ASB6-W,M BM-W HS-W,M
 MG-W,M VA-W,M
Children's Seating Rhyme
 NF-W
Children's Song of the Nativity
 OB-W,M
Child's Dream

JF-W,M
Child's Dreamland
AmH-W,M
Child's Evensong
ASB3-W,M
Child's Lullaby (Beth Raebeck)
GM-M
Child's Prayer
ASB2-W,M
Child's Thanksgiving
MG-W,M
Chilled by the Blasts of Adverse
Fate
AHO-W,M
Chilly Waters
DD-W,M
Chilly Winds
WU-W,M
Chilly Winds (of Chicago)
TOM-W,M
Chim Chim Cher-ee
GOI7-W,M NI-W,M OnT1-W,M
OTJ-W,M OTO-W RW-W,M
SBS-W,M WD-W,M
Chimes
ASB1-W,M ASB2-W,M
Chimes of Dunkirk
MAR-W,M
Chimes of Freedom
FoR-W,M
Chimes of Normandy
AmH-M
Chimney Swallow
Oz3-W
Chimney Sweeper
DD-W,M Me-W,M SG-W,M
Chin Up, Ladies!
Mo-W,M NM-W,M OTO-W
China
EA-W,M SHS-W,M
**China Syndrome Theme see
Somewhere in Between**
Chinatown (Theme)
AT-M LM-W,M
Chinatown, My Chinatown
MF-W,M RC-W,M
Chinese
GB-W,M
Chinese Baby Song
HSD-W,M
Chinese Chicken
OTJ-W,M
Chinese Girls
ASB4-W,M
Chinese Hymn
SL-W,M
Chinese Kung Fu
DDH-W,M
Chinese Lullaby
ASB6-W,M SCL-W,M
Chinese Serenade
AmH-M
Ching-a-Ring Chaw
OA2-W,M
Chipmunk Song
BCS-W,M OPS-W,M OTJ-W,M
Chippy, Get Your Hair Cut
AH-W,M
Chiquilla
TI1-W,M (Spanish Only)
Chiquita Banana (Jingle)
NoS-W,M
**Chiquita Banana (Jingle) see also
I'm Chiquita Banana**
Chisholm Trail
RW-W,M SoC-W
Chit Chat

HAS-W,M
Chitty Chitty Bang Bang
SBS-W,M
Chivalrous C.S.A.
SiS-W
Chivalrous Knight of France
MPP-W,M
Chivalrous Shark
FW-W OHO-W,M
Chlo-e
HLS1-W,M T-W,M
Chloe Found Amyntas Lying
SR-W,M
Chock Full o' Nuts Is That
Heavenly Coffee
GSM-W,M
Choc'late Candy
OTJ-W,M
Choclo see El Choclo
Choctaw and Cherokee
ESU-W
Choo Choo Ch' Boogie
OnT6-W,M
Chopin's Polonaise
TI1-M
**Chopin's Polonaise see also
Polonaise**
Chopo
SoC-W,M
Chopsticks
MAR-M
Choral (Schumann)
ASB1-M
Choral Bells
GeS-W,M
Choral Fanfare
GeS-W,M
Choral Fantasy (Beethoven,
adapted by Molzer)
MuM-W,M
Choral Harp
FHR-W,M
Choral Prayer
LoS-W
Choral Prelude (from Loomis'
Cinderella)
FSA1-W,M
Choral Sanctus (Alfred Gaul)
SL-W,M TF-W,M
Chorale from Wagner's Hans
Sachs
GUM2-W,M
Chorale 146 (Bach)
BMC-M
Chords
SoP-W,M
Chorus Girl Blues
TS-W
Chorus of Blessed Spirits
TF-W,M
Chorus of Liberty
GrM-W,M
Chorus of Peers
TH-W,M
Chorus of the Norwegian Sailors
MMM-W,M
Chorus Sung before General
Washington
MPP-W,M
Choruses from Patriotic Songs
ASB1-W,M
Chosen Kalle Mazeltov
OTJ-W,M (Yiddish Only)
Chosen Reservoir
AF-W
Chosen Three on Mountain Height
AHO-W,M

Choucoune
LaS-W,M MHB-W,M
Choumi Maritza
SiP-W,M (Bulgarian)
Christ Arose
AME-W,M GH-W,M OM-W,M
Christ Be with Me
FiS-W,M
Christ Child
SiB-W,M
Christ Day
CCM-W,M
Christ for Me
GH-W,M
Christ for the World We Sing
AHO-W,M AME-W,M FH-W,M
Hy-W,M
Christ from Whom All Blessings
Flow
AME-W,M
Christ Is Coming
GH-W,M
Christ Is Made the Sure
Foundation
AME-W,M CEM-W,M Hy-W,M
Christ Is My Redeemer
GH-W,M
Christ Is Risen
GH-W,M
Christ Is the World's Redeemer
Hy-W,M
Christ Is the World's True Light
Hy-W,M
Christ Liveth in Me
GH-W,M
Christ My All
GH-W,M
Christ My Beloved
ER-W,M
Christ of All My Hopes the Ground
Hy-W,M
Christ of the Upward Way
Hy-W,M
Christ Receiveth Sinful Men
GH-W,M
Christ Returneth
GH-W,M
Christ Shall Have Dominion
Hy-W,M
Christ the Fountain
GH-W,M
Christ the Lord Is Risen
ER-W,M OB-W,M TF-W,M
Christ, the Lord, Is Risen Again
AME-W,M SJ-W,M
Christ the Lord Is Risen To-day
AME-W,M
Christ the Lord Is Risen Today
CEM-W,M IH-M JBF-W,M OS-W
SHP-W,M SiB-W,M SL-W,M
TB-W,M VB-W,M
Christ Was Born on Christmas Day
BCS-W,M
Christ, Whose Glory Fills the Skies
Hy-W,M
Christi Eleison
Boo-W,M (Greek Only)
Christian, The
SHS-W,M
Christian Aid
GBC-W,M
Christian Band
WN-W,M
Christian, Be Up
AHO-W,M
Christian Commission
SiS-W

Christian Conflicts
SHS-W,M
Christian Cowboy's Creed
HOH-W
Christian, Dost Thou See Them
Hy-W,M SJ-W
Christian Prospect
ATS-W SHS-W,M
Christian Soldier
SHS-W,M
Christian Song
SHS-W,M
Christian, Walk Carefully
GH-W,M
Christian Warfare
SHS-W,M
Christians, Awake
HSD-W,M
Christians, Awake, Salute the
Happy Morn
YC-W,M
Christian's Farewell
SHS-W,M
Christian's Good-Night
GH-W,M
Christian's Hope
SHS-W,M
Christine Leroy
Oz4-W,M
C-H-R-I-S-T-M-A-S
BCS-W,M OGC2-W,M TI1-W,M
UFB-W,M
Christmas
SiR-W,M
Christmas (While Shepherds
Watch'd Their Flocks by Night)
BC1-W,M
**Christmas (While Shepherds
Watch'd Their Flocks by Night)
see also While Shepherds
Watched Their Flocks (by Night)**
Christmas (Is the Happiest Time of
All)
TI1-W,M UFB-W,M
Christmas Auld Lang Syne
DC-W,M MF-W,M
Christmas Bells
MES1-W,M MES2-W,M Y-W,M
Christmas Bells (Are Ringing,
Ringing Soft and Low)
SoP-W,M
Christmas Bells (The Bells in the
Steeple Are Ringing Today)
ASB1-W,M
Christmas Bells (Chiming from the
Tower, in a Silver Shower)
FSA1-W,M
Christmas Bells (Ding Dong!
Merrily on High)
RS-W,M
Christmas Bells (The Merry Bells of
Christmas Ring)
STS-W,M
Christmas Bells (Oh, Christmas
Bells)
MAS-W,M
Christmas Bells (Over the Snow, O
the Cold Frosty Snow)
JOC-W,M
Christmas Bells (Ring the Merry,
Merry Bells)
MH-W,M
Christmas Bells Ring Sweet and
Clear
MF-W,M
Christmas Candle
GBC-W,M

Christmas Candles
SCL-W,M
Christmas Carol
LA-W,M (Spanish) MU-W,M
(Latin)
Christmas Caroling Song
TF-W,M VA-W,M
Christmas Cheer
CSG-W,M
Christmas Chimes
MH-W,M
Christmas Chorale
MU-W,M
Christmas Comes Again
CCH-W,M CCM-W,M
Christmas Comes 'Round
CSB-W,M
Christmas Day (Bells and Drums
and Soldiers Tall)
MH-W,M
Christmas Day (Christmas Is So
Jolly!)
KS-W,M
Christmas Day (David/Bacharach)
Mo-W,M OTO-W
Christmas Day (There Was a Pig
Went Out to Dig)
GBC-W,M
Christmas Day in the Morning
CCH-W,M MC-W,M
Christmas Day Is Just around the
Corner
MF-W,M
Christmas Eve
CCH-W,M MC-W,M OB-W,M
Christmas Fantasy
SAC-W,M
Christmas Greeting
MAS-W,M SFB-W,M SL-W,M
Christmas Holidays
ASB1-W,M
Christmas Hymn
GP-W,M
Christmas in Killarney
BCh-W,M MF-W,M MR-W,M
Christmas Is
TI1-W,M UFB-W,M
Christmas Is A-Comin'
TI2-W,M
Christmas Is A-Coming
Le-W,M
Christmas Is Coming
ASB3-W,M BMC-W,M Boo-W,M
LMR-W,M MAS-W,M MC-W,M
Christmas Is for Children
RW-W,M
Christmas Is Here
CCM-W,M
Christmas Luau
HSA-W,M
Christmas Lullaby
OnT6-W,M
Christmas Mem'ries
MF-W,M
Christmas Morning
RS-W,M
Christmas on the Moon
GG3-W,M
Christmas Prayer
MU-W,M
Christmas Present
OnT6-W,M
Christmas Round
BMC-W,M
Christmas Song
AST-W,M MH-W,M OTJ-W,M
Christmas Song (Chestnuts

Roasting on an Open Fire)
BCh-W,M Mo-W,M NM-W,M
RDT-W,M TI2-W,M
**Christmas Song (Chestnuts
Roasting on an Open Fire) see
also Chestnuts Roasting on an
Open Fire**
Christmas Star
SiR-W,M
Christmas Story
SoP-W,M
Christmas Time
KS-W,M
Christmas Tree (The Holly's Up,
the House Is All Bright)
OB-W,M
Christmas Tree (What Tree Is
There So Fair to See)
ASB1-W,M
Christmas Turkey
NF-W
Christmas Waltz
BCS-W,M FrS-W,M MF-W,M
Christmas Will Come Again
OTJ-W,M
Christmas Wish
ASB3-W,M
Christmas's Lamentation
GBC-W,M
Christopher Columbus (Mister
Christopher Columbus Sailed the
Sea without a Compass)
Mo-W,M NM-W,M TI2-W,M
Christopher Columbus (What
Captain Crossed the Ocean Blue)
ASB3-W,M
Christopher Street
TW-W
Christ's Life Our Code
AHO-W,M
Chronicles of the Pope
MSB-W
Ch'u T'ou Ko (Song of the Hoe)
FD-W,M (Chinese)
Chuck Wagon Races
HB-W
Chuck Wagon's Stuck
HB-W,M
Chuck Will's Widow Song
NF-W
Chug a Lug
CMG-W,M CSp-W,M
Chula La Manana
LA-W,M (Spanish)
Chumbara
PaS-W,M RSL-W,M
Ch'un Hsin (Spring Tidings)
FD-W,M (Chinese)
Chung Ch'iu Kuei Yuan (Love's
Lament in Mid-Autumn)
FD-W,M (Chinese)
Church
FF-W
Church across the Way
Oz4-W
Church Bells (Bells Ringing in the
Church Steeple High)
MH-W,M
Church Bells (To and Fro the
Church Bells Swing)
SoP-W,M
Church in the Wildwood
Bo-W CEM-W,M HHa-W,M
OBN-W,M
**Church in the Wildwood see also
Little Brown Church in the Vale**
Church Is Moving On

AME-W,M
Church Is Wherever God's People
  Are Praising
  SHP-W,M
Church of God
  RF-W,M
Church's One Foundation
  AME-W,M FH-W,M Hy-W,M
  WiS7-W,M
Churning Song
  GUM1-W,M
Chussen Kalle Mazel Tov
  MF-W,M (Yiddish Only)
Ciao, Ciao, Bambina
  GG5-W,M GSN3-W,M (Italian)
  HLS3-W,M (Italian) RW-W,M
  Sta-W,M
Cicirinella
  VA-W,M (Italian)
Cielito Lindo
  ATS-W,M FW-W (Spanish Only)
  GuC-W,M (Spanish) HS-W,M
  (Spanish) LaS-W,M (Spanish)
  LoS-W,M (Spanish) MG-W,M
  (Spanish) OTJ-W,M (Spanish
  Only) PaS-W,M UF-W,M
Cielito Lindo Is My Lady
  FrF-W,M (Spanish)
Cigareetes, Whusky and Wild, Wild
  Women
  OGC2-W,M
Cigarettes Will Spoil Yer Life
  NeA-W,M
Cimarron
  FC-W,M
Cinco Pollitos
  CDM-W,M (Spanish)
Cinco Robles
  TI1-W,M
Cinderelatives
  GOB-W,M
Cinderella
  FSA1-W,M OHT-W,M OTJ-W,M
**Cinderella Waltz see So This Is
  Love (Cinderella Waltz)**
Cinderella's Song
  FSA1-W,M
Cindy
  FG2-W,M FPG-W,M FW-W
  FWS-W,M GeS-W,M GuC-W,M
  HS-W,M LoS-W,M MES2-W,M
  OFS-W,M OS-W OTJ-W,M
  POT-W,M RW-W,M SG-W,M
  SiB-W,M VA-W,M WU-W,M
**Cindy see also Get Along Home,
  Cindy**
Cindy in the Summertime
  FVV-W,M
Cindy, Oh Cindy
  TI2-W,M
Cinnamon Girl
  ERM-W,M MF-W,M
Cinq Pieds Deux
  CaF-W (French Only)
Cinquantaine see La Cinquantaine
Circle Four in London
  Oz3-W,M
Circle in the Sand
  RoE-W,M
Circle of Two
  VB-W,M
Circle Round
  GM-W
Circuit Rider's Home
  HB-W,M
Circumstances Alter Cases
  AL-W

Circus
  FSA1-W,M MH-W,M
Circus Comes to Town
  CSS-W
Ciribiribin
  AmH-M OBN-W,M OTJ-W,M
  RW-W,M TI1-M UF-W,M UFB-M
Cisco Kid
  DP-W,M GrH-W,M
Citadel
  RoS-W,M
Cities Are Burning
  IHA-W,M JF-W
City Comin' Down
  AG-W,M
City Cowboy
  SoC-W
City Flowers
  FSA1-W,M
City Four-Square
  AME-W,M
City Horses
  KS-W,M
City Lights
  TI2-W,M UBF-W,M
City, Lord, Where Thy Dear Life
  AHO-W,M
City Mouse, Country Mouse
  PF-W,M
City o' Babylon
  MoM-W,M
City of Angels Theme
  MF-W,M
City of God, How Broad and Far
  Hy-W,M
City of the Refuge
  AN-W
City of Winnepeg
  SoC-W
Civil War
  AWB-W
Civil War Song
  BMM-W,M FMT-W
Civilization
  OTJ-W,M
Civilization (Bongo, Bongo, Bongo)
  Mo-W,M NM-W,M TI2-W,M
  UBF-W,M
Clack-a-Lack
  ASB5-W,M
Clair De Lune
  FPS-M MF-M NCB-W,M PoG-M
  RW-M WGB/O-M WGB/P-W,M
Clancy Lowered the Boom
  MF-W,M
Clandestine Letter
  NF-W
Clanking Spurs
  MHB-W,M (Polish)
Clap, Clap, Clap
  IL-W,M
Clap for the Wolfman
  DP-W,M
Clap Hands! Here Comes Charley!
  OHB-W,M
Clap, Snap, Tap, Rap
  GM-W
Clap Yo' Hands
  GOB-W,M LSO-W MF-W,M
  NYT-W,M
Claremont
  SHS-W,M
Clarinet Marmalade
  HLS1-M
Clarinet Polka
  MF-M OBN-M PT-M TI1-M
Class

CMV-W,M
Classical Gas
  GO17-M GSN4-M
Claudette
  TFC-W,M
Clavelitos
  MSS-W,M (Spanish)
Clay and Frelinghuysen
  MPP-W,M
Clay Parody on Yankee Doodle
  ATS-W
Clayton's Grand March
  Mo-M
Clean Clothes Song
  SSo-W,M
Clean Heart
  AME-W,M
Clean Up
  GM-W
Cleanse Me
  OM-W,M
Cleansing Fountain
  GH-W,M
Clear Brook
  LA-W,M (Spanish)
Clear the Kitchen
  TMA-W,M
Clear the Track
  MPP-W SA-W,M WS-W,M
Clear the Way, or the Song of the
  Wagon Road
  OHG-W,M
Clementine
  ATS-W,M BaB-W,M (French)
  BMC-W,M Bo-W,M CSo-W,M
  FSB1-W,M FW-W FWS-W,M
  HAS-W,M HS-W,M IL-W,M
  LMR-W,M LoS-W,M MAS-W,M
  MES1-W,M MES2-W,M RW-W,M
  SBF-W,M SoC-W TI1-W,M U-W
  UFB-W,M VA-W,M
**Clementine see also My Darling
  Clementine and Oh, My Darling
  Clementine**
Clever Fair Lass of Islington
  SR-W,M
Click Go the Shears
  ATM-W,M
Clickety-Clack
  KH-W,M
Climb Ev'ry Mountain
  CEM-W,M DBC-W,M HC1-W,M
  HLS8-W,M OTJ-W,M OTO-W
  RW-W,M RDF-W,M SM-W,M
  TI1-W,M Tr-W,M UBF-W,M
  UFB-W,M
Climbing Jacob's Ladder
  AN-W
Climbing over Rocky Mountain
  MGT-W,M
Climbing up the Golden Stair
  TMA-W,M
Climbin' up the Golden Stairs
  Oz2-W
**Climbing up Thine Hill see Er
  Clim'in' up Thine Hill**
Climbing up Zion's Hill
  WN-W,M
Clime beneath Whose Genial Sun
  HSD-W,M
Clinch Mountain
  Oz3-W
Cling to the Bible
  GH-W,M
Clinging Vine
  TI1-W,M UFB-W,M
Cloches Du Monastere see Les

Cloches Du Monastere
Clock
FWS-W,M
Clock, The (The Clock Stands in
the Corner)
CSG-W,M
Clock, The (Clock upon the
Landing)
ASB3-W,M
Clock, The (There Was a Man,
There Was a Clock)
FSA2-W,M
Clock, The (Tick-Tock, Tick-Tock,
Goes the Little Clock)
ASB1-W,M
Clock, The (With a Tick and a
Tock)
AST-W,M
Clock Canon
OTJ-W,M
Clock Carol
GBC-W,M
Clock Store
ASB2-W,M
Clocks
SiR-W,M
Clocks (A Clock in the Kitchen)
MH-W,M
Clocks (Ding Ding Ding Dong!)
ASB5-W,M
Clog Dance
AmH-M
Close As Pages in a Book
DBC-W,M HC1-W,M TI1-W,M
TW-W UBF-W,M UFB-W,M
Close By
BSo-W,M
Close Encounters of the Third Kind
(Theme)
TOM-M
Close Enough to Perfect
TOC82-W,M
Close His Eyes! His Work Is Done
MPP-W
Close of Day
ASB5-W,M
Close, Open
OTJ-W,M
Close Support Missions
AF-W
Close to Thee
AME-W,M GH-W,M
Close to You (They Long to Be)
BDF-W,M HD-W,M MCG-W,M
MF-W,M On-W,M RDT-W,M
RW-W,M
Close Up the Ranks
SiS-W
Close Up to My Darlin'
FSF-W (French)
Close Your Eyes (Baby, Night
Shadow Falls)
ASB2-W,M
Close Your Eyes (Rest Your Head
on My Shoulder and Sleep)
GSO-W,M HLS2-W,M
Closer and Closer and Closer
OTO-W
Closer I Get to You
HSe-W,M OBN-W,M WGB/P-W,M
Closer, Lord, to Thee
GH-W,M
Closer Than a Brother
BSG-W,M BSP-W,M
Closer Than a Kiss
Mo-W,M NM-W,M
Closer Than Close

TTH-W,M
Closer You Get
TOC83-W,M
Closing Hymn
SL-W,M
Closing Ode
AL-W
Closing Song
AL-W GrM-W,M
Clothes-Pole Man
Me-W,M
Cloud Shadows
AS-W,M
Cloud Ships
ASB5-W,M
Cloud, Where Do You Fly?
MML-W,M
Clouds
SiR-W,M
Clouds (Are Only Dewdrops That
Once Kissed a Rose)
WDS-W,M
Clouds (Cloud, Cloud, Riding the
Sky)
ASB2-W,M
Clouds (Gay Little White Clouds
Go Sailing By)
MH-W,M
Clouds (Go Sailing Softly By)
GM-W,M
Clouds Send Rain
Boo-W,M
Clown, The (I Like to See the
Spotted Clown)
GM-W,M
Clown, The (See That Crazy
Fellow)
ASB3-W,M
Cluck Old Hen
AFS-W,M
Clyde
TOH-W,M
C'mon Everybody
SRE2-W,M
C'mon Marianne
ToO76-W,M
Coach
FSA1-W,M
Coaching
FSA2-W,M
Coal Baron's Song
AL-W,M
Coal Creek Rebellion
AL-W
Coal Creek Trouble
AL-W BMM-W
**Coal's Miner's Song see Mose
Preston's Mine Ballad**
Coal Owner and the Pitman's Wife
LW-W,M
Coast Artillery Marching Song
GO-W
Coast Artillery Song
GO-W
**Coast Guard Song see Semper
Paratus**
Coast of Peru
FW-W SA-W,M
Coasting (Coasting, down the Hill
We Go)
MH-W,M
Coasting (Down the Hill We're
Sliding)
ASB1-W,M
Coasting (From Below, Up We Go)
ASB3-W,M
Coasting (It's Snowing, It's

Snowing)
ASB2-W,M
Coasting (Run Your Sleds over the
Snow)
FSA2-W,M
Coasting (When the Ground Is
Covered with Snow)
SOO-W,M
Coasting Song
SSe-W,M
Coat of Faded Gray
SiS-W
Coat of Many Colors
BDP-W,M
Coax Me
FSN-W,M
Coaxing Polly
VA-W,M
Cobbler
ASB1-W,M ASB3-W,M IS-W,M
Cobbler and the Crow
FSA1-W,M
Cobbler, Cobbler
SMa-W,M
Co-ca-che-lunk
ATS-W HAS-W,M HSD-W,M
SiS-W
**Coca-Cola Jingle see Fifty Million
Times a Day, It's the Real Thing,
and Things Go Better with Coke**
Cocaine Bill
IL-W,M
Cocaine Bill and Morphine Sue
FW-W
Cocaine Blues
FW-W
Cocaine Habit
NH-W
Cock a Doodle Doo
ASB2-W,M OTJ-W,M SMa-W,M
Cock Robin
CSo-W,M GuC-W,M OTJ-W,M
Cockeyed Optimist
HC2-W,M L-W OTJ-W,M OTO-W
SP-W,M TI1-W,M UBF-W,M
UFB-W,M
Cockies of Bungaree
IS-W,M
Cockles and Mussels
CA-W,M CSo-W,M FBI-W,M
GuC-W,M HS-W,M LMR-W,M
OBN-W,M OTJ-W,M SFB-W,M
SMY-W,M U-W WU-W,M
Cocksucker Blues
RoS-W,M
Cocktail Party
L-W
Cocktails for Two
AT-W,M LM-W,M
Cocoanut Grove
FMT-W OTO-W
Cocoanut Sweet
Mo-W,M NM-W,M OTO-W
UBF-W,M
Cod Liver Oil
FW-W
Code of the Mountains
ITP-W,M
Codfish Shanty
SA-W,M
Coe Loyalty
CoS-W,M
Coed and the Cadet
AF-W
C-O-F-F-E-E
Boo-W,M
Coffee Blues

DBL-W
Coffee Break
UBF-W,M
Coffee Grows on White Folks'
Trees
NF-W
Coffee Grows on White Oak Trees
FMT-W FoM-W,M
Coffee Song
MF-W,M TI1-W,M UFB-W,M
Coffin to Bind Me Down
WN-W,M
Cois Araglain
VP-W (Gaelic Only)
Cois Ariglen
VP-W (Gaelic Only)
Cold, Cold Clay
Oz4-W
Cold, Cold Heart
FOC-W,M HW-W,M TI2-W,M
Cold, Cold Snow
LC-W
Cold-Hearted Mama
LC-W
Cold Rainy Day
NeA-W,M
Cold Water
PSN-W,M
Cold's the Wind and Wet's the
Rain
SSP-W
Cole Younger
FW-W HB-W,M LSR-W,M
Oz2-W,M
Coleen Bawn
Oz1-W,M
**Colgate Toothpaste Jingle see
Brush Your Teeth with Colgate**
Colinda
CLaL-W,M
Colin's Cattle
SeS-W,M
College Hornpipe
AmH-M
College Medley
WU-W,M
College on Broadway
TS-W
College Ox
NF-W
College Swing
OTO-W
Collegiate
MF-W,M NoS-W,M TI1-W,M
UFB-W,M
Collier Laddie
BB-W
Collier Swell
MSB-W
Collies Run-l-O
SoC-W
Collinet and Phebe
EA-W,M SAR-W,M SBA-W
Colonel Shelby
Oz2-W
Colonel's Lament
AF-W
Colony Times
OHO-W,M
Color Him Father
RY-W,M RYT-W,M
Colorado Love Call
LMS-W,M
Colorado Trail
FoS-W,M FSD-W,M FW-W
HWS-W,M MM-W,M NeA-W,M
SBF-W,M

Colored Volunteer
MPP-W
Colorful
Mo-W,M NM-W,M OTO-W
Coloring Song
VB-W,M
Colors of My Life
MF-W,M
Colour My World
BR-W,M GOI7-W,M GSN4-W,M
Colour of Love
CFB-W,M
Colt 45
TVT-W,M
Columbia
AWB-W
Columbia Rules the Sea
ANS-W
Columbia, the Gem of the Ocean
AAP-W,M AH-W,M ASB5-W,M
ATS-W CSS-W ESB-W,M FW-W
HS-W,M NAS-W,M OS-W
OTJ-W,M RW-W,M SL-W,M
STR-W,M TH-W,M
Columbia, Trust the Lord
AHO-W,M
Columbian Independence
ESU-W
Columbia's Call
SiS-W
Columbine
FSA1-W,M
Columbus
SiR-W,M
Columbus (Columbus Sailed the
Ocean Blue)
ASB2-W,M
Columbus (Know Ye the Tale of
Italia's Gallant Mariner)
FSA1-W,M SL-W,M
Columbus (O, Once I Had a
Glorious View)
SHS-W,M
Columbus (O Sing to Columbus)
MH-W,M
Columbus (There Lived Long Ago
in a Land Far Away)
GM-W,M
Columbus Stockade
FPG-W,M
Columbus Stockade Blues
BIS-W,M BSo-W,M FSSC-W,M
FW-W
Columbus Was a Sailor
MH-W,M
Come
GH-W,M
Come a Little Bit Closer
Mo-W,M
Come Again
Gu-W,M OH-W,M
Come All Ye Fair and Tender
Ladies
LW-W,M OTJ-W,M
**Come All Ye Fair and Tender
Ladies see also Come All You Fair
and Tender Ladies**
Come All Ye Fair and Tender
Maidens
OFS-W,M Oz1-W,M
Come All Ye Faithful
HSD-W,M
**Come All Ye Faithful see also
Adeste Fideles and O Come All
Ye Faithful**
Come All Ye False Lovers
FSU-W

**Come All Ye Jolly Boatmen Boys
see Blow the Candle Out**
Come All Ye Jolly Shepherds
SeS-W,M
Come All Ye Jolly Soldiers
SG-W,M
Come All Ye Lads Who Sail the
Sea
BMM-W
Come All Ye Lonesome Cowboys
Oz2-W,M
Come All Ye Maids
SCa-W,M
Come All Ye Maids and Pretty Fair
Maidens
SCa-W
Come All Ye Mourning Pilgrims
AHO-W,M
Come All Ye People
AHO-W,M
Come All Ye Poor Men of the
North
BSC-W
Come All Ye Pretty Maids
SG-W,M
Come All Ye Shepherds
CSF-W
Come All Ye Unmarried Men
SCa-W,M
Come All Ye Western Cowboys
HB-W,M
Come All Ye Young Men
OTJ-W,M
Come All You Bold Canadians
SI-W,M
Come All You Fair and Handsome
Girls
SCa-W,M
Come All You Fair and Tender
Ladies
FoS-W,M FW-W SCa-W,M
**Come All You Fair and Tender
Ladies see also Come All Ye Fair
and Tender Ladies**
Come All You Hardy Miners
AFP-W
Come All You Makers
GBC-W,M
Come All You Young Men
Oz3-W,M
Come All You Young of Wary Age
Oz4-W
Come Along
SRE2-W,M
Come Along All You Cowboys
Le-W,M
Come Along and Join Our Song
SOO-W,M
Come Along and Shout Along
WN-W,M
Come Along Home
RBO-W
Come Along Moses
NSS-W WN-W,M
Come Along My Own True Love
SCa-W
Come an' Go wit' Me (Dis Ole
Worl' Is Not Ma Home)
BDW-W,M
Come and Drink
ASB5-W,M
Come and Follow Me
PIS-W,M
Come and Get It
Be2-W,M
Come and Go with Me to That
Land

FW-W JF-W,M SFF-W,M
Come and Kiss Me, Robin
    Oz4-W
Come and Ride
    MAR-W,M
Come and Run
    SD-W,M
Come and See
    VB-W,M
Come and Sing Praises
    OGR-W,M
Come and Taste with Me
    SHS-W,M
Come, Annemarijke, and Show Me
    the Town
    ID-W,M
Come, Annemarijke, Say Where
    Have You Been
    ID-W,M
Come Away, Come Sweet Love
    EL-W,M
Come Away, Melinda
    TO-W,M
Come Back, Baby
    LC-W
Come Back to Erin
    AmH-W,M CSo-W,M HSD-W,M
    WiS8-W,M
Come Back to Me
    ILT-W,M OTO-W TI1-W,M
    UBF-W,M UFB-W,M
Come Back to Sorrento
    HLS1-W,M (Italian) MF-M
    OTJ-W,M RW-M TI1-M UFB-M
Come Back with the Same Look in
    Your Eyes
    UBF-W,M
Come Believing
    GH-W,M
Come, Blessed Peace
    MuM-W,M
Come, Bring with a Noise
    GUM2-W,M
Come Brothers All
    AL-W
Come Brothers Come
    AL-W
Come Buy My Cherries
    Boo-W,M
Come Buy My Flowers
    UF-W,M
Come by Here
    JF-W,M SFF-W,M
Come Celebrate Jesus
    VB-W,M
Come, Christians, Join to Sing
    Hy-W,M SHP-W,M
Come, Come Away
    Boo-W,M
Come, Come Away to the Tavern,
    I Say
    Boo-W,M
Come, Come Delightful Spring
    Boo-W,M
Come, Come to Jesus
    GH-W,M
Come, Come, Ye Saints
    ATS-W,M
Come, Comrades, Come
    AL-W
Come Comrades, Let Us Begin Our
    Joyful Singing
    SiM-W,M (German)
Come Count the Time for Me
    Boo-W,M
Come Dance
    CSD-W,M (French)

Come Dance and Sing
    GB-W,M
Come Dance with Me
    MF-W,M SD-W,M
Come, Dearest Lord, Descend and
    Dwell
    Hy-W,M
Come Down, Angel, and Trouble
    the Water
    NSS-W
Come Down, Ma Evenin' Star
    FSTS-W,M
Come Down, Sinner
    RF-W,M
Come Downtown
    TW-W
Come Drink, My Friend Tom
    Boo-W,M
Come Drink to Me
    Boo-W,M
Come, Ever Smiling Liberty
    MML-W,M
Come Every Joyful Heart
    GH-W
Come Every Soul
    AHO-W,M
Come Ev'ry Soul by Sin Oppressed
    AME-W,M
Come, Fair Rosina
    EA-W,M
Come Fly with Me
    FrS-W,M MF-W,M
Come Follow
    OHO-W,M OTJ-W,M RW-W,M
    TF-W,M
Come Follow Me
    MG-W,M
Come Follow Me, Follow Me in
    This Round
    Boo-W,M
Come Follow Me to the
    Greenwood Tree
    Boo-W,M
Come Follow Me with Merry Glee
    Boo-W,M
Come, for the Feast Is Spread
    GH-W,M
Come, Friends and Neighbors,
    Come
    AHO-W,M
Come, Friends, Come Right In
    OTJ-W,M
Come, Gang Awa' with Me
    Oz4-W,M
Come, Gentle Spring
    ASB6-W,M
Come Go with Me
    DRR-W,M ILF-W,M MF-W,M
    TI2-W,M
Come, Good Wind
    NAS-W,M
Come, Great Deliverer
    GH-W,M
Come, Happy Children
    AHO-W,M
Come, Happy Souls, Approach
    Your God
    AME-W,M
Come Harken unto Me
    AHO-W,M
Come Here, Vitu
    LA-W,M (Spanish)
Come Hither, Tom
    Boo-W,M
Come, Holy Ghost, Our Souls
    Inspire
    AME-W,M Hy-W,M SJ-W,M

Come Holy Harlequin
    GBC-W,M
Come, Holy Spirit
    GH-W,M WiS7-W,M
Come, Holy Spirit, Come
    AME-W,M
Come, Holy Spirit, Dove Divine
    AHO-W,M
Come, Holy Spirit, God and Lord
    SJ-W,M
Come, Holy Spirit, Heavenly Dove
    AME-W,M GH-W Hy-W,M
Come Home
    A-W,M
Come Home Dewey
    OHG-W,M
Come Home, Father
    AH-W,M ATS-W EFS-W,M
    HSD-W,M OHG-W,M
Come Home, Hine, Come Home
    SNZ-W,M (Maori)
Come, Honest Friends
    Boo-W,M
Come In from the Rain
    MF-W,M TI2-W,M
Come In, Loving Henery
    SCa-W
Come In Out of the Draft or How
    Are You, Conscript
    Sin-W,M SiS-W
Come In, Stranger
    OGC2-W,M
Come into the Garden, Maud
    EL-W,M
Come, Jesus, Holy Child, to Me
    SHP-W,M
Come Join with Me
    Boo-W,M
Come, Jolly Harvey
    ESU-W
Come, Josephine, in My Flying
    Machine
    HLS1-W,M MF-W,M OAP-W,M
    TI1-W,M UFB-W,M
Come, Kingdom of Our God
    AME-W,M
Come Kiss Your Man
    Lo-W,M
Come, Labor On
    Hy-W,M
Come, Landlord, Fill the Flowing
    Bowl
    CSo-W,M IL-W,M
Come, Lasses and Lads
    CSo-W,M ESB-W,M
Come, Lay Aside Your Sighing
    Boo-W,M
Come, Leave Your Work
    GBC-W,M
Come, Let Our Voices Join to
    Raise
    AME-W,M
Come, Let Us All A'maying Go
    Boo-W,M
Come Let Us All This Day
    BMC-W,M
Come Let Us Cast the Dice
    Boo-W,M
Come, Let Us Dance
    SiR-W,M
Come, Let Us Gaily Wander
    TH-W,M
Come, Let Us Join Our Cheerful
    Songs
    AME-W,M SJ-W,M
Come, Let Us Join with One
    Accord

AME-W,M
Come, Let Us Laugh
  Boo-W,M
Come, Let Us to the Lord Our God
  Hy-W,M
Come, Let Us Tune Our Loftiest
  Song
  AHO-W,M
Come, Let's Be Merry
  SiR-W,M
Come, Let's Laugh
  Boo-W,M
Come, Let's Sing a Merry Round
  Boo-W,M
Come, Let's to Bed
  MH-W,M
Come Life, Shaker Life
  GB-W,M
Come List to a Ranger
  Oz2-W,M
Come, Little Children
  Y-W,M
**Come, Little Children see also O
  Come, Little Children**
Come, Little Leaves
  SSe-W,M
Come Live with Me
  EL-W,M MF-W,M
Come Live with Me and Be My
  Love
  OH-W,M SSP-W
Come Live Your Life with Me
  OTO-W WGB/P-W,M
Come, Lord, and Tarry Not
  Hy-W,M
Come, Love We God
  MC-W,M OB-W,M
Come, Merry Men
  Boo-W,M
Come Mother's Sons and
  Daughters
  GB-W,M
Come, My Hearts, Let's Now Be
  Merry
  Boo-W,M
Come, My Soul, Thou Must Be
  Waking
  ESB-W,M Hy-W,M TH-W,M
Come, My Soul, Thy Suit Prepare
  GH-W Hy-W,M
Come near Me
  GH-W,M
Come Now, Let Us Jovial Be
  Boo-W,M
Come Now, Let Us Merry Be
  Boo-W,M
Come Now My Dear Brethren
  WN-W,M
Come Now, Saith the Lord
  GH-W,M
Come, O Come, Thou Quickening
  Spirit
  SJ-W,M
Come, O Come with Me
  HSD-W,M
Come, O My Soul, in Sacred Lays
  AME-W,M
Come, O Sabbath Day
  AHO-W,M Bo-W,M
Come, O Swallow
  FSA1-W,M
Come O Thou All Victorious Lord
  AME-W,M
Come o'er the Bourne Bessy
  SSP-W
Come On
  HR-W

Come On and Join into the Game
  WSB-W,M
Come On and Join the Air Corps
  GO-W
Come On Baby, Let the Gook
  Heads Roll
  VS-W,M
Come On Down to My Boat
  Mo-W,M
Come On Eph
  B-W,M BI-W,M
**Come On Everybody see C'mon
  Everybody**
Come On, Let's Go
  BHO-W,M
**Come On Marianne see C'mon
  Marianne**
Come On Over to the L & M Side
  GSM-W,M
Come On Scabs If You Want to
  Hear
  AFP-W WW-W,M
Come On Strong
  Mo-W,M
Come Out! Come Out!
  SSe-W,M
Come Out into the Sunshine
  SOT-W,M
Come Out, Ye Continentalers
  ATS-W SSS-W,M
**Come over the Bourne Bessy see
  Come o'er the Bourne Bessy**
Come, Polly, Pretty Polly
  TBF-W,M
Come Praise the Lord
  GH-W,M
Come, Precious Soul
  AHO-W,M
Come Pretty Maidens, What Will
  You Buy?
  Boo-W,M
Come Prima
  TI1-W,M (Italian)
Come, Prodigal, Come
  GH-W,M
Come Rain or Come Shine
  DBC-W,M DJ-W,M FrS-W,M
  HC2-W,M HLS8-W,M LM-W,M
  OHF-W OTO-W RW-W,M
  TI1-W,M ToS-W,M UBF-W,M
  UFB-W,M
Come Raise Me in Your Arms,
  Dear Brother
  Oz2-W,M
Come Roam in the Woodland
  TH-W,M
Come, Rouse Up! Brave Boys
  SiS-W
Come Rowing with Me
  BMC-W,M
Come, Said Jesus' Sacred Voice
  GH-W
Come Saturday Morning
  AT-W,M ILT-W,M IPH-W,M
  LM-W,M OTJ-W,M OTO-W
Come Shake Your Dull Noodles
  EA-W,M SSS-W,M
Come Sing Along with Me
  Boo-W,M
Come Sing and Be Merry
  SOT-W,M
Come Sing with Us
  CA-W,M
Come, Sinner, Come
  GH-W,M NH-W
Come Sinners, to the Gospel Feast
  AME-W,M

Come, Sister Dear
  LA-W,M (Spanish)
Come Softly, Walk Gently
  SFP-W,M
Come Soon
  MHB-W,M (German)
Come Summer
  Mo-W,M OTO-W
Come Sunday
  GMD-W,M
Come Swallow Your Bumpers, Ye
  Tories
  ATS-W,M
Come, Thou Almighty King
  AME-W,M ASB5-W,M BM-W
  Bo-W,M CA-W,M CEM-W,M
  ESB-W,M GH-W,M HS-W,M
  HSD-W,M Hy-W,M IL-W,M
  OPS-W,M OS-W SiR-W,M
  SL-W,M TB-W,M TH-W,M
  WiS7-W,M
Come, Thou Desire of All Thy
  Saints
  AME-W,M
Come, Thou Fount
  GH-W,M
Come, Thou Fount of Every
  Blessing
  CEM-W,M HSD-W,M Hy-W,M
Come, Thou Fount of Ev'ry
  Blessing
  AME-W,M WiS7-W,M
Come, Thou Long-Expected Jesus
  AME-W,M CEM-W,M Hy-W,M
  SHP-W,M
Come to Calvary's Holy Mountain
  AME-W,M
Come to Jesus! Come Away
  GH-W,M
Come to Jesus, Come to Jesus
  AME-W,M
Come to Jesus Just Now
  GH-W,M
Come to Me
  FiS-W,M
Come to Me, Bend to Me
  LL-W,M OnT1-W,M RW-W,M
  STP-W,M
Come to Me Grief For Ever
  MU-W,M
Come to My Love
  TOH-W,M
Come to the Bower
  VP-W,M
Come to the Fair
  LoS-W,M
Come to the Fountain
  GH-W,M
Come to the Land
  ASB6-W,M
Come to the Moon
  ReG-W,M
Come to the Old Oak Tree
  Boo-W,M ESB-W,M
Come to the Savior Make No Delay
  AME-W,M
Come to the Saviour
  GH-W,M
Come to the Saviour Now
  Hy-W,M
Come to the Sea
  RW-W,M
Come to the Table
  VB-W,M
Come Together
  BBe-W,M Be2-W,M TWS-W
Come Trembling Down

AAF-W,M WN-W,M
Come under My Plaidie
  AmH-M
Come unto Him
  MML-W,M
Come unto Me
  GH-W,M GrM-W,M
Come unto Me and Rest
  GH-W,M
Come unto Me, When Shadows
  Darkly Gather
  AHO-W,M
Come unto Me, Ye Weary
  Hy-W,M RDF-W,M
Come unto These Yellow Sands
  FSS-W,M LMR-W,M SSB-W,M
Come Up, Horsey
  AFS-W,M
Come Up to Kool
  GSM-W,M
Come Up to My Place
  TW-W
Come We That Love the Lord
  AME-W,M Hy-W,M
Come What May
  SRE1-W,M
Come Where My Love Lies
  Dreaming
  FHR-W,M HSD-W,M SSF-W,M
  SSFo-W,M TF-W,M WiS8-W,M
Come Where Shall We Walk
  Boo-W,M
Come with All Believers True
  GBC-W,M (Latin)
Come with Gladness
  Boo-W,M
Come with Me
  MAR-W,M
Come with Me (Let's Go Skating)
  SOO-W,M
Come with Me (Lorenz Hart)
  TS-W TW-W
Come with Thy Sweet Voice Again
  FHR-W,M SSF-W,M
Come, Ye Disconsolate
  AME-W,M AmH-W,M CEM-W,M
  GH-W,M HSD-W,M OM-W,M
  SHS-W,M WiS7-W,M
Come, Ye Disconsolate, Where'er
  Ye Languish
  Hy-W,M
Come, Ye Faithful
  TF-W,M
Come, Ye Faithful, Raise the Strain
  Hy-W,M
Come, Ye People, Rise and Sing
  Hy-W,M
Come, Ye Sinners
  GH-W,M Oz4-W,M
Come, Ye Thankful
  LoS-W,M
Come, Ye Thankful People
  ASB6-W,M
Come, Ye Thankful People, Come
  AME-W,M BM-W CEM-W,M ESB-
  W,M HS-W,M Hy-W,M IH-W,M
  LT-W,M MAB1-W MAS-W,M
  MES1-W,M MES2-W,M MML-
  W,M MSA1-W MuM-W,M SBF-
  W,M SHP-W,M SiB-W,M SJ-W
  VA-W,M
Come Ye That Fear the Lord
  WN-W,M
Come Ye That Fear the Lord and
  Hear
  Hy-W,M
Come Ye That Know and Fear the

Lord
  AME-W,M
Come Ye That Love the Lord
  WN-W,M
Come You Knights of the Table
  Round
  FSF-W (French)
Come You Not from Newcastle
  F3-W,M
Comedy Tonight
  DBC-W,M OTO-W TI1-W,M
  TW-W UBF-W,M UFB-W,M
Comely Dame of Islington
  SR-W,M
Comely Swain
  MML-W,M
Comely Youth
  FMT-W FoM-W,M
Comes Love
  TI1-W,M UFB-W,M
Comes Once in a Lifetime
  TI1-W,M UFB-W,M
Comes the Broken Flower
  GiS-W,M
Comes the Moment to Decide
  TH-W,M
Comes the Pretty Young Bride
  GiS-W,M
Comfort and Tidings of Joy
  FW-W
Comfort, Comfort Ye, My People
  SJ-W,M
Comfort, Ye Ministers of Grace
  AME-W,M
Comforter Has Come
  AME-W,M
Comical Ditty
  BSC-W
Comical Dreamer
  SR-W,M
Comin' Ag'in By an' By
  BDW-W,M
Comin' down de Line
  BDW-W,M
Comin' Dung with You' Bunch o'
  Roses
  SGT-W,M
Comin' In on a Wing and a Prayer
  CS-W,M
Comin' 'round the Mountain
  LoS-W,M
**Comin' 'round the Mountain see
also She'll Be Comin' round the
Mountain**
Comin' thro' the Rye
  AL-W AmH-W,M HSD-W,M
  MF-W,M NAS-W,M OTJ-W,M
  SeS-W,M WiS8-W,M
Comin' through the Rye
  BMC-W,M FM-W,M FW-W
  IL-W,M MAB1-W,M MSA1-W
  OFS-W,M OS-W TH-W,M
  VA-W,M
Coming Around Again
  TTH-W,M
Coming Down Again
  RoS-W,M
Coming Home
  SiS-W
Coming Home from the Old Camp
  Ground
  SiS-W
Coming Home Tonight
  GH-W,M
Coming In and Out of Your Life
  TI1-W,M TI2-W,M UFB-W,M
Coming of Spring

MG-W,M TH-W,M
Coming of the Maori
  SNZ-W,M (Maori)
Coming To-day
  GH-W,M
Commandments
  FH-W,M
Comme Ci, Comme Ca
  TI2-W,M (French)
Commissioner's Report
  PO-W,M
Commodore Rodgers
  ANS-W
Common Bill
  AmS-W,M FMT-W FW-W Oz1-W
  RW-W,M SCa-W,M
Common Man
  TOC83-W,M
Common Prayer for the Times
  SBA-W
Common Sense Exercises
  AL-W
Commonwealth of Toil
  FW-W SWF-W,M
Communion
  SHS-W,M
Communion Hymn
  FiS-W,M
Commuters' Special
  VA-W,M
Como Cada Noche
  TI1-W,M (Spanish Only)
Como El Alamo Al Comino
  TI1-W,M (Spanish Only)
Como Una Estrella Fugaz
  LA-W,M (Spanish)
Compact
  OG-W,M
Compagnons De La Marjolaine
  CaF-W (French Only)
Companions, Draw Nigh
  Oz4-W,M
Company
  OTO-W TI2-W,M TW-W
  UBF-W,M
Company Way
  TW-W
Company's Comin'
  CMF-W,M HLS9-W,M
Comper' Lapin
  CSD-W,M (French)
Compere Et Commere
  CUP-W,M (French Only)
Compere Guilleri
  MP-W,M (French Only)
**Competition Love Theme see
People Alone**
Complainer
  SHS-W,M
Complainte Pour Marie-Jacques
  SSN-W,M (French)
Complete in Thee, No Work of
  Mine
  AHO-W,M
Complicated
  RoS-W,M
Compromise Song
  Sin-W,M
Comrades (Comrades, Ever Since
  We Were Boys)
  ATS-W BH-W,M EFS-W,M
  FSN-W,M
Comrades (Here's the Road, We'll
  Tramp Together)
  MML-W,M
Comrades, Fill No Glass for Me
  FHR-W,M SSFo-W,M

Comrades, Hasten to the Battle
SiS-W
Comrades, I Am Going Home
SiS-W
Comrades! Join the Flag of Glory
AWB-W
Comrades' Last Brave Charge
Oz2-W
Con Amore
AmH-M
Con Medio Peso
CDM-W,M (Spanish)
Con Razon O Sin Razon
TI1-W,M (Spanish Only)
Concerning Travel
MH-W,M
Concert Goers' Carol
GBC-W,M
Concerto in F (Gershwin)
BI-M NYT-M
Concord
SHS-W,M
Condemned without Trial
OGC1-W,M
Condescension
SHS-W,M
Conditor Kirie
Boo-W,M (Latin Only)
Conductor's Call
ASB1-W,M
Coney Island U.S.A.
Mo-W,M NM-W,M OTO-W
Confederate Flag
SCo-W,M SiS-W
Confederate Song
SiS-W
Confederate Transposed to a
Petticoat
SiS-W
Confederate Yankee Doodle
Oz2-W
Confess It to Your Heart
TI2-W,M
Confess We All before the Lord
AHO-W,M
Confession (Howard Dietz)
TW-W
Confession (I Used to be a
Gambler)
ATS-W,M
Confidence
SHS-W,M WN-W,M
Confidences to the Perfume River
VS-W,M
Confirmation
TI1-M UFB-M
Congaudeat
OB-W,M
Congotay
SGT-W,M
Congratulations
PS-W,M RoS-W,M
Congress
SAR-W,M SI-W,M
Conjugal Love
SR-W,M
Connais Tu Le Pays
AmH-W,M MU-W,M (French)
Connecticut State Song
Fif-W,M
Connection
RoS-W,M
Connubial Bliss
OG-W,M
Conquered Banner
MPP-W SCo-W,M SiS-W
Conquered Flag

SiS-W
Conquering Kings Their Titles Take
SJ-W,M
Conquistador
MF-W,M
Conscript
SiS-W
Conscription Ramp
VS-W,M
Conscript's Mother
SiS-W
Consecration
JS-W,M (Hebrew)
Consecration of Rhadames
MU-W,M
Consent at Last
SR-W,M
Consequences
FSA2-W,M
Consider the Lilies
GrM-W,M
Consider Yourself
DBC-W,M O-W,M TI1-W,M
UBF-W,M UFB-W,M
Consideration
GrG-W,M
Consolation (Liszt, No. 5)
AmH-M
Consolation (Mendelssohn)
AmH-M RW-M
Consolation (Watts)
OTJ-W,M SHS-W,M
**Consolation (Watts) see also Once
More, My Soul, the Rising Day**
Consolation New
SHS-W,M
Constance
LA-W,M (Spanish)
Constant Bass
NO-W,M
Constant Wife
BSC-W
Constantly
OTO-W
Constellation and the Insurgente
AWB-W
Constitution and Guerriere
AWB-W ESU-W FW-W MAS-W,M
MPP-W SA-W,M
Constitution and the Guerriere
ANS-W SI-W,M
Constitution's Last Fight
ANS-W
Conte see Un Conte
Contemplation
GeS-W,M
Contented Camel
FSA2-W,M
Contented Lover
EL-W,M
Contented Soldier
SHS-W,M
Contentment (McGinley/
Beethoven)
MHB-W,M
Contentment (Weeks/Mozart)
MML-W,M
Contes d'Hoffman (Selection)
AmH-M
Continental
BBB-W,M HFH-W,M MF-W,M
NK-W,M
Continuing Story of Bungalow Bill
TWS-W
Contraband Now
SiS-W
Contraband of Port Royal

SiS-W
Contraband's Jubilee
SiS-W
Contraband's Song of Freedom
SiS-W
Contrary Owl
ASB4-W,M
Conundrum Song
TMA-W,M
Conversation between Two
Emigrants
SE-W (Swedish)
Conversation Peace
VB-W,M
Conversation with Death
Oz4-W
Converted Thief
SHS-W,M
Convict Maid
ATM-W,M
Convict of Clonmel
IS-W,M VP-W
Conviction of the Wise Men in
Jerusalem
MoM-W
Convoy
DP-W,M
Coo Coo
LMS-W,M
Cookey Darling
MSB-W
Cookham
SHS-W
Cooking Dinner
NF-W
Cool, Calm and Collected
RoS-W,M
Cool Water
OGC2-W,M FC-W,M FPS-W,M
HLS9-W,M TI1-W,M UFB-W,M
Coon Huntin' Song
BMM-W
Cooperative Song
AL-W
Cooper's Song
FSA2-W,M HSD-W,M
Coorie Doon
TO-W,M
Cootie Song
GO-W
Copacabana (At the Copa)
RW-W,M
Cope Sent a Letter Frae Dunbar
SeS-W,M
Copenhagen
Mo-W,M NM-W,M
Co-pilot's Lament
AF-W SoC-W
Coplas
FW-W (Spanish)
Copper Campaign Song
AL-W
**Coppertone Suntan Lotion Jingle
see Tan, Don't Burn, Get a
Coppertone Tan**
Cops of the World
VS-W,M
Copulation Round
PAJ-W,M
Coquette
GST-W,M HLS2-W,M MF-W,M
RW-W,M
Coqui see El Coqui
Cora Dean
FHR-W,M SSFo-W,M
Coral Reef
MF-M

Corduroy Road
  W-W,M
Cordwainers' Rallying Song
  AL-W
Cordwainers' Song
  AL-W
Corichie or the Hill of Fare
  SBB-W
Corinna
  FW-W LC-W
Cork Leg
  ATS-W MSB-W
Corn Bread Rough
  Le-W,M
Corn Cobs Twist Your Hair
  MPP-W,M
Corn Dance Song
  VA-W,M
Corn Grinding Song
  ATS-W,M
Corn Pone
  AFP-W,M
Corn Shuckin' Song
  NFS-W,M
Corn Shucking
  ATS-W
Corn Song
  ESB-W,M
Cornball Matching Test
  OHO-W,M
Cornell Alma Mater
  IL-W,M
Cornell Song
  ESB-W,M
Cornerstone
  HHa-W,M OGR-W,M VB-W,M
Cornfield Medley
  WiS8-W,M
Cornstalk Fiddle
  VA-W,M
Cornwallis Burgoyned
  EA-W,M SAR-W,M SBA-W
  SI-W,M
Cornwallis' Country Dance
  EA-W,M SI-W SSS-W,M
Coronation
  SHS-W,M SL-W,M
Coronation March (Meyerbeer's Le
  Prophete)
  AmH-M
Corporal
  GI-W GO-W
Corporal Schnapps
  Sin-W,M SiS-W
Corporal's Musket
  SiS-W
Correspondence
  PSN-W,M
Corrido De La Canelera
  LA-W,M (Spanish)
Corrido De Macario Romero
  LA-W,M (Spanish)
Corrido De Modesta Ayala
  LA-W,M (Spanish)
Corrina, Corrina
  OFS-W,M
**Corvette Song see One I Loved
  Back Then**
Cose, Cose, Cose
  LaS-W,M (Spanish)
Cosher Bailey
  PO-W,M
Cosher Bailey's Engine
  FW-W
Cosmetic Surgery (or the Saga of
  Kate)
  WF-W,M

Cossack Lullaby
  OTJ-W,M
Cossack Song
  CA-W,M
Cossack's Lullaby
  SMY-W,M TH-W,M
Costa see La Costa
Cottage for Sale
  TI1-W,M UFB-W,M
Cottage in the Country
  WDS-W,M
Cott'n Dance Song
  NFS-W,M
Cott'n Picking Song
  NFS-W,M
**Cott'n Picking Song see also
  Cotton Picking Song**
Cotton Blossom
  SB-W,M
Cotton Candy
  TI1-M UFB-M
Cotton Crop Blues
  DBL-W
**Cotton Dance Song see Cott'n
  Dance Song**
Cotton Dress
  OFS-W,M
Cotton-Eyed Joe
  FW-W J-W,M NF-W SG-W,M
  VA-W,M
Cotton Farmer Blues
  AFP-W,M
Cotton Field Blues
  LC-W
Cotton Fields
  TI1-W,M UFB-W,M
Cotton Fields see also Cotton Song
Cotton Mill Girls
  BF-W,M LW-W,M WW-W,M
Cotton Needs Pickin'
  OU-W,M SSe-W,M
Cotton Needs Picking
  HS-W,M
Cotton Pickin' Time
  OBN-M
Cotton Picking Song
  WS-W,M
**Cotton Picking Song see also
  Cott'n Picking Song**
Cotton Song (Cotton Fields)
  Le-W,M TI1-W,M UFB-W,M
Cotton the Kid
  Oz2-W
Could I Have This Dance
  CoH-W,M FOC-W,M TI2-W,M
  TOH-W,M
Could I Leave You?
  Fo-W,M UBF-W,M
Could It Be Forever
  MCG-W,M
Could It Be Love
  TOC82-W,M
Could It Be Magic
  DP-W,M
Could It Be You
  ML-W,M
Could You Use Me?
  GOB-W,M LSO-W MF-W,M
Couldn't Hear Nobody Pray
  LoS-W,M NAS-W,M NFS-W,M
  UF-W,M
**Couldn't Hear Nobody Pray see
  also I Couldn't Hear Nobody Pray**
Couldn't Raise No Sugar Corn
  Oz2-W,M
Could've Been
  CFB-W,M

Coulee Dam
  AFP-W
Count
  MES2-W,M
Count 'Em
  MF-M
Count Every Star
  BeL-W,M TI2-W,M
Count Me In
  VB-W,M
Count of Cabra
  LA-W,M (Spanish)
Count of Sory, Why What of He!
  Boo-W,M
Count the Cost
  VB-W,M
Count Your Blessings
  U-W
Counter-Charm
  SL-W,M TF-W,M
Countersigns
  SA-W,M
Countess of Laurel
  LA-W,M (Spanish)
Counties of Arkansas
  Oz4-W
Counting Game
  CSG-W,M
Counting Out
  FSA1-W,M
Counting Song
  MMY-W,M
Country Boy (at Heart)
  EC-W,M
Country Boy (Who Rolled the Rock
  Away)
  TTH-W,M
Country Boy (You Got Your Feet
  in L.A.)
  ToO76-W,M
Country Boy Can Survive
  TOC83-W,M
Country Chorus
  ASB3-W,M
Country Clodhoppers
  SMY-W,M
Country Dance (Beglarian)
  GM-M
Country Fair
  OTO-W
Country Fiddler
  ASB3-W,M
Country Gardens
  MF-M OTJ-M
Country Girl
  OTO-W
Country Honk
  RoS-W,M
Country Hop, Hop, Hop
  OTJ-W,M
Country Music Holiday
  OTO-W
Country Statutes
  MSB-W
Country Style
  TI1-W,M UFB-W,M
Country Sunshine
  FOC-W,M TI2-W,M
Country's in the Very Best of
  Hands
  OHF-W
County Fair (Torme/Wells)
  Mo-W,M
County Fair, The (Singing a Song,
  We're Dancing Along)
  RS-W,M
County Fair, The (Welcome, Right

Welcome)
FSA2-W,M
Couplets of the Kings
MU-W,M
Courrier, Courrier, Qu'y A-t-il De
Nouveau
FSO-W,M (French)
Courrier, Courrier, Say What News
Hast There?
FSO-W,M (French)
Courtesy Song
GM-W
Courtin' Cage
SCa-W,M
Courting Boy
NF-W
Courting Cage
Oz3-W,M
Courting Jessie
Oz1-W,M
Courting Song
Oz3-W,M
Courtship
NF-W
Cousin Jedediah
HAS-W,M NAS-W,M OS-W
Cousine Lili see La Cousine Lili
Cousins (Patty Duke Show Theme)
GTV-W,M
Cove Who Went A-Sailin'
GC-W,M
Covenant of Sinai
JS-W,M
Coventry Carol
BCh-W,M BCS-W,M GBC-W,M
Gu-W,M GUM2-W,M JOC-W,M
MC-W,M MG-W,M OB-W,M
RW-W,M WSB-W,M Y-W,M
YC-W,M
Cover Me
OGR-W,M
Coverdale's Carol
OB-W,M
Covington
SCa-W
Cow Chase
SBA-W SSS-W,M
Cow Cow Yicky Yicky Yea
Le-W,M
Cow Needs a Tail in Fly Time
NF-W
Cow Patti
NoS-W,M
Coward of the County
PoG-W,M
Cowboy
SD-W,M
Cowboy (All Day on the Prairie in a
Saddle I Ride)
HOH-W,M HWS-W,M
Cowboy (As I Rode Down to
Letheric Barren)
BSC-W
Cowboy (The Bloody Sunburnt
Cowboy Sat)
AF-W GI-W,M
Cowboy (It Were Down by Tom
Sherman's Bar-Room)
SCa-W,M
Cowboy (One Day a Lone Cowboy
Was Loafing)
ASB5-W,M
Cowboy (Over the Prairie the
Cowboy Will Ride)
ASB2-W,M
Cowboy and the Lady
TOC82-W,M

Cowboy at Church
HOH-W,M
Cowboy Camp Meetin'
OGC2-W,M
Cowboy in Church
HB-W,M
Cowboy Jack
HB-W,M HWS-W,M ITP-W,M
SoC-W
Cowboy Jack's Last Ride
SoC-W
Cowboy Meditations
FMT-W FoM-W,M
Cowboy Night Song
VA-W,M
Cowboy #1
HB-W,M
Cowboy #2
HB-W,M
Cowboy Serenade
FC-W,M
Cowboy Song
ITP-W,M Oz2-W SCa-W
Cowboy Victimized
SoC-W
Cowboy Wishes, The
GA-W
Cowboy with the White Hat
SoC-W
Cowboys
MES1-W,M MES2-W,M
Cowboy's Best Friend Is His Horse
SoC-W
Cowboy's Call to Prayer
HOH-W
Cowboy's Challenge
BSC-W
Cowboy's Christmas Ball
HB-W,M HWS-W,M SoC-W,M
Cowboy's Deck of Cards
CCS-W,M
Cowboy's Dream
FW-W HOH-W,M Oz2-W
SoC-W,M
Cowboy's Faith
HOH-W
Cowboy's Gettin' Up Holler
VA-W,M
Cowboy's Hat
SoC-W,M
Cowboy's Heaven
FC-W,M HOH-W,M
Cowboy's Hymn
SoC-W
Cowboy's Lament
ATS-W,M BSC-W HOH-W,M
HS-W,M HWS-W,M Oz2-W
SoC-W,M
**Cowboy's Lament see also Streets
of Laredo**
Cowboy's Last Ride
HOH-W
Cowboy's Life
GM-W HB-W,M SoC-W,M
Cowboy's Meditation
ATS-W,M CA-W,M HOH-W,M
Cowboy's Mother
HOH-W SoC-W
Cowboy's New Years Dance
SoC-W
Cowboy's Nightherd Thoughts
HOH-W
Cowboy's Prayer
GA-W HB-W HOH-W,M
Cowboy's Prayer at Twilight
HOH-W,M
Cowboy's Salvation Song

HOH-W,M
Cowboy's Sweet Bye and Bye
Bo-W CSS-W GA-W,M HWS-W,M
SoC-W
Cowboy's Thoughts
SoC-W
Cowboys Victimized
SoC-W
Cowboy's Vision
HOH-W SoC-W
Cowboy's White Hat
SoC-W
Cowgirl
Oz2-W
Cowgirl and the Dandy
TOH-W,M
Cowhand's Lament
HOH-W,M
Cowhand's Last Ride
LJ-W,M
Cowman's Prayer
HB-W,M HOH-W HWS-W,M
Cows
FF-W
Cow's Advice
FSA1-W,M
Cows and Sheep
ASB1-W,M
Coxey Army
AFP-W AL-W
Coxey's on the Grass
AL-W
Coyote's Song
ASB3-M
Cozy Bordello
TW-W
Cozy Nook Trio
LSO-W
Crab
ASB6-W,M
Crabbed Age and Youth (The
Passionate Pilgrim)
FSS-W,M
Crabbiness Survey
YG-W,M
Crabfish
SaS-W,M
Crabtree Still
BMM-W
Crackers
TOH-W,M
Cracklin' Rosie
GrS-W,M TI2-W,M
Cradle
OB-W,M
Cradle Croon
FSA1-W,M
Cradle Hymn (Isaac Watts)
FoS-W,M WiS7-W,M
**Cradle Hymn (Isaac Watts) see
also Cradle Song (Isaac Watts),
Hush My Babe, and Watts' Cradle
Hymn (Song)**
Cradle Hymn (Martin Luther)
ASB3-W,M CCH-W,M
**Cradle Hymn (Martin Luther) see
also Away in a Manger**
Cradle on the Bough
FSA2-W,M
Cradle Song (Aruru, My Nino)
ASB2-W,M (Spanish)
Cradle Song (Baby Mine, a Star Is
Peeping in the Sky)
STS-W,M
Cradle Song (Brahms)
FSY-W,M (German) OS-W
SD-W,M TI1-M WiS8-W,M

**Cradle Song (Brahms) see also
   Brahms' Lullaby**
Cradle Song (Cole Porter)
   ML-W,M
Cradle Song (Grieg)
   MH-M
Cradle Song (Hush Now, Hush
   Now, All Be Quiet Now)
   GM-W,M
Cradle Song (Isaac Watts)
   BMC-W,M
**Cradle Song (Isaac Watts) see also
   Cradle Hymn (Isaac Watts)**
Cradle Song (Light and Rosy Be
   Thy Slumbers)
   HSD-W,M
Cradle Song (Miska Hauser)
   AmH-M MH-M
Cradle Song (My Sweet Little
   Darling, My Comfort and Joy)
   GBC-W,M
Cradle Song (Nightingale, Come
   Winging)
   ASB6-W,M
Cradle Song (Schubert)
   HS-W,M SFB-W,M TF-W,M
   TH-W,M
Cradle Song (Schumann)
   MH-M
Cradle Song (Sleep, Baby, Sleep!
   Thy Father Guards the Sheep)
   BBF-W,M HSD-W,M
Cradle Song (Sleep, My Heart's
   Darling, in Slumber Repose)
   HSD-W,M OTJ-W,M
Cradle Song (Traditional)
   MH-W,M
**Cradle Song (Traditional) see also
   Rockaby, Baby**
Cradle Song (Von Wilm)
   MH-W
Cradle Song of the Poor
   AL-W
Cradle Time
   MH-W,M
Crafty Cat
   CoF-W,M
Crap-Shootin' Charley
   SSo-W,M
Crash
   ASB2-W,M
Crash On, Artillery
   GO-W
Crawdad
   FG2-W,M FGM-W,M FW-W
   FPG-W,M POT-W,M
Crawdad Man
   ITP-W,M
Crawdad Song
   FSB1-W,M GuC-W,M OFS-W,M
   OTJ-W,M RW-W,M
Crawlin' Baby Blues
   LC-W
Crawling and Creeping
   AF-W
Crazy (for Lovin' You)
   CMG-W,M CoH-W,M FOC-W,M
   TI2-W,M WNF-W
Crazy (They Say I'm Crazy, Just a
   Little Bit Out of Whack)
   TOM-W,M
Crazy Blue Eyes
   TOH-W,M
Crazy 'Cause I Love You
   OGC2-W,M
Crazy for You
   HFH-W,M

Crazy Horses
   BR-W,M
Crazy Mama
   RoS-W,M
Crazy on You
   ToO76-W,M
Crazy Rhythm
   HC1-W,M TI2-W,M
Crazy She Calls Me
   AO-W,M NK-W,M
Crazy Song
   SiB-W,M
Create in Me a Clean Heart, O God
   Hy-W,M SJ-W
Creation
   AN-W MAS-W,M Oz2-W,M
Creation's Lord, We Give Thee
   Thanks
   AHO-W,M AME-W,M
Creator Alme Siderum
   SL-W,M (Latin Only)
Creator of Infinities
   AHO-W,M
Credo (Robert Sherwood)
   GI-W
Creek Ribbon Dance
   HSA-W,M
Creole Love Call
   GMD-W,M
Creole Waltz
   VA-W,M
**Cricket Cigarette Lighter Jingle see
   Catch a Cricket**
Cricket on the Hearth
   Sw-W,M
Cries of London
   MSB-W
Crime of the D'Autremont Brothers
   LSR-W,M
Criminal Cried
   MGT-W,M
Crimson and Clover
   AO-W,M GAR-W,M ILS-W,M
   MF-W,M RY-W,M
Criole Candjo
   AAF-W,M (French)
Cripple Creek
   BIS-W,M FSB-W,M FW-W
   OFS-W,M POT-W,M
Crisis
   MSB-W
Cristofor Colombo
   GI-W GO-W,M
Cro-Challain Would Gie Me
   SeS-W,M
Crocodile Rock
   TI2-W,M
Crocodile Song
   AFS-W,M RSL-W,M
Crocuses
   SSe-W,M
Crocuses Are Blooming
   KS-W,M
Croodin Doo see Lord Randal
Crooked Little Man
   OTJ-W,M
Crooked Nose Jane
   NF-W
Crooked Rifles
   Boo-W,M
Crooked Trail to Holbrook
   HWS-W,M SoC-W
Crooked Whiskey
   SY-W,M
Croon Spoon
   TW-W
Croppies Lie Down

VP-W,M
Croppy Boy
   BSC-W FW-W IS-W,M Oz1-W
   VP-W,M
Croquet
   HAS-W,M
Cross and Crown
   GH-W,M
Cross-Eyed Gopher
   AFS-W,M
Cross-Eyed Mary
   BJ-W,M
Cross-Eyed Sally
   NH-W
Cross Eyed Sue
   FAW-W,M
Cross Me Over
   NH-W
**Cross Me Over see also Cross-er
   Me Over**
Cross of Christ
   SHS-W,M
Cross of Jesus
   GH-W,M
Cross of Jesus, Cross of Sorrow
   Hy-W,M
Cross of the South
   SCo-W,M SiS-W
Cross over the Bridge
   MF-W,M
Cross Purposes
   CA-W,M
Cross-er Me Over
   BDW-W,M
**Cross-er Me Over see also Cross
   Me Over**
Crossing a Footlog
   NF-W
Crossing the Bar
   ESB-W,M FiS-W,M TF-W,M
   TH-W,M
Crossing the Brook
   LA-W,M (Spanish)
Crossing the Divide
   HOH-W
Crossing the Grand Sierras
   ATS-W
Crossing the River
   NF-W
Crossing the Street
   ASB1-W,M
Crow
   MH-W,M
Crow Song
   Oz2-W,M TBF-W,M
Crowd
   TFC-W,M
Crown Him
   GH-W,M
Crown Him with Many Crowns
   AME-W,M Hy-W,M IH-M TB-W,M
   WiS7-W,M
Crown of Roses
   JOC-W,M OB-W,M
Crowning Day
   GH-W,M
Crows in the Garden
   FMT-W
Crucifixion
   SHS-W,M WiS7-W,M
Crucifixus
   FiS-W,M (French)
Cruel Brother
   FMT-W ITP-W
Cruel Jews
   BDW-W,M
Cruel Mother

BB-W BCT-W,M BT-W,M FW-W
SCa-W,M
Cruel Shadow
ASB6-W,M
Cruel Ship's Carpenter
SCa-W,M
Cruel Sisters
FSA1-W,M
Cruel to Be Kind
ToO79-W,M
Cruel War
BF-W,M FGM-W,M LW-W,M
Cruel War Is Over, Jenny
SiS-W
Cruel War Is Raging
FW-W
Cruel Wife
SCa-W
Cruel Youth
LW-W,M
Cruella De Ville
NI-W,M
Cruiscin Lan
IS-W,M
Cruise of Bigler
SA-W,M
Cruise of the Fair American
ANS-W
Cruisin'
ToO79-W,M
Cruising down the River
MAB1-W MSA1-W,M OnT1-W,M
PB-W,M RDT-W,M TI2-W,M
U-W
Crumpets
Boo-W,M
Crunchy Granola Suite
TI2-W,M
Crusaders
MML-W,M
Crusaders' Hymn
GUM2-W,M HS-W,M SiR-W,M
Crush on You
TTH-W,M
Cry
HLS3-W,M MF-W,M TI1-W,M
UFB-W,M
Cry Baby Cry
TWS-W
Cry Just a Little Bit
EC-W,M
Cry Like the Wind
DR-W,M
Cry Me a River
DJ-W,M RW-W,M ToS-W,M
Cry Myself to Sleep
TTH-W,M
Cry of the Toilers
AL-W
Cry the Beloved Country
LS-W,M
Cry to Arms
AWB-W
Cryes of London
SSP-W
Cryin' Heart Blues
OGC2-W,M
Crying
HR-W TFC-W,M
Crying in the Chapel
HLS3-W,M HLS9-W,M ILS-W,M
OGC1-W,M RDF-W,M RW-W,M
TI1-W,M UFB-W,M
Crying My Heart Out over You
TI2-W,M
Crying of Water
NA-W,M

Crying Time
CMG-W,M
Crying Won't Help You
DBL-W
Crystal Blue Persuasion
ILS-W,M MF-W,M
Crystal Candelabra
CF-W,M
Crystal Day
VA-W,M
Crystal Palace
MSB-W
Cu-Cu Cantaba La Rana
SCL-W,M (Spanish)
Cu-Cu Sang the Frog
SCL-W,M (Spanish)
**Cuando Calienta El Sol see Love
Me with All Your Heart**
Cuando Vuelva A Amanecer
TI1-W,M (Spanish Only)
**Cuando Vuelva A Tu Lado see
What a Diff'rence a Day Made**
**Cuatro Generales see Los Cuatro
Generales**
Cub Scout Advancement Song
CSS-W
Cub Scout Booster Song
CSS-W
Cub Scout Marching Song
CSS-W
Cub Scout Prayer
CSS-W
Cub Scout Welcome Song
CSS-W
Cub Scouts
ASB3-W,M
Cuban Overture
NYT-M
Cuban Pete
LaS-W,M OnT6-W,M
Cubbing Along Together
CSS-W
Cubbing in the Morning
CSS-W
Cubs Whistle While They Work
CSS-W
Cucaracha see La Cucaracha
Cuckoo
MSH-W,M SCL-W,M
Cuckoo (Awake, Awake, Ye
Dreamers)
TH-W,M
Cuckoo, The (Cuckoo, from the
Woods Sing)
UF-W,M
Cuckoo, The (Cuckoo! Welcome
Your Song)
ASB2-W,M
Cuckoo, The (Is a Funny Bird)
FW-W
Cuckoo, The (Is a Pretty Bird)
Oz1-W,M
Cuckoo, The (Oh, I Went to the
Flowing Spring)
HS-W,M MG-W,M
Cuckoo, The (She's a Pretty Bird)
AH-W,M BT-W,M DD-W,M
Cuckoo Clock
ASB1-W,M ASB2-W,M MAR-W,M
SiR-W,M
Cuckoo Fallera
VA-W,M
Cuckoo, Good Neighbors Help Us
Boo-W,M
Cuckoo She's a Pretty Bird
SG-W,M
Cuckoo's Career

FSA2-W,M
Cuddle Buggin' Baby
OGC2-W,M
Cuddle Up a Little Closer
U-W
Cuddle Up a Little Closer, Lovey
Mine
MF-W,M OAP-W,M
Cuentame see Speak Up Mambo
Cuffee's War Song
SiS-W
Cujus Animam
AmH-W,M FSA1-W,M
Culloden
SBB-W
Cultivator
GrM-W,M
Cultivator Blues
LC-W
Cumberland Gap
BIS-W,M DD-W,M FSB2-W,M
FW-W HAS-W,M IHA-W,M
Oz3-W POT-W,M Re-W,M
Cumberland's Crew
Sin-W,M
Cumha Mhontroise
SBB-W
Cumparsita see La Cumparsita
Cup of Coffee, a Sandwich and
You
MF-W,M OHB-W,M
Cup of Rejoicing
GB-W,M
Cupboard
MH-W,M SiR-W,M
Cupid, Make Your Virgins Tender
EL-W,M
Cupid the Cunnin' Paudeen
E-W,M
Curfew
MMM-W,M
Curiosity
TTH-W,M
Curious Story
ASB1-M
Curious Things
ASB2-W,M
Curlew's Song
IS-W,M
Curly Locks
OTJ-W,M SMa-W,M
Curs'd Be the Wretch
Boo-W,M
Curse of an Aching Heart
BH-W,M OS-W
Cut It Down
GH-W,M
Cute
MF-M TI2-W,M
Cutter to Houston (Theme)
TV-M
Cutty Sark
BMC-W,M
Cutty Wren
AFP-W FW-W SWF-W,M
Cygne see Le Cygne
Cymbals
ASB1-W,M GM-W
Czardas
MAR-W,M
Czarine see La Czarine

D

D-Day Dodgers
FW-W

D-I-V-O-R-C-E
TI2-W,M
D-2 Horse Wrangler
GA-W SoC-W
Da Doo Ron Ron
GAR-W,M
Dabbling in the Dew
LW-W,M
Daddy (Hey! Daddy! I Want a
Di'mond Ring)
BBB-W,M TI2-W,M
Daddy (Take My Head on Your
Shoulder, Daddy)
AmH-W,M TMA-W,M
Daddy Daddy
HRB1-W,M
Daddy Don't You Walk So Fast
TI1-W,M TI2-W,M UFB-W,M
Daddy Frank (the Guitar Man)
NMH-W,M
Daddy MacNeven's Somerset
AL-W
Daddy Sang Bass
BSG-W,M BSo-W,M BSP-W,M
CEM-W,M CMG-W,M FOC-W,M
GCM-W,M HHa-W,M OTJ-W,M
RDF-W,M RW-W,M TI2-W,M
Daddy Shot a Bear
AFS-W,M
Daddy Was an Old Time Preacher
Man
BDP-W,M
Daddy Wouldn't Buy Me a Bow
Wow
U-W
Daddy's Hands
AWS-W,M CoH-W,M FOC-W,M
TTH-W,M
Daddy's Home
ILS-W,M MF-W,M
Daddy's Little Boy
OTJ-W,M TI2-W,M
Daddy's Little Girl
OBN-W,M OnT1-W,M TI2-W,M
Dad's a Millionaire
EFS-W,M
Daemon Lover see James Harris
Daffodillies
SOO-W,M SSe-W,M
Daily Growing
FW-W
Daily Guidance
SS-W
Daily Records
WA-W,M
Dainty Fine Aniseed Water
Boo-W,M
Dairy Maids
BMC-W,M
**Dairy Queen Jingle see
Scrumpdillyishus Day**
Daisies
FSA2-W,M NA-W,M
Daisies Won't Tell
BH-W,M EFS-W,M OS-W
Daisy
RuS-W,M (Russian)
Daisy a Day
GrH-W,M
Daisy Bell
ATS-W BH-W,M FSN-W,M
FSTS-W,M FW-W FWS-W,M
IL-W,M MAB1-W
MSA1-W OAP-W,M
OTJ-W,M
**Daisy Bell see also Daisy Daisy and
Bicycle Built for Two**

Daisy Chain
CSG-W,M
Daisy Daisy
CSS-W U-W
**Daisy Daisy see also Daisy Bell and
Bicycle Built for Two**
Daisy Jane
MF-W,M
Dakota Land
FW-W HB-W,M
Dallas (Theme)
TV-M
Dallas Blues
B-W,M Bl-W,M Mo-W,M NM-W,M
Dallas County Jail
Oz2-W,M
Dame Get Up
HS-W,M MH-W,M SMa-W,M
Dame Get Up and Bake Your Pies
CSo-W,M OTJ-W,M
Dame Lend Me a Loaf
Boo-W,M
Damon
AS-W,M (German)
Damon's Winder
DD-W,M
Dan D'Irisleabhar Na Gaeilge
VP-W (Gaelic Only)
Dan Gran' Chimin
CSD-W,M (French)
Dan Ragg
AL-W
Dance
RoS-W,M
Dance, A
GUM1-W,M
Dance, The (Cornwallis Led a
Country Dance)
AWB-W SBA-W
Dance a Cachucha
MGT-W,M
Dance All Night with a Bottle in
Your Hand
FVV-W,M
Dance and Sing
TF-W,M
Dance Children Do
ASB3-W,M
Dance Dance Dance
ILS-W,M
Dance Here and Dance There
PIS-W,M
Dance Little Bird
MF-M NoS-M
Dance Little Sister
RoS-W,M
Dance Mamma Dance Pappa
Dance
RW-W,M
Dance of Greeting
MAR-W,M
Dance of the Candy Fairy
OTJ-M
Dance of the Elves
FSA2-W,M
Dance of the Guests
CoF-W,M
Dance of the Infidels
MF-M
Dance of the Marionettes
NaM-W,M
Dance of the Reed Flutes
OTJ-W,M
Dance of the Slave Maidens
RW-M
Dance of the Sugar-Plum Fairy
RW-M

Dance of the Tumblers
LD-W,M
Dance Only with Me
UBF-W,M
Dance Song
GUM2-W,M
Dance: Ten; Looks: Three
CL-W,M UBF-W,M
Dance Thumbkin Dance
ASB1-W,M MG-W,M
Dance to the Golden Calf
SoM-W,M
Dance to the Music
MF-W,M
Dance to Your Daddy
FW-W OTJ-W,M
Dance Up
BSC-W
Dance with a Dolly
TI1-W,M UFB-W,M
Dance with Me
HRB4-W,M ToO76-W,M
Dance with Me Henry
FRH-W,M
Dancers, The (Come Where the
Viols Are Singing)
TF-W,M
Dancers, The (On with the Dance!)
FSA1-W,M
Dancin' on de Green
TMA-W,M
Dancing
SCL-W,M
Dancing (As Long As You're
Dancing, the World Seems to
Dance Along)
Mo-W,M NM-W,M OTO-W
TI2-W,M
Dancing around the Christmas Tree
AST-W,M
Dancing Doll
AmH-M ASB1-M
Dancing Dolly
ASB1-W,M
Dancing in a Ring
ASB1-W,M
Dancing in the Barn
TMA-W,M
Dancing in the Dark
DBC-W,M MF-W,M TW-W
Dancing in the Garden
GUM1-W,M
Dancing in the Moonlight
WDS-W,M
Dancing in the Rain
OTJ-W,M
Dancing in Vienna
MuM-W,M
Dancing on My Tippy-Tippy Toes
W-W,M
Dancing on the Ceiling
FrS-W,M HC1-W,M MF-W,M
OHB-W,M TS-W
Dancing on the Green
FSA1-W,M
Dancing Queen
GrS-W,M TI1-W,M UFB-W,M
Dancing Shoes
GOB-W,M
Dancing the Gavotte
ASB5-W,M
Dancing Together
LMR-W,M
Dancing Will Keep You Young
MPM-W,M
Dancing with Alice
Mo-W,M NM-W,M OTO-W

Dancing with Mr. D
RoS-W,M

Dancing with Rosa
BMC-W,M

Dancing with Tears in My Eyes
MF-W,M OHB-W,M

Dancing with the Mountains
PoG-W,M

Dandelion (Gay Blossom of the
Field)
ASB6-W,M

Dandelion (I'm a Happy Little
Thing)
SSe-W,M

Dandelion (In the Early Days of
Spring)
ASB2-W,M

Dandelion (Jagger/Richards)
RoS-W,M

Dandelions (The Little Stars Came
Down Last Night)
ASB4-W,M

Dandelions (on the Lawn)
GM-W,M

Dandelion Seed
ASB2-W,M

Dandelions
ASB3-W,M GM-W

Dandoo
BSC-W Oz1-W,M TBF-W

Dandy Jim from Caroline
DE-W,M

Dang Me
CMG-W,M CSp-W,M

Danger Zone
TTH-W,M

Daniel (Is Trav'ling Tonight on a
Plane)
TI2-W,M

Daniel (You Call Yourself Church-
Member)
NSS-W

**Daniel (You Call Yourself Church-
Member) see also O Daniel**

Daniel Boone
ASB5-W,M FSA1-W,M

Daniel Boone (Theme)
GTV-W,M

Daniel Saw the Stone
RF-W,M

Daniel's in de Lion's Den
BDW-W,M

Danish National Hymn
AmH-W,M (Danish) HSD-W,M

Danke Schoen
MF-W,M

Danny
SRE1-W,M SRE2-W,M

Danny Boy
EP-W,M FW-W

Danny Winters
Oz3-W,M

Dans La Foret Lointaine
Boo-W,M (French Only)

Dans La Louisianne
Lo-W,M (French Only)

Dans Le Berceau
FSO-W,M (French)

Dans Les Chantiers
CFS-W,M (French)

Dans Les Chantiers Nous
Hivernerons
FSO-W,M (French)

Dans Les Prisons De Nantes
CFS-W,M (French)

Dans Tes Beaux Yeux
CaF-W (French Only)

Dans Tous Les Cantons
CFS-W,M (French)

**Danse Des Gorets see La Danse
Des Gorets**

Danse Ronde
FSO-W,M (French)

Dansero
OTJ-W,M

Dansez Codaine
BaB-W,M (French)

Dansons La Capucine
Ch-W (French Only)

Danube Garland
RuS-W,M (Russian)

Danube River
HSD-W,M SL-W,M

Danville Girl
BF-W,M FW-W

Dapper Dan
T-W,M

Dar He Goes Dats Him
DE-W,M

Darby and Joan
AmH-W,M HSD-W,M

Darby Ram
BMC-W,M FGM-W,M FW-W

Darby's Castle
SuS-W,M

Dardanella
T-W,M

Dare to Be a Daniel
GH-W,M

Dare to Be a Union Man
AL-W

Dare to Be Brave
FH-W,M

Dark Alley Blues
LC-W

Dark and Dreary Weather
Oz4-W,M

Dark As a Dungeon
AFP-W,M FG1-W,M SWF-W,M

Dark-Eyed Girl
Oz4-W

Dark-Eyed Sailor
BB-W FW-W

Dark Eyes
OTJ-W,M RW-W,M TI1-W,M
UFB-W,M

Dark Girl Dressed in Blue
Oz3-W

Dark Hollow
BSo-W,M

Dark Hollow, The
Oz4-W,M

Dark Hollow Blues
ITP-W,M

Dark Interlude
BMC-M

Dark Is the Desert
ITP-W,M

Dark Is the Night
GH-W,M

Dark Muddy Bottom
DBL-W

Dark Side of My Life
TW-W

Dark Song
BRB-W

Dark the Night
OB-W,M

Dark Was the Night
AME-W,M

Darkechoh
JS-W,M (Hebrew Only)

Dark'cho
MU-W,M (Hebrew)

Darker the Night
VB-W,M

Darkies' Rally
SiS-W

Darkies' Rallying Song
SiS-W

Darkness
TH-W,M

Darkness Is under His Feet
VB-W,M

Darkness on the Delta
TI2-W,M

Darkness on the Edge of Town
RV-W

Darkness on the Face of the Earth
WNF-W

Darktown Poker Club
MR-W,M

Darktown Strutters' Ball
GSN1-W,M HLS1-W,M RW-W,M
STW-W,M

Darky Matrons
CSD-W,M (French)

Darky Sunday School
HAS-W,M

Darlin'
AFB-W,M FW-W MF-W,M

Darlin' Corey
FW-W LW-W,M WSB-W,M

**Darlin' Corey see also Darling
Corey**

Darlin' Corrie
IHA-W,M

Darlin' You Can't Love but One
FWS-W,M

Darling Be Home Soon
MCG-W,M THN-W,M TI2-W,M

Darling Corey
BSo-W,M FSB2-W,M

**Darling Corey see also Darlin'
Corey**

Darling Cory
FG1-W,M FG2-W,M

Darling Je Vous Aime Beaucoup
LM-W,M TI1-W,M

Darling Little Joe
Oz4-W,M

Darling Nellie Gray
FU-W,M FuB-W,M HSD-W,M
POT-W,M

Darling Nelly Gray
AmH-W,M ATS-W BH-W,M
FW-W NAS-W,M PoS-W,M
WiS8-W,M

Darling of L.S.U.
SLS-W,M

Darn It Baby That's Love
UBF-W,M

Darn That Dream
MF-W,M RoE-W,M TI1-W,M
UFB-W,M

Dar's a Better Day A-Comin'
WN-W,M

**Darth Vader's Theme see Imperial
March**

Dartmouth Our Dartmouth
IL-W,M

Dartmouth's in Town Again
IL-W,M

Darwin
GI-W

Das Veilchen see Violet

Dashing Away with the Smoothing
Iron
FSA1-W,M

Dashing White Sergeant
OH-W,M

Dat Ol' Boy
L-W
Dat Ol' Time Religion
WiS7-W,M
Dat Ol' Time Religion see also That Old-Time Religion
Dat Sabbath Hath No End
NH-W
Dat Same Train
BDW-W,M
Dat Suits Me
Me-W,M
Dat Water Million
CA-W,M
Date of Thirty-Nine
ANS-W
Dat's Love
L-W
Dat's My Philosphy
SiS-W
Daughter of Peggy O'Neil
RW-W,M
Daughter of Rosie O'Grady
MF-W,M WDS-W,M
Daughters Will You Marry?
FW-W
David and Goliath
VS-W,M
David, David, Yes, Yes
BMM-W,M
David's Lamentation
EA-W,M SHS-W,M SiM-W,M
David's Psalm
Mo-W,M NM-W,M
Davis
SHS-W,M
Davy Crockett
ASB6-W,M BSC-W FSU-W
Oz3-W,M
Davy Crockett--King of the Wild Frontier (Theme) see Ballad of Davy Crockett
Dawn Comes Softly
CA-W,M
Dawn (Matins)
SBF-W,M
Dawn of a New Day
AL-W
Dawn of Love
Fi-W,M
Dawn of Maytime
SL-W,M TF-W,M
Dawn of Tomorrow
OS-W
Dawn Song
GUM2-W,M
Dawning Fair, Morning Wonderful
AHO-W,M (Spanish)
Dawsonville Jail
FVV-W,M
Day after Day
SoF-W,M TI1-W,M UFB-W,M
Day and Night
OTJ-W,M
Day before Spring
LL-W,M
Day by Day
CEM-W,M DBC-W,M FrS-W,M
G-W,M GS1-W HC1-W,M
Hy-W,M On-W,M OTJ-W,M
OTO-W RDF-W,M TI2-W,M
UBF-W,M
Day Dream
GMD-W,M
Day He Wore My Crown
VB-W,M
Day I Lef' My Home

NH-W
Day I Met Your Father
TW-W
Day I Played Baseball
SoC-W
Day In Day Out
FrS-W,M HLS2-W,M MF-W,M
OHF-W
Day in the Life
BBe-W,M Be2-W,M RV-W
TWS-W WG-W,M
Day in the Life of a Fool
DJ-W,M HLS5-W,M RT6-W,M
RW-W,M TI1-W,M UFB-W,M
Day Is Breaking
Boo-W,M
Day Is Done
BM-W Boo-W,M LoS-W,M
Day Is Dying in the West
AHO-W,M AME-W,M Bo-W
CEM-W,M ESB-W,M Hy-W,M
OS-W TF-W,M VA-W,M YS-W,M
Day Is Past and Gone
AHO-W,M AME-W,M
Day-O see Banana Boat Song
Day of God! Thou Blessed Day
AHO-W,M
Day of Judgement
SHS-W,M
Day of Labor
AL-W
Day of Liberty's Comin'
SiS-W
Day of Resurrection
AME-W,M FH-W,M Hy-W,M
Day That the Circus Left Town
Mo-W,M OTJ-W,M
Day the Rain Came
TI2-W,M
Day Thou Gavest, Lord, Is Ended
AME-W,M
Day Thou Givest, Lord, Is Ended
Hy-W,M
Day Tripper
BBe-W,M Be1-W,M SwS-W,M
TWS-W
Day Will Come
AL-W
Day without You
OTO-W
Day You Came Along
OTO-W
Dayaynu
SBJ-W,M (Hebrew Only)
Dayaynu see also Dayenu and Deyainu
Daybreak (Adamson/Grofe)
GSF-W,M GSN2-W,M
Daybreak (Barry Manilow)
RW-W,M TOF-W,M
Daybreak (Dunbar/Silcher)
MHB-W,M
Daybreak (Longfellow/Dubois)
FSA1-W,M
Daybreak in the Alps
FSA2-W,M
Daydream
RYT-W,M THN-W,M TI2-W,M
Daydream Believer
GAR-W,M MF-W,M
Daydreamer
Mo-W,M OTO-W
Daydreaming
ASB4-W,M
Daydreams about Night Things
TI2-W,M
Dayenu

HSA-W,M (Hebrew)
Dayenu see also Dayaynu and Deyainu
Days and Weeks and Months Pass By
SHP-W,M
Day's Farewell
ASB4-W,M
Days Gone By
OTO-W
Day's Happenings
NF-W
Days of Forty-Nine
FW-W LMR-W,M Oz2-W,M
Days of the Past Are Gone
HB-W,M
Days of the Week (Sunday, Sunday, First Day Is Sunday)
MAR-W,M
Days of the Week (Today Is Monday, Don't You Know)
GM-W,M
Days of the Week (Which of the Days Do You Like the Best)
ASB1-W,M
Days of Wine and Roses
EY-W,M HFH-W,M MF-W,M
OHF-W RoE-W,M
Dayspring
SHS-W,M SL-W,M
Daytime Friends
HLS9-W,M MF-W,M
Daytime Nightime Suffering
PMC-W,M
Dazz (Disco Jazz)
ToO76-W,M
De (The) see next word in title
De Bezem
Boo-W,M (Dutch Only)
De Colores
JF-W,M (Spanish)
De Trop
Fi-W,M
Deacon Henshaw
NSS-W
Deacons for Defense and Justice
BRB-W
Dead and Gone
FVV-W,M
Dead Flowers
RoS-W,M
Dead from the Dust
AFP-W
Dead Horse
NAS-W,M
Dead Man's Curve
HR-W
Dead March and Monody
MPP-W,M OHG-W,M
Dead Skunk
WF-W,M
Deaf Woman's Courtship
MAS-W,M MG-W,M MHB-W,M
SaS-W,M VA-W,M
Dean Martin Show Theme see Everybody Loves Somebody
Dean Rusk Song
VS-W,M
Dear Brethren Are Your Harps in Tune?
AHO-W,M
Dear Charming Beauty
OTJ-W,M
Dear Companion
D-W,M FW-W
Dear Do Not Your Fair Beauty

Wrong
OH-W,M
Dear Doctor
RoS-W,M
Dear Draft Dodger
AF-W
Dear Evelina
AmH-W,M ATS-W MAS-W,M
Dear Evelina Sweet Evelina
HSD-W,M WiS8-W,M
Dear Father Hear Our Prayer to
Thee
SHP-W,M
Dear Father, the Girl
Boo-W,M
Dear Friend
OTO-W
Dear Friend Whose Presence in the
House
AHO-W,M
Dear God Be near Me through the
Day
SHP-W,M
Dear Happy Souls
AHO-W,M
Dear Heart
PoG-W,M WG-W,M
Dear Hearts and Gentle People
MAB1-W,M Mo-W,M MSA1-W
NM-W,M OS-W OTJ-W,M
RDF-W,M
Dear I Love You So
CSD-W,M (French)
Dear Jewell
Oz1-W
Dear John
TI1-W,M UFB-W,M
Dear Judge
OGC1-W,M
Dear Katie
TMA-W,M
Dear Land of the South
SiS-W SY-W,M
Dear Little Birdie
SoP-W,M
Dear Little Cafe
BS-W,M
Dear Little Girl
ReG-W,M
Dear Little Girl Who Is Good
M-W,M
Dear Lord and Father of Mankind
AHO-W,M AME-W,M CA-W,M
FH-W,M HF-W,M Hy-W,M
MAS-W,M OM-W,M SJ-W,M
TB-W,M
Dear Lord Behold Thy Servants
AHO-W,M
Dear Mother, I've Come Home to
Die
SiS-W
Dear Mother, the Battle Is Over
SiS-W
Dear Mrs. Applebee
OnT1-W,M
Dear Old Comrade Soldiers
BMM-W,M
Dear Old Farm
GrM-W,M
Dear Old Girl
BH-W,M FSN-W,M OS-W
RW-W,M
Dear Old Nebraska U
Mo-W,M TI2-W,M
Dear Old Sunny South by the Sea
LJ-W,M
Dear Old Syracuse

TS-W
Dear Old White and Gold
CoS-W,M
Dear One, Believe
LMR-W,M (Italian) SL-W,M
(Italian)
**Dear One, Believe see also Caro
Mio Ben and Dearest Believe**
Dear Prudence
BBe-W,M Be2-W,M TWS-W
Dear Santa
GM-W
Dear Santa Have You Had the
Measles?
CSB-W,M
Dear Savior If These Lambs Should
Stray
AHO-W,M
Dear Uncle Sam
RB-W
Dear Wife, I'm with You Once
Again
SiS-W
Dear Willie
HCY-W,M
Dear World
Mo-W,M OTO-W TI2-W,M
UBF-W,M
Dearer Than Life
FHR-W,M
Dearest Believe
AS-W,M (Italian) FSY-W,M
(Italian)
**Dearest Believe see also Caro Mio
Ben and Dear One, Believe**
Dearest Mae
HSD-W,M
Dearest Spot
NAS-W,M
Dearest Spot Is Home
HSD-W,M
Dearest Wilt Thou Bid Me Go?
SiS-W
Dearie
OTJ-W,M
Dearly Beloved
OHF-W TI1-W,M UFB-W,M
Death
BSC-W
Death Ain't You Got No Shame
WN-W,M
Death and Resurrection
GBC-W,M
Death Blues
LC-W
Death Goin' t' Lay His Col' Icy
Han' on Me
BDW-W,M
Death Is a Long Long Sleep
Boo-W,M
Death Is a Melancholy Call
BSC-W
Death Is in Dis Land
NH-W
Death Letter Blues
NeF-W
Death of a Romish Lady
FMT-W Oz4-W,M
Death of Bernard Friley
BMM-W
Death of Crockett
ATS-W
Death of Fan McCoy
BMM-W,M
Death of General Warren
ESU-W
Death of General Wolfe

EA-W,M
Death of Harry Simms
AFP-W,M PSN-W,M
Death of Jesse James
SoC-W
Death of Lula Vires
BMM-W
Death of Molly Bender
SCa-W
Death of Mother Jones
SWF-W,M
Death of Ned Kelly
ATM-W,M
Death of Nelson
OH-W,M
Death of Parcy Reed
SBB-W
Death of Parker
MSB-W
Death of Poor Bill Brown
MSB-W
Death of Queen Jane
AA-W,M BT-W,M
**Death of Roy Rickey see Little Roy
Rickey**
**Death of Samuel Adams see Labor
Trouble Murder**
Death of the Brave
ESU-W
Death of the Right Honourable Sir
Robert Peel
MSB-W
Death of Wellington
MSB-W
Death of William and Nancy
BSC-W
Death or Freedom
AL-W
Death Song of an Indian Chief
EA-W,M
Death, 'Tis a Melancholy Day
Oz4-W
Debil and the Farmer's Wife
LW-W,M
**Debil and the Farmer's Wife see
also Devil and the Farmer's Wife**
Debout, Sainte Cohorte
CUP-W,M (French Only)
Decatur's Victory
ANS-W MPP-W,M OHG-W,M
Deceitful Brownskin
LC-W
December Day
WNF-W
December 1963 (Oh What a Night)
ToO76-W,M
Decision in the Gypsy's Warning
Oz4-W
Deck the Hall
BCh-W,M BCS-W,M BeB-W,M
CC-W,M CI-W,M CSF-W FW-W
FWS-W,M GBC-W,M IL-W,M
MAS-W,M MC-W,M MML-W,M
OE-W,M OTJ-W,M RW-W,M
SCS-W SMa-W,M TH-W,M
UF-W,M YS-W,M
Deck the Halls
CEM-W,M DC-W,M HS-W,M
MF-W,M OAP-W,M OPS-W,M
PoG-W,M TI1-W,M UFB-W,M
Deck the Halls with Boughs of
Holly
FM-W,M
Deck Thyself with Joy and
Gladness
SJ-W,M
Declaration D'Amour see La

Declaration D'Amour
Declaration of Love
FSO-W,M (French)
Decree
OB-W,M
Dedicated to Old Party Voters
AL-W
Dedicated to the One I Love
DRR-W,M TI2-W,M
Dedication (Robert Franz)
FSY-W,M (German) LMR-W,M
TM-W,M WGB/O-W,M
Dedication (Robert Schumann)
MU-W,M
Dedication (Von Wilm/Strauss)
AS-W,M (German) FSY-W,M
**Dedication (Von Wilm/Strauss) see
also To You (Zueignung)**
Dedication Hymn
AL-W
Dedication Ode
GrM-W,M
'Deed I Do
TI2-W,M
Deedle Dumpling
NF-W
Deep (Theme)
TOM-M
Deep Blue Sea
FGM-W,M FW-W GuC-W,M
OHO-W,M Oz4-W,M
Deep Deep South
LMR-W,M
Deep Down Inside
Mo-W,M NM-W,M OTO-W
Deep Fork River Blues
RBO-W,M
Deep Henderson
Mo-W,M NM-W,M
Deep in a Dream
MF-W,M
Deep in Love see Girl Died for Love
Deep in the Heart of Harlem
RB-W
Deep in the Heart of Texas
WiS9-W,M
Deep in Your Heart
Mo-W,M NM-W,M OTO-W
Deep Purple
GSN2-W,M GSO-W,M HLS2-W,M
OP1-W,M RDT-W,M RW-W,M
Sta-W,M
Deep River
AH-W,M ATS-W ETB-W,M
FN-W,M FW-W JF-W,M LoS-W,M
NAS-W,M NSS-W OAP-W,M
OFS-W,M OTJ-W,M RF-W,M
RW-W,M SFM-W SpS-W,M
TF-W,M TH-W,M TI1-W,M
UFB-W,M WiS7-W,M
Deep River Blues
B-W,M (Spanish) BI-W,M
(Spanish) FPG-W,M
Deep Sea Blues
SSo-W,M
Deep Water
FW-W
Deep Were His Wounds and Red
SJ-W,M
Deeper Than the Holler
GCM-W,M
Deeper Than the Night
ToO79-W,M
Deer
LA-W,M (Spanish)
Deer Hunter (Theme) see Cavatina
Deer Song

AFS-W,M
Defeat and Victory
ANS-W
Defend Us Lord from Every Ill
AHO-W,M
Defenders
SiS-W
De'il Cam' Fiddlin' thro' the Toun
SeS-W,M
De'il Take the War
SR-W,M
De'il's Awa' wi' the Exciseman
SeS-W,M
Dein Eigen see Thine Own
Deja Vu
TI1-W,M UFB-W,M
Dejala
TI1-W,M (Spanish Only) UFB-
W,M (Spanish Only)
DeKalb Blues
Le-W,M NeF-W
Delaissee see La Delaissee
Delaware
TI2-W,M
Delay Not a Moment
ESU-W
**Delco Jingle see More You Know,
the More You'll Want Delco**
Delia
FG1-W,M J-W,M
Delia Gone
LaS-W,M
Delia Holmes
FSSC-W,M
Delia's Gone
FW-W OHO-W,M
Delicado (Baiao)
MF-W,M
Delicatessen Store
MH-W,M
Delicious see Delishious
Delicta Quis
Boo-W,M (Latin Only)
Delie
AN-W
Delight
SHS-W,M
Delilah
MCG-W,M RYT-W,M
Delishious
NYT-W,M ReG-W,M
Deliver the Goods
SMW-W,M WS-W,M
Deliverance Will Come
GH-W,M
Dell on the Mountain
LC-W
Delta Blues
SFF-W,M
Delta Dawn
AO-W,M GrH-W,M HLS9-W,M
RW-W,M RY-W,M
Delta Is Ready When You Are
GSM-W,M
Dem Bones Gonna Rise Again
OHO-W,M
Demagogue's Song
AL-W
Demand for Perseverance
AL-W
Democrat Blues
DBL-W
Democratic Ode
MPP-W
Demon Lover
ATS-W
Demonstrating G.I.

SFF-W,M
Den My Little Soul Will Shine
AN-W
Den of Iniquity
TW-W
Den Olycklige Emigranten
SE-W,M (Swedish)
Den Svenske Emigrantens
Afskedswisa Fran Sin Hemort
SE-W,M (Swedish)
Den Swenska Flickan Nils Som
Wille Resa Till Amerika
SE-W,M (Swedish)
Dengozo
AmH-M
Denmark's Verdant Meadows
SiP-W,M (Danish)
Dentist
WF-W,M
Departure (Li Ch'ing)
FD-W,M (Chinese)
Deportee
TI1-W,M UFB-W,M
**Deportee see also Plane Wreck at
Los Gatos**
Deportees
JF-W,M
Depression Blues
LC-W
Depth of Mercy
GH-W,M OM-W,M
Depth of Mercy Can There Be
AME-W,M Hy-W,M
Der Deitcher's Dog
HS-W,M PoS-W,M
**Der Deitcher's Dog see also Oh
Where Has My Little Dog Gone
and Where Has My Little Dog
Gone**
Der Musikanter
FWS-W,M (German Only)
YS-W,M (Dutch Only)
Der Sturmische Morgen
AS-W,M (German)
Der Tod Und Das Madchen
SBF-W,M (German)
Der XXIII Psalm
BC1-W,M (German Only)
Derby Ram
BSC-W HS-W,M LMR-W,M
OH-W,M Oz1-W,M SA-W,M
Dere Is a Mighty Shoutin'
BDW-W,M
Dere's a Little Wheel A-Turnin' in
My Heart
RF-W,M
Dere's a Mighty War in de Hebben
BDW-W,M
Dere's No One Lak Jesus
NH-W
Dere's No Rain to Wet You
NSS-W
Derrick
SHS-W,M
Derriere Chez Nous
FSF-W (French)
Derry Ding Ding Dasson
Bo-W,M
'Des Hold My Hand Tonight
OTJ-W,M
Des Noms
CaF-W (French Only)
Desafinado
BeL-W,M DJ-W,M TI1-W,M
TWD-W,M
**Desafinado see also Slightly Out of
Tune**

Descent on Middlesex
SBA-W
Description of a Scab
VP-W
Desde Que To Te Has Ido
TI1-M UFB-M
Dese All Er Ma Father's Chillun
BDW-W,M
Dese All My Fader's Children
NSS-W
Dese Bones
MAS-W,M
Desert Blues
LJ-W,M
Desert Song
DS-W,M HC2-W,M MF-W,M
Deserted Lover
Oz4-W,M
Deserted Rebel Mansion
SiS-W
Design for Dedication
HCY-W,M
Designing Dancing Master
SR-W,M
Desire
OTO-W TI1-W,M UFB-W,M
Desiree
TI2-W,M
Desires of My Heart
OGR-W,M
Desperado, (Why Don't You Come
to Your Senses)
DC-W,M DPE-W,M ERM-W,M
Desperado, The (There Was a
Desperado from the Wild and
Wooly West)
FGM-W,M FW-W
Desponding Negro
MPP-W,M
Destined to Win
VB-W,M
Destinies of Good and Bad
Children
NF-W
Destiny of All
VS-W,M
Destitute Former Slave Owners
NF-W
Destroyer Song
GI-W,M GO-W SSo-W,M
Destruction of the Tea
SI-W,M
Detour
HLS9-W,M OGC1-W,M RW-W,M
TI1-W,M UFB-W,M
Detroit
OnT6-W,M SHS-W,M
Detroit City
BSo-W,M CMG-W,M FOC-W,M
RB-W TI2-W,M
Devil and Ganger McGlynn
IFM-W
Devil and the Farmer's Wife
FW-W GuC-W,M OHO-W,M
WSB-W,M
**Devil and the Farmer's Wife see
also Debil and the Farmer's Wife**
Devil and the School Child
ITP-W,M
**Devil Cam' Fiddlin' thro' the Town
see De'il Cam' Fiddlin' thro' the
Town**
Devil Came to My Door
Oz3-W,M
Devil in a Sleeping Bag
WNF-W
Devil in Disguise see You're the

Devil in Disguise
Devil or Angel
HRB3-W,M
**Devil Take the War see De'il Take
the War**
Devil Wore a Crucifix
JF-W,M
Devilish Mary
FW-W LW-W,M Oz3-W,M
Devilish Pigs
NF-W
**Devil's Awa' wi' the Exciseman
see De'il's Awa' wi' the
Exciseman**
Devil's Brigade March (I Want a
Woman)
RW-W,M
Devil's Dream
AmH-M POT-M
Devil's Mad and I Am Glad
Oz2-W
Devil's Nine Questions
ITP-W,M
**Devil's Questions see Riddles
Wisely Expounded**
Devil's Song
ITP-W
Devinez
CE-W,M (French)
Devoted
TI2-W,M
Devoted to You
MF-W,M
Devotion
SHS-W,M
Dey Hab a Camp Meetin'
DE-W,M
Dey Said We Wouldn't Fight
SiS-W
Deyainu
MF-W,M (Hebrew Only)
**Deyainu see also Dayaynu and
Dayenu**
Dezlaissee see La Dezlaissee
Dh' Fhalbh Mo Leannan Fhein
SeS-W,M
**Dia De Tu Santo see El Dia De Tu
Santo**
Dialogue
SL-W,M
Dialogue between a Believer and
His Soul
WN-W,M
Diamanto
UF-W,M
Diamon' in da Ring A'ready
SGT-W,M
Diamon' Joe
NH-W
Diamond in My Eye
BB-W
Diamonds Are a Girl's Best Friend
RoE-W,M TI2-W,M TW-W V-W,M
Diamonds Are Forever
MCG-W,M
Diamonds from the Crown of the
Lord
GrG-W,M
Diane
FPS-W,M GG5-W,M HLS5-W,M
OP1-W,M RW-W,M
Diane Is
Mo-W,M NM-W,M OTO-W
Dick and Doll
SR-W,M
Dick German the Cobbler
Oz1-W,M

Dick Myers Jig
DE-WM
Dick Van Dyke Show (Theme)
GTV-M
Dickie
Mo-W,M OTO-W
Dicklicker's Holler
NeF-W
Dickory Dickory Dock
AmH-W,M MH-W,M
**Dickory Dickory Dock see also
Hickory Dickory Dock**
Did Christ o'er Sinners Weep
AME-W,M GH-W
Did I Ever Really Live?
ILT-W,M
Did I Remember
CS-W,M HLS5-W,M RW-W,M
WDS-W,M
**Did You Ever (Get One of Them
Days) see Didja' Ever**
Did You Ever? (See a Mouse Paint
a House)
MAR-W,M
Did You Ever Cross Over to
Sneden's
Mo-W,M
Did You Ever Have to Make Up
Your Mind
TI2-W,M
Did You Ever See a Dream
Walking?
HC2-W,M LM-W,M OTO-W
TI1-W,M
Did You Ever See a Lassie
BBF-W,M BM-W HS-W,M
(German) MH-W,M OTJ-W,M
Did You Feed My Cow?
NF-W
Did You Hear How Dey Crucified
My Lord?
RF-W,M
Did You Steal My Money?
WA-W,M
Did You Stop to Pray This Morning
HLS7-W,M
Did Your Mother Come from
Ireland?
RW-W,M TI1-W,M UFB-W,M
Diddle Diddle Dumpling
HS-W,M
Didja' Ever
SRE1-W,M
Didn't He Ramble?
FW-W
Didn't He Shine
CEM-W,M
Didn't It Rain?
NH-W,M
**Didn't It Rain? see also Oh Didn't
It Rain**
Didn't My Lord Deliver Daniel
AH-W,M AHO-W,M FW-W
OTJ-W,M WiS7-W,M
Didn't Old John
Le-W,M
Didn't We
DC-W,M GOI7-W,M GSN4-W,M
HSi-W,M On-W,M
Dido's Song
OH-W,M
Die an Old Maid
SCa-W,M
**Die Beiden Grenadiere see Two
Grenadiers**
Die Bekehrte
AS-W,M (German)

Die Finkelach
WW-W,M (Yiddish)
Die Gedanken Sind Frei
SBF-W,M SWF-W,M (German)
WSB-W,M (German)
Die Greene Koseene (My Little
Country Cousin)
MF-W,M (Yiddish Only)
Die in the Pig Pen Fighting
NF-W
Die Kleine Heerde Zeugen
AHO-W,M (German)
Die Nacht
MM-W,M (German)
Die Sonn Ist Wieder Aufgegangen
AHO-W,M (German)
Die Wacht Am Rhein
SiP-W,M (German)
Dieciseis Anos
TI1-W,M (Spanish Only) UFB-
W,M (Spanish Only)
Diego's Bold Shores
SA-W,M
Dies Irae, Dies Illa (Benjamin Carr)
AHO-W,M
**Diet Rite Cola Jingle see
Everybody Likes It**
Different Bites for Different Likes
GSM-W,M
Different Way
AG-W,M
Dig a Pony
TWS-W
Dig Deep Children
RTH-W
Dig It
TWS-W
Dig My Grave
AAF-W,M FW-W
Dig My Grave with a Silver Spade
LC-W
Diggin'
SSo-W,M
Digging Your Scene
TTH-W,M
Diggins, O
MSB-W
Digue Dindaine
CFS-W,M (French)
Dim Narrow Trail
SoC-W
Dimples
Mo-W,M NM-W,M OTO-W
Dinah
ASB3-W,M GSN2-W,M HS-W,M
LoS-W,M MAR-W,M Mo-W,M
NM-W,M On-W,M OTJ-W,M
TI2-W,M U-W VA-W,M
**Dinah see also I've Been Workin'
on the Railroad**
Dinah's Dinner Horn
NF-W
Ding-A-Ding-Dain-A
CFS-W,M (French)
Ding Ding Ding Dong Bell
Boo-W,M
Ding Dong
ASB3-W,M
Ding Dong Bell
OTJ-W,M SMa-W,M SOO-W,M
Ding Dong Dollar
FW-W
Ding Dong Merrily on High
GBC-W,M JOC-W,M
Ding Dong the Witch Is Dead
GG3-W,M RW-W,M THN-W,M
WO-W,M

Dinge Dong
DP-W,M
Dink's Song
FW-W
Dinky
Oz2-W,M
Dinner for One, Please James
TI1-W,M UFB-W,M
Dinner with My Friends
MF-M
Dip Your Fingers in the Water
J-W,M
Diploma
A-W,M
Dirge
MPP-W
Dirge for a Soldier
KH-W,M
Dirge of St. Malo
AL-W
Dirt Song
GO-W
Dirty Dirty Feelin'
MF-W,M
Dirty Dishes
OU-W,M
Dirty Dozens
LC-W
Dirty Gertie from Bizerte
GI-W,M GO-W
Dirty Old Egg-Sucking Dog
CSp-W,M
Dis Flower
L-W
Dis Mornin' Dis Evenin' So Soon
AmS-W,M
**Dis Mornin' Dis Evenin' So Soon
see also This Mornin' This Evenin'
So Soon**
Disappointed Fisherman
FSA1-W,M
Disappointment
SR-W,M
Disciple
SHS-W,M
Disco Baby
DDH-W,M
Disco Lady
ToO76-W,M
Disco Mickey Mouse
NI-W,M
Disco Nights
ToO79-W,M
Discontented
TW-W
Disguises
WA-W,M
Disgustingly Rich
TS-W
Dish-Washing Song
MH-W,M
Dismission of the Devil
GB-W,M
Dissertation on the State of Bliss
LSO-W Mo-W,M NM-W,M OTO-W
Dissonance
FSY-W,M
Distant Melody
Mo-W,M NM-W,M OTO-W
Distress (So Fades the Lovely,
Blooming Flow'r)
ATS-W,M SHS-W,M
Disturb Not the Plover
Boo-W,M
Dites-Moi
OTJ-W,M OTO-W SP-W,M
TI1-W,M (French) UBF-W,M

UFB-W,M (French)
Dive Ducks Dive
SOO-W,M
Divers Never Gave Nothing to the
Poor
MoM-W
Divertissement
DR-W,M
Dives and Lazarus
AFP-W GBC-W,M OB-W,M
Divide the Day
AL-W
Dividing Line
Oz4-W
Diving
SiR-W,M
Division Street Jig
E-W,M
D-I-V-O-R-C-E
TI2-W,M
Divorce
Su-W,M
Dixiana Rise
HJ-W,M
Dixie
AAP-W,M ASB5-W,M AWB-W
Bo-W CSS-W DC-W,M FM-W,M
FW-W FWS-W,M HS-W,M
HSD-W,M IHA-W,M IL-W,M
LoS-W,M MAS-W,M MF-W,M
OFS-W,M OS-W PIS-W,M
Re-W,M SiS-W SL-W SMW-W,M
SoF-W,M TF-W TH-W TI1-W,M
UFB-W,M
**Dixie see also Dixie Land, Dixie's
Land, and I Wish I Was in Dixie**
Dixie after Dark
Sta-W,M
Dixie Doodle
SiS-W
Dixie Land
AmH-W,M DE-W,M ESB-W,M
NAS-W,M OTJ-W,M RW-W,M
UF-W WiS8-W,M
Dixie Rose
ReG-W,M
Dixie the Land of King Cotton
Sin-W,M SiS-W
Dixie War Song
SiS-W
Dixieland Band
OHF-W
Dixieland Combo
NO-W,M
Dixieland Delight
EC-W,M GCM-W,M MF-W,M
Dixie's Land
AH-W,M ATS-W MPP-W PoS-
W,M SCo-W,M Sin-W,M
Dixie's Nurse
SiS-W
Dixon and Johnson
Oz1-W,M
Dizzy Miss Lizzie
GAR-W,M
Dizzy's Business
MF-M
Djerag the Shark
ATM-W,M
Do Da Day
HS-W,M
**Do Da Day see also Camptown
Races**
Do Do Do
GOB-W,M LSO-W MF-W,M
NYT-W,M OHB-W,M
Do I Hear a Waltz?

TI1-W,M UBF-W,M UFB-W,M
Do I Like It
　OGC2-W,M
Do I Love You?
　HC2-W,M ML-W,M NF-W OTO-W
Do I Love You (Because You're
　Beautiful)
　HC2-W,M OTJ-W,M OTO-W
　TI1-W,M UBF-W,M UFB-W,M
Do I Trust You
　VB-W,M
Do It ('Til You're Satisfied)
　SoH-W,M ToO76-W,M
Do It Again
　NYT-M ReG-W,M RoE-W,M
Do It Again a Little Bit Slower
　THN-W,M
Do It Any Way You Wanna
　DDH-W,M
Do It for Love
　TTH-W,M
Do It in the Name of Love
　DP-W,M
Do It or Die
　ToO79-W,M
Do Lord
　MAR-W,M SNS-W
Do Lord Remember Me
　BDW-W,M WN-W,M
Do My Brudder O Yes Yes Member
　NSS-W
Do My Johnny Booker
　RW-W,M
Do Not Care
　UF-W,M
Do Not Disturb
　SRE2-W,M
Do Not Forsake Me
　GG2-W,M RT5-W,M
**Do Not Forsake Me see also High
　Noon**
Do Not Go My Love
　FSY-W,M
Do Not Grieve for Thy Dear Mother
　SiS-W
Do Not Mortgage the Farm
　GrM-W,M
Do Not Rumple My Topknot
　SR-W,M
Do Nothin' Till You Hear from Me
　DJ-W,M GMD-W,M GSN3-W,M
　MF-W,M RW-W,M ToS-W,M
Do-Re-Mi
　DBC-W,M FPS-W,M HC1-W,M
　OTJ-W,M OTO-W RW-W,M
　SM-W,M TI1-W,M UBF-W,M
　UFB-W,M
Do-Re-Mi-Fa
　Boo-W,M
Do 'Round My Lindy
　FVV-W,M
Do Something Now
　VB-W,M
Do They Know It's Christmas?
　BCS-W,M
Do They Miss Me at Home?
　Oz4-W
Do They Miss Me in the Trench?
　SiS-W
Do They Think of Me at Home?
　AmH-W,M HSD-W,M WiS8-W,M
Do Wah Diddy
　ERM-W,M GAR-W,M
Do What the Spirit Say Do
　SFF-W,M
Do What You Do
　ReG-W,M

Do Ya
　ELO-W,M
Do You Believe in Magic
　MCG-W,M THN-W,M TI2-W,M
Do You Believe the Johnson Line?
　VS-W,M
Do You Care?
　OnT1-W,M
Do You Ever Dream of Vienna
　LMS-W,M
Do You Ever Think of Me
　GSN2-W,M HLS2-W,M RW-W,M
Do You Fear the Wind?
　MML-W,M
Do You Hear the People Sing
　UBF-W,M
Do You Know the Way to San
　Jose
　BDF-W,M HD-W,M MF-W,M
　OTJ-W,M
Do You Know What It Means to
　Miss New Orleans
　Mo-W,M NM-W,M OTO-W
　TI1-W,M UFB-W,M
Do You Know Where You're Going
　To?
　DPE-W,M HFH-W,M MF-W,M
　TOM-W,M ToO76-W,M
Do You Know You Are My
　Sunshine
　CMG-W,M PoG-W,M WG-W,M
**Do You Love Me (from Sunny) see
　D'ye Love Me**
Do You Love Me? (Harnick/Bock)
　OTO-W TW-W UBF-W,M
Do You Remember
　WGB/P-W,M
Do You Think There's a Prairie in
　Heaven?
　HOH-W
Do You Wanna Dance?
　RB-W
Do You Wanna Go to Heaven
　TOH-W,M
Do You Want to Dance?
　DRR-W,M FRH-W,M On-W,M
Do You Want to Know a Secret?
　BBe-W,M ILS-W,M RW-W,M
　RY-W,M RYT-W,M TWS-W
Do Your Ears Hang Low?
　CSS-W
Dock of the Bay
　GSN4-W,M RB-W TOC82-W,M
Doctor Doctor
　TI2-W,M
Dr. Eisenbart
　SiB-W,M
Dr. Freud
　FW-W Mo-W,M NM-W,M OTO-W
　PO-W,M WF-W,M
Dr. Hekok Jig
　DE-W,M
Doctor Ironbeard
　ASB5-W,M
Doctor Is In
　YG-W,M
Dr. Jimmy
　WA-W,M
**Dr. Kildare (Theme) see Three
　Stars Will Shine Tonight**
Doctor Lawyer Indian Chief
　Mo-W,M NM-W,M OTO-W
Doctor Monro
　ESU-W
**Dr. Pepper Jingle see It Tastes Too
　Good to Be True, Most
　Misunderstood Soft Drink, and**

Most Original Soft Drink Ever
Dr. Robert
　TWS-W
**Doctor Zhivago (Lara's Theme) see
　Somewhere My Love**
Doctor's Orders
　TTH-W,M
Dodger
　OA1-W,M SWF-W,M
Dodger Song
　FW-W PSN-W,M
Dodgin' Joe
　SoC-W
Doer of the Word
　VB-W,M
Doers of the Word
　GH-W,M
Does Anybody Really Know What
　Time It Is?
　GOI7-W,M
Does Fort Worth Ever Cross Your
　Mind
　AWS-W,M
Does It Make Any Diff'rence to
　You?
　BSG-W,M BSP-W,M
Does Jesus Care
　AME-W,M OM-W,M
Does Money Talk?
　NF-W
Does the Spearmint Lose Its Flavor
　on the Bed Post Overnight
　TI2-W,M
Does Your Chewing Gum Lose Its
　Flavor
　NoS-W,M
Does Your Heart Beat for Me
　TI2-W,M
Doffing Mistress
　VP-W,M
Dog and Gun
　BSC-W,M DD-W,M FMT-W
　FoM-W,M SCa-W,M
Dog Catcher's Child
　HAS-W,M
Dog Dog
　SFF-W,M
Dog Eat Dog
　Mo-W,M NM-W,M OTO-W
Dog Me Around
　DBL-W
**Doggie in the Window see How
　Much Is That Doggie in the
　Window**
Doggie's Bath
　MH-W,M
Doggone It Baby I'm in Love
　OGC1-W,M
Dogie Song
　Bo-W,M HS-W,M SL-W,M
**Dogie Song see also Git Along
　Little Dogies and Whoopee Ti-Yi-
　Yo**
Dog's Appetite
　ASB3-W,M
Dogs Kids Love to Bite
　GSM-W,M
Dogs of Alabama
　RBO-W,M
Doin' the Best I Can
　SRE1-W,M
Doin' the Crazy Walk
　GMD-W,M
Doing Good
　Mo-W,M NM-W,M OTO-W
Doing My Time
　BIS-W,M

Doing Nothing but Sing
SCL-W,M
Doing What We Do Best
BNG-W,M
Dolcy Jones
FHR-W,M SSFo-W,M
Doll
SCL-W,M SD-W,M
Doll Dance
GG5-W,M TI2-W,M
Dolly and Her Mama
OTJ-W,M
Dolly Day
FHR-W,M SSF-W,M SSFo-W,M
Dolly Lullaby
ASB1-W,M
Dolly Mois
SGT-W,M
Dolly Sisters (Theme) see I Can't Begin to Tell You
Dolly's Brae
VP-W,M
Dolly's Lullaby
MH-W,M
Dolores
AT-W,M OTO-W
Dolores (Love Theme from Pirates)
TTH-W,M (Spanish Only)
Dom Pedro
SA-W,M
Domestic Workers' Song
LW-W,M
Domesticated Artillery Man
GO-W
Domine Fili Dei Vivi
Boo-W,M (Latin Only)
Domine Fili Unigenite
SiM-W,M (Latin)
Dominique
MF-W,M OTJ-W,M RDF-W,M
(French) RW-W,M SSN-W,M
(French) TI1-W,M UFB-W,M
Domino
MF-W,M TI2-W,M
Don Jose Ole
LaS-W,M
Don Ramon
LA-W,M (Spanish)
Dona Ana Esta Aqui
LA-W,M (Spanish)
Dona Anna
LA-W,M (Spanish)
Dona Nobis (Round)
OHO-W,M OTJ-W,M (Latin Only)
PSN-W,M (Latin)
Dona Nobis Pacem (Round)
BM-W Boo-W,M (Latin Only) HS-
W,M (Latin Only) LMR-W,M (Latin
Only) MAS-W,M (Latin Only) MG-
W,M (Latin Only) SBF-W,M (Latin
Only) SCL-W,M (Latin Only)
Don'cha Bother Me
RoS-W,M
Don'cha Go 'Way Mad
MF-W,M
Doncha Love Me No Mo'
NeF-W,M
Donde Vas Alfonso Doce?
LA-W,M (Spanish)
Donderback's Machine
Oz3-W
Done Found the Way at Last see Dun Found de Way at Las'
Done Laid Around
WSB-W,M
Done wid Driber's Dribin'
AAF-W,M NSS-W,M

Donec A Boire
Boo-W,M (French Only)
Doney Gal
FW-W,M HWS-W,M LT-W,M
VA-W,M WU-W,M
Donkey
SOO-W,M
Donkey, The
BM-W,M HS-W,M
Donkey Is Jackass
LaS-W,M
Donkey Riding
HS-W,M SCL-W,M SiR-W,M
Donkey's Carol
GBC-W,M
Donna
BNG-W,M H-W,M HR-W,M
MF-W,M
Donna Che Un Sasso Prese
Boo-W,M (Italian Only)
Donna E Mobile see La Donna E Mobile
Donnelly and Cooper
VP-W,M
Don't
GAR-W,M MF-W,M SRE2-W,M
Don't Ask Me Questions
NF-W
Don't Be a Dropout
RB-W
Don't Be a Woman If You Can
LSO-W
Don't Be Angry
WDS-W,M
Don't Be Ashamed of Your Age
OGC1-W,M
Don't Be Cruel
CFB-W,M DRR-W,M ILF-W,M RW-
W,M RY-W,M RYT-W,M TI1-W,M
UFB-W,M
Don't Be Idle
FHR-W,M
Don't Be That Way
GG5-W,M RW-W,M Sta-W,M
Don't Be Weary Traveller
NSS-W RF-W,M
Don't Bet Your Money on de
Shanghai
FHR-W,M SSFo-W,M
Don't Blame Me
GG4-W,M GSO-W,M HLS2-W,M
OP2-W,M RW-W,M
Don't Bother Me
TI2-W,M TWS-W
Don't Bother Me, I Can't Cope
DB-W,M
Don't Break the Heart That Loves
You
ILS-W,M MF-W,M
Don't Bring Lulu
MF-W,M MR-W,M OHB-W,M
Don't Call de Roll
RF-W,M
Don't Cheat in Our Home Town
TI2-W,M
Don't Close Dose Gates
SSo-W,M
Don't Come Oh Lord
RTH-W
Don't Count the Rainy Days
TOC83-W,M
Don't Count Your Chickens
Oz3-W
Don't Cry for Me Argentina
DBC-W,M TI2-W,M UBF-W,M
Don't Cry Joe
MF-W,M

Don't Cry Lady
PO-W,M
Don't Cry Out Loud
MF-W,M TI1-W,M ToO79-W,M
UFB-W,M
Don't Dilly Dally on the Way
U-W
Don't Disturb This Groove
CFB-W,M
Don't Do Anything I Wouldn't Do
WDS-W,M
Don't Explain
LSB-W,M ToS-W,M
Don't Fear the Reaper see Reaper
Don't Fence Me In
FC-W,M MF-W,M
Don't Forget Me (When I'm Gone)
TTH-W,M
Don't Forget Me, Little Darling
Oz4-W
Don't Forget 127th Street
Mo-W,M NM-W,M OTO-W
Don't Forget the Lilac Bush
SSA-W,M
Don't Forget the Union Label
AL-W
Don't Get Around Much Anymore
BBB-W,M CS-W,M DJ-W,M
GG5-W,M GMD-W,M GSF-W,M
GSN3-W,M HLS3-W,M MF-W,M
NK-W,M RW-W,M
Don't Get Weary
RF-W,M WN-W,M
Don't Give Up the Ship
MR-W,M
Don't Go Away without Jesus
BSG-W,M BSP-W,M
Don't Go Breaking My Heart
TI2-W,M
Don't Go Out into the Rain
RW-W,M THN-W,M
Don't Go Out Tonight, My Darling
Oz2-W
Don't Go Ridin' down That Old
Texas Trail
FVV-W,M
Don't Go, Tommy
Oz4-W
Don't I Wish I Was a Single Girl
Again
LW-W,M
Don't It Break Your Heart
TOC82-W,M
Don't It Make My Brown Eyes Blue
CMG-W,M GrS-W,M HLS9-W,M
RW-W,M
Don't Just Stand There
OGC1-W,M
Don't Laugh at Me
DBL-W
Don't Leave Me Lord
RF-W,M
Don't Leave Me Now
SRE1-W,M
Don't Let Go the Coat
WA-W,M
Don't Let Me Be Lonely Tonight
GrS-W,M
Don't Let Me Down
BBe-W,M Be2-W,M SwS-W,M
TWS-W
Don't Let the Deal Go Down
ITP-W,M
Don't Let the Rain Fall Down on
Me
MCG-W,M THN-W,M
Don't Let the Stars Get in Your

Eyes
RW-W,M
Don't Let the Sun Catch You
Crying
TI2-W,M
Don't Let the Sun Go Down on Me
GrS-W,M TI2-W,M
Don't Let Your Deal Go Down
BSo-W,M FW-W
Don't Lie to Me
RoS-W,M
Don't Like Goodbyes
Mo-W,M NM-W,M OTO-W
UBF-W,M
Don't Look at Me
FO-W,M
Don't Look at Me That Way
TW-W
Don't Look Back
VB-W,M
Don't Look Now
OGC1-W,M
Don't Lose Your Eye
DBL-W
Don't Love Me Like Othello
TS-W
Don't Make Me Over
HD-W,M MF-W,M
Don't Marry Me
UBF-W,M
Don't Never Git One Woman on
Your Mind
NH-W
Don't Never Marry a Drunkard
Oz2-W
Don't Never Trust a Sailor
Oz4-W
Don't Nobody Bring Me No Bad
News
Wi-W,M
Don't Pass Me By
TWS-W
Don't Plan on Sleeping Tonight
TOC83-W,M
Don't Put Her Down, You Helped
Put Her There
BSo-W,M
Don't Rain on My Parade
HC1-W,M HSi-W,M TI1-W,M
UBF-W,M UFB-W,M
Don't Rob Another Man's Castle
OGC1-W,M
Don't Run Away
VB-W,M
Don't Say Goodbye If You Love
Me
SF-W,M
Don't Say No Tonight
EC-W,M
Don't Sell Him Any More Rum
Oz2-W,M
Don't Send My Boy to Berlin
AF-W
Don't Shed a Tear
CFB-W,M
Don't Shoot the Salt, Peter
GI-W
Don't Sing before Breakfast
NF-W
Don't Sing Love Songs
FW-W
Don't Sit under the Apple Tree
FPS-W,M GSF-W,M MF-W,M
RW-W,M
Don't Sleep in the Subway
TI2-W,M
Don't Sleep Too Long

Le-W,M
Don't Slip
SiB-W,M
Don't Stand So Close to Me
TTH-W,M
Don't Stand Still
HCY-W,M
Don't Start Me to Talkin'
DBL-W
Don't Stay after Ten
Oz3-W,M
Don't Stay Away (O Brother! Don't
Stay Away)
VA-W,M
Don't Stay Away ('Till Love Grows
Cold)
OGC1-W,M
Don't Take Your Guns to Town
OGC2-W,M TI1-W,M UFB-W,M
Don't Take Your Love from Me
HLS9-W,M TI1-W,M UFB-W,M
Don't Tax the Millionaire
AL-W
Don't Tell All You Know
NF-W
Don't Tell Mama
C-W,M
Don't Tell Me Your Name
TW-W
Don't Tell the Society
ESU-W
Don't the Moon Look Pretty
LC-W
Don't Think the Future
GSM-W,M
Don't This Road Look Rough and
Rocky
BSo-W,M
Don't Trifle on Your Sweetheart
OGC2-W,M
Don't Turn Around
AFP-W
Don't Underestimate My Love for
You
EC-W,M GCM-W,M
Don't Wait 'til the Night before
Christmas
CSF-W
Don't Wake Up the Kids
HR-W
Don't Walk Away
TTH-W,M
Don't Want to Go Home
SiR-W,M
Don't Worry, Be Happy
CFB-W,M
Don't Worry 'bout Me
TI2-W,M
Don't Worry 'bout Me Baby
TOC82-W,M
Don't You Be Like the Foolish
Virgin
AHO-W,M
**Don't You Bother Me see Don'cha
Bother Me**
**Don't You Go Away Mad see
Don'cha Go 'Way Mad**
Don't You Go Tommy
SY-W,M
Don't You Grieve after Me
BDW-W,M Oz2-W,M
Don't You Just Know It
FRH-W,M
Don't You Know
HRB2-W,M
Don't You Know How Much I Love
You

HRB1-W,M TOC83-W,M
Don't You Let Nobody Turn You
Around
FN-W,M
**Don't You Love Me No More see
Doncha Love Me No Mo'**
Don't You Miss the Train
TW-W
Don't You Push Me
PSN-W,M
Don't You See
AN-W
Don't You See That Ship A-Sailin'
NSS-W
Don't You See What a Shape I'm
In
LC-W
Don't You View Dat Ship A-Come
A-Sailin'
RF-W,M
Don't You Want Me
CFB-W,M MF-W,M
Don't You Weep after Me
FW-W
Don't You Wish You Were in
Hebben?
BDW-W,M
Don't You Write Her Off
ToO79-W,M
Don't Your Mem'ry Ever Sleep at
Night
TOC83-W,M
Doo Doo Doo Doo Doo
RoS-W,M
Doodle Doo Doo
CS-W,M GST-W,M RW-W,M
STW-W,M TI2-W,M
Doodlin'
MF-M
Doodlin' Song
Mo-W,M NM-W,M
Doom of Floyd Collins
BMM-W
Door Is Open
BSG-W,M BSP-W,M
Door of My Dreams
RM-W,M
Doorstep to Heaven
OGC1-W,M
Dorothy (Old English Dance)
AmH-M
Dorthula's Song
SNS-W
Dose for the Tories
SI-W
Dose of Rock and Roll
ToO76-W,M
Dost Thou Know That Sweet Land
TH-W
Dost Thou Love Me, Sister Ruth
HSD-W,M
Dost Thou Not Remember, Ned
Boo-W,M
D'ou Viens-tu Bergere
CE-W,M (French) CFS-W,M
(French) CUP-W,M (French Only)
FSO-W,M (French)
Double Breasted Mansion of the
Square
SoC-W
Double or Nothing
HFH-W,M
Double Your Pleasure
GSM-W,M
**Doublemint Chewing Gum Jingle
see Double Your Pleasure and
Doublemint Will Do It**

Doublemint Will Do It
TI1-W,M UFB-W,M
Doubly Good to You
VB-W,M
Douglas Tender and True
HSD-W,M
Douglas Tragedy
ITP-W
Doug's Communique
AF-W
Douze Mulets
CaF-W (French Only)
Dove (La Paloma)
AmH-W,M BSC-W FSY-W,M
(Spanish) LMR-W,M MF-W,M
MH-W,M MML-W,M (Spanish)
OTJ-W,M SL-W,M TI1-M UFB-M
WiS8-W,M
Dove of Peace
SHS-W,M
Doves
ASB5-W,M
Dowie Dens of Yarrow
FW-W
Down among the Cane Brakes
FHR-W,M SSF-W,M SSFo-W,M
Down among the Dead Men
CSo-W,M OH-W,M
Down among the Sheltering Palms
BH-W,M GG5-W,M HLS1-W,M
MF-W,M RW-W,M TI1-W,M
UFB-W,M
Down Argentine Way
GSF-W,M
Down at Carmel
MML-W,M
Down at the Cross
AME-W,M
Down at the Old Bull and Bush
U-W
Down at the Station
MES2-W,M OTJ-W,M RSL-W,M
Down by the Greenwood Side
Oz1-W,M SCa-W,M
Down by the Lazy River
BR-W,M
Down by the O-hi-o
OAP-W,M TI1-W,M UFB-W,M
Down by the Old Mill Stream
FPS-W,M GSN1-W,M IL-W,M
OAP-W,M RoE-W,M
Down by the River
OTO-W RF-W,M
Down by the Riverside
FWS-W,M IF-W,M IL-W,M
IPH-W,M MAB1-W,M MF-W,M
MSA1-W OAP-W,M OBN-W,M
OTJ-W,M TI1-M UFB-M WN-W,M
Down by the Sally Gardens
FGM-W,M FW-W
Down by the Sea-Shore
Oz1-W,M
Down by the Side of the River
GrG-W,M
Down by the Station
Bo-W,M CSS-W IL-W,M STS-W,M
Down by the Stream
BSB-W,M
Down by the Waterfall
LC-W
Down Bye Street
NA-W,M
Down Came an Angel
AH-W,M
Down Child
DBL-W
Down Down

RSL-W,M
Down, Down Derry Down
AmS-W,M
Down, Down, Down Derry Down
Oz3-W
Down Home
P-W,M
Down Home Girl
DBL-W
Down Home Town
ELO-W,M
Down in a Coal Mine
AL-W ATS-W BH-W,M
FSA1-W,M HS-W,M SWF-W,M
Down in a Dungeon Deep
Boo-W,M
Down in a Licensed Saloon
Oz2-W
Down in Alabam'
PoS-W,M
Down in Arkansas
Oz3-W
Down in Arkansaw
GeS-W,M
Down in Dixie
SL-W,M
Down in Mississippi
DBL-W
Down in Mobile
TF-W,M
Down in the Alley
HRB3-W,M
Down in the Coal Mine
IHA-W,M
Down in the Depths on the
Ninetieth Floor
ML-W,M OTO-W UBF-W,M
Down in the Forest
Gu-W,M
Down in the Hole
RoS-W,M
Down in the Lonesome Garden
NF-W
Down in the Tules
HB-W,M
Down in the Valley
ASB6-W,M ATS-W,M BF-W,M
BIS-W,M BM-W BMC-W,M
Bo-W,M BSC-W FG1-W,M
FSB1-W,M FU-W,M FuB-W,M
FW-W FWS-W,M GuC-W,M
HS-W,M IL-W,M IPH-W,M
LH-W,M LoS-W,M LT-W,M
MAB1-W,M MAR-W,M MAS-W,M
MES1-W,M MES2-W,M MG-W,M
MSA1-W MU-W,M OFS-W,M
OTJ-W,M Oz4-W,M RW-W,M
SBF-W,M SG-W,M UF-W,M
VA-W,M WU-W,M
Down in the Valley to Pray
WN-W,M
Down in the Wilderness
PIS-W,M
Down in the Willow Garden
BSo-W,M FG2-W,M FSt-W,M
FW-W
Down in Yon Forest
FW-W GBC-W,M OB-W,M
Down Mobile
BSB-W,M LMR-W,M SL-W,M
Down on MacConnachy Square
HSS-W,M HST-W,M OU-W,M
Down on Me
MCG-W,M RYT-W,M SFF-W,M
Down on Penny's Farm
SWF-W,M
Down on Roberts' Farm

AFP-W
Down on the Banks of the Ohio
Oz2-W,M
Down on the Big Ranch
LA-W,M (Spanish)
Down on the Corner
TOC83-W,M
Down on the Pichelo Farm
Oz3-W
Down on 33rd and 3rd (Thoidy
Thoid and Thoid)
MF-W,M
Down She Comes All Dressed in
Silk
OTJ-W,M
Down South
FSA2-W,M
Down the Field
CoS-W,M IL-W,M
Down the Line
Mo-W,M
Down the Mother Volga
RSC-W,M (Russian Only)
Down the Ohio
TMA-W,M
Down the River
MAS-W,M MG-W,M Oz3-W
SCL-W,M
Down the River of Golden Dreams
CS-W,M
Down the Road
BIS-W,M BSo-W,M GCM-W,M
RW-W,M
Down the Ruhr Valley
AF-W
Down the Stream
VA-W,M
Down to the Sacred Wave
AHO-W,M
Down Went McGinty
ATS-W BH-W,M EFS-W,M FSN-
W,M FSTS-W,M HAS-W,M OHG-
W,M STR-W,M
Down with Darkness
SSe-W,M
Down with It
VP-W
Down with Love
UBF-W,M
Down with the Money King
AL-W
Down with the Old Canoe
FSSC-W,M
Down with the Traitor's Serpent
Flag
SiS-W
Down Yonder
FVV-W,M
Downfall of Paris
SG-W,M
Downfall of Tythes at Slievenamon
VP-W
Downtown
RDT-W,M TI2-W,M
Downtown Suzie
RoS-W,M
Downward Road Is Crowded
NH-W
**Downward Road Is Crowded see
also Oh, de Downward Road Is
Crowded**
Downy Cheek
ESU-W
Doxology
AME-W,M AmH-W,M GH-W,M
HF-W,M HS-W,M IH-M JBF-W,M
NAS-W,M

Speeding)
ASB4-W,M
Drummer Boy, The (from War
Came Marching Gaily)
ASB5-W,M
Drummer Boy of Antietam
SiS-W
Drummer Boy of Shiloh
Oz2-W Sin-W,M
Drummond
SHS-W,M
Drunk As I Could Be
SRS-W,M
Drunk Last Night
FW-W IL-W,M
Drunkard
Oz2-W,M TBF-W,M
Drunkard's Child
ITP-W,M Oz2-W SY-W,M
Drunkard's Doom
AmS-W,M BSC-W,M FW-W
Drunkard's Dream
BSC-W ITP-W,M Oz2-W,M
SCa-W,M
Drunkard's Hell
Oz2-W,M
Drunkard's Hiccoughs
Oz3-W,M
Drunkard's Home Made Sweet
ESU-W
Drunkard's Horse
Oz2-W,M
Drunkard's Lone Child
Oz2-W,M TMA-W,M
Drunkard's Ragged Wee Ane
TBF-W,M
Drunkard's Song
BMM-W SCa-W,M
Drunkard's Story
Oz2-W
Drunkard's Wife
Oz2-W
Drunken Pilot
AF-W
Drunken Sailor
GuC-W,M IL-W,M RSW-W,M
RW-W,M SA-W,M TMA-M
**Drunken Sailor see also What Are
You Going to Do with a Drunken
Sailor? and What Shall We Do
with the Drunken Sailor**
Dry Bones
BeB-W,M FoS-W,M Me-W,M
Dry Bones Goin' Rise
NH-W
Dry Bones Goin' t' Rise Ag'in
BDW-W,M
Dry Dock Omnibus
ESU-W
**Du Bist Wie Eine Blume see Thou
Art So Like a Flower**
Du, Du, Liegst Mir Im Herzen
FW-W (German Only) GuC-W,M
(German) OFS-W,M (German
Only)
**Du, Du, Liegst Mir Im Herzen see
also Home (Home, Why Did I
Leave Thee?)**
**Du Kannst Nicht Treu Sein see You
Can't Be True, Dear**
Dublin
SHS-W,M
Dublin Bay
Oz4-W,M
Dublin Jack of All Trades
IFM-W
Duchess

LMR-W,M
Duck and the Hen
MH-W,M
Duck Dance Songs (Creek Indian)
IF-M
Duck in the Meadow
BMC-W,M
Ducks
ASB1-W,M SCL-W,M
Ducks Are Flying
RuS-W,M (Russian)
Ducks in the Mill Pond
Oz3-W
Dudley
SHS-W,M
Duelin' Banjo
BR-M On-M OPS-M
Duet
ASB5-W,M
Duermete, Nino Lindo
FW-W (Spanish)
Dugway Lament
SoC-W
Duke A-Riding
SG-W,M
Duke Marlborough
NAS-W,M
Duke of Earl
DRR-W,M HR-W TI1-W,M
TRR-W,M UFB-W,M
Duke of Marlborough
GUM2-W,M
Duke Street
SHS-W,M
Duke William's Frolic
MSB-W
**Dukes of Hazzard Theme see Good
Ol' Boys**
Dulcinea
MLM-W,M
Dumb Wife
UF-W,M
Dumb Wife Cured
Oz3-W,M
Dumbarton's Drums
FW-W
Dummy Line
TMA-W,M
Dump the Bosses off Your Back
AFP-W
Dun Found de Way at Las'
BDW-W,M
Duncan
PS-W,M
Duncan and Brady
Le-W,M
Dundai
SBF-W,M (Hebrew Only)
Dundee
NAS-W,M
Dunderbeck
FW-W OHO-W,M
D'une Rive Lointeine
CaF-W,M (French Only)
Dungaree Doll
FRH-W,M TI2-W,M
Dunlap's Creek
SHS-W,M
Durazno see El Durazno
Durham Lockout
BB-W
Dusky Stevedore
Mo-W,M NM-W,M
Dust
FC-W,M
Dust an' Ashes
RF-W,M

Dust Pneumonia Blues
AFB-W,M
Dutch Carol
OB-W,M
Dutch Company
HSD-W,M
Dutch Dance
ASB4-W,M
Dutch National Hymn
AmH-W,M (Dutch)
Dutch National Song
HSD-W,M
Dutch Song
SBA-W
Dutch Warbler
HAS-W,M
Dweller in My Deathless Dreams
EL-W,M
D'ye Love Me
Su-W,M
**Dyevooshkoo Chakoi Zovoot see
"Seagull" the Maiden Is Named**
Dying Boy
Oz4-W
Dying British Sergeant
SI-W,M
Dying Brother
BSC-W
Dying Californian
FMT-W Oz2-W,M
Dying Christian's Last Farewell
BC1-W,M
Dying Coon
MPP-W
Dying Cowboy (As I Walked Out
on the Streets of Laredo)
SCa-W,M SoC-W TBF-W,M
**Dying Cowboy (As I Walked Out
on the Streets of Laredo) see also
Cowboy's Lament and Streets of
Laredo**
Dying Cowboy (Oh Bury Me Not
on the Lone Prairie)
Bo-W,M BSC-W CA-W,M
HOH-W,M ITP-W,M MHB-W,M
NAS-W,M OTJ-W,M TH-W,M
**Dying Cowboy (Oh Bury Me Not
on the Lone Prairie) see also Oh
Bury Me Not on the Lone Prairie**
Dying Cowboy (The Sun Was
Settin' in the West)
Oz2-W,M
Dying Drunkard
ESU-W
Dying Flag Bearer
SiS-W
Dying Girl
FVV-W,M Oz4-W,M
Dying Girl's Message
Oz4-W,M
Dying Hobo
FMT-W ITP-W,M LSR-W,M
Oz4-W
Dying Knight's Farewell
SG-W,M
Dying Lineman
SoC-W
Dying Message
BSC-W
Dying Nun
BSC-W,M Oz4-W,M
Dying on the Battlefield
SiS-W
Dying Poet
AmH-M
Dying Polly
SCa-W,M

Dying Preacher
Oz4-W,M
Dying Ranger
HB-W,M SoC-W
Dying Skier
SoC-W
Dying Soldier
Oz2-W,M SiS-W
Dying Stockman
ATM-W,M
Dying Volunteer
HSD-W,M SiS-W
Dying Volunteer of the 6th
Massachusetts
SiS-W
Dying Youth
Oz4-W,M
Dynasty (Theme)
TV-M
Dynomite Part 1
DDH-W,M

E

E Pari Ra
SNZ-W,M (Maori)
E Pluribus Unum
ATS-W
E Tan' Patat' La Cuit'
CSD-W,M (French)
E Tan Patat' La Cuit' see also Et
Tan Patate La Cuite
Each and Every Day of the Year
RoS-W,M
Each Minute I Look at You
LA-W,M (Spanish)
Each Step I Take
BSG-W,M BSP-W,M JBF-W,M
Each Tomorrow Morning
Mo-W,M OTO-W
Eagle and Me
TW-W
Eagle and the Hawk
PoG-W,M
Eagle Song
VB-W,M
Eagles They Fly High
PO-W,M
Eamann An Chnoic
IS-W,M (Gaelic Only)
Earl Brand
BT-W,M FMT-W FW-W
Earl of Moray
IS-W,M
Early
SCa-W,M
Early Aborts
AF-W
Early and Late
FSA2-W,M
Early Autumn
DJ-W,M MF-W,M TI1-W,M
UFB-W,M
Early Autumn Christmas Card
OHF-W
Early Days of Spring
ASB5-W,M
Early, Early in the Spring
BSC-W Oz1-W,M SCa-W
Early Frost
ASB4-W,M
Early in de Mornin'
NH-W
Early in the Mornin'
LC-W
Early in the Morning

TI2-W,M
Early in the Spring
FMT-W SCa-W,M
Early Mornin' Rain
DPE-W,M MF-W,M
Early Morning
DBL-W
Early One Morning
CSo-W,M FW-W Gu-W,M
HS-W,M LMR-W,M LTL-W,M
OH-W,M OTJ-W,M
Early Spring
MH-W,M
Early to Bed
HS-W,M NAS-W,M
Early to Bed and Early to Rise
Boo-W,M
Earsdon Sword Dance Song
BB-W
Earth Angel
DRR-W,M ERM-W,M FRH-W,M
GAR-W,M MF-W,M
Earth Is Full
SHP-W,M
Earth Now Is Green
ER-W,M
Earth Rejoice
MG-W,M
Earth with All That Dwell Therein
Hy-W,M
Earthly Friends
OB-W,M
Ease On down the Road
BNG-W,M EY-W,M HFH-W,M
MF-W,M TOM-W,M Wi-W,M
Ease That Trouble in the Mind
Oz2-W
East of Eden (Theme)
HFH-M
East of the Sun (and West of the
Moon)
HLS2-W,M RW-W,M TI1-W,M
UFB-W,M
East Ohio Miners' Strike
AFP-W
East St. Louis
B-W,M
East Side, West Side
LoS-W,M
East Side, West Side see also
Sidewalks of New York
East Virginia
FG1-W,M FW-W
East Virginia Blues
BIS-W,M RW-W,M
Eastbound Train
LSR-W,M
Easter
SiR-W,M
Easter (The Bells in Ev'ry Steeple
Chime)
ASB6-W,M
Easter (From Ev'ry Heart a Song
Pours Out)
FSA2-W,M
Easter (Is a Happy Time)
FF-W
Easter (Now the Long Cold Night,
So Deep, So Dark)
SL-W,M
Easter Anthem
SHS-W,M
Easter Bells
SiR-W,M
Easter Canticle
MU-W,M
Easter Carol

GBC-W,M OB-W,M
Easter Day Carol
GBC-W,M
Easter Egg
SOO-W,M
Easter Eggs (Give to Him That
Begs)
OB-W,M
Easter Eggs (Red Eggs for Easter)
AST-W,M
Easter Eggs (What a Pretty Sight)
MH-W,M
Easter Eggs Are Rolling
HSA-W,M
Easter Lilies
OTJ-W,M
Easter Song
VB-W,M
Easter Time (Flowers Bloom at
Easter Time)
SOO-W,M
Easter Time (Is Here Again)
MH-W,M
Eastern and Western Love
DS-W,M
Eastern Gate
HHa-W,M
Easy and Familiar Lesson for Two
Performers on One Piano Forte
BC1-M
Easy Come Easy Go
MF-W,M
Easy Does It
FG2-M
Easy Living
LM-W,M
Easy Lovin'
OTO-W
Easy Loving
CMG-W,M GOI7-W,M HLS9-W,M
N-W,M RW-W,M
Easy on the Eyes
OGC2-W,M
Easy Question
SRE1-W,M
Easy Rider
FW-W LC-W Le-W,M TO-W,M
Easy Street
RW-W,M TI2-W,M UBF-W,M
Easy to Be Hard
H-W,M RY-W,M RYT-W,M
Easy to Love
HC1-W,M HFH-W,M ML-W,M
OTO-W TI1-W,M UFB-W,M
Easy to Please
TTH-W,M
Eat a Little Something
TW-W
Eat Drink and Be Merry
CMF-W,M
Eating Goober Peas
HAS-W,M MAS-W,M PSN-W,M
Eating Goober Peas see also
Goober Peas
Eating Out of Your Hand
BSo-W,M
Ebb Tide
GG4-W,M GSN3-W,M HLS5-W,M
RT6-W,M RW-W,M THN-W,M
Ebony and Ivory
TI2-W,M
Ebony Eyes
HR-W
Echo
MES1-W,M MES2-W,M
Echo (Beattie/Wolverton)
ASB3-W,M

Echo (Winthrop/Loomis)
  SL-W,M
Echo, The (Kathleen Uhler)
  SMa-W,M
Echo Boy
  FSA1-W,M
Echo Canon
  CSB-W,M
Echo of Your Footsteps
  OGC1-W,M
Echoes
  FSA1-W,M
Echoes of Harlem
  GMD-W,M
Echoes of the Ballroom
  AmH-M
Echoing Horn
  MPP-W,M
Ecossaises
  ASB1-M
Ecumenical March
  PO-W,M
Ed Hawkins---Murderer
  BMM-W,M
Ed Hawkins' Piece
  BMM-W
Eddie My Love
  FRH-W,M
Eddy Jones
  NH-W
Eddystone Light
  FW-W OU-W,M PSN-W,M
  WSB-W,M
Edelweiss
  DBC-W,M HC1-W,M OTJ-W,M
  OTO-W RW-W,M SM-W,M
  TI1-W,M UBF-W,M UFB-W,M
Eden of Love
  SHS-W,M
Edinburgh Town
  FMT-W
Edna's Song
  BT-W,M
Edom
  SHS-W,M
Edson's Raiders
  GI-W
Educated Feller
  SoC-W
Edward
  AA-W,M BT-W,M FMT-W
  FSSC-W,M FW-W SCa-W,M
  TBF-W,M
Edward Hollander
  BSC-W,M
Eelam More Jig
  DE-W,M
Eency Weency Spider
  FP-W,M HS-W,M OTJ-W,M
  SOO-W,M
Ef de Lord Calls You
  RTH-W
Ef My Mudder Will Go
  WN-W,M
Ef You Want to Get to Hebben
  RF-W,M
Eggs and Marrowbone
  FG2-W,M FW-W LW-W,M
Eglatine
  FSA2-W,M
Egmont (Overture)
  LMR-M
Eh Cumpari
  RW-W,M (Italian Only)
Eh Ma Blanche Chanterai-Je
  CaF-W (French Only)
Eh My Little Boy

SNS-W
Eho Eho
  F2-W,M (French)
Eia Eia
  OB-W,M
Eight and Sixty Thousand
  AL-W
Eight Bells
  FSA2-W,M RSW-W,M SaS-W,M
Eight Days a Week
  BBe-W,M Be1-W,M DRR-W,M
  TWS-W
Eight Hour Day
  AL-W SWF-W,M
Eight Hour Lyrics
  AL-W
Eight Hour Song
  AL-W WW-W,M
Eight Hours
  AL-W,M PSN-W,M
Eight Hours a Day
  AL-W
Eight Hours the Work Day
  AL-W
Eight Is Enough
  WG-W,M
Eight Miles High
  RB-W
**Eight Shillings a Wee see Present
  Times**
1881 Rent Agitation
  VP-W
Eighteen Wheels and a Dozen
  Roses
  GCM-W,M
Eighth Naval Victory
  ANS-W
Eighty-Six Pilots
  AF-W
Eileen Alannna Asthore
  E-W,M
Eileen Aroon
  IS-W,M
Eilidh Bhan
  SeS-W,M
Ein Lammlein Geht
  AHO-W,M (German)
Ein Petit Bonhomme
  CaF-W (French Only)
Ein Semaine
  CaF-W (French Only)
Ein Von Gott Geborner Christ
  AHO-W,M (German)
Eine Belle Bergere
  SAF-W (French Only)
Eine Kleine Nachtmusik (Theme)
  BMC-M
**El Amor Llamo see Moon Was
  Yellow**
El Bodeguero
  RW-W,M (Spanish Only)
El Capitan
  OBN-M RW-M
El Capotin
  LA-W,M (Spanish)
El Cefiro
  LaS-W,M (Spanish) MSS-W,M
  (Spanish)
El Charro
  LA-W,M (Spanish)
El Choclo
  LaS-M MF-M TI1-M UFB-M
El Coqui
  CDM-W,M (Spanish)
El Dia De Tu Santo
  SBF-W,M (Spanish Only)
El Durazno

LA-W,M (Spanish)
El Hijo Del Conde
  CDM-W,M (Spanish)
El Himno De Riego
  SiP-W,M (Spanish)
El Manton De Manila
  MML-W,M
El Mole Rachamim
  JS-W,M (Hebrew Only)
El Nino or the Soldier Child
  SoC-W
El Noroh Aliloh
  JS-W,M (Hebrew Only)
El Paso
  FC-W,M FOC-W,M HLS9-W,M
  RYT-W,M RW-W,M TI1-W,M
  UFB-W,M
El Patio De Mi Casa
  LA-W,M (Spanish)
El Pescador
  RW-W,M (Spanish Only)
**El Quinto Regimiento see Venga
  Jaleo**
El Rancho Grande
  GuC-W,M (Spanish)
El Relicario
  LaS-M MF-W,M TI2-W,M
  (Spanish)
El Rio Rey
  SoC-W
El Shaddai
  OGR-W,M VB-W,M
El Sombrero
  W-W,M
El Toro Moro
  SoC-W
El Venadito
  LA-W,M (Spanish)
El Watusi
  ILS-M
Elam Moore Jig
  DE-W,M
Elanoy
  FW-W OS-W
Eldorado
  ELO-W,M NA-W,M
Eleanor Rigby
  BBe-W,M Be1-W,M JF-W,M
  PMC-W,M RV-W SwS-W,M
  TWS-W WG-W,M
Eleanor's Tour
  AF-W
Eleazer Wheelock
  IL-W,M
Election Returns
  OT-W,M
Election the People's Right
  MPP-W,M OHG-W,M
Electric Avenue
  TI2-W,M
Electric Blue
  CFB-W,M
Electric Chair Blues
  LC-W
**Electric Horseman (Theme) see
  Mammas Don't Let Your Babies
  Grow Up to Be Cowboys**
Electric Tram
  VP-W
Electricity and All
  Am-W,M
Elegance
  Mo-W,M NM-W,M OTO-W
Elegie
  FSY-W,M (French) RW-M
Elegy
  WiS8-W,M

Elegy for Marie Jacques
SSN-W,M (French)
Elegy in a Country Churchyard
ESB-W,M
Elements
WF-W,M
Elephant (Lumbers Along on the
Road)
ASB2-W,M
Elephant (Mister Wrinkled
Elephant, Are You Very Old)
MH-W,M
Elephant (My Mammy Gimme
Fifteen Cents)
NF-W
Elephant (One Elephant Began to
Play)
BMC-W,M
Elephant and the Flea
OTJ-W,M
Elephant Song
MAR-W,M RSL-W,M
Elephant Walk
MF-M
Elephants or the Force of Habit
Boo-W,M
Eleven Cent Cotton
SWF-W,M
11:59
PL-W,M
Eleventh Armored
GO-W
Eleventh of November 1887
AL-W
Elfin Dance
RW-M
Elfin Knight
BT-W,M ITP-W,M
Elfland Horns
FSA2-W,M
Eli Yale
IL-W,M
Elijah (Introduction)
LMR-W,M
Elijah (Richard Mullins)
VB-W,M
Eliyohu Hannovi
JS-W,M (Hebrew)
Eliza
ESU-W
Eliza Jane
AN-W
Eliza's Flight
OHG-W,M SY-W,M
Elks' Parade
RW-M
Ella Dare
Oz4-W
Ella Lea
BSC-W
Ella Rhee
Oz4-W
Ella Speed
NeF-W
Elle Descend De La Montagne
CE-W,M (French Only)
Ellen Bayne
ASB6-W,M FHR-W,M SSF-W,M
SSFo-W,M
Ellen Smith
FSU-W FVV-W,M ITP-W,M
Ellen Smith Ballet
FMT-W
Ellsworth
MPP-W
Ellsworth Avengers
Sin-W,M

Elmer's Tune
GSF-W,M GSN3-W,M HLS2-W,M
Elnora
NeF-W
Elogie
MF-M
Elohenu
JS-W,M (Hebrew Only)
Eltham
SHS-W,M
Elves and Gnomes
PIS-W,M
Elves' Dance
CoF-W,M
Elysian
SHS-W,M
Emancipation
Sin-W,M
Emancipation from British
Dependence
AWB-W
Embargo
ANS-W MPP-W
Embarrassment
HSD-W,M
Embraceable You
BNG-W,M DC-W,M FrS-W,M
GOB-W,M HC1-W,M LSO-W
MF-W,M NYT-W,M (French,
Spanish) OHB-W,M RoE-W,M
TW-W
Emerald Point N.A.S.
TVT-M
Emgann Sant-Kast
AAF-W,M (French)
Emigrant
SE-W (Swedish)
Emigrant Waltz
SE-W (Swedish)
Emigrantangaren Geisers
Undergang
SE-W (Swedish)
Emigranten
SE-W (Swedish)
Emigrantens Afsked Farval O
Moder Svea
SE-W,M (Swedish)
Emigranternas Afsked Till Hemmet
SE-W (Swedish)
Emigrant's Dying Child
SY-W,M
Emigrant's Farewell
SE-W,M (Swedish) VP-W
Emigrant's Farewell or Farewell O
Mother Sweden
SE-W,M (Swedish)
Emigrant's Farewell to Donegal
VP-W
Emigrant's Farewell to Their Home
SE-W (Swedish)
Emigrant's Song
SE-W (Swedish)
Emigrant's Song, a Word of
Caution to the Emigrant
SE-W,M (Swedish)
Emigrantvalsen
SE-W (Swedish)
Emilia Polka
PT-W,M TI2-W,M
Emily
OHF-W RT6-W,M
Emitte Lucem Tuam
Boo-W,M (Latin Only)
Emmanuel
VB-W,M
Emmanuelle (Theme)
TOM-M

Emmanuel's Land see Immanuel's
Land
Emmet's Lullaby
AmH-W,M EFS-W,M HSD-W,M
OTJ-W,M
Emotion
SoH-W,M TI1-W,M UFB-W,M
Emotional Rescue
RoS-W,M
Emperor Waltz
ID-W,M MU-W,M RW-M TI1-M
UFB-M
Emperor's Waltz
OTJ-W,M
Empire of the West
ESU-W
Emptiest Arms in the World
NMH-W,M
Empty
VS-W,M
Empty Arms
RW-W,M
Empty Bed Blues
PO-W,M
Empty Chairs at Empty Tables
UBF-W,M
Empty Garden
TI2-W,M
Empty Heart
RoS-W,M
Empty Litter and the Wazir's Spies
Ki-W,M
Empty Nest
ASB1-W,M
Empty Pockets Blues
FG2-W,M TO-W,M
Empty Saddles
FC-W,M
Empty Sleeve
SiS-W
En Arriere De Soi Mon Pere
Lo-W,M (French Only)
En Avant Grenadiers
BaB-W,M (French)
En El Madrid De Anos Atras
ESB-W,M (Spanish)
En Emigrants Afsked
SE-W,M (Swedish)
En Evan' Grenadie
CSD-W,M (French)
En Habana
LA-W,M (Spanish)
En Haut
CaF-W (French Only)
En Kelohenu
JS-W,M (Hebrew)
En Komochoh
JS-W,M (Hebrew Only)
En Mi Viego San Juan
CDM-W,M (Spanish)
En Ny Amerika-visa
SE-W (Swedish)
En Ny Amerikavisan
SE-W (Swedish)
En Ny Och Wacker Sjomanswisa
Om En Brigg Som Gick Forlorad I
Nordsjon
SE-W (Swedish)
En Ny Wisa Om Utwandringen Till
Amerika
SE-W,M (Swedish)
En Passant Par La Lorraine
CUP-W,M (French Only) MP-W,M
(French Only)
En Revenant De Rivote
CaF-W (French Only)
En Roulant Ma Boule

ATS-W,M
En Roulant Ma Boule Roulant
  CFS-W,M (French)
En Todo El Tiempo Pasado
  LA-W,M (Spanish)
En Visa Jag Diktat
  SE-W,M (Swedish)
Enchanted Isle
  HSD-W,M
Enchanter
  MLM-W,M
Enchanting Childhood
  LMR-W,M (Portuguese)
Enchantment
  FSA1-W,M
Enclosed, One Broken Heart
  OGC1-W,M
Encompassed in an Angel's Frame
  ESU-W
End, The (At the End of the
  Rainbow)
  TI1-W,M UFB-W,M
End, The (James Reed)
  DBL-W
End, The (Jim Morrison)
  RV-W
End, The (Lennon/McCartney)
  TWS-W
End Game
  OTO-W
End of a Love Affair
  TI2-W,M ToS-W,M
End of Bill Snyder
  AFP-W
End of Ten Little Negroes
  NF-W
End of the Book
  VB-W,M
End of the World (Why Does the
  Sun Go On Shining)
  MAB1-W,M MSA1-W OnT6-W,M
  TI1-W,M UFB-W,M
Ending with a Kiss
  OTO-W
Endless Love
  HFH-W,M TI2-W,M
Endless Sleep
  FRH-W,M HR-W
Endlessly
  FRH-W,M ILF-W,M LWT-W,M
  MF-W,M RW-W,M TI1-W,M
  UFB-W,M
Ends of All the Earth Shall Hear
  Hy-W,M
Endsong
  TW-W
Energy for a Strong America
  TI1-W,M UFB-W,M
Enfield Gun
  SiS-W
Engine
  ASB1-W,M FW-W
Engine Engine Number Nine
  TI2-W,M
Engine of Love
  UBF-W,M
Engine 143
  FSt-W,M LSR-W,M
Engineer O.C.S. Song
  GI-W GO-W
Engineer Rigg
  AN-W
Engineers
  GI-W
Engineer's Child
  LSR-W,M
Engineer's Song

GO-W
Engines
  MH-W,M
England Swing
  CSp-W,M
England Swings
  ATC1-W,M CMG-W,M
English Chantey
  HSD-W,M
**English National Hymn see God
  Save the King**
English Neutrality
  SiS-W
Enjoy Yourself (It's Later Than You
  Think)
  MF-W,M Mo-W,M NM-W,M
  On-W,M TI2-W,M
Enough for You
  SuS-W,M
Enough Is Enough
  PoG-W,M
Enraptured I Gaze
  AH-W,M NAS-W,M
Entendez-Vous
  Boo-W,M (French Only)
Enter His Gates with Thanksgiving
  SHP-W,M
Enter Laughing
  OnT6-W,M
Enter, Rejoice, and Come In
  JF-W,M
Enterprise and Boxer
  ANS-W ESU-W
Enterre Moi Dans Le Coin De Ta
  Cour
  CaF-W (French Only)
Entertainer, The
  BNG-M FSB3-M GOI7-M HLS5-M
  LM-W,M MF-M MoA-M On-W,M
  OPS-W,M OTJ-M PoG-M TI1-M
  ToO76-M UFB-M
Entertainment Tonight (Theme)
  TV-M
**Entombed Here Lies Good Sir Harry
  see Intombed Here Lies Good Sir
  Harry**
Entre Les Etoiles
  SSN-W,M (French)
Entre Paris Et Saint-Denis
  CFS-W,M (French)
Entreat Me Not see Intreat Me Not
Entreat Me Not to Leave Thee
  (Gounod)
  TM-W,M WGB/O-W,M
Entreat Me Not to Leave Thee
  (Sibelius)
  TH-W,M
Entreaty
  LA-W,M (Spanish)
Entreaty (Night Blues)
  RuS-W,M (Russian)
Entrei Na Roda
  LA-W,M (Spanish)
Environment--Heredity
  TW-W
Envoyons D'l'avant Nos Gens
  CFS-W,M (French)
Epigram
  AL-W
Epilogue
  SAR-W SBA-W
Episode in Havana
  LA-W,M (Spanish)
Episode of the Swing
  MA-W,M
Epistle to the Troops in Boston
  SBA-W

Equal Rights for All
  AL-W
Equinoxial and Phoebe
  LW-W,M
Er Clim'in' up Thine Hill
  AN-W
Ere Space Exists
  SBJ-W,M
Ere You Ask a Girl to Leave Her
  Happy Home
  Oz4-W
Eres Alta
  WSB-W,M (Spanish)
Eres Tu (Touch the Wind)
  GrS-W,M NCB-W,M (Spanish)
  TI1-W,M UFB-W,M WGB/P-W,M
  (Spanish)
E-ri-e
  FW-W
Erie Canal
  ASB6-W,M BeB-W,M BF-W,M
  FSB2-W,M FW-W FWS-W,M
  HS-W,M IHA-W,M IL-W,M
  MAS-W,M MG-W,M OFS-W,M
  OHO-W,M OTJ-W,M RW-W,M
  SAm-W,M SFM-W SMY-W,M
  WS-W,M
Erin Go Braugh
  FW-W
Erin! the Tear and the Smile in
  Thine Eyes
  RW-W,M
Erin's Green Shore
  BSC-W Oz1-W,M
Erin's Lovely Home
  Oz1-W,M
Es Hat Nicht Sollen Sein
  AmH-W,M
Es Ist Ein' Ros' Entsprungen
  OB-W,M (German Only)
**Es Ist Ein' Ros' Entsprungen see
  also Lo, How a Rose E'er
  Blooming**
Escape from Slavery of Henry Box
  Brown
  AFP-W AL-W
Escape of John Webb
  OHO-W,M
Escape of Old John Webb and Billy
  Tenor
  OTJ-W,M
Escape of Old John Webber
  SI-W,M
Escuela Linda
  CDM-W,M (Spanish)
Eskimo
  ASB3-W,M
Eskimo Baby
  SiR-W,M
Eskimo Hunter
  ASB1-W,M
Esmeralda (Hesitation Waltz)
  AmH-M
Espani Cani
  RW-M
Essay
  SHS-W,M
Esso Refinery Blues
  LC-W
Esta Noche Es Noche Buena
  HSA-W,M (Spanish)
Esthete on Clark Street
  MF-M
Estrellita
  MSS-W,M (Spanish)
Estudiantina
  AmH-M CA-W,M LaS-M OBN-M

RW-M
Estudio
LaS-M
Et In Spiritum Sanctum (Franck)
MMM-W,M (Latin Only)
Et In Terra Pax (John Benaglia)
Boo-W,M (Latin Only)
Et Maintenant see What Now My Love
Et Moi Je M'enfouiyais
CFS-W,M (French)
Et Tan' Patate La Cuite
CLaL-W,M (French)
Et Tan Patate La Cuite see also E Tan Patat' La Cuit'
Eternal Father! Strong to Save
CEM-W,M GeS-W,M Hy-W,M
LT-W,M MAS-W,M OM-W,M
RDF-W,M SJ-W,M VA-W,M
WiS9-W,M
Eternal Father! Strong to Save see also Navy Hymn
Eternal Flame
RoE-W,M
Eternal God How They're Increased
AHO-W,M
Eternal God Whose Power Upholds
AHO-W,M Hy-W,M
Eternal King
TH-W,M
Eternal Spirit, God of Truth
AME-W,M
Eternal Spirit, Source of Light
AHO-W,M
Eternally
ILT-W,M TI1-W,M UFB-W,M
Eternity
GH-W,M
Etiquette
SBA-W SI-W,M
Eton
SHS-W,M
Etude (Chopin)
MF-M
Etz Chayim
JS-W,M (Hebrew Only)
Eulalie
FHR-W,M SSFo-W,M
Eumerella Shore
ATM-W,M
Eureka
Oz3-W,M
Eutaw Springs
AWB-W
Evangelist's Song
BMM-W
Eve of Destruction
RB-W
Evelina
UBF-W,M
Even Me
AME-W,M GH-W,M OM-W,M
Even the Mountains Praise You
OGR-W,M
Evenin'
Sta-W,M
Evening (At Evening When the Thrushes Call)
FSA2-W,M
Evening (Comes with Rustling Leaves)
AS-W,M (German)
Evening (In the West the Sun Declining)
TH-W,M
Evening and Morning

FiS-W,M
Evening Bells
ASB5-W,M RSC-W,M (Russian Only) SBF-W,M
Evening Fair see Beau Soir
Evening Hymn
SiR-W,M
Evening Hymn (Again, As Evening's Shadow Falls)
JS-W,M
Evening Hymn (The Day Thou Gavest, Lord, Is Ended)
Mu-W,M
Evening Hymn (Glory to Thee, My God, This Night)
WiS7-W,M
Evening Hymn (Hear Us, Father, As We Pray)
OTJ-W,M
Evening in Paris
MF-M
Evening in Port
RuS-W,M (Russian)
Evening in the Garden
SiR-W,M
Evening in the Tropics
SL-W,M
Evening Prayer
BSG-W,M BSP-W,M
Evening Prayer (Father, in Thy Keeping)
ASB6-W,M
Evening Prayer (God, Who Sendest Night and Day)
SL-W,M
Evening Prayer (If I Have Wounded Any Soul To-day)
HLS7-W,M
Evening Prayer (Now I Lay Me Down to Sleep)
FSA1-W,M SiB-W,M
Evening Prayer (Now I Lay Me Down to Sleep) see also Now I Lay Me Down to Sleep
Evening Prayer (Savior, Breathe an Evening Blessing)
AME-W,M GH-W,M
Evening Prayer (Thou, Who Watcheth Ev'ry Sparrow's Flight)
ASB5-W,M
Evening Prayer (When I Lay Me Down in Bed)
WiS7-W,M
Evening Reflection
NSS-W
Evening Shade
SHS-W,M
Evening Song (Eichendorff/Franz)
MHB-W,M (German)
Evening Song (Lights of Evening, Petals Closing)
SL-W,M
Evening Song (Like Fireflies That Glitter and Wink in the Night)
GM-W,M
Evening Song (Lord, I Lay to Rest Another Day with You)
VB-W,M
Evening Song (Slowly Gather the Shadows)
ASB6-W,M
Evening Song (Sun, Sun, Golden Sun at Evening)
BMC-W,M
Evening Star (from Wagner's Tannhauser)
AmH-W,M HSD-W,M RW-W,M

WiS7-W,M
Evening Star (O Evening Star, with Peaceful Eye She Glows Afar)
SMa-W,M
Evening Star (Schumann)
SMY-W,M
Evening Sun Yodel
LJ-W,M
Evening Train
LSR-W,M
Evensong
BeB-W,M
Ever After On
B-W,M Bl-W,M
Ever Never Lovin' You
TOC83-W,M
Ever of Thee
AmH-W,M HSD-W,M
WGB/O-W,M
Ever of Thee I'm Fondly Dreaming
ATS-W,M
Ever Sowing
GrM-W,M
Ever the Winds
IS-W,M
Everett, November Fifth
AFP-W
Evergreen
BNG-W,M CSp-W,M DC-W,M
DPE-W,M EY-W,M HFH-W,M
MF-W,M
Evergreen see also Star Is Born (Love Theme)
Everlasting
MF-W,M
Everlasting Arms
Mo-W,M
Everlasting Hills of Oklahoma
FC-W,M OGC2-W,M
Everlasting Love
TI1-W,M UFB-W,M
Evermore and a Day
BS-W,M
Every... see also Ev'ry...
Every Breath You Take
TI2-W,M
Every Christian Born of God
AHO-W,M (German)
Every Christmas Morning
BCh-W,M
Every Christmas Night
SCL-W,M
Every Day
NH-W
Every Day a Little Death
LN-W,M
Every Day Help Me Say
SHP-W,M
Every Day of the Week
FSSC-W
Every Day the Movement's Gettin' Stronger
VS-W,M
Every Day Will I Bless
GH-W,M
Every Day's a Holiday
OTO-W
Every Little Movement
MF-W,M
Every Little Nothing
LMS-W,M
Every Little Thing
BBe-W,M Be1-W,M TWS-W
Every Lover Must Meet His Fate
Sw-W,M
Every Man His Own Politician
AFP-W AL-W

Every Morning Mercies New
OS-W

Every Night
Be2-W,M LT-W,M

Every Night When the Sun Goes In
FG2-W,M FoS-W,M FW-W
WSB-W,M

**Every Night When the Sun Goes In
see also Ev'ry Night When the
Sun Goes Down**

Every Night When You Say a
Prayer
LWT-W,M

Every Road Leads Back to You
WG-W,M

Every Star--Thirty Four
SiS-W

Every State Is My Home
RSW-W,M

Every Step of the Way
VB-W,M

Every Time I Feel the Spirit
FW-W HS-W,M JBF-W,M
OTJ-W,M WN-W,M

**Every Time I Feel the Spirit see
also Ev'ry Time I Feel the Spirit
and O Ev'ry Time I Feel de Spirit**

Every Time I Think of You
PoG-W,M WG-W,M

Every Time Two Fools Collide
CMG-W,M

**Every Time You Cross My Mind
see Everytime You Cross My
Mind**

**Every Time You Go Outside... see
Everytime You Go Outside...**

Every Which Way but Loose
TI2-W,M ToO79-W,M

Every Woman in the World
TI1-W,M UFB-W,M

Everybody... see also Ev'rybody...

Everybody
MAR-W,M

Everybody Come Aboard
SRE2-W,M

Everybody Do This
FP-W,M

Everybody Does It in Hawaii
LJ-W,M

Everybody Likes It (Diet Rite Cola)
TI1-W,M UFB-W,M

Everybody Loves a Nut
CSp-W,M

Everybody Loves My Baby
TI2-W,M

Everybody Loves Saturday Night
FW-W GuC-W,M JF-W,M
OTJ-W,M SWF-W,M

Everybody Loves Somebody
MF-W,M TVT-W,M

Everybody Plays the Fool
SoH-W,M

Everybody Plays the Fool
Sometime
TI2-W,M

Everybody Rejoice
Wi-W,M

Everybody Sing Freedom
SFF-W,M

Everybody Wants to Know
DBL-W

Everybody Will Be Happy
HHa-W,M

Everybody Works but Father
FSN-W,M

**Everybody's Been Down on Me
see Ev'ybody Bin Down on Me**

Everybody's Dixie
Sin-W,M

Everybody's Dream Girl
TOC83-W,M

Everybody's Got a Home but Me
OTJ-W,M OTO-W TI1-W,M
UBF-W,M UFB-W,M

Everybody's Got a Right to Live
JF-W,M

Everybody's Got Something to
Hide Except Me and My Monkey
TWS-W

Everybody's Had the Blues
NMH-W,M

Everybody's Reaching Out for
Someone
CEM-W,M

Everybody's Talkin' (Theme from
Midnight Cowboy)
DPE-W,M MCG-W,M MF-W,M
RW-W,M RY-W,M RYT-W,M

**Everybody's Talkin' see also
Midnight Cowboy (Theme)**

Everyday
TTH-W,M

Everyday Dirt
FPG-W,M FW-W

Everyday People
ERM-W,M GAR-W,M

**Everyone Says I Love You see
Ev'ryone Says I Love You**

Everything... see also Ev'rything...

Everything
Ro-W,M

Everything a Man Could Ever Need
OTO-W

Everything Beautiful Happens at
Night
OHT-W,M

Everything but You
GMD-W,M

Everything Happens to Me
NK-W,M RoE-W,M TI1-W,M
ToS-W,M UFB-W,M

Everything I Have Is Yours
GG4-W,M GSN2-W,M GSO-W,M
HLS5-W,M RW-W,M

Everything I Want
NM-W,M

**Everything I Want see also
Ev'rything I Want**

Everything in the World
Mo-W,M NM-W,M OTO-W

Everything Is Beautiful
CEM-W,M CMG-W,M MF-W,M
On-W,M OTJ-W,M

**Everything Is Beautiful see also
Ev'rything Is Beautiful**

Everything Is Turning to Gold
RoS-W,M

Everything I've Always Wanted
TI1-W,M UFB-W,M

Everything Put Together Falls
Apart
PS-W,M

Everything That Happens to You
Happens to Me
MLS-W,M

Everything's Alright
UBF-W,M

Everything's Coming Up Roses
DBC-W,M HC1-W,M HLS8-W,M
OTJ-W,M OTO-W RW-W,M TI1-
W,M TW-W UBF-W,M UFB-W,M

Everything's Great
Mo-W,M NM-W,M OTO-W

Everytime You Cross My Mind

(You Break My Heart)
TOC82-W,M

Everytime You Go Outside I Hope
It Rains
WF-W,M

Everywhere I Go
VB-W,M

Eve's Mirror
Ap-W,M

Evil Blues
DBL-W

Evil-Hearted Man
FW-W

Evil-Hearted Me
J-W,M

Evil Ways
BR-W,M LM-W,M

Evil Woman
ELO-W,M

Evolution
FSA2-W,M

Ev'ry... see also Every...

Ev'ry Day of My Life
MCG-W,M RW-W,M

Ev'ry Day We Wash Our Hands
AST-W,M

Ev'ry Day Will Be Sunday By and
By
GrG-W,M

Ev'ry Hour on the Hour (I Fall in
Love with You)
Mo-W,M NM-W,M OTO-W

Ev'ry Night When the Sun Goes
Down
GeS-W,M

**Ev'ry Night When the Sun Goes
Down see also Every Night When
the Sun Goes In**

Ev'ry Play Must Have a Villain
CoF-W,M

Ev'ry Street's a Boulevard (in Old
New York)
OTO-W TI1-W,M UFB-W,M

Ev'ry Time (When We Are Gone)
RBO-W,M

Ev'ry Time I Feel the Spirit
ETB-W,M FN-W,M MuM-W,M
OU-W,M RDF-W,M RF-W,M
WiS7-W,M

**Ev'ry Time I Feel the Spirit see also
Every Time I Feel the Spirit and O
Ev'ry Time I Feel de Spirit**

Ev'ry Time We Say Goodbye
HC1-W,M ML-W,M OTO-W
TI1-W,M UBF-W,M UFB-W,M

Ev'rybody... see also Everybody...

Ev'rybody Has the Right to Be
Wrong
MF-W,M

Ev'rybody Knows I Love
Somebody
ReG-W,M

Ev'rybody Laugh
CA-W,M

Ev'rybody Wants to Be a Cat
NI-W,M

Ev'rybody's Somebody's Fool
MF-W,M

Ev'ryone Says I Love You
OTO-W

Ev'rything... see also Everything...

Ev'rything I Love
ML-W,M

Ev'rything I Want
Mo-W,M OTO-W

**Ev'rything I Want see also
Everything I Want**

Ev'rything Is Beautiful
RDF-W,M
Ev'rything Is Beautiful see also Everything Is Beautiful
Ev'rything I've Got
OTO-W TI1-W,M TS-W UBF-W,M
UFB-W,M
Ev'ybody Bin Down on Me
NH-W
Ewing Brooks
Oz2-W,M
Exactly Like You
GSN2-W,M HC1-W,M HLS2-W,M
MF-W,M RoE-W,M TI1-W,M
UFB-W,M
Exaudi Domine
Boo-W,M (Latin Only)
Excelsior
SY-W,M
Except the Lord That He for Us
Had Been
AHO-W,M
Exciseman Outwitted
MSB-W
Excuses
AG-W,M
Executive
SYB-W,M
Exercise Song
SoP-W,M
Exeunt Gypsies
MPM-W,M
Exhilaration
SHS-W,M
Exhiliration (Tango-Maxixe)
AmH-M
Exile King
BMM-W
Exiled Canadian see Un Canadien Errant
Exodus Song
EY-W,M HFH-W,M HLS5-W,M
OTJ-W,M OTO-W RT6-W,M
TI1-W,M UFB-W,M VB-W,M
Expectation Waltz
RW-M
Expedition to Rhode Island
SBA-W
Expert Girl
Oz2-W
Expostulation
GH-W,M
Express
DP-W,M ToO76-W,M
Express Office
Oz4-W,M
Expressive Glances
MGT-W,M
Extended on a Cursed Tree
AME-W,M
Extolled Be the Living God
JS-W,M (Hebrew)
Extremes
MH-W,M
Exultation
SHS-W,M
Exxon Corporation Jingle see Energy for a Strong America
Eye Hath Not Seen
FiS-W,M
Eye of Faith
GH-W,M
Eye of the Tiger (Rocky III Theme)
BNG-W,M HFH-W,M MF-W,M
Eyes of Blue
OTO-W
Eyes of God

FSA2-W,M
Eyes of Laura Mars (Love Theme)
TI2-W,M
Eyes of Love
TI2-W,M
Eyes of Texas
FW-W OTJ-W,M
Eyes That See in the Dark
TI2-W,M
Eyesight to the Blind
DBL-W
Ezekiel Saw de Wheel
CA-W,M IL-W,M OTJ-W,M
RF-W,M
Ezekiel Saw the Wheel
BSB-W,M FN-W,M FW-W
JBF-W,M

F

F.F.V.
BMM-W
F Troop (Theme)
TVT-W,M
Fable
SBA-W
Face in the Crowd
Mo-W,M NM-W,M OTO-W
Face It Girl It's Over
Mo-W,M
Face Lost in the Crowd
BSo-W,M
Face on the Dime
TW-W
Face the Flag
JW-W,M
Face to Face
OM-W,M SS-W
Face to Face with Christ My Savior
AME-W,M
Fact Can Be a Beautiful Thing
Mo-W,M OTO-W
Factory Bell
AL-W
Factory Girl (I Am a Poor Little
Factory Girl)
AL-W
Factory Girl (Jagger/Richards)
RoS-W,M
Factory Girl (No More Shall I Work
in the Factory)
FW-W LW-W,M WW-W,M
Factory Girl (She Wasn't the Least
Bit Pretty)
AL-W
Factory Girl ('Twas on a Wintry
Morning)
AL-W
Factory Girl's Come-All-Ye
AL-W
Factory Slave
AL-W
Factory Song
AL-W
Facts of Life (Theme)
TV-W,M
Fade Away and Radiate
PL-W,M
Faded Coat of Blue
ATS-W FMT-W HSD-W,M SiS-W
Faded Flowers
BSC-W
Faded Gray Jacket
SiS-W
Faded Love
OGC1-W,M TI1-W,M UFB-W,M

Faded Roses
MLS-W,M
Fading, Still Fading
HSD-M
Faier's Faire
FSB3-M
Faint Falls the Gentle Voice
AHO-W,M
Faint Heart Never Won Fair Lady
MGT-W,M
Faint Yet Pursuing
GH-W,M
Fair, The
ASB1-M
Fair and Free Elections
FW-W PSN-W
Fair and Handsome Girls
SCa-W,M
Fair and Tender Ladies
BSo-W,M
Fair and Tender Maidens
ITP-W,M
Fair Annie
FSU-W
Fair Annie of Lochyran
AmS-W,M
Fair Are My Fields
SoF-W,M
Fair at Batesland
HB-W
Fair Caroline
TBF-W,M
Fair Charlotte
BSC-W TBF-W,M
Fair Ellen
SCa-W,M
Fair Ellender
FMT-W FW-W Oz1-W RW-W,M
SCa-W
Fair Emily
Oz2-W
Fair Fannie Moore
BSC-W Oz2-W,M
Fair Glows the Earth
SL-W,M
Fair Harvard
AmH-W,M ESB-W,M HSD-W,M
IL-W,M
Fair Helen of Kirkconnel
SeS-W,M
Fair Indian Lass or Little Mohee
DD-W,M
Fair Indian Lass or Little Mohee see also Indian Lass, Lass of Mohea, Little Mohea, and Pretty Mauhee (Mohea)
Fair Is the Summer
BM-W
Fair Kate
BMM-W
Fair Lady of the Plains
Oz2-W,M
Fair Maid
Oz2-W
Fair Maid and the Soldier
SRS-W,M
Fair Margaret and Sweet William
ATS-W,M FMT-W SCa-W,M
Fair Moon
SMa-W,M
Fair Morn
Boo-W,M
Fair Morn Ascends
Boo-W,M
Fair Phoebe and Her Dark-Eyed
Sailor
SCa-W,M

Fair Princess Royal
  SA-W,M
Fair Prospect
  AL-W
Fair Sally
  Oz1-W,M
Fair Ursley
  Boo-W,M
Fair Waitress
  BMM-W
Fair Young Mary
  SeS-W,M
Fairchild Abortion
  AF-W
Fairest Beloit
  CoS-W,M
Fairest Lord Jesus
  AME-W,M ASB6-W,M CEM-W,M
  FH-W,M FWS-W,M HS-W,M
  Hy-W,M IH-M JBF-W,M LoS-W,M
  LTL-W,M MAS-W,M OTJ-W,M
  SHP-W,M TB-W,M WiS7-W,M
  YS-W,M
Fairest of Ten Thousand
  VB-W,M
Fairfield
  SHS-W,M
Fairies' Music
  ASB2-W,M
Fairies' Song
  FSA2-W,M
Fairy Belle
  FHR-W,M NAS-W,M SSF-W,M
  SSFo-W,M
Fairy Circle
  FSA2-W,M
Fairy Friends
  SL-W,M
Fairy Lullaby
  SeS-W,M
Fairy Shoes
  CoF-W,M
Fairy Tales Are All Unfair
  TW-W
Faisdodo
  Lo-W,M
Fait Do Do
  CaF-W (French Only)
Faith (George Michael)
  CFB-W,M
Faith (Lawrence/Freeman)
  Mo-W,M NM-W,M OTO-W
Faith (Pierpont/Mozart)
  FSA1-W,M TF-W,M
Faith Can Move Mountains
  HLS7-W,M SUH-W,M
Faith Is a Living Power from
  Heaven
  GH-W,M
Faith Is the Victory
  GH-W,M
Faith of Our Fathers
  AME-W,M ASB6-W,M BMC-W,M
  BNG-W,M Bo-W BSG-W,M
  BSP-W,M CEM-W,M DC-W,M
  FH-W,M FS-W,M HF-W,M
  HS-W,M Hy-W,M IH-M JBF-W,M
  MAB1-W,M MF-W,M MML-W,M
  MSA1-W NAS-W,M OS-W OTJ-
  W,M TB-W,M TF-W,M
Faith of Our Fathers Living Still
  SL-W,M
Faith Takes a Vision
  VB-W,M
Faith Thou Beacon
  Boo-W,M
Faith Undying

UF-W,M
Faith Unlocks the Door
  TI2-W,M
Faith unto Death
  SMW-W,M
Faith Walkin' People
  VB-W,M
Faithful
  OTO-W
Faithful Forever
  OTO-W
Faithful Johnny
  ASB5-W,M
Faithful Lover
  FMT-W,M
Faithful Soldier
  SHS-W,M
Faithless Husband
  Oz4-W
Faithless Nelly Gray
  ESU-W
Faking Love
  TOC83-W,M
Falan-Tiding
  OB-W,M
Falcon Crest (Theme)
  TV-M
**Fall Guy Theme see Ballad of the
Unknown Stuntman**
Fall of Sumter
  SiS-W
Fall of the Year
  GBC-W,M
Fallin' (Al Jarreau)
  BOA-W,M
Fallin' (Sager/Hamlisch)
  TP-W,M UBF-W,M
Fallin' in Love (Again)
  ToO76-W,M
Falling
  TFC-W,M
Falling in Love
  RW-W,M
Falling in Love Again (Can't Help
  It)
  AT-W,M ILT-W,M LM-W,M
  OTO-W WGB/P-W,M
Falling in Love with Love
  DBC-W,M FrS-W,M HC1-W,M
  HLS8-W,M OTO-W RW-W,M
  TI1-W,M TS-W UFB-W,M
Falling in Love with You
  UBF-W,M
Falling Leaf
  Oz4-W,M
Falling Leaves (Red Leaves Falling
  Down)
  STS-W,M
Falling Leaves (Softly from the
  Tree Tops)
  ASB1-W,M
Falling Rain Blues
  DBL-W
Falls of Minnehaha
  FSA2-W,M
False Alarm
  NH-W
False Face
  RSL-W,M
False-Hearted Lover
  BSC-W
False Knight upon the Road
  BSC-W BT-W,M
False Lamkin
  Oz1-W,M
False Lover
  Oz4-W

False Lying True Love
  SCa-W,M
False Sir John
  TBF-W,M
False True Love
  FW-W
False Young Man
  Oz4-W SCa-W,M
Falstafferel
  Boo-W,M
Fame (Lennon/Bowie)
  DDH-W,M
Fame (Theme)
  MoA-W,M TV-W,M
Fame and Fortune
  SRE1-W,M
Family
  FF-W RoS-W,M
Family Bible
  SHS-W,M WNF-W,M
Family of God
  BSG-W,M BSP-W,M FS-W,M
Family Tree
  GI-W
Famine Song
  VP-W,M
Famous Wedding
  FVV-W,M
Fan Mail
  VB-W,M
Fanchon
  FSF-W (French)
Fancies
  FSA1-W,M
Fancy Forgetting
  OTO-W
Fancy Free
  Mo-W,M NM-W,M OTO-W
Fancy Meeting You Here
  Mo-W,M NM-W,M
Fancy Passes
  LSB-W,M
Fannie and Angeline's Song
  SNS-W
Fannie Moore
  BSC-W
Fannin Street
  Le-W,M
Fanny (Folk Song)
  FSF-W (French)
Fanny (Harold Rome)
  TI1-W,M TW-W UBF-W,M
  UFB-W,M
Fanny Be Tender with My Love
  TI1-W,M UFB-W,M
Fanny Mae
  MF-W,M
Fantaisie Impromptu
  MF-M RW-M TI1-M UFB-M
Fantasy Island (Theme)
  TV-M
Far above Cayuga's Waters
  ESB-W,M FW-W OTJ-W,M
  TI2-W,M
Far Away
  HSD-W,M ML-W,M
Far Away, The
  RSC-W,M (Russian Only)
Far Away Eyes
  RoS-W,M
Far Away, Far Away
  Oz4-W
Far Away from Home
  SRS-W,M
Far down the Ages Now
  AME-W,M
Far Far Away

AL-W BMC-W,M
Far from Our Friends
AHO-W,M
Far from the Home I Love
OTO-W TW-W UBF-W,M
Far from These Scenes of Night
AME-W,M
Far Northland
Bo-W,M
Far Off I See the Goal
Hy-W,M
Far Off Is Our Land
SMW-W,M (German)
Far-Off Sweetheart
RuS-W,M (Russian)
Far Out (the Dream Goes On)
Mo-W,M
Far over Yon Hills
SeS-W,M
Faraway Airman
AF-W
Farce
SSS-W,M
Fare Thee Well
OTJ-W,M WU-W,M
Fare Thee Well Cisco
RBO-W,M
Fare Thee Well Enniskillen
IS-W,M
Fare Thee Well My Honey
FoS-W,M
Fare Thee Well My Love
OFS-W,M
Fare Thee Well to Harlem
OHF-W
Fare Thee Well You Sweethearts
SSS-W,M
Fare Ye Well Old Ely Branch
AFP-W
Fare You Well, My Darling
BSC-W Oz4-W
Farewell (Come Christians, Be
Valiant)
SHS-W,M
Farewell (Dykema/Saxony Folk
Song)
LMR-W,M
Farewell (My Darling, Farewell)
NH-W
Farewell (Ruckert/Brahms)
MU-W,M
Farewell (Russian Folk Song)
RSC-W,M (Russian)
Farewell (Sigmund Romberg)
DS-W,M
Farewell (Zick/Silcher)
HSD-W,M
Farewell Anthem
BC1-W,M SHS-W,M
Farewell Dear Love
FSS-W,M SSP-W
Farewell Dear Rosanna
FSU-W
Farewell, Father, Friend and
Guardian
MPP-W Sin-W,M SiS-W
Farewell Forever to the Star-
Spangled Banner
SiS-W,M
Farewell Hymn Dedicated to the
Officers
ANS-W
Farewell Mother Dear
FHR-W,M
Farewell My Dearest Katy
SiS-W
Farewell My Lilly Dear

FHR-W,M SSF-W,M SSFo-W,M
Farewell My Lily Dear
RW-W,M
Farewell My Own
HSD-W,M MGT-W,M
Farewell O Earth
MuM-W,M
**Farewell O Mother Sweden see
Emigrant's Farewell or Farewell O
Mother Sweden**
Farewell Old Cottage
FHR-W,M SSFo-W,M
Farewell Song (Comrades, We
Must Part Now)
FSA1-W,M
Farewell Song (A Last Goodbye!)
HSD-W,M
Farewell Song to Swedish
Emigrants
SE-W (Swedish)
Farewell Sweet Mother
FHR-W,M
Farewell Sweetheart
Oz4-W,M
Farewell, Thou Delaware, Thou
Pennsylvania Stream
SE-W (Swedish)
Farewell to Carter County
BMM-W
Farewell to Grog
HAS-W,M SiS-W
Farewell to Innsbruck
MU-W,M
Farewell to Ireland
IFM-W
Farewell to Judges and Juries
MSB-W
Farewell to Lochaber
SeS-W,M
Farewell to Summer
GrM-W,M
Farewell to the Forest
TF-W,M TH-W,M
Farewell to the Native Land
SE-W (Swedish)
**Farewell to the Protestant Ethic
see Sam's Soliloquy**
Farewell to the Star Spangled
Banner
MPP-W
Farewell to the Woods
MHB-W,M
Farewell to Thee see Aloha Oe
Farewell We Sing
Boo-W,M
Farm
ASB2-W,M
Farm Blues
LC-W
Farmer
BM-W
Farmer (I Sell Butter, I Sell Cheese)
MH-W,M
Farmer (Shall I Show You How the
Farmer)
ASB1-W,M
Farmer and His Animals
AST-W,M
Farmer and His Bride
TBF-W,M
Farmer and the Cowman
TGO-W,M UBF-W,M
Farmer and the Shanty Boy
BSC-W,M
Farmer Built a House for His Cow
AST-W,M
Farmer Comes to Town

WS-W,M
Farmer Feeds Them All
GrM-W,M
Farmer Feeds Us All
GrM-W,M
Farmer He Must Feed Them All
Oz3-W
Farmer in the Dell
AH-W,M BBF-W,M BM-W
GUM1-W,M HS-W,M MF-W,M
MG-W,M OTJ-W,M RW-W,M
TMA-W,M
Farmer Is an Honest Man
SOT-W,M
Farmer Is the Man
AFP-W FW-W IHA-W,M
SWF-W,M WU-W,M
Farmer of North Bend
MPP-W OHG-W,M
Farmer Went Riding
ASB1-W,M
Farmer Went to Market
SiR-W,M
Farmer's Boy
BSC-W CSo-W,M Oz1-W,M
Farmer's Curst Wife
AA-W,M BT-W,M FMT-W
PSN-W,M RW-W,M
Farmer's Daughter
Oz4-W
Farmer's in His Den
CSG-W,M
Farmers' March
GrM-W,M
Farmer's Song (All Walk Along and
Swing the Hoe)
ASB6-W,M
Farmer's Song (Oh, Happy Is the
Farmer's Life)
UF-W,M
Farming (Cole Porter)
ML-W,M
Farming (The King He Left Me an
Acre of Land)
FSA2-W,M
Farmyard Cabaret
T-W,M
Farther Along
FGM-W,M FPG-W,M FW-W
HHa-W,M
Farwal, Du Delawar, Du
Pennsylvani Trom
SE-W (Swedish)
Farwal Till Fosterjorden
SE-W (Swedish)
Fascinating Rhythm
GOB-W,M HC2-W,M LSO-W
MF-W,M NYT-W,M
Fascination
HLS1-M MF-M OAP-M OBN-W,M
OPS-M RW-M TI1-W,M TM-W,M
UFB-W,M WGB/O-W,M
WGB/P-W,M
Fascist Rally
BRB-W
Fashionable Beau
ESU-W
Fashionable Belle
ESU-W
Fashions
ESU-W
Fast Break (Theme) see Go for It
Fast Car
CFB-W,M
Fast Lanes and Country Roads
TTH-W,M
Fast Life Woman

LC-W
Fasten Your Seat Belts
Ap-W,M Mo-W,M OTO-W
VSA-W,M
Fat Man
BJ-W,M
Fatal Rose of Red
Oz4-W
Fatal Run
LSR-W,M
Fatal Wedding
BSC-W,M FMT-W ITP-W,M
Oz4-W,M
Fatal Wedding Morn
Oz4-W
Fate
Ki-W,M
Fate of Harry Young
Oz2-W
Fate of John Burgoyne
AWB-W SAR-W,M SBA-W
SI-W,M
Fate of Old Strawberry Roan
HB-W
Fated to Be Mated
UBF-W,M
Father Abraham
AAF-W,M BDW-W,M
Father Abraham's Reply
SiS-W
Father Almighty, Bless Us
ESB-W,M
Father Almighty, Bless Us with
Thy Blessing
AME-W,M
Father and Mother Dear
MML-W,M (Czech)
Father Bless the Gifts We Bring
Thee
SHP-W,M
Father, Dear Father, Come Down
with the Stamps
HAS-W,M
Father, Dear Father, Come Home
with Me Now
FW-W Oz2-W,M
Father Eternal, Ruler of Creation
Hy-W,M
Father Figure
CFB-W,M
Father Fill Us with Thy Love
Hy-W,M
Father Gander's Melodies
AL-W
Father Give Thy Benediction
Hy-W,M
Father Grumble
ASB5-W,M BCT-W,M OTJ-W,M
Oz1-W,M SCa-W,M
Father Hear the Prayer We Offer
AHO-W,M AME-W,M
Father How Long
AFP-W
Father I Own Thy Voice
AHO-W,M
Father I Stretch My Hands to Thee
AME-W,M RW-W,M
Father in Thy Mysterious Presence
Kneeling
AHO-W,M Hy-W,M
Father Is Drinking Again
Oz2-W
Father James' Song
GB-W,M
Father Lead Me Day by Day
AME-W,M Hy-W,M SiR-W,M
SOO-W,M

Father, Long before Creation
Hy-W,M
Father Murphy
VP-W,M
Father Noah
ASB4-W,M
Father of All Our Mercies
AME-W,M
Father of Mercies in Thy Word
AME-W,M Hy-W,M
Father of Peace and God of Love
Hy-W,M
Father of the Bride
I-W,M
Father Paul
Mo-W,M
Father Put the Cow Away, for I
Cannot Milk Tonight
Oz4-W
Father Take My Hand
GH-W,M
Father the Watches of the Night
Are O'er
Hy-W,M
Father Time
WU-W,M
Father Was Killed by the Pinkerton
Men
AL-W
Father We Greet Thee, God of
Love Whose Glory
Hy-W,M
Father We Praise Thee, Now the
Night Is Over
Hy-W,M
Father We Thank Thee
BM-W FH-W,M
Father We Thank Thee for the
Night
Bo-W,M Hy-W,M SHP-W,M
**Father We Thank Thee for the
Night see also Morning Hymn
(Father We Thank Thee for the
Night)**
Father We'll Rest in Thy Love
GrM-W,M
Father Who Mak'st Thy Suff'ring
Sons
AHO-W,M
Father Whose Will Is Life and Good
Hy-W,M
Fatherhood of God and the
Brotherhood of Man
MPP-W,M
Father's a Drunkard and Mother Is
Dead
SY-W,M
Father's Birthday
SOO-W,M
Father's Day
OTJ-W,M
Father's Eyes
VB-W,M
Father's Grave
SFF-W,M
Father's Valentine
SOO-W,M
Father's Whiskers
FW-W OFS-W,M OHO-W,M
OTJ-W,M TMA-W,M
Fatigue Call
ATS-W,M GI-W GO-W
Fattening Frogs for Snakes
DBL-W NF-W
Faucet Song
SOO-W,M
Faultless Bride

BSC-W
Favorite Christmas Hymn
EA-W,M
Favorite New Federal Song
MPP-W,M
Fawn Awake's Song
FSA2-W,M
Fay Mi Fa Re
Boo-W,M
Fear
LS-W,M
Fear No More the Heat o' the Sun
FSS-W,M
Fear Not
GH-W,M
Fear Not, Poor Weary One
AHO-W,M
Fear Thou Not
GH-W,M
**Feast of Gold see California or the
Feast of Gold**
Feast of Lanterns
TF-W,M
Feasting by the Ocean
CA-W,M VA-W,M
Feat of Clay
VS-W,M
Feather or Fur
SSe-W,M
Feather Your Nest
CS-W,M
Feather's Nest
MF-W,M
Feathery Passage
SoC-W
Fed from the Tree of Knowledge
NF-W
Federal Constitution
ESU-W
Federal Constitution and Liberty
Forever
BC1-W,M EA-W,M MPP-W,M
SAR-W,M SY-W,M
Federal Convivial Song
MPP-W
Federal March
BC1-M
Federal Song
MPP-W
Feed It to the Fish
Lo-W,M
Feed the Birds
NI-W,M OTJ-W,M SBS-W,M
WD-W,M
Feeding the Animals
ASB1-W,M
Feeding the Birds
MH-W,M
Feeding the Horses
GUM1-W,M
Feel Like Makin' Love
DP-W,M
Feel Right
TOC83-W,M
Feel So Right
MF-W,M
Feelin' Free
GSM-W,M
Feelin' Stronger Every Day
BR-W,M
Feeling Good
TI1-W,M UBF-W,M UFB-W,M
Feeling I'm Falling
GOB-W,M
Feeling We Once Had
Wi-W,M
Feelings

GrS-W,M GSN4-W,M (Spanish)
IPH-W,M LaS-W,M OBN-W,M
OPS-W,M RW-W,M TI1-W,M
ToO76-W,M (Spanish) UFB-W,M
Feels Alright
AG-W,M
Feels So Right
EC-W,M
Felix the Soldier
SI-W,M
Fella Bird
OTJ-W,M
Fellars of Us-tralia
AF-W
Fellow Needs a Girl
A-W,M L-W OTJ-W,M OTO-W
TI1-W,M UBF-W,M UFB-W,M
Fellow That Looks Like Me
Oz3-W
Fellow Workers Pay Attention
AFP-W
Fellowship (Here's to Comrades in
All Kinds of Weather)
MML-W,M
Fellowship (One for All! Friendship
Never Ending)
MU-W,M
Female Auctioneer
ATS-W,M
Female Convict
SHS-W,M
Female Patriots
SSS-W,M
Female Smuggler
MSB-W
Female Warrior
ESU-W
Femme Fatality
TW-W
Fence Painting
TW-W
Fender Mender
OTJ-W,M
Fengyang Drum
MG-W,M
Fenian Hope of Independence
VP-W
Ferdinand the Bull
HST-W,M
Ferguson Brothers Killing
AFP-W
Fernando
DPE-W,M MF-W,M TI1-W,M
ToO76-W,M UFB-W,M
Ferry (Round)
TF-W,M
Ferry Boat
STS-W,M
Ferry Boat Serenade
RW-W,M
Ferry Cross the Mersey
TI2-W,M
Festival Carol
OB-W,M
Festival of Lights
ASB4-W,M
Festival of Spring
MMY-W,M
Festive Wine Cup
SBJ-W,M
Feudin' and Fightin'
TI1-W,M UFB-W,M
Fever
DJ-W,M OnT6-W,M TI2-W,M
Few Days
WN-W,M
Few Negroes by States

NF-W
Fhir A Bata
SeS-W,M
Fichermont Mon Beau Domaine
SSN-W,M (French)
Fickle Finger of Fate
Mo-W,M NM-W,M OTO-W
Fiddle and I
AmH-W,M MH-W,M WiS8-W,M
Fiddle Blues
LC-W
Fiddle Dee Dee
HS-W,M RW-W,M
Fiddle Faddle
FR-W,M
Fiddle-I-Fee
RW-W,M
Fiddle Rag
POT-M
Fiddler
ASB6-W,M
Fiddler on the Roof
DBC-W,M HC1-W,M LM-W,M
On-W,M OTJ-W,M OTO-W
SBF-W,M TI2-W,M TW-W
UBF-W,M
Fiddlers of Ophir Creek
CMG-W,M
Fiddles and Horns
MH-W,M
Fidelity Fiduciary Bank
OnT6-W,M WD-W,M
Fides Est Animae Vita
Boo-W,M (Latin Only)
Fidgety Feet
GOB-W,M MF-W,M
Fiducia
SHS-W,M
Field Artillery Song
TI1-W,M UFB-W,M
**Field Artillery Song see also
Caisson Song and Caissons Go
Rolling Along**
Field Daisy
MH-W,M
Field of Bannockburn
SBB-W
Field of Monterey
HSD-W,M Oz4-W,M
Field of Wheat
LMR-W,M
Field Song (South Dakota
University)
CoS-W,M
Fields of Vietnam
IFM-W VS-W,M
Fier, My Savior, Fier
NSS-W
Fierce Raged the Tempest o'er the
Deep
AME-W,M
Fiesta
OU-W,M
Fifteen Glorious Years
PAJ-W,M
Fifteen Years on the Erie Canal
ATS-W,M
Fifth Nocturne
AmH-M
Fifth of Beethoven
ToO76-M
Fifth Symphony Theme
(Tchaikovsky)
MF-M
Fifty Million Times a Day
GSM-W,M
Fifty Ways to Leave Your Lover

GrS-W,M ToO76-W,M
Fifty Years I've Known a
Woodland
BMM-W
Fight Ames Fight
CoS-W,M
Fight at Bunker Hill
BSC-W
Fight 'Em Washington
CoS-W,M
Fight Fight Fight for University of
Akron
CoS-W,M
Fight for Cornell
IL-W,M
Fight for L.S.U.
SLS-W,M
Fight for Our Dear Old T.T.
CoS-W,M
Fight for the Nigger
SiS-W
Fight of the Armstrong Privateer
ANS-W
Fight On
Mo-W,M TO-W,M
Fight On Pennsylvania
IL-W,M
Fight over Me
NN2-W,M
Fight Siwash
CoS-W,M
Fight Song
Mo-W,M NM-W,M OTO-W
Fight Song (Lake Forest College)
CoS-W,M
Fight the Good Fight
CA-W,M
Fight the Good Fight with All Thy
Might
Hy-W,M
**Fight Them Washington see Fight
'Em Washington**
Fighter Pilot's Hymn
AF-W
Fighter Pilot's Hymn II
AF-W
Fightin' Mad
SoC-W
Fightin' Side of Me
NMH-W,M
Fighting for My Rights
SFF-W,M
Fighting for Pharaoh
DB-W,M TW-W
Fighting On
RF-W,M
Fighting Q.M.C.
GI-W
Fighting Seventy-Ninth
GI-W,M
Fileuse
F2-W,M (French)
Fil-i-mi-oo-ree-ay
TO-W,M
Filipino Hombre
ATS-W
**Fill' Du Roi D'Espagne see La Fill'
Du Roi D'Espagne**
Fill in the Words
TP-W,M UBF-W,M
Fill My Cup Lord
BSG-W,M BSP-W,M HHa-W,M
**Fille De La Meuniere see La Fille De
La Meuniere**
**Fille De Parthenay see La Fille De
Parthenay**
Fille De Quinze Ans see Une Fille

De Quinze Ans
Filled with Life
   JF-W,M
Filles De Roi see Les Filles De Roi
Fillimeecriay
   FGM-W,M
Finally
   TOC82-W,M VB-W,M
Find a Hurt and Heal It
   VB-W,M
Find a Reason to Believe
   TI2-W,M
Find a Way
   GP-W,M VB-W,M
Fine and Dandy
   DBC-W,M HC1-W,M OHB-W,M
   RoE-W,M
Fine and Mellow
   LSB-W,M TI2-W,M
Fine Flowers in the Valley
   SeS-W,M
Fine Knacks for Ladies
   SSP-W TF-W,M
Fine Mess
   TTH-W,M
Fine Old Country Gentleman
   CA-W,M
Fine Old English Gentleman
   CSo-W,M
Fine Ould Irish Gentleman
   SY-W,M
Fine Plaster
   NF-W
Fine Romance
   BeL-W,M RW-W,M TI1-W,M
   UFB-W,M
Finger Play No. 1
   OTJ-W,M
Finger Play No.2
   OTJ-W,M
Fingerprint File
   RoS-W,M
Fingers and Toes
   GI-W,M
Finian's Exit
   FR-W,M
Finkelach see Die Finkelach
Finlandia
   HS-W,M LMR-M MF-M MML-W,M
   OTJ-W,M RW-M TI1-M UFB-M
Finnegan's Wake
   FW-W
Fire (Cling Clang! Cling Clang!
   Trucks Go Rushing By)
   ASB3-W,M
Fire (Fire, Fire, Fire! See the Engine
   Going)
   MH-W,M
Fire (Jimi Hendrix)
   PoG-W,M
Fire (Ohio Players)
   SoH-W,M
Fire and Rain
   IHA-W,M
Fire-Can Song
   AF-W
Fire Department
   ASB1-W,M
Fire Down Below
   FW-W OTJ-W,M SA-W,M
Fire Engine
   GM-W
Fire in My Meditation Burned
   AHO-W,M
Fire in the Mountain
   CSG-W,M
Fire My Savior Fire see Fier My

Savior Fier
Fire Tragedy
   ITP-W,M
Fireflies
   VA-W,M
Firefly
   MF-W,M Mo-W,M NM-W,M
   OTJ-W,M SOO-W,M TI2-W,M
Fireman (I'd Like to Be a Fireman)
   SOO-W,M
Fireman (with the Engine Goes)
   MH-W,M
Fireman's Anniversary Song
   OHG-W,M
Fireman's Song (The Sailor at Sea,
   and the Soldier on Land)
   SY-W,M
Fireman's Song (When the Lurid
   Flame at Night)
   AL-W
Fireship
   FW-W LW-W,M PO-W,M
   PSN-W,M
Firestone Where the Rubber Meets
   the Road
   GSM-W,M
Fireworks
   DR-W,M
Firm Names
   FSA1-W,M
Firmly Stand My Native Land
   Boo-W,M HSD-W,M
First Chair Player
   SiR-W,M
First Christmas Night
   ASB2-W,M
First for Good Reason
   GSM-W,M
First Fruits in 1812
   ANS-W
First Green
   FSA2-W,M
First Gun Is Fired
   SiS-W,M
First Mazurka (Theme)
   MH-W,M
First Noel
   AME-W,M BCh-W,M BCS-W,M
   BM-W CCH-W,M CCM-W,M
   CEM-W,M CI-W,M FM-W,M
   FW-W HS-W,M Hy-W,M IL-W,M
   MF-W,M MML-W,M OAP-W,M
   OPS-W,M OTJ-W,M RW-W,M
   SAC-W,M SCS-W SiR-W,M
   TI1-W,M UFB-W,M Y-W,M
First Nowell
   CC-W,M FSA1-W,M GBC-W,M
   Gu-W,M HSD-W,M JOC-W,M
   MC-W,M OB-W,M SL-W,M U-W
First Nowell the Angel Did Say
   YC-W,M
First of May
   MU-W,M (Provencal)
First Pledge
   ESU-W
First Pythic Ode
   MU-W,M (Greek)
First Signs of Spring
   BMC-W,M
First Snowdrops
   UF-W,M
First Star
   FSA1-W,M
First Stone
   VB-W,M
First Thing Each Morning
   TOH-W,M

First Thing I Do Every Morning
   BSG-W,M BSP-W,M FS-W,M
First Thing Monday Morning
   P-W,M
First Things First
   Mo-M
First Time (Ebb/Kander)
   UBF-W,M
First Time (Michel Legrand)
   MLS-W,M
First Time (She Was a Honey, She
   Was One of the Best)
   AF-W
First Time Ever I Saw Your Face
   DPE-W,M FW-W GrH-W,M
   GrS-W,M GSN4-W,M ILT-W,M
   MF-W,M RW-W,M WG-W,M
First Time I Heard a Bluebird
   MLS-W,M
First Tulip
   ASB5-W,M
Fish and Tea
   SI-W,M
Fisherman (Dip the Oars in the
   Water Blue)
   ASB1-W,M
Fisherman (In Winter When It's
   Raining)
   FSA1-W,M
Fisherman (Lightly Floats My Little
   Boat)
   UF-W,M
Fisherman's Church
   AL-W
Fisherman's Daughter
   Oz4-W
Fisherman's Girl
   ESU-W
Fisherman's Song
   SBF-W,M
Fishermen (O Fishermen,
   Fishermen, Pull for the Sea)
   ASB5-W,M
Fishermen's Song
   IN-W,M
Fisher's Hornpipe
   AmH-M POT-M
Fishin' Creek Blues
   FSB3-M
Fishin' Hole
   GTV-W,M
Fishin' Song
   LaS-W,M
Fishing Simon
   NF-W
Fishing Song
   UF-W,M
Fit As a Fiddle
   RW-W,M
Fitches and Austins
   BMM-W
Five and Ten Cent Store
   MH-W,M
Five Angels
   RSL-W,M
Five Brothers
   TI1-M UFB-M
Five Can't Ketch Me and Ten Can't
   Hold Me
   NSS-W
Five Currant Buns
   OTJ-W,M
5-D
   RB-W
Five Fat Turkeys
   RSL-W,M
Five Fifteen

WA-W,M
Five Foot Two, Eyes of Blue
 BBB-W,M GG2-W,M GG5-W,M
 GSN2-W,M GST-W,M HLS2-W,M
 MAB1-W MF-W,M MSA1-W
 PB-W,M RDT-W,M RW-W,M
 TI2-W,M
Five-Four Blues
 Mo-M
Five Hundred Hats
 ASB5-W,M
Five Hundred Miles
 FVV-W,M GOI7-W,M OPS-W,M
 OTJ-W,M
Five Little Campers (Cowboys,
 Pumpkins, Snowflakes,
 Spacemen)
 MAR-W,M
Five Little Flowers
 GM-W
Five Little Pumpkins
 MES1-W,M MES2-W,M SiR-W,M
Five Little Soldiers
 FP-W,M
Five Little Squirrels
 FF-W
Five Little White Mice
 MH-W,M
Five Long Years
 DBL-W
Five Minutes More
 Mo-W,M NM-W,M TI2-W,M
Five Nights Drunk (You Old Fool)
 TO-W,M
Five O'Clock Drag
 GMD-W,M
Five O'Clock World
 MF-W,M
Five Short Minutes
 JC-W,M
5-10-15 Hours
 HRB1-W,M
Five to My Five
 FVV-W,M
Five Were Foolish
 AHO-W,M
Fix Your Eyes upon Jesus
 GH-W,M
Fixin' to Die Rag
 VS-W,M
Fixing a Hole
 BBe-W,M PMC-W,M TWS-W
Flag
 ASB5-W,M
Flag Ceremony
 MuM-W,M
Flag Day
 MH-W,M
Flag of Columbia
 AAP-W,M Sin-W,M
Flag of Fort Sumter
 SiS-W
Flag of Liberty
 ASB6-W,M
Flag of Our Union
 ATS-W,M MPP-W SY-W,M
Flag of Texas
 MPP-W,M OHG-W,M
Flag of the Constellation
 AWB-W
Flag of the Free
 ESB-W,M WiS8-W,M
Flag of the Regiment
 SiS-W
Flag of the Sunny South
 SiS-W
Flag Song

OTJ-W,M
Flag Song (Brave, Martial Music on
 the Highway Sounding)
 SL-W,M
Flag Song (Out on the Breeze o'er
 Land and Seas)
 ASB4-W,M
Flag with the Thirty-Four Stars
 BSC-W
Flagman
 MH-W,M
Flak in the Night
 AF-W
Flak Showers
 AF-W
Flambeau, Jeanette, Isabelle see
 Un Flambeau, Jeanette, Isabelle
Flaming Agnes
 I-W,M
Flamingo
 Mo-W,M TI2-W,M
Flamingo Stew
 TW-W
Flap Jacks
 NF-W
Flash Bang Wallop
 OTO-W
Flash Frigate
 ANS-W
Flashdance (Love Theme)
 TI2-M
Flashdance (What a Feeling)
 HFH-W,M TI2-W,M
Flat Foot Floogee
 TI1-W,M UFB-W,M
Flat Top
 CCS-W,M
Flatiron
 FSB3-M
Flatt'rer
 AmH-M
Flawless
 VB-W,M
Flaxwheel
 FSA1-W,M
Flee As a Bird
 ATS-W,M HSD-W,M RDF-W,M
Flemish Carol
 OB-W,M
Fleur De Cactus
 SSN-W,M (French)
Flight
 RoS-W,M
Flight, The
 GUM1-W,M
Flight of the Foo Birds
 MF-M
Flight '76
 ToO76-M
Fling Out the Banner
 AHO-W,M
Fling Out the Banner! Let It Float
 Hy-W,M
Fling to the Breeze Our Banner
 AL-W
Flip, Flop and Fly
 HRB3-W,M
Flipper (Theme)
 GTV-W,M
Floatin' Down to Cotton Town
 Mo-W,M NM-W,M
Floats
 MaG-W,M
Flodden Field
 SBS-W
Floods Swell around Me, Angry,
 Appalling

AHO-W,M
Flop-Eared Mule
 FPG-M POT-M
Flora Gave Me Fairest Flowers
 OH-W,M
Flora MacDonald's Lament
 SeS-W,M
Florella
 FMT-W
Florence
 LSO-W
Florian's Song
 AmH-W,M LMR-W,M TH-W,M
 WiS8-W,M
Florida
 SHS-W,M
Florida Blues
 B-W,M Bl-W,M
Flow Gently, Sweet Afton
 ESB-W,M FM-W,M FW-W
 Gu-W,M HSD-W,M LTL-W,M
 MAB1-W MSA1-W NAS-W,M
 OFS-W,M OS-W OTJ-W,M
 RW-W,M SeS-W,M SL-W
 TH-W,M WiS8-W,M
Flow, River
 ASB6-W,M
Flow, River, Flow
 MHB-W,M (Russian)
Flow, Thou Regal Purple Stream
 ESU-W
Flower Carol
 OB-W,M
Flower Drum (Hua Ku Ko)
 FD-W,M (Chinese) SBF-W,M
 (Chinese Only)
Flower Gardens
 UF-W
Flower Ghosts
 FSA2-W,M
Flower Girl
 FSA1-W,M
Flower of Changunga
 MHB-W,M (Spanish)
Flower of Dawn
 Mo-W,M NM-W,M
Flower Song (Gustav Lange)
 AmH-M
Flower Song (Herbert/Bach)
 FSA2-W,M SL-W,M
Flowers Are Dying
 Boo-W,M
Flowers for Mother
 ASB3-W,M
Flowers for Sale
 SiR-W,M
Flowers' Lullaby
 ASB2-W,M
Flower's Message
 SoP-W,M
Flowers of the Forest
 SBB-W
Flowers on the Wall
 CMG-W,M TI1-W,M UFB-W,M
Flowers That Bloom in the Spring
 GiS-W,M HSD-W,M MGT-W,M
 OTJ-W,M WiS8-W,M
Flow'ret
 AmH-M
Floyd Collins
 ITP-W,M
Floyd Frazier
 FSU-W
Fluffy
 ASB1-W,M
Flushed from the Bathroom of Your
 Heart

WF-W,M
Fluttering Leaves
MH-W,M
Fly, The
GM-W
Fly Around My Blue-Eyed Gal
FW-W POT-W,M
Fly Away
CJ-W,M PoG-W,M TI1-W,M
UFB-W,M WG-W,M
Fly Bird Fly
ASB5-W,M
Fly Eagle
ASB5-W,M
Fly into Love
TOC83-W,M
Fly Kite
MH-W,M
Fly Me to the Moon
DJ-W,M FPS-W,M NK-W,M
TI1-W,M TWD-W,M UFB-W,M
Fly, My Affection
LA-W,M (Spanish)
Fly Now, O Song I'm Singing
MML-W,M
Fly She Sat
Boo-W,M
Fly Song
GI-W,M
Flying
TWS-W
Flying Cloud
SA-W,M
Flying Cranes
UF-W,M
Flying Down to Rio (If Offered Any
Transportation to the Place
Where I Would Go)
ASB6-W,M
Flying Down to Rio (Where There's
Rhythm and Rhyme)
TI1-W,M UFB-W,M
Flying Dutchman (Overture)
LMR-M
Flying for Me
CJ-W,M
Flying Home
TI1-W,M UFB-W,M
Flyin' Home to Nashville
CMG-W,M
Flying Trapeze
OGH-W,M PoS-W,M
Flynn of Virginia
OHG-W,M
Fo' Day Worry Blues
NeF-W
Foes and Friends
Sin-W,M SiS-W
Foggy Day (in London Town)
DJ-W,M FPS-W,M FrS-W,M
HC2-W,M LM-W,M LSO-W
NYT-W,M OTO-W TI1-W,M
TW-W UFB-W,M
Foggy Dew
FSU-W FW-W IS-W,M Oz1-W,M
PO-W,M
Foggy, Foggy Dew
AmS-W,M F3-W,M FW-W
GG2-W,M IHA-W,M IL-W,M
OTJ-W,M SAm-W,M
Foggy Mountain Top
BIS-W,M BSo-W,M FW-W
Fohty Days an' Nights
NH-W
Fola Fola Blakken
MG-W,M
Fold My Hands and Tie My Feet

RTH-W
Folk Dances
FSA1-W,M
Folk Song
MHB-W,M
Folks Who Live on the Hill
L-W
Follow Me
HCY-W,M
Follow Me (John Denver)
CJ-W,M PoG-W,M WG-W,M
Follow Me (Lerner/Loewe)
LL-W,M OTO-W TI1-W,M
UBF-W,M UFB-W,M
Follow Me (Round)
Boo-W,M
Follow Me, Boys
OnT1-W,M
Follow Me, Full of Glee
AmH-W,M
Follow Me Quickly
Boo-W,M
Follow On (Come Along, Sing
Along, Follow Me)
HS-W,M VA-W,M
Follow On! (Down in the Valley,
with My Saviour I Would Go)
GH-W,M
Follow That Dream
SRE1-W,M TI1-W,M UFB-W,M
Follow the Drinkin' Gourd
IHA-W,M SFM-W WSB-W,M
Follow the Drum
SiS-W
Follow the Leader (Follow Me
Wherever I Go)
MH-W,M
Follow the Leader (Play This
Morning at Follow the Leader)
FSA2-W,M
Follow the Swallow to Hideaway
Hollow
Mo-W,M NM-W,M
Follow Washington
SSS-W,M
Follow Your Heart
PF-W,M
Followers of the Lamb
GB-W,M
Following Fully
GH-W,M
Following the King
VB-W,M
Following the Leader
NI-W,M
Following You
VB-W,M
Folsom Prison Blues
CMG-W,M OGC2-W,M RW-W,M
TI1-W,M UFB-W,M
Fond Affection
BB-W BSC-W
Fond Appeal
EL-W,M
Fond of Chewing Gum
Oz3-W,M
Fontaine see La Fontaine
Food, Glorious Food
O-W TI1-W,M UFB-W,M
Fool (If You Think It's Over)
PoG-W,M
Fool, Fool, Fool
HRB1-W,M
Fool for Your Love
TOC83-W,M
Fool on the Hill
BBe-W,M Be2-W,M FPS-W,M

PMC-W,M SwS-W,M TWS-W
Fool That I Am
TI1-W,M UFB-W,M
Fool to Cry
RoS-W,M
Fooled by a Feeling
TOH-W,M ToO79-W,M
Foolin' Around
CSp-W,M
Foolish Beat
CFB-W,M
Foolish Boy
TBF-W,M
Foolish Little Girl
MF-W,M
Foolish Pride
TTH-W,M
Foolish Questions
OHO-W,M
Foolish Senorita
LMR-W,M
Fools Fall in Love
HRB3-W,M MF-W,M
Fools Rush In
FrS-W,M MF-W,M OHF-W
RoE-W,M
Foot Traveler
SCL-W,M
Foot Traveller
FSD-W,M
Football
ASB6-W,M
Football Song (Eighteen Hundred
and Sixty-One, Football, Football)
Oz2-W,M
Football Song (Oh, Soccer Is
Played in Old England)
VA-W,M
**Footloose Love Theme see Almost
Paradise**
Footprints in the Snow
BIS-W,M BSo-W,M
Fopp
DP-W,M
For a Winter World of White
SHP-W,M
For All My Sin
BSG-W,M BSP-W,M
For All the Blessings of the Year
AME-W,M
For All the Saints
OM-W,M SJ-W,M
For All the Saints Who from Their
Labors Rest
Hy-W,M
For All the Wrong Reasons
TOC82-W,M
For All Thy Gifts of Love
SHP-W,M
For All We Know
FPS-W,M GrS-W,M GSO-W,M
MF-W,M RW-W,M TI1-W,M
TI2-W,M UFB-W,M
For Baby
CJ-W,M PoG-W,M WG-W,M
For Bales
SCo-W,M Sin-W,M SiS-W,M
For Bobbie
PoG-W,M WG-W,M
For Carlos
OnT6-M
For Every Fish
TW-W
For Every Man There's a Woman
Mo-W,M NM-W,M OTO-W
TI2-W,M
For Health and Strength

Fount of Glory
SHS-W,M
Fountain
GC-W,M
Fountain (Into the Sunshine, Full of
the Light)
FSA2-W,M
Fountain (O How Fresh and Pure
the Rippling, Chattering Fountain)
ASB6-W,M
Fountain (Upon the Terrace Where
I Play)
MH-W,M
Fountain in the Park
FSN-W,M
**Fountain in the Park see also While
Strolling through the Park**
Four and Twenty
RV-W
Four Brothers (Jimmie Giuffre)
TI2-M
Four Brothers (I Had Four Brothers
over the Sea)
Oz1-W
**Four Day Worry Blues see Fo' Day
Worry Blues**
Four-F Charlie
GI-W,M
Four Faces
ASB6-W,M
Four-Finger Rag
FG2-M
Four Freedoms
LMR-W,M
Four Generals
LaS-W,M SMW-W,M (Spanish)
Four Green Fields
IS-W,M
Four in the Middle
Oz3-W,M
**Four Insurgent Generals see Los
Cuatro Generales**
Four Little Angels of Peace
TW-W
Four Little Cats
AST-W,M
Four Maries
FW-W PSN-W,M
Four Marys
BF-W,M FGM-W,M Oz1-W
Four Mothers
TI1-M UFB-M
Four Nights Drunk
FW-W LW-W,M PO-W,M
Four O'Clock
LS-W,M
Four Pence a Day
FW-W
**Four Pence a Day see also
Fourpence a Day**
Four Runaway Negroes; Whence
They Came
NF-W
Four Seasons
MH-W,M
Four Sixes
SoC-W
Four Strong Winds
ERM-W,M
Four Walls
RW-W,M
Four Weavers
VA-W,M
Four Winds (Blow, Blow, Breezes
of Spring!)
ASB5-W,M
Four Winds (The Winds Blow

South, the Winds Blow North)
SL-W,M
Fourfold Amen
LMR-W,M
Fourpence a Day
BB-W SWF-W,M
**Fourpence a Day see also Four
Pence a Day**
Fourteen Ninety-Two
ASB4-W,M
Fox, The
BF-W,M FW-W GuC-W,M IL-W,M
OTJ-W,M RDT-W,M TBF-W,M
Fox and Geese
NF-W
Fox and Goose
SOO-W,M
Fox and Rabbit Drinking
Propositions
NF-W
Fox and the Grapes
FSA1-W,M
Fox Chase
SCa-W
Fox Has Left His Lair
Su-W,M
Fox on the Run (Mannfred Mann)
BSo-W,M
Fox on the Run (Sweet)
ToO76-W,M
Fox Walked Out
Oz1-W,M
Foxy Lady
PoG-W,M
Fragment
SBA-W
Fragment of a Chanted Negro
Sermon
AN-W
Fran Nordens Sorgbundna Dalar
SE-W (Swedish)
Fran Sveas Vanner, En Doende
Cowboy
SoC-W,M (Swedish)
Frank and Jesse James
NH-W
Frank James, the Burglar
SCa-W
Frank Little
AFP-W
Frank Mills
H-W,M
Frank Pierce's Soliloquy
MPP-W
**Frank Sinatra Show Theme see Put
Your Dreams Away (for Another
Day)**
Frankfort Special
SRE2-W,M
Frankfort Town
AFP-W
Frankie
FMT-W
Frankie and Albert
AmS-W,M AN-W BSC-W NeF-W
Frankie and Johnnie
GI-W,M
Frankie and Johnny
AFB-W,M AmS-W,M BF-W,M
BH-W,M FG1-W,M FW-W
GG2-W,M HLS1-W,M IHA-W,M
IL-W,M IPH-W,M LJ-W,M
LW-W,M MF-W,M NO-W,M
OPS-W,M OTJ-W,M Oz2-W,M
RW-W,M SRE2-W,M TI1-W,M
UFB-W,M
Frankie Blues

AmS-W,M
Frankie Dupree
ITP-W,M
Frankie Silver
Oz2-W,M
Franklin D. Roosevelt
BMM-W
Franklin D. Roosevelt's Back Again
FW-W
Franklin Slaughter Ranch
HB-W,M
Franklin's Crew
SA-W,M
Fray Martin
GM-W
Frazier
OHF-W
Freckles
SoC-W
Fred on Bed
BRB-W
Freddie Freeloader
MF-M
Freddy and His Fiddle
SN-W,M
Freddy Frog
GM-W
Freddy, My Love
Gr-W,M Mo-W,M OTO-W TW-W
Free Again
LC-W
Free America
ATS-W,M AWB-W EA-W,M
FW-W HSD-W,M IHA-W,M
SI-W,M TMA-W
Free Amerikay
SSS-W,M
Free at Las'
BDW-W,M
Free at Last
AH-W,M FW-W JF-W,M Me-W,M
OTJ-W,M
Free Bird
TI2-W,M
Free Born Man
BSo-W,M
Free Concert
FSA1-W,M
Free Free My Lord
NH-W
Free, Go Lily
FVV-W,M
Free Little Bird
BSC-W FW-W
Free Lunch Cadets
OHG-W,M
Free Man
DDH-W,M
Free Silver
AL-W,M BMM-W
Free the People
MCG-W,M RW-W,M
Free Trade and a Misty Moon
E-W,M
Freedman's Song
SiS-W
Freedom (Bread Is Freedom,
Freedom Bread)
AL-W
Freedom (Everybody Sing
Freedom)
JF-W,M
Freedom (Freedom's in the State
of Mind)
OTO-W Sh-W,M UBF-W,M
Freedom (I Want Freedom Now)
SRS-W,M

Freedom (Land Where the Banners
  Wave Last in the Sun)
  VA-W,M
Freedom (Man's Got to Make His
  Own)
  SBS-W,M
Freedom Is a Constant Struggle
  FW-W JF-W,M SFF-W,M
Freedom Isn't Free
  HCY-W,M
Freedom Now
  JF-W SFF-W,M
Freedom of Election
  MPP-W
Freedom Overspill
  TTH-W,M
Freedom Rider
  IHA-W,M
Freedom Road
  J-W,M
Freedom Train A-Comin'
  SFF-W,M
Freedom's Comin' and It Won't Be
  Long
  SFF-W,M
Freedom's Era
  NSS-W
Freedom's Muster Drum
  SiS-W
Freedom's Sons
  IS-W,M
Freeman Blues
  LC-W
Freight Boats
  ASB6-W,M
Freight Handler's Strike
  AFP-W AL-W
Freight Train (Freight Train, Run So
  Fast)
  BSo-W,M FAW-W,M FG1-M
  FW-W LSR-W,M
Freight Train (Is Coming Along
  the Track)
  ASB1-W,M
Freight Train Blues
  LC-W LSR-W,M
Freight Train Joe
  OnT6-M
Freight Wreck at Altoona
  LSR-W,M
Freiheit
  FW-W (German)
Fremont Campaign
  SY-W,M
French Broad
  SHS-W,M
French Connection (Theme)
  MF-M
French Cradle Song
  SOO-W,M
**French National Song see La
  Marseillaise**
Frere Jacques
  BBF-W,M FW-W (French)
  Boo-W,M (French, Spanish)
  CUP-W,M (French Only) FW-W
  (French) HS-W,M (French)
  MP-W,M (French Only) OTJ-W,M
  (French Only) RW-W,M (French
  Only) SBF-W,M (French) TI1-W,M
  (French Only) UFB-W,M (French
  Only)
**Frere Jacques see also Are You
  Sleeping and Brother John**
Fresa Salvaje
  TI1-W,M (Spanish Only)
  UFB-W,M (Spanish Only)

Freshmen Get Together
  A-W,M
Friday Night
  IFM-W
Friday Night Blues
  TOH-W,M
Friday on My Mind
  THN-W,M
Friend, a Friend
  Boo-W,M
Friendless Blues
  B-W,M Bl-W,M
Friendly Beasts
  BCS-W,M CCM-W,M HS-W,M
  KS-W,M SFB-W,M
Friendly Cow
  MH-W,M
Friendly Cricket
  ASB5-W,M
Friendly Fire
  VB-W,M
Friendly Island
  Mo-W,M
Friendly Islands
  NM-W,M
Friendly Persuasion
  HLS5-W,M MF-W,M RT5-W,M
  RW-W,M
Friends
  OTJ-W,M
Friends (Michael W. Smith)
  GP-W,M VB-W,M
Friends (Theme from Kate and
  Allie)
  BNG-W,M DC-W,M TVT-W,M
Friends and Lovers (Both to Each
  Other)
  DC-W,M GCM-W,M MF-W,M
  RoE-W,M
Friends for Tea
  MH-W,M
Friends Forever
  TVT-W,M
Friends! Friends! Friends!
  SHP-W,M
Friends Goodbye
  LC-W
Friends of Temperance
  Oz2-W
Friends with You
  PoG-W,M
Friendship (Cole Porter)
  FPS-W,M HC2-W,M ML-W,M
  OTO-W TI1-W,M TW-W UBF-
  W,M UFB-W,M
Friendship (Lapland Tune)
  FSA1-W,M
Friendship (Marzials)
  AmH-W,M
Friendship (Mozart)
  ASB6-W,M
Friggin' Falcon
  PO-W,M
Frightened Away from a Chicken
  Roost
  NF-W NH-W
Frisco Rag Time
  NH-W
Frisco Strike Saga
  AFP-W
Frisky Jim
  Oz3-W
Fritz Truan, a Great Cowboy
  HB-W
Frog and Owl
  ASB4-W,M
Frog and the Mouse

MG-W,M TBF-W,M
Frog He Did A-Wooing Ride
  BSC-W,M
Frog He Went A-Courting
  SCa-W,M
Frog He Would A-Wooing Go
  HS-W,M TBF-W,M
Frog in a Mill
  NF-W
Frog Music
  VA-W,M
Frog Pond
  OTJ-W,M
Frog Round
  FSA1-W,M
Frog Went A-Courtin'
  ASB4-W,M BMC-W,M BSC-W,M
  DD-W,M HAS-W,M HS-W,M
  NF-W Oz1-W RW-W,M SCa-W,M
  TBF-W,M VA-W,M
**Frog Went A-Courtin' see also
  Froggie Went A-Courtin', and Mr.
  Frog Went A-Courtin' and He Did
  Ride**
Frog Went Co'tin'
  MHB-W,M
Froggie
  SD-W,M
Froggie, Jump
  GM-W
Froggie Went A-Courtin'
  FW-W ITP-W,M J-W,M OTJ-W,M
  SAm-W,M
**Froggie Went A-Courtin' see also
  Frog Went A-Courtin'**
Frogs (Round)
  BCS-W,M TF-W,M
Frogs at Night
  ASB2-W,M
Frogs at School
  MH-W,M
Frog's Courtship
  BT-W,M FMT-W Oz1-W,M
From a Jack to a King
  EP-W,M
From a Window
  Be1-W,M
From Age to Age They Gather
  AHO-W,M AME-W,M
From All That Dwell below the
  Skies
  AME-W,M GH-W Hy-W,M
**From All That Dwell below the
  Skies see also Alleluia (From All
  That Dwell below the Skies)**
From Alpha to Omega
  ML-W,M
From Countless Hearts
  AHO-W,M
From Cradle to Altar
  L-W
From Depths of Swedish Hearts
  SiP-W,M (Swedish)
From Every Kind of Man
  GiS-W,M MGT-W,M
From Every Spire on Christmas Eve
  CSF-W
From Every Stormy Wind That
  Blows
  AME-W,M Hy-W,M
From Graceland to the Promised
  Land
  NMH-W,M
From Greenland's Icy Mountains
  AH-W,M AME-W,M FH-W,M
  SJ-W,M WiS7-W,M
From Heart to Heart

AHO-W,M
From Heaven Above
LMR-W,M SJ-W,M
From Heaven Above to Earth I
Come
CCM-W,M
From Heaven High I Come to You
CC-W,M YC-W,M
From Here to Eternity
FrS-W,M
From His Canadian Home
CFS-W,M (French)
From Ill Do Thou Defend Me
MML-W,M
From Me to You
BBe-W,M ILS-W,M MF-W,M
OPS-W,M TWS-W
From My Album
AL-W
From My Father's Collection
SNS-W
From Now On
ReG-W,M
From Ocean unto Ocean
Hy-W,M
From Paris to St. Denis, See
CFS-W,M (French)
From Russia with Love
HLS5-W,M RT6-W,M RW-W,M
From Slavery
NF-W
From the Bottle to the Bottom
SuS-W,M
From the British Light Infantry
SBA-W
From the Candy Store on the
Corner to the Chapel on the Hill
TI1-W,M UFB-W,M
From the Declaration of
Independence
LMR-W,M
From the Fair Lavinian Shore
SSP-W
From the Land of the Sky Blue
Water
Mo-W,M NM-W,M
From the Moon
GB-W,M
From the Northland's Grieving
Valleys
SE-W (Swedish)
From the Red Battlefield
SiS-W
From the Rubaiyat
Ki-W,M
From the Sea
MMM-W,M
From the Sunny Spanish Shore
GiS-W,M
From Thee All Skill and Science
Flow
Hy-W,M
From This Day On
LL-W,M OnT6-W,M TW-W
From This Moment
VB-W,M
From This Moment On
DBC-W,M DJ-W,M HC2-W,M
ML-W,M OTO-W TI1-W,M
UBF-W,M UFB-W,M
From Town
HOH-W
From Whence Doth This Union
Arise
AHO-W,M
Frost
UF-W,M

Frost Pictures (Frost upon the
Window Glass)
ASB3-W,M
Frost Pictures (In Wintertime an
Artist Comes)
ASB2-W,M
Frosty the Snow Man
BCS-W,M RW-W,M TI1-W,M
UFB-W,M
Frowns That She Gave Me
Oz4-W
Frozen Girl
AmS-W,M BSC-W,M
Frozen Logger
FW-W WSB-W,M
Fruitful Fields Are Waving
Boo-W
Fruits and Vegetables
BMC-W,M
Fruits on Your Trees
LC-W,M
Fugitive (Theme)
GTV-M
Fugitive Breakdown
BIS-W,M
Fugue for Tinhorns
TI2-W,M TW-W UBF-W,M
Fugue in Three Voices (from
Bach's Well-Tempered Clavier)
BMC-M
Fulfilment
WN-W,M
Full Fathom Five
SSB-W,M
Full Fathom Five Thy Father Lies
FSS-W,M
Full Many Shall Come from the
East and the West
SJ-W,M
Full Moon and an Empty Heart
OTO-W
Full Moon and Empty Arms
HLS3-W,M MF-W,M
Full Pocketbook
NF-W
Fuller and Warren
BSC-W,M FMT-W Oz2-W,M
Fully Persuaded
GH-W,M
Fully Trusting
GH-W,M
Fum Fum Fum
BeB-W,M CEM-W,M GBC-W,M
HS-W,M (Spanish) MC-W,M
Fumbler's Wife's Cat
SR-W,M
Fun in Our Garden
SOO-W,M
Fun on the Farm
GUM1-W,M
Funeral Anthem
SHS-W,M
Funeral Dirge on the Death of
General George Washington
EA-W,M
Funeral Elegy
BC1-W,M
Funeral March (Chopin)
AmH-M RW-M WiS7-M
Funeral March of a Marionette
AmH-M
Funeral March of the Marionettes
BNG-M
Funeral Thought
SHS-W,M
Funiculi, Funicula
AmH-W,M ESB-W,M IL-W,M

MF-W,M NAS-W,M OFS-W,M
OTJ-W,M TI1-M UFB-M
WiS8-W,M
Funkytown
TI1-W,M UFB-W,M
Funny Clown
SiR-W,M
Funny Face
GOB-W,M NYT-W,M RW-W,M
Funny Girl
OTO-W TI1-W,M UBF-W,M
UFB-W,M
Funny Honey
CMV-W,M
Funny How Time Slips Away
CMG-W,M TI2-W,M WNF-W
Funny Little Bunny
MM-W,M
Funny Little Sailor Men
Ne-W,M
Funny Little Squirrel
SOO-W,M
Funny Old Clown
SOO-W,M
Funny Old Hills
OTO-W
Funny Song
AST-W,M
Funny Thing Happened
TW-W
Funny Witches
ASB1-W,M
Fur Elise
AmH-M MF-M RW-M TI1-M
UFB-M
Fur Trader
FSA1-W,M
Furry Day Carol
OB-W,M
Furry Sings the Blues
RV-W
Furtive Tear
WiS7-W,M
Futile Serenade
SiB-W,M
Future America
AL-W
Future Mrs. 'Awkins
AmH-W,M WiS8-W,M
Fuzzy Caterpillar
SiR-W,M
Fyvie-O
TO-W,M

G

G.I. Blues (I Don't Want No More
of Army Life)
GI-W GO-W
**G.I. Blues (I Don't Want No More
of Army Life) see also Army Life**
G.I. Blues (They Give Us a Room
with a View of the Beautiful
Rhine)
RW-W,M SRE1-W,M TI1-W,M
UFB-W,M
G.I. Insomnia
GI-W
G.I. Jive
OHF-W
G.I. Joe
GI-W
G.I. March
GI-W
GTO
RB-W

G Suits and Parachutes
AF-W
Gabie
Mo-W,M NM-W,M OTO-W
Gabriel's Message
ER-W,M GUM2-W,M OB-W,M
Gadabouts
ASB3-W,M
Gaelic Lullaby
ASB6-W,M
Gage's Proclamation
SSS-W,M
Gai Lon La, Gai Le Rosier
CFS-W,M (French)
Gaily the Troubadour
HSD-W,M NAS-W,M
Gaily thro' Life Wander
TH-W,M
Gaily Tripping
GiS-W,M MU-W,M
Gaines
WN-W,M
Gal from Joe's
GMD-W,M
Gal I Left behind Me
FMT-W FW-W POT-W,M
Gal I Left in Arkansas
Oz1-W
Gal in Calico
MF-W,M
Gal That Got Stuck on Everything
She Saw
LW-W,M
Gal Who Invented Kissin'
OGC1-W,M
Gal with the Balmoral
HAS-W,M OHG-W,M
Gale
ANS-W
Gallant Girl That Smote the
Dastard Tory, Oh
SiS-W
Gallant Old Hero
MPP-W
Gallery Carol
OB-W,M
Galley Slave
ESU-W
Gallis Pole
Le-W,M
Gallis Pole see also Gallows Pole
Galloping Horses
KS-W,M
Galloping Randy Dandy O
SA-W,M
Gallows Pole
FW-W
Gallows Pole see also Gallis Pole
Gallows Tree
Oz1-W
Galman Day
RTH-W
Galway Bay
MAB1-W,M MSA1-W RDT-W,M
TI2-W,M U-W
Galway City
IS-W,M
Galway Piper
YS-W,M
Galway Races
IS-W,M
Gamale Norge
NAS-W,M
Gambler
BSC-W FW-W
Gambler (Theme)
TOM-W,M ToO79-W,M

Gambler's Blues
RW-W,M
Gambler's Sweetheart
Oz4-W
Gambling Man
Oz4-W
Gambling on the Sabbath
HOH-W,M
Gambling on the Sabbath Day
Oz2-W,M
Gambling Polka Dot Blues
LJ-W,M
Game
MH-W,M
Game of Love (The Purpose of a
Man Is to Love a Woman)
MF-W,M
Game of Love (Victor Herbert)
Sw-W,M
Game of Poker
Mo-W,M NM-W,M OHF-W
OTO-W
Games People Play
MCG-W,M RY-W,M
Games That Lovers Play
GG3-W,M RW-W,M THN-W,M
Gandy Dancer's Ball
OTH-W,M
Gang Songs
NH-W
Gang That Sang Heart of My Heart
GG2-W,M GSN2-W,M HLS2-W,M
RDT-W,M RW-W,M
Gantz's Jig
DE-W,M
Garbage (Folk Song)
IHA-W,M
Garbage (Jerry Herman)
Mo-M OTO-W
Garbage Man
GM-W
Garden Helper
GM-W
Garden Hymn
LMR-W,M SHS-W,M
Garden Melody
ASB6-W,M
Garden of Dreams
FSA1-W,M
Garden of Jesus
OB-W,M
Garden of Love
AS-W,M (French)
Garden of My Dreams
CoF-W,M
Garden Party
GrS-W,M
Garden Song
PoG-W,M
Gardener (A-Riding, A-Riding a
Steed White As Snow)
MHB-W,M (German)
Gardener (Out in the Garden,
Watering Flow'rs)
MH-W,M
Gardening
ASB3-W,M
Gardens
FSA1-W,M
Gardens in the Sea
ASB3-W,M
**Gardez Piti Milatte see La Gardez
Piti Milatte**
Garfield
FVV-W,M
Garibaldi's War Hymn
AmH-W,M (Italian) SiP-W,M

(Italian) SMW-W,M (Italian)
**Garibaldi's War Hymn see also
Italian National Hymn (Song)**
Garrick Gaieties Opening
TW-W
Garry Owen
UF-W,M
Garryowen
POT-W,M
Gary, Indiana
TI2-W,M
Gascon Carol
CCH-W,M
Gate Ajar for Me
AME-W,M GH-W,M
Gather the Cherished Ones
GrM-W,M
Gather Them In
GH-W,M
Gather Ye Rosebuds
TH-W,M
Gather Ye Rosebuds While Ye May
CSo-W,M
Gather Your Rosebuds
OH-W,M
Gather Your Rosebuds Whilst You
May
EL-W,M
Gathering Flowers for the Master's
Bouquet
BIS-W,M
Gathering Flowers from the Hillside
BIS-W,M
Gathering Home
GH-W,M
Gathering Nuts in May
Oz3-W,M
Gaudeamus Domino
SM-W,M (Latin Only)
Gaudeamus Igitur
HSD-W,M (Latin) IL-W,M (Latin
Only) MML-W,M (Latin Only)
OTJ-W,M (Latin Only)
Gauguin's Shoe
TW-W
Gavotte (Arditi)
FSA1-W,M
Gavotte (Bach)
RW-M
Gavotte (Gossec)
AmH-M MH-M
Gavotte (Handel)
MH-M
Gavotte (Martini)
ASB5-W,M
Gavotte (Old French)
MH-M
Gavotte (Von Gluck)
MH-M
Gavotte in D (Von Wilm)
MH-M
Gay and Happy
SiS-W,M
Gay Caballero
PO-W,M
Gay Girl Marie
Oz1-W
Gay, La La, Gay Is the Rose
CFS-W,M (French)
Gay Musician
MAR-W,M
Gay Ranchero
TI2-W,M
Gay Spanish Maid
FSU-W
Gay Spanish Mary
Oz1-W

Gay West Wind
SOT-W,M
Gay Young Lad
LaS-W,M
Gebenedyt Sey Allzeit
AHO-W,M (German)
**Gedanken Sind Frei see Die
Gedanken Sind Frei**
Gee Baby Ain't I Good to You
NK-W,M
Gee but I Wanna Go Home
FGM-W,M
Gee but I Want to Go Home
FW-W OTJ-W,M
**Gee but I Want to Go Home see
also Army Life and I Don't Want
No More of Army Life**
Gee but It's Great to Meet a Friend
PB-W,M
Geisha
TW-W
Gems of Day
OB-W,M
General Armstrong
ANS-W
General Electric Company Theme
(Bring Good Things To Life)
BNG-W,M
General Lee's Grand March
SCo-W,M
General Lee's Surrender
SiS-W
General Monroe
VP-W,M
General Roll Call
WN-W,M
General Strike
AFP-W AL-W
General Sullivan's Song
SBA-W
**General Tires Jingle see Sooner or
Later You'll Own Generals**
General Toast
ESU-W
General Wayne's New March
MPP-W,M
Generation of Peace
RW-W,M
Generique see Borsalino (Theme)
Generous Heart
SL-W
Genocide
VS-W,M
Gentian
FSA2-W,M
Gentil Coquelicot
Ch-W (French Only) MP-W,M
(French Only)
Gentle and Sweet Musette
AS-W,M (French)
Gentle Annie
AH-W,M ASB6-W,M FHR-W,M
HSD-W,M NAS-W,M Oz4-W,M
SSF-W,M SSFo-W,M TF-W,M
Gentle Hands
VB-W,M
Gentle Lena Clare
FHR-W,M SSFo-W,M
Gentle Mary Laid Her Child
Hy-W,M
Gentle on My Mind
AT-W,M CMG-W,M IPH-W,M
MCG-W,M
Gentle Rain
RW-W,M
Gentle Shepherd
SBA-W

Gentleman Frog
SCa-W,M
Gentleman Is a Dope
A-W,M HC1-W,M L-W OTJ-W,M
OTO-W TI1-W,M UBF-W,M
UFB-W,M
Gentleman Jimmy
UBF-W,M
Gentleman Still
Oz4-W
Gentlemen of Ireland
VP-W
Gentleness
GrM-W,M
Gently, Johnny My Jingalo
FGM-W,M FW-W
Gently to the Listening Ear
LMR-W,M
Geordie
BT-W,M FW-W ITP-W SCa-W,M
Geordie see also Georgia (Geordie)
George Allien (Allin)
SCa-W
George Barnwell
BB-W
George Collins
BB-W FSSC-W,M FW-W ITP-W,M
Oz1-W,M RW-W,M SCa-W,M
George Collum
FMT-W FoM-W,M
George E. Wedlock
Oz1-W
George Fox
GBC-W,M JF-W,M
George Promer
FMT-W
George the Third's Soliloquy
SBA-W
George Washington (A Soldier
True, A Hero Great)
ASB2-W,M ASB3-W,M
George Washington (Washington
Forever! Hurrah!)
FSA1-W,M
Georgia
SSo-W,M
Georgia (Geordie)
BSC-W
Georgia (Geordie) see also Geordie
Georgia (Return, O God of Love,
Return)
SHS-W,M
Georgia (State Song)
Fif-W,M
Georgia on My Mind
FPS-W,M GSN2-W,M
Georgia Skin
LC-W
Georgie see Geordie
Georgie Jeems
Oz1-W,M
Georgie Porgie
DRR-W,M OTJ-W,M
**Georgie Porgie see also Georgy
Porgy**
Georgie the Engineer
Oz4-W,M
Georgy Barnwell
MSB-W
Georgy Girl
HFH-W,M OTO-W RT6-W,M
TI1-W,M UBF-W,M
Georgy-O
SCa-W,M
Georgy Porgy
SiR-W,M
Georgy Porgy see also Georgie

Porgie
Geraniums in the Winder
TG-W,M
**Gerber Baby Food Jingle see
Gerber Knows How Babies Grow
and Bringing Up Baby**
Gerber Knows How Babies Grow
GSM-W,M
German Folk Song
BMC-M
**German National Song see Watch
on the Rhine**
Gershwin at the Keyboard
NYT-W,M
Get a Horse see Git a Horse
Get a Job
DRR-W,M HR-W RB-W
Get a Little Dirt on Your Hands
TOH-W,M
Get a Load of That
SSA-W,M
Get Along Home, Cindy
Oz3-W,M
**Get Along Home, Cindy see also
Cindy**
**Get Along John see Git Along
John**
Get Along Little Dogies
HS-W,M
**Get Along Little Dogies see also
Dogie Song and Git Along Little
Dogies**
**Get Along Liza Jane see Git Along
Liza Jane**
Get Along, Mah Cindy
PIS-W,M
Get Back
BBe-W,M Be2-W,M PMC-W,M
SwS-W,M TWS-W WG-W,M
Get Dancin'
DDH-W,M
Get Down Tonight
ToO76-W,M
Get Gone see Git Gone
Get Happy
MF-W,M MR-W,M
Get in the Union
NH-W
Get into Reggae Cowboy
TOC82-W,M
Get It On
TWD-W,M
Get It Right Next Time
ToO79-W,M
Get It Up
TOH-W,M ToO79-W,M
Get Me to the Church on Time
DBC-W,M HC1-W,M HLS3-W,M
HLS8-W,M LL-W,M OTO-W
RW-W,M TI1-W,M TM-W,M
UBF-W,M UFB-W,M
Get Off of My Cloud
RoS-W,M
Get off the Track
AFP-W AL-W MPP-W SY-W,M
Get on Board
GuC-W,M HS-W,M JF-W,M
LSR-W,M MG-W,M
Get on Board Little Children
FW-W OTJ-W,M SFF-W,M
WN-W,M
**Get on Board Little Children see
also Git on Board Little Children
and Gospel Train (Is Coming)**
**Get on Board o' Ship o' Zion see
Git on Board o' Ship o' Zion**
Get on de Boat Little Chillun see

Git on de Boat Little Chillun
Get on the Right Thing
  PMC-W,M
Get Out of Mexico
  MPP-W SY-W,M
Get Out of Town
  HC2-W,M ML-W,M TI1-W,M
  ToS-W,M UBF-W,M UFB-W,M
Get Out the Gotkes
  PO-W,M
Get outta My Dreams, Get into My
  Car
  CFB-W,M
Get That Money
  NH-W
Get the Money
  NeA-W,M
Get Thee behind Me Satan
  AFB-W,M FW-W SWF-W,M
Get Together
  JF-W,M
Get Up and Bar the Door
  FSU-W
Get Up and Shut the Door
  Oz1-W,M
Get Up, My Ox
  LA-W,M (Spanish)
Get Wildroot Cream Oil, Charlie
  GSM-W,M
Get Your Rights Jack
  SFF-W,M
Gettin' in Tune
  WA-W,M
Gettin' Late in the Evenin'
  LC-W,M
Getting Better
  BBe-W,M TWS-W
Getting Closer
  PMC-W,M
Getting Married Today
  Co-W,M
Getting Ten Negro Boys Together
  NF-W
Getting to Know You
  BeL-W,M DBC-W,M FPS-W,M
  HC1-W,M HLS8-W,M ILT-W,M
  OTJ-W,M OTO-W RW-W,M
  TI1-W,M UBF-W,M UFB-W,M
Getting Up Song
  SOO-W,M
Ghana
  MF-M
Ghost Dance Song
  UF-W,M
Ghost of a Chance see I Don't
  Stand a Ghost of a Chance with
  You
Ghost Song
  SSo-W,M
Ghost Song (The Woman Stood at
  the Old Church Door)
  HSA-W,M
Ghost's High Noon
  BeB-W,M
Giannina Mia
  Fi-W,M
Giant (This Then Is Texas)
  HFH-W,M MF-W,M
Giant's Shoes
  RSL-W,M
Gidget
  TI1-W,M UBF-W,M
Gif' ob Gawd Is Eternal Life
  BDW-W,M
Gift, The
  TI2-W,M
Gift of Love

MF-W,M
Gigi
  BeL-W,M FPS-W,M HC1-W,M
  HFH-W,M LL-W,M LM-W,M
  OTO-W RT5-W,M RW-W,M
  TI1-W,M UBF-W,M UFB-W,M
Gilding the Guild
  TS-W
Giles Collins
  FMT-W
Giles Jolt, As Sleeping
  Boo-W,M
Giles Scroggins
  SCa-W
Giles Scroggin's Ghost
  MSB-W
Gillette Razor Blades Jingle see To
  Look Sharp
Gilligan's Island Theme see Ballad
  of Gilligan's Isle
Gilly Gilly Ossenfeffer Katzenellen
  Bogen by the Sea
  NoS-W,M
Gimme a Little Kiss (Will Ya Huh?)
  RoE-W,M RW-W,M TI1-W,M
  UFB-W,M
Gimme a Pigfoot (and a Bottle of
  Beer)
  LSB-W,M
Gimme Little Sign
  OnT6-W,M
Gimme Some
  Mo-W,M NM-W,M OTO-W
Gimme Some Lovin'
  TRR-W,M
Gimme That Old Time Religion
  MF-W,M
Gimme That Old Time Religion see
  also Gimmie That Ole Time
  Religion
Gimmie Shelter
  RoS-W,M
Gimmie Song
  SSo-W,M
Gimmie That Ole Time Religion
  MoM-W,M OTJ-W,M
Gimmie That Ole Time Religion see
  also Gimme That Old Time
  Religion and Give Me That Old
  Time Religion
Gin a Body Meet a Body
  SeS-W,M
Gin a Body Meet a Body see also
  Comin' thro' (through) the Rye
Ginger Blue
  Oz2-W
Gingerbread Boy
  STS-W,M
Gingerbread Man
  SCL-W,M
Gino's Gives You Freedom of
  Choice
  GSM-W,M
Gipsy... see also Gypsy...
Gipsy
  CSG-W,M
Gipsy (Mazurka) see La Zingana
Gipsy in da Moonlight
  SGT-W,M
Gipsy John
  SL-W,M
Gipsy John see also Gypsy John
Gipsy June
  LMR-W,M
Gipsy Life
  SL-W,M
Gipsy Life see also Gypsy Life

Gipsy Rondo
  AmH-M
Gipsy Song
  SL-W,M
Gipsy Song see also Gypsy Song
Gipsy's Life
  FSA2-W,M
Gipsy's Warning
  TMA-W,M
Gipsy's Warning see also Gypsy's
  Warning
Giraffe
  ASB3-W,M
Gird on the Sword
  GH-W,M
Girl
  BBe-W,M Be1-W,M TWS-W
  WG-W,M
Girl Died for Love
  SCa-W
Girl Freed from the Gallows
  FMT-W
Girl Friend
  TS-W
Girl Friend of the Whirling Dervish
  OHF-W
Girl from Ipanema
  DJ-W,M RDT-W,M TI2-W,M
Girl from Parthenay
  FSF-W (French)
Girl Girl Girl
  OTO-W
Girl I Left Behind
  Oz1-W,M
Girl I Left behind Me
  AmH-W,M ASB6-W,M FBI-W,M
  FW-W GeS-W,M HS-W,M
  HSD-W,M HWS-W,M IL-W,M
  LMR-W,M MAS-M NAS-W,M
  OTJ-W,M Oz3-W,M TMA-W,M
  WiS8-W,M
Girl I Left in Missouri
  HB-W,M
Girl I Love
  Mo-W,M NM-W,M
Girl I Loved in Sunny Tennessee
  Oz4-W
Girl Like You
  THN-W,M TOC82-W,M
Girl Named Tamiko
  OTO-W
Girl of Constant Sorrow
  FW-W
Girl of the Mist
  SNZ-W,M (Maori)
Girl of the Moment
  LD-W,M
Girl on Page Forty-Four
  RB-W
Girl on the Greenbriar Shore
  FW-W
Girl on the Prow
  Ne-W,M
Girl Volunteer
  FSU-W
Girl with the Sun in Her Hair
  Mo-W,M
Girl with the Waterfall
  Oz3-W,M
Girl You'll Be a Woman Soon
  TI2-W,M
Girls and Boys Come Out to Play
  OTJ-W,M SOO-W,M
Girls around Cape Horn
  SA-W,M
Girls Can Never Change Their
  Nature

IL-W,M
Girls Dancing on the Deck
RuS-W,M (Russian)
Girls Girls Girls
MF-W,M
Girls in Love
THN-W,M
Girls Just Want to Have Fun
DC-W,M MF-W,M
Girls of Madeira
FSA1-W,M
Girls Who Sit and Wait
Mo-W,M NM-W,M OTO-W
Git a Horse
OHG-W,M
Git Along John
NSS-W
Git Along Little Dogies
ATS-W,M CSS-W FW-W
IHA-W,M NAS-W,M OTJ-W,M
SiB-W,M SoC-W TO-W,M
VA-W,M YS-W,M
**Git Along Little Dogies see also
Dogie Song and Get Along Little
Dogies**
Git Along Liza Jane
AN-W
Git Gone
VS-W,M
Git on Board Little Children
RF-W,M
**Git on Board Little Children see
also Get on Board Little Children**
Git on Board o' Ship o' Zion
MoM-W
Git on de Boat Little Chillun
BDW-W,M
Gitchy Goomy
TI2-W,M
Give a Little Whistle (from
Pinocchio)
NI-W,M TI1-W,M UFB-W,M
Give a Little Whistle (from Wildcat)
Mo-W,M NM-W,M OTO-W
TI2-W,M W-W,M
Give Ear, O God, to My Loud Cry
AHO-W,M
Give Ear, O Heavens, to That
Which I Declare
AHO-W,M
Give Ear O Lord
SiP-W,M (Hebrew)
Give Ear O Ye Heavens
SoM-W,M
Give It Back to the Indians
TS-W TW-W
Give It What You Got
DDH-W,M DP-W,M
**Give Me... see also Gimme... and
Gimmie...**
Give Me a Little Buttermilk
NH-W
Give Me a Little Cosy Corner
U-W
Give Me a Little Old Fashion Love
OGC1-W,M
Give Me a Place in the Sun
SFB-W,M
Give Me All Night
CFB-W,M
Give Me All Your Love
BHO-W,M
Give Me Back My Cool Clean
Water
CMG-W,M
Give Me Back That Wig
DBL-W

Give Me Jesus
NH-W WN-W,M
**Give Me Jesus see also Give-er Me
Jesus**
Give Me Just a Little More Time
SoH-W,M
Give Me Louisiana
Fif-W,M
Give Me Love (Give Me Peace on
Earth)
BR-W,M
Give Me More More More
OGC1-W,M
Give Me, O Lord, a Heart of Grace
AME-W,M
Give Me That Old Time Religion
FW-W GS1-W HLS7-W,M
OFS-W,M SpS-W,M TI1-W,M
UFB-W,M
**Give Me That Old Time Religion
see also Gimmie That Ole Time
Religion**
Give Me the Gourd to Drink Water
SFF-W,M
Give Me the Simple Life
DJ-W,M MF-W,M TOM-W,M
Give Me the Sweet Delights of
Love
Bo-W,M
Give Me the Wings of Faith
GH-W,M
Give Me Thine Heart
GH-W,M
Give Me Three Grains of Corn,
Mother
AmS-W,M SCa-W,M
Give Me Wings
TTH-W,M
Give Me Your Hand
BSo-W,M
Give Me Your Tired, Your Poor
FWS-W,M RDF-W,M
Give Mother My Crown
CEM-W,M
Give My Love to Nell
ITP-W,M
Give My Regards to Broadway
FSN-W,M FWS-W,M GSN1-W,M
HLS1-W,M MF-W,M OAP-W,M
OTJ-W,M RW-W,M TI1-W,M
TW-W UBF-W,M UFB-W,M
Give My Regards to Saigon
VS-W,M
Give of Your Best to the Master
AME-W,M
Give Peace in These Our Days, O
Lord
AHO-W,M
Give Peace, O God, the Nations
Cry
AHO-W,M
Give Peace to Us
SCL-W,M
Give Praise to God Who Made the
Day
SHP-W,M
Give the Dutch Room
BSC-W
Give the People What They Want
DDH-W,M
Give the Stranger Happy Cheer
FHR-W,M
Give Them All to Jesus
VB-W,M
Give This to Mother
FHR-W,M SiS-W,M
Give to the Winds Thy Fears

AME-W,M Hy-W,M
Give Up
CEM-W,M GS1-W
Give Us Peace
SBF-W,M
Give Us This Day
HLS7-W,M RDF-W,M
Give Us This Day Our Daily Bread
FHR-W,M
Give-er Me Jesus
BDW-W,M
**Give-er Me Jesus see also Give Me
Jesus**
Give-er Me Jesus W'en I Die
BDW-W,M
Giving (Santa's Theme)
BCS-W,M
Giving (See the Rivers Flowing)
FSA1-W,M
Giving Thanks
ASB4-W,M
Gizmo (Gremlins Theme)
HFH-M MF-M
Glad Am I
Boo-W,M
Glad Christmas Bells
CSF-W RW-W,M
Glad Glad Day
SoP-W,M
Glad I Am to Live
SHP-W,M
Glad I Got Religion
NH-W
Glad Is My Heart This Day
SHP-W,M
Glad News
CCM-W,M
Glad Praises Sing to God
SHP-W,M
Glad Song
SoP-W,M
Glad Tidings (Shalom Chaverim)
WSB-W,M (Hebrew)
**Glad Tidings see also Shalom
Chaverim**
Glad to Be Unhappy
FrS-W,M OTO-W TS-W UBF-W,M
Glad Welcome to the Morning
SHP-W,M
Gladiator March
RW-M
Gladly Lift We Hearts and Voices
SHP-W,M
Glasgow
SHS-W,M
**Glass Menagerie (Lara's Theme)
see Blue Roses**
**Glass Menagerie Main Title Theme
see Tom's Theme**
Glass Onion
TWS-W
Glasses Sparkle on the Board
ESU-W
Gleaner
GrM-W,M
Gleaners' Song
UF-W,M
Glee Club Rhearsal
YG-W,M
Glee Reigns in Galilee
JF-W,M
Glendy Burk
ASB5-W,N FHR-W,M GuC-W,M
HS-W,M MHB-W,M OTJ-W,M
SSF-W,M SSFo-W,M VA-W,M
Glendy Burke
WiS8-W,M

Glenn Miller Story (Theme) see
  Adios
Glenogie
  SeS-W,M
Glider
  ASB3-W,M
Glimmer on the Sea
  TH-W,M
Glitter and Be Gay
  TW-W
Gloom Is Cast o'er All the Land
  SiS-W
Gloomy Night of Sadness
  AHO-W,M
Gloria (Bigazzi and Tozzi)
  TI2-W,M
Gloria (Harnick and Bock)
  TW-W
Gloria (Mozart)
  SL-W,M (Latin)
Gloria (Van Morrison)
  DRR-W,M TRR-W,M
Gloria, Gloria (Haydn)
  MuM-W,M (Latin)
Gloria in Excelsis
  LMR-W,M SJ-W
Gloria in Excelsis (Mozart)
  MuM-W,M (Latin)
Gloria in Excelsis (Old Scottish
  Chant)
  AME-W,M
Gloria in Excelsis Deo (Carl Stein)
  MuM-W,M (Latin Only)
Gloria in Excelsis Deo (John
  Benaglia)
  Boo-W,M (Latin Only)
Gloria Patri
  AME-W,M GH-W,M SJ-W
Gloria Patri (Charles Ellerton)
  FSA1-W,M
Gloria Patri (Palestrina)
  MU-W,M (Latin Only)
Glorious Forever
  TH-W,M
Glorious Fourth
  HSD-W,M
Glorious Gates of Righteousness
  Hy-W,M
Glorious Morning
  GH-W,M
Glorious Morning, Glorious
  Morning
  NSS-W
Glorious Naval Victory Obtained by
  Commodore Bainbridge
  NS-W
Glorious Repeal Meeting Held at
  Tara
  VP-W
Glorious Things of Thee Are
  Spoken
  AME-W,M CEM-W,M CSo-W,M
  Hy-W,M MHB-W,M OM-W,M
  SL-W,M WiS7-W,M
Glorious Victory
  AL-W
Glory (Sing to the Lord)
  AHO-W,M
Glory Alleluia
  OTJ-W,M
Glory an' Honor
  BDW-W,M
Glory and Honor
  NSS-W
Glory and Love to the Men of Old
  ESB-W,M
Glory and Peace

FSA1-W,M
Glory Be to God on High
  AME-W,M Hy-W,M
Glory Be to Jesus
  SJ-W,M
Glory Be to Jesus' Name
  GH-W,M
Glory Be to the Father
  AME-W,M GH-W,M Hy-W,M
Glory Be to Thee, O Lord
  AME-W,M Hy-W,M
Glory Ever Be to Jesus
  GH-W,M
Glory for Dartmouth
  IL-W,M
Glory, Glory
  SiS-W
Glory Glory for Columbia
  IL-W,M
Glory Glory Hallelujah
  PoS-W,M
Glory Glory Hallelujah see also
  John Brown's Body
Glory Hallelujah
  OHG-W,M SiS-W
Glory Hallelujah see also John
  Brown's Body
Glory Now to Thee Be Given
  LMR-W,M SL-W,M
Glory of Love, The
  HLS5-W,M MF-W,M RDT-W,M
  RT6-W,M TI1-W,M TTH-W,M
  UFB-W,M
Glory of Love (Theme from Karate
  Kid Part II)
  GSN5-W,M MF-W,M
Glory of the Light
  MMM-W,M
Glory Row
  BJ-W,M
Glory to God (Handel)
  SiM-W,M
Glory to God (Rachmaninoff)
  CA-W,M
Glory to God in the Highest
  AME-W,M
Glory to God on High
  GH-W
Glory to Heaven
  MuM-W,M
Glory to Him (Fay/
  Rachmaninoff)
  SL-W,M TF-W,M
Glory to the Steel
  GrM-W,M
Glory to Thee My God
  CSo-W,M
Glory Trail
  GA-W SoC-W
Gloucester Wassail
  MC-W,M
Gloucestershire Wassail
  JOC-W,M OB-W,M
Glow-Worm
  BBB-W,M OHF-W RW-M TI1-M
  TI2-W,M UFB-M
Gluckselger Ist Uns Doch Keine
  Nacht
  AHO-W,M (German)
Gnomes' Dance
  FSA2-W,M
Go Ahead
  SFF-W,M
Go and Call
  WN-W,M
Go and I Go wid You
  NH-W

Go and Leave Me
  Am-W,M
Go Away from My Window
  OFS-W,M OTJ-W,M
Go Away from My Window see
  also Go 'Way from My Window
Go Away Girls
  MPM-W,M
Go Away Little Girl
  MF-W,M OnT6-W,M
Go Away Old Man see Go 'Way
  Old Man
Go Away Sister Nancy
  SCa-W,M
Go Back You Fool
  OGC1-W,M
Go Bring Me, Said the Dying Fair
  AHO-W,M
Go Bury Thy Sorrow
  GH-W,M
Go Call the Doctor--Be Quick or
  Anticalomel
  SY-W,M
Go Down Death
  Me-W,M
Go Down Moses
  ATS-W BM-W ESB-W,M ETB-
  W,M FN-W,M FW-W HS-W,M
  IL-W,M JBF-W,M JF-W,M
  LT-W,M MAS-W,M MES1-W,M
  MF-W,M MML-W,M NFS-W,M
  NSS-W OTJ-W,M RDF-W,M
  RF-W,M RW-W,M SL-W,M
  SoF-W,M SS-W SWF-W,M
  TF-W,M TH-W,M WiS7-W,M
  WN-W,M
Go Down Moses see also Let My
  People Go and When Israel was in
  Egypt's Land
Go Down Ol' Hannah
  NeF-W
Go Down Old Hannah
  Le-W,M SFF-W,M
Go Down You Murderers
  FW-W
Go Elijah see Go 'Lija
Go Fly a Kite
  OTJ-W,M OTO-W
Go for It
  TOM-W,M
Go Forth Ye Heralds in My Name
  AME-W,M
Go from My Window
  SSP-W
Go Home
  TTH-W,M
Go in and out the Window
  GM-W HS-W,M OTJ-W,M Oz3-W
  TMA-W,M
Go Labor On; Spend and Be Spent
  AME-W,M Hy-W,M
Go Learn of the Ant
  Boo-W,M
Go 'Lija
  RTH-W
Go Lovely Rose
  EL-W,M
Go Mary an' Toll de Bell
  RF-W,M
Go Mississippi
  Fif-W,M
Go Mustangs Go
  Mo-W,M
Go Northwestern Go
  Mo-W,M TI2-W,M
Go On Bruins
  Mo-W,M TI2-W,M

Go On Old Gator
  AFS-W,M
Go On Train
  ASB6-W,M
Go Preach My Gospel Saith the
  Lord
  AME-W,M
Go Slow, Boys
  Oz2-W,M
Go Tell
  PSN-W,M
Go Tell Aunt Gracie
  SNS-W
Go Tell Aunt Nancy
  SOO-W,M
Go Tell Aunt Rhodie
  D-W,M GuC-W,M MG-W,M
Go Tell Aunt Rhody
  ASB2-W,M FSB1-W,M FSt-W,M
  FWS-W,M HS-W,M IHA-W,M
  LH-W,M Oz2-W,M RW-W,M
**Go Tell Aunt Rhody see also Aunt
  Rhody**
Go Tell It
  LoS-W,M
Go Tell It on de Mountain
  FoS-W,M RF-W,M WN-W,M
Go Tell It on the Mountain
  GuC-W,M HS-W,M MF-W,M
  OAP-W,M OFS-W,M PaS-W,M
  PoG-W,M RW-W,M SCL-W,M
  SFF-W,M SpS-W,M
Go Tell It on the Mountains
  CCM-W,M ETB-W,M FW-W
  JF-W,M MAS-W,M OTJ-W,M
  RS-W,M WSB-W,M YS-W,M
Go Tell Young Henry
  AFP-W
Go to Bed
  NF-W
Go to Dark Gethsemane
  Hy-W,M SJ-W,M
Go to Helen Hunt for It
  Oz3-W
Go to It
  SL-W,M
Go to Joan Glover
  Boo-W,M
Go to New York
  TW-W
Go to Sleep (Go to Sleepy, Little
  Baby)
  AFS-W,M
Go to Sleep (Little Boys, Little
  Girls, Go to Sleep)
  STS-W,M
Go to Sleep Lena Darling
  AmH-W,M HSD-W,M WiS8-W,M
Go to Sleep Whatever You Are
  TW-W
Go to Sleepy
  WU-W,M
Go to Sleepy, Little Baby
  PSD-W,M
Go 'Way from My Window
  J-W,M
**Go 'Way from My Window see
  also Go Away from My Window**
Go 'Way Old Man
  HSD-W,M
Go West
  ToO79-W,M
Go Where Glory Waits Thee
  MML-W,M
Go Where I Send Thee
  JF-W,M MM-W,M PSN-W,M
Go Work in My Vineyard

GH-W,M
Go Work in the Union
  AL-W
Go Ye into All the World
  GH-W,M
Goat (One Day My Goat Was
  Feeling Fine)
  RSL-W,M
Goat (There Was a Animal Called a
  Goat)
  DBL-W
Goat (There Was a Man, Now
  Please Take Note)
  BSB-W,M OTJ-W,M
Goat Herders
  ASB6-W,M
Goat Kid
  ASB4-W,M
Gobble
  ASB1-W,M
Gobble Gobble Gobble
  SiR-W,M
Goblin Lives in Our House
  SOO-W,M
Goblins and Witches
  SiR-W,M
God and God Alone
  GP-W,M
God and Our Rights
  SiS-W
God and Yet a Man
  GBC-W,M
God Be in My Head
  Hy-W,M
God Be Merciful to Me
  Hy-W,M
God Be Merciful unto Us
  AME-W,M
God Be Our Guide
  ASB6-W,M
God Be with You
  GH-W,M HLS7-W,M HSD-W,M
  OM-W,M RS-W,M U-W
God Be with You Till We Meet
  Again
  AHO-W,M AME-W,M CEM-W,M
  Hy-W,M NAS-W,M NSS-W
**God Be with You Till We Meet
  Again see also Mizpah (God Be
  with You Till We Meet Again)**
God Bless America
  Bo-W,M CSS-W FWS-W,M
  RDF-W,M RDT-W,M
God Bless My Boy Tonight
  SiS-W
God Bless Our Brave Young
  Volunteers
  SiS-W
God Bless Our Land
  VA-W,M
God Bless Our Native Land
  AME-W,M ESB-W,M Hy-W,M
  OTJ-W,M
God Bless Our Southern Land
  SiS-W
God Bless Our Union
  AL-W
God Bless the Child
  DJ-W,M LSB-W,M RDT-W,M
  TI2-W,M ToS-W,M
God Bless the Human Elbow
  Mo-W,M NM-W,M OTJ-W,M
  TO-W
God Bless the Old Sixth Corps
  Sin-W,M
God Bless the Prince of Wales
  CSo-W,M

God Bless the U.S.A.
  AG-W,M AWS-W,M CoH-W,M
  FOC-W,M
God Bless Us Every One
  OTJ-W,M
God Bless You
  GH-W,M
God Called Adam
  JF-W
God Cares for His People
  SHP-W,M
God Cares for Me
  SCL-W,M
God Defendeth the Right
  SiS-W
God Ever Glorious
  SL-W,M TF-W,M TH-W,M
God for Poland
  SiP-W,M (Polish)
God from His Throne with Piercing
  Eyes
  AHO-W,M
God Got Plenty o' Room
  NSS-W
God Has Heard My Prayer
  MMW-W,M
God Has Made a Beautiful World
  SHP-W,M
God Has Made the Changing
  Seasons
  SHP-W,M
God Help Me
  AL-W
God Himself Is Present
  SJ-W,M
God Himself Is with Us
  Hy-W,M
God Is a Good God
  BSG-W,M BSP-W,M
God Is Always near Me
  GM-W
God Is Ascended
  OB-W,M
God Is Calling Yet
  GH-W,M
God Is Ever beside Me
  HLS7-W,M
God Is God
  OTJ-W,M
God Is Here
  JF-W,M
God Is in His Holy Temple
  SBJ-W,M
God Is Love (His Word Proclaims
  It)
  GH-W,M
God Is Love (Praise Him, Praise
  Him, All You Little Children)
  MAR-W,M
**God Is Love (Praise Him, Praise
  Him, All You Little Children) see
  also Praise Him, Praise Him! (All
  Ye Little Children)**
God Is Love (So the Bible Tells)
  Sop-W,M
God Is Love, His Mercy Brightens
  AME-W,M GH-W,M HSD-W,M
  Hy-W,M OTJ-W,M WiS7-W,M
God Is Love, Oh God Is Love
  SoP-W,M
God Is My Strong Salvation
  Hy-W,M
God Is Our Refuge and Our
  Strength
  Hy-W,M
God Is the Loving Father
  SHP-W,M

God Is with Me Every Day
SHP-W,M
God Is Working His Purpose Out
Hy-W,M
God Isn't Dead
BSG-W,M BSP-W,M
God Knows It's Time
NH-W
God Listens As I Pray
SHP-W,M
God Lives
Mo-W,M
God Made Our Hands
OTJ-W,M
God Made Us All
AFP-W
God Moves in a Mysterious Way
AME-W,M Hy-W,M SJ-W
God of Abraham Praise
ESB-W,M
God of Abrah'm Praise
AME-W,M
God of All Nature
SL-W,M
God of Bethel Heard Her Cries
AHO-W,M
God of Compassion in Mercy
Befriend Us
Hy-W,M
God of Grace and God of Glory
AME-W,M Hy-W,M
God of Love That Hear'st Pray'r
AME-W,M
God of Might
JS-W,M (Hebrew) SBJ-W,M
God of My Life
AHO-W,M
God of My Life thro All My Days
AME-W,M
God of Our Fathers
AHO-W,M AME-W,M ASB6-W,M
CEM-W,M FWS-W,M HS-W,M
Hy-W,M LoS-W,M NAS-W,M
OM-W,M OU-W,M SBF-W,M
SoF-W,M TF-W,M VA-W,M
**God of Our Fathers see also God
of Our Fathers Whose Almighty
Hand and National Hymn**
God of Our Fathers Bless This Our
Land
AHO-W,M
God of Our Fathers Known of Old
ESB-W,M
God of Our Fathers Whose
Almighty Hand
AHO-W,M ESB-W,M
**God of Our Fathers Whose
Almighty Hand see also God of
Our Fathers and National Hymn**
God of Our Life through All the
Circling Years
Hy-W,M
God of Peace in Peace Preserve Us
AHO-W,M
God of the Free
AL-W
God of the Nations
AHO-W,M
God of the Nations Near and Far
AHO-W,M
God of the Prophets Bless the
Prophets' Sons
AHO-W,M Hy-W,M
God of the Strong, God of the
Weak
AHO-W,M
God of the World Thy Glories

Shine
AHO-W,M
God Preserve His Majesty
Boo-W,M
God Preserve Our Noble Emperor
SiP-W,M (German)
God Rest Ye Merry, Gentlemen
BCh-W,M BCS-W,M CC-W,M
CCM-W,M CI-W,M CSB-W,M
CSF-W FW-W IL-W,M JOC-W,M
MAS-W,M OAP-W,M OTJ-W,M
PoG-W,M SCS-W SL-W,M
TI1-W,M UFB-W,M
God Rest You Merry, Gentlemen
CEM-W,M DC-W,M GBC-W,M
HS-W,M Hy-W,M MF-W,M
OB-W,M RW-W,M U-W YC-W,M
God Save America
AME-W,M MPP-W,M OTJ-W,M
SI-W,M SY-W,M
God Save Ireland
VP-W,M
God Save Our President
OTJ-W,M
God Save Our States
SSS-W,M
God Save the Czar
SiP-W,M (Russian)
God Save the King
AmH-W,M MPP-W,M NAS-W,M
SiP-W,M
God Save the Nation
SiS-W
God Save the Queen
CSo-W,M
God Save the South
MPP-W OHG-W,M SCo-W,M
Sin-W,M SiS-W,M
God Save the Thirteen States
EA-W,M SI-W
God Save the Volunteers
SiS-W
God Set Us Here
AHO-W,M (Dutch)
God Shall Wipe All Tears Away
AME-W,M
God Shall Wipe Away All Tears
FiS-W,M
God So Loved the World
TH-W,M
God Speed the Right
HSD-W,M
God Stelt Ons Hier
AHO-W,M (Dutch)
God Supreme to Thee We Pray
AHO-W,M
God That Madest Earth and
Heaven
Hy-W,M
God the All-Merciful
ESB-W,M FH-W,M
God, the Lord, a King Remaineth
Hy-W,M
God the Master of All Pagans
EA-W,M
God the Omnipotent King Who
Ordainest
Hy-W,M
God to Thee We Humbly Bow
AHO-W,M
God Understands
OM-W,M
God Who Made the Earth
Hy-W,M SHP-W,M
God Who Touchest Earth with
Beauty
Hy-W,M

God Whose Name Is Love
SHP-W,M
God-Why-Don't-You-Love-Me
Blues
Fo-W,M OTO-W UBF-W,M
God Will Take Care of You
AME-W,M HF-W,M OM-W,M
**Godfather Love Theme see Speak
Softly Love**
Godfather II Theme
AT-M HSe-M OTO-M TM-M
Godfather Waltz
AT-M OTO-M
Godly Sorrow at the Cross
NSS-W
God's A-Gwine Ter Move All de
Troubles Away
NFS-W,M
God's Book
SoP-W,M
God's Counsel Is My Wisdom
SiM-W,M (German)
God's Dear Son
OB-W,M
God's Goin' Set This World on Fire
NeA-W,M
God's Goin' Wake Up the Dead
NH-W
**Gods Going to Move All the
Troubles Away see God's A-
Gwine ter Move All de Troubles
Away**
God's Gonna Do the Same
AG-W,M
God's Green World
LL-W,M
God's House, God's Day
SoP-W,M
God's Little Candles
HLS7-W,M SUH-W,M
God's Own Fool
VB-W,M
God's Own Son
GBC-W,M
God's People All round the World
SHP-W,M
God's Time Now
GH-W,M
God's Wonderful People
HHa-W,M VB-W,M
Goin' see also Going and Gwine
Goin' Away to See-er Ma Lord
BDW-W,M
Goin' Back and Talk to Mama
DBL-W
Goin' Back to New Orleans
LC-W
Goin' Back to Texas
FC-W,M
Goin' down Highway 51
DBL-W
Goin' down That Long Long
Lonesome Road
B-W,M Bl-W,M
Goin' down the Road
FoS-W,M
Goin' down the Road Feelin' Bad
AFP-W FSB2-W,M
**Goin' down the Road Feelin' Bad
see also Going down the Road
Feeling Bad**
Goin' down This Road
Am-W,M
Goin' down This Road Feelin' Bad
FVV-W,M
Goin' Down to Jordan
NH-W

Goin' Down to Town
OTJ-W,M
Goin' Down Town
D-W,M ITP-W,M
Goin' Downtown Boogie
LC-W,M
Goin' Fishin'
DBL-W
Goin' Home
RoS-W,M WNF-W
Goin' Home Boys
J-W,M
Goin' Mobile
WA-W,M
Goin' Out of My Head
ILS-W,M RDT-W,M TI1-W,M
UFB-W,M
Goin' to Boston
AH-W,M D-W,M FSD-W,M FW-W
VA-W,M
Goin' to Georgia
FVV-W,M
Goin' to Outshine the Sun
NH-W
Goin' to School
PIS-W,M
Goin' to See My Sarah
B-W,M BI-W,M
Goin' to Shout All over God's
Heav'n
FN-W,M RF-W,M
**Goin' to Shout All over God's
Heav'n see also All God's
Children, Heab'n, and Heaven (I
Got a Robe)**
Going see also Goin' and Gwine
Going down the Road Feeling Bad
FG1-W,M FGM-W,M SWF-W,M
**Going down the Road Feeling Bad
see also Goin' down the Road
Feelin' Bad**
Going for a Pardon
LSR-W,M Oz4-W
Going Home Alone
TW-W
Going Home Song
SSo-W,M
Going round the Horn
ANS-W
Going to Be Good Slaves
NF-W
Going to Boston
HS-W,M
Going to Church (Round)
TF-W,M
Going to Heaven
RF-W,M
Going to Pull My War Clothes
FSSC-W,M
Going to School in the Rain
MH-W,M
Going to Study War No More
SWF-W,M
**Going to Study War No More see
also Ain't Gonna Study War No
More, I Ain't Goin' to (Gwine)
Study War No More, and Study
War No More**
Going to the Fair
HS-W,M
Going to the Mexican War
FMT-W
Going to the Wars
SiS-W
Going to the Zoo
RBO-W,M
Going Where the Lonely Go

NMH-W,M
Gold
BSC-W
Gold and Silver Waltz
MF-M RW-M
Gold Bugs Go Down before Bryan
AL-W
Gold Digger's Song
HFH-W,M MF-W,M OHB-W,M
Gold Fever Theme see Alaskans
Gold Rush Is Over
OGC1-W,M
Gold Strike
FVV-W,M
Gold Watch and Chain
BIS-W,M
Gol-darned Wheel
HB-W,M
Golden Axe
Oz2-W,M
Golden Boy
Mo-W,M NM-W,M OTO-W
Golden Brown Blues
B-W,M
Golden Carol
OB-W,M
Golden Choir of Melchior, Casper
and Balthazar
CSF-W
Golden Curls
JD-W,M
Golden Dreams and Fairy Castles
FHR-W,M
Golden Earrings
AT-W,M LM-W,M OnT1-W,M
OTO-W
Golden Glove
BSC-W,M FMT-W SCa-W,M
Golden Helmet of Mambrino
MLM-W,M
Golden Leaves
ASB1-W,M
Golden Light, Serene and Bright
SJ-W,M
Golden Mornings
OB-W,M
Golden Rocket
OGC2-W,M
Golden Rule
FSA2-W,M
Golden Rule Song
OTJ-W,M
Golden Sheaves
OB-W,M
Golden Slippers
FW-W GuC-W,M HS-W,M
**Golden Slippers see also Oh, Them
Golden Slippers**
Golden Slumbers (Kiss Your Eyes)
ASB6-W,M CSo-W,M OTJ-W,M
SiR-W,M TH-W,M
Golden Slumbers (Lennon/
McCartney)
BBe-W,M Be2-W,M TWS-W
Golden Slumbers Kiss Your Eyes
BM-W TF-W,M
Golden Thread
JF-W,M
Golden Vanity
BSC-W BT-W,M FSt-W,M FW-W
Gu-W,M IF-W,M OHO-W,M
SA-W,M SCa-W SFM-W TBF-W,M
**Golden Wedding Anniversary see
La Cinquantaine**
Golden Willow Tree
ITP-W,M OA2-W,M SCa-W,M
Golden Years

OTO-W
Goldenrod Is Yellow
SiR-W,M
Goldfinger
HLS5-W,M ILS-W,M RT6-W,M
RW-W,M
Goldsmith's Rant
OHG-W,M
Goliath
VB-W,M
Gomer Pyle Theme
GTV-M
Gomper
RoS-W,M
Gondolier
ASB6-W,M
Gone (Mary Came unto the Tomb
of Jesus)
HHa-W,M
Gone (Since You've Gone)
OGC2-W,M TI1-W,M UFB-W,M
Gone Before
WN-W,M
Gone Case
AL-W
Gone Is Autumn's Kindly Glow
Boo-W,M
Gone Long Ago
Oz2-W,M
Gone Too Far
TOH-W,M
Gone with the Cowboys
NB-W
Gone with the Wind
DJ-W,M ILT-W,M TI1-W,M
UFB-W,M
Gonna Be a Meeting over Yonder
SFF-W,M
Gonna Be Another Hot Day
OHT-W,M
Gonna Build a Mountain
BeL-W,M CEM-W,M DBC-W,M
HC2-W,M HLS8-W,M MF-W,M
TI1-W,M UBF-W,M UFB-W,M
Gonna Fly Now
GrS-W,M RW-W,M
Gonna Get Along without Ya Now
ILF-W,M TI1-W,M UFB-W,M
Gonna Get Back Home Somehow
SRE2-W,M
Gonna Get Together in the Live
Oak
Am-W
Gonna Give Her All the Love I've
Got
THN-W,M
Gonna Have a Party
TOC83-W,M
Gonna Live the Life I Sing About
J-W,M
Gonna Move My Baby
LC-W
Gonna Sing My Lord
JF-W,M
Goober Peas
AAP-W,M AH-W,M FW-W
IHA-W,M OFS-W,M OTJ-W,M
PoS-W,M Re-W,M RW-W,M
SCo-W,M SiB-W,M Sin-W,M
SiS-W,M
**Goober Peas see also Eating
Goober Peas**
Gooch's Song
Mo-W,M NM-W,M OTO-W TW-W
Good Advice
FSA1-W,M
Good Bait

MF-M
Good Bookkeeping
  FSA2-W,M
Good Christian Men Rejoice
  BCh-W,M BCS-W,M CC-W,M
  CEM-W,M CSF-W OAP-W,M
  SJ-W,M VA-W,M YC-W,M
Good Christian Men, Rejoice and
  Sing
  SJ-W,M
Good Clean Fun
  OTO-W
Good Comrade
  ASB6-W,M
Good Dagobert
  ASB6-W,M
Good Day Sunshine
  BBe-W,M Be1-W,M OnT6-W,M
  TWS-W
Good Evening Everybody
  DBL-W
Good Exercise
  FSA1-W,M
Good Friends
  Ap-W,M Mo-W,M OTO-W
  VSA-W,M
Good Green Acres of Home
  MR-W,M
Good Hearted Woman
  TI2-W,M
Good Humor
  FSA1-W,M
Good Intentions
  Mo-W,M NM-W,M OTO-W
Good King Wenceslas
  BCh-W,M BMC-M CC-W,M
  CCH-W,M CEM-W,M CSF-W
  ESB-W,M FSA1-W,M FW-W
  HS-W,M IL-W,M JOC-W,M
  MAS-W,M MC-W,M OB-W,M
  OPS-W,M OTJ-W,M PoG-W,M
  RW-W,M SAC-W,M TF-W,M
  TH-W,M U-W YC-W,M
Good Life
  MF-W,M TI2-W,M
Good Lord Dun Been Here
  BDW-W,M
Good Lord in de Manshans Above
  NSS-W
Good Lord Shall I Ever Be de One
  RF-W,M
Good Lovin'
  DRR-W,M TRR-W,M
Good Lovin' Man
  TOH-W,M
Good Luck Charm
  SRE1-W,M
Good Man Is Hard to Find
  Mo-W,M NM-W,M TI2-W,M
  ToS-W,M
Good Manners
  MAR-W,M
Good Mornin'
  OTJ-W,M
Good Mornin' (Sam Coslow)
  OTO-W
Good Morning! (Good Morning, All,
  on This New Day)
  MH-W,M
Good Morning (Good Morning!
  Good Morning! And Here Is Come
  Another Day)
  FSA2-W,M
Good Morning (Good Morning,
  Good Morning, Good Morning to
  You)
  ASB1-W,M

Good Morning (Good Morning,
  Good Morning, It's a Good, Good,
  Good, Good Morning)
  GM-W,M
Good Morning (High in the
  Heavens Rises the Sun)
  ASB6-W,M
Good Morning (We've Danced the
  Whole Night Thru)
  TI1-W,M UFB-W,M
Good Morning Blues
  AFB-W,M FG1-W,M FW-W
  Le-W,M
Good Morning Carrie
  EFS-W,M
Good Morning, Good Morning
  SoP-W,M TWS-W
Good Morning Happy Children
  MH-W,M
Good Morning Heartache
  LSB-W,M
Good Morning Merry Sunshine
  OTJ-W,M Oz4-W,M
Good Morning Mister Railroadman
  OTJ-W,M
Good Morning Mr. Zip-Zip-Zip
  RW-W,M
Good Morning Sky
  SOO-W,M
Good Morning Song
  RSL-W,M SoP-W,M
Good Morning Starshine
  H-W,M HLS8-W,M ILS-W,M
  MCG-W,M RW-W,M
Good Morning to All
  SCL-W,M
Good Morning to You
  SHP-W,M
Good Morrow Good Lover
  MGT-W,M
Good Morrow Good Mother
  GiS-W,M
Good Morrow Gossip Joan
  TH-W,M
Good Morrow My Lover
  GiS-W,M
Good News (Chariot's A-Comin')
  BF-W,M FGM-W,M FoS-W,M
  FW-W GeS-W,M OTJ-W,M
  SiB-W,M
Good News (from Heav'n, Good
  News for Thee)
  GH-W,M
Good News (I Got a Letter This
  Morning My Wife Had a Brand
  New Baby Girl)
  DBL-W
Good News! (Winter's Coming!)
  GM-W,M
Good News (You're Bound to Do
  Me Good)
  TI1-W,M UBF-W,M UFB-W,M
Good News Chariot's Comin'
  NFS-W,M
Good News de Chariot's Comin'
  RF-W,M WN-W,M
Good News Member
  AFP-W NSS-W
Good News to Tell
  SHP-W,M
Good Night see also Goodnight
Good Night
  BM-W
Good Night (A Fair Little Girl Sat
  under a Tree)
  MH-W,M
Good Night (Good Night, My Own

True Heart)
  MML-W,M
Good Night (Good Night, Sleep
  Well My Dearest One)
  MG-W,M
Good Night (Lennon/McCartney)
  TWS-W
Good Night (Now, Good Night,
  Hearts and Voices All Unite)
  GrM-W,M
Good Night ('Tis Growing Late,
  Yes 'Tis Growing Late)
  MU-W,M
Good Night (to You All, and Sweet
  Be Thy Sleep)
  ASB6-W,M HS-W,M NAS-W,M
Good Night and Christmas Prayer
  CCH-W,M
Good Night Beloved
  TF-W,M TH-W,M
**Good Night Beloved see also
  Serenade (Good Night! Good
  Night, Beloved!)**
Good Night Cub Scouts
  CSS-W
Good Night Cubbers
  CSS-W
Good Night Farewell
  HSD-W,M
Good Night Good Night
  Boo-W,M
Good Night Ladies
  AmH-W,M ATS-W BSB-W,M
  CSo-W,M FU-W,M FuB-W,M
  FW-W HSD-W,M IL-W,M
  MAB1-W MM-W,M MSA1-W
  NAS-W,M OTJ-W,M RW-W,M
  TI1-W,M TMA-M UFB-W,M
  VA-W,M WiS8-W,M
**Good Night Ladies see also
  Goodnight Ladies**
Good Night Little Girl of My
  Dreams
  Mo-W,M
Good Night Mister Moon
  SSN-W,M (French)
Good Night Song
  FSA2-W,M
Good Night Sweetheart
  GSN2-W,M GSO-W,M HLS2-W,M
  RW-W,M
**Good Night Sweetheart see also
  Goodnight Sweetheart**
Good Night to You All
  SCL-W,M SMY-W,M
Good Night's Love
  TOC83-W,M
Good Ol' Boys
  BNG-W,M TOC82-W,M TOH-W,M
  TV-W,M TVT-W,M
Good Old Bowling Green
  TO-W,M
Good Old Days of Adam and Eve
  BSC-W
Good Old Rebel
  FW-W
Good Old Union Feeling
  Am-W
Good Old Union Wagon
  SiS-W
Good Old Way
  SHS-W,M
Good Physician
  SHS-W,M
Good Reuben James
  SMW-W,M
Good Ship Came A-Sailing

ITP-W,M
Good Sweet Ham
  HAS-W,M
Good, the Bad, and the Ugly
  RW-M
Good Thing Blues
  DBL-W
Good Thing Going
  MF-W,M UBF-W,M
Good Things
  JW-W,M
Good Things to Life
  BNG-W,M
Good Time Charlie's Got the Blues
  MF-W,M
Good Time Coming
  AL-W
Good Time Man Like Me Ain't Got
  No Business
  JC-W,M
Good Times Bad Times
  RoS-W,M
Good Times Come at Last or the
  Race to California
  OHG-W,M
Good Timin'
  HR-W ILS-W,M
Good Unexpected
  Boo-W,M
Goodby (I Thank You for the Fun)
  GM-W,M
Good-by Andy
  MPP-W
Good-by City o' Babylon
  MoM-W,M
Goodby Gambler
  WN-W,M
Good-by Liza Jane
  AmS-W,M ATS-W FW-W
  TMA-W,M
Good-by Song
  MH-W,M
Good-by Winter
  GM-W
Goodbye
  GC-W,M SD-W,M
Goodbye (Falling Leaf, and Fading
  Tree)
  AmH-W,M FSY-W,M TH-W,M
  WiS8-W,M
Goodbye (Farewell, Farewell Is a
  Lonely Sound)
  HSD-W,M
Goodbye (God Bless the Master of
  This House)
  OB-W,M
Goodbye(Lennon/McCartney)
  SwS-W,M WG-W,M
Goodbye Again
  CJ-W,M
Good-Bye Broadway, Hello France
  OS-W RW-W,M
Good-Bye Brother
  NSS-W,M
Goodbye Columbus
  OTO-W
Goodbye Cruel World
  TRR-W,M
Goodbye Darlin'
  TW-W
Goodbye Dolly Gray
  OTJ-W,M U-W
Good-Bye Fare You Well
  SA-W,M
Goodbye for Now
  TOM-W,M
Goodbye Girl

DC-W,M DPE-W,M EY-W,M
  HFH-W,M
Goodbye Girls I'm Through
  SLB-W,M
Good-Bye Jeff
  SiS-W
Goodbye Kisses
  CCS-W,M
Goodbye Little Bonnie Blue Eyes
  FVV-W,M Oz4-W,M
Goodbye Little Bonnie Goodbye
  FW-W RW-W,M
Goodbye Little Dream Goodbye
  ML-W,M
Goodbye Little Girl
  Mo-W,M NM-W,M
Goodbye Liza Jane
  ATS-W
**Goodbye Liza Jane see also
  Good-by Liza Jane**
Goodbye My Coney Island Baby
  TI2-W,M
Goodbye My Darling
  MAR-W,M
Good-Bye My Lady Love
  FSN-W,M OTJ-W,M
Goodbye My Lover Goodbye
  BSB-W,M FW-W HS-W,M IL-W,M
  MAS-W,M OFS-W,M SA-W,M
  TMA-W,M WiS8-W,M
Goodbye My Sweet Johnny
  CMG-W,M
Good-Bye Old Arm
  SiS-W
Good-Bye Old Booze
  BMM-W
Good-Bye Old Glory
  Sin-W,M SiS-W
Goodbye Old Paint
  ASB4-W,M FAW-W,M FW-W
  HS-W,M HWS-W,M NAS-W,M
  WS-W,M
Goodbye Ring
  NF-W
Good-Bye Song
  SoP-W,M
Goodbye Stranger
  ToO79-W,M
Goodbye Susan Jane
  Oz3-W
Good-Bye Sweetheart Good-Bye
  HSD-W,M
Good-Bye Tennessee
  SSo-W,M
Good-Bye to America
  SSS-W,M
Goodbye to Love
  ILT-W,M
**Goodbye to Naples see Napule Ve
  Salute**
Good-Bye to the Plains
  HOH-W,M
Goodbye Wife
  NF-W
Goodbye Yellow Brick Road
  TI2-W,M
Goodnight see also Good Night
Goodnight (Jones/Smith)
  I-W,M
Goodnight (Roy Orbison)
  TFC-W,M
Goodnight Irene
  FG2-W,M FSP-W,M MF-W,M
  RW-W,M SBF-W,M TI1-W,M
  TWD-W,M UFB-W,M WSB-W,M
Goodnight It's Time to Go
  ILF-W,M TI1-W,M UFB-W,M

Goodnight Ladies
  ATS-W LH-W,M OBN-W,M U-W
**Goodnight Ladies see also Good
  Night Ladies**
Goodnight My Love
  HLS5-W,M
Goodnight My Someone
  DBC-W,M TI2-W,M TW-W
  UBF-W,M
Goodnight Sweetheart
  RDT-W,M
**Goodnight Sweetheart see also
  Good Night Sweetheart**
Goodnight Tonight
  PMC-W,M TI2-W,M
Goodtime Lonesome Blues
  LC-W
Goody Bull
  HAS-W,M SSS-W,M
Goody Goody
  FPS-W,M FrS-W,M MF-W,M
  OHF-W OnT6-W,M RW-W,M
Goofus
  RW-W,M
Goose Girl
  MHB-W,M (Czech)
Goose Hangs High
  BSC-W
Goose Never Be a Peacock
  Mo-W,M NM-W,M OTO-W
Goose Round
  LoS-W,M
Gooseberry Wine
  NF-W
Goosey Goosey Gander
  OTJ-W,M
Goosie Gander Play Rhyme
  NF-W
Gorgeous Alexander
  Ne-W,M
Gory Gory
  OHO-W,M
Gospel Bells
  GH-W,M
Gospel Calls
  GH-W,M
Gospel Cannonball
  LSR-W,M
Gospel Changes
  CMG-W,M
Gospel of Thy Grace
  GH-W,M
Gospel Pool
  AN-W
Gospel Tidings
  SHS-W,M
Gospel Train
  BDW-W,M ETB-W,M MoM-W
  NH-W PaS-W,M WiS7-W,M
Gospel Train Is Coming
  GrG-W,M LSR-W,M
**Gospel Train Is Coming see also
  Get on Board (Little Children)**
Gospel Trumpet
  SHS-W,M
Gospel Trumpets
  GH-W,M
Gosport Tragedy see Oh Polly!
Gossip Rabbit
  CSD-W,M (French)
Gossips
  TW-W
Got a Date with an Angel
  TI1-W,M UBF-W,M UFB-W,M
Got a Home at Las'
  My-W,M
Got a Lot o' Livin to Do

SRE2-W,M
Got a Rainbow
ReG-W,M
Got Glory an' Honor
MoM-W,M
Got My Mind Set on You
CFB-W,M
Got My Mojo Working
EP-W,M
Got No Mo' Home Dan a Dog
B-W,M
Got No More Home Dan a Dawg
Bl-W,M
Got Nowhere to Lay My Weary
Head
NH-W
Got to Get You into My Life
BBe-W,M Be1-W,M PMC-W,M
TWS-W WG-W,M
Got to Let It Go
VB-W,M
Got to Let You Go
DBL-W
Got to Tell Somebody
VB-W,M
Gott Erhalte Franz Den Kaiser
AmH-W,M (German) SiP-W,M
(German)
**Gott Erhalte Franz Den Kaiser see
also Austrian Hymn**
Gotta Get Away
RoS-W,M
Gotta Get Me Somebody to Love
Mo-W,M NM-W,M OTO-W
Gotta Have Me Go with You
LSO-W Mo-W,M NM-W,M
Gotta Have Me to Go with You
OTO-W
Gotta Have the Real Thing
VB-W,M
Gotta Learn to Love without You
TTH-W,M
Gotta Shake 'Em Up an' Go
LC-W
Gotta Travel On
CMG-W,M WG-W,M
Gouge of Armour Avenue
B-W,M Bl-W,M
Government Issue
GI-W,M
Government Street Blues
LC-W
Governor General or a Hobo
ATS-W
Governor O.K. Allen
NeF-W
Governor Pat Neff
NeF-W
Gowans Are Gay
FSU-W
**Goya Love Theme see Till I Loved
You**
Grabe Sinkin' Down
WN-W,M
Grace
Bo-W,M CSo-W,M SCL-W,M
Grace after the Meal
SBJ-W,M (Hebrew Only)
Grace and Truth Shall Mark the
Way
Hy-W,M
Grace at Table
FF-W,M
Grace before Meals
GH-W,M
Grace before Meat
ASB6-W,M

Grace before Meat at Hampton
RF-W,M
Grace Song
Bo-W,M
Grace 'Tis a Charming Sound
AME-W,M
Graceful and Easy
BSB-W,M
Graceful Dance
FSA1-W,M
Gracious Saviour We Adore Thee
AHO-W,M
Gracious Spirit Dwell with Me
Hy-W,M
Gracious Spirit Holy Ghost
SJ-W,M
Gracious Spirit Love Divine
AME-W,M
Grade Song
NH-W
Graduates' Farewell
HSD-W,M
Graduation Day
HR-W RW-W,M
Graduation Song
LMR-W,M
Grafted into the Army
ATS-W MAS-W,M MPP-W
Sin-W,M SiS-W SY-W,M
Granada
AO-W,M TOM-W,M
Granadinas
MSS-W,M (Spanish)
Grand Ball
MaG-W,M
Grand Constitution
MPP-W
Grand Dieu Nous Te Benissons
CUP-W,M (French Only)
Grand Dieu Que Je Suis-t-a Mon
Aise
CaF-W (French Only)
Grand Labor Cause
AL-W
Grand March from Aida
OBN-M
Grand Old Duke of York
CSG-W,M CSS-W
Grand Roundup
HOH-W SoC-W
Grandad
GA-W,M
Grandfather's Clock (So Straight
and Tall)
ASB2-W,M
Grandfather's Clock (Was Too
Large for the Shelf)
AmH-W,M ATS-W EFS-W,M
FW-W FSt-M IL-W,M NAS-W,M
OFS-W,M OHG-W,M OTJ-W,M
PoS-W,M SD-W,M SiB-W,M
WiS8-W,M
Grandfather's Hat
ATS-W
Grandfather's Song
SiR-W,M
Grandma
TBF-W,M
Grandma Grunts
MuM-W,M
Grandma Harp
NMH-W,M
Grandma's Advice
TMA-W,M
Grandma's Feather Bed
CJ-W,M CMG-W,M PoG-W,M
Grandmaw's Advice

Oz1-W,M
Grandmother
SOO-W,M
Grandmother Complains
FSO-W,M (French)
Grandmother's Old Armchair
SCa-W,M
Grandpa (Tell Me 'bout the Good
Old Days)
AWS-W,M CoH-W,M FOC-W,M
Granny Wales
SSS-W,M
Granny's Old Arm Chair
Oz3-W,M
Grant
ATS-W
Grant National Campaign Song
ATS-W
Grant Pill
SiS-W
Grant Those Glances (Mirame Asi)
MSS-W,M (Spanish)
Grant Us Peace
SBF-W,M
Grant Us Thy Peace
RS-W,M
Grass Is Always Greener
UBF-W,M
Grass of Uncle Sam
GA-W,M
Grasshopper
FSA2-W,M
Grasshopper and the Ant
MHB-W,M
Grasshopper and the Ants
GM-W,M
Grasshopper Sense
NF-W
Grasshopper Sitting on a Sweet
Potato Vine
NF-W
Grave of Wolfe Tone
VP-W,M
Grave Robber
VB-W,M
**Grave Sinkin' Down see Grabe
Sinkin' Down**
Gravedigger Blues
LC-W
Grave-Diggers
SSo-W,M
Gravedigger's Song
IFM-W
Gray and Black Horses
NF-W
Gray Goose
AFS-W,M FW-W J-W,M RW-W,M
Gray Goose see also Grey Goose
Gray Hills Taught Me Patience
AHO-W,M
Gray Pony
MH-W,M
Gray Squirrel
MH-W,M
Gray Squirrels
GM-W MH-W,M
Graybacks So Tenderly Clinging
SiS-W
Grease
Gr-W,M TI1-W,M UFB-W,M
Greased Lightnin'
Gr-W,M Mo-W,M OTO-W
Greasy Greens
NH-W
Greasy Wops and Yankee Boys
GO-W
Great American Bum

FW-W

Great American Chocolate Bar see
  Hershey Is the Great American
  Chocolate Bar
Great American Dream
  RBO-W,M
Great American Game
  LMR-W,M
Great and Fair Is She Our Land
  ESB-W,M
Great and Mighty Wonder
  YC-W,M
Great Baby Show
  FHR-W,M
Great Balls of Fire
  DRR-W,M FOC-W,M ILF-W,M
  OGC1-W,M TI1-W,M UFB-W,M
Great Bells of Oseney
  Boo-W,M
Great Camp Meetin'
  SNS-W
Great Campmeetin'
  AAF-W,M
Great Campmeeting
  MU-W,M
Great Caruso (Theme) see Granada
Great Compromise
  RV-W
Great Conspiracy
  BRB-W
Great Country
  AL-W
Great Day (Great Day the
  Righteous Marching)
  FW-W SWF-W,M
Great Day (There's Gonna Be a
  Great Day)
  GSN2-W,M HLS8-W,M MF-W,M
  RW-W,M
Great Day for Me
  SFF-W,M
Great Getting Up Morning
  FW-W
Great God Attend While Zion Sings
  AME-W,M
Great God How Frail a Thing Is
  Man
  AHO-W,M
Great God How Infinite Art Thou
  AME-W,M
Great God Preserver of All Things
  AHO-W,M
Great God the Followers of Thy
  Son
  AHO-W,M
Great God Thy Works
  AHO-W,M
Great God We Sing That Mighty
  Hand
  Hy-W,M
Great God We Sing Thy Mighty
  Hand
  SL-W,M
Great Grandad
  ATS-W HAS-W,M
Great Grand-Dad
  Oz3-W,M
Great Grandma
  ATS-W,M GA-W
Great Hallelu
  JF-W,M
Great Is the Lord
  GP-W,M OGR-W,M VB-W,M
Great Is Thy Faithfulness
  BSG-W,M BSP-W,M HLS7-W,M
Great Is Your Faithfulness
  OGR-W,M

Great Jehovah We Adore Thee
  AME-W,M
Great Judgment
  Oz4-W,M
Great Judgment Day
  NH-W
Great King of Nations Hear Our
  Prayer
  AME-W,M
Great Lord of All Whose Work of
  Love
  AHO-W,M
Great Millennial Day's before Us
  ESU-W
Great Northern Blues
  LC-W
Great Owl's Song
  NF-W
Great Physician
  GH-W,M
Great Physician Now Is Near
  AME-W,M
Great Pretender
  TOM-W,M
Great Roundup
  HOH-W,M SoC-W
Great Shepherd of Thy People Hear
  AME-W,M
Great Ship
  SCa-W
Great Silkie
  FGM-W,M FW-W
Great Speckled Bird
  FW-W Oz4-W,M
Great Spirit
  HCY-W,M
Great Titanic
  AN-W Oz4-W
Great Titanic see also Titanic, The
  (It Was Sad When That Great
  Ship Went Down)
Great Tom Is Cast
  Boo-W,M
Greater Is He That Is in Me
  VB-W,M
Greatest Gift of All
  BCS-W,M
Greatest Love of All
  GSN5-W,M TOM-W,M TTH-W,M
Greatest Performance of My Life
  MF-W,M
Greatest Show on Earth
  LD-W,M OTJ-W,M OTO-W
Greatest Story Ever Told
  RW-M
Greatly Rejoice
  OGR-W,M
Greeley and Gratz Campaign Song
  MPP-W
Greeley Pill
  MPP-W
Green Acres
  MF-W,M
Green and Yellow Basket
  OTJ-W,M
Green and Yellow Basket see also
  A-Tisket, A-Tasket and I-Tisket,
  I-Tasket
Green Beds
  BSC-W
Green Berets
  VS-W,M
Green Bus
  ASB4-W,M
Green Carnations
  BS-W,M
Green Corn

BF-W,M FW-W Le-W,M NeF-W
  OTJ-W,M Oz2-W,M
Green Door
  TI2-W,M
Green Eyes (Aquellos Ojos Verdes)
  FPS-W,M (Spanish) TOM-W,M
  (Spanish Only)
Green Fields (How Tedious and
  Tasteless the Hours)
  SHS-W,M
Green Fields see also Greenfields
Green Fields of America
  VP-W
Green for the Mountain-Side
  MML-W,M
Green Grass Grew All Around
  FW-W
Green Grass Grew All Round
  Oz3-W
Green Grass Growing All Around
  RW-W,M
Green Grass Starts to Grow
  GOI7-W,M HD-W,M MF-W,M
Green Gravel
  OTJ-W,M Oz3-W,M TMA-W,M
Green Green
  IPH-W,M
Green Green Grass of Home
  ATC1-W,M CMG-W,M CoH-W,M
  CSp-W,M FOC-W,M GOI7-W,M
  MCG-W,M OnT1-W,M RB-W
  TI2-W,M
Green Green Green
  UF-W,M
Green Grow the Lilacs
  AH-W,M ATS-W,M BF-W,M
  BM-W FGM-W,M FW-W
  GuC-W,M HS-W,M OFS-W,M
  OTJ-W,M RSW-W,M
Green Grow the Rushes O
  CSo-W,M
Green Grow the Rushes Oh
  Bo-W,M FW-W OHO-W,M
  OTJ-W,M
Green Groweth the Holly
  GBC-W,M
Green Grows the Laurel
  SCa-W,M
Green Grow'th the Holly
  OB-W,M
Green Leaves of Summer
  RT5-W,M RW-W,M THN-W,M
Green Light
  KS-W,M
Green Mountain Yankee
  SY-W,M
Green Mountaineer
  SSS-W,M
Green Oak Tree! Rocky-O
  NF-W
Green Plumes of Royal Palms
  AHO-W,M
Green Sleeves
  OH-W,M
Green Sleeves see also
  Greensleeves and My Lady
  Greensleeves
Green Tambourine
  RW-W,M
Green Willow Tree
  ITP-W,M TBF-W,M
Greenback
  FVV-W,M
Greenback Boys Are Waking
  AL-W
Greenback Dollar Blues
  LC-W

Greenback Yankee Medley
AL-W
Greenbacks
HRB2-W,M SY-W,M
Greenberg Shop Is Moving South
AFP-W
Greenberg's Shop Is Moving South
WW-W,M
Greene Koseene see Die Greene Koseene
Greenfield (God Is Our Refuge in Distress)
SHS-W,M
Greenfields
AH-W,M
Greenfields see also Green Fields
Greenhorn
SoC-W
Greenhorn Cowboy
SoC-W
Greenhorn's Experience
SoC-W
Greenland
SHS-W,M
Greenland Fisheries
FGM-W,M FW-W OHO-W,M
Greenland Fishery
SA-W,M
Greenland Whale Fishery
BB-W MSB-W WSB-W,M
Greensleeves
FSS-W,M FW-W Gu-W,M
GuC-W,M GUM2-W,M HLS1-W,M
HS-W,M LW-W,M MC-W,M
MF-W,M MG-W,M OB-W,M
OE-W,M OPS-M OTJ-W,M
PSN-W,M RW-W,M SBF-W,M
SSP-W TI1-W,M U-W UFB-W,M
Greensleeves see also Green Sleeves and My Lady Greensleeves
Green-Up Time
UBF-W,M
Greenwood Side see Down by the Greenwood Side
Greeting
TF-W,M
Greeting Song
SCL-W,M
Greeting Song (Caldara)
SMY-W,M
Greeting Song (Now the Busy Day Is Done)
GrM-W,M
Greeting Song (Where Is Larry?)
MAR-W,M
Greeting to Spring
TH-W,M
Greeting to Visitors
MH-W,M
Greetings
OTJ-W,M TH-W,M
Gremlin
ASB5-W,M
Gremlins Theme see Gizmo
Grenadiers
MaG-W,M
Gresford Disaster
BB-W
Grey Goose
AFP-W Le-W,M NeF-W
Grey Goose see also Gray Goose
Grey October
VS-W,M
Greyhound's in Touch with America
GSM-W,M

Gridiron King
IL-W,M Mo-W,M TI2-W,M
Grievance Blues
DBL-W
Grieved Soul
WN-W,M
Grinding Corn
ASB2-W,M
Grinner's Lament
AL-W
Grizzly Bear
FW-W
Grocery Man
ASB2-W,M
Groovin'
GG3-W,M ILS-W,M MCG-W,M
RW-W,M RY-W,M RYT-W,M
THN-W,M TI2-W,M TRR-W,M
Groovin' for Nat
MF-M
Groovy Kind of Love
MF-W,M
Grosebeck Blues
DBL-W
Ground Crew Song
AF-W
Groundhog
BIS-W,M FW-W OHO-W,M
Ground-Hog
D-W,M ITP-W,M
Ground-Hog Day
ASB4-W,M
Ground-Hog Song
Oz3-W,M
Grow Old Along with Me
WiS9-W,M
Growing Pains
TW-W
Growing Pains (Theme) see As Long As We Got Each Other
Growing Up Is Learning to Say Good Bye
OTO-W
Growing Up Is Learning to Say Goodbye
Mo-W,M NM-W,M OTJ-W,M
Grown Up Wrong
RoS-W,M
Grumbellin People
Me-W,M
Grumbling Mother-in-Law (T'an Ch'in Chia)
FD-W,M (Chinese)
Grundys
MPP-W
Guanica Guanica
LaS-W,M (Spanish)
Guantanamera
FW-W (Spanish) JF-W,M
(Spanish) LaS-W,M OBN-W,M
OTJ-W,M (Spanish) RW-W,M
(Spanish Only) RYT-W,M TO-W,M
WG-W,M
Guarantees
Mo-W,M NM-W,M OTO-W
Guardian Angel
FS-W,M
Guardian Angels
OTJ-W,M
Guardian Beauty Contest
PO-W,M
Gue-Gue
CLaL-W,M (French)
Gue-Gue Solingaie
BaB-W,M (French)
Guerilla Boy
BSC-W

Guerilla Song
SMW-W,M (Serbo-Croatian)
Guerrilla Man
Oz4-W,M
Guess I'll Hang My Tears Out to Dry
FrS-W,M UBF-W,M
Guess Who
FRH-W,M
Guess Who I Saw Today
DJ-W,M ToS-W,M TW-W
Guest from Heaven
CCM-W,M
Guide Me
GH-W,M
Guide Me O Thou Great Jehovah
AME-W,M HOH-W,M Hy-W,M
Guide My Feet While I Run This Place
SFF-W,M
Guillannee see La Guillannee
Guilty (Bee Gees)
TI1-W,M UFB-W,M
Guilty (Kahn/Whiting, Akst)
GSO-W,M MF-W,M OPS-M
RW-W,M
Guilty Eyes
TTH-W,M
Guinea Gall
NF-W
Guitar
OU-W,M
Guitar Boogie Shuffle
TI1-M UFB-M
Guitar Man
EP-W,M RB-W
Guitars, Cadillacs
GCM-W,M
Gum Chewer's Song see I'm Gonna Dance wit de Guy Wot Brung Me
Gum Tree Canoe
Oz4-W TMA-W,M
Gundagai
U-W
Gunner's Song
AF-W
Gunpowder Tea
SI-W,M
Gunsmoke
FC-W,M
Gusto Blusto
TTH-W,M
Guter Gott Dir Ich Befehle
AHO-W,M (German)
Guthrie on Relativity
AFP-W
Guts of the Army
GO-W
Guy Is a Guy
TI1-W,M UFB-W,M
Guys and Dolls
TI2-W,M TW-W UBF-W,M
Gwine Dig a Hole to Put de Devil In
NeF-W
Gwine into the Wilderness
NSS-W
Gwine Lay Down My Life for My Lord
NH-W
Gwine to de Mill
DE-W,M
Gwine to Live Humble to de Lord
RF-W,M
Gwine to March Away in de Gold Band
NSS-W

Gwine to Run All Night
  FHR-W,M PoS-W,M SSFo-W,M
**Gwine to Run All Night see also
  Camptown Races**
Gwine Up
  RF-W,M
Gypsia Song
  SCa-W
Gypsy... see also Gipsy...
Gypsy, The (Along the Road As I
  Take My Way)
  TH-W,M
Gypsy, The (From Smiling Fields of
  Rakosh)
  MML-W,M
Gypsy, The (In a Quaint Caravan
  There's a Lady They Call the
  Gypsy)
  TI2-W,M
Gypsy Baron Waltz
  RW-M
Gypsy Davy
  BF-W,M FW-W LW-W,M
  Oz1-W,M SCa-W,M TBA-W
Gypsy in da Moonlight
  HSA-W,M
Gypsy Is a Gentleman
  IFM-W
Gypsy Jan
  FT-W,M
Gypsy John
  GC-W,M
Gypsy John see also Gipsy John
Gypsy Laddie
  BT-W,M FMT-W IF-W,M Oz1-W
  SCa-W,M
Gypsy Life
  CA-W,M
Gypsy Life see also Gipsy Life
Gypsy Love Song
  FSN-W,M MF-W,M MuM-W,M
  OTJ-W,M RW-W,M SFB-W,M
  TW-W
**Gypsy Love Song see also Slumber
  On, My Little Gypsy Sweetheart**
Gypsy Lover
  Oz1-W,M
Gypsy Maid
  Oz1-W
Gypsy Rondo
  RW-M
Gypsy Rover
  FGM-W,M FW-W OTJ-W,M
Gypsy Song (Gypsies, Making
  Camp on Field and Heather)
  ASB4-W,M
Gypsy Song (Reinhold)
  ASB1-M
Gypsy Song (Sigmund Romberg)
  MPM-W,M
Gypsy Song (Two Romany Fellows
  Were Banished Far)
  ATS-W
Gypsy Song see also Gipsy Song
Gypsy without a Song
  GMD-W,M
Gypsy Woman
  DBL-W
Gypsy's Answer
  IFM-W
Gypsys Tramps and Thieves
  On-W,M
Gypsy's Warning
  ITP-W,M Oz4-W,M TBF-W,M
**Gypsy's Warning see also Gipsy's
  Warning**
Gyptian Laddie

BSC-W

H

H & T Blues
  MF-M
**H.F.C. (Household Finance
  Corporation) Jingle see Never
  Borrow Money Needlessly**
Ha Cha Cha
  CF-W,M
Ha Ha My Darlin' Chile
  LMR-W UF-W,M
Ha Ha This-a-Way
  FW-W Le-W,M MAR-W,M
Ha Ha Thisaway
  NeF-W
Ha Ni An Be
  SiP-W,M (Arabic)
Ha! We to the Other World
  Boo-W,M
Habanera
  AmH-W,M FSA2-W,M FSY-W,M
  (French) LaS-M MF-M RW-M
  WiS7-W,M
Hackney Coachman
  ESU-W
Had a Big Fight in Mexico
  FMT-W FoM-W,M
Had a Little Dog
  ASB5-W,M
Had Gadya
  SBJ-W,M (Hebrew Only)
Had I Wings
  WN-W,M
Had She Not Care Enough
  Boo-W,M
Had You Been Around
  LSB-W,M
Haec Est Vita Aeterna
  Boo-W,M (Latin Only)
Haere Mai
  SNZ-W,M (Maori)
Haere Ra E Hine
  SNZ-W,M (Maori)
Haere Ra My Love
  SNZ-W,M (Maori)
Haida
  GuC-W,M (Hebrew Only)
Haiku
  SiM-W,M
Hail America
  ESU-W
Hail and Farewell
  ESB-W,M FSA2-W,M
Hail Bright Easter
  TF-W,M
Hail Cadmus Hail
  MMM-W,M
Hail Columbia
  AAP-W,M AH-W,M AmH-W,M
  ANS-W AWB-W EA-W,M
  ESB-W,M HA-W,M HSD-W,M
  MAS-W,M MPP-W,M NAS-W,M
  OHG-W,M OTJ-W,M SAR-W,M
  SHS-W,M SI-W,M SiP-W,M
  SL-W,M WiS8-W,M
Hail Columbia Happy Land
  OHG-W,M
Hail Evening Bright
  MML-W,M
Hail Great Aloha State
  Fif-W,M
Hail Hail
  GI-W
Hail Hail Green Fields

Boo-W,M
Hail Hail Hail
  RF-W,M
Hail Hail Scouting Spirit
  Bo-W
Hail Hail the Gang's All Here
  BH-W,M Bo-W,M CSS-W IL-W,M
  IPH-W,M OTJ-W,M RW-W,M
  TI1-W,M UFB-W,M
Hail Hail the P.T.A.
  LoS-W
Hail Holy Land
  AHO-W,M
Hail John's Army Ben' Down an'
  Die
  BDW-W,M
Hail Liberty Thy Sweetest Bliss
  OHG-W,M
Hail Loyola
  CoS-W,M
Hail Minnesota
  CoS-W,M Fif-W,M Mo-W,M
  TI2-W,M
Hail O King of a Golden Land
  GiS-W,M
Hail Oh Hail to the King
  AHO-W,M
Hail on the Pine Trees
  SiR-W,M
Hail Our Gracious Emperor
  UF-W,M
Hail Our Incarnate God
  AHO-W,M
Hail Our Queen
  ID-W,M
Hail Pennsylvania
  Fif-W,M IL-W,M
Hail Purdue
  Mo-W,M TI2-W,M
Hail Sinners! Hail-lo!
  RTH-W
Hail Slovaks
  NAS-W,M
Hail South Dakota
  Fif-W,M
Hail the Crown
  ETB-W,M
Hail the Day That Sees Him Rise
  AME-W,M
Hail the Glorious Golden City
  AHO-W,M
Hail the March of Prohibition
  GrM-W,M
Hail Thou Once Despised Jesus
  AME-W,M Hy-W,M
Hail to Cubbing
  CSS-W
Hail to Old I.U.
  CoS-W,M
Hail to Old Tippecanoe
  MPP-W
Hail to Our Chief
  GC-W,M
Hail to Our Country
  MuM-W,M
Hail to the Brightness of Zion's
  Glad Morning
  AHO-W,M AME-W,M Hy-W,M
Hail to the Chief
  AAP-W,M HA-W,M HSD-W,M
  NAS-W,M OTJ-W,M RW-M
  STR-W,M TI1-M UFB-M
Hail to the Chief Lady of the Lake
  MPP-W,M
Hail to the Eight-Hour Day
  AL-W
Hail to the Elm

MML-W,M
Hail to the Harvest
  GrM-W,M
Hail to the Joyous Day
  AHO-W,M
Hail to the Lord's Annointed
  Hy-W,M
Hail to the Queen
  AHO-W,M
Hail to the Sabbath Day
  AHO-W,M AME-W,M
Hail Tranquil Hour of Closing Day
  AHO-W,M
Hail Vermont
  Fif-W,M
Hail You Fighter Pilots
  AF-W
Hair
  H-W,M RW-W,M
Halcyon Days of Old England
  SAR-W,M SBA-W SI-W,M
Hale in the Bush
  SSS-W,M
Halelu
  JS-W,M (Hebrew)
Haleluia Haleluia
  Boo-W,M
Half a Sixpence
  OTO-W TI1-W,M UBF-W,M
  UFB-W,M
Half a Stranger
  DBL-W
Half a World Away
  TT-W,M
Half an Hour past Twelve O'Clock
  Boo-W,M
Half and Half
  TW-W
Half As Big As Life
  Mo-W,M OTO-W
Half-Breed
  On-W,M
Half Has Never Been Told
  MoM-W
Half-Moon
  FSA2-W,M
Half-Moon Street
  MF-M
Half of It, Dearie, Blues
  GOB-W,M LSO-W
Half past Jumpin' Time
  MF-M
Half Step Down, Please
  MF-W,M
Half the Battle
  Mo-W,M NM-W,M OTO-W
Half the Way
  ToO79-W,M
Half Was Never Told
  GH-W,M
Half-Way Doings
  NF-W
Halifax Station
  ANS-W
Hall of Song
  FSA2-W,M
Hall of the Mountain King
  ASB1-M
Halleluia Chorus (Handel)
  TF-W,M
Halleluia Chorus (Handel) see also
  Hallelujah Chorus
Halleluiah to de Lamb
  BDW-W,M
Halleluja
  TI1-W,M UBF-W,M
Hallelujah

SBF-W,M SSN-W,M (French)
Hallelujah (And Let This Feeble
  Body Fail)
  SHS-W,M
Hallelujah (Hallelujah! I Do Belong
  to That Band)
  WN-W,M
Hallelujah (Hayes)
  Boo-W,M
Hallelujah (He Comes! He Comes!
  the Judge Severe)
  SHS-W,M
Hallelujah (Sing Hallelujah!
  Hallelujah! and You'll Shoo the
  Blues Away)
  MF-W,M OHB-W,M TI2-W,M
  TW-W
Hallelujah Amen
  MU-W,M
Hallelujah Bless His Name
  GH-W,M
Hallelujah Chorus (Handel)
  JF-W WiS7-M
Hallelujah Chorus (Handel) see also
  Halleluia Chorus
Hallelujah Christ Is Risen
  GH-W,M
Hallelujah for the Cross
  GH-W,M
Hallelujah I Love Him (Her) So
  HRB3-W,M TI1-W,M UFB-W,M
Hallelujah I'm a Bum
  AFP-W FW-W GO-W HB-W,M
  IL-W,M SWF-W,M WS-W,M
Hallelujah I'm A-Travelin'
  FW-W SFF-W,M
Hallelujah Praise the Lord
  AHO-W,M
Hallelujah 'Tis Done
  AME-W,M GH-W,M
Halleluyoh
  JS-W,M (Hebrew)
Hallo in Forest Track
  Boo-W,M
Hallowed Hour of Prayer
  GH-W,M
Halloween
  OTJ-W,M SiR-W,M
Halloween (Hot Jack-o'-Lantern,
  It's Halloween)
  Mo-W,M NM-W,M OTO-W
Halloween (Little Orange Pumpkin,
  You're Happy I Can See)
  FF-W,M
Halloween (Pumpkins Are Gay on
  Halloween Day)
  STS-W,M
Halloween ('Tis the Night of
  Halloween)
  SOO-W,M
Halloween (Tonight We'll See
  Some Big Black Cats)
  MH-W,M
Halloween (When the Moon Is Hid)
  FSA2-W,M
Halloween (Witches and Goblins
  with Jack-o'-Lanterns Bright)
  ASB4-W,M
Hallowe'en Carol
  GBC-W,M
Hallowe'en Fun
  MES1-W,M MES2-W,M
Hallowe'en Is Coming
  MAR-W,M SOO-W,M
Halloween Night
  ASB3-W,M MH-W,M RSL-W,M
Halloween Time

GM-W
Hallowe'en's Here
  SCL-W,M
Halls
  AmH-W,M
Halls of Ivy
  TI1-W,M UFB-W,M
Halls of Montezuma
  IL-W,M
Halls of Montezuma see also
  Marines' Hymn
Halo Everybody Halo
  GSM-W,M
Ham and Eggs
  Bo-W,M Le-W,M
Ham Beats All Meat
  NF-W
Hamburger Fair
  Oz3-W
Hame Hame Hame
  SeS-W,M
Hamline March
  CoS-W,M
Hamma-Tamma Damma-Ramma
  FVV-W,M
Hammer and Saw
  IL-W,M
Hammer Song
  SAm-W,M SBF-W,M SD-W,M
  SFF-W,M SFM-W
Hammer Song see also If I Had a
  Hammer
Hammerin' Song
  NFS-W,M
Hammock
  ATS-W,M
Han Skal Leve
  YS-W,M (Danish Only)
Hand Game
  ASB2-M
Hand Loom Versus the Power
  Loom
  BB-W
Hand Me Down My Walkin' Cane
  ATS-W,MBH-W,M FW-W
  GeS-W,M MAS-W,M OS-W
  OTJ-W,M
Hand Me Down My Walking Cane
  Fu-W,M FuB-W,M FVV-W,M
Hand of Fate
  RoS-W,M
Hand of Fate, The
  Ki-W,M
Hand That Holds the Bread
  GrM-W,M
Hand That Rocks the World
  GrM-W,M
Handbag Is Not a Proper Mother
  Mo-W,M NM-W,M
Handel's Water Piece
  BC1-M
Handful of Earth
  EFS-W,M
Handful of Keys
  UBF-W,M
Handkerchief Dance
  UF-W,M
Handkerchief Strike Song
  WW-W,M
Hands across the Table
  Sta-W,M TI2-W,M
Hands of Time
  MLS-W,M TOM-W,M TVT-W,M
Hands of Time see also Brian's
  Song
Handsome Cabin Boy
  FW-W LW-W,M

Handsome Harry
  ESU-W TMA-W,M
Handsome Molly
  BSo-W,M FW-W
Handwriting on the Wall
  GH-W,M
Handy Man
  GSN4-W,M ILS-W,M RW-W,M
Hang Down Your Head Tom
  Dooley
  FGM-W,M
**Hang Down Your Head Tom
  Dooley see also Tom Dooley**
Hang 'Em High
  RW-M
Hang Fire
  RoS-W,M
Hang Him on the Sour Apple Tree
  SiS-W
Hang On Sloopy
  Mo-W,M OTJ-W,M TI1-W,M
  UFB-W,M
Hang On to Me
  GOB-W,M
Hang Out the Moon
  CoF-W,M
**Hang Them High see Hang 'Em
  High**
Hangin' over Hell
  NH-W
Hanging Johnny
  FW-W GI-W,M SA-W,M
Hanging on a Heart Attack
  TTH-W,M
Hanging on the Telephone
  PL-W,M
Hanging Out the Linen Clothes
  AmS-W,M
**Hangman see Maid Freed from the
  Gallows**
Hangman, Hold Your Rope
  SCa-W,M
Hangman's Son
  SCa-W,M
Hangman's Song
  FMT-W FoM-W,M
Hangman's Tree
  BSC-W,M
Hangs-a-Man
  ITP-W,M
Hangtown Gals
  ATS-W,M FW-W IHA-W,M
Hank
  N-W,M
Hannukah Song
  MuM-W,M (Hebrew)
**Hannukah Song see also Chanukah
  Song and Hanuka Song**
Hanover
  SHS-W,M
Hanover Loyalty
  CoS-W,M
Hans Beimler
  FW-W (German)
Hansel and Gretel (Selection)
  AmH-M
Hansel and Gretel Dance
  HS-W,M
Hanuka Song (Chanukah Song)
  TI1-M UFB-M
**Hanuka Song see also Chanukah
  Song and Hannukah Song**
Hanukkah O Hanukkah
  HSA-W,M (Yiddish)
**Hanukkah, O Hanukkah see also
  Chanuke, O Chanuke**
Happening, The

THN-W,M
Happiest Girl in the Whole U.S.A.
  HLS9-W,M TI1-W,M UFB-W,M
Happiness
  SBF-W,M
Happiness (Is Finding a Pencil)
  TW-W YG-W,M
Happiness (No More beneath th'
  Oppressive Hand)
  SHS-W,M
Happiness (A Spring Day, with
  Lilacs in Bloom)
  MMY-W,M
Happiness Is
  TI2-W,M
Happiness Is a Thing Called Joe
  GSF-W,M HLS3-W,M RT4-W,M
  RW-W,M
Happiness Is a Warm Gun
  BBe-W,M TWS-W
Happy (Jagger and Richards)
  RoS-W,M
Happy (Love Theme from Lady
  Sings the Blues)
  LSB-W,M MLS-W,M TOM-W,M
Happy (Michaels and Gorman)
  THN-W,M
Happy Are They
  VA-W,M (Hebrew)
Happy Birthday
  NI-W,M
Happy Birthday (Happy Birthday,
  Happy Birthday to You)
  SOO-W,M
Happy Birthday (Huddie Ledbetter)
  Le-W,M
Happy Birthday (John Has a
  Birthday)
  ASB4-W,M
Happy Birthday (to You)
  HS-W,M TI1-M UFB-M
**Happy Birthday (to You) see also
  Happy Birthday to You**
Happy Birthday Greetings
  CoF-W,M
Happy Birthday My Darling
  MF-W,M
Happy Birthday Sweet Sixteen
  MF-W,M
Happy Birthday to Me
  OTJ-W,M
Happy Birthday to Me (Ebb/Kander)
  OTO-W UBF-W,M
Happy Birthday to Me (Leikin/
  Rubin)
  TOM-W,M
Happy Birthday to You
  AAP-W,M ATS-W MF-W,M
  OTJ-W,M
**Happy Birthday to You see also
  Happy Birthday (to You)**
Happy Builders
  ASB2-W,M
Happy Child
  MH-W,M
Happy Clown
  OTJ-W,M
Happy Contraband
  SiS-W
Happy Day
  AME-W,M GH-W,M
**Happy Day see also O Happy Day
  and Oh Happy Day**
Happy Day Will Soon Appear
  AHO-W,M
Happy Days (I Been Havin'
  Trouble, Ever Since I Was Two

Feet High)
  LC-W
Happy Days (Theme)
  AT-W,M HSe-W,M TV-W,M
Happy Days (Tread the Road
  beyond Your Door)
  SL-W,M
Happy Days Are Here Again
  MF-W,M OHB-W,M U-W
Happy Ending
  Fa-W,M
Happy Ever After
  OHF-W
Happy Family
  SL-W,M
Happy Farmer
  RW-M
Happy Feet
  MF-W,M
Happy Goodmorning
  SSe-W,M
Happy Guy
  Mo-W,M OTO-W
Happy Habit
  Mo-W,M NM-W,M OTO-W
Happy, Happy Birthday, Baby
  DP-W,M ILF-W,M TI1-W,M
  UFB-W,M
Happy Hours
  GrM-W,M
Happy Hours at Home
  FHR-W,M SFF-W,M
Happy Is the Nation
  SHP-W,M
Happy Jack
  WA-W,M
Happy Journey
  GB-W,M
Happy Kittens
  GM-W
Happy Land (Stephen Foster)
  FHR-M
Happy Land (There Is a Happy
  Land Far, Far Away)
  HSD-W,M SHS-W,M
Happy Land of Canaan
  Oz2-W,M
Happy Landing
  GO-W
Happy Little Ones Are We
  FHR-W,M
Happy Miller
  OTJ-W,M
Happy Music
  SD-W,M
Happy New Year (Jerome Kern)
  SB-M
Happy New Year (Let Us Say
  When We Meet on New Year's
  Day)
  MH-W,M
Happy New Year (to Everyone
  Here)
  STS-W,M
Happy New Year to Commodore
  Rodgers
  ANS-W
Happy Peasants
  GrM-W,M
Happy Reform
  MSB-W
Happy River
  SOO-W,M
Happy, Savior, Would I Be
  AHO-W,M
Happy School Days
  ASB3-W,M

Happy Shepherd
FSA2-W,M
Happy Song
FSA1-W,M
Happy Talk
HC2-W,M L-W OTJ-W,M OTO-W
SP-W,M TI1-W,M UBF-W,M
UFB-W,M
Happy the Man Who Finds the
Grace
AME-W,M
Happy Thoughts
FSA1-W,M
Happy Time
OTO-W TI2-W,M UBF-W,M
Happy to Be Themselves
OTO-W
Happy to Make Your Acquaintance
TW-W
Happy Together
RYT-W,M THN-W,M TI2-W,M
Happy Tomorrows
SBS-W,M
Happy Trails
FC-W,M IPH-W,M OTJ-W,M
RDF-W,M
Happy Wanderer
Bo-W CSS-W FWS-W,M
HSS-W,M HST-W,M MM-W,M
OTJ-W,M OU-W,M PT-W,M
RW-W,M STP-W,M TI1-W,M
UFB-W,M VA-W,M
Happy with the Blues
Mo-W,M NM-W,M
Harbor Bell
GH-W,M
Harbor Lights
TI1-W,M UFB-W,M
Harbor of Love
RC-W,M
Harbour Lights
T-W,M
Hard Ain't It Hard
FG1-W,M FPG-W,M FSt-W,M
FW-W WSB-W,M
Hard-Boiled Herman
RM-W,M
Hard by the Crystal Fountain
SoF-W,M
Hard Candy Christmas
BCS-W,M
Hard Crackers Come Again No
More
ATS-W Sin-W,M
Hard Day's Night
BBe-W,M Be1-W,M TWS-W
Hard Heart of Mine
AHO-W,M
Hard Hearted Hannah
MF-W,M OHB-W,M TI2-W,M
WF-W,M
**Hard Hearted Hannah see also
Hardhearted Hannah**
Hard Is the Fate
Boo-W,M
Hard Is the Fortune of All
Womankind
FGM-W,M FW-W LW-W,M
Hard Knocks
SRE1-W,M
Hard Luck
SRE2-W,M
Hard of Hearing
BSC-W
Hard Time Blues
J-W,M LC-W
Hard Time for Lovers

ToO79-W,M
Hard Time Losin' Man
JC-W,M
Hard Time Lovin' Blues
LC-W
Hard Times
AL-W BSC-W DBL-W DE-W,M
ESB-W,M ESU-W FMT-W
Hard Times at Little New River
AFP-W
Hard Times, Come Again No More
AmH-W,M ATS-W FHR-W,M
HSD-W,M NAS-W,M SSF-W,M
SSFo-W,M WiS8-W,M
Hard Times in Colman's Mines
AFP-W,M
Hard Times in the Mill
AFP-W IHA-W,M SFM-W
SWF-W,M WW-W,M
Hard to Say I'm Sorry
GSN5-W,M
Hard Travelin'
JF-W,M SFF-W,M
Hard Traveling
FW-W SWF-W,M WSB-W,M
Hard Trials
BDW-W,M RF-W,M
Hard Up and Broken Down
Oz4-W,M
Hard Way
OTO-W
Hard Way Every Time
JC-W,M
Hard-Working Miner
AL-W SFM-W
Harden My Heart
MF-W,M
Hardhearted Hannah
FPS-W,M
**Hardhearted Hannah see also Hard
Hearted Hannah**
**Hardy Boys Theme see Love and
Let Love**
**Hardy Boys Theme see Wheels
(Keep on Turning)**
Hardy Horseman
HSD-W,M
Hardyknute or the Battle of Largs
SBB-W
Hare and Hounds
FSA1-W,M
Hare and the Tortoise
FSA2-W,M
Hark and Hear My Trumpet
Sounding
AHO-W,M
Hark from the Tomb
Oz4-W,M
Hark from the Tombs a Doleful
Sound
AME-W,M
Hark, Hark, Hark to the Curfew
Boo-W,M
Hark, Hark, My Soul
AME-W,M GH-W,M Hy-W,M
WiS7-W,M
Hark, Hark, My Soul! Angelic
Songs
ESB-W,M
Hark! Hark! the Bonny Christ
Church Bells
OTJ-W,M
Hark, Hark, the Dogs Do Bark
MH-W,M OTJ-W,M
Hark! Hark! the Lark
AmH-W,M ESB-W,M FSS-W,M
SL-W,M SSB-W,M TH-W,M

WiS8-W,M (German)
Hark! Hark! with Harps of Gold
AHO-W,M
Hark, How the Watchmen Cry
AME-W,M
Hark, How the Woods
Boo-W,M
Hark! I Hear a Voice
HSD-W,M
Hark! I Hear the Hunters
Boo-W,M
Hark, Listen to the Trumpeters
WN-W,M
Hark, My Soul, It Is the Lord
AME-W,M Hy-W,M
Hark, Ten Thousand Harps and
Voices
AME-W,M
Hark! the Bell is Ringing
Boo-W,M
Hark the Bonny Christ Church Bells
CSo-W,M
Hark! the Herald Angels Sing
AME-W,M AmH-W,M BCh-W,M
BCS-W,M CC-W,M CCH-W,M
CCM-W,M CEM-W,M CI-W,M
CSB-W,M CSF-W DC-W,M
FM-W,M FW-W FWS-W,M
HS-W,M Hy-W,M IL-W,M
JOC-W,M LoS-W MAB1-W
MC-W,M MF-W,M MSA1-W,M
OAP-W,M OM-W,M OPS-W,M
OTJ-W,M RW-W,M SAC-W,M
SCS-W U-W SiR-W,M TI1-W,M
UFB-W,M WiS7-W,M YC-W,M
Hark! the Merry Bells Are Ringing
Boo-W,M
Hark, the Nightingale
Boo-W,M
Hark! the Summons
ESB-W,M
Hark the Vesper Hymn
ESB-W,M
Hark! the Vesper Hymn Is Stealing
PaS-W,M
Hark! the Voice of Jesus Calling
FH-W,M
Hark! the Voice of Jesus Crying
AME-W,M SJ-W,M
Hark! the Voice of Love and Mercy
AME-W,M
Hark, There Comes a Whisper
AME-W,M
Hark! 'Tis the Cuckoo's Voice
Boo-W,M
Hark! 'Tis the Indian Drum
Boo-W,M
Hark! 'Tis the Saviour of Mankind
AHO-W,M
Hark! 'Tis the Shepherd's Voice I
Hear
AME-W,M
Hark! to Arms!
SiS-W
Hark to Me
BMC-W
Hark to the Mill Wheel
SoF-W,M
Hark, What a Sound, and Too
Divine for Hearing
Hy-W,M
Hark! Without
Boo-W,M
Harlem Blues
B-W,M Bl-W,M
Harlem Butterfly
OHF-W

Harlem Nocturne
  BBB-W,M RoE-W,M TI1-W,M
  UFB-W,M
Harlem River Chanty
  LSO-W
Harlem Serenade
  ReG-W,M
Harlem Shuffle
  TTH-W,M
Harlem Song
  RB-W
Harmonious Blacksmith
  OTJ-M
Harmonious Coons
  MPP-W
Harmony (All Music Is but Three
  Parts Vied)
  FSA1-W,M
Harmony (The Time Has Come Let
  Us Begin)
  AAP-W,M
Harmony Greeting
  LoS-W,M
Harninu
  JS-W,M (Hebrew Only)
Harold the Bootblack
  IFM-W
Harp of the South, Awake
  SiS-W
Harp on the Willow
  Oz4-W
Harp That Once
  CSo-W,M
Harp That Once through Tara's
  Halls
  FW-W NAS-W,M
Harper Valley P.T.A.
  CMG-W,M GOI7-W,M TI1-W,M
  UFB-W,M
Harrigan
  RDT-W,M TI2-W,M UBF-W,M
Harrison Song
  MPP-W SY-W,M
Harrison Town
  Oz2-W,M
Harry Bluff
  ESU-W
Harry Clay
  ESU-W
Harry Come Back
  LaS-W,M
Harry Dale
  BSC-W
Harry the Hairy Ape
  HR-W
Hart, He Loves the High Wood
  Boo-W,M
Hart to Hart (Theme)
  TV-M
Haru Ga Kita
  SCL-W,M (Japanese)
Harvard Student
  Oz3-W,M
Harvest
  VA-W,M
Harvest Dawn Is Near
  AHO-W,M
Harvest Home
  FSA1-W,M LMR-W,M TF-W,M
  UF-W,M
Harvest Hymn (Blessed with
  Plentiful Orchard and Field)
  ASB5-W,M
Harvest Hymn (Harvest Time Has
  Come Once More)
  UF-W,M
Harvest Song

Harvest Song (Las' Year Wus a
  Good Crop Year)
  NF-M
Harvest Song (March)
  GrM-W,M
Harvest Time
  ASB3-W,M
Harvest War Song
  AFP-W
Harvester
  GrM-W,M
Harwell
  SHS-W,M
Has Anybody Here Seen Basie
  MF-M
Has Anybody Here Seen Kelley?
  FSTS-W,M
Has Anybody Here Seen Kelly?
  U-W
Has Anybody Seen Our Ship?
  OTO-W
Has Sorrow Thy Young Day
  Shaded?
  LMR-W,M
Hast Thou Heard It, O My Brother
  AHO-W,M AME-W,M
Hasta Manana
  TI1-W,M UFB-W,M
Haste Thee, Nymph
  Boo-W,M CSo-W,M OTJ-W,M
  TF-W,M
Haste to the Wedding
  POT-M
Hasten, Brothers, to the Battle
  SiS-W
Hasten Shepherds
  ASB5-W,M
Hasten Sinner to Be Wise
  GH-W,M
**Hatari (Theme) see Baby Elephant
  Walk**
Hated Blackbird and Crow
  NF-W
Hatikvah
  MF-W,M (Hebrew Only) RW-W,M
  (Hebrew Only) SBJ-W,M (Hebrew
  Only) TI1-W,M (Hebrew Only)
  UFB-W,M (Hebrew Only)
Hats Make the Woman
  M-W,M
Hattie Hattie
  SNS-W
Hatzi Kaddish
  SBJ-W,M (Hebrew Only)
Haughs o' Cromdale
  SBB-W
Haul Away, Joe
  ATM-W,M FW-W Le-W,M
  MM-W,M OHO-W,M SA-W,M
  SAm-W,M SiR-W,M
Haul on the Bowlin'
  ASB4-W,M CSo-W,M HSD-W,M
  NAS-W,M TH-W,M
Haul on the Bowline
  FW-W OHO-W,M SA-W,M
  WS-W,M
Haunted Heart
  UBF-W,M
Hava Na Shira
  FW-W (Hebrew Only) OHO-W,M
Hava Nagila
  FW-W (Hebrew Only) GuC-W,M
  (Hebrew) JF-W,M (Hebrew Only)
  LM-W,M PoG-W,M (Hebrew)
  SBJ-W,M (Hebrew Only)
Havah Nagilah

MF-W,M (Hebrew Only) OTJ-W,M
  (Hebrew Only) RW-W,M (Hebrew
  Only) SBF-W,M TI1-W,M (Hebrew
  Only) UFB-W,M (Hebrew Only)
Havdala Service
  SBJ-W,M (Hebrew Only)
Have a Little Faith in Me
  MF-W,M
Have Courage, My Boy
  GH-W,M
Have I Got a Girl for You
  Co-W,M TW-W
Have I Got a Heart for You
  TTH-W,M
Have I Told You Lately That I Love
  You
  TI2-W,M
Have Mercy
  TTH-W,M
Have Patience and Hope
  GrM-W,M
Have Pity on Me
  RSC-W,M (Russian Only)
Have Thine Affections Been Nail'd
  to the Cross
  AME-W,M
Have Thine Own Way, Lord
  AME-W,M HF-W,M Hy-W,M
  OM-W,M
Have You Any Room
  GH-W,M
Have You Any Work for a Tinker
  Boo-W,M
Have You Ever
  DBL-W
Have You Ever Been Lonely?
  HLS2-W,M MF-W,M TI1-W,M
  UFB-W,M
Have You Ever Seen the Rain
  OTJ-W,M
Have You Got Any Dreams for
  Sale?
  MCG-W,M
Have You Heard How They
  Crucified Our Lord
  WN-W,M
Have You Looked into Your Heart
  TI1-W,M UFB-W,M
Have You Met Miss Jones?
  HC2-W,M OTO-W TI1-W,M TS-W
  UBF-W,M UFB-W,M
Have You Never Been Mellow
  GrS-W,M
Have You Observed
  Boo-W,M
Have You Seen
  UF-W,M
Have You Seen but a White Lily
  Grow
  Gu-W,M SSP-W
Have You Seen Her
  SoH-W,M
Have You Seen Sam?
  MPP-W
Have You Seen the Ghost of John
  OTJ-W,M
Have You Seen Your Mother, Baby
  RoS-W,M
Have You Sir John Hawkins Hist'ry
  Boo-W,M
Have You Sought
  GH-W,M
Have You Struck Ile
  OHG-W,M SY-W,M
Have You Tried Wheaties
  GSM-W,M
Have Yourself a Merry Little

Christmas
GSF-W,M RW-W,M

Haven of Rest
AME-W,M

Hawaii
RW-W,M

Hawaii Five-O
RY-M

Hawaii Ponoi
Fif-W,M

Hawaiian Boat Song
BMC-W,M

Hawaiian Butterfly
CS-W,M

Hawaiian Eye
TVT-W,M

Hawaiian Farewell Song
AmH-W,M

Hawaiian Night
ASB5-W,M

**Hawaiian Punch Jingle see Seven
Kinds of Fruit in Hawaiian Punch**

Hawaiian War Chant
RW-W,M (Hawaiian Only)

Hawaiian Wedding Song
TI2-W,M (Hawaiian)

Hawk and Buzzard
NF-W

Hawk and Chickens
NF-W

Hawk and Chickens Play
NF-W

Hawker
FSA2-W,M

Hawthorn Tree
OH-W,M

Hay Cuttin' Song
LC-W

Haydn's Music
ASB4-W,M

Haying Time
SiR-W,M

Hayom Teamtzenu
JS-W,M (Hebrew Only)

Hayride
BMC-W,M

Hayseed
AmS-W,M FW-W

Hayseed Like Me
AFP-W

Hazel
TVT-W,M

Hazel Dell
HSD-W,M

He
BCS-W,M HHa-W,M HLS3-W,M
HLS7-W,M PB-W,M RDF-W,M
RW-W,M TI2-W,M Tr-W,M

He Ain't Heavy...He's My Brother
BR-W,M GAR-W,M MF-W,M
On-W,M OTJ-W,M

He and She
TS-W

He Arose
WN-W,M

He Bought My Soul at Calvary
HLS7-W,M

He Came from His Palace Grand
NeA-W,M

He Came to Bethany
GH-W,M

He Can Do It
P-W,M

He Can't Diddle Me
PO-W,M

He Come Down This Morning
R-W,M

He Died for Thee
GH-W,M

He Don't Love You (Like I Love
You)
DP-W,M ILS-W,M ToO76-W,M

**He Don't Love You (Like I Love
You) see also He Will Break Your
Heart**

He Got His Orders
AF-W

He Has Gone
SiS-W

He Hasn't a Thing except Me
LSO-W

He Hides within the Lily
AHO-W,M

He Holds the Key
GH-W,M

He Holds the Keys
VB-W,M

He Is an Englishman
GiS-W,M MGT-W,M MML-W,M

He Is Born
MHB-W,M (Bulgarian)

He Is Born, the Divine Christ Child
MC-W,M

**He Is Born, the Divine Christ Child
see also Born Is He, Born Is Jesus
the Infant King, and Il Est Ne (Le
Divin Enfant)**

He Is Coming
GH-W,M

He Is King of Kings
RF-W,M

He Is My Horse
NF-W

He Is Sleeping in a Manger
SHP-W,M

He Is the Way, the Truth, the Life
BSG-W,M BSP-W,M

He Is Waiting
NH-W

He Knows
GH-W,M

He Leadeth Me
AME-W,M CEM-W,M GH-W,M
HF-W,M HLS7-W,M HSD-W,M
Hy-W,M IH-M TB-W,M

He Leadeth Me beside Still Waters
FHR-W,M

He Leadeth Me, Oh Blessed
Thought
AHO-W,M FH-W,M

He Lives
OM-W,M Tr-W,M

He Los' He Coat
NSS-W

He Loved Us and Sent His Son
SoP-W,M

He Loves and She Loves
DC-W,M GOB-W,M NYT-W,M

He Loves Sugar and Tea
NF-W

He Never Came Back
Oz3-W,M

He Never Said a Mumblin' Word
J-W,M Me-W,M

He Nui Taku Aroha
SNZ-W,M (Maori)

He Paid Me Seven (Parody)
NF-W

He Passed
ESU-W

He Puti Puti Pai
SNZ-W,M (Maori)

He Raise-a Poor Lazarus
AHO-W,M

**He Raise-a Poor Lazarus see also
Oh, He Raise-a Poor Lazarus**

He Rode the Strawberry Roan
HB-W

He Rolled Away the Stone
VB-W,M

He Says Yes--She Says No
Fi-W,M

He Scarcely Thinks As Children
Think
ESU-W

He Set Me Free
HHa-W,M

He Set My Life to Music
VB-W,M

He Shall Feed His Flock
ASB6-W,M ESB-W,M FiS-W,M
HS-W,M LMR-W,M MML-W,M
RS-W,M

He Stopped Loving Her Today
FOC-W,M TI2-W,M TOH-W,M

He That Believes and Is Baptized
SJ-W,M

He That Believeth
GH-W,M

He That Drinks Is Immortal
Boo-W,M

He That Goeth Forth
GrM-W,M

He That Goeth Forth with Weeping
AME-W,M

He That Keepeth Israel
FiS-W,M

He That Reads This Verse
Boo-W,M

He That Will an Alehouse Keep
Boo-W,M

He the Pearly Gates Will Open
OM-W,M

He Touched Me
BSG-W,M BSP-W,M FS-W,M
Tr-W,M

He Turned Water into Wine
CEM-W,M

He Walked Right In
OTJ-W,M

He Was a Friend of Mine
FW-W

He Was Not Afraid to Die
SiS-W

He Was Sorry That He Did It
GI-W

He Was Such a Nice Young Man
MSB-W

He Was There All the Time
VB-W,M

He Was Too Good to Me
MF-W,M TS-W

He Wears a White Hat
Oz3-W

He Who Knows the Way
UBF-W,M

He Who Would Valiant Be
Hy-W,M

He Who'd Lead a Happy Life
Boo-W,M

He Will Break Your Heart
TI1-W,M UFB-W,M

**He Will Break Your Heart see also
He Don't Love You (Like I Love
You)**

He Will Carry You
VB-W,M

He Will Get Mr. Coon
NF-W

He Will Hide Me
GH-W,M

He Will Meet My Needs
  OGR-W,M
He Will Not Come Again
  SiS-W
He Will Set Your Fields on Fire
  BSo-W,M
He Will Understand
  YL-W,M
Heab'n (I Got Shoes)
  OS-W
Heab'n see also All God's Children,
  Goin' to Shout All over God's
  Heav'n, and Heaven (I Got a
  Robe)
Head and Shoulders, Knees and
  Toes
  CSS-W
Head, Shoulders
  RSL-W,M
Head That Once Was Crowned
  with Thorns
  AME-W,M Hy-W,M
Headin' down the Wrong Highway
  OGC1-W,M RW-W,M
Headless Horseman
  Mo-W,M NM-W,M OTJ-W,M
  OTO-W
Headlines
  TTH-W,M
Headquarters Troop Song
  GI-W,M
Heads
  SBA-W SI-W
Heal Me, Jesus
  NH-W
Healer of Broken Hearts
  BSG-W,M BSP-W,M
Healing Hands of Time
  WNF-W
Health Song
  GM-W
Health to John T. Williams
  BMM-W
Hear de Angels Singin'
  RF-W,M
Hear de Lambs A-Cryin'
  RF-W,M
Hear Dem Bells
  OTJ-W,M
Hear, Hear, O Ye Nations
  AHO-W,M
Hear Me, Blessed Jesus
  GH-W,M
Hear My Words, O Gracious Lord
  Hy-W,M
Hear, O Israel
  SHP-W,M
Hear Our Prayer, O Lord
  AME-W,M Hy-W,M
Hear the Angels Singing see Hear
  de Angels Singin'
Hear the Bells Ring
  GM-W
Hear the Blessed
  GH-W,M
Hear the Call
  GH-W,M
Hear the Christmas Bells
  SOO-W,M
Hear the Lambs Crying see Hear de
  Lambs A-Cryin'
Hear the Lively Song of the Frogs
  Boo-W,M
Hear the Noisy Wind
  SL-W,M
Hear the Rain
  SOO-W,M

Hear the Voice of Spring see Voici
  Le Printemps
Hear Them Bells see Hear Dem
  Bells
Hear Thou in Love, O Lord, Our
  Cry
  AME-W,M
Hear Thou My Prayer
  Boo-W,M GH-W,M
Hear Us, Heavenly Father
  AME-W,M
Hear Us, O Saviour
  GH-W,M
Hearsay
  NF-W
Hearse Song
  FW-W GI-W GO-W HAS-W,M
Heart
  RW-W,M
Heart and Soul
  AT-W,M GSN2-W,M OTO-W
  RDT-W,M WGB/P-W,M
Heart Beatin' Like a Hammer
  LC-W
Heart Bowed Down
  AmH-W,M HSD-W,M NAS-W,M
Heart Full of Love
  OGC1-W,M
Heart Is Quicker Than the Eye
  TS-W
Heart of a Clown
  OGC2-W,M
Heart of a Sailor
  HSD-W,M
Heart of Glass
  PL-W,M
Heart of Mine
  HSe-W,M
Heart of My Heart
  OTJ-W,M
Heart of My Heart see also Story
  of the Rose
Heart of Oak
  CSo-W,M
Heart of Stone
  RoS-W,M
Heart of the Country
  PMC-W,M
Heart of the Seeker
  VB-W,M
Heart Strings (Merle Moore)
  OGC2-W,M
Heart That Forms for Love
  Oz4-W
Heart to Heart
  WG-W,M
Heartaches
  TI2-W,M
Heartaches by the Number
  CMG-W,M FOC-W,M FPS-W,M
  MAB1-W,M MSA1-W TI2-W,M
Heartaches of a Fool
  TOC82-W,M
Heart-achin' Blues
  LC-W
Heartbeat
  TTH-W,M
Heartbeat, It's a Lovebeat
  AO-W,M
Heartbreak Express
  TOC82-W,M
Heartbreak Hotel
  CMG-W,M DRR-W,M FOC-W,M
  HR-W RB-W SRE2-W,M TI2-W,M
Heartbreaker (Bee Gees)
  TI2-W,M
Heartbreaker (Sager and Wolfert)

RW-W,M TI1-W,M TI2-W,M
  UFB-W,M
Heartless Lady
  Oz1-W
Heartlight
  MF-W,M
Hearts and Flowers
  FSN-W,M
Heart's Ease
  FSS-W,M
Hearts of Oak
  MML-W,M
Hearts of Oak Are We Still
  SI-W
Hearts of Stone
  TI1-W,M UFB-W,M
Heart's on Fire
  TTH-W,M
Heartsease
  NA-W,M
Heartstrings (Stuart Hoppin)
  LMR-W,M
Hearty Welcome Home
  SiS-W
Heat Wave (Love Is Like a Heat
  Wave)
  ToO76-W,M
Heathen Chinee
  OHG-W,M
Heather on the Hill
  HLS8-W,M LL-W,M OnT1-W,M
  OU-W,M
Heave and Ho, Rumbelow
  Boo-W,M
Heave and Ho, Rumbelow see also
  Turn Again Whittington
Heave Away
  SA-W,M
Heave Away, My Johnny
  LMR-W,M TF-W,M
Heave-a-Hora
  NH-W
Heaven (Bryan Adams)
  GSN5-W,M
Heaven (I Got a Robe)
  Me-W,M
Heaven (I Got a Robe) see also All
  God's Children, Goin' to Shout All
  over God's Heav'n, Heab'n, and
  Heaven, Heaven
Heaven (In Childhood I Heard of a
  Heaven)
  BSo-W,M
Heaven (Jagger/Richards)
  RoS-W,M
Heaven (Well, There Are Sinners
  Here and Sinners There)
  NH-W
Heaven and Earth
  ESB-W,M OTJ-W,M
Heaven and Earth and Sea and Air
  Hy-W,M
Heaven and Hell
  WNF-W
Heaven and Ocean
  WiS7-W,M
Heaven Bell A-Ring
  NSS-W
Heav'n Bells A-Ringin' in Mah Soul
  ETB-W,M
Heaven Came Down and Glory
  Filled My Soul
  BSG-W,M BSP-W,M
Heaven Fell Like Rain (When He
  Spoke)
  VB-W,M
Heaven, Heaven

IL-W,M OFS-W,M TH-W,M
Heaven, Heaven see also Heaven (I Got a Robe)
Heaven, Heaven, Heaven Is the Place
　AHO-W,M
Heaven in Your Eyes
　TTH-W,M
Heaven Is a Place on Earth
　BHO-W,M
Heaven Is A-Shinin' see Hebben Is A-Shinin'
Heaven Is Here
　AHO-W,M
Heaven Is My Home
　HSD-W,M WiS7-W,M
Heaven Knows
　TI1-W,M ToO79-W,M UFB-W,M
Heaven Must Be Missing an Angel
　SoH-W,M ToO76-W,M
Heaven Must Have Sent You
　ToO79-W,M
Heaven on Earth
　SNZ-W,M (Maori)
Heaven Shall-a Be My Home
　NSS-W
Heavenly Aeroplane
　Oz4-W
Heav'nly Aida
　AmH-W,M WiS7-W,M
Heav'nly Aida see also Celeste Aida
Heavenly Armour
　SHS-W,M
Heavenly Bodies
　TOC83-W,M
Heavenly Canaan
　GH-W,M
Heavenly Display
　GB-W,M
Heavenly Father
　VB-W,M
Heavenly Father Cares for Me
　SoP-W,M
Heavenly Land
　GH-W,M
Heavenly March
　AH-W,M SHS-W,M
Heavenly Vision
　SHS-W,M
Heavens Are Declaring
　ESB-W,M
Heavens Are Telling
　OGR-W,M TF-W,M
Heavens Declare Thy Glory, Lord
　Hy-W,M
Heavens Do Declare
　AHO-W,M
Heaven's Jubilee
　HHa-W,M
Heaven's Just a Sin Away
　HLS9-W,M
Heavens Resound
　LMR-W,M
Heavy Metal (Theme) see Takin' a Ride
Heavy the Beat of the Weary Waves
　SeS-W,M
Hebben Is A-Shinin'
　BDW-W,M
Hebben Is A-Shinin' see also Oh de Hebben Is Shinin'
Hebrew Children
　ATS-W,M SHS-W,M
Hebron
　SHS-W,M

Heel and Toe
　ASB3-W,M
Heelin' Bill
　HB-W
Heffalumps and Woozles
　OTJ-W,M
Heidelberg Victory March
　CoS-W,M
Heiden-Roslein
　Gu-W,M (German)
Heigh-Ho
　IL-W,M NI-W,M OTJ-W,M
　TI1-W,M UFB-W,M
Heigh-Ho! for a Husband
　FSS-W,M SSP-W
Heigh Ho, Heigh Hi see Quand J'etais Chez Mon Pere
Heimweh see Longing for Home
Heiraten see Married
Heirlooms
　VB-W,M
Heissa Kathreinele
　SCL-W,M (German)
Helen Wheels
　PMC-W,M TI2-W,M
Helena Polka
　MF-M OBN-M PT-M TI1-M UFB-M
Hell and High Water
　TTH-W,M
Hell and Texas
　Oz2-W,M
He'll Come Home
　FHR-W,M
Hell in Texas
　SoC-W
He'll Never Let You Fall
　BSG-W,M BSP-W,M
Hell No! I Ain't Gonna Go
　VS-W,M
Hell No! We Won't Go
　VS-W,M
Hell of an Engineer see Helluvan Engineer
He'll Shine His Light on You
　VB-W,M
He'll Understand and Say Well Done
　SUH-W,M
Hell-Bound Train
　AF-W GI-W,M HB-W,M HOH-W,M
　LSR-W,M Oz4-W,M
Hello (What Shall We Do Today?)
　RSL-W,M
Hello Beautiful
　WDS-W,M
Hello Broadway
　LSB-W,M
Hello Central, Give Me Heaven
　BH-W,M EFS-W,M
Hello City Limits
　BSo-W,M
Hello Dolly
　DBC-W,M GOl7-W,M HC1-W,M
　MAB1-W Mo-W,M MSA1-W
　NM-W,M OTJ-W,M OTO-W
　RDT-W,M TI2-W,M UBF-W,M
Hello Girls
　AmS-W,M OTJ-W,M
Hello Goodbye
　BBe-W,M Be2-W,M TWS-W
Hello Hello
　Bo-W,M Boo-W,M CSS-W U-W
Hello! Hello! Telephone Girlie
　NN2-W,M
Hello! Hello! Telephone Girlie see also Telephone Girlie
Hello in There

RV-W
Hello Ma Baby
　AH-W,M BH-W,M FSN-W,M
　HLS1-W,M MF-W,M OAP-W,M
　RW-W,M
Hello Ma Baby see also Hello My Baby
Hello Mary Lou
　PoG-W,M TI2-W,M
Hello Mudduh, Hello Fadduh
　NoS-W,M
Hello My Baby
　FW-W OTJ-W,M TI1-W,M
　UFB-W,M
Hello My Baby see also Hello Ma Baby
Hello Spring
　GM-W
Hello Texas
　TOH-W,M
Hello Trees
　GSM-W,M
Hello Twelve
　JP-W,M
Hello Twelve, Hello Thirteen, Hello Love
　CL-W,M
Hello Walls
　CMG-W,M TI2-W,M WNF-W
Hello Young Lovers
　DBC-W,M HC1-W,M OTJ-W,M
　OTO-W RW-W,M TI1-W,M TW-W
　UBF-W,M UFB-W,M
Helluvan Engineer
　GI-W,M GO-W
Help!
　BBe-W,M Be1-W,M JF-W,M
　TWS-W
Help It On
　ESB-W,M GrM-W,M
Help, Lord, Because the Godly Man
　AHO-W,M
Help Me
　DBL-W
Help Me, God, to Praise Thee
　SHP-W,M
Help Me Make It through the Night
　CMG-W,M SuS-W,M
Help Me My Brother
　VB-W,M
Help, Neighbor
　Mo-W,M NM-W,M
Help Thy Servant
　AHO-W,M
Help Yourself
　AT-W,M (Italian)
Helping
　MAR-W,M
Helping Mother Bake a Cake
　SiR-W,M
Helping Song
　SoP-W,M
Helter Skelter
　BBe-W,M TWS-W
Hem of His Garment
　GH-W,M
Henry Clay
　FMT-W
Henry Clay's Remonstrance
　MPP-W
Henry George Campaign Song
　AL-W
Henry Green
　BSC-W Oz2-W,M
Henry Joy McCracken
　VP-W,M
Henry Martin

BB-W BF-W,M FW-W
Henry Sweet Henry
  OnT6-W,M
Henry's Swing Club
  DBL-W
Her Beautiful Eyes
  LMR-W,M
Her Blanket
  MAS-W,M
Her Bright Smile
  SA-W,M
Her Bright Smile Haunts Me Still
  HSD-W,M
Her Eyes Don't Shine Like
  Diamonds
  FSN-W,M
Her Eyes Don't Shine Like
  Diamonds--Three Little Lads' Love
  Story
  FSTS-W,M
Her Hair
  MLS-W,M
Her Majesty
  TWS-W
Her Mouth Makes Roses
  TW-W
Her Own Brave Volunteer
  SiS-W
Her White Bosom Bare
  Oz4-W
Herald of Happiness
  SL-W,M
Heralds of Christ
  AHO-W,M
Heralds of Christ Who Bear the
  King's Commands
  Hy-W,M
Herald's Song
  FSA1-W,M
Herb Carol
  GBC-W,M
Herd Bells
  MML-W,M
Herdsman
  Bo-W,M VA-W,M
Herdsman's Mountain Home
  TH-W,M
Here Am I
  SoM-W,M
Here Am I Broken Hearted see
  Broken Hearted
Here Am I, Send Me
  GH-W,M
Here Are Mother's Knives and
  Forks
  FP-W,M
Here betwixt Ass and Oxen Mild
  YC-W,M
Here Come the British
  OHF-W
Here Come the River Boats
  MaG-W,M
Here Comes a Young Man
  Courting
  NF-W
Here Comes Another Song about
  Texas
  Mo-W,M NM-W,M
Here Comes Cookie
  NoS-W,M TI1-W,M UFB-W,M
Here Comes My Baby
  CSp-W,M
Here Comes Santa Claus
  BCh-W,M CI-W,M RW-W,M
Here Comes Summer
  TI1-W,M UFB-W,M
Here Comes That Rainy Day

Feeling Again
  TI2-W,M
Here Comes the Bride
  PoG-M
Here Comes the Bride see also
  Bridal Chorus and Bridal March
Here Comes the Flag
  MML-W,M
Here Comes the King (Budweiser)
  TI1-W,M UFB-W,M
Here Comes the Show Boat
  TI1-W,M UFB-W,M
Here Comes the Star
  Mo-W,M
Here Comes the Sun
  BBe-W,M TWS-W
Here Flat on Her Back
  Boo-W,M
Here He Comes with My Heart
  VB-W,M
Here I Am
  VB-W,M
Here I Go
  Boo-W,M
Here I Go Again
  RoE-W,M
Here I Stand
  NF-W
Here I Stand All Ragged and Dirty
  Oz3-W
Here I'll Stay
  TI1-W,M UBF-W,M UFB-W,M
Here in My Arms
  TS-W TW-W
Here in Sweet Sleep
  Boo-W,M
Here in the Real World
  GCM-W,M
Here Innocence and Beauty Lies
  Boo-W,M
Here Is a Big Train
  SOO-W,M
Here Is a Song
  AHO-W,M
Here Is the Bee Hive
  FP-W,M SOO-W,M
Here Is the Church
  AST-W,M MAR-W,M
Here Lies a Woman
  Boo-W,M
Here Lies, Here Lies
  Boo-W,M
Here Lies Poor Teague
  Boo-W,M
Here Lord, Retired, I Bow in Prayer
  AHO-W,M
Here, O My Lord, I See Thee Face
  to Face
  Hy-W,M
Here on His Back Doth Lay
  Boo-W,M
Here Pleasures Are Few
  Boo-W,M
Here Sits a Monkey
  SiR-W,M
Here Stand I
  Boo-W,M
Here There and Everywhere
  BBe-W,M Be1-W,M PMC-W,M
  TWS-W
Here Today
  TI2-W,M
Here We Come A-Caroling
  MC-W,M RS-W,M RW-W,M
Here We Come A-Wassailing
  ASB5-W,M BCh-W,M BCS-W,M
  OE-W,M TI1-W,M UFB-W,M

YC-W,M
Here We Go A-Riding on a Train
  SOO-W,M
Here We Go Looby-Loo
  FW-W OTJ-W,M SMa-W,M
Here We Go Looby-Loo see also
  Looby Loo
Here We Go round the Mulberry
  Bush
  OTJ-W,M
Here We Go Skating Along
  SOO-W,M
Here We Have Idaho
  Fif-W,M
Here We Rest
  AFP-W WW-W,M
Here Where Rippling Waters
  Boo-W,M
Here You Come Again
  EC-W,M
Hereford Carol
  OB-W,M
Here's a Ball for Baby
  FP-W,M
Here's a First Rate Opportunity
  SL-W,M
Here's a Health
  Boo-W,M
Here's a Health to Thee, Tom
  Breese
  ANS-W
Here's a Health unto His Majesty
  CSo-W,M OH-W,M
Here's a How-De-Do
  GiS-W,M MGT-W,M
Here's Adieu to All Judges and
  Juries
  SCa-W
Here's How
  OG-W,M
Here's That Rainy Day
  DJ-W,M FPS-W,M ILT-W,M
  RoE-W,M TI1-W,M ToS-W,M
  UFB-W,M
Here's the Beehive
  RSL-W,M
Here's the Bottle She Loved So
  Much
  ESU-W
Here's the Bower
  ESU-W
Here's the Man A-Coming
  MSB-W
Here's to Baker
  CoS-W,M
Here's to Good Old Brown
  IL-W,M
Here's to My Lady
  MF-W,M Mo-W,M NM-W,M
  OHF-W
Here's to the Boy Scouts
  Bo-W,M
Here's to the Land We Love, Boys
  OG-W,M
Here's to the Losers
  Mo-W,M NM-W,M
Here's to the Maiden
  OH-W,M
Here's to the Maiden of Bashful
  Fifteen
  CSo-W,M
Here's to the Man Who Wears the
  D
  CoS-W,M
Here's to Us
  Mo-W,M NM-W,M OTO-W
Here's to You Harry Clay

MPP-W
Here's to You, My Sparkling Wine
BP-W,M
Here's What I'm Here For
Mo-W,M NM-W,M
Here's Your Mule
SCo-W,M Sin-W,M SiS-W
Hernando's Hideaway
HC1-W,M
Hero of Fort Sumter
SiS-W
Hero Rewarded
FMT-W
Heron
NAS-W,M
Herons
ASB5-W,M
Herons Homeward Flying
MML-W,M
Hero's Grave
SiS-W
Herr Doktor, Die Periode
LW-W,M (German)
Herrick's Carol
OB-W,M
Herrick's Ode
OB-W,M
Herring the King
VP-W,M
**Hershey Chocolate Bar Jingle see
Hershey Is the Great American
Chocolate Bar and There's
Nothing Like the Face of a Kid
Eating a Hershey Bar**
Hershey Is the Great American
Chocolate Bar
TI1-W,M UFB-W,M
He's a Big Fat Turkey
SOO-W,M
He's a Burden-Bearer
SSo-W,M
He's a Devil in His Own Home
Town
SLB-W,M
He's a Fool
FW-W
He's a Heartache
TOC83-W,M
He's a Rag Picker
SLB-W,M
He's a Railroad Man
LC-W
He's a Rebel
RB-W
He's a Tramp
NI-W,M OTJ-W,M OTO-W
He's a V.I.P.
DR-W,M
He's Alive
VB-W,M
He's Coming to Us Dead
LSR-W,M
He's Gone Away
AmS-W,M FoS-W,M FW-W
LMR-W,M MuM-W,M NeA-W,M
SRS-W,M
He's Gone, He's Gone up the Trail
HOH-W,M
He's Gone to the Arms of
Abraham
Sin-W,M SiS-W
He's Gone up the Trail
HOH-W
**He's Good for Me see He's (She's)
Good for Me**
He's Got His Discharge from the
Army

SiS-W
He's Got the Whole World
HHa-W,M MAR-W,M
He's Got the Whole World in His
Hands
BNG-W,M Bo-W,M CEM-W,M
FoS-W,M FS-W,M FWS-W,M
FW-W GS1-W GuC-W,M
HLS1-W,M HLS7-W,M HS-W,M
JBF-W,M MAB1-W MF-W,M
MG-W,M MSA1-W On-W,M
OPS-W,M OTJ-W,M PoG-W,M
RDF-W,M RW-W,M SFB-W,M
SpS-W,M SUH-W,M TI1-W,M
Tr-W,M UFB-W,M
He's in Love
Ki-W,M UBF-W,M
He's My Friend
AME-W,M
He's Only a Prayer Away
BSG-W,M BSP-W,M FS-W,M
HLS7-W,M MF-W,M VB-W,M
He's (She's) Good for Me
MF-W,M
He's Somebody's Darling
SiS-W
He's Still Working on Me
AG-W,M HHa-W,M
He's Sure the Boy I Love
HR-W RB-W
He's Taken My Feet from the Mire
WN-W,M
He's the Last Word
WDS-W,M
He's the Lily of the Valley
RF-W,M WiS7-W,M
He's the One
AME-W,M
He's the Wizard
Wi-W,M
Hesitating Blues
B-W,M Bl-W,M FW-W
Hesitation Blues
LC-W
Hesitation Waltz see Esmeralda
Hevenu Shalom Alayhem
SBJ-W,M (Hebrew Only)
Hey Ba-Ba-Re-Bop
TI2-W,M
Hey Baby
TOC82-W,M
Hey Baby! They're Playin' Our
Song
OnT6-W,M
Hey Betty Martin
AH-W,M ATS-W,M FW-W
HS-W,M MAS-W,M MG-W,M
OHO-W,M SCL-W,M
Hey Boy
FSA1-W,M
Hey Bulldog
TWS-W
Hey Diddle Diddle
AmH-W,M HS-W,M MH-W,M
OTJ-W,M
Hey Doll Baby
HRB2-W,M
Hey Down a Down, Behold and
See
Boo-W,M
Hey Fightin' Tigers
Mo-W,M
Hey Girl (I Know He Put You
Down)
OnT6-W,M
Hey Girl (I Want You to Know)
ERM-W,M ToO79-W,M

Hey Girl, Come and Get It
DDH-W,M
Hey Good Lookin'
HW-W,M TI1-W,M TI2-W,M
UFB-W,M
Hey Hey! Let 'Er Go
ReG-W,M
Hey Ho, Anybody Home
HS-W,M MG-W,M
Hey Ho, Behold I Will Show
Boo-W,M
Hey Ho, Nobody at Home
Boo-W,M SSP-W
Hey Ho, Nobody Home
FGM-W,M FW-W GuC-W,M
SWF-W,M
Hey Ho! to the Greenwood
BMC-W,M Boo-W,M UF-W,M
Hey Jealous Lover
MF-W,M
Hey Jim Along
ASB1-W,M
Hey Joe
RY-W,M RYT-W,M
Hey Jude
BBe-W,M Be2-W,M PMC-W,M
SwS-W,M TRR-W,M TWS-W
Hey Liley, Liley Lo
TI1-W,M UFB-W,M
Hey Little Girl (in the High School
Sweater)
FRH-W,M
Hey Little One
MF-W,M
Hey Lolly Lolly
OTJ-W,M
Hey Look Me Over
HC1-W,M MAB1-W MF-W,M
Mo-W,M MSA1-W NM-W,M
OTJ-W,M OTO-W TI2-W,M
UBF-W,M W-W,M
Hey Love
Mo-W,M NM-W,M OTO-W
Hey Lucky Lady
BDP-W,M
Hey, Mable, Black Label
GSM-W,M
Hey Miss Fanny
HRB2-W,M
Hey Mr. Banjo
TI2-W,M
Hey Mr. Bluebird
OGC1-W,M
Hey Mr. Echo
GM-W
Hey Mister Hacha
SMW-W,M (Czech)
Hey Motswala
SBF-W,M
Hey Negrita
RoS-W,M
Hey Okie
AFP-W
Hey Robin, Jolly Robin
SSP-W
Hey There
HC1-W,M
Hey There Lonely Girl
AT-W,M IPH-W,M
Hey Tomorrow
JC-W,M
**Hey Won't You Play Another
Somebody Done Somebody
Wrong Song see Another
Somebody Done Somebody
Wrong Song**
Hi Cheerily Ho

Boo-W,M
Hi-Diddle-Dee-Dee
  NI-W,M TI1-W,M UFB-W,M
Hi Diddle Diddle
  YS-W,M
Hi for the Beggarman
  IS-W,M
Hi-Heel Sneakers
  DRR-W,M EP-W,M TI2-W,M
Hi Hi Hi
  TI2-W,M
Hi-Ho Hi-Ho
  GO-W
Hi Ho, Nobody Home
  Bo-W,M CSS-W
Hi Ho, the Holly
  Y-W,M
Hi-Lee Hi-Lo Hi-Lup-Up-Up
  TI1-W,M UFB-W,M
Hi-Lili, Hi-Lo
  EAG2-W,M GG1-W,M GSN3-W,M
  HLS5-W,M RDT-W,M RT5-W,M
  RW-W,M STW-W,M
Hi Neighbor
  PB-W,M
Hi There, Cub
  CSS-W
Hi-Yo Witzi
  UF-W,M
Hiawatha
  FSTS-W,M SSe-W,M
Hiawatha's Brothers
  FSA1-W,M
Hiawatha's Sailing
  GC-W,M
Hiawatha's Wooing
  NAS-W,M
Hibiscus
  Mo-W,M NM-W,M
Hic, Haec, Hoc
  Mo-W,M (Latin Only) NM-W,M
  (Latin Only) OTO-W (Latin Only)
Hickory Dickory Dock
  BBF-W,M CSo-W,M FF-W GM-W
  HS-W,M MG-W,M OTJ-W,M
  SiR-W,M SMa-W,M
Hickory Dickory Dock see also
  Dickory Dickory Dock
Hick's Farewell
  FSSC-W,M SHS-W,M
Hide and Seek
  STS-W,M
Hide Me
  GH-W,M
Hide Me in Thy Bosom
  GrG-W,M
Hide Thou Me
  AME-W,M BSG-W,M BSP-W,M
  GH-W,M
Hide Your Heart Little Hippie
  JF-W,M
Hide Your Love
  RoS-W,M
Hiding in Thee
  GH-W,M
Hie Away Home
  HAS-W,M
Hieland Laddie
  FW-W
Hieland Laddie see also Highland
  Laddie
Hier Apres-Midi
  CaF-W (French Only)
Hier Sur Le Pont D'Avignon
  CFS-W,M (French)
Higgledy Piggledy
  ASB1-W,M

Higgledy, Piggledy, My Black Hen
  OTJ-W,M
High and Blue the Sky
  SSe-W,M
High and Dry
  RoS-W,M
High and Low
  TW-W
High and the Mighty
  HFH-W,M MF-W,M
High Barbaree
  FW-W OTJ-W,M SA-W,M
High Barbary
  ANS-W SSP-W
High, Betty Martin
  SiR-W,M
High Chin Bob
  HB-W,M HWS-W,M SoC-W
High Crime
  BOA-W,M
High Daddy
  DE-W,M
High Germany
  FW-W
High Hat
  GOB-W,M
High Heel Sneakers see Hi-Heel
  Sneakers
High Hopes
  EY-W,M FrS-W,M HFH-W,M
  MF-W,M
High Noon
  FC-W,M GG2-W,M HLS5-W,M
  MF-W,M RT5-W,M RW-W,M
High on His Everlasting Throne
  AME-W,M
High on Sierra Morena
  MuM-W,M
High o'er the Hills
  AHO-W,M
High School Cadets
  RW-M
High School U.S.A.
  RB-W
High Sheriff of Hazard
  RBO-W,M
High Society
  TI2-W,M
High-Stepping Horses
  ASB3-W,M
High-Tail Blues
  AF-W
High upon a Mountain
  Mo-W,M NM-W,M
Higher and Higher
  DPE-W,M MF-W,M
Higher Ground
  OM-W,M
Higher Love
  LOM-W,M
Higher the Plum Tree
  TH-W,M
Highest Judge of All
  L-W TG-W,M
Highland Fling
  AmH-M FSA2-W,M
Highland Lad
  TH-W,M
Highland Laddie
  SA-W,M
Highland Laddie see also Hieland
  Laddie
Highway Blues
  LC-W
Highway Boy
  SoC-W
Highway 40 Blues

TI2-W,M
Highway of Regret
  BSo-W,M
Highways and Byways
  MHB-W,M
Hijo Del Conde see El Hijo Del
  Conde
Hiking
  Bo-W,M
Hiking Song
  GUM1-W,M
Hiking Song (Above a Plain of Gold
  and Green)
  UF-W,M
Hiking Song (I Have Broken Do on
  My Clarinet)
  ASB4-W,M
Hilariter
  OB-W,M
Hill of Dreams
  SN-W,M
Hill of Fare see Corichie
Hill Street Blues Theme
  GSN5-M TV-M
Hills of God, Break Forth in Singing
  AHO-W,M
Hills of Ixopo
  LS-W,M
Hills of Mexico
  HWS-W,M SoC-W
Hills of Old Wyomin'
  FC-W,M OTO-W
Hills of Roan County
  BIS-W,M
Hills of the North, Rejoice
  Hy-W,M SJ-W,M
Hilltop Song
  ASB2-W,M
Hilo! Hilo!
  AFP-W
Himno De Riego see El Himno De
  Riego
Himno Nacional (Argentina)
  SiP-W,M (Spanish)
Hinder Me Not
  NSS-W
Hindu Song
  MML-W,M
Hine
  SNZ-W,M (Maori)
Hine E Hine
  SNZ-W,M (Maori)
Hine Ma Tov
  SBJ-W,M (Hebrew Only) TO-W,M
  (Hebrew Only)
Hineh Mah Tov
  GuC-W,M (Hebrew)
Hinemoa and Tutanekai
  SNZ-W,M (Maori)
Hiney Matov
  JF-W,M (Hebrew)
Hinky Dinky Parlay-Voo
  HAS-W,M IHA-W,M SMW-W,M
Hinky Dinky Parlay-Voo see also
  Mademoiselle from Armentieres
Hinky Dinky Parley-Voo
  MF-W,M
Hinky Dinky Parlez-Vous
  SWF-W,M
Hint to the Wise
  NH-W
Hip! Hip! for Eight Hours
  AL-W
Hippety Hop
  ASB1-W,M SOO-W,M
Hiram Hubbert
  FSU-W

Hiram's Menagerie
MPP-W
Hiring Fairs of Ulster
VP-W,M
Hi-ro Jerum
OHO-W,M
Hirondelles see Les Hirondelles
His Blood Still Sets Men Free
HHa-W,M
His Eye Is on the Sparrow
AME-W,M BSG-W,M BSP-W,M
FS-W,M HLS7-W,M J-W,M
JBF-W,M MF-W,M RDF-W,M
Tr-W,M
His Eyes, Her Eyes
MLS-W,M
His Grace Is Greater
VB-W,M
His Latest Flame
SRE2-W,M TI1-W,M UFB-W,M
His Love Comes A-Tricklin' Down
RTH-W
His Name Is Wonderful
BSG-W,M BSP-W,M RDF-W,M
His Praises I Will Sing
GH-W,M
His Rocking Horse Ran Away
OTJ-W,M OTO-W
His Sheep Am I
BSG-W,M BSP-W,M JBF-W,M
His Way with Thee
OM-W,M
His Word a Tower
GH-W,M
His Word Will Stand
OGR-W,M
History ob de World
SY-W,M
History of the World
Oz2-W,M TMA-W,M
Hit at the Times
ESU-W
Hit 'Em in the Head with Love
NB-W
Hit the Line
SL-W,M
Hit the Line of Wittenberg
CoS-W,M
Hit the Road to Dreamland
LM-W,M OHF-W OTJ-W,M
OTO-W
Hitch-Hiker
CMG-W,M
Hither Come
GrM-W,M
Hither We Come, Our Dearest Lord
AHO-W,M
Hitler Ain't Dead
VS-W,M
Hitler Song
Le-W,M
Ho, Boys, de Time Am Come
SiS-W
Ho Every One That Thirsts
WN-W,M
Ho, Every Sleeper, Waken
ASB5-W,M SMY-W,M
Ho for California
ASB5-W,M WS-W,M
Ho for the Kansas Plains
SY-W,M
Ho Ho
NH-W
Ho Ho Ho
GB-W,M
Ho! Westward Ho!
SY-W,M

Ho! Workingmen!
AL-W
Ho! Ye Townsmen
FT-W,M
Hobbies
IHA-W,M SI-W,M
Hobble and Bobble
ATS-W,M
Hobby Derry Dando
MuM-W,M
Hobo Bill's Last Ride
LSR-W,M
Hobo Blues
LC-W
Hobo Diddle De Ho
Oz3-W
Hobo Worried Blues
LC-W
Hobo's Blues
PS-W,M
Hobo's Death
FMT-W
Hobo's Lullaby
FW-W RW-W.M
Hobo's Meditation
LJ-W,M
Hocus Pocus
MF-M
Hoday, Hoday, Hoday
NeF-W
Hodge in London
MSB-W
Hodie Christus Natus Est
MMW-W,M (Latin)
Hodo
JS-W,M (Hebrew Only)
Hodo Al Erets
SBJ-W,M (Hebrew Only)
Hodu
JS-W,M (Hebrew Only)
Hoe Cake
NF-W
Hoea Ra
SNZ-W,M (Maori)
Hoffmann Hoffmann
Boo-W,M
Hoffnung see When the Roses Bloom
Hog Drovers
FMT-W FoM-W,M
Hog-Eye Man
SA-W,M
Hog Rovers
Oz3-W,M
Hoist Up the Flag
SiS-W
Hoki Hoki
SNZ-W,M (Maori)
Hoki Hoki Tonu Mai
SNZ-W,M (Maori)
Hoki Mai
SNZ-W,M (Maori)
Hol' de Win'
SNS-W
Hol' Out to de En'
BDW-W,M
Hold 'Em Joe
TI1-W,M UFB-W,M
Hold Fast Till I Come
GH-W,M
Hold Me
GG5-W,M GSO-W,M OP1-W,M
RW-W,M TI1-W,M UFB-W,M
Hold Me, Thrill Me, Kiss Me
GSN3-W,M
Hold Me Tight
Be1-W,M TWS-W

Hold Me 'Til the Mornin' Comes
TI2-W,M
Hold On
FW-W VB-W,M
Hold On Abraham
SiS-W
Hold On I'm Coming
TOC83-W,M
Hold On to the Night
WG-W,M
Hold Out to the End see Hol' Out to de En'
Hold the Fort
FG2-W,M FW-W GH-W,M
RDF-W,M Sin-W,M SiS-W
SWF-W,M
Hold the Wind see Hol' de Win'
Hold Them Joe see Hold 'Em Joe
Hold Thou My Hand
FiS-W,M GH-W,M TM-W,M
WGB/O-W,M
Hold Thy Peace
Boo-W,M SL-W,M TF-W,M
Hold Tight, Hold Tight
NoS-W,M
Hold Tight to Your Girl
FSF-W (French)
Hold Your Hands, Old Man
Oz1-W,M
Hold Your Light
AN-W FSSC-W,M
Holdin' On
TOC82-W,M
Holding Back the Years
TTH-W,M
Hole in the Ground
VS-W,M
Hole in the Wall
DBL-W
Holiday
OnT6-W,M
Holiday, A
FSA2-W,M
Holiday for Strings
DC-M MF-M
Holiness
VB-W,M
Holla-Hi, Holla-Ho
PaS-W,M
Holland
EA-W,M
Holland Windmill
FSA1-W,M
Holland's National Hymn
AmH-W,M (Dutch)
Hollow Eyes
VB-W,M
Holly and the Ivy
BCS-W,M BT-W,M CEM-W,M
FW-W GBC-W,M Gu-W,M
GUM2-W,M HS-W,M JOC-W,M
OB-W,M OE-W,M OU-W,M
SMY-W,M U-W YC-W,M
Holly Boy
OTJ-W,M
Holly Holy
TI2-W,M
Holly Jolly Christmas
BCh-W,M BCS-W,M MF-W,M
TI1-W,M UFB-W,M
Holly Twig
FMT-W
Hollywood Party
TS-W
Holmes and Watson
Mo-W,M NM-W,M OTO-W
Holtoyo

UF-W,M

Holy Child (For a Manger Lowly,
Shepherds Leave Their Flocks)
ASB4-W,M

Holy Child (Mother, See Who's at
the Doorway)
RW-W,M

Holy City
FS-W,M MuM-W,M SS-W U-W

Holy Father, Great Creator
AHO-W,M

Holy Ghost with Light Divine
AME-W,M GH-W,M HSD-W,M
OM-W,M

Holy God We Praise Thy Name
AHO-W,M CEM-W,M ESB-W,M
MAS-W,M RDF-W,M WiS9-W,M

Holy Ground
GP-W,M IS-W,M OGR-W,M
VB-W,M

Holy, Holy
VB-W,M

Holy, Holy, Holy
AME-W,M AmH-W,M CEM-W,M
FH-W,M GH-W,M HF-W,M
HLS7-W,M HSD-W,M IH-M
MAB1-W MML-W,M MSA1-W
OS-W OTJ-W,M OU-W,M
RDF-W,M RW-W,M TB-W,M
TF-W,M TH-W,M WiS7-W,M

Holy, Holy, Holy, Lord God
Almighty
AME-W,M ESB-W,M Hy-W,M
OPS-W,M SHP-W,M SJ-W,M

Holy, Holy, Holy, Lord God of
Hosts
Hy-W,M

Holy Hour
SS-W

Holy Is His Name
VB-W,M

Holy Is the Lord
GH-W,M

Holy Manna
SHS-W,M WN-W,M

Holy Mother Give to Me
GB-W,M

Holy Night
AmH-W,M

Holy Night, Peaceful Night
CCH-W,M FH-W,M WiS7-W,M

Holy Order
GB-W,M

Holy Savior Call
GB-W,M

Holy Season
MHB-W,M (Serbo-Croatian)

Holy Spirit, Faithful Guide
AHO-W,M AME-W,M GH-W,M

Holy Spirit from on High
AME-W,M

Holy Spirit Hear Us
AME-W,M

Holy Spirit, Teacher Thou
GH-W,M

Holy Spirit, Truth Divine
AHO-W,M AME-W,M Hy-W,M

Holy Well
GBC-W,M OB-W,M

Home (Charlie Smalls)
Wi-W,M

Home (Franz Lehar)
TW-W

Home (Home, Can I Forget Thee?)
HS-W,M (German)

**Home (Home, Can I Forget Thee?)
see also Du, Du, Liegst Mir Im**

Herzen

Home Again
ATS-W HSD-W,M

Home Again in My Heart
EC-W,M

Home and Dry
ToO79-W,M

Home at Last
GH-W,M

Home, Boys, Home
FW-W GI-W,M GO-W,M

Home Call
LJ-W,M

Home Came the Old Man
FoS-W,M

Home Cookin'
OTO-W

Home Corral
HOH-W SoC-W

Home, Dearie, Home
OHO-W,M SA-W,M

Home for the Holidays
BCh-W,M BCS-W,M CI-W,M
MF-W,M OPS-W,M OTJ-W,M
RW-W,M TI1-W,M UFB-W,M

Home from the War
SiS-W

Home Heavenly Home
FHR-W

**Home Home Home see Hame
Hame Hame**

Home, Home on the Base
GI-W

Home in Glory
WN-W,M

Home in That Rock
FW-W J-W,M WSB-W,M

Home Is Waiting
FSA1-W,M SL-W,M

Home Is Where You're Happy
WNF-W

Home Means Nevada
Fif-W,M

Home of the Brave
RB-W

Home of the Soul
GH-W,M

Home on Furlough
SiS-W

Home on High
GH-W,M

Home on the Range
ATS-W BH-W,M Bo-W,M CSS-W
Fif-W,M FU-W,M FuB-W,M FW-W
FWS-W,M GeS-W,M GuC-W,M
HOH-W,M HS-W,M HWS-W,M
IL-W,M LoS-W,M LT-W,M
MAB1-W MAS-W,M MF-W,M
MG-W,M MML-W,M MSA1-W
NAS-W,M OBN-W,M OFS-W,M
OS-W OTJ-W,M Oz2-W,M
PaS-W,M RW-W,M SiR-W,M
SoC-W SoF-W,M U-W UF-W,M
WiS9-W,M

Home Over There
AME-W,M GH-W,M

Home, P.T.A. Home
LoS-W,M

Home Rule
VP-W

Home Sweet Home
AH-W,M AmH-W,M ATS-W
BH-W,M BIS-W,M ESB-W,M
FM-W,M FW-W HS-W,M
HSD-W,M IPH-W,M MAB1-W
MF-W,M MSA1-W NAS-W,M
OBN-W,M OHG-W,M OS-W

OTJ-W,M PoS-W,M RW-W,M
SiP-W,M TH-W U-W UF-W
WiS8-W,M

Home to Emily
ToO76-W,M

Home to Our Mountains
HSD-W,M TH-W,M WiS7-W,M

Home Where I Belong
VB-W,M

Homecoming
DPE-M

Homeland
SL-W,M

Homeland, The
HSD-W,M

Homeless Man
ASB6-W,M

Homesick Blues
V-W,M

Homesick That's All
Mo-W,M NM-W,M

Homesickness
GI-W

Homesickness Blues
BI-W,M

Homespun Dress
FMT-W IHA-W,M Oz2-W,M
SCo-W,M Sin-W,M SiS-W

Homestead on the Farm
BIS-W,M

Homestead Strike
AL-W

Homestead Struggle
AL-W

Hometown Band
TI1-W,M UFB-W,M

Hometown Gossip
EC-W,M

Homeward Bound (Oh! to
Pensacola Town We'll Bid Adieu)
ANS-W

Homeward Bound (Out on an
Ocean All Boundless We Ride)
HSD-W,M WiS7-W,M

Homing Heart
NA-W,M

Hommes, Prenez Courage, Jesus
Est Ne
AHO-W,M (Algonquin, French)

**Honda Automobile Jingle see First
for Good Reason and Hello Trees**

Honest Man
Mo-W,M NM-W,M OTO-W

Honest Old Abe
OHG-W,M

Honest Ploughman, or 90 Years
Ago
MSB-W

Honest Policeman of Mitcham
MSB-W

Honest Workingman
AL-W

Honestly Sincere
Mo-W,M NM-W,M OTO-W

Honey (and Honey I Miss You)
AO-W,M ATC1-W,M CMG-W,M
CSp-W,M HLS9-W,M RW-W,M
TI1-W,M UFB-W,M

Honey (I'm in Love with You
Honey)
CS-W,M GSN2-W,M GST-W,M
HLS2-W,M RW-W,M

Honey Ant Song of Ljaba
ATM-W,M

Honey Babe
SCa-W

Honey Baby

Me-W,M
Honey Be There
CMG-W,M
Honey Bee
DBL-W SL-W,M
Honey Bun
HC1-W,M OTJ-W,M OTO-W
SP-W,M TI1-W,M UBF-W,M
UFB-W,M
Honey for the Bees
TTH-W,M
Honey, Honey
DP-W,M TI1-W,M UBF-W,M
Honey Love
HRB2-W,M
Honey Pie
BBe-W,M Be2-W,M PMC-W,M
TWS-W WG-W,M
Honey Song
Mo-W,M NM-W,M
Honey Take a One on Me
NH-W
Honey Take a Whiff on Me
NH-W
Honeybee
ASB1-W,M
Honeycomb
HLS9-W,M RW-W,M TTH-W,M
Honeyfoglin' Time
Mo-W,M NM-W,M
Honeymoon Is Over
I-W,M
Honeysuckle Rose
BeL-W,M DJ-W,M GSN2-W,M
RW-W,M TI1-W,M UBF-W,M
UFB-W,M
Honky Cat
TI2-W,M
Honky Tonk Train
FPS-M
Honky Tonk Women
RoS-W,M
Honor and Arms
FiS-W,M
Honor, Honor
NSS-W
Honor Our Commitment
VS-W,M
Honor to Our Workmen
AL-W
Honor to Sheridan
Sin-W,M
Honor to the Hills
WN-W,M
Honza I Love You
SMY-W,M
Hoodoo Blues
LC-W
Hoodoo, Hoodoo
DBL-W
Hooked on a Feeling
ATC1-W,M MF-W,M
Hookin' Cow Blues
BI-W,M
Hooking Cow Blues
B-W,M
Hoop De Dooden Do
HSD-W,M
Hoop-Dee-Doo
PT-W,M TI2-W,M
Hoops My Dears
TMA-W,M
Hooray for Captain Spaulding
MF-W,M TVT-W,M
Hooray for Hollywood
EY-W,M HFH-W,M MF-W,M
Hooray for Love

Mo-W,M NM-W,M OTO-W
TI2-W,M
Hooray for Spinach Christmas Card
OHF-W
Hoosen Johnny
AFS-W,M FW-W
Hoot Owl Song
ITP-W,M
Hooversville
Am-W
Hop Light Loo
DE-W,M
Hop o'er the Fields
SiR-W,M
Hop Right
NH-W
Hop Up and Jump Up
GB-W,M
Hop Up My Ladies
AFS-W,M FoS-W,M POT-W,M
Hopak
FSA2-W,M MHB-W,M MML-W,M
Hopak Dancing
ASB4-W,M
Hope
SHS-W,M
Hope and Faith
SL-W,M
Hope and Persevere
GrM-W,M
Hope Carol
SL-W,M TF-W,M
Hope for the Toiling
AL-W
Hope I Jine de Ban'
BDW-W,M
Hope of the World, Thou Christ of
Great Compassion
Hy-W,M
Hope On
GH-W,M
Hope That We Can Be Together
Soon
DDH-W,M
Hopelessly Devoted to You
Gr-W,M TI1-W,M UBF-W,M
Hopewell
SHS-W,M
**Hopewell see also Jesus, My All,
to Heaven Is Gone**
Hopsa Lisella
GBC-W,M
Hop-Scotch Polka
MF-W,M PT-W,M TI1-W,M
Hopsha Diri
WSB-W,M (Serbo-Croatian Only)
Horace and No Relations
MPP-W
Horiu
JS-W,M (Hebrew)
Horn Music
SL-W,M
Hornet
ANS-W
Hornpipe
MAS-W
Horrors of Libby Prison
BMM-W
Horse Named Bill
FW-W NeA-W,M RW-W,M
Horse Thief
Oz2-W,M
Horse to Trot, to Trot I Say
Boo-W,M
Horse Traders' Song
Oz3-W,M
Horse with No Name

DPE-W,M ERM-W,M
Horse Wrangler
SoC-W,M
Horses Carry Tails
Mo-W,M NM-W,M
Horses Run Around
Bo-W,M OTJ-W,M
Horticultural Wife
SY-W,M
Horton
WN-W,M
Hosanna (Didiee/Granier)
AmH-W,M FiS-W,M (French)
WiS7-W,M
Hosanna (Michael and Deborah
Smith)
OGR-W,M VB-W,M
Hosanna (Palestrina)
MML-W,M (Latin)
Hosanna (Rice/Webber)
UBF-W,M
Hosanna (Tricia Walker)
OGR-W,M
Hosanna, Gloria
VB-W,M
Hosanna Hosanna Sang the Happy
People
SHP-W,M
Hosanna in Excelsis (Palestrina)
SiM-W,M (Latin)
Hosanna, Loud Hosanna (Threlfall)
AME-W,M Hy-W,M
Hosannah
Boo-W,M
Hosannah in the Highest (Gounod)
AME-W,M
Hospitality and Rescue
FSA1-W,M
Host and His Guests
FSA2-W,M
Hostler Joe
Oz4-W
Hot Canary
TI2-M
Hot Codlings
MSB-W
Hot Codlins
ESU-W
Hot Corn see Little Katy
Hot Corn, Cold Corn
BSo-W,M
Hot Cross Buns
BM-W BMC-W,M GM-W HS-W,M
OTJ-W,M SMa-W,M SOO-W,M
Hot Dog
GAR-W,M MF-W,M
Hot Fun in the Summertime
GAR-W,M
Hot Line
SoH-W,M
Hot Lover
GV-W,M
Hot Spice Gingerbread
Boo-W,M
Hot Stuff
RoS-W,M SI-W,M SoH-W,M
TOH-W,M ToO79-W,M
Hot Time in the Old Town
AH-W,M FSN-W,M FSTS-W,M
Hot Time in the Old Town Tonight
RW-W,M
**Hot Time in the Old Town Tonight
see also There'll Be a Hot Time in
the Old Town Tonight**
Hotel (Theme)
TV-M
Hotel California

DPE-W,M
Hottes' Bran' Goin'
  LC-W
Hound Dog
  AO-W,M CMG-W,M DRR-W,M
  ERM-W,M Gr-W,M ILF-W,M
  RW-W,M SRE2-W,M TI1-W,M
  UFB-W,M
Hound Dog Song
  Oz3-W,M
Hour for Thee and Me
  FHR-W,M SSF-W,M
Hour Glass
  FSA2-W,M
Hour She Let Me In
  SR-W,M
Hour's Arrived
  SiS-W
House-Burning in Carter County
  BMM-W
House Carpenter
  AmS-W,M ATS-W BSC-W
  DD-W,M ESU-W FMT-W FSSC-W
  ITP-W,M Oz1-W,M SCa-W,M
  TBF-W,M
House Carpenter's Wife
  FW-W TBF-W,M
House I Live In
  CEM-W,M FrS-W,M HFH-W,M
  J-W,M RDF-W,M
House Is Not a Home
  HD-W,M ILT-W,M
House of Bamboo
  TI1-W,M UFB-W,M
House of Blue Lights
  RW-W,M
House of Daynees
  CSD-W,M (French)
House of Flowers
  Mo-W,M NM-W,M OTO-W
  UBF-W,M
House of Peers and the Home Rule
  Bill
  VP-W
House of the Rising Sun
  FW-W GOI7-W,M GSN4-W,M
  ILS-W,M J-W,M Le-W,M On-W,M
  OPS-W,M OTJ-W,M PoG-W,M
  RW-W,M WSB-W,M
House What's Built wit'out Han's
  BDW-W,M
Household Finance Corporation
Jingle see Never Borrow Money
Needlessly
Housekeeping
  MH-W,M OTJ-W,M
Housewife Terrorists
  VS-W,M
Housewife's Lament
  FW-W LW-W,M
Houston
  TI1-W,M UFB-W,M
Hovu Ladonoi
  SBJ-W,M (Hebrew Only)
How About You?
  GG4-W,M GSN3-W,M HLS5-W,M
  RT4-W,M RW-W,M
How Am I to Know
  GST-W,M
How Are Things in Glocca Morra
  BeL-W,M DBC-W,M HC1-W,M
  HLS8-W,M OTO-W RW-W,M
  TI1-W,M UBF-W,M UFB-W,M
How Are Thy Servants Blest, O
  Lord
  RW-W,M
How Are You, Conscript

Sin-W,M SiS-W
How Are You, Exempt?
  SiS-W
How Are You Greenbacks?
  MPP-W SiS-W
How Are You John Morgan
  MPP-W
How Are You, Mister Little Mac?
  SiS-W
How Are You, Telegraph
  SiS-W,M
How Are Your Green-Backs?
  SY-W,M
How Beauteous Are Their Feet
  AME-W,M
How Beautiful Heaven Must Be
  HHa-W,M
How Beautiful Is the Flag see Que
Bonita Bandera
How Beautiful Is the Green Earth
  SHP-W,M
How Big Is God
  HHa-W,M
How Blest Is He Whose Trepass
  Hy-W,M
How Bright Appears the Morning
  Star
  LMR-W,M
How Brightly Beams
  ASB5-W,M OB-W,M
How Brightly Beams the Morning
  Star
  CC-W,M SJ-W,M
How Brightly Shines the Morning
  Star
  BMC-W,M
How Can a Sinner Know
  AME-W,M
How Can I Be Sure
  TI2-W,M
How Can I Keep from Singing?
  FW-W
How Can I Leave Thee?
  AmH-W,M HSD-W,M NAS-W,M
  OFS-W,M OS-W RW-W,M
  TH-W,M WiS8-W,M
How Can I Leave You Again
  CJ-W,M
How Can I Tell?
  Mo-W,M NM-W,M OTO-W
How Can I Tell Her (about You)
  AT-W,M
How Can I Wait?
  LL-W,M TW-W
How Can Love Survive?
  SM-W,M UBF-W,M
How Can They Live without
  Jesus?
  VB-W,M
How Can You Do It Alone?
  WA-W,M
How Can You Mend a Broken
  Heart
  TI1-W,M UFB-W,M
How Can You Tell an American?
  KH-W,M
How Clear Is the Trumpet
  Boo-W,M
How Come That Blood on Your
  Shirt Sleeve?
  ITP-W,M
How Come You Do Me Like You
  Do
  TI2-W,M
How Could I Ever Say No
  VB-W,M
How Could I Know?

OTO-W
How Could Red Riding Hood?
  WF-W,M
How Creatures Move
  ASB4-W,M
How Dear to Me, O Lord of Hosts
  Hy-W,M
How Deep Is Down?
  TT-W,M
How Deep Is Your Love
  TI1-W,M UFB-W,M
How Did My Heart Rejoice to Hear
  AME-W,M
How Did You Feel?
  SFF-W,M
How Do You Do?
  Bo-W,M CSS-W
How Do You Do, My Partner
  MAR-W,M
How Do You Jump So High?
  OTJ-W,M
How Do You Keep the Music
  Playing?
  DC-W,M EY-W,M HFH-W,M
  MF-W,M MLS-W,M RoE-W,M
How Do You Like It, Jefferson D?
  MPP-W
How Do You Preach?
  SYB-W,M
How Do You Raise a Barn
  PF-W,M
How Do You Speak to an Angel?
  OTO-W UBF-W,M
How Does a Child Grow?
  SYB-W,M
How Does the Ballad End?
  TW-W
How Dry I Am
  BSB-W,M
How D'ye Do?
  OTJ-W,M
How D'ye Do and Shake Hands
  NI-W,M OTJ-W,M
How Excellent Is Thy Name
  GP-W,M VB-W,M
How Excellent Thy Name
  SoM-W,M
How Far Away Is Far Away
  Mo-W,M
How Far Is It to Bethlehem
  CCM-W,M CSB-W,M RS-W,M
  YC-W,M
How Firm a Foundation
  AME-W,M ESB-W,M FH-W,M
  FoS-W,M Hy-W,M OS-W TB-W,M
  WiS7-W,M
How Five and Twenty Shillings
  Were Expended in a Week
  MSB-W
How Gentle God's Commands
  AME-W,M HSD-W,M Hy-W,M
  WiS7-W,M
How Glad I Am Each Christmas
  SHP-W,M
How Glorious Are the Morning
  Stars
  AHO-W,M
How Good It Is to Thank the Lord
  SBJ-W,M
How Goodly Is Thy House
  AHO-W,M
How Great the Wisdom, Pow'r and
  Grace
  AME-W,M
How Great Thou Art
  BSG-W,M BSP-W HHa-W,M
  JBF-W,M RDF-W,M Tr-W,M

How Happy Are They
WN-W,M
How Happy Are We
GH-W,M
How Happy Ev'ry Child of Grace
AME-W,M
How Happy the Soldier
EA-W,M HAS-W,M SI-W,M
How High the Moon
DBC-W,M DJ-W,M DP-W,M
HC2-W,M OTO-W RW-W,M
TI1-W,M UBF-W,M UFB-W,M
How I Feel
OTO-W UBF-W,M
How I Love My Home
VA-W,M
How I Love Thy Law, O Lord
Hy-W,M
How Imperfect Is Expression
ESU-W
How Insensitive
DJ-W,M TI2-W,M
How It Lies, How It Lies, How It
Lies
Mo-W,M NM-W,M
How It Rains
UF-W,M
How It Tis-a with Me
AN-W
How Laughable It Is
Mo-W,M NM-W,M OTO-W
UBF-W,M
How Little We Know
MF-W,M Mo-W,M NM-W,M
OHF-W
How Long
DDH-W,M TI2-W,M
How Long Blues
LC-W
How Long de Train Been Gone?
FN-W,M
**How Long de Train Been Gone?
see also How Long the Train
Been Gone?**
How Long Has It Been
BSG-W,M BSP-W,M HHa-W,M
How Long Has This Been Going
On?
GOB-W,M LSO-W MF-W,M
RoE-W,M
How Long, How Long Blues
LSR-W,M
How Long Jehovah?
AHO-W,M
How Long the Train Been Gone?
FVV-W,M
**How Long the Train Been Gone?
see also How Long de Train Been
Gone?**
How Long Will It Take
OGC1-W,M
How Lovely Are the Messengers
FS-W,M SL-W,M SOO-W,M
TF-W,M
How Lovely to Be a Woman
Mo-W,M NM-W,M OTO-W
How Majestic Is Your Name
GP-W,M OGR-W,M VB-W,M
How Many
FSA1-W,M
How Many Times Do I Love Thee,
Dear?
NCB-W,M WGB/P-W,M
How Mistaken Is the Lover
EL-W,M
How Mountain Girls Can Love
BIS-W,M BSo-W,M

How Much Is That Doggie in the
Window
MAB1-W MSA1-W RDT-W,M
How Often Do We Say Thank God
FS-W,M
How Sad It Is to Part
MMM-W,M
How Shall the Young Direct Their
Way
Hy-W,M
How Shall We Escape?
GH-W,M
How Should I Sing Well?
Boo-W,M
How Should I Your True Love
Know?
Gu-W,M SSP-W
How Silent Is Our Village
GeS-W,M
How Sleep the Brave
FSA1-W,M
How Solemn Are the Words
GH-W
How Stands the Glass Around?
EA-W,M SI-W,M
How Still the Baby's Lying
ESU-W
How Strong and Sweet My
Father's Care
SHP-W,M
How Strong Thine Arm Is, Mighty
God
AME-W,M
How Sweet Is the Language of
Love
AHO-W,M
How Sweet It Is (to Be Loved by
You)
ToO76-W,M
How Sweet the Name
U-W
How Sweet the Name of Jesus
Sounds
AME-W,M Hy-W,M
How Tedious and Tasteless the
Hours
AME-W,M Oz4-W,M
How the Workers Can Be Free
AL-W
How to Be a Millionaire
TTH-W,M
How to Become Rich
AL-W
How to Get to Glory Land
NF-W
How to Handle a Woman
HC2-W,M LL-W,M OTO-W
UBF-W,M
How to Keep or Kill the Devil
NF-W
How to Kiss Your Girl
Oz3-W,M
How to Make It Rain
NF-W
How to Murder Your Wife
RW-W,M
How to Plant and Cultivate Seeds
NF-W
How to Please a Preacher
NF-W
How to Reach the Masses
AME-W,M
How We Burned the Philadelphia
ANS-W
How Will I Know
TTH-W,M
How Would You Like to Be

SRE1-W,M
How Ya Gonna Keep 'Em Down on
the Farm?
FPS-W,M OTJ-W,M T-W,M
TI2-W,M WDS-W,M
Howlin' at the Moon
HW-W,M
Hraly Dudy
IF-W,M (Czech)
Hsiao Ho Shang (Little Monk)
FD-W,M (Chinese)
Hsiao Pai Ts'ai (Little Cabbage)
FD-W,M (Chinese)
Hua Ku Ko (The Flower Drum)
FD-W,M (Chinese) SBF-W,M
(Chinese Only)
Huckleberry Finn
ASB6-W,M
Huckleberry Hunting
SA-W,M
Hugh McGeehan
AL-W
Hugh of Lincoln
SCa-W
Hull and Victory
MPP-W,M
Hullabaloo Belay
FGM-W,M FW-W GeS-W,M
Hull's Victory
OHG-W,M POT-M
Hull's Victory or Huzza for the
Constitution
ANS-W
Hully Gully
HR-W SFF-W,M
Human Body
BM-W
Humble Heart
GB-W,M
Humble Penitent
SHS-W,M
Humblin' Rack
AFP-W
Humming Bird
ASB4-W,M ASB5-W,M HS-W,M
Humoreske
AmH-M
Humoresque
PO-W,M RW-M TI1-M UFB-M
Humours of Bartlemy Fair
MSB-W
Humours of Donnybrook
VP-W,M
Humours of the Races
MSB-W
Humphrey Duggins
MSB-W
Humpty Dumpty
AmH-W,M Boo-W,M HS-W,M
MH-W,M OTJ-W,M RW-W,M
Humpty Dumpty Heart
OGC1-W,M
Hundert Mann Gebt Ihr Befehl
VS-W,M
Hundred Million Miracles
UBF-W,M
Hundred Pipers
ESB-W,M
Hundred Pounds of Clay
ERM-W,M GAR-W,M ILS-W,M
MF-W,M OTJ-W,M
Hundred Years Ago
MPP-W
Hundred Years Hence
MPP-W
Hundred Years on the Eastern
Shore

SA-W

Hundreds of Girls
OTO-W

Hungarian Dance No. 4
RW-M

Hungarian Dance No. 5
AmH-M FSA1-W,M RW-M

Hungarian National Hymn
AmH-W,M

Hungarian Rhapsody No. 2
RW-M

Hungarian Round
GuC-W,M

Hungaria's Hussars
FT-W,M

Hungry Confederate's Song
FMT-W

Hungry Eyes
NMH-W,M

Hungry Like the Wolf
TI2-W,M

Hungry Men
OHT-W,M

Hungry Ragged Blues
AFP-W,M

Hungry Years
TI2-W,M

Hunt Ball
Su-W,M

Hunt Is Up
GUM2-W,M SSP-W

Hunt Regiment
NSS-W

Hunt Till You Find Him, Hallelujah
NSS-W

Hunter (The Hounds Have Scented
Reynard's Trail)
ASB6-W,M

Hunter (Maidens Fair in Summer
Hours)
TH-W,M

Hunter and Rabbit
ASB4-W,M

Hunter from Kentucky
Oz4-W,M

Hunter Regiment
NSS-W

Hunters
TT-W,M

Hunter's Horn
BMC-W,M

Hunters of Kentucky
AH-W,M ATS-W,M FW-W
IHA-W,M MPP-W,M OHG-W,M

Hunting
VK-W,M

Hunting Camp
NF-W

Hunting Chorus
MML-W,M

Hunting for a City
WN-W,M

Hunting Horn (How Clear
Resounds thro' Forest Bounds)
FSA1-W,M

Hunting Horn (Merrily Merrily Greet
the Morn)
OTJ-W,M

Hunting Horns
ASB5-W,M

Hunting of the Cheviot or Chevy
Chase
SBB-W

**Hunting of the Cheviot see also
Chevy Chase**

Hunting of the Coney
SR-W,M

Hunting Song (The Morn Is Rosy
on the Hill)
TH-W,M

Hunting Song (Reinecke, Op. 77)
ASB1-M

Huntington
SHS-W,M

Huntsman Sound the Winding Horn
Boo-W,M

Huntsman's Song
AS-W,M (German)

Hupane Kaupane
SNZ-W,M (Maori)

Hurdy-Gurdy
KS-W,M MH-W,M

Hurdy-Gurdy Man
MHB-W,M (German)

Huron Carol
BMC-W,M MC-W,M

Huron Christmas Chant
NAS-W,M

Hurrah Boys
ESU-W

Hurrah for Father Mathew's Mill
MSB-W

Hurrah for Henry Clay
MPP-W,M

Hurrah for Our Boys in Blue
AL-W

Hurrah for the Hero of Tippecanoe
ESU-W

Hurrah for the Noble Carpenter
AL-W

Hurrah for the Old Flag
SiS-W

Hurrah for the Temperance Flag
ESU-W

Hurrah for the Union
SiS-W

Hurrah Hurrah
Boo-W,M

Hurricane Audrey Blues
LC-W

Hurry Back
Mo-W,M OTO-W VSA-W,M

Hurry, Hurry, Hurry
SSe-W,M

Hurry! It's Lovely Up Here
OTO-W

Hurry Little Horsey
HSA-W,M

Hurry On My Weary Soul
AHO-W,M NSS-W

Hurry Up, Conscripts
SiS-W

Hurry Up, Fellows
MHB-W,M (Polish)

Hurt
HLS3-W,M RW-W,M TTH-W,M

Hurt Bowed Down
AmH-W,M

Hurt So Bad
ILS-W,M TI1-W,M UFB-W,M

Hurtin' Inside
MF-W,M

Hurting Each Other
TI1-W,M UFB-W,M

Husband and Wives
CSp-W,M

**Husband Goes to War see Chang
Fu Ch'u Tang Ping**

Husband Lamenting the Death of
the Wife
BSC-W

Husband with No Courage in Him
FW-W LW-W,M

Husbandman

GrM-W,M

Husbandman's Welcome
GrM-W,M

Husbands and Wives
ATC1-W,M

Husband's Departure
BSC-W

**Husband's Dream see Drunkard's
Dream**

Hush
OnT6-W,M

Hush Hush
KH-W,M

Hush! Hush! My Soul Be Calm and
Still
AME-W,M

Hush Li'l Baby
SCL-W,M SHP-W,M

Hush Little Baby
BF-W,M FoS-W,M FSB1-W,M
FW-W GuC-W,M HS-W,M
IHA-W,M OFS-W,M OTJ-W,M
RSL-W,M RW-W,M SBF-W,M
WSB-W,M

**Hush Little Baby see also Mocking
Bird (Hush Up Baby, Don't Say a
Word)**

Hush My Babe
DD-W,M HSD-W,M

**Hush My Babe see also Cradle
Hymn (Isaac Watts) and Watts'
Cradle Hymn (Song)**

Hush My Baby
SiR-W,M SOO-W,M

**Hush My Baby see also Cradle
Hymn (Isaac Watts)**

Hush Thee, Princeling
AHO-W,M

Hush Ye, My Bairnie
SeS-W,M

Hushaby
ASB3-W,M

Hushaby Baby
ASB2-W,M

Hush-a-by, Darling
SeS-W,M

Hushabye
ILF-W,M TI1-W,M UFB-W,M

Hush-a-bye Baby
SMa-W,M

Hush-a-bye Island
Mo-W,M NM-W,M OTO-W

Hushabye Mountain
SBS-W,M

Hushed Was the Evening Hymn
FH-W,M

Hussars
RSC-W,M (Russian Only)

Hustle, The
MF-M

Hut Sut Song
NoS-W,M

Hutch's Ballad
AF-W

Huxley
LD-W,M

Huzza for Commodore Rodgers
ANS-W

Huzza for Liberty
EA-W,M

Huzza for the Constellation
MPP-W,M OHG-W,M

Huzza for the Constitution
ANS-W

Huzza Huzza Forever for the Land
of Coal Mines
AL-W

Hyah, Rattler
NFS-W,M
Hyde Park Frolic
SR-W,M
Hymn
VB-W,M
Hymn, A
SBA-W
Hymn--Arise
GrM-W,M
Hymn for a Sunday Afternoon
NM-W,M
Hymn for a Sunday Evening
Mo-W,M OTO-W
Hymn for Christmas
BC1-W,M
Hymn for Christmas Day
CCH-W,M
Hymn for Nations
FW-W
Hymn for the Nations
SoF-W,M
Hymn for the Unfortunate
AL-W
Hymn of Betrothal
SN-W,M
Hymn of Thanksgiving
ESB-W,M IH-M
Hymn of the Proletariat
AL-W
Hymn of the Slavs
NAS-W,M
Hymn to Freedom
SiP-W,M (Greek)
Hymn to Joy
CEM-W,M LMR-W,M
Hymn to Man
MM-W,M
Hymn to Shiva
SBF-W,M (Sanskrit Only)
Hymn to the Muse
GUM2-W,M
Hymn to the Sun
ASB6-W,M RW-M
Hymn to Zeus
GUM2-W,M
Hymne
DC-M DPE-M MF-M
Hymno Nacional (Brazil)
SiP-W,M (Portuguese)
Hymno Nacional (Portugal)
SiP-W,M (Portuguese)
Hymnusz
SiP-W,M (Hungarian)
Hyphen
JW-W,M
Hypocrite and Concubine
NSS-W

I

I L D Song
AFP-W,M
I.O.U.
CoH-W,M TI2-W,M
I Ain't A-Gonna Grieve
AF-W
I Ain't Bother Yet
NH-W
I Ain't Down Yet
DBC-W,M TI2-W,M UBF-W,M
I Ain't Goin' to Study War No
More
NH-W RF-W
**I Ain't Goin' to Study War No
More see also Ain't Gonna Study**

**War No More, Going to Study
War No More, I Ain't Gonna
(Gwine) Study War No More, and
Study War No More**
I Ain't Gonna Grieve My Lord No
More
FWS-W,M OTJ-W,M
**I Ain't Gonna Grieve My Lord No
More see also Ain't Gonna Grieve
My Lord (No More)**
I Ain't Gonna Study War No More
LH-W,M
**I Ain't Gonna Study War No More
see also I Ain't Goin' to Study
War No More**
I Ain't Got No Business Doing
Business Today
TOH-W,M
I Ain't Got No Home in This World
Anymore
Am-W,M FG2-W,M
**I Ain't Got No Home in This World
Anymore see also I Can't Feel at
Home in This World Anymore**
I Ain't Got Nobody
NM-W,M
I Ain't Got Nothin' but the Blues
NM-W,M
I Ain't Got Time to Tarry
DE-W,M
I Ain't Gwine Er Trus' Nobody
BDW-W,M
I Ain't Gwine Study War No More
TF-W,M
I Ain't Gwine to Study War No
More
SL-W,M
**I Ain't Gwine to Study War No
More see also I Ain't Goin' to
Study War No More**
I Ain't Marchin' Any More
IHA-W,M
I Ain't No Stranger Now
AFP-W
I Ain't Scared a' Your Jail
SFF-W,M
I Almost Called Your Name
FrF-W,M (Spanish)
I Almost Lost My Mind
HLS9-W,M RDT-W,M TI1-W,M
UFB-W,M
I Am a Brisk and Sprightly Lad
KS-W,M
I Am a Cuckoo
SY-W,M
I Am a Done-Up Man
Oz3-W,M
I Am a Girl of Constant Sorrow
AFP-W,M LW-W,M PSN-W,M
I Am a Great Complainer
Oz4-W
I Am a Man of Consequence
SOT-W,M
I Am a Man of Constant Sorrow
RW-W,M
**I Am a Man of Constant Sorrow
see also I'm a Man of Constant
Sorrow and Man of Constant
Sorrow**
I Am a Pilgrim
FW-W
I Am a Pirate King
SL-W,M
I Am a Poor Girl
SG-W,M
I Am a Poor Wayfaring Pilgrim
FVV-W,M

I Am a Poor Wayfaring Pilgrim see
also Wayfaring Pilgrim
I Am a Prussian
SiP-W,M (German)
I Am a 'round Town Gentleman
NF-W
I Am a Tree
GM-W,M
I Am A-Trouble in de Mind
NSS-W
**I Am A-Trouble in de Mind see also
I'm Troubled in Mind**
I Am a Union Woman
AFP-W IHA-W,M LW-W,M
I Am a Young Musician
OTJ-W,M
I Am Alone
WiS7-W,M
I Am an American
Mo-W,M NM-W,M OTJ-W,M
I Am Athirst
Boo-W,M
I Am Bound for the Promised Land
IHA-W,M NSS-W
**I Am Bound for the Promised Land
see also Bound for the Promised
Land, I'm Bound for the Promised
Land, On Jordan's Stormy Banks
(I Stand), and Promised Land (I
Am Bound for the Promised Land)**
I Am Coming
GH-W,M
I Am Coming to a King
MoM-W
I Am Coming to the Cross
GH-W,M Hy-W,M
I Am Courtier Grave and Serious
MGT-W,M
I Am de Light uv de Worl'
NH-W
I Am de Truth an' de Light
BDW-W,M
I Am Free
BDW-W,M UBF-W,M
I Am Goin' to Join in This Army
RF-W,M
I Am Happy When I'm Hiking
CSS-W
I Am He
VB-W,M
I Am He That Liveth
GH-W,M
I Am Huntin' for a City to Stay
Awhile
NSS-W
I Am, I Am
SRS-W,M
I Am...I Said
GrS-W,M TI2-W,M
I Am Learning to Read the Bible
SHP-W,M
I Am Loved (Cole Porter)
ML-W,M OTO-W UBF-W,M
I Am Loved (Gaither/Gaither)
VB-W,M
I Am Not Alone
CEM-W,M
I Am Not Going to Hobo Any More
NF-W
I Am on the Shining Pathway
AME-W,M
I Am Praying for You
GH-W,M
**I Am Praying for You see also I'm
Praying for You**
I Am Seekin' for a City
RF-W,M

I Am So Glad Each Christmas Eve
CCM-W,M SJ-W,M
I Am So Glad That Our Father in
Heaven
AME-W,M
I Am So Weary
Boo-W,M
I Am Sold and Going to Georgia
AFP-W AL-W
I Am Sure
VB-W,M
I Am the Captain of the Pinafore
GiS-W,M MGT-W,M SL-W,M
I Am the Door
GH-W,M
**I Am the Light of the World see I
Am de Light uv de Worl'**
I Am the Lord
AHO-W,M (German)
I Am the Monarch of the Sea
GiS-W,M MGT-W,M OTJ-W,M
SL-W,M
I Am the Starlight
UBF-W,M
**I Am the Truth and the Light see I
Am de Truth an' de Light**
I Am the Very Model of a Modern
Major-General
GiS-W,M
I Am the Walrus
BBe-W,M Be2-W,M TWS-W
I Am the Way
GH-W,M
I Am the Wind
MH-W,M
I Am Thine, O Lord
AME-W,M CEM-W,M GH-W,M
Hy-W,M
I Am Thy Heart
NA-W,M
I Am Trusting Thee
GH-W,M
I Am Trusting Thee, Lord Jesus
OM-W,M
I Am Waiting
RoS-W,M
I Am Weary of My Groaning
Boo-W,M
I Am Weary of Straying
AHO-W,M
I Am What I Am
TI2-W,M
I Am Who I Am
JC-W,M
I Am with Thee
SoP-W,M
I Am Woman
BR-W,M GOI7-W,M GrS-W,M
On-W,M
I an' Satan Had a Race
NSS-W
I Apologize
TI1-W,M UBF-W,M
I Ask You
Boo-W,M
I Asked the Lord
BSG-W,M BSP-W,M CEM-W,M
FS-W,M HLS7-W,M MF-W,M
I Attempt from Love's Sickness to
Fly
EL-W,M OH-W,M
I Ax All Dem Brudder Roun
NSS-W
I Been A-Listenin'
BDW-W,M
**I Been A-Listenin' see also I've
Been A-Listening All de Night**

Long
I Been 'Buked an' I Been Scorned
My-W,M
I Been in the Storm So Long
SFF-W,M
**I Been in the Storm So Long see
also Been in the Storm So Long**
I Believe
CEM-W,M MF-W,M RDF-W,M
TI1-W,M TWD-W,M UFB-W,M
I Believe (in a Hill Called Mt.
Calvary)
BSG-W,M BSP-W,M
I Believe He Died for Me
CEM-W,M
I Believe in Jesus
SHP-W,M
I Believe in Love
RW-W,M
I Believe in Miracles
BSG-W,M BSP-W,M CS-W,M
I Believe in Music
DPE-W,M EC-W,M GCM-W,M
MF-W,M RDF-W,M
I Believe in Santa Claus
MF-W,M
I Believe in You
RW-W,M TI2-W,M TW-W
UBF-W,M
I Believe Less Than You
SYB-W,M
I Believe O Lord
Boo-W,M
I Believe This Dear Old Bible
Oz4-W
I Belong to Jesus
GH-W,M
I Belong to You
VB-W,M
I Better Go Now
DBL-W
I Bind My Heart This Tide
Hy-W,M
I Bless Thee Lord for Sorrows Sent
AHO-W,M
I Bought Me a Cat
OA1-W,M
I Bought Me a Rooster
Oz3-W,M
I Bow My Forehead to the Dust
Hy-W,M
I Bowed on My Knees and Cried
Holy
AG-W,M HLS7-W,M
I Bring My Sins to Thee
GH-W,M
I Build My House upon a Rock
NSS-W
I Cain't Get Offa My Horse
WF-W,M
I Cain't Say No
L-W OTJ-W,M OTO-W TGO-W,M
TI1-W,M TW-W UFB-W,M
UFB-W,M
I Call Your Name
Be1-W,M TWS-W
I Called to My Loving Wife
SCa-W,M
I Called You My Sweetheart
STW-W,M
I Can
Mo-W,M NM-W,M OTO-W
I Can Do That
CL-W,M JP-W,M TI2-W,M
UBF-W,M
I Can Dream, Can't I
HC2-W,M OTO-W RW-W,M

TI1-W,M UBF-W,M UFB-W,M
I Can Hear My Savior Calling
AME-W,M
I Can Help
HLS9-W,M
I Can Make It Happen
UBF-W,M
I Can Play and Sing
SOO-W,M
I Can Recall Spain
BOA-W,M
I Can See
VB-W,M
I Can See Clearly Now
GrH-W,M GrS-W,M
I Can See for Miles
TI1-W,M TRR-W,M UFB-W,M
WA-W,M
I Can See It
Fa-W,M OTO-W TW-W
I Can See My Father
TW-W
I Can Tell by the Way You Dance,
Dear
K-W,M
I Cannot Be a Slave
WW-W,M
I Cannot Bid Thee Go, My Boy
SiS-W
I Cannot Call Her Mother
Oz4-W,M
I Cannot Come
JF-W,M
I Cannot Drift
AME-W,M
I Cannot Leave the Battlefield
SiS-W
I Cannot Sing the Old Songs
AmH-W,M HSD-W,M WiS8-W,M
I Cannot Sing This Catch
Boo-W,M
I Cannot Sing Tonight
FHR-W,M
I Cannot Stay Here by Myself
NH-W
I Cannot Tell
GiS-W,M
I Cannot Tell How Precious
GH-W,M
I Cannot Tell What This Love May
Be
MGT-W,M
I Can't Be Bothered Now
LSO-W OTO-W
I Can't Be Satisfied
DBL-W
I Can't Begin to Tell You
HFH-W,M MAB1-W,M MF-W,M
MSA1-W TOM-W,M
I Can't Believe I'm Losing You
ILT-W,M TI1-W,M UFB-W,M
I Can't Do That Sum
BMC-W,M OTJ-W,M
I Can't Feel at Home in This World
Anymore
FW-W
**I Can't Feel at Home in This World
Anymore see also I Ain't Got No
Home in This World Anymore**
I Can't Get Enough of You
TOH-W,M
**I Can't Get Off My Horse see I
Cain't Get Offa My Horse**
I Can't Get No Satisfaction
RoS-W,M
I Can't Get Over You (Gettin' Over
Me)

TOC83-W,M
I Can't Get Started
  DBC-W,M FPS-W,M FrS-W,M
  HC2-W,M LM-W,M LSO-W
  TI1-W,M ToS-W TW-W
  UBF-W,M UFB-W,M
I Can't Give You Anything but
  Love
  BBB-W,M GSN2-W,M NK-W,M
  RDT-W,M TI2-W,M TW-W
I Can't Help but Wonder (Where
  I'm Bound)
  CMG-W,M FW-W RBO-W,M
I Can't Help It (If I'm Still in Love
  with You)
  HW-W,M TI2-W,M
I Can't Live with You
  CMF-W,M
I Can't Love You Anymore (Any
  More Than I Do)
  MF-W,M
I Can't Make Up My Mind
  HAS-W,M
I Can't Put My Arms around a
  Memory
  FrF-W,M
I Can't Say No see I Cain't Say No
I Can't See the Wind
  SSe-W,M
I Can't Stan' de Fire
  NSS-W
I Can't Stand It No More
  ToO79-W,M
I Can't Stay Away
  BDW-W,M My-W,M
I Can't Stay Behind, My Lord
  NSS-W
I Can't Stop Loving You
  GSN3-W,M
I Charge Ye, O Daughters of
  Jerusalem
  Boo-W,M
I Climb the Mountains
  SeS-W,M
I Close My Eyes
  GM-W,M
I Come and Stand at Every Door
  FW-W
I Come to the Garden Alone
  AME-W,M
I Come to Thee
  TM-W,M WGB/O-W,M
I Concentrate on You
  HC1-W,M ML-W,M OTO-W
  RT4-W,M TI1-W,M ToS-W,M
  UFB-W,M
I Could Be Happy with You
  OTO-W
I Could Get Used to You
  TTH-W,M
I Could Go On Singing
  Mo-W,M NM-W,M OTO-W
I Could Have Danced All Night
  DBC-W,M HC1-W,M HLS3-W,M
  HLS8-W,M LL-W,M OTO-W
  RT6-W,M RW-W,M TI1-W,M
  UBF-W,M UFB-W,M
I Could Love You in a Heartbeat
  TTH-W,M
I Could Never Be Ashamed of You
  HW-W,M
I Could Not Find My Baby-O
  NeA-W,M
I Could Write a Book
  DBC-W,M FrS-W,M OTO-W
  RW-W,M TI1-W,M TS-W
  UBF-W,M UFB-W,M

I Couldn't Get High
  RB-W
I Couldn't Git In
  NH-W
I Couldn't Hear Nobody Pray
  FW-W MHB-W,M RF-W,M
  SBF-W,M WiS7-W,M
**I Couldn't Hear Nobody Pray see
  also Couldn't Hear Nobody Pray**
I Couldn't Sleep a Wink Last Night
  TI1-W,M UFB-W,M
I Count the Tears
  HRB4-W,M
I Courted for Love
  Oz1-W,M
I Cover the Waterfront
  FrS-W,M MF-W,M
I Cried a Tear
  HRB4-W,M
I Cried for You
  BBB-W,M GST-W,M HLS2-W,M
  LSB-W,M RW-W,M TI2-W,M
  ToS-W,M
I Cried to God
  GH-W,M
I Dedicate All My Love to You
  OGR-W,M VB-W,M
I Did View One Angel
  NSS-W
I Didn't Know What Time It Was
  OTO-W TI1-W,M TS-W UBF-W,M
  UFB-W,M
I Dig a Pony
  TWS-W
I Do (a Wedding Song)
  TM-W,M WGB/O-W,M
  WGB/P-W,M
I Do Believe
  AME-W,M
I Do, I Do
  I-W,M TI1-W,M UBF-W,M
I Do, I Do, I Do, I Do, I Do
  MF-W,M TI1-W,M ToO76-W,M
  UFB-W,M
I Do Like to Be beside the Seaside
  U-W
I Do Love de Lamb
  RTH-W
I Do Not Know a Day I Did Not
  Love You
  UBF-W,M
I Do What I Do
  TTH-W,M
I Done Done
  SNS-W
I Done What Yer Tole Me ter Do
  NSS-W
I Don't Believe I'll Fall in Love
  Today
  CSp-W,M
I Don't Care
  FSN-W,M MF-W,M
I Don't Care for Riches
  NH-W
I Don't Care If the Sun Don't Shine
  AT-W,M FOC-W,M TI1-W,M
  UFB-W,M
I Don't Do Like That No More
  TOH-W,M
I Don't Feel Weary and Noways
  Tired
  NSS-W
I Don't Hurt Anymore
  HLS9-W,M OGC1-W,M
I Don't Intend to Die in Egypt Land
  J-W,M
I Don't Know Enough about You

OnT1-W,M
I Don't Know How I Do It, but I Do
  Sw-W,M
I Don't Know How to Love Him
  DBC-W,M GrS-W,M TI2-W,M
  UBF-W,M
I Don't Know How We Made It
  Over
  FVV-W,M
I Don't Know If It's Right
  WG-W,M
I Don't Know Where to Start
  TOC82-W,M
I Don't Know Why (I Just Do)
  BeL-W,M FPS-W,M NK-W,M
  RW-W,M TI1-W,M UFB-W,M
I Don't Know You
  RW-W,M
I Don't Like No Railroad Man
  NeA-W,M
I Don't Mind at All
  BHO-W,M
I Don't Mind the Thorns (If You're
  the Rose)
  DC-W,M EC-W,M
I Don't Remember Loving You
  TOC82-W,M
I Don't See It
  SiS-W
I Don't See Why I Love Him
  Oz4-W
I Don't Stand a Ghost of a Chance
  with You
  TI2-W,M ToS-W,M
I Don't Stand Alone
  VS-W,M
I Don't Think I'll End It All Today
  Mo-W,M NM-W,M OTO-W
I Don't Think I'll Fall in Love Today
  GOB-W,M LSO-W,M
I Don't Think She's in Love
  Anymore
  TOC82-W,M
I Don't Wan' to Be Buried in de
  Stawm
  NeA-W,M
I Don't Wanna Be Kissed
  Mo-W,M
I Don't Wanna Be Kissed (by
  Anyone but You)
  NM-W,M
I Don't Wanna Go On with You
  Like That
  CFB-W,M
I Don't Wanna Play House
  TI1-W,M UFB-W,M
I Don't Want Any More France
  SSo-W,M
I Don't Want No Black Woman
  LC-W,M
I Don't Want No More Army
  GI-W,M GO-W,M HAS-W,M
I Don't Want No More of Army Life
  HSA-W,M
**I Don't Want No More of Army Life
  see also Army Life, G.I. Blues (I
  Don't Want No More of Army
  Life), and Gee but I Wanna Go
  Home**
**I Don't Want to Be Buried in the
  Storm see I Don't Wan' to Be
  Buried in de Stawm**
I Don't Want to Be Lost in the
  Slums
  SFF-W,M
I Don't Want to Be Right
  ToO79-W,M

I Don't Want to Get Adjusted
FW-W WSB-W,M
I Don't Want to Go
SSo-W,M
I Don't Want to Know
Mo-W,M OTO-W UBF-W,M
I Don't Want to Live without You
CFB-W,M
I Don't Want to Lose You
TOH-W,M
I Don't Want to Play in Your Yard
ATS-W BH-W,M EFS-W,M
FSN-W,M OTJ-W,M RW-W,M
STR-W,M
I Don't Want to Set the World on
Fire
OnT1-W,M TI1-W,M UFB-W,M
I Don't Want to Spoil the Party
BBe-W,M Be1-W,M TWS-W
I Don't Want to Stay Here No
Longer
RF-W,M
I Don't Want to Walk without You
AT-W,M IPH-W,M MAB1-W
MSA1-W WGB/P-W,M
I Don't Want Your Millions, Mister
FW-W JF-W,M SWF-W,M
I Dream of Jeannie Theme see
Jeannie
I Dream of Thee
SiS-W
I Dream Too Much
TW-W
I Dreamed a Dream
DBC-W,M UBF-W,M
I Dreamed I Saw St. Augustine
RV-W
I Dreamed My Boy Was Home
Again
SiS-W
I Dreamed of Home
GrM-W,M
I Dreamed of My True Lover
Oz1-W,M
I Dreamt I Dwelt in Marble Halls
AmH-W,M
I Dreamt That I Dwelt in Marble
Halls
HSD-W,M WiS7-W,M
I Engineer
TTH-W,M
I Enjoy Being a Girl
BeL-W,M DBC-W,M HC2-W,M
OTJ-W,M OTO-W TI1-W,M
UBF-W,M UFB-W,M
I Envy Not the Mighty Great
Boo-W,M
I Faint, I Die
Boo-W,M
I Fall in Love Too Easily
FrS-W,M HLS3-W,M RT4-W,M
RW-W,M
I Fall to Pieces
CMG-W,M FOC-W,M TI2-W,M
I Fear Thy Kisses
EL-W,M
I Feel a Song Comin' On
GG5-W,M HLS5-W,M RW-W,M
TW-W
I Feel at Home with You
TS-W
I Feel Fine
BBe-W,M Be1-W,M TWS-W
WG-W,M
I Feel It
OnT6-W,M
I Feel It with You

TOC82-W,M
I Feel Like a Feather in the Breeze
OTO-W
I Feel Like Dyin' in Dis Army
BDW-W,M
I Feel Like My Time Ain't Long
WN-W,M
I Feel Like Travelin' On
HHa-W,M
I Feel That I've Known You
Forever
SRE1-W,M
I Feel the Earth Move
DPE-W,M MF-W,M
I Feel the Winds of God
RS-W,M
I Fight mit Sigel
Oz2-W,M
I Fight mit Sigel see also I Goes to
Fight mit Sigel
I Fold Up My Arms and I Wonder
Me-W,M
I Forgive You
SYB-W,M
I Forgot More Than You'll Ever
Know
RW-W,M
I Forgot to Be Your Lover
TTH-W,M
I Found a Four Leaf Clover
ReG-W,M
I Found a Friend
HLS7-W,M
I Found a Million Dollar Baby
MF-W,M MR-W,M NK-W,M
OHB-W,M
I Found a Peach in Orange, New
Jersey
Mo-W,M NM-W,M
I Found Someone
TTH-W,M
I Found the Answer
BSG-W,M BSP-W,M CEM-W,M
FS-W,M MF-W,M RDF-W,M
I Found the Lord
SSN-W,M (French)
I Gave My Life for Thee
AME-W,M GH-W,M
I Gave My Love a Cherry
FW-W OFS-W,M OTJ-W,M
RW-W,M TI2-W,M UBF-W,M
I Gave My Love a Cherry see also
Riddle Song
I Get a Kick Out of You
DC-W,M EY-W,M FrS-W,M
HC1-W,M MF-W,M ML-W,M
OHB-W,M RoE-W,M TW-W
I Get Along without You Very Well
AT-W,M ILT-W,M LM-W,M
I Get Carried Away
TW-W
I Get Weak
BHO-W,M
I Go Before My Darling
MMW-W,M
I Go My Merry Way
SSN-W,M (French)
I Goes to Fight mit Sigel
Sin-W,M SiS-W
I Goes to Fight mit Sigel see also I
Fight mit Sigel
I Goin' Put On My Golden Shoes
NH-W
I Goin' t' Ware That Starry Crown
Over There
AN-W
I Goin' Try the Air

NH-W
I Got a Gal in Baltimore
Oz3-W
I Got a Home
NH-W
I Got a Home in de Rock
Me-W,M
I Got a Home in That Rock
FN-W,M
I Got a Letter from Jesus
NeA-W,M
I Got a Marble and a Star
SSA-W,M
I Got a Mother
AN-W
I Got a Name
HFH-W,M JC-W,M MF-W,M
PM-W,M
I Got a Robe
ETB-W,M LoS-W,M
I Got a Robe see also All God's
Children
I Got a Rose between My Toes
WF-W,M
I Got a Shoe
OTJ-W,M
I Got a Woman
TI1-W,M UFB-W,M
I Got a Woman Crazy for Me see
She's Funny That Way
I Got a Woman on Sourwood
Mountain
FVV-W,M
I Got It Bad and That Ain't Good
GMD-W,M GSF-W,M GSN3-W,M
HLS3-W,M NK-W,M RW-W,M
ToS-W,M
I Got Life
H-W,M
I Got Love
P-W,M
I Got Lucky
SRE2-W,M
I Got Lucky in the Rain
OnT6-W,M
I Got Ma 'Ligion on de Way
BDW-W,M
I Got Me Flowers
ER-W,M
I Got Mine
NH-W
I Got Plenty o' Nuthin'
LSO-W
I Got Plenty o' Nuttin'
HC1-W,M MF-W,M NYT-W,M
On-W,M OTJ-W,M OTO-W
TI1-W,M UBF-W,M UFB-W,M
I Got Rhythm
DBC-W,M DC-W,M EY-W,M
GOB-W,M HC1-W,M LSO-W
MF-W,M NYT-W,M OHB-W,M
TW-W
I Got Shoes
AN-W Bo-W,M SiB-W,M
I Got the Blues
RoS-W,M
I Got the Feelin' (Oh No No)
TI2-W,M
I Got Two Wings
Me-W,M
I Got You (I Feel Good)
DRR-W,M TRR-W,M
I Got You Babe
ERM-W,M GAR-W,M MF-W,M
I Gotta Get Drunk
WNF-W
I Gotta Keep Moving

TI2-W,M
I Know a Youth
MGT-W,M
I Know about Love
DR-W,M
I Know an Old Lady
RSL-W,M
I Know an Old Lady see also Old Lady
I Know but I Don't Know
PL-W,M
I Know Him So Well
DBC-W,M
I Know How to Do Time
LC-W
I Know I Have Another Building
FN-W,M
I Know I Love Thee Better
GH-W,M
I Know It Can Happen Again
A-W,M
I Know Moonlight
J-W,M
I Know My God Can Do It
AG-W,M
I Know My Heavenly Father Knows
AME-W,M
I Know My Love
FW-W WU-W,M
I Know My Mother Weeps for Me
SiS-W
I Know My Mother's Hand
SiS-W
I Know My Time Ain't Long
NH-W
I Know Not How That Bethlehem's Babe
AHO-W,M AME-W,M Hy-W,M
I Know Not Where the Road Will Lead
AHO-W,M
I Know That My Redeemer Lives
AME-W,M SJ-W,M
I Know That My Redeemer Liveth
FiS-W,M GH-W,M
I Know That You Know
MF-W,M
I Know the Lord Will Make a Way for Me
HHa-W,M
I Know the Lord's Laid His Hands on Me
AME-W,M RF-W,M
I Know the Lord's Laid His Hands on Me see also Oh, I Know the Lord Laid His Hands on Me
I Know Where I'm Going
EC-W,M FW-W RW-W,M
TI2-W,M UBF-W,M WSB-W,M
I Know Who Holds Tomorrow
HHa-W,M
I Know Whom I Have Believed
GH-W,M
I Know Why (and So Do You)
GSF-W,M
I Know You Rider
FW-W
I Know You're Married but I Love You Still
BSo-W,M BIS-W,M
I Lay with an Old Man
Boo-W,M
I Learned about Horses from Him
HB-W,M
I Learned All about Cheatin' from You
TOH-W,M

I Left It All with Jesus
GH-W,M
I Left My Darling Lying Here
SeS-W,M
I Left My Heart in San Francisco
DC-W,M FPS-W,M GOI7-W,M
IPH-W,M MAB1-W MF-W,M
MSA1-W OBN-W,M OnT1-W,M
OPS-W,M RW-W,M TI1-W,M
UFB-W,M
I Left My Soul to God
AME-W,M
I Left My Sugar Standing in the Rain
OnT1-W,M
I Let a Song Go Out of My Heart
GMD-W,M
I Lie in the American Land
AL-W
I Lift My Eyes unto Heaven Above
SJ-W,M
I Lift My Eyes Up to the Hills
AHO-W,M
I Lift My Heart to Thee
AHO-W,M
I Like Chiclets
GSM-W,M
I Like Dreamin'
RW-W,M TI2-W,M
I Like Him
Mo-W,M OTO-W
I Like It Like That
ERM-W,M MF-W,M
I Like the Likes of You
MF-W,M RoE-W,M
I Like to Do It
ToO76-W,M
I Like to Recognize the Tune
OTO-W TS-W
I Like to Ride the Elevator
RSL-W,M
I Like to Sing
GM-W,M
I Like to Think of Jesus
SHP-W,M
I Like Winter
SSe-W,M
I Like You
RSL-W,M TW-W
I Likes a Drop of Good Beer
MSB-W
I Loathe That I Did Love
SSP-W
I Long to See the Girl I Left Behind
FSTS-W,M
I Look for Jesus All My Days
NH-W
I Look o'er Yander
AAF-W,M
I Look to Thee in Every Need
Hy-W,M
I Looked to Jesus
GH-W,M
I Love (Little Baby Ducks)
CoH-W,M TI1-W,M UFB-W,M
I Love a Lonely Day
VB-W,M
I Love a New Yorker
Mo-W,M NM-W,M
I Love a Nobody
Oz4-W,M
I Love a Parade
MF-W,M
I Love a Rainy Day
TOH-W,M
I Love Bosco
GSM-W,M

I Love Everybody
SFF-W,M
I Love Her Mind
TOC83-W,M
I Love How You Love Me
MF-W,M OnT1-W,M TOC83-W,M
I Love, I Love Thee, Lord Most High
AME-W,M
I Love Jesus
WN-W,M
I Love Little Willie
Oz3-W,M
I Love Louisa
MF-W,M TW-W
I Love Lucy
TI2-W,M
I Love My Baby
T-W,M TI1-W,M UFB-W,M
I Love My Father
GV-W,M
I Love My Jesus Quite Alone
AHO-W,M (German)
I Love My Love in the Morning
RW-W,M
I Love My Rancho Grande
FrF-W,M (Spanish Only)
I Love My Rooster
ITP-W,M
I Love My Union
AFP-W
I Love My Wife
HLS8-W,M I-W,M UBF-W,M
I Love New England
OnT6-W,M
I Love New York
TI1-W,M UFB-W,M
I Love Paris
DBC-W,M FPS-W,M HC1-W,M
ML-W,M OTO-W TI1-W,M
UBF-W,M UFB-W,M
I Love School
SiB-W,M
I Love Somebody
NF-W
I Love Susie Brown
Oz3-W
I Love That Man, O God I Do
NH-W
I Love That Word Hello
CSS-W
I Love the Ladies
Mo-W,M NM-W,M OTO-W
I Love the Lord
AHO-W,M
I Love the Lord; He Heard My Cries
AME-W,M
I Love the Lord, His Strength Is Mine
Hy-W,M
I Love the Summer Time
SoP-W,M
I Love the Sunny South
SiS-W
I Love Thee
AmH-W,M FSY-W,M (German)
MML-W,M (Danish) NCB-W,M
(German) TM-W,M WGB/O-W,M
WGB/P-W,M WiS8-W,M (German)
I Love Thy Kingdom, Lord
AHO-W,M AME-W,M GH-W,M
Hy-W,M
I Love to Cry at Weddings
RW-W,M SC-W,M TW-W
I Love to Hear the Pealing Bells
Boo-W,M
I Love to Hear the Train

SiR-W,M
I Love to Laugh
 NI-W,M WD-W,M
I Love to Rhyme
 OTO-W
I Love to Steal Awhile Away
 AHO-W,M
I Love to Tell the Story
 AME-W,M CEM-W,M GH-W,M
 Hy-W,M IH-M JBF-W,M MAB1-W
 MSA1-W RDF-W,M RW-W,M
 TB-W,M
I Love What I'm Doing
 V-W,M
I Love You (Gershwin)
 GOB-W,M
I Love You (Grant/Smith)
 VB-W,M
I Love You (Porter)
 HC2-W,M ML-W,M OTO-W TI1-
 W,M TW-W UBF-W,M UFB-W,M
I Love You (Thompson/Archer)
 GSN1-W,M HLS2-W,M OP1-W,M
 RW-W,M
I Love You (Wright/Forrest)
 SN-W,M TI1-W,M UBF-W,M
 UFB-W,M
I Love You (and You Love Me)
 Mo-W,M
I Love You This Morning
 LL-W,M
I Love You Truly
 FSN-W,M FWS-W,M GSN1-W,M
 HLS1-W,M MF-W,M NCB-W,M
 OAP-W,M OBN-W,M RW-W,M
 TI1-W,M TM-W,M UFB-W,M
 WGB/O-W,M WGB/P-W,M
I Love You Well
 Oz4-W,M
I Loved 'Em Every One
 TI2-W,M
I Loved Her Too
 SSA-W,M
I Loved You Better Than You Knew
 Oz4-W
I Loved You Once in Silence
 DBC-W,M LL-W,M OTO-W
 TI1-W,M UBF-W,M UFB-W,M
I Loves You Porgy
 DJ-W,M NYT-W,M OTO-W
 UBF-W,M
I Made It through the Rain
 TI1-W,M UFB-W,M
I Married a Wife
 OTJ-W,M
I Married an Angel
 HLS2-W,M RT4-W,M RW-W,M
I Married Me a Wife
 Oz3-W,M
I May Be Wrong (but I Think
 You're Wonderful)
 MF-W,M OHB-W,M
I May Never Pass This Way Again
 RDF-W,M TI2-W,M
I Me Mine
 TWS-W
I Met a Girl
 TW-W
I Might Grow Fond of You
 Su-W,M
I Minded God
 AHO-W,M
I Missed the Last Rainbow
 LM-W,M OTO-W
I Must Be Doing Something Right
 MF-W,M
I Must Be Dreaming

RW-W,M
I Must Tell Jesus
 OM-W,M
I Must Tell Jesus All of My Trials
 AME-W,M
I Need a Garden
 GOB-W,M
I Need Thee Every Hour
 AME-W,M ATS-W CEM-W,M
 GH-W,M HF-W,M Hy-W,M IH-M
 OM-W,M RDF-W,M RW-W,M
 TB-W,M WiS7-W,M
I Need to Feel Your Touch Again
 OGR-W,M
I Need You
 TWS-W
I Need You Now
 GG5-W,M
I Need You So
 HRB1-W,M
I Need Your Love Tonight
 EP-W,M FRH-W,M SRE1-W,M
I Needed God
 SOW1-W,M SOW2-W,M
I Needs to Be Bee'd With
 MF-M
I Never Can Forget the Day
 AME-W,M
I Never Felt More Like Praising
 HHa-W,M
I Never Felt This Way Before
 GMD-W,M
I Never Has Seen Snow
 Mo-W,M NM-W,M OTO-W
I Never Heard a Man
 SNS-W
I Never Knew
 GST-W,M RW-W,M TI1-W,M
 UFB-W,M
I Never Knew You
 GH-W,M
I Never Met a Rose
 LM-W,M OTO-W
I Never Promised You a Rose
 Garden
 GOI7-W,M
I Never Said I Love You
 ToO79-W,M
I Never Saw a Moor
 YS-W,M
I Never Walk Alone
 BSG-W,M BSP-W,M
I Never Will Marry
 BF-W,M CMG-W,M FGM-W,M
 FPG-W,M FSt-W,M FW-W
 OFS-W,M WG-W,M WSB-W,M
I Once Had a Sweetheart
 Oz1-W
I Once Loved a Lass
 IS-W,M
I Once Was a Carman
 SoC-W,M
I Only Have Eyes for You
 DC-W,M FrS-W,M HFH-W,M
 MF-W,M RoE-W,M T-W,M
I Only Want to Say (Gethsemane)
 UBF-W,M
I Ought to Be in Pictures (Theme)
see One Hello
I Pass All My Hours
 OH-W,M
I Pick Up My Hoe
 SSe-W,M
I Planted My Wheat
 SSe-W,M
I Points to Mineself
 Bo-W,M

I, Poor and Well
 Boo-W,M
I Pretend
 Mo-W,M
I Promise You
 Mo-W,M NM-W,M OTO-W
I Promise You a Happy Ending
 OTO-W
I Put a Spell on You
 ILF-W,M
I Put My Arms Up High
 GM-W,M
I Put My Hand In
 Mo-W,M NM-W,M OTO-W
I Really Don't Want to Know
 HLS3-W,M HLS9-W,M
 OGC1-W,M RW-W,M
I Really Like Him
 MLM-W,M
I Rejoice in the Cross
 GB-W,M
I Remember Calvary
 AME-W,M
I Remember It Well
 BeL-W,M LL-W,M OTO-W
 TI1-W,M UBF-W,M UFB-W,M
I Remember the Hour
 SiS-W
I Remember You
 AT-W,M GSN3-W,M OTO-W
I Ride an Old Paint
 AH-W,M AmS-W,M BF-W,M
 FGM-W,M FW-W HWS-W,M
 NAS-W,M OTJ-W,M
I Roll the Ball
 RSL-W,M
I Said My Pajamas
 TI2-W,M
I Said No
 OTO-W
I Said the Donkey
 GBC-W,M
I Sang Dixie
 GCM-W,M
I Saw a Man
 HLS7-W,M
I Saw a Way-Worn Traveler
 AME-W,M
I Saw de Beam in My Sister's Eye
 NSS-W
I Saw de Light
 FN-W,M
I Saw Her Standing There
 BBe-W,M BR-W,M ERM-W,M
 ILS-W,M MF-W,M OPS-W,M
 TI2-W,M TWS-W
I Saw Him Standing There
 BHO-W,M
I Saw Mommy Kissing Santa Claus
 BCS-W,M TI1-W,M UFB-W,M
I Saw the Light (Hank Williams)
 FOC-W,M TI2-W,M Tr-W,M
I Saw Three Ships
 BCh-W,M BCS-W,M CC-W,M
 CI-W,M GBC-W,M HS-W,M
 JOC-W,M OAP-W,M OB-W,M
 RW-W,M SMa-W,M Y-W,M
I Saw Three Ships Come Sailing In
 FW-W
I Say a Little Prayer
 BDF-W,M HD-W,M MF-W,M
 On-W,M OTJ-W,M
I Say to All Men Far and Near
 SHP-W,M
I Scream You Scream We All
 Scream for Ice Cream
 NoS-W,M

GI-W

I Want a Woman see Devil's Brigade March

I Want All the World to Know
K-W,M

I Want an Easter Bunny
Mo-W,M NM-W,M OTJ-W,M

I Want My Freedom
SFF-W,M

I Want My Mama
RW-W,M

I Want Some Valiant Soldier Here
NSS-W

I Want to... see also I Wanna...

I Want to Be a Clone
VB-W,M

I Want to Be a Cowboy's Sweetheart
FC-W,M

I Want to Be Free
GAR-W,M MF-W,M

I Want to Be Happy
FPS-W,M MF-W,M NN2-W,M NN7-W,M

I Want to Be Loved (but by Only You)
Mo-W,M NM-W,M

I Want to Be Ready
FN-W,M JF-W,M NAS-W,M RF-W,M

I Want to Be Strong
HCY-W,M

I Want to Be with You
Mo-W,M NM-W,M OTO-W

I Want to Be with You Always
OGC1-W,M

I Want to Be Your Man (Larry Troutman)
CFB-W,M

I Want to Climb
ASB5-W,M

I Want to Climb up Jacob's Ladder
NSS-W

I Want to Die A-Shouting
WN-W,M

I Want to Die Like-a Lazarus Die
NSS-W

I Want to Go Back to Michigan
SLB-W,M

I Want to Go Home
AF-W GO-W,M

I Want to Go to Heaven When I Die
NSS-W

I Want to Hold Your Hand
BBe-W,M DRR-W,M RDT-W,M TI2-W,M TRR-W,M TWS-W

I Want to Join the Union
AFP-W

I Want to Know Christ
VB-W,M

I Want to Know What Love Is
BNG-W,M

I Want to Live
CJ-W,M PoG-W,M WG-W,M

I Want to Make a Difference
VB-W,M

I Want to Marry a Male Quartet
K-W,M

I Want to See Jesus in de Mornin'
BDW-W,M

I Want to See the Old Home
WiS8-W,M

I Want to Spend My Life with You (Paper Chase Love Theme)
MF-W,M

I Want to Talk to the Heavenly Father
SoP-W,M

I Want to Tell You
TWS-W

I Want to Tell You, Bossman
LC-W

I Want to Walk You Home
ILF-W,M

I Want to Wish You a Merry Christmas
BCh-W,M

I Want What I Want When I Want It
M-W,M

I Want You ('Cause When I See Your Eyes, Then I Know I Want You)
TTH-W,M

I Want You (My Friend, to Be True, My Friend)
Mo-W,M NM-W,M

I Want You (She's So Heavy)
BBe-W,M TWS-W

I Want You (Three Little Words, As Sweet As a Kiss, I Want You)
Mo-W,M NM-W,M OTO-W

I Want You, I Need You, I Love You
SRE1-W,M TI1-W,M UFB-W,M

I Want You to Be My Girl
MF-W,M RY-W,M

I Want You to Want Me
ToO79-W,M

I Wanted Wings
AF-W GI-W

I Wanted Wings II
AF-W

I Was Born about Four Thousand Years Ago
Oz3-W,M

I Was Born about Ten Thousand Years Ago
BF-W,M FGM-W,M FW-W GO-W,M OTJ-W,M

I Was Born in Love with You
MLS-W,M

I Was Born on the Day before Yesterday
Wi-W,M

I Was Borned and Raised in Covington
SCa-W,M

I Was Country When Country Wasn't Cool
TI2-W,M

I Was Doing All Right
OTO-W

I Was Drunk Last Night
Oz3-W,M

I Was Glad When They Said to Me
SHP-W,M

I Was Having Trouble Seeing Mary
PO-W,M

I Was Made for Dancing
ToO79-W,M

I Was Made for Loving You
ToO79-W,M

I Was Once Far Away from the Savior
AME-W,M

I Was Seeing Nelly Home
AmH-W,M

I Was So Young
GOB-W,M

I Was the One
OGC1-W,M SRE2-W,M

I Was There

CMG-W,M

I Wash My Face in a Golden Vase
BCT-W,M

I Went Down Sing Polka
NSS-W

I Went down 61 Highway
LC-W

I Went down the Road
NF-W

I Went Home One Night
Oz1-W,M

I Went to Atlanta
AFP-W

I Went to Your Wedding
OGC2-W,M

I Went Upstairs
SiR-W,M

I Wept and Chastened Myself
Boo-W,M

I Whistle a Happy Tune
DBC-W,M HLS8-W,M OTJ-W,M OTO-W TI1-W,M UBF-W,M UFB-W,M

I Will! (God Helping Me, I Will Be Thine)
GH-W,M

I Will (Lennon/McCartney)
BBe-W,M Be2-W,M PMC-W,M TWS-W

I Will Always Love You
BDP-W,M CMG-W,M TOC82-W,M TOM-W,M

I Will Arise
WN-W,M

I Will Be in Love with You
TI2-W,M

I Will Be True to Thee
FHR-W,M

I Will Bow and Be Simple
GB-W,M

I Will Care for Mother Now
SiS-W

I Will Clap My Hands
RSL-W,M

I Will Follow You
Mo-W,M NM-W,M OTO-W TI2-W,M

I Will Give Thanks to the Lord
SHP-W,M

I Will Go to the Fast Running River
RSC-W,M (Russian Only)

I Will Go to the Swift River
RuS-W,M (Russian)

I Will Lift Up Mine Eyes
GH-W,M

I Will Love Thee Always
Oz4-W,M

I Will Never Marry
SBF-W,M

I Will Never Pass This Way Again
GrH-W,M HLS7-W,M RDF-W,M

I Will Overcome
SFF-W,M

I Will Pass over You
GH-W,M

I Will Say Goodbye
MLS-W,M

I Will Serve Thee
BSG-W,M BSP-W,M FS-W,M HLS7-W,M

I Will Sing a Lullaby
UF-W,M

I Will Sing the Wondrous Story
GH-W,M

I Will Sing to the Lord As Long As I Live
SHP-W,M

I Will Sleep Away
RTH-W
I Will Survive
SoH-W,M ToO79-W,M
I Will Tell You My Troubles
SoC-W
I Will Trust in the Lord
AME-W,M
I Will Wait for You
BeL-W,M MLS-W,M RDT-W,M
TI1-W,M UFB-W,M
I Wish
ToO76-W,M MH-W,M
I Wish I Didn't Love You So
OTO-W
I Wish I Had a Fat Contract
SiS-W
I Wish I Had a Girl
BH-W,M HLS1-W,M RW-W,M
I Wish I Knew
MF-W,M
I Wish I Was
MAR-W,M
I Wish I Was a Little Bird
BSC-W
**I Wish I Was a Little Rock see I
Wish I Wuz a Little Rock**
I Wish I Was a Mole in the Ground
FoS-W,M FVV-W,M
**I Wish I Was a Mole in the Ground
see also Mole in the Ground**
**I Wish I Was an Ant see I Wisht I
Was an Ant**
I Wish I Was an Apple
NF-W
I Wish I Was at Home
Oz2-W
I Wish I Was Eighteen Again
TI2-W,M
I Wish I Was in Dixie
MPP-W
**I Wish I Was in Dixie see also
variant titles below and Dixie**
I Wish I Was in Dixie Land
OHG-W,M
I Wish I Was in Dixie's Land
DE-W,M MG-W,M SiS-W
I Wish I Was in Love Again
UBF-W,M
I Wish I Was Single Again
AmS-W,M ATS-W,M BF-W,M
BSC-W FAW-W,M FW-W IL-W,M
OFS-W,M OTJ-W,M Oz3-W,M
TMA-W,M
I Wish I Were a Little Sparrow
Oz1-W
I Wish I Were a Sailor
GUM1-W,M
I Wish I Were an Oscar Mayer
Wiener
GSM-W,M
**I Wish I Were an Oscar Mayer
Wiener see also Oscar Mayer
Wiener Song**
I Wish I Were in Love Again
HC2-W,M LM-W,M OTO-W
TI1-W,M TS-W UFB-W,M
I Wish I Were Where Helen Lies
SeS-W,M
I Wish I Wuz a Little Rock
TMA-W,M
I Wish I'd Bought a Half a Pint and
Stayed in the Wagon Yard
FVV-W,M
I Wish They Didn't Mean Goodbye
Mo-W,M
I Wish You a Merry Christmas

SOO-W,M
**I Wish You a Merry Christmas see
also Merry Christmas (I Wish You
a Merry Christmas)**
I Wish You Could Have Turned My
Head (and Left My Heart Alone)
TI2-W,M TOC82-W,M
I Wish You Knew
BIS-W,M
I Wish You Love
RDT-W,M TI2-W,M
I Wished on the Moon
OTO-W
I Wisht I Was an Ant
LC-W
I Woke at Dawn
LA-W,M (Spanish)
I Wonder As I Wander
GBC-W,M JOC-W,M SBF-W,M
I Wonder, I Wonder, I Wonder
GSF-W,M
I Wonder If I Take You Home
TTH-W,M
I Wonder If They Ever Think of Me
NMH-W,M
I Wonder What Became of Me
OHF-W
I Wonder What It's Like
OTO-W UBF-W,M
I Wonder What the King Is Doing
Tonight?
LL-W,M OTO-W UBF-W,M
I Wonder What's Become of Sally
MF-W,M OHB-W,M
I Wonder When I Shall Be Married
AH-W,M VA-W,M
I Wonder Where My Baby Is
Tonight
WDS-W,M
I Wonder Where You Are Tonight
BIS-W,M
I Wonder Who's Kissing Her Now
FSTS-W,M GSN1-W,M OAP-W,M
(French) TI2-W,M
I Wonder Why
FRH-W,M
I Wonder Why You Said Goodbye
OGC2-W,M
I Won't Be a Nun
BSC-W,M Oz3-W,M
I Won't Be Home No More
HW-W,M
I Won't Be Yo' Lowdown Dog No
Mo'
LC-W
I Won't Dance
BBB-W,M TI1-W,M UFB-W,M
I Won't Die No Mo'
BDW-W,M
I Won't Fight Another Man's War
VS-W,M
I Won't Forget You
CFB-W,M
I Won't Grow Up
Mo-W,M NM-W,M OTJ-W,M
OTO-W UBF-W,M
I Won't Last a Day without You
ILT-W,M
I Won't Let You Get Away
V-W,M
I Won't Send Roses
OTO-W UBF-W,M
I Worship Thee, O Holy Ghost
AHO-W,M
I Would Be True
AME-W,M CEM-W,M FH-W,M
OM-W,M

I Would If I Could but I Can't
Sta-W,M
I Would Like to Change My Name
SiS-W
I Would Like to Read
RF-W,M
I Would Not Be Alone
FMT-W
I Would Not Die in Spring Time
FHR-W,M
I Would Not Die in Summer Time
FHR-W,M
I Would Not Live Alway
AHO-W,M
I Would Not Live Always
Oz4-W,M
I Would Not Marry a Black Girl
NF-W
I Would Not Marry a Yellow or a
White Negro Girl
NF-W
I Would That My Love
AmH-W,M (German) HSD-W,M
TF-W,M WiS8-W,M
I Wouldn't Change You If I Could
TOC83-W,M
I Wouldn't Have Missed It for the
World
TI2-W,M TOC82-W,M
I Wouldn't Marry
BSC-W
I Write the Songs
GrS-W,M PoG-W,M RW-W,M
WG-W,M
I Wrote the Book
UBF-W,M
I Yawn So
SiR-W,M
I, Yi, Yi, Yi, Yi
GSF-W,M
Ice Box Song
SOO-W,M
Ice Castles (Theme)
GSN5-W,M ToO79-W,M
Ice Cream
MF-W,M TW-W
Ice Cream Man
GM-W,M SOO-W,M
Ice Cream Sextet
SSA-W,M
Iceland
SiP-W,M (Icelandic)
Ich Bin Ein Herr
AHO-W,M (German)
Ich Bin Ein Preusse
SiP-W,M (German)
Ich Liebe Dich see I Love Thee
Ich Liebe Jesus Noch Allein
AHO-W,M (German)
Ich Weiss Nicht
Boo-W,M (German Only)
Icicles
SSe-W,M
Icicles (High)
ASB1-W,M
Icicles (That Come by Night)
ASB3-W,M
I'd 'Ave Baked a Cake
OTJ-W,M
I'd Be a Fairy
FHR-W,M
I'd Be Lost without You
WDS-W,M
I'd Climb the Highest Mountain
TI1-W,M UFB-W,M
I'd Do Anything
O-W,M TI1-W,M UBF-W,M

UFB-W,M
I'd Do Anything for You
  TOH-W,M
I'd Give a Million Tomorrows
  MF-W,M
I'd Give Everything for
  Herzogovina
  VS-W,M
**I'd Have Baked a Cake see I'd 'Ave
  Baked a Cake**
I'd Like to Be
  SSN-W,M (French)
I'd Like to Be a Farmer
  MH-W,M
I'd Like to Be in Texas When They
  Round Up in the Spring
  FC-W,M
I'd Like to Marry
  PIS-W,M
I'd Like to Teach the World to Sing
  AAP-W,M GrH-W,M GSN4-W,M
  HLS7-W,M HLS9-W,M MCG-W,M
  RDF-W,M RW-W,M RYT-W,M
I'd Love Just Once to See You
  RB-W
**I'd Love You Better, My Husband
  see J't'aim'rais Mieux, Mon Mari**
I'd Love You to Want Me
  On-W,M
I'd Rather Be a Negro Than a Poor
  White Man
  NF-W
I'd Rather Be a Panther
  AFS-W,M
I'd Rather Be Blue over You
  TI1-W,M UFB-W,M
I'd Rather Be Right
  UBF-W,M
I'd Rather Be Sorry
  SuS-W,M
I'd Rather Believe in You
  VB-W,M
I'd Rather Charleston
  ReG-W,M
I'd Rather Have Jesus
  HHa-W,M OM-W,M
I'd Rather Leave While I'm in Love
  MF-W,M TI1-W,M UFB-W,M
I'd Really Love to See You Tonight
  ToO76-W,M
I'd Trade All of My Tomorrows
  OGC1-W,M
Ida Marina
  VA-W,M
Ida Red
  FW-W ITP-W,M Oz3-W,M
  POT-W,M
Ida! Sweet As Apple Cider
  FSN-W,M GSN1-W,M HLS1-W,M
  MF-W,M OAP-W,M RW-W,M
Ida Was a Twelvemonth Old
  MGT-W,M
Idaho
  Oz3-W SY-W,M TI2-W,M
Idle Dreams
  ReG-W,M
Idols of Silver and Gold
  JF-W,M
Idumea
  SHS-W,M
Idylle (Valse Boston)
  AmH-M
If (a Picture Paints a Thousand
  Words)
  BNG-W,M DC-W,M DPE-W,M
  MF-W,M RoE-W,M
If (They Made Me a King)

RDT-W,M TI1-W,M UFB-W,M
If a Girl Isn't Pretty
  UBF-W,M
If a Hard and Weary Task
  Boo-W,M
If All Be True That I Do Think
  Boo-W,M
If All the World Were Paper
  OTJ-W,M SMa-W,M
If All the Young Men
  RuS-W,M (Russian)
If Anybody Ask You Who I Am
  Me-W,M
If Anybody Had a Heart
  TTH-W,M
If Birds That Neither Sow Nor Reap
  AHO-W,M
If E'er I Should Wish to Get
  Married
  ESU-W
If Eve Had Left the Apple on the
  Bough
  E-W,M
**If Ever I See You Again (Theme)
  see California (Movie Theme)**
If Ever I Would Leave You
  DBC-W,M HC1-W,M HLS8-W,M
  HSi-W,M LL-W,M OTO-W
  RW-W,M TI1-W,M TW-W
  UBF-W,M UFB-W,M
If Every Day Was Like Christmas
  EP-W,M
If Father a Hero Fell
  RuS-W,M (Russian)
If God Be for Us
  GH-W,M
If He Walked into My Life
  DBC-W,M Mo-W,M NM-W,M
  OTO-W TI2-W,M UBF-W,M
If Here Where All Is Dark and
  Silent
  MU-W,M
If Hungry My Nose
  Boo-W,M
If I Became the President
  LSO-W
If I Can
  SNS-W
If I Can Give
  CEM-W,M
If I Can Help Somebody
  RDF-W,M
If I Can Stop One Heart from
  Breaking
  AHO-W,M
If I Can't Have You
  SoH-W,M TI1-W,M UFB-W,M
If I Could Be with You
  MF-W,M OHB-W,M
If I Could Fly
  SL-W,M
If I Could Plant a Tiny Seed of
  Love
  U-W
If I Could've Been
  UBF-W,M
If I Didn't Care
  TI2-W,M
If I Die in Arkansas
  NH-W Oz3-W
If I Ever Fall in Love Again
  GCM-W,M
If I Fell
  BBe-W,M Be1-W,M TWS-W
If I Gave You
  UBF-W,M
If I Give My Heart to You

HLS3-W,M
If I Had a Donkey Wot Wouldn't
  Go
  MSB-W
If I Had a Hammer
  IHA-W,M JF-W,M RDF-W,M
  TI1-W,M TO-W,M TWD-W,M
  UFB-W,M
**If I Had a Hammer see also
  Hammer Song**
If I Had a Million
  UBF-W,M
If I Had a Scolding Wife
  Oz2-W,M
If I Had a Talking Picture of You
  HC2-W,M MF-W,M
If I Had a Wishing Ring
  Mo-W,M NM-W,M
If I Had an Armadillo
  OU-W,M
If I Had but a Voice of Song
  GrM-W,M
If I Had My Druthers
  OHF-W
If I Had My Life to Live Over
  TI1-W,M UFB-W,M
If I Had My Way
  MM-W,M RoE-W,M
If I Had Wings Like Nora's Dove
  NeA-W,M
If I Had You
  GSN2-W,M GST-W,M HLS2-W,M
  OP1-W,M RW-W,M TW-W
If I Know What You Know
  Boo-W,M
If I Lose
  BSo-W,M
If I Love Again
  MF-W,M
If I Loved You
  L-W TG-W,M TI1-W,M TW-W
  UFB-W,M
If I May
  NK-W,M
If I Needed Someone
  TWS-W
If I Only Had a Brain
  TW-W WO-W,M
If I Ruled the World
  DBC-W,M HC2-W,M OTJ-W,M
  OTO-W TI1-W,M UBF-W,M
  UFB-W,M
If I Should Lose You
  OTO-W
If I Should Wander Back Tonight
  BIS-W,M
If I Sing Ahead of You
  Boo-W,M
If I Was a Mourner
  NH-W
If I Were a Bell
  DBC-W,M TI2-W,M UBF-W,M
If I Were a Carpenter
  MCG-W,M RYT-W,M TI2-W,M
If I Were a Dancer (Dance Part 2)
  RoS-W,M
If I Were a Rich Man
  HC2-W,M On-W,M OTJ-W,M
  OTO-W TI2-W,M TOM-W,M
  TW-W UBF-W,M
If I Were Anybody Else but Me
  NaM-W,M
If I Were King of the Forest
  WO-W,M
If I Were Not I, Love
  SOT-W,M
If I Were on the Stage

FSN-W,M M-W,M TW-W

If I Were on the Stage see also Kiss Me Again

If I Were the Man
Mo-W,M NM-W,M OTO-W
UBF-W,M

If I Were You
Mo-W,M NM-W,M OTO-W

If I'd As Much Money
MH-W,M

If It Takes All Night
TOC83-W,M

If It Was Easy
TOC83-W,M

If Jack Were Only Here see Mother Was a Lady

If Looks Could Kill
TTH-W,M

If Love Were All
BS-W,M

If Music Be the Food of Love, Play On
FSS-W,M

If My Complaints Could Passion Move
EL-W,M

If My Friends Could See Me Now
HLS5-W,M HLS8-W,M MF-W,M
RW-W,M SC-W,M TW-W

If My Mother Will Go see Ef My Mudder Will Go

If My Old Top Were a Dancing Man
CFS-W,M (French)

If Neither Brass Nor Marble
Boo-W,M

If One Won't Another Will
ITP-W,M

If Only (Oh Daddy If Only You Could Know)
VB-W,M

If Only (the Bells of Joy Were Ringing)
GBC-W,M

If Only I Had Known
TI2-W,M

If Our Fathers Want to Go
WN-W,M

If She Forsake Me
OH-W,M

If Somebody There Chanced to Be
MGT-W,M

If That Is So
GiS-W,M

If That Isn't Love
HHa-W,M

If the Lord Calls You see Ef de Lord Calls You

If There Is Someone Lovelier Than You
MF-W,M TW-W

If This Isn't Love
DBC-W,M HC1-W,M OTO-W
R-W,M RW-W,M TI1-W,M
UBF-W,M UFB-W,M

If Thou Art an Honest Friend
Boo-W,M

If Thou but Suffer God to Guide Thee
CEM-W,M Hy-W,M

If Thou Wilt Hear
AHO-W,M

If We Can't Be the Same Old Sweethearts
BH-W,M RW-W,M

If We Could See beyond Today
BSG-W,M BSP-W,M

If We Don't Stop Rushing
Lo-W,M

If We Make It through December
NMH-W,M

If We Must Part
EL-W,M

If We Only Have Love
HLS7-W,M RDF-W,M (French)
TI1-W,M UFB-W,M

If We Were in Love
HFH-W,M

If We Will, We Can Be Free
AFP-W

If We're Not Back in Love by Monday
NMH-W,M

If We're Weak Enough to Tarry
MGT-W,M

If with All Your Heart
LMR-W,M

If with All Your Hearts
FiS-W,M TF-W,M

If Ye Would Hear
OB-W,M

If You Ain't Got Nothin'
TOC82-W,M

If You Ain't Lovin'
CSp-W,M

If You Are but a Dream
MF-W,M

If You Are Tired of Your Load of Sin
AME-W,M

If You Ask Me to Toast You
ESU-W

If You Believe
Wi-W,M

If You Believe in Make Believe
SBS-W,M

If You Can't Come Send One Angel Down
Me-W,M

If You Can't Rock Me
RoS-W,M

If You Catch Me Stealin'
AFP-W

If You Come Only Come with Me
BS-W,M

If You Could Read My Mind
DPE-W,M ERM-W,M GrS-W,M

If You Could See Her
C-W,M OTO-W UBF-W,M

If You Cry
HRB4-W,M

If You Don't Like the Way I Work
NH-W

If You Fly an "89"
AF-W

If You Frown
NF-W

If You Give Me Your Attention
MGT-W,M

If You Go Away
TI2-W,M

If You Gotta Go, Go Now
FoR-W,M

If You Happy Would Be
AHO-W,M (Spanish)

If You Knew Susie
FPS-W,M HLS2-W,M MF-W,M
TI1-W,M UFB-W,M

If You Know of a Heart
SOT-W,M

If You Know What I Mean
RV-W,M ToO76-W,M

If You Leave
TTH-W,M

If You Leave Me Now
ToO76-W,M

If You Let Me
RoS-W,M

If You Let Me Make Love to You Then Why Can't I Touch You?
UBF-W,M

If You Look up de Road You See Fader Mosey
NSS-W

If You Love God, Serve Him
RF-W,M

If You Love Me (Let Me Know)
EP-W,M

If You Love Me, Carmen
MU-W,M

If You Love Me, Really Love Me
TI2-W,M

If You Miss Me from the Back of the Bus
SFF-W,M

If You Really Knew Me
TP-W,M UBF-W,M

If You Really Loved Me
SNZ-W,M (Maori)

If You Really Want to Be My Friend
RoS-W,M

If You Remember Me
TI1-W,M UFB-W,M

If You Say My Eyes Are Beautiful
TTH-W,M

If You See Johnny (If You See Sally)
STW-W,M

If You Should Ever Feel in a Peculiar Frame of Mind
SOT-W,M

If You Should Need Me
SNZ-W,M (Maori)

If You Take the Gun
VS-W,M

If You Talk in Your Sleep (Don't Mention My Name)
WF-W,M

If You Wanna Be Happy
DRR-W,M

If You Want a Receipt
GiS-W,M

If You Want to Get to Heaven see Ef You Want to Get to Hebben

If You Want to Go A-Courtin'
NH-W

If You Want to Know
ASB5-W,M

If You Want to Know Where the Privates Are
HAS-W,M

If You Want to Know Who We Are
GiS-W,M MGT-W,M

If You Want to Marry
NH-W

If You Want to Write Me see Si Me Quieres Escribir

If You Were a Woman (and I Was a Man)
TTH-W,M

If You Were an Eskimo
GUM1-W,M

If You Were My True Love
ITP-W,M

If You Were the Only Girl in the World
MF-W,M TI2-W,M U-W

If You Will Drink for Pleasure
Boo-W,M

If You Would Hear see If Ye Would Hear

If Your Foot Is Pretty, Show It
  SY-W,M
If Your Heart Isn't in It
  TTH-W,M
If You're a Girl
  GM-W,M
If You're Anxious for to Shine
  GiS-W,M MGT-W,M
If You're Happy
  Bo-W,M CSS-W GM-W,M
  MAR-W,M
If You're So Smart How Come You
  Ain't Rich?
  WF-W,M
If You've Got the Time, We've Got
  the Beer
  GSM-W,M
If You've Only Got a Moustache
  FHR-W,M
Ifca's Castle
  BMC-W,M MG-W,M
Il A Tout Dit
  CE-W,M (French)
Il Bacio (The Kiss)
  MF-M
Il Court, Il Court, Le Furet
  CUP-W,M (French Only) MP-W,M
  (French Only)
Il Est Midi
  CE-W,M (French)
Il Est Ne
  CE-W,M (French) JOC-W,M
Il Est Ne, Le Divin Enfant
  CUP-W,M (French Only)
  SHP-W,M
Il Est Ne, Le Divin Enfant see also
  He Is Born, the Divine Christ Child
Il Est Quelqu'un Sur Terre (There's
  Someone in My Fancy)
  F2-W,M (French)
Il Etait Trois Petits Enfants
  MP-W,M (French Only)
Il Etait Un' Bergere
  CUP-W,M (French Only)
Il Etait Un Petit Homme
  MP-W,M (French Only)
Il Etait Un Petit Navire
  Ch-W (French Only) MP-W,M
  (French Only)
Il Etait Une Bergere
  FSO-W,M (French) MP-W,M
  (French Only)
Il Etait Une Dame Tartine
  MP-W,M (French Only)
Il Faut Aller En Guerre
  FSO-W,M (French)
Il Faut Rire
  CaF-W (French Only)
Il Pleut Bergere
  Ch-W (French Only)
Il Pleut Il Pleut Bergere
  CUP-W,M (French Only)
Ilkla Moor Baht Hat
  OHO-W,M
Ilkley Moor Baht'at
  FW-W
Ill Wind
  Mo-W,M NM-W,M TI2-W,M
  ToS-W,M
I'll Always Be Glad to Take You
  Back
  OGC2-W,M
I'll Always Be in Love with You
  MF-W,M TI1-W,M UFB-W,M
I'll Always Love You
  CFB-W,M OTO-W
I'll Be a Buoyant Girl

DS-W,M
I'll Be a Soldier
  FHR-W,M SiS-W
I'll Be All Right
  SFF-W,M
I'll Be All Smiles Tonight
  Oz4-W TMA-W,M
I'll Be Around
  MF-W,M TI1-W,M ToS-W,M
  TWD-W,M UFB-W,M
I'll Be Back
  BBe-W,M Be1-W,M SRE2-W,M
  TWS-W
I'll Be Coming Back for More
  TOH-W,M
I'll Be Free
  NSS-W
I'll Be Happy When the Preacher
  Makes You Mine
  WDS-W,M
I'll Be Home
  TI1-W,M UFB-W,M
I'll Be Home for Christmas
  BCh-W,M BCS-W,M MF-W,M
  OPS-W,M OTJ-W,M TI1-W,M
  UFB-W,M
I'll Be Home Tomorrow
  FHR-W,M
I'll Be on My Way
  RW-W,M
I'll Be Seeing You
  FPS-W,M FrS-W,M HC1-W,M
  RW-W,M TI1-W,M UBF-W,M
  UFB-W,M
I'll Be There
  OGC1-W,M
I'll Be There in the Morning
  RF-W,M
I'll Be Your Baby Tonight
  EC-W,M
I'll Be Your Man around the House
  TOC82-W,M
I'll Be Your Sweetheart
  U-W
I'll Bid You Farewell
  ITP-W,M
I'll Bomb Cologne
  AF-W
I'll Build a Stairway to Paradise
  GOB-W,M MF-W,M NYT-W,M
I'll Build My Log Cabin on a
  Mountain So High
  SCa-W,M
I'll Buy an Egg
  SOO-W,M
I'll Buy That Dream
  Mo-W,M NM-W,M OTO-W
I'll Buy You a Star
  TW-W
I'll Catch the Sun (Peter's Theme)
  MF-W,M
I'll Cry Instead
  BBe-W,M Be1-W,M TWS-W
I'll Dance at Your Wedding
  AT-W,M
I'll Do It All Over Again
  RW-W,M
I'll Eat When I'm Hungry
  FMT-W NF-W
Ill Fares the Family
  Boo-W,M
I'll Fly Away
  HHa-W,M OHO-W,M Tr-W,M
I'll Follow My Secret Heart
  OTO-W UBF-W,M
I'll Follow the Sun
  BBe-W,M Be1-W,M TWS-W

WG-W,M
I'll Forgive but I'll Never Forget
  RW-W,M
I'll Get By (As Long As I Have You)
  DC-W,M MF-W,M RW-W,M
  T-W,M TI1-W,M UFB-W,M
I'll Get You
  TWS-W
I'll Get You, Rabbit
  NF-W
I'll Give You One More As You Go
  Oz3-W,M
I'll Go Home with Bonnie Jean
  TW-W
I'll Go Stepping Too
  BIS-W,M
I'll Go to My Grave Loving You
  CMG-W,M PoG-W,M
I'll Hang My Harp on a Willow Tree
  HSD-W,M
I'll Hang My Stocking
  ASB1-W,M
I'll Have a New Life
  HHa-W,M
I'll Have to Say I Love You in a
  Song
  JC-W,M MF-W,M PM-W,M
  RW-W,M
I'll Know
  ILT-W,M TI2-W,M TW-W
  UBF-W,M
I'll Live for Him
  AME-W,M
I'll Marry
  Fa-W,M
I'll Meet You in the Evening
  Oz2-W,M
I'll Need Someone to Hold Me
  (When I Cry)
  TI2-W,M
I'll Never Be Lonely Again
  UBF-W,M
I'll Never Be Yours
  Oz2-W
I'll Never Fall in Love Again
  BDF-W,M GOI7-W,M HC2-W,M
  HD-W,M ILT-W,M Mo-W,M
  OTO-W RDT-W,M TI1-W,M
  UFB-W,M
I'll Never Find Another You
  TI1-W,M UFB-W,M
I'll Never Get Out of This World
  Alive
  HW-W,M
I'll Never Let You Go
  EP-W,M
I'll Never Love This Way Again
  GSN5-W,M ToO79-W,M
I'll Never Make the Same Mistake
  Again
  Mo-W,M NM-W,M
I'll Never Say "Never Again" Again
  MF-W,M
I'll Never Say No
  UBF-W,M
I'll Never Smile Again
  TI2-W,M
I'll Never Stop Loving You
  HLS3-W,M RT5-W,M RW-W,M
I'll Never Wear the Red Any More
  Oz3-W
I'll Only Miss Her When I Think of
  Her
  MF-W,M
I'll Paint You a Song
  AT-W,M OTO-W
I'll Pay the Check

TW-W

I'll Remember see In the Still of the Night (I'll Remember)

I'll Remember April
DJ-W,M TI2-W,M

I'll Remember You Love in My Prayers
HOH-W,M

I'll Rest and Sleep
ASB1-W,M

I'll Sail upon the Dog-Star
OH-W,M

I'll See You Again
BS-W,M HC1-W,M MF-W,M

I'll See You in My Dreams
FPS-W,M GSN2-W,M GST-W,M
HLS2-W,M RW-W,M

I'll Show Him
PF-W,M

I'll Sing Thee Songs of Araby
TF-W,M WiS8-W,M

I'll Sing You a Thousand Love Songs
MF-W,M

I'll Stand by You
GH-W,M

I'll Step Aside
OGC1-W,M

I'll Still Be Loving You
CFB-W,M DPE-W,M GCM-W,M
TTH-W,M

I'll String Along with You
MF-W,M OHB-W,M

I'll Swim Away
MMM-W,M

I'll Take a Back Seat for You
OGC1-W,M

I'll Take a Leg from Some Old Table
IL-W,M

I'll Take Romance
RoE-W,M TI1-W,M UFB-W,M

I'll Take You Home Again, Kathleen
AH-W,M ATS-W BH-W,M
FSTS-W,M FW-W LMR-W,M
MAB1-W MF-W,M MSA1-W
OAP-W,M OS-W OTJ-W,M
PoS-W,M TI1-W,M U-W
UFB-W,M

I'll Tell It Wherever I Go
GrG-W,M

I'll Tell My Mother
Boo-W,M

I'll Tell You Where They Were
GI-W,M GO-W,M

I'll Try Anything
THN-W,M

I'll Try to Prove Faithful
WN-W,M

I'll Wait, Mr. Greene
TW-W

I'll Walk Alone
GOI7-W,M Mo-W,M NM-W,M
OTO-W TI2-W,M

I'll Walk with God
MF-W,M

I'll Walk with You
TW-W

I'll Wear Me a Cotton Dress
NF-W

Ill Wind
Mo-W,M NM-W,M TI2-W,M
ToS-W,M

Illegitimate Daughter
LSO-W OT-W,M

Illinois

Fif-W,M OS-W

Illinois Loyalty
Mo-W,M TI2-W,M

Illinois' Response
SiS-W

Illusion of Love
TW-W

Ilona
OTO-W

I'm... see also I'se...

I'm a Believer
ERM-W,M GAR-W,M MF-W,M
OnT1-W,M

I'm a Brass Band
MF-W,M SC-W,M

I'm a Child of Grace
FN-W,M

I'm a Child of the King
TB-W,M

I'm a Cranky Old Yank
GO-W,M

I'm a Ding Dong Daddy from Dumas
RW-W,M

I'm a Dreamer, Aren't We All
HC2-W,M MF-W,M TI1-W,M
UFB-W,M

I'm a Family Man
ESU-W

I'm a Fool to Want You
MF-W,M

I'm a Freeborn Man
IFM-W

I'm a Gamblin' Man
LC-W

I'm a Gent
MSB-W

I'm a Gigolo
TW-W

I'm a Good Old Rebel
FMT-W Oz2-W,M SiS-W

I'm a Good Old Rebel see also O I'm a Good Old Rebel

I'm a Jayhawk
Mo-W,M TI2-W,M

I'm a Jesus Fan
AG-W,M

I'm a Little Christmas Tree
SOO-W,M

I'm a Little Scholar
ITP-W,M

I'm a Little Teapot
FP-W,M GM-W,M OTJ-W,M

I'm a Lonely Little Petunia
NoS-W,M OnT1-W,M TI2-W,M

I'm A-Looking for a Home
PSN-W,M

I'm a Loser
BBe-W,M Be1-W,M TWS-W

I'm a Man
GAR-W,M TI1-W,M TRR-W,M
UFB-W,M

I'm a Man of Constant Sorrow
FPG-W,M

I'm a Man of Constant Sorrow see also I Am a Man of Constant Sorrow and Man of Constant Sorrow

I'm a Man That Done Wrong to His Parents
Oz4-W,M

I'm a Memory
WNF-W

I'm a Natu'al-Bohn Eastman
NH-W

I'm a Natural Woman
Lo-W,M

I'm a Nut
HSA-W,M

I'm a Pilgrim
BSo-W,M FiS-W,M GH-W,M
HSD-W,M WiS7-W,M

I'm a Pilgrim (I'm a Stranger)
GrG-W,M

I'm a Po' Li'l Orphan
My-W,M

I'm a Poor Wayfarin' Stranger
OFS-W,M

I'm a Poor Wayfarin' Stranger see also I'm Just a Poor Wayfarin' Stranger and Wayfaring Stranger

I'm a Prowlin' Ground Hog
LC-W

I'm A-Rolling
BeB-W,M RF-W,M TH-W,M
WiS7-W,M

I'm a Rover
TH-W,M

I'm a Scotch Bonny Wee One
GB-W,M

I'm a Shepherd Born to Sorrow
TF-W,M

I'm a Soldier of de Cross in de Army of My Lord
Me-W,M

I'm a Solger in de Army ob de Lord
BDW-W,M

I'm a Stranger Here
FW-W

I'm A-Tramping
MuM-W,M

I'm A-Trav'ling to the Grave
RF-W,M

I'm a Warrior
SSo-W,M

I'm a Woman
ERM-W,M MF-W,M

I'm a Yankee Doodle Dandy
OTJ-W,M UBF-W,M

I'm a Yankee Doodle Dandy see also Yankee Doodle Boy and Yankee Doodle Dandy

I'm Agoing to Lay Down My Sword
AHO-W,M

I'm All I've Got
Mo-W,M NM-W,M OTO-W

I'm All Out an' Down
NeF-W

I'm All Right
RoS-W,M

I'm All Smiles
Mo-W,M NM-W,M OTO-W
UBF-W,M

I'm Almost Done Traveling see I'm Mos' Dun Travelin'

I'm Alone
MA-W,M

I'm Always Chasing Rainbows
BH-W,M EAG2-W,M GG4-W,M
GrH-W,M HLS1-W,M HLS8-W,M
OS-W RT4-W,M RW-W,M T-W,M

I'm Always on a Mountain When I Fall
NMH-W,M

I'm an Australian, 20 Years Old
VS-W,M

I'm an Old Cowhand
FC-W,M HLS5-W,M MF-W,M
OHF-W OnT6-W,M RW-W,M

I'm an Old Man
OGC1-W,M

I'm an Ordinary Man
TW-W

I'm Back for More
TOH-W,M

I'm Beginning to See the Light
TI1-W,M UFB-W,M

I'm Bitin' My Fingernails and
Thinking of You
OGC1-W,M

I'm Blind
SiS-W

I'm Blue As a Man Can Be
LC-W

I'm Bound Away
SoF-W,M

I'm Bound for the Promised Land
AME-W,M Oz4-W,M

**I'm Bound for the Promised Land
see also Bound for the Promised
Land, and I Am Bound for the
Promised Land**

I'm Bringing a Red, Red Rose
WDS-W,M

I'm Building Up to an Awful Let
Down
OHF-W

I'm Called Little Buttercup
AmH-W,M GiS-W,M MGT-W,M
OTJ-W,M SL-W,M WiS8-W,M

I'm Calling to You
GM-W,M

I'm Certainly Living a Ragtime Life
POT-W,M

I'm Chiquita Banana
GSM-W,M

**I'm Chiquita Banana see also
Chiquita Banana (Jingle)**

I'm Climbin'
AN-W

I'm Coming Back Home to Live
with Jesus
GrG-W,M

I'm Coming Home
Mo-W,M

I'm Coming, Virginia
GST-W,M

I'm Confessin' (That I Love You)
TI1-W,M UFB-W,M

I'm Counting on You
CMF-W,M EP-W,M OGC1-W,M

I'm Day Dreamin' Tonight
CMF-W,M

I'm Despised for Being Poor
BSC-W

I'm Down
TWS-W

I'm Down on Double Quick
SiS-W

I'm Dreaming of a White Mistress
GO-W

I'm Dreaming of a Wonderful Night
BP-W,M

I'm Drifting Back to Dreamland
Mo-W,M NM-W,M

I'm Dying Far from Those I Love
SiS-W

I'm Dying for Some One to Love
Me
Oz3-W,M

I'm Easy
TI2-W,M ToO76-W,M

I'm Falling in Love Again
WNF-W

I'm Falling in Love with Some One
NaM-W,M

I'm Falling in Love with Someone
MF-W,M TW-W

I'm Fascinating
Mo-W,M NM-W,M OTO-W

I'm Flying
Mo-W,M NM-W,M OTJ-W,M
OTO-W UBF-W,M

I'm Flying High
MF-W,M

I'm Forever Blowing Bubbles
MF-W,M RC-W,M U-W

I'm Free (from the Chain Gang
Now)
LJ-W,M

I'm Free (Jagger/Richards)
RoS-W,M

I'm Free (Pete Townshend)
WA-W,M

I'm from Chicago
BP-W,M

I'm Getting Sentimental over You
GSN2-W,M TI2-W,M

I'm Glad I'm Not Young Anymore
LL-W,M OTO-W UBF-W,M

I'm Glad I'm Six
SHP-W,M

I'm Glad There Is You
Mo-W,M NM-W,M TI2-W,M
ToS-W,M

I'm Glad to Know about the World
SHP-W,M

I'm Goin' Back
NH-W

I'm Goin' Back to Good Ol'
Birmingham
FVV-W,M

I'm Goin' Back to Mississippi
LC-W

I'm Goin' Home on a Cloud
Me-W,M

I'm Goin' t' Stay in de Battle Fiel'
BDW-W,M

I'm Goin' Where Dere Aint No Mo'
Dyin'
BDW-W,M

**I'm Going Away see I'm Going
'Way**

I'm Going Away to Texas
Oz3-W,M

**I'm Going Back to Dixie see I'se
Gwine Back to Dixie**

I'm Going Back to Old Kentucky
BIS-W,M

I'm Going Down
RoS-W,M

I'm Going down This Road Feeling
Bad
FW-W

I'm Going Home
GH-W,M OTJ-W,M

I'm Going Home to Die No More
LSR-W,M

I'm Going Home to Dixie
DE-W,M

**I'm Going over the Mountains see
I'm Gwine ober de Mountains**

**I'm Going to Alabama see I'm
Gwine to Alabamy**

I'm Going to Cross the Sea
Oz3-W

I'm Going to Join the Army
FSU-W

**I'm Going to Join the Great
Association see I'm Gwine to Jine
de Great 'Sociation**

I'm Going to Land on the Shore
WN-W,M

**I'm Going to Lay Down My Sword
see I'm Agoing to Lay Down My
Sword**

I'm Going to Leave Old Texas Now

HWS-W,M

I'm Going to My New Jail
Tomorrow
SCa-W

**I'm Going to Put On My Golden
Shoes see I Goin' Put On My
Golden Shoes**

**I'm Going to Say Good Bye see
I'se Goin' to Say Good Bye**

I'm Going to the Limelight to Die
RBO-W,M

**I'm Going to Try the Air see I
Goin' Try the Air**

**I'm Going to Wear That Starry
Crown see I Goin' t' Ware That
Starry Crown**

**I'm Going to Weep No More see
I'se Gwine to Weep No More**

I'm Going 'Way
NH-W

I'm Gonna Be Boss
OGC2-W,M

I'm Gonna Build Me a Castle
LC-W

I'm Gonna Dance wit de Guy Wot
Brung Me (Gum Chewer's Song)
WF-W,M

I'm Gonna Fly
VB-W,M

I'm Gonna Get Him Back
TW-W

I'm Gonna Laugh You Right Out of
My Life
MF-W,M

I'm Gonna Love You Just a Little
More, Baby
SoH-W,M

I'm Gonna Love You Too
PL-W,M

I'm Gonna Make You Love Me
MF-W,M

I'm Gonna Quit You, Baby
DBL-W

I'm Gonna Sing
FoS-W,M RS-W,M

I'm Gonna Sit at the Welcome
Table
SFF-W,M

I'm Gonna Sit Right Down and Cry
EP-W,M

I'm Gonna Sit Right Down and
Write Myself a Letter
FRH-W,M MF-W,M NK-W,M
RDT-W,M RoE-W,M TI2-W,M
UBF-W,M

I'm Gonna Wash That Man Right
Out of My Hair
OTO-W

I'm Gonna Wash That Man Right
Out'a My Hair
SP-W,M

I'm Gonna Wash That Man Right
Outa My Hair
OTJ-W,M TI1-W,M UBF-W,M
UFB-W,M

I'm Growing Older
LC-W

I'm Gwine ober de Mountains
DE-W,M

I'm Gwine to Alabamy
AAF-W,M

**I'm Gwine to Alabamy see also Oh
I'm Gwine to Alabamy**

I'm Gwine to Jine de Great
'Sociation
RF-W,M

I'm Happy Just to Dance with You

BBe-W,M Be1-W,M TWS-W
I'm Happy When I'm Hiking
  Bo-W,M
I'm Henry VIII, I Am
  GAR-W,M GG2-W,M
I'm Home
  Mo-W,M NM-W,M
I'm Hurt Too Much to Cry
  JD-W,M
I'm Hurtin'
  TFC-W,M
I'm in Love Again
  ILF-W,M RW-W,M
I'm in Love, I'm in Love
  OTO-W Ro-W,M
I'm in Love with a Wonderful Guy
  SP-W,M
I'm in Love with Miss Logan
  TW-W
I'm in the Mood for Love
  EAG2-W,M GG5-W,M GSN2-W,M
  GSO-W,M HLS5-W,M OP1-W,M
  RDT-W,M RW-W,M TW-W
I'm in Trouble, Lord, I'm in Trouble
  NSS-W
I'm into the Bottle (to Get You Out
  of My Mind)
  TOH-W,M
I'm Just a Country Boy
  CMG-W,M MF-W,M RW-W,M
  TI1-W,M UFB-W,M
I'm Just a Lucky So and So
  GMD-W,M
I'm Just a Poor Wayfarin' Stranger
  SAm-W,M
**I'm Just a Poor Wayfarin' Stranger
see also I'm a Poor Wayfarin'
Stranger and Wayfaring Stranger**
I'm Just a Rebel Soldier
  Re-W,M
I'm Just a Singer (in a Rock and
  Roll Band)
  TI2-W,M
I'm Just from the Fountain
  Oz4-W,M
I'm Just Wild about Harry
  HC2-W,M MF-W,M OHB-W,M
  TW-W U-W
Im Kahne see In the Boat
I'm Late
  OTJ-W,M NI-W,M
I'm Leavin'
  SRE2-W,M
I'm Leavin' You Baby
  DBL-W
I'm Leaving It (All) Up to You
  CMG-W,M
I'm Like a New Broom
  TW-W
I'm Living a Lie
  RW-W,M
I'm Lonely and Blue
  LJ-W,M
I'm Lonesome Blues
  LC-W,M
**I'm Looking for a Home see I'm A-
Looking for a Home**
I'm Looking over a Four Leaf
  Clover
  BBB-W,M MF-W,M MR-W,M
  OHB-W,M U-W
I'm Looking through You
  BBe-W,M TWS-W
I'm Lovely
  TW-W
I'm Me! I'm Not Afraid
  TW-W

**I'm Mighty Tired see I'se Mighty
Tired**
I'm Mos' Dun Travelin'
  BDW-W,M
I'm Movin' On
  OGC1-W,M
I'm My Own Grandpaw
  WF-W,M
I'm Nine Hundred Miles from My
  Home
  ITP-W,M
I'm Nobody's Baby
  RW-W,M TI2-W,M
I'm Nobody's Darling on Earth
  Oz4-W,M
I'm Not a Fool Anymore
  FrF-W,M (Spanish)
I'm Not a Well Man
  TW-W
I'm Not Afraid
  NB-W
I'm Not Ashamed to Own My Lord
  Hy-W,M
I'm Not Ashamed to Own the Lord
  AME-W,M
I'm Not Finished Yet
  Mo-W,M NM-W,M OTO-W
I'm Not Lisa
  TI2-W,M ToO76-W,M
I'm Not Strong, Sir
  Boo-W,M
I'm Not Through Loving You Yet
  FrF-W,M
I'm Nothing but a Plain Old Soldier
  FHR-W,M SiS-W
I'm Off to Port (Voy A Partir)
  MSS-W,M (Spanish)
I'm Old Fashioned
  OHF-W TI1-W,M UFB-W,M
I'm on My Journey Home
  FoS-W,M NH-W SFB-W,M
I'm on My Last Go-Round
  NH-W
I'm on My Last Old Train
  RBO-W,M
I'm on My Way
  AFP-W,M FW-W GG1-W,M
  JF-W,M LL-W,M OHO-W,M
  OTJ-W,M
I'm on My Way to Canaan
  AHO-W,M
I'm on My Way to Canada
  AL-W
I'm on My Way to the Freedom
  Land
  SFF-W,M
I'm on the Way see I'se on de Way
I'm on Your Side
  OTO-W
I'm Only Dreaming
  YL-W,M
I'm Only in It for the Love
  TI2-W,M TOC83-W,M
I'm Only Sleeping
  TWS-W
I'm Only Thinking of Him
  MLM-W,M
I'm Popeye the Sailor Man
  AT-W,M HSe-W,M IPH-W,M
  LM-W,M OTJ-W,M TOM-W,M
I'm Praying for You
  AME-W,M
**I'm Praying for You see also I Am
Praying for You**
I'm Putting Me in Your Hands
  Mo-W,M NM-W,M
I'm Riding on the Moon and

Dancing on the Stars
  GMD-W,M
I'm Rolling see I'm A-Rolling
I'm Sad and I'm Lonely
  FW-W
I'm Seventy-Two Today
  Oz3-W
I'm Shadowing You
  OHF-W
I'm Sitting on Top of the World
  BBB-W,M GG2-W,M GSN2-W,M
  GST-W,M RW-W,M STW-W,M
  TI2-W,M
I'm So Deep in Trouble
  AFP-W
I'm So Glad
  BDW-W,M SFF-W,M
I'm So Glad Today I'm Ready
  ITP-W,M
I'm So Glad Trouble Don't Last
  Alway
  RF-W,M
I'm So Glad Troubles Don't Last
  Always
  FN-W,M
I'm So in Love with You
  GMD-W,M
I'm So Lonesome I Could Cry
  TI2-W,M
I'm So Tired
  TWS-W
I'm Soon Going Home
  HHa-W,M
I'm Sorry (for Myself, 'Cause
  You're Not Here with Me)
  CJ-W,M PoG-W,M
I'm Sorry (So Sorry, That I Was
  Such a Fool)
  TI2-W,M
I'm Sorry for You, My Friend
  HW-W,M
I'm Sorry I Made You Cry
  BH-W,M CS-W,M GSN1-W,M
  HLS1-W,M OS-W RW-W,M
I'm Sorry--I Want a Ferrari
  Mo-W,M NM-W,M
I'm Standing Guard
  SiS-W,M
I'm Standing on the Outside of
  Your Shelter
  TO-W,M
I'm Standing on the Solid Rock
  HHa-W,M
I'm Stepping Out with a Memory
  Tonight
  MF-W,M
I'm Stickin' with You
  RY-W,M
I'm Sticking to the Murphys
  Oz2-W
I'm Still Here
  Fo-W,M UBF-W,M
I'm Still in Love with You
  HRB1-W,M
I'm Still Standing
  TI2-W,M
I'm Talking to My Pal
  TS-W
I'm Tall, I'm Small
  GM-W,M
I'm Telling You Now
  GG3-W,M Mo-W,M NM-W,M
  OTO-W
I'm the Boy see I'se the B'y
I'm the 47th All-Weather Man
  GG2-W,M
I'm the Greatest Star

OTO-W UBF-W,M
I'm the Man from Krakow
  UF-W,M
I'm the Man That Built the Bridges
  RBO-W,M
I'm the Man That Rote Ta Rarra
  Bumdia
  Oz3-W,M
I'm the One Who Loves You
  OGC1-W,M
I'm Through with Roaming Romeos
  HJ-W,M
I'm Throwing Rice
  OGC1-W,M
I'm Thru with Love
  GG5-W,M RW-W,M
I'm Tramping see I'm A-Tramping
**I'm Traveling to the Grave see I'm
  A-Trav'ling to the Grave**
I'm Troubled
  FoS-W,M
I'm Troubled in Mind
  AFP-W RF-W,M WN-W,M
**I'm Troubled in Mind see also I'm
  A-Trouble in de Mind**
I'm Up
  VB-W,M
I'm Using My Bible for a Roadmap
  BSo-W,M
I'm Walkin'
  ILF-W,M RW-W,M RY-W,M
  RYT-W,M
I'm Walking behind You
  TI2-W,M
I'm Walking the Dog
  OGC2-W,M
I'm Wearin' Awa', Jean
  SeS-W,M
I'm Wearing Awa', Jean
  HSD-W,M
I'm Wishing
  NI-W,M TI1-W,M UFB-W,M
I'm with a Crowd but So Alone
  OGC1-W,M
Imagination
  HSS-W,M HST-W,M RoE-W,M
  TI1-W,M UFB-W,M
Imagine
  WG-W,M
Imandra
  SHS-W,M
Immanuel see Emmanuel
Immanuel's Land
  GH-W,M
Immensity
  SHS-W,M
Immigrant
  TI2-W,M
Immortal Babe
  OB-W,M
Immortal, Invisible, God Only Wise
  Hy-W,M SJ-W,M
Immortal Love, Forever Full
  AHO-W,M Hy-W,M
Imogen
  SiS-W
Impatience
  CA-W,M MU-W,M
Impeachment Song
  MPP-W,M
Imperial March (Darth Vader's
  Theme)
  TOM-M
Impossible (Hammerstein/Rodgers)
  TW-W UBF-W,M
Impossible (Steve Allen)
  NK-W,M

Impossible Dream
  HC1-W,M HSi-W,M MLM-W,M
  OnT1-W,M OTJ-W,M PoG-W,M
  RDF-W,M RW-W,M WG-W,M
Impressions
  FSB3-M
Impressment of Seamen
  MPP-W,M
Imprevu
  GSM-W,M
Imprison'd Once at Nantes
  CFS-W,M (French)
Impromptu
  MPP-W
In a Boxcar around the World
  LSR-W,M
In a Fine Castle
  SGT-W,M
In-A-Gadda-Da-Vida
  MF-W,M
In a Hurry
  K-W,M
In a Little Dutch Kindergarten
  STP-W,M
In a Little Spanish Town
  BBB-W,M CS-W,M EAG2-W,M
  GST-W,M HLS2-W,M RW-W,M
  TI2-W,M
In a Little While
  VB-W,M
In a Lonely Graveyard Many Miles
  Away
  AME-W,M
In a Lowly Manger Sleeping
  AME-W,M
In a Manger He Is Lying
  CSF-W
In a Mellow Tone
  GSF-W,M
In a Mulberry Tree
  NF-W
In a Rush
  NF-W
In a Sentimental Mood
  GMD-W,M TI2-W,M
In a Shanty in Old Shanty Town
  BeL-W,M MAB1-W MF-W,M
  MSA1-W OnT1-W,M TI2-W,M
In a Simple Way I Love You
  MF-W,M UBF-W,M
In a Stable Far Away
  SHP-W,M
In All My Vast Concerns with Thee
  AME-W,M
In All the Country Round
  CFS-W,M (French)
In All the Magic of Christmas-Tide
  AHO-W,M
In an 18th Century Drawing Room
  TI1-M UFB-M
In and Out Those Dusty Bluebells
  CSG-W,M
In Another Land
  RoS-W,M
In April (Green April, Altho' 'Tis
  Surely Flowertime)
  FSA2-W,M
In April (in April, My Garden
  Bloomed So Sweet)
  SMa-W,M
In Arizona
  FSA1-W,M
In Arkansas
  Oz3-W,M
In Autumn We Should Drink, Boys
  ESU-W
In Bahia

ASB6-W,M PIS-W,M
In Battle
  AL-W
In Bethlehem, That Fair City
  OB-W,M
In Bethlehem, the Lowly
  CSF-W
In Bibberley Town
  SaS-W,M
In Bright Mansions Above
  MuM-W,M RF-W,M
In Buddy's Eyes
  Fo-W,M OTO-W UBF-W,M
In Capulet's Tomb
  RJ-W,M
In Christ There Is No East or West
  FH-W,M Hy-W,M SJ-W,M
In Comes the Farmer
  OTJ-W,M
"In" Crowd, The
  TI1-W,M UFB-W,M
In Darkness
  Boo-W,M
In Dat Great Gittin'-Up Morning
  RF-W,M
In Dat Mornin' All Day
  NSS-W
In de Mornin'
  BDW-W,M SA-W,M
**In de Mornin' see also In the
  Morning**
In de Mornin When I Rise
  NSS-W
In de Vinter Time
  NeA-W,M
In Dem Long Hot Summer Days
  NeF-W
In Dreams
  TFC-W,M
In Dulci Jubilo
  CCH-W,M GBC-W,M JOC-W,M
  OB-W,M OE-W,M UF-WM
In Early April
  ASB5-W,M
In Egern on the Tegern See
  L-W MA-W,M
In Eighteen Forty-Nine
  Oz4-W,M
In Eighteen Hundred and Sixty
  Oz3-W,M
In Eighteen Hundred and Sixty-One
  Oz2-W,M
In Elvas
  SiR-W,M
In Enterprise of Martial Kind
  GiS-W,M MGT-W,M
In Erin's Isle
  E-W,M
In Every Trying Hour
  AME-W,M
In Evil Long I Took Delight
  AME-W,M
In Excelsis Gloria
  OB-W,M
In Fairyland
  MH-W,M
In Father's Lovely Garden
  SiR-W,M
In Finding You I Found Love
  TVT-W,M
In Flanders' Fields
  GC-W,M
In France
  ASB3-W,M
In Freedom We're Born
  SSS-W,M
In God We Trust

CEM-W,M
In God's Eternity
  AHO-W,M
In God's Eyes
  WNF-W
In God's Holy House
  SoP-W,M
In Good Old Colony Times
  BSC-W MAS-W,M
**In Good Old Colony Times see also
  In the Good Old Colony Times**
In Great-Grandma's Day
  ASB3-W,M
In Happy Moments
  FSA1-W,M
In Happy Moments Day by Day
  AmH-W,M WiS7-W,M
In Hawaii
  FSA1-W,M SL-W,M
In Heaven Above
  SJ-W,M
In Heaven Soaring Up
  AHO-W,M
In Heavenly Love Abiding
  Hy-W,M WiS7-W,M
In Heavenly Pastures
  GH-W,M
In Heaven's Eyes
  GP-W,M
In Heaven's Vault above Me
  AS-W,M (Swedish)
In Hindustan
  FSA1-W,M
In His Name
  VB-W,M
In His Steps
  SOW1-W,M SOW2-W,M
In Izzenschnooken on the Lovely
  Essenzook Zee
  LMS-W,M
In Japan
  GUM1-W,M
In Jersey City
  SCa-W,M
In Jessie's City
  BSC-W
In Jesus
  OM-W,M
In Jesus' Blood
  WN-W,M
In Jesus' Face
  GH-W,M
In Johnson City
  SCa-W
In Kansas
  AFP-W FW-W
In Love with a Fool
  Mo-W,M OTO-W
In Marion
  ASB5-W,M
In May (Away, Lads, Away, Lads)
  FSA1-W,M
In May (We Hail the Happy
  Maytime)
  ASB3-W,M
In Me Ye Shall Have Peace
  GH-W,M
In Memoriam
  ASB5-W,M SL-W,M
In Mercy, Lord, Incline Thine Ear
  AHO-W,M
In Mexico
  FSA1-W,M
In My Attic
  AS-W,M
In My Bark Canoe
  ASB6-W,M

In My Garden Is a Hazel Tree
  MHB-W,M (Ukrainian)
In My Heart see In-a My Heart
In My Heart There Rings a Melody
  OM-W,M
In My Life
  BBe-W,M Be1-W,M TWS-W
  UBF-W,M WG-W,M
In My Merry Oldsmobile
  AH-W FSN-W,M GSN1-W,M
  HLS1-W,M MAB1-W MF-W,M
  MSA1-W OAP-W,M OBN-W,M
  OTJ-W,M RW-W,M
In My Name Written
  GH-W,M
In My Own Lifetime
  OTO-W Ro-W,M
In My Own Little Corner
  UBF-W,M
In My Right Hand I Have a Rose
  SGT-W,M
In My Robe of White
  AG-W,M HHa-W,M
In My Younger Days
  DBL-W
In Old Madrid
  AmH-W,M ESB-W,M (Spanish)
  HSD-W,M WiS8-W,M
In Old Versailles
  SL-W,M
In Old Vienna
  ASB5-W,M
In Olden Times
  LA-W,M (Spanish)
**In Other Words see Fly Me to the
  Moon**
In Our Little Home, Sweet Home
  MPM-W,M
In Our Little Salon for Two
  Mo-W,M
In Our United States
  LSO-W
In Pilgrim Life Our Rest
  AHO-W,M
In Pleasant Lands Have Fallen the
  Lines
  AHO-W,M
In Praise of Friendship
  LMR-W,M
In Praise of May
  GUM2-W,M
In Praise of the Pudding
  SR-W,M
In Praise of Women
  LN-W,M TW-W
In Sapphire Seas
  Fi-W,M
In School
  ASB1-W,M
In Scotland
  FSA2-W,M
In Seventy-Six
  NF-W
In Some Way or Other the Lord
  Will Provide
  AHO-W,M
In Someone's Shadow
  NB-W
In Spring
  MMW-W,M
In Summer
  SL-W,M
In Sweet Communion, Lord, with
  Thee
  Hy-W,M
In Switzerland
  ASB4-W,M

In Te Domine Speravi
  Boo-W,M (Latin Only)
In That Beautiful World on High
  RF-W,M
**In That Great Getting-Up Morning
  see In Dat Great Gittin'-Up
  Morning**
In That Morning
  SHS-W,M
**In That Morning All Day see In Dat
  Mornin' All Day**
In the Armor
  MU-W,M
In the Army
  AL-W
In the Baggage Coach Ahead
  FSN-W,M FSTS-W,M LSR-W,M
In the Beginning
  SHP-W,M
In the Bleak Midwinter
  GBC-W,M SJ-W,M
In the Boat
  CA-W,M LMR-W,M MHB-W,M
  TH-W,M
In the Bond
  UF-W,M
In the Candlelight
  Mo-W,M NM-W,M
In the Center
  BRB-W
In the Chapel in the Moonlight
  HLS2-W,M MF-W,M RDT-W,M
  TI1-W,M UFB-W,M
In the Christian's Home in Glory
  AME-W,M
In the Convent They Never Taught
  Me That
  Sw-W,M
In the Cool, Cool, Cool of the
  Evening
  AT-W,M MAB1-W MSA1-W
  OHF-W OnT1-W,M OTO-W
In the Cross of Christ
  GH-W,M
In the Cross of Christ I Glory
  AME-W,M Hy-W,M
In the Crowds That Came to Jesus
  SHP-W,M
In the Days of the Maccabees
  JS-W,M
In the Days When We Went Gold-
  Hunting
  SY-W,M
In the Distress upon Me
  AHO-W,M
In the Early Morning
  ASB6-W,M
In the Evening
  OTJ-W,M
In the Evening by the Moonlight
  ATS-W BH-W,M Bo-W,M
  BSB-W,M EFS-W,M FSTS-W,M
  FU-W,M FuB-W,M FW-W
  MAS-W,M OAP-W,M OS-W
  PoS-W,M RW-W,M TI1-W,M
  UFB-W,M
**In the Evening by the Moonlight
  see also Southern Memories**
In the Eye Abides the Heart
  FHR-W,M
In the Forest
  SL-W,M
In the Garden
  BSG-W,M BSP-W,M CEM-W,M
  HF-W,M HLS7-W,M JBF-W,M
  RDF-W,M RW-W,M Tr-W,M
In the Ghetto

GAR-W,M
In the Glen
  Fa-W,M
In the Gloaming
  AmH-W,M ATS-W BH-W,M
  FW-W HSD-W,M IL-W,M
  MAS-W,M NAS-W,M OS-W
  RW-W,M TH-W,M WiS8-W,M
In the Glow of Moonlight
  FSO-W,M (French)
In the Good Old Colony Times
  Oz1-W,M
In the Good Old Colony Times see also In Good Old Colony Times
In the Good Old Summertime
  Bo-W,M FSN-W,M FSTS-W,M
  FW-W FWS-W,M GSN1-W,M
  HLS1-W,M MAB1-W MF-W,M
  MSA1-W OAP-W,M OBN-W,M
  OTJ-W,M PoG-W,M RW-W,M
  TI1-W,M UFB-W,M
In the Good Ole Picket Line
  WW-W,M
In the Greenwood
  MML-W,M
In the Heaven Stars Are Shining
  SMa-W,M
In the Hills of Tennessee
  LJ-W,M
In the Hollow of His Hand
  GH-W,M
In the Hour of Trial
  AME-W,M FH-W,M Hy-W,M
In the Jailhouse Now
  LJ-W,M
In the Kingdom
  RF-W,M
In the King's Garden
  V A-W,M
In the Land of Fadeless Day
  AME-W,M
In the Looking Glass of Francis
  GBC-W,M
In the Mandarin's Orchid Garden
  LSO-W ReG-W,M
In the Manger
  FSO-W,M (French)
In the Merry Marianas
  AF-W
In the Middle of a Kiss
  OTO-W
In the Middle of an Island
  Mo-W,M NM-W,M
In the Middle of the Eighteenth
  Century
  TW-W
In the Midnight Hour
  MF-W,M
In the Misty Moonlight
  HLS9-W,M RW-W,M
In the Mood
  BBB-W,M GSN2-W,M MF-W,M
  TI1-W,M UFB-W,M
In the Morning
  ATS-W,M BSB-W,M Mo-W,M
  NH-W
In the Morning see also In de Mornin'
In the Morning by the Bright Light
  Oz2-W
In the Morning I Will Pray
  AHO-W,M
In the Morning When I Rise see In de Mornin When I Rise
In the Name of the Lord
  GP-W,M VB-W,M
In the Navy

ToO79-W,M
In the Night
  SRS-W,M
In the North Countree
  FSA2-W,M
In the Open
  FSA1-W,M
In the Orchard
  STS-W,M
In the Park
  MH-W,M
In the Park in Paree
  OTO-W
In the Pine
  ITP-W,M
In the Pines
  BIS-W,M BSo-W,M FPG-W,M
  FW-W LSR-W,M
In the Presence of the Lord
  GH-W,M
In the Promised Land
  VB-W,M
In the Rain
  SSe-W,M
In the Rain (Tony Hester)
  MCG-W,M
In the Reign of Justice
  AL-W
In the Shade of the Old Apple Tree
  FSN-W,M MAB1-W MF-W,M
  MSA1-W OAP-W,M OBN-W,M
  RC-W,M RW-W,M U-W
In the Shadow of His Wings
  GH-W,M
In the Silent Midnight
  GH-W,M
In the Silent Midnight Watches
  AHO-W,M
In the Starlight
  NAS-W,M
In the State of Arkansas
  SoC-W
In the Still of the Night
  DJ-W,M FrS-W,M HC1-W,M
  ML-W,M MU-W,M OTO-W
  TI1-W,M UFB-W,M
In the Still of the Night (I'll
  Remember)
  DRR-W,M
In the Sweet By and By
  AME-W,M FW-W HF-W,M
  HLS1-W,M HLS7-W,M HSD-W,M
  RDF-W,M RW-W,M SoC-W
  WiS7-W,M
In the Time of Roses
  NAS-W,M
In the Town
  OB-W,M
In the Toy Shop
  ASB2-W,M
In the Upper Room
  BSG-W,M BSP-W,M FS-W,M
In the Valley
  BT-W,M
In the Valley of the Moon
  Mo-W,M NM-W,M
In the Window Stands a Red Rose
  RuS-W,M (Russian)
In the Winter Time see In de Vinter Time
In the Wood
  MH-W,M
In the Woods
  MHB-W,M (German)
In Thee I Put My Trust
  MML-W,M
In Them Long Hot Summer Days

see In Dem Long Hot Summer
Days
In This Life
  Mo-W,M
In This Stable
  CCM-W,M
In This Street
  LA-W,M (Spanish)
In Three-Quarter Time
  LSO-W
In Thy Cleft, O Rock of Ages
  AME-W,M
In Times Like These (Barbara
  Mandrell)
  TOC83-W,M
In Times Like These (You Need a
  Savior)
  OM-W,M
In Union's Might
  AL-W
In Veradero
  MF-M
In Vernali Tempore
  GBC-W,M (Latin)
In Whispers Soft and Light
  TH-W,M
In Winter
  FSA2-W,M
In Your Arms
  SRE1-W,M
In Your Hands
  OGR-W,M
In Your Nest
  ASB3-W,M
In-a My Heart
  WN-W,M
In-A-Gadda-Da-Vida
  MF-W,M
Inca
  FSA2-W,M
Inch Worm
  TI2-W,M
Inchin' Along
  CA-W,M
Incidents in the Life of Pierce
  MPP-W
Include Me Out
  VS-W,M
Incognito Serenader
  SoF-W,M
Income Tax
  MSB-W
Inconsequence
  SL-W,M
Indeed I Do see 'Deed I Do
Indeed I Would
  IFM-W
Independence
  SBA-W
Independence Day
  AL-W ESU-W SSS-W,M
Independence Day Hora
  Mo-W,M NM-W,M OTO-W
Independent
  NF-W
Independent Farmer
  HSD-W,M
Independent Man
  AL-W
India Tea
  SBA-W
Indian Chant
  BMC-W,M
Indian Convert
  SHS-W,M
Indian Cradle Song
  ASB3-W,M

Indian Dance (Indians Dance with
Feathers)
GM-W,M
Indian Dance (Shake Your Rattles
High)
ASB1-W,M
Indian Fighters
Oz2-W,M
Indian Flea
NF-W
Indian Flute
LA-W,M (Spanish)
Indian Girl
RoS-W,M
Indian Hunter
Oz4-W,M
Indian Lake
HLS9-W,M
Indian Lass
SCa-W,M
**Indian Lass see also Fair Indian
Lass, Lass of Mohea, Little
Mohea, and Pretty Mauhee
(Mohea)**
Indian Love
EL-W,M (German)
Indian Love Call
HC2-W,M MF-W,M OHB-W,M
RM-W,M
Indian Mother's Song
ASB2-W,M
Indian Names
ASB6-W,M
Indian Song
BMM-W BSC-W
Indian Summer (An Indian on a
Lonely Hill)
ASB6-W,M
Indian Summer (Summer, You Old
Indian Summer)
MF-W,M
Indian Tom-Toms
OBN-M
Indian War Song
SSS-W,M
Indiana (Back Home Again in
Indiana)
BBB-W,M DJ-W,M TI1-W,M
TI2-W,M UFB-W,M
Indiana, Our Indiana
Mo-W,M TI2-W,M
Indians
MAR-W,M
Indian's Farewell
SHS-W,M
Indian's over the Border, The
SSS-W,M
Indian's Petition
ATS-W SHS-W,M
Indische Liebe
EL-W,M (German)
Indiscreet
Mo-W,M NM-W,M OTO-W
Industrial Emancipation
AL-W
Industrial Freedom
AL-W
Industrial Workers of the World
AFP-W
Ine Vine Violet
GB-W,M
Infant Holy
Hy-W,M JOC-W,M
Infant in the Stall
GBC-W,M
Infant So Gentle
CSF-W

Infantry
GI-W,M GO-W,M
Infantry, King of the Highway
GO-W
Infinite Light
OB-W,M
Inflammatus
WiS7-M
Ingle Nook
SL-W,M
Ingrate
VS-W,M
Injy Rubber Overcoat
Oz2-W,M
Inka Dinka Doo
TI1-W,M UFB-W,M
Innamorata
OTO-W WGB/P-W,M
Inner Light
TWS-W
Inner Thoughts
Ap-W,M
Innocent Eyes
TTH-W,M
Innocent Ingenue Baby
GOB-W,M
Innocent Lonesome Blue Baby
ReG-W,M
Innsbruck
MU-W,M
Insect Blues
LC-W
Inseparable
DP-W,M TI1-W,M UFB-W,M
Inside
TOC83-W,M
Inspector Clouseau Theme
RW-M
Inspiration
BMM-W
Installation Ode
GrM-W,M
Instant Karma
Be2-W,M WG-W,M
Instruments
LoS-W,M
**Instruments De Musique see Les
Instruments De Musique**
Integer Vitae
ESB-W,M (Latin) HSD-W,M (Latin)
LMR-W,M (Latin) TF-W,M (Latin)
Intelligent Contraband
SiS-W
Intende Voci Orationis Meae
Boo-W,M (Latin Only)
Interceding
HHa-W,M
Intercession
SHS-W,M
Intermezzo (A Love Story)
HLS5-W,M MF-W,M TI1-W,M
UFB-W,M
Intermezzo (from Mascagni's
Cavalleria Rusticana)
OBN-M
Intermezzo Russe
AmH-M
Intermission Riff
TI1-W,M UFB-W,M
Internationale
FW-W WW-W,M
Interplanetary Chastushki
RuS-W,M (Russian)
Interrogation
SHS-W,M
Interrupted Hope
MMM-W,M

Interrupted Melody
FSA1-W,M
Into the Tomb of Ages Past
SBJ-W,M
Into the Woods
EY-W,M
Into the Woods My Master Went
AHO-W,M
Intombed Here Lies Good Sir Harry
Boo-W,M
Intoxicated Rat
FW-W
Intreat Me Not (Maurits Kesnar)
WGB/P-W,M
**Intreat Me Not to Leave Thee see
Entreat Me Not to Leave Thee**
Intry Mintry
SiR-W,M
Invalid Corps
Sin-W,M SiS-W
Invictus
WiS9-W,M
Invisible
TTH-W,M
Invisible Hands
HLS7-W,M SUH-W,M
Invitation (Come, Ye Sinners, Poor
and Wretched)
SHS-W,M WN-W
Invitation (Theme)
HLS3-M RT5-M
Invitation (Will You Go, Pretty
Maid)
FSA2-W,M
Invitation, The
SBA-W
Invitation to North America
SI-W,M
Invitation to the Dance
RW-M
Invited to Take the Escort's Arm
NF-W
Invocation (Bortniansky)
MU-W,M
Invocation (Rise, My Soul, and
Stretch Thy Wings)
SHS-W,M
Invocation of Orpheus
MU-W,M (Italian)
Ionia
SHS-W,M
Iowa Corn Song
CoS-W,M Mo-W,M TI2-W,M
Ireland Must Be Heaven
CS-W,M RW-W,M
Ireland, Poor Ireland
VP-W
Ireland's Hurling Men
VP-W,M
Irene
HLS8-W,M Le-W,M NeF-W
RW-W,M
Irish Ballad
WF-W,M
Irish Carol
OB-W,M
Irish Girl
BSC-W
Irish Have a Great Day To-night
E-W,M
Irish Jubilee
EFS-W,M Oz3-W,M
Irish Labourer
VP-W,M
Irish Lady
BSC-W
Irish Love Song

LMR-W,M SL-W,M
Irish National Song see St. Patrick's Day
Irish Peddler see Peddler and His Wife
Irish Rover
  IS-W,M
Irish Trainman's Chant
  SoC-W
Irish Trot
  HSA-W,M
Irish Volunteer
  SiS-W
Irish Wake
  Oz3-W,M
Irish Washerwoman
  AmH-M BSC-W MF-M OTJ-M
  Oz3-W POT-M TI1-M UFB-M
  WN-W,M
Irishman's Epistle
  SI-W,M
Irishman's Epistle to the Officers and Troops at Boston
  SAR-W,M
Irishman's Observations on British Politics
  ANS-W
Irma La Douce
  UBF-W,M
Irma La Douce Theme (Look Again)
  RW-W,M
Iron Horse
  OHG-W,M
Iron! Iron! Iron!
  Sw-W,M
Iron Mountain Baby
  BSC-W
Ironing Day
  MH-W,M
Irresistible (Tango)
  AmH-M
Is Forever Longer Than Always
  BDP-W,M
Is He Satisfied
  HLS7-W,M
Is I Gotta Go to School, Ma?
  Mo-W,M NM-W,M OTJ-W,M
Is It a Race War?
  VS-W,M
Is It Only Cause You're Lonely
  TOH-W,M
Is It Really Me
  OHT-W,M
Is It True
  MoM-W
Is It True What They Say about Dixie
  OTJ-W,M
Is Jesus Able to Redeem?
  GH-W,M
Is Life a Boon?
  GiS-W,M MGT-W,M
Is My Name Written There
  AME-W,M
Is She Really Going Out with Him
  ToO79-W,M
Is That All There Is?
  TI2-W,M
Is That Mother Bending o'er Me?
  SiS-W
Is That My Mother?
  SiS-W
Is There Anyone Can Help Us
  AME-W,M
Is There No Balm in Christian Lands?
  AHO-W,M

Is This Land Your Land
  FW-W
Is This Love
  BHO-W,M
Is This Where I Wake Up
  OTO-W
Is Thy Cruse of Comfort Failing
  GH-W,M
Is Thy Heart Right with God
  AME-W,M
Is You Is, or Is You Ain't (My Baby)
  TI2-W,M
Is Your Lamp Burning
  GH-W,M
Isabeau Se Promene
  FSO-W,M (French)
Isabeau Went A-Strolling
  FSO-W,M (French)
Isabel
  TI1-W,M UFB-W,M
Isalei
  MML-W,M
I'se Goin' to Say Good Bye
  TMA-W,M
I'se Gwine Back to Dixie
  EFS-W,M WiS8-W,M
I'se Gwine to Weep No More
  TMA-W,M
I'se Mighty Tired
  My-W,M
I'se on de Way
  SiS-W
I'se the B'y
  FW-W
Isla Bonita see La Isla Bonita
Island (Iceland)
  SiP-W,M (Icelandic)
Island Girl
  GrS-W,M TI2-W,M
Island in the Sun
  OTJ-W,M
Island in the West Indies
  LSO-W
Island of Love
  SRE2-W,M
Island of the Mind
  TT-W,M
Islands in the Stream
  AWS-W,M CoH-W,M FOC-W,M
  TI2-W,M
Islay Maiden
  SeS-W,M
Isle of Beauty
  TF-W,M
Isle of Capri
  TI1-W,M UFB-W,M
Isle of St. Helena
  BSC-W
Isles of the South
  SHS-W,M
Isn't It a Pity
  GOB-W,M NYT-W,M RoE-W,M
Isn't It Cozy Here
  Mo-W,M OTO-W
Isn't It Fun
  MAR-W,M
Isn't It Grand, Boys
  IS-W,M
Isn't It Romantic
  AT-W,M HC2-W,M LM-W,M
  OTO-W TS-W WGB/P-W,M
Isn't She Lovely
  GSN5-W,M ToO76-W,M
Israel
  MF-M
Israeli Lullaby

OTJ-W,M SBF-W,M
Istanbul (Not Constantinople)
  NoS-W,M TI1-W,M UFB-W,M
It
  DS-W,M
It Ain't Cool to Be Crazy about You
  TTH-W,M
It Ain't Easy Bein' Easy
  EC-W,M TOC82-W,M
It Ain't Gonna Rain No Mo'
  OTJ-W,M
It Ain't Me Babe
  FoR-W,M
It Ain't Necessarily So
  DBC-W,M HC2-W,M LM-W,M
  LSO-W MF-W,M NYT-W,M
  OTO-W RW-W,M TI1-W,M
  UBF-W,M UFB-W,M
It Ain't No Harm to Trust in Jesus
  AN-W
It Ain't No Sin see 'Taint No Sin
It Ain't Nobody's Bizness see 'Tain't Nobody's Bizness
It Ain't What You Do see 'Taint What You Do
It All Depends on You
  FrS-W,M HC1-W,M MF-W,M
  OTO-W TI1-W,M UFB-W,M
It Amazes Me
  MF-W,M Mo-W,M NM-W,M
It Builds Its Coral Palaces
  ESU-W
It Came upon a Midnight Clear
  CEM-W,M FM-W,M FWS-W,M
  MF-W,M
It Came upon the Midnight Clear
  AHO-W,M AME-W,M AmH-W,M
  BCh-W,M BCS-W,M CC-W,M
  CCH-W,M CCM-W,M CI-W,M
  CSB-W,M CSF-W ESB-W,M
  FH-W,M HS-W,M Hy-W,M
  JOC-W,M MAB1-W MC-W,M
  MSA1-W OAP-W,M OM-W,M
  OPS-W,M OTJ-W,M RW-W,M
  SCS-W TH-W,M TI1-W,M
  UFB-W,M WiS7-W,M YC-W,M
It Can't Be Wrong
  HFH-W,M MF-W,M
It Could Be a Wonderful World
  SWF-W,M
It Could Happen to You
  AT-W,M ILT-W,M OTO-W
It Couldn't Be Done
  FSA2-W,M
It Couldn't Please Me More
  C-W,M
It Depends on What You Pay
  Fa-W,M
It Doesn't Have to Be That Way
  JC-W,M
It Don't Mean a Thing (If It Ain't Got That Swing)
  GMD-W,M TI2-W,M
It Fell upon a Summer Day
  Hy-W,M
It Goes Like It Goes
  HFH-W,M TOM-W,M
It Had to Be You
  MF-W,M RoE-W,M
It Happened in Monterey
  RW-W,M
It Happened in Sun Valley
  GSF-W,M
It Happens Every Spring
  MF-W,M
It Happens to the Best of Friends
  Sta-W,M

It Is Better to Laugh Than to Be
Sighing
MU-W,M
It Is Enough
FiS-W,M
It Is Finished
BSC-W GH-W,M
It Is Good
OGR-W,M VB-W,M
It Is Good to Be Alive
FSA2-W,M
It Is Good to Sing Thy Praises
Hy-W,M
It Is Hard to Love
NF-W
It Is I, Be Not Afraid
GrM-W,M
It Is Light
Boo-W,M
It Is No Secret (What God Can Do)
RDF-W,M TI2-W,M
It Is Not That I Love You Less
OH-W,M
It Is Thanksgiving Time Again
SHP-W,M
It Is the Oar That Impels Us On
CFS-W,M (French)
It Is Thy Servant's Prayer, Amen
GrG-W,M
It Is Well with My Soul
AME-W,M GH-W,M HF-W,M
It Isn't Easy to Love Like That
SYB-W,M
It Isn't Nice
JF-W,M SFF-W,M
It Just Suits Me
NH-W
It Keeps Right on A-Hurtin'
EP-W,M
It Looks Like a Big Night Tonight
RC-W,M
It Looks Like Rain in Cherry
Blossom Lane
MF-W,M OPS-W,M RDT-W,M
It Makes No Difference Now
JD-W,M SF-W,M
It May Be a Good Idea
A-W,M
It May Be Lon Chaney
HFH-W,M
It Might As Well Be Spring
DBC-W,M HC1-W,M HFH-W,M
L-W OTJ-W,M OTO-W TI1-W,M
TW-W UBF-W,M UFB-W,M
It Must Be
Boo-W,M
It Must Be Him
BHB-W,M MCG-W,M RW-W,M
It Never Entered My Mind
FrS-W,M HC1-W,M ILT-W,M
TI1-W,M TS-W UBF-W,M
UFB-W,M
It Never, Never Can Be Love
NaM-W,M
It Never Rains in Southern
California
GrS-W,M
It Never Was You
KH-W,M UBF-W,M
It Only Takes a Minute
ToO76-W,M
It Only Takes a Moment
HC2-W,M Mo-W,M NM-W,M
OTO-W TI2-W,M UBF-W,M
It Passeth Knowledge
GH-W,M
It Rained a Mist

ASB3-W,M
It Seems Like Old Times
MAB1-W,M MSA1-W
It Seems That God Bestowed
Somehow
AHO-W,M
It Should Be Easier Now
WNF-W
It Singeth Low in Every Heart
AME-W,M
It Started in Naples
OTO-W
It Sure Was
SuS-W,M
It Takes a Great Big Irish Heart to
Sing an Irish Song
RW-W,M
It Takes a Whole Lot of Human
Feeling
DB-W,M UBF-W,M
It Takes a Woman
Mo-W,M NM-W,M OTO-W
It Takes Love to Make a Home
Mo-W,M NM-W,M OTO-W
It Tastes Too Good to Be True
GSM-W,M
It Took a Miracle
HLS7-W,M
**It Was a Canadian Boy see 'Twas
a Canadian Boy**
It Was a Dream
MML-W,M TH-W,M
It Was a Good Time
HLS5-W,M MCG-W,M
It Was a Lover and His Lass
CSo-W,M EL-W,M FSS-W,M
FW-W Gu-W,M MML-W,M
OH-W,M SSB-W,M SSP-W
It Was a Very Good Year
GOI7-W,M OnT1-W,M OPS-W,M
It Was Almost Like a Song
HD-W,M TI2-W,M
**It Was at the Siege of Vicksburg
see 'Twas at the Siege of
Vicksburg**
It Was Dunois the Young and
Brave
SiP-W,M (French)
**It Was Early in the Spring see
'Twas Early in the Spring**
It Was Enough
OGR-W,M VB-W,M
It Was Good Enough for Grandma
TW-W
**It Was Nine Years Ago see 'Twas
Nine Years Ago**
It Was Not So to Be
AmH-W,M WiS8-W,M
**It Was on a Night Like This see In
a Little Spanish Town**
It Was on One Monday Morning
BSC-W
**It Was on That Night When
Doomed to Know see 'Twas on
That Night When Doomed to
Know**
**It Was on the Way to Bethlehem
see 'Twas on the Way to
Bethlehem**
It Was Poor Little Jesus
PSN-W,M
It Was Sad
AF-W
It Was Sad, Oh It Was Sad
AF-W
It Was Saturday Night
IL-W,M

**It Was Sunset in a Garden see
'Twas Sunset in a Garden**
**It Was the Night Before Christmas
see 'Twas the Night before
Christmas**
**It Was Winter and Blue Tory Noses
see 'Twas Winter and Blue Tory
Noses**
It Was Written in the Stars
Mo-W,M NM-W,M OTO-W
UBF-W,M
It Wasn't God Who Made Honky
Tonk Angels
CMG-W,M
It Wasn't Rainin' (When Noah Built
the Ark)
AG-W,M
It Were All Green Hills
OTO-W
**It Will Never Do to Give It Up So
see Twill Nebber Do to Gib It Up
So**
**It Will Not Be Long see Twill Not
Be Long**
It Wonders Me
PF-W,M
It Won't Be Long
BBe-W,M Be1-W,M TWS-W
It Won't Mean a Thing
Su-W,M
It Won't Seem Like Christmas
(without You)
TI1-W,M UFB-W,M
It Won't Stop
HLS7-W,M
It Would Have Been Wonderful
LN-W,M
Italia Beloved
TF-W,M
Italian National Hymn
HSD-W,M
Italian National Song
AmH-W,M
**Italian National Song see also
Garibaldi's War Hymn**
Italian Street Song
MF-W,M NaM-W,M
Itazuke Ort
AF-W
Itchin' for My Baby
CMF-W,M
Itik Besenda Gurau
SCL-W,M (Indonesian)
It'll Be Her
TOC82-W,M
It'll Be Me
TTH-W,M
It's
Mo-W,M NM-W,M
It's a Beautiful Day for a Ball Game
OTJ-W,M
It's a Big Wide Wonderful World
HC2-W,M Mo-W,M OTJ-W,M
PB-W,M TI2-W,M
It's a Blue World
TI1-W,M UFB-W,M
It's a Boy
Sh-W,M WA-W,M
It's a Deal
R-W,M
It's a Dirty Job
TOC83-W,M
It's a Fine Life
O-W,M
It's a Good Day
TI1-W,M UFB-W,M
It's a Good Thing to Join a Union

FW-W
It's a Good Time to Get Together
  LoS-W
It's a Grand Night for Singing
  BeL-W,M DBC-W,M HC1-W,M
  L-W OTJ-W,M OTO-W TI1-W,M
  UBF-W,M UFB-W,M
It's a Great Day for the Irish
  MAB1-W MSA1-W RW-W,M
It's a Hap-Hap-Happy Day
  AT-W,M OTJ-W,M OTO-W
It's a Happening World
  OnT6-W,M
It's a Happy Day
  GM-W,M
It's a Heartache
  TI2-W,M
It's a Helluva Way to Run a Love
  Affair
  PF-W,M
It's a Laugh
  WG-W,M
It's a Little Dolly
  SHP-W,M
It's a Long, Long Way to Tipperary
  FPS-W,M OS-W OTJ-W,M
  TI1-W,M UFB-W,M
It's a Long Way There
  ToO76-W,M
It's a Long Way to Daytona
  MF-W,M
It's a Long Way to the Top of the
  World
  BSo-W,M
It's A-Me O Lord
  NAS-W,M RW-W,M
It's A-Me O Lord see also It's Me
  O Lord, Standin' in the Need of
  Prayer, and 'Tis Me, O Lord
It's a Most Unusual Day
  GSN3-W,M HLS3-W,M RT4-W,M
  RW-W,M TI1-W,M UFB-W,M
It's a New World
  Mo-W,M NM-W,M OTO-W
It's a Nice Face
  SC-W,M
It's a Pity to Say Goodnight
  BBB-W,M TI2-W,M
It's a Scandal! It's an Outrage!
  TGO-W,M
It's a Short Life
  GO-W
It's a Sin to Tell a Lie
  MAB1-W MF-W,M MSA1-W
  T-W,M
It's a Small World
  NI-W,M On-W,M OTJ-W,M
  RW-W,M SBS-W,M
It's a Way We Have at Old Harvard
  HSD-W,M IL-W,M
It's a Well Known Fact
  I-W,M
It's a Windy Day on the Battery
  MPM-W,M
It's a Woman's Prerogative
  OHF-W
It's a Wonderful World
  SRE1-W,M
It's About That Time see It's 'Bout
  That Time
It's All in the Game
  MF-W,M TI2-W,M TOC83-W,M
It's All in the Movies
  NMH-W,M
It's All Right with Me
  DBC-W,M DJ-W,M FrS-W,M
  HC1-W,M LM-W,M ML-W,M

OTO-W TI1-W,M UBF-W,M
UFB-W,M
It's All the Same
  MLM-W,M
It's All Too Much
  TWS-W
It's All Up in Dixie
  SiS-W
It's All Yours
  TW-W
It's Almost Day
  FW-W
It's Almost Done
  FW-W
It's Always No, No, No
  NN2-W,M
It's Always You
  OTO-W
It's Been a Great Afternoon
  NMH-W,M
It's Been a Long Long Time
  Mo-W,M NM-W,M On-W,M
  OTO-W TI2-W,M
It's Been So Long
  WDS-W,M
It's Been So Long, Darlin'
  OGC2-W,M
It's Beginning to Look a Lot Like
  Christmas
  TI2-W,M
It's Better with a Union Man
  WW-W,M
It's 'Bout That Time
  MF-M
It's Christmas All over the World
  BCS-W,M
It's Christmas Once Again
  HSS-W,M HST-W,M
It's Christmas Time All over the
  World
  BCh-W,M
It's Delightful Down in Chile
  V-W,M
It's De-Lovely
  DBC-W,M ML-W,M OTO-W
  TI1-W,M UBF-W,M UFB-W,M
It's Delovely
  TW-W
It's D'Lovely
  HC1-W,M
It's Easter
  MAR-W,M
It's Easter Today
  ASB1-W,M
It's Easy to Remember
  AT-W,M FPS-W,M LM-W,M
  OTO-W TS-W WGB/P-W,M
It's Easy to Say
  HFH-W,M
It's for You
  Be1-W,M
It's Fun to Pick Potatoes
  SOO-W,M
It's Fun to Think
  Mo-W,M NM-W,M OTO-W
It's Getting Harder All the Time
  OnT6-W,M
It's G-L-O-R-Y to Know That I'm
  S-A-V-E-D
  FW-W
It's Going to Take Some Time
  MF-W,M
It's Got to Be Love
  TS-W
It's Hard, Ain't It Hard
  OFS-W,M
It's Hard to Be a Nigger

AFP-W
It's How We Drive the Winter Out
  OTJ-W,M
It's Impossible
  FPS-W,M (Spanish) LM-W,M
  MCG-W,M On-W,M RW-W,M
It's in Every One of Us
  DPE-W,M
It's in His Kiss
  TI2-W,M
It's in His Kiss see also Shoop
  Shoop Song
It's in My Mind to Ramble
  BSo-W,M
It's Jolly to Swing
  Boo-W,M
It's Just a House without You
  TI2-W,M
It's Just a Matter of Time
  ATC1-W,M FRH-W,M TI2-W,M
It's Just the First Farewell
  VB-W,M
It's Legitimate
  DR-W,M
It's Lookin' fer Railroad Bill
  NH-W
It's Magic
  MF-W,M
It's Me
  JF-W,M
It's Me O Lord
  FN-W,M FW-W TH-W,M
It's Me O Lord see also It's A-Me
  O Lord, Standin' in the Need of
  Prayer, and 'Tis Me, O Lord
It's Movin' Day
  NH-W
It's My Party
  DRR-W,M PoG-W,M TI2-W,M
  TRR-W,M
It's My Turn
  TOM-W,M
It's No Business of Mine
  Oz3-W,M
It's Not a Song
  VB-W,M
It's Not Cricket to Picket
  TW-W
It's Not Easy (from Peter Pan)
  NI-W,M
It's Not Easy (Jagger/Richards)
  RoS-W,M
It's Not for Me to Say
  MF-W,M
It's Not for Me to Understand
  WNF-W
It's Not Love (but It's Not Bad)
  NMH-W,M
It's Not So Easy Leavin'
  PoG-W,M
It's Not Supposed to Be That Way
  WNF-W
It's Not the First Mile
  BSG-W,M BSP-W,M WN-W,M
It's Not Unusual
  TI2-W,M
It's Not Where You Start
  MF-W,M
It's Now or Never
  FOC-W,M TI1-W,M UFB-W,M
It's Only a Paper Moon
  FPS-W,M FrS-W,M HC1-W,M
  MF-W,M OHB-W,M TI1-W,M
  TW-W UFB-W,M
It's Only Love
  BBe-W,M Be1-W,M TWS-W
It's Only Make Believe

DRR-W,M
It's Only Rock 'n Roll
  RoS-W,M
It's Our Little Secret
  Mo-W,M OTO-W
It's Out of This World
  AG-W,M
It's Over
  ELO-W,M TFC-W,M
It's Pretty Soft for Simon
  NaM-W,M
It's Raining
  ASB1-W,M SSe-W,M
It's Raining on Prom Night
  Gr-W,M Mo-W,M OTO-W
It's Simple
  TW-W
It's Snowing
  SOO-W,M
It's So Easy
  TI2-W,M
It's So Easy to Say
  ILF-W,M
It's So Nice to Have a Man around
  the House
  Mo-W,M NM-W,M TI2-W,M
It's Spring
  SOO-W,M
It's Such a Pretty World Today
  CSp-W,M
It's Super Nice
  Mo-W,M NM-W,M OTO-W
It's Superman
  Mo-W,M NM-W,M OTJ-W,M
  OTO-W
It's That Bad Railroad Bill
  NH-W
It's the Bible against the Bottle
  GS1-W
It's the Hard-Knock Life
  TI2-W,M UBF-W,M
It's the Little Things in Texas
  UBF-W,M
It's the Real Thing
  GSM-W,M
It's the Same Old Shillelagh
  RW-W,M TI1-W,M UFB-W,M
It's the Same the Whole World
  Over
  GO-W,M HAS-W,M PO-W,M
It's the Syme the Whole World
  Over
  FW-W
It's the Talk of the Town
  MF-W,M OPS-W,M PB-W,M
  TI2-W,M
It's Time I Was a Bride
  Oz2-W
It's Time to Start
  HJ-W,M
It's Today
  Mo-W,M NM-W,M
It's Too Late
  MF-W,M
It's Too Soon to Know
  Mo-W,M NM-W,M
It's Tragic
  AF-W
It's Tulip Time in Holland
  MR-W,M
It's 1200 Miles from Palm Springs
  to Texas
  Mo-W,M NM-W,M
It's Up to You and Me
  OTJ-W,M
It's Who You Love
  TOC82-W,M

It's Wonderful see 'S Wonderful
It's You
  TOC83-W,M
It's You or No One
  MF-W,M
It's Your Fault
  Mo-W,M NM-W,M OTO-W
It's Your Life
  DBL-W
Itsy Bitsy Spider
  CSS-W
Itsy Bitsy Teenie Weenie Yellow
  Polkadot Bikini
  DRR-W,M GAR-W,M HR-W
  MF-W,M NoS-W,M TI2-W,M
Ivan Skizavitzsky Skivar
  Bo-W,M
I've a Longing in My Heart for You,
  Louise
  EFS-W,M
I've a Message f'om Ma Lord
  BDW-W,M
I've a Message from the Lord,
  Hallelujah
  AME-W,M
I've Been A-List'ning All de Night
  Long
  RW-W,M
**I've Been A-List'ning All de Night
  Long see also I Been A-Listenin'**
I've Been Everywhere
  OGC2-W,M TI2-W,M
I've Been Lying in a Foxhole
  GI-W
I've Been Roaming
  OH-W,M
I've Been to Gather Mussels
  FSF-W (French)
I've Been Toilin' at de Hill
  RF-W,M
I've Been with Jesus
  HLS7-W
I've Been Workin' on de Railroad
  IL-W,M
I've Been Workin' on the Railroad
  ATS-W BMC-W,M Bo-W CSS-W
  FW-W MAS-W,M OTJ-W,M
  RSD-W,M VA-W,M WU-W,M
I've Been Working on the Railroad
  EFS-W,M FU-W,M FuB-W,M
  FWS-W,M GuC-W,M HS-W,M
  LSR-W,M TI1-W,M UFB-W,M
**I've Been Working on the Railroad
  see also Dinah**
I've Built Me a Neat Little Cot,
  Darling
  Oz4-W
I've Come to Wive It Wealthily in
  Padua
  TW-W
I've Confessed to the Breeze
  NN2-W,M NN7-W,M
I've Danced So Much
  FSO-W,M (French)
I've Done My Work
  SS-W
I've Fallen in the Battle
  SiS-W
I've Found a Friend
  GH-W,M
I've Found a Friend, O Such a
  Friend
  AME-W,M Hy-W,M
I've Got a Crush on You
  DC-W,M FPS-W,M FrS-W,M
  GOB-W,M LSO-W MF-W,M
  NYT-W,M OHB-W,M

I've Got a Feelin' You're Foolin'
  RW-W,M
I've Got a Feeling
  TWS-W
I've Got a Feeling I'm Falling
  RW-W,M
I've Got a Gal in Kalamazoo
  HFH-W,M MF-W,M TOM-W,M
I've Got a Little List
  GiS-W,M MGT-W,M
I've Got a Lovely Bunch of
  Cocoanuts
  NoS-W,M OTJ-W,M TI2-W,M
I've Got a Mother in de Heaven
  RF-W,M
I've Got a Pocketful of Dreams
  HLS2-W,M MAB1-W MSA1-W
  RW-W,M
I've Got a Shoe
  SoF-W,M
I've Got a Tiger by the Tail
  HLS9-W,M
I've Got a Woman
  HRB2-W,M
I've Got a Wonderful Future behind
  Me
  WNF-W
I've Got Five Dollars
  OHB-W,M TS-W
I've Got Love on My Mind
  SoH-W,M TI1-W,M UFB-W,M
I've Got Mine
  Lo-W,M
I've Got My Questionnaire
  LC-W
I've Got No Strings
  NI-W,M TI1-W,M UFB-W,M
I've Got No Use for the Women
  GeS-W,M HWS-W,M
I've Got Rings on My Fingers
  MF-W,M
I've Got Sixpence
  AF-W
I've Got Tears in My Ears (from
  Lyin' on My Back in My Bed
  While I Cry over You)
  WF-W,M
I've Got That Cub Scout Spirit
  CSS-W
I've Got That Joy
  JF-W,M
I've Got That Scouting Spirit
  Bo-W
I've Got the World on a String
  MF-W,M NK-W,M TI2-W,M
I've Got to Be There
  ReG-W,M
I've Got to Find My Baby
  SRE2-W,M
I've Got to Get a Message to You
  TI1-W,M UFB-W,M
**I've Got to Get a Message to You
  see also I've Gotta Get a
  Message to You**
I've Got to Know
  FW-W
I've Got You under My Skin
  BeL-W,M DJ-W,M FrS-W,M
  HC2-W,M LM-W,M ML-W,M
  OTO-W TI1-W,M UFB-W,M
I've Got Your Number
  MF-W,M Mo-W,M NM-W,M
  OTO-W TI2-W,M UBF-W,M
I've Gotta Crow
  Mo-W,M NM-W,M OTO-W
  UBF-W,M
I've Gotta Get a Message to You

TRR-W,M

**I've Gotta Get a Message to You
see also I've Got to Get a
Message to You**

I've Grown Accustomed to Her
Face
DBC-W,M HC2-W,M HLS3-W,M
ILT-W,M LL-W,M OTO-W
RW-W,M TI1-W,M TW-W
UBF-W,M UFB-W,M

I've Had a Beautiful Time
NMH-W,M

I've Had My Moments
WDS-W,M

I've Heard about a City
HLS7-W,M

I've Heard It All Before
OTO-W Sh-W,M

I've Heard That Song Before
HC2-W,M MF-W,M Mo-W,M
NM-W,M OTO-W TI2-W,M

I've Heard the Thunder
VB-W,M

I've Just Come from the Fountain
WN-W,M

I've Just Got In across the Plains
BSC-W

I've Just Seen a Face
BBe-W,M TWS-W

I've Just Seen Her (As Nobody
Else Has Seen Her)
Mo-W,M NM-W,M OTO-W

I've Just Seen Jesus
VB-W,M

I've Left the Snow-Clad Hills
HSD-W,M

I've Lost My Mistress, Horse, and
Wife
Boo-W,M

I've Never Been in Love Before
ILT-W,M TI2-W,M TW-W
UBF-W,M

I've Never Been to Me
TOC82-W,M

I've Never Forgotten
Mo-W,M NM-W,M OTO-W

I've Never Loved Him Better
HHa-W,M

I've Never Said I Love You
Mo-W,M OTO-W

I've No Time to Be A-Sighin'
SL-W,M

I've Only Loved Three Women
LJ-W,M

I've Passed the Cross
GH-W,M

I've Reached the Land of Corn and
Wine
AHO-W,M

I've Seen the Lightning Flashing
AME-W,M

I've Seen the Smiling
Boo-W,M

I've Set My Face for Zion's
Kingdom
GB-W,M

I've Still Got My Health
ML-W,M TW-W

I've Told Ev'ry Little Star
L-W MA-W,M RW-W,M TI1-W,M
UFB-W,M

I've Vowed to Die a Maid
SR-W,M

I've Wandered Far Away from God
AME-W,M

I've Worked Eight Hours This Day
EFS-W,M

Ivory Palaces
BSG-W,M BSP-W,M HLS7-W,M

Ivory Tower
Mo-W,M NM-W,M TI2-W,M

Ivy
Mo-W,M NM-W,M TI2-W,M

Ivy and the Oak
Sw-W,M

Ivy Green
ESB-W,M

J

J.A.G. Song
GI-W

J.B. Marcum
FSU-W

J.C. Holmes Blues
LSR-W,M

J C U B A K
Boo-W,M

Ja-Da
BH-W,M GG2-W,M GSN1-W,M
HLS1-W,M OS-W RDT-W,M
RW-W,M

Ja Posejah Lubenice
HSA-W,M (Serbo-Croatian)

Ja Vi Elsker Dette Landet
SiP-W,M (Norwegian)

Jack and Dinah Want Freedom
NF-W

Jack and Gill
HSD-W,M

Jack and Jean
FSA2-W,M

Jack and Jill
AmH-W,M ASB2-W,M BBF-W,M
Boo-W,M CSo-W,M HS-W,M
LMR-W,M

Jack and Jill Went up the Hill
OTJ-W,M

Jack and Joe
Oz4-W

Jack, Be Nimble
ASB3-W,M MH-W,M OTJ-W,M

Jack Binnacle and Queen Victoria
MSB-W

Jack Boy, Ho
Boo-W,M

Jack, Can I Ride
AFS-W,M

Jack Combs
FSU-W

Jack Combs' Death Song
SoC-W

Jack Combs' Murder
SoC-W

Jack Cramer
ANS-W

Jack Donahoo
FMT-W

Jack Frost
GM-W,M SOO-W,M SSe-W,M

**Jack Hammer John see
Jackhammer John**

Jack-in-the-Box
AST-W,M MAR-W,M MH-W,M
RSL-W,M

**Jack-in-the-Box Restaurants Jingle
see Take Life a Little Easier**

Jack-in-the-Pulpit
MH-W,M

Jack Is Every Inch a Sailor
FW-W

Jack Mainmast
ANS-W

Jack Munroe
BSC-W

Jack-o'-Lantern
SSe-W,M

Jack-o'-Lantern (Burns His Candle)
SOO-W,M

Jack-o'-Lantern (Jack, Jack-o'-
Lantern, I Wonder If You Know)
ASB2-W,M

Jack-o'-Lantern (To Scare Some
Folks on Halloween)
MAR-W,M

Jack of Diamonds
FMT-W RW-W,M

Jack Returned from Sea
MSB-W

Jack Robinson
MSB-W

Jack Sprat
OTJ-W,M

Jack the Miller
Oz1-W,M

Jack the Sailor
BSC-W

Jack Thou'rt...Come, Come
Boo-W,M

Jack Was Every Inch a Sailor
FW-W

Jackaroe
SCa-W

Jackass Song
SSo-W,M

Jackhammer John
Am-W,M TO-W,M

Jackie Frazier
SCa-W

**Jackie Frazier see also Jacky
Freasher**

**Jackie Gleason Show (Theme) see
Melancholy Serenade**

Jackson (Oh Jackson's on the
Sea, Jackson's on the Shore)
ATS-W,M FW-W

Jackson (We Got Married in a
Fever)
CSp-W,M GAR-W,M GCM-W,M
MF-W,M

Jackson and Liberty
AL-W

Jackson Put the Kettle On
NF-W

Jacky Freasher
SCa-W,M

Jacob, Drink
NAS-W

Jacob the Pilgrim
ITP-W,M

Jacob's Ladder
ASB5-W,M BM-W Bo-W,M
CA-W,M CCH-W,M FSU-W FW-W
GBC-W,M GuC-W,M HS-W,M
LoS-W,M MG-W,M NSS-W
OB-W,M Oz2-W,M RDF-W,M
SoF-W,M YS-W,M

Jacques D'Iraque
OTO-W UBF-W,M

Jag Reser Nu Bort
SE-W (Swedish)

Jagdlied
AS-W,M (German)

J'ai Cueilli La Belle Rose
CFS-W,M (French)

J'ai Du Bon Tabac
Ch-W (French Only)

J'ai Encore Un Tel Pate
GUM2-W,M

J'ai Fais Tou' L' Tour

CLaL-W,M (French)
J'ai Fait Longtemps La Vie De Fille
CaF-W (French Only)
J'ai Fait Une Maitresse
FSO-W,M (French)
J'ai Passe Devant Ta Porte
CLaL-W,M (French)
J'ai Rencontre Trois Jolies
Demoiselles
CaF-W (French Only)
J'ai Tant Danse
FSO-W,M (French)
J'ai Tant D'Enfants A Marier
FSO-W,M (French)
J'ai 'Te Au Bal
CLaL-W,M (French)
J'ai Travaille Chez Des Rousseau
CaF-W (French Only)
J'ai Trouve Le Seigneur
SSN-W,M (French)
J'ai Trouve Une Maitresse
FSO-W,M (French)
Jail House
SSo-W,M
Jailer's Daughter
SCa-W,M
Jailhouse Blues
Le-W,M NeF-W,M
Jailhouse Rock
ERM-W,M EY-W,M GAR-W,M
HFH-W,M ILF-W,M MF-W,M
RB-W RW-W,M SRE1-W,M
TI1-W,M UFB-W,M
Jaime's Blues
FSB3-M
Jake and Roanie
HB-W,M
Jalousie (Jealousy)
MF-W,M
Jam at Gerry's Rock
TBF-W,M
Jam Factory
GI-W,M
Jam on Gerry's Rock
FW-W IHA-W,M
Jam Up Twist
HRB2-M
Jamaica Farewell
GuC-W,M LaS-W,M OFS-W,M
OPS-W,M OTJ-W,M PB-W,M
Jambalaya (on the Bayou)
FOC-W,M HW-W,M TI2-W,M
Jamboree Hymn see Camporee
Jamboree Jones
OHF-W
James (Hold the Ladder Steady)
HR-W
James Bird
BSC-W SI-W,M
James Bond Theme
RW-M
James Brown
AFP-W AL-W
James Harris (The Daemon Lover)
FMT-W SCa-W,M
Jamestown Homeward Bound
SA-W,M
Jamie's on the Stormy Sea
HSD-W,M SY-W,M
Jane an' Louisa
SGT-W,M
Jane, Jane
FW-W OTJ-W,M
Janey
OTO-W
Janice and Jarvis and Me
TW-W

Janie Sharp Ballet
FMT-W
January
MH-W,M SiR-W,M
January and February
MH-W,M SSe-W,M
January Carol
OB-W,M
**Japanese National Song see
Kimigayo**
Japanese Rain Song
RSL-W,M
Japanese Sandman
MF-W,M RC-W,M T-W,M
Japanese War Chant
AF-W
Jarabe
ASB5-W,M
Jarabe Tapatio
CA-W,M
Jarama Valley
FW-W
**Jardin D'Amour see Le Jardin
D'Amour**
Jargon
EA-W,M
Jasmine
Mo-W,M NM-W,M
Jasmine Flower
MML-W,M SCL-W,M
Java
OPS-M
Java Jive
MF-W,M
J'avais Jure Dedans Ma Jeunesse
CaF-W (French Only)
J'avais Une Vielle Grand'mere
FSO-W,M (French)
Jawbone
NF-W
Jawbone Song
Oz2-W,M
Jay Bird (Jay Bird, Sittin' on a
Limb)
TMA-W,M
Jay Bird (Pulling a Two Mule Plow)
SCa-W,M
Jay Gooze
NH-W
Jay Gould's Daughter
FW-W IHA-W,M
Jaybird (De Jaybird Jump from
Lim' to Lim')
NF-W
Jaybird Died with the Whooping
Cough
NF-W
Jaybird's Altar
Oz3-W
Jazz Corner
MF-M
Jazz Me Blues
TI2-W,M
Jazzman
MF-W,M ToO76-W,M
Je Chante, Je Bois, Et Je Mange
CaF-W (French Only)
Je M'ai Fait Une Maitresse
CaF-W (French Only)
Je Me Suis Retourne
CaF-W (French Only)
Je M'en Fiche Du Sex-Appeal
TS-W
Je M'en Vais Au Chez Des Iles
CaF-W (French Only)
Je Passe Du Long La Mer
CaF-W (French Only)

Je Pense A Toi Ma Bien-Amiee
CaF-W (French Only)
Je R'commence Eine Fois Dans Ma
Vie
CaF-W (French Only)
Je Suis Deserte
CaF-W (French Only)
Je Suis Grand Galle
CaF-W (French Only)
Je Suis Plu' Amant
CaF-W (French Only)
Je Suis Plus Fiere Que Charles
D'Espagne
CaF-W (French Only)
Je Veux M' Marier
CLaL-W,M (French)
Je Voudrais
SSN-W,M (French)
Jealous
TI2-W,M
Jealous Brothers
Oz1-W,M
Jealous Lover
BSC-W FMT-W ITP-W,M
Oz2-W,M TBF-W.M
Jealous Lover of Lone Green
Valley
Oz2-W
Jealousy see Jalousie
Jean
DC-W,M HFH-W,M MF-W,M
TOM-W,M
Jean Harlow
Le-W,M
Jeanie with the Light Brown Hair
ASB5-W,M ATS-W BH-W,M
EFS-W,M FHR-W,M FW-W
HS-W,M IL-W,M MAB1-W
MF-W,M MHB-W,M MSA1-W
OAP-W,M OS-W OTJ-W,M
RW-W,M SL-W,M SoF-W,M
SSF-W,M SSFo-W,M U-W
UF-W,M WiS8-W,M
Jeanneton Prend Sa Faucille
FSF-W (French)
Jeannette and Her Little Wooden
Shoes
Sw-W,M
Jeannie
TVT-W,M
Jeannine (I Dream of Lilac Time)
GG2-W,M HLS2-W,M OP1-W,M
RW-W,M
Jeep Is Jumpin'
GMD-W,M
Jeepers
GI-W
Jeepers Creepers
MF-W,M OHB-W,M OHF-W
Jeff Buckner
AFP-W
Jeff Davis' Dream
Sin-W,M SiS-W
Jeff Davis in Crinoline
SiS-W
Jeff in Petticoats
HAS-W,M SiS-W
Jefferson
SHS-W,M
Jefferson and Liberty
FW-W IHA-W,M MPP-W,M
SWF-W,M
Jefferson D
SiS-W
Jefferson Davis in Prison
SiS-W
Jeffersons (Theme) see Movin' On

Up
Jefferson's Violin
ASB5-W,M

Jeg Elsker Dig see I Love Thee
Jehovah
OGR-W,M VB-W,M
Jehovah, God, Who Dwelt of Old
AHO-W,M
Jehovah Has Triumph, Messiah Is
King
MoM-W
Jehovah, Herr Und Majestat
AHO-W,M (German)
Jehovah, Lord and Majesty
AHO-W,M (German)
Jehoviah Hallelujah
NSS-W
Jelly Roll
LC-W,M
Jennie Jenkins
HS-W,M SCL-W,M
**Jennie Jenkins see also Jenny
Jenkins and Jinny Jenkins**
Jennie Johnson
TMA-W,M
Jennie, the Flower of Kildare
FoM-W,M
Jennie's Coming o'er the Green
FHR-W,M
**Jennie's Coming o'er the Green
see also Jenny's Coming o'er the
Green**
Jenny
EL-W,M UBF-W,M
Jenny, Come Tie My Tie
SOO-W,M
Jenny Jenkins
FW-W IHA-W,M LW-W,M
OHO-W,M OTJ-W,M RW-W,M
**Jenny Jenkins see also Jennie
Jenkins and Jinny Jenkins**
Jenny Jones
OTJ-W,M
Jenny June
FHR-W,M
Jenny Lind Mania
SY-W
Jenny Lind Polka
PT-M
Jenny, My Blithest Maid
SR-W,M
Jenny Went Out Cutting Rushes
FSF-W (French)
Jenny's Coming o'er the Green
SSFo-W,M
**Jenny's Coming o'er the Green see
also Jennie's Coming o'er the
Green**
Jerdan's Mills A-Grinding
NSS-W
Jeremiah, Blow the Fire
OTJ-W,M
Jericho (From the Burning of the
Desert Came the People of the
Lord)
VB-W,M
Jericho (God Said to His People,
Possess the Promised Land)
AG-W,M
Jerry, Go and Oil That Car
SWF-W,M
Jerry, Go Ile That Car
LSR-W,M
Jerry Hall
SOO-W,M
Jersey Bounce
MF-W,M RW-W,M TI1-W,M

UFB-W,M
Jersey City
SCa-W
Jerusalem (Charles Gounod)
SL-W,M
Jerusalem (Henry Parker)
AmH-W,M HSD-W,M WiS7-W,M
Jerusalem (I'm on My Journey
Home, to the New Jerusalem)
SHS-W,M
Jerusalem (William Blake)
U-W
Jerusalem, Jerusalem
LM-W,M OTJ-W,M TI1-W,M
UFB-W,M
Jerusalem Mornin'
RF-W,M
Jerusalem My Happy Home
AME-W,M GH-W,M SJ-W,M
Jerusalem the Golden
AME-W,M AmH-W,M CEM-W,M
ESB-W,M HSD-W,M Hy-W,M
SL-W,M WiS7-W,M
Jerusalem! Thou That Killest the
Prophets
FiS-W,M (German)
Jes Like John
BDW-W,M
Jesous Ahatonhia
AHO-W,M (Algonquin, French)
FoS-W,M SFB-W,M
Jesse James
AH-W,M BIS-W,M BSo-W,M
FAW-W,M FG1-W,M FMT-W
FPG-W,M FSB1-W,M FVV-W,M
FW-W GuC-W,M HWS-W,M
LSR-W,M OTJ-W,M Oz2-W,M
PG1-W,M SoC-W
Jessica's Day
MF-M
Jessica's Theme
DC-M HFH-M
Jesu, Come on Board
AHO-W,M (German)
Jesu, Joy of Man's Desiring
JBF-M LMR-W,M MU-W,M TI1-M
UFB-M WGB/P-M WiS9-W,M
**Jesu, Joy of Man's Desiring see
also Joy (Jesu, Joy of Man's
Desiring)**
Jesu, Komm Herein
AHO-W,M (German)
Jesu, to Thee My Heart I Bow
AHO-W,M
Jesus a Child His Course Begun
AHO-W,M
Jesus and Shall It Ever Be
AME-W,M GH-W
Jesus, at Whose Supreme
Command
AME-W,M
Jesus Born in Bethlehem
GBC-W,M
Jesus Borned in Bethlea
SAm-W,M SHP-W,M
Jesus Call Your Lambs
VB-W,M
Jesus Calls Thee
GH-W,M
Jesus Calls Us
IH-M OM-W,M
Jesus Calls Us o'er the Tumult
AME-W,M CEM-W,M FH-W,M
Hy-W,M
Jesus Came on Christmas Day
SHP-W,M
Jesus Came the Heavens Adoring

AME-W,M
Jesus Cares for Me
CEM-W,M
Jesus Christ (Woody Guthrie)
AFP-W JF-W,M PSN-W
Jesus Christ Is Passing By
GH-W,M
Jesus Christ Is Risen
SHP-W,M
Jesus Christ Is Risen Today
AME-W,M FH-W,M Hy-W,M
SHP-W,M SJ-W,M
Jesus Christ Is Risen To-day
WiS7-W,M
Jesus Christ Our Saviour
GH-W,M
Jesus Demands This Heart of Mine
AME-W,M
Jesus Don't Give Up on Me
CEM-W,M
Jesus Enthroned and Glorified
AHO-W,M
Jesus, Friend, So Kind and Gentle
Hy-W,M
Jesus Goin' to Make Up My Dyin'
Bed
Me-W,M MoM-W,M
Jesus Gonna Make Up My Dyin'
Bed
J-W,M
Jesus Got His Business Fix
RTH-W
Jesus Great Shepherd of the
Sheep
AME-W,M
Jesus Hail! Enthroned in Glory
GH-W
Jesus Heal de Sick
AAF-W,M
Jesus Healed the Crippled Children
SHP-W,M
Jesus, I Come
AME-W,M GH-W,M
Jesus, I Come to Thee
AHO-W,M
Jesus, I Live to Thee
AHO-W,M
Jesus, I Love and Praise and Adore
AME-W,M
Jesus I Love Thy Charming Name
AME-W,M
Jesus, I My Cross Have Taken
AME-W,M Hy-W,M OM-W,M
Jesus, I Will Trust Thee
GH-W,M
Jesus, in Sickness and in Pain
AHO-W,M
Jesus in Your Heart
VB-W,M
Jesus Is a Rock
Oz4-W
Jesus Is All the World to Me
AME-W,M
Jesus Is All You Need
BSG-W,M BSP-W,M
Jesus Is Calling
AME-W,M BNG-W,M GH-W,M
Jesus Is Coming
GH-W,M
Jesus Is Coming Again
BSG-W,M BSP-W,M
Jesus Is Coming Soon
BSG-W,M BSP-W,M HHa-W,M
**Jesus Is Going to Make Up My
Dying Bed see Jesus Goin' to
(Gonna) Make Up My Dyin' Bed**
Jesus Is King of All the Church

SHP-W,M
Jesus Is Lord
VB-W,M
Jesus Is Mighty to Save
GH-W,M
Jesus Is Mine
GH-W,M
Jesus Is My Saviour
GH-W,M
Jesus Is Tenderly Calling
CEM-W,M
Jesus Is Tenderly Calling Thee
Home
AME-W,M Hy-W,M
Jesus Is Your Ticket to Heaven
AG-W,M TOC82-W,M
Jesus, Jesus, Rest Your Head
JOC-W,M
Jesus, Keep Me near the Cross
AHO-W,M AME-W,M Hy-W,M
**Jesus, Keep Me Near the Cross
see also Near the Cross**
Jesus, Kneel beside Me
Hy-W,M
Jesus Knows Thy Sorrow
GH-W,M
Jesus, Lead the Way
Hy-W,M
Jesus Lives
WiS7-W,M
Jesus, Lord to Me
GP-W,M OGR-W,M VB-W,M
Jesus, Lover of My Soul
AME-W,M AmH-W,M CEM-W,M
FH-W,M GH-W,M HF-W,M
Hy-W,M IH-M JBF-W,M
NAS-W,M RDF-W,M TB-W,M
WiS7-W,M
Jesus Loves Even Me
AME-W,M GH-W,M
Jesus Loves Me
BNG-W,M FH-W,M GH-W,M
MAB1-W MSA1-W OTJ-W,M
Jesus Loves Me This I Know
AHO-W,M AME-W,M Hy-W,M
Jesus Loves the Little Children
RDF-W,M
Jesus' Lullaby
CC-W,M
Jesus Made Me Higher
CEM-W,M
Jesus Master, O Discover
AHO-W,M
Jesus, Meine Zuversicht
LTL-W,M (German Only)
Jesus Merciful
Hy-W,M
Jesus Merciful and Mild
AHO-W,M
Jesus, My All
GH-W,M
Jesus, My All, to Heaven Is Gone
AME-W,M
**Jesus, My All, to Heaven Is Gone
see also Hopewell**
Jesus, My Great High Priest
AME-W,M
Jesus, My Lord, My God, My All
WiS9-W,M
Jesus, Name All Names Above
SJ-W,M
Jesus Never Fails
VB-W,M
Jesus of Nazareth
GH-W,M
Jesus of the Manger
OB-W,M

Jesus Only
GH-W,M
Jesus, Only Jesus
GH-W,M
Jesus Only, When the Morning
GH-W
Jesus Our Brother, Strong and
Good
SHP-W,M
Jesus Our Loving Friend
SHP-W,M
Jesus Paid It All
AME-W,M HF-W,M OM-W,M
Jesus, Priceless Treasure
CEM-W,M Hy-W,M
Jesus Remembers When Others
Forget
GrG-W,M
Jesus Rode to the City
SHP-W,M
Jesus Rollin' in-er His Arms
BDW-W,M
Jesus Rose Again
GrG-W,M
Jesus Saves
GH-W,M
Jesus Saves from Sin
HOH-W,M
Jesus, Savior, Pilot Me
AME-W,M OM-W,M
Jesus, Saviour, Pilot Me
AHO-W,M CEM-W,M GH-W,M
Hy-W,M
Jesus Shall Reign
GH-W,M
Jesus Shall Reign Where'er the
Sun
AME-W,M FH-W,M Hy-W,M
SHP-W,M
Jesus, Shepherd of Thy Sheep
AHO-W,M
Jesus Sittin' on de Waterside
FN-W,M
**Jesus Sittin' on de Waterside see
also King Jesus Sittin' on de
Water Side**
Jesus, Son of God, Most Holy
SHP-W,M
Jesus Spreads His Banner o'er Us
AHO-W,M
Jesus, Stand among Us
AME-W,M Hy-W,M
Jesus, Tender Shepherd, Hear Me
FH-W,M SJ-W,M
Jesus the Master
BSG-W,M BSP-W,M
Jesus the Name High over All
AME-W,M
Jesus, the Very Thought of Thee
AME-W,M GH-W,M HSD-W,M
Hy-W,M WiS7-W,M
Jesus, These Eyes Have Never
Seen
AHO-W,M
Jesus, Thou Divine Companion
AHO-W,M
Jesus, Thou Joy of Loving Hearts
Hy-W,M
Jesus, Thy Boundless Love to Me
Hy-W,M
Jesus, Thy Name I Love
AME-W,M GH-W,M
Jesus Walked This Lonesome
Valley
FSB2-W,M
Jesus Wants Me for a Sunbeam
RDF-W,M

Jesus Was a Capricorn
SuS-W,M
Jesus Was a Loving Teacher
SHP-W,M
Jesus Watch and Guide Me
SS-W
Jesus We Look to Thee
AME-W,M
Jesus Went Alone to Pray
SHP-W,M
Jesus Wept! Those Tears Are Over
AME-W,M GH-W
Jesus Whom Ev'ry Saint Adores
ER-W,M
Jesus Wore the Crown
NH-W
Jeszcze Polska
SiP-W,M (Polish)
Jet
PMC-W,M TI2-W,M
Jet Pilots in the Sky
AF-W
J'Etais Dans Ein Logis
CaF-W (French Only)
J'Etais En Guerre
CaF-W (French Only)
Jewish Lover
Oz2-W
Jew's Daughter
ITP-W
Jew's Daughter see also Sir Hugh
Jew's Garden
BSC-W FMT-W Oz1-W,M
Jezebel
TI1-W,M UFB-W,M
Jig Along Home
PSN-W,M WSB-W,M
Jig, Jig, to the Hirings
MSB-W
Jiggity Jog
SOO-W,M
Jigsaw Puzzle
RoS-W,M
Jijibo
GOB-W,M
Jilson Setters' Ballad of the C.I.O.
BMM-W
Jilted, Jilted
LSO-W
Jim
HJ-W,M TI2-W,M
Jim Along Josey
DE-W,M
Jim Along Josie
ASB1-W,M ATS-W Oz3-W
TMA-W,M
Jim Blake's Message
LSR-W,M
Jim Bret Harte
OHG-W,M
Jim Crack Corn
IHA-W,M MF-W,M PoS-W,M
**Jim Crack Corn see also Blue Tail
Fly, Jimmie Crack Corn, and
Jimmy Crack Corn**
Jim Crow
HAS-W,M MSB-W OHG-W,M
TMA-M
Jim Crow Blues
Le-W,M
Jim Crow Train
J-W,M
Jim Dandy
FRH-W,M MF-W,M
Jim Fisk
ATS-W,M BSC-W LSR-W,M
Jim Hatfield's Son

BMM-W,M
Jim the Carter-Lad
  BB-W
Jimmie Brown the Newsboy
  BIS-W,M
Jimmie Brown the Newsboy see also Jimmy Brown the Newsboy
Jimmie Crack Corn
  OTJ-W,M
Jimmie Crack Corn see also Blue Tail Fly, Jim Crack Corn, and Jimmy Crack Corn
Jimmie Rodgers Visits the Carter Family
  LJ-W,M
Jimmie the Kid
  LJ-W,M
Jimmie's Mean Mama Blues
  LJ-W,M
Jimmie's Texas Blues
  LJ-W,M
Jimmy
  FMT-W FoM-W,M
Jimmy Brown the Newsboy
  CMG-W,M
Jimmy Brown the Newsboy see also Jimmie Brown the Newsboy
Jimmy Crack Corn
  FW-W HS-W,M
Jimmy Crack Corn see also Blue Tail Fly, Jim Crack Corn, and Jimmie Crack Corn
Jimmy Hutter
  SNS-W
Jimmy Mack
  TTH-W,M
Jimmy Randal
  AH-W,M ITP-W
Jimmy Valentine
  MF-W,M
Jine de Army ob de Lord
  BDW-W,M
Jing Jang
  ASB1-W,M
Jingle at the Window
  MG-W,M Oz3-W,M PIS-W,M
  SiR-W,M SOO-W,M
Jingle Bell Rock
  BCS-W,M OGC2-W,M RW-W,M
  TI1-W,M UFB-W,M
Jingle Bell Travelogue
  CSB-W,M
Jingle Bells
  AmH-W,M ASB1-W,M ATS-W,M
  BCh-W,M BCS-W,M BMC-W,M
  CI-W,M CSF-W DC-W,M FM-W,M
  FW-W FWS-W,M GuC-W,M
  HS-W,M HSD-W,M IL-W,M
  LoS-W,M MAB1-W MAS-W,M
  MF-W,M MSA1-W NAS-W,M
  OAP-W,M OHG-W,M OPS-W,M
  OTJ-W,M PoS-W,M RW-W,M
  SAC-W,M SCS-W TH-W,M
  TI1-W,M UFB-W,M WiS8-W,M
Jingle Berry Tea
  Oz3-W,M
Jingle Jangle Jingle
  AT-W,M FC-W,M MM-W,M
  OTJ-W,M OTO-W
Jingle Jingle
  ASB1-W,M
Jingle Jingle Jingle
  BCh-W,M
Jingle Medley
  MHB-W,M
Jingle Sticks
  GM-W,M

Jinkin the Jester
  Bo-W,M
Jinny Go Round and Round
  Oz2-W,M
Jinny Jenkins
  PSN-W,M
Jinny Jenkins see also Jennie Jenkins and Jenny Jenkins
Jitterbug
  WO-W,M
Jive at Five
  MF-M
Jive Talkin'
  TI1-W,M UFB-W,M
Jive Talking
  GrS-W,M
Jivin' Sister Fanny
  RoS-W,M
Jo-Ann
  ILF-W,M
Joan, Come Kiss Me Now
  Boo-W,M
Joan of Arc
  FSA2-W,M HCY-W,M
Joan's Ale Is Good
  ESU-W
Joan's Song see Poor People of Paris
Job
  OB-W,M
Job of Work to Do
  RBO-W,M
Jo-buh-see-bus
  Me-W,M
Jock o' Hazeldean
  SeS-W,M SoF-W,M
Jock o' the Side
  SBB-W
Jock of the Side
  BT-W,M
Jockey Hat and Feather
  SY-W,M
Jockey Hat and Feathers
  Oz3-W
Jody
  TTH-W,M
Jody and the Kid
  SuS-W,M
Joe and Jess
  SiR-W,M
Joe and Malinda Jane
  NF-W
Joe Bowers
  ATS-W BSC-W FMT-W FW-W
  OTJ-W,M Oz2-W,M SoC-W
  TBF-W,M
Joe Hardy
  ATS-W
Joe Hill
  IHA-W,M SWF-W,M
Joe Hill's Last Will
  AFP-W
Joe Hillstrom
  Am-W,M
Joe Jacobs
  B-W,M BI-W,M
Joe Jimmy Murphy
  BSC-W
Joe Stiner
  Oz2-W
Joe Turner
  AFB-W,M FGM-W,M NH-W
Joe Turner Blues
  B-W,M BI-W,M LC-W RSL-W,M
Joey, Joey, Joey
  TI2-W,M TW-W UBF-W,M
Jog on, Jog on the Footpath Way

SSP-W
Jogo Blues
  B-M BI-M
Johanna
  MF-W,M UBF-W,M
John Adkin's Farewell
  NeA-W,M
John Anderson, My Jo
  FW-W HSD-W,M
John Anderson, My Jo, John
  SeS-W,M
John B. Sails
  AmS-W,M FG1-W,M FW-W
  NeA-W,M
John Barleycorn
  BB-W
John Belly Grow
  SGT-W,M
John Bramble
  SAm-W,M
John Brown
  MPP-W,M NSS-W
John Brown Had a Little Indian
  Oz3-W SOO-W,M
John Brown's Baby
  CSS-W
John Brown's Body
  ATS-W CSo-W,M ETB-W,M
  FG1-W,M FG2-W,M FW-W
  HSD-W,M IHA-W,M LH-W,M
  MAB1-W MSA1-W NSS-W
  OTJ-W,M SiS-W SMW-W,M
  SWF-W,M U-W
John Brown's Body see also Glory Glory Hallelujah and Glory Hallelujah
John Brown's Body (Parody)
  Sin-W,M
John Bull's Taxes
  VP-W
John Cherokee
  SA-W,M
John Chinaman
  AL-W
John Cooper Was Boring
  Boo-W,M
John Dory
  GUM2-W,M
John Dunbar Theme
  MF-M
John Garner's Trail Herd
  SoC-W
John Hall
  Oz2-W
John Hardy
  BIS-W,M BSo-W,M FPG-W,M
  FSB3-W,M FSt-W,M FW-W
  ITP-W,M Oz2-W,M
John Henry
  AFP-W AmS-W,M AN-W BIS-W,M
  BSo-W,M FG2-W,M FSB3-W,M
  FSU-W FVV-W,M FW-W
  GuC-W,M IF-W,M IHA-W,M
  ITP-W,M LJ-W,M Le-W,M
  LSR-W,M MAS-W,M MSH-W,M
  NF-W OHO-W,M OTJ-W,M
  RSW-W,M SAm-W,M SBF-W,M
  SoF-W,M SWF-W,M WS-W,M
John Henry Blues
  B-W,M BI-W,M
John Jacob Jingleheimer Schmidt
  Bo-W,M CSS-W FW-W FWS-W,M
  OHO-W,M OTJ-W,M RSL-W,M
John, John, de Holy Member
  NSS-W
John, John, John
  RBO-W,M

John, John, wid de Holy Order
NSS-W
John Marshall
Oz2-W,M
John Morgan
Oz3-W,M
John of Hazel Green
SCa-W,M
John over the Hazel Green
SCa-W,M
John Peel
ASB6-W,M CSo-W,M FW-W
IL-W,M MML-W,M OFS-W,M
OH-W,M OTJ-W,M TH-W,M U-W
John Ran
Boo-W,M
John Riley
FGM-W,M FW-W OTJ-W,M
Oz1-W,M
John Riley II
ITP-W,M
John Riley's Courtship
Oz1-W
John Saw
AG-W,M HHa-W,M RF-W,M
John Saw de Holy Numbah
BDW-W,M M-W,M
John Sawr-O
NSS-W
John Smith
ASB1-W,M
John the Boy, Hello
Oz3-W,M
John the Rabbit
RSL-W,M
**John the Rabbit see also Oh, John
the Rabbit**
John the Revelator
HHa-W,M
Johnnie
BSC-W
Johnnie Armstrong
SBB-W
Johnnie Cope
SBB-W SeS-W,M
Johnnie Doyle
FoM-W,M
**Johnnie Doyle see also Johnny
Doyle**
Johnnie, I Hardly Knew Ye
VP-W,M
**Johnnie, I Hardly Knew Ye see
also Johnny, I Hardly Knew Ye**
Johnnie Randle
FMT-W
**Johnnie Randle see also Johnny
Randall**
Johnnie Verbeck
Bo-W,M
**Johnnie Verbeck see also Johnny
Berbeck**
Johnnie, Won'tcha Ramble
AFP-W
Johnnie's Comin' Home
Mo-W,M
Johnny Angel
DRR-W,M GSN4-W,M ILS-W,M
Johnny Appleseed
ASB6-W,M SAm-W,M
Johnny Appleseed's Song
FSA2-W,M
Johnny B. Goode
HR-W RB-W TI1-W,M UFB-W,M
Johnny Berbeck
Oz3-W
**Johnny Berbeck see also Johnnie
Verbeck**

Johnny Big-Foot
NF-W
Johnny Bobeens
TBF-W
Johnny Boker
FW-W SA-W,M
**Johnny Boker see also Jonny
Boker**
Johnny Bull, My Jo, John
FW-W
Johnny Bull's Big Guns
ANS-W
Johnny Come down de Hollow
AFP-W
Johnny Come Down to Hilo
SA-W,M
Johnny Come Home
TTH-W,M
Johnny Comes Marching Home
BMM-W
Johnny Dile
SCa-W,M
Johnny Doyle
Oz1-W,M FMT-W SCa-W,M
**Johnny Doyle see also Johnnie
Doyle**
Johnny Dyers
Oz1-W
Johnny Fell Down in the Bucket
Oz3-W,M
Johnny Fill Up the Bowl
MPP-W
Johnny Fool
Oz3-W
Johnny German
BSC-W
Johnny Get Your Gun
PoS-W,M
Johnny Git Your Gun
AH-W,M
Johnny Has Gone for a Soldier
AH-W,M EA-W,M LMR-W,M
OTJ-W,M SI-W,M
Johnny, I Hardly Knew Ye
IS-W,M JF-W,M
**Johnny, I Hardly Knew Ye see also
Johnnie, I Hardly Knew Ye**
Johnny, I Hardly Knew You
FW-W GuC-W,M
Johnny Is a Roving Blade
IS-W,M
Johnny Is Gone for a Soldier
AAP-W,M Sin-W,M SiS-W
Johnny Is My Darling
FGM-W,M OTJ-W,M
Johnny, Johnny
Boo-W,M
Johnny Jump-Up
GC-W,M
Johnny Lad
BB-W
Johnny Morgan
TMA-W,M
Johnny Must Fight
Oz1-W,M
Johnny One Note
LM-W,M OTJ-W,M OTO-W
TI1-W,M TS-W TW-W UBF-W,M
UFB-W,M
Johnny Randall
BSC-W
**Johnny Randall see also Johnnie
Randle**
Johnny Randolph
Oz1-W,M
Johnny Ringo
SoC-W

Johnny Sands
ATS-W,M BSC-W FMT-W
HSD-W,M Oz4-W,M
Johnny Schmoker
GuC-W,M HAS-W,M HS-W,M
(German) SiR-W,M SY-W,M
UF-W,M
Johnny the Sailor
Oz1-W,M
Johnny Todd
BB-W FW-W
Johnny Works with One Hammer
FP-W,M
Johnny's Comin' Home
NM-W,M
Johnny's So Long at the Fair
TMA-W,M
**Johnny's So Long at the Fair see
also Oh Dear What Can the
Matter Be**
Johnny's Theme (Tonight Show
with Johnny Carson Theme)
TI2-M
John's on de Island on His Knees
BDW-W,M
Johnson
FW-W
Johnson Boys
FPG-W,M FSB3-W,M FW-W
WSB-W,M
Johnson Rag
GSN1-W,M HLS1-W,M RW-W,M
TI2-W,M
Johnson's Ale
FW-W OHO-W,M
Johnson's Motor Car
FW-W
Join All the Glorious Names
AME-W,M
Join, Brethren, Join Us O
NSS-W
Join de Heaven wid de Angels
NH-W
Join 'Em All, Join for Jesus
NSS-W
Join in Singing Hallelujah
Boo-W,M
Join in the Game
FP-W,M
Join into the Game
WSB-W,M
Join, O Maritza
SiP-W,M (Bulgarian)
**Join the Army of the Lord see Jine
de Army ob de Lord**
Join the Circle
LA-W,M (Spanish)
**Join the Heaven with the Angels
see Join de heaven wid de
Angels**
Join Them All... see Join 'Em All...
Join We All to Swell the Song
Boo-W,M
Joint Is Jumpin'
TI2-W,M UBF-W,M
Joke
ASB2-W,M
Joker, The (Lee Morgan)
MF-M
Joker, The (There's Always a
Joker in the Pack)
TI1-W,M UBF-W,M UFB-W,M
Jolene
BDP-W,M CMG-W,M ToO76-W,M
Joli Tambour see Le Joli Tambour
Jolie Fleur De Rosier
FSO-W,M (French)

RF-W,M SHS-W,M
Judgment Day
  WN-W,M
Judgment Day Is Rolling Around
  Oz4-W,M
Judgment Day Is Tryin' Time
  BDW-W,M
Judiciary
  AL-W
Judith
  OTO-W
Judy's Turn to Cry
  HR-W
Jug of Punch
  FGM-W,M FW-W
Jug of Wine
  LL-W,M
Juggler
  ASB3-W,M
Juice of the Forbidden Fruit
  BSC-W ITP-W,M Oz3-W,M
Juicy Fruit Gum (Jingle) see Let's Pick a Pack
Juif Errant see Le Juif Errant
Juke Box Saturday Night
  HC1-W,M TI1-W,M TTH-W,M
  UBF-W,M UFB-W,M
Jukebox in My Mind
  GCM-W,M
Jula Waters
  NH-W
Juley
  SA-W,M
Julia (Lennon/McCartney)
  BBe-W,M Be2-W,M TWS-W
Julia (A Sailor Has One Pleasure Dear)
  UF-W,M
Julida Polka
  PT-M TI1-M UFB-M
Julie Ann Johnson
  Le-W,M NeF-W
Juliet's Song
  IFM-W
Julius Caesar
  TW-W
Jullien's Grand Polka
  MSB-W
July's Garden
  FSA1-W,M
Jump de Broom
  Mo-W,M OTO-W
Jump Jim Crow
  ASB2-W,M ATS-W,M MPM-W,M
  NF-W Oz2-W,M
Jump, Jump
  ASB1-W,M
Jump Shout Boogie
  TOF-W,M
Jump the Broom see Jump de Broom
Jump Up
  GM-W,M
Jumpin' at the Woodside
  MF-W,M
Jumpin' Jack Flash
  RoS-W,M
Jumpin' with Symphony Sid
  TI1-W,M UFB-W,M
June
  RW-M
June Comes Around Every Year
  Mo-W,M NM-W,M OTO-W
June in January
  AT-W,M OTO-W
June Is Bustin' Out All Over
  L-W TG-W,M TI1-W,M UFB-W,M

June, Lovely June
  Boo-W,M
June Night
  BBB-W,M EAG2-W,M GSN2-W,M
  GST-W,M HLS2-W,M RW-W,M
  TI2-W,M
Jungle Drums
  TI2-W,M
Jungle Love
  OTO-W
Jungleland
  RV-W
Junior's Farm
  PMC-W,M
Juniper Tree
  Oz3-W,M
Junto Song
  SAR-W,M SI-W,M
Jupiter Symphony (Theme)
  LTL-M
Jurame (Promise, Love)
  FSY-W,M (Spanish)
Just a Closer Walk
  HHa-W,M
Just a Closer Walk with Thee
  BSG-W,M BSP-W,M FS-W,M
  FW-W HLS7-W,M JBF-W,M
  MAB1-W MSA1-W OAP-W,M
  OFS-W,M RDF-W,M RW-W,M
  SUH-W,M TI1-W,M Tr-W,M
  UFB-W,M
Just a Cottage Small
  MF-W,M
Just a Dream
  FRH-W,M
Just a Dream of You, Dear
  FWS-W,M
Just a Gigolo
  TI1-W,M UFB-W,M
Just a Little Bit South of North Carolina
  OnT1-W,M
Just a Little Lonesome
  OGC1-W,M
Just a Little Lovin'
  OGC1-W,M TI1-W,M UFB-W,M
Just a Little Tack in the Shingle of Your Roof
  FVV-W,M
Just a Little Talk with Jesus
  HHa-W,M
Just a Memory
  MF-W,M
Just a Moment More
  OTO-W
Just a Song at Twilight
  ATS-W
Just a Song at Twilight see also Love's Old Sweet Song
Just a Woman
  TTH-W,M
Just a Word for Jesus
  GH-W,M
Just after the Battle
  SiS-W
Just Another Day
  JC-W,M
Just Another Polka
  PT-W,M TI2-W,M
Just Another Rhumba
  OTO-W
Just Anything
  ITP-W,M
Just As I Am
  GH-W,M HF-W,M HSD-W,M
  JBF-W,M TB-W,M WiS7-W,M
Just As I Am, Thine Own to Be

AME-W,M Hy-W,M
Just As I Am, without One Plea
  AME-W,M CEM-W,M Hy-W,M
Just As Thou Art
  AHO-W,M
Just Ask Him
  BSG-W,M BSP-W,M
Just A-Wearyin' for You
  OBN-W,M
Just Because
  PT-W,M TI2-W,M
Just Because She Made Dem Goo-Goo Eyes
  ATS-W,M BH-W,M EFS-W,M
Just Before I Sleep Tonight
  SCL-W,M SHP-W,M
Just Before the Battle, Mother
  ATS-W FW-W HSD-W,M
  NAS-W,M PoS-W,M Sin-W,M
  SiS-W
Just Call Me Lonesome
  OGC2-W,M
Just Can't Stay
  DBL-W
Just for a Thrill
  ToS-W,M
Just for Fun
  OTO-W
Just for the Bride and Groom
  Mo-W,M NM-W,M OTO-W
Just for Today
  BSG-W,M BSP-W,M FS-W,M
Just for Tonight
  OTO-W TP-W,M UBF-W,M
Just for You
  OTO-W
Just Forty Years Ago
  ITP-W,M
Just Friends
  HLS2-W,M
Just Give Me a June Night, the Moonlight and You see June Night
Just Give Me Operations
  AF-W
Just Go Away
  PL-W,M
Just Go to the Movies
  UBF-W,M
Just Hold My Hand Tonight see 'Des Hold My Hand Tonight
Just Imagine
  MF-W,M OTO-W TI1-W,M
  UFB-W,M
Just in Time
  DBC-W,M DJ-W,M FrS-W,M
  HC1-W,M HLS3-W,M HLS8-W,M
  ILT-W,M LM-W,M OTO-W
  TI1-W,M TW-W UBF-W,M
  UFB-W,M
Just Leave Everything to Me
  Mo-W,M OTO-W
Just Like a Man
  GG3-W,M
Just Like John see Jes Like John
Just Like Paradise
  BHO-W,M
Just Like Starting Over
  TI2-W,M
Just Like the Ivy
  U-W
Just Like Tom Thumb's Blues
  FoR-W,M
Just One Girl
  Oz4-W
Just One Look
  DRR-W,M

Just One More Chance
AT-W,M OnT1-W,M OTO-W
Just One of Those Things
DC-W,M DJ-W,M FrS-W,M
HC1-W,M MF-W,M ML-W,M
OHB-W,M
Just One Person
UBF-W,M
Just Our Luck (Theme)
TV-W,M
Just Out of Reach
FrF-W,M HLS9-W,M
Just Plain Folks
Oz4-W
Just Set a Light
Oz4-W
Just Squeeze Me
GSF-W,M
Just Tell Her Jim Said Hello
MF-W,M SRE1-W,M
Just Tell Them That You Saw Me
BH-W,M EFS-W,M FSN-W,M
Just the Other Side of Nowhere
SuS-W,M
Just the Way You Are
GrS-W,M RW-W,M
Just to Be Close to You
ToO76-W,M
Just to Know You Are Mine
ReG-W,M
Just to Satisfy You
TOC82-W,M
Just to See Her
CFB-W,M
Just Tread on the Tail of Me Coat
Oz3-W,M
Just Wait a Little While
GrG-W,M
Just Walkin' in the Rain
HLS9-W,M
Just Walking in the Rain
OPS-W,M PB-W,M
Just Want to See His Face
RoS-W,M
Just Wearyin' for You see Just A-Wearyin' for You
Just When I Needed You Most
ToO79-W,M
Just Whistle a Bit
VA-W,M
Just Win a Pretty Widow
BP-W,M
Just You, Just Me
GSN2-W,M HLS2-W,M RW-W,M
Just You Wait
UBF-W,M
Justice Has Stricken the Chains
from the Slave
SiS-W
Justicia En Marcha
JF-W,M (Spanish)
Juvenile Greeting Song
GrM-W,M

K

K.C.
NH-W
K.C. Loving
GAR-W,M
K.C. Railroad
LSR-W,M
K-14 Tower
AF-W
K-K-K-Katy
BH-W,M GSN1-W,M HLS1-W,M

OS-W RW-W,M
K.P. Blues
GO-W
K.P. Guy
GI-W
K.P.'s Are Scrubbing Along
GI-W
Ka-lu-a
TI1-W,M
Kamate Kamate
SNZ-W,M (Maori)
Kambia
SHS-W,M
Kangaroo (An Animal Strange Is
the Kangaroo)
ASB3-W,M
Kangaroo (A Kangaroo Sat on an
Oak)
OTJ-W,M
Kangaroo (To Do the Kangaroo,
You Hop)
Mo-W,M NM-W,M OTO-W
Kanohi Tiaho
SNZ-W,M (Maori)
Kansas Boys
AmS-W,M FW-W
Kansas City (Hammerstein/
Rodgers)
L-W TGO-W,M TI2-W,M
UBF-W,M
Kansas City (Leiber/Stoller)
ERM-W,M GAR-W,M
Kansas City Blues
BI-W,M FW-W
Kansas City Kitty
WDS-W,M
Kansas City Lights
TOC82-W,M
Kansas City Railroad Blues
LSR-W,M
Kansas Line
SoC-W
**Karate Kid Part II (Theme) see
Glory of Love (Theme from Karate
Kid Part II)**
Karen
TTH-W,M
Kashmiri Song
RW-W,M
**Kate and Allie (Theme) see Friends
(Theme from Kate and Allie)**
Kate and Her Horns
FSU-W
Kate and the Clothier
SU-W
Kate's Young Man
MSB-W
Katey's Letter
HSD-W,M
Kathleen Aroon
HSD-W,M
Kathleen Mavourneen
AmH-W,M BH-W,M EFS-W,M
FW-W HSD-W,M NAS-W,M
OTJ-W,M SCo-W,M TH-W,M
WiS8-W,M
Katie
U-W
Katie and Willie
BSC-W
Katie Lee and Willie Gray
Oz4-W
Katie Mae
DBL-W
Katie the Kangaroo
SiB-W,M
Katie Went to Haiti

ML-W,M OTO-W
Katie's Secret
Oz4-W,M
Katinka
K-W,M
Katiusha
BF-W,M LW-W,M (Russian)
Katiusha see also Katusha
Katrina's Wedding Waltz
VA-W,M
Katsumi Love Theme
MF-M
Katusha
RSC-W,M (Russian Only)
Katusha see also Katiusha
Katy Bell
FHR-W,M SSF-W,M SSFo-W,M
Katy Cline
FW-W
Katy Cruel
AH-W,M FW-W LW-W,M
Katy Daley
BSo-W,M
Katy Dear, or Willie Darling
SCa-W
Katy Wells
Re-W,M
Kaw-Liga
HW-W,M TI2-W,M
Kay's Theme
OTO-W
Kedron
SHS-W,M
Kedusha
SBJ-W,M (Hebrew Only)
Kedushoh
JS-W,M (Hebrew Only)
Kee Mitseeyon
SBJ-W,M (Hebrew Only)
Keel Row
ASB6-W,M CSo-W,M OTJ-W,M
SMY-W,M
Keemo Kimo
AN-W
Keep A-Goin'
SL-W
Keep A-Inchin' Along
RF-W,M
**Keep A-Inchin' Along see also
Keep Inchin' Along**
Keep A-Inching Along
WiS7-W,M
Keep A-Knockin'
TI2-W,M
Keep Dat 'Possum Warm
TMA-W,M
Keep de Ark A-Movin'
BDW-W,M
Keep Goin' see Keep A-Goin'
Keep in the Middle ob de Road
MML-W,M
Keep in the Middle of the Road
HS-W,M
Keep Inchin' Along
NH-W
**Keep Inchin' Along see also Keep
A-Inchin' Along**
Keep It a Secret
TI1-W,M UFB-W,M
Keep It before the People
AL-W
Keep It Clean
GI-W
Keep It Dark
Oz3-W
Keep It Gay
OTJ-W,M OTO-W

Keep It Up Baby
BRB-W
Keep Knockin' see Keep A-Knockin'
Keep Me from Sinkin' Down
RF-W,M
Keep Me from Sinking Down
SpS-W,M
Keep My Mem'ry in Your Heart
OGC2-W,M
Keep My Skillet Good and Greasy
FW-W
Keep off the Grass
YL-W,M
Keep On Dancing
TI1-W,M UFB-W,M
Keep On Loving You
MF-W,M
Keep On Pushing
SFF-W,M
Keep On Singing
TI2-W,M
Keep On Smiling
ST-W,M
Keep On the Sunny Side
BIS-W,M FSt-W,M RDF-W,M
Keep Politics off Your Farm
GrM-W,M
Keep Right On to the End of the Road
U-W
Keep Singing, Keep Humming
KS-W,M
Keep Smiling at Trouble
MF-W,M
Keep Steady
AFP-W
Keep That Possum Warm see Keep Dat 'Possum Warm
Keep the Ark Moving see Keep de Ark A-Movin'
Keep the Ball Rollin'
OnT6-W,M
Keep the Flame Burning
OGR-W,M VB-W,M
Keep the Home Fires Burning
OS-W
Keep Them Rolling
GO-W
Keep This Bible near Your Heart
SiS-W
Keep to the Work
Boo-W,M
Keep Us, O Lord
SL-W,M
Keep Woman in Her Sphere
LW-W,M
Keep Your Eye on the Prize
JF-W,M
Keep Your Eyes on the Prize
FW-W SFF-W,M
Keep Your Feet Still, Geordie Hinny
SoC-W
Keep Your Garden Clean
DD-W,M Oz1-W,M
Keep Your Hands off Her
Le-W,M
Keep Your Hands to Yourself
BHO-W,M
Keep Your Lamp Trimmed and Burning
FGM-W,M FW-W
Keep Your Lamps Trimmed
WN-W,M
Keep Your Saddle Tight
HB-W,M
Keeper, The

FW-W HS-W,M MES1-W,M MES2-W,M OHO-W,M OTJ-W,M WSB-W,M
Keeper of My Heart
OGC2-W,M
Keepin' My Eyes on You
VB-W,M
Keepin' Out of Mischief Now
Mo-W,M NM-W,M
Keepin' Power
TOC83-W,M
Keeping On
SL-W,M
Keller's American Hymn
ATS-W ESB-W,M HSD-W,M NAS-W,M SL-W,M
Kelley's Irish Brigade
BSC-W
Kelly Field Song
AF-W
Kelly's Irish Brigade
VP-W
Kelly's Love
NH-W
Kemo Kimo
Oz2-W
Kenny Madland
HB-W
Kenny Wagner
FMT-W ITP-W,M
Kenny Wagner's Surrender
FMT-W
Kent Gij Dat Volk Vol Heldenmoed
SiP-W,M (Afrikaans)
Kent State Massacre
FW-W
Kentucky
SiS-W
Kentucky Babe
BeB-W,M FSN-W,M FWS-W,M HS-W,M IL-W,M LMR-W,M MF-W,M Mo-W,M NM-W,M OBN-W,M OPS-W,M OTJ-W,M SFB-W,M
Kentucky Bootlegger
FW-W RW-W,M
Kentucky Fried Chicken Jingle see Real Goodness from Kentucky Fried Chicken
Kentucky Moonshiner
AH-W,M
Kentucky Rain
TI1-W,M UFB-W,M
Kentucky Woman
TI2-W,M
Keokuk Culture Club
M-W,M
Kept Busy
NF-W
Kercie
FSO-W,M (French)
Kern River
NMH-W,M
Kerry Dance
HSD-W,M MF-W,M OFS-W,M OTJ-W,M POT-W,M RW-W,M TF-W,M TH-W,M WiS8-W,M
Kerry Recruit
FW-W
Kevin Barry
AmS-W,M FW-W SMW-W,M SWF-W,M
Kevin Conway
VS-W,M
Key Largo
TOC82-W,M
Key to the Highway

LC-W
Keys of Heaven
Oz3-W,M
Keys of the Kingdom
BB-W
Keys to the Kingdom
HLS7-W,M SUH-W,M
Kharitosha the Mailman
RSC-W,M (Russian Only)
Khedival Hymn
SiP-W,M (Arabic)
Ki Lekach Tov
JS-W,M (Hebrew Only)
Ki Onu Amechoh
JS-W,M (Hebrew Only)
Ki Vayom Hazze
JS-W,M (Hebrew Only)
Kia Ora, E Arohanui
SNZ-W,M (Maori)
Kia Ora Katoa
SNZ-W,M (Maori)
Kicker
Oz3-W
Kickin' Mule
BIS-W,M
Kickin' the Clouds Away
GOB-W,M
Kicking Mule
AFS-W,M
Kid, The
TI1-M UFB-M
Kiddio
MF-W,M
Kidd's Lament
FMT-W
Kiddush
JS-W,M (Hebrew Only)
SBJ-W,M (Hebrew Only)
Kids
OTJ-W,M
Kids (What's the Matter with Kids Today)
HC1-W,M Mo-W,M NM-W,M OTO-W UBF-W,M
Kids Are Alright, The
WA-W,M
Kids Say the Darndest Things
Mo-W,M N-W,M NM-W,M OTJ-W,M
Kilgary Mountain
GG1-W,M OHO-W,M
Kill for Peace
VS-W,M
Killarney
AmH-W,M ASB6-W,M CSo-W,M ESB-W,M HSD-W,M NAS-W,M OTJ-W,M
Killiecrankie
FMT-W SBB-W
Killin' in the Gap
BMM-W
Killing Ground
VS-W,M
Killing Me Softly with His Song
AO-W,M DC-W,M DPE-W,M GrH-W,M GrS-W,M GSN4-W,M MF-W,M RW-W,M
Kim Ga Yo
SiP-W,M (Japanese)
Kimi-Ga-Yo
SL-W,M
Kimigayo
AmH-W,M (Japanese)
Kimonaro
BSC-W
Kind Captain, I've Important Information

MGT-W,M
Kind Friends Are Near Her
SiS-W
Kind of a Drag
RY-W,M RYT-W,M
Kind of Loving
TT-W,M
Kind of Man a Woman Needs
Mo-W,M NM-W,M OTO-W
UBF-W,M
Kind Sir
SCa-W,M
Kind Words Are Dear to All
HSD-W,M
Kind Words Can Never Die
AHO-W,M
Kinda Sorta Doing Nothing
Mo-W,M NM-W,M OTO-W
Kindle the Taper
AHO-W,M
Kindly Act
FSA1-W,M
Kindness to Animals
FSA2-W,M
Kine
Boo-W,M
King Alcohol
SY-W,M
King and the Sailor
MSB-W
King and West Countryman
MSB-W
King Andrew
MPP-W,M
King Arthur
OH-W,M OTJ-W,M
King Arthur Had Three Sons
FBI-W,M
King Bee without a Queen
LC-W
King Christian
AmH-W,M (Danish)
King Christian Stood beside the
Mast
SiP-W,M (Danish)
King Creole
GAR-W,M SRE2-W,M TI1-W,M
UFB-W,M
King Edwards
SA-W,M
King Emanuel
RF-W,M
King for a Day
TTH-W,M
King George IV's Welcome to
Scotland
MSB-W
King Henry
VS-W,M
King Henry V's Conquest of France
BT-W,M
King Herod and the Cock
BT-W,M OB-W,M OE-W,M
King Herod's Song
UBF-W,M
King in Glory
OB-W,M
King Is Coming
Tr-W,M
**King Is Gone A-Hunting see Le Roi
S'en Va-t'en Chasse**
King Jesus Is the Rock
NH-W
King Jesus Lit de Candle
NSS-W
King Jesus Sittin' on de Water
Side

BDW-W,M
**King Jesus Sittin' on de Water
Side see also Jesus Sittin' on de
Waterside**
King Lear and His Three Daughters
SSP-W
King Matty and Blair
MPP-W
King of All Kings
CEM-W,M RDF-W,M
King of France
MH-W,M OTJ-W,M TF-W,M
King of Glory
SL-W,M
King of Glory Standeth
Hy-W,M
King of Kings
TH-W,M
King of Love (My Shepherd Is)
FH-W,M GC-W,M U-W
King of Love My Shepherd Is
ESB-W,M Hy-W,M
King of My Life I Crown Thee Now
AME-W,M
King of Pain
TI2-W,M
King of Peace
SHS-W,M
King of the Ball
FSO-W,M (French)
King of the Road
ATC1-W,M CMG-W,M CoH-W,M
CSp-W,M FOC-W,M GOI7-W,M
OnT1-W,M RB-W RYT-W,M
TI2-W,M
King of Who I Am
AG-W,M VB-W,M
King of Yvetot
SL-W,M
King Porter Stomp
Mo-M TI2-M
King Richard's Prison Song
MU-W,M (French)
King Rooster
ASB4-W,M
King Shall Come When Morning
Dawns
Hy-W,M
King Shall Reign in Righteousness
AHO-W,M
King Stephen Was a Worthy Peer
SSP-W
King William
FMT-W FoM-W,M SiR-W,M
King William, Duke Shambo
FVV-W,M
King William Was King James's
Son
Oz3-W,M
Kingdom
OB-W,M
Kingdom Comin'
HAS-W,M
Kingdom Coming
AmH-W,M AN-W HSD-W,M
MPP-W PoS-W,M POT-W,M
SCo-W,M Sin-W,M SiS-W,M
WiS8-W,M
**Kingdom Coming see also Year of
Jubilo**
Kingdom of Love
VB-W,M
Kings
OB-W,M
Kings' Daughters
ITP-W,M
King's Hunt

OH-W,M
Kings of Orient
JOC-W,M OB-W,M
King's Own Regulars
SAR-W,M SI-W
King's Seven Daughters
FoM-W,M
Kingwood
SHS-W,M
Kinmont Willie
SBB-W
Kiss, The
ESU-W
Kiss an Angel Good Mornin'
EC-W,M HLS9-W,M MCG-W,M
MF-W,M RW-W,M RYT-W,M
TI1-W,M UFB-W,M
Kiss and Say Goodbye
SoH-W,M
Kiss for Cinderella
LSO-W
Kiss Her Now
Mo-W,M OTO-W UBF-W,M
Kiss Him Goodbye (Na Na Hey
Hey)
CFB-W,M
**Kiss Him Goodbye (Na Na Hey
Hey) see also Na Na Hey Hey
Kiss Him Goodbye**
Kiss in the Dark
MF-W,M
Kiss Me (from The Cosby Show)
TTH-M
Kiss Me (Noel Coward)
BS-W,M
Kiss Me Again
MF-W,M
**Kiss Me Again see also If I Were
on the Stage**
Kiss Me Before I Die, Mother
SiS-W
Kiss Me Dear Mother
FHR-W,M
Kiss Me, Father, Ere I Die
SiS-W
Kiss Me First
MF-W,M
Kiss Me Good-Bye for Mother
SiS-W
Kiss Me Goodnight, Sergeant
Major
U-W
Kiss Me, Mother, and Let Me Go
SiS-W
Kiss Me, Mother, Ere I'm Dead
SiS-W
Kiss Me Quick
SRE1-W,M
Kiss Me Quick and Go
HSD-W,M TMA-W,M
Kiss of Fire
TI2-W,M
Kiss the World Goodbye
SuS-W,M
Kiss to Build a Dream On
HLS5-W,M RT5-W,M RW-W,M
Kiss Waltz
MF-W,M
Kisses Sweeter Than Wine
IHA-W,M MF-W,M TI1-W,M
UFB-W,M WSB-W,M
Kissin' Cousins
MF-M RW-W,M
Kissing in the Dark
DBL-W FHR-W,M
Kissing Song (A Sleish o' Bread an'
Butter Fried)

NF-W
Kissing Song (When a Man Falls in
Love with a Little Turtle Dove)
DD-W,M HAS-W,M
**Kissing Song (When a Man Falls in
Love with a Little Turtle Dove)
see also When a Man Falls in
Love with a Little Turtle Dove**
Kissin's No Sin
OU-W,M
Kit and Tom Child
Boo-W,M
Kit Carson
LMR-W,M
Kitchen Clock
SD-W,M
Kitchen Kalendar
MHB-W,M
Kitchen Kops
GI-W
Kitchen Police
GO-W
Kite
YG-W,M
Kites Are Flying
MHB-W,M
Kitten
ASB1-W,M
Kitten in School
AST-W,M
Kitty, Caint You Come Along Too?
Oz2-W,M
Kitty Cat
FF-W,M MES1-W,M MES2-W,M
Kitty Clover
TMA-W,M
Kitty Tyrrell
HSD-W,M
Kitty White
MH-W,M
Kiwi
FSA1-W,M
Ki-wi Song
AF-W GO-W
**Kleenex Tissues Jingle see Soft,
Strong, Pops Up Too**
Klein Klein Kleuterken
SiR-W,M
**Kleine Heerde Zeugen see Die
Kleine Heerde Zeugen**
**Kleine Nachtmusik see Eine Kleine
Nachtmusik**
Kneel on This Carpet
NF-W
Knife Grinder's Song
ASB5-W,M
Knight of the Woeful Countenance
MLM-W,M
Knight That Would Not When He
Might
SR-W,M
Knights of Labor
AFP-W AL-W
Knights of Labor New Year Song
AL-W
Knights of Labor Song
AL-W
Knights of Labor Strike
AL-W
Knitting Song
MPP-W SiS-W
Knock at the Door
MH-W,M
Knock, Knock
SOO-W,M
Knock on the Door
NA-W,M

Knock on Wood (Floyd/Cropper)
ToO79-W,M
Knock on Wood (Sylvia Fine)
OTO-W
Knock Song
OTJ-W,M
Knock Three Times
HLS9-W,M MCG-W,M RW-W,M
TI2-W,M
Knock'd 'Em in the Old Kent Road
AmH-W,M WiS8-W,M
Knockin' on Heaven's Door
GrS-W,M
Knocking, Knocking
GH-W,M
Knocking, Knocking, Who Is There
AME-W,M
Knots Landing (Theme)
TV-M
Know Ye That Race of Hero Mold
SiP-W,M (Afrikaans)
Knowest Thou That Dear Land?
MU-W,M (French)
Knowing Me, Knowing You
TI1-W,M UFB-W,M
Knowing When to Leave
ILT-W,M Mo-W,M OTO-W TW-W
Known by the Scars
VB-W,M
Know'st Thou That Fair Land
AmH-W,M
Know'st Thou Yonder Land
WiS7-W,M
Knoxville
SHS-W,M
Knoxville Gal
SCa-W
Knoxville Girl
BIS-W,M BSo-W,M FW-W
Oz2-W,M SCa-W,M
Knuts to Knudsen
AFP-W
Ko Ko Mo (I Love You So)
LWT-W,M
K'o Lien Ti Ch'iu Hsiang (Poor
Ch'iu Hsiang)
FD-W,M (Chinese)
Kochae-Bushi
SBF-W,M (Japanese Only)
Kodak Makes Your Pictures Count
GSM-W,M
Kohala's Breezes
VA-W,M
Kokomo
CFB-W,M
Kokomo, Indiana
MF-W,M
Kol Dodi
SBF-W,M (Hebrew Only)
Kol Nidre
JS-W,M OTJ-W,M
Kol Nidrei
AmH-M WiS7-M
Kong Christian Stod Ved Hoien
Mast
SiP-W,M (Danish)
Kongo Kate
GOB-W,M
Kookaburra
BMC-W,M FW-W HS-W,M
IL-W,M OHO-W,M OTJ-W,M
Kookaburra see also Kuckaburro
Kookie, Kookie (Lend Me Your
Comb)
TVT-W,M
**Kool Cigarettes Jingle see Come
Up to Kool**

Koom Ba Yah
BMC-W,M GeS-W,M
**Koom Ba Yah see also Kum Ba
Ya(h) and Kumbaya**
Korea
AF-W
Korean Christmas Carol
AF-W
Korner's Battle Prayer
HSD-W,M
Kotuku
SNZ-W,M (Maori)
Krakowiak
MHB-W,M
**Kramer vs. Kramer Theme see
Vivaldi Concerto in C Major**
K-ra-zy for You
GOB-W,M
Krazy Kat
BI-M
Kris Kringle's Travels
MH-W,M
Kuckaburro
ASB6-W,M
Kuckaburro see also Kookaburra
Kuhl, Nicht Lau
Boo-W,M (German)
Kuiama
ELO-W,M
Kukuck
SCL-W,M
Ku-ku-ri-ku!
SOO-W,M
Kum Ba Ya
On-W,M RDF-W,M RW-W,M
Kum Ba Yah
Bo-W,M FW-W,M GOI7-W,M
GuC-W,M IPH-W,M MG-W,M
OFS-W,M OPS-W,M OTJ-W,M
SBF-W,M
**Kum Ba Yah see also Koom Ba Yah
and Kumbaya**
Kum Bachur Atzel
WSB-W,M (Hebrew)
Kumbaya
WSB-W,M
**Kumbaya see also Koom Ba Yah
and Kum Ba Ya(h)**
Kunarri and Antung
AF-W
Kung Fu Fighting
DP-W,M
Kye Song
TF-W,M
Kyrie
LMR-W,M MU-W,M (Greek)
Kyrie Eleison (Lotti)
SiM-W,M (Greek)
Kyrie Eleison (Mozart)
Boo-W,M (Greek Only)
Kyrie Eleison (Yugoslav Carol)
MHB-W,M (Serbo-Croatian)
Kyrie from the Holy Mass of the
Blessed Trinity
BC1-M

L

**L&M Cigarettes Jingle see Come
On Over to the L&M Side and
This Is the L&M Moment**
L. and N.
NH-W
L & N Special
AN-W
L.B.J.

IFM-W
LBJ Looks After Me
  IFM-W VS-W,M
LBJ, What Do You Say?
  VS-W,M
L-O-V-E
  MF-W,M OnT1-W,M
L.S.U. Alma Mater see Alma Mater (L.S.U.)
L.S.U. Cadets on Parade
  SLS-W,M
L.S.U. Memory Song
  SLS-W,M
La Bamba
  BHO-W,M (Spanish Only)
  BNG-W,M (Spanish Only)
  DC-W,M (Spanish Only)
  HFH-W,M (Spanish Only) JF-W,M
  (Spanish) LaS-W,M MF-W,M
  (Spanish Only) OAP-W,M
  (Spanish Only) OPS-W,M
  OTJ-W,M
La Bas Dans Ces Vallons
  CaF-W (French Only)
La Bas Sur Ces Montagnes
  CFS-W,M (French)
La Bebe Et Le Gaimbleur
  CaF-W (French Only)
Le Belle Au Bois Dormant
  CUP-W,M (French Only)
La Belle Est Au Jardin D'Amour
  (Beauty in Love's Garden)
  FW-W,M (French)
La Belle S'en Va Au Jardin
  D'Amour
  CaF-W (French Only)
La Bonne Aventure
  OTJ-W,M (French Only)
La Brabanconne
  AmH-W,M (French) NAS-W,M
  SiP-W,M (French) SMW-W,M
  (French)
La Cage Aux Folles
  UBF-W,M
La Carmagnole
  SiP-W,M (French) SMW-W,M
  (French)
La Chanson D'Eine Vielle Fille
  CaF-W (French Only)
La Chanson Des Metamorphoses
  FSO-W,M (French)
La Ci Darem
  MU-W,M (Italian)
La Cinquantaine (The Golden
  Wedding Anniversary)
  AmH-M MF-M
La Costa
  WG-W,M
La Cousine Lili
  CaF-W (French Only)
La Cucaracha
  BeB-W,M FWS-W,M GuC-W,M
  (Spanish) LaS-M OTJ-W,M
  TI1-W,M
La Cumparsita
  LaS-M MF-W,M OTJ-M RW-M
La Czarine
  AmH-M FSA1-W,M
La Danse Des Gorets
  CUP-W,M (French Only)
La Declaration D'Amour
  FSO-W,M (French)
La Delaissee
  CE-W,M (French)
La Dezlaissee
  CaF-W,M (French Only)
La Donna E Mobile

AmH-W,M FSY-W,M (Italian)
  MF-W,M (Italian Only) PaS-W,M
  RW-W,M (Italian Only) WiS7-W,M
La Fiesta
  OBN-M VA-W,M
La Fill' Du Roi D'Espagne
  CFS-W,M (French)
La Fille De La Meuniere
  FSF-W (French)
La Fille De Parthenay
  FSF-W (French)
La Fontaine
  AmH-M
La Gardez Piti Milatte
  BaB-W,M (French)
La Golondrina
  LaS-M RW-M STR-M TI1-W,M
  UFB-W,M
La Golondrina see also O Swallow Swift
La Guignolee
  BSC-W,M
La Guillannee
  FSO-W,M (French)
La Isla Bonita
  BHO-W,M
La Jesucita
  LaS-W,M MAR-M
La-La-La-Lies
  WA-W,M
La La La Mi
  Boo-W,M
La-La-Lu
  NI-W,M OTJ-W,M
La La Song
  FSA2-W,M
La Le Padraic 1913
  VP-W
La Linda Manita
  CDM-W,M (Spanish)
La Maison Denise
  CSD-W,M (French)
La Marche D'la Noce
  CaF-W (French Only)
La Marguerite
  CUP-W,M (French Only)
La Marseillaise
  AmH-W,M (French) CUP-W,M
  (French Only) ESB-W,M (French)
  FW-W (French) MML-W,M
  (French) OTJ-W,M (French) RW-
  M SiP-W,M (French) SMW-W,M
  (French) STR-W,M SWF-W,M
  (French)
La Mer see Beyond the Sea
La Mer' Michel
  CUP-W,M (French Only)
La Mere Acadie
  CE-W,M (French)
La Mere Michel
  MP-W,M (French Only) OTJ-W,M
  (French Only)
La Mouche Et La Fourmi
  CUP-W,M (French Only)
La Muneca
  SCL-W,M (Spanish) SHP-W,M
La Musique Est Un Art
  Boo-W,M (French Only)
La Noel Passee (The Orphan and
  King Henry)
  F2-W,M (French)
La Nouvelle Annee
  CaF-W (French Only)
La Nuit Palit
  Boo-W,M (French Only)
La Paloma (The Dove)
  AmH-W,M BSC-W FSY-W,M

(Spanish) LMR-W,M MF-W,M
  MH-W,M MML-W,M (Spanish)
  OTJ-W,M SL-W,M TI1-M UFB-M
  WiS8-W,M
La Peregrinacion
  JF-W,M (Spanish)
La Polichinelle
  CUP-W,M (French Only)
La Raspa
  LaS-M MAR-W,M
La Raspe
  HS-W,M
La Sorella
  AmH-M LaS-M MF-M
La Spagnola
  LaS-M OBN-M
La Tour Prends Garde
  CUP-W,M (French Only)
La Valse Criminelle
  CaF-W (French Only)
La Valse De Not'e Village
  CaF-W (French Only)
La Valse Des Creoles
  CaF-W (French Only)
La Veille De Vot'e Fete
  CaF-W (French Only)
La Verse De Basile
  CaF-W (French Only)
La Verse Qui M'a Po'te A Ma
  Fosse
  CaF-W (French Only)
La Vie En Rose
  MF-W,M RoE-W,M
La Violetera
  LaS-M
La Visite Du Jour De L'an
  CFS-W,M (French)
La Viudita
  LA-W,M (Spanish)
La Viudita Del Conde Laurel
  LA-W,M (Spanish)
La Zingana
  AmH-M
Laat Ons Den Herre Singen
  AHO-W,M (Dutch)
Labor (Labor's Noble! Labor's
  Holy!)
  AL-W
Labor (There's a Never-Dying
  Chorus)
  AL-W
Labor ('Tis Toil That over Nature
  Gives Man His Proud Control)
  GrM-W,M
Labor Chant
  AL-W
Labor Day Song
  AL-W
Labor Free for All
  AL-W
Labor Hymn
  AL-W
Labor in Want
  AL-W
Labor Is Honor
  AL-W
Labor Is King
  GrM-W,M
Labor, Land, and Freedom
  AL-W
Labor On
  GH-W,M
Labor Song
  AL-W
Labor Trouble Murder
  BMM-W
Laborer

GrM-W,M
Laborer's Battle Hymn
   AL-W,M
Laborer's Lament
   AL-W
Laborers of Christ, Arise
   AHO-W,M GH-W,M
Laboring and Heavy Laden
   AHO-W,M
Labor's Chorus
   AL-W
Labor's Demand
   AL-W
Labor's Harvest Home
   AL-W
Labor's Marseillaise
   AL-W
Labor's Ninety and Nine
   AL-W
Labor's Yankee Doodle
   AL-W
Lacrimoso Son Io
   Boo-W,M (Italian Only)
Ladder
   Fa-W,M
Laden with Guilt and Full of Fears
   AME-W,M
Ladies Auxiliary
   LW-W,M (Spanish)
Ladies of Brisbane
   ATM-W,M
Ladies of the Town
   BS-W,M
Ladies Patriot Song
   MPP-W,M
Ladies Patriotic Song
   OHG-W,M
Ladies to the Center
   Oz3-W
Ladies' Triumph
   POT-M
Ladies Who Lunch
   Co-W,M OTO-W TW-W
Lady (Graham Goble)
   TI2-W,M
Lady (Kusik, Singleton/Kaempfert,
   Rehbein)
   OnT1-W,M
Lady Alice
   FMT-W ITP-W,M SCa-W,M
Lady and the Dragoon
   SCa-W,M
Lady Blue
   ToO76-W,M
Lady Bug
   ASB3-W,M
Lady Bug, Lady Bug
   SiR-W,M
Lady Came from Baltimore
   RB-W TI2-W,M
Lady Chatterly's Lover
   LW-W,M PO-W,M
Lady, Come Down and See
   Boo-W,M OTJ-W,M
Lady Daffadown
   MH-W,M
Lady Fair
   Oz1-W,M
Lady from L.A.
   OTO-W
Lady Gay
   ITP-W,M Oz1-W,M
Lady Godiva
   GAR-W,M
Lady, If You So Spite Me
   EL-W,M
Lady in Blue

GMD-W,M
Lady in Red
   MF-W,M MR-W,M
Lady in the Blue Mercedes
   TOH-W,M
Lady Is a Tramp
   DBC-W,M DJ-W,M FrS-W,M
   HC2-W,M LM-W,M OTO-W
   RT4-W,M RW-W,M TI1-W,M
   TS-W TW-W UBF-W,M UFB-W,M
Lady Is Love
   TTH-W,M
Lady Isabel and the Elf Knight
   FMT-W FW-W IF-W,M SCa-W
Lady Jane
   RoS-W,M
Lady Lay Down
   TOC82-W,M
Lady Lost Her Glove
   SCa-W,M
Lady Madonna
   BBe-W,M Be2-W,M SwS-W,M
   TWS-W WG-W,M
Lady Maggie
   FMT-W
Lady Maisry
   SCa-W
Lady Margaret
   BSC-W FW-W Oz1-W,M
   SCa-W,M
Lady Margarette
   BSC-W
Lady Moon
   FSA1-W,M SL-W,M TF-W,M
Lady Moon see also O Lady Moon
Lady Must Live
   TS-W
Lady Needs a Change
   TW-W
Lady of Carlisle
   FW-W
Lady of Spain
   LaS-W,M MuM-W,M OBN-W,M
   OnT1-W,M RW-W,M STP-W,M
   T-W,M TI1-W,M UFB-W,M
Lady Play Your Mandolin
   MF-W,M
Lady, She's Right
   TOC83-W,M
Lady Sings the Blues
   LSB-W,M
**Lady Sings the Blues (Love Theme)
   see Happy (Love Theme from
   Lady Sings the Blues)**
Lady Smiles
   OnT1-W,M
Lady Soul
   TTH-W,M
Lady Walpole's Reel
   LMR-M
Lady Washington's Lamentation
   ESU-W
Lady Who Came to Dinner
   AF-W
Lady Willpower
   MF-W,M
Ladybird, Ladybird, Fly Away
   Home
   OTJ-W,M
Ladybird's Lullaby
   VS-W,M
Lady's Daughter of Paris
   SCa-W,M
Lady's Disgrace
   SCa-W,M
Lady's in Love with You
   OTO-W

Lady's Man
   OGC2-W,M
Lady's Not for Sale
   SuS-W,M
Laird o' Cockpen
   HSD-W,M SeS-W,M
Lak Jeem
   RM-W,M
Lake
   GeS-W,M
Lake at Night
   FSA1-W,M SL-W,M
Lam', Lam', Lam'
   EFS-W,M
Lamb Blood Dun Wash Me Clean
   BDW-W,M
Lamb Is the Light
   GH-W,M
Lamb of Glory
   GP-W,M VB-W,M
Lamb of God (Twila Paris)
   GP-W,M VB-W,M
Lambeth Walk
   DBC-W,M UBF-W,M
Lambs in the Valley
   VB-W,M
Lame Crane
   FSA2-W,M
Lament
   BMC-M
Lament for Brendan Behan
   IS-W,M
Lament of Ian the Proud
   NA-W,M
Lament of the Troubadour
   GUM2-W,M
Lament to Love
   ILT-W,M
Lamentation over Boston
   BC1-W,M MPP-W,M
Lamento Borincano
   CDM-W,M (Spanish) PSN-W,M
Lamm Gottes Abgeschlachtet
   AHO-W,M (German)
**Lammlein Geht see Ein Lammlein
   Geht**
L'Amour Est Bleu see Love Is Blue
L'Amour Toujours L'Amour (Love
   Everlasting)
   MF-W,M
Lamp Is Low
   GSO-W,M (French)
Lamp of Our Feet, Whereby We
   Trace
   Hy-W,M
Lamplighter
   LA-W,M (Spanish) SiR-W,M
Lamplighter's Hornpipe
   POT-M
Lancashire May Song
   BB-W
Land I Love
   RS-W,M SFB-W,M
Land League's Advice to the
   Tenant Farmers of Ireland
   VP-W
Land o' the Leal
   HSD-W,M SeS-W,M
Land of a Thousand Dances
   DRR-W,M TRR-W,M
Land of Beulah
   GH-W,M
Land of Cotton
   TOH-W,M
Land of Counterpane
   MH-W,M
Land of Dreams

LWT-W,M
Land of Flowers
FSA2-W,M
Land of Freedom
SoF-W,M
Land of Hope and Glory
FWS-W,M U-W
Land of La La
TTH-W,M
Land of My Youth
BV-W,M
Land of Nod
ASB3-W,M
Land of Opportunitee
LSO-W
Land of Our Birth
SoF-W,M
Land of Our Fathers
AL-W
Land of Pleasure
SHS-W,M
Land of Rest
WN-W,M
**Land of the Leal see Land o' the
Leal**
Land of the Long White Cloud
SNZ-W,M (Maori)
Land of the Midnight Sun
FSA2-W,M SL-W,M
Land of the Noonday Night
AFP-W
Land of the Silver Birch
SSe-W,M VA-W,M
Land of the South
SiS-W
Land of the Swallows
GrM-W,M
Land-Sighting
GC-W,M
Land Song
AL-W
Land That Gives Birth to Freedom
AL-W
Land We Love Is Calling
ESB-W,M
Landholders' Victory
AFP-W
Landing of the Pilgrims
CA-W,M ESB-W,M MML-W,M
TF-W,M
Landless
AL-W
Landlord, Fill the Flowing Bowl
FW-W HSD-W,M OFS-W,M
Lane County Bachelor
AmS-W,M
L'ane Et Le Loup
CUP-W,M (French Only)
Language Barrier
TW-W
Lantern
RoS-W,M
Lanterns Glowing
MHB-W,M
**Lara's Theme (Dr. Zhivago) see
Somewhere My Love**
**Lara's Theme from the Glass
Menagerie see Blue Roses**
Larboard Watch
HSD-W,M
Lardy Dah
HAS-W,M
Largo (Dvorak)
MF-M RW-M
Largo (Handel)
AmH-M ESB-W,M MF-M SL-W,M
WiS7-M

Largs
SBB-W
Lark (In Misty Gray the Night Is
Slowly Drifting)
FSA2-W,M
Lark (The Lark Now Leaves His
Wat'ry Nest)
MMY-W,M
Lark (Oh, Swan of Slenderness,
Dove of Tenderness)
TH-W,M
Lark and the Magpie
RW-W,M
**Lark Cigarettes Jingle see There Is
Nothing Like a Lark**
Lark in the Morn
BMC-W,M BT-W,M
Lark in the Morning
Oz3-W,M
Lark, Linnet and Nightingale
Boo-W,M
Larry O'Gaff
POT-M
Larry's Good-Bye
FHR-W,M SiS-W
Las Chipanecas
LaS-M
Las Cuatro Milpas
GuC-W,M (Spanish)
Las Mananitas
GuC-W,M (Spanish) HS-W,M
(Spanish)
Las Posadas
LaS-W,M (Spanish Only)
Lass Canadian
ASB6-W,M
Lass from the Low Country
OTJ-W,M
Lass of Lynn's Lament
SR-W,M
Lass of Mohea
SA-W,M
Lass of Mohee
SCa-W
**Lass of Mohee see also Fair Indian
Lass, Indian Lass, Little Mohea,
and Pretty Mauhee (Mohea)**
Lass of Richmond Hill
CSo-W,M OH-W,M OTJ-W,M
Lass of Roch Royal
FMT-W FSU-W FW-W SCa-W
Lass with the Delicate Air
FSY-W,M OTJ-W,M
Lassie from Lancashire
U-W
Last Cake of Supper
ATS-W
Last Call
MoM-W
Last Chance Texaco
RV-W
Last Cowboy Song
TOH-W,M
Last Dance (Cole Porter)
BS-W,M
Last Dance (Paul Jabara)
MoA-W,M
Last Drink with Don
VS-W,M
Last Farewell
Oz4-W,M SCa-W
Last Friday Evening
BSC-W
Last General March
AL-W
Last Kiss
HR-W

Last Longhorn
HWS-W,M
Last Mile
FSA2-W,M
Last Mile of the Way
BSG-W,M BSP-W,M
Last Month of the Year
BCS-W,M
Last Night (the Nightingale Woke
Me)
AmH-W,M ESB-W,M HSD-W,M
TF-W,M WiS8-W,M
Last Night I Had the Strangest
Dream
IHA-W,M TI1-W,M UFB-W,M
WSB-W,M
Last Night I Held a Little Hand
AF-W
Last Night on the Back Porch
RDT-W,M TI1-W,M UFB-W,M
Last of Jack
NF-W
Last of the Alabama
SiS-W
Last Ride
HOH-W
Last Rose of Summer
AmH-W,M BH-W,M CSo-W,M
FSY-W,M (Italian) FW-W
HSD-W,M NAS-W,M OFS-W,M
OS-W OTJ-W,M RW-W,M
TH-W,M WiS7-W,M
Last Round-Up
FC-W,M MF-W,M SoC-W
Last Roundup
HOH-W
Last Serenade
Oz4-W,M
Last Song
BSo-W,M
Last Thing I Needed (the First
Thing This Morning)
TOC83-W,M
Last Thing on My Mind
RBO-W,M
Last Time
RoS-W,M
Last Time I Felt Like This
TI1-W,M UFB-W,M
Last Time I Saw Paris
BeL-W,M HLS8-W,M L-W
TI1-W,M UFB-W,M
Last Token
Oz4-W
Last Train to Clarksville
GAR-W,M MF-W,M
Last Waltz (Stephen Sondheim)
LN-W,M
Last Waltz, The (The Ballroom Was
Empty, the Hour Was Three)
OGC2-W,M
Last Waltz, The (I Wondered
Should I Go or Should I Stay)
GG3-W,M
Last Week I Took a Wife
ATS-W
Last Will
AL-W
Last Word in Lonesome Is Me
ATC2-W,M CSp-W,M
Late Last Night (Way Downtown)
BSo-W,M
Late, Late Show
DR-W,M NK-W,M
Lately Song
HFH-W,M
Later

LN-W,M TW-W
Latest Thing from Paris
Fi-W,M
Laudate Dominum
MU-W,M (Latin)
Laudate Nomen
Boo-W,M (Latin Only)
Laudate Nomen Domini
Boo-W,M (Latin Only)
Laugh! Clown! Laugh!
MF-W,M MR-W,M
Laughin' Fool
JF-W,M
Laughing Catch
Boo-W,M
Laughing Ho, Ho!
SOO-W,M
Laughing, Laughing, Laughing
Boo-W,M
Laughing on the Outside
MF-W,M PB-W,M
Laughing Polka
OTJ-M
Laughing Song
MMY-W,M MuM-W,M SL-W,M
Laughing Spring
MML-W,M
Laughter
FSA2-W,M
Laughter in the Rain
TI2-W,M
Laughter Makes the World Go
Round
Boo-W,M
Launch
MPP-W
Launch, The
ANS-W
Laura (Mercer/Raksin)
GG5-W,M GSF-W,M GSN3-W,M
HLS5-W,M OHF-W RDT-W,M
RT4-M RW-W,M
Laura (What's He Got That I Ain't
Got)
TI1-W,M UFB-W,M
Laura Lee
FHR-W,M SSF-W,M SSFo-W,M
Laura's Grave
ESU-W
Lauriger Horatius
HSD-W,M
Lauterbach
AS-W,M (German)
Lavender Blue (Dilly Dilly)
FW-W IL-W,M MAB1-W MSA1-W
Lavender Blue (from Walt Disney's
So Dear to My Heart)
HLS3-W,M NI-W,M RT4-W,M
RW-W,M
Lavender Cowboy
FW-W
Lavender's Blue
FBI-W,M HS-W,M MG-W,M
OTJ-W,M SMa-W,M SOO-W,M
TF-W,M UF-W,M
Law
MSB-W
Law and Order
SL-W,M
Law Is for Protection of the People
SuS-W,M
Law Is the True Embodiment
GiS-W,M MGT-W,M SL-W,M
Lawdy, Lawdy, Lawdy
NH-W
Lawdy, Miss Clawdy
GG3-W,M THN-W,M

Lawman
TVT-W,M
Lawn As White As the Driven
Snow
FSS-W,M SSP-W
Lawn Mower Song
SOO-W,M
Lawrence of Arabia (Theme)
HFH-M TOM-M
Lawyers
TW-W
Lay By the Corn
LC-W
Lay Dis Body Down
FSSC-W,M
Lay Dis Body Down see also Lay
This Body Down
Lay Down, Dogies
ATS-W
Lay Down My Sword and Shield
JF-W,M
Lay Down Sally
TI1-W,M UFB-W,M
Lay Down Your Staffs
VA-W,M
Lay Me Down
MF-W,M
Lay Me Down and Save the Flag
SiS-W
Lay Me Low
GB-W,M
Lay Some Happiness on Me
THN-W,M
Lay This Body Down
WN-W,M
Lay This Body Down see also Lay
Dis Body Down
Layla
GrS-W,M
Lazarus
SaS-W,M
Lazarus and the Rich Man
Oz4-W
Lazarus Come Forth
VB-W,M
Lazy
MU-W,M
Lazy Afternoon
TI1-W,M ToS-W,M TW-W
UBF-W,M UFB-W,M WU-W,M
Lazy Cat
MH-W,M
Lazy Clouds
ASB2-W,M
Lazy Day (Powers/Fischoff)
BHB-W,M OnT6-W,M
Lazy Days
MBS-W,M
Lazy Man and the Busy Man
SCL-W,M
Lazy Mary
ASB1-W,M OTJ-W,M
Lazy Mary, Will You Get Up
BBF-W,M RW-W,M SOO-W,M
Lazy Mood
OHF-W
Lazy River
AO-W,M FPS-W,M GSN2-W,M
RW-W,M
Lazy Robin
FBI-W,M
Lazy Sheep, Pray Tell Me Why
OTJ-W,M
Lazy Young Man
Oz3-W,M
Lazybones
OHF-W WiS9-W,M

Le Bel Age
TTH-W,M
Le Chant Du Depart
CUP-W,M (French Only)
Le Cygne see Swan, The (Saint-
Saens)
Le Forgeron
CUP-W,M (French Only)
Le Freak
SoH-W,M
Le Grand Boom Boom
Mo-W,M NM-W,M OTO-W
Le Jardin D'Amour
AS-W,M (French)
Le Joli Tambour
CUP-W,M (French Only)
Le Juif Errant
CaF-W (French Only)
Le Lendemain De Noces
FSO-W,M (French)
Le Long De La Grande Mer
CaF-W (French Only)
Le Long D'eine Grande Mer
CaF-W (French Only)
Le Moulin
CUP-W,M (French Only)
Le Nez De Martin
CUP-W,M (French Only)
Le Petit Navire
CUP-W,M (French Only)
Le Petit Nigaud
MP-W,M (French Only)
Le Pont De Morlaix
FSF-W (French)
Le Portrait
FSF-W (French)
Le Premier Soir De Mes Noces
CaF-W (French Only)
Le Premiere Jour De Janvier
CaF-W (French Only)
Le Retour Du Marin
SA-W,M (French Only)
Le Roi A Fait Battre Tambour
FSF-W (French)
Le Roi Dagobert
Ch-W (French Only) CUP-W,M
(French Only) MP-W,M (French
Only)
Le Roi Du Bal
FSO-W,M (French)
Le Roi S'en Va-t'en Chasse (The
King Is Gone A-Hunting)
F2-W,M (French)
Le Rosier
CUP-W,M (French Only)
Le Secret
AmH-M
Le Soldat Francais
CUP-W,M (French Only)
Le Tic-Tac Du Moulin
OTJ-W,M (French Only)
Le Vieux Soulard Et Sa Femme
CaF-W (French Only)
Lead Her Up and Down
MAS-W,M Oz3-W,M
Lead Her Up and Down see also
Rosa Becka Lina
Lead, Kindly Light
AME-W,M AmH-W,M CEM-W,M
ESB-W,M FiS-W,M GH-W,M
HF-W,M HSD-W,M Hy-W,M IH-M
NAS-W,M OTJ-W,M RDF-W,M
RW-W,M SL-W,M TB-W,M
TH-W,M WiS7-W,M
Lead Me Gently Home, Father
AME-W,M
Lead Me, Guide Me

HLS7-W,M SUH-W,M TI1-W,M
UFB-W,M
Lead Me, Lord, Lead Me in Thy
Righteousness
Hy-W,M
Lead Me On (Come On and Lead
Me On, Come On and Tease Me
All Night Long)
ToO79-W,M
Lead Me On (Trav'ling to the
Better Land)
GH-W,M
Lead Me, Saviour
GH-W,M
Lead Me to Calvary
AME-W,M
Lead Me to the Rock That's Higher
Than I
GrG-W,M
Lead On
CA-W,M
Lead On, O King Eternal
AHO-W,M AME-W,M CEM-W,M
Hy-W,M
Lead Poison on the Wall
SFF-W,M
Lead Us, Heavenly Father, Lead Us
Hy-W,M
Lead Us, O Father, in the Paths of
Peace
AHO-W,M Hy-W,M
Leadbelly Is a Hard Name
Am-W
Leader of the Pack
ERM-W,M GAR-W,M MF-W,M
Leading the Horses
GUM1-W,M
Leaf
YG-W,M
Leaf by Leaf the Roses Fall
TMA-W,M
Leah
TFC-W,M
Lean on Me
BHO-W,M DC-W,M LOM-W,M
Leander
SHS-W,M
Leanin' on de Lord
RF-W,M
Leanin' on the Ole Top Rail
FC-W,M
Leaning on a Lamp-Post
DBC-W,M UBF-W,M
Leaning on the Everlasting Arms
AME-W,M
Leap for Life
ASB1-M
Leap Frog
BBB-W,M TI2-W,M
Learn Me to Let All Women Alone
NH-W
Learn to Count
NF-W
Learn to Croon
LM-W,M OTO-W
Learn to Pray Ev'ry Day
BSG-W,M BSP-W,M
Learn Your Lessons Well
OTJ-W,M
Learn Your Lessons Well (Stephen
Schwartz)
G-W,M On-W,M OTO-W UBF-W,M
Learnin' the Blues
MF-W,M
Learning a Rhythm
SD-W,M
Learning to Knit

SiR-W,M
Learning to Lean
HHa-W,M
Learning to Swing
ASB1-W,M
Leather Bottle
OH-W,M
Leather Breeches
DD-W,M MHB-M
Leatherwing Bat
FW-W
Leave Her, Johnny
AFP-W AL-W ASB5-W,M FW-W
SA-W,M SWF-W,M
Leave It There
OM-W,M
Leave Me Alone (Ruby Red Dress)
AO-W,M TI1-W,M UFB-W,M
Leave Me with My Mother
FHR-W,M
Leave Them Boys Alone
TOC83-W,M
Leaves (Blades of Grass and Fern
Fronds)
FSA2-W,M
Leaves (New Leaves Come in
Spring)
ASB1-W,M
Leaves Are Gone
MH-W,M
Leaves in Autumn
MN-W,M
Leaves of Love
Mo-W,M
Leavin' Blues
LC-W Le-W,M
Leavin' Here, Don't Know Where
I'm Goin'
FVV-W,M
Leaving of Liverpool
FW-W IS-W,M
Leaving on a Jet Plane
CJ-W,M FPS-W,M MCG-W,M
PoG-W,M WG-W,M
Leaving the Party
AL-W
L'Echo Des Montagnes De
Bethleem
ESB-W,M (French Only)
Lechoh Adonoy
JS-W,M (Hebrew Only)
Lechoh Dodi
JS-W,M (Hebrew Only)
Lee Hays
PSN-W,M
Lee's Ferry
HB-W,M
Leezie Lindsay
AS-W,M TBF-W,M UF-W,M
**Leezie Lindsay see also Will Ye
Gang to the Hielands, Leezie
Lindsay?**
Left All Alone Again Blues
Bl-W,M
Left Hand, Right Hand
GM-W,M
Left Right Out of Your Heart
TI1-W,M UFB-W,M
Left to the Window
FP-W,M
Legacy (When in Death I Shall
Recline)
FSSC-W,M SHS-W,M
Legend
SN-W,M
**Legend, The (Tchaikovsky) see
Crown of Roses**

Legend of Bonnie and Clyde
NMH-W,M
Legend of Danville
SFF-W,M
Legend of St. Nicolas
ASB6-W,M
Legend of the Rebel Soldier
BSo-W,M
Legende De Saint Nicolas
OTJ-W,M (French Only)
**L'eggs Hose Jingle see Our L'eggs
Fit Your Legs**
Leis An Lurgainn
SeS-W,M
Lelei
SNZ-W,M (Maori)
Lemon Tree
OTJ-W,M
Lemon Twist
Mo-W,M NM-W,M
Lena
SHS-W,M
Lena Our Loved One Is Gone
FHR-W,M
Lenora
Oz4-W
Lenox
SHS-W,M
L'Envoi
RF-W,M
Leonard
NMH-W,M
Leroy
HR-W
Les Anges Dans Nos Campagnes
CE-W,M (French)
Les Belles Filles
CaF-W (French Only)
Les Bicyclettes De Belsize
MF-W,M
Les Canards
CUP-W,M (French Only)
Les Cloches Du Monastere
AmH-M
Les Filles De Roi
CaF-W (French Only)
Les Hirondelles
CaF-W (French Only)
Les Instruments De Musique
CUP-W,M (French Only)
Les Jours Me Sont Durs
CaF-W (French Only)
Les Maragouins
CaF-W (French Only)
Les Marionettes
GM-W,M OTJ-W,M
Les Noches Du Papillon
CUP-W,M (French Only)
Les Raftsmen
FW-W (French)
Les Tracas Du Hobo Blues
CaF-W (French Only)
Lesson from the Desert
FSA2-W,M
Lessons in Love
CFB-W,M
Lestoil
GSM-W,M
Let a Smile Be Your Umbrella
BBB-W,M OnT1-W,M PB-W,M
TI2-W,M
Let All Created Things
AHO-W,M
Let All Mortal Flesh Keep Silence
Hy-W,M
Let All the World in Every Corner
Sing

Hy-W,M SJ-W,M
Let All Who Enter Here
  Hy-W,M
Let All with Dutch Blood in Their
  Veins
  SiP-W,M (Dutch)
Let Brotherly Love Continue
  AL-W
Let Christian Hearts Rejoice Today
  AHO-W,M (Algonquin, French)
Let de Church Roll On
  BDW-W,M
Let de Heaven Light Shine on Me
  RF-W,M
Let 'Em Eat Cake
  GOB-W,M NYT-W,M
Let 'Em In
  PMC-W,M TI2-W,M
Let Everything That Breathes
  Praise the Lord
  SHP-W,M
Let Her Not Be Beautiful
  Mo-W,M NM-W,M OTO-W
Let Him Go, Let Him Tarry
  U-W
Let Him with Kisses of His Mouth
  AHO-W,M
Let It Be
  BBe-W,M Be2-W,M PMC-W,M
  RDF-W,M TWS-W WG-W,M
Let It Be Me
  RDT-W,M TI2-E,M
Let It Bleed
  RoS-W,M
Let It Loose
  RoS-W,M
Let It Rock
  HR-W
Let It Snow! Let It Snow! Let It
  Snow!
  BCh-W,M BCS-W,M MF-W,M
  OPS-W,M OTJ-W,M TI1-W,M
  UFB-W,M
Let Jesus Come into Your Heart
  AME-W,M OM-W,M
Let Love Come between Us
  OnT6-W,M
Let Me Be a Man
  WNF-W
Let Me Be the One
  ILT-W,M
Let Me Be There
  EP-W,M
Let Me Be Your Mirror
  MLS-W,M
Let Me Be Your Side Track
  LJ-W,M
Let Me Call You Sweetheart
  FWS-W,M HLS1-W,M MF-W,M
  MM-W,M OAP-W,M RDT-W,M
  RoE-W,M TI1-W,M UFB-W,M
Let Me Carry Your Cross for
  Ireland, Lord
  VP-W
Let Me Come In
  OTO-W UBF-W,M
Let Me Day Dream
  WDS-W,M
Let Me Down Easy
  TTH-W,M
Let Me Dream Again
  HSD-W,M TH-W,M
Let Me Entertain You
  DBC-W,M HC1-W,M LM-W,M
  OTJ-W,M OTO-W RW-W,M
  TI1-W,M UBF-W,M UFB-W,M
Let Me Fly

FGM-W,M FW-W
Let Me Give
  OGR-W,M
Let Me Go (Barry Manilow)
  TOF-W,M
Let Me Go (Jagger/Richards)
  RoS-W,M
Let Me Go Home Whiskey
  LC-W,M
Let Me Go, Lover
  OGC2-W,M TI1-W,M UFB-W,M
Let Me Go Where Saints Are Going
  AHO-W,M
Let Me Have Mother's Gospel
  GB-W,M
Let Me In
  GAR-W,M TOH-W,M
Let Me Kiss Him for His Mother
  SiS-W,M
Let Me Know (I Have a Right)
  ToO79-W,M
Let Me Lay My Funk on You
  DDH-W,M
Let Me Love You To-night
  HLS3-W,M RW-W,M
Let Me Make Love to You
  DDH-W,M
Let Me Rove Free
  OTJ-W,M
Let Me Sleep in Your Tent Tonight,
  Beal
  AFP-W
Let Me Sleep This Night Away
  Boo-W,M
Let Me Tell You What Is Nat'rally
  de Fac'
  NSS-W
Let My People Go
  BMC-W,M
Let Not Love on Me Bestow
  EL-W,M
Let Now the Harp
  VA-W,M
Let Old Nellie Stay
  HB-W,M
Let Our Gladness Know No End
  MC-W,M
Let Our Voices Be Heard
  HCY-W,M
Let Our Voices Now Ring Out
  Boo-W,M
Let Peace Endure
  SL-W,M
Let Simon's Beard Alone
  Boo-W,M OTJ-W,M
Let the Bells Ring Out
  SHP-W,M
Let the Bright Seraphim
  ESB-W,M
**Let the Church Roll On see Let de
Church Roll On**
Let the Deep Organ Swell
  AHO-W,M
Let the Good Times Roll
  DRR-W,M TI1-W,M TI2-W,M
  UFB-W,M
**Let the Heaven Light Shine on Me
see Let de Heaven Light Shine on
Me**
Let the Little Ones Come unto Me
  AME-W,M
Let the Lower Lights Be Burning
  AME-W,M CEM-W,M GH-W,M
  IH-M OM-W,M
Let the Rest of the World Go By
  FC-W,M MF-W,M
Let the River Run

LOM-W,M
Let the Savior Bless Your Soul
  Right Now
  GrG-W,M
Let the Song Last Forever
  WG-W,M
Let the Sun Shine Forever
  RuS-W,M (Russian)
Let the Sunshine In
  H-W,M HLS8-W,M ILS-W,M
  RW-W,M
Let the Whole Creation Cry
  SJ-W,M SL-W,M
Let the Whole World Sing
  VB-W,M
Let the Wind Blow (High or Low)
  Boo-W,M
Let the Wind Blow (There's a
  Storm on the Horizon)
  VB-W,M
Let the Words of My Mouth
  AME-W,M Hy-W,M
**Let Them Eat Cake see Let 'Em Eat
Cake**
Let Them Go
  VB-W,M
Let Them In see Let 'Em In
Let Them Wear Their Watches Fine
  AFP-W WW-W,M
Let There Be Light
  AHO-W,M MU-W,M
Let There Be Light, Lord God of
  Hosts
  Hy-W,M
Let There Be Love
  BBB-W,M DJ-W,M NK-W,M
  TI1-W,M UFB-W,M
Let There Be Peace on Earth
  BCh-W,M BSG-W,M BSP-W,M
  CEM-W,M FS-W,M JBF-W,M
  NCB-W,M On-W,M OPS-W,M
  OTJ-W,M WGB/O-W,M
Let There Be Planters
  GSM-W,M
Let There Be Praise
  VB-W,M
Let There Be You
  TI2-W,M
Let Things Be Like They Always
  Was
  SSA-W,M
Let Thy Kingdom
  AHO-W,M
Let Thy Word Abide in Us
  Hy-W,M
Let Tyrants Shake Their Iron Rod
  AHO-W,M
**Let Tyrants Shake Their Iron Rod
see also Chester**
Let Us All Speak Our Minds
  LW-W,M SWF-W,M
Let Us All Speak Our Minds If We
  Die for It
  SY-W,M
Let Us Be Merry in Our Old Clothes
  Boo-W,M
Let Us Begin
  CJ-W,M
Let Us Break Bread Together
  FoS-W,M FW-W Hy-W,M LT-W,M
Let Us Break the Bread Together
  AHO-W,M
Let Us Cheer the Weary
  B-W,M
Let Us Cheer the Weary Traveler
  AHO-W,M RF-W,M SpS-W,M
Let Us Crown Him

GH-W,M
Let Us Draw Near
  OGR-W,M
**Let Us Drink, Knights of the Round
  Table see Chevaliers De La Table
  Ronde**
Let Us Go Back to God
  GrG-W,M
Let Us Go Down to Jerden
  BDW-W,M
Let Us Go Forth
  GH-W,M
Let Us Play a Gay Musette
  VA-W,M
Let Us Praise Gawd
  NSS-W
Let Us Praise Him
  RF-W,M WN-W,M
Let Us with a Gladsome Mind
  ESB-W,M Hy-W,M RW-W,M
  SHP-W,M SJ-W,M
Let Your Fingers Do the Walking
  GSM-W,M
Let Your Living Water Flow
  AG-W,M
Let Your Love Flow
  GrS-W,M ToO76-W,M
Let's All Bring in a Member
  LoS-W
Let's All Sing Like the Birdies Sing
  PB-W,M TI2-W,M
Let's Be Buddies
  ML-W,M OTO-W UBF-W,M
Let's Be Lonesome Together
  GOB-W,M
Let's Be Sweethearts Again
  JD-W,M OnT1-W,M
Let's Build a Tower
  GM-W,M
Let's Call the Whole Thing Off
  HC1-W,M HFH-W,M LM-W,M
  LSO-W NYT-W,M OTO-W
  TI1-W,M UFB-W,M
Let's Cast Away Care and Merrily
  Sing
  Boo-W,M
Let's Chase Each Other around the
  Room
  NMH-W,M
Let's Dance (Baldridge)
  BBB-W,M TI2-W,M
Let's Dance (Bowie)
  TI2-W,M
Let's Do It (Let's Fall in Love)
  DC-W,M EY-W,M HC2-W,M MF-
  W,M ML-W,M OHB-W,M
Let's Do Something Cheap and
  Superficial
  WF-W,M
Let's Drink to All Our Wives
  Boo-W,M
Let's Fall in Love
  HST-W,M RoE-W,M TI1-W,M
  UFB-W,M
Let's Find Each Other Tonight
  TOC83-W,M
Let's Fly Away
  TW-W
Let's Get Away from It All
  OnT1-W,M TI1-W,M UFB-W,M
Let's Get It While the Getting Is
  Good
  TOH-W,M
Let's Get Lost
  OTO-W
Let's Get over Them Together
  TOC83-W,M

Let's Get Together
  OTJ-W,M
Let's Get Together
  (Sherman/Sherman)
  NI-W,M SBS-W,M
Let's Go
  Mo-W,M NM-W,M OTO-W
Let's Go Dancing
  SBF-W,M
Let's Go Fly a Kite
  NI-W,M OTJ-W,M OTO-W
  SBS-W,M WD-W,M
Let's Go Get Stoned
  ERM-W,M
Let's Go to the Store
  GM-W,M
Let's Go Walking
  AST-W,M RSL-W,M
Let's Hang On
  MF-W,M
Let's Have a Party
  AF-W PaS-W,M
Let's Have a Peal
  Boo-W,M
Let's Have a Peal for John Cooke's
  Soul
  Boo-W,M
Let's Have an Old Fashioned
  Christmas
  BCh-W,M Mo-W,M NM-W,M
Let's Keep America Beautiful
  VA-W,M
Let's Keep It That Way
  TOH-W,M
Let's Kiss and Make Up
  GOB-W,M
Let's Lift Him High
  OGR-W,M
Let's Live for Today
  TRR-W,M
Let's Lock the Door
  Mo-W,M
Let's March around the Wall
  FVV-W,M
"Let's Marry" Courtship
  NF-W
Let's Misbehave
  MF-W,M
Let's Not Talk about Love
  ML-W,M UBF-W,M
Let's Not Waste a Moment
  Mo-W,M NM-W,M OTO-W
Let's Pick a Pack (Juicy Fruit Gum)
  TI1-W,M UFB-W,M
Let's Play Band
  SiR-W,M
Let's Pretend
  RBO-W,M
Let's Put Out the Lights and Go to
  Sleep
  MF-W,M
Let's Say Goodbye Like We Said
  Hello
  OGC1-W,M
Let's Say Good-Night
  Su-W,M
Let's Spend the Night Together
  RoS-W,M
Let's Squiggle
  CMF-W,M
Let's Take a Walk around the
  Block
  MF-W,M
Let's Take the Long Way Home
  Mo-W,M NM-W,M OTO-W
Let's Talk Dirty in Hawaiian
  WF-W,M

Let's Turn Back the Years
  HW-W,M
Let's Twist Again
  DRR-W,M
Letter, The
  SBA-W
Letter, The (My Baby Just Wrote
  Me a Letter)
  GAR-W,M ILS-W,M MCG-W,M
  MF-W,M RW-W,M RY-W,M
  RYT-W,M
Letter Edged in Black
  EFS-W,M FW-W Oz4-W,M
Letter from Home
  ITP-W,M
Letter from the King
  LA-W,M (Spanish)
Letter Has Come to Me
  VS-W,M
Letter Home
  GCM-W,M
Letter in the Candle
  Oz4-W,M
Letter That Never Came
  EFS-W,M
Letters
  ITP-W,M
Letters and Names
  RSL-W,M
Letters Have No Arms
  OGC1-W,M
Letting Go
  PMC-W,M
Levee Camp Blues
  LC-W
Levee Camp Song
  LC-W
Levee Song
  NAS-W,M
Levon
  TI2-W,M
L'Hamidie
  SiP-W,M (Turkish)
L'ho Adonai Hagdulo
  SBJ-W,M (Hebrew Only)
L'ho Dodee
  SBJ-W,M (Hebrew Only)
L'Homme Arme
  SFM-W
L'hu Neraneno
  SBJ-W,M (Hebrew Only)
Li Ch'ing (Departure)
  FD-W,M (Chinese)
Liaisons (Stephen Sondheim)
  LN-W,M TW-W
Libera Me (Gabriel Faure)
  MMM-W,M (Latin) SiM-W,M
  (Latin)
Libera Me Domine A
  Persequentibus (Pammelia)
  Boo-W,M (Latin Only)
Liberated Woman's Husband's
  Talking Blues
  LW-W,M
Liberation, Now!
  LW-W,M
Liberator Blues
  AF-W
Liberty
  SHS-W,M
Liberty Bird
  SiS-W
Liberty Song
  AAP-W,M AH-W,M EA-W,M
  HA-W,M MPP-W,M RW-W,M
  SAR-W,M SI-W,M
Liberty Tree

AWB-W BMM-W,M MPP-W,M
SBA-W SSS-W,M
Liberty's Call
SBA-W
Liberty's Reveille
SiS-W
Lida Rose
DBC-W,M TI2-W,M UBF-W,M
Lieb Und Leid
EL-W,M
Liebestraum
HLS1-W,M MF-M RW-M TI1-M
TM-M WGB/O-M
Liebestraume
OBN-M OTJ-W,M
Liechtensteiner Polka
PB-W,M PT-W,M (German Only)
TI1-W,M (German Only) TI2-W,M
(German Only) UFB-W,M (German
Only)
Lies (Jagger/Richards)
RoS-W,M
Lies (That Made Me Happy)
TI1-W,M UFB-W,M
Lies (We Took a Vow to Be Ever
True)
CFB-W,M
Lies, Lies, Lies
OTO-W
Life and Trial of Palmer
MSB-W
Life Boat
Oz4-W,M
Life Can Be Beautiful
Mo-W,M NM-W,M OTO-W
**Life Could Be a Dream see
Sh-Boom**
Life Goes On
TOH-W,M ToO79-W,M
Life I Lead
OnT6-W,M WD-W,M
Life in a Looking Glass
TTH-W,M
Life Is see Zorba (Theme)
Life Is a Battle
IFM-W
Life Is a Jest
Boo-W,M
Life Is a Long Winter's Day
Mo-W,M OTO-W
Life Is a Song (Let's Sing It
Together)
MF-W,M
Life Is a Toil
SWF-W,M
Life Is for Living
Mo-W,M NM-W,M
Life Is Just a Bowl of Cherries
HC2-W,M MF-W,M OTO-W
RW-W,M TI1-W,M UBF-W,M
UFB-W,M
Life Is Just What You Make It
BR-W,M
Life Is Like a Mountain Railroad
AFP-W AME-W,M BSo-W,M
FW-W
Life Is So Peculiar
OTO-W
Life of a Rose
ReG-W,M
Life of Ages, Richly Poured
AHO-W,M
Life of Georgia
BSC-W
Life of Georgie
Oz1-W,M
Life of the Mannings

MSB-W
Life on the Ocean Wave
FW-W HSD-W,M LMR-W,M
OTJ-W,M TH-W,M TMA-W,M
Life on the Vicksburg Bluff
ATS-W Sin-W,M SiS-W
Life Savers
GSM-W,M
Life That's Free
SMY-W,M
Life upon the Wicked Stage
SB-W,M
Life without Her
OTO-W UBF-W,M
Life's a Game (So What the Heck)
Mo-W,M NM-W,M OTJ-W,M
OTO-W
Life's a Game at Best
E-W,M
Life's Little Ups and Downs
GCM-W,M
Life's Onward Current
GrM-W,M
Life's Railway to Heaven
AME-W,M LSR-W,M
Life's Sea Is Oft'times Dark and
Dreary
AME-W,M
Lift Every Voice and Sing
FW-W JF-W
Lift Ev'ry Voice and Sing
RDF-W,M TI2-W,M
Lift Him Up
AME-W,M VB-W,M
Lift Thine Eyes
TF-W,M
Lift Up, Lift Up Your Voices Now
AME-W,M
Lift Up Our Hearts, O King of Kings
Hy-W,M
Lift Up the Voice
LMR-W,M (Italian)
Lift Up Your Heads
SJ-W,M
Lift Up Your Heads, Rejoice
AME-W,M
Lift Up Your Heads, Ye Mighty
Gates
Hy-W,M
Lift Up Your Hearts
Hy-W,M
Lift Your Glad Voices in Triumph
on High
AHO-W,M
Light
SL-W,M
Light after Darkness
GH-W,M
Light and Joy
JS-W,M (Hebrew)
Light As a Swallow
LA-W,M (Spanish)
Light at the End of the Tunnel
UBF-W,M
Light Cavalry Overture
RW-W
Light Is Breaking
AL-W
Light o' Love
FSS-W,M SSP-W
Light of God Is Falling
Hy-W,M
Light of Israel
JS-W,M (Hebrew)
Light of Light, Enlighten Me
Hy-W,M
Light of the World

G-W,M GH-W,M On-W,M OTO-W
UBF-W,M
Light of the World, We Hail Thee
AME-W,M Hy-W,M
Light Sings
OTO-W UBF-W,M
Light the Candles
GM-W,M
Light upon the Shore
GH-W,M
Lighthouse
HHa-W,M KS-W,M
Lighthouse Song
KS-W,M
Lighting of the Hanukkah Candles
SBJ-W,M (Hebrew Only)
Lighting of the Sabbath Candles
SBJ-W,M (Hebrew Only)
Lightly Laugh and Gaily Sing
GrM-W,M
Lightly Row
BM-W BMC-W,M HS-W,M
HSD-W,M OFS-W,M SiR-W,M
Lightnin' Blues
LC-W,M
Lightning Express
LSR-W,M
Lights Out
SNZ-W,M (Maori)
Like a Feather in the Wind
RTH-W
Like a Good Neighbor
GSM-W,M
Like a Rolling Stone
FoR-W,M RV-W
Like a Rough and a Rolling Sea
RF-W,M
Like a Sad Song
CJ-W,M PoG-W,M
Like a Shooting Star
LA-W,M (Spanish)
Like a Straw in the Wind
Mo-W,M NM-W,M
Like As a Father
Boo-W,M TF-W,M
Like Flowers We Spring Up Fair
ER-W,M
Like No Other Night
TTH-W,M
Like Noah's Weary Dove
AHO-W,M
Like Nothing Ever Happened
TOC82-W,M
Like Pretty Birds
GB-W,M
Like Silver Lamps
CCH-W,M
Like Someone in Love
RoE-W,M TI1-W,M UBF-W,M
Like the Lark
TH-W,M
Like to the Grass That's Green
Today
AHO-W,M
Likes and Dislikes
NF-W
Li'l Boy Name David
MoM-W,M
Li'l Darlin' (Neal Hefti)
MF-M
Li'l David Play on Yo' Hawp
Me-W,M
**Li'l David Play on Yo' Hawp see
also Little David Play on Yo' Harp**
Li'l Jasmine Bud
Ba-W,M
Li'l Liza Jane

BH-W,M ETB-W,M FSA2-W,M
FW-W MAS-W,M NAS-W,M
OFS-W,M OTJ-W,M PIS-W,M
POT-W,M RW-W,M TF-W,M

**Li'l Liza Jane see also Little Liza
Jane and Liza Jane**

Lilacs
FSY-W,M (German) MMY-W,M

Lilacs in the Rain
ASB6-W,M

Lili Marleen
GI-W,M

Lili Marlene
LMR-W,M T-W,M TI1-W,M

Lilies of the Field (Theme)
RW-M

Lilli Burlero
FW-W

Lilli Marlene
TI2-W,M U-W

Lilliburlero
SiP-W,M

Lilly
NH-W

Lilly and the Nightingale
FT-W,M

Lilly Dale
AH-W,M ATS-W,M BSC-W
FoS-W,M HSD-W,M

Lilly Fair Damsel
SCa-W,M

Lily Bells
MH-W,M

Lily Fair Damsel
SCa-W

Lily Lee
Oz1-W,M

Lily, Lily Oh
Oz1-W

**Lily Marlene see Lili Marleen, Lili
Marlene, and Lilli Marlene**

Lily of Arkansas
Oz1-W,M

Lily of Laguna
U-W

Lily of the Valley
AME-W,M GH-W,M SoC-W

Lily of the West
BSC-W FVV-W,M FW-W
NeA-W,M OFS-W,M Oz2-W,M

Lily Ray
FHR-W,M SSFo-W,M

Limehouse Blues
DJ-W,M MF-W,M

Limehouse Nights
GOB-W,M

Limerick
SiB-W,M

Limericks (A Canner, Exceedingly
Canny)
TF-W,M

Limericks (A Merchant Addressing
a Debtor)
CA-W,M

Limericks (There Was an Old Lady
from Fife)
ATS-W,M

Lincoln (The Day Is Hallowed)
FSA1-W,M SL-W,M

Lincoln (In Memoriam)
SiS-W

Lincoln (O Lincoln, Lincoln, Kind
and Brave)
ASB2-W,M

Lincoln (Old Abe Is Coming Down
to Fight)
ATS-W

Lincoln (We Love the Name of
Lincoln)
MH-W,M

Lincoln and Liberty
AH-W,M FGM-W,M FW-W

Lincoln Campaign Song
NeA-W,M

Lincoln Marching Song
SL-W,M

Lincoln's Land
FSA2-W,M

Lincolnshire Dance
SG-W,M

Lincolnshire Poacher
CSo-W,M FGM-W,M FW-W
OH-W,M

Linda
OnT1-W,M TI2-W,M

Linda Has Departed
FHR-W,M

Linda Mujer
RW-M

Linda on My Mind
CMG-W,M

Lindau
SHS-W,M

Lindbergh Baby
BMM-W

Linden Tree
HS-W,M (German) OTJ-W,M

Line for Lyons
TI1-M UFB-M

Line Up! Count Off!
MuM-W,M

Lineman's Hymn
SoC-W

Linen Clothes
ATS-W

Lines on the Phoenix Park Tragedy
VP-W

Lines on the Reduction of Pay
AL-W

Ling Ting Tong
HRB2-W,M

Linger Awhile
CS-W,M GST-W,M HLS2-W,M
OP1-W,M RW-W,M TI2-W,M

Linger in Blissful Repose
FHR-W,M SSFo-W,M

Linstead Market
FW-W OFS-W,M

Lion Sleeps Tonight
DRR-W,M TI1-W,M TRR-W,M
TWD-W,M UFB-W,M

Lion Tamer
MS-W,M

Lips That Touch Liquor Shall Never
Touch Mine
Oz2-W

Lips to Find You
TTH-W,M

Lipstick
AT-M

Lipstick on Your Collar
TI1-W,M UFB-W,M

Lipton Whistle Song
GSM-W,M

Lisbon
SHS-W,M

Lis'en to de Lam's
TH-W,M

**Lis'en to de Lam's see also Listen
to de Lambs and Listen to the
Lambs**

Lisetto
LMR-W,M

Lisnagade

VP-W,M

Lisping Lovers see Wery Pekooliar

List and Learn
GiS-W,M

List to the Sound
Boo-W,M

Listen (Listen! What Did You Hear
Just Now?)
MAR-W,M

Listen (to the Waves Breaking)
GBC-W,M

Listen to de Lambs
NFS-W,M RF-W,M

**Listen to de Lambs see also Lis'en
to de Lam's and Listen to the
Lambs**

Listen to My Song
TW-W

Listen to the Lambs
MuM-W,M YS-W,M

**Listen to the Lambs see also Lis'en
to de Lam's and Listen to de
Lambs**

Listen to the Mocking Bird
AmH-W,M FW-W HSD-W,M
LoS-W,M MF-W,M NAS-W,M
OTJ-W,M PoS-W,M WiS8-W,M

Listen to the Mockingbird
POT-W,M RW-W,M

Listen to the Music
DPE-W,M

Listen to the Watermill
GrM-W,M

Listen to What the Man Said
PMC-W,M TI2-W,M

Listening to the Rain
BSo-W,M

Litany
JF-W

Literary Dustman
MSB-W

Little Adobe Casa
SoC-W

Little Adobe Shack Way out West
SoC-W

Little Ah Sid
ATS-W

Little Alice Summers
Oz4-W

Little Angel with a Dirty Face
OGC2-W,M

Little Annie Rooney
BH-W,M EFS-W,M FSN-W,M
FSTS-W,M FU-W,M FuB-W,M
LoS-W,M MF-W,M OS-W Oz4-W

Little April Shower
NI-W,M SSe-W,M

Little at a Time
TOC83-W,M

Little Babes in the Woods
BSC-W

Little Baby Duckies
SOO-W,M

Little Baby in the Manger, I Love
You
SoP-W,M

Little Ball
FP-W,M

Little Ball of Yarn
FW-W

Little Ballad Girl
FHR-W,M

Little Ballerina Blue
TI2-M

Little Bell at Westminister
Boo-W,M

Little Belle Blair

FHR-W,M SSFo-W,M
Little Bells
SOO-W,M
Little Bells of Westminster
OTJ-W,M
Little Bessie
BSo-W,M
Little Betty Blue
MH-W,M
Little Billy Woodcock
ATS-W
Little Bird (I Can See You, Little Bird)
SMa-W,M
Little Bird (Peep Said the Little Bird)
ASB1-W,M
Little Bird, Little Bird
OTJ-W,M
Little Bird of the Cliff
LA-W,M (Spanish)
Little Bird Told Me
TI1-W,M UFB-W,M
Little Birdie
BIS-W,M BSo-W,M FW-W
ITP-W,M
Little Birdie Told Me So
TS-W
Little Birds
AST-W,M
Little Birds' Ball
ASB2-W,M
Little Biscuit
Mo-W,M NM-W,M OTO-W
Little Bit Independent
OPS-W,M
Little Bit Me, a Little Bit You
GAR-W,M
Little Bit More
ToO76-W,M TTH-W,M
Little Bit Now
OnT6-W,M
Little Bit of Good
CMV-W,M
Little Bit of Heaven (Shure They Call It Ireland)
MF-W,M OAP-W,M SLB-W,M WiS9-W,M
Little Bit of Soap
OnT6-W,M
Little Bit off the Top
PO-W,M
Little Bit Older
Sta-W,M
Little Bitty Baby
OTJ-W,M
Little Bitty Pretty One
FRH-W,M ILF-W,M
Little Black Bull
AFS-W,M ITP-W,M
Little Black Mustache
ITP-W,M Oz3-W
Little Black Train
AN-W LSR-W,M MG-W,M
Little Blossom
Oz2-W,M
Little Bo-Peep
AmH-W,M BBF-W,M Boo-W,M
CSo-W,M HS-W,M HSD-W,M
MF-W,M OTJ-W,M SOO-W,M
TF-W,M
Little Boat
TI2-W,M
Little Boxes
FW-W IHA-W,M JF-W,M
Little Boy, The
Mo-W,M NM-W,M OTJ-W,M

Little Boy and the Sheep
SMa-W,M
Little Boy Blew
BC1-W,M
Little Boy Blue
AmH-W,M ASB1-W,M HS-W,M
OTJ-W,M SOO-W,M
Little Boy in Galilee
SHP-W,M
Little Boy, Little Boy
AFP-W,M
Little Boy Lost
HLS5-W,M RW-W,M
Little Boy Lost see also Pieces of Dreams
Little Boy Named David see Li'l Boy Name David
Little Boy Threw His Ball So High
SCa-W
Little Boy Went Walking
GM-W,M
Little Boy Who Couldn't Count Seven
NF-W
Little Boy's Walk
IL-W,M
Little Brand New Baby
RBO-W,M
Little Brass Wagon
FW-W
Little Brother, Dance with Me
KS-W,M
Little Brown Church
MAB1-W MSA1-W NAS-W,M
Little Brown Church in the Vale
ATS-W LMR-W,M MAS-W,M
OS-W RDF-W,M
Little Brown Church in the Vale see also Church in the Wildwood
Little Brown Dog
AFS-W,M FW-W
Little Brown Jug
BH-W,M BMC-W,M BSC-W
CSo-W,M FW-W GG1-W,M
HAS-W,M IL-W,M IPH-W,M
MAB1-W MF-W,M MSA1-W
OFS-W,M OTJ-W,M Oz3-W,M
PoS-W,M RW-W,M TI1-W,M U-W
UFB-W,M
Little Bunch of Cactus on the Wall
SoC-W
Little Bunny
STS-W,M
Little Bunny Rabbit
AN-W MH-W,M
Little by Little
RoS-W,M
Little Cabbage (Hsiao Pai Ts'ai)
FD-W,M (Chinese)
Little Cabin Home on the Hill
BIS-W,M
Little Charlie Went A-Fishing
SY-W,M
Little Chicken
FF-W
Little Chickens in the Garden
Oz4-W,M
Little Child
Be1-W,M TWS-W
Little Child (Daddy Dear)
Mo-W,M NM-W,M OTJ-W,M
Little Child, Good Child
SiR-W,M
Little Children, Can You Tell
CSF-W
Little Children's Blues
Le-W,M

Little Chillun You Better Believe
BDW-W,M
Little Communist
AL-W
Little Cowgirl
SoC-W
Little Creek
ASB3-W,M
Little Dance
SD-W,M
Little Darlin' (Maurice Williams)
EP-W,M ERM-W,M FRH-W,M
Little Darling
Oz4-W,M
Little Darling Pal of Mine
BIS-W,M
Little David
ASB5-W,M BDW-W,M FW-W
PaS-W,M SFM-W SpS-W,M
VA-W,M
Little David Blues
AFP-W,M
Little David Play on Yo' Harp
BDW-W,M FN-W,M
Little David Play on Yo' Harp see also Li'l David Play on Yo' Hawp
Little David Play on Your Harp
ETB-W,M HS-W,M MAS-W,M
RF-W,M WN-W,M YS-W,M
Little David, Play Yo' Harp
AN-W
Little Deuce Coupe
HR-W
Little Dicky Bird
SOO-W,M
Little Dog Named Right
AFS-W,M
Little Dogs
NF-W
Little Donkey
BCh-W,M OTJ-W,M
Little Doogie
Oz2-W,M
Little Drops of Rain
Mo-W,M NM-W,M OTO-W
Little Drummer Boy
BCh-W,M
Little Duck
MES1-W,M MES2-W,M
Little Duckie Waddles
MES1-W,M
Little Ducklings
MG-W,M
Little Ducky Duddle
SOO-W,M
Little Dustman
NAS-W,M
Little Eau Pleine
IHA-W,M
Little Ella
FHR-W,M SSFo-W,M
Little Ella's an Angel
FHR-W,M
Little Eva
MPP-W
Little Eva Song
OTJ-W,M
Little Factory Girl to a More Fortunate Playmate
AL-W
Little Fairy Tale (Kabalevsky)
GM-M
Little Fall of Rain
UBF-W,M
Little Family
BSC-W BT-W,M FMT-W Oz4-W,M
SCa-W

Little Fiddler
ASB3-W,M
Little Fight in Mexico
Oz3-W,M
Little Fish
GM-W,M MAR-W,M
Little Fishermaiden
AmH-W,M
Little Fishes
MH-W,M
Little Flight Music
RSL-M
Little Flower see Petite Fleur
Little Folk Song
MHB-W,M (German)
Little Frog
MES1-W,M MES2-W,M
SOO-W,M
Little Fugue
BMC-W,M
Little Girl
TI2-W,M
Little Girl and the Dreadful Snake
BSo-W,M
Little Girl Blue
DJ-W,M TI1-W,M ToS-W,M TS-W
TW-W UFB-W,M
Little Girl from Little Rock
V-W,M
Little Girl Gone
AO-W,M On-W,M
Little Girl of Mine
ILF-W,M RY-W,M RYT-W,M
Little Girls
UBF-W,M
Little Glass of Wine
BSo-W,M
Little Goblin
MH-W,M
Little Good News
AWS-W,M TI2-W,M VB-W,M
Little Gossip
MLM-W,M TW-W
Little Gray Donkey
AST-W,M
Little Gray House
LS-W,M
Little Green Apples
AO-W,M ATC1-W,M CMG-W,M
CSp-W,M FOC-W,M ILS-W,M
RW-W,M TI1-W,M UFB-W,M
Little Grey Squirrel
SiR-W,M
Little Hands
UBF-W,M
Little Harry the Drummer Boy
SiS-W
Little Hatchet
LA-W,M (Spanish)
Little Horses
OA2-W,M
Little Indian
GM-W,M
Little Jack Horner
AmH-W,M HS-W,M MF-W,M
MH-W,M OTJ-W,M TF-W,M
Little Jar
ASB6-W,M
**Little Jasmine Bud see Li'l
Jasmine Bud**
Little Jazz Bird
GOB-W,M MF-W,M
Little Jenny Dow
FHR-W,M
Little Jesus, Sweetly Sleep
SHP-W,M
Little Joe

BSo-W,M Oz4-W
Little Joe the Wrangler
FW-W HWS-W,M MHB-W,M
Oz2-W SiB-W,M SoC-W,M
Little Joe the Wrangler's Sister Nell
HB-W,M Oz2-W SoC-W
Little Johnny
ASB2-W,M
Little Johnny Green's First
Experiment on Stilts
OTJ-W,M
Little Katie
SMa-W,M
Little Katy, or Hot Corn
SY-W,M
Little Kingdom I Possess
AHO-W,M
Little Kiss Each Morning
MF-W,M
Little Known Facts
YG-W,M
Little Lamb
OTJ-W,M TW-W UBF-W,M
Little Lap-Dog Lullaby
AFS-W,M
Little Lark
FSO-W,M (French)
Little Lights
GH-W,M
Little 'Liza Jane
GuC-W,M HS-W,M RS-W,M
**Little 'Liza Jane see also Li'l Liza
Jane and Liza Jane**
Little Lost Child
FSTS-W,M
Little Love
TI2-W,M
Little Mac
SiS-W
Little Mac, Little Mac, You're the
Very Man
FHR-W,M
Little Maggie
BIS-W,M BSo-W,M FPG-W,M
FSB2-W,M FSt-W,M FW-W
Little Maid Milking Her Cow
TMA-W,M
Little Major
Sin-W,M SiS-W
Little Man
OTO-W
Little Man in the Wood
BMC-W,M
Little Mary Phagan
FVV-W,M
Little Mary Sunshine
LMS-W,M OTO-W UBF-W,M
Little Mathy Groves
Oz1-W,M
Little Matthew Groves
FSSC-W
Little Matthy Groves
BSC-W,M
Little Matty Grove
ITP-W,M
**Little Matty Grove see also Matty
Groves**
Little Maumee
TBF-W,M
Little Me
Mo-W,M NM-W,M OTO-W
Little Miss Muffet
AmH-W,M Boo-W,M MH-W,M
OTJ-W,M
Little Mr. Banjo
MaG-W,M
Little Mocking Bird

AST-W,M
Little Mohea
FMT-W
Little Mohee
BF-W,M FW-W HS-W,M
NAS-W,M SAm-W,M
**Little Mohee see also Fair Indian
Lass, Indian Lass, Lass of Mohea,
and Pretty Mauhee (Mohea)**
Little Monk (Hsiao Ho Shang)
FD-W,M (Chinese)
Little Moon Came Out
Boo-W,M
Little More Cider
HSD-W,M
Little More Cider Too
TMA-W,M
Little More Faith in Jesus
BMM-W WN-W,M
Little More Grape, Captain Bragg
MPP-W
Little More Love
ToO79-W,M
Little Mose Groves
SCa-W,M
Little Moses
FGM-W,M FSt-W,M FW-W Oz4-W
Little Musgrave and Lady Barnard
BT-W,M SCa-W,M
Little Music
EL-W,M
Little Negro Fly
NF-W
Little Nellie Meeks
Oz2-W
Little New Log Cabin in the Hills
SoC-W
Little Nigger Baby
AFP-W
Little Night Music
MF-M UBF-W,M
Little Night Wind
ASB4-W,M
Little Nut Tree
SMa-W,M
Little of One with Tother
SR-W,M
Little Old Fashioned Karma
TOC83-W,M
Little Old Lady
HC1-W,M OTO-W UBF-W,M
Little Old Lady (from Pasadena)
ERM-W,M GAR-W,M HR-W
MF-W,M
Little Old Log Cabin by the Stream
SoC-W
Little Old Log Cabin in the Lane
FVV-W,M SoC-W TMA-W,M
Little Old Sod Shanty
AmS-W,M IHA-W,M
Little Old Sod Shanty on the Claim
FW-W GA-W,M Oz2-W,M
SoC-W,M
Little Old Sod Shanty on the Plain
ATS-W
Little Ole
ASB4-W,M SCL-W,M
Little Omie
Oz2-W
Little Ommie Wise
FMT-W
**Little Ommie Wise see also Oma
Wise, Omie Wise, and Poor Oma
Wise**
Little Ona
Oz2-W
Little Orphan Girl

SCa-W,M
Little Page Boy
  Oz1-W,M
Little Peter Rabbit
  CSS-W
Little Phoebe
  FW-W
Little Pickaninny
  NF-W
Little Pig (Man and a Woman
  Bought a Little Pig)
  AFS-W,M
Little Pig (There Was an Old
  Woman and She Had a Little Pig)
  FSA1-W,M
Little Pine Tree
  ASB4-W,M
Little Polly Flinders
  OTJ-W,M SMa-W,M
Little Pony
  MF-M
Little Prince
  AT-W,M LM-W,M OTO-W
Little Princess (Princesita)
  MSS-W,M (Spanish)
Little Rabbit
  FF-W
Little Raindrops
  MH-W,M
Little Red Caboose
  SiR-W,M
Little Red Caboose behind the
  Train
  LSR-W,M SoC-W
Little Red Hat
  OHT-W,M
Little Red Hen
  GM-W,M MH-W,M NF-W
Little Red Lark
  MHB-W,M
Little Redbird in the Tree
  MG-W,M
Little Robin Red Breast
  FP-W,M
Little Rock Atop the Mountain
  Crest
  FSO-W,M (French)
Little Rooster
  NF-W
Little Rose
  GC-W,M
Little Rosebud Fair
  FSO-W,M (French)
Little Rosewood Casket
  BSC-W DD-W,M FW-W ITP-W,M
  Oz4-W,M TBF-W,M
Little Roy Rickey
  BMM-W
Little Sailboat
  ASB6-W,M
Little Sally More
  MAR-W,M
Little Sally Racket
  FW-W LW-W,M
Little Sally Walker
  FMT-W FVV-W,M FW-W Le-W,M
Little Sally Waters
  OTJ-W,M
Little Sandy Girl
  SGT-W,M
Little Scotch-ee
  AmS-W,M
Little Seaside Village
  Oz4-W,M
Little Sergeant
  SSS-W,M
Little Shamrock

OTJ-W,M
Little Sheep
  ASB1-W,M
Little Shepherd
  ASB4-W,M
Little Ship
  FVV-W,M LTL-W,M
Little Shoemaker (In the
  Shoemaker's Shop This
  Refrain Would Never Stop)
  TI1-W,M UFB-W,M
Little Shoemaker (There's a Little
  Wee Man in a Little Wee House)
  HS-W,M SOO-W,M
Little Short Legs
  ASB2-W,M
Little Sir Echo
  LoS-W,M MF-W,M
Little Sir Hugh
  SCa-W
Little Sir Hugh see also Sir Hugh
Little Sir William
  F1-W,M
Little Sister
  SRE1-W,M
Little Sister, Won't You Marry Me
  NF-W
Little Sleeping Negroes
  NF-W
Little Snowflake
  SSe-W,M
Little Sparrow
  DD-W,M FMT-W
Little Star
  ERM-W,M ILF-W,M MF-W,M
Little Star (Estrellita)
  MSS-W,M (Spanish)
Little Star Creeps o'er the Hill
  SHP-W,M
Little Still
  AF-W
Little Strawberry Girl
  SY-W,M
Little Street Where Old Friends
  Meet
  Mo-W,M NM-W,M TI2-W,M
Little Sun, a Little Rain
  SL-W,M
Little T & A
  RoS-W,M
Little Thief
  ASB3-W,M
Little Things (Little Drops of Water)
  AmH-W,M OTJ-W,M
Little Things (Stephen Sondheim)
  Co-W,M
Little Things (Willie Nelson)
  WNF-W
Little Things Mean a Lot
  HLS3-W,M RW-W,M
Little Things You Do Together
  OTO-W TW-W UBF-W,M
Little Tin Box
  TI2-W,M TW-W
Little Tom Tinker
  BM-W HS-W,M
Little Tommy Tinker
  CSS-W
Little Tommy Tucker
  OTJ-W,M
Little Topsy's Song
  SY-W,M
Little Trouble Goes a Long, Long
  Way
  Mo-W,M NM-W,M
Little Trouble Goes a Long Way
  OTO-W

Little Trumpet
  GB-W,M
Little Tune
  SSe-W,M
Little Turtle Dove
  BT-W,M SoF-W,M VA-W,M
Little Vanny
  MPP-W
Little Vine-Clad Cottage on the
  Claim
  SoC-W
Little Wheel A-Turnin'
  MML-W,M
Little Wheel A-Turnin' in My Heart
  AH-W,M WiS7-W,M
Little Wheel A-Turning
  HS-W,M
Little While
  GH-W,M
Little White Church
  BSo-W,M
Little White Church on the Hill
  HLS7-W,M
Little White Duck
  MF-W,M OTJ-W,M RW-W,M
Little White Gardenia
  AT-W,M OTO-W
Little White Lies
  WDS-W,M
Little Widow Dunn
  ATS-W
Little Willie
  Oz4-W,M PSN-W,M SCa-W,M
Little Wind
  SSe-W,M
Little Yellow Dog
  Oz1-W,M
Liturgy Plainsong
  PAJ-W,M
Live and Let Die
  AO-W,M GrH-W,M RW-W,M
  TI2-W,M
Live and Let Live
  BIS-W,M
Live for Life
  GG4-W,M RW-W,M
Live for To-day
  NaM-W,M
Live Humble
  RF-W,M
Live In
  Mo-W,M NM-W,M OTO-W
Live Is Life
  TTH-W,M
Live, Laugh, Love
  Fo-W,M TW-W
Live with Me
  RoS-W,M
Liverpool
  SHS-W,M
Liverpool Dock
  Oz1-W,M
Liverpool Hornpipe
  POT-M
Livery Stable Blues
  Mo-W,M NM-W,M
Livin' in All Men
  JF-W,M
Livin' It Up (Friday Night)
  ToO79-W,M
Livin' on a Prayer
  BHO-W,M
Livin' Thing
  ELO-W,M
Living for Jesus
  OM-W,M
Living in America

TTH-W,M
Living in Laodicea
　VB-W,M
Living in the Past
　BJ-W,M
Living in the Whitehouse
　DBL-W
Living Simply
　Mo-W,M NM-W,M OTO-W
Living Years
　LOM-W,M
Livingstone, Addie
　SiS-W
Livrochoh
　JS-W,M (Hebrew Only)
Liza (All the Clouds'll Roll Away)
　GOB-W,M MF-W,M NYT-W,M
　RoE-W,M
Liza Jane
　AmS-W,M ASB6-W,M DD-W,M
　GC-W,M HAS-W,M NFS-W,M
　OS-W Oz3-W,M SG-W,M
Liza Jane see also L'il Liza Jane
and Little Liza Jane
Liza Lee
　SA-W,M
Lizzie Borden
　TW-W
Lizzie Dies Tonight
　FHR-W,M
Lizzie's Comin' Home
　OHT-W,M
Llama
　ASB5-W,M
Llorona
　FG2-W,M (Spanish Only)
Lo, As the Potter Molds His Clay
　SBJ-W,M
Lo! He Comes with Clouds
　Descending
　Hy-W,M
Lo! Heaven and Earth
　CSo-W,M
Lo, How a Rose
　SJ-W,M
Lo, How a Rose E'er Blooming
　CCH-W,M CI-W,M GeS-W,M
　Hy-W,M UF-W,M
Lo, How a Rose E'er Blooming see
also Es Est Ein' Ros' Entsprungen
Lo, I Shall Never Want
　MML-W,M
Lo Mucho Que Te Quiero
　OnT1-W,M (Spanish)
Lo, the Winter Is Past
　SHP-W,M
Lo, We Walk a Narrow Way
　SoF-W,M
Lo, What a Branch of Beauty
　SL-W,M TF-W,M
Lo! What a Glorious Sight Appears
　AME-W,M
Lo, What Enraptured Songs of
　Praise
　AHO-W,M
Loaf of Bread
　AL-W
Loath to Depart
　SSP-W
Lobet Den Herrn Alle Seine
　Heerschaaren
　BC1-W,M (German Only)
Lobet Und Preiset
　SHP-W,M
Lobster Quadrille
　MuM-W,M
Local Memory

WNF-W
Loch Lomond
　ASB6-W,M BeB-W,M CSo-W,M
　FBI-W,M FW-W GC-W,M HS-W,M
　HSD-W,M IL-W,M MF-W,M
　NAS-W,M OFS-W,M OS-W
　OTJ-W,M RW-W,M SL-W
　STR-W,M TH-W,M U-W VA-W,M
Loch Lomond see also By Yon
Bonnie Banks
Lochaber No More
　SeS-W,M
Lock and Key
　SiR-W,M
Lock the Door, Larriston
　SBB-W
Locked in the Atom
　GBC-W,M
Locked in the Walls of Prison
　Oz2-W,M
Locked Out Boogie
　DBL-W
Locks and Bolts
　FW-W
Loco Polk-O Convention
　MPP-W
Loco-Motion
　ERM-W,M GAR-W,M ToO76-W,M
Locomotive Breath
　BJ-W,M
Loema Tombe
　AAF-W,M (French Only)
Log of the Lost
　AL-W
Logan County Jail
　FSU-W Oz2-W,M
Logger Lover
　OTJ-W,M
Logical Song
　ToO79-W,M
Logie O'Buchan
　FMT-W MHB-W,M
Lohengrin (Selection)
　AmH-M
Lohengrin's Entrance
　MU-W,M
Loin Du Bal
　AmH-M
Lollipop (I Call Her Lollipop)
　DRR-W,M TI2-W,M
Lollipops and Roses
　BeL-W,M TI2-W,M
Lolly Too-Dum
　FW-W WU-W,M
Lollytoodum
　FoS-W,M
Lolotte
　AH-W,M
London Bridge
　AmH-W,M BBF-W,M BM-W
　FSB1-W,M GM-W,M HS-W,M
　MES1-W,M MES2-W,M MF-W,M
　MG-W,M MH-W,M OTJ-W,M
　RW-W,M SMa-W,M SOO-W,M
London Bridge Is Falling Down
　Oz3-W TMA-W,M
London Merchant
　MSB-W
London Mourning in Ashes
　BB-W
London Street
　OTJ-W,M
London Town (Paul McCartney)
　PMC-W,M TI2-W,M
London Town (There Once Was an
　English Maid)
　AF-W

Londonderry Air
　FBI-W,M FSY-W,M OAP-W,M
　OTJ-W,M RW-W,M TI1-W,M
　U-W UFB-W,M WiS8-W,M
London's Burning
　Bo-W,M
Lone Fish-Ball
　HSD-W,M
Lone Fishball
　HAS-W,M LMR-W,M
Lone Pilgrim
　SHS-W,M
Lone Prairie
　SoF-W,M TBF-W,M
Lone Star Ranger
　Oz2-W
Lone Star Trail
　ASB4-W,M BMC-W,M FAW-W,M
　GuC-W,M HS-W,M MG-W,M
Lone the Plow-Boy
　Oz1-W,M
Lone Widow
　BSC-W
Lone Wild Fowl
　AHO-W,M
Lone, Wild Fowl in Lofty Flight
　Hy-W,M
Loneliest Boy in the World
　TI2-W,M
Loneliness
　MF-M
Lonely Accordion
　RSC-W,M (Russian Only)
Lonely Banna Strand
　VP-W,M
Lonely Days
　TI1-W,M UFB-W,M
Lonely Goatherd
　OTJ-W,M OTO-W SM-W,M
　TI1-W,M UBF-W,M UFB-W,M
Lonely House
　SSA-W,M TW-W
Lonely Is the Hogan
　VA-W,M
Lonely Little Kiwi
　SNZ-W,M (Maori)
Lonely Man
　SRE2-W,M
Lonely Miner of Wilkes-Barre
　AL-W
Lonely One
　LMR-W,M
Lonely Room
　L-W TGO-W,M TW-W
Lonely Shepherd
　ASB4-W,M
Lonely Street
　HLS9-W,M
Lonely Teardrops
　TI1-W,M UFB-W,M
Lonely Things
　TT-W,M
Lonely Town
　MF-W,M TW-W
Lonely Wine
　OGC2-W,M
Lonesome Blues
　LC-W
Lonesome Cabin
　DBL-W
Lonesome Cowboy
　SRE1-W,M
Lonesome Dove
　DD-W,M IF-M ITP-W,M Oz4-W,M
　SG-W,M
Lonesome Grove
　AH-W,M

Lonesome Home
DBL-W
Lonesome House Blues
FG2-W,M
Lonesome Hungry Hash House
FVV-W,M
Lonesome Jailhouse Blues
AFP-W
Lonesome Loser
TI2-W,M
Lonesome Low
Oz1-W,M
Lonesome River
BSo-W,M
Lonesome Road
AT-W,M FWS-W,M LMR-W,M
OFS-W,M OTJ-W,M TI1-M UFB-M
Lonesome Road Blues
BSo-W,M
Lonesome Roving Wolves
SoC-W
Lonesome Scenes of Winter
BSC-W
Lonesome Town
FRH-W,M
Lonesome Traveler
BF-W,M JF-W,M TI1-W,M
UFB-W,M WSB-W,M
Lonesome Valley
FSt-W,M FW-W GuC-W,M
HS-W,M JF-W,M Me-W,M
Long about Midnight
LC-W
Long Ago (and Far Away)
BBB-W,M DJ-W,M FPS-W,M
LSO-W SHP-W,M SJ-W,M
TI1-W,M UFB-W,M
Long Ago (Do Not These Words
Recall Past Years)
HSD-W,M
Long Ago (Winds through the Olive
Trees)
BM-W BMC-W,M SOO-W,M
**Long Ago (Winds through the Olive
Trees) see also Wind through the
Olive Trees**
Long Ago Day
FHR-W,M
Long Ago the Lilies Faded
AME-W,M
Long Ago the Little Children
SHP-W,M
Long an' Tall an' Chocolate to the
Bone
NH-W
Long and Lasting Love
DC-W,M DPE-W,M EC-W,M
GCM-W,M
Long and Short of It
LoS-W
Long and Winding Road
BBe-W,M Be2-W,M PMC-W,M
TWS-W WG-W,M
Long As the Darkening Cloud
Abode
AHO-W,M
Long Before I Knew You
HC2-W,M TI1-W,M TW-W
UBF-W,M UFB-W,M
Long Black Veil
BSo-W,M CMG-W,M TI2-W,M
Long Day Closes
GC-W,M
**Long De La Grande Mer see Le
Long De La Grande Mer**
**Long D'eine Grande Mer see Le
Long D'eine Grande Mer**

Long Distance Blues
MAS-W,M
Long Distance Call
DBL-W
Long Gone
B-W,M Bl-W,M SSo-W,M
Long Grass Ripples
Boo-W,M
Long-Haired Kings
AL-W,M
Long-Handled Shovel
AFB-W,M
Long Hot Summer (Theme)
GTV-W,M
Long John
FW-W OHO-W,M
Long Journey Home, or Two Dollar
Bill
BIS-W,M BSo-W,M
Long-Legged Lula's Back in Town
FVV-W,M
Long-Line Skinner
AFB-W,M FW-W
Long Live Canadian Maidens
SiP-W,M (French)
Long Live Our Noble King
SiP-W,M (Romanian)
Long Live the King
Boo-W,M
Long Lonesome Highway
TI2-W,M
Long, Long Ago (Tell Me the Tales
That to Me Were So Dear)
ATS-W FU-W,M FuB-W,M
HS-W,M HSD-W,M IPH-W,M
NAS-W,M OFS-W,M PaS-W,M
PoS-W,M WiS8-W,M
Long, Long, Long
TWS-W
Long, Long Trail
U-W
Long, Long Way
TW-W
Long, Long Weary Day
HSD-W,M
Long, Long While
RoS-W,M
Long Road
MML-W,M
Long Run
DPE-W,M
Long Sought Home
SHS-W,M
Long Strike
AL-W
Long Tall Mama Blues
LJ-W,M
Long Tall Sally
DRR-W,M
Long the Days of Sorrow
Oz3-W
Long Time Ago (Away Down
South Where I Was Born)
SA-W,M
Long Time Ago (I Thought I'd Join
the Black Ball Line)
OTJ-W,M
Long Time Ago (Jesus Died on
Calvary's Mountain, Long Time
Ago)
SHS-W,M
Long Time Ago (Near the Lake
Where Drooped the Willow)
OA1-W,M TMA-W,M
Long Time Ago (on an Island in
Mid-Pacific)
GI-W GO-W

Long Time Ago (Seems Like Such
a Long Time Ago)
JC-W,M
Long Way from Home
LC-W
Long Way from Texas
DBL-W
Longest Train
LSR-W,M
Longfellow Serenade
TI2-W,M ToO76-W,M
Longfellow's Carol
GBC-W,M
Longing
EL-W,M (German)
Longing for Home
AmH-M UF-W,M
Longshoreman's Strike
AFP-W AL-W
Longside of the Santa Fe Trail
HB-W,M
Looby Loo
ASB1-W,M BBF-W,M BM-W
BMC-W,M HS-W,M MES2-W,M
MH-W,M SOO-W,M
**Looby Loo see also Here We Go
Looby-Loo**
Look
MLS-W,M
**Look Again see Irma La Douce
Theme**
Look and Live
AME-W,M
Look at Me, I'm Sandra Dee
Gr-W,M Mo-W,M OTO-W
Look at That Face
ILT-W,M
Look at the Ears on Him
AF-W
Look Away
RF-W,M
Look Away in the Heaven
Le-W,M
Look Away to Jesus
GH-W,M
Look down Dat Lonesome Road
AFP-W
Look for a Sky of Blue
LMS-W,M
Look for Small Pleasures
Mo-W,M NM-W,M OTO-W
UBF-W,M
Look for the Silver Lining
RDF-W,M RDT-W,M TI1-W,M
TW-W UFB-W,M
Look for the Sky of Blue
TW-W
Look How Far You've Come
VB-W,M
Look in the Mirror
MAR-W,M
Look in Your Eyes
OnT6-W,M
Look, Neighbors, Look
Boo-W,M
Look of Love
BDF-W,M BHB-W,M DPE-W,M
HD-W,M HFH-W,M MF-W,M
OnT6-W,M
Look Out Below
ATM-W,M
Look to the Rainbow
CEM-W,M DBC-W,M FR-W,M
HC2-W,M HLS3-W,M OTJ-W,M
OTO-W RDF-W,M RW-W,M
TI1-W,M UBF-W,M UFB-W,M
Look unto Me

SJ-W,M
Lord Jesus Christ, We Humbly
Pray
AHO-W,M
Lord Jesus, I Long to Be Perfectly
Whole
AME-W,M
Lord Jesus Plants His Garden
GBC-W,M
Lord Jesus, Think on Me
Hy-W,M
Lord Keep Watch
GH-W,M
Lord! Lead the Way the Savior
Went
AHO-W,M
Lord, Let Me Live Today
SOW1-W,M SOW2-W,M
Lord, Lord, You've Been So Good
to Me
MAS-W,M SG-W,M
Lord Lovel
AmS-W,M BT-W,M FMT-W
FoM-W,M FSSC-W,M FW-W
ITP-W NAS-W,M Oz1-W,M
SCa-W,M SG-W,M TBF-W,M
Lord Make Me More Patient
WN-W,M
Lord, Many Times Thou Pleased
Art
AHO-W,M
Lord My Ford
N-W,M
Lord My Pasture Shall Prepare
LMR-W,M
Lord My Shepherd Is
SJ-W,M
Lord, My Weak Thought in Vain
Would Climb
AHO-W,M
Lord Nelson
IS-W,M MSB-W
Lord North's Recantation
SBA-W
Lord, Now Lettest Thou Thy
Servant Depart in Peace
Hy-W,M
Lord of All (Did Reign Supreme)
JS-W,M (Hebrew)
**Lord of All (Did Reign Supreme)
see also Adon Olom**
Lord of All (You Have Always Been
and Always Will Be Lord of All)
GP-W,M
Lord of All Being, Throned Afar
AHO-W,M Hy-W,M NAS-W,M
Lord of Each Soul
AHO-W,M
Lord of Glory
VB-W,M
Lord of Health, Thou Life within Us
Hy-W,M
Lord of Life, All Praise Excelling
AHO-W,M
Lord of Life and All Creation
MU-W,M (Italian)
Lord of Light
SL-W,M
Lord of My Heart's Elation
AHO-W,M
Lord of the Dance
GBC-W,M JF-W,M VB-W,M
Lord of the Earth
BeB-W,M
Lord of the World
SBJ-W
Lord of the Worlds Above

Hy-W,M
Lord of the Worlds Below
AHO-W,M
Lord Our God Alone Is Strong
AHO-W,M
Lord Randal
AA-W,M BSC-W,M BT-W,M
FW-W IL-W,M J-W,M SCa-W
Lord Reigneth
JS-W,M
Lord Rendal
BT-W,M OH-W,M
**Lord Spare Me Over Till Another
Year see Oh Death**
Lord, Speak to Me
SOW1-W,M SOW2-W,M
Lord, Speak to Me, That I May
Speak
Hy-W,M
Lord, Teach Me How to Pray
AME-W,M
Lord, Teach Thy Servants How to
Pray
AME-W,M
Lord Thomas
BSC-W FSSC-W,M FVV-W,M
ITP-W,M Oz1-W,M SCa-W,M
Lord Thomas and Fair Annet
BT-W,M FMT-W SCa-W,M
Lord Thomas and Fair Eleanor
ATS-W,M BSC-W
Lord Thomas and Fair Ellen
BSC-W DD-W,M SCa-W,M
Lord Thomas and Fair Ellender
BCT-W,M SCa-W
Lord Thomas and the Brown Girl
Oz1-W
Lord, Thou Hast Been Our Dwelling
Place
Hy-W,M
Lord, Thou Hast Promised
AHO-W,M
Lord, Thou Hast Searched and
Seen Me Thro'
AME-W,M
Lord, Thy Word Abideth
Hy-W,M
Lord Ullin's Daughter
SG-W,M
Lord, Until I Reach My Home
RF-W,M
Lord, Vouchsafe Thy Loving
Kindness
TH-W,M
Lord Watch between Me and Thee
AME-W,M
Lord Wetram
TBF-W,M
Lord, Who throughout These Forty
Days
Hy-W,M
Lord, Who's the Happy Man
AHO-W,M
Lord Will Come and Not Be Slow
Hy-W,M
Lord Will Provide
GH-W,M WN-W,M
Lord, with Undying Love
SL-W,M
Lords of Creation
BSC-W
Lords of Creation Men We Call
HAS-W,M
Lord's My Shepherd, I'll Not Want
AHO-W,M GH-W,M Hy-W,M
SHP-W,M
Lord's My Shepherd, I'll Not Want

see also Lord Is My Shepherd
Lord's Prayer
AME-W,M FiS-W,M FS-W,M
HSD-W,M LoS-W,M OBN-W,M
SFB-W,M TM-W,M WGB/O-W,M
Lord's Prayer see also Our Father
Lordy, Turn Your Face
AFP-W SSo-W,M
Lorelei (Gershwin)
GOB-W,M LSO-W MF-W,M
NYT-W,M OTO-W
Lorelei (Styne)
V-W,M
Lorelei, The
AmH-W,M ESB-W,M (German
Only) OFS-W,M (German Only)
Loreley, The
AmH-W,M HSD-W,M MML-W,M
(German) NAS-W,M WiS8-W,M
Lorena
ATS-W,M BSC-W FW-W
HSD-W,M IHA-W,M PoS-W,M
Re-W,M SCo-W,M Sin-W,M
SiS-W
Lorena and Paul Vane
Oz4-W,M
Lorena's Answer
Oz4-W,M
Lorna's Here
Mo-W,M NM-W,M OTO-W
Lorraine Blues
LC-W
Los Angeles
OTO-W
Los Cuatro Generales
FW-W (Spanish)
Los' My Glove on a Satu'day Night
SGT-W,M
Los Tres Santos Reyes
SHP-W,M
Lose That Long Face
LSO-W Mo-W,M NM-W,M
Losing Game
VB-W,M
Losing Kind of Love
TOH-W,M
Losing My Mind
Fo-W,M OTO-W UBF-W,M
Loss of the Earl Moira
VP-W
Loss of the Hornet
ESU-W
Loss of the Kilpatrick
BB-W
Lost
Mo-W,M NM-W,M OTO-W
Lost and Found
MF-W,M
Lost April
NK-W,M
Lost Child
Oz4-W
Lost Chord
AmH-W,M BSG-W,M BSP-W,M
ESB-W,M FS-W,M FSY-W,M
HSD-W,M JBF-W,M LMR-W,M
MuM-W,M RDF-W,M SS-W
TH-W,M WiS7-W,M
Lost Creek Miners
AFP-W
Lost Doll
OTJ-W,M
Lost Girl
Oz1-W,M
Lost He Wanders
Boo-W,M
Lost in Meditation

GMD-W,M
Lost in the Feeling
TOC83-W,M
Lost in the Fifties Tonight
AWS-W,M EC-W,M GCM-W,M
Lost in the Flood
RV-W
Lost in the Stars
CEM-W,M HC1-W,M TI1-W,M
TW-W UBF-W,M UFB-W,M
Lost Is Found
GBC-W,M
Lost John
NH-W
**Lost My Glove on a Saturday Night
see Los' My Glove on a Satu'day
Night**
Lost on the Lady Elgin
Oz4-W,M
Lost Rosabel
ESU-W
**Lost Sheep see Ninety and Nine or
Lost Sheep**
Lost Soldier
VS-W,M
Lost Song
FSA2-W,M
Lost War-Sloop
ANS-W
Lost without Your Love
ToO76-W,M
Lot of Livin' to Do
HC2-W,M Mo-W,M NM-W,M
OTJ-W,M OTO-W TI2-W,M
UBF-W,M
Lots of Worms
RSL-W,M
Lotta Love
DPE-W,M
Lotte Walked
VA-W,M
Lottery (Main Title Theme)
TV-M
**Lottery Theme Song see Turn of
the Cards**
Lou Baylero
FSF-W (French)
Lou Bye-Lairo
FSF-W (French)
Loudly Let the Trumpet Bray
GiS-W,M MGT-W,M
Lough Neagh Fishers
IS-W,M
Louie, Louie
DRR-W,M TRR-W,M
Louis Charles Zenobie Salvador
Maria
Boo-W,M
Louis Kossuth
SMW-W,M (Hungarian)
Louise (Ev'ry Little Breeze Seems
to Whisper Louise)
AT-W,M HC2-W,M LM-W,M
OnT1-W,M OTO-W RDT-W,M
Louise (Is the Sweetest Gal I
Know)
LC-W
Louisian'
CCS-W,M
Louisiana (Come, Little Children,
Now We May Partake a Little
Morsel)
SHS-W,M
Louisiana! (Louisian', the Best
State in the Land)
LoS-W,M
Lou'siana Belle

FHR-W,M SSFo-W,M
Louisiana Blues
DBL-W
Louisiana Girls
UF-W,M
Louisiana Hayride
MF-W,M OHB-W,M
Louisiana Lou
SLS-W,M
**Louisiana Low Grounds see
Loozyanna Low Grounds**
Louisiana Lullaby
MaG-W,M SCL-W,M
Lou'siana Man
Lo-W,M
Louisiana Woman, Mississippi Man
N-W,M
Lou'siana Young
CMG-W,M
Louisville Burglar
Oz2-W,M
Loupy Lou
Oz3-W,M
Louse Song
GI-W GO-W
Lovana
BSC-W
L-O-V-E
MF-W,M OnT1-W,M
Love (Blane/Martin)
GSF-W,M RT4-W,M
Love (Huddleston/Burns)
NI-W,M On-W,M
Love (Can Make You Happy)
TI1-W,M UBF-W,M
Love (Your Spell Is Everywhere)
TI1-W,M UFB-W,M
Love Again
CJ-W,M
Love Ain't for Keepin'
WA-W,M
Love Alone
FPG-W,M
Love Always
TTH-W,M
Love and Ashes
VS-W,M
Love and Blessing
GB-W,M
Love and Brandy
ESU-W
Love and Friendship
EL-W,M
Love and Grief
EL-W,M (German)
Love and Learn
MLS-W,M
Love and Let Love
TVT-W,M
Love and Marriage
FrS-W,M MF-W,M RoE-W,M
Love and Oysters
OHG-W,M
Love at First Sight
BMM-W CMF-W,M
Love Ballad
TI1-W,M UFB-W,M
Love Bites
CFB-W,M
Love Boat (Main Title Theme)
DC-W,M MF-W,M TV-W,M
Love Busted
TOC82-W,M
Love Calling
VB-W,M
Love Came for Me
NI-W,M

Love, Come Home
BIS-W,M
Love, Come Take Me Again
UBF-W,M
Love Come Tricklin' Down
Me-W,M
Love Comes Quickly
TTH-W,M
Love Divine, All Love Excelling
AME-W,M FH-W,M Hy-W,M
OS-W
Love Divine, All Loves Excelling
CEM-W,M RDF-W,M SJ-W,M
Love Don't Turn Away
OHT-W,M
**Love Everlasting see L'Amour
Toujours L'Amour**
Love Every Day
OnT6-W,M
Love Everybody in the World
VB-W,M
Love for Sale
DC-W,M DJ-W,M HC2-W,M
MF-W,M ML-W,M OHB-W,M
RoE-W,M TW-W VK-W,M
Love Found a Way
OGR-W,M VB-W,M
Love God with All Your Soul and
Strength
SHP-W,M
Love Goddess
OTO-W
Love Gregory
Oz1-W
Love Hangover
ToO76-W,M
Love Has a Way
OTO-W
Love Has Brought Me to Despair
FSU-W
Love Has Driven Me Sane
GV-W,M
Love Has Eyes
OH-W,M
Love Has Taken Its Time
TOH-W,M
Love Held Lightly
Mo-W,M NM-W,M OTO-W
Love Hurts
ToO76-W,M
Love I Bear to Thee
FHR-W,M
Love in a Goldfish Bowl
OTO-W
Love in Any Language
VB-W,M
Love in Bloom
AT-W,M LM-W,M OnT1-W,M
OTO-W
Love in the Afternoon
OHF-W
Love in Vain
RoS-W,M
Love Is a Bable
EL-W,M
Love Is a Carousel
Mo-W,M NM-W,M
Love Is a Chance
Mo-W,M NM-W,M OTO-W
Love Is a Four Letter Word
Mo-W,M NM-W,M
Love Is a Many-Splendored Thing
GG5-W,M GSN3-W,M HLS5-W,M
RT5-W,M RW-W,M
Love Is a Plaintive Song
MGT-W,M
Love Is a Simple Thing

HLS3-W,M RT5-W,M TI1-W,M
UFB-W,M
Love Is a Song
NI-W,M OTJ-W,M
Love Is a Very Light Thing
TW-W
Love Is All Around
TVT-W,M
Love Is All We Need
RW-W,M
Love Is Blue
GOI7-W,M (French) On-W,M
RDT-W,M TI2-W,M
Love Is Come Again
OB-W,M
Love Is Eternal
Mo-W,M NM-W,M
Love Is Here to Stay
FrS-W,M HC1-W,M ILT-W,M
LM-W,M LSO-W NYT-W,M
OTO-W TI1-W,M UFB-W,M
Love Is Just a Thing of Fancy
NF-W
Love Is Just around the Corner
AT-W,M ILT-W,M OTO-W
Love Is Like a Butterfly
BDP-W,M
Love Is Like a Firefly
Fi-W,M
**Love Is Like a Heat Wave see Heat
Wave**
Love Is on a Roll
TOC83-W,M
Love Is Only Love
Mo-W,M OTO-W
Love Is Quite a Simple Thing
L-W Ne-W,M
Love Is Sweeping the Country
GOB-W,M LSO-W MF-W,M
NYT-W,M OT-W,M TW-W
Love Is the Answer
DDH-W,M ToO79-W,M
Love Is the Foundation
N-W,M
Love Is the Reason
TW-W
Love Is the Sweetest Thing
MF-W,M
Love Is Thicker Than Water
TI1-W,M UFB-W,M
Love Is Where You Find It
GSF-W,M
Love Isn't Everything
I-W,M
Love Letter
OHG-W,M
Love Letters
AT-W,M OnT1-W,M OTO-W
Love Letters in the Sand
FPS-W,M TI1-W,M UFB-W,M
Love Like This
OTO-W
Love-Line
Mo-W,M NM-W,M OTO-W
Love, Look Away
OTJ-W,M OTO-W TI1-W,M
UBF-W,M UFB-W,M
Love, Look in My Window
Mo-W,M OTO-W
Love, Love, Love
GB-W,M
Love, Love, Sweet Love
Boo-W,M
Love Machine
ToO76-W,M
Love Makes the World Go 'Round
GG1-W,M HLS8-W,M RW-W,M

UBF-W,M
Love May Go Hang
BeB-W,M
Love Me
GAR-W,M MF-W,M
Love Me, and the World Is Mine
FSTS-W,M MF-W,M
Love Me Do
BBe-W,M BR-W,M DPE-W,M
MF-W,M RY-W,M RYT-W,M
TWS-W
Love Me Just a Little Bit
HSi-W,M
Love Me Little, Love Me Long
OH-W,M
Love Me, Love My Dog
M-W,M
Love Me or Leave Me
HC1-W,M MF-W,M OPS-W,M
T-W,M TW-W WDS-W,M
Love Me or No
BSC-W
Love Me Tender
CMG-W,M DRR-W,M HLS5-W,M
HLS9-W,M ILF-W,M RT5-W,M
RW-W,M RYT-W,M SRE2-W,M
TI1-W,M UFB-W,M
Love Me Tonight
TI2-W,M TS-W
Love Me To-night Duet
VK-W,M
Love Me with All Your Heart
AO-W,M HLS3-W,M (Spanish)
Love Nest
MF-W,M
Love Never Fails
VB-W,M
Love Not
HSD-W,M
Love of a Wife
GOB-W,M
Love of Another Kind
VB-W,M
Love of God
BSG-W,M BSP-W,M OM-W,M
Love of My Life
LL-W,M Mo-W,M NM-W,M
OTO-W TW-W
Love of the Common People
CMG-W,M
Love or Something Like It
CMG-W,M PoG-W,M WG-W,M
Love Parade
CF-W,M
Love, Please Come Home
BSo-W,M
Love Potion Number Nine
ERM-W,M GAR-W,M RB-W
WF-W,M
Love Power
BHO-W,M DPE-W,M MF-W,M
Love, Reign o'er Me
WA-W,M
Love Rollercoaster
DP-W,M
Love Said Goodbye
AT-W,M OTO-W
**Love Sidney Theme see Friends
Forever**
Love So Right
GrS-W,M
Love Somebody
FoS-W,M RS-W,M
Love Somebody (but I Won't Tell
Who)
OFS-W,M
Love Somebody Yes I Do

FW-W OTJ-W,M
Love Song (Lee Greenwood)
TI2-W,M
Love Song of the Waterfall
OGC2-W,M
Love Story Theme (Where Do I
Begin?)
AT-W,M GOI7-M GrS-W,M
ILT-W,M LM-W,M MoA-W,M
OBN-W,M On-W,M OTO-W
RDT-W,M TM-W,M TOM-W,M
WGB/P-W,M
Love Takes Time
ToO79-W,M
Love That Gave Jesus
GH-W,M
Love That Is Hoarded
JF-W,M
Love That's Pure, Itself Disdaining
AHO-W,M (German)
Love the Lord
NH-W
Love Them While We Can
VB-W,M
Love Theme from The Godfather
On-W,M
**Love Theme from The Godfather
see also Speak Softly Love**
Love Thoughts
WiS8-W,M
Love Thy Neighbor
HC2-W,M OTO-W
Love to Love You, Baby
SoH-W,M
Love Touch
TTH-W,M
Love Train
SoH-W,M
Love Trouble Blues
LC-W
Love Walked In
FrS-W,M HC2-W,M ILT-W,M
LM-W,M LSO-W NYT-W,M
OTO-W TI1-W,M UFB-W,M
Love Will Find a Way
Oz1-W RW-W,M
Love Will Find Out the Way
OH-W,M
Love Will Keep Us Together
TI2-W,M
Love Will See Us Through
Fo-W,M
Love Will Turn You Around
TOC82-W,M
Love with the Proper Stranger
AT-W,M OTO-W
Love Won't Let You Get Away
Mo-W,M
Love You Inside Out
TI1-W,M UFB-W,M
Love You Madly
GMD-W,M
Love You Save (May Be Your
Own)
RB-W
Love You Too
TWS-W
Love Your Hair
GSM-W,M
Lovebug Itch
OCG1-W,M
Loved One
NM-W,M
Loveland (Charles Friml)
YL-W,M
Loveland (Stephen Sondheim)
Fo-W,M

Loveless Love
  B-W,M BI-W,M
Lovelier Than Ever
  UBF-W,M
Loveliest Night of the Year
  HLS5-W,M OP1-W,M RT5-W,M
Lovelorn Youth
  SAm-W,M
Lovely
  UBF-W,M
Lovely Albert
  MSB-W
Lovely Appear
  LMR-W,M TF-W,M
Lovely Creature
  OTJ-W,M
Lovely Cuba, 'Tis You
  MHB-W,M (Spanish)
Lovely Evening
  ASB6-W,M BM-W EFS-W,M
  HS-W,M LoS-W,M MG-W,M
  UF-W,M VA-W,M
Lovely Flowers, I Pray
  AmH-W,M WiS7-W,M
Lovely Hula Girl
  TI1-W,M UFB-W,M
Lovely Hula Hands
  TI1-W,M UFB-W,M
Lovely Is She
  OTO-W
Lovely Meadows
  ASB6-W,M
Lovely Meadows see also Ah,
  Lovely Meadows
Lovely Messengers
  ASB6-W,M
Lovely Monarch
  ID-W,M
Lovely Nancy
  DD-W,M Oz1-W,M SCa-W,M
  SG-W,M
Lovely Night (Chwatal)
  HSD-W,M
Lovely Night (Offenbach's Tales of
  Hoffmann)
  AmH-W,M WiS7-W,M
Lovely Night, A
  UBF-W,M
Lovely Night to Go Dancing
  Mo-W,M NM-W,M
Lovely Polly
  SCa-W,M
Lovely Rita
  BBe-W,M OnT6-W,M TWS-W
Lovely Rosebush
  UF-W,M
Lovely to Look At
  RW-W,M TI1-W,M UFB-W,M
Lovely Way to Spend an Evening
  TI1-W,M UFB-W,M
Lovely Weather for Ducks
  OTJ-W,M
Lovely William
  Oz1-W,M
Lover (Hart/Rodgers)
  AT-W,M HC2-W,M LM-W,M
  RDT-W,M TM-W,M TS-W
  WGB/P-W,M
Lover, Come Back to Me
  DJ-W,M EY-W,M HC2-W,M L-W
  LSB-W,M MF-W,M Ne-W,M
  OHB-W,M TW-W
Lover Doll
  EP-W,M
Lover Man (Oh Where Can You
  Be?)
  FPS-W,M LSB-W,M TI2-W,M

Lover of the Lord
  WN-W,M
Lovers Again
  TOC83-W,M
Lovers' Carol
  GBC-W,M
Lover's Cross
  JC-W,M PM-W,M
Lovers' Goodnight
  NF-W
Lover's Lament
  AmS-W,M BSC-W NA-W,M
  SCa-W,M
Lover's Lament for Her Sailor
  BSC-W
Lovers, Mother, I'll Have None
  SY-W,M
Lovers Never Say Goodbye
  FRH-W,M
Lovers on the Rebound
  TOC83-W,M
Lover's Question
  DRR-W,M HRB4-W,M MF-W,M
  TI2-W,M
Lover's Song
  Oz4-W,M
Lover's Test
  FMT-W
Love's a Worrisome Thing
  Mo-W,M NM-W,M
Love's Been Good to Me
  OPS-W,M WGB/P-W,M
Love's Dream
  MU-W,M
Love's Dream after the Ball
  AmH-M
Love's Dreamland
  AmH-M
Love's Gonna Fall Here Tonight
  TOC82-W,M
Love's Greeting
  AmH-M SL-W,M
Love's Greetings
  TF-W,M
Love's Lament in Mid-Autumn see
  Chung Ch'iu Kuei Yuan
Loves Me Like a Rock
  On-W,M
Love's Old Sweet Song
  AmH-W,M ESB-W,M FSN-W,M
  FSY-W,M GSN1-W,M HLS1-W,M
  HSD-W,M MF-W,M NAS-W,M
  OBN-W,M OS-W RW-W,M SL-W
  TF-W TH-W,M TM-W,M U-W
  WGB/O-W,M WiS8-W,M
Love's Old Sweet Song see also
  Just a Song at Twilight
Love's Own Kiss
  HJ-W,M
Love's Revenge
  GV-W,M
Love's the Tune
  WiS8-W,M
Love's Theme
  PoG-M SoH-W,M TI1-M TI2-M
  TOM-M UFB-M WG-W,M
Love's Young Dream
  HSD-W,M
Lovest Thou Me (More Than
  These?)
  BSG-W,M BSP-W,M
Lovewell's Fight
  AWB-W
Lovey Dovey
  HRB3-W,M
Lovin' a Livin' Dream

TOH-W,M
Lovin' Al
  UBF-W,M
Lovin' Henry
  ITP-W,M
Lovin' Henry see also Loving
  Henery
Lovin' Things
  ATC2-W,M
Lovin', Touchin', Squeezin'
  ToO79-W,M
Loving Cajun Style
  FrF-W,M (Spanish)
Loving Care
  SOO-W,M
Loving Cup
  RoS-W,M
Loving Girl
  Oz4-W,M
Loving Henery
  SCa-W,M
Loving Henery see also Lovin'
  Henry
Loving Her Was Easier Than
  Anything I'll Ever Do Again
  SuS-W,M
Loving Kindness
  GH-W,M
Loving Me, Loving You, Loving Me
  MLS-W,M
Loving Up a Storm
  TOH-W,M
Loving You
  ERM-W,M GAR-W,M MF-W,M
  OTO-W SRE1-W,M TI1-W,M
  UFB-W,M
Loving You Has Made Me Bananas
  WF-W,M
Low-Backed Car
  HSD-W,M LMR-W,M NAS-W,M
Low-Back'd Car
  WiS8-W,M
Low Bridge, Everybody Down
  SWF-W,M
Low-Down Blues
  FVV-W,M
Low in a Manger, Dear Little
  Stranger
  AME-W,M
Low in the Grave He Lay
  AME-W,M
Low Rider
  DP-W,M
Lowe Bonnie
  FSSC-W,M
Lowell Factory Girl
  AFP-W AL-W
Lowland Home
  TH-W,M
Lowlands
  BSC-W FW-W OTJ-W,M SA-W,M
Lowlands Low
  FMT-W Oz1-W,M SoF-W,M
Lowlands of Holland
  FSU-W IS-W,M
Loyal Hearts Will Gather round Her
  SiS-W
Loyal York
  SBA-W
L'shana Habaa
  SBJ-W,M (Hebrew Only)
Lubin Loo
  CSG-W,M
Lubly Fan, Will You Cum Out
  Tonight?
  AH-W,M
Luci Had a Baby

VS-W,M

Lucia di Lammermoor (Selection)
AmH-M

Lucille
CMG-W,M FOC-W,M HLS9-W,M
RW-W,M

Luck Be a Lady
HC2-W,M TI2-W,M UBF-W,M

Luck to Sell
Mo-W,M OTO-W

Luckenbach, Texas
TI2-W,M

Lucky Day
MF-W,M

Lucky Escape
IHA-W,M

Lucky in Love
HC2-W,M OTO-W UBF-W,M

Lucky Jim
TMA-W,M

Lucky Number
FSA2-W,M

Lucky to Be Me
MF-W,M TW-W

Lucy and the Stranger
TOC82-W,M

Lucy Clark's Exaltation
GB-W,M

Lucy in the Sky with Diamonds
BBe-W,M Be2-W,M OnT6-W,M
TWS-W

Lucy Locket
OTJ-W,M

Lucy Long
Oz4-W,M TMA-W,M

Ludella
DBL-W

Ludlow Massacre
AFP-W,M FW-W

Luke and Leia (from Return of the
Jedi)
MF-M

Lukey's Boat
HS-W,M VA-W,M

Lula Is Gone
FHR-W,M SSFo-W,M

Lula Vower
ITP-W,M

Lula Walls
Oz3-W,M

Lullaby (Bentley)
BMC-W,M

Lullaby (Brahms)
ASB4-W,M BM-W BMC-M
HS-W,M (German) MF-M OBN-M
SiR-M SL-W,M TF-W,M TH-W,M

**Lullaby (Brahms) see also Brahms'
Lullaby**

Lullaby (Dunbar/Kwalwasser)
TH-W,M

Lullaby (Erminie)
WiS8-W,M

Lullaby (Jacobowski)
HSD-W,M

Lullbay (Kwalwasser/Iljynski)
TH-W,M

Lullaby (Little Baby, Hear Me
Singing)
MHB-W,M (Japanese)

Lullaby (Scotch Folk Song)
BM-W

Lullaby (Whittaker)
BMC-M

Lullaby and Goodnight
AME-W,M

Lullaby from Jocelyn (Berceuse)
AmH-W,M FSY-W,M (French)

MML-W,M (French) TF-W,M
WiS7-W,M

Lullaby League and Lollypop Guild
WO-W

Lullaby of Birdland
BNG-W,M MF-W,M RW-W,M

Lullaby of Broadway
DBC-W,M MF-W,M

Lullaby of Life
SL-W,M

Lullaby of the Christ Child
SMa-W,M

Lullaby of the Leaves
DJ-W,M HST-W,M TI1-W,M
TI2-W,M UFB-W,M

Lullaby Press
AL-W

Lullaby Round
MG-W,M SCL-W,M

Lullaby to Myself
GM-W,M

Lullay My Liking
OB-W,M

Lullay, Thou Little Tiny Child
CEM-W,M CSF-W

Lulloo Lullay
WSB-W,M

Lully, Lullay
OU-W,M

Lulu Gal
AN-W

Lulu Is Our Darling Pride
HSD-W,M

Lulu's Back in Town
HFH-W,M MF-W,M

Lundstroms Erfarenheter I Amerika
SE-W (Swedish)

Lundstrom's Experiences in
America
SE-W (Swedish)

Lush Life
ToS-W,M

Lusty Month of May
LL-W,M OTO-W UBF-W,M

Lusty Young Smith
SR-W,M

Lute Book Lullaby
Gu-W,M OB-W,M

Luther
SHS-W,M

Lutzow's Wild Hunt
HSD-W,M

Luxury
RoS-W,M

Lyddy Margot
FMT-W

Lydia Pinkham
GI-W,M GO-W,M HAS-W,M
LW-W,M

Lyin' Eyes
MF-W,M

Lying Here with Linda on My Mind
CMG-W,M

Lying in Calcutta Gutter
PO-W,M

Lynchburg Town
AN-W

Lyndon Johnson Told the Nation
VS-W,M

Lyndon's Lullaby
VS-W,M

Lyrical Song
LMR-W,M

Lysistrata's Oath
TW-W

M

M Is for Mary
MAR-W,M

M*A*S*H Theme Song
BNG-M DC-W,M EY-W,M HFH-
W,M MF-W,M TOM-W,M ToO76-
W,M TVT-W,M

MIG 15's
AF-W

M-I-S-S-I-S-S-I-P-P-I
BH-W,M HLS1-W,M

M-O-T-H-E-R
BH-W,M CS-W,M GSN1-W,M
HLS1-W,M OS-W RW-W,M

M.P., The
GI-W GO-W

M.T.A. Song
TI1-W,M UFB-W,M

Ma! (He's Making Eyes at Me)
RDT-W,M TI2-W,M U-W

Ma Bella Bimba
PaS-W,M

Ma Belle Est Comme Ein Badinage
CaF-W (French Only)

Ma Belle S'a Sauvee
CaF-W (French Only)

Ma Brune
FSO-W,M (French)

Ma Chere 'Tite Fille
CaF-W (French Only)

Ma Cherie
MBS-W,M

Ma Commere
CLaL-W,M (French)

Ma L'il Batteau
Ba-W,M

Ma-Ma-Ma Belle
ELO-W,M

Ma Mourri
AAF-W,M (French)

Ma Negresse M'a Quitt'e
LC-W (French)

Ma Nishtano
SBJ-W,M (Hebrew Only)

Ma Normandie
FSF-W (French)

Ma Sister You'll Be Called On
BDW-W,M

Ma Soul's Determin'
BDW-W,M

Mabellene
DP-W,M HR-W RB-W TI1-W,M
UFB-W,M

Mac Will Win the Union Back
SiS-W

McAfee's Confession
BSC-W TBF-W,M

**McAfee's Confession see also
McFee's Confession**

MacArthur Park
ERM-W,M

McClellan for President
MPP-W

MacCrimmon's Lament
SeS-W,M

McDonald
FSSC-W

**McDonald's Restaurants Jingle see
You Deserve a Break Today and
You, You're the One**

MacDonald's Return to Glencoe
Oz1-W

Macedon Youth
Boo-W,M

McFee's Confession
Oz2-W,M

AT-W,M HD-W,M ILT-W,M
MF-W,M
Make It Real
CFB-W,M
Make It with You
DPE-W,M MF-W,M
Make Love to Me
Mo-W,M NM-W,M
Make Me a Bed on the Floor
BF-W,M
**Make Me a Bed on the Floor see
also Make Me a Pallet on Your
Floor**
Make Me a Captive, Lord
Hy-W,M
Make Me a Cowboy Again
HB-W,M
Make Me a Miracle
MF-W,M
Make Me a Palat on de Flo'
NH-W
Make Me a Pallet on Your Floor
LC-W
**Make Me a Pallet on Your Floor
see also Make Me a Bed on the
Floor and Make Me One Pallet on
Your Floor**
Make Me Forget
MLS-W,M
Make Me No Gaudy Chaplets
HSD-W,M
Make Me One Pallet on Your Floor
B-W,M
**Make Me One Pallet on Your Floor
see also Make Me a Pallet on
Your Floor**
Make Me Rainbows
RW-W,M
Make Me Smile
BR-W,M GOI7-W,M
Make Me Yours
OnT6-W,M
Make My Heart Your Home
VB-W,M
Make New Friends
GuC-W,M
Make Ole Massa Hum
SiS-W
Make Someone Happy
DBC-W,M DR-W,M HC1-W,M
ILT-W,M OTO-W RDF-W,M
TI1-W,M UBF-W,M UFB-W,M
Make the Man Love Me
TW-W
Make the World Go Away
CMG-W,M CoH-W,M FOC-W,M
GOI7-W,M MAB1-W MSA1-W
TI2-W,M
Make Up My Heart
UBF-W,M
Make Us Gods to Go before Us
SoM-W,M
Make We Joy
OB-W,M
Make We Merry
OB-W,M
Make Ye a Joyful Sounding Noise
AHO-W,M
Maker of My Heart
VB-W,M
Makin' Love Ukulele Style
Mo-W,M
Makin' Whoopee
MF-W,M OPS-W,M TW-W
WDS-W,M
Making a Snow-Man
MH-W,M

Making a Valentine
MH-W,M
Making History
FSA2-W,M
Making Love
MF-W,M TI2-W,M
Making Memories
THN-W,M
Making Our Dreams Come True
AT-W,M
Making Plans
BSo-W,M
Making Valentines
ASB1-W,M
Mala Femmena
MF-W,M (Italian Only) RW-W,M
(Italian Only)
Malaguena
FPS-M
Malaguena Salerosa
FG2-W,M (Spanish Only)
Malbrough
MP-W,M (French Only)
Malbrough see also Marlborough
Malbrough S'en Va-t'en Guerre
CUP-W,M (French Only)
OTJ-W,M (French Only)
Malbrouk S'en Va-t-en Guerre
SiP-W,M (French)
Malbrouk to War Is Going
SiP-W,M (French)
**Malbrouk to War Is Going see also
To War Has Gone Duke
Marlborough**
Malt's Come Down
Boo-W,M
Mama, a Rainbow
OTO-W UBF-W,M
Mama and Daddy Broke My Heart
OGC2-W,M
Mama Can't Buy You Love
ToO79-W,M
Mama Don't 'Low
FGM-W,M FW-W GuC-W,M
OFS-W,M OTJ-W,M
**Mama Don't 'Low see also
Mammy Don't 'Low**
Mama He's Crazy
AWS-W,M GCM-W,M
Mama Inez
TI2-W,M
Mama Rita in Hollywood
Lo-W,M
Mama Told Me Not to Come
TI2-W,M
Mama Tried
NMH-W,M
Maman
Mo-W,M UBF-W,M
Maman, Find Me a Husband
LA-W,M (Spanish)
Maman, Les P'tits Bateaux
Ch-W (French Only) MP-W,M
(French Only)
Mama's Baby Child
DBL-W
Mama's Bible
CEM-W,M
Mama's Christmas Song
OTJ-W,M
Mambru
CDM-W,M (Spanish)
Mambru Is with the Army
LA-W,M (Spanish)
Mambru Se Fue A La Guerra
LA-W,M (Spanish)
Mame

DBC-W,M HC1-W,M Mo-W,M
NM-W,M OTO-W RDT-W,M
TI2-W,M UBF-W,M
Mame Ou Toi T'es?
CaF-W (French Only)
Mamenu
WW-W,M (Yiddish)
Mamie Is Mimi
V-W,M
Mamma, Mamma, Have You
Heard?
Oz3-W,M
Mamma Mia
TI1-W,M
Mamma's Darling
NF-W
Mammas Don't Let Your Babies
Grow Up to Be Cowboys
CMG-W,M CoH-W,M FOC-W,M
TI2-W,M TOM-W,M
Mammy Blue
On-W,M
Mammy Don't 'Low
OHO-W,M
**Mammy Don't 'Low see also
Mama Don't 'Low**
Mammy Loves
AH-W,M
Mammy's Little Baby
OTJ-W,M
Mam'selle
GG5-W,M HLS3-W,M RW-W,M
Man about Town
SYB-W,M
Man and a Woman
OHT-W,M TI2-W,M
Man around My Door
DBL-W
Man behind the Armor-Plated Desk
AF-W
Man Called Noon
OTO-W
**Man Could Get Killed (Theme) see
Strangers in the Night**
Man Frank Weems
AFP-W
Man from Snowy River
HFH-M MF-M
Man from U.N.C.L.E. (Theme)
GTV-M
Man Has Dreams
WD-W,M
Man I Love
BNG-W,M DBC-W,M DC-W,M
GOB-W,M HC2-W,M LSO-W
MF-W,M NYT-W,M (French,
Spanish) OHB-W,M RoE-W,M
Man in a Raincoat
ToS-W,M
Man in Blue
RSL-W,M
Man in My Life
Mo-W,M NM-W,M OTO-W
Man in the Middle
AG-W,M VB-W,M
Man in the Mirror
BHO-W,M CFB-W,M LOM-W,M
Man in the Moon (Came Down Too
Soon)
OTJ-W,M SL-W,M
Man in the Moon (Have You Ever
Seen the Man in the Moon?)
MH-W,M
Man in the Moon (Is a Lady)
Mo-W,M NM-W,M
Man in the Moon (Is As Round As
Can Be)

SOO-W,M
Man in the Ring
IFM-W
Man Needs to Know
CEM-W,M
Man of Constant Sorrow
BSo-W,M FSt-W,M FW-W
**Man of Constant Sorrow see also I
Am a Man of Constant Sorrow**
Man of Double Deed
IS-W,M
Man of La Mancha
MLM-W,M OTJ-W,M
Man of My Type
L-W
Man of the People
MPP-W
Man of Words
NF-W
Man Oh Manischewitz
GSM-W,M
Man on a Subway Train
TW-W
Man on the Flying Trapeze
ATS-W BH-W,M BMC-W,M FW-W
HAS-W,M MAS-W,M MF-W,M
OS-W OTJ-W,M RSL-W,M
RW-W,M
Man Once Said
Mo-W,M NM-W,M
Man Say
R-W,M
Man Size Love
TTH-W,M
Man That Broke the Bank at Monte
Carlo
ATS-W
**Man That Broke the Bank at Monte
Carlo see also Man Who Broke
the Bank at Monte Carlo**
Man That Doth in Secret Place
AME-W,M
Man That Got Away
HC2-W,M HFH-W,M LSO-W
Mo-W,M NM-W,M OTO-W
TI2-W,M ToS-W,M
Man That Is Me
JC-W,M
Man That Waters the Workers'
Beer
FW-W JF-W,M SWF-W,M
**Man That Waters the Workers'
Beer see also Man Who Waters
the Workers' Beer**
Man Upstairs
RDF-W,M
Man We Love So Dearly
MPP-W
Man Who Broke the Bank at Monte
Carlo
BH-W,M EFS-W,M FSN-W,M
FSTS-W,M FW-W OFS-W,M U-W
**Man Who Broke the Bank at Monte
Carlo see also Man That Broke
the Bank at Monte Carlo**
Man Who Comes Around
PO-W,M
Man Who Couldn't Walk Around
J-W,M
Man Who Shot Liberty Valance
HD-W,M OTO-W
Man Who Thinks He's Good
L-W
Man Who Waters the Workers'
Beer
PO-W,M
Man Who Waters the Workers'

Beer see also Man That Waters
the Workers' Beer
Man Who Wears the Star
GSM-W,M
Man Who Would Woo a Fair Maid
MGT-W,M
Man Who Wouldn't Hoe Corn
FMT-W
Man with the Microphone
PO-W,M
Man without a Woman
AF-W FWS-W,M IL-W,M
MM-W,M OFS-W,M
Man without Love
TI2-W,M
Man You Don't Meet Every Day
Oz3-W
Managua, Nicaragua
TI1-W,M UFB-W,M
Manana
OTJ-W,M TI1-W,M
Manassa Junction
Oz2-W,M
Manassas
AWB-W
Manchester England
RY-W,M
Mandandiran
ASB4-W,M
Mandoline
MMM-W,M
Mandy
DPE-W,M MF-W,M On-W,M
TI1-W,M ToO76-W,M UFB-W,M
Mandy Is Two
OHF-W
Mandy Lee
ATS-W
Mane Nobiscum
Boo-W,M (Latin Only)
Maneater
TI2-W,M
Maneuver Song
GO-W
Mang Chiang Ngu (Meng Chiang
Nu's Lament)
FD-W,M (Chinese)
Manger Throne
CCH-W,M
Mango Walk
OTJ-W,M
**Manha De Carnaval see Day in the
Life of a Fool**
Manhattan
DJ-W,M HC2-W,M MU-W,M
RDT-W,M T-W,M TI2-W,M TS-W
TW-W
Manhattan Melodrama
TS-W
Manhattan Merry-Go-Round
Mo-W,M NM-W,M
Manhattan Serenade
RW-W,M
Manhattan's Dear Isle
ANS-W
Maniac
TI2-W,M
Manila Pom-Pom Song
AF-W
**Manischewitz Wine Jingle see Man
Oh Manischewitz**
Mannix
AT-M
Man's a Man for A' That
AL-W FW-W SWF-W,M
Man's Life's a Vapor
TH-W,M

Mansion
GV-W,M
Mansion Builder
VB-W,M
Mansion of Aching Hearts
BH-W,M
Mansion over the Hilltop
HHa-W,M HLS7-W,M RDF-W,M
Tr-W,M
Mansions Above
WN-W,M
Mantle So Green
Oz1-W,M
**Manton De Manila see El Manton
De Manila**
Manu Rere
SNZ-W,M (Maori)
Many a New Day
L-W OTJ-W,M OTO-W TGO-W,M
UBF-W,M
Many Happy Returns of the Day
MF-W,M
Many Mansions
GH-W,M
Many, Many Children
SHP-W,M
Many Moons Ago
TW-W
Many Say I Am Too Noisy
Oz4-W,M
Many Thousand Go
AAF-W,M IHA-W,M
Many Thousand Gone
AAF-W,M AFP-W,M AL-W
FN-W,M FSSC-W,M FW-W
Many Years Ago
GiS-W,M
Maori Farewell Song
FPS-W,M TI1-M UFB-M
**Maori Farewell Song see also Now
Is the Hour**
Maori Style
SNZ-W,M (Maori)
Maoriland
SNZ-W,M (Maori)
Maoz Tsur
SBJ-W,M (Hebrew)
**Map of Virginia see Richmond, or
the Map of Virginia**
Maple Leaf
SiP-W,M
Maple Leaf Forever
AmH-W,M CSo-W,M NAS-W,M
Maple Leaf Rag
MF-M Mo-M OAP-M On-M OPS-M
OTJ-M POT-M TI2-M
Maple on the Hill
BIS-W,M BSo-W,M ITP-W,M
Maple Tree
FSA1-W,M
Maple Trees
ASB5-W,M
Mapleton High Chorale
LD-W,M
M'appari see Ah! So Pure
Mapuna
SNZ-W,M (Maori)
Maragouins see Les Maragouins
Marais Bouleur
CaF-W (French Only)
Marama
SNZ-W,M (Maori)
Maranoa Lullaby
ASB6-W,M
Marat, Marat
PAJ-W,M
Marat We're Poor

PAJ-W,M
Marathon Man (Theme)
　AT-M
Marcelina
　FSA1-W,M
March (Bartok)
　GM-M
March (Nutcracker Suite)
　OTJ-M RW-M
**March (Nutcracker Suite) see also
　Nutcracker Suite March**
March Along
　RTH-W
March Down to Jerdon
　My-W,M
March in Three Beats
　ASB6-W,M
March! March! March!
　AL-W
March Militaire
　OBN-M
March of Civilization
　SL-W,M
March of Labor
　AL-W
March of Liberation
　VS-W,M
March of the Armoured Corps
　GO-W,M
March of the Dwarfs
　OTJ-M
March of the Kings
　MC-W,M
March of the Men of Harlech
　NAS-W,M SMW-W,M
March of the Siamese Children
　TI1-M UBF-M
March of the Signaleers
　GO-W
March of the Three Kings
　ASB6-W,M
March of the Tin Soldiers
　ASB1-M OTJ-M
March of the Titans
　CoS-W,M
March of the Toilers
　AL-W
March of the Toys
　BCS-M MF-W,M OTJ-W,M RW-M
　TI1-M UBF-M
March of the Workers
　AL-W
March of Turenne
　CA-W,M
March of Union Labor
　AL-W
March of United Labor
　AL-W
March On, O Soul, with Strength
　Hy-W,M
March Slav
　RW-M
March to Victory
　ATS-W
March Wind (Blow, Blow, Old
　March Wind!)
　ASB5-W,M
March Wind (The March Wind Is
　Blowing the Kites in the Sky)
　ASB3-W,M
Marcha Real
　SiP-W,M (Spanish)
Marche
　TM-M WGB/O-M
Marche Des Rois
　CUP-W,M (French Only)
Marche D'la Noce see La Marche

D'la Noche
Marche Militaire
　RW-M
Marcheta
　HLS1-W,M WiS9-W,M
Marching
　MH-W,M
Marching Along
　ATS-W,M HSD-W,M SiS-W,M
Marching Along Together
　OP2-W,M
Marching and Running
　SiR-W,M
Marching down the Street
　GM-W,M
Marching on Georgia
　TMA-W,M
Marching round the Gum Stump
　Oz3-W
Marching round the Levee
　FMT-W FoM-W,M
Marching Scouts
　ASB4-W,M
Marching Soldiers
　ASB2-W,M
Marching Song
　SiR-W,M
Marching Song (As We Go
　Marching Two by Two)
　MG-W,M
Marching Song (In Our Poverty and
　Toil)
　AL-W
Marching Song (Now the Bugle Is
　Sounding)
　SL-W,M
Marching Song (See Here Comes
　the Big Procession)
　STS-W,M
Marching Song (With a Song
　Swing Along)
　FSA2-W,M
Marching thro' Georgia
　SMW-W,M
Marching through Georgia
　AH-W,M AmH-W,M CSo-W,M
　ETB-W,M FW-W HSD-W,M
　MPP-W OFS-W,M OTJ-W,M
　PoS-W,M Sin-W,M SiS-W
　TMA-W,M U-W
Marching thru' Berlin
　SWM-W,M
Marching to Freedom
　AL-W
Marching to Pretoria
　FW-W MG-W,M OHO-W,M
　RSL-W,M TO-W,M
Marching Tune
　GB-W,M
Marching with Coxey
　AL-W
Marchons Avec Joie
　CUP-W,M (French Only)
Mardi Gras
　CE-W,M (French) FSA1-W,M
　MaG-W,M MU-W,M NO-W,M
Margaret's Cradle Song
　TH-W,M
Margate Hoy
　MSB-W
Margery, Serve Well the Black Sow
　Boo-W,M
Margie
　GSN1-W,M RDT-W,M TI2-W,M
　U-W
Margot
　DS-W,M

Marguerite
　FSTS-W,M
Marguerite, La see La Marguerite
Maria
　OTJ-W,M OTO-W
Maria (Hammerstein/Rodgers)
　SM-W,M TI1-W,M UBF-W,M
　UFB-W,M
Maria (Sondheim/Bernstein)
　DBC-W,M HC1-W,M TW-W
Maria, Marie
　WiS8-W,M
Maria Martita
　LaS-W,M (Spanish Only)
Marianina
　CA-W,M SL-W,M TF-W,M
　VA-W,M
Mariann' S'en Va-t-au Moulin
　CFS-W,M (French) FSO-W,M
　(French)
Marianne
　OTJ-W,M
Marianne (Hammerstein/Romberg)
　Ne-W,M
Marianne (Oh Marianne, Oh Won't
　You Marry Me?)
　RW-W,M
Marianne Goes to the Mill
　ASB6-W,M
Marianne Wanders to the Mill
　CFS-W,M (French)
Marianne's Going to the Mill
　FSO-W,M (French)
Marianson, Dame Joli'
　FSO-W,M (French)
Marianson, My Lady Fair
　FSO-W,M (French)
Marie-Clemence
　AAF-W,M (French Only)
Marie! Marie!
　OTJ-W,M
Marie Mine
　WiS8-W,M
Marie Trempe Ton Pain
　MP-W,M (French Only)
Marie's Law
　TW-W
Mariez-Moi, Ma Petite Maman
　LA-W,M (Spanish)
**Mariko's Love Theme see
　Forbidden**
Marine Corps Flying Song
　GI-W
Marine Marching Cadence
　MAS-W,M
Marinela
　MSS-W,M (Spanish)
Mariner
　HSD-W,M
Marines' Hymn
　AAP-W,M ANS-W EFS-W,M
　FU-W,M FuB-W,M FWS-W,M
　GO-W HA-W,M HS-W,M IPH-W,M
　LT-W,M MAS-W,M NAS-W,M
　OTJ-W,M PoG-W,M RW-W,M
　SiB-W,M SMW-W,M TI1-W,M
　UFB-W,M VA-W,M WiS9-W,M
**Marines' Hymn see also Halls of
　Montezuma**
Marion Massacre
　AFP-W
Marion Strike
　AFP-W WW-W,M
Marionettes see Les Marionettes
Marion's Men
　SSS-W,M
Marion's Theme

TOM-M
Mario's Tune
  FSB3-M
Maritana (Selection)
  AmH-M
Mark My Mother Gave Me
  SR-W,M
Mark Where the Bee
  Boo-W,M
Market Day (Come, Get Up! The
  Clock Is Ringing)
  ASB4-W,M
Market Day (Now 'Tis Basso Porto
  Market Day)
  FSA1-W,M
Market Man
  STS-W,M
Market Song
  FSA2-W,M
Market Street Blues
  FVV-W,M
Marksville Blues
  CaF-W (French Only)
Marlboro Cigarettes Jingle see You
  Get a Lot to Like with a Marlboro
Marlborough
  SMW-W,M (French)
Marlborough see also Malbrough
Marmalade, Molasses and Honey
  LM-W,M OTO-W
Marriage Rite Is Over
  Oz4-W
Marriage Type Love
  UBF-W,M
Marriage Vow
  OGC1-W,M
Married (Ebb/Kander)
  C-W,M OTO-W TI2-W,M TW-W
  UBF-W,M
Married by the Bible, Divorced by
  the Law
  OGC1-W,M
Married I Can Always Get
  TI2-W,M
Married Life
  YL-W,M
Married Man
  FSU-W
Married Sweet
  SGT-W,M
Married Woman's Lament
  Oz3-W,M
Marry the Man Today
  TW-W
Marry Young
  Mo-W,M NM-W,M
Marryin' Blue Yodel
  AFB-W,M
Marseillaise see La Marseillaise
Marseillaise Hymn
  HSD-W,M NAS-W,M
Marshmallow World
  BCS-W,M HLS3-W,M MF-W,M
  TI1-W,M UBF-W,M
Marta (Rambling Rose of the
  Wildwood)
  TI2-W,M
Martha (Selection)
  AmH-M
Martha and Mary
  BMM-W,M
Martha Dexter
  BSC-W
Martha My Dear
  BBe-W,M PMC-W,M TWS-W
  WG-W,M
Martial Trumpet

SHS-W,M
Martian Love Song see My True
  Love
Martin Said to His Man
  SSP-W
Martin Van of Kinderhook
  MPP-W
Martina
  MLS-W,M
Martinique Love Song
  AAF-W,M (French)
Martini's March
  BC1-M
Marty
  RSL-W,M
Marty Inglehart
  DE-W,M
Martyrs of Baltimore
  SiS-W
Martyrs Tune
  EA-W,M
Marvelous Toy
  PoG-W,M RBO-W,M
Mary Alone
  NA-W,M
Mary and Martha
  BMC-W,M GuC-W,M HS-W,M
  NAS-W,M
Mary and Willie
  BSC-W FMT-W Oz1-W,M
Mary Ann
  FW-W LaS-W,M MG-W,M
  OFS-W,M
Mary-Anne
  RW-W,M
Mary Arnold, the Female Monster
  MSB-W
Mary Blain
  FoM-W,M
Mary, Doncha Weep
  NeF-W
Mary Don't You Weep
  JF-W,M
Mary Don't You Weep see also
  O Mary Don't You Weep
Mary Golden Lee
  TBF-W
Mary Had a Baby
  ASB5-W,M FW-W MAR-W,M
  RW-W,M WU-W,M
Mary Had a Boy-Child
  GBC-W,M
Mary Had a Little Lamb
  AmH-W,M BBF-W,M BM-W
  GM-W,M HS-W,M HSD-W,M
  MF-W,M MG-W,M OTJ-W,M
  Oz3-W,M RW-W,M SOO-W,M
  TI2-W,M
Mary Had a Little Lot
  AL-W
Mary Hamilton
  BT-W,M FSU-W
Mary in the Morning
  TI2-W,M
Mary Lifted from the Dead
  AHO-W,M
Mary Lou
  TI2-W,M
Mary Loves the Flowers
  FHR-W,M SSFo-W,M
Mary, Mary
  OnT1-W,M
Mary, Mary, Quite Contrary
  MH-W,M OTJ-W,M
Mary Middling
  SiR-W,M
Mary of Argyle

HSD-W,M
Mary of the Wild Moor
  BSC-W TBF-W,M
Mary on the Wild Moor
  FSSC-W,M
Mary Tyler Moore Show Theme
  see Love Is All Around
Mary Wore Three Links of Chain
  AH-W,M NeA-W,M
Mary, You're a Little Bit Old
  Fashioned
  RC-W,M
Maryland, My Maryland
  AAP-W,M AmH-W,M ATS-W
  ESB-W,M Fif-W,M HSD-W,M
  MPP-W OHG-W,M OTJ-W,M
  PoS-W,M SCo-W,M Sin-W,M
  SiS-W WiS8-W,M
Maryland, My Maryland (A
  Northern Reply)
  Sin-W,M
Maryland Resolves
  SBA-W SSS-W,M
Mary's a Grand Old Name
  FSN-W,M GSN1-W,M HLS1-W,M
  MF-W,M OAP-W,M OTJ-W,M
  RW-W,M TI1-W,M UBF-W,M
  UFB-W,M
Mary's Child
  GBC-W,M
Mary's Dream
  SeS-W,M
Mary's Little Boy
  BCh-W,M
Mary's Little Boy Child
  TI1-W,M UBF-W,M
Mary's Little Lot
  AFP-W
Mary's Lullaby
  ASB6-W,M FSD-W,M HS-W,M
Mary's Prayer
  CFB-W,M
Mary's Tooth
  GM-W,M
Mary's Wandering
  OB-W,M
Marysville
  SHS-W,M
Mascot of the Troop
  M-W,M
M*A*S*H Theme Song
  BNG-M DC-W,M EY-W,M
  HFH-W,M MF-W,M TOM-W,M
  ToO76-W,M TVT-W,M
Masked Valentines
  HSA-W,M
Masquerade
  RW-W,M TVT-W,M UBF-W,M
Masquerade Is Over
  MF-W,M
Masquerades
  FSA2-W,M
Massa Dear
  SL-W,M
Massa Had a Yaller Gal
  AN-W
Massachusetts
  TI1-W,M UFB-W,M
Massachusetts Liberty Song
  EA-W,M SI-W
Massachusetts Line
  AWB-W
Massachusetts Song of Liberty
  MPP-W,M
Massa's in de Cold, Cold Ground
  HSD-W,M
Massa's in de Cold Ground

AmH-W,M ATS-W SSF-W,M
SSFo-W,M TH-W,M WiS8-W,M
Massa's in the Cold, Cold Ground
RW-W,M
Massa's in the Cold Ground
ESB-W,M NAS-W,M
Master, Come Help Me
Boo-W,M
Master Is Six Feet One Way
NF-W
Master Killed a Big Bull
NF-W
Master McGrath
IS-W,M VP-W,M
Master, No Offering
AHO-W,M Hy-W,M
Master of the House
UBF-W,M
Master of the Sea
HHa-W,M
Masterpiece, The (Masterpiece
Theater Theme)
BeL-M BNG-M GSN4-M MF-M
TI1-M TV-M TVT-M UFB-M
Masters in This Hall
FW-W JOC-W,M LMR-W,M
MC-W,M OB-W,M SBF-W,M
SiB-W,M
Master's Stolen Coat
NF-W
Mata Hari
LMS-W,M
Matarile
LA-W,M (Spanish)
Matchbox Blues
LC-W
Matchmaker
DBC-W,M HC1-W,M On-W,M
OTO-W TI2-W,M UBF-W,M
Matchmaker, Matchmaker
FPS-W,M
Mate to a Cock
Boo-W,M
Matilda
LaS-W,M MF-W,M SBF-W,M
SMa-W,M TI1-W,M UFB-W,M
Matilda, Matilda!
RDT-W,M
Matin
CUP-W,M (French Only)
Matin Song
SL-W,M
Mating Season
OTO-W
Matona
SL-W,M TF-W,M
Matron
GrM-W,M
Matt Houston
TVT-M
Matter of Trust
TTH-W,M
Matterhorn
BSo-W,M
Matthew, Mark, Luke and John
GM-W,M
Mattie Mae
DBL-W
Mattinata
RW-M
Matty Groves
FW-W
**Matty Groves see also Little Mathy
Groves and the following variant
titles**
Maudit Sois-Tu Carillonneur
Boo-W,M (French Only)

Maverick
TVT-W,M
Mawhee
SCa-W,M
Mawhee see also Little Mohea
Maxim's
TS-W
Maxwell's Doom
BSC-W
Maxwell's Silver Hammer
BBe-W,M Be2-W,M OnT1-W,M
PMC-W,M TWS-W WG-W,M
Maxwellton Braes Are Bonnie
SeS-W,M
Maxy
MPP-W
May
FSA2-W,M
May and January
KH-W,M
May Basket
MH-W,M
May Bells
ASB4-W,M
May Breezes (Mendelssohn)
GM-M
May Brings Round
Boo-W,M
May Carol
GUM2-W,M OB-W,M
May Dance
SL-W,M
May Day
MH-W,M
May Day Carol
LMR-W,M
May Day Carol (Robin Hood and
Little John, They Both are Gone
to the Fair, O)
ASB4-W,M
May Day Carol (We have Been
Rambling Half the Night)
GBC-W,M
May-Day Garland
OB-W,M
May Does Ev'ry Fragrance
Boo-W,M
May Each Day
GTV-W,M
May Flight
UF-W,M
May God Save the Union
Sin-W,M
May Hit the Road a Welt Yourself
AL-W
May I?
OTO-W
May I Sleep in Your Barn Tonight
Mister?
ITP-W,M
**May I Sleep in Your Barn Tonight
Mister? see also Can I Sleep in
Your Barn Tonight?**
May I throughout This Day of
Thine
AME-W,M
May I Woo the Lassie?
SaS-W,M
May in Flower
SL-W,M
May Irwin's Bully Song
EFS-W,M FSTS-W,M
May Irwin's Frog Song
EFS-W,M
May Night
MHB-W,M (German)
May Our Lord Long Reign

SiP-W,M (Japanese)
May Peace Abide with You
MU-W,M
May Queen
FSA1-W,M MU-W,M (French)
May Queen's Plaint
Boo-W,M
May Song
GUM2-W,M MML-W,M
May the Bird of Paradise Fly up
Your Nose
WF-W,M
May the Good Lord Bless and Keep
You
RDF-W,M RDT-W,M TI2-W,M
May the Grace of Christ Our Savior
AME-W,M
May the Grace of Christ Our
Saviour
Hy-W,M
May the Queen Live Long
Boo-W,M
May the Words
JS-W,M SBJ-W,M (Hebrew Only)
May There Be Peace on Earth This
Christmas
CI-W,M
May Time see also Maytime
May Time (When the Spring with
Magic Finger)
MML-W,M
May You All Prosper
RuS-W,M (Russian)
May You Always
PB-W,M TI1-W,M UFB-W,M
Maybe (from Annie)
HLS8-W,M TI2-W,M UBF-W,M
Maybe (Gershwin)
GOB-W,M GST-W,M MF-W,M
NYT-W,M
Maybe (If I Prayed Ev'ry Night,
You'd Come Home to Me)
ILF-W,M RY-W,M RYT-W,M
Maybe (You'll Think of Me, When
You Are All Alone)
HLS2-W,M RW-W,M
Maybe Baby
TI2-W,M
Maybe I'm a Fool
ToO79-W,M
Maybe I'm Amazed
Be2-W,M
Maybe It's the Moon
WDS-W,M
Maybe This Time
HC1-W,M ILT-W,M On-W,M
OTO-W ToS-W,M UBF-W,M
Maybe Your Baby's Got the Blues
GCM-W,M
Mayday! Mayday! Mayday!
AF-W
Maypole Dance
FSA1-W,M TF-W,M
Maytime see also May Time
Maytime (Birds on the Tree Sing a
Sunlight Song)
FSA1-W,M
Mazurek
NAS-W,M
Mazurka (Chopin, Op. 7, No. 1)
AmH-M FSA2-W,M
Mazurka (Godard, Op. 54, No. 2)
AmH-M
Mazurka (Hark! the Music Is
Sounding Its One-Two-Three)
FSA1-W,M
Mazurka (Now We Dance in

Measure Sprightly)
SL-W,M
Me a Heap Big Injun
LMS-W,M
Me about You
THN-W,M
Me an' My Boss
L-W
Me and Bobby McGee
CMG-W,M CSp-W,M SuS-W,M
Me and Crippled Soldiers
NMH-W,M
Me and Dorothea
TW-W
Me and Jesus
CEM-W,M TI1-W,M UFB-W,M
Me and Julio Down by the
Schoolyard
GrS-W,M PS-W,M
Me and Mrs. Jones
SoH-W,M
Me and My Arrow
BR-W,M
Me and My Baby
CMV-W,M
Me and My Boss see Me an' My
Boss
Me and My Captain
AFP-W
Me and My Girl
UBF-W,M
Me and My Lover
NF-W
Me and My R C
GSM-W,M
Me and My Shadow
FPS-W,M HSS-W,M T-W,M
TI1-W,M UFB-W,M
Me and Paul
WNF-W
Me and the Cat
TT-W,M
Me and You and a Dog Named Boo
AT-W,M OTJ-W,M
Me Bless the Cross
GB-W,M
Me Darlin' Ben
LaS-W,M
Me Johnny Mitchell Man
AL-W
Me Stone Is the Stone
SGT-W,M
Meadowland (Red Army Song)
FW-W
Meadowland (Red Army Song) see
also Cavalry of the Steppes
Meadowlands
RW-M VA-W,M
Meadow-Larks
NA-W,M
Mean
Mo-W,M NM-W,M OTO-W
Mean Mr. Mustard
BBe-W,M TWS-W
Mean Mistreatin' Woman
LC-W
Mean Ole Frisco
LC-W
Mean Ole Lion
Wi-W,M
Mean to Me
FPS-W,M LSB-W,M MF-W,M
RW-W,M TI1-W,M ToS-W,M
TWD-W,M UFB-W,M
Mean Trouble Blues
LC-W
Mean Woman Blues

RW-W,M SRE2-W,M TFC-W,M
Meanest Man in the World
RBO-W,M
Meantime
TT-W,M
Mear
SHS-W,M
Measles in the Spring
AFS-W,M Oz3-W,M
Measure the Valleys
R-W,M TW-W
Meat-Pie Seller
ASB6-W,M (Spanish)
Mechanic
AL-W
Mechanic's Appeal to the Public
MSB-W
Mechanic's Song
AL-W
Me'credi Soir Passe
CaF-W (French Only)
Med Gud Och Hans Vanscap
AHO-W,M (Swedish)
Medic Theme see Blue Star
Medic's Chant
GI-W
Medic's Song
GO-W
Meditation (Bach/Gounod)
AmH-M OBN-M
Meditation (Gimbel/Jobim)
DJ-W,M TI2-W,M
Meditation (Massenet)
TM-M WGB/O-M
Meditation (Today, If You Hear His
Voice)
SHS-W,M
Mee Homoho
SBJ-W,M (Hebrew Only)
Mee Y'malayl
SBJ-W,M (Hebrew)
Meeks Family
BSC-W
Meeks Murder
BSC-W,M Oz2-W,M
Meerschaum Pipe
AmH-W,M ATS-W HSD-W,M
Meeskite
C-W,M
Meet Benny Bailey
MF-M
Meet Me at the Fair
Oz3-W
Meet Me by Moonlight
OH-W,M Oz4-W
Meet Me in St. Louis
FWS-W,M MAB1-W MSA1-W
OBN-W,M
Meet Me in St. Louis, Louis
FSN-W,M FSTS-W,M FW-W
GG2-W,M GSN1-W,M HLS1-W,M
MF-W,M OAP-W,M OTJ-W,M
RW-W,M
Meet Me in the Bottom
LC-W,M
Meet Me in the Moonlight
SCa-W,M
Meet Me There
GH-W,M
Meet Me Tonight
Oz4-W,M
Meet Me To-night in Dreamland
HLS1-W,M MF-W,M TI1-W,M
UFB-W,M
Meet Me Tonight in Dreamland
OAP-W,M RoE-W,M
Meet Mother in the Skies

AME-W,M
Meeting at the Building
FW-W Le-W,M
Meeting Here Tonight
WN-W,M
Meg Merriles
FSA2-W,M
Meggie's Theme see Anywhere the
Heart Goes
Mehe Manu Rere
GuC-W,M (Maori)
Mein Glaubiges Herze see My
Heart Ever Faithful
Mein Herr
OTO-W UBF-W,M
Mein Hut
HS-W,M (German) RS-W,M
SHP-W,M
Mein Yiddishe Meidele
MF-W,M (Yiddish Only)
Meine Lieder
AS-W,M (German)
Melancholy Cowboy
SoC-W,M
Melancholy, Folly
Boo-W,M
Melancholy Music Man
THN-W,M
Melancholy Rhapsody
MF-W,M
Melancholy Serenade
GTV-W,M
Melina
TI1-W,M (Spanish Only)
UFB-W,M (Spanish Only)
Melinda
TW-W
Melinda May
FHR-W,M SSFo-W,M
Melisande
OHT-W,M
Mellow Horn
ESB-W,M
Melody
RoS-W,M
Melody from the Sky
OTO-W
Melody in F
AmH-W,M MF-M RW-M TI1-M
UFB-M
Melody of Love
HLS1-W,M MF-W,M OAP-M
OBN-M OPS-M TI1-W,M TM-M
UFB-W,M WGB/O-M
Melos
CF-W,M
Melt the Bells
Sin-W,M SiS-W
Meltdown (at Madame Tussaud's)
VB-W,M
'Member Me
BDW-W,M
Members and Guests
LoS-W
Membership Song
LoS-W
Memo from Turner
RoS-W,M
Memorial Day
ASB4-W,M
Memorial Flowers
SiS-W
Memorial Song
GrM-W,M
Memories (from Top Gun)
TTH-M
Memories (Memories, Dreams of

Love So True)
MF-W,M Mo-W,M OTO-W
Memories (O'er the Valley and the
Mountain When the Hush of
Evening Falls)
GrM-W,M
Memories (Pressed between the
Pages of My Mind)
TI1-W,M UFB-W,M
Memories (We Cherish of Days
Fled for Aye)
FSA1-W,M
**Memories of Days Gone By see
Wus Geven Is Geven Un Nitu**
Memories of Earth
GH-W,M
Memories of Maoriland
SNZ-W,M (Maori)
Memories of Mother and Dad
BSo-W,M
Memories of You
RoE-W,M TI1-W,M UFB-W,M
Memory (Andrew Lloyd Webber)
DBC-W,M TI2-W,M UBF-W,M
Memory Lane
MF-W,M
Memory Motel
RoS-W,M
Memory of Your Smile
BSo-W,M
Memory's Flowers
FSA1-W,M
Memphis Blues
B-W,M
Memphis in June
Mo-W,M NM-W,M OTO-W
TI2-W,M
Memphis, Tennessee
TI1-W,M UFB-W,M
Men
V-W,M
Men and Children Everywhere
SHP-W,M
Men into Plowshares
OHO-W,M
Men of Auld Lang Syne
AL-W
Men of Dartmouth
IL-W,M
Men of Harlech
AmH-W,M CSo-W,M FBI-W,M
OTJ-W,M SiP-W,M (Welsh)
Men of Pennsylvania
Mo-W,M TI2-W,M
Men of the North and West
AWB-W
Men of the Soil
SWF-W,M
Men on the Flying Trapeze
AF-W
Men Who Work
AL-W
Men Whose Boast It Is
SoF-W,M
Menagerie
HAS-W,M NAS-W,M
Menagerie Song
ATS-W
Mendelssohn's Wedding March
RW-M
**Mendelssohn's Wedding March
see also Wedding March
(Mendelssohn)**
Meng Chiang Nu's Lament (Mang
Chiang Ngu)
FD-W,M (Chinese)
Men's Clothes I Will Put On

Oz1-W,M
Mental Arithmetic
ASB5-W,M
Mention My Name in Sheboygan
TI2-W,M
Menuchoh Vesimchoh
JS-W,M (Hebrew)
Menuet A L'Antique (Theme)
MF-M
**Menuet A L'Antique (Theme) see
also Minuet A L'Antique**
Menuetto Pastorale
SL-W,M
Meow
SL-W,M
Meow Mix Theme
BNG-W,M
Mer' Michel see La Mer' Michel
Merchants' Carol
OB-W,M
Merchant's Daughter
TBF-W,M
Mercy, Mercy, Mercy
DJ-M
Mercy's Free
GH-W,M SHS-W,M
Mermaid, The
BMM-W CSo-W,M ESB-W,M
FMT-W FW-W GI-W,M GO-W,M
HSD-W,M OHO-W,M SCa-W
Mermaid's Song
MMW-W,M
Merrily Fuddle Thy Nose
ESU-W
Merrily, Merrily
MML-W,M
Merrily, Merrily Greet the Morn
Boo-W,M
Merrily, Merrily, On We Ride
Boo-W,M
Merrily Sing (Away with
Melancholy, Nor Doleful Changes
Ring)
TH-W,M
Merrily Sing (Our Happy Evening
Song)
GrM-W,M
Merrily We Ride Along
SFB-W,M
Merrily We Roll Along
FSB1-W,M LT-W,M MF-W,M
Merrily We Shepherds Live
Boo-W,M
Merry Are the Bells
SiR-W,M
Merry Bells of Hamburg Town
Boo-W,M
Merry Christmas (I Wish You a
Merry Christmas)
MAS-W,M
**Merry Christmas (I Wish You a
Merry Christmas) see also I Wish
You a Merry Christmas**
Merry Christmas (Merry Christmas,
on This Bright and Happy Day)
MH-W,M
Merry Christmas (Merry, Merry
Christmas)
FF-W,M
Merry Christmas (On Christmas
Eve the Bells Were Rung)
OB-W,M
Merry Christmas (We Wish You a
Merry Christmas)
ASB5-W,M
**Merry Christmas (We Wish You a
Merry Christmas) see also We**

Wish You a Merry Christmas
Merry Christmas, A
JOC-W,M SCL-W,M
Merry Christmas and Happy New
Year
CA-W,M
Merry Christmas Baby
HRB1-W,M
Merry Christmas Bells
SiR-W,M
Merry Christmas, My Darling
OnT6-W,M
Merry Christmas Polka
PT-W,M TI1-W,M
Merry Christmas Time-ee-o
OTJ-W,M
Merry Christmas to You
MAR-W,M
Merry-Go-Round
OTO-W SiR-W,M
Merry-Go-Round (The Animals
Riding the Merry-Go-Round)
ASB4-W,M
Merry-Go-Round (Far down the
Street I Can Hear a Gay Sound)
ASB2-W,M
Merry-Go-Round (Oh, Camels and
Bears and Ponies Are Found)
MH-W,M
Merry-Go-Round (When I Go Out
on a Merry-Go-Round)
GM-W,M
Merry-Go-Round Broke Down
MF-W,M
Merry Golden Tree
BSC-W Oz1-W,M
Merry Green Fields of the Lowland
Oz3-W,M
Merry Hunter
BMC-M
Merry Is the Morning
LA-W,M (Spanish)
Merry Life, A
NAS-W,M OS-W TH-W,M
Merry Little Birds Are We
FHR-W,M
Merry Little Minuet
TW-W
Merry Little Soldier
MPP-W
Merry Men
FSA1-W,M
Merry, Merry Christmas
Boo-W,M
Merry, Merry Month of May
FHR-W,M SSF-W,M
Merry Month of May
EL-W,M
Merry Old Land of Oz
WO-W,M
Merry Roundelay
Boo-W,M
Merry Singer
OHG-W,M
Merry Widow Waltz
AmH-W,M BH-W,M MF-M RW-M
TI1-M UFB-M
**Merry Widow Waltz see also Waltz
Song (Merry Widow)**
Merseburg
AF-W
Mess Call
ATS-W,M GI-W GO-W MAS-W,M
Mess-Kit Blues
AF-W
Mess of Blues
SRE1-W,M

Message (Mari, When We Two Are
  Parted)
  LA-W,M (Spanish)
Message (A Message Came to a
  Maiden Young)
  OB-W,M
Message to Michael
  ERM-W,M HD-W,M
Messenger
  SL-W,M
Messiah
  SHS-W,M VB-W,M
Mesu Mefre Agya, Katakyie
  SBF-W,M (Ghanaian Only)
Metaphor
  TW-W
Methodist Pie
  Oz2-W,M
Mets Ton Joli Jupon
  SSN-W,M (French)
Meunier Tu Dors
  Ch-W (French Only) MP-W,M
  (French Only)
Meurs Si Tu Veux
  CaF-W (French Only)
Mewsette
  Mo-W,M NM-W,M OTO-W
Mexicali Rose
  FC-W,M (Spanish) OnT1-W,M
  RW-W,M TI2-W,M
Mexican Blues
  FG1-M
Mexican Christmas Procession
  CCM-W,M
Mexican Hat Dance
  LaS-M MF-M OTJ-M PoG-M
  RW-M TI1-M
Mexican Road Race
  OnT6-M
Mexican Serenade
  AmH-M
Mexico City
  WDS-W,M
Mi Caballo Blanco
  FW-W (Spanish) WSB-W,M
  (Spanish)
Mi Casa, Su Casa
  RW-W,M
Mi Chomochoh
  JS-W,M (Hebrew Only)
Mi Hamaca
  LaS-W,M (Spanish Only)
Mi Mama Me Aconsejaba
  LA-W,M (Spanish)
Mi Y'malel
  FW-W (Hebrew) WSB-W,M
  (Hebrew)
Miami Beach Rhumba
  TI2-W,M
Michael Finnegan
  Bo-W,M
Michael Finnigan
  FW-W FWS-W,M OHO-W,M
  SFB-W,M SiB-W,M
Michael Haul Your Boat Ashore
  JF-W,M
Michael Row the Boat Ashore
  Bo-W,M FSSC-W,M FW-W
  GuC-W,M LH-W,M MAB1-W
  MF-W,M MSA1-W OAP-W,M
  OTJ-W,M PoG-W,M RDT-W,M
  RW-W,M SBF-W,M SpS-W,M
  WSB-W,M
Michael Roy
  ATS-W,M HSD-W,M
Michael's Theme
  OTO-W

Michelle
  BBe-W,M Be1-W,M OnT1-W,M
  PMC-W,M SwS-W,M TWS-W
  WG-W,M
**Michelob Beer Jingle see
  Weekends Were Made for
  Michelob**
Michie Banjo
  CLaL-W,M (French)
**Michie Banjo see also Mister Banjo,
  Monsieur Banjo, M'sieu Bainjo,
  Musieu Bainjo, O Mu'sieu Banjo,
  and Oh Mister Banjo**
Michie Preval
  AAF-W,M (French Only)
  BaB-W,M (French)
Michigan Dixie
  SiS-W
Michigan-I-O
  SoC-W
Michigan, My Michigan
  Fif-W,M
Mick McGuire
  IS-W,M
Mickey Free and the Fashions
  VP-W
Mickey Mouse March
  NI-W,M On-W,M OTJ-W,M
  RW-W,M
Midas Touch
  TTH-W,M
Middle Years
  TW-W
Middlebury
  SHS-W,M
Midgets
  MF-M
Midnight (Hush'd a Thousand
  Voices, Gone the Noontide Glare)
  MML-W,M
Midnight (Under This Sod Lies a
  Great Bucking Hoss)
  HB-W
Midnight at the Onyx
  Sta-W,M
Midnight Bells
  ReG-W,M
Midnight Blue
  TI2-W,M
Midnight Blues
  LC-W
Midnight Cowboy (Theme)
  GOI7-M Mo-W,M RW-M TI2-W,M
**Midnight Cowboy (Theme) see also
  Everybody's Talkin'**
Midnight Cry
  HHa-W,M SHS-W,M
Midnight Express (Theme)
  MoA-W,M
Midnight Fire
  TOC83-W,M
Midnight Hour
  HRB1-W,M
Midnight in Heaven
  CCS-W,M
Midnight in Moscow
  TI1-M UFB-M
Midnight in Paris
  STP-W,M TI2-W,M
Midnight Murder of the Meeks
  Family
  Oz2-W
Midnight Oil
  SBS-W,M
Midnight on the Stormy Deep
  BSo-W,M
Midnight Rambler

LC-W RoS-W,M
Midnight Special
  AFB-W,M AmS-W,M FW-W
  GG1-W,M IHA-W,M J-W,M
  JF-W,M Le-W,M LSR-W,M NeF-W
  OFS-W,M OTJ-W,M Oz2-W,M
  PoG-W,M RDT-W,M TI1-W,M
  UFB-W,M WSB-W,M
Midnight Sun
  DJ-W,M OHF-W ToS-W,M
Midnight Sun Will Never Set
  LM-W,M MF-W,M
Midnight Train to Georgia
  GrS-W,M SoH-W,M
Midshipmite
  HSD-W,M
Midsummer Night (Come, Boys,
  Now We'll Light the Fires)
  UF-W,M
Midsummer Night (Moonlight Falls
  o'er Quiet Hill and Valley)
  FSA1-W,M
Midsummer's Eve
  SN-W,M
Midwestern Summer
  TW-W
Mid-Winter
  OB-W,M
MIG 15's
  AF-W
Mighty Day
  FW-W
Mighty Fortress
  FH-W,M GH-W,M SJ-W,M
  SMW-W,M (German) VB-W,M
Mighty Fortress Is Our God
  AME-W,M CEM-W,M DC-W,M
  HF-W,M HLS7-W,M Hy-W,M
  IH-M JBF-W,M RW-W,M
  SBF-W,M TB-W,M WiS7-W,M
  YS-W,M
Mighty God, While Angels Bless
  Thee
  Hy-W,M
Mighty Lak' a Rose
  FSN-W,M MF-W,M OTJ-W,M
  RW-W,M
Mighty Lord
  VB-W,M
Mighty One, before Whose Face
  AHO-W,M
Mighty Oregon
  Mo-W,M TI2-W,M
Mighty River
  VS-W,M
Mighty to Save
  GH-W,M
Mighty Wings
  TTH-W,M
Mignonette
  K-W,M YL-W,M
Migrant's Letter to His Mother
  VP-W
Mikado (Selection)
  AmH-M
Milatres Cou'ri
  CSD-W,M (French)
Milenburg Joys
  Mo-W,M NM-W,M TI2-W,M
Milestones
  MF-M
Milford Sound
  SNZ-W,M (Maori)
Military Dancing Drill
  GOB-W,M
Military Glory of Great Britain
  (Chorus)

BC1-W,M
Military Molly
  AmH-M
Military Song
  SBA-W
Milk and Honey
  Mo-W,M NM-W,M OTJ-W,M
  OTO-W UBF-W,M
Milk Is a Natural
  GSM-W,M
Milk Wagon
  ASB2-W,M
Milking Maid
  Oz1-W,M
Milking Song
  GUM1-W,M
Milkmaid
  FMT-W
Milkman
  GM-W,M
Milkman's Horse
  KS-W,M
Milkmen's Matinee
  Mo-W,M NM-W,M
Mill, The (Busy Hands at the Work)
  FSA2-W,M
Mill, The (Go to the Top of the
  Path of the Garden)
  ASB5-W,M
Mill Has Shut Down
  AFP-W AL-W
Mill Mother's Lament
  AFP-W LW-W,M WW-W,M
Mill Was Made of Marble
  AFP-W,M JF-W,M (Spanish)
  SWF-W,M WW-W,M
Milledgeville
  SHS-W,M
Millennium
  SHS-W,M
Miller, The
  FW-W TBF-W
Miller, a Miller
  Boo-W,M
Miller and His Sons
  TBF-W
**Miller Beer Jingle see If You've Got
  the Time, We've Got the Beer**
Miller Boy
  Oz3-W,M TMA-W,M
Miller of Dee
  F3-W,M
Miller of the Dee
  CSo-W,M ESB-W,M HSD-W,M
Miller's Advice to His Three Sons
  SCa-W,M
Miller's Daughter
  Boo-W,M FSF-W (French)
Miller's Daughters
  Oz1-W,M
Miller's Flowers
  MML-W,M
Miller's Son
  LN-W,M TW-W
Miller's Will
  BSC-W
Million Goes to Million
  Mo-W,M NM-W,M
Million Miles from Your Heart
  OGC1-W,M
Mill-Wheel
  OTJ-W,M
Millwheel
  SMa-W,M
Milord
  TI2-W,M
Milton Berle Show Theme see Near

You
Milwaukee Blues
  LSR-W,M
Milwaukee Here I Come
  BSo-W,M
Mimi
  AT-W,M HC2-W,M OTO-W TS-W
Mince Pie or a Pudding
  GB-W,M
Mind--a Labor Chant
  AL-W
Mind Games
  TI2-W,M
Mind If I Make Love to You
  ML-W,M
Mind Your Manners, Boys
  VS-W,M
Mine (Love Is Mine)
  GOB-W,M LSO-W MF-W,M
  NYT-W,M
Mine! (What Rays of Glory Bright)
  GH-W,M
**Mine Eyes Have Seen the Glory
  see Battle Hymn of the Republic**
Mine Is the Mourning Heart
  FHR-W,M
Miner
  AL-W
Miners' Bewail and Expected
  Triumph
  AL-W
Miner's Dream of Home
  U-W
Miner's Flux
  AFP-W
Miner's Life
  SWF-W,M
Miner's Life Is Like a Sailor's
  AFP-W
Miner's Lifeguard
  AL-W FW-W
Miner's Song
  BSC-W
Mingled Melodies
  LMR-W,M TF-W,M
Minimum Love
  TOC83-W,M
Minister's Farewell
  SHS-W,M
Minka
  TH-W,M
Minki
  LT-W,M
Minnesang
  MU-W,M (German)
Minnie the Moocher
  NoS-W,M
Minnie's Yoo Hoo
  NI-W,M
Minstrel Band
  MaG-W,M
Minstrel Boy
  AmH-W,M CSo-W,M FBI-W,M
  FW-W Gu-W,M GUM2-W,M
  NAS-W,M OFS-W,M OTJ-W,M
  TF-W,M TH-W,M
Minstrel in the Gallery
  BJ-W,M
Minstrel's Return from the War
  OHG-W,M
Minuet (Bach)
  MF-M PoG-M
Minuet (Boccherini)
  MF-M
Minuet (Mozart)
  AmH-M BMC-M GM-M RW-M
Minuet A L'Antique

AmH-M
**Minuet A L'Antique see also
  Menuet A L'Antique**
Minuet in G (Beethoven)
  MF-M
Minueto
  TI1-W,M (Spanish Only)
  UFB-W,M (Spanish Only)
Minute Men, Form
  SiS-W
Minute Waltz
  AmH-M TI2-W,M
Mione
  BSC-W
Mira
  TW-W
Miracle Happened to Me
  BSG-W,M BSP-W,M FS-W,M
  MF-W,M
Miracle Man
  VB-W,M
Miracle of Miracles
  OTO-W TI2-W,M TW-W
  UBF-W,M
Miracles (If Only You Believe in
  Miracles Baby, So Would I)
  ToO76-W,M
Miracles (Miracles, That's What
  Life's About)
  TI2-W,M
Miraculous Harvest
  OB-W,M
Mirame Asi
  MSS-W,M (Spanish)
Miranda
  Mo-W,M NM-W,M OTO-W
Mirror of Your Heart
  VB-W,M
Mis Raices Estan Aqui (My Roots
  Are Buried Here)
  JW-W,M
Mischa, Jascha, Toscha, Sascha
  GOB-W,M LSO-W NYT-W,M
Mischiefs of Drinking
  ESU-W
Miserable with You
  TW-W
Miserables
  CaF-W (French Only)
Miserere
  ESB-W,M GI-W MML-W,M (Latin
  Only)
Miserere (Il Trovatore)
  MU-W,M (Italian)
Miserere Nostri Domine Secundum
  Boo-W,M (Latin Only)
Miserere Nostri Domine Viventium
  Boo-W,M (Latin Only)
Misery (Lennon/McCartney)
  BR-W,M MF-W,M OPS-W,M
  TWS-W
Misery and Gin
  NMH-W,M
Misery Loves Company
  TOC82-W,M TOH-W,M
Misirlou
  DP-W,M TI1-W,M (Spanish)
  UFB-W,M (Spanish)
Mis'ry River
  TOC82-W,M
Miss Amanda Jones
  RoS-W,M
Miss America
  NoS-W,M TI2-W,M
Miss Bailey
  ESU-W
Miss Bailey's Ghost

RV-W
Mistress Daisy
  SOT-W,M
Mistress Mary
  SMa-W,M
Mistress Shady
  TF-W,M
Misty
  BNG-W,M DC-W,M DJ-W,M
  FPS-W,M GSN3-W,M MF-W,M
  TI2-W,M ToO76-W,M ToS-W,M
Misty Night Is Falling
  ID-W,M
Mitchel's Address
  VP-W,M
Mitten Song
  SSe-W,M
Mix a Pancake
  MH-W,M
Mizay Marie
  SGT-W,M
Mizpah (God Be with You Till We
  Meet Again)
  FSA2-W,M
**Mizpah (God Be with You Till We
  Meet Again) see also God Be with
  You (Till We Meet Again)**
Mizpah (I Can't Believe That
  Once Again It's Time for Us to
  Go)
  VB-W,M
MMM, MMM, Good
  GSM-W,M
Mo L'aime Toi Chere
  CE-W,M (French)
Mo Nighean Chruinn, Donn
  SeS-W,M
Mo Nighean Donn, Bhoidheach
  SeS-W,M
Moanin' Low
  MF-W,M
Moanin' the Blues
  RW-W,M
Moanish Lady
  AmS-W,M
Mobile Bay
  SA-W,M
Moccasin Game Song
  IF-M
Mockin' Bird Hill
  CMG-W,M FPS-W,M MF-W,M
  TI1-W,M TWD-W,M UFB-W,M
Mocking Bird (Hush Up Baby,
  Don't Say a Word)
  KS-W,M
**Mocking Bird (Hush Up Baby,
  Don't Say a Word) see also Hush
  Little Baby**
Mocking Bird (I Love to Roam in
  the Woodland)
  FSA2-W,M
Mocking Bird (Of All the Singing
  Birds I Know)
  MH-W,M
Mocking, Mocking
  Boo-W,M
Mockingbird (Everybody Have You
  Heard?)
  GSN4-W,M RW-W,M
Model Church
  GH-W,M
Model Grange
  GrM-W,M
Model of a Modern Major-General
  MGT-W,M OTJ-W,M
Modern Heroism
  AL-W

Modern Hinky-Dinky
  GO-W
Modern Love
  TI2-W,M
Modern Major-General
  WF-W,M
Modern Missionary Zeal
  AL-W
Modern Woman
  TTH-W,M
Modesty Answer
  TBF-W,M
Modoc Indian Song
  IF-M
Modulation
  GG3-W,M
Mogayn Ovos
  SBJ-W,M (Hebrew Only)
Mogen Ovos
  JS-W,M (Hebrew Only)
Moi, Je Suis Ein Homme
  CaF-W (French Only)
Molasses to Rum
  TW-W
Mole End Carol
  GBC-W,M
Mole in the Ground
  AFS-W,M FW-W
**Mole in the Ground see also I Wish
  I Was a Mole in the Ground**
Moliendo Cafe
  RW-W,M (Spanish Only)
**Mollie Bonder see Song Ballet of
  Mollie Bonder**
Mollie Dear, Go Ask Your Mother
  SCa-W
Mollie Lou, Sweet Mollie Mine
  SoC-W
Mollie Vaughn
  SCa-W
**Mollie Vaughn see also Molly
  Vaughn**
Mollie's Love Song
  BMM-W
Molly and the Baby
  Oz2-W
Molly Bendon and Jimmy Randolph
  Oz1-W
Molly Brannigan
  FW-W LW-W,M
Molly Brooks
  Oz3-W,M
Molly Cottontail
  NF-W
Molly Darling
  OGC2-W,M
Molly Dear, Good Night
  FHR-W,M SSFo-W,M
Molly! Do You Love Me?
  FHR-W,M
Molly Malone
  FW-W IL-W,M RW-W,M WU-W,M
Molly O!
  EFS-W,M RW-W,M
Molly O'Malley
  WDS-W,M
Molly, Put the Kettle On
  TMA-W,M
Molly Vaughn
  FMT-W Oz1-W,M
**Molly Vaughn see also Mollie
  Vaughn**
Molly Vonder
  Oz1-W
Mom and Dad's Waltz
  OGC1-W,M
Moment Musical

AmH-M RW-M
Moment of Madness
  MF-W,M
Moment to Moment
  PoG-W,M WG-W,M
Moments Like This
  OTO-W
Moments to Remember
  MF-W,M TI2-W,M
Momma, Look Sharp
  TW-W
Mommie Dearest (Theme)
  TOM-M
Mommy, Mommy, Mommy
  BRB-W
Mommy Please Stay Home with
  Me
  OGC2-W,M
Momzel Zi Zi
  CLaL-W,M (French)
Momzel Zizi
  CSD-W,M (French)
Momzelle Zizi
  CE-W,M (French)
Mon Ami, My Friend
  UBF-W,M
Mon Amour
  FSO-W,M (French) MLS-W,M
Mon Amour Est Barre
  CE-W,M (French)
Mon Ane, Mon Ane
  MP-W,M (French Only)
Mon Beau Sapin
  CE-W,M (French)
Mon Berger
  FSO-W,M (French)
Mon Bon Vieux Mari
  CE-W,M (French)
Mon Cher Bebe Creole
  CaF-W (French Only)
Mon Coeur Appelle Pou'toi
  CaF-W (French Only)
**Mon Coeur S'ouvre A Ta Voix see
  My Heart at Thy Sweet Voice
Mon Homme see My Man**
Mon Joli Coeur De Rosier
  FSO-W,M (French)
Mon Per' M'a Donne Un Mari
  CUP-W,M (French Only)
Mon Pere, Il Me Marie
  CaF-W (French Only)
Mona
  AmH-W,M WiS8-W,M
Mona Lisa
  AT-W,M GSN3-W,M LM-W,M
  MAB1-W MSA1-W OTO-W
  RDT-W,M TOM-W,M
Monastery Bells
  AmH-M
Monday, Monday
  BR-W,M MCG-W,M RW-W,M
  TI2-W,M TRR-W,M
**Monday Night Baseball Theme No.
  3 see Slugger Theme**
Monday, Tuesday
  SMa-W,M
Monday's Child
  YS-W,M
Mondo Cane Theme see More
Money (O Money Is the Meat in
  the Cocoanut)
  AmS-W,M NeA-W,M
Money (Pink Floyd)
  TWD-W,M
Money Am a Hard Thing to Borrow
  SY-W,M
Money for Nothing

TTH-W,M
Money Honey
  HR-W RB-W
Money Is King
  FW-W
Money Isn't Everything
  A-W,M
Money Isn't Ev'rything
  L-W
Money, Marbles and Chalk
  DBL-W
Money Money
  OTO-W TI2-W,M UBF-W,M
Money, Money, Money
  TI1-W,M UFB-W,M
Money, Money, Oh Sweet Money
  Oz3-W,M
Money, Money, 'Tis That Only
  Boo-W,M
Money Musk
  AmH-M BC1-M POT-M
Money Power Arraigned
  AL-W
Money Taking Woman
  DBL-W
Moneyless Children
  Am-W,M
'Mongst Other Folks
  Boo-W,M
Monica
  OTO-W
Monkees (Theme)
  OnT1-W,M TVT-W,M
Monkey (George Michael)
  CFB-W,M
Monkey, The (Monkeys Hang by
  Hands or Tails)
  MH-W,M
Monkey in the Mango
  TW-W
Monkey Man
  RoS-W,M
Monkey See, Monkey Do
  MF-W,M
**Monkey Song see I Wan'na Be Like
  You**
Monkey Turned Barber
  BSC-W
Monkey Ward Can't Make a
  Monkey Out of Me
  AFP-W
Monkey's Wedding
  AmS-W,M ATS-W OHG-W,M
  WU-W,M
Monks of Bangor's March
  ESB-W,M
Monmouth Victory
  CoS-W,M
Monoshee Range
  BMC-W,M
Monsieur Banjo
  LA-W,M (Spanish)
**Monsieur Banjo see also Michie
  Banjo, Mister Banjo, M'sieu
  Bainjo, Musieu Bainjo, O Mu'sieu
  Banjo, and Oh Mister Banjo**
Monster Mash
  NoS-W,M
Monster's Holiday
  OTJ-W,M
Montana
  Fif-W,M
Montana Song
  RV-W
Monterey
  AWB-W
Montgomery

SHS-W,M
Month of January
  IS-W,M
Month of Sundays
  BeL-W,M
Mony, Mony
  BHO-W,M ERM-W,M ILS-W,M
  MF-W,M
Mood Indigo
  GMD-W,M GSN2-W,M NK-W,M
  TI2-W,M
Moody River
  HR-W
Mooje Moccasin
  MAS-W,M (Ojibway Only)
Mooley Cow Red
  MH-W,M
Moon (Have You Seen the Moon
  Pass By)
  ASB4-W,M
Moon (I Saw the Lovely Moon at
  Night)
  FF-W,M
Moon (Lady Moon, Lady Moon,
  Where Are You Roving)
  FSA1-W,M SL-W,M
Moon (The Moon Goes Softly up
  the Sky)
  ASB5-W,M
Moon (My Heart Is Like the
  Gloomy Night)
  AS-W,M (German)
Moon and I
  MGT-W,M
Moon Balloon
  ASB4-W,M
Moon-Cradle's Rocking
  SOO-W,M
Moon-Faced, Starry-Eyed
  SSA-W,M UBF-W,M
Moon Had Climbed the Highest Hill
  SeS-W,M
Moon Is Risin'
  LC-W
Moon Is Up
  Boo-W,M
Moon Love
  AT-W,M TI1-W,M UFB-W,M
Moon of Manakoora
  TI2-W,M UBF-W,M
Moon of My Delight
  TS-W
Moon of Wintertime
  ASB5-W,M
Moon on My Pillow
  NM-W,M
Moon over Miami
  MF-W,M OPS-W,M RDT-W,M
  RW-W,M
Moon River
  AT-W,M GOl7-W,M IPH-W,M
  LM-W,M MAB1-W MM-W,M
  MSA1-W OBN-W,M OHF-W
  OnT1-W,M OTJ-W,M OTO-W
  RDT-W,M SBF-W,M TOM-W,M
Moon Shepherd
  OTJ-W,M
Moon Shines Bright
  GBC-W,M GUM2-W,M
Moon Ship
  SiR-W,M
Moon Song
  BM-W
Moon Song (That Wasn't Meant
  for Me)
  OTO-W
Moon Was Yellow (El Amor Llamo)

MF-W,M RoE-W,M
Moondance
  MF-W,M
Moonfall
  EY-W,M
Moonglow
  BBB-W,M GSN2-W,M MF-W,M
  RDT-W,M TI2-W,M
Mooning
  Gr-W,M Mo-W,M
Moonlight
  MES1-W,M MES2-W,M
Moonlight (Dreaming in the
  Moonlight, I Lingered near a
  Wood)
  ASB4-W,M
Moonlight (See What a Night of
  Moonlight)
  UF-W,M
Moonlight (When the Moon Is Big
  and Bright)
  MH-W,M
Moonlight (When the Tranquil Eve
  Descends upon the Woodland)
  FSA2-W,M
Moonlight and Roses (Bring
  Wonderful Mem'ries of You)
  HLS2-W,M RW-W,M TI1-W,M
  UFB-W,M
Moonlight and Roses (Mem'ries of
  You)
  WDS-W,M
Moonlight and Shadows
  AT-W,M OTO-W
Moonlight and Skies
  HB-W,M LJ-W,M
Moonlight Attack on Curtin's
  House
  VP-W,M
Moonlight Bay
  MF-W,M OAP-W,M RoE-W,M
  TI2-W,M
Moonlight Becomes You
  AT-W,M LM-W,M OTO-W
Moonlight Gambler
  Mo-W,M NM-W,M
Moonlight in Vermont
  DJ-W,M NK-W,M TI1-W,M
  UFB-W,M
Moonlight Mile
  RoS-W,M
Moonlight Music
  FSA1-W,M
Moonlight on the Ganges
  TI2-W,M
Moonlight Serenade
  GSN2-W,M HLS2-W,M RW-W,M
  SL-W,M Sta-W,M
Moonlight Sonata
  TM-M WGB/O-M
Moonlight Song
  NA-W,M
Moonlighting (Theme)
  BHO-W,M BNG-W,M BOA-W,M
  DC-W,M MF-W,M
Moonrise
  SBF-W,M
Moonshine Blues
  DBL-W
Moonshiner
  FSU-W FW-W
Moos Tzur
  JS-W,M (Hebrew)
Morality
  SHS-W,M
More (Than the Greatest Love the
  World Has Known)

RDT-W,M TI2-W,M
More about Jesus
OM-W,M
More about Jesus I Would Know
AME-W,M Hy-W,M
More I Cannot Wish You
UBF-W,M
More I Know of You
VB-W,M
More I See of Others, Dear, the
Better I Like You
OG-W,M
More I See You
HFH-W,M MF-W,M TOM-W,M
More Love
AHO-W,M GB-W,M
More Love Than Your Love
Mo-W,M NM-W,M
More Love to Thee
HF-W,M OM-W,M
More Love to Thee, O Christ
AHO-W,M AME-W,M GH-W,M
Hy-W,M
More, More, More (Part 1)
ToO76-W,M
More of Jesus
GH-W,M
More Power to Ya
VB-W,M
More Secure Is No One Ever
OM-W,M
More Than a Bedroom Thing
TOH-W,M
More Than a Feeling
ToO76-W,M
More Than a Woman
SoH-W,M TI1-W,M UFB-W,M
More Than Anything Else in the
World
OGC1-W,M
More Than I Can Say
MF-W,M RoE-W,M
More Than Physical
TTH-W,M
More Than Tongue Can Tell
GH-W,M
More Than Wonderful
AG-W,M VB-W,M
More Than You Know
DJ-W,M GG4-W,M GST-W,M
HLS2-W,M HLS8-W,M MF-W,M
RW-W,M TI1-W,M ToS-W,M
UFB-W,M
More to Follow
GH-W,M
More Today Than Yesterday
ERM-W,M ILS-W,M TI1-W,M
UFB-W,M
More We Get Together
Bo-W CSS-W HS-W,M LoS-W
MES2-W,M PaS-W,M
More Yet
Le-W,M
More You Know, the More You'll
Want Delco
TI1-W,M UFB-W,M
Moreton Bay
ATM-W,M
Morgana Jones
PoG-W,M
Morgen
TI2-W,M
Morlaix Bridge
FSF-W (French)
Mormons
Oz3-W
Morn Doth Break

Boo-W,M
Morn of May
SL-W,M
Mornin'
BOA-W,M
Mornin' on ze Bayou
Ba-W,M
Mornin's Come
SRS-W,M
Morning
OTO-W
Morning (Excerpt from Grieg's Peer
Gynt)
FSA1-M
Morning (I Like to Have It Morning)
MH-W,M
Morning (Morning's Golden Light Is
Breaking)
MML-W,M
Morning (When the First Flush of
the East Glows)
FSA2-W,MM
Morning After, The (If I Didn't
Have to Face the Morning After)
Mo-W,M NM-W,M
Morning After, The (There's Got to
Be a Morning After)
HFH-W,M TOM-W,M
Morning and Evening
ASB1-W,M
Morning Bells I Love to Hear
Boo-W,M
Morning Bright, with Rosy Light
AHO-W,M
Morning Carnival
FSA1-W,M
Morning Comes Too Early
TOH-W,M
Morning Dance
ToO79-W,M
Morning Glories
ASB3-W,M
Morning Has Broken
Hy-W,M IPH-W,M On-W,M
OPS-W,M OTJ-W,M WGB/P-W,M
Morning Hymn (Father We Thank
Thee for the Night)
OTJ-W,M
**Morning Hymn (Father We Thank
Thee for the Night) see also
Father We Thank Thee for the
Night and Morning Prayer**
Morning Hymn (Now with
Creation's Morning Song)
TH-W,M
Morning Hymn (Richard Rodgers)
SM-W,M (Latin Only)
Morning in Marken
ASB4-W,M
Morning Is Come
Boo-W,M SCL-W,M
Morning Light Is Breaking
AHO-W,M AME-W,M Hy-W,M
Morning Lights
GH-W,M
**Morning on the Bayou see Mornin'
on ze Bayou**
Morning Papers
Boo-W,M
Morning Praise
BM-W MHB-W,M
Morning Prayer (Father Hear Our
Morning Prayer)
MH-W,M
Morning Prayer (Father We Thank
Thee for the Night)
OS-W

**Morning Prayer (Father We Thank
Thee for the Night) see also
Morning Hymn**
Morning Prayer (Lord We Ask Thy
Blessing for This Day)
SiB-W,M
Morning Serenade
ASB5-W,M
Morning Song
SiR-W,M
Morning Song (Awake and Greet
the Morning Fair)
MHB-W,M
Morning Song (Blessed Lord of
Night and Morning)
ASB1-W,M
Morning Song (I Awake to the Day
on a Mountain High)
VA-W,M
Morning Song (Shines o'er All
Morn's Bright Ray)
FSA2-W,M
Morning Star
SHS-W,M
Morning Star, O Cheering Sight
AHO-W,M
Morning Sun
SiR-W,M
Morning Train (Nine to Five)
TI2-W,M
Morning Trumpet (How Long, O
Lord, How Long)
JF-W,M
Morning Trumpet (Oh When Shall I
See Jesus)
SHS-W,M
Morning Worship
SHS-W,M
**Morning's Come see Mornin's
Come**
Morris Dance
GUM2-W,M
Mortals Learn Your Lives to
Measure
Boo-W,M
Mortar Song
GI-W
Moscow Nights (How I Miss the
Moscow Nights)
OTJ-W,M
Moscow Nights (You'll Cherish,
Dear, through the Passing Years,
This Most Beautiful Moscow
Night)
FW-W RuS-W,M (Russian)
Mose Preston's Mine Ballad
BMM-W
Moses in the Bulrushes
BSC-W SiR-W,M
Most Beautiful Girl
AO-W,M HLS9-W,M HSe-W,M
On-W,M
Most Beautiful Girl in the World
BBB-W,M RW-W,M TI1-W,M
TS-W UFB-W,M
Most Brilliant Naval Victory on
Lake Erie
ANS-W
Most Done Suffering
AN-W
Most Done Trabelling
RF-W,M
**Most Done Trabelling see also
Almost Done Traveling**
Most Gentlemen Don't Like Love
ML-W,M OTO-W
Most Glorious Lord of Life

ER-W,M
Most Misunderstood Soft Drink
  GSM-W,M
Most of All Why
  BDP-W,M
Most Original Soft Drink Ever
  GSM-W,M
Most Perfect Is the Law of God
  Hy-W,M
Most Wonderful Day of the Year
  BCh-W,M BCS-W,M
Moste Strange Weddinge of the
  Frogge and the Mouse
  SCa-W,M
Moth and the Flame
  FSN-W,M FSTS-W,M Oz4-W
M-O-T-H-E-R
  BH-W,M CS-W,M GSN1-W,M
  HLS1-W,M OS-W RW-W,M
Mother and Baby
  SiR-W,M
Mother and Child Reunion
  On-W,M
Mother and Father
  MH-W,M
Mother Ann's Song
  GB-W,M
Mother Bloor
  LW-W,M
Mother, Can I Go
  SiS-W
Mother Country
  GSM-W,M MPP-W
Mother Dear, O Pray for Me
  AHO-W,M
Mother Earth
  FSA2-W,M
Mother Goose
  Sw-W,M
Mother Hen
  STS-W,M
Mother-in-Law
  ILS-W,M RY-W,M
Mother, Is Massa Gwine to Sell
  Us?
  RF-W,M
Mother, Is the Battle Over
  Oz2-W SiS-W
Mother, I've Come Home to Die
  MPP-W
Mother Jones
  AFP-W LW-W,M
Mother Kissed Me in My Dream
  SiS-W
Mother-Love
  FSY-W,M
Mother Loves Me
  MAR-W,M
Mother Lucy's Birthday Song
  GB-W,M
Mother Machree
  MF-W,M
Mother, May I Go Out to Swim
  OTJ-W,M
Mother Nature's Son
  Be2-W,M TWS-W
Mother o' Mine
  OTJ-W,M
Mother of Men
  IL-W,M
Mother of the Soldier Boy
  SiS-W
Mother Pin a Rose on Me
  EFS-W,M FSN-W,M
Mother, Put Out Your Service Star
  AF-W
Mother Says Go On Dear Children

GB-W,M
Mother Says I Am Six Years Old
  NF-W
Mother, Take In Your Service Flag
  GO-W
Mother, the Queen of My Heart
  LJ-W,M
Mother, Thou'rt Faithful to Me
  ATS-W,M FHR-W,M SSFo-W,M
Mother Volga
  SL-W,M
Mother Was a Lady
  FSN-W,M OBN-W,M
Mother Went Out on a Party
  ITP-W,M
Mother Would Comfort Me
  Sin-W,M SiS-W
Motherhood March
  Mo-W,M NM-W,M OTO-W
Mothering Sunday
  OB-W,M
Motherless Child
  JF-W,M
**Motherless Child see also
  Sometimes I Feel Like a
  Motherless Child**
Motherless Children
  FW-W LC-W
Motherless Children Have a Hard
  Time
  LC-W
Mother's Call
  ASB2-W,M
Mother's Day
  GM-W,M
Mother's Farewell
  SiS-W
Mother's Knives and Forks
  GM-W,M HS-W,M
Mother's Letter to Her Son
  VP-W
Mother's Little Helper
  RoS-W,M
Mothers' Lullaby
  GrM-W,M
Mother's Old Red Shawl
  AmH-W,M
Mother's Prayer
  SiS-W
Mother's Song
  ASB2-W,M BMM-W
Mother's Valentine
  ASB3-W,M
Motor Boat
  SOO-W
Motor Car
  MH-W,M
Motor School Song
  GO-W
Motorized Field Artillery Song
  GO-W
Motsi
  SBJ-W,M (Hebrew Only)
**Mouche Et La Fourmi see La
  Mouche Et La Fourmi**
Mouldering Vine
  SHS-W,M
Moulin see Le Moulin
**Moulin Rouge Song see Song from
  Moulin Rouge**
Mound of Your Grave
  AFP-W
Mount Sinai
  SoM-W,M
Mount Vernon
  BC1-W,M EA-W,M
Mount Zion

SHS-W,M
Mountain
  MH-W,M
Mountain Boy
  FSA2-W,M
Mountain Brook
  SL-W,M
Mountain Dew
  BIS-W,M BSo-W,M FPG-W,M
  FW-W OHO-W,M POT-W,M
Mountain Greenery
  HC1-W,M MF-W,M OHB-W,M
  TS-W
Mountain Hornpipe
  POT-M
Mountain March
  ASB1-M
Mountain Music
  EC-W,M GCM-W,M
Mountain of Love
  Mo-W,M TI2-W,M
Mountain Picture
  SL-W,M
Mountain Romance
  SL-W,M
Mountain Shepherd
  FSA2-W,M
Mountain Top (I'd Love to Live on
  a Mountain Top, Fellowshipping
  with the Lord)
  VB-W,M
Mountain Top (I'll Go Up on the
  Mountain Top and Grow Me a
  Patch of Cane)
  AmS-W,M
Mountain Top Blues
  BI-W,M
Mountaineer
  FSA2-W,M
Mountaineer's Song
  ESU-W
Mountains
  FSA1-W,M
Mountains o' Mourne
  OTJ-W,M
Mounties
  RM-W,M
Mourn Anglia
  Boo-W,M
Mourner's Lamentation
  WN-W,M
Mourning Slave Fiancees
  NF-W
Mourning Souls
  BSC-W
Mouse Cousins
  MH-W,M
Move Away
  TTH-W,M
Move Eastward, Happy Earth
  FSA2-W,M
Move Like This
  GM-W,M
Move On Over
  SFF-W,M
Move Over, America
  Mo-W,M NM-W,M OTO-W
Move Over, New York
  Mo-W,M NM-W,M
Move Slow, Dogies, Move Slow
  GA-W,M
Movies Were Movies
  OTO-W
Movin' On Up
  TV-W,M
Movin' Out
  RW-W,M

Moving Day
ASB2-W,M
Moving On
SFF-W,M
Moving On Song
IFM-W
Moving Up to Gloryland
AG-W,M
Mower
BSC-W
Mowing Machine
HB-W,M
Mozart Number 40
On-M
Mozart's Lullaby
OTJ-W,M
Moze Haymar Jig
DE-W,M
Mr. see Mister
Mrs. Bond
OTJ-W,M
Mrs. Ladybird
VS-W,M
Mrs. McGrath
FW-W
Mrs. Monday
MSB-W
Mrs. Murphy's Chowder
OHO-W,M
**Mrs. Murphy's Chowder see also
Who Threw the Overalls in Mrs.
Murphy's Chowder**
Mrs. Rockett's Pub
IS-W,M
M'sieu Bainjo
VA-W,M
**M'sieu Bainjo see also Michie
Banjo, Mister Banjo, Monsieur
Banjo, Musieu Bainjo, O Mu'sieu
Banjo, and Oh Mister Banjo**
Much More
Fa-W,M OTO-W TW-W
Much, Much Greater Love
ToO79-W,M
Mud Pies
GM-W,M
Muddy Water
UBF-W,M
Mudlog Pond
NF-W
Mudsills Are Coming
SiS-W
**Mueller's Egg Noodles Jingle see
Nothing Goes with Everything
Like Mueller's**
Muffin Man
HS-W,M MH-W,M OTJ-W,M
SMa-W,M
Mugford's Victory
ANS-W
Mulberry Bush
AmH-W,M ASB1-W,M BBF-W,M
CSG-W,M HS-W,M MH-W,M
OTJ-W,M STR-W,M
Mulberry Gap
FVV-W,M
Mulberry Springs
TW-W
Mule
TMA-W,M
Mule Blues
LC-W,M
Mule Skinner Blues
AFB-W,M FG1-W,M FGM-W,M
FW-W
Mule Skinner's Holler
PSN-W,M

Mule Song
GO-W NH-W
Mule's Kick
NF-W
Mule's Nature
NF-W
Mull of Kintyre
PMC-W,M TI2-W,M
Mulligan Guard
AH-W,M ATS-W,M LMR-W,M
Mulligan Guards
FSTS-W,M HAS-W,M
Mummers' Song
FSA1-W,M
Munchkinland
WO-W,M
Muppet Show Theme
WG-W,M
Murder, He Says
OTO-W
Murder in Parkwold
LS-W,M
Murder of Charley Stacey
Oz2-W
Murder of Pearl Bryan
BMM-W
Murder of Stell Kenny
BMM-W
Murder on the Orient Express
(Theme)
OTO-W
Murder on the Road in Alabama
SFF-W,M
Murdered Brother
SCa-W,M
Murmuring Zephyrs
AmH-M
Musetta's Waltz
MF-M
Mush, Mush
AmH-W,M
Mushrooms
FSA2-W,M
Music
FSA1-W,M
Music Alone Shall Live
FW-W GuC-W,M HS-W,M
(German) LT-W,M MG-W,M
(German)
Music and the Mirror
CL-W,M JP-W,M
Music at the Mill
FSA1-W,M
Music Box
ASB2-W,M OBN-M
Music Box Dancer
GSN5-M OPS-M OTJ-M
Music Eternal
FSA2-W,M
Music Everywhere
FSA1-W,M
Music Everywhere, That's Why I
Love It So
FHR-W,M
Music from across the Way
TI2-W,M
Music Goes 'Round and Around
HLS2-W,M RW-W,M TI1-W,M
UFB-W,M
Music in China
FSA1-W,M SL-W,M
Music in the Air
BM-W FSA2-W,M MG-W,M
TF-W,M
Music, Maestro Please
TI1-W,M UFB-W,M
Music Magic

ASB4-W,M
Music Makin' Mama from Memphis
OGC2-W,M
Music! Music! Music!
MF-W,M PT-W,M RW-W,M
TI1-W,M TWD-W,M UFB-W,M
Music of Goodbye (Love Theme
from Out of Africa)
BOA-W,M
Music of His Steps
AHO-W,M
Music of Home
UBF-W,M
Music of the Night
UBF-W,M
Music That Makes Me Dance
UBF-W,M
Music to Watch Girls By
TI1-W,M UFB-W,M
Musical Alphabet
SY-W,M
Musical Clocks
SiB-W,M
Musical Mirror
SiB-W,M
Musical Snore
YL-W,M
Musical Wife
ESU-W
Musieu Bainjo
AAF-W,M (French) AH-W,M
HAS-W,M LA-W,M (Spanish)
NAS-W,M
**Musieu Bainjo see also Michie
Banjo, Mister Banjo, Monsieur
Banjo, M'sieu Bainjo, O Mu'sieu
Banjo, and Oh Mister Banjo**
Musikanter see Der Musikanter
Musing Mine Own Self
Boo-W
Muskoka
SoC-W
Muskrat
AFS-W,M FSA1-W,M FW-W
Muskrat Love
ToO76-W,M
Muskrat Ramble
OTJ-M
Muss I Denn
FW-W (German)
Musselburgh Field
SBB-W
**Must I Be Bound or Must I Go Free
see Girl Died for Love**
Must I Go, and Empty Handed
GH-W,M
Must I Then see Muss I Denn
Must It Be Love?
Mo-W,M NM-W,M OTO-W
UBF-W,M
Must Jesus Bear the Cross Alone
AME-W,M Hy-W,M
**Mustang Automobile Jingle see
Only Mustang Makes It Happen**
Mustang Gray
HWS-W,M SoC-W
Mutt and Jeff
MF-M
Mutual Admiration Society
OTJ-W,M TI1-W,M UBF-W,M
UFB-W,M
Mutual Love
SHS-W,M
Mutual of Omaha, People You Can
Count On
GSM-W,M
My Adobe Hacienda

My Elusive Dreams
ATC2-W,M CMG-W,M FOC-W,M
MAB1-W MSA1-W TI2-W,M
My Emmet's No More
VP-W,M
My Evaline
BSB-W,M
My Everything
CMF-W,M OGC1-W,M
My Eyes Adored You
ToO76-W,M
My Fair Lady
GOB-W,M
My Fair Teresa
SR-W,M
My Faith Looks Up to Thee
AHO-W,M AME-W,M AmH-W,M
CEM-W,M GH-W,M HF-W,M
HSD-W,M Hy-W,M NAS-W,M
OM-W,M RDF-W,M RW-W,M
SJ-W,M TB-W,M WiS7-W,M
My Faith Still Clings
GH-W,M
My Faithfu' Johnnie
GC-W,M
My Farm
MG-W,M (Spanish) RSL-W,M
My Father Gave Me a Lump of
Gold
Oz4-W,M
My Father Is Rich
AME-W,M
My Father Reigns Eternal
GrM-W,M
My Father Was a Gambler
Oz2-W,M
My Father Was Born a Hebrew
PO-W,M
My Father's House
Bo-W,M RSL-W,M
My Fault
DBL-W
My Favorite Memory
NMH-W,M
My Favorite Things
BCh-W,M BCS-W,M DBC-W,M
HC1-W,M HLS8-W,M OTJ-W,M
OTO-W RW-W,M SM-W,M
TI1-W,M UBF-W,M UFB-W,M
My Fiddle
NF-W
My Filipino Rose
OGC1-W,M
My Finest Hour
VB-W,M
My Fire Engine
MH-W,M
My First and My Second Wife
NF-W
My First Dressing Room
TW-W
My First Jig
DE-W,M
My First Taste of Texas
TOC83-W,M
My Fisherman, My Laddy-O
TO-W,M
My Flag
ASB4-W,M
My Flute
MH-W,M
My Folks and Your Folks
NF-W
My Foolish Heart
HLS5-W,M RT4-W,M RW-W,M
TI1-W,M ToS-W,M UFB-W,M
My Fortune's Been Bad

SCa-W,M
My Friend
MHB-W,M (Ukrainian)
My Friend and I
BSG-W,M BSP-W,M
My Friend John
SiR-W,M
My Friends and Relations
HB-W,M
My Friends Do Not Worry
SBF-W,M UF-W,M
My Funny Valentine
DBC-W,M DJ-W,M FPS-W,M
FrS-W,M HC1-W,M HLS8-W,M
OTJ-W,M OTO-W RW-W,M
TI1-W,M ToS-W,M TS-W TW-W
UBF-W,M UFB-W,M
My Future Just Passed By
OTO-W
My Gal
AN-W
My Gal Is a High Born Lady
BH-W,M EFS-W,M FSTS-W,M
My Gal Sal
FSN-W,M FWS-W,M GSN1-W,M
HLS1-W,M MAB1-W MF-W,M
MM-W,M MSA1-W OAP-W,M
OBN-W,M OTJ-W,M RW-W,M
My Garden
FF-W
My Generation
TI1-W,M TWD-W,M UFB-W,M
WA-W,M
My Girl Bill
AT-W,M
My Girl Josephine
ILS-W,M
My God and I
BSG-W,M BSP-W,M HHa-W,M
My God and My All
GH-W,M
My God, How Endless Is Thy Love
AME-W,M
My God, How the Money Rolls In
AF-W FW-W
My God I Have Found
GH-W
My God, I Thank Thee
AHO-W,M
My God, I Thank Thee, Who Hast
Made
Hy-W,M
My God Is Real
HLS7-W,M SUH-W,M TI1-W,M
UFB-W,M
My God, My Father, Blissful Name
AME-W,M
My God, My God, to Thee I Cry
AME-W,M
My God, the Spring of All My Joys
AME-W,M
My Good Gal's Gone Blues
LJ-W,M
My Good Lord Has Been Here
MoM-W,M
My Goose
ASB5-W,M
My Grandfather Had Some Very
Fine Ducks
SY-W,M
My Grandfather's Clock
U-W
My Grandma's Advice
ATS-W,M HSD-W,M
My Grandmother Lived on Yonder
Green
SCa-W,M

My Great, Great Grandfather
Mo-W,M
My Greenstone Island
SNZ-W,M (Maori)
My Guy
TOH-W,M
My Hands
GM-W,M
My Handy Man
Mo-W,M NM-W,M
My Happy Little Home in Arkansas
Oz4-W
My Harding County Home
HB-W,M
My Hat
HS-W,M (German) SHP-W,M
My Hat Has Three Corners
CSS-W
My Hat It Has Three Corners
KS-W,M
My Heart
TOH-W,M
My Heart at Thy Dear Voice
MU-W,M
My Heart at Thy Sweet Voice
AmH-W,M FSY-W,M (French)
MF-M OBN-W,M RW-M
WiS7-W,M
My Heart Be Still
RuS-W,M (Russian)
My Heart Belongs to Daddy
DBC-W,M HC2-W,M ML-W,M
OTO-W RW-W,M TI1-W,M TW-W
UBF-W,M UFB-W,M
My Heart Belongs to Me
TI2-W,M
My Heart Cries for You
HLS3-W,M TI1-W,M UFB-W,M
My Heart Ever Faithful
FiS-W,M (German) FSY-W,M
(German) MG-W,M TM-M
WGB/O-M
My Heart Has a Mind of Its Own
MF-W,M
My Heart, How Very Hard It's
Grown
AHO-W,M
My Heart Is an Open Book
DRR-W,M
My Heart Is Like a Singing Bird
EL-W,M
My Heart Is Resting, O My God
Hy-W,M
My Heart, Once As Light As a
Feather
Boo-W,M
My Heart Stood Still
FrS-W,M HC2-W,M MF-W,M
OHB-W,M TS-W TW-W
My Heart Would Know
HW-W,M
My Heart's in the Highlands
GC-W,M MML-W,M TF-W,M
My Heav'nly Father Knows
AME-W,M
My Heav'nly Father Watches over
Me
AME-W,M
My Hen
MH-W,M
My Hero
MF-W,M
My High Tower
GH-W,M
My Homeland (Forests of Maple on
Hillsides Green)
ASB6-W,M

My Homeland (I Journey Eastward
   at Sunset)
   MHB-W,M (Swedish)
My Homeland (In My Homeland I
   Long to Be)
   MG-W,M
My Home's across the Smokey
   Mountains
   BF-W,M FGM-W,M FPG-W,M
   FW-W
My Home's in Alabama
   TOC82-W,M
My Home's in Charlotte, North
   Carolina
   FVV-W,M
My Home's in Montana
   HB-W,M PaS-W,M SHP-W,M
   SoC-W
My Honey's Loving Arms
   MF-W,M TI2-W,M
My Hope Is Built (on Nothing Less)
   AME-W,M CEM-W,M Hy-W,M
My Hope Is Built (on Nothing Less)
   see also Solid Rock, The
My Hope Is in the Everlasting
   FiS-W,M
My Hopes Have Departed Forever
   FHR-W,M
My Horses Ain't Hungry
   ASB5-W,M ATS-W,M FW-W
   SCa-W,M
My, How the Time Goes By
   Mo-W,M NM-W,M
My Husky Dog
   ASB5-W,M
My Ideal
   AT-W,M MM-W,M OTO-W
My Inspiration
   MF-M
My Island
   ASB6-W,M
My Isle of Golden Dreams
   MF-W,M
My Jesus, As Thou Wilt
   AME-W,M GH-W,M HSD-W,M
   Hy-W,M
My Jesus, I Love Thee
   AME-W,M GH-W,M Hy-W,M
   OM-W,M
My Joe
   L-W
My Kind of Country
   OTO-W
My Kind of Girl
   ILT-W,M NK-W,M TI1-W,M
   UFB-W,M
My Kind of Town
   EY-W,M FrS-W,M HFH-W,M
   MF-W,M
My Kinda Love
   HLS2-W,M
My Kite (High on the Hilltop I Fly
   My New Kite)
   ASB2-W,M
My Kite (Little Kite, So High in
   April Sky)
   ASB4-W,M
My Kite (Up in the Sky So Very
   High)
   MH-W,M
My Kitty (I Have a Little Kitty)
   GM-W,M
My Kitty (Kitty Runs In)
   ASB2-W,M
My Lady
   GOB-W,M
My Lady and Her Maid

Boo-W,M
My Lady Greensleeves
   SMY-W,M
My Lady Greensleeves see also
   Green Sleeves and Greensleeves
My Lady's a Wild Flying Dove
   RBO-W,M
My Last Cigar
   HSD-W,M NAS-W,M
My Last Gold Dollar
   Oz4-W,M
My Latest Sun Is Sinking Fast
   AHO-W,M
My Lawd Gawd Rockin' in de
   Weary Land
   Me-W,M
My Life
   Am-W
My Life I Give Thee
   AME-W,M
My Life Is an Open Book
   TI2-W,M
My Life's a Dance
   TTH-W,M
My Lips Are Sealed
   OGC1-W,M
My Little Batteau see Ma Li'l
   Batteau
My Little Bimbo
   WDS-W,M
My Little Boat
   GrM-W,M
My Little Boy
   AL-W
My Little Corner of the World
   TI1-W,M UFB-W,M
My Little Country Cousin see Die
   Greene Koseene
My Little Dog Has Ego
   UBF-W,M
My Little Georgie May
   SoC-W
My Little German Home across the
   Sea
   Oz4-W,M
My Little Girl
   TG-W,M
My Little Grass Shack in
   Kealakekua, Hawaii
   RW-W,M
My Little Irish Rose
   E-W,M
My Little Lady
   OTJ-W,M
My Little Maid
   ASB5-W,M
My Little Old Home Down in New
   Orleans
   LJ-W,M
My Little One's Waiting for Me
   Oz4-W,M
My Little Pig
   NF-W
My Little Pony
   MAR-W,M RSL-W,M
My Little Red Book
   HD-W,M RW-W,M
My Little Red Wagon
   ASB1-W,M
My Little Town
   ToO76-W,M
My Liza Jane
   AN-W
My Lodging It Is on the Cold
   Ground
   OH-W,M
My Lone Rock by the Sea

Oz4-W,M
My Longing Desire
   SR-W,M
My Lord Delibered Daniel
   RF-W,M
My Lord God see My Lawd Gawd
My Lord God Rockin' in the Weary
   Land see My Lawd Gawd Rockin'
   in de Weary Land
My Lord What a Mornin'
   FN-W,M OTJ-W,M
My Lord What a Morning
   ATS-W,M BMC-W,M RF-W,M
   SpS-W,M VA-W,M
My Lord What a Morning see also
   Oh What a Mornin', Stars Begin
   to Fall, What a Mornin', and
   When the Stars Begin to Fall
My Lord, What a Mourning
   FW-W
My Lord's A-Riding All the Time
   RF-W,M
My Lord's Comin' Again
   NH-W
My Love (Folk Song)
   FSO-W,M (French)
My Love (Hatch)
   TI2-W,M
My Love (LaTouche, Wilbur/
   Bernstein)
   TW-W
My Love (McCartney)
   GrS-W,M On-W,M PMC-W,M
   TI2-W,M
My Love (Martin/Leonard)
   Mo-W,M NM-W,M
My Love, Forgive Me
   MF-W,M (Italian) OPS-W,M
   TI2-W,M (Italian)
My Love Gifts
   SoP-W,M
My Love He Is a Zou-Zu
   SiS-W
My Love Is a Cowboy
   SoC-W
My Love Is a Married Man
   LL-W,M
My Love Is a Rider
   FW-W HB-W,M HWS-W,M
   SoC-W,M
My Love Is Black
   BRB-W
My Love Is Gone to Sea
   EA-W,M
My Love Is Like a Red, Red Rose
   FW-W GC-W,M
My Love Is Like a Red, Red Rose
   see also O, My Love Is Like a
   Red, Red Rose
My Love Is Like a Rose
   WGB/O-W,M
My Love, My Love
   RW-W,M
My Love, She's but a Lassie Yet
   SeS-W,M
My Love to My Bride
   SeS-W,M
My Loved One and My Own
   FHR-W,M
My Lovely Annina
   MU-W,M
My Lovely Sailor Boy
   Oz4-W,M
My Love's an Arbutus
   TH-W,M
My Lovin' Father
   Oz4-W,M

My Lovin' Gal, Lucille
LJ-W,M
My Mammy
TI1-W,M TI2-W,M UFB-W,M
WDS-W,M
My Man
GST-W,M HLS2-W,M HLS8-W,M
LSB-W,M OP1-W,M RT6-W,M
RW-W,M
My Man Blues
UBF-W,M
My Man John
SaS-W,M TF-W,M
My Man's Gone Now
NYT-W,M OTO-W UBF-W,M
My Mary
JD-W,M
My Mary Anne
HSD-W,M
My Maryland
MPP-W Re-W,M
My Master
YS-W,M
My May Basket
ASB1-W,M
My Melancholy Baby
MF-W,M OAP-W,M OPS-W,M
RoE-W,M TI2-W,M
My Melody of Love
BeL-W,M MF-W,M PT-W,M
RW-W,M ToO76-W,M
My Miss Mary
UBF-W,M
My Mistress Will Not Be Content
Boo-W,M
My Mistress's Cunny
SR-W,M
My Mocking Bird
ASB3-W,M
My Model Girl
BP-W,M
My Most Important Moments Go
By
TW-W
My Mother
ASB2-W,M
**My Mother and Father Are Gone
see My Mother'n Father Are Gone**
My Mother Bids Me Bind My Hair
FSY-W,M (German) LMR-W,M
My Mother Chose My Husband
LW-W,M PO-W,M
My Mother Got a Letter
NH-W
My Mother-In-Law
Oz3-W
My Mother 'n Father Are Gone
LC-W
My Mother the Car (Theme)
GTV-W,M
My Mother Would Love You
UBF-W,M
My Mother's Advice
LA-W,M (Spanish)
My Mother's Bible
HSD-W,M SY-W,M
My Mother's Contribution
SNS-W
My Mother's Eyes
GST-W,M RW-W,M STW-W,M
My Mother's Face
GM-W,M
My Mother's Hands
ITP-W,M
My Mother's in Heaven
RTH-W
My Mother's Picture

FSA1-W,M
My Mother's Prayer
AME-W,M GH-W,M
My Mother's Weddin' Day
LL-W,M
My Moustache
HSD-W,M
My Mule
NF-W
My Name
O-W,M
My Name Is Allan-a-Dale
ITP-W
My Name Is John Wellington Wells
MGT-W,M
My Native Land
CA-W,M
My Native Land, Quang Binh
VS-W,M
My Nellie's Blue Eyes
TMA-W,M
My Nelly's Blue Eyes
ATS-W,M BH-W,M
My New Celebrity Is You
OHF-W
My North Dakota Home
TI1-W,M UFB-W,M
My Number Will Be Changed
FVV-W,M
My Object All Sublime
GiS-W,M MGT-W,M SL-W,M
My Obsession
RoS-W,M
My Offering
GH-W,M
My Ohio Home
WDS-W,M
My Old Brown Coat and Me
TBF-W,M
My Old Daddy
DE-W,M
My Old Dog Tray
HSD-W,M OTJ-W,M
My Old Dutch
AmH-W,M WiS8-W,M
My Old Flame
AT-W,M OTO-W
My Old Hen's a Good Old Hen
AFS-W,M
My Old Kentucky Home
AH-W,M AmH-W,M ATS-W
BH-W,M BSB-W,M CSo-W,M
ESB-W,M ETB-W,M FHR-W,M
Fif-W,M FSY-W,M FW-W HS-W,M
HSD-W,M IL-W,M MAB1-W
MF-W,M MSA1-W NAS-W,M
OS-W PoS-W,M RW-W,M SL-W
SoC-W SoF-W,M STR-W,M TF-W
TH-W,M U-W UF-W WiS8-W,M
My Old Kentucky Home, Good
Night
SSF-W,M SSFo-W,M
My Old Pinto Pal
HB-W,M
My One and Only
GOB-W,M NYT-W,M
My One and Only Highland Fling
LSO-W
My One and Only Love
MF-W,M TI2-W,M ToS-W,M
My Only Brother's Gone
SiS-W
My Own Best Friend
CMV-W,M UBF-W,M
My Own Business
SYB-W,M
My Own Country see My Ain

Countree
My Own Dear One's Gone
SeS-W,M
My Own Home
OTJ-W,M
My Own Kind of Hat
TOH-W,M
My Own Loved Home Again
SiS-W
My Own Peculiar Way
WNF-W
My Own True Love
DC-W,M MF-W,M TVT-W,M
**My Own True Love see also Tara
Theme**
My Pa
Mo-W,M NM-W,M OTJ-W,M
OTO-W
My Pappy He Will Scold Me
Oz3-W,M
My Paradise
K-W,M
My Particular Prince
TW-W
My Personal Property
SC-W,M
My Pet Horse
SoC-W
My Pigeon House
FP-W,M
My Place
AL-W
My Plane Tree
ESB-W,M
**My Plane Tree see also Largo
(Handel)**
My Pony (Can Gallop and Gallop
All Day)
ASB1-W,M
My Pony (Here Comes That Little
Black Pony of Mine)
MH-W,M
My Pony (Hop, Hop, Hop! Nimble
As a Top)
OTJ-W,M
My Pony (Old Jim, Runs Up When
I Call)
ASB4-W,M
My Pony (One Morning Bright and
Early)
Oz3-W
My Pony (Trot, My Pony, Trot)
MG-W,M
My Pony Boy
FC-W,M
My Prayer (I Would Not Ask for My
Burden to Be Lightened)
SOW1-W,M SOW2-W,M
My Prayer (Is to Linger with You)
DRR-W,M ERM-W,M FPS-W,M
HLS2-W,M MF-W,M TI1-W,M
UFB-W,M
My Prayer (More Holiness Give Me)
GH-W,M
My Pretty Cabocla
MHB-W,M (Portuguese)
My Pretty Mary
SeS-W,M
My Radio
ASB3-W,M
My Ramblin' Boy
CMG-W,M FW-W IHA-W,M
TO-W,M
My Rambling Young Son
BSC-W
My Rayon Coat
MES1-W,M MES2-W,M

My Redeemer
GH-W,M
My Redeemer Lives
HHa-W,M
My Restless Heart
TW-W
My Reverie
GSO-W,M (French) HLS2-W,M
RW-W,M
My Rhythm Sticks
ASB1-W,M
My Romance
DJ-W,M HLS8-W,M TI1-W,M
TS-W UFB-W,M
My Rooster
SiR-W,M
**My Roots Are Buried Here see Mis
Raices Estan Aqui**
My Sailor Lad
SOT-W,M
My Saviour
GH-W,M
My Saviour Tells Me So
GH-W,M
My Scooter
MH-W,M
My Shadow
SiB-W,M
My Shadow and I
ASB4-W,M
My Shaw!
TI2-W,M
My Sheep Were Grazing
CSF-W
My Shepherd
FSO-W,M (French)
My Shepherd Is the Living Lord
AHO-W,M
My Shepherd Is the Lord Most
High
AME-W,M
My Shepherd, Thou
SOW1-W,M SOW2-W,M
My Shingle Boat
MH-W,M
My Shining Hour
Mo-W,M NM-W,M OHF-W
OTO-W TI2-W,M
My Ship (Has Sails That Are Made
of Silk)
DJ-W,M LD-W,M LM-W,M
LSO-W OTO-W TI1-W,M TW-W
UBF-W,M UFB-W,M
My Ship (O Ship, a Great
Adventure Calls)
SL-W,M
My Shoes Keep Walking Back to
You
OGC2-W,M TI1-W,M UFB-W,M
My Silent Love
OnT1-W,M
My Sin
TI1-W,M UFB-W,M
My Sins Are Blotted Out, I Know
OM-W,M
My Sister, Ain't You Mighty Glad
MoM-W,M
My Sister Kate
BSC-W
My Sister Sam (Theme)
DC-W,M
My Sister, She Works in a Laundry
GI-W GO-W
**My Sister You'll Be Called On see
Ma Sister You'll Be Called On**
My Son-in-Law
LSO-W TW-W

My Son Joshua
ITP-W,M
My Son Ted
IS-W,M
My Song Forever Shall Record
Hy-W,M
My Song Is from Franconia
MU-W,M (German)
My Song Is Love Unknown
SJ-W,M
My Song of Songs
BSG-W,M BSP-W,M
My Song Shall Be of Jesus
GH-W,M
My Songs
AS-W,M (German)
My Soul, Be on Thy Guard
AME-W,M GH-W,M Hy-W,M
My Soul before Thee Prostrate Lies
AHO-W,M
My Soul Desire
VB-W,M
My Soul Doth Magnify the Lord
Hy-W,M
**My Soul Doth Magnify the Lord
see also Magnificat**
My Soul Feels Better Right Now
GrG-W,M
My Soul in Sad Exile
AME-W,M
My Soul Is a Witness
FN-W,M
My Soul Is Athirst for God
FiS-W,M
My Soul Repeat His Praise
AME-W,M
My Soul Wants Something That's
New
RF-W,M
My Soul Wants to Go Home to
Glory
Me-W,M
My Soul, Weigh Not Thy Life
AHO-W,M
My Soul Will Overcome
GH-W,M
My Soul with Expectation
Hy-W,M
My Soul Would Fain Indulge a
Hope
AHO-W,M
**My Soul's Determined see Ma
Soul's Determin'**
My Soul's Goin' to Heaven
NH-W
My Southern Soldier Boy
SiS-W
My Southern Sunny Home
SiS-W
My Souvenirs of Maoriland
SNZ-W,M (Maori)
My Special Angel
ATC2-W,M GAR-W,M MF-W,M
My Speckled Hen
NF-W
My Spirit Longs for Thee
Hy-W,M
My Star (I Have a Star, a Special
Magic Star)
Mo-W,M NM-W,M OTO-W
My Star (When Night Is Calm and
Dark and Clear)
FSA1-W,M
My Stetson Hat
HB-W,M
**My Stone Is the Stone see Me
Stone Is the Stone**

My Sunshine
FSY-W,M (Italian) NAS-W,M
SL-W
My Sunshine see also O Sole Mio
My Sweet Ipo
SNZ-W,M (Maori)
My Sweet Lady
CJ-W,M PoG-W,M WG-W,M
My Sweet Lord
GOI7-W,M TM-W,M
My Sweet Sailor Boy
Oz1-W,M
My Sweetheart Is a Cowboy
SoC-W
My Sweetheart Went Down with
the Maine
Oz4-W
My Sweetheart's a Mule in the
Mines
PO-W,M
My Sweetheart's the Man in the
Moon
BH-W,M EFS-W,M FSTS-W,M
MF-W,M OBN-W,M OS-W
My Sweetheart's the Mule in the
Mines
FW-W IHA-W,M SWF-W,M
VA-W,M
My Swing
ASB2-W,M
My Tambourine (I Play on My
Tambourine)
STS-W,M
My Tambourine (Listen to My
Tambourine)
ASB1-W,M
My Task
FS-W,M JBF-W,M
My Teddy Bear
MH-W,M
My Tennessee Mountain Home
BDP-W,M
My Thing Is My Own
SR-W,M
My Thoughts Surmount These
Lower Skies
AME-W,M
My Three Friends
SOO-W,M
My Time Ain't Long
LJ-W,M
My Time Is Your Time
MF-W,M
My Time of Day
TW-W
My Top
SCL-W,M
My Treasure (Becucci)
AmH-M
My Treasure (I Sail'd and I Sail'd
the Seven Seas)
FSA2-W,M
My Trip to Mexico
SoC-W
My Trouble Is Hard
NH-W
My True Love (Martian Love Song)
WSB-W,M
My True Love Hath My Heart
EL-W,M
My True Love Is a Cowboy
SoC-W
My Trundle Bed
HSD-W,M SY-W,M
My Uncle Abel
Lo-W,M
My Very Good Friend

TW-W
My Violin
  ASB3-W,M
My Vote
  AL-W
My Wagon
  VA-W,M
My Warrior Boy
  SiS-W
My Way
  BR-W,M FrS-W,M TI2-W,M
My Way's Cloudy
  RF-W,M
My Week
  MAS-W,M
My White Horse see Mi Caballo
  Blanco
My White Mouse
  RSL-W,M
My Wife Done Joined the Club
  LC-W
My Wife Has a Tongue
  Boo-W,M
My Wife Is a Knowing Woman
  FHR-W,M
My Wife Won't Let Me see Waiting
  at the Church
My Wild Eyed Cadet
  AF-W GI-W GO-W
My Wild Irish Rose
  FSN-W,M FW-W GSN1-W,M
  MAB1-W MF-W,M MSA1-W
  OAP-W,M OBN-W,M RW-W,M
My Wish
  ASB1-W,M UBF-W,M
My Wonderful Travel
  NF-W
My World Begins and Ends with
  You
  TOH-W,M
My Yiddishe Momme
  OTJ-W,M TI1-W,M
My Zither
  MH-W,M
My Zlaty Rodice see Father and
  Mother Dear
Mynheer Vandunck
  ESU-W
Myself I Planted My Garden
  RSC-W,M (Russian Only)
Mysterious Face-Washing
  NF-W
Mysterious Presence! Source of All
  AHO-W,M
Mystery of Number Five
  LJ-W,M
Mystic Warrior (Theme) see Song
  of the Land

N

NCAA Champions
  RW-M
N-E-S-T-L-E'-S
  GSM-W,M
N.Y.C.
  TI2-W,M UBF-W,M
Na Na Hey Hey Kiss Him Goodbye
  NoS-W,M TI1-W,M TRR-W,M
  UFB-W,M
Na Na Hey Hey Kiss Him Goodbye
  see also Kiss Him Goodbye (Na
  Na Hey Hey)
Nacht see Die Nacht
Nadia's Theme
  BNG-M DC-M DPE-W,M MF-M

ToO76-M TVT-M
Nadine (Is It You?)
  ILS-W,M
Nae Mair We'll Meet Again
  SeS-W,M
Nagasaki
  MF-W,M MR-W,M OHB-W,M
Name of Jesus Is So Sweet
  AME-W
Name of the Game
  TI1-W,M UFB-W,M
Namely You
  HFH-W,M
Nancy (with the Laughing Face)
  FrS-W,M MF-W,M
Nancy Lee
  AmH-W,M ESB-W,M HSD-W,M
  NAS-W,M OTJ-W,M TH-W,M
Nancy Whiskey
  IS-W,M
Nanette
  CFS-W,M (French)
Naomi Wise
  FSSC-W,M
Napalm Sue
  VS-W,M
Naples
  MML-W,M
Napoleon (I Have a Horse I Call
  Napoleon)
  OTJ-W,M
Napoleon (Napoleon's a Pastry,
  Bismark Is a Herring)
  Mo-W,M NM-W,M OTO-W
Napule Ve Salute (Goodbye to
  Naples)
  OTO-W
Nar Jag Blef Sjutton Ar see When I
  Was Seventeen
Nar Som Jag Fyllde Sjutton Ar
  SE-W,M (Swedish)
Nar Vil Du, Jesu, Min Elandes
  Vandring Besluta?
  AHO-W,M (Swedish)
Naranjas Dulces
  CDM-W,M (Spanish)
Narrow and Strait
  GH-W,M
Narrow Way
  SHS-W,M
Nasby's Lament over the New
  York Nominations
  MPP-W
Nashville (I Love the Volume of
  Thy Word)
  SHS-W,M
Nashville (Ray Stevens)
  N-W,M
Nashville Cats
  RB-W TI2-W,M
Nashville Ladies
  NF-W
Nashville Nightingale
  ReG-W,M
Nat Turner
  AFP-W AL-W
Natasha's Theme
  PoG-W,M
Nathan Hale
  AWB-W SI-W,M SL-W,M
Nation in Tears
  OHG-W,M
Nation Mourns Her Chief
  SiS-W
Nation Mourns Her Martyr'd Son
  SiS-W
National Anthem (U.S.) see Star

Spangled Banner
National Anthem--God of the Free
  AL-W
National Defense Blues
  Le-W,M
National Grass Plot
  AFP-W AL-W
National Hymn
  MML-W
National Hymn see also God of Our
  Fathers and God of Our Fathers
  Whose Almighty Hand
National Hymn, A (Thou Hast Ever
  Led Our People, Thou, Our
  Father's God!)
  AL-W
National Hymn (Argentina)
  SiP-W,M (Spanish)
National Hymn (Brazil)
  SiP-W,M (Portuguese)
National Hymn (Hungary)
  SiP-W,M (Hungarian)
National Hymn (Portugal)
  SiP-W,M (Portuguese)
National Interest March
  VS-W,M
National Jubilee
  MPP-W
National Whig Song
  MPP-W
Nation's Orphans
  SiS-W
Nations That Long in Darkness
  Walked
  AHO-W,M
Natural Girl for Me
  RBO-W,M
Natural High
  NMH-W,M UBF-W,M
Natural History
  FSA1-W,M
Natural Woman
  BHB-W,M OnT6-W,M
Nature Boy
  NK-W,M OTJ-W,M TI1-W,M
  UFB-W,M
Nature's Beauty
  TH-W,M
Nature's Music
  FSA1-W,M
Nature's Praise
  ASB5-W,M
Naughty Baby
  ReG-W,M
Naughty Bird
  SMa-W,M
Naughty Lady of Shady Lane
  OTJ-W,M
Naughty Marietta
  NaM-W,M
Naughty, Naughty Nancy
  LMS-W,M
Naughty Soap Song
  ASB2-W,M
Nautical Philosophy
  ESU-W
Navajo
  ASB1-W,M
Navajo Happy Song
  SMY-W,M (Navajo Only)
Naval Academy Graduate's Song
  ANS-W
Naval Recruiting Song
  ANS-W
Naval Song
  MPP-W
Naval Song: Charge the Can

Cheerily
ANS-W
Naval Song: Pillar of Glory
ANS-W
Naval Song: Rise, Columbia, Brave
and Free
ANS-W
Naval Victory by the United States
Frigate Constitution
ANS-W
Navy Blue and Gold
Mo-W,M TI2-W,M
Navy Blue and White
CoS-W,M
Navy Fragment
GI-W
Navy Hymn
AAP-W,M SBJ-W,M
**Navy Hymn see also Eternal
Father! Strong to Save**
Navy Prayer
AF-W
Nazareth (Though Poor Be the
Chamber)
AmH-W,M CCH-W,M ESB-W,M
SL-W,M
Ne Nkansu
SBF-W,M (Tshiluba Only)
Neapolitan Boat Song
MML-W,M
Neapolitan Love Song
MF-W,M
Neapolitan Nights
TI1-W,M UFB-W,M
Near Our Old Home
FSF-W (French)
Near the Cross
GH-W,M
**Near the Cross see also Jesus
Keep Me Near the Cross**
Near to the Heart of God
OM-W,M
Near You
EC-W,M MF-W,M TVT-W,M
Nearer and Dearer
Mo-W,M NM-W,M OTO-W
Nearer Home
GrM-W,M
Nearer My God to Thee
AME-W,M AmH-W,M ATS-W
CEM-W,M CSo-W,M FH-W,M
FM-W,M FW-W GH-W,M HF-W,M
HLS7-W,M HSD-W,M Hy-W,M
IH-M MAB1-W MF-W,M MSA1-W
NAS-W,M RDF-W,M RW-W,M
STR-W,M TB-W,M WiS7-W,M
Nearness of You
AT-W,M GSN2-W,M ILT-W,M
LM-W,M MAB1-W MSA1-W
'Neath... see also Beneath...
'Neath Our Flag
SL-W,M
'Neath the Elms
ESB-W,M
'Neath the Southern Moon
NaM-W,M
'Neath This Window
SL-W,M
Nebraska
Mo-W,M NM-W,M OTO-W
Necessity
FR-W,M TW-W
Ned Kendall's Hornpipe
POT-M
Needle's Eye
FMT-W FoM-W,M Oz3-W,M
SiR-W,M

Needles and Pins
GSN4-W,M TTH-W,M
Negra Consentida
TI2-W,M (Spanish)
Negro and the Policeman
NF-W
Negro Baker Man
NF-W
Negro Bum
NH-W
Negro Emancipation Song
SiS-W
Negro Jig
DE-W,M
**Negro National Anthem see Lift
Every (Ev'ry) Voice and Sing**
Negro Soldiers' Civil War Chant
NF-W
Negro Song
EA-W,M
Negroes Never Die
NF-W
Negro's Dream
NSS-W
Neighborhood Song
Mo-W,M NM-W,M OTO-W
Neighbours
RoS-W,M
Neither Do I Condemn Thee
GH-W,M
Neither One of Us
SoH-W,M
Nel Blu, Dipinto Di Blu see Volare
Nell and I
FHR-W,M SSF-W,M SSFo-W,M
Nell Flaherty's Drake
IS-W,M
Nellie Dean
U-W
Nellie Was a Lady
RW-W,M
Nellie's Lament
BSC-W
Nelly Bly
AmH-W,M ASB5-W,M FHR-W,M
FW-W HS-W,M IHA-W,M
LMR-W,M MHB-W,M OTJ-W,M
RW-W,M SSF-W,M SSFo-W,M
WiS8-W,M
Nelly Was a Lady
AmH-W,M FHR-W,M SSF-W,M
SSFo-W,M WiS8-W,M
Neptune
MHB-W,M (Swedish)
Nerves
SiS-W
Nervy Woman Blues
DBL-W
Nest of Doves
FSA1-W,M
Nesta Rua
LA-W,M (Spanish)
Nesting
NF-W
Never
TTH-W,M
Never a Care I Know
TH-W,M
Never a Day Goes By
WDS-W,M
Neve' a Man Speak Like This Man
AAF-W,M
Never Be the Same
BCC-W,M
Never Been So Loved (in All My
Life)
TI2-W,M

Never Been to Spain
MCG-W,M On-W,M
Never Borrow Money Needlessly
GSM-W,M
Never Can Say Goodbye
ToO76-W,M
Never Ending
SRE1-W,M
Never Ending Song of Love
RYT-W,M
Never for You
Ne-W,M
Never Forget the Dear Ones
Sin-W,M SiS-W
Never Forget What God Has Done
SHP-W,M
Never Gonna Cry
Mo-W,M
Never Hit Your Grandma with a
Shovel
WF-W,M
Never Leave Me Alone
GrG-W,M
Never Let a Man
Boo-W,M
Never Let Me Go
OTO-W
Never Mind
FSA1-W,M
Never Mind the Why and
Wherefore
GiS-W,M MGT-W,M
Never Murmuring
Boo-W,M
Never My Love
DPE-W,M GAR-W,M MF-W,M
Never Never Gonna Give You Up
SoH-W,M
Never Never Land
Mo-W,M NM-W,M OTJ-W,M
OTO-W UBF-W,M
Never No Mo' Blues
LJ-W,M
Never on Sunday
GOI7-W,M GSN4-W,M
HLS5-W,M OBN-W,M RT6-W,M
RW-W,M TI2-W,M
Never Part Again
SHS-W,M
Never Say Goodbye
DPE-W,M
Never Say No
Fa-W,M OTO-W UBF-W,M
Never Say Yes
SRE2-W,M
Never Seen a Mountain So High
TOH-W,M
Never Shone a Light
GH-W,M
Never Smile at a Crocodile
NI-W,M OTJ-W,M
Never So Beautiful
OTO-W
Never Steal Anything Small
Mo-W,M NM-W,M OTO-W
Never Thought (That I Could Love)
CFB-W,M
Never Till Tomorrow Leave
Boo-W,M
Never Too Much Love
SFF-W,M
Never Turn Back
GrM-W,M
Never Turn Back Any More
WN-W,M
Never Turn Back No More
WN-W,M

Never Was a Child So Lovely
BCT-W,M
Never Weather-Beaten Sail
OH-W,M SSP-W
Never Will I Marry
UBF-W,M
Nevertheless (I'm in Love with
You)
FrS-W,M TI1-W,M UFB-W,M
New Alphabetical Song on the
Corn Law Bill
MSB-W
New America Song
SE-W (Swedish)
New and Beautiful Sailor's Song
about a Brig Which Was Lost in
the North Sea
SE-W (Swedish)
New Ashmolean Marching Society
and Students Conservatory Band
TI2-W,M UBF-W,M
New Assistant for the Piano-Forte
BC1-M
New Baby
SoP-W,M
New Ballad
SBA-W
New Ballad of Lord Lovell
SiS-W
New Bedford Whaler
OHO-W,M
New Beginnings
TW-W
New Bonnet
MH-W,M
New Britain
SHS-W,M
New Columbia
ESU-W
New Crawlin' King Snake
DBL-W
New Created World
SiR-W,M
New Day
JF-W,M VB-W,M
New Day Yesterday
BJ-W,M
New Dial
OB-W,M
New Electric Light
Oz3-W
New England Ballad
SI-W,M
New Every Morning Is the Love
Hy-W,M
New Fangled Preacher Man
P-W,M TW-W
New Fashioned Farmer
MSB-W
New Freedom Bell
BSo-W,M
New Harmony
WN-W,M
New Hat
ASB4-W,M
New Haven
SHS-W,M
New Heart
VB-W,M
New Highway
ASB6-W,M
New Hunting Song
MSB-W
New Jail
SCa-W,M
New Jerusalem (And Did Those
Feet in Ancient Time)

FW-W SWF-W,M TO-W,M
New Jerusalem (My Gracious
Redeemer I Love)
SHS-W,M
New Jubilee
AL-W
New Kind of Love
GCM-W,M
New Liberty Song
SAR-W
New Life
GBC-W,M
New Looks from an Old Lover
TOC83-W,M
New Love Is Old
CF-W,M
New Loyal Song against Home
Rule
VP-W,M
New Market Wreck
LSR-W,M
New Massachusetts Liberty Song
MPP-W SAR-W
New Moon
FSA1-W,M
New Moon on Monday
TI2-W,M
New Naked City Theme
TVT-M
New National Anthem
AL-W
New Organ
Oz4-W
New Orleans (Guida/Royster)
DRR-W,M
New Orleans (Why Do We Mourn
Departing Friends)
SHS-W,M
New Orleans Blues
LC-W
New Orleans Jeunesse Doree
NaM-W,M
New Orleans Nightfall
NO-W,M
New Oysters
SSP-W
New Oysters, New Oysters
Boo-W,M
New Party
MPP-W
New-Plymouth
EA-W,M
New Prince, New Pomp
OB-W,M
New River Train
BSo-W,M FW-W GuC-W,M
ITP-W,M LSR-W,M RSL-W,M
RW-W,M
New Rocks of Bawn
IFM-W
New Shoes
MES1-W,M MES2-W,M
New Skedaddle
SiS-W
New Skedaddle Song
MPP-W
New Song (Americans Swarming
by Thousands on Shore)
MPP-W
New Song (As Near Beauteous
Boston Lying)
MPP-W
New Song (But If Changed in
Demeanor We Look for the Brave)
AL-W
New Song (Come, All Ye Good
People)

MPP-W
New Song (Come Honies of
Congress)
MPP-W
New Song (Come Jolly Sons of
Liberty)
AL-W
New Song (Democrats, Your
Country Calls)
AL-W
New Song (The Frenchmen Came
upon the Coast)
SBA-W
New Song (God Save the Rights of
Man)
MPP-W
New Song (I Will Sing Him a New
Song)
VB-W
New Song (James Madison My
Joe)
MPP-W
New Song (A Plan Is Proposed)
MPP-W
New Song (Rejoice, Columbia's
Sons Rejoice)
AL-W
New Song (Sing to the Lord a New
Song)
JF-W,M
New Song (When Britain
Determined to Tax Us)
MPP-W
New Song (You Simple Bostonians)
MPP-W
New Song, The (With Harps and
with Viols)
GH-W,M
New Song about the Emigration to
America
SE-W,M (Swedish)
New Song against Rack Renting
VP-W
New Song Called the Hiring Day
VP-W
New Song Entitled the Kerry
Eviction
VP-W
New Song on Michael Davitt
VP-W
New Song on the Birth of the
Prince of Wales
MSB-W
New Song on the Census of 1891
VP-W
New Song on the Corn Bill
MSB-W
New Song on the Cutting Machine
VP-W
New Song on the Hiring of the
Servants
VP-W
New Song on the Home Rule
Association
VP-W
New Song on the Races of
Roscommon
VP-W
New Song on the Rotten Potatoes
VP-W
New Song on the Taxes
VP-W,M
New Song Sympathising with
Fenian Exiles
VP-W
New Song to an Old Tune (O, Take
Your Time, Ye Bosses)

AL-W
New Song to an Old Tune (What a
  Court Hath Old England, of Folly
  and Sin)
  ESU-W SAR-W SBA-W
New Song Written by a Soldier
  SI-W,M
New Songs Ring with Gladness
  SSe-W,M
New Stranger's Blues
  AFB-W,M
New Sun in the Sky
  TW-W
New Texas Dixie
  OHG-W,M
New Tomorrow
  HCY-W,M
New Topia (Young People All,
  Attention Give)
  SHS-W,M
New Tory Ballad
  SI-W
New Town Is a Blue Town
  TW-W
New War Song
  MPP-W SAR-W,M SBA-W
New Will Never Wear Off of You
  TOC83-W,M
New World in the Morning
  RDT-W,M
New Yankee Doodle
  ATS-W ESU-W Oz2-W
New Yealand
  Oz1-W
New Year (Eternity Draws Nigh)
  SHS-W,M
New Year (Hear the Ringing
  Steeple Bell)
  ASB4-W,M
New Year (O, I Am the Little New
  Year)
  MH-W,M
New Year (The Old Year Is Dying,
  Fast Dying Away)
  ASB5-W,M MML-W,M
New Year Bells
  HSA-W,M
New Year Carol
  VA-W,M
New Year's Day
  SBA-W
New Year's Day Visit
  CFS-W,M (French)
New Year's Eve
  SL-W,M
New Year's Sermon
  BSC-W
New Year's Song
  FSA1-W,M
New York City
  PSN-W,M
New York Mets Victory and
  Commiseration Song
  RBO-W,M
New York, New York (a Helluva
  Town)
  DC-W,M MF-W,M TW-W
New York, New York (Start
  Spreadin' the News)
  FrS-W,M
New York, O What a Charming
  City
  ATS-W,M NeA-W,M OHG-W,M
New York, or Oh, What a
  Charming City
  AH-W,M SY-W,M
New York, Our Empire State

Fif-W,M
New York Times (Home Delivery)
  GSM-W,M
New York Town
  BF-W
New York Trader
  MSB-W
New York's Not My Home
  JC-W,M PM-W,M
New Zealand's Christmas Tree
  SNZ-W,M (Maori)
Newburgh
  SHS-W,M
**Newe Ballade see Ballad of
  Thomas Appletree**
Newhart (Theme)
  TV-M
Newly Weds
  NF-W
News Frae Moidart Cam' Yestreen
  SeS-W,M
Newsboy
  MH-W,M
Newton Jig
  DE-W,M
Newtopia see New Topia
Next Best Thing to Your Good
  Cooking
  GSM-W,M
Next Is Me
  SR-W,M
Next Man That I Marry
  JC-W,M
Next Market Day
  FW-W
Next Time I Fall
  TTH-W,M
Next Time I Love
  Mo-W,M NM-W,M OTO-W
Next Time, This Time
  JC-W,M
Next to Lovin' (I Like Fightin' Best)
  Sh-W,M
Next to Texas I Love You
  TW-W
Next Voice You Hear
  Mo-W,M NM-W,M
Next Year in Jerusalem
  SBJ-W,M (Hebrew Only)
**Nez De Martin see Le Nez De
  Martin**
Niagara Falls
  ATS-W,M
Nibblety Nibblety, Nib
  SiR-W,M
Nice and Easy see Nice 'n' Easy
**Nice and Naasty see Nice 'n'
  Naasty**
Nice Boy
  AF-W
Nice Dreams
  TOM-W,M
Nice Girls Don't Chase the Boys
  SaS-W,M SMY-W,M
Nice 'n' Easy
  MF-W,M
Nice 'n' Naasty
  ToO76-W,M
Nice, Nice, Very Nice
  HSe-W,M
Nice People
  TW-W
Nice Place to Visit
  TW-W
Nice Work If You Can Get It
  DJ-W,M FrS-W,M HC2-W,M
  LSO-W NYT-W,M OTO-W

RT5-W,M TI1-W,M UFB-W,M
Nice Young Man
  ESU-W SY-W,M
Nicholas and Alexandra (Theme)
  TOM-M
Nicholas Raven's Trip to America
  and Homesickness
  SE-W (Swedish)
Nick and a Nock
  ASB4-W,M
Nickel under the Foot
  TW-W
Nickety Nackety
  ITP-W,M
Nicodemus
  AL-W
Nicodemus Johnson
  SiS-W
Nicolas and Marie
  ASB6-W,M
Nicolas Sous Cet Ombrage
  CaF-W (French Only)
Nigger and White Man
  AFP-W
Nigger Be a Nigger
  AFP-W
Nigger 'Lasses
  SoC-W
Nigger on de Wood Pile
  DE-W,M
Nigger on the Brain
  SiS-W
Niggers Get the Turpentine
  AFP-W
Night (Daylight Dying, and Swiftly
  Flying)
  OS-W
Night (Duparc)
  OU-W,M
Night and Day
  DBC-W,M DC-W,M DJ-W,M
  EY-W,M (French) FrS-W,M
  (French) HC1-W,M MF-W,M
  MHB-W,M ML-W,M OHB-W,M
Night Before
  Be1-W,M TWS-W
Night before Christmas
  RW-W,M
Night before Christmas Song
  BCh-W,M BCS-W,M
Night before the Battle
  SiS-W
Night Breezes
  MMW-W,M
Night Chicago Died
  TI2-W,M
Night Club
  Co-W,M
Night Express
  LSR-W,M
Night Fever
  TI1-W,M UFB-W,M
Night Flies By
  MA-W,M
Night Games
  TOC83-W,M
Night Has a Heart of Its Own
  TTH-W,M
Night Has a Thousand Eyes
  GC-W,M
Night Herding Song
  ASB5-W,M BMC-W,M FGM-W,M
  HOH-W,M HS-W,M HWS-W,M
  MAS-W,M WS-W,M
Night in June
  FSA2-W,M
Night in the City

ELO-W,M
Night in Tunisia
TI2-M
Night Is Filled with Wonderful
Sounds
Mo-W,M NM-W,M OTO-W
Night Is Serene
ATS-W,M
Night Is Young
OnT1-W,M TI2-W,M
Night Letter
GV-W,M
Night Life
TOH-W,M WNF-W
Night Lights
NK-W,M
Night of My Nights
Ki-W,M
Night of Wonder
SBF-W,M
Night Song
Mo-W,M NM-W,M OTO-W
Night Take-Offs in Weather
AF-W
Night They Drove Old Dixie Down
RV-W
Night They Invented Champagne
DBC-W,M HC2-W,M LL-W,M
LM-W,M OTO-W RT5-W,M
TI1-W,M UBF-W,M UFB-W,M
Night Thought
WN-W,M
Night Time (Creeping, Creeping
Comes the Night Time)
ASB1-W,M
Night Time (The Setting Sun Has
Turned to Red)
ASB4-W,M
Night Time (Soft the Breezes Blow)
ASB2-W,M
Night Time in Araby
GOB-W,M
Night Time Is the Right Time
LC-W
Night Train
GOI7-W,M
Night Voyage
FSA2-W,M
Night Waltz (Sun Won't Set)
LN-W,M
Night Was Made for Love
CF-W,M TI1-W,M UFB-W,M
Night Watch
OGC2-W,M
Night We Called It a Day
ILT-W,M
Night Will Never Stay
MHB-W,M
Night Wind
GC-W,M
Night Wind's Lullaby
SiR-W,M
Nightfall
ASB5-W,M
Nightingale (Folk Song)
BT-W,M DD-W,M FW-W Oz1-W
TBF-W,M
**Nightingale (Folk Song) see also
One Morning in May**
Nightingale (the Merry Nightingale)
Boo-W,M
Nightingale (The Sunrise Wakes
the Lark to Sing)
TH-W,M
Nightingale (When the Daylight Is
Gently Waning)
MHB-W,M

Nightingale and the Star
M-W,M
Nightingale Sang in Berkeley
Square
BBB-W,M TI1-W,M UFB-W,M
Nightlife
Mo-W,M NM-W,M OTO-W
Nightrider
ELO-W,M
Nights in White Satin
GrS-W,M MF-W,M TI1-W,M
TWD-W,M UFB-W,M
Nights of Splendor
STP-W,M
Nights on Broadway
GrS-W,M
Nighttime see Night Time
Niklas Korps Resa Till Amerika Och
Hemlangtan
SE-W (Swedish)
Nile
ASB6-W,M
**Nils Who Will Travel to America
see Swedish Girl**
Nina Never Knew
NK-W,M
Ninas Hermosas
LA-W,M (Spanish) SCL-W,M
(Spanish)
Nine Girls
ASB6-W,M
Nine Hundred Miles
FG2-W,M FSB3-W,M FW-W
OTJ-W,M POT-W,M RW-W,M
Nine Hundred Miles from Home
LSR-W,M
999, The
TMA-W,M
Nine Pound Hammer
BIS-W,M BSo-W,M FG2-W,M
FGM-W,M FW-W LSR-W,M
OGC2-W,M PB-W,M
Nine to Five (Theme)
TOM-W,M TV-W,M TVT-W,M
Nineteen Birds
MH-W,M SiR-W,M
1982
AWS-W,M
1900--The Bugles
AL-W
Nineteen Hundred and Eighty Five
PMC-W,M
Nineteen Thirteen Massacre
AFP-W,M FW-W
19th Nervous Breakdown
RoS-W,M
Nineties' Serenade
MuM-W,M
Ninety and Nine, The
ATS-W FW-W GH-W,M
WiS7-W,M
Ninety and Nine or Lost Sheep
OHG-W,M
Ninety Fifth Psalm
SHS-W,M
Ninety Nine and a Half Won't Do
SFF-W,M
Ninety-Nine Blue Bottles
Oz3-W,M
Ninety-Nine Bottles of Beer
OHO-W,M
99 Miles from L.A.
HD-W,M
Ninety-Nine Years
Oz2-W
Ninety-Third Psalm
SHS-W,M

90 Years Ago see Honest
Ploughman
Nino see El Nino
Nipper's Song
IFM-W
No Arms Can Ever Hold You (Like
These Arms of Mine)
MF-W,M
No Beautiful Chamber
AME-W,M
No Can Do
TI1-W,M UFB-W,M
No Devil in Our Lan'
BDW-W,M
No Drunkard
ITP-W,M
No Easy Way Out
TTH-W,M
No Expectations
RoS-W,M
No Flag but the Old Flag
SiS-W
No Fooling
GI-W
No Golden Harvest
GrM-W,M
No Goodbyes
OTO-W UBF-W,M
No Greater Love
HLS3-W,M
No Hay Arbol
LA-W,M (Spanish)
No Hiding Place
FGM-W,M FW-W
No Home, No Home
FHR-W,M SY-W,M
No Hope in Jesus
GH-W,M
No I Aint Ashame
BDW-W,M
No Irish Need Apply
AFP-W,M AL-W FW-W
No Is My Answer
MHB-W,M (Slovak)
No John
FW-W,M
**No John see also O No, John and
Oh, No John, No**
No Land Like Ours
SL-W,M
No Letter Blues
LC-W
No Liar Can Stan'
BDW-W,M
No Man Can Find the War
RB-W
No Man Is an Island
HSS-W,M HST-W,M RDF-W,M
TI1-W,M UFB-W,M
No Matter What Happens
MLS-W,M
No Moon at All
TI2-W,M
No More (Do I See the Starlight
Caress Your Hair)
SRE2-W,M
No More (Well, You Had Your
Way! No More)
Mo-W,M NM-W,M OTO-W
No More Auction Block
RF-W,M SWF-W,M
No More beneath the Oppressive
Hand
AHO-W,M
No More Blues (Chega De
Saudade)
TI1-W,M UFB-W,M

No More Cane on This Brazos
IHA-W,M
No More Dams I'll Make for Fish
FSS-W,M
No More Good Time
NH-W
No More Johnson
VS-W,M
No More Mournin'
AFP-W
No More Night
OGR-W,M VB-W,M
No More Rain Fall for Wet You
NSS-W
No More Shall I Work in the
Factory
AFP-W
No More Tears
PoG-W,M
**No More We'll Meet Again see Nae
Mair We'll Meet Again**
No Never Alone
AME-W,M
No, Never, No
HSD-W,M
No Nickel Won't Buy No Wine
LC-W
No Night There
AME-W,M FS-W,M JBF-W,M
No Nights by Myself
DBL-W
No! No! A Thousand Times No!
BH-W,M RW-W,M
No, No Fair Heretic, It Cannot Be
EL-W,M
No, No Mister Bear
ASB2-W,M
No, No, Nanette
MF-W,M NN2-W,M NN7-W,M
No, No, No, It Must Not Be
EL-W,M
No Not Much
ATC2-W,M
No One Ever Cared for Me Like
Jesus
HHa-W,M
No One Is Alone
EY-W,M
No One to Cry To
OGC1-W,M
No One to Love
HSB-W,M
No One Understands Like Jesus
BSG-W,M BSP-W,M
No Orchids for My Lady
ToS-W,M
No Other Love
BeL-W,M HC2-W,M OTJ-W,M
OTO-W TI1-W,M UBF-W,M
UFB-W,M
No Other Moon
SBF-W,M
No Other Name
GH-W,M
No Other Name but Jesus
OGR-W,M VB-W,M
No Particular Place to Go
GAR-W,M TI1-W,M UFB-W,M
No Reply
BBe-W,M Be1-W,M TWS-W
No Room at the Hotel
FVV-W,M
No Room in the Inn
AME-W,M FW-W OB-W,M
No Room to Poke Fun
NF-W
No Shadows Yonder

WiS7-W,M
No Shortage
VB-W,M
No, Sir
ITP-W,M
No Sir! No Sir!
Oz3-W,M
No Slave beneath That Starry Flag
SiS-W
No Sorrow There
WN-W,M
No Special Rider
LC-W
No Strings
OTJ-W,M OTO-W TI1-W,M
UBF-W,M UFB-W,M
No Surrender
MPP-W SiS-W VP-W
No Tell Lover
ToO79-W,M
No Time for Talk
BCC-W,M
No Time Like the Present
GrM-W,M
No Tree but Has a Shadow
LA-W,M (Spanish)
No Two People
TI2-W,M
No Use in Crying
RoS-W,M
No, Ve Vouldn't Gonto Do It
KH-W,M
No Way to Go but Up
OnT1-W,M
No Way to Stop It
SM-W,M
Noah Built the Ark
BMM-W
Noah Found Grace in the Eyes of
the Lord
CEM-W,M
Noah's Ark (Old Noah He Built
Himself an Ark)
ATS-W BMC-W,M GuC-W,M
HAS-W,M HS-W,M NAS-W,M
Noah's Ark (Tell Me Who Built
the Ark)
OTJ-W,M
Noah's Dove
AH-W,M
Nobby Head of Hair
MSB-W
Nobility
FSA2-W,M
Noble Duke
DD-W,M
Noble Duke of York
ASB3-W,M FW-W MAR-W,M
Noble Knights of Labor
AFP-W AL-W
Noble Lads of Canada
ESU-W SI-W,M
Noble Ribbon Boys
VP-W,M
Nobleman's Daughter
BSC-W
Nobody (I Ain't Never Done
Nothin' to Nobody)
OTJ-W,M
Nobody (If to Force Me to Sing It
Be Your Intention)
HAS-W,M
Nobody (Sittin' in a Restaurant,
She Walked By)
TOC82-W,M TOC83-W,M
Nobody at Home
SL-W,M

Nobody but You
GOB-W,M NYT-M
Nobody Cares for Me
Oz4-W,M
Nobody Does It Better
RW-W,M
Nobody Doesn't Like Sara Lee
GSM-W,M
Nobody Home
MES1-W,M MES2-W,M
Nobody Knows (de Trouble I've
Seen)
AFP-W LoS-W,M RTH-W
**Nobody Knows (de Trouble I've
Seen) see also Nobody Knows de
Trouble I've Seen**
Nobody Knows (the Sound of My
Voice)
MLS-W,M
Nobody Knows (Winds of the
Morning, Bending the Grasses)
ASB4-W,M
Nobody Knows but Me
LJ-W,M
Nobody Knows but Mother
SiR-W,M
Nobody Knows de Trouble I See
FN-W,M
Nobody Knows de Trouble I'se
Seen
TH-W,M
Nobody Knows de Trouble I've
Had
AH-W,M NSS-W
Nobody Knows de Trouble I've
Seen
AAF-W,M AHO-W,M RF-W,M
WiS7-W,M
**Nobody Knows de Trouble I've
Seen see also Nobody Knows (de
Trouble I've Seen)**
Nobody Knows the Trouble I See
AAF-W,M ETB-W,M MAS-W,M
TF-W,M WN-W,M
Nobody Knows the Trouble I've
Had
RW-W,M
Nobody Knows the Trouble I've
Seen
ATS-W FW-W Gu-W,M GuC-W,M
HS-W,M IHA-W,M IL-W,M
LT-W,M NAS-W,M OBN-W,M
OFS-W,M OS-W OTJ-W,M
Nobody Knows You
LC-W
Nobody Knows You When You're
Down and Out
J-W,M WSB-W,M
Nobody Likes Sad Songs
TI2-W,M
Nobody Looking
NF-W
Nobody Loves No Baby (Like My
Baby Loves Me)
WDS-W,M
Nobody Makes a Pass at Me
TW-W WW-W,M
Nobody Told Me (John Lennon)
TI2-W,M
Nobody Told Me (Richard Rodgers)
OTJ-W,M OTO-W
Nobody Wins
SuS-W,M
Nobody's Bizness but Mine
NH-W
Nobody's Chasing Me
TW-W

Nobody's Darling
ATS-W
Nobody's Darling but Mine
SF-W,M
Nobody's Heart
TS-W
Nobody's Lonesome for Me
HW-W,M
Nobody's Perfect
I-W,M
Nobody's Perfekt
TOM-W,M
Nobody's Sweetheart
TI2-W,M
Noces Du Papillon see Les Noces
Du Papillon
Nocturne (Borodin)
RW-M
Nocturne (Chopin, Op. 9, No. 2)
AmH-M Mo-W,M NM-W,M
OBN-M OTO-W RW-M
Nocturne (Chopin, Op. 55, No. 1)
RW-M
Nocturne (Mendelssohn)
RW-M
Nocturne in ze Lan' of Ol' Bayou
MBS-W,M
Noel
MU-W,M (Latin)
Noel De Thevet
GBC-W,M
Noel Des Ausels
CCH-W,M
Noel Girl, The
Oz2-W,M
Noel! Noel!
BMC-W,M MF-W,M OPS-W,M
RW-W,M
Noel, Raise the Roof
GBC-W,M
Noelle's Theme
TOM-M
Noisy March
ASB2-W,M
Noisy Wind
ASB5-W,M
Nola
OTJ-W,M RW-M TI1-W,M
UFB-W,M
Nomination Song
SiS-W
Noms see Des Noms
Non Dimenticar
MF-W,M NK-W,M (Italian)
TI1-W,M
Non E Ver ('Tis Not True)
WiS8-W,M
Non Nobis, Domine
LMR-W,M (Latin Only) MML-W,M
(Latin) SBF-W,M (Latin Only)
TF-W,M (Latin only)
Non-Committal Song
MPP-W
None but Christ
GH-W,M
None but the Lonely Heart
CA-W,M MF-W,M OAP-M
None Shall Part Us
MGT-W,M SL-W,M
None Shall Weep a Tear for Me
FHR-W,M
Nonsense Song
FSA1-W,M
Non-Union Chorus
AL-W
Nor Costly Domes
ESB-W,M

Nor Love Thy Life
Boo-W,M
Nor Will I Sin
Oz2-W
Nora O'Neal
HSD-W,M
Norfolk Girls
ANS-W
Norma Rae (Theme) see It Goes
Like It Goes
Norma's Awake Now
TW-W
Norman
HR-W
Normandy
FSF-W (French)
North and South (Ah, Wherefore
Woulds't Thou Leave Our Band)
SiS-W
North and South (List Ye That Low
and Plaintive Wail)
AL-W
North and South (Theme)
BNG-M
North Argentinian Folk Dance
SBF-W,M (Spanish Only)
North Carolina
TI1-W,M UFB-W,M
North Carolina Call to Arms
SiS-W
North Dakota Hymn
Fif-W,M
North Dakota University
CoS-W,M
North Star
ASB3-W,M
North to Alaska
RW-W,M
North Wind (Is Blowing)
ASB1-W,M
North Wind (Loud Calls the North
Wind and Clear)
ASB2-W,M
North Wind Doth Blow
MH-W,M OTJ-W,M
Northern Lights
FSA2-W,M
Northern Swans
ASB4-W,M SCL-W,M
Northern Winter
ASB5-W,M
Northfield (How Long, Dear Jesus,
Oh! How Long)
SHS-W,M TO-W,M
Northmen's Marseillaise
SiS-W
Norwegian Dance
AmH-M BMC-M RW-M
Norwegian Hymn
ESB-W,M
Norwegian National Song
AmH-W,M (Norwegian)
Norwegian Summer
ASB5-W,M
Norwegian Wood
BBe-W,M Be1-W,M TWS-W
WG-W,M
Nos Galan
OB-W,M
Nostalgia
Mo-M
Not a Day Goes By
MF-W,M UBF-W,M
Not a Day More Than Thirty
Boo-W,M
Not a Moment Too Soon
Mo-W,M

Not a Second Time
TWS-W
Not All the Blood of Beasts
AME-W,M
Not Alone for Mighty Empire
AHO-W,M ESB-W,M Hy-W,M
Not Anymore
R-W,M
Not by Might, Not by Power
VB-W,M
Not Far from the Kingdom
GH-W,M
Not for Joe
ATS-W
Not Guilty
HHa-W,M
Not Half Has Ever Seen
GH-W,M
Not Mine
OTO-W
Not My Own
GH-W,M
Not My Will
HLS7-W,M
Not Now, but Later
HJ-W,M
Not Now, My Child
GH-W,M
Not of This World
VB-W,M
Not One Single Word
OU-W,M
Not Only Where God's Free Winds
Blow
AHO-W,M
Not Since Nineveh
Ki-W,M
Not So in Haste, My Heart
Hy-W,M
Not to Us, Not unto Us, Lord
AHO-W,M
Not to Us, O Lord
VB-W,M
Not Try, but Trust
GH-W,M
Not What These Hands Have Done
GH-W,M OM-W,M
Not While I'm Around
UBF-W,M
Noted Cowboy
SoC-W
Nothin' Improves My Day
OGR-W,M
Nothing
CL-W,M JP-W,M
Nothing behind You, Nothing in
Sight
TOC82-W,M
Nothing between My Soul and the
Savior
AME-W,M
Nothing but a Soldier
SFF-W,M
Nothing but Leaves
GH-W,M
Nothing but Leaves! the Spirit
Grieves
AME-W,M
Nothing but the Blood
GH-W,M MAB1-W MSA1-W
VB-W,M
Nothing but the Blood of Jesus
AME-W,M
Nothing but the Radio On
TOC82-W,M
Nothing but Time
CSp-W,M

Nothing Can Stop Me Now
TI1-W,M UBF-W,M UFB-W,M
Nothing for Christmas see Nuttin'
for Christmas
Nothing Goes with Everything Like
Mueller's
GSM-W,M
Nothing Improves My Day see
Nothin' Improves My Day
Nothing in Common
Mo-W,M NM-W,M OTO-W
TTH-W,M
Nothing in the World
MF-W,M NK-W,M
Nothing Is Easy
BJ-W,M
Nothing Like Grog
ESU-W HAS-W,M
Nothing Serious
SL-W,M
Nothing's Gonna Change My Love
for You
BHO-W,M DC-W,M DPE-W,M
Nothing's Gonna Stop Us Now
BHO-W,M LOM-W,M
Notre Dame, Our Mother
Mo-W,M
Notre Dame Victory March
Mo-W,M RDT-W,M TI2-W,M
Nottingham Fair
Oz3-W,M
Nous Etions Dix Filles A Marier
MP-W,M (French Only)
Nous N'irons Plus Au Bois
Ch-W (French Only) CUP-W,M
(French Only) MP-W,M (French
Only) OTJ-W,M (French Only)
Nouvelle Annee see La Nouvelle
Annee
November (The Flow'rs Are Dead
and the Birds Are Fled)
FSA2-W,M
November (Trees Bare and Brown,
Dry Leaves Ev'rywhere)
MH-W,M
November Days (Are Here Again,
the Winds Are Chill and Cold)
ASB6-W,M
November Days (When Days Are
Short and Nights Are Cold)
ASB3-W,M
November Winds
ASB1-W,M
Novgorod Lyrical Melody
RuS-W,M (Russian)
Now (Robert Wright)
SN-W,M
Now (Stephen Sondheim)
LN-W,M TW-W
Now All the Bells Are Ringing
SL-W,M
Now and Forever (You and Me)
EC-W,M TTH-W,M
Now and the Not Yet
OGR-W,M VB-W,M
Now Be the Gospel Banner
AHO-W,M
Now Behold the Saviour Pleading
AHO-W,M
Now Comes the Hour
SMY-W,M
Now Evening Puts Amen to Day
AHO-W,M
Now from Labor and from Care
AHO-W,M
Now Give Three Cheers
TH-W,M

Now Glad of Heart
OB-W,M
Now God Be with Old Simeon
Boo-W,M
Now God Be with Us, for the Night
Is Closing
Hy-W,M
Now Goodnight
MH-W,M
Now Help Us, Lord
AHO-W,M
Now I Am a Big Boy
Oz3-W
Now I Am Married
Boo-W,M
Now I Belong to Jesus
BSG-W,M BSP-W,M OM-W,M
Now I Journey Away
SE-W (Swedish)
Now I Lay Me Down to Sleep (I
Pray the Lord My Soul to Keep)
OTJ-W,M SOO-W,M
Now I Lay Me Down to Sleep (I
Pray the Lord My Soul to Keep)
see also Evening Prayer (Now I
Lay Me Down to Sleep)
Now I Lay Me Down to Sleep (the
Words I Used to Say)
Mo-W,M NM-W,M
Now I Lay Me Down to Sleep--
Parody
NF-W
Now in the Days of Youth
Hy-W,M
Now Is the Hour
FPS-W,M TI2-W,M U-W
Now Is the Hour see also Maori
Farewell Song
Now Is the Month of Maying
HS-W,M OH-W,M OTJ-W,M
SL-W,M TF-W,M TH-W,M
Now Is the Time
L-W
Now Israel May Say, and That in
Truth
Hy-W,M
Now Israel May Say, and That
Truly
AHO-W,M
Now It's Christmas Time
SOO-W,M
Now It's Happy Autumn Time
SHP-W,M
Now I've Got a Witness
RoS-W,M
Now, Jurymen, Hear My Advice
GiS-W,M
Now Just a Word for Jesus
AME-W,M
Now Kiss the Cup, Cousin
Boo-W,M
Now Let All the Heavens Adore
Thee
MC-W,M
Now Let Our Hearts Their Glory
Wake
AHO-W,M
Now My Dear Companions
GB-W,M
Now, O Now, I Needs Must Part
OH-W,M
Now, on Land and Sea Descending
AME-W,M Hy-W,M
Now or Never
VB-W,M
Now, Robin, Lend to Me Thy Bow
LMR-W,M SSP-W

Now Run Along Home
SCL-W,M
Now Sleep My Little Child So Dear
AHO-W,M (German)
Now Thank We All Our God
AME-W,M CEM-W,M ESB-W,M
HF-W,M HS-W,M Hy-W,M
MML-W,M SBF-W,M SHP-W,M
SJ-W,M
Now That I Need You
OTO-W
Now That It's Ended
ILT-W,M
Now That the Buffalo's Gone
IHA-W,M
Now the Blacksmith's Arm
Boo-W,M
Now the Day Is Nearly Done
Boo-W,M
Now the Day Is Over
AME-W,M CEM-W,M ESB-W,M
FH-W,M FWS-W,M GeS-W,M
GH-W,M HS-W,M HSD-W,M
Hy-W,M LoS-W MAS-W,M
MML-W,M MuM-W,M NAS-W,M
OTJ-W,M RW-W,M SL-W,M
SoF-W,M TB-W,M TF-W,M
WiS7-W,M YS-W,M
Now the Hungry Lion Roars
FSS-W,M
Now the Kings Are Coming
SHP-W,M
Now the Last Load
Boo-W,M
Now the Time Has Come for Play
MH-W,M
Now the Winter's Come to Stay
CFS-W,M (French)
Now There Once Was a Young Girl
NeA-W,M
Now to All a Kind Goodnight
Boo-W,M
Now to the Banquet We Press
MGT-W,M
Now to the Lord a Noble Song
AME-W,M
Now We Are Met
Boo-W,M
Now We Are Met and Humors
Agree
Boo-W,M
Now We Say Farewell
Boo-W,M
Now We'll Make the Rafters Ring
Boo-W,M
Now What Is Love
EL-W,M
Now When the Summer's Fruits
Boo-W,M
Now Woods and Wolds Are
Sleeping
Hy-W,M SHP-W,M
Now You Has Jazz
TI1-W,M UFB-W,M
Nowdays
CMV-W,M
Nowell, Sing We
GBC-W,M
Nowhere Man
BBe-W,M Be1-W,M JF-W,M
SwS-W,M TWS-W
Nuit Etoilee
CE-W,M (French)
Nullification--A Song
AL-W
#9 Dream
TI2-W,M

Number 12 Train
AFB-W,M FG1-W,M
Number Twelve Train
FW-W J-W,M
Number Twenty-Nine
ATS-W,M CA-W,M
Numberless As the Sands
GH-W,M
Nun Schlaff Du Liebes Kindelein
AHO-W,M (German)
Nunca Mi Amaron Asi
TI1-W,M (Spanish Only)
UFB-W,M (Spanish Only)
Nur Wer Die Sehnsucht Kennt see One Who Has Yearn'd, Alone
Nurse Pinched the Baby
NeA-W,M
Nursery Rhymes for the Poor
AL-W
Nurse's Song
SR-W,M
Nut Brown Maiden
HSD-W,M NAS-W,M WiS8-W,M
Nutcracker Suite March
TI1-M UFB-M
Nutcracker Suite March see also March (Nutcracker Suite)
Nuts in May
CSG-W,M
Nuttin' for Christmas
BCS-W,M TI1-W,M UFB-W,M
Nutting
FSA1-W,M
Nymphs and Shepherds
OH-W,M

O

007
RW-M
O.P.A. Ditty
NeA-W,M
O... see also Oh...
O (Oh)
HLS3-W,M
O Adam
BSC-W
O Adam, Where Are You
NSS-W
O A-Hunting We Will Go
SCL-W,M
O, Ale Ab Alendo
Boo-W,M
O Ask of the Stars above You
(Preguntale A Las Estrellas)
MSS-W,M (Spanish)
O Babe
NH-W
O Bambino
OnT6-W,M
O Be Joyful in the Lord
Hy-W,M
O Beautiful for Spacious Skies
AME-W,M FH-W,M Hy-W,M
O Beautiful for Spacious Skies see also America the Beautiful
O Beautiful My Country
AHO-W,M
O Bienheureuse Nuit
CCH-W,M
O Black and Unknown Bards
NSS-W
O Bless the Lord
On-W,M
O Bless the Lord, My Soul
G-W,M OTO-W UBF-W,M

O Blessed Word
GH-W,M
O Blest Estate, Blest from Above
AHO-W,M
O Blowden, My True Love
WiS8-W,M
O Bone Jesu
LMR-W,M (Latin Only)
O Bread of Life for All Men Broken
Hy-W,M
O Brother, Life's Journey
GH-W,M
O Brother Man, Fold to Thy Heart
Thy Brother
Hy-W,M
O Brothers Lift Your Voices
Hy-W,M
O Can Ye Sew Cushions?
F1-W,M
O Can Ye Sew Cushions? see also Can You Sew Cushions?
O Canaan, Sweet Canaan
NSS-W
O Canada
FW-W (French)
O Capital to Thee We Pledge
Devotion
CoS-W,M
O Captain, My Captain
GC-W,M
O Cease, My Wand'ring Soul
GH-W,M
O Chester
Bo-W
O Child of God
GH-W,M
O Child of Lowly Manger Birth
AHO-W,M AME-W,M
O Children, Would You Cherish
AHO-W,M (German)
O Christ of Bethlehem
AHO-W,M
O Christmas Babe
CCM-W,M
O Christmas Night
AHO-W,M (Dutch)
O Christmas Pine
NAS-W,M
O Christmas Tree
BCh-W,M BCS-W,M CI-W,M
CSF-W GBC-W,M HS-W,M
(German) MC-W,M MF-W,M
OAP-W,M OPS-W,M OTJ-W,M
RW-W,M SAC-W,M SCS-W
TI1-W,M UFB-W,M Y-W,M
O Christmas Tree see also O Tannenbaum, Oh Tannenbaum, and Tannenbaum
O Coaly Coaly Dear
FSF-W (French)
O Columbia the Gem
ESB-W,M
O Columbia, We Love Thee
GrM-W,M
O Come All Ye Children
GSB-W,M
O Come All Ye Faithful
AmH-W,M BCh-W,M BCS-W,M
Bo-W CC-W,M CCH-W,M
CCM-W,M CEM-W,M CI-W,M
CSF-W,M CSo-W,M DC-W,M
ESB-W,M FW-W FWS-W,M
GeS-W,M HS-W,M (Latin)
Hy-W,M IH-M JOC-W,M
LoS-W,M MAB1-W MAS-W,M
MC-W,M MF-W,M MML-W,M
(Latin) MSA1-W OAP-W,M

OGR-W,M OTJ-W,M PoG-W,M
(Latin) RW-W,M SCS-W SHP-W,M
SJ-W,M SMa-W,M SOO-W,M
TB-W,M TH-W,M TI1-W,M U-W
UF-W,M UFB-W,M VB-W,M
WiS7-W,M YC-W,M
O Come All Ye Faithful see also Adeste Fideles and Come All Ye Faithful
O Come and Mourn with Me
Awhile
AME-W,M Hy-W,M SJ-W,M
O Come and Sing unto the Lord
Hy-W,M
O Come, Beloved
JS-W,M (Hebrew Only)
O Come, Come Away
HSD-W,M SHS-W,M
O Come Emmanuel
JF-W,M
O Come, Let Us Sing
SHP-W,M
O Come, Let Us Sing unto the Lord
Hy-W,M
O Come, Little Children
ASB2-W,M CC-W,M CSF-W
HS-W,M SHP-W,M SiR-W,M
O Come, Little Children see also Come, Little Children
O Come My Brethren and Sisters
Too
NSS-W
O Come My People to My Law
Hy-W,M
O Come, O Come, Emmanuel
AJ-W BCh-W,M BMC-W,M
CSF-W ESB-W,M GUM2-W,M
HS-W,M Hy-W,M MC-W,M
MG-W,M (Latin) OAP-W,M
SHP-W,M SJ-W,M TF-W,M
Y-W,M YC-W,M
O Come, O Come, My Dearest
EL-W,M
O Come, Poor Folk and Lowly
CSB-W,M GeS-W,M
O Come, Sinner, Come There's
Room for Thee
AME-W,M
O Come, Sweet Music
Boo-W,M
O Come to the Merciful
GH-W,M
O Come to the Savior
GH-W,M
O Come unto Me
TH-W,M
O Come with Joy and Worship
God
SHP-W,M
O Come with Me
GM-W,M
O Could I Find from Day to Day
AHO-W,M
O Could I Speak the Matchless
Worth
AME-W,M Hy-W,M
O Crown of Rejoicing
GH-W,M
O Cuba (Tu)
MSS-W,M (Spanish)
O Cuba see also Tu
O Dad o' Mine
Bo-W
O Dad, Poor Dad
OTJ-W,M
O Dad, Poor Dad see also Oh Dad, Poor Dad

O Daniel
WN-W,M
**O Daniel see also You Call
Yourself Church-Member**
O Day of God
JS-W,M (Hebrew)
O Day of God, Draw Nigh
AHO-W,M
O Day of Light and Gladness
AHO-W,M
O Day of Rest and Gladness
GH-W,M Hy-W,M OM-W,M
O de Lamb Done Been Down Here
an' Died
NSS-W
O de Vinter
NSS-W
O Dearest Lord
Hy-W,M SHP-W,M
O Dieu, S'il Faut Qu'on Te Craigne
CUP-W,M (French Only)
O Divine Redeemer
FiS-W,M (French, Latin)
O Do Not Let the Word Depart
AME-W,M
O Don't You Hear the Heaven Bells
A-Ringing over Me
NSS-W
O Du Frohliche
SHP-W,M
O Du Lieber Augustin
AmH-W,M (German Only)
O Earnest Be
AHO-W,M (German)
O Ev'ry Time I Feel de Spirit
NFS-W,M
**O Ev'ry Time I Feel de Spirit see
also Ev'ry Time I Feel the Spirit**
O Fair New Mexico
Fif-W,M
O Fare You Well, My Brudder
NSS-W
O Fir Tree Tall
SSe-W,M
O Fly With Me
TH-W,M
O for a Closer Walk with God
AME-W,M Hy-W,M OM-W,M
O for a Faith That Will Not Shrink
AME-W,M GH-W RW-W,M
O for a Glance of Heavenly Day
AME-W,M
O for a Heart of Praise My God
AME-W,M
O for a Heart to Praise My God
GH-W Hy-W,M
O for a Shout of Sacred Joy
ER-W,M
O for a Thousand Seraph Tongues
AME-W,M
O for a Thousand Tongues
AG-W,M HHa-W,M OGR-W,M
O for a Thousand Tongues to Sing
AME-W,M Hy-W,M
O for the Happy Hour
AHO-W,M
O Freedom
AH-W,M FW-W JF-W,M
SWF-W,M TO-W,M
O Freedom see also Oh Freedom
O Give Me a Home by the Sea
HSD-W,M
O Give Me a Hut
ATM-W,M
O Give Thanks
Boo-W,M
O Give Thanks to the Lord, for He

Is Good
SHP-W,M
O Glad and Glorious Gospel
GH-W,M
O Gladsome Light, O Grace of God
Hy-W,M
O Glorious Fountain
GH-W,M
O God, above the Drifting Years
AHO-W,M
O God, Accept the Sacred Hour
AHO-W,M
O God, beneath Thy Guiding Hand
AHO-W,M ESB-W,M HS-W,M
Hy-W,M NAS-W,M
O God, Creator of All Things
SHP-W,M
O God, Great Father, Lord and
King
AHO-W,M
O God, I Cried, No Dark Disguise
AHO-W,M
O God in Whom the Flow of Days
AHO-W,M
O God in Whose Great Purpose
AHO-W,M
O God, May the Whole World
Praise Thee
SHP-W,M
O God of Bethel by Whose Hand
Hy-W,M
O God of Earth and Altar
Hy-W,M
O God of Hosts
TH-W,M
O God of Light, Thy Word, a Lamp
Unfailing
Hy-W,M
O God of Love, O King of Peace
ESB-W,M Hy-W,M
O God of My Salvation, Hear
AHO-W,M
O God of Stars and Distant Space
AHO-W,M
O God of Youth
AHO-W,M
O God, Our Help
GH-W,M
O God, Our Help in Ages Past
AME-W,M CA-W,M CEM-W,M
CSo-W,M FH-W,M Hy-W,M
LMR-W,M MML-W,M RS-W,M
SJ-W,M WiS7-W,M
O God, Regard My Humble Plea
Hy-W,M
O God, Send Men
AHO-W,M
O God, the Rock of Ages
AME-W,M Hy-W,M
O God, Thou Art the Father
Hy-W,M
O God, through Countless Worlds
of Light
AHO-W,M
O God, We Give Thanks
SHP-W,M
O God, We Lift Our Hearts to Thee
AME-W,M
O God, Who Art the Only Light
SMY-W,M
O God, Who Workest Hitherto
AME-W,M
O God Whose Presence Glows in
All
AHO-W,M
O God, Whose Smile Is in the Sky
AME-W,M

O Gracious Father of Mankind
AHO-W,M
O Gracious God, Forsake Me Not
Hy-W,M
O Gracious Jesus, Blessed Lord
AHO-W,M
O Grant Us Light, That We May
Know
Hy-W,M
O Graveyard
AAF-W,M
O Had I Jubal's Lyre
FSA2-W,M
O Had I Wings Like to á Dove
MU-W,M
O Hail Mary, Hail
NSS-W
O Hanukkah
HS-W,M MG-W,M
O Happy Day
CEM-W,M JBF-W,M OM-W,M
On-W,M
**O Happy Day see also Oh Happy
Day**
O Happy Day, That Fixed My
Choice
AME-W,M
O Happy Day When We Shall
Stand
SJ-W,M
O Happy Home, Where Thou Art
Loved the Dearest
Hy-W,M
O Happy, O Happy
Boo-W,M
O Healing River
JF-W,M
O Hear My Prayer, Lord
AHO-W,M
O Hearken and I Will Tell You How
SeS-W,M
O Heaven Indulge
AHO-W,M
O Heavenly Jerusalem
ESB-W,M
O Holy Child
GeS-W,M
O Holy City Seen of John
AHO-W,M Hy-W,M
O Holy, Holy, Holy Lord
AHO-W,M
O Holy Night
BCh-W,M BCS-W,M BeB-W,M
Cl-W,M CSB-W,M CSF-W
FWS-W,M MF-W,M OAP-W,M
PoG-W,M RW-W,M TI1-W,M
UFB-W,M
O Holy One
VB-W,M
O Holy Saviour, Friend Unseen
Hy-W,M
O Holy Spirit, Come
GH-W
O How He Loves
GH-W,M
O How I Love Jesus
AME-W,M
O Hush Thee, My Babie
ESB-W,M SMY-W,M TF-W,M
TH-W,M
**O Hush Thee, My Babie see also
Oh Hush Thee, My Baby**
O I Am So Happy
WN-W,M
O I Am So Happy in Jesus
GH-W,M
O I Believe in Jesus

WN-W,M
O I Love Mother
  GB-W,M
O I Love to Talk with Jesus
  GH-W,M
O I Would Live in a Dairy
  SL-W,M
O I'm a Good Old Rebel
  MPP-W OHG-W,M SCo-W,M
  Sin-W,M
O I'm a Good Old Rebel see also
  I'm a Good Old Rebel
O I'm Not Weary Yet see O Me No
  Weary Yet
O Jesu So Meek, O Jesu So Kind
  SJ-W,M
O Jesus at Thy Feet We Wait
  AME-W,M
O Jesus Christ, Our Lord Most
  Dear
  Hy-W,M
O Jesus Christ, True Light of God
  AHO-W,M
O Jesus, Crucified for Man
  AME-W,M
O Jesus, I Have Promised
  AME-W,M Hy-W,M
O Jesus, My Saviour, I Know Thou
  Art Mine
  AHO-W,M
O Jesus So Sweet
  CC-W,M
O Jesus, Thou Art Standing
  AME-W,M AmH-W,M FH-W,M
  Hy-W,M SJ-W,M WiS7-W,M
O Jesus, We Adore Thee
  Hy-W,M
O Johnny's on the Water
  D-W,M
O Kairos Adelphoi
  SiP-W,M (Greek)
O Kersnacht
  AHO-W,M (Dutch)
O King of Saints, We Give Thee
  Praise and Glory
  AHO-W,M
O Lady Moon
  Boo-W,M
O Lady Moon see also Lady Moon
O Lamb of God
  SJ-W,M
O Lamb of God, That Taketh Away
  the Sins of the World
  Hy-W,M
O Land of the Blessed
  GH-W,M
O Lawd, How Long?
  Me-W,M
O Lawd, When I Die
  NSS-W
O Leave Your Sheep
  LMR-W,M
O Let My Supplicating Cry
  Hy-W,M
O Let Us Be Glad Today
  RW-W,M
O Life That Maketh All Things New
  AHO-W,M
O Light Whose Beams Illumine All
  Hy-W,M
O Li'l Liza Jane
  PSD-W,M
O Li'l Liza Jane see also Li'l Liza
  Jane, Little Liza Jane, and Liza
  Jane
O Lillie, O Lillie
  FMT-W

O Listen to the Voice of Love
  EL-W,M
O Little One
  OB-W,M
O Little Rock
  CFS-W,M (French)
O Little Shepherd
  SMa-W,M
O Little Town
  LoS-W,M OB-W,M
O Little Town of Bethlehem
  AHO-W,M AME-W,M BCh-W,M
  BCS-W,M CCH-W,M CCM-W,M
  CEM-W,M CI-W,M CSB-W,M
  CSF-W FH-W,M FW-W GBC-W,M
  HF-W,M HS-W,M Hy-W,M
  IL-W,M MAB1-W MAS-W,M
  MC-W,M MF-W,M MSA1-W
  OAP-W,M OPS-W,M OTJ-W,M
  PoG-W,M RW-W,M SCS-W
  SiR-W,M SL-W,M TB-W,M
  TI1-W,M UFB-W,M YC-W,M
O Lord, Almighty God
  AHO-W,M
O Lord, Be Merciful
  FiS-W,M
O Lord, Bow Down Thine Ear
  AHO-W,M
O Lord, by Thee Delivered
  Hy-W,M
O Lord! Correct Me
  TH-W,M
O Lord God
  SoM-W,M
O Lord, How Long? see O Lawd,
  How Long?
O Lord, How Lovely Is the Place
  AHO-W,M
O Lord in Thee Is All My Trust
  Boo-W,M
O Lord, Make Haste to Hear My
  Cry
  Hy-W,M
O Lord Most High, with All My
  Heart
  Hy-W,M
O Lord Most Holy
  SL-W,M SS-W
O Lord, My God, Most Earnestly
  Hy-W,M
O Lord, My God, Thou Art So
  Great
  SHP-W,M
O Lord, My Inmost Heart and
  Thought
  Hy-W,M
O Lord of Beauty
  BeB-W,M
O Lord of Heaven and Earth and
  Sea
  SJ-W,M
O Lord of Life
  AHO-W,M
O Lord of Life, to Thee We Lift
  Hy-W,M
O Lord on High
  FiS-W,M
O Lord on Whom I Do Depend
  Boo-W,M
O Lord, Open Thou Our Eyes
  Hy-W,M
O Lord Our God, Thy Mighty Hand
  AHO-W,M
O Lord, Our Lord, in All the Earth
  Hy-W,M
O Lord, That Art My God and King
  AHO-W,M

O Lord, Thou Art My God and King
  Hy-W,M
O Lord, Thou Hast Been to the
  Land
  AHO-W,M
O Lord, Turn Not Away Thy Face
  AHO-W,M
O Lord, When I Die see O Lawd,
  When I Die
O Love Divine and Golden
  Hy-W,M
O Love Divine, O Matchless Grace
  AME-W,M
O Love Divine, That Stooped to
  Share
  AHO-W,M FH-W,M Hy-W,M
O Love How Deep, How Broad,
  How High
  CEM-W,M
O Love of God Most Full
  Hy-W,M
O Love That Lights the Eastern
  Sky
  AHO-W,M
O Love That Wilt Not Let Me Go
  AME-W,M Hy-W,M TB-W,M
O, Lovely, Budding Rose-Tree
  FSO-W,M (French)
O Lovely May
  SiM-W,M (German)
O Loving Father
  VA-W,M (Latin)
O Loving Heart, Trust On
  HSD-W,M
O Ma Tendre Musette
  AS-W,M (French)
O Madam, I Have a Fine Little
  Horse
  FMT-W
O Magnify the Lord
  GP-W,M OGR-W,M VB-W,M
O Mary, Don't You Weep
  AHO-W,M AN-W FW-W
  MML-W,M OHO-W,M
O Mary, Don't You Weep see also
  Mary Doncha (Don't You) Weep
O Mary, What You Weepin'
  About?
  Me-W,M
O Mary Where Is Yo' Baby?
  Me-W,M
O Master, Let Me Walk with Thee
  AHO-W,M AME-W,M CEM-W,M
  Hy-W,M TB-W,M
O Master Workman of the Race
  AHO-W,M Hy-W,M
O Me No Weary Yet
  NSS-W
O Member Will You Linger
  NSS-W
O Mistress Mine
  EL-W,M FSS-W,M OH-W,M
  SSB-W,M SSP-W
O Molly Dear
  ITP-W,M
O Morning Land
  GH-W,M
O Morning Star, How Fair and
  Bright
  Hy-W,M
O Mother Dear, Jerusalem
  ESB-W,M
O Mother I Believe
  NSS-W
O Mourner, Let's Go Down
  NSS-W
O Music

HSD-W,M
O Mu'sieu Banjo
  CSD-W,M (French)
O Mu'sieu Banjo see also Michie Banjo, Mister Banjo, Monsieur Banjo, M'sieu Bainjo, Musieu Bainjo and Oh Mister Banjo
O My Babe, Won't You Come Home?
  NH-W
O My Body Rock 'Long Fever
  NSS-W
O My Body's Racked with de Fever
  NSS-W
O My Child
  FHR-W,M
O My Darling, O My Pet
  MGT-W,M
O My Fearful Dreams
  Boo-W,M
O My King Emanuel, My Emanuel Above
  NSS-W
O My Lord, What Shall I Do?
  MoM-W,M
O My Sister Light de Lamp, and de Lamp Light de Road
  NSS-W
O My Soul, Bless God the Father
  SHP-W,M
O My Soul, Bless Thou Jehovah
  GH-W
O No, John
  BeB-W,M FSA1-W,M IL-W,M
  MML-W,M NAS-W,M TF-W,M
O No, John see also No John and Oh, No John, No
O No Man, No Man, No Man Can Hinder Me
  NSS-W
O No, No! Not I!
  ESU-W
O Paradise! (O Paradise! Who Doth Not Crave for Rest?)
  AmH-W,M HSD-W,M WiS7-W,M
O Paradise! (Sweet Paradise, from Scenes of Earth We Long to Rise)
  GH-W,M
O Perfect Love
  FS-W,M HLS1-W,M JBF-W,M
  NCB-W,M OBN-W,M OM-W,M
  TM-W,M WGB/O-W,M
  WGB/P-W,M
O Perfect Love, All Human Thought Transcending
  Hy-W,M
O Peter, Go Ring Them Bells
  BeB-W,M
O Peter Go Ring-a Dem Bells
  ETB-W,M GC-W,M
O Peter, Go Ring-a Dem Bells see also Peter, Go Ring Dem Bells
O Polly Dear
  FMT-W
O Praise Him
  GH-W,M
O Praise the Lord
  SiM-W,M
O Praise the Lord All Ye Nations
  MU-W,M (Latin)
O Praise the Lord Our Master
  SL-W,M
O Precious Word
  GH-W,M TM-W,M
O Render Thanks
  Boo-W,M
O Rest in the Lord

AmH-W,M BMC-W,M ESB-W,M
FiS-W,M FSY-W,M MML-W,M
SL-W,M TF-W,M TH-W,M
WiS7-W,M
O Revive Us by Thy Word
  GH-W,M
O Ride On, Jesus
  AHO-W,M NFS-W,M
O Ride On, Jesus see also Ride On, Jesus
O Risen Lord upon the Throne
  AHO-W,M
O Rock of Ages
  GH-W,M
O Rock-a My Soul
  WN-W,M
O Rock-a My Soul see also Rock o' My Soul in de Bosom of Abraham, Rocka My Soul, and Rock-er Ma Soul
O Ruddier Than the Cherry
  LMR-W,M
O Run, Mary, Run
  NSS-W
O Run, Mary, Run see also Run, Mary, Run
O Sacred Head
  WiS9-W,M
O Sacred Head Now Wounded
  AME-W,M CEM-W,M Hy-W,M
  OM-W,M
O Sanctissima
  BCh-W,M
O San-nisk-a-na
  GB-W,M
O Savior Sweet
  ASB6-W,M MHB-W,M (German)
O Saviour, Hear Me
  FiS-W,M
O Saviour of a World Undone
  AHO-W,M
O Saviour, Precious Saviour
  GH-W,M
O Say Can You See through Fierce Faction's Dark Night
  ESU-W
O Say Not Woman's Love Is Bought
  ESU-W
O, Search Ye Well the Lists, Mother
  SiS-W
O Seid Im Arnscht
  AHO-W,M (German)
O Shenandoah
  UF-W,M
O Shenandoah see also Shenandoah and Wide Missouri
O Shout, O Shout, O Shout Away
  NSS-W
O Silent Stars
  SOT-W,M
O Sin I So?
  OU-W,M
O Sing a New Song to the Lord
  Hy-W,M
O Sing a Song of Bethlehem
  Hy-W,M
O Sing of His Mighty Love
  GH-W,M
O Sing to Me of Heaven
  AHO-W,M
O Sinner, Now Is de Time for to Pray
  MoM-W,M
O Sion, Haste, Thy Mission High Fulfilling

AHO-W,M
O Sion, Haste, thy Mission High Fulfilling see also O Zion Haste, Thy Mission High Fulfilling
O Soldier, Soldier
  MML-W,M
O Soldier, Soldier see also Soldier, Soldier
O Sole Mio
  AmH-W,M FSY-W,M (Italian)
  HLS1-W,M (Italian) MF-W,M
  (Italian Only) NAS-W,M OP2-M
  OTJ-W,M RW-W,M (Italian Only)
  TH-W,M TI1-M UFB-M WiS8-W,M
O Sole Mio see also My Sunshine
O Some Tell Me That a Nigger Won't Steal
  NSS-W
O Son of Man, Our Hero Strong and Tender
  Hy-W,M
O Son of Man, Thou Madest Known
  AHO-W,M AME-W,M
O Sons and Daughters, Let Us Sing
  Hy-W,M SJ-W,M
O Speed Thee, Christian, on Thy Way
  AME-W,M
O Spirit of the Living God
  AME-W,M Hy-W,M
O Spirit Sweet of Summer-Time
  SMa-W,M
O Splendor of God's Glory Bright
  Hy-W,M
O Spread the Tidings Round
  AME-W,M
O Star Divine
  SL-W,M
O Stay in the Field
  WN-W,M
O Stay in the Field see also Stay in de Field
O Susanna see Oh! Susanna
O Susanna! (I Was Born along Old Sweden's Coast)
  SE-W,M (Swedish)
O Susanna! (Jag Ar Fodd Vid Gamla Sveriges Kust)
  SE-W,M (Swedish)
O Swallow Swift
  LMR-W,M
O Swallow Swift see also La Golondrina
O, Sweden
  SE-W (Swedish)
O Sweet Simplicity
  Boo-W,M
O, Swerge!
  SE-W (Swedish)
O Take Me Back to Switzerland
  NAS-W,M
O Tannenbaum
  GuC-W,M (German) HS-W,M
  (German) NAS-W,M TI1-W,M
O Tannenbaum see also O Christmas Tree, Oh Tannenbaum, and Tannenbaum
O Tell Me Have You Met My Love?
  SOT-W,M
O Tempora! O Mores
  ESB-W,M FSA1-W,M LMR-W,M
O Tender Moon
  TH-W,M
O That I Knew the Secret Place
  AME-W,M

O the Crown, the Glory
  GH-W,M
O the Great Joy That I Find in His
  Service
  AME-W,M
O the Lamb see O de Lamb
O the Sad Day
  OH-W,M
O the Simple Gifts of God
  GB-W,M
O the Wily, Wily Fox with His
  Many Wily Mocks
  Boo-W,M
O They Tell Me of a Home
  AME-W,M
O Think of the Home Over There
  AME-W,M
O Thou, in All Thy Might So Far
  Hy-W,M
O Thou, in Whose Presence
  AME-W,M
O Thou Joyful Day
  WiS7-W,M
O Thou Joyous Day
  SHP-W,M
O Thou Most High Who Rulest All
  AHO-W,M
O Thou, My Savior, Brother, Friend
  AME-W,M
O Thou My Soul, Bless God the
  Lord
  Hy-W,M
O Thou Who Didst Ordain the
  World
  AHO-W,M
O Thou Who Hearest Every
  Heartfelt Prayer
  Hy-W,M
O Thou Who Makest Souls to
  Shine
  Hy-W,M
O Thou Whose Feet
  TF-W,M
O Thou Whose Feet Have Climbed
  Life's Hill
  AHO-W,M Hy-W,M SJ-W,M
O Thou Whose Gracious Presence
  Shone
  AHO-W,M
O Thou Whose Own Vast Temple
  Stands
  AHO-W,M
O Thou Whose Presence Went
  Before
  AHO-W,M
O Tixo, Tixo Help Me
  LS-W,M
O to Be Nothing
  GH-W,M
O to Be Over Yonder
  GH-W,M
O, Touch Not My Sister's Picture
  SiS-W
O Trinity of Blessed Light
  Hy-W,M
O Turn Thee
  TF-W,M
O Turn Ye, O Turn Ye
  AHO-W,M
O Victorious People
  SL-W,M
O Vinter'll Soon Be Ober
  NSS-W
O Vinter'll Soon Be Ober see also
  Winter'll Soon Be Ober
O Vos Omnes
  SiM-W,M (Latin)

O Walk Jordan Long Road
  NSS-W
O Waly, Waly
  F3-W,M Gu-W,M RW-W,M
O Wasn't That a Mighty Day
  MoM-W
O Weary Feet
  HSD-W,M
O Wert Thou in the Cauld Blast
  SMY-W,M TF-W,M
O Wert Thou in the Cauld Blast see
  also Oh Wert Thou in the Cauld
  Blast
O Western Wind
  LMR-W,M SL-W,M
O Western Wind see also Westron
  Wynde
O What a Saviour
  GH-W,M
O What Amazing Words of Grace
  AME-W,M
O What Their Joy and Their Glory
  Must Be
  Hy-W,M
O Where Are Kings and Empires
  Now
  Hy-W,M SJ-W,M
O Where Are the Reapers
  GH-W,M
O Where Shall Rest Be Found?
  AME-W,M Boo-W,M
O Who Will o'er the Downs
  ESB-W,M
O Who Will o'er the Downs see
  also Who Will o'er the Downs?
O Why Not Tonight?
  AME-W,M
O Why Not Tonight? see also Why
  Not Tonight?
O Will You Meet Us at the Stile?
  SOT-W,M
O Willow, Willow
  TH-W,M
O Winter Will Soon Be Over see O
  Vinter'll Soon Be Ober
O Wonderful Word
  GH-W,M
O Wondrous Land
  GH-W,M
O Wondrous Name
  GH-W,M
O Wondrous Type, O Vision Fair
  Hy-W,M
O Word of God Incarnate
  AME-W,M Hy-W,M
O Worship the King
  AME-W,M Bo-W GeS-W,M
  GH-W,M Hy-W,M OS-W
  RDF-W,M RW-W,M SBJ-W,M
O Worship the King see also Oh,
  Worship the King
O Ye Dwellers of the Earth
  JS-W,M
O Ye Heavens
  CCM-W,M
O Ye Tears
  HSD-W,M
O! Yes, O! Yes, O! Yes
  Boo-W,M
O Yonder's My Ole Mother
  NSS-W
O Young and Fearless Prophet
  AHO-W,M
O Young Gal Go round da Ring
  SGT-W,M
O Zion, Best City
  ESB-W,M

O Zion Haste, Thy Mission High
  Fulfilling
  AME-W,M Hy-W,M
O Zion Haste, Thy Mission High
  Fulfilling see also O Sion, Haste,
  Thy Mission High Fulfilling
O Zion That Bringest Good Tidings
  CCH-W,M
Oak and the Ash
  FW-W OH-W,M SoF-W,M
Oak and the Ash see also Oh the
  Oak and the Ash
Oak from a Small Acorn
  Boo-W,M
Oak Trees
  MH-W,M
Oaken Leaves
  Boo-W,M
Oakie Boogie
  OGC2-W,M
Oath of Freedom
  AWB-W
Oats and Beans and Barley Grow
  SiR-W,M
Oats, Peas, Beans
  GM-W,M HS-W,M
Oats, Peas, Beans, and Barley
  BBF-W,M CSG-W,M
Oats, Peas, Beans and Barley
  Grow
  BM-W GUM1-W,M OTJ-W,M
Ob Ich Deiner Schon Vergiss
  AHO-W,M (German)
Ob-La-Di, Ob-La-Da
  BBe-W,M Be2-W,M TWS-W
  WG-W,M
Object of My Affection
  TI1-W,M UFB-W,M
Obstination (Resolve)
  FSY-W,M (French) WiS8-W,M
Obstruction
  VP-W
Ocean
  SHS-W,M
Ocean Burial
  PoS-W,M
Ocean-Fight
  ANS-W
Ocean Is Wide
  Oz3-W
Oceans of Love
  Mo-W,M NM-W,M
Och, Och, Mar Tha Mi
  SeS-W,M
O'Connell's Dead
  VP-W
O'Connell's New Song on
  Emancipation
  VP-W
October and November
  SSe-W,M
October in Oxnard
  WF-W,M
October Music
  FSA2-W,M
Octopus's Garden
  BBe-W,M TWS-W
Odd Couple
  AT-M
Odd Fellows Hall
  NH-W
Odder Side of Jordan
  SNS-W
Odder Side of Jordan see also
  Other Side of Jordan
Ode for American Independence
  EA-W,M SAR-W,M

Ode for General Hamilton's Funeral
MPP-W,M
Ode for the Fourth of July
AL-W ESU-W SAR-W,M
Ode on Science
SHS-W,M
Ode to America
VA-W,M
Ode to Billy Joe
CMG-W,M PoG-W,M WG-W,M
Ode to Columbia's Favourite Son
MPP-W,M
Ode to Freud
TW-W
Ode to Joy
CA-W,M JBF-W,M MF-M On-W,M
OPS-W,M OTJ-W,M PoG-M
SBF-W,M WGB/O-W,M WGB/P-
W,M
Ode to New Jersey
Fif-W,M
Ode to St. Crispin
AL-W
Ode Triumphant
MML-W,M
Odes for Locals
AL-W
O'Donnel Abu
IS-W,M
O'Donnell Aboo
FW-W
O'Donovan Rossa's Farewell to
Dublin
VP-W,M
Odorono
WA-W,M
O'er Continent and Ocean
AHO-W,M
O'er Coolin's Face the Night Is
Creeping
SeS-W,M
O'er the Crossing
AAF-W,M
O'er the Hills Away
FSA2-W,M
O'er the Horizon
ASB6-W,M
O'er the Season Vernal
GiS-W,M
O'er Waiting Harp-Strings of the
Mind
AHO-W,M
Of Alfred the Great
Boo-W,M
Of All the Beast-es
AFS-W,M
Of All the Birds
OH-W,M SSP-W
Of All the Brave Birds
MML-W,M
Of All the Causes
ESU-W
Of All the Instruments
Boo-W,M
Of All the Torments
EL-W,M
Of All the Young Ladies I Know
GiS-W,M MGT-W,M
Of Jesus' Love That Sought Me
AME-W,M
Of Merrie England I'll Tell a Tale
BMM-W
Of the Father's Love Begotten
Hy-W,M SJ-W,M
Of Thee I Sing
GOB-W,M LSO-W MF-W,M
NYT-W,M OHB-W,M OT-W,M

Off from Richmond
NF-W
Off She Goes
TBF-M
Off Shore
TI1-W,M UFB-W,M
Off the Hook
RoS-W,M
Off the Record
TS-W
Off to Bed, Now
OTJ-W,M
Off to the Sea
SSe-W,M
Off to the Woods
SiR-W,M
Offertory Song
SoP-W,M
**Officer and a Gentleman (Theme)
see Up Where We Belong**
Officer's Funeral
SiS-W
Officers of Dixie
SiS-W
Offset for the Chesapeake
ANS-W
Offshore see Off Shore
Oft in the Stilly Night
ATS-W,M HSD-W,M
Oginga Odinga
SFF-W,M
Oh... see also O...
Oh, a Private Buffoon
MGT-W,M
Oh, Absalom, My Son
Boo-W,M FW-W
Oh Argentine
ST-W,M
Oh, Babe, It Ain't No Lie
FW-W
Oh, Babe, What Would You Say?
TI1-W,M UFB-W,M
Oh Baby
DDH-W,M WDS-W,M
Oh, Baby Doll
HR-W
Oh Baby Mine (I Get So Lonely)
Mo-W,M NM-W,M TI2-W,M
Oh Bess, Oh Where's My Bess
OTO-W
Oh Better Far to Live and Die
GiS-W,M MGT-W,M
Oh, Blue
AFS-W,M
Oh Boy!
TI2-W,M
Oh! Boys, Carry Me 'Long
AmH-W,M ATS-W CA-W,M
FHR-W,M MF-M SSF-W,M SSFo-W,M
WiS8-W,M
Oh, Bring My Brother Back to Me
SiS-W
Oh, Brother, Did You Weep
IFM-W
Oh, Brother Will You Meet Me?
BMM-W
Oh Brothers, Don't Get Weary
AFP-W NSS-W
Oh Buddha
VB-W,M
Oh Bury Me Not
BSC-W NAS-W,M
Oh Bury Me Not on the Lone
Prairie
AmS-W,M ATS-W,M FAW-W,M
FMT-W HWS-W,M OFS-W,M
Oz2-W,M RW-W,M

Oh Bury Me Not on the Lone
Prairie see also Dying Cowboy
(Oh Bury Me Not on the Lone
Prairie)
Oh Calcutta
RW-W,M
Oh California
SoC-W
Oh Captain, Captain, Tell Me True
SCa-W,M
Oh! Carol
MF-W,M
Oh, Charlie Is My Darling
SeS-W,M
**Oh, Charlie Is My Darling see also
Charlie Is My Darling**
Oh, Cherish Love
SL-W,M
Oh Come Along John
DE-W,M
Oh Come and Go Back My Pretty
Fair Miss
SCa-W
Oh, Come You from the
Battlefield?
SiS-W
Oh Coony, Coony Clay
MPP-W
Oh Dad, Poor Dad
OnT1-W,M
**Oh Dad, Poor Dad see also O Dad,
Poor Dad**
Oh Dan Tucker
DE-W,M
**Oh Dan Tucker see also
Ol'/Old/Ole Dan Tucker**
Oh! Darling
BBe-W,M Be2-W,M TWS-W
Oh Day of Days
AHO-W,M
Oh, de Downward Road Is
Crowded
RF-W,M
**Oh, de Downward Road Is
Crowded see also Downward
Road Is Crowded**
Oh de Hebben Is Shinin'
RF-W,M
**Oh de Hebben Is Shinin' see also
Hebben Is A-Shinin'**
Oh, de Red Sea
ATS-W
Oh Dear!
MAR-W,M
Oh Dear What Can the Matter Be?
CSo-W,M DD-W,M EA-W,M EFS-
W,M FBI-W,M FW-W HS-W,M
HSD-W,M MF-W,M NAS-W,M
OFS-W,M OS-W OTJ-W,M RW-
W,M SMY-W,M TF-W,M TH-W,M
**Oh Dear What Can the Matter Be?
see also Johnny's So Long at the
Fair**
Oh Deat' He Is a Little Man
NSS-W
Oh Death
BMM-W,M
Oh Dem Golden Slippers
AH-W,M AmH-W,M ATS-W
BH-W,M HAS-W,M OS-W
PoS-W,M WiS8-W,M
**Oh Dem Golden Slippers see also
Oh Them Golden Slippers and
Them Golden Slippers**
Oh Didn't It Rain
OU-W,M
Oh Didn't It Rain see also Didn't It

Rain?
Oh Doctor, My Period see Herr Doktor, Die Periode
Oh! Don't You Remember Sweet Alice
  HSD-W,M
Oh! Ever against Eating Cares
  Boo-W,M
Oh Fabulous One
  LD-W,M
Oh, Fairest Maid
  Boo-W,M
Oh, Foolish Fay
  MGT-W,M
Oh, Fred, Tell Them to Stop
  ATS-W
Oh Freedom
  RF-W,M SFF-W,M
Oh Freedom see also O Freedom
Oh Gee! Oh Joy!
  ReG-W,M
Oh, Gentlemen, Listen
  MGT-W,M
Oh, Gentlemen, Listen I Pray
  GiS-W,M
Oh Girl
  SoH-W,M
Oh! Give Thanks
  SL-W,M
Oh, Give Us a Navy of Iron
  SiS-W
Oh, Give Us Pleasure in the Flowers Today
  AHO-W,M
Oh, Give Way, Jordan
  RF-W,M
Oh, Happy Christmas Morning
  GM-W,M
Oh Happy Day
  AO-W,M BNG-W,M GrH-W,M
  GS1-W HLS7-W,M MCG-W,M
  OPS-W,M RDF-W,M RW-W,M
  WiS7-W,M
Oh Happy Day see also Happy Day and O Happy Day
Oh, He Raise-a Poor Lazarus
  RF-W,M
Oh, He Raise-a Poor Lazarus see also He Raise-a Poor Lazarus
Oh Heart
  EC-W,M
Oh, Heaven Is Shining see Oh, de Hebben Is Shinin'
Oh, Here Is Miss Pussy
  MH-W,M
Oh, How Beautiful the Sky
  CCM-W,M
Oh, How He Lied
  FW-W,M IL-W,M
Oh, How He Loves You and Me
  VB-W,M
Oh How, How Oh
  ATS-W
Oh! How I Hate to Get Up in the Morning
  Bo-W
Oh, How I Love Him
  HHa-W,M
Oh, How I Miss You Tonight
  OPS-W,M TI2-W,M
Oh How Joyfully
  CSF-W
Oh, How Lovely Is the Evening
  Boo-W FW-W IL-W,M
  OHO-W,M OTJ-W,M RW-W,M
  SiB-W,M
Oh, Hush Thee, My Baby

HSD-W,M
Oh, Hush Thee, My Baby see also O Hush Thee, My Babie
Oh, I Am a Merry Sailor Lad
  ANS-W
Oh, I Know the Lord Laid His Hands on Me
  OTJ-W,M
Oh, I Know the Lord Laid His Hands on Me see also I Know the Lord's Laid His Hands on Me
Oh, I Never Shall Forget the Day
  BSG-W,M BSP-W,M
Oh I Shall Wear a Uniform
  SiS-W
Oh! I Should Like to Marry
  SY-W,M TMA-W,M
Oh, I Wish the War Were Over
  SiS-W
Oh, I'd Be a Soger Boy
  SiS-W
Oh I'm Gwine to Alabamy
  NSS-W
Oh I'm Gwine to Alabamy see also I'm Gwine to Alabamy
Oh, I'm So Glad It's Snowing
  KS-W,M
Oh, Is There Not One Maiden Breast
  MGT-W,M
Oh, Italia Beloved
  TF-W,M
Oh Jeff, Oh Jeff, How Are You Now?
  SiS-W
Oh, Jerusalem
  RF-W,M
Oh, John the Rabbit
  SCL-W,M SHP-W,M
Oh, John the Rabbit see also John the Rabbit
Oh, Johnny, Oh
  MF-W,M TI1-W,M UFB-W,M
Oh Johnny, Oh Johnny Oh
  FPS-W,M
Oh Julie
  FRH-W,M
Oh, Kay
  GOB-W,M
Oh Ladies All
  DE-W,M
Oh, Lady Be Good
  DC-W,M GOB-W,M HC2-W,M
  LSO-W MF-W,M NYT-W,M
  OHB-W,M RoE-W,M
Oh Leave Your Sheep Good Shepherds
  FSD-W,M
Oh! Lemuel
  CA-W,M FHR-W,M SSFo-W,M
Oh, Let Me Shed One Silent Tear
  SiS-W
Oh, Let the Girls Sit Down
  AL-W
Oh Lily, Dear Lily
  Oz4-W,M
Oh, Little Chillun
  RTH-W
Oh! Look at Me Now
  MF-W,M TI1-W,M UFB-W,M
Oh, Lord, Chastise Me Not
  Boo-W,M
Oh Lord Have Mercy on Me
  BDW-W,M
Oh Lord, How Long
  Oz4-W,M
Oh Lord, I Want Some Valiant

Soldier
  NSS-W
Oh Lord, Send Us a Blessing
  Oz4-W
Oh Lord, the Sun Is Shinin'
  LC-W
Oh Lord You're Beautiful
  VB-W,M
Oh, Love Will Venture In
  SeS-W,M
Oh, Mah Lindy
  BSB-W,M
Oh, Marie
  RW-W,M TI1-W,M UFB-W,M
Oh Marie Di Jolie
  CaF-W (French Only)
Oh, Massa's Gone to Washington
  SiS-W
Oh, Meadowland
  CA-W,M
Oh! Meet Me, Dear Mother
  FHR-W,M
Oh Mein Papa see Oh! My Pa-Pa
Oh, Mirk, Mirk Is the Midnight Hour
  SeS-W,M
Oh Mister Banjo
  CSD-W,M (French)
Oh Mister Banjo see also Michie Banjo, Mister Banjo, Monsieur Banjo, M'sieu Bainjo, Musieu Bainjo, and O Mu'sieu Banjo
Oh Mother, Take the Wheel Away
  Oz4-W
Oh Music, Sweet Music
  Boo-W,M
Oh, My Aunt Came Back
  RSL-W,M
Oh, My Darling Clementine
  AmH-W,M BH-W,M FM-W,M
  FU-W,M FuB-W,M IPH-W,M
  MF-W,M OS-W PoS-W,M
  WiS8-W,M
Oh, My Darling Clementine see also Clementine and My Darling Clementine
Oh My God Them Taters
  AFP-W,M
Oh, My Lindy see Oh, Mah Lindy
Oh, My Little Darling
  RW-W,M
Oh, My Love
  Boo-W,M
Oh, My Love Is Like a Red, Red Rose
  SeS-W,M
Oh, My Love Is Like a Red, Red Rose see also My Love Is Like a Red, Red Rose
Oh, My Luve's Like a Red, Red Rose
  TF-W,M
Oh, My Old Man Has Gone to the War
  SiS-W
Oh! My Pa-pa
  TI1-W,M
Oh! My Papa
  MF-W,M
Oh, My Sweetheart
  RuS-W,M (Russian)
Oh Name Him Not
  ESU-W
Oh, No! I'll Never Mention Him
  ESU-W
Oh, No John, No
  Gu-W,M

Oh, No John, No see also No John
  and O No, John
Oh-Oh I'm Falling in Love Again
  MF-W,M
Oh! Oh! Oh! It's a Lovely War
  GI-W GO-W
Oh! Oh! Where Shall I Fly To
  MPP-W
Oh, Once I Had a Fortune
  Oz2-W,M
Oh One Day As Anoder
  NSS-W
Oh, People
  TTH-W,M
Oh, Polly
  SCa-W,M
Oh, Praise the Lord, Ye That Fear
  Him
  Boo-W,M
Oh, Pretty Woman
  GSN4-W,M TFC-W,M
Oh, Pretty Woman see also Pretty
  Woman
Oh Pritchett, Oh Kelly
  SFF-W,M
Oh Promise Me
  FS-W,M FSN-W,M FSTS-W,M
  HLS1-W,M JBF-W,M LMR-W,M
  MF-W,M MuM-W,M NCB-W,M
  TM-W,M WGB/O-W,M
  WGB/P-W,M
Oh, Religion Is a Fortune
  RF-W,M
Oh! Rock Me! Julie
  AAF-W,M
Oh! Roll Your Leg Over
  GI-W
Oh, Sainte Catarina
  CaF-W (French Only)
Oh Santisimo
  SHP-W,M
Oh, Send Me One Flower from His
  Grave
  SiS-W
Oh, Send My Old Man Home Again
  SiS-W
Oh, Sing to God
  AHO-W,M (Dutch)
Oh, Sinner Man
  BF-W,M SBF-W,M
Oh, Sinner Man see also Sinner
  Man
Oh, Sinner, You'd Better Get
  Ready
  RF-W,M
Oh, So Nice
  ReG-W,M
Oh, Sometimes the Shadows Are
  Deep
  AME-W,M
Oh, Stand the Storm
  RF-W,M
Oh, Stand the Storm see also
  Stand the Storm
Oh! Susanna
  AH-W,M ASB4-W,M ATS-W
  BF-W,M BH-W,M BMC-W,M
  Bo-W FGM-W,M FHR-W,M
  FSB1-W,M FU-W,M FuB-W,M
  FW-W GuC-W,M HAS-W,M
  HS-W,M HSD-W,M KS-W,M
  LH-W,M LoS-W,M MAB1-W
  MAS-W,M MSA1-W NAS-W,M
  OH-W,M OS-W OTJ-W,M
  PaS-W,M PoS-W,M RW-W,M
  SMa-W,M SoC-W SoF-W,M
  SSF-W,M SSFo-W,M STR-W,M

VA-W,M WiS8-W,M
Oh Susannah
  MF-W,M
Oh Suzanna
  AN-W
Oh Take Me Home to Die
  SiS-W
Oh Tannenbaum
  FW-W (German)
Oh Tannenbaum see also O
  Christmas Tree, O Tannenbaum,
  and Tannnenbaum
Oh! Tell Me of My Mother
  FHR-W,M SSFo-W,M
Oh! That Kiss
  ESU-W
Oh, That My Head Were Waters
  Boo-W,M
Oh, the Beautiful Treasures
  GB-W,M
Oh, the Downward Road Is
  Crowded see Oh, de Downward
  Road Is Crowded
Oh, the Fog
  RuS-W,M (Russian)
Oh the Oak and the Ash
  CSo-W,M
Oh the Oak and the Ash see also
  Oak and the Ash
Oh, the Red Sea see Oh, de Red
  Sea
Oh the Rocks and the Mountains
  RF-W,M
Oh, the Sunshine
  NH-W
Oh, Them Golden Slippers
  GG1-W,M OTJ-W,M POT-W,M
  RW-W,M SpS-W,M
Oh, Them Golden Slippers see also
  Golden Slippers, Oh Dem Golden
  Slippers, and Them Golden
  Slippers
Oh, There's a Dark Secession Wag
  SiS-W
Oh There's No Such Girl As Mine
  FHR-W,M
Oh, Thou from Whom All Blessings
  Come
  MU-W,M
Oh! 'Tis Glorious
  FHR-W,M
Oh, to Be a Gypsy
  FSA1-W,M
Oh! Turn Sinner
  SHS-W,M
Oh! Turn Sinner see also Turn
  Sinner
Oh, Varmeland
  BMC-W
Oh, Vreneli
  LMR-W,M
Oh, Vreneli see also Vreneli
Oh, Wallace (You Never Can Jail
  Us All)
  SFF-W,M
Oh, Wasn't Dat a Wide Riber?
  RF-W,M
Oh, We Miss You at Home
  SiS-W
Oh, We're the Boys
  AF-W
Oh Wert Thou in the Cauld Blast
  ESB-W,M TH-W,M
Oh Wert Thou in the Cauld Blast
  see also O Wert Thou in the
  Cauld Blast
Oh, What a Beautiful Mornin'

DBC-W,M HC1-W,M HLS8-W,M
  L-W OTJ-W,M OTO-W RDF-W,M
  RW-W,M TGO-W,M TI1-W,M
  U-W UBF-W,M UFB-W,M
Oh, What a Day
  HHa-W,M
Oh, What a Hard Time
  NH-W
Oh, What a Horrible Morning
  GI-W
Oh What a Mournin'
  NSS-W
Oh What a Mournin' see also My
  Lord What a Mornin', Stars Begin
  to Fall, What a Mornin', and
  When the Stars Begin to Fall
Oh, What a Night
  GI-W,M
Oh, What a Night for Love
  MF-W,M
Oh, What a Pal Was Whoozis
  BH-W,M
Oh, What Did Delaware, Boys
  MAS-W,M
Oh, What Did Delaware, Boys see
  also What Did Delaware?
Oh, What Is Man
  JS-W,M
Oh! What It Seemed to Be
  MAB1-W MF-W,M MSA1-W
  TI1-W,M UFB-W,M
Oh, When I Get t' Heaven
  RF-W,M
Oh When I Go A-Ploughing
  SOO-W,M
Oh, When Shall I See Jesus?
  AHO-W,M
Oh Where Has My Little Dog Gone
  BM-W RW-W,M
Oh, Where Is Mary Gone?
  RTH-W
Oh Where Is My Little Dog Gone?
  ASB1-W,M
Oh Where, Oh Where Is My Little
  Dog Gone?
  BBF-W,M OTJ-W,M PoS-W,M
  SMa-W,M SOO-W,M
Oh Where, Oh Where Is My Little
  Dog Gone? see also Der
  Deitcher's Dog, Oh Where Has
  (Is) My Little Dog Gone, and
  Where Has My Little Dog Gone
Oh Where, Tell Me Where
  SeS-W,M
Oh Who Will Shoe My Foot
  Oz1-W,M
Oh! Who's Going to Shoe Your
  Pretty Little Foot?
  BCT-W,M
Oh! Who's Going to Shoe Your
  Pretty Little Foot? see also
  Who's Gonna Shoe Your Pretty
  Little Foot
Oh! Why Am I So Happy?
  FHR-W,M
Oh Why Left I My Hame?
  SeS-W,M
Oh! Willie, We Have Miss'd You
  HSD-W,M
Oh! Willie, We Have Miss'd You
  see also Willie We Have Missed
  You
Oh! Wonderful Star
  FF-W,M
Oh, Won't You Sit Down?
  LoS-W,M SMY-W,M
Oh, Worship the King

ASB6-W,M CEM-W,M MML-W,M
OS-W SoF-W,M TH-W,M
Oh, Worship the King see also O
Worship the King
Oh! Ya! Ya!
Mo-W,M NM-W,M
Oh Ye Young, Ye Gay, Ye Proud
DD-W,M Oz4-W,M
Oh, Yea
GI-W GO-W
Oh, Yes!
RF-W,M
Oh Yes, I'm Goin' Up
RTH-W
Oh, Yes, Yonder Comes My Lord
RF-W,M
Oh! You Beautiful Doll
BBB-W,M GSN1-W,M MF-W,M
OAP-W,M RC-W,M RoE-W,M
TI2-W,M U-W
Oh You Caint Go to Heaven
Oz2-W
Oh, You Crazy Moon
DC-W,M MF-W,M
Oh You Who Are Able
Oz2-W
Oh Zion Halleluiah
BDW-W,M
Ohio
MF-W,M UBF-W,M
Ohio Canal
ASB6-W,M
Ohio State
CoS-W,M
Oi Bethlehem
LaS-W,M (Spanish Only)
Oid Den Oireachtas Mor I Mbaile
Ath Cliath 1897
VP-W (Gaelic Only)
Oil on the Brain
HAS-W,M
Oil Station Man
SiR-W,M
Okie Boogie see Oakie Boogie
Okie from Muskogee
CMG-W,M HLS9-W,M N-W,M
NMH-W,M RW-W,M
Oklahoma
DBC-W,M Fif-W,M HC2-W,M
HLS8-W,M L-W OTJ-W,M OTO-W
RW-W,M TGO-W,M TI1-W,M
UBF-W,M UFB-W,M
Oklahoma Hills
CMG-W,M FC-W,M
Okolo Trebone
IF-W,M (Czech)
Ol' Dan Tucker
GeS-W,M
Ol' Dan Tucker see also
Oh/Old/Ole Dan Tucker
Ol' Darkie, Ol' Mule
WiS9-W,M
Ol' Man River
DJ-W,M FrS-W,M L-W SB-W,M
TI1-W,M TW-W UBF-W,M
Olaf Trygvason
TF-W,M
Olaynu
SBJ-W,M (Hebrew Only)
Olcott's Lullaby
OTJ-W,M
Old Abe and His Fights
MPP-W
Old Abe Has Gone and Did It, Boys
SiS-W
Old Abe Lies Sick
Re-W,M

Old Abe Lincoln
OTJ-W,M
Old Abe Lincoln Came Out of the
Wilderness
FW-W NeA-W,M
Old Abe They Said Was an Honest
Man
SiS-W
Old Abe's Elected
Oz2-W
Old Abram Brown
Boo-W,M OTJ-W,M
Old Akela Had a Pack
CSS-W
Old Ark A-Moverin' Along
NAS-W,M
Old Ark Is Movin'
BMM-W
Old Ark's A-Moverin'
FW-W GC-W,M LoS-W,M
OTJ-W,M
Old Ark's A-Moverin' see also Ole
Ark A-Moverin' Along
Old Arm Chair
HSD-W,M OHO-W,M
Old Army Mule
Am-W,M
Old Aunt Kate
NF-W OTJ-W,M
Old Bachelor
BSC-W Oz3-W
Old Bangum
FW-W Oz1-W,M SCa-W,M
Old Bangum see also Bangum and
the Boar, and Ole Bangum
Old Bark Hut
ATM-W,M
Old Bell'd Yoe
AFS-W,M
Old Betty Larkin
D-W,M
Old Black Booger
Oz1-W,M
Old Black Gnats
NF-W
Old Black Joe
AmH-W,M BSB-W,M ESB-W,M
ETB-W,M FHR-W,M HSD-W,M
IL-W,M MML-W,M NAS-W,M
NSS-W OFS-W,M OHG-W,M
OS-W PoS-W,M RW-W,M
SSF-W,M SSFo-W,M STR-W,M
TF-W TH-W,M WiS8-W,M
Old, Blind, Drunk John
FMT-W FoM-W,M
Old Blue
BIS-W,M FMT-W FW-W OTJ-W,M
Oz2-W,M RW-W,M
Old Bombardment Group
AF-W
Old Brass Wagon
ASB4-W,M HS-W,M OFS-W,M
OTJ-W,M Oz3-W,M TMA-W,M
Old Brown Coat
Oz4-W
Old Brown Shoe
TWS-W
Old Buck-a-roo
FC-W,M
Old Bucks County
RW-W,M
Old Bumpy
Oz3-W,M
Old Cabin Home
AmH-W,M HSD-W,M WiS8-W,M
Old Camp Kettle
SiS-W

Old Cape Cod
MF-W,M RW-W,M TI2-W,M
Old Chape: The Troubadour of Red
Fork Ranch
SoC-W
Old Chieftain
SiS-W
Old Chisholm Trail
AFS-W,M Bo-W,M FG1-W,M
FW-W HS-W,M HWS-W,M
IHA-W,M MF-W,M MHB-W,M
NAS-W,M OFS-W,M OTJ-W,M
Oz2-W,M SAm-W,M SoC-W
SWF-W,M
Old Chuck Wagon
SoC-W
Old Church Yard
Oz4-W,M WN-W,M
Old Colony Times
AH-W,M ASB5-W,M IHA-W,M
WU-W,M
Old Contraband
MPP-W SiS-W
Old Convention Song
AG-W,M
Old Cow Died
AFS-W,M FW-W
Old Cross Road
ITP-W
Old Crumbly Crust
BSC-W
Old Dame
PIS-W,M
Old Dan
KS-W,M
Old Dan Tucker
AH-W,M ASB5-W,M ATS-W
BF-W,M FSB2-W,M FW-W
HS-W,M HSD-W,M LMR-W,M
OS-W OTJ-W,M Oz3-W,M
PoS-W,M POT-W,M RW-W,M
VA-W,M
Old Dan Tucker see also
Oh/Ol'/Ole Dan Tucker
Old Darkie, Old Mule see Ol'
Darkie, Ol' Mule
Old Deuteronomy
UBF-W,M
Old Devil Moon
DBC-W,M DJ-W,M FR-W,M
HC1-W,M OTO-W TI1-W,M
UBF-W,M UFB-W,M
Old Dirge from the Isle of Mull
SeS-W,M
Old Dobbin
ASB2-W,M
Old Dog Tray
AmH-W,M FHR-W,M FW-W
HS-W,M NAS-W,M OS-W
RW-W,M SSF-W,M SSFo-W,M
TF-W,M WiS8-W,M
Old Dogs, Children and
Watermelon Wine
TI1-W,M UFB-W,M
Old Dominion
ASB5-W,M
Old Dumpty Moore
Oz3-W,M
Old Elm Tree
BSC-W Oz4-W
Old England Forty Years Ago
SI-W
Old Farm Gate
Oz4-W,M
Old Farmer in the Countree
BSC-W,M
Old Fashioned Love Song

GrS-W,M
Old Fashioned Way
  TI1-W,M UFB-W,M
Old Father Gray
  Oz3-W,M
Old Father Grimes
  Oz3-W,M
Old Father Thames
  U-W
Old Fisherman
  ASB4-W,M
Old Fisherman (Pan Ch'iao Tao
  Ch'ing)
  FD-W,M (Chinese)
Old Flag
  SiS-W
Old Folks At Home
  AmH-W,M ASB3-W,M ATS-W
  BH-W,M BM-W CSo-W,M
  ESB-W,M ETB-W,M FHR-W,M
  FM-W,M FW-W HS-W,M
  HSD-W,M IL-W,M LoS-W,M
  LT-W,M MAB1-W MF-W,M
  MG-W,M MSA1-W NAS-W,M
  OHG-W,M OS-W PoS-W,M
  RW-W,M SiR-W SL-W SMa-W,M
  SoF-W,M SSF-W,M SSFo-W,M
  TF-W TH-W,M U-W UF-W
  WiS8-W,M
Old Folks at Home see also
  Swanee River and Way Down
  upon the Swanee River
Old Folks at Home (Humoresque)
  GC-W,M
Old Folks Quadrilles
  FHR-W,M
Old Fox
  AFS-W,M
Old Fox Walked Out
  Oz1-W
Old Friend
  UBF-W,M
Old Fumbler
  SR-W,M
Old General Lane
  Oz3-W,M
Old General Price
  Oz2-W,M
Old Georgy
  Oz2-W,M
Old Girder Bill
  BMM-W
Old Glory
  OTO-W
Old Gold
  CoS-W,M
Old Gospel Ship
  FW-W
Old Grampus
  FMT-W
Old Granite State
  MPP-W SY-W,M
Old Gray Cat
  RSL-W,M
Old Gray Goose
  HS-W,M
Old Gray Goose see also Ole Gray
  Goose
Old Gray Horse
  Oz2-W,M
Old Gray Mare
  AmS-W,M ASB4-W,M BH-W,M
  FuB-W,M FW-W GI-W IL-W,M
  MF-W,M OTJ-W,M RW-W,M
  TI1-W,M UFB-W,M
Old Gray Mink
  NF-W

Old Grey Mare
  FU-W,M OBN-W,M
Old Grimes
  ATS-W
Old Grimes Is Dead
  BSC-W,M
Old Ground Hog
  AFS-W,M
Old Grumble
  BSC-W,M Oz1-W,M
Old Grumbler
  BSC-W
Old Gumbie Cat
  UBF-W,M
Old Hannah
  FW-W
Old Hen Cackled
  NF-W
Old Hen Cackled and the Rooster
  Laid the Egg
  AFS-W,M
Old Home Ain't What It Used to Be
  SiS-W
Old Honest Abe
  BSC-W
Old Hundred
  AmH-W,M ATS-W FW-W
  GH-W,M HSD-W,M MAS-W,M
  MML-W,M SHS-W,M WiS7-W,M
Old Hundredth
  AH-W,M CSo-W,M ESB-W,M
  HS-W,M NAS-W,M
Old Hundred(th) see also Doxology
  and Praise God from Whom All
  Blessings Flow
Old Ironsides
  ANS-W AWB-W TF-W,M
Old Jeff Davis Tore Down the
  Government
  BMM-W
Old Joe
  DE-W,M
Old Joe Clark
  ATS-W BIS-W,M D-W,M DD-W,M
  FSB3-W,M FW-W GuC-W,M
  HAS-W,M HS-W,M ITP-W,M
  LMR-W,M MAS-W,M OTJ-W,M
  Oz3-W,M POT-W,M RS-W,M
Old John Braddleum
  OTJ-W,M
Old John Brown
  NSS-W
Old John Brown Had a Little Indian
  TMA-W,M
Old John Henry Died on the
  Mountain
  FVV-W,M
Old John Jones see Get Up and
  Bar the Door
Old Jubiter
  TMA-M,W
Old Kent Road
  AmH-M
Old Kentucky
  BMM-W
Old Kentucky Home
  ESB-W,M NAS-W,M OFS-W,M
Old King Cole
  AmH-W,M ASB5-W,M BM-W
  FW-W MH-W,M OTJ-W,M
  PO-W,M
Old Lady
  OTJ-W,M
Old Lady see also I Know an Old
  Lady
Old Lady Goose
  AFS-W,M

Old Lamplighter
  BBB-W,M TI1-W,M UFB-W,M
Old Laredo
  BSC-W
Old Leather Bonnet
  Oz3-W,M
Old Lee Blues
  ITP-W,M
Old Lord by the Northern Sea
  MSH-W,M
Old Lord of Northern Sea
  OHO-W,M
Old Love Letters
  BIS-W,M LJ-W,M
Old Love Song
  Oz1-W
Old Ma Bell
  SWF-W,M
Old MacDonald
  ATS-W IL-W,M MES2-W,M
  OTJ-W,M
Old MacDonald Had a Farm
  BMC-W,M CSS-W FW-W HS-W,M
  IPH-W,M RW-W,M SiR-W,M
Old Maid and the Burglar
  FMT-W
Old Maid Song
  OTJ-W,M TBF-W,M
Old Maid's Song
  FW-W Oz3-W,M
Old Man
  GM-W
Old Man Atom
  IHA-W,M
Old Man Came Tumbling Home
  FSSC-W
Old Man from the Mountain
  NMH-W,M
Old Man He Come Dancin' Out
  AFP-W
Old Man in the North Country
  BSC-W
Old Man in the Old Country
  Oz1-W,M
Old Man in the Wood
  FW-W LMR-W,M
Old Man Know-All
  NF-W
Old Man Noah
  MAS-W,M MuM-W,M
Old Man River see Ol' Man River
Old Man under the Hill
  Oz1-W,M
Old Man Who Lived in the West
  FoM-W,M
Old Man Who Lived in the Wood
  FMT-W FoM-W,M
Old Man Who Lived in the Wood
  see also Ole Man Who Lived in
  the Wood
Old Man Will Your Dog Catch a
  Rabbit?
  Le-W,M
Old Man Winter
  ASB3-W,M
Old Man's Comforts
  ESU-W
Old Man's Courtship
  BSC-W
Old Man's Rubble
  VB-W,M
Old Memories
  FHR-W,M SSF-W,M SSFo-W,M
Old Miller
  DD-W,M SCa-W
Old Miller's Will
  OHO-W,M

Old Miner's Refrain
  AL-W
Old Missouri
  CoS-W,M Oz3-W
Old Mister Elephant
  ASB1-W,M
Old Molly Hare
  NF-W Oz2-W,M SCL-W,M
Old Moses Smote de Waters
  Oz2-W,M
Old Mother Flip-Flop
  Oz1-W,M
Old Mother Hubbard
  BMC-W,M OTJ-W,M
Old Mother Wind
  MH-W,M
Old Mountain Dew
  OFS-W,M
Old Music Master
  OHF-W OTO-W
Old Napper
  FMT-W FoM-W,M
Old Nassau
  ESB-W,M IL-W,M
Old Navy
  GI-W GO-W,M
Old Nelson
  BMM-W
Old New Hampshire
  Fif-W,M
Old North State
  Fif-W,M SiS-W
Old Norway
  NAS-W,M
Old Oaken Bucket
  AmH-W,M ATS-W BH-W,M
  FW-W HSD-W,M NAS-W,M
  OTJ-W,M PoS-W,M RW-W,M
  WiS8-W,M
Old Old House
  BSo-W,M
Old Orange Flute
  FW-W IS-W,M
Old Packingham
  BSC-W,M
Old Paint
  Bo-W,M Gu-W,M MHB-W,M
  WSB-W,M
Old Plantation
  SiS-W
Old Polish Religious Song
  LMR-W,M
Old Pompey
  ASB3-W,M
Old Portrait
  FSA1-W,M
Old Rags, Bottles, Rags
  NFS-W,M
Old Rattler
  FW-W NeF-W OHO-W,M
Old Reilly
  FW-W
Old Riley
  Le-W,M WSB-W,M
Old Robin's Ballad
  BMM-W
Old Roger Is Dead
  CSG-W,M SiR-W,M
Old Rosin the Beau
  AH-W,M BSC-W FW-W HSD-W,M
  OHG-W,M PoS-W,M TMA-W,M
Old Rosin the Bow
  BSC-W Oz4-W,M
Old Ruben
  FSB3-W,M
Old Rugged Cross
  AHO-W,M AME-W,M BSG-W,M

BSP-W,M CEM-W,M DC-W,M
  HF-W,M HLS7-W,M JBF-W,M
  OS-W RDF-W,M TB-W,M Tr-W,M
  WiS9-W,M
Old Rustic Bridge by the Mill
  U-W
Old Sailor's Song
  SA-W
Old Santa's Coming
  SOO-W,M
Old Satan Told Me to My Face
  NSS-W
Old Sawbucks
  AFP-W
Old Sayings
  TMA-W,M
Old Scout's Lament
  HB-W
Old Section Boss
  BSC-W NF-W
Old Sexton
  AmH-W,M HSD-W,M
Old Shady
  HSD-W,M
Old Shady see also Ole Shady
Old Shep
  OnT1-W,M OTJ-W,M RW-W,M
Old Ship of Zion
  AN-W FW-W LMR-W,M WN-W,M
**Old Ship of Zion see also Ole Ship
of Zion**
Old Skibbereen
  VP-W,M
Old Slew Foot
  BIS-W,M
**Old Slew Foot see also Ole Slew
Foot**
Old Smokie
  SCa-W,M
Old Smoky
  BM-W GuC-W,M II-W,M LoS-W,M
  SCa-W,M TBF-W,M
**Old Smoky see also Ole Smokey
and On Top of Old Smokey**
Old Soldier
  OTJ-W,M
Old Soldier's Prayer
  ESU-W
Old Soldiers Never Die
  AF-W FW-W PO-W,M
Old Soldiers of the King
  SSS-W,M
Old Song
  AL-W BSC-W
Old Songs
  FSA2-W,M
Old Sow
  AFS-W,M
Old Spice
  GSM-W,M
Old Spinnning Wheel
  MF-W,M
Old Stepstone
  Oz4-W
Old Stonewall
  SiS-W
Old Stormy
  SAm-W,M
Old Texas
  BM-W BMC-W,M GuC-W,M HS-
  W,M MES1-W,M MES2-W,M
  MG-W,M OTJ-W,M
Old Thompson's Mule
  OTJ-W,M
Old Tikhvin Melody
  RuS-W,M (Russian)
Old Time Cowboy

HB-W,M SoC-W
Old-Time Favorites
  MuM-W,M
Old Time Gambler's Song
  SoC-W
Old Time Religion
  AH-W,M CEM-W,M IL-W,M
  Oz4-W,M RW-W,M WN-W,M
**Old Time Religion see also Ole
Time Religion**
Old Time Rock and Roll
  ToO79-W,M
Old Tippecanoe
  ESU-W
Old Tom Bolen
  Oz3-W,M
Old Toy Trains
  BCS-W,M
Old Triangle
  PO-W,M
Old Uncle Ned
  FHR-W,M SSF-W,M SSFo-W,M
Old Union Wagon
  MPP-W OHG-W,M SiS-W
Old Vienna
  MU-W,M
Old Vienna see also Emperor Waltz
Old Wabash
  CoS-W,M
Old Wagoner
  Oz2-W,M
Old Wife
  FSU-W
Old Woman
  MH-W,M
Old Woman All Skin and Bone
  BSC-W
Old Woman and the Devil
  BSC-W
Old Woman and the Peddler
  ASB4-W,M
Old Woman in the Hills
  NF-W
Old Woman, Old Woman
  Oz3-W,M
Old Woman Taught Wisdom
  SI-W
Old Woman's Courtship
  HSA-W,M
Old Year and the New
  SBA-W
Old Zip Coon
  AH-W,M AmH-M Oz2-W,M
Old Zip Coon see also Zip Coon
Old Zip Lyda Coon
  Oz3-W
Older and Bolder
  OCG2-W,M
Older Women
  TI2-W,M
Oldest Established
  TW-W
Ole Ark
  SSo-W,M
Ole Ark A-Moverin' Along
  RF-W,M
**Ole Ark A-Moverin' Along see also
Old Ark A-Moverin' Along**
Ole Bangum
  SCa-W
**Ole Bangum see also Bangum and
the Boar, and Old Bangum**
Ole Buttermilk Sky
  Mo-W,M NM-W,M OTO-W
  TI2-W,M
Ole Dan Tucker
  NAS-W,M

Ole Dan Tucker see also
  Oh/Ol'/Old Dan Tucker
Ole Faithful
  FC-W,M
Ole Gray Goose
  AH-W,M DE-W,M
Ole Gray Goose see also Old Gray
  Goose
Ole Jaw Bone
  DE-W,M
Ole Joe Golden
  DE-W,M
Ole Man Who Lived in the Wood
  BSC-W
Ole Man Who Lived in the Wood
  see also Old Man Who Lived in
  the Wood
Ole Massa
  UF-W,M
Ole Massa on His Trabbels Gone
  SiS-W
Ole Massa Was a Stingy Man
  AN-W
Ole Miss
  B-M
Ole Mule
  Me-W,M
Ole Mule Breakin' Blues
  LC-W
Ole Pee Dee
  DE-W,M
Ole! Santa
  MF-W,M
Ole Satan Is a Busy Ole Man
  NSS-W
Ole Shady
  NAS-W,M SiS-W
Ole Shady see also Old Shady
Ole Sheep Done Know de Road
  Re-W,M
Ole Ship of Zion
  MoM-W NH-W
Ole Ship of Zion see also Old Ship
  of Zion and 'Tis the Ole Ship of
  Zion
Ole Slew Foot
  BSo-W,M
Ole Slew Foot see also Old Slew
  Foot
Ole Smokey
  SAm-W,M
Ole Smokey see also Old Smoky
  and On Top of Old Smokey
Ole Sow Had de Measles
  SNS-W
Ole Tare River
  DE-W,M
Ole Time Religion
  NH-W RF-W,M
Ole Time Religion see also Old
  Time Religion
Ole Uncle Abrum's Comin'
  SiS-W
Oleana
  AL-W BF-W,M FGM-W,M FW-W
  OHO-W,M
O'Leary's Bar
  AF-W
Olive Shade
  SHS-W,M
Olive Tree
  FSA1-W,M SL-W,M
Oliver
  MF-W,M O-W,M
Oliver Cromwell
  F1-W,M
Olive's Brow

GH-W,M
Olney
  SHS-W,M
Olympia
  TI2-W,M
Olympic Fanfare and Theme
  TVT-M
Olympic Theme--U.S.A. vs. the
  World
  TVT-M
Om Utwandringen
  SE-W (Swedish)
Oma Wise
  BSC-W
Oma Wise see also Omie Wise
Omega
  EA-W,M
Omie Wise
  FW-W ITP-W,M
Omie Wise see also Little Omie,
  Oma Wise, and Poor Oma Wise
On a Carousel
  TI2-W,M
On a Clear Day (You Can See
  Forever)
  DBC-W,M HC2-W,M HSi-W,M
  OTO-W RW-W,M TI1-W,M TW-W
  UBF-W,M UFB-W,M
On a Cold Frosty Morning
  Oz2-W,M
On a Desert Island with Thee
  TS-W
On a Faded Violet
  NA-W,M
On a Hill Far Away
  AHO-W,M AME-W,M
On a Hog
  NH-W
On a Little Street in Singapore
  BBB-W,M TI1-W,M UFB-W,M
On a Long Summer Day
  VA-W,M
On a Monday
  Le-W,M
On a Rainy Day
  GM-W,M SOO-W,M
On a Raven-Black Horse
  FPG-W,M (Russian) RuS-W,M
  (Russian)
On a Saturday Night
  BH-W,M EFS-W,M OS-W
On a Slow Boat to China
  TI2-W,M
On a Summer Eve
  AFP-W
On a Summer Morning
  SSe-W,M
On a Sunday Afternoon
  FSN-W,M MAB1-W MSA1-W
  OAP-W,M OBN-W,M TI1-W,M
  UFB-W,M
On a Tree by a River
  GiS-W,M
On and On
  BIS-W,M
On and On (Love Song)
  VB-W,M
On and On and On
  LSO-W ReG-W,M
On Behalf of the Visiting Fireman
  MF-W,M
On Behalf of the Visiting Firemen
  OHF-W
On Broadway
  ERM-W,M GAR-W,M MF-W,M
  RB-W
On Buena Vista's Battlefield

Oz2-W
On Canaan Shore
  SL-W,M
On Christ the Solid Rock I Stand
  see My Hope Is Built (on Nothing
  Less) and Solid Rock, The
On Christmas Day in the Morning
  CSB-W,M
On Christmas Night
  GBC-W,M OE-W,M
On Days Like These
  AT-W,M
On Disbanding the Army
  SBA-W
On Earth There Is a Lamb So Small
  AHO-W,M (German)
On Entend Partout
  CUP-W,M (French Only)
On Fieldmount Spring
  Oz3-W,M
On Friday Morning We Set Sail
  ANS-W
On Green Dolphin Street
  GSF-W,M GSN3-W,M HLS3-W,M
  RW-W,M
On Guard
  SiS-W
On Her Majesty's Secret Service
  RW-M
On His Bronco the Gay Caballero
  SMY-W,M
On Ilkla Moor Baht'at
  U-W
On Independence
  SBA-W SI-W,M
On Iowa
  Mo-W,M
On Johnny Mitchell's Train
  AL-W
On Jordan's Banks the Baptist's
  Cry
  SJ-W,M
On Jordan's Stormy Banks
  GH-W,M OM-W,M
On Jordan's Stormy Banks I Stand
  AME-W,M NSS-W Re-W,M
On Jordan's Stormy Banks I Stand
  see also I Am Bound for the
  Promised Land and Promised
  Land (I Am Bound for the
  Promised Land)
On Lake Como
  FSA1-W,M
On Lake Titicaca
  ASB5-W,M
On Mobile Bay
  RC-W,M
On Mondays I Never Go to Work
  PO-W,M
On Mother Kelly's Doorstep
  U-W
On Mules
  OTJ-W,M
On Mules We Find
  Boo-W,M
On My Head
  FP-W,M
On My Honor
  Bo-W,M
On My Journey
  WSB-W,M
On My Journey Home
  MuM-W,M WN-W,M
On My Mind the Whole Night Long
  ReG-W,M
On My Own
  BNG-W,M DBC-W,M DPE-W,M

MF-W,M UBF-W,M
On My Way
  Am-W,M VB-W,M
On My Way to Mexico
  Oz3-W
On My Way to You
  MLS-W,M
On, On, On, the Boys Came
  Marching
  SiS-W,M
On One Condition
  VB-W,M
On Our Way Rejoicing
  Hy-W,M
On Parade
  ASB3-W,M Sw-W,M
On Patrol
  ASB6-W,M
On Picket Duty
  SiS-W
On, Roll On, My Ball I Roll On
  CFS-W,M (French)
On Second Thought
  Mo-W,M NM-W,M
On Silver Sands
  SSe-W,M
On Sunday Mornin' I Seek My Lord
  NSS-W
On That Day
  JS-W,M
On That Other Bright Shore
  Oz4-W,M
On the Atchison, Topeka and the
  Santa Fe
  GG4-W,M GSF-W,M GSN3-W,M
  HLS3-W,M OHF-W RT4-W,M
  RW-W,M
On the Atlantic
  FSA1-W,M
On the Banks of A-Dundee
  BSC-W
On the Banks of Jordan
  MuM-W,M
On the Banks of Sweet Dundee
  Oz1-W,M
On the Banks of the Ohio
  SAm-W,M
On the Banks of the Old
  Tennessee
  Oz4-W,M
On the Banks of the Railroad
  AL-W
On the Banks of the Sacramento
  OTJ-W,M
**On the Banks of the Sacramento
see also Banks of Sacramento
and Banks of the Sacramento**
On the Banks of the Wabash
  FW-W FWS-W,M MF-W,M
  OBN-W,M OTJ-W,M RW-W,M
On the Banks of the Wabash, Far
  Away
  AH-W,M Fif-W,M FSN-W,M
  FSTS-W,M
On the Bayou see Jambalaya
On the Beach at Bali Bali
  Mo-W,M NM-W,M
On the Beach at Waikiki
  HLS1-W,M RW-W,M
On the Beautiful Blue Danube
  AmH-M
On the Boardwalk (in Atlantic City)
  MAB1-W MF-W,M MSA1-W
On the Bridge
  SMa-W,M
On the Bridge of Avignon
  CSG-W,M

**On the Bridge of Avignon see also
Bridge of Avignon and Sur Le
Pont D'Avignon**
On the Brigantine Privateer Prince
  De Neufchatel
  ANS-W
On the British Blockade and
  Expected Attack
  ANS-W
On the Broad Volga
  RSC-W,M (Russian Only)
On the Bus
  MH-W,M
On the Capture of the Guerriere
  ANS-W
On the Capture of the United
  States Frigate Essex
  ANS-W
On the Chapel Steps
  IL-W,M
On the Death of a Little Child after
  a Very Short Illness
  ESU-W
On the Death of Captain Nicholas
  Biddle
  ANS-W
On the Dodge
  SoC-W
On the Dummy Line
  LSR-W,M
On the Eve of Battle, Sister
  SiS-W
On the Eve of Christmas Day
  FSD-W,M
On the Good and Faithful
  Hy-W,M
On the Good Ship Lollipop
  OTJ-W,M STP-W,M TI1-W,M
  UFB-W,M
On the Ground Here I Lie
  SiR-W,M
**On the Hearth see Oyfn
Pripetshuck**
On the High Road to Dijon
  FSF-W (French)
On the Hinky Dinky Double D Farm
  OTJ-W,M
On the Isle of Capri
  AF-W
On the Jericho Road
  BSo-W,M HLS7-W,M
On the Lake Expeditions
  ANS-W
On the Lake Where Drooped the
  Willow
  ATS-W,M
On the Late Royal Sloop-of-War
  General Monk
  ANS-W
On the Launching of the Frigate
  Constitution
  ANS-W
On the Launching of the Seventy-
  Four Gun Ship Independence
  ANS-W
On the Line
  SWF-W,M
On the Ling, Ho!
  FSA1-W,M
On the Loss of the Privateer
  Brigantine General Armstrong
  ANS-W
On the Memorable Victory
  Obtained by the Gallant Captain
  Paul Jones
  ANS-W
On the Mountain's Top Appearing

AME-W,M
On the Murder of Hamilton
  MPP-W
On the Naval Attack near
  Baltimore
  ANS-W
On the New American Frigate
  Alliance
  ANS-W
On the Nodaway Road
  OHF-W
On the Other Hand
  AWS-W,M FOC-W,M TTH-W,M
On the Other Side of Jordan
  FN-W,M
On the Other Side of the Tracks
  Mo-W,M NM-W,M OTO-W
  TI2-W,M UBF-W,M
On the Radio
  PoG-W,M
On the Road
  CSD-W,M (French)
On the Road Again
  DBL-W MF-W,M TOH-W,M
  TOM-W,M
On the Road to Valencia
  LA-W,M (Spanish)
On the Rock Where Moses Stood
  BIS-W,M
On the Seashore
  ASB2-W,M
On the Shelf
  WG-W,M
On the South Side of Chicago
  TI1-W,M UFB-W,M
On the Square
  Mo-M
On the Street Where You Live
  DBC-W,M FPS-W,M HC2-W,M
  HLS3-W,M LL-W,M OTO-W
  RT6-W,M RW-W,M TI1-W,M
  UBF-W,M UFB-W,M
On the Sunny Side of the Rockies
  STP-W,M
On the Sunny Side of the Street
  BBB-W,M GSN2-W,M HC1-W,M
  HLS2-W,M MF-W,M RDT-W,M
  TI1-W,M TW-W UFB-W,M
On the Swing Shift
  OHF-W
On the Town
  HFH-W,M
On the Trail
  RW-M
On the Water
  VB-W,M
On the Way Home
  GS1-W HLS7-W,M
On the Way to School
  MH-W,M
On the Willows
  G-W,M OTO-W UBF-W,M
On the Wings of Love
  GSN5-W,M
On This Happy Easter
  SHP-W,M
On Tiptoe
  FSA1-W,M
On to Charleston
  SiS-W
On to Savannah
  SiS-W
On to the Battle
  ESB-W,M
On to Victory (Valparaiso
  University)
  CoS-W,M

On to Washington
AFP-W AL-W

On Tom Big Bee River
Oz4-W

On Top of Old Baldy
AF-W

On Top of Old Fuji
AF-W

On Top of Old Pyongyang
AF-W

On Top of Old Rainier
AF-W

On Top of Old Smokey
BMC-W,M FG1-W,M FW-W
FWS-W,M IPH-W,M MAB1-W
MAS-W,M MSA1-W OFS-W,M
OTJ-W,M SBF-W,M WSB-W,M
YS-W,M

On Top of Old Smoky
FAW-W,M FGM-W,M FSB1-W,M
FU-W,M FuB-W,M GSN1-W,M
HS-W,M MF-W,M OAP-W,M
RW-W,M

**On Top of Old Smoky see also Old
Smoky and Ole Smokey**

On Top of Spaghetti
FAW-W,M FPS-W,M WF-W,M

On Top of the Pot
NF-W

On Wings of Song
ASB6-W,M OTJ-W,M RW-M

On Wisconsin
Fif-W-M Mo-W,M PB-W,M
TI2-W,M

On with the Show
RoS-W,M

On Your Toes
TS-W UBF-W,M

On Zion and on Lebanon
AHO-W,M

Once a Little Bluebell
SOT-W,M

Once for All
GH-W,M OM-W,M

Once for Us a Boy Was Born
SHP-W,M

Once I Had a Sweetheart
OFS-W,M OTJ-W,M

Once I Had an Old Grey Mare
FVV-W,M

Once I Led a Happy Life
HOH-W,M

Once I Lived a Happy Life
HOH-W

Once I Loved a Maiden Fair
OH-W,M

Once I Loved Thee, Mary Dear
FHR-W,M SSFo-W,M

Once I Was Dead in Sin
GH-W

Once I Was Happy
Oz4-W,M

Once I Went Swimming
OTJ-W,M

Once in a Blue Moon
LMS-W,M UBF-W,M

Once in a Lifetime
HLS8-W,M MF-W,M RW-W,M
TI1-W,M UBF-W,M UFB-W,M

Once in a While
GSN2-W,M GSO-W,M HLS2-W,M
OP1-W,M RW-W,M

Once in Arcadia
Boo-W,M

Once in Love with Amy
DBC-W,M RW-W,M TI2-W,M
UBF-W,M

Once in Our Lives
Boo-W,M

Once in Royal David's City
BCS-W,M CCH-W,M FH-W,M Hy-
W,M JOC-W,M U-W YC-W,M

Once Is Enough
SRE1-W,M

Once Is Not Enough
AT-W,M

Once More at Home
SiS-W

Once More, My Soul, the Rising
Day
AME-W,M

**Once More, My Soul, the Rising
Day see also Consolation (Watts)**

Once More O Lord
AHO-W,M

Once More, Our God, Vouchsafe
to Shine
AHO-W,M

Once More the Rebel's Bugle
SiS-W

Once on a Lonely Hill
BeB-W,M

Once There Was a Garden Fair
SHP-W,M

Once There Were Three Fishermen
FW-W

Once to Every Man and Nation
CA-W,M ESB-W,M Hy-W,M
SBF-W,M SFB-W,M

Once upon a Dream
NI-W,M

Once upon a Song
OU-W,M

Once upon a Summertime
MLS-W,M OHF-W TI2-W,M

Once upon a Time
HC2-W,M HLS8-W,M MMY-W,M
Mo-W,M NM-W,M OTO-W
RW-W,M

Once Upon a Time in America
HFH-M

Once You Get the Feel of It
TOC83-W,M

Once You Lose Your Heart
UBF-W,M

Once You've Been in Love
MLS-W,M

Onconstant Lover
BSC-W

**Onconstant Lover see also
Unconstant Lover**

One
CL-W,M JP-W,M OPS-W,M
OTO-W TI2-W,M UBF-W,M
WG-W,M

One after Nine-O-Nine
TWS-W

One Alone
EY-W,M HC2-W,M MF-W,M

One and Only
HSe-W,M WGB/P-W,M

One and Two Are Three
SiR-W,M

One Arabian Night
Mo-W,M

One at a Time
MLS-W,M

One Bad Apple
BR-W,M

One Bad Stud
GAR-W,M

One Boy
Mo-W,M NM-W,M OTO-W
UBF-W,M

One Button, Two Buttons
UF-W,M

One Cold Freezing Morning
NSS-W

One Dawson
AL-W

One Day
MLS-W,M

One Day at a Time
CEM-W,M GS1-W TOH-W,M

One Day at a Time (Theme)
TV-W,M

One Day for Recreation
VP-W,M

One Day It Will Come to Pass
PAJ-W,M

One Day Old and No Damn Good
AFP-W

One Day We Dance
Mo-W,M NM-W,M OTO-W
W-W,M

One Dollar Bill, Baby
NeF-W

One Dozen Roses
AT-W,M OnT1-W,M

One Evening Having Lost My Way
MMM-W,M

One Evening in the Moonlight
FSF-W (French)

One Fine Day
MF-W,M ToO79-W,M

One Finger, One Thumb
Bo-W,M CSS-W LoS-W,M
SHP-W,M

One Fish Ball
FW-W

One Flag or No Flag
SiS-W

One Foot, Other Foot
A-W,M

One for My Baby (and One More
for the Road)
FrS-W,M Mo-W,M NM-W,M
OHF-W,M OTO-W TI2-W,M

One for the Money
SiR-W,M

One Gift Works Many Wonders
OnT6-W,M

One God
JS-W,M (Hebrew)

One Good Boy Gone Wrong
DS-W,M

One Grain of Sand
SBF-W,M

One Hallowe'en
Ap-W,M Mo-W,M VSA-W,M

One Happy Swede
SWF-W,M

One Has My Name, the Other Has
My Heart
FPS-W,M

One Heart, One Mind
AmH-M

One Hello
TOM-W,M

One Hit (to the Body)
TTH-W,M

One Horse Open Sleigh
PoS-W,M

**One Horse Open Sleigh see also
Jingle Bells**

One Horse Shay
MSB-W

One Hundred Children
OTJ-W,M

One Hundred Days Men
SiS-W

One Hundred Easy Ways to Lose a
Man
TW-W
100 Psalm Tune New
BC1-W,M EA-W,M
100 Years Ago
RoS-W,M
One I Loved Back Then (Corvette
Song)
TTH-W,M
One in a Million
OnT6-W,M TI2-W,M
One Indispensable Man
KH-W,M
One Industrious Insect
Boo-W,M
One Kiss
MF-W,M Ne-W,M
One Kiss Too Many
OGC1-W,M
One Last Goodbye
VB-W,M
One Last Kiss
Mo-W,M NM-W,M OTO-W
One Less Bell to Answer
BDF-W,M GOI7-W,M HD-W,M
ILT-W,M MF-W,M
One Less Set of Footsteps
JC-W,M PM-W,M
One Life to Live
LD-W,M LSO-W ToO79-W,M
TVT-W,M TW-W
One Little Brown Bird
GM-W,M
One Little Candle
RDF-W,M YS-W,M
One Little Frog
Oz3-W
One Little Word Before We Part
ESU-W
One Little World Apart
Mo-W,M NM-W,M OTO-W
One Love
Mo-W,M NM-W,M
One Man (Ain't Quite Enough)
Mo-W,M NM-W,M OTO-W
One Man's Hands
JF-W,M SFF-W,M
One Man's Woman
PoG-W,M
One Meat Ball
J-W,M OTJ-W,M
One Mint Julep
DJ-M HRB1-W,M TI1-W,M
UFB-W,M
One Minute to One
CS-W,M
One Misty, Moisty Morning
SiR-W,M SL-W,M
One Mo' Rounder Gone
NH-W
One Moment Alone
CF-W,M
One Moment in Time
LOM-W,M MF-W,M
One More Battle to Fight
AL-W
One More Dance
MA-W,M
One More Day
SA-W,M
One More Day's Work
GH-W,M
One More Day's Work for Jesus
AHO-w,M
One More Drink for the Four of Us
HAS-W,M

One More Hour
TOM-W,M
One More Kiss
Fo-W,M OTO-W UBF-W,M
One More Night
BNG-W,M DC-W,M DPE-W,M
One More River
HS-W,M OTJ-W,M Oz2-W,M
RW-W,M
One More River to Cross
ETB-W,M FW-W OTJ-W,M
SpS-W,M WN-W,M
**One More Rounder Gone see One
Mo' Rounder Gone**
One More Song for Jesus
CEM-W,M
One More Song for You
VB-W,M
One More Try
CFB-W,M RoS-W,M
One Morning in June
BSC-W
One Morning in May
BSC-W,M FW-W Oz1-W,M
SCa-W,M Sta-W,M TBF-W,M
**One Morning in May see also
Nightingale (Folk Song)**
One Morning, One Morning, One
Morning in May
SCa-W
One Night
SRE2-W,M
One Night As I Lay on the Prairie
Oz2-W,M
One Note Samba
DJ-W,M TI2-W,M
One O'Clock Jump
RW-M
One of a Kind
Ap-W,M Mo-W,M OTO-W
TOH-W,M VSA-W,M
One of a Kind (Love Affair)
SoH-W,M
One of a Kind Pair of Fools
EC-W,M
One of the Boys
ESU-W
One of the Girls
UBF-W,M
One of These Days
BSG-W,M BSP-W,M DBL-W
One of These Fine Days
TW-W
One of Those Songs
TI2-W,M
One of Us Will Be a Queen
GS-W,M
One on One
TI2-W,M
One on the Right Is on the Left
CSp-W,M
One Paddle, Two Paddle
TI2-W,M
One Parting Word, Dear Mother
SiS-W
One Person
Mo-W,M OTO-W
One Potato, Two Potatoes
SOO-W,M
One Promise Come True
Mo-W,M NM-W,M OTO-W
One Room
Ro-W,M
One Song
HSS-W,M HST-W,M NI-W,M
TI1-W,M UFB-W,M
One Step Beyond

WNF-W,M
One Step into Love
BP-W,M
One Summer Dream
ELO-W,M
One Sweetly Solemn Thought
AHO-W,M AmH-W,M FiS-W,M
FSY-W,M HSD-W,M WiS7-W,M
One Thing I of the Lord Desire
AME-W,M
One Thing Leads to Another
VB-W,M
One Tin Soldier
TI2-W,M
One Touch of Alchemy
KH-W,M
One-Tune Piper
ASB6-W,M
One, Two
ASB3-W,M MAR-W,M
One, Two, Buckle My Shoe
OTJ-W,M SOO-W,M
One, Two, Three
ASB2-W,M ASB4-W,M Boo-W,M
GM-W,M SOO-W,M
One, Two, Three, Four
RW-W,M SiR-W,M SOO-W,M
One, Two, Three, Four, Five
OTJ-W,M
One, Two, Three, O'Leary
BMC-W,M
One, Two, Three Steps
GB-W,M
One Way or Another
PL-W,M
One Who Has Yearn'd, Alone
FSY-W,M (German)
One Who Will Understand
K-W,M
Onion Song
GUM1-W,M
Only a Beam of Sunshine
GH-W,M
Only a Brakeman
Oz4-W,M
Only a Kiss
RM-W,M
Only a Little Way
GH-W,M
Only a Little While
GH-W,M
Only a Man in Overalls
AL-W
Only a Miner
Oz4-W,M
Only a Northern Song
TWS-W
Only a Rose
AT-W,M VK-W,M
Only a Step to Jesus
AME-W,M GH-W,M
Only an Armor Bearer
GH-W,M
Only Another Boy and Girl
TW-W
Only Believe
BSG-W,M BSP-W,M
Only Child
VB-W,M
Only for Thee
GH-W,M
Only Home I Know
Sh-W,M
Only in America
RB-W
Only in My Dreams
CFB-W,M

Only in the Play
FT-W,M
Only Love
ILT-W,M UBF-W,M
Only Love Can Break a Heart
HD-W,M MF-W,M WG-W,M
Only Mustang Makes It Happen
GSM-W,M
Only One Girl in the World for Me
EFS-W,M
Only One Love in My Life
MF-W,M
Only One Man Killed Today
SiS-W
Only One You
TOC82-W,M
Only, Only Love
Mo-W,M NM-W,M
Only Remembered
GH-W,M Oz4-W,M
Only Road to Freedom
AL-W
Only Sixteen
ToO76-W,M
Only Son Is Going Now
SiS-W
Only the Lonely
TFC-W,M
Only the Lonely Heart
MHB-W,M (German)
Only the Sad of Heart
WiS8-W,M
Only Thing I Want for Christmas
MF-W,M
Only Trust Him
AME-W,M GH-W,M
Only Trusting in My Saviour
GH-W,M
Only Waiting
GH-W,M
Only When I Laugh (Theme)
TOM-W,M
Only You (and You Alone)
BeL-W,M DBC-W,M ILF-W,M
MF-W,M TI1-W,M TWD-W,M
UBF-W,M UFB-W,M
Onnoh
JS-W,M (Hebrew)
Onnoh Adonoy
JS-W,M (Hebrew Only)
Onward
ESB-W,M GrM-W,M
Onward Brothers
AL-W
Onward, Christian
GH-W,M
Onward Christian Soldiers
AME-W,M AmH-W,M Bo-W
CEM-W,M FH-W,M FM-W,M
FW-W HF-W,M HLS7-W,M
HSD-W,M Hy-W,M IH-M IL-W,M
LMR-W,M MAB1-W MAS-W,M
MSA1-W NAS-W,M OPS-W,M
OTJ-W,M PoG-W,M RDF-W,M
RW-W,M SiB-W,M SL-W,M
TB-W,M TI1-W,M U-W UFB-W,M
WiS7-W,M YS-W,M
Onward Go
GH-W,M
Onward Marching
GrM-W,M
Onward, Onward, Men of Heaven
AHO-W,M
Onward to Victory
MU-W,M
Onward! Upward!
GH-W,M

Onward, Upward, Homeward
GH-W,M
Onward We Go
AFP-W
Ooby Dooby
TFC-W,M
Oo-De-Lally
NI-W,M On-W,M
Ooh, Do You Love You!
Mo-W,M NM-W,M OTO-W
Ooh My Feet
TW-W
Ooh Poo Pah Doo
RY-W,M
Ooh, That Kiss
OnT1-W,M
Ooh! What You Said
NM-W,M
Oom-Pah-Pah
O-W,M
Ooo Baby Baby
ToO79-W,M
Open a New Window
Mo-W,M NM-W,M OTO-W TW-W
Open Arms
VB-W,M
Open Arms, Open Heart
SNZ-W,M (Maori)
Open My Eyes That I May See
AME-W,M Hy-W,M
Open Now Thy Gates of Beauty
Hy-W,M RW-W,M
Open Road
UF-W,M
Open Secret
FSA1-W,M
Open, Shut Them
GM-W,M RSL-W,M
Open the Door, Richard!
NoS-W,M TI2-W,M
Open the Gates of the Temple
FS-W,M SS-W
Open Thy Lattice, Love
ATS-W,M FHR-W,M OHG-W,M
SSF-W,M SSFo-W,M
Opening
TW-W
Opening Ode for Knights of Labor
AL-W,M
Opening Song
AL-W
Operatives' March
MSB-W
Operator
JC-W,M PM-W,M TI1-W,M
UFB-W,M
Operator, Long Distance Please
TOC82-W,M
Ophelia Letter Blow 'Way
SGT-W,M
Opon de Rock
AAF-W,M
Opossum Hunt
NF-W NH-W
Opportunities (Let's Make Lots of
Money)
TTH-W,M
Oppossum
OTJ-W,M
Optimistic Voices
WO-W,M
Opus One
BBB-W,M TI1-W,M UFB-W,M
Or Let the Merry Bells
MU-W,M
Ora Et Labora
Boo-W,M (Latin Only)

Ora Pro Nobis
AmH-W,M
Orange and Blue
Oz1-W,M
Orange and the Black
IL-W,M
Orange and the Blue
SCa-W,M
Orange Blossom Special
IPH-W,M
Orange Colored Sky
MF-W,M NK-W,M
Orange Merchant
ASB5-W,M
Orange on an Apple Tree
GM-W,M
Oranges and Lemons
OTJ-W,M
Orchestra
BM-W HS-W,M TF-W,M YS-W,M
Orchestra Song
HS-W,M MuM-W,M PIS-W,M
**Orchestra Wives (Theme) see I've
Got a Gal in Kalamazoo**
Orchids in the Moonlight
HLS5-W,M TI1-W,M UFB-W,M
Ordinary Blues
LC-W
Ordinary Couple
SM-W,M UBF-W,M
Ordinary People
VB-W,M
Ordination Anthem
BC1-W,M
Oregon Grape
VA-W,M
Oregon State Song
Fif-W,M
Oregon Trail
LMR-W,M
Organ Grinder
ASB4-W,M FSA2-W,M
Organ Grinder's Swing
Sta-W,M
Organ Man
ASB2-W,M MH-W,M
Organize the Hosts of Labor
AL-W
Orient Express
AT-M TW-W
Oriental Romance
MML-W,M
Oriental Song
FSA1-W,M
Orientis Partibus
GBC-W,M (Latin)
Origin of the Snake
NF-W
Origin of the Stars and Bars
SiS-W
Origin of Yankee Doodle
ATS-W
Original Song
AL-W
Original Talking Blues
FSSC-W,M PSN-W
**Original Talking Blues see also
Talking Blues**
Oriole
ASB1-W,M
Oriole's Nest
MH-W,M
Orleans, Beaugency
Boo-W,M
Ornithology
TI1-M UFB-M
Oro, Se Do Bheatha 'Bhaile

S-W,M (Gaelic Only)

Orphan and King Henry see La Noel Passee

Orphan Boys
HSD-W,M

Orphan Child
Oz4-W,M

Orphan Girl
ASB6-W,M BSC-W,M Oz4-W

Orphan Song
AL-W Oz4-W,M

Orpheus with His Lute
ESB-W,M FSS-W,M SSB-W,M

Orson's Theme
MLS-M

Ortonville
SHS-W,M

Oscar Mayer Wiener Song
BNG-W,M

Oscar Mayer Wiener Song see also I Wish I Were an Oscar Mayer Wiener

Other Guy
TI2-W,M

Other Half of Me
Mo-W,M NM-W,M OTO-W

Other Side of Dixie
SiS-W

Other Side of Jordan
FW-W Oz2-W

Other Side of Jordan see also Odder Side of Jordan

Other Side of Midnight (Theme) see Noelle's Theme

Other Side of the World
TTH-W,M

Other Woman
ToS-W,M

Other World Is Not Like This see Udder Worl' Is Not Lak Dis

Ou-Vas Tu Basile?
MP-W,M (French Only)

Our Airplane
ASB2-W,M

Our Ancient Liberties
KH-W,M

Our Baby
HSD-W,M

Our Band
SOO-W,M

Our Banner
SiS-W

Our Battle Hymn for Children
LoS-W

Our Battle Song
AL-W

Our Beautiful Flag
SiS-W

Our Bondage It Shall End
AHO-W,M

Our Boy Is a Warrior Now
SiS-W

Our Boys Afloat
SiS-W

Our Boys Are All Gone to the War
SiS-W

Our Boys Are Coming Home
SiS-W

Our Boys Are Home to Stay
SiS-W

Our Boys in Camp
SiS-W

Our Boys Will Shine
BMC-W,M

Our Boys Will Shine Tonight
FU-W,M FuB-W,M IPH-W,M
MAS-W,M OS-W

Our Brave Boys in Blue
SiS-W

Our Brave Little Band
AL-W

Our Bright, Bright Summer Days Are Gone
SSFo-W,M

Our Bright, Summer Days Are Gone
FHR-W,M SSF-W,M

Our Brother Is Born
OB-W,M

Our Brutus
SiS-W

Our California Hills
OHG-W,M

Our Cause
AL-W

Our Chicago
CoS-W,M

Our Children
Mo-W,M NM-W,M OTO-W

Our Children They Were Sickly
AFP-W

Our Church Proclaims God's Love and Care
SHP-W,M

Our Color Guard
SiS-W

Our Comrade Has Fallen
Sin-W,M

Our Concerto
OnT6-W,M

Our Cottage by the Glen
GrM-W,M

Our Country
ASB5-W,M MML-W,M

Our Country's Call
AWB-W

Our Country's Gratitude
AL-W

Our Darling Kate
FHR-W,M

Our Day Will Come
TI2-W,M

Our Dear New England Boys
SiS-W

Our Delaware
Fif-W,M

Our Delight
MF-M

Our Director
OTJ-M

Our Director March
TI1-M UFB-M

Our Doorbell
GM-W,M

Our Family
ASB2-W,M

Our Father
JF-W,M PoG-W,M

Our Father see also Lord's Prayer

Our Father, by Whose Name
AHO-W,M

Our Father, God
AHO-W,M

Our Father in Heaven
AHO-W,M

Our Father Which in Heaven Art
AHO-W,M

Our Father! While Our Hearts Unlearn
AHO-W,M

Our Father's Church
AME-W,M

Our Fathers' God
AHO-W,M

Our First President's Quickstep
SCo-W,M

Our Flag
ASB1-W,M ASB2-W,M
ASB6-W,M FSA2-W,M
MAR-W,M MH-W,M

Our Flag Is There
ANS-W OTJ-W,M SL-W,M

Our Flag Is Up
MPP-W

Our Flag o'er Georgia Floats Again
SiS-W

Our Garden
ASB1-W,M ASB4-W,M

Our God
JS-W,M

Our God, Our Help
NeA-W,M

Our God, Our Help in Ages Past
ESB-W,M SCL-W,M

Our God Reigns
OGR-W,M

Our God, to Whom We Turn
Hy-W,M

Our Goodman
BSC-W FMT-W SCa-W,M

Our Great Savior
OM-W,M

Our Heavenly Father, Hear
AME-W,M

Our Helpers
SoP-W,M

Our Heritage
SL-W,M

Our Heroes
FSA1-W,M

Our History Sings
BMC-W,M

Our Home Is on the Mountain's Brow
SY-W,M

Our Instruments
GM-W,M

Our Journey Home
SHS-W,M

Our Kind Creator
AHO-W,M

Our Lady of the Hospital
SiS-W

Our Lamps Are Burning
WN-W,M

Our Land, Our Fatherland
SiP-W,M (Finnish)

Our Language of Love
TI1-W,M UBF-W,M UFB-W,M

Our L'eggs Fit Your Legs
GSM-W,M

Our Little Cowgirl
SoC-W

Our Lord Has Risen
ITP-W,M

Our Love
SoH-W,M TI1-W,M UFB-W,M

Our Love Affair
GSF-W,M

Our Love and Aloha
TI1-W,M UFB-W,M

Our Love Is on the Faultline
TOC83-W,M

Our Love Was, Is
WA-W,M

Our March
MAR-M

Our Master Hath a Garden
LMR-W,M

Our Native Song
HSD-W,M

Our Navy
  AWB-W
Our Neutral Friend
  SiS-W
Our Noble Chief Has Passed Away
  SiS-W
Our Old Mule
  NF-W
Our Orchestra
  ASB3-W,M
Our Piano
  GM-W,M
Our Private World
  MF-W,M
Our Refuge
  GH-W,M
Our Rosebush
  ASB2-W,M
Our Saviour King
  GH-W,M
Our School Now Closes Out
  AHO-W,M
Our School Will Shine
  FSA1-W,M
Our Soldier
  SiS-W
Our Song of Thanks
  ASB3-W,M
Our Southern Flag
  SiS-W
Our State Fair
  UBF-W,M
Our States, O Lord
  AHO-W,M
Our Street Car
  BMM-W
Our Teacher
  GM-W,M
Our Tense and Wintry Minds
  AHO-W,M
Our Thirty-Four Bright Stars
  SiS-W
Our Thoughts Go round the World
  SHP-W,M
Our Two-Year Boys
  SiS-W
Our Veteran Fathers
  SiS-W
Our Waltz
  MF-W,M
Our Wedding Prayer
  FS-W,M TM-W,M WGB/O-W,M
Our Willie Dear Is Dying
  FHR-W,M
Our Women
  SBA-W
Our Young Soldier's Grave
  SiS-W
Ours
  ML-W,M
Ours Is the World
  CA-W,M
Out among the Fir Trees
  SiR-W
Out among the Red Men
  MAS-W,M MML-W,M
Out and About
  OnT6-W,M
Out Here on My Own
  GSN5-W,M
Out in the Cold World, or Bring
  Back My Wandering Boy
  BIS-W,M
Out in the Meadows
  SSe-W,M
Out in the Moonlight
  Oz4-W,M

Out in the Streets
  RB-W
Out in This Terrible War
  SiS-W
Out in West Texas
  LC-W
**Out of Africa Love Theme see
  Music of Goodbye**
Out of Breath
  OHF-W
Out of Darkness into Light
  GH-W,M
**Out of My Bondage, Sorrow and
  Night see Jesus, I Come**
Out of My Dreams
  L-W OTJ-W,M OTO-W UBF-W,M
Out of Nowhere
  AT-W,M OnT1-W,M
Out of Sight, Out of Mind
  ILF-W,M RY-W,M
Out of the Ark
  GH-W,M
Out of the Blue
  CFB-W,M
Out of the Dawn
  WDS-W,M
Out of the Deep Have I Called unto
  Thee
  FiS-W,M
Out of the Depths
  SiM-W,M SoM-W,M
Out of the Dreams
  BV-W,M
Out of the Orient
  GBC-W,M
Out of the Wilderness
  Oz3-W,M WN-W,M
Out of This World
  Mo-W,M NM-W,M OHF-W
  UBF-W,M
Out of Time
  RoS-W,M
Out-of-Towners
  OTO-W
Out of Work
  AH-W,M SY-W,M
Out of Your Pocket
  PSN-W,M
Out of Your Sleep
  OB-W,M
Out on the Deep
  ESB-W,M HSD-W,M TH-W,M
Out on the Meadow
  UF-W,M
Out on the Ocean
  BSo-W,M
Out Run the Sun
  TOH-W,M
Out There on Yonder Mountains
  CFS-W,M (French)
Out They Come
  AL-W
Out Walking
  ASB6-W,M
Out with Winter
  HSA-W,M
Outcast, a Sad Song
  Oz4-W
Outlaw Broncho
  GA-W,M
Outlaw Dunny
  HB-W
Outlaws' Song
  FSA2-W,M
**Outrun the Sun see Out Run the
  Sun**
Outrunning the Devil

  NF-W
Outside My Window
  Mo-W,M NM-W,M
Outside the Holy City
  AHO-W,M
Outskirts of Town
  J-W,M
Outward Bound
  SL-W,M
Oven Bird
  ASB3-W,M
Over and Over
  AST-W,M DRR-W,M FRH-W,M
  Mo-W,M OTO-W
**Over Continent and Ocean see
  O'er Continent and Ocean**
**Over Coolin's Face the Night Is
  Creeping see O'er Coolin's Face
  the Night Is Creeping**
Over-Courteous Knight
  SR-W,M
Over Here
  OTO-W UBF-W,M
Over Hill, over Dale
  FSS-W,M
Over in the Meadow
  MG-W,M SOO-W,M
Over Jordan
  GH-W,M
Over Land and over Sea
  GO-W
Over My Head
  SFF-W,M ToO76-W,M
Over My Meadow
  ASB5-W,M
Over Song
  AF-W
Over Tatra
  NAS-W,M
Over the Banister
  WiS8-W,M
Over the Bright Blue Sea
  SL-W,M
**Over the Crossing see O'er the
  Crossing**
Over the Garden Wall
  HSD-W,M Oz4-W
Over the Grave
  TH-W,M
Over the Hill
  OTO-W Sh-W,M
Over the Hill to the Poorhouse
  EFS-W,M
Over the Hills
  TO-W,M
Over the Hills at the Poorhouse
  BSC-W
**Over the Hills Away see O'er the
  Hills Away**
**Over the Horizon see O'er the
  Horizon**
Over the Line
  ANS-W GH-W,M
Over the Meadows
  SSe-W,M
Over the Mountain
  VB-W,M
Over the Mystic Sea
  GrM-W,M
Over the Ocean Wave
  AME-W,M GH-W,M
Over the Rainbow
  CS-W,M EAG2-W,M GG2-W,M
  GSO-W,M HLS5-W,M RDF-W,M
  RW-W,M STW-W,M T-W,M
  TW-W WO-W,M
Over the River

FHR-W,M
Over the River and through the
  Woods
  HS-W,M OFS-W,M OS-W
  OTJ-W,M RW-W,M SOO-W,M
  STR-W,M TI1-W,M UFB-W,M
Over the River, Charlie
  D-W,M
Over the River, Faces I See
  AME-W,M
**Over the Season Vernal see O'er
  the Season Vernal**
Over the Stars There Is Rest
  AmH-W,M WiS7-W,M
Over the Summer Sea
  TH-W,M
Over the Sunset Mountains
  BSG-W,M BSP-W,M
Over the Trail
  HOH-W
Over the Waves
  OBN-M OTJ-W,M RW-M TI1-M
  UFB-M
Over There
  FMT-W GSN1-W,M HA-W,M
  HLS1-W,M OS-W RW-W,M
Over There Hills Waltz
  OGC2-W,M
**Over Waiting Harp-Strings of the
  Mind see O'er Waiting Harp-
  Strings of the Mind**
Over You
  HFH-W,M
Overcoats
  ASB3-W,M
Overjoyed
  TTH-W,M
Overland Stage
  SoC-W
Overlookin' and Underthinkin'
  RW-W,M
Overtures from Richmond
  FGM-W,M
Ovinu Malkenu
  JS-W,M (Hebrew)
Ovos, Amida
  SBJ-W,M (Hebrew Only)
Owed to Middle Age
  TW-W
Owl
  MH-W,M
Ox-Driver
  FW-W
Oxford
  SI-W,M
Oxford Girl
  BSC-W FMT-W
Oye Como Va
  AO-M MF-M RW-W,M (Spanish
  Only)
Oye Negra
  RW-M
Oyfn Pripetshuk
  FW-W (Yiddish)
Oysters, Sir
  SY-W,M

P

P.S. I Love You
  BBe-W,M BR-W,M DPE-W,M
  ERM-W,M GAR-W,M HLS2-W,M
  MF-W,M RY-W,M RYT-W,M
  TI2-W,M TWS-W
P.T.A.
  LoS-W

P.T.A. Round
  LoS-W
P.T.A. Song
  LoS-W,M
Pabst Blue Ribbon Beer
  GSM-W,M
Pace-Egging Song
  BB-W GBC-W,M
**Pachelbel's Canon see Canon in D
  and Canon in D Major**
Pack, Clouds, Away
  SL-W,M
Pack Up Your Sorrows
  FSt-W,M JF-W,M
Pack Up Your Troubles
  Bo-W OS-W U-W
Pack Up Your Troubles in Your Old
  Kitbag
  CSo-W,M
Pack Up Your Troubles in Your Old
  Kitbag and Smile, Smile, Smile
  TI1-W,M UFB-W,M
Packenham
  BSC-W
Packing Ham
  BSC-W
Pacolet
  SHS-W,M
Paddle Song
  Bo-W,M
Paddle Your Own Canoe
  BH-W,M HSD-W,M OTJ-W,M
Paddlin' Madelin' Home
  RoE-W,M TI1-W,M UFB-W,M
Paddling My Canoe
  KS-W,M SSe-W,M
Paddy Darry
  BSC-W
Paddy Doyle
  SA-W,M
Paddy Doyle's Boots
  FSA1-W,M IS-W,M
Paddy on the Railway
  SoF-W,M
Paddy on the Turnpike
  HB-W,M
Paddy Ryan
  HB-W,M
Paddy Shannon
  ESU-W
Paddy Works on the Railway
  FG1-W,M HAS-W,M LSR-W,M
  SA-W,M VP-W,M
Paddy's Curiosity Shop
  TMA-W,M
Paddy's Own Good Irish Stew
  VP-W
Padre
  TI1-W,M
Padstow May Song
  BB-W
Paean
  OB-W,M
Pagan Love Song
  GST-W,M HLS5-W,M OP1-W,M
  RW-W,M
Page Sat in the Lofty Tower
  EL-W,M
Pageant
  FSA2-W,M
Page's Geese
  NF-W
Paint It Black
  RoS-W,M
Paint Me a Rainbow
  Mo-W,M NM-W,M OTO-W
Painted Ladies

AO-W,M
Painter
  ASB3-W,M GM-W,M LA-W,M
  (Spanish) LMR-W,M
Painting the Clouds with Sunshine
  MF-W,M
Pajarillo Barranqueno
  LA-W,M (Spanish)
Pal of My Cradle Days
  RW-W,M STW-W,M
Pal of My Dreams
  EFS-W,M
Pal That I Loved Stole the Gal That
  I Loved
  STW-W,M
Palapala
  MHB-W,M (Spanish)
Pale Moonlight
  ITP-W,M
**Paleface (Theme) see Buttons and
  Bows**
Palisades Park
  ILS-W,M
Pallet on Your Floor
  BSo-W,M
Palm Branches
  WiS7-M
Palmetto State Song
  MPP-W
Palms
  AmH-W,M FiS-W,M (French)
  SL-W,M WiS7-W,M
Palms and Myrtles
  JS-W,M
Palms of Victory
  Oz4-W,M
Paloma see La Paloma
Paloma Blanca
  MF-W,M PT-W,M
Pan Am Makes the Goin' Great
  GSM-W,M
Pan Ch'iao Tao Ch'ing (Old
  Fisherman)
  FD-W,M (Chinese)
Pancho
  OTO-W
Pancho and Lefty
  TOC83-W,M
Pancho Lopez
  OnT6-W,M
Pania of the Reef
  SNZ-W,M (Maori)
Panic Is On
  PO-W,M
Panis Angelicus
  BCh-W,M MHB-W,M (Latin)
  NCB-W,M (Latin Only) TM-M
  WGB/O-M WiS9-W,M (Latin)
Pans o' Biscuit
  NH-W
Pansies
  MH-W,M
Pansy
  MML-W,M
Papa and Mama Had Love
  Lo-W,M
Papa, Can You Hear Me?
  MLS-W,M
Papa Died Old
  Lo-W,M
Papa Hobo
  PS-W,M
Papa Joe's
  Mo-W,M
Papa Loves Mambo
  TI1-W,M UFB-W,M
Papa Oom Mow Mow

HR-W
Papageno
  FSA1-W,M
Papa's Billy Goat
  LSR-W,M
Papa's Gonna Make It Alright
  Sh-W,M
Papaya Mama
  RW-W,M
Papaya Tree
  BMC-W,M
**Paper Chase Love Theme see I
  Want to Spend My Life with You**
Paper Cup
  TI2-W,M
Paper Doll
  BeL-W,M RDT-W,M TI2-W,M
Paper Dolls
  MH-W,M
Paper Mache
  HD-W,M
Paper of Pins
  ASB3-W,M BSC-W DD-W,M
  FMT-W FW-W HS-W,M IS-W,M
  LoS-W,M MSH-W,M OTJ-W,M
  Oz3-W,M RS-W,M RW-W,M
  SCa-W,M SG-W,M SRS-W,M
Paper Roses
  AO-W,M BR-W,M CMG-W,M
  EC-W,M HLS9-W,M MF-W,M
  On-W,M OnT6-W,M OPS-W,M
  RW-W,M TI1-W,M UFB-W,M
Paperback Writer
  BBe-W,M Be1-W,M TWS-W
Paper'd-Up Hair
  MSB-W
Papillon
  LA-W,M (Spanish)
Pap's Old Billy Goat
  ITP-W,M
Par Derrier' Chez Ma Tant'
  CFS-W,M (French)
Par Derrier' Chez Mon Pere
  FSO-W,M (French)
Par Ein Beau Lundi
  CaF-W (French Only)
Par Ein Lundi Matin
  CaF-W (French Only)
Para Los Rumberos
  MF-W,M (Spanish Only)
Parachute Woman
  RoS-W,M
Parade
  ASB2-W,M ASB3-W,M
  ASB4-W,M FSA1-W,M MH-W,M
Parade of the Wooden Soldiers
  BCS-W,M TI2-W,M
Paradise (Come with Me to
  Paradise)
  GH-W,M
Paradise (Down by the Green River
  Where Paradise Lay)
  BSo-W,M
Paradise (She Takes Me to
  Paradise)
  CS-W,M HLS2-W,M OP1-W,M
  RW-W,M
Paradise Garden
  Ki-W,M
Paradise, Hawaiian Style
  SRE1-W,M
Paradise Tonight
  TOC83-W,M
Paranoia Blues
  PS-W,M
Paratroopers' Lament
  GI-W

Parchman Parodies
  SFF-W,M
Pardon Came Too Late
  Oz4-W
Pardon My Southern Accent
  MF-W,M OHF-W
Pardon, Peace, and Power
  GH-W,M
Pardon Renied Again
  LC-W
Pardoning Love
  SHS-W,M
**Paris after Dark (Theme) see
  Besame Mucho**
Paris Blues
  GMD-W,M RW-W,M
Paris, France
  Mo-W,M NM-W,M OTO-W
Paris Here I Come
  FSF-W (French)
Paris Holiday
  Mo-W,M NM-W,M OTO-W
Paris in the Spring
  HC2-W,M
Paris Is a Lonely Town
  Mo-W,M NM-W,M OTO-W
Paris Loves Lovers
  UBF-W,M
Paris Was Made for Lovers
  MLS-W,M
Parisian Pierrot
  T-W,M
Parisian Thoroughfare
  MF-M
Parking a Car
  Boo-W,M
Parks of Paris
  Mo-W,M NM-W,M OTO-W
Parlez-Moi Du Soleil
  SSN-W,M (French)
Parlez-Vous L'English
  TW-W
Parliament of England
  ATS-W
Parlor
  TMA-W,M
Parody
  SBA-W
Parody of the Banks of the Dee
  SAR-W,M SSS-W,M
Parody on the Liberty Song
  SAR-W
Parody on Wat'ry God
  SAR-W,M
Parody Parodized
  SBA-W
Parody upon a Well-Known Liberty
  Song
  SI-W
Parrot
  ASB6-W,M
Parson Fuller
  NSS-W
Parson Jones
  SCa-W
Part in Peace: Christ's Life Was
  Peace
  Hy-W,M
Part of Me That Needs You Most
  TTH-W,M
Partant Pour La Syrie
  SiP-W,M (French)
Parthenia to Ingomar
  FHR-W,M SSF-W,M
Part-Time Servant
  OGR-W,M
Parting

MML-W,M
Parting Friends
  SHS-W,M
Parting Glass
  IS-W,M
Parting Hand
  SHS-W,M
Parting Hour
  SL-W,M
Parting Hymn
  GH-W,M GrM-W,M
Parting Hymn We Sing
  AHO-W,M Hy-W,M
Parting Song
  CSS-W SL-W,M
Partner Come and Dance with Me
  HS-W,M
Party
  SRE1-W,M
Party Doll
  GAR-W,M ILF-W,M MF-W,M
  RY-W,M
Party in Tacoma
  AF-W
Party's Over
  DBC-W,M HC1-W,M LM-W,M
  OTO-W TI1-W,M ToS-W,M TW-W
  UBF-W,M UFB-W,M
Pas Loin De Chez Moi
  CE-W,M (French)
Pass Around the Bottle
  AF-W GI-W
Pass It On
  GH-W,M
Pass Me By
  Mo-W,M NM-W,M OTJ-W,M
  OTO-W RDT-W,M TI2-W,M
Pass Me Not
  GH-W,M
Pass Me Not, O Gentle Savior
  AME-W,M
Pass That Peace Pipe
  TI1-W,M UBF-W,M UFB-W,M
Pass the Cross to Me
  Sh-W,M
Pass under the Rod
  Oz4-W
Passant Par Paris
  FSF-W (French)
Passin' the Faith Along
  VB-W,M
Passing
  TH-W,M
Passing By (I May Never Pass This
  Way Again)
  Mo-W,M NM-W,M
Passing By (Purcell)
  FSY-W,M LMR-W,M SFB-W,M
Passing Once thru' Fair Lorraine
  SMW-W,M (French)
Passing through Seville
  LA-W,M (Spanish)
Passion Play Edit #8
  BJ-W,M
Passion Play Edit #9
  BJ-W,M
**Passionate Pilgrim see Crabbed
  Age and Youth**
Past Is Dark with Sin and Shame
  AHO-W,M
Past, Present, and Future
  BMM-W,M
Past Ten O'Clock the Watchman's
  Call
  Boo-W,M
Past Three O'Clock
  JOC-W,M LMR-W,M

Pastime with Good Company
　SSP-W
Pastoral
　SL-W,M
Pastoral Elegy
　SHS-W,M
Pastorale
　GUM2-W,M
Pastourelle (Poulenc)
　GM-M
Pastures Green
　OTJ-W,M
Pastures of Plenty
　AFP-W Am-W,M FG2-W,M
　TI-W,M TO-W,M UFB-W,M
Pat Malloy
　SCa-W,M
Pat Works on the Railway
　AFP-W AL-W ASB5-W,M FW-W
　GuC-W,M LT-W,M SWF-W,M
　WS-W,M
Pat-a-Cake
　OTJ-W,M RSL-W,M RW-W,M
Pat-a-Cake Man
　SOO-W,M
Pat-a-Pan
　HS-W,M VA-W,M
Patapan
　OB-W,M SFB-W,M
Patches
　HR-W
Patient Joe
　ESU-W
Patio De Mi Casa see El Patio De Mi Casa
Patrick's Day Parade
　ATS-W OHG-W,M
Patriot Flag
　SiS-W
Patriot Game
　FW-W
Patriot Mother
　LW-W,M
Patriotic Diggers
　AL-W ATS-W,M ESU-W SI-W,M
Patriotic Exultation on Lyon's
　Release
　MPP-W
Patriotic Sky
　ASB3-W,M
Patriotic Song (Mexico)
　SiP-W,M (Spanish)
Patron's Chain
　GrM-W,M
Patron's Standard
　GrM-W,M
Patsy-ory-ory-ay
　IL-W,M
Patter-Roll roun' Me
　NSS-W
Patton Theme
　HFH-M
Pattonia, the Pride of the Plains
　Oz2-W
Patty Duke Show Theme see Cousins
Paul and Silas
　NH-W
Paul and Silas, Bound in Jail
　NSS-W
Paul Bunyan
　SAm-W,M
Paul Jones
　ANS-W SAR-W SI-W,M
Paul Jones' Victory
　ANS-W AWB-W SI-W,M
Paul Revere

HCY-W,M
Paul Revere's Ride
　ASB4-W,M AWB-W
Paul Said to the Corinthians
　SBF-W,M UF-W,M
Paul Vane
　Oz4-W,M SiS-W
Pauv' Piti Mom'zelle Zizi
　BaB-W,M (French)
Paw-Paw Patch
　BMC-W,M Bo-W,M FW-W
　MES2-W,M RW-W,M SG-W,M
Pawpaw Patch
　HS-W,M
Paw-Paw Peeling
　Oz3-W,M
Pax Vobiscum
　MU-W,M
Pay Day at Coal Creek
　FW-W
Pay Me My Money Down
　FG1-W,M FGM-W,M FW-W
　GuC-W,M WSB-W,M
Payday Song
　GO-W
Paying Debts with Kicks
　NF-W
Pea-Patch Jig
　DE-W,M
Pea Ridge Battle
　Oz2-W,M
Peace
　OGR-W,M
Peace--1815
　ESU-W
Peace! Be Still!
　GH-W,M
Peace Be with All
　SL-W,M
Peace Breaking People
　DBL-W
Peace Has Come
　SiS-W
Peace Hymn
　MML-W,M
Peace in the Valley
　HLS7-W,M HLS9-W,M RDT-W,M
　SUH-W,M TI1-W,M Tr-W,M
　UFB-W,M
Peace in the Valley see also There'll Be Peace in the Valley for Me
Peace Is the Mind's Old Wilderness
　AHO-W,M
Peace Jubilee
　SiS-W
Peace Like a River
　PS-W,M
Peace of the River
　SMY-W,M
Peace on Earth
　FS-W,M MuM-W,M PSN-W,M
Peace, Peace Is Mine
　GH-W,M
Peace, Perfect Peace, in This Dark World of Sin
　Hy-W,M
Peace Pipe
　DP-W,M
Peace Pipe Song
　ASB2-W,M
Peace Song
　AL-W
Peace to All
　MHB-W,M (Serbo-Croatian)
Peace to the Brave
　ANS-W

Peaceful
　BR-W,M
Peaceful Easy Feeling
　DPE-W,M
Peach
　LA-W,M (Spanish)
Peach on the Beach
　NN7-W,M
Peach Picking Time Down in Georgia
　LJ-W,M
Peacherine Rag
　On-M
Peacock Stung by the Hornet
　ANS-W
Pealing Bells
　SiR-W,M
Peanut Pickin' Song
　NAS-W,M NFS-W,M UF-W,M
Peanut Song
　GeS-W,M
Peanut Vendor
　TI2-W,M
Pear Tree
　FSA2-W,M RuS-W,M (Russian)
Pearl
　FSA2-W,M MHB-W,M (Spanish)
　SL-W,M
Pearl Bright
　Oz2-W
Pearl Bryan
　FSU-W ITP-W,M
Pearl of Greatest Price
　GH-W,M
Pearls
　Mo-W,M OTO-W
Pearly Shells
　TI1-W,M (Hawaiian) UFB-W,M (Hawaiian)
Peas, Beans, Oats, and Barley
　UF-W
Peasant Chorus (Faust)
　SMY-W,M
Peasant Dance
　SL-W,M
Peasant's Vesper Song
　MHB-W,M
Peasants' Wedding March
　CA-W,M
Pease Porridge Hot
　OTJ-W,M
Peat Bog Soldiers
　FW-W SMW-W,M (German)
　SWF-W,M
Pecaste Sin Maldad
　LaS-W,M (Spanish Only)
Pecos Bill
　FC-W,M SAm-W,M
Pecos River Queen
　SoC-W
Pecos Stream
　SoC-W
Peddler
　FSA2-W,M MG-W,M
Peddler and His Wife
　FSU-W
Peddler's Pack
　MHB-W,M
Peek-a-Boo
　EFS-W,M HR-W TMA-W,M
Peeler and the Goat
　VP-W,M
Peel's Jig
　DE-W,M
Peep Squirrel
　AFS-W,M FSA1-W,M NF-W
Peepin' thru' the Keyhole

OGC2-W,M
Peerless Maiden
  SeS-W,M
Peg o' My Heart
  BH-W,M EAG2-W,M FPS-W,M
  GG2-W,M GSN1-W,M HLS1-W,M
  MAB1-W MSA1-W OAP-W,M
  OS-W RW-W,M
Peg O'Ramsay
  FSS-W,M SSP-W
Peggy-O
  FW-W
Peggy O'Neil
  BH-W,M CS-W,M GST-W,M
  HLS1-W,M OS-W RW-W,M U-W
Peggy Sue
  DRR-W,M TI2-W,M
Peggy, the Pearl of Pensacola
  LW-W,M PO-W,M
Peggy Walker
  BSC-W
Peigin Leitir Mor
  VP-W (Gaelic Only)
Pelle's Fanciful Yankee Doodle
  SE-W,M (Swedish)
Pelles Fantasifyllda Yankee Doodle
  SE-W,M (Swedish)
Pelot De Betton
  FSF-W (French)
Pendulum
  FSA1-W,M
Penguin
  ASB4-W,M
Penitentiary Blues
  LC-W,M
Penitent's Prayer
  SHS-W,M
Pennies from Heaven
  HLS5-W,M MAB1-W MSA1-W
  RDT-W,M RW-W,M TI1-W,M
  UFB-W,M
Pennsylvania
  BC1-W,M
Pennsylvania Miner
  AL-W
Pennsylvania Polka
  MF-W,M PT-W,M TI1-W,M
Pennsylvania 6-5000
  GSF-W,M GSN3-W,M RW-W,M
Pennsylvania Song
  SBA-W
Penny by Penny
  MLS-W,M
Penny Candy
  TW-W
Penny for Your Thoughts
  CCS-W,M FHR-W,M
Penny Lane
  BBe-W,M Be2-W,M OnT1-W,M
  PMC-W,M SwS-W,M TWS-W
Penny Problems
  SOO-W,M
Pennzoil Please
  GSM-W,M
Penthouse Serenade
  AT-W,M OnT1-W,M RDT-W,M
Pentland Hills see Rullion Green
People
  DBC-W,M HC2-W,M HSi-W,M
  ILT-W,M OTJ-W,M OTO-W
  RT6-W,M RW-W,M TI1-W,M
  UBF-W,M UFB-W,M
People, The
  JW-W,M
People Alone
  TOM-W,M
People Are Strange

RB-W
People Awake
  SMW-W,M (Serbo-Croatian)
People Called Christians
  GB-W,M
People Get Ready
  SFF-W,M
People Got to Be Free
  MCG-W,M TI2-W,M TRR-W,M
People in a Box
  VB-W,M
People in Me
  OnT1-W,M
People Like You
  GG4-W,M
People, Look East
  YC-W,M
People Need Love
  TI1-W,M UFB-W,M
People Need the Lord
  GP-W,M VB-W,M
People of the Way
  SHP-W,M
People Will Say We're in Love
  DBC-W,M HC1-W,M HLS8-W,M
  L-W OTJ-W,M OTO-W TGO-W,M
  TI1-W,M UBF-W,M UFB-W,M
People's Friend
  MPP-W,M
People's Party Song
  AFP-W AL-W
People's Rally Cry
  AFP-W AL-W
People's Reaction
  PAJ-W,M
Pepita
  ReG-W,M
Pepper Grinders
  OU-W,M
Pepper Head Woman
  DBL-W
Peppermint Stick
  GM-W,M
Peppermint Twist
  ILS-W,M MF-W,M RY-W,M
Pepsi-Cola Hits the Spot
  GSM-W,M
Pepsi-Cola Jingle see Feelin' Free,
  Pepsi-Cola Hits the Spot, and
  Pepsi's Got a Lot to Give
Pepsi's Got a Lot to Give, You've
  Got a Lot to Live
  GSM-W,M
Pepsodent Toothpaste Jingle see
  You'll Wonder Where the Yellow
  Went
Perdido
  LaS-W,M
Pere Michel
  CaF-W (French)
Perfect Day
  OS-W
Perfect Man
  Mo-W,M NM-W,M OTO-W
Perfect Nanny
  OnT6-W,M WD-W,M
Perfect Rose
  NAS-W,M
Perfect State
  TW-W
Perfect Strangers
  TOH-W,M
Perfect Time to Be in Love
  TW-W
Perfection
  Mo-W,M NM-W,M OTO-W
Perfectly Marvelous

C-W,M
Perfume De Amor
  RW-M
Perhaps Love
  CJ-W,M
Periwinkle
  NF-W
Permit Us, Lord, to Consecrate
  AHO-W,M
Perpetual Anticipation
  LN-W,M
Perrie Merrie Dixie Dominie
  ITP-W
Perry's Victory
  ANS-W AWB-W SI-W,M
Persephone
  TW-W
Persia's Crew
  SA-W,M
Personality (Burke/Van Heusen)
  TI1-W,M UFB-W,M
Personality (Victor Herbert)
  OG-W,M
Personality (You've Got)
  FRH-W,M
Personally
  TI2-W,M TOC82-W,M
  TOC83-W,M
Personent Hodie
  OB-W,M (Latin Only)
Pesach Hymn
  JS-W,M
Pesach Lonu Shaar
  JS-W,M (Hebrew Only)
Pescador see El Pescador
Pesky Sarpent
  AH-W,M
Pet Bird
  MH-W,M
Pete from Betton
  FSF-W (French)
Pete Knight
  HB-W,M
Pete Knight, the King of the
  Cowboys
  HB-W
Pete Knight's Last Ride
  HB-W
Peter
  J-W,M
Peter and the Wolf
  RW-M
Peter Cottontail
  TI1-W,M UFB-W,M
Peter, Go Ring Dem Bells
  FN-W,M WiS7-W,M
Peter, Go Ring Dem Bells see also
  O Peter, Go Ring Dem Bells
Peter Gray
  FW-W HSD-W,M MAS-W,M
Peter Gunn
  PoG-M
Peter Gunn Style
  TTH-M
Peter Johnson, or the Trip to
  America
  SE-W,M (Swedish)
Peter Keenan's Song
  IFM-W
Peter on the Sea
  FN-W,M RF-W,M
Peter Parker
  SSS-W,M
Peter Paul Candy Bars Jingle see
  Different Bites for Different Likes
  and Sometimes I Feel Like a Nut
Peter, Peter, Pumpkin Eater

OTJ-W,M SiR-W,M
Peter Piper
  LMR-W,M
Peter Porter
  SMa-W,M
Peter Rabbit, Ha! Ha!
  PSD-W,M
Peter Story
  DE-W,M
Peter Story Jig
  DE-W,M
Peter White
  Boo-W,M
Peterborough
  SHS-W,M
Peter's Theme see I'll Catch the Sun
Petit Bonhomme see Ein Petit Bonhomme and Un Petit Bonhomme
Petit Navire see Le Petit Navire
Petit Rocher
  CFS-W,M (French)
Petit Rocher De La Haute Montagne
  FSO-W,M (French)
Petite Fleur
  TI1-M UFB-M
Petite Waltz
  TI2-W,M
Petition
  SL-W,M
Petter Jonsson Resan Till Amerika
  SE-W,M (Swedish)
Petticoat High
  Mo-W,M NM-W,M OTO-W
Petticoats of Portugal
  TI2-W,M
Peyote Song
  IF-M
Peyton Place (Theme) see For Those Who Are Young
Phantom of the Opera
  UBF-W,M
Pharaoh's Army
  AN-W
Phenomenon
  FSA1-W,M MMW-W,M
Phfft! You Were Gone!
  BIS-W,M
Phfft! You Were Gone! (Gospel Version)
  BIS-W,M
Philadelphia
  NB-W
Philadelphia Freedom
  GrS-W,M TI2-W,M
Philadelphia Lawyer
  AFP-W
Philadelphia Riots
  VP-W
Philip Morris Cigarettes Jingle see Call for Philip Morris
Philippine Convoy
  GO-W
Philippines
  SL-W,M
Philmont Grace
  Bo-W
Philmont Hymn
  Bo-W,M
Philosophic Love Song
  MPP-W
Phoebus
  BC1-W,M
Phony King of England
  On-W,M

Photographs and Memories
  JC-W,M MF-W,M PM-W,M
Physician
  TW-W
Piano Blues
  LC-W
Piano Concerto in A Minor Theme (Grieg)
  RW-M
Piano Concerto in B Flat Minor (Tschaikovsky)
  RW-M
Piano Concerto in B Flat Minor, Second Movement (Tschaikovsky)
  RW-M
Piano Concerto No. 1 (Tschaikovsky)
  MF-M
Piano Concerto No. 2 Theme (Rachmaninoff)
  RW-M
Piano Concerto No. 2 Second Theme (Rachmaninoff)
  RW-M
Piano Concerto Theme (Schumann, Op. 54)
  RW-M
Piano Man
  GrS-W,M
Piano Sonata (Beethoven Op. 2, No. 3)
  LTL-M
Piano Sonata in A Major (Mozart)
  LTL-M
Picasso Summer Theme
  EY-W,M
Picasso Summer Theme see also Summer Me, Winter Me
Picayune Butler
  AL-W NeA-W,M
Piccolo Pete
  TI2-W,M
Pick a Bale o' Cotton
  NeF-W
Pick a Bale of Cotton
  Bo-W,M FW-W Le-W,M MG-W,M
  OFS-W,M OHO-W,M OTJ-W,M
  RW-W,M WU-W,M
Pick a Pocket or Two
  O-W,M
Pick and Shovel Song
  NH-W
Pick 'Em Up Higher
  LC-W
Pick Up the Tempo
  WNF-W
Pick Yourself Up
  TI1-W,M UFB-W,M
Pickers Are Comin'
  OTO-W Sh-W,M
Picket Guard
  SiS-W
Picket Line Blues see C.I.O.
Picket-Line Song
  FW-W
Picking Lint
  SiS-W
Picking Peaches
  ST-W,M
Picnic
  TI1-W,M UFB-W,M
Picnic Song
  GrM-W,M
Picnic Theme
  MF-W,M
Picnics

SL-W,M
Picture from Life's Other Side
  FW-W Oz4-W,M
Picture No Artist Can Paint
  Oz4-W
Picture That Is Turned toward the Wall
  EFS-W,M FSTS-W,M
Picture This
  PL-W,M
Pictureland
  FSA1-W,M
Pictures of Lily
  WA-W,M
Piddlin' Pup
  GI-W
Pie
  ASB6-W,M
Pie in the Sky
  FW-W HAS-W,M IHA-W,M
  SFM-W TO-W,M
Piece of Ground
  JF-W,M
Piece of Sky
  MLS-W,M
Pieces of April
  TI2-W,M
Pieces of Dreams
  MLS-W,M
Pieces of Dreams see also Little Boy Lost
Piedra Sobre Piedra
  TI1-W,M (Spanish Only)
  UFB-W,M (Spanish Only)
Pierrot's Song
  Gu-W,M
Pietas Omnium Virtutum
  Boo-W,M (Latin Only)
Pig in a Pen
  BIS-W,M
Pig-in-a-Polk
  MPP-W
Pig in the Parlor
  Oz3-W,M
Pigalle
  TI2-W,M
Pigeon Is Never Woe
  Boo-W,M
Pigeons
  GM-W,M MH-W,M
Pigeons and Fairies
  UF-W,M
Piggies
  TWS-W
Piggy-Wig and Piggy-Wee
  MH-W,M
Piggyback Ride
  GM-W,M
Pigmeat
  Le-W,M
Pigtail
  NF-W
Pigtown Fling
  POT-M
Pike's Dixie
  SiS-W
Pilate's Dream
  UBF-W,M
Pilgrim
  MHB-W,M SHS-W,M
Pilgrim: Chapter 33
  SuS-W,M
Pilgrim Fathers
  FSA2-W,M
Pilgrims' Chorus
  SL-W,M
Pilgrim's Farewell

SHS-W,M
Pilgrim's Legacy
 SY-W,M
Pilgrim's Lot
 SHS-W,M WN-W,M
Pilgrims of Love
 Sw-W,M
Pilgrim's Song
 ASB6-W,M NH-W RF-W,M
 SHS-W,M WN-W,M
Pilgrim's Triumph
 WN-W,M
Pill
 CMG-W,M
Pill Oll Helle
 IF-W,M (Estonian)
Pillar of Glory see Naval Song:
 Pillar of Glory
Pillsbury Says It Best
 GSM-W,M
Pilot's Lament
 AF-W
Pinball Wizard
 WA-W,M
Pinball Wizard/See Me, Feel Me
 Medley
 BR-W,M
Pine Cones and Holly Berries
 TI2-W,M UBF-W,M
Pine Top
 LC-W
Pine Top's Boogie
 Mo-W,M NM-W,M
Pine Tree
 AS-W,M
Pine Tree Song
 BMC-W,M SiR-W,M
Pineapple Princess
 SBS-W,M
Pinery Boy
 WS-W,M
Pinetop's Blues
 LC-W
Pinewood Derby Song
 CSS-W
Piney Wood Hills
 OnT6-W,M
Pink Elephants on Parade
 NI-W,M
Pink Pajamas
 Bo-W
Pink Panther
 PoG-W,M WG-W,M
Pinkville Helicopter
 IHA-W,M
Pinocchio
 OTJ-W,M
Pintor De Cannahy
 LA-W,M (Spanish)
Pioneer Preacher
 FMT-W
Pioneers
 SL-W,M
Pipeline
 DRR-M
Piper of Dundee
 SoF-W,M
Piper of Hamelin
 ASB5-W,M
Pique La Baleine
 FSF-W (French)
Pirate Days
 OBN-W,M
Pirate Lover
 ESU-W
Pirates' Chorus
 HSD-W,M

Pirates Love Theme see Dolores
 (Love Theme from Pirates)
Piri-Miri-Dictum Domini
 MSH-W,M
Pisgah
 SHS-W,M WN-W,M
Piss on Johnson's War
 VS-W,M
Pistol Packin' Mama
 LWT-W,M TI1-W,M UFB-W,M
Pit-a-Pat
 SiR-W,M
Pitch It in the Blue Whale
 FSF-W (French)
Pitite
 CaF-W (French Only)
Pitter Patter
 ASB2-W,M GM-W,M
Pity, Lord, Pity
 SoM-W,M
Pity the Downtrodden Landlord
 FW-W JF-W,M PO-W,M
Pizzicato (Sylvia)
 AmH-M
Pizzicato Polka
 MF-M PT-M TI1-M UFB-M
Place of Bittersweet
 MLS-W,M
Place to Fall Apart
 NMH-W,M
Plain We Live
 PF-W,M
Plains of Manassas
 Re-W,M
Plains of Waterloo
 BB-W
Plaisir D'Amour
 Gu-W,M (French Only)
Plane Wreck at Los Gatos
 AFP-W TI1-W,M UFB-W,M
Plane Wreck at Los Gatos see also
 Deportee
Planets
 ASB5-W,M
Plant a Radish
 Fa-W,M OTJ-W,M OTO-W
 UBF-W,M
Plantation Boogie
 OGC2-W,M
Planters Peanuts Jingle see Let
 There Be Planters
Planting My Garden
 ASB1-W,M
Planting Rice
 HSA-W,M MG-W,M SWF-W,M
Plantons La Vigne
 CUP-W,M (French Only)
Plaster
 NF-W
Plastic Jesus
 FW-W PO-W,M
Platonia
 HB-W,M
Play a Simple Melody
 OAP-W,M SLB-W,M
Play Another Slow Song
 TOH-W,M
Play, Fiddle, Play
 TI2-W,M
Play Me
 TI2-W,M
Play Me or Trade Me
 TOC82-W,M
Play Song
 Oz3-W
Play the Bugle
 ASB5-W,M

Play the Game
 FSA2-W,M
Play with Fire
 RoS-W,M
Playboy's Theme
 Mo-W,M NM-W,M TI2-W,M
Playin' Dominoes and Shootin'
 Dice
 OGC1-W,M
Playing a Tune
 SOO-W,M
Playing Ball
 MH-W,M
Playing Circus
 MH-W,M
Playing Croquet
 LMS-W,M
Playing in the Band
 MH-W,M
Playing in the Sun
 SOO-W,M
Playing Indian
 MH-W,M
Playing the Bugle
 MH-W,M
Playing the Flute and Drum
 BMC-W,M SiR-W,M
Playing the Races
 DBL-W
Playing Together
 ASB3-W,M
Playing Train
 ASB1-W,M
Playing with Baby
 MH-W,M
Playing with the Boys
 TTH-W,M
Pleasant Are Thy Courts Above
 Hy-W,M
Pleasant Hill
 SHS-W,M
Please
 AT-W,M LM-W,M OnT1-W,M
 OTO-W
Please Be Kind
 MF-W,M
Please Buy My Record
 RB-W
Please Daddy (Don't Get Drunk
 This Christmas)
 CMG-W,M
Please Don't Drag That String
 Around
 SRE1-W,M
Please Don't Eat the Daisies
 (Theme)
 GTV-M
Please Don't Go
 ToO79-W,M
Please Don't Go Girl
 CFB-W,M
Please Don't Let This Harvest Pass
 WN-W,M
Please Don't Stop Loving Me
 BDP-W,M SRE2-W,M
Please Don't Talk about Me When
 I'm Gone
 MF-W,M MR-W,M OHB-W,M
Please Don't Tell Me How the
 Story Ends
 FrF-W,M HLS9-W,M SuS-W,M
Please Don't Think I'm Nosey
 DBL-W
Please Forgive Me
 GMD-W,M
Please Give Me Black an' Brown
 LC-W

Please Go Home
  RoS-W,M
Please Go 'Way and Let Me Sleep
  OBN-W,M
Please Help Me, I'm Falling
  OGC2-W,M
Please Let Me Stay with You
  RBO-W,M
Please Love Me Forever
  BHB-W,M OnT6-W,M
Please, Mister Conductor
  LSR-W,M Oz4-W,M
Please Mr. Postman
  ToO76-W,M
Please Please Me
  BBe-W,M TI2-W,M TWS-W
Please, Take Me Back to the Army
  GO-W
Please Throw This Dog a Bone
  LC-W
Pleasure and Pain
  TTH-W,M
Pleasure It Is
  Boo-W,M OB-W,M
Pledge
  ASB5-W,M GM-W,M
Pledge Now Thy Hand
  MU-W,M (Italian)
Pledge of Allegiance
  GeS-W,M JW-W,M MM-W,M
Pledge of Allegiance to the Flag
  AAP-W,M
Pledge the Canadian Maiden
  CFS-W,M (French)
Plenary
  SHS-W,M
Plenty of Pennsylvania
  PF-W,M
Plenty of Time
  HHa-W,M
Pleyel's Hymn
  WiS7-W,M
Plight of a Miner's Widow
  AL-W
Plough Boy
  F3-W,M OH-W,M
Ploughshare
  GBC-W,M
Plow Deep's the Motto
  GrM-W,M
Plow, Spade and Hoe
  GrM-W,M
Plume De Radis
  SSN-W,M (French)
Plunged in a Gulf of Dark Despair
  AME-W,M
Plymouth Is Out to Win You Over
  GSM-W,M
Plymouth Rock
  MF-M
Po' Boy (I'm the Po' Boy)
  LC-W,M
Po' Boy Long Way from Home
  NH-W
Po' Folks
  RB-W
Po' Howard
  NeF-W
Po' Howard see also Poor Howard
Po Li'l Jesus
  Me-W,M NSS-W
Po Li'l Jesus see also Poor Little
  Jesus
Po' Mona, You Shall Be Free
  RTH-W
Po River Valley
  AF-W

Po' Sinner Die
  NH-W
Po' Sinner Fare You Well
  BDW-W,M
Poacher
  OTJ-W,M
Poacher's Fate
  SCa-W,M
Pobre Cega
  LA-W,M (Spanish)
Pocahontas
  RV-W
Pocketful of Miracles
  MF-W,M
Pod Huger Times
  OHO-W,M
Poems, Prayers and Promises
  CJ-W,M PoG-W,M
Poet and Peasant (Overture)
  AmH-M
Poet and the Slave Girls
  Ki-W,M
Poetry
  LMR-W,M OTJ-W,M TF-W,M
Poetry in Motion
  ILS-W,M LWT-W,M TI1-W,M
  UFB-W,M
Poinciana
  TI1-W,M
Point of No Return
  BHO-W,M UBF-W,M
Pointe Aux Pins
  Lo-W,M (French)
Pointing
  MAR-W,M
Poison Ivy
  HRB4-W,M RB-W
Poison Love
  OGC1-W,M
Poisoning Pigeons in the Park
  WF-W,M
Poisoning the Students' Minds
  PO-W,M
Pokarekare
  SNZ-W,M (Maori)
Poker
  ELO-W,M
Poker Polka
  OHT-W,M
Polar Bear
  ASB4-W,M
Police Story (Theme)
  TVT-M
Police Woman
  TVT-M
Policeman
  GM-W,M
Policeman's Lot Is Not a Happy
  One
  GiS-W,M MGT-W,M SL-W,M
Polichinelle see La Polichinelle
Polident Denture Cleanser Jingle
  see Stay Close to Someone
Polish Composer
  FSA1-W,M
Polish Dance (Scharwenka, Op. 3,
  No. 1)
  AmH-M
Polish National Anthem
  SMW-W,M (Polish)
Polish National Hymn
  AmH-W,M (Polish)
Polish National Song
  SiP-W,M (Polish)
Politeness
  MH-W,M
Politician's Alphabet

IFM-W
Politics and Poker
  OTO-W TW-W UBF-W,M
Polka
  FSA1-W,M
Polka Dots and Moonbeams
  DJ-W,M FPS-W,M RoE-W,M
  TI1-W,M UFB-W,M
Poll Your Vote
  AL-W
Polliwog
  ASB3-W,M
Pollution
  WF-W,M
Polly and William
  BSC-W
Polly and Willie
  Oz1-W,M
Polly Kimo
  TMA-W,M
Polly, Put the Kettle On
  FSA1-W,M HS-W,M OTJ-W,M
  SMa-W,M
Polly Van
  FMT-W
Polly Wolly Doodle
  AmH-W,M ATS-W BH-W,M
  BM-W BSB-W,M CSo-W,M
  ESB-W,M FSB1-W,M FW-W
  GuC-W,M HAS-W,M HS-W,M
  HSD-W,M IL-W,M MAS-W,M
  MES1-W,M MES2-W,M MF-W,M
  NAS-W,M OS-W OTJ-W,M
  POT-W,M RW-W,M SiB-W,M
  SiR-W,M SoC-W U-W VA-W,M
  WiS8-W,M
Polly's Piano
  MH-W,M
Polonaise (Chopin, Op. 53)
  MF-M RW-M
Polonaise (Chopin, Op. 53) see
  also Chopin's Polonaise
Polovetzian Dance
  TI1-M UFB-M
Polynesian Stick Game
  RSL-W,M
Polythene Pam
  BBe-W,M TWS-W
Pomp and Circumstance
  MF-M OTJ-M RW-M TI1-M
  UFB-M
Pomp's Soliloquy
  AN-W
Pompton Turnpike
  TI1-W,M UFB-W,M
Ponsaw Train
  Oz4-W,M
Pont De Morlaix see Le Pont De
  Morlaix
Pony
  FF-W,M
Pony Ride
  ASB3-W,M GM-W,M
Pony Song
  HS-W,M SD-W,M STS-W,M
Poor... see also Po...'
Poor Anzo
  FSSC-W
Poor Aviator Lay Dying
  AF-W GI-W,M GO-W,M
Poor Baby
  Co-W,M
Poor Black Boy
  BC1-W,M
Poor Boy (Bow Down Your Head
  and Cry, Poor Boy)
  BF-W,M FW-W

Poor Boy (Elvis Presley)
SRE2-W,M
Poor Boy (Hey There, Poor Boy)
LWT-W,M
Poor Boy (Razzy Bailey)
TOC83-W,M
Poor Boy (They'll Put You in the
Penitentiary, Poor Boy)
AmS-W,M
**Poor Boy Long Way from Home
see Po' Boy Long Way from
Home**
Poor Butterfly
MF-W,M
Poor Ch'iu Hsiang (K'o Lien Ti
Ch'iu Hsiang)
FD-W,M (Chinese)
Poor Drooping Maiden
FHR-W,M
Poor Ellen Smith
BSo-W,M
Poor Everybody Else
TW-W
Poor Ex-Soldier
FVV-W,M
Poor Folks see Po' Folks
Poor Goins
BMM-W FSU-W
Poor Howard
FG1-W,M FGM-W,M FW-W
Le-W,M WSB-W,M
Poor Howard see also Po' Howard
Poor Joe
A-W,M
Poor John
NH-W
**Poor Jud see Pore Jud and Pore
Jud Is Daid**
Poor Jude
MPP-W
Poor Lisa
TO-W,M
**Poor Little Country Maid see
Streets of Cairo**
Poor Little Darlin'
OGC1-W,M
Poor Little Fool
FRH-W,M
Poor Little Hollywood Star
Mo-W,M NM-W,M OTO-W
Poor Little Jesus
FW-W WSB-W,M
**Poor Little Jesus see also Po Li'l
Jesus**
Poor Little Joe
Oz4-W TBF-W,M
Poor Little Pierrette
OTO-W
Poor Little Zizi
MaG-W,M
Poor Lonesome Cowboy
HWS-W,M NeA-W,M
Poor Man Blues
FW-W
Poor Man, O Poor Man
TBF-W,M
Poor Man, Poor Man
Oz1-W
Poor Man's Family
AL-W PSN-W,M
Poor Marat in Your Bathtub Seat
PAJ-W,M
Poor Mary
SCa-W,M
Poor Miner's Farewell
AFP-W
Poor Mona, You Shall Be Free see

Po' Mona, You Shall Be Free
Poor Mourner's Found a Home
WN-W,M
Poor Old Joe
CSo-W,M
Poor Old Man
SA-W,M TH-W,M
Poor Old Marat
PAJ-W,M
Poor Old Slave
Wis8-W,M
Poor Old Soul
CSD-W,M (French)
Poor Oma Wise
Oz2-W,M
Poor Omie
FMT-W
**Poor Omie see also Little Omie,
Oma Wise, and Omie Wise**
Poor Owen
Boo-W,M
Poor People of Paris
TI1-W,M UFB-W,M
Poor Peter
LMR-W,M
Poor Pilgrim
Oz4-W RF-W,M WN-W,M
Poor Polly
Oz4-W
Poor Polly the Mad Girl
ESU-W
Poor Ralpho
Boo-W,M
Poor Robin Redbreast
Boo-W,M
Poor Rosy, Poor Gal
NSS-W
Poor Side of Town
RYT-W,M TI2-W,M
Poor Sinner Die see Po' Sinner Die
**Poor Sinner Fare You Well see Po'
Sinner Fare You Well**
Poor Smuggler's Boy
MSB-W
Poor Snow-Man
MH-W,M
Poor Stranger a Thousand Miles
from Home
BSC-W
Poor Thing
FMT-W
Poor Tramp Has to Live
LSR-W,M
Poor Voter on Election Day
AL-W,M
Poor Wandering One
GiS-W,M MGT-W,M WiS8-W,M
Poor Wayfaring Stranger
MAS-W,M NeA-W,M WU-W,M
Poor White Slave
AL-W
Poor Whites
NSS-W
Poor Working Girl
IHA-W,M
Pop, Goes the Question
TMA-W,M
Pop Goes the Weasel
AH-W,M ASB1-W,M ASB4-W,M
CA-W,M FW-W GuC-W,M
HS-W,M IHA-W,M MES2-W,M
MF-W,M OTJ-W,M Oz3-W,M
PoS-W,M POT-W,M SG-W,M
Pop Goes the World
BHO-W,M
Pop Musik
ToO79-W,M

Popcorn
TI1-M UFB-M
Popcorn Song
SSe-W,M
Pope
IL-W,M
**Popeye (Theme) see I'm Popeye
the Sailor Man**
Poplar Trees
SL-W,M
Poppyland
GOB-W,M
Popular Creed
AL-W
Popular Gag Song
Oz3-W
Popular Wobbly
FW-W
Por Una Mujer
TI1-W,M (Spanish Only)
UFB-W,M (Spanish Only)
Pore Jud
OTJ-W,M OTO-W
Pore Jud Is Daid
L-W TGO-W,M
Pore Red
LC-W
Porters' Calls
MAS-W,M
Porter's Love Song
Mo-W,M
Porter's Love Song (to a
Chambermaid)
NM-W,M
Portlairge
IS-W,M (Gaelic Only)
Portland County Jail
FW-W
Portland Fancy
LMR-W,M
Portrait see Le Portrait
Portrait of My Love
OnT1-W,M
Portugal
SHS-W,M
Portuguese Hymn
GH-W,M SHS-W,M
**Poseidon Adventure (Theme) see
Morning After, The**
Positively 4th Street
FoR-W,M
Possessions
FSA2-W,M
Possum see Opossum
Possum and the Banjo
Oz2-W,M
Possum Song
Oz2-W
Possum Sop and Polecat Jelly
Oz3-W,M
Possum up a Gum Stump
NF-W Oz2-W,M
Possum Valley
TMA-W,M
Posterity Is Just around the Corner
OT-W,M
Postman
ASB1-W,M ASB2-W,M BMC-M
MH-W,M SOO-W,M STS-W,M
Postman's Whistle
MH-W,M
Posy
CSG-W,M
Potato
VP-W,M
Potato Cake Woman
Me-W,M

Potato Harvest
SSe-W,M
Poteen, Good Luck to Ye, Dear
VP-W
Potential New Boyfriend
TOC83-W,M
Pou' Ein Charivari
CaF-W (French Only)
Pou' Eine Fete
CaF-W (French Only)
Poupee Valsante
AmH-M
Pour Me Another Tequila
TOH-W,M
Pour, O Pour the Pirate Sherry
GiS-W,M
Pour On the Power
VB-W,M
Pour Out My Insides
Lo-W,M
Pourquoi
TBF-W,M
Pov' Piti Lolotte
AAF-W,M (French Only)
Poverty
JOC-W,M OB-W,M
Poverty and Wealth
AL-W
Poverty Train
RB-W
Pow! Bam! Zonk!
Mo-W,M NM-W,M OTO-W
Pow, Pow, Powerful
GSM-W,M
Powder River Jack
HB-W
Powder River Let 'Er Buck
HB-W,M
Power in Jesus' Name
OGR-W,M
Power of Love
TTH-W,M
Power of the Human Eye
FT-W,M
Power of Thought
AL-W
Practice Cruise
ANS-W
Prairie
W-W,M
Prairie Flower
ATS-W
Prairie Grove
Oz2-W,M
Prairie of Love
SF-W,M
Prairie Schooner
ASB5-W,M
Praise
FSA1-W,M OGR-W,M SL-W,M
Praise Be to Thee, O Christ
Hy-W,M
Praise de Lamb
BDW-W,M
Praise God
NAS-W,M SL-W,M
Praise God from Whom All
Blessings Flow
AME-W,M CEM-W,M FH-W,M
HS-W,M Hy-W,M RDF-W,M
RW-W,M SHP-W,M TH-W,M
Praise God from Whom All
Blessings Flow see also Doxology
and Old Hundred(th)
Praise God, Tell His Grace
GBC-W,M
Praise God Who Sent Us Jesus

SHP-W,M
Praise God, Ye Servants of the
Lord
Hy-W,M
Praise Him! Praise Him! (All Ye
Little Children)
SoP-W,M
Praise Him! Praise Him! (All Ye
Little Children) see also God Is
Love (Praise Him, Praise Him, All
You Little Children)
Praise Him! Praise Him! (Jesus,
Our Blessed Redeemer)
AME-W,M GH-W,M
Praise Him Who Makes Us Happy
AHO-W,M
Praise Jehovah
AME-W,M
Praise, Member, Praise God
NSS-W
Praise My Soul
U-W
Praise, My Soul, the King of
Heaven
AME-W,M CSo-W,M ESB-W,M
GH-W,M Hy-W,M
Praise Now Your God
AHO-W,M
Praise of Christmas
OB-W,M
Praise of Islay
SeS-W,M
Praise Our Father for This Sunday
Hy-W,M
Praise the Lamb see Praise de
Lamb
Praise the Lord (Beethoven)
LMR-W,M
Praise the Lord (Constantini)
MMY-W,M
Praise the Lord (Haydn)
SL-W,M TH-W,M
Praise the Lord (Stephen Foster)
FHR-W,M
Praise the Lord and Pass the
Ammunition
OTJ-W,M
Praise the Lord, for He Is Good
Hy-W,M
Praise the Lord, He Never Changes
VB-W,M
Praise the Lord, His Glories Show
Hy-W,M SHP-W,M
Praise the Lord, O Ye Servants
Boo-W,M
Praise the Lord, Ye Heavens Adore
Him
Hy-W,M LMR-W,M
Praise the Saviour
GH-W,M
Praise to God
OB-W,M
Praise to God and Thanks We
Bring
SL-W,M
Praise to God, Immortal Praise
ESB-W,M SMY-W,M
Praise to the King
VB-W,M
Praise to the Living God
MAS-W,M SBJ-W,M SHP-W,M
Praise to the Lord
HS-W,M SJ-W,M
Praise to the Warlike Whigs
ESU-W
Praise Ye, Praise Ye the Lord
Hy-W,M

Praise Ye the Lord
CEM-W,M GH-W,M SCL-W,M
Praise Ye the Lord, for It Is Good
Hy-W,M
Praise Ye the Lord Most High
MuM-W,M
Praise Ye the Lord, O Celebrate His
Fame
AHO-W,M
Praise Ye the Lord, the Almighty,
the King of Creation
Hy-W,M SHP-W,M
Praise Ye the Lord, Ye Immortal
Choirs
AME-W,M
Prancin' Horses
BDW-W,M
Praties
FW-W PSN-W,M
Pray All de Member
NSS-W
Pray All Night
RTH-W
Pray, Brethren, Pray
GH-W,M
Pray for Forgiveness
SSo-W,M
Pray for Me
VB-W,M
Pray God Bless
MES1-W,M MES2-W,M
SMY-W,M
Pray, Maiden, Pray
SCo-W,M Sin-W,M SiS-W
Pray On, Pray On
NSS-W
Pray Papa
HAS-W,M
Pray, Remember
Boo-W,M
Pray Tony, Pray Boy, You Got de
Order
NSS-W
Prayer (from Hansel and Gretel)
LoS-W,M SiB-W,M
Prayer (Hart)
TS-W
Prayer (Kern)
MA-W,M
Prayer (Massenet)
WiS7-W,M
Prayer (Thank You for the World
So Sweet)
SOO-W,M
Prayer (Von Weber)
MML-W,M WiS7-W,M
Prayer, A (Dvorak)
TH-W,M
Prayer, A (Gregorian Chant)
ASB4-W,M
Prayer, A (Wagner)
SL-W,M
Prayer Book in Cards see Rattlin'
Joe Prayer
Prayer for Announcement of New
Moon
JS-W,M (Hebrew)
Prayer for Peace
ASB4-W,M MHB-W,M (German)
VS-W,M
Prayer for Rain
ASB5-W,M
Prayer Is Appointed to Convey
AME-W,M
Prayer Is de Key of Heaven
RF-W,M
Prayer Is the Soul's Sincere Desire

AH-W,M D-W,M FGM-W,M
FMT-W FSD-W,M FW-W
OTJ-W,M Oz4-W,M SCa-W,M
Pretty Things
  RM-W,M
Pretty to Walk With
  Mo-W,M NM-W,M OTO-W
Pretty Widow
  LA-W,M (Spanish)
Pretty Woman
  HR-W
**Pretty Woman see also Oh, Pretty
  Woman**
Pretty Women
  MF-W,M UBF-W,M
Prettye Bessie
  FSA2-W,M
Price of Freedom
  AL-W
Pride of the Prairie
  FC-W,M HB-W,M
Priests' March
  AmH-M
Prima Donna
  UBF-W,M
**Prime of Miss Jean Brodie (Theme)
  see Jean**
Primrose
  SHS-W,M
Primrose Lane
  TI1-W,M UFB-W,M
Primroses
  EA-W,M
Primus Lan'
  SMY-W,M
Primus Land
  WN-W,M
**Primus Land see also Promised
  Land (I Have a Father in the
  Promised Land)**
Prince Charles He Is King James's
  Son
  Oz1-W
Prince Charley
  DD-W,M
Prince Charlie
  SG-W,M
Prince Charming
  Mo-W,M
Prince Charming's Wooing
  FSA1-W,M
Prince Eugene
  SMW-W,M (German)
Prince of Peace His Banner
  Spreads
  AHO-W,M
Prince Robert
  FSU-W
Prince William
  TMA-W,M
Prince William of Old Nassau
  SiP-W,M (Dutch)
Prince's Three Daughters
  FSO-W,M (French)
Princesita
  MSS-W,M (Spanish)
Princess and the Horseman
  SD-W,M
Princess Leia's Theme
  MF-M TOM-M
Princess of Pure Delight
  LD-W,M LSO-W TW-W
Princess Salamanca
  CFS-W,M (French)
Princeton Cannon Song
  IL-W,M
Princeton Marines' Hymn

GI-W
Printer's Song
  AL-W
Priosun Cluain Meala
  VP-W (Gaelic Only)
Prison without Walls
  OGC1-W,M
Prisoner at the Bar
  ITP-W,M Oz4-W,M
Prisoner for Life
  Oz2-W,M
Prisoner of Love
  GOI7-W,M Mo-W,M NM-W,M
  TI2-W,M
Prisoner of War
  SiS-W
Prisoner-of-War Blues
  AF-W
**Prisoner's Hope see Tramp, Tramp,
  Tramp**
Prisoner's Lament
  SiS-W
Prisoner's Love Song
  SoC-W
Prisoner's Release
  SiS-W
Prisoner's Return
  SiS-W
Prisoner's Song
  SCa-W TBF-W,M TI1-W,M
  UFB-W,M
Prisoner's Talking Blues
  LC-W
Prithee, Pretty Maiden
  GiS-W,M MGT-W,M SL-W,M
Prithee Why So Sad?
  Boo-W,M
Private
  GI-W
Private Buffoon Is a Lighthearted
  Loon
  GiS-W,M
Private Eyes
  TI2-W,M
Private Number
  TTH-W,M
Private Song
  GO-W
Privateer
  ASB5-W,M
Privateering and Pirateering
  ANS-W
Private's Lament
  GI-W
Prize of the Margaretta
  ANS-W
Prize Song
  FSA2-W,M
Problema Social
  PSN-W,M (Spanish)
Proclaim the Glory of the Lord
  GP-W,M OGR-W,M VB-W,M
Proclaim the Lofty Praise
  AHO-W,M
Proclamation
  SBA-W
Prodigal
  VB-W,M
Prodigal Child
  GH-W,M
Prodigal Comes Home
  GBC-W,M
Prodigal Son
  SaS-W,M
Prodigal's Return
  GH-W,M
Producer's Election Hymn

AL-W
Producer's Hymn
  AL-W
Professor's Lament
  SoC-W
Progress of Sir Jack Brag
  AWB-W
Prologue (Beautiful Girls)
  UBF-W,M
**Prologue (Beautiful Girls) see also
  Beautiful Girls**
Promise and Law
  CSS-W
Promise Her Anything
  LM-W,M OTO-W
Promise, Love (Jurame)
  FSY-W,M (Spanish)
Promised Land (Chuck Berry)
  GAR-W,M
Promised Land (I Am Bound for the
  Promised Land)
  SHS-W,M
**Promised Land (I Am Bound for the
  Promised Land) see also I Am
  Bound for the Promised Land and
  On Jordan's Stormy Banks (I
  Stand)**
Promised Land (I Have a Father in
  the Promised Land)
  HSD-W,M
**Promised Land (I Have a Father in
  the Promised Land) see also
  Primus Lan'**
Promised Land (Where, Oh Where
  Are the Good Old Patriarchs?)
  BSC-W,M
Promises
  TI2-W,M VB-W,M
Promises of Freedom
  NF-W
Promises of Something New
  HCY-W,M
Promises, Promises
  GOI7-W,M HC2-W,M HD-W,M
  MF-W,M Mo-W,M OTO-W TW-W
Promises to Keep
  JF-W,M
Propa P.H.
  GSM-W,M
Prophecy
  FSA1-W,M
Prophecy of a SNCC Field
  Secretary
  SFF-W,M
Prophets
  FSA2-W,M
Prophet's Old Dog, or Mr. Jeremy
  Clarke's Old Dog Spott
  Boo-W,M
Prospect
  SHS-W,M
Prospect of Heaven
  SHS-W,M
Prospecting Dream
  FW-W
Prostrate, Dear Jesus, at Thy Feet
  AME-W,M
Protect the Freedman
  SiS-W
Protester's Carol
  GBC-W,M
Proud Mary
  BR-W,M GOI7-W,M GSN4-W,M
  HSi-W,M MCG-W,M On-W,M
  RY-W,M
Proudly As the Eagle
  LMR-W,M

Proudly Proclaim o'er Land and
  Sea
  SoF-W,M
Psalm
  MLM-W,M
Psalm 5
  ATS-W,M
Psalm of Labor for the
  Workingmen
  AL-W
Psalm of Sammy Tilden
  MPP-W
Psalm of Sion
  OB-W,M
Psalm of the Son of Man
  SL-W,M
Psalm 3
  ATS-W,M
Psaume 68: Que Dieu Se Montre
  Seulement
  CUP-W,M (French Only)
Pskov Lyrical Melody
  RuS-W,M (Russian)
Public Spirit of the Women
  SAR-W SBA-W
Pudgy Legs
  A-W,M
Puer Natus
  OB-W,M
Puer Nobis
  JOC-W,M OB-W,M
Puhi Huia
  SNZ-W,M (Maori)
Pull for the Shore
  GH-W,M
Pullet
  FSO-W,M (French)
Pullman Strike
  AFP-W AL-W
Pump Up the Volume
  BHO-W,M
Pumpkin Pies That Mother Used to
  Make
  OTJ-W,M
Pumpkins
  ASB1-W,M
Punch in the Presence of the
  Passenjare
  OHG-W,M
Pupil's Song
  TMA-W,M
Puppet on a String
  SRE1-W,M
Puppets
  RSL-W,M
Puppy Dog Song
  SSe-W,M
Puppy Love
  TI2-W,M
Pupu U Ewa see Pearly Shells
Pure and Easy
  WA-W,M
Pure As Snow
  AmH-M
Pure Religion
  BDW-W,M
Pure Stream of Eden
  ESU-W
Pure, the Bright, the Beautiful
  FHR-W,M
Purim Song
  JS-W,M (Hebrew)
Purlie
  P-W,M TW-W
Purling Streams
  Boo-W,M
Purple Bamboo (Tzu Chu Tiao)

FD-W,M (Chinese)
Purple Haze
  PoG-W,M
Purple People Eater
  DRR-W,M NoS-W,M
Pusan University
  AF-W
Push Boat
  BMM-W,M SG-W,M
Push de Button
  Mo-W,M NM-W,M OTO-W TW-W
  UBF-W,M
Push the Hog's Feet under the Bed
  NF-W
Puss
  MH-W,M
Pussy Cat
  HS-W,M
Pussy Cat, Pussy Cat
  OTJ-W,M
Pussy Willow
  ASB1-W,M RSL-W,M SiR-W,M
Pussycat, Pussycat
  MG-W,M
Put a Little Love in Your Heart
  GrH-W,M GSN4-W,M MCG-W,M
  RDF-W,M RW-W,M RYT-W,M
Put a Tic Tac in Your Mouth
  GSM-W,M
**Put Another Nickel In see Music!
  Music! Music!**
Put 'Em in a Box, Tie 'Em with a
  Ribbon
  MF-W,M
Put Forth, O God, Thy Spirit's
  Might
  AHO-W,M Hy-W,M
Put In All! Put In All!
  SR-W,M
Put It on the Ground
  JF-W,M PO-W,M
Put John on de Islan'
  RF-W-M
Put Me in My Little Bed
  TMA-W,M
Put Me to the Test
  LSO-W
Put My Little Shoes Away
  BIS-W,M ITP-W,M Oz4-W,M
Put My Name Down
  FW-W
Put Off and Row wi' Speed
  SeS-W,M
Put On a Happy Face
  GOI7-W,M HC1-W,M MAB1-W
  Mo-W,M MSA1-W NM-W,M
  OTJ-W,M OTO-W RDF-W,M
  RSL-W,M TI2-W,M UBF-W,M
Put On Your Old Grey Bonnet
  FWS-W,M MF-W,M RC-W,M
Put On Your Pretty Dress
  SSN-W,M (French)
Put on Your Sunday Clothes
  Mo-W,M NM-W,M OTO-W
  UBF-W,M
Put the Traffic Down
  Oz2-W,M
Put Yo' Honey Lovin' Mind on Me
  MoM-W,M
Put Your Arms around Me, Honey
  OAP-W,M RoE-W,M TI2-W,M
Put Your Clothes Back On
  TOH-W,M
Put Your Dreams Away (for
  Another Day)
  MF-W,M TI1-W,M TVT-W,M
  UFB-W,M

Put Your Finger in the Air
  MAR-W,M RSL-W,M
Put Your Hand in the Hand
  BSG-W,M BSP-W,M CEM-W,M
  EC-W,M GCM-W,M HHa-W,M
  MAB1-W MCG-W,M MF-W,M
  MSA1-W RDF-W,M
Put Your Hand on Your Shoe
  RSL-W,M
Put Your Little Foot
  ASB4-W,M HB-W,M MES1-W,M
Putting On Airs
  Oz3-W
Putting On the Style
  BF-W,M FW-W OHO-W,M
  OTJ-W,M Oz3-W,M PO-W,M
Putting On the Style--Ski Version
  OHO-W,M
Puzzling Questions
  ASBS-W,M
Pythic Ode
  GUM2-W,M

Q

Quadrophenia
  WA-M
Quail
  FSA2-W,M
Quaker's Courtship
  Oz3-W
Quaker's Wife
  HS-W,M
Quaker's Wooing
  AmS-W,M
Quan Mote Jeune
  CSD-W,M (French)
**Quan' Patate La Cuite see When
  Your Potato's Done**
Quand Biron Voulut Danser
  MP-W,M (French Only)
Quand J'ai Parti De Ce Nouveau
  Pays
  CaF-W (French Only)
Quand J'ai Parti De Mon Pays
  CaF-W (French Only)
Quand J'ai Quitte Pou' Le Texas
  CaF-W (French Only)
Quand J'etais Chez Mon Pere
  F2-W,M (French)
Quand J'etais 'Ti Garcon
  CaF-W (French Only)
**Quand On N'a Que L'Amour see If
  We Only Have Love**
Quand Trois Poules Vont Au
  Champ
  MP-W,M (French Only)
Quando, Quando, Quando (Tell Me
  When)
  MF-W,M
Quantrell
  BT-W,M
Quantrell Side
  PSN-W,M
Quartermaster Corps
  IL-W,M
Quartermaster Song
  GO-W
Quartermaster's Band
  SiS-W
Quartermaster's Store
  Bo-W,M FW-W PO-W,M
Quartet, The
  MML-W,M
Quartet in G Major (Mozart, K.
  387)

LTL-M
Quay in Brussels
　CF-W,M
Que Bonita Bandera
　FPG-W,M (Spanish Only) FW-W
　(Spanish)
Que Bonita Eres (Al Pasar El
　Arroyo)
　LA-W,M (Spanish)
Que Llueva
　CDM-W,M (Spanish)
Que Ne Suis-Je La Fougere
　Gu-W,M (French)
Que Preciosas Mananitas
　AHO-W,M (Spanish)
Que Sera, Sera (Whatever Will Be,
　Will Be)
　FPS-W,M FRH-W,M MAB1-W MF-
　W,M MSA1-W PB-W,M PoG-W,M
　TI1-W,M UFB-W,M WG-W,M
Que Voulez-Vous, La Belle?
　CUP-W,M (French Only)
Queen and the Coal Exchange
　MSB-W
Queen Elizabeth
　TS-W
Queen Jane
　FW-W SCa-W,M
Queen Lucy
　YG-W,M
Queen Mary
　CSG-W,M
Queen of Elfan's Nourice
　BT-W,M
Queen of Hearts
　FW-W
Queen of the Carnival
　VA-W,M (Spanish)
Queen of the Night
　FSA1-W,M
Queen Victoria
　MSB-W
Queenie's Bally-Hoo
　SB-W,M
Queenland Drover
　ATM-W,M
Queen's Dream
　MSB-W
Queen's Maries see Mary Hamilton
Queen's Marriage
　MSB-W
Queen's Visit to France
　MSB-W
Queer Little Man
　ESU-W
Quel Petit Homme
　CaF-W (French Only)
Quem Pastores
　OB-W,M (Latin Only)
Quest
　OB-W,M
**Quest (from Man of La Mancha)
　see Impossible Dream**
Questions
　ASB2-W,M DB-W,M FSA1-W,M
　TW-W
Questions and Answers
　ASB4-W,M
**Qui Sola Vergin Rosa see Last
　Rose of Summer**
Qui Veut Manger Du Lievre
　FSO-W,M (French)
Quicksilver
　Mo-W,M
Quicquid Petieritis Patrem
　Boo-W,M (Latin Only)
Quiero

TI1-W,M (Spanish Only)
UFB-W,M (Spanish Only)
Quiet As the River Flowing
　BV-W,M
Quiet Is the Night
　BMC-W,M SOO-W,M
Quiet, Lord
　GH-W,M
Quiet Love
　VB-W,M
Quiet Night
　TS-W UBF-W,M
Quiet Nights of Quiet Stars
　DJ-W,M RDT-W,M TI2-W,M
Quiet One
　WA-W,M
Quiet Place
　VB-W,M
Quiet Village
　TI1-W,M UFB-W,M
Qu'il Fait Chaud
　CE-W,M (French)
Quilting Bee
　TO-W,M
Quilting Party
　AH-W,M AmH-W,M BH-W,M
　HSD-W,M NAS-W,M OBN-W,M
　RW-W,M WiS8-W,M
Quincy's Boogie
　MF-M
Quintessence
　MF-M
Quis Est Homo?
　MMW-W,M (Latin)
Quodlibet (What You Will)
　SMY-W,M
Quotation
　FSA1-W,M
Quoth John to Joan
　SSP-W
Quoth Roger to Nelly
　Boo-W,M

R

**R C Cola Jingle see Me and My
　R C**
R.F.C.
　BMM-W
R.O.M.'s Lament
　GI-W
RON Song
　AF-W
ROTC
　AF-W
R2D2, We Wish You a Merry
　Christmas
　TI1-W,M UFB-W,M
Rabbit
　ASB1-W,M MH-W,M
Rabbit Came
　ASB2-W,M
Rabbit Chasing
　YG-W,M
Rabbit Hash
　NF-W
Rabbit in the Log (Feast Here
　Tonight)
　BSo-W,M
Rabbit Soup
　NF-W
Rabbit Town
　GM-W,M
Rabbits Eat Lettuce
　MES1-W,M MES2-W,M
Rabble Soldier

NeA-W,M
**Rabble Soldier see also Rebel
　Soldier**
Raccoon and Opossum Fight
　NF-W
Raccoon and Possum
　AFS-W,M
Raccoon's Got a Bushy Tail
　FW-W
Race Is On
　VB-W,M
Race of the Terrapin and the Deer
　BSC-W,M
Race-Starter's Rhyme
　NF-W
Race That Long in Darkness Pined
　AME-W,M Hy-W,M
**Race to California see Good Times
　Come at Last**
Rachmaninoff Concerto Theme
　TI1-M UFB-M
Racing with the Moon
　GSF-W,M RW-W,M
Rackets around the Blue Mountain
　Lake
　FW-W
Rackety Coo
　K-W,M
Radieu La Fleur De Ma Jeunesse
　CaF-W (French Only)
Radio
　FSA1-W,M
Radio Operator's Lament
　AF-W
Raftmen
　CFS-W,M (French)
Raftsmen
　FW-W (French)
Rag Doll
　ASB1-W,M
Rag Mop
　NoS-W,M OGC2-W,M TI1-W,M
　UFB-W,M
Rag Pat
　Oz2-W,M
Ragged Coat
　MSB-W
Raggedy
　FW-W PSN-W,M
Raggedy Raggedy
　AFP-W
Raggle-Taggle
　NeA-W,M
Raggle Taggle Gypsies, O
　TBF-W,M
Raggletaggletown Singers
　SiR-W,M
Raghupati
　WSB-W,M (Hindi)
**Ragtime (Theme) see One More
　Hour**
Ragtime Annie
　POT-M
Ragtime Cowboy Joe
　FC-W,M FW-W RW-W,M
Ragupati Ragava Rajah Ram
　FW-W (Hindi)
Rahadlakum
　Ki-W,M
Raid of the Reidswire
　SBB-W
Raiders
　OTJ-W,M
Raiders' Lament
　GI-W
Raiders March (Raiders of the Lost
　Ark Theme)

ToM-M
Raiders' Song
  GI-W
Rail Cutters
  AF-W
Railroad Bill
  BIS-W,M FG1-M FSt-W,M
  FVV-W,M FW-W LSR-W,M
  NH-W OFS-W,M RW-W,M
Railroad Blues
  LSR-W,M
Railroad Boomer
  LSR-W,M
Railroad Bum
  FMT-W
Railroad Chorus
  ATS-W,M
Railroad Corral
  FW-W HWS-W,M SMY-W,M
Railroad Daddy Blues
  BMM-W
Railroad Flagman
  Oz4-W,M
Railroad Police Blues
  LSR-W,M
Railroad Track Mender's Song
  Me-W,M
Railroader
  BSC-W Oz3-W,M
Railroader for Me
  LSR-W,M
Railroading on the Great Divide
  LSR-W,M
Railway
  VP-W
Railway Spiritualized
  LSR-W,M
Railway Station
  CSG-W,M
Rain (Dancing on the Roof-Tops)
  ASB3-W,M
Rain (Eugene Ford)
  GST-W,M RW-W,M
Rain (Hayne/McKay)
  LMR-W,M
Rain (Lennon/McCartney)
  BBe-W,M Be1-W,M TWS-W
Rain (Pitter, Pitter Pat)
  FF-W,M
Rain and Snow
  RBO-W,M
Rain and the River
  LMR-W,M
Rain Drops see also Raindrops
Rain Drops (Feels Like Rain Drops
  Falling from My Eyes)
  TI1-W,M UFB-W,M
Rain Drops, The (I Like to Hear the
  Rain Come Down)
  SoP-W,M
Rain Fall and Wet Becca Lawton
  NSS-W
Rain in April
  MH-W,M
Rain in Spain
  DBC-W,M HC2-W,M LL-W,M
  OTJ-W,M OTO-W TI1-W,M
  UBF-W,M UFB-W,M
Rain in Summer
  MH-W,M
Rain in the Night
  SOO-W,M
Rain on the Roof
  Fo-W,M TI2-W,M
Rain, Rain, Rain
  SiR-W,M
Rain, Rain, Rain Came Down,

Down, Down
  OTJ-W,M
Rain Rattles
  AST-W,M
Rain Sometimes
  Mo-W,M
Rain Song
  GM-W,M MG-W,M OHT-W,M
  SD-W,M STS-W,M
Rain, Summer Rain
  LMR-W,M
Rainbow
  ASB4-W,M
Rainbow and the Rose
  CCS-W,M
Rainbow Blues
  BJ-W,M
Rainbow Gold
  FSA1-W,M
Rainbow in My Heart
  OGC1-W,M
Rainbow Stew
  NMH-W,M
Raindrop
  ASB2-W,M
Raindrops see also Rain Drops
Raindrops, The ("Patter" Said the
  Raindrops)
  SMa-W,M
Raindrops Keep Fallin' on My Head
  BDF-W,M GOI7-W,M HD-W,M
  MF-W,M OTJ-W,M OTO-W
  RDT-W,M
Raining in My Heart
  TI1-W,M UFB-W,M
Raining in My Sunshine
  OnT1-W,M
Raining on the Inside
  VB-W,M
Rainmaker
  OTO-W
Rainy Day
  BMC-W,M
Rainy Day, A
  ASB1-W,M MH-W,M
Rainy Day, The
  HSD-W,M
Rainy Day Woman
  TI2-W,M
Rainy Days and Mondays
  GrS-W,M GSN4-W,M ILT-W,M
Rainy Night in Georgia
  HLS9-W,M
Raise a Ruckus
  FoS-W,M J-W,M
Raise a Ruckus Tonight
  FW-W LW-W,M NF-W
Raise High the Song
  GH-W,M
Raise the Flag of Dixie
  Sh-W,M
Raise the Iron
  NH-W
Raise the Window
  BSC-W
Raise Up the Banner
  SiS-W
Raising, The
  MPP-W
Raising: A New Song for Federal
  Mechanics
  AL-W
Raising Old Harry
  MPP-W
Raisins and Almonds
  FAW-W,M UF-W,M
Rakes of Mallow

AmH-M OTJ-W,M POT-W,M
Rakoczi March
  SMW-W,M (Hungarian)
Rally, Boys, for Greenbacks
  AL-W
Rally, Boys, Rally
  FMT-W
Rally Boys Rally for Reconstruction
  OHG-W,M
Rally for the Union
  SiS-W
Rally 'round the Flag
  SiS-W TO-W,M
Rally 'round the Flag, Boys
  MPP-W
Rally Song
  AL-W GuC-W,M (Turkish Only)
Rallying Song
  AL-W
Rallying Song of the Eight-Hour
  League
  AL-W
Ram of Dalby
  AFS-W,M ATM-W,M
Ram of Derby
  FMT-W
Ram Sam Sam
  Boo-W,M
Rama Lama Ding Dong
  NoS-W,M
Rambler from Clare
  IFM-W
Ramblin' Fever
  NMH-W,M
Ramblin' Man
  HW-W
Ramblin' Rose
  OPS-W,M WG-W,M
Ramblin' Round
  MF-W,M
Rambling Beauty
  BSC-W
Rambling Boy
  BSC-W FSU-W JF-W,M Oz2-W,M
  RBO-W,M
Rambling, Gambling Man
  FW-W
Rambling Irishmen
  IFM-W
Rambling Miner
  BMM-W
Rambling Wreck from Georgia
  Tech
  CoS-W,M Mo-W,M TI2-W,M
Ramon Del Alma Mia
  LA-W,M (Spanish)
Ramona
  CS-W,M GST-W,M HLS2-W,M
  RW-W,M
**Rancho Grande see El Rancho
Grande**
Rand Hymn
  PO-W,M
Randal, My Son
  SCa-W
**Randal, My Son see also Lord
Randal**
Randsome Tantsome
  NF-W
Randu's Holiday
  SBF-W,M
Range Is Heaven to Me
  SoC-W
Range of the Buffalo
  LMR-W,M RSW-W,M SL-W,M
  SoC-W
Range Rider's Appeal

HOH-W,M
Range Rider's Soliloquy
  HOH-W
Rangers' Command
  FG2-W,M
Ranger's Prayer
  HB-W
Rangiora
  SNZ-W,M (Maori)
Rank Stranger
  BSo-W,M
Rankin Tree
  PSN-W,M
Ransomed Spirit to Her Home
  AHO-W,M
Rantin Laddie
  FSU-W
Rap-a-Tap-Tap
  CoF-W,M
Rap, Tap, Tap
  PO-W,M
Rapid Roy
  JC-W,M PM-W,M
Rapid Transit Galop
  OHG-W,M
Rapparee
  IS-W,M
Rapture
  SHS-W,M
Rascal
  NF-W
'Raslin' Jacob
  RF-W,M
**'Raslin' Jacob see also Wrasslin'
  Jacob**
Rat Coon, Rat Coon
  Oz2-W,M
Rat Race
  MF-M
Ratcatcher's Daughter
  MSB-W
Ratcliffe Highway in 1842
  MSB-W
Rather Too Much for a Shilling
  SiS-W
Ratification Song
  MPP-W
Ration Day
  NF-W
Rattle the Drum
  FSF-W (French)
Rattler
  NF-W
Rattlesnake Song
  Oz3-W
Rattlety Train
  GM-W,M
Rattlin' Joe Prayer
  HOH-W
Raunchy
  OHT-W,M
Rave On
  TI2-W,M
Raven Visits Rawhide
  HOH-W
Ravioli
  CSS-W
Ravishing Ruby
  TI1-W,M UFB-W,M
Raw Head and Bloody Bones
  NF-W
Raw Recruit
  ATS-W Sin-W,M
Ray That Beams Forever
  ESU-W
Rayito De Luna
  LaS-W,M (Spanish Only)

Raymon-Raymon
  CSD-W,M (French)
Raz-Ma-Taz-A-Ma-Tee
  Oz3-W,M
Razzle Dazzle
  CMV-W,M UBF-W,M
Reach for the Top
  TOM-W,M
Reach Out for Me
  HD-W,M MF-W,M
Reaching and Winding
  Boo-W,M
Reaching for Someone
  WDS-W,M
Read 'Em and Weep
  TI2-W,M
Read in de Bible
  UF-W,M
Read, Sweet, How Others Strove
  AHO-W,M
Ready for School
  MH-W,M
Ready for the Times to Get Better
  RW-W,M
Ready or Not
  RW-W,M
Ready Teddy
  TI1-W,M UFB-W,M
Ready to Take a Chance Again
  GSN5-W,M OBN-W,M TOM-W,M
Real American Folk Song (Is a Rag)
  LSO-W NYT-W,M OTO-W
  UBF-W,M
Real Goodness from Kentucky
  Fried Chicken
  GSM-W,M
Real Live Girl
  MAB1-W MF-W,M Mo-W,M
  MSA1-W NM-W,M OTO-W
  TI2-W,M UBF-W,M
Real Me
  WA-W,M
Real New Year
  FSA2-W,M
Real Nice Clambake
  TG-W,M
Real Old Mountain Dew
  FW-W
Real Slow Drag
  UBF-W,M
Real Work
  MH-W,M
Reaper, The
  ToO76-W,M
Reaper on the Plain
  SY-W,M
Reapers
  SL-W,M
Reaper's Song
  ASB1-M BMC-M
Reaping Song
  ASB6-W,M
Reason to Live
  BHO-W,M
Reason Why
  MH-W,M SiS-W
Reasons for Drinking
  ESU-W
Reasons to Quit
  NMH-W,M
Rebecca of Sunny-Brook Farm
  RC-W,M
Rebel, The (Theme)
  TVT-W,M
Rebel Girl
  FW-W LW-W,M WW-W,M
Rebel Kingdom Falling

SiS-W
Rebel March (University of
  Mississippi)
  TI2-W,M
Rebel Rouser
  DRR-M
Rebel Soldier
  Oz2-W
**Rebel Soldier see also Rabble
  Soldier**
Rebel without a Cause (Theme)
  HFH-M
Rebellion's Weak Back
  SiS-W
Rebels
  SAR-W,M SBA-W
Rebel's Grave
  SiS-W
Recado Bossa Nova
  TI2-W,M (Portuguese Only)
Recently
  JC-W,M
Recess
  SBA-W
Recessional
  ESB-W,M MML-W,M MuM-W,M
  TM-M WGB/O-M
Recognition Song
  CSS-W
Reconsider Me
  HLS9-W,M
Recruit
  GI-W,M GO-W
Red and Black (Cincinnati
  University)
  CoS-W,M
Red and Black (Ohio Wesleyan
  University)
  CoS-W,M
Red and Blue
  IL-W,M
Red and Green Signal Lights
  LSR-W,M
Red Apple Juice
  FW-W LW-W,M
Red Apples
  VA-W,M
Red Ball Express
  TW-W
Red Balloon
  Mo-W,M OTJ-W,M
Red Bandana
  NMH-W,M
Red Baron
  YG-W,M
Red Bird
  FW-W Le-W,M
Red Cross Sto'
  NeF-W
Red Flag
  AL-W FW-W SWF-W,M
Red Flag Is Unfurled
  AL-W
Red-Headed Woodpecker
  NF-W
Red Iron Ore
  FW-W HS-W,M SoF-W,M
Red Light
  KS-W,M
Red Light Saloon
  LW-W,M PO-W,M
Red-Nose MIG's
  AF-W
Red Raven Polka
  PT-M
Red, Red Is the Path to Glory
  SeS-W,M

Red, Red Rose
  SL-W,M
Red, Red Wine
  CFB-W,M TI2-W,M
Red River
  J-W,M
Red River Valley
  AmS-W,M ATS-W,M BeB-W,M
  BF-W,M BH-W,M BM-W Bo-W,M
  BSB-W,M FSB1-W,M FSt-W,M
  FU-W,M FuB-W,M FW-W
  GG1-W,M GuC-W,M HOH-W,M
  HS-W,M HWS-W,M IHA-W,M
  IL-W,M LH-W,M LoS-W,M
  MAS-W,M OFS-W,M OS-W
  OTJ-W,M Oz4-W,M POT-W,M
  RW-W,M SAm-W,M SBF-W,M
  SoC-W
Red Rocking Chair
  BIS-W,M FPG-W,M
Red Roses for a Blue Lady
  HLS3-W,M HLS9-W,M RDT-W,M
  RW-W,M TI1-W,M UFB-W,M
Red Sails in the Sunset
  GSN2-W,M HLS2-W,M MF-W,M
  NK-W,M RDT-W,M RoE-W,M
  T-W,M TI1-W,M UFB-W,M
Red Sea Parted
  VB-W,M
Red Silk Stockings and Green
  Perfume
  Mo-W,M NM-W,M
Red Top
  TI2-W,M
Red, White and Blue
  AmH-W,M ESB-W,M HSD-W,M
  MPP-W NAS-W,M SCa-W,M
  TMA-W,M WiS8-W,M
Red Wing
  BIS-W,M FWS-W,M
Redeemed
  AN-W GH-W,M
Redeeming Grace
  SHS-W,M
Redemption
  GH-W,M SHS-W,M
Redemption Draweth Nigh
  HHa-W,M
Redemption Ground
  GH-W,M
Redmond O'Hanlon
  IS-W,M
Redneck Girl
  TOC82-W,M
**Reds (Theme) see Goodbye for
  Now**
Reelin' and Rockin'
  HR-W ILF-W,M TI1-W,M
  UFB-W,M
**Reese's Peanut Butter Cups Jingle
  see Two Great Tastes**
Reflections
  ASB4-W,M FSA2-W,M
Reflex
  TI2-W,M
Refrain, Audacious Tar
  MGT-W,M
Refugee Song
  SAR-W
Regular Army, Oh
  HAS-W,M
Reid at Fayal
  ANS-W
Reign, Massa Jesus
  RF-W,M
Reign, Master Jesus,
  Reign--Parody

NF-W
Reign, Messa Jesus
  RF-W,M
Reign of Labor
  AL-W
Reilly, Ace of Spies (Theme)
  TVT-M
Reilly's Daughter
  FW-W
Reine Liebe Sucht Nicht Sich
  Selber
  AHO-W,M (German)
Rejected by Eliza Jane
  NF-W
Rejoice
  VB-W,M
Rejoice All Ye Believers
  AME-W,M SJ-W,M
Rejoice and Be Glad
  GH-W,M
Rejoice and Be Merry
  GBC-W,M
Rejoice and Sing, the Lord Is King
  AME-W,M
Rejoice in the Lord
  OGR-W,M
Rejoice in the Lord Alway
  GH-W,M
Rejoice, Let Alleluias Ring
  AHO-W,M
Rejoice Rejoice
  SHP-W,M
Rejoice, Rejoice, Believer
  GH-W,M
Rejoice, Rejoice, Believers
  Hy-W,M
Rejoice, Rejoice on Easter Day
  SHP-W,M
Rejoice, the Lord Is King
  Hy-W,M
Rejoice with Me
  GH-W,M
Rejoice, Ye People of the Way
  SHP-W,M
Rejoice, Ye Pure in Heart
  AME-W,M Hy-W,M LMR-W,M
  SJ-W,M WiS9-W,M YS-W,M
Rejoice! Ye Saints
  GH-W,M
Rejoice, Ye Shepherds
  FoS-W,M
Relax
  SRE2-W,M
Release Me
  GG3-W,M HLS9-W,M MCG-W,M
  RW-W,M THN-W,M
Release Me (from My Sin)
  GS1-W HLS7-W,M
Relicario see El Relicario
Religion Is the Best of All
  Oz4-W
Remember
  OB-W,M
Remember?
  LN-W,M UBF-W,M
Remember All the People
  Hy-W,M SHP-W,M SJ-W,M
Remember de Dyin' Lamb
  BDW-W,M
Remember Me
  GH-W,M NSS-W SHS-W,M
  WN-W,M
**Remember Me see also 'Member
  Me**
Remember Me?
  MF-W,M
Remember September

SSe-W,M
Remember, Sinful Youth
  AHO-W,M
Remember That I Care
  SSA-W,M
Remember the Alamo
  ATS-W,M
**Remember the Dying Lamb see
  Remember de Dyin' Lamb**
Remember the Good Times
  WNF-W
Remember Thy Creator Now
  AHO-W,M
Remember When
  OnT1-W,M
Remembering
  OTO-W
Remembering When
  TW-W
Remembrance
  AS-W,M
Remington Steele (Theme)
  TV-M
Reminiscing
  MF-W,M TI2-W,M
Remon, Remon
  AAF-W,M (French Only)
  CSD-W,M (French)
Renegade
  ToO79-W,M
Reno Nevada
  FoR-W,M
Rent Strike Blues
  SFF-W,M
Repeal of the Union
  VP-W
Repent Ye
  GH-W,M
Repentance
  SHS-W,M
Repetition
  MF-M
Repetitive Regret
  TTH-W,M
Reply to the Bonnie Blue Flag
  SiS-W
Reply to the Little Old Sod Shanty
  SoC-W
Repose
  SHS-W,M
Repossession Blues
  DBL-W
Request to Sell
  NF-W
Requiem (Stevenson/Homer)
  AS-W,M
Requiem (Stevenson/Woodman)
  MML-W,M
Requiem for Everyone
  Mo-W,M NM-W,M
Requiem for Jeff Davis
  SiS-W
Rescue the Perishing
  AME-W,M FH-W,M GH-W,M IH-M
Reservist's Lament
  AF-W
Resident Power
  VB-W,M
Resignation
  SHS-W,M
Resolve (Obstination)
  FSY-W,M (French) WiS8-W,M
Resonet In Laudibus
  GBC-W,M (Latin)
Respect
  JF-W,M TTH-W,M
Respectable

RoS-W,M
Response
SL-W,M
Rest for the Toiling Hand
AME-W,M
Rest for the Weary
AME-W,M GH-W,M HSD-W,M
WiS7-W,M WN-W,M
Rest for the Weary Traveler
WN-W,M
Rest, Martyr, Rest
SiS-W
Rest, Noble Chieftain
SiS-W
Rest Sweet Nymphs
EL-W,M
Rested Body Is a Rested Mind
Wi-W,M
Restless
TTH-W,M
Restoration
SHS-W,M
Resurrection
SSN-W,M (French)
Resurrection Morn
GH-W,M
Resurrection Morning
WN-W,M
Retour Du Marin see Le Retour Du Marin
Retreat
HSD-W,M NA-W,M
Retreat (Cries My Heart)
TI2-W,M
Return, O Wanderer
GH-W,M
Return of the Red Baron
OnT6-W,M OTJ-W,M
Return to Sender
TI1-W,M UFB-W,M
Returned Soldier
BSC-W
Retzey
JS-W,M (Hebrew Only)
Reuben and Rachel
ASB5-W,M ATS-W EFS-W,M
FSA1-W,M HAS-W,M HS-W,M
NAS-W,M OFS-W,M OS-W
OTJ-W,M PoS-W,M RW-W,M
VA-W,M
Reuben James
ANS-W
Reuben Ranzo
ASB6-W,M FW-W NAS-W,M
SA-W,M
Reuben, Reuben
FW-W
Reuben's Train
FPG-W,M LSR-W,M
Reunion Song
GrM-W,M
Reunited
SoH-W,M ToO79-W,M
Reveille
ASB6-W,M ATS-W,M GI-W,M
GO-W HS-W,M MAS-W,M
VA-W,M
Revenge
Mo-W,M NM-W,M OTO-W
Revenge Is Sweet
CoF-W,M
Reverie (Debussy)
MF-M TI1-M UFB-M
Reveries
E-W,M
Revery
FSA2-W,M

Reviewing the Situation
O-W,M
Revive Thy Work
GH-W,M
Revive Us Again
FW-W
Revive Us, Oh Lord
VB-W,M
Revolution (Do You Know Me, O You Masses?)
AL-W
Revolution (I Come Like a Comet Newborn)
AL-W
Revolution (Lennon/McCartney)
BBe-W,M Be2-W,M SwS-W,M
TWS-W
Revolution Nine
TWS-W
Revolution One
TWS-W
Revolutionary Alphabet
SSS-W,M
Revolutionary Tea
AH-W,M FGM-W,M IHA-W,M
SI-W,M TBF-W,M
Rexford Girl
Oz2-W
Reynold's Letter on the American Civil War
VP-W
Rhapsody in Blue
BI-M MF-M NYT-M
Rheingold Beer Jingle see My Beer Is Rheingold the Dry Beer
Rheinlied
SiP-W,M (German)
Rhiannon
ToO76-W,M
Rhine Song
SiP-W,M (German)
Rhinestone Cowboy
EC-W,M GCM-W,M MF-W,M
ToO76-W,M
Rhode Island
Fif-W,M SHS-W,M
Rhode Island Algerines' Appeal to John Davis
AFP-W
Rhode Island Is Famous for You
UBF-W,M
Rhode Island to the South
AWB-W
Rhumba Boogie
OGC1-W,M
Rhumboogie
TI2-W,M
Rhyfelgyrch Gwyr Harlech
SiP-W,M (Welsh)
Rhyme for Angela
LSO-W
Rhymes and Chimes
ATS-W ESU-W
Rhymes and Reasons
CJ-W,M
Rhymes Have I
Ki-W,M
Rhyming Alphabet
Oz4-W
Rhythm Game
GM-W,M
Rhythm of Life
SC-W,M
Rhythm of the Rain
MF-W,M
Rhyvelgyrch Cadpen Morgan
AAF-W,M (Welsh)

Ribbon of Darkness
FoR-W,M
Ribbons down My Back
Mo-W,M NM-W,M OTO-W
UBF-W,M
Rice
Mo-W,M NM-W,M
Rice Crispies Cereal Jingle see Snap, Crackle & Pop
Rice Planting Song
SCL-W,M (Tagalog)
Rice Pudding
LA-W,M (Spanish)
Rice with Milk
ASB5-W,M
Rich, The
TW-W
Rich and Rambling Boy see Rambling Boy
Rich and Rare Were the Gems She Wore
MU-W,M
Rich Irish Lady
BSC-W
Rich Lady
Oz1-W
Rich Lady from London
FoM-W,M Oz1-W,M
Rich Man
WN-W,M
Rich Man and the Poor Man
FW-W SWF-W,M
Richmond, or the Map of Virginia
ESU-W
Richmond Falls
SiS-W
Richmond Has Fallen
MPP-W
Richmond Is a Hard Road to Travel
SiS-W
Richmond Is Ours
SiS-W
Richmond on the James
SiS-W
Richmond Prisoner
SiS-W
Rickett's Hornpipe
DD-W,M
Ricky Don't Lose That Number see Rikki Don't Lose That Number
Rico Vacilon
LaS-M OPS-M
Ricochet
RW-W,M
Ricochet Romance
MF-W,M
Riddle
ASB2-W,M KS-W,M SR-W,M
TH-W,M
Riddle: My Man John
Boo-W,M
Riddle of Spring
SL-W,M
Riddle Song
BF-W,M BT-W,M FW-W
GG2-W,M Gu-W,M GuC-W,M
HS-W,M IHA-W,M IL-W,M ITP-
W,M J-W,M LT-W,M SAm-W,M
WU-W,M
Riddle Song see also I Gave My Love a Cherry
Riddles
FSA1-W,M
Riddles Wisely Expounded
BCT-W,M BT-W,M
Ride a Cock-Horse to Banbury Cross

Rise 'n' Shine
MF-W,M

**Rise 'n' Shine see also Rise an'
Shine**

Rise Now, Oh Shepherds
BMC-W,M

Rise, O Servians
SiP-W,M (Serbo-Croatian)

Rise Old Snapper
DE-W,M

Rise, Sugar, Rise
PSD-W,M

Rise to Greet the Sun
OU-W,M

Rise Up, and Hasten
GH-W,M

Rise Up, O Flame
VA-W,M

Rise Up, O Men of God
AHO-W,M AME-W,M Hy-W,M

Rise Up Shepherd
JF-W,M

Rise Up, Shepherd, an' Foller
RF-W,M

Rise Up, Shepherd, and Follow
FW-W HS-W,M MAS-W,M

Rise Up, Shepherds
CSB-W,M

Rise Up, Shepherds, and Foller
CSF-W VA-W,M

Rise, Ye Children
AHO-W,M (German)

Rise Ye Up
Oz1-W,M

Rising Early in the Morning
GiS-W,M MGT-W,M

Rising of the Lark
FSA2-W,M MML-W,M SMY-W,M

Rising of the Moon
FW-W VP-W,M

Rising Song
FSA1-W,M

Risselty Rasselty
ITP-W,M

Risselty Rosselty
FW-W

Risselty, Rosselty, Now, Now,
Now
Oz3-W,M

Rival Vendors
FSA1-W,M

River
On-W,M

River, The
ASB2-W,M MH-W,M SL-W,M

River Deep--Mountain High
ERM-W,M GAR-W,M

River in the Rain
DBC-W,M UBF-W,M

River Is Wide
OTJ-W,M

River King
SoC-W

River Kwai March
MF-M OTO-W TI1-M UFB-M

River Lea
SA-W,M

River of Love
CMG-W,M

River of Time
GrM-W,M

River Ran Red
AF-W

River Runs
RuS-W,M (Russian)

River Seine
MF-W,M

River Song
SBS-W,M SOO-W,M

River, Stay 'Way from My Door
TI1-W,M UFB-W,M

River That in Silence Windest
Boo-W,M

Riverboat Shuffle
Sta-W,M

Riviera
MF-W,M Mo-W,M

Rivington's Reflections
SSS-W,M

Road Is Rugged, but I Must Go
FSSC-W,M

Road Runner (Theme)
TVT-M

Road Song see Tshotsholosa

Road to Heaven
Oz4-W RTH-W

Road to Morocco
AT-W,M OTO-W

Road to Paradise
MPM-W,M

Road to Richmond
DE-W,M

Road to Zion
VB-W,M

Road You Didn't Take
Fo-W,M

Roamin' in the Gloamin'
MF-W,M U-W

Roaming o'er the Meadows
Boo-W,M

Roar, Lion Roar
IL-W,M

Roaring Twenties
TV-W,M

Roast Beef of Old England
OH-W,M

Robbins' Nest
TI1-M UFB-M

Robe of Calvary
SUH-W,M

**Robert Hall Clothes Jingle see
When the Values Go Up**

Roberta
NeF-W

Roberts' Farm
FW-W

Robin
MH-W,M

Robin, The
ASB1-W,M STS-W,M

Robin Adair
AmH-W,M HSD-W,M MML-W,M
NAS-W,M OTJ-W,M SeS-W,M
WiS8-W,M

Robin Hood
Mo-W,M NM-W,M

Robin Hood and the Bishop of
Hereford
BT-W,M

Robin Hood and the Pedlar
BT-W,M

Robin in the Rushes
SR-W,M

Robin Redbreast
GM-W,M

Robin Ruff
HSD-W,M

Robins' Call
ASB1-W,M

Robinson Crusoe
ASB2-W,M FSA1-W,M TMA-W,M

Roc-a-Chicka
OGC2-W,M

Roch Royal

Oz1-W

Rochester
SHS-W,M

Rock, The
SHS-W,M

Rock About My Saro Jane
FGM-W,M FW-W

Rock All Our Babies to Sleep
LJ-W,M Oz3-W,M

Rock and Roll Is Here to Stay
DRR-W,M Gr-W,M

Rock & Roll Music
ILF-W,M TI1-W,M UFB-W,M

**Rock & Roll Music see also Rock 'n
Roll Music**

Rock around the Clock
DRR-W,M ERM-W,M GAR-W,M
OTJ-W,M

Rock Freak see Disco Nights

Rock Gently
NB-W

Rock Island Blues
LC-W

Rock Island Line
FW-W GuC-W,M Le-W,M
LSR-W,M MF-W,M OFS-W,M
OTJ-W,M TI1-W,M UFB-W,M
WSB-W,M

Rock Me Amadeus
TTH-W,M (German Only)

Rock Me, Mama
LC-W

Rock Me to Sleep
SCo-W,M

Rock Me to Sleep Mother
HSD-W,M

Rock Mount Sinai
Me-W,M

Rock 'n Roll Music
HR-W

**Rock 'n Roll Music see also Rock &
Roll Music**

Rock 'n' Roll Party Queen
Gr-W,M Mo-W,M OTO-W

Rock 'n' Roll to the Rescue
TTH-W,M

Rock 'n' Row Me Over
FW-W

Rock o' Jubilee
MAS-W,M

Rock o' Jubilee, Poor Fallen Soul
NSS-W

Rock o' My Soul in de Bosom of
Abraham
NSS-W

**Rock o' My Soul in de Bosom of
Abraham see also O Rock-a My
Soul, Rocka My Soul, and Rock-er
Ma Soul**

Rock of Ages
AmH-W,M ATS-W CEM-W,M
FW-W GH-W,M HF-W,M
HLS7-W,M HSD-W,M IH-M
JBF-W,M MAB1-W MSA1-W
OS-W OTJ-W,M RDF-W,M
Re-W,M RW-W,M SHS-W,M
TB-W,M TI1-W,M Tr-W,M
UFB-W,M VA-W,M WiS7-W,M

Rock of Ages (for the Feast of
Lights)
HS-W,M (Hebrew) JS-W,M
(Hebrew) LMR-W,M SBJ-W,M

Rock of Ages, Cleft for Me
AME-W,M DC-W,M FM-W,M
Hy-W,M

**Rock of Jubilee see Rock o'
Jubilee**

Rock of Rubies
NA-W,M
Rock of Strength
UF-W,M
Rock Show
PMC-W,M
Rock Solid
VB-W,M
Rock That Is Higher Than I
AME-W,M
Rock the Cradle
GBC-W,M
Rock Well Blues
LC-W
Rock with Me
TV-W,M
Rocka My Soul
ASB6-W,M BDW-W,M GuC-W,M
LoS-W,M LT-W,M MG-W,M
OTJ-W,M
Rocka My Soul see also O Rock-a
My Soul, Rock o' My Soul in de
Bosom of Abraham, and Rock-er
Ma Soul
Rockaby
ASB5-W,M MH-W,M
Rockaby, Baby
ASB1-W,M BBF-W,M FW-W
Rockaby, Baby see also Cradle
Song (Traditional)
Rockabye Basie
MF-M
Rock-a-Bye My Soul
FW-W
Rock-a-Bye Your Baby
OBN-W,M
Rock-a-Bye Your Baby with a Dixie
Melody
BeL-W,M GSN1-W,M HC1-W,M
OTJ-W,M TI2-W,M
Rock-a-Hula Baby
RW-W,M
Rockaria!
ELO-W,M
Rockaway Land
MH-W,M
Rockbridge
SHS-W,M
Rock'd in the Cradle of the Deep
PoS-W,M WiS7-W,M
Rocked in the Cradle of the Deep
AmH-W,M ATS-W HSD-W,M
NAS-W,M RW-W,M
Rock-er Ma Soul
BDW-W,M
Rock-er Ma Soul see also O Rock-a
My Soul, Rock o' My Soul in de
Bosom of Abraham, and Rocka
My Soul
Rocket Man
TI2-W,M
Rockin' around the Christmas Tree
BCh-W,M BCS-W,M MF-W,M
TI1-W,M UFB-W,M
Rockin' Chair (Hoagy Carmichael)
TI2-W,M
Rockin' Good Way (to Mess
Around and Fall in Love)
MF-W,M
Rockin' in Rhythm
GMD-W,M
Rockin' Jerusalem
JF-W,M
Rockin' Pneumonia and the Boogie
Woogie Flu
FRH-W,M
Rockin' Robin

DRR-W,M FRH-W,M MCG-W,M
RYT-W,M
Rocking
AST-W,M JOC-W,M OB-W,M
Rocking Carol
GBC-W,M
Rocking Chair (Christenson/Spear)
ASB2-W,M
Rocking Horse
ASB1-W,M MH-W,M
Rocking the Cradle
OTJ-W,M
Rockingham
SHS-W,M
Rockpile Blues
BI-W,M
Rocks and Gravel
FW-W
Rocks in de Mountens
SA-W,M
Rocks of Bawn
IS-W,M
Rocks Off
RoS-W,M
Rocky Island
ITP-W,M
Rocky Mountain High
CJ-W,M GrS-W,M PoG-W,M
WG-W,M
Rocky Mountain Way
On-W,M
Rocky Raccoon
BBe-W,M Be2-W,M TWS-W
Rocky Road to Dublin
IS-W,M
Rocky Road to Georgia
Oz3-W,M
Rocky III (Theme) see Eye of the
Tiger
Rocky Top
CoH-W,M FOC-W,M MF-W,M
OPS-W,M TI2-W,M
Roddy M'Corley
FW-W
Rodeo
WG-W,M
Rodeo Joe
BeB-W,M
Rodeo Rider's Lament
UF-W,M
Rodgers and Bingham
ANS-W
Rodgers and Victory
ANS-W
Rodgers & Victory: Tit for Tat
ANS-W
Roger the Tinker Man
Oz3-W,M
Rogue River Valley
Mo-W,M OTO-W
Roi A Fait Battre Tambour see Le
Roi A Fait Battre Tambour
Roi Du Bal see Le Roi Du Bal
Roll Along Covered Wagon
HSS-W,M OGC2-W,M
Roll Along! Roll Along!
MPP-W
Roll an' Rock
BDW-W,M
Roll Call Song
RSL-W,M
Roll de Cotton Down
UF-W,M
Roll de Cotton Down see also Roll
the Cotton Down
Roll de Ole Chariot Along
RF-W,M

Roll de Ole Chariot Along see also
Roll the Chariot Along
Roll in My Sweet Baby's Arms
BIS-W,M BSo-W,M FPG-W,M
FW-W POT-W,M
Roll Jordan
RTH-W WN-W,M
Roll, Jordan, Roll
AAF-W,M AHO-W,M AN-W
Bo-W,M FW-W LMR-W,M
MuM-W,M NSS-W OHO-W,M
OTJ-W,M Oz2-W RF-W,M
RW-W,M SpS-W,M SSo-W,M
WiS7-W,M
Roll Me Nelly
SGT-W,M
Roll Muddy River
BSo-W,M
Roll My Ball
ASB5-W,M
Roll, Nancy Gal, Roll
OTJ-W,M
Roll On
WN-W,M
Roll On Buddy
BSo-W,M
Roll On, Columbia
FG2-W,M IHA-W,M PSN-W,M
TO-W,M VA-W,M
Roll On Dogies
HOH-W,M SoC-W,M
Roll On, Silver Moon
Oz4-W
Roll on the Ground
FGM-W,M FW-W
Roll Out, Cowboy
ATS-W
Roll Out! Oh, Heave That Cotton
OTJ-W,M
Roll Out the Barrel
T-W,M TI1-W,M U-W UFB-W,M
Roll Out the Barrel see also Beer
Barrel Polka
Roll Over
FW-W OHO-W,M OTJ-W,M
RSL-W,M
Roll Over, Beethoven
ILF-W,M
Roll the Chariot Along
BMM-W
Roll the Chariot Along see also Roll
de Ole Chariot Along
Roll the Cotton Down
SA-W,M SoF-W,M
Roll the Cotton Down see also Roll
de Cotton Down
Roll the Pumpkin Out
GM-W,M
Roll the 'Tater
Oz3-W
Roll the Union On
AFP-W FW-W SWF-W,M
WW-W,M
Roll Them Down
FSA1-W,M
Roll Them Simelons
FMT-W FoM-W,M
Roll Up the Ribbons
I-W,M
Roller
ToO79-W,M
Roller Coaster
Mo-M
Roller Derby Queen
JC-W,M PM-W,M
Roller Skating
ASB1-W,M ASB3-W,M

ASB4-W,M SiR-W,M
Rollicking Band of Pirates We
GiS-W,M
Rollin' in Jesus' Arms
BDW-W,M
Rollin' Mill
NH-W
Rollin' Stone
LC-W
Rolling Along
RSL-W,M
Rolling down the Highway
VA-W,M
Rolling Down to Old Maui
SA-W
Rolling Home
FW-W OTJ-W,M
Rolling King
ASB4-W,M SA-W,M
Rolling Stone
Oz2-W,M
Rolly Trudam
FMT-W NeA-W,M Oz3-W,M
Roman Lady
BSC-W
Romance (Debussy)
MMW-W,M
Romance (Harbach,
   Hammerstein/Romberg)
DS-W,M
Romance (Leslie/Donaldson)
WDS-W,M
Romance (Louise Mandrell)
TOC82-W,M
Romance (Prokofieff)
MMM-W,M
Romance (Rubinstein)
TI1-M TM-M UFB-M WGB/O-M
Romancing the Stone
TI2-W,M
Romany Life
FT-W,M RW-M
Rome (Beautiful, Wonderful,
   Fabulous)
Mo-W,M NM-W,M OTO-W
Rome Will Never Leave You
RW-W,M
Romeo and Juliet (Gounod)
FSA2-W,M
**Romeo and Juliet (Love Theme)
see Time for Us**
Romeo and Juliet (Theme-
   Tschaikovsky)
MF-M OBN-M RW-M TI1-M TM-M
UFB-M WGB/O-M
Romeo's Foreboding
RJ-W,M
Romish Lady
BSC-W SCa-W,M SHS-W,M
RON Song
AF-W
Ronald
Oz1-W,M
Rondo
EA-W,M
Rondo III
BC1-M
Roof Garden
BOA-W,M
Rookie
GI-W HAS-W,M
Room at the Cross for You
OM-W,M
Room Enough for Two
DC-W,M
Room for Thee
GH-W,M

Room Full of Roses
HLS9-W,M OGC2-W,M TI1-W,M
UFB-W,M
Room in Bloomsbury
OTO-W
Room in Dar
FSSC-W
Room 222 (Theme)
TVT-M
Room with a View
OTO-W UBF-W,M
Rooster's Call
ASB1-W,M
Root, Abe, or Die
BSC-W
Root Hog or Die
AFP-W BSC-W FW-W Oz2-W
Oz3-W,M SiS-W
Root Hog or Die Jig
DE-W,M
Roots (Theme)
TVT-M
Roots of My Raising
NMH-W,M
Ropesman
DD-M,W
Rorate
OB-W,M
Rory O'Moore
AmH-M HSD-W,M POT-M
Rory O'More Turned Teetotal
MSB-W
Rosa
NAS-W,M SiR-W,M UF-W,M
Rosa Becka Lina
MAS-W,M SG-W,M
**Rosa Becka Lina see also Lead Her
Up and Down**
Rosa Betsy Lina
Oz3-W,M
Rosa Lee
HSD-W,M WiS8-W,M
Rosalie
ATS-W GOB-W,M HSD-W,M
OTO-W Oz4-W TI1-W,M
UFB-W,M
Rosary
ATS-W FSN-W,M TM-W,M
Rose, The
BNG-W,M DC-W,M DPE-W,M
EC-W,M EY-W,M GCM-W,M
HFH-W,M MF-W,M RoE-W,M
SL-W,M TOM-W,M
Rose Colored Glasses
EC-W,M GCM-W,M
Rose Connoley
ITP-W,M
Rose Garden
GOI7-W,M MCG-W,M
Rose in the Snow
MLS-W,M
Rose Leaves Are Falling Like Rain
NA-W,M
Rose Marie
HC2-W,M MF-W,M OHB-W,M
RM-W,M
Rose of Alabama
HSD-W,M
Rose of Ardeen
FMT-W
Rose of Madrid
ReG-W,M
Rose of Sharon
SHS-W,M
Rose of Tralee
FW-W MF-W,M OAP-W,M OTJ-
W,M RW-W,M TI1-W,M U-W

UFB-W,M
Rose of Washington Square
HLS2-W,M MF-W,M TI1-W,M
UFB-W,M
Rose Room
GG5-W,M GSN1-W,M HLS1-W,M
OP1-W,M RW-W,M
Rose, Rose
GuC-W,M OHO-W,M
Rose, Rose, Rose
Boo-W,M
Roseate Clouds of Evening Drift
AS-W,M (German)
Rosemary Fair
VP-W,M
Rosemary's Baby
TW-W
Rosen Fra Fyn
GuC-W,M (Danish)
Rosenthal's Goat
LSR-W,M
Roses
OGC2-W,M SL-W,M
Roses Are Red
BMC-W,M OTJ-W,M SiR-W,M
Roses Are Red (My Love)
FrF-W,M ILS-W,M RW-W,M
RYT-W,M
Roses for Remembrance
Mo-W,M NM-W,M
Roses in December
NCB-W,M
Roses of Picardy
TI1-W,M UFB-W,M
Roses Red
NF-W
Roses Red--Violets Blue
Mo-W,M NM-W,M OTO-W
Rose's Turn
TW-W
Roses White and Roses Red
MGT-W,M
Rosetta
Mo-W,M NM-W,M TI2-W,M
Rosewood Casket
FSt-W,M FW-W
Rosh Hashonoh Hymn
JS-W,M (Hebrew)
Rosie
Mo-W,M NM-W,M OTO-W
UBF-W,M
Rosie Nell
AmS-W,M
Rosier see Le Rosier
Rosin the Beau
SoC-W
Rosin the Bow
FMT-W
Rosina
ASB4-W,M
Rosita
LaS-W,M
Rosy Apple
OTJ-W,M
**Rosy's Theme see It Was a Good
Time**
Rote Abendwolken Zieh'n
AS-W,M (German)
Rothesay, O
FW-W
Rothschild and Sons
Ro-W,M
Roto-Rooter
GSM-W,M
Rough Dried Woman
DBL-W
Round... see also Around...

Round, a Round
  Boo-W,M
Round about the Mountain
  AAF-W,M
'Round and 'Round
  Fa-W,M
Round and round Hitler's Grave
  FW-W
Round and round the Levee
  Oz3-W,M
Round and round the Village
  BBF-W,M MH-W,M SOO-W,M
Round Dance
  FSO-W,M (French)
Round Her Neck She Wears a
  Yeller Ribbon
  OS-W
'Round Her Neck She Wears a
  Yellow Ribbon
  MF-W,M OTJ-W,M RW-W,M
'Round Her Neck She Wears a
  Yellow Ribbon see also Around
  Her Neck She Wore a Yellow
  Ribbon and She Wore a Yellow
  Ribbon
Round Her Neck She Wore a
  Golden Locket
  OTJ-W,M
Round Her Neck She Wore a
  Yellow Ribbon
  FW-W
Round Her Neck She Wore a
  Yellow Ribbon see also Round
  Her Neck She Wears a Yeller
  (Yellow) Ribbon
'Round Midnight
  MF-W,M
Round of Thanks
  MES1-W,M MES2-W,M SCL-W,M
Round, Round, Round see Blue
  Rondo A La Turk
Round the Bay of Mexico
  FW-W OTJ-W,M
Round the Corner
  SA-W,M
Round the Mulberry Bush
  MF-W,M TMA-W,M
Round the Pear Tree
  SOO-W,M
Round the Village
  ASB1-W,M
Round Up in Glory
  SoC-W
Round Up Saloon
  TOC82-W,M
Rounded Up in Glory
  HOH-W,M
Roundel
  SL-W,M
Roundelay
  FSA2-W,M
Roundup in the Spring
  HB-W,M
Roundup Lullaby
  ASB6-W,M HOH-W,M
Rouse and Rally
  AL-W
Rouse, Britons
  SSS-W,M
Roustabout
  SRE2-W,M
Route 66
  Mo-W,M NM-W,M TI2-W,M
Route 66 (Theme)
  TVT-M
Rovers
  FSA2-W,M

Rovers Meet the Winders
  VP-W,M
Rovin' Gambler
  FAW-W,M FVV-W,M
Roving Cowboy
  BMC-W,M
Roving Gambler
  BSo-W,M FG1-W FSB2-W,M
  ITP-W,M OTJ-W,M
Roving Gambler see also Rovin'
  Gambler
Roving Gambler Blues
  FW-W
Roving Journeyman
  Oz4-W
Roving Kind
  MF-W,M TI1-W,M UFB-W,M
  WSB-W,M
Roving Soldier
  BSC-W,M
Row Boat
  STS-W,M
Row, Bullies, Row
  SA-W,M
Row, Row, Row
  LWT-W,M TI1-W,M UFB-W,M
Row, Row, Row Your Boat
  BM-W BMC-W,M Bo-W,M
  Boo-W,M CSS-W EFS-W,M
  ESB-W,M FW-W GUM1-W,M
  HS-W,M IL-W,M IPH-W,M
  MES2-W,M OTJ-W,M RW-W,M
  SOO-W,M TH-W,M
Row the Boat
  SL-W,M
Row Your Boat
  ASB4-W,M MES1-W,M
Rowan County Crew
  FSU-W ITP-W,M Oz2-W,M
  TBF-W,M
Rowan County Troubles
  BMM-W,M DD-W,M
Rowan County War see Rowan
  County Crew
Rowan Tree
  RSC-W,M (Russian)
Rowdy Rat
  AF-W
Rowing
  ASB2-W,M ASB5-W,M
Rowing against the Tide
  GrM-W,M
Rows and Rows of Carrots
  GUM1-W,M
Roxanne
  ToO79-W,M
Roxie
  CMV-W,M
Roxie Ann
  Oz3-W,M
Royal Adventurer
  AWB-W
Royal Anthem
  PAJ-W,M
Royal Garden Blues
  TI1-W,M UFB-W,M
Royal March
  SiP-W,M (Spanish)
Royal Proclamation
  SHS-W,M
Royal Summer Comes Apace
  SL-W,M
Roy's Wife of Aldivalloch
  HSD-W,M
Rozhinkes Mit Mandlen
  FW-W (Yiddish Only)
Rub-a-Dub-Dub

GM-W,M OTJ-W,M
Rubbers
  ASB2-W,M
Ruby
  HLS5-W,M RT5-W,M RW-W,M
  Sta-W,M
Ruby and the Pearl
  OTO-W
Ruby Baby
  DRR-W,M HRB3-W,M TI1-W,M
  UFB-W,M
Ruby, Don't Take Your Love to
  Town
  CMG-W,M FOC-W,M TI2-W,M
Ruby Red Dress (Leave Me Alone)
  TI1-W,M UFB-W,M
Ruby Tuesday
  RoS-W,M
Rudolph the Red-Nosed Reindeer
  BCh-W,M BCS-W,M FPS-W,M
  MF-W,M TI1-W,M UFB-W,M
  Y-W,M
Rue
  FW-W
Rue Raphenel
  AF-W
Rufus Mitchell's Confession
  BMM-W
Rule, Britannia
  CSo-W,M MPP-W,M NAS-W,M
  SiP-W,M
Rule of Three
  FSA1-W,M
Rules of the Road
  Mo-W,M NM-W,M SA-W
  TI2-W,M
Rules of the Road at Sea
  ANS-W
Rullion Green or Pentland Hills
  SBB-W
Rum and Coca-Cola
  GSF-W,M GSN3-W,M HLS3-W,M
  RW-W,M
Rum Saloon Shall Go
  Oz2-W
Rumanian Christmas Carol
  IF-W,M
Rumba Jumps
  NM-W,M OHF-W
Rumbling in the Land
  RBO-W,M
Rumpled, Tumbled and Jumbled
  SR-W,M
Rumsty Ho!
  TF-W,M
Run a Little
  AST-W,M
Run and Catch the Wind
  HCY-W,M
Run and Walk
  SOO-W,M
Run, Baby Chick
  MES2-W,M
Run, Brook, Run
  ASB3-W,M
Run, Come See
  FW-W
Run Come See Jerusalem
  TO-W,M
Run for Your Life
  BBe-W,M Be1-W,M TWS-W
Run Here Jeremiah
  BDW-W,M
Run Little Chick
  MES1-W,M
Run, Mary, Run
  RF-W,M

Run, Mary, Run see also O Run, Mary, Run
Run, Mona, Run
  J-W,M
Run Mo'ner Run
  BDW-W
Run, Neighbors, to the Crib
  SiR-W,M
Run, Nigger, Run
  AN-W NF-W NSS-W Oz2-W,M
Run Sally Run
  RY-W,M RYT-W,M
Run, Tell Aunt Nancy
  PSD-W,M
Run That Body Down
  PS-W,M
Run to Him (Her)
  MF-W,M
Run to Jesus
  AFP-W AL-W RF-W,M
Run to Jesus, Shun the Danger
  NSS-W
Run to Me
  TI1-N,M UFB-W,M
Run Up the Sail
  Boo-W,M
Run with the Bullgine
  SA-W,M
Run with the Power
  VB-W,M
Runaround Sue
  GAR-W,M TRR-W,M
Runaway
  DRR-W,M EP-W,M TI1-W,M
  TRR-W,M TTH-W,M UFB-W,M
Rune
  ASB6-W,M
Runner
  VB-W,M
Runnin', Runnin'
  PSN-W,M
Runnin' to Meet the Man
  R-W,M
Runnin' Wild
  GST-W,M MF-W,M RW-W,M
Running and Walking
  SiR-W,M SOO-W,M
Running Bear
  HR-W TI1-W,M TRR-W,M
  UFB-W,M
Running Scared
  TFC-W,M
Running Song
  GM-W,M SD-W,M
Runo
  UF-W,M
Rush Light
  MSB-W
Rush the Business On
  CSG-W,M
Russian Hymn
  ESB-W,M
Russian Lullaby
  OHO-W,M
Russian Maiden
  LMR-W,M
Russian National Hymn
  AmH-W,M (Russian)
Russian Sailor's Dance
  RW-M
Russian Sleigh Ride
  ASB5-W,M
Russians Are Coming
  RW-M
Rustic Reel
  POT-M
Rusting in the Rain

TT-W,M
Rustlin' Gambler
  BMM-W
Rusty Jiggs and Sandy Sam
  HAS-W,M
Rusty Old Halo
  OTJ-W,M
Rye Straw
  POT-M
Rye Waltz
  ASB3-W,M
Rye Whiskey
  FW-W HAS-W,M HWS-W,M
  PSN-W,M
Rye Whiskey, Rye Whiskey
  Oz3-W,M
Ryner Dyne see Rinordine

S

S-A-V-E-D
  TO-W,M
S-H-I-N-E
  MF-W,M TI1-W,M UFB-W,M
S.O.S.
  DP-W,M GI-W MF-W,M
  ToO76-W,M
S. P. Train
  LC-W
S.S. Vancouver
  VS-W,M
S.W.A.T. (Theme)
  ToO76-M
'S Wonderful
  BNG-W,M DBC-W,M DC-W,M
  GOB-W,M HC1-W,M LSO-W
  MF-W,M NYT-W,M OHB-W,M
Sa Huo K'ei Lei? (What Flow'r Blooms?)
  FD-W,M (Chinese)
Sabbath Bells
  FSA2-W,M
Sabbath Day Was By
  AHO-W,M
Sabbath Prayer
  OTO-W TI2-W,M UBF-W,M
Sabbath Queen
  JS-W,M (Hebrew)
Sabbath's Balm
  JS-W,M (Hebrew)
Sabre Dance
  MF-M
Sabre Jet Chant
  AF-W
Sabre Song
  DS-W,M
Sabrina
  OTO-W
Sacramento
  FW-W GuC-W,M HS-W,M
  RS-W,M SA-W,M
Sacramento Gals
  OTJ-W,M
Sacred Lines for Thanksgiving Day
  BC1-W,M
Sacred Mountain
  FSA2-W,M
Sacred Refuge for Federals
  ANS-W
Sacred War
  RuS-W,M (Russian)
Sacrifice of Praise
  HHa-W,M
Sacrifices of God
  JS-W,M
Sacrifices of God Are a Broken

Spirit
  Hy-W,M
Sad Am I and Sorrow-Laden
  SeS-W,M
Sad Calypso
  LaS-W,M
Sad Christmas
  FSA1-W,M
Sad Day
  RoS-W,M
Sad-Eyed Lady of the Lowlands
  RV-W
Sad Eyes
  ToO79-W,M
Sad Mother Nature
  ASB4-W,M
Sad Music
  SD-W,M
Sad News from Home
  SY-W,M
Sad Song
  Oz4-W,M
Sad Songs (Say So Much)
  TI2-W,M
Sad Songs and Waltzes
  WNF-W
Saddest Thing of All
  DP-W,M MLS-W,M
Sadie
  AmS-W,M
Sadie Ray
  Oz4-W,M
Sadie, Sadie
  TI1-W,M UBF-W,M UFB-W,M
Sadly to Mine Heart Appealing
  FHR-W,M
Saeynu
  WSB-W,M (Hebrew)
Safe
  VB-W,M
Safe Home in Port
  GH-W,M
Safe in the Arms of Jesus
  AME-W,M GH-W,M
Safe in the Promised Land
  FoS-W,M
Safe Side
  MML-W,M
Safehand Mail
  AF-W
Safely through Another Week
  Hy-W,M NAS-W,M
Safety First
  MH-W,M
Saga of Big Pete
  AF-W
Saga of Jenny
  LD-W,M LSO-W
Saga of Kate see Cosmetic Surgery
Saga of the Swede
  AF-W
Sail Along, Silv'ry Moon
  TI1-W,M UFB-W,M
Sail Around
  AFS-W,M
Sail Away
  DPE-W,M ERM-W,M MF-W,M
  ToO79-W,M
Sail Away for Lullabye Bay
  WDS-W,M
Sail Away Ladies
  B-W,M BI-W,M FW-W NF-W
  OHO-W,M POT-W,M
Sail Boat
  STS-W,M
Sail, O Believer, Sail

NSS-W
Sail On
  HCY-W,M TOH-W,M ToO79-W,M
  VB-W,M
Sail the Summer Winds
  OTO-W
Sailin' Over Yonder
  BDW-W,M
Sailing
  AmH-W,M BCC-W,M BH-W,M
  DPE-W,M GUM1-W,M HS-W,M
  HSD-W,M MES2-W,M OS-W
  SiR-W,M TH-W,M WiS8-W,M
Sailing at High Tide
  OTJ-W,M
Sailing at the High Tide
  VA-W,M
Sailing Away
  HHa-W,M
Sailing down Life's River
  GrM-W,M
Sailing for San Francisco
  ATS-W,M
Sailing Men
  FSA2-W,M
Sailing on the Sea of Your Love
  VB-W,M
Sailing, Sailing
  FW-W IL-W,M OTJ-W,M
Sailing the Union Way
  AFP-W
Sailor
  DD-W,M SCa-W,M
Sailor and the Soldier
  FoM-W,M
Sailor Boy
  BSC-W Oz1-W,M
Sailor Boy's Farewell
  ANS-W
Sailor Boys Have Talk to Me in
  English
  Mo-W,M NM-W,M
Sailor Cut Down in His Prime
  SoC-W
Sailor Lad
  LaS-W,M SL-W,M
Sailor Maid
  ASB6-W,M
Sailor on the Deep Blue Sea
  FW-W
Sailors
  FSA2-W,M
Sailors Aboard
  ASB5-W,M
Sailor's Address
  SI-W
Sailors' and Soldiers' Memorial
  Day
  ANS-W
Sailors' Come-All-Ye
  SA-W
Sailors' Farewell
  MuM-W,M
Sailor's Farewell to the Sea
  AL-W
Sailor's Grave
  ANS-W SA-W,M SY-W,M
Sailor's Home
  SHS-W,M
Sailor's Home Song
  SL-W,M
Sailor's Hornpipe
  POT-M
Sailor's Life for Me
  ANS-W
Sailor's Plea
  LJ-W,M

Sailor's Return
  BSC-W GI-W SaS-W,M SMY-W,M
Sailor's Song
  VS-W,M
Sailor's Sweetheart
  Oz1-W,M Oz4-W,M
Sailor's Tear
  ESU-W
Sailor's Trade
  BSC-W
Saint, The (Theme)
  GTV-M RW-M
St. Anthony's Chorale
  MU-W,M
St. Bridget
  NM-W,M OTO-W
St. Brigit
  Mo-W,M
St. Elsewhere (Theme)
  TV-M
St. James Infirmary
  AFB-W,M FAW-W,M FW-W
  ITP-W,M SoC-W,M
St. James's and St. Giles's
  MSB-W
St. James's Hospital
  AH-W,M
St. Louis Blues
  B-W,M BI-W,M OAP-W,M
  SLB-W,M
Saint Louis, Bright City
  Oz2-W,M
Saint Malo's Sands
  FSA1-W,M
Saint Nicholaes Goed Heilig Man
  ATS-W (Dutch Only)
Saint Patrick Was a Gentleman
  SiP-W,M
Saint Patrick's Day
  AmH-W,M SiP-W,M VA-W,M
Saint Patrick's Day in the Morning
  POT-M
St. Patrick's Day Jig
  AmH-M
St. Patrick's Potato Race
  HSA-W,M
Saint Paul's Steeple
  FSA2-W,M
Saint Stephen
  OB-W,M
St. Therese of the Roses
  OPS-W,M
St. Valentine's Day
  ASB4-W,M FSA1-W,M SiR-W,M
Saints Bound for Heaven
  SHS-W,M
Saints Day Carol
  GBC-W,M
Saint's Delight
  SHS-W,M
Saints Go Marchin' In
  JF-W,M
Saints in Glory, We Together
  AHO-W,M
Saints Will Rise
  AG-W,M
Sal
  CCS-W,M
Sal Got a Meatskin
  FW-W
Salamander
  MMY-W,M
Salangadou
  CLaL-W,M (French) CSD-W,M
  (French) FW-W (French) SoF-W,M
Sale of a Wife
  MSB-W

Salem
  SHS-W,M
Salem Cigarettes Jingle see You
  Can take Salem Out of the
  Country, But ...
Salerno Fishermen
  ASB6-W,M
Salley Gardens
  Gu-W,M
Sallie
  NF-W
Sally
  T-W,M U-W
Sally Ann
  FVV-W,M FW-W
Sally Brown
  ASB6-W,M FW-W SA-W,M
  TF-W,M
Sally Buck
  AFS-W,M
Sally Come Up
  HSD-W,M WiS8-W,M
Sally G
  TI2-W,M
Sally Gardens
  F1-W,M
Sally Go Round
  BM-W
Sally Go round the Chimney Pot
  TMA-M,W
Sally Go round the Moon
  OTJ-W,M
Sally Gooden
  SNS-W
Sally Goodin
  FSB3-W,M FVV-W,M FW-W
  Oz3-W,M POT-W,M
Sally in Our Alley
  AmH-W,M CSo-W,M FW-W
  HSD-W,M NAS-W,M WiS8-W,M
Sally My Dear
  FW-W
Sally O
  IS-W,M
Sally Sailsworth
  BSC-W,M
Salon and Saloon
  JC-W,M
Salt of the Earth
  RoS-W,M
Salt Peanuts
  TI2-M
Salt-Rising Bread
  NF-W
Salt Spray
  LMR-W,M
Salty Dog
  BIS-W,M FG2-W,M Le-W,M
  POT-W,M
Salty Dog Blues
  FW-W
Salty Dog Rag
  OGC2-W,M
Salut D'Amour
  AmH-M RW-M
Salutation
  SHS-W,M
Salutation Carol
  OB-W,M
Salute the Flag
  FSA2-W,M MH-W,M
Salute to Life
  FW-W
Salute to the Flag
  SL-W,M
Salute to the Medical Corps
  GO-W

Salvation
GH-W,M SHS-W,M
Salvation! O the Joyful Sound
AME-W,M GH-W
Salve Jesu Pastor Bone
AHO-W,M
Sam
TI2-W,M
Sam and Delilah
GOB-W,M LSO-W
Sam Bass
ATS-W BSC-W FW-W HWS-W,M
SoC-W
Sam Hall
FW-W J-W,M
Sam Is a Clever Fellow
NF-W
Sam Slick the Pedlar
ATS-W
Sam Slick, the Yankee Pedlar
ESU-W
Sam Stone
RV-W
Sam, the Old Accordion Man
WDS-W,M
Sam, You Made the Pants Too
Long
NoS-W,M TI1-W,M UFB-W,M
Samanthra
SHS-W,M
Samba De Orfeu
TI1-W,M (Portuguese Only)
UFB-W,M (Portuguese Only)
Sambo Rainey
SGT-W,M
Sambo's Opinion
AL-W
Sambo's Right to Be Kilt
SiS-W
Same Merry-Go-Round
PSN-W,M
Same Old Song
VS-W,M
Same Old Summer
Mo-W,M NM-W,M
Same Old You
THN-W,M
Same Ole Me
TOC82-W,M
Same One
MF-W,M
Same Train
ASB5-W,M LSR-W,M NH-W
UF-W,M
Samiotissa
ASB6-W,M
Samiotissa see also Samyotisa
Sam's Soliloquy, or Farewell to the
Protestant Ethic
TW-W
Samson
JF-W,M
Samson's Wife Sot on His Knees
RTH-W
Samtal Emellan Twenne
Utwandrare
SE-W (Swedish)
Samuel Hall
IL-W,M
Samyotisa
FPG-W,M (Greek Only)
Samyotisa see also Samiotissa
San
Mo-W,M NM-W,M TI2-W,M
San Antonio
FC-W,M
San Antonio Rose

FC-W,M FPS-W,M HSS-W,M
TI1-W,M UFB-W,M
San Fernando Valley
NM-W,M
San Francisco
GSN2-W,M GSO-W,M HLS5-W,M
RW-W,M
San Francisco (Be Sure to Wear
Some Flowers in Your Hair)
MCG-W,M TI2-W,M
San Francisco Bay Blues
TI1-W,M UFB-W,M
San Sereni
LA-W,M (Spanish) MG-W,M
(Spanish)
Sanct Escriture
Boo-W,M (French Only)
Sanctified
CEM-W,M
Sanctofy Me
NSS-W
Sanctus
SBF-W,M (Latin Only)
Sanctus (Gounod)
SL-W,M (Latin)
Sanctus (Michael Haydn)
SiM-W,M (Latin)
Sanctus (Schubert)
LMR-W,M
Sand and the Sea
NK-W,M
Sand in My Shoes
OTO-W
**Sand Pebbles Theme see And We
Were Lovers**
Sandford Barnes
Oz3-W
**Sandford Barnes see also Sanford
Barnes**
Sandgate Girl's Lament
BB-W
Sandman
ASB4-W,M ASB5-W,M MH-W,M
OTJ-W,M TF-W,M TH-W,M
**Sandpiper (Love Theme) see
Shadow of Your Smile**
Sands of Time
GH-W,M UBF-W,M
Sandy
Gr-W,M
Sandy Daw
CSG-W,M
Sandy Gibson's
DE-W,M
Sandy Land
BMC-W,M HS-W,M MG-W,M
Sandy McNab
Boo-W,M
Sandy Sam and Rusty Jiggs
TMA-W,M
Sanford Barnes
SoC-W
**Sanford Barnes see also Sandford
Barnes**
Sang For Danske
SiP-W,M (Danish)
Sano Duso
WSB-W,M (Serbo-Croatian)
Sans Day Carol
OB-W,M
Sans Souci
IL-W,M
Sanska Emigrantangaren Norges
Undergang I Atlanten
SE-W (Swedish)
Santa Anna
ATS-W,M

Santa Anna see also Santy Anna
Santa Anna's Retreat from Buena
Vista
FHR-W,M
Santa, Bring My Baby Back (to Me)
BCS-W,M TI1-W,M UFB-W,M
Santa Claus
DBL-W STS-W,M
Santa Claus Blues
PSN-W,M
Santa Claus Comes
ASB2-W,M
Santa Claus Is Back in Town
GAR-W,M MF-W,M
Santa Claus Is Comin' to Town
CSF-W GG3-W,M GM-W,M
MF-W,M RDT-W,M RW-W,M
SCS-W
Santa Claus Is Coming
GM-W,M MAR-W,M
Santa Fe Trail
MML-W,M
Santa Lucia
BF-W,M ESB-W,M FM-W,M
FW-W GuC-W,M HS-W,M (Italian)
HSD-W,M IL-W,M MF-W,M
MG-W,M NAS-W,M OS-W
OTJ-W,M PaS-W,M RW-W,M
TH-W,M TI1-M UFB-M WiS8-W,M
Santa Lucia Di Lammermoor
TF-W
Santa Maria
CDM-W,M (Spanish)
Santa, Santa, Santa Claus
BCh-W,M
Santa's Coming
CSS-W
Santa's Theme see Giving
Santiago
AmH-M
Santy Anna
FW-W SA-W,M SMY-W,M
Santy Anna see also Santa Anna
Santy Maloney
HS-W,M PIS-W,M
Sapphic Ode
FSY-W,M (German)
**Sara Lee Desserts Jingle see
Nobody Doesn't Like Sara Lee**
Sara Smile
TI1-W,M UFB-W,M
Sarah Jane
SGT-W,M
Sarasponda
MG-W,M OHO-W,M YS-W,M
Saratoga
Mo-W,M NM-W,M OTO-W
Sarava
PoG-W,M WG-W,M
Sardina
SHS-W,M
Saskatchewan
HB-W,M
Satan
NF-W
Satan Rules
UBF-W,M
Satin Doll
BBB-W,M DJ-W,M GMD-W,M
GSN3-W,M LM-W,M OHF-W
OPS-W,M TI2-W,M
Satin Sheets
FOC-W,M
Satisfaction
RoS-W,M
Satisfaction Guaranteed
OGC1-W,M

Satisfied
  GH-W,M MML-W,M NH-W
  OM-W,M
Satisfied Mind
  BSo-W,M RDF-W,M TI2-W,M
  TOC83-W,M
Saturday
  ASB4-W,M
Saturday in the Park
  BR-W,M GOI7-W,M
Saturday Morning in Angel Lane
  IFM-W
Saturday Night at the Movies
  RB-W
Saturday Night Fish Fry
  OTJ-W,M
Saturday Night Is the Loneliest
  Night of the Week
  BBB-W,M FrS-W,M MF-W,M
  TI1-W,M UFB-W,M
Saturday Night Songs Written on
  Board
  ANS-W
Saturday Night's Alright (for
  Fighting)
  TI2-W,M
Saucy Anna Lee
  Oz4-W,M
Saucy Sailor
  SaS-W,M
Sauerkraut see Sourkraut
Saute Crapaud
  CaF-W (French Only) CLaL-W,M
  (French)
Savanna
  Mo-W,M NM-W,M OTO-W
Savannah Song
  SSS-W,M
Save de Union
  MPP-W
Save, Jesus, Save
  GH-W,M
Save My Father's Picture from the
  Sale
  Oz4-W,M
Save the Bones for Henry Jones
  TI1-W,M UFB-W,M
Save the Last Dance for Me
  DRR-W,M HRB4-W,M ILS-W,M
  RY-W,M TI1-W,M TI2-W,M
  TRR-W,M UFB-W,M
Save the People
  G-W,M On-W,M OTJ-W,M
  OTO-W,TW-W UBF-W,M
Save the Union see Save de Union
Saved
  MF-W,M
S-A-V-E-D
  TO-W,M
Saved by Grace
  OM-W,M
Saved by the Blood
  GH-W,M
Savez-Vous Planter Les Choux?
  CUP-W,M (French Only) MP-W,M
  (French Only) OTJ-W,M (French
  Only)
Saving All My Love for You
  BNG-W,M DC-W,M DPE-W,M
Savior, Again to Thy Dear Name
  AME-W,M WiS9-W,M
Savior, Breathe an Evening
  Blessing
  AME-W,M
**Savior, Breathe an Evening
  Blessing see also Saviour, Breathe
  an Evening Blessing**

Savior, Hear Us through Thy Merit
  AME-W,M
Savior Is Waiting
  BSG-W,M BSP-W,M
Savior, Lead Me, Lest I Stray
  AME-W,M
Savior, More Than Life to Me
  AME-W,M
**Savior, More Than Life to Me see
  also Saviour, More Than Life**
Saviour, Again
  GH-W,M
Saviour, Again to Thy Dear Name
  Hy-W,M
Saviour, Breathe an Evening
  Blessing
  Hy-W,M
**Saviour, Breathe an Evening
  Blessing see also Savior, Breathe
  an Evening Blessing**
Saviour Came in Search of Me
  BSG-W,M BSP-W,M
Saviour, Hear Us, We Pray
  AME-W,M
Saviour, I Look to Thee
  AME-W,M
Saviour, Like a Shepherd
  GH-W,M
Saviour, Like a Shepherd Lead Us
  AME-W,M CEM-W,M Hy-W,M
Saviour, More Than Life
  GH-W,M
**Saviour, More Than Life see also
  Savior, More Than Life to Me**
Saviour, of the Sin-Sick Soul
  AME-W,M
Saviour, Sprinkle Many Nations
  AHO-W,M
Saviour, Teach Me, Day by Day
  Hy-W,M SJ-W,M
Saviour, Thy Dying Love
  AHO-W,M AME-W,M Hy-W,M
Saviour Visit Thy Plantation
  GH-W
Saviour, Who Thy Flock Art
  Feeding
  AHO-W,M
Saviour's Face
  GH-W,M
Saviour's Universal Prayer
  GB-W,M
Saviour's Work
  OB-W,M
Savoy Truffle
  TWS-W
Saw, The
  ASB5-W,M (French)
Sawyer's Exit
  FSSC-W,M
Say a Little Prayer for Me
  GrG-W,M
Say a Prayer for Me Tonight
  LL-W,M
Say, Are You Ready
  GH-W,M
Say Au Revoir, but Not Goodbye
  BH-W,M BSB-W,M EFS-W,M
  FSN-W,M FSTS-W,M MAS-W,M
Say Brothers
  WN-W,M
Say Forever You'll Be Mine
  BDP-W,M
Say, Has Anybody Seen My Sweet
  Gypsy Rose
  On-W,M OTJ-W,M
Say Hello
  BMC-W,M

Say It (Over and Over Again)
  OTO-W
Say It Loud--I'm Black and I'm
  Proud
  RB-W
Say Not Those Happy Days Can
  Never Return
  FHR-W,M
Say Oh! Beware
  BSC-W
Say Say Say
  TI2-W,M
Say Si,Si
  TI2-W,M
Say So!
  ReG-W,M
Say the Words
  TOF-W,M
Say Uncle
  LMS-W,M
Say You Love Me
  ToO76-W,M
Say You Will
  BHO-W,M CFB-W,M
Say You'll Be Mine
  BCC-W,M
Scabs Crawl In
  AFP-W PSN-W,M SWF-W,M
Scab's Death
  AL-W
Scab's Lament
  AL-W
Scale, The
  MHB-W,M TF-W,M TH-W,M
Scales and Arpeggios
  NI-W,M SBS-W,M
Scalp Song
  MPP-W
Scandal Walk
  ReG-W,M
Scandalize My Name
  FW-W OU-W,M
Scandalon
  VB-W,M
Scarborough Banks
  BB-W
Scarborough Fair
  FGM-W,M FW-W IPH-W,M
  OAP-W,M OPS-W,M OTJ-W,M
  PoG-W,M RW-W,M
Scarce Is Barley
  VA-W,M
Scarecrow
  ASB1-W,M ASB2-W,M
Scarecrow and Mrs. King (Theme)
  BNG-M TVT-M
Scarf Dance
  AmH-M
Scarlet and Cream
  CoS-W,M
Scarlet Poppies
  OBN-M
Scarlet Ribbons (for Her Hair)
  GSN3-W,M RDT-W,M
Scarlet Tree
  FSSC-W
Scars
  KH-W,M
Scat! Scat!
  SOO-W,M
Scat Song
  Sta-W,M
Scatter-Brain
  MF-W,M
Scatter Seeds of Kindness
  GH-W,M
Scenes from an Italian Restaurant

RV-W
Scenes of Wusih (Vu Si Ching)
 FD-W,M (Chinese)
Scenes That Are Brightest
 AmH-W,M TH-W,M
Schaefer Is the One Beer
 GSM-W,M
Schenectady
 SHS-W,M
Schnitzelbank
 OTJ-W,M (German Only)
School Dance
 RB-W
School Day
 HR-W RB-W TI1-W,M UFB-W,M
School Days
 BMM-W DBL-W FW-W
 GSN1-W,M MF-W,M OTJ-W,M
 TI1-W,M UFB-W,M
School Days of Long Ago
 Oz4-W
School Flag
 ASB3-W,M
School Is for Everyone
 LoS-W,M
School Orchestra
 FSA2-W,M
School, Sweet School
 ESU-W
School Time
 ASB1-W,M
School Verses
 RSC-W,M (Russian Only)
Schoolgirls We
 GiS-W,M
Schoolhouse Blues
 BI-W,M
Schoolhouse Fire
 BIS-W,M
Schoolroom Helpers
 ASB2-W,M
Schroeder
 YG-W,M
Schultz and Schultz
 SB-W,M
Scissor Bill
 AFP-W
Scissor Man
 SOO-W,M
Scissors and String
 OTJ-W,M
Scissors Grinder
 MHB-W,M (Italian)
Scissors Grinder's Bell
 ASB1-W,M
Scolding Wife
 FMT-W Oz3-W
Scoot
 MF-M
Scotch and Soda
 TOC83-W,M
Scotch Archer's Song
 VK-W,M
Scotch Poem
 RW-M
Scotland
 SL-W,M
Scotland's Burning
 ASB4-W,M BMC-W,M Boo-W,M
 FW-W IL-W,M MG-W,M
 NAS-W,M OHO-W,M OTJ-W,M
 SMa-W,M
Scots Wh' Ha'e wi' Wallace Bled
 SeS-W,M
Scots Wha Hae
 ESB-W,M SBB-W SiP-W,M
Scots Wha Hae wi' Wallace Bled

CSo-W,M FW-W NAS-W,M
 SMW-W,M
**Scottish National Song see
 Campbells Are Coming**
Scottish Wedding
 SeS-W,M
Scottsboro
 AFP-W
Scour and Scrub
 GB-W,M
Scout Benediction
 CSS-W
Scout Hearted Men
 Bo-W
Scout Leader's Prayer
 Bo-W,M
Scout Vesper
 Bo-W
Scout Vesper Song
 CSS-W
Scouting Marches On
 Bo-W,M
Scouting We Go
 Bo-W,M CSS-W
Scout's Good Night Song
 Bo-W,M CSS-W
Scrapple from the Apple
 TI1-M UFB-M
Scratch
 SSo-W,M
Scrumpdillyishus Day
 GSM-W,M
Se Canto
 FSF-W (French)
Se Gnori Z' Apo Tin Kopsi
 SiP-W,M (Greek)
Sea
 MH-W,M
Sea and Land Victories
 ANS-W AWB-W
Sea Birds
 LMR-W,M
Sea Captain or, the Maid on the
 Shore
 BT-W,M
**Sea Captain or, the Maid on the
 Shore see also Maid on the Shore**
Sea Captain and the Squire
 FSU-W
Sea Chantey
 TH-W,M
Sea Cruise
 FRH-W,M
Sea Fever
 AS-W,M MML-W,M
Sea Hunt (Theme)
 RW-M
Sea Line
 BMM-W,M
Sea of Heartbreak
 HD-W,M
Sea of Love
 DRR-W,M TI2-W,M
Sea Scout Chantey
 FSA1-W,M
Sea Shell
 ASB4-W,M
Sea Song
 AL-W SL-W,M
Sea Song from the Shore
 MH-W,M
Sea, the Sea!
 ANS-W
"Seagull" the Maiden Is Named
 LW-W,M (Russian) RuS-W,M
Seal Us, O Holy Spirit
 Hy-W,M

Sealed with a Kiss
 GSN4-W,M ILS-W,M RW-W,M
 RY-W,M
Seals
 GM-W,M
Seamen's Loyal Standard
 AL-W
Search, The
 LS-W,M
Search Is Over
 DPE-W,M LOM-W,M
Search Is Through
 LSO-W Mo-W,M NM-W,M OTO-W
Search Me, O Lord
 GH-W,M
Search Ye Your Camps
 GB-W,M
Searchin' (Leiber/Stoller)
 DRR-W,M HRB3-W,M TI1-W,M
 UFB-W,M
Searching (for Someone Like You)
 OGC2-W,M
Sears Where America Shops
 GSM-W,M
Seasons
 ASB1-W,M ASB3-W,M GrM-W,M
 MAR-W,M
Seasons and Times
 ER-W,M
Seasons Change
 BHO-W,M
Seasons in the Sun
 GrS-W,M TI2-W,M
Second Chance
 RW-W,M
Second-Hand Rose
 FPS-W,M TI2-W,M
Second Rhapsody
 NYT-M
Second Star to the Right
 NI-W,M OTJ-W,M
Second Terzetto
 BMC-M
Second Thoughts
 FSA1-W,M
Second Time Around
 FrS-W,M GG4-W,M HLS5-W,M
 PoG-W,M RT6-W,M RW-W,M
Second Time in Love
 Mo-W,M NM-W,M
Secret
 MH-W,M
Secret, Le see Le Secret
Secret Agent
 GOI7-M
Secret Agent Man
 OTJ-W,M
Secret Flower
 OB-W,M
Secret Love
 EY-W,M FrF-W,M HFH-W,M
 MF-W,M MR-W,M
Secret Lovers
 TTH-W,M
Secret of Christmas
 RW-W,M
Secretary Is Not a Toy
 UBF-W,M
Secretly
 ILF-W,M MF-W,M RY-W,M
 RYT-W,M
Security
 VA-W,M
See Afar Yon Hill Ardmore
 SeS-W,M
See Amid the Winter's Snow
 JOC-W,M

See at Your Feet
HSD-W,M
See da Robbers Passin' By
SGT-W,M
See Fo' and Twenty Elders
RF-W,M
See How I'm Jumping
SHP-W,M
See How the Rising Sun
AHO-W,M
See If I Care
GCM-W,M
See Me, Feel Me
WA-W,M
See Me, Feel Me see also Pinball Wizard/See Me, Feel Me Medley
See Miss Lilian So Fresh 'n Gay
SGT-W,M
See Saw
MH-W,M PIS-W,M
See Saw, Margery Daw
AmH-W,M GM-W,M HS-W,M
MM-W,M OTJ-W,M
See Saw Marjorie Daw
MF-W,M
See Saw, Sacra Down
GM-W,M OTJ-W,M
See Saw Song
AmH-W,M
See Saw Waltz Song
HSD-W,M
See See Rider see C.C. Rider
See, the Conquering Hero Comes
ESB-W,M LMR-W,M
See the Elephant Jump the Fence
AFS-W,M
See, the Gallant Hero Comes
MuM-W,M
See, the Harvest Moon Is Shining
SOT-W,M
See the Raindrops
Boo-W,M
See the Robbers Passing By see See da Robbers Passin' By
See the Show Again
TOF-W,M
See the U.S.A. in Your Chevrolet
GSM-W,M
See the Waters Gliding
SCa-W,M
See the Woman at the Well
BMM-W,M
See Those Poor Fellows
Boo-W,M
See What Happens
RoS-W,M
See What Love
SiM-W,M
See You in September
ERM-W,M FRH-W,M ILT-W,M
ToO79-W,M
See You Later, Alligator
ILF-W,M OTJ-W,M TI1-W,M
UFB-W,M
Seeds of Love
BT-W,M OTJ-W,M
Seein' the Elephant
ATS-W,M
Seeing Nellie Home
FW-W NAS-W,M
Seeing Things
OTO-W UBF-W,M
Seek and Ye Shall Find
FHR-W,M RF-W,M
Seek and You Shall Find
JF-W,M
Seeker, The

BDP-W,M
Seeking for Me
GH-W,M
Seeking to Save
GH-W,M
Seems Like Old Times
BBB-W,M HLS3-W,M MF-W,M
RW-W,M TOM-M TVT-W,M
Seesaw (from the musical)
MF-W,M
Sehnsucht
EL-W,M (German)
Seize Joy
JF-W,M
Selach Noh
JS-W,M (Hebrew Only)
Self-Banished
Gu-W,M OH-W,M
Self-Control
NF-W
Selfish Carol
CSB-W,M
Selling Gowns
MPM-W,M
Selling the Cow
ITP-W,M
Selling the Cow see also Yorkshire Bite
Semaine see Ein Semaine
Semaria Says
WW-W,M
Semaria Says He Loves His Girls
AFP-W
Semons La Salade
CUP-W,M (French Only)
Semper Fidelis
AAP-M MF-M OTJ-M RW-M
Semper Paratus
HA-W,M MAS-W,M TI1-W,M
UFB-W,M VA-W,M
Sen' Dem Angels Down
BDW-W,M
Sen' er One Angel Down
BDW-W,M
Senate
OT-W,M
Senator from Minnesota
OT-W,M
Send Down Thy Truth
BMC-W,M
Send Down Thy Truth, O God
AME-W,M
Send for Me
NK-W,M
Send Forth, O God, Thy Light and Truth
AHO-W,M
Send Forth Your Spirit Lord
JF-W,M
Send Her On Along
CFS-W,M (French)
Send in the Clowns
DBC-W,M DC-W,M EY-W,M
GrS-W,M LN-W,M MF-W,M
UBF-W,M
Send It to Me
RoS-W,M
Send Me the Pillow You Dream On
HLS9-W,M RW-W,M TOC83-W,M
Send My Baby Back to Me
Mo-W,M NM-W,M
Send One Angel Down see Sen' er One Angel Down
Send Out Thy Light
TH-W,M
Send Out Thy Light and Thy Truth
AME-W,M

Send Them Angels Down see Sen' Dem Angels Down
Senhora Viuva
LA-W,M (Spanish)
Senorita What's Her Name
LaS-W,M
Sensation
HLS1-M
Sentence
SL-W,M TF-W,M
Sentimental Gentleman from Georgia
Sta-W,M
Sentimental Journey
BBB-W,M IFM-W MAB1-W
Mo-W,M MSA1-W NM-W,M
On-W,M TI2-W,M
Sentimental Me (Cassin/Morehead)
TI1-W,M UFB-W,M
Sentimental Me (and Romantic You)
TS-W
Sentimental Rhapsody
HLS2-M
Sentry's Song
OTJ-W,M
Senza Mama (without a Mother)
OTO-W
Seoul City Sue
AF-W
Separate Lives
BNG-W,M GSN5-W,M HFH-W,M
MoA-W,M
Separation
SHS-W,M
September
FSA1-W,M SiR-W,M SoH-W,M
ToO79-W,M
September in the Rain
FrS-W,M HFH-W,M MF-W,M
September Morn
TI2-W,M
September Song
DBC-W,M FPS-W,M FrS-W,M
HC2-W,M HLS8-W,M ILT-W,M
KH-W,M LM-W,M MF-W,M
OTO-W TI1-W,M TW-W
TWD-W,M UBF-W,M UFB-W,M
September Thoughts
FSA1-W,M
Sequel to Grandfather's Clock
OHG-W,M
Sequel to Lorena
Oz4-W,M
Sequel to Nine-Nine Years
Oz2-W
Ser Como El Aire Libre
JF-W,M (Spanish)
Serenade (Donnelly/Romberg)
MF-W,M
Serenade (Good Night! Good-Night, Beloved!)
WiS9-W,M
Serenade (Good-Night! Good-Night, Beloved!) see also Good Night Beloved
Serenade (Pierne)
AmH-M
Serenade (Schubert)
AmH-W,M FSY-W,M (German)
Gu-W,M (German) GUM2-W,M
MF-W,M MHB-W,M OBN-M
SL-W,M TH-W,M TI1-W,M TM-
W,M UFB-M VA-W,M VK-W,M
WGB/O-W,M WiS8-W,M
Serenade in Blue
HFH-W,M MF-W,M

Serenade of the Bells
  Mo-W,M NM-W,M TI2-W,M
Serenade to a Lemonade
  Mo-W,M NM-W,M
Serenade to Nita
  MML-W,M
Serenade to the Moon
  FSA1-W,M
Serenata
  AmH-M TI2-W,M
Serene Is the Night
  NAS-W,M
Sergeant
  GI-W GO-W
Sergeant Champe
  EA-W,M SBA-W SI-W,M
**Sergeant Champe see also Ballad
  of Sergeant Champe**
Sgt. Pepper's Lonely Hearts Club
  Band
  BBe-W,M Be2-W,M TWS-W
Sergeant's Face
  GI-W
Sermonette
  MF-M OPS-W,M
Serpico (Theme)
  HSe-M OTO-W
Servant of God, Well Done
  AME-W,M
Serve the Lord with Joy and
  Gladness
  SHP-W,M
Servian National Hymn
  AmH-W,M (Serbo-Croatian)
Service for Others
  LoS-W
Service of Supplies
  GI-W
Service of the Lord
  WN-W,M
Set Down, Servant
  FoS-W,M FW-W GeS-W,M
  SAm-W,M
Set 'Em Up
  SYB-W,M
Set You Down, My Own True Love
  SCa-W
Settin' Down by de Side of de
  Lamb
  RTH-W
Seu Sheorim
  JS-W,M (Hebrew Only)
Seven Blessings of Mary
  FW-W ITP-W,M WSB-W,M
Seven Cent Cotton and Forty Cent
  Meat
  FW-W
Seven Daffodils
  TO-W,M
Seven Days' Pass
  GI-W
Sev'n Great Towns of Greece
  Boo-W,M
Seven Joys of Mary
  BCh-W,M
Seven Kinds of Fruit in Hawaiian
  Punch
  GSM-W,M
Seven Kings' Daughters
  BSC-W Oz1-W
Seven Little Girls
  RW-W,M
Seven Little Girls Sitting in the
  Back Seat
  DRR-W,M HR-W ILF-W,M
7 Rooms of Gloom
  THN-W,M

Seven Spanish Angels
  AWS-W,M DC-W,M EC-W,M
  GCM-W,M
Seven Steps
  ASB1-W,M PIS-W,M UF-W,M
Seven Steps to Heaven
  MF-M
Seven Virgins
  GBC-W,M OB-W,M
Seventeen
  RB-W
Seventeen and Twenty-One
  ReG-W,M
Seventh Dawn
  RW-W,M
Seventh Son
  TI1-W,M UFB-W,M
Seventy-Four
  FVV-W,M
Seventy-Four Blues
  DBL-W,M
77 Sunset Strip
  MF-W,M TVT-W,M
77 Sunset Strip Theme (Kookie,
  Kookie)
  TVT-W,M
Seventy-Six Trombones
  DBC-W,M HC2-W,M TI2-W,M
  UBF-W,M
Sewanee Sweetheart
  Mo-W,M
Sewing Machine
  AL-W
Sex Laugh
  NF-W
Sextet (Lucia Di Lammermoor)
  TF-W,M
Sextette from Lucia
  WiS7-W,M
Sexy
  DDH-W,M
Sexy + 17
  TI2-W,M
Sexy Sadie
  BBe-W,M TWS-W
Sh-Boom (Life Could Be a Dream)
  HRB2-W,M ILF-W,M TI1-W,M
  UFB-W,M
Sh Ta Dah Day (Irish Lullaby)
  AmS-W,M
Sh Ta Ra Dah Day (Irish Lullaby)
  AmS-W,M
Sh Tara Dah Day
  PSN-W,M
Sha, Sha, Der Rebbe Gait
  MF-W,M (Yiddish Only)
Shabbat Shalom
  SBJ-W,M (Hebrew Only)
Shabby De-Rue
  BSC-W
Shaded Grove
  Mu-W,M (French)
Shades of Gray
  OnT1-W,M
Shadow Dance
  FSA2-W,M
Shadow Dancing
  TI1-W,M UFB-W,M
Shadow of the Rock
  GH-W,M
Shadow of Your Smile
  FPS-W,M GG5-W,M HLS5-W,M
  OP2-W,M RT6-W,M RW-W,M
  STW-W,M THN-W,M
Shadow Pictures
  FSA2-W,M
Shadow Waltz

  MF-W,M MR-W,M OHB-W,M
Shadows in the Moonlight
  TI1-W,M UFB-W,M
Shadows of the Evening Hours
  AME-W,M
Shadowy Wood
  SoF-W,M
Shady Grove
  AH-W,M BIS-W,M D-W,M
  FSB3-W,M FVV-W,M FW-W
  OTJ-W,M RW-W,M
Shady Lady Bird
  TW-W
Shake 'Em On Down
  LC-W
Shake Hands, Mary
  PSD-W,M
Shake Hands with Uncle Sam
  SiS-W
Shake Off the Flesh
  GB-W,M
Shake, Rattle and Roll
  HRB2-W,M ILF-W,M TI1-W,M
  UFB-W,M
Shake, Shake, Mama
  LC-W
Shake, Shake, Mattie Blues
  LC-W
Shake That Little Foot
  ASB4-W,M
Shake That Little Foot, Dinah-O
  AFS-W,M
Shake That Tambourine
  SRE2-W,M
Shake the Apple Tree
  SiR-W,M SOO-W,M
Shake the Persimmons Down
  NF-W
Shake You Down
  CFB-W,M
Shake Your Booty
  ToO76-W,M
Shake Your Groove Thing
  SoH-W,M ToO79-W,M
Shake Your Love
  CFB-W,M
Shakedown
  HFH-W,M MoA-W,M
Shakespeare's Carol
  OB-W,M
Shakespeare's Willow
  BC1-W,M
Shall I Come, Sweete Love, to
  Thee
  OH-W,M
Shall I Wasting in Despair
  BSB-W,M
Shall Man, O God of Light
  AHO-W,M
Shall We Dance?
  HC1-W,M LSO-W OTO-W
  TI1-W,M UBF-W,M UFB-W,M
Shall We Gather at the River
  AH-W,M AHO-W,M AME-W,M
  AmH-W,M CEM-W,M WiS7-W,M
Shall We Go On to Sin
  AME-W,M
Shall We Meet
  GH-W,M HSD-W,M
Shall We Meet beyond the River?
  AME-W,M WiS7-W,M
Shall You? Shall I?
  GH-W,M
Shallo Brown
  SA-W,M
Shalom
  HC2-W,M Mo-W,M NM-W,M

OTJ-W,M OTO-W TI2-W,M
UBF-W,M
Shalom Aleichem
  FW-W (Hebrew Only) JF-W,M
  (Hebrew)
Shalom Aleichem see also Sholom
  Alaichem
Shalom Chaverim
  Boo-W,M (Hebrew Only) FW-W
  (Hebrew) GuC-W,M (Hebrew
  Only) MG-W,M (Hebrew)
  WSB-W,M (Hebrew)
Shalom Havayreem
  JF-W,M (Hebrew)
Shalom Haverim
  SBF-W,M (Hebrew Only)
Shame
  PoG-W,M WG-W,M
Shame on You
  OGC1-W,M
Shamrock and the Heather
  SMY-W,M
Shamrocks over Korea
  AF-W
Shamus O'Brien
  Oz4-W,M TMA-W,M
Shan Van Vocht
  VP-W,M
Shan Van Voght
  FW-W
Shanghai Breezes
  CJ-W,M
Shangri-La
  ELO-W,M GSF-W,M GSN3-W,M
  GTV-W,M HLS3-W,M OP2-W,M
  RW-W,M
Shannon and Chesapeake
  ANS-W
Shannon and the Chesapeake
  SI-W
Shanteyman's Life
  LMR-W,M SoC-W
Shanty-Boy and the Pine
  WS-W,M
Shanty-Man's Life
  SoF-W,M
Shape of Things
  TW-W
Sharayah
  VB-W,M
Share Your Love with Me
  TI2-W,M
Sharecropper Song
  Am-W,M
Sharing
  TOH-W,M
Sharon
  SHS-W,M
Sharon's Getting Betrothed
  FR-W,M
Shattered
  RoS-W,M
Shavua Tov
  SBJ-W,M (Hebrew Only)
She
  TI1-W,M TT-W,M UFB-W,M
She Appeared to Be Eighteen or
  Nineteen Years Old
  BIS-W,M
She Believes in Me
  PoG-W,M WG-W,M
She Came In through the
  Bathroom Window
  BBe-W,M Be2-W,M TWS-W
She Didn't Say Yes
  CF-W,M TI1-W,M UFB-W,M
She Drunk

LC-W
She Fooled Me
  DBL-W
She Got the Goldmine (and I Got
  the Shaft)
  TOC82-W,M
She Had Been Drinkin'
  LC-W
She Hangs Out in Our Alley
  GOB-W,M
She Hugged Me and Kissed Me
  NF-W
She Is More to Be Pitied
  IL-W,M
She Is More to Be Pitied Than
  Censured
  FSN-W,M FW-W RW-W,M
She Is More to Be Pitied Than
  Censured see also She's More to
  Be Pitied Than Censured
She Is Not Thinking of Me see
  Waltz at Maxim's
She Isn't You
  OTO-W
She Just Started Likin' Cheatin'
  Songs
  TOH-W,M
She Left Love All over Me
  TOC82-W,M
She Likes Basketball
  Mo-W,M OTO-W
She Loves Me
  DBC-W,M ILT-W,M MF-W,M
  OTO-W TI2-W,M
She Loves You
  BBe-W,M BR-W,M ERM-W,M
  GAR-W,M ILS-W,M MF-W,M
  TI2-W,M TWS-W
She May Have Seen Better Days
  BH-W,M EFS-W,M FSN-W,M
She Never Blamed Him, Never
  ESU-W
She Never Gets Got
  LaS-W,M
She Never Knew Me
  RW-W,M
She Never Thinks 'Tis Mine
  ESU-W
She Never Told Her Love
  FSS-W,M
She Roll Dem Two White Eyes
  NH-W
She Said She Said
  TWS-W
She Said She Was Only Flirting
  Oz4-W,M
She Said the Same to Me
  AmS-W,M
She Says It with Her Eyes
  HJ-W,M
She Smiled Sweetly
  RoS-W,M
She That Will Eat Her Breakfast in
  Her Bed
  Boo-W,M
She Thinks I Still Care
  EP-W,M
She Touched Me
  DBC-W,M HC2-W,M HSi-W,M
  Mo-W,M OTO-W TI2-W,M
  UBF-W,M
She Was a Woman Didn't Mean
  No One Man No Good
  LC-W
She Was All the World to Me
  FHR-W,M
She Was Bred in Old Kentucky

FSN-W,M FSTS-W,M
She Was Happy Till She Met You
  AH-W,M BH-W,M EFS-W,M
  LJ-W,M Oz4-W
She Was Just a Sailor's
  Sweetheart
  BH-W,M
She Was One of the Early Birds
  U-W
She Was Only Seventeen
  HR-W
She Was Poor but She Was Honest
  RW-W,M
She Weepeth Sore
  Boo-W,M
She Won't Get Up
  Oz3-W
She Wore a Yellow Ribbon
  TI1-W,M UFB-W,M
She Wore a Yellow Ribbon see
  also 'Round Her Neck She Wears
  (Wore) a Yellow Ribbon
Shear the Sheep
  MH-W,M
Sheathe the Sword, America
  SiS-W
She'd Rather Be with Me
  THN-W,M
Sheep and Goat
  NF-W
Sheep Dog
  FSA1-W,M
Sheep Shell Corn
  NF-W
Sheep's Eyes For Ever
  MSB-W
Sheepshearing
  HS-W,M
Sheepskin and Beeswax
  Oz3-W,M
Sheepwasher
  ATM-W,M
Sheffield Apprentice
  BSC-W
Sheik of Araby
  BBB-W,M TI2-W,M
Shein Vi Di L'Vone
  MF-W,M (Yiddish Only)
Shelby County Blues
  DBL-W
She'll Always Remember
  TI1-W,M UFB-W,M
She'll Be Comin' round the
  Mountain
  BF-W,M BH-W,M Bo-W,M
  FM-W,M FP-W,M FSB2-W,M
  FW-W FWS-W,M IL-W,M
  MAB1-W MAS-W MF-W,M
  MSA1-W OFS-W,M OS-W
  OTJ-W,M PaS-W,M RW-W,M
  TMA-W,M
She'll Be Coming round the
  Mountain
  FU-W,M FuB-W,M HS-W,M
  LH-W,M POT-W,M
She'll Be Coming round the
  Mountain see also Comin' 'round
  the Mountain
Shells of the Ocean
  Oz1-W,M
Shelter from the Storm
  GrS-W,M
Shelter in the Time of Storm
  GH-W,M OM-W,M
Shelter of His Eyes
  CEM-W,M
Sheltered in the Arms of God

Shoemaker and the Elves
SOO-W,M
Shoemaker Dance
SiR-W,M
Shoemakers
AL-W
Shoemaker's Dance
MAR-W,M
Shoemaker's Song
AL-W
Shoes
NA-W,M
Shoes, Boots and Leggins
Oz1-W,M
Shoes with Wings On
LSO-W
Shofet Kol Hooretz
JS-W,M (Hebrew)
Shogun (Love Theme) see Forbidden
Sholom Alaichem (Peace to All)
MF-W,M
Sholom Alayhem
SBJ-W,M (Hebrew Only)
Sholom Alechem
JS-W,M (Hebrew)
Sholom A'leychem
Bo-W,M (Hebrew Only)
Sholom A'leychem see also Shalom Aleichem
Shomor V'zohor
SBJ-W,M (Hebrew Only)
Shoo Fly
ASB3-W,M ITP-W,M MAR-W,M
Oz2-W,M
Shoo Fly, Don't Bother Me
BH-W,M FW-W HAS-W,M
HS-W,M IL-W,M MAS-W,M
MU-W,M OS-W RW-W,M
Shoo Fly, Don't Bother Me see also Shew! Fly, Don't Bother Me
Shoo Fly Pie and Apple Pan Dowdy
NoS-W,M TI2-W,M
Shoo, My Love
SNS-W
Shoo! Shoo!
NF-W
Shool
HAS-W,M
Shoop Shoop Song
DRR-W,M TRR-W,M
Shoop Shoop Song see also It's in His Kiss
Shoot the Buffalo
ASB5-W,M FMT-W IHA-W,M
Oz3-W,M TMA-W,M
Shoot the Turkey Buzzard
FVV-W,M
Shootin' with Rasputin
FW-W PO-W,M
Shooting of His Dear
FMT-W
Shop Around
HR-W ToO76-W,M
Shop Windows
FSA1-W,M
Shoppin' Around
SRE2-W,M
Shopping
ASB1-W,M
Shopping List
VB-W,M
Short and Curlies
RoS-W,M
Short Creek Raid
HB-W,M
Short Haired Woman

DBL-W
Short Letter
NF-W
Short Life of Trouble
BSo-W,M
Short Rations
MPP-W OTJ-W,M SCo-W,M
Sin-W,M SiS-W
Short, Short Is the Pain
Boo-W,M
Shortnin' Bread
AN-W BMC-W,M FWS-W,M HAS-
W,M HS-W,M IL-W,M MAS-W,M
OFS-W,M OTJ-W,M Oz2-W,M
RW-W,M UF-W,M
Shorty George
FW-W Le-W,M NeF-W PSN-W,M
Shotai
SiP-W,M (Japanese)
Shotgun Willie
WNF-W
Should Auld Acquaintance Be Forgot see Auld Lang Syne
Should He Upbraid
OH-W,M
Should I
GST-W,M HLS5-W,M RW-W,M
Should I Come Back Home to You
OGC2-W,M
Should I Come Home
TOH-W,M
Shoulder Arms
SiS-W
Shoulder Straps
SiS-W
Shoulder to Cry On
N-W,M
Shoulder to Shoulder
CA-W,M SMW-W,M (German)
Shouldn't I Know
HRB1-W,M
Shout (Isley Brothers)
ERM-W,M FRH-W,M ILF-W,M
MF-W,M
Shout for Joy
JF-W
Shout It Out
SRE1-W,M
Shout Jerusalem
BDW-W,M
Shout, Lulu
FVV-W,M
Shout of Protest
AL-W,M
Shout On, Chil'en, You Never Die
NSS-W
Shout On, Pray On
WN-W,M
Shout, Shout, We're Gaining Ground
Oz4-W,M
Shouting Mac and Freedom
SiS-W
Shouting the Battle-Cry of Labor
AL-W
Shovel and Broom
MSB-W
Shovuos Hymn
JS-W,M
Show a Room see Shew a Room
Show Me
HC1-W,M LL-W,M OTO-W
TI1-W,M TW-W UBF-W,M
UFB-W,M
Show Me the Way
AN-W GrS-W,M
Show Me the Way Back to Your

Heart
OGC2-W,M
Show Me the Way to Go Home
RDT-W,M U-W
Show Pity, Lord
Oz4-W,M
Show Pity, Lord, O Lord Forgive
AME-W,M
Showboat Go-Boat
HCY-W,M
Showdown
ELO-W,M
Showers of Blessing
AME-W,M
Shreveport Jail
NeF-W
Shrimp Boats
OnT6-W,M OTJ-W,M
Shriner's Convention
TOH-W,M
Shrove Tuesday Carol
GBC-W,M
Shtil Di Nacht
FW-W (Yiddish)
Shucking of the Corn
HS-W,M
Shuffle Off to Buffalo
HFH-W,M MF-W,M
Shuffle Song
TOH-W,M
Shuffling Song
GB-W,M
Shule Aron
FMT-W
Shule Aroon
BSC-W
Shule, Shule
Oz1-W,M
Shusti Fiddli
UF-W,M
Shut Down
HR-W
Shut That Gate
OGC2-W,M
Shut the Door
TI1-W,M UFB-W,M
Shut Up in the Mines of Coal Creek
ITP-W,M
Shutters and Boards
TI1-W,M UFB-W,M
Shy Incognita
UF-W,M
Shy Violet
ASB6-W,M
Si Algun Cadete
LA-W,M (Spanish)
Si Cantemo
RW-W,M (Spanish Only)
Si Feliz Quieres Ser
AHO-W,M (Spanish)
Si Le Roi M'avait Donne
CUP-W,M (French Only)
Si Les Garcons S'raient Sou' Las Ponts
CaF-W (French Only)
Si Me Quieres Escribir
FW-W (Spanish) WSB-W,M (Spanish)
Si Mes Vers Avaient Des Ailes see Were My Song with Wings Provided
Si Non Paruisti
Boo-W,M (Latin Only)
Siamese Cat Song
NI-W,M OTJ-W,M
Siboney

GG5-W,M RW-W,M
Sic Him, Towse
Oz3-W,M
Sich a Gitting up Stairs
AH-W,M
Sicilian Tarantella
PoG-M
Siciliana
AmH-W,M WiS7-W,M
Sicilienne
ASB1-M
Sick Call
ATS-W,M GI-W GO-W
Sick Tune
SSP-W
Sick Wife
NF-W
Side by Side
BBB-W,M GSN2-W,M HLS2-W,M
MF-W,M RDT-W,M TI1-W,M U-W
UFB-W,M
Side by Side by Side
Co-W,M OTO-W UBF-W,M
Sidewalk Talk
TTH-W,M
Sidewalk Tree
R-W,M TW-W
Sidewalks of Cuba
Sta-W,M
Sidewalks of New York
AH-W,M FSN-W,M FW-W
FWS-W,M GSN1-W,M HLS1-W,M
MF-W,M OAP-W,M OS-W
OTJ-W,M RC-W,M RW-W,M
TI1-W,M UFB-W,M
**Sidewalks of New York see also
East Side, West Side**
Sidewalks of New York City
HS-W,M
Sidney Allen
BMM-W FMT-W
Siege of Tripoli
ANS-W
Siembamba
ASB4-W,M
Sierra Sue
FC-W,M
Sierry Petes
GA-W,M HB-W,M
Sigh No More Ladies
FSS-W,M OH-W,M SSB-W,M
Sight for a Father
MSB-W
Sign of de Judgment
MAS-W,M
Signal
GOB-W,M
Signing the Pledge
Oz2-W,M
Signor Abbate
Boo-W,M
Signor Mons Muldoni
FT-W,M
Signs
MCG-W,M
Signs of Autumn
ASB3-W,M MH-W,M
Signs of Spring
SSe-W,M
Signs of the Weather
ASB5-W,M
Silence Is Golden
Mo-W,M NM-W,M
Silence on the Line
TOH-W,M
**Silent Is the Night see Shtil Di
Nacht**

Silent Love
VB-W,M
Silent Night
ASB4-W,M BBF-W,M BCS-W,M
BM-W BMC-W,M CCH-W,M
(German) CCM-W,M CEM-W,M
CSF-W DC-W,M FW-W FWS-W,M
GBC-W,M Gu-W,M GuC-W,M
HS-W,M (German) HSD-W,M
IL-W,M IPH-W,M JOC-W,M
LoS-W,M MAB1-W MAS-W,M
MC-W,M MES1-W,M MES2-W,M
MSA1-W NAS-W,M OTJ-W,M
OU-W,M RW-W,M SAC-W,M
SCS-W SL-W,M SMa-W,M
SOO-W,M TF-W TH-W,M
TI1-W,M U-W UFB-W,M YS-W,M
Silent Night, Holy Night
AME-W,M BCh-W,M CC-W,M
CI-W,M ESB-W,M HF-W,M
Hy-W,M IH-M MML-W,M
OAP-W,M OPS-W,M PoG-W,M
SHP-W,M SJ-W,M TB-W,M
YC-W,M
Silent Partner
VB-W,M
Silent Things
GM-W,M
Silent to Thee
MMM-W,M
Silent Weeper
VB-W,M
Silently Now We Bow
SOW1-W,M SOW2-W,M
Silently the Shades of Evening
AME-W,M
Silhouette
MF-M
Silhouettes
GAR-W,M HR-W ILF-W,M
TI1-W,M UFB-W,M
Silicosis Blues
J-W,M
Silk Merchant's Daughter
FMT-W ITP-W,M Oz1-W,M
Silk Stockings
TI1-W,M UFB-W,M
Silk Worm
MH-W,M
Silly Love Songs
PMC-W,M TI2-W,M
Silly Ole Woman She Walks Alone
SGT-W,M
Silver and Gold
BCh-W,M BCS-W,M
Silver Bell
MR-W,M
Silver Bells
AT-W,M BCh-W,M FWS-W,M
GOI7-W,M LM-W,M MM-W,M
OBN-W,M OnT6-W,M OTJ-W,M
OTO-W Y-W,M
Silver Bells of Memory
TMA-W,M
Silver Dagger
BSC-W,M FMT-W ITP-W,M
OFS-W,M OTJ-W,M Oz2-W,M
Silver Dollar
IL-W,M TI1-W,M UFB-W,M
Silver Jack
FMT-W
**Silver Spoons (Theme) see
Together (Theme from Silver
Spoons)**
Silver Street
SHS-W,M
Silver Swan

Boo-W,M OH-W,M
Silver Threads among the Gold
ATS-W BH-W,M FSTS-W,M
FW-W MF-W,M OAP-W,M
PoS-W,M RW-W,M STR-W,M
U-W WiS8-W,M
Silver-Tongued Devil and I
SuS-W,M
Silver Train
RoS-W,M
Silvered Is the Raven Hair
GiS-W,M MGT-W,M
Silvery Moon
Oz4-W,M
Silvery Tide
Oz1-W,M
Sim and the Widow
BSC-W
Sim Courted the Widow
Oz3-W,M
Simchas Torah Hymn
JS-W,M
Simon Says
RYT-W,M
Simon Slick
AN-W
Simon Slick's Mule
NF-W NH-W
Simon the Cellarer
HSD-W,M
Simple Aveu
AmH-M
Simple Gifts
AH-W,M GB-W,M JF-W,M
MG-W,M OA1-W,M OTJ-W,M
SBF-W,M TT-W,M
Simple Joys of Maidenhood
OTO-W UBF-W,M
Simple Little Things
OHT-W,M
Simple Lullaby
OTJ-W,M
Simple Simon
OTJ-W,M
Simple Song for a Mighty God
OGR-W,M
Simply Wonderful
Mo-W,M
Simpson Bush--Murderer
BMM-W
Sin No More
GH-W,M
Sin-Sick Soul
WN-W,M
Sinbad
SA-W,M
Since Christ My Soul from Sin Set
Free
AME-W,M
Since First I Saw Your Face
CSo-W,M EL-W,M OH-W,M
SSP-W
Since I Fell for You
DPE-W,M ERM-W,M GCM-W,M
MF-W,M
Since I Left Arkansas
Oz3-W,M
Since I Met You Baby
FrF-W,M HRB3-W,M TI1-W,M
UFB-W,M
Since Jesus Came into My Heart
AME-W,M RDF-W,M
Since Jesus Is My Friend
AME-W,M Hy-W,M
Since My Daughter Plays on the
Typewriter
OHG-W,M

Since My Loved One Has Gone
SeS-W,M
Since Robin Hood
BMC-W,M
Since the Chinese Ruint the Trade
AL-W
Since Time So Kind
Boo-W,M
Since We Parted
AS-W,M
Since Wine, Love, Music Present
Are
Boo-W,M
Since You're Not Around
OTO-W UBF-W,M
Sincerely
DRR-W,M GAR-W,M ILF-W,M
TI1-W,M UFB-W,M
Sincerely Yours
VB-W,M
Sincerity
SHS-W,M
Sinful to Flirt
ITP-W,M
Sing!
CL-W,M FPS-W,M FSA1-W,M
JP-W,M
Sing-a-Ling-a-Ling
HS-W,M TF-W,M
Sing a Song
ASB2-W,M ASB5-W,M
Sing a Song of Charleston
MPP-W
Sing a Song of Merry-Go-Round
SOO-W,M
Sing a Song of Sixpence
AmH-W,M HS-W,M MF-W,M
OTJ-W,M SMa-W,M SOO-W,M
Sing a Song of Spring
SSe-W,M
Sing a Song to Our Navy
GO-W
Sing about the Sunshine
SSN-W,M (French)
Sing Again That Sweet Refrain
BH-W,M EFS-W,M
Sing, All Creation
BeB-W,M
Sing Along
LoS-W,M
Sing Amalgamated
WW-W,M
Sing and Dance
ASB4-W,M
Sing and Dance It
MMY-W,M
Sing and Pray
GH-W,M
Sing As We Go
U-W
Sing at Your Work
FSA1-W,M
Sing 'Em Low see Chantez Les Bas
Sing for Joy
OGR-W,M
Sing for the Wide, Wide Fields
VA-W,M
Sing for Your Supper
OTO-W TS-W UBF-W,M
Sing Good Night
ASB6-W,M
Sing Hallelujah
CEM-W,M
Sing It Over
Boo-W,M
Sing Ivy
OTJ-W,M

Sing Lullaby
GBC-W,M
Sing Me a Baby Song
STW-W,M
Sing Me a Song
MH-W,M
Sing Me a Song with Social
Significance
UBF-W,M
**Sing Me a Song with Social
Significance see also Sing Us a
Song with Social Significance**
Sing Me Another
Boo-W,M
Sing Me Back Home
NMH-W,M
Sing Me Not a Ballad
LSO-W UBF-W,M
Sing, My Soul
AHO-W,M
Sing, My Tongue, the Glorious
Battle
SJ-W,M
Sing, O Heavens
CCH-W,M
Sing, O Sing
STS-W,M
Sing, O Ye Ransom'd of the Lord
AME-W,M
Sing of Fire
RDT-W,M
Sing of My Redeemer
WN-W,M
Sing of Spring A-Coming
RS-W,M
Sing O-hi-o (Marching Song)
CoS-W,M
Sing On
SL-W,M
Sing On in Glory Someday
HHa-W,M
Sing One, Two, Three
Boo-W,M
Sing Out Express
HCY-W,M
Sing Praise to God Who Reigns
Above
Hy-W,M
Sing, Said the Mother
KH-W,M MH-W,M
Sing Sally O
SA-W,M
Sing, Sing, Sing
RW-W,M
Sing, Sing Together
GuC-W,M
Sing, Smile, Slumber
HSD-W,M
Sing Something Simple
MF-W,M
Sing the Glory of His Name
OGR-W,M VB-W,M
Sing the Praises o' My Dearie
SeS-W,M
Sing the Wondrous Love Of Jesus
AME-W,M
Sing Them Over Again to Me
AME-W,M Hy-W,M
Sing Them, Songs of Labor
AL-W
Sing This All Together
RoS-W,M
Sing This Grave and Simple Strain
Boo-W,M
Sing Till the Power of the Lord
Comes Down
SFF-W,M

Sing to God
ASB4-W,M
Sing to God in Joyful Voice
SCL-W,M
Sing to the Lord
VB-W,M
Sing to the Lord Most High
AHO-W,M
Sing to the Lord the Children's
Hymn
SJ-W,M
Sing to the Seasons
MHB-W,M
Sing Together
HS-W,M SiR-W,M
Sing unto Him
VB-W,M
Sing unto the Lord
GH-W,M
Sing Us a Song with Social
Significance
TW-W
**Sing Us a Song with Social
Significance see also Sing Me a
Song with Social Significance**
Sing We Noel
CCH-W,M
Sing We Now
MuM-W,M
Sing We Now of Christmas
Y-W,M
Sing We Now Our Morning Song
Boo-W,M
Sing We This Roundelay
Boo-W,M
Sing with All the Sons of Glory
AME-W,M
Sing with Joy
OGR-W,M
Sing with Thy Mouth
Boo-W,M
Sing Ye Sweetly
Y-W,M
Sing Ye to the Lord
SoM-W,M
Sing You Now after Me
Boo-W,M
Sing You Sinners
OTO-W
Sing Your Praise to the Lord
OGR-W,M VB-W,M
Sing Your Way Home
BeB-W,M BM-W
Singer
My-W,M VB-W,M
Singer, Not the Song
RoS-W,M
Singin' in the Rain
BH-W,M EAG2-W,M GG1-W,M
GST-W,M HLS5-W,M OS-W
RT5-W,M RW-W,M
Singin' Johnny
FSA2-W,M
Singing a Love Song
VB-W,M
Singing All Day and Dinner on the
Ground
BSo-W,M
Singing All the Time
GH-W,M
Singing Along
SiR-W,M
Singing Around
AST-W,M
Singing As We Journey
GH-W,M
Singing Bird

FSA1-W,M
Singing Christian
SHS-W,M
Singing on the Old Church Ground
WN-W,M
Singing River
OTJ-W,M
Singing the Blues
GSN3-W,M
Singing Time
AST-W,M
Singing Top
ASB1-W,M RSL-W,M
Singing with Grace
GH-W,M
Single Girl
AH-W,M FW-W IHA-W,M
LW-W,M ITP-W,M RW-W,M
SCa-W,M
Single Women
TOC82-W,M
Sinking in the Atlantic of the
Danish Emigrant Steamship Norge
SE-W (Swedish)
Sinking of the Emigrant Steamer
Geiser
SE-W (Swedish)
Sinking of the Reuben James
WSB-W,M
Sinking of the Titanic
BB-W WN-W,M
**Sinking of the Titanic see also Ship
Titanic and Titanic, The**
Sinner and the Song
AME-W,M
Sinner Die
NH-W
Sinner Forgiven
GH-W,M
Sinner, Is Thy Heart at Rest?
AHO-W,M
Sinner Like Me
AME-W,M GH-W,M
Sinner Man
AH-W,M FW-W GuC-W,M
RW-W,M WSB-W,M
**Sinner Man see also Oh, Sinner
Man**
Sinner, Please
NSS-W
Sinner, Please Don't Let This
Harvest Pass
FN-W,M LMR-W,M NeA-W,M
OU-W,M
Sinner Was Wandering at Eventide
AME-W,M
Sinner Where Will You Stand
WN-W,M
Sinner Why Will You Die
WN-W,M
Sinners, Obey the Gospel Word
AME-W,M
Sinners Prayer
HRB1-W,M
Sinners' Redemption
OB-W,M
Sinners, Turn
WN-W,M
Sinners, Turn, Why Will Ye Die
AME-W,M GH-W
Sinner's Warning
BSC-W
Sinners Will Call for the Rocks and
the Mountains
Oz4-W
Sinners, Will You Scorn the
Message

AHO-W,M   AME-W,M
Sion's Daughter
OB-W,M
Sioux City Sue
FC-W,M Mo-W,M NM-W,M
TI2-W,M
Sippin' Bourbon through a Straw
AF-W
Sipping Cider through a Straw
FW-W OFS-W,M
Sir Christmas
OB-W,M
Sir Hugh
FMT-W
Sir Hugh, or the Jew's Daughter
BSC-W SCa-W,M
**Sir Hugh, or the Jew's Daughter
see also Jew's Daughter**
Sir Lionel
BSC-W SCa-W,M
Sir Peter Parker
SI-W,M
Sir Walter, Enjoying His Damsel
One Night
Boo-W,M
Sirup Is So Sweet
MHB-W,M (French Creole)
Sis Mary Wore Three Links of
Chain
AN-W
Sisotowbell Lane
RV-W
Sister Adele
SSN-W,M (French)
Sister Carrie
Sin-W,M
Sister Christian
TI2-W,M
Sister Golden Hair
DPE-W,M
Sister Mary's Twelve Blessings
WN-W,M
Sister Morphine
RoS-W,M
Sister Rosy, You Get to Heaven
Before I Go
NSS-W
Sister Suffragette
OnT6-W,M WD-W,M
Sister Susie's Sewing Shirts for
Soldiers
SLB-W,M
Sister, Thou Wast Mild and Lovely
NeA-W,M
Sister's Husband see Fair Annie
Sit Down You're Rockin' the Boat
TI2-W,M UBF-W,M
Sittin' on a Fence
RoS-W,M
**Sittin' on the Dock of the Bay see
Dock of the Bay**
Sitting
GrM-W,M
Sitting by My Own Cabin Door
FHR-W,M
**Sitting Down by the Side of the
Lamb see Settin' Down by de
Side of de Lamb**
Sitting in Jail
KH-W,M
Sitting on Top of the World
BSo-W,M OTJ-W,M
Sitting Pretty
C-W,M
Six Feet of Earth
AFP-W
Six King's Daughters

TBF-W,M
Six Little Dogs
SiR-W,M
Six Little Ducks
LoS-W,M SHP-W,M
Six Men Riding
RBO-W,M
Six O'Clock
THN-W,M
Six Questions
PO-W,M
Six, Six, Six
VB-W,M
634-5789
TOC83-W,M
Six to Six
AFP-W AL-W
Sixteen Candles
PoG-W,M TI2-W,M
Sixteen Going on Seventeen
OTJ-W,M OTO-W SM-W,M
TI1-W,M UBF-W,M UFB-W,M
Sixteen Reasons (Why I Love You)
TI1-W,M UFB-W,M
Sixteen Tons
FOC-W,M HLS3-W,M HLS9-W,M
OTJ-W,M PB-W,M RW-W,M
SWF-W,M TI1-W,M UFB-W,M
16th Avenue
TOC82-W,M
Sixth Naval Victory
ANS-W
61 Highway
LC-W
Sixty-Six Highway Blues
SBF-W,M
Sixty-Three Is the Jubilee
SiS-W
Size 12
Mo-W,M NM-W,M
Skaters, The
AmH-M OBN-M
Skaters' Waltz
ASB1-M HS-W,M RW-M TI1-M
UFB-M
Skating
ASB1-W,M ASB3-W,M
FSA2-W,M MH-W,M MML-W,M
SOO-W,M
Skating Away (on the Thin Ice of
the New Day)
BJ-W,M
Skating Song
ASB2-W,M SY-W,M
Skedaddle
SiS-W
Skeptic's Daughter
ITP-W,M Oz4-W,M
Skewbald Black
SoC-W
Skidikiscatch
K-W,M
Skillet Good and Greasy
FPG-W,M PO-W,M
Skimbleshanks: The Railway Cat
UBF-W,M
Skin-and-Bone Woman
Oz1-W,M
Skip to My Lou
ASB2-W,M ATS-W,M BM-W
BMC-W,M FG1-M FG2-M
FGM-W,M FMT-W FoM-W,M
FSB1-W,M FU-W,M FuB-W,M
FW-W FWS-W,M GuC-W,M
HS-W,M IHA-W,M IPH-W,M
J-W,M Le-W,M LMR-W,M
LT-W,M MAR-W,M MF-W,M

OTJ-W,M Oz3-W,M SCL-W,M
SFM-W SiR-W,M SRS-W,M
TMA-W,M WU-W,M
Skip Turn a Loo
UF-W,M
Skipper
ASB1-W,M ASB3-W,M
Skippin' and Steppin'
RSL-M
Skipping
ASB2-W,M
Skipping and Galloping
SiR-W,M SOO-W,M
Skipping and Walking
SOO-W,M
Skipping Is Fun
MAR-W,M
Skipping Rope
GM-W,M
Skokiaan
TI1-W,M
Sky Boat
FSA1-W,M
Sky Boat Song
OTJ-W,M
Sky High
SoC-W
Sky over Vietnam
VS-W,M
Sky Pictures
SiR-W,M
Skye Boat Song
FBI-W,M Gu-W,M HS-W,M
LMR-W,M MG-W,M STP-W,M
TH-W,M
Skylark
DJ-W,M MF-W,M TI2-W,M
Skylark Christmas Card
OHF-W
Skyliner
TI1-W,M UFB-W,M
Sky's the Limit
VB-W,M
Slack Your Rope
TBF-W,M
Slago Town
FSU-W
Slain Lamb of God
AHO-W,M (German)
Slap That Bass
LSO-W OTO-W
Slaughter on Tenth Avenue
TI2-M UBF-M
Slav Ho
SA-W,M
Slave
RoS-W,M
Slave Marriage Ceremony
Supplement
NF-W
Slave Song
MES1-W,M MES2-W,M
Slave to the Rhythm
TTH-W,M
Slavery Chain
AFP-W AL-W RF-W,M
Slavery Chain Done Broke at Last
FW-W
Slaves Appeal
AFP-W
Slave's Dream
NSS-W
Slave's Revenge
AL-W
Sleds Go Zooming
SSe-W,M
Sleep

OBN-M OP1-W,M RW-M
Sleep Baby Sleep
EFS-W,M HS-W,M MG-W,M
NAS-W,M OTJ-W,M SL-W,M
SMa-W,M
Sleep, Beloved, Sleep
HSD-W,M
Sleep, Holy Babe
BCh-W,M CCH-W,M CSB-W,M
Sleep, Little One
WU-W,M
Sleep, Little One, Sleep
MML-W,M
**Sleep My Child see Shlof Mayn
Kind, Shlof Keseyder**
Sleep, Noble Hearts
TF-W,M
Sleep, Sleep, Sleep
FWS-W,M
Sleep, Sleep Well
Boo-W,M
Sleep, Soldiers
FSA2-W,M
Sleep, Sweet Babe
OTJ-W,M
Sleep Sweetly
AHO-W,M
Sleep Wayward Thoughts
Gu-W,M
Sleepin' Bee
Mo-W,M NM-W,M OTO-W
UBF-W,M
Sleeping Beauty
OBN-M RW-M
Sleeping Beauty Waltz
MF-M
Sleeping Dolls
MH-W,M
Sleeping for the Flag
SiS-W
Sleeping in the Battlefield
SiS-W
Sleeping in the Valley
SiS-W
Sleeping Princess
ASB2-W,M HS-W,M
Sleeping Single in a Double Bed
TI2-W,M
Sleepwalk
TI2-M
Sleepy City
RoS-W,M
Sleepy Head
WDS-W,M
Sleepy-Head Sun
ASB3-W,M
Sleepy Lagoon
LM-W,M TI1-W,M UFB-W,M
Sleepy Latrine
GI-W
Sleepy Song
SOO-W,M
Sleepy Time
ASB1-W,M
Sleepy Time Gal
CS-W,M GSN2-W,M HLS2-W,M
OPS-W,M PB-W,M RW-W,M
STW-W,M
Sleigh Bell Carol
JOC-W,M
Sleigh Ride
BCh-W,M HLS3-W,M SiR-W,M
Sta-W,M
Slicin' Sand
SRE1-W,M
Slide, The
ASB1-W,M ASB2-W,M

Slide Off of Your Satin Sheets
RW-W,M
Slide Some Oil to Me
Wi-W,M
Slidin' Around
FG2-M
Sliding
ASB4-W,M
Sliding Jenny Jig
DE-W,M
Slightly Out of Tune
MF-W,M TI1-W,M
**Slightly Out of Tune see also
Desafinado**
Slip Kid
WA-W,M
Slipper and the Rose Waltz
SBS-W,M
Slippin' and A-Slidin' with My New
Shoes On
FVV-W,M
Sloop John B.
FG2-W,M GuC-W,M OFS-W,M
OTJ-W,M TI2-W,M
Slovak Dance
ASB4-W,M
**Slovak Industrial Song see Aja
Lejber Man**
Slow Down Old World
WNF-W
Slow Hand
EC-W,M GCM-W,M
Slow Walking Song
SD-W,M
Slowly
RY-W,M
Slowly but Surely
SRE1-W,M
Slowly, by God's Hand Unfurled
AHO-W,M
Slugger Theme (ABC Monday
Night Baseball Theme No.3)
TVT-M
Slum and Beans
GI-W
Slumber Boat
HS-W,M MG-W,M
Slumber My Darling
FHR-W,M
Slumber On, My Little Gypsy
Sweetheart
FT-W,M FWS-W,M
**Slumber On, My Little Gypsy
Sweetheart see also Gypsy Love
Song**
Slumber Song
ASB3-W,M (Portuguese)
ASB4-W,M (Spanish) ASB6-W,M
GeS-W,M SiR-W,M
Slumbering Cathedral
ASB6-W,M
Sly Mongoose
LaS-W,M
Smack Dab in the Middle
MF-W,M
Small Fry
LM-W,M OTO-W
Small Talk
TW-W
Small World
DBC-W,M HC2-W,M OTO-W
TI1-W,M UBF-W,M UFB-W,M
Smarty Pants
WDS-W,M
Smashing of the Van
VP-W,M
Smellin' of Vanilla

Mo-W,M NM-W,M OTO-W
Smile
  FSA1-W,M NK-W,M RDF-W,M
  TI1-W,M UFB-W,M
Smile a Little Smile for Me
  PoG-W,M TI2-W,M
Smile, Darn Ya, Smile
  TI1-W,M UFB-W,M
Smile Na Sae Sweet, My Bonnie
  Babe
  SeS-W,M
Smile Song
  Bo-W
Smile Will Go a Long, Long Way
  Mo-W,M NM-W,M
Smiles
  GI-W MF-W,M OS-W
Smiling Phases
  TI1-W,M
Smiling Spring
  ASB6-W,M
Smithfield Mountain
  IHA-W,M
Smitten Rock
  GH-W,M
Smoke Gets in Your Eyes
  DJ-W,M ILF-W,M MU-W,M
  RDT-W,M RW-W,M TI1-W,M
  TW-W UFB-W,M
Smoke Goes up the Chimney
  SiR-W,M
Smoke Like Lightnin'
  LC-W
Smoke Rings
  TI2-W,M
Smoke Stack Lightnin'
  DBL-W
Smokey Joe's Cafe
  HRB3-W,M
Smokin' Reefers
  TW-W
Smoky Mountain Rain
  FOC-W,M TI2-W,M TOH-W,M
Smoky Mountains
  ASB5-W,M
Smooth Sailing
  TOH-W,M
Smoothly Glide
  Boo-W,M
Smorgasbord
  RW-W,M SRE2-W,M
Smuggler's Song
  UF-W,M
Snail, Snail
  FMT-W FoM-W,M
Snail's Reply
  NF-W
Snake Baked a Hoecake
  AFS-W,M
Snake in the Grass
  OTO-W Oz4-W
Snakey Blues
  B-M BI-M
Snap, Crackle & Pop
  GSM-W,M
Snapdragon Song
  RSL-W,M
Snapoo
  SA-W
Snapshot
  TOC83-W,M
Snatched from the Cradle
  YL-W,M
Sneaky Snake
  TI1-W,M UFB-W,M
Sneezing Song
  GM-W,M

Snob and the Bottle
  MSB-W
Snoopy
  TW-W YG-W,M
Snoopy vs. the Red Baron
  OTJ-W,M
Snow
  ASB3-W,M SiR-W,M
Snow Blanket
  FSA2-W,M
Snow Feathers
  ASB4-W,M
Snow Flakes see also Snowflakes
Snow Flakes (Gently Falling Down)
  STS-W,M
Snow Flakes (Gershwin)
  ReG-W,M
Snow in the Street
  LMR-W,M OB-W,M
Snow Lay on the Ground
  YC-W,M
Snow Lies Thick
  OB-W,M
Snow Man
  KS-W,M STS-W,M
Snow Song
  SD-W,M
Snow Storm
  SY-W,M
Snow-White Little Burro
  SiR-W,M
Snowball Tree Is Blooming
  RSC-W,M (Russian)
Snowbird
  ASB4-W,M EC-W,M FVV-W,M
  GOI7-W,M MCG-W,M MF-W,M
Snowbirds
  MH-W,M
Snowfall
  BCh-W,M
Snowflake Feathers
  MH-W,M
Snowflakes see also Snow Flakes
Snowflakes
  SiR-W,M
Snowflakes (George L. Wright)
  MH-M
Snowflakes (Little White Feathers
  Filling the Air)
  MH-W,M
Snowflakes (The Snow Is Falling
  Down)
  KS-W,M
Snowflakes (The Snow Is Flying
  All the Night Long)
  SOO-W,M
Snowflakes (Snowflakes Are
  Dancing About in the Air)
  ASB2-W,M
Snowflakes (Whirling, Swirling,
  Rushing, Twirling)
  RSL-W,M
Snowman
  MH-W,M SSe-W,M
Snug 'neath the Fir Trees
  VA-W,M
Snuggled on Your Shoulder
  OnT1-W,M
So Am I
  GOB-W,M
So Are You!
  ReG-W,M
So Bad
  TI2-W,M
So, Brother
  OB-W,M
So Close

  MF-W,M
So Close Yet So Far
  SRE2-W,M
So Come! So Come!
  Boo-W,M
So Doggone Lonesome
  OGC2-W,M
So Doggone Soon
  NeF-W
So Early in de Morning
  CSo-W,M
So Early in the Morning
  ETB-W,M
So Emotional
  BHO-W,M DPE-W,M MF-W,M
So Far
  A-W,M HC1-W,M UBF-W,M
So Far So Good
  TTH-W,M
So Fine
  FRH-W,M
So Glad
  VB-W,M
So Glad I Know
  VB-W,M
So Go to Him
  GiS-W,M
So Good, So Right
  ToO79-W,M
So Great Salvation
  BSG-W,M BSP-W,M
So Handy
  SA-W
So I Can Write My Name
  My-W,M
So I Wheel About, I Turn About
  NSS-W
So in Love
  TI1-W,M TTH-W,M UBF-W,M
  UFB-W,M
So Let Our Lips and Lives Express
  Hy-W,M
So Little Time
  DB-W,M
So Long, Big Guy
  Mo-W,M NM-W,M OTO-W
So Long, Big Time
  Mo-W,M NM-W,M
So Long Blues
  DBL-W
So Long Dad
  RB-W
So Long, Dearie
  Mo-W,M NM-W,M OTO-W
So Long, Farewell
  SM-W,M TI1-W,M UBF-W,M
  UFB-W,M
So Long, It's Been Good to Know
  You
  AFP-W,M BF-W,M FPS-W,M
  IHA-W,M RSL-W,M SWF-W,M
  VA-W,M WSB-W,M
So Long It's Been Good to Know
  Yuh
  TI1-W,M UFB-W,M
So Long San Francisco
  TT-W,M
So Many White Dresses
  LA-W,M (Spanish)
So Much Blues
  FSB3-M
So Much to Do
  WNF-W
So Much to Do in New York
  UBF-W,M
So Much World
  Mo-W,M

So Near and Yet So Far
ML-W,M
So Nice (Summer Samba)
BeL-W,M DJ-W,M TI2-W,M
So Peaceful Rests
Boo-W,M
So Praise Him
OGR-W,M
So Rare
GSN2-W,M HLS2-W,M RW-W,M
So Sad to Be Lonesome
DBL-W
So Soon in the Mornin'
J-W,M
So the Story Goes
Mo-W,M NM-W,M
So This Is Love?
TTH-W,M
So This Is Love (Cinderella Waltz)
NI-W,M OTJ-W,M OTO-W
So Touch Our Hearts with
Loveliness
AHO-W,M
So What (Gershwin)
ReG-W,M
So What (Kander/Ebb)
C-W,M
So What (Miles Davis)
MF-M
So What's the Big Blonde Boy of
Freedom Doing Now?
VS-W,M
So Will Ich's Aber Heben An
IF-W,M (German Only)
So You Want to Be a Rock and
Roll Star
RB-W
So You Wanted to See the Wizard
Wi-W,M
Soap Bubbles
ASB3-W,M
Social Band
ATS-W,M SHS-W,M
Social Freedom
AL-W
Social Orchestra
FHR-W,M
Socialist Wagon
AL-W
Socialists Are Coming
AL-W
Society the Life of Man
Boo-W,M
Society's Child
IHA-W,M RV-W
Society's Excited
NN2-W,M
Soeur Adele
SSN-W,M (French)
Soft and Warm
Mo-M
Soft Is Their Slumber
MML-W,M
Soft Music
OTO-W
Soft Shoe Song
TI1-W,M UFB-W,M
Soft, Soft Music Is Stealing
HSD-W,M
Soft, Strong, Pops Up Too
GSM-W,M
Softly and Tenderly
AME-W,M GH-W,M IH-M
MAB1-W MSA1-W
Softly, As I Leave You
GG3-W,M HLS3-W,M RW-W,M
Softly As in a Morning Sunrise

HC1-W,M MF-W,M Ne-W,M
Softly Fades the Twilight Ray
AHO-W,M
Softly, Now Tenderly, Lift Him
with Care
SiS-W
Softly Now the Light of Day
AHO-W,M AME-W,M HSD-W,M
Hy-W,M WiS7-W,M
Softly the Shade of Evening Falls
TH-W,M
Softly Tread, the Child Is Sleeping
OU-W,M
Soir Au Clair De Lune see Un Soir
Au Clair De Lune
Soir En Me Promenant see Un Soir
En Me Promenant
Soiree Polka
FHR-W,M SSFo-M
Soiridh
SeS-W,M
Sol Tropical
RW-M
Sold Off to Georgy
AL-W
Soldat Francais see Le Soldat
Francais
Soldier
BSC-W SFB-W,M
Soldier and the Sailor
PO-W,M
Soldier at Home
SBA-W
Soldier Boy
BSC-W OTJ-W,M SCa-W,M
Soldier Boys
BSC-W
Soldier Bride's Lament see
Lowlands of Holland
Soldier Child see El Nino
Soldier Coming Home
SiS-W
Soldier Cut Down in His Prime
SoC-W
Soldier from Missouri
Oz2-W,M
Soldier, I Stay to Pray for Thee
SiS-W
Soldier in de Colored Brigade
FHR-W,M SiS-W
Soldier Man Blues
GI-W,M GO-W,M SSo-W,M
Soldier of Love
TTH-W,M
Soldier Rode from the East to the
West
Oz1-W,M
Soldier, Sailor, Tinker, Tailor
SR-W,M
Soldier, Soldier
FoS-W,M HS-W,M VA-W,M
Soldier, Soldier see also O Soldier,
Soldier
Soldier, Soldier, Marry Me
Oz1-W,M
Soldier, Soldier, Will You Marry Me
SAm-W,M
Soldier, Soldier, Won't You Marry
Me
AH-W,M FW-W
Soldier to His Mother
SiS-W
Soldier, Will You Marry Me
ASB6-W,M
Soldier, Won't You Marry Me
IL-W,M
Soldiers' Chorus

CSo-W,M ESB-W,M FSA1-W,M
TH-W,M
Soldier's Dream Song
SiS-W
Soldier's Farewell
BSB-W,M HSD-W,M NAS-W,M
SCo-W,M SiS-W TH-W,M
Soldier's Field
IL-W,M
Soldier's Good Bye
MPP-W
Soldier's Grave
SCo-W,M SiS-W
Soldier's Home
FHR-W,M SiS-W
Soldier's Homeless Boy
BSC-W
Soldier's Joy
IF-M POT-W,M
Soldier's Lamentation
SI-W
Soldier's Last Letter
OGC1-W,M
Soldier's Letter
Oz2-W
Soldier's Life
TBF-W,M
Soldier's Life Is the Life We Love
SiS-W
Soldiers' March
ASB1-M RW-M
Soldier's Mother
SiS-W
Soldiers of Christ, Arise
AME-W,M Hy-W,M
Soldiers of the Plough
LMR-W,M
Soldier's Poor Little Boy
BSC-W Oz4-W,M TBF-W,M
Soldier's Return
ITP-W,M SCa-W,M SHS-W,M
Soldier's Suit of Grey
SCo-W,M SiS-W
Soldier's Sweetheart
SCa-W,M
Soldier's Tear
ESU-W HSD-W,M
Soldiers Three
Gu-W,M
Soldier's Widow
SiS-W
Soldier's Wife
SiS-W
Solemn Thought
SHS-W,M
Solfa Canon
OTJ-W,M
Solicitude
SHS-W,M
Solid Gold (Theme)
TV-W,M
Solid Rock (Pop Instrumental)
GOl7-M
Solid Rock, The
AME-W,M GH-W,M OM-W,M
Solid Rock, The see also My Hope
Is Built (on Nothing Less)
Solid Silver Platform Shoes
MS-W,M
Solidaridad Por Siempre
JF-W,M (Spanish)
Solidarity Forever
AFP-W FW-W JF-W,M SWF-W,M
WW-W,M
Soliloquy
FrS-W,M GA-W
Solitaire

TI2-W,M
Solitary Man
  TI2-W,M
Solitude
  BBB-W,M FPS-W,M GMD-W,M
  RoE-W,M TI2-W,M
Solitude New
  SHS-W,M
Solo
  TT-W,M
Solo and Chorus of Peers
  TH-W,M
Solomon Isaacs
  SoC-W
Solomon Levi
  AmH-W,M HAS-W,M OS-W
  WiS8-W,M
Solomon's Song
  MMM-W,M
Solvejg's Song
  FSY-W,M (German) LMR-W,M
Solvieg's Song
  MMY-W,M
Som-Som-Beni
  FSF-W (French)
Sombrero see El Sombrero
Some Children See Him
  CSB-W,M TI1-W,M UFB-W,M
Some Churches Are on
  Mountainsides
  SHP-W,M
Some Come Cripple
  AAF-W,M
Some Day
  AT-W,M HSD-W,M VK-W,M
Some Day I'll Wander Back Again
  EFS-W,M
Some Day My Prince Will Come
  HST-W,M NI-W,M
Some Days Are Diamonds (Some
  Days Are Stone)
  TI2-W,M
Some Days It Rains All Night Long
  TOC82-W,M
Some Enchanted Evening
  DBC-W,M HC1-W,M HLS8-W,M
  L-W OTJ-W,M OTO-W RW-W,M
  SP-W,M TI1-W,M TW-W
  UBF-W,M UFB-W,M
Some Far-Away Someone
  ReG-W,M
Some Folks
  ATS-W FHR-W,M OFS-W,M
  OTJ-W,M SiB-W,M SSF-W,M
  SSFo-W,M
Some Folks Do
  CSo-W,M PaS-W,M
Some Folks Say
  AN-W
Some Folks Say John Was a
  Baptist
  Oz4-W,M
Some Girls
  RoS-W,M
Some Girls Have All the Luck
  TTH-W,M
Some Got Six Months
  LC-W,M
Some Have Fathers Gone to Glory
  ITP-W,M
Some Have Fathers Over Yonder
  FVV-W,M
Some Like It Hot
  RW-W,M
Some Memories Just Won't Die
  TOC82-W,M
Some Must Win

SF-W,M
Some of These Days
  ToS-W,M
Some of Us Belong to the Stars
  OTO-W
Some Other Time
  TW-W
Some People
  TI1-W,M TW-W UBF-W,M
  UFB-W,M
Some Rain Must Fall
  GOB-W,M
Some Sweet Day, By and By
  GH-W,M
Some Things for Christmas
  OTJ-W,M
Some Things for Xmas
  Mo-W,M
Some Things Just Stick in Your
  Mind
  RoS-W,M
Some Time
  ST-W,M
Some Wonderful Sort of Someone
  GOB-W,M
Somebodies Coming to See Me
  Tonight
  FHR-W,M
Somebody
  NeA-W,M
Somebody Bad Stole de Wedding
  Bell
  Mo-W,M NM-W,M
Somebody Believed
  VB-W,M
Somebody Bigger Than You and I
  BSG-W,M BSP-W,M CEM-W,M
  EP-W,M FS-W,M HLS7-W,M
  JBF-W,M MF-W,M RDF-W,M
Somebody Else Is Taking My Place
  BBB-W,M TI1-W,M UFB-W,M
Somebody Else's Fire
  TTH-W,M
Somebody from Somewhere
  ReG-W,M
Somebody Knockin' at Yo' Door
  FN-W,M
**Somebody Knockin' at Yo' Door
  see also Somebody's Knockin' at
  Your Door**
Somebody Like You
  TTH-W,M
Somebody Loves Me
  DBC-W,M FSTS-W,M GOB-W,M
  MF-W,M NYT-W,M RoE-W,M
Somebody Loves You
  BBB-W,M Mo-W,M NM-W,M
Somebody, Somewhere
  TW-W
Somebody Stole My Gal
  RW-W,M
Somebody Touched Me
  AG-W,M HHa-W,M
Somebody Wants Me Out of the
  Way
  TTH-W,M
Somebody Who Cares
  TI2-W,M
Somebody's Always Saying
  Goodbye
  TI2-W,M
Somebody's Been Beatin' My Time
  OGC1-W,M
Somebody's Brother
  VB-W,M
Somebody's Calling My Name
  ASB6-W,M

**Somebody's Coming to See Me
  Tonight see Somebodies Coming
  to See Me Tonight**
Somebody's Darling
  Re-W,M SCo-W,M Sin-W,M
  SiS-W
Somebody's Gonna Love You
  TOC83-W,M
Somebody's Knockin'
  TI1-W,M TI2-W,M UFB-W,M
Somebody's Knockin' at Your Door
  JF-W,M WiS7-W,M
**Somebody's Knockin' at Your Door
  see also Somebody Knockin' at
  Yo' Door**
Somebody's Knocking at Your
  Door
  ETB-W,M LMR-W,M RF-W,M
  RSL-W,M
Somebody's Prayin'
  VB-W,M
Somebody's Sweetheart I Want to
  Be
  FSN-W,M
Somebody's Tall and Handsome
  Oz3-W,M
Somebody's Waiting for Me
  BH-W,M
Somebody's Wrong about Dis Bible
  B-W,M BI-W,M
Someday (You'll Want Me to Want
  You)
  TI2-W,M
Someday I'll Find You
  HC2-W,M OTO-W TI1-W,M
  UBF-W,M UFB-W,M
Someday I'm Gonna Fly
  Mo-W,M NM-W,M OTJ-W,M
  OTO-W
Someday My Prince Will Come
  DJ-W,M RoE-W,M TI1-W,M
  UFB-W,M
Someday There'll Be No Tomorrow
  HLS7-W,M
Someday We'll Meet Again
  MF-W,M
Someday When Jesus Comes
  BSG-W,M BSP-W,M
Someday When Things Are Good
  NMH-W,M
Somehow I Never Could Believe
  SSA-W,M
Somehow It Seldom Comes True
  ReG-W,M
Someone at Last
  NM-W,M Mo-W,M OTO-W
Someone Believes in You
  GOB-W,M
Someone Could Lose a Heart
  Tonight
  TOC82-W,M
Someone Is Waiting
  Co-W,M OTO-W TW-W UBF-W,M
Someone Like You
  UBF-W,M
Someone Loves You, Honey
  RW-W,M
Someone Needs Me
  I-W,M
Someone Nice Like You
  TI1-W,M UBF-W,M UFB-W,M
Someone Saved My Life Tonight
  TI2-W,M
Someone to Light Up My Life
  MF-W,M TI1-W,M UFB-W,M
Someone to Watch over Me
  BNG-W,M DBC-W,M (French)

DC-W,M FrS-W,M GOB-W,M
HC1-W,M LSO-W MF-W,M
NYT-W,M (French) OHB-W,M
RoE-W,M TW-W

Someone Told My Story
NMH-W,M

Someone's Rocking My Dreamboat
MF-W,M

Someone's Waiting for You
NI-W,M

Somerset Carol
OB-W,M

Somerset Wassail
OB-W,M

Somethin' Cute
MF-M

Somethin' Stupid
GG3-W,M GOI7-W,M OPS-W,M
THN-W,M

Somethin' Wrong with My
Machine
LC-W

Something
BBe-W,M BR-W,M Fi-W,M
OnT1-W,M TM-W,M TWS-W

Something about Love
ReG-W,M

Something Cold to Drink
Mo-W,M OTO-W

Something for Jesus
GH-W,M

Something for the Boys
UBF-W,M

Something Good
TI2-W,M

Something Got Hold of Me
Oz4-W,M

Something Greater
Ap-W,M Mo-W,M VSA-W,M

Something Happened to Me
Yesterday
RoS-W,M

Something Has Happened
I-W,M

Something I Dreamed Last Night
OTO-W

Something in His Eyes
Mo-W,M OTO-W

Something More
UBF-W,M

Something New
SHS-W,M WN-W,M

Something New in My Life
MLS-W,M

Something Old, Something New
OGC1-W,M

Something Seems Tingle-Ingleing
HJ-W,M

Something Sort of Grandish
FR-W,M OTO-W UBF-W,M

Something to Do with Spring
UBF-W,M

Something to Live For
GMD-W,M

Something to Remember You By
MF-W,M TW-W

Something Wonderful
OTJ-W,M OTO-W TI1-W,M
UBF-W,M UFB-W,M

Something Worth Living For
BSG-W,M BSP-W,M FS-W,M

Something You Got
MF-W,M

Something's Coming
TW-W

Something's Got a Hold on Me
RY-W,M RYT-W,M

Something's Gotta Give
HFH-W,M MF-W,M OHF-W
OnT6-W,M RT5-W,M

Sometimes
WG-W,M

Sometimes (I Just Can't Stand
You)
Mo-W,M

Sometimes a Day Goes By
MF-W,M UBF-W,M

Sometimes a Light Surprises
Hy-W,M

Sometimes I Feel Like a Motherless
Child
ATS-W BeB-W,M FoS-W,M FW-W
OFS-W,M OTJ-W,M RF-W,M
SiB-W,M SpS-W,M WiS7-W,M

**Sometimes I Feel Like a Motherless
Child see also Motherless Child**

Sometimes I Feel Like a Motherless
Chile
FN-W,M

Sometimes I Feel Like a Nut
GSM-W,M

Sometimes I'm Happy
BBB-W,M MF-W,M TI2-W,M

Sometimes She's a Little Girl
OnT6-W,M

Sometimes When Morning Lights
the Sky
SHP-W,M

Sometimes When We Touch
WG-W,M

Sometimes You Just Can't Win
TOC82-W,M

Sometimes Your Eyes Look Blue to
Me
OTO-W

**Sometimes Your Eyes Look Blue to
Me see also Whoever You Are, I
Love You**

Someway, Somehow, Sometime,
Somewhere
GrG-W,M

Somewhere
DBC-W,M GrM-W,M

Somewhere a Child Is Singing
BM-W BMC-W,M

Somewhere along the Way
MF-W,M NK-W,M

Somewhere around a Throne
FN-W,M

Somewhere between Right and
Wrong
TOC83-W,M

Somewhere in America
TTH-W,M

Somewhere in Between
TOM-W,M

Somewhere in New Guinea
GI-W

Somewhere in Old Wyoming
Mo-W,M NM-W,M

Somewhere in the Night
ToO79-W,M

Somewhere in the World
TW-W

Somewhere Just beyond
Tomorrow
HCY-W,M

Somewhere My Love (Lara's
Theme)
FPS-W,M GG2-W,M GrH-W,M
HLS5-W,M OP2-W,M RT6-W,M
RW-W,M STW-W,M THN-W,M

Somewhere the Sun Is Shining
AME-W,M

Somewhere Up in Starland
SSN-W,M (French)

Somos Novios see It's Impossible

Son--Child
OTJ-W,M

Son of a Gambler
AmS-W,M

Son of a Gam-bo-leer
SoC-W

Son of a Gambolier
IL-W,M POT-W,M

Son of a Louisiana Man
Lo-W,M

Son of a Preacher Man
OnT1-W,M TI2-W,M

Son of God Goes Forth to War
AME-W,M FH-W,M HSD-W,M
Hy-W,M SL-W WiS7-W,M

Son of Man
GBC-W,M

Son of the Beach
GI-W Go-W

Son Who Was His Mother's Pride
SiS-W

Sonata (Beethoven, Op. 14, No. 2)
ASB1-M

Sonata No. 3 (Mozart)
MF-M

Sonatina (Mozart)
BMC-M

Song
SBA-W

Song about a Captain
RuS-W,M (Russian)

Song about a Rabbit
AST-W,M

Song about an Elephant
AST-W,M

Song about Charleston
SAR-W SBA-W

Song about the Captain
RSC-W,M (Russian Only)

Song and a Smile
FSA2-W,M

Song and Dance
GBC-W,M Oz2-W,M

Song Angels Cannot Sing
HHA-W,M

Song at Dusk
SFB-W,M SiR-W,M

Song Ballad
Oz4-W

Song Ballet of Mollie Bonder
Oz1-W

Song Ballet of Young Shollity
Oz4-W

Song for Adolf
GO-W

Song for All Good Men
AL-W

Song for August
FSA2-W,M

Song for Cass and Butler
MPP-W

Song for Freedom
ASB6-W,M

Song for Hatters
AL-W

Song for Our Times
VP-W

Song for Robin
SMa-W,M

Song for the Bank Men
AL-W

Song for the 5th of March
MPP-W

Song for the Million

Song of the Night Watch
  SL-W,M
Song of the Nuns of Chester
  OB-W,M (Latin Only) OE-W,M
Song of the Open Air
  SMY-W,M
Song of the Pennsylvania Miners
  AL-W
Song of the Pigeon
  ASB6-W,M
Song of the Proletaire
  AL-W
Song of the Range
  SoC-W
Song of the Rooster
  UF-W,M
Song of the Sea
  HSD-W,M
Song of the Seabees
  GO-W
Song of the Seasons
  ASB3-W,M
Song of the Shell
  ASB2-W,M
Song of the Shepherd Lehl
  LMR-W,M MHB-W,M
Song of the Ship
  OB-W,M
Song of the Shirt
  AL-W WW-W,M
Song of the Signal Corps
  GO-W
Song of the Six Hundred Thousand
  see To Canaan
Song of the Soldiers
  SiS-W
Song of the South
  SiS-W
Song of the Spirit
  OB-W,M
Song of the Starving
  AL-W
Song of the Street Car
  GUM1-W,M
Song of the Ten Hour Workingman
  AL-W
Song of the Texas Rangers
  SiS-W
Song of the Times
  AL-W BSC-W
Song of the Toilers
  AL-W
Song of the Tomatoes and
  Potatoes
  GUM1-W,M
Song of the Traffic Squad
  ASB5-W,M
Song of the Triton
  TF-W,M
Song of the Trust
  AL-W
Song of the Unenfranchised
  AL-W
Song of the Vagabonds
  MM-W,M VK-W,M
Song of the Vikings
  GC-W,M
Song of the Volga Boatman
  LMR-W,M OTJ-W,M
Song of the Volga Boatmen
  FSY-W,M (Russian) TF-W,M
  WiS8-W,M
Song of the Volga Boatmen see
  also Volga Boatmen
Song of the Wagon Road see Clear
  the Way
Song of the West

VA-W,M
Song of the Workers
  AL-W
Song of Toil
  AL-W
Song of Transformation
  FSO-W,M (French)
Song on Captain Barney's Victory
  ANS-W
Song on Liberty
  SAR-W,M
Song on the Brave General
  Montgomery
  SI-W
Song on the Sand
  DBC-W,M TI2-W,M UBF-W,M
Song Story
  ASB2-W,M
Song Sung Blue
  GrS-W,M TI2-W,M
Song--the Emigrant's Home
  AL-W
Song to Ivan
  FSA2-W,M
Song to Mother
  ASB1-W,M
Song to Oshima
  MHB-W,M (Japanese)
Song to the Christmas Tree
  GBC-W,M
Song to the Good Old Plow
  GrM-W,M
Song to the Nightingale
  SL-W,M
Song to the Runaway Slave
  NF-W
Song to the Shepherds
  MMW-W,M
Song to the Sultan
  SiP-W,M (Turkish)
Song without Words
  RW-M
Song Written at Corientes on the
  American Fleet
  ANS-W
Song Written for the Fourth of July
  1828
  AL-W
Songbird
  RW-W,M TI1-W,M TI2-W,M
  UFB-W,M
Songs from Brigadoon (Medley)
  OU-W,M
Songs from the Alps
  MuM-W,M
Songs from the Nursery
  WU-W,M
Songs My Mother Taught Me
  FSY-W,M (German) RW-M
  TH-W,M WiS8-W,M
Songs of Brotherhood
  AL-W
Songs of Gladness
  GH-W,M
Songs of Long Ago
  ReG-W,M
Songs of the Rails
  MuM-W,M
Songs of the Saddle
  MuM-W,M
Songs of the Socialists
  AL-W
Songs We Sang upon the Old
  Camp Ground
  Sin-W,M SiS-W
Sonn Ist Wieder Aufgegangen see
  Die Sonn Ist Wieder Aufgegangen

Sonner Af Norge
  SiP-W,M (Norwegian)
Sonnet XL
  EL-W,M
Sonnet LXX
  EL-W,M
Sonny Boy
  HC1-W,M OTJ-W,M TI1-W,M
  UFB-W,M
Sons
  Ro-W,M
Sons of Art
  AL-W
Sons of Liberty
  SI-W,M
Sons of Norway
  SiP-W,M (Norwegian)
Sons of Old Grinnell
  CoS-W,M
Soolaimon
  TI2-W,M
Soon
  GOB-W,M HOH-W,M LN-W,M
  LSO-W MF-W,M Mo-W,M
  NM-W,M NYT-W,M OTO-W
Soon and Very Soon
  VB-W,M
Soon As I Get Home
  Wi-W,M
Soon As We May
  GiS-W,M
Soon Comes the Day
  SiR-W,M
Soon I Will Be Done
  RF-W,M
Soon It's Gonna Rain
  Fa-W,M OTJ-W,M OTO-W
  TI1-W,M TW-W UBF-W,M
  UFB-W,M
Soon, One Mornin'
  FVV-W,M
Soon We Shall Land on Canaan's
  Shore
  WN-W,M
Sooner or Later You'll Own
  Generals
  TI1-W,M UFB-W,M
Sophia
  OTO-W
Sophisticated Lady
  GMD-W,M Sta-W,M
Sophisticated Swing
  Sta-W,M TI2-W,M
Sorceror's Apprentice
  BNG-M
Sorella see La Sorella
Sororite
  LW-W,M
Sorrow (Bartok)
  GM-M
Sorrow Shall Come Again No More
  FHR-W,M
Sorrowful Lament for Callaghan,
  Greally & Mullen
  VP-W,M
Sorry (I Ran All the Way Home)
  RY-W,M
Sorry--Grateful
  Co-W,M OTO-W TW-W UBF-W,M
Sorry Her Lot
  MGT-W,M
Sorry Seems to Be the Hardest
  Word
  TI2-W,M
Sorta on the Border
  Mo-W,M NM-W,M
So's Your Old Man

Su-W,M
Soul and Inspiration
    DPE-W,M
Soul Bossa Nova
    LaS-M OPS-M
Soul Survivor
    RoS-W,M
Soulita
    MF-M
Souls of Men, Why Will Ye
    GH-W,M
Sound His Praise
    VB-W,M
Sound in Your Mind
    WNF-W
Sound of Money
    TW-W
Sound of Music
    DBC-W,M HC2-W,M HLS8-W,M
    OTJ-W,M OTO-W RDF-W,M
    RW-W,M SM-W,M TI1-W,M
    UBF-W,M UFB-W,M
Sound of Philadelphia
    SoH-W,M
Sound of Silence
    GSN4-W,M RV-W
Sound Off
    TI1-W,M UFB-W,M
Sound Off for Chesterfield
    GSM-W,M
Sound, Sound the Truth Abroad
    GH-W
Sound the Alarm
    GH-W,M
Sound the Clarion
    Boo-W,M
Sound the High Praises
    GH-W,M
Sound the Strain Again
    Boo-W,M
Sounds
    OTO-W UBF-W,M
Sounds I Hear
    MAR-W,M
Sounds of Morning
    SiR-W,M
Soup Song
    FW-W SWF-W,M
Sour Apple Tree
    MPP-W OHG-W,M SiS-W
Sourire D'Avril
    AmH-M
Sourkraut
    DD-W,M HAS-W,M
Sourwood Mountain
    AmS-W,M ASB6-W,M ATS-W,M
    DD-W,M FSB1-W,M FW-W
    HAS-W,M HS-W,M NAS-W,M
    OTJ-W,M Oz3-W,M POT-W,M
    SAm-W,M STR-W,M VA-W,M
    WU-W,M
**Sous Les Ponts De Paris see Under
the Bridges of Paris**
South, The
    MPP-W SiS-W
South America, Take It Away
    MF-W,M
South Australia
    FW-W
South Carolina, The
    ANS-W
South in New Orleans
    OGC1-W,M
South of the Border
    FC-W,M TI1-W,M UFB-W,M
South Our Country
    SiS-W

South Sea Isles
    GOB-W,M
South Street
    TRR-W,M
Southerly Wind
    Boo-W,M
Southern Blues
    LSR-W,M
Southern Boys
    SiS-W
Southern Captive
    SiS-W
Southern Contraband
    SiS-W
Southern Cross
    Mo-W,M OTO-W SiS-W
Southern Encampment
    Oz2-W,M
Southern Girl
    Sin-W,M
**Southern Girl see also Homespun
    Dress**
Southern Home
    ITP-W,M
Southern Jack
    AN-W
Southern Marseillaise
    SiS-W
Southern Memories
    IL-W,M LMR-W,M TF-W,M
**Southern Memories see also In the
    Evening by the Moonlight**
Southern Moon
    MBS-W,M
Southern Nights
    DPE-W,M MF-W,M
Southern Oath
    BSC-W
Southern Paean
    SiS-W
Southern Roses
    TI1-M UFB-M
Southern Soldier Boy
    Oz2-W,M Sin-W,M SiS-W,M
    SY-W
Southern Wagon
    BSC-W SiS-W
Southron's Chaunt of Defiance
    SCo-W,M SiS-W
Southwark Rebolution
    VP-W
Southwel New
    EA-W,M
Souvenirs
    WG-W,M
Sovereign and Transforming Grace
    AHO-W,M
Sow Took the Measles
    FW-W RS-W,M SRS-W,M
Sowers
    FSA1-W,M
Sowing and Reaping
    GrM-W,M
Sowing in the Morning
    AME-W,M
Sowing on the Mountain
    FW-W
Sowing the Seed
    GrM-W,M
Sowing the Seeds of Love
    EL-W,M
Space Oddity
    GrS-W,M TWD-W,M
Spacey Jones
    IHA-W,M
Spacious Firmament
    SBF-W,M

Spacious Firmament on High
    AME-W,M ESB-W,M Hy-W,M
    SL-W,M SMY-W,M
Spaghetti Rag
    TI1-W,M UFB-W,M
Spain
    BOA-W,M
Spanish and American War
    Oz4-W,M
Spanish Carol
    OB-W,M
Spanish Cavalier
    OS-W POT-W,M WiS8-W,M
Spanish Dance (Mozkowski)
    AmH-M
Spanish Eyes
    DPE-W,M MF-W,M OnT1-W,M
Spanish Flea
    GOI7-M OnT1-M
Spanish Guitar
    GeS-W,M LaS-W,M OTJ-W,M
    PaS-W,M SBF-W,M VA-W,M
Spanish Harlem
    BeL-W,M DRR-W,M HLS3-W,M
    HRB4-W,M ILS-W,M MCG-W,M
    RB-W RW-W,M RYT-W,M
    TI1-W,M UFB-W,M
Spanish Is the Loving Tongue
    FW-W
Spanish Ladies
    OTJ-W,M SMY-W,M
Spanish Lady
    SSP-W
Spanish Maid
    ST-W,M
Spanish Moss
    Lo-W,M
Spanish National Hymn
    AmH-W,M (Spanish)
Spare Us, O Lord, Aloud We Pray
    AHO-W,M
Sparking on Sunday Night
    Oz3-W,M
Sparking or Courting
    NF-W
Sparking Sunday Night
    Oz3-W
Sparkling and Bright
    ATS-W,M ESU-W
Sparrow Watcher
    VB-W,M
Sparrows
    GM-W,M
Speak His Name
    HHa-W,M
Speak in Silence
    Mo-W,M NM-W,M
Speak Low
    DBC-W,M DJ-W,M FrS-W,M
    HC2-W,M MF-W,M TI1-W,M
    TW-W UBF-W,M UFB-W,M
Speak Out
    AL-W
Speak Softly
    NF-W
Speak Softly Love
    AT-W,M FPS-W,M GrS-W,M
    ILT-W,M IPH-W,M LM-W,M
    OBN-W,M OTO-W TM-W,M
    TOM-W,M WGB/P-W,M
**Speak Softly Love see also Love
    Theme from The Godfather**
Speak to Me, My Love
    EL-W,M
Speak Up Mambo
    TI1-W,M (Spanish) UFB-W,M
    (Spanish)

Speakers Didn't Mind
  AFP-W
Special Agent
  LSR-W,M
Special Delivery
  VB-W,M
Speckles
  SoC-W
Speech
  Mo-W,M NM-W,M OTO-W
Speech Fugue
  RSL-W,M
Speed Away
  GH-W,M TF-W,M
Speed Away! Speed Away
  HSD-W,M
Speed Ball
  MF-M
Speed, My Reindeers
  UF-W,M
Speed Our Republic
  ESB-W,M NAS-W,M SL-W,M
Speed, Speed the Temperance
  Ship
  ESU-W
Speed the Plough
  POT-M
Speed Up
  TF-W,M
Speedball Tucker
  JC-W,M
Spellbound
  TI1-W,M UFB-W,M
Spelling Lesson
  FSA1-W,M
Spelling Song
  Oz4-W,M
Spencer the Rover
  BB-W
Spenser: for Hire (Theme)
  BNG-M DC-M
Spider and Spout
  GM-W,M
Spider and the Fly
  Boo-W,M OTJ-W,M RoS-W,M
  TF-W,M
Spill the Wine
  DP-W,M MCG-W,M RYT-W,M
Spin It On
  PMC-W,M
Spin, Spin, My Darling Daughter
  BMC-W,M
Spin, Spin, Spin
  JC-W,M
Spinner
  MH-W,M
Spinning Song
  ASB4-W,M ASB5-W,M
  FSA1-W,M SMa-W,M
Spinning Wheel
  BR-W,M MCG-W,M RW-W,M
  RY-W,M RYT-W,M TRR-W,M
Spinout
  SRE2-W,M
Spirit
  BOA-W,M
Spirit, The
  OB-W,M
Spirit Breathes upon the Word
  AME-W,M Hy-W,M
Spirit Divine, Attend Our Prayers
  Hy-W,M
Spirit in Our Hearts
  AHO-W,M AME-W,M
Spirit Is Movin'
  JF-W,M
Spirit o' the Lord Done Fell on Me

My-W,M
Spirit of God, Descend upon My
  Heart
  AME-W,M Hy-W,M
Spirit of Life, in This New Dawn
  AHO-W,M
Spirit of My Song
  FHR-W,M
Spirit of Summer Time
  FSA2-W,M
Spirit of Truth, O Let Me Know
  GH-W
Spirit of Twilight
  LMR-W,M SL-W,M
Spirit Wings
  OGR-W,M
Spiritual Sailor
  SHS-W,M
Splendor in the Grass (Theme)
  HFH-M MF-M
Splish Splash
  DRR-W,M HR-W ILF-W,M
  RW-W,M RY-W,M
Spooky
  ToO79-W,M
Spoon River
  SRS-W,M
Spoonful of Sugar
  NI-W,M OTJ-W,M OTO-W
  SBS-W,M WD-W,M
Sportin' Life Blues
  AFB-W,M
Sporting Cowboy
  HB-W,M
Sporting Life Blues
  FW-W
Sporting Races of Galway
  VP-W,M
S'posin'
  Mo-W,M NM-W,M RDT-W,M
  TI2-W,M
Spot Promotion
  AF-W
Spotted Crow
  ASB5-W,M
Sprague
  SHS-W,M
Spread, O Spread, Thou Mighty
  Word
  SJ-W,M
Spread the Light
  AL-W
Spreadin' Like Wildfire
  VB-W,M
Spreading All over the World
  VB-W,M
Spring (Foxwell/Silcher)
  MML-W,M
Spring (Gibault/Schubert)
  ASB3-W,M
Spring (Netherlands Folk Song)
  ASB4-W,M
Spring (Rossetti/Ware)
  MH-W,M
Spring (Swedish Folk Song)
  MHB-W,M (Swedish)
Spring, The
  HSD-W,M NAS-W,M
Spring and Youth
  FSA2-W,M SL-W,M
Spring Awakes
  ASB4-W,M
Spring Beauty
  ASB5-W,M
Spring Calls
  UF-W,M
Spring Can Really Hang You Up

the Most
  DJ-W,M ToS-W,M
Spring Carol
  OTJ-W,M
Spring Comes to the Resistance
  Camp
  VS-W,M
Spring Dance
  FSA2-W,M
Spring Dawn see Springdawn
Spring Day
  LMR-W,M
Spring Flowers
  MH-W,M
Spring Greeting
  MML-W,M
Spring Has Come
  OB-W,M
Spring in Maine
  Mo-W,M NM-W,M
Spring Is a New Beginning
  Mo-W,M NM-W,M OTJ-W,M
  OTO-W
Spring Is Come
  Boo-W,M
Spring Is Crowned Queen Tonight
  BV-W,M
Spring Is Here
  ASB1-W,M GG4-W,M GSN2-W,M
  GSO-W,M HLS2-W,M HLS8-W,M
  RT4-W,M RW-W,M TS-W TW-W
Spring Is in My Heart Again
  OHF-W
Spring of the Next Year
  Mo-W,M OTO-W
Spring of the Year
  AST-W,M
Spring Secret
  SSe-W,M
Spring Song
  AmH-M ASB2-W,M ASB6-W,M
  FSA2-W,M MH-W,M OBN-M
  SD-W,M SoP-W,M STS-W,M
Spring, Spring, Spring
  OHF-W
Spring Tidings see Ch'un Hsin
Spring Time (Is Garden Time)
  AST-W,M
Spring Victorious
  FSA2-W,M
Spring Will Be a Little Late This
  Year
  ILT-W,M TI2-W,M UBF-W,M
Springdawn
  FSA1-W,M
Springfield Burglar
  Oz2-W
Springfield Mountain
  ASB5-W,M FMT-W FW-W
  GuC-W,M OHO-W,M Oz3-W,M
  RW-W,M TBF-W,M VA-W,M
Spring's Apology
  FSA2-W,M
Spring's First Song
  ASB6-W,M
Spring's Herald
  FSA1-W,M
Spring's Magic
  LMR-W,M
Springtime
  SiR-W,M
Springtime (Now the Sprightly,
  Laughing Springtime)
  BMC-W,M
Springtime (Sunshine, Happy
  Playtime)
  ASB5-W,M

Springtime Has Come
SCL-W,M
Springtime in Alaska
GO-W
Springtime on the River
BV-W,M
Spurn Not the Nobly Born
MGT-W,M
Square Dance
LMR-W,M
Square in the Social Circle
WF-W,M
Square Order Shuffle
GB-W,M
Squeeze Box
WA-W,M
Squib
AL-W
Squid-Jiggin' Ground
FW-W
Squirrel
FW-W   MH-W,M
Squirrel Has a Bushy Tail
ASB1-W,M
Squirrel Is a Pretty Thing
ATS-W,M
Squirrel's Eyes
ASB2-W,M
Stabat Mater
SiM-W,M (Latin)
Stabat Mater Dolorosa
SL-W,M (Latin Only)
Stable Call
ATS-W,M GI-W GO-W
Stack o' Dollars
LC-W
Stackabones Own Song
Am-W
Stackolee
FSB3-W,M
Stadole Pum-pa
YS-W,M (Czech)
Stadole Pum-pa see also Stodola Pumpa
Stagger Lee
HLS9-W,M HR-W ILF-W,M
RW-W,M RY-W,M RYT-W,M
Stagolee
FW-W   NH-W
Stagolee Done Kill Dat Bully Now
NH-W
Stagolee Was a Bully
FVV-W,M
Stairway to Heaven
BNG-W,M DC-W,M DPE-W,M
Stairway to Paradise
LSO-W
Stairway to the Stars
GSO-W,M HLS5-W,M RT5-W,M
RW-W,M Sta-W,M
Stammatina E Morto
VS-W,M
Stamp Act Repeal
SBA-W
Stan' Steady
My-W,M
Stan' Up an' Fight
L-W
Stand Back, Black Man
NF-W
Stand Back, Old Man, Get Away
Oz3-W,M
Stand by Me
AME-W,M DC-W,M DRR-W,M
ERM-W,M FOC-W,M ILS-W,M
LOM-W,M MF-W,M TI1-W,M
TRR-W,M UFB-W,M

Stand by Us
AL-W
Stand by Your Man
ATC2-W,M TI1-W,M UFB-W,M
Stand Columbia
IL-W,M
Stand for the Right
AL-W
Stand Out, Ye Miners
AL-W
Stand Steady see Stan' Steady
Stand Tall
Fif-W,M
Stand the Storm
WN-W
Stand the Storm see also Oh, Stand the Storm
Stand to Your Glasses
AF-W
Stand Up
AL-W   TTH-W,M
Stand Up and Fight see Stan' Up an' Fight
Stand Up for Jesus
GH-W,M WiS9-W,M
Stand Up for Jesus see also Stand Up, Stand Up for Jesus
Stand Up for the Flag
FHR-W,M
Stand Up for the Truth
FHR-W,M
Stand Up for Uncle Sam My Boys
SiS-W
Stand Up Like Soldiers
MoM-W
Stand Up, Stand Up for Jesus
AHO-W,M CEM-W,M FH-W,M
Hy-W,M RDF-W,M RW-W,M
SJ-W,M
Stand Up, Stand Up for Jesus see also Stand Up for Jesus
Standard Bearer
SiS-W
Standchen see Serenade (Schubert)
Standin' at That Greyhound Bus Station
LC-W
Standin' in the Need of Prayer
NAS-W,M WU-W,M YS-W,M
Standin' in the Need of Prayer see also It's A-Me O Lord, It's Me O Lord, Standing in the Need of Prayer, and 'Tis Me, O Lord
Standin' on de Sea ob Glass
BDW-W,M
Standing at That Greyhound Bus Station see Standin' at That Greyhound Bus Station
Standing at the Portal
ESB-W,M
Standing in the Need of Prayer
OFS-W,M OTJ-W,M SpS-W,M
Standing in the Need of Prayer see also Standin' in the Need of Prayer
Standing in the Rain
GBC-W,M
Standing on Our Threshold Threadbare
GBC-W,M
Standing on the Corner
TI2-W,M UBF-W,M
Standing on the Edge of Town
RBO-W,M
Standing on the Mountain
BSo-W,M UF-W,M

Standing on the Promises
OM-W,M
Standing on the Sea of Glass see Standin' on de Sea ob Glass
Stanton
SHS-W,M
Star, The
MH-W,M
Star Carol
BCh-W,M BCS-W,M FSA1-W,M
Star Dust
GSN2-W,M (French) HLS2-W,M
RDT-W,M Sta-W,M
Star Eyes
GSF-W,M
Star in Heaven
UF-W,M
Star in the East
FoS-W,M SHS-W,M
Star Is Born (Love Theme)
DC-W,M DPE-W,M EY-W,M
MF-W,M
Star Is Born (Love Theme) see also Evergreen
Star Is Never Lost
FSA1-W,M
Star Light, Star Bright
SiR-W,M
Star of Bethlehem
AmH-W,M
Star of Columbia
SHS-W,M
Star of Hope
BCh-W,M CEM-W,M
Star of Peace
ASB6-W,M
Star of the East
BCh-W,M CI-W,M FS-W,M
Star of the Morning
VB-W,M
Star of the Summer Night
BM-W
Star of the Twilight
HSD-W,M
Star of the Western Skies
HOH-W
Star Spangled Banner
AAP-W,M AL-W AME-W,M
AmH-W,M ASB4-W,M ASB5-W,M
ASB6-W,M ATS-W AWB-W
BM-W Bo-W DC-W,M ESB-W,M
FM-W,M FWS-W,M GC-W,M
HCY-W,M HS-W,M HSD-W,M
LMR-W,M LoS-W,M MAB1-W
MF-W,M MML-W,M MPP-W,M
MSA1-W MU-W,M MuM-W,M
NAS-W,M NSS-W OHG-W,M
OPS-W,M OS-W OTJ-W,M
RW-W,M SBF-W,M SI-W,M
SiP-W,M SiR-W,M SL-W,M
SMW-W,M SoF-W,M SOO-W,M
TF-W TH-W,M TI1-W,M
TMA-W,M UF-W UFB-W,M
VA-W,M WiS8-W,M WS-W,M
YS-W,M
Star Spangled Cross
SiS-W
Star Spangled Rhythm (Theme) see That Old Black Magic
Star Star
RoS-W,M
Star Trek (Theme)
HSe-W,M
Star Trek II (Theme)
TOM-M
Star Wars (Cantina Band) see Cantina Band

Star Wars (Main Theme)
EY-M HFH-M MF-M TOM-M
Star Wars (Main Title Theme)
BNG-M
**Star Wars (Princess Leia's Theme)
see Princess Leia's Theme**
Starflakes
SOO-W,M
Starlight
ELO-W,M FSA1-W,M HB-W
SL-W,M
Starlight Express
DBC-W,M UBF-W,M
Starlit Hour
HLS2-W,M
Starmaker
TI2-W,M
Starry, Starry Night see Vincent
Stars
ASB5-W,M SOO-W,M
Stars and Rosebuds
E-W,M
Stars and Stripes
AWB-W
Stars and Stripes Are Still Unfurled
SiS-W
Stars and Stripes Forever
AAP-M Bo-W,M HA-W,M MF-M
OTJ-M RW-M SFB-W,M
Stars and Stripes of Old
SiS-W
Stars Begin to Fall
FSSC-W,M
**Stars Begin to Fall see also My
Lord What a Mornin' and When
the Stars Begin to Fall**
Stars Fell on Alabama
GSN2-W,M Sta-W,M TI2-W,M
Stars in the Elements
RF-W,M
Stars of Ice
CCM-W,M
Stars of Our Banner
SiS-W
Stars of the Summer Night
ESB-W,M FSA2-W,M GC-W,M
HSD-W,M MML-W,M NAS-W,M
OS-W SiB-W,M SL-W,M
WiS8-W,M
Start Me Up
RoS-W,M
Started to Leave
NH-W
Starting Again
PoG-W,M
Starting Over
TI2-W,M
Starting Today
SRE1-W,M
Starvation
LC-W
Starved in Prison
SiS-W
Starving to Death on a
Government Claim
FW-W Oz2-W,M
**State Farm Insurance Jingle see
Like a Good Neighbor**
State of Arkansas
BMM-W DD-W,M FW-W
Oz3-W,M PSN-W,M WSB-W,M
State of El-a-noy
SRS-W,M
State of Maine Song
Fif-W,M
State of the Heart
TTH-W,M

Stately Mansion
MuM-W,M
Stately Southerner
SA-W,M
Stately Structure of This Earth
AHO-W,M
States and Capitals
Oz4-W,M
Statue at Tsarkoie-Selo
LMR-W,M
Stay
DRR-W,M TRR-W,M
Stay As Sweet As You Are
HC1-W,M OTO-W TI1-W,M
UFB-W,M
Stay Awake
OnT6-W,M OTJ-W,M OTO-W
SBS-W,M WD-W,M
Stay Away from Lonely Places
WNF-W
Stay Close to Someone
GSM-W,M
Stay, Father, Stay
Oz2-W
Stay in de Field
RF-W,M
**Stay in de Field see also O Stay in
de Field**
Stay, Master Stay, upon This
Heavenly Hill
AME-W,M
Stay on the Farm
GrM-W,M Oz4-W TMA-W,M
Stay Summer Breath
FHR-W,M
Stay, Thou Insulted Spirit, Stay
GH-W,M
Stay Well
LS-W,M
Stay with Me
MF-W,M TI1-W,M UFB-W,M
Stay with the Happy People
Mo-W,M NM-W,M
Stayin' Alive
TI1-W,M UFB-W,M
Staying Together
CFB-W,M
Steadfast, Loyal and True
GAR-W,M MF-W,M
Steady, Steady
Mo-W,M NM-W,M OTO-W
Steal Apples for Me
Oz3-W
Steal Away
ATS-W FN-W,M FW-W
HLS7-W,M HS-W,M LT-W,M
MuM-W,M NAS-W,M NH-W
NSS-W OGC1-W,M OTJ-W,M
SUH-W,M TH-W,M WiS7-W,M
Steal Away to Jesus
AME-W,M ETB-W,M RF-W,M
Stealin', Stealin'
FW-W
Stealing a Ride
NF-W
Steam Doctor
BSC-W
Steam Engine
KS-W,M
Steamboat
HRB2-W,M
Steamboat Bill
FW-W
Steamboat's Comin'
OTJ-W,M
Steel Battalions
SMW-W,M (Spanish)

Steel-Driving Man see John Henry
Steel Guitar Rag
TI1-W,M
Steel-Linin' Chant
SAm-W,M
Steeple Bell
AST-W,M
Steeplejack
FSA2-W,M
Stein Song
IL-W,M
Stella by Starlight
AT-W,M GSN3-W,M LM-W,M
OnT1-W,M RDT-W,M
Stella Kenny
ITP-W,M
Stella, the Belle of Fedela
GI-W,M
Stenka Rasin
FW-W RSC-W,M (Russian Only)
Step Back
TOC82-W,M
Step in Time
NI-W,M OnT6-W,M OTJ-W,M
OTO-W RSL-W,M WD-W,M
Step into My Neighbor's Shoes
SYB-W,M
Step into the Water
AG-W,M HHa-W,M
Step It Up and Go
FW-W
Step to the Rear
HLS8-W,M
Stephanie
AmH-M
Stephano's Songs
SSP-W
Stepmother
Oz4-W,M
Steppin' in the Valley
LC-W
Steppin' Out, I'm Gonna Boogie
Tonight
On-W,M
Steppin' Out of Line
SRE2-W,M
Steppin' Stones
BSo-W,M
Steps of Those Whom He
Approves
Hy-W,M
Stepsisters' Lament
UBF-W,M
Stereophonic Sound
ML-W,M
Stereotomy
TTH-W,M
Sterling Price
BSC-W
Stern Old Bachelor
Oz3-W
Sterret's Sea Fight
ANS-W
Steve O'Donnel's Wake
AF-W
Stewball
ATS-W,M FPG-W,M FW-W
Le-W,M TO-W,M
Stick Around
Mo-W,M NM-W,M OTO-W
Stick Close to Your Bedding
Ground
HOH-W,M
Stick to Your Mother, Tom
Oz4-W,M
Stick to Your Union
AL-W

Stick-a-ma-stew
NF-W

Stiff Upper Lip
LSO-W

Still
GSN5-W,M OnT6-W,M
ToO79-W,M

Still a Fool
DBL-W

Still As the Night
AmH-W,M WiS8-W,M (German)

Still As the Night see also Calm As the Night

Still Crazy after All These Years
ToO76-W,M

Still for Thy Loving Kindness
AME-W,M

Still in the Ring
TOC83-W,M

Still Rolls the Stone
VB-W,M

Still Small Voice
OTJ-W,M

Still, Still, Still
GM-W,M

Still, Still with Thee
AHO-W,M AME-W,M ESB-W,M
OM-W,M

Still Water Creek
NF-W

Still Water Runs Deep
NF-W

Still Wie Die Nacht see Calm As the Night and Still As the Night

Stille Nacht
ESB-W,M (German)

Stille Nacht, Heilige Nacht
SHP-W,M (German)

Stille Nacht, Heilige Nacht see also Silent Night (Holy Night)

Stingaree Blues
B-W,M Bl-W,M

Stir Crazy (Theme) see Crazy

Stir It Up and Serve It
RY-W,M

Stir the Pudding
LW-W,M PSN-W,M

Stockholm Sweetnin'
MF-M

Stockyard Blues
DBL-W

Stodola Pumpa
MAR-W,M MG-W,M

Stodola Pumpa see also Stadole Pum-pa

Stolen Baby
BMM-W

Stolen Bride
BMM-W

Stompin' at the Savoy
DJ-W,M GG4-W,M RW-W,M
TI2-W,M

Stone That Goes Rolling Will Gather No Moss
Oz2-W,M

Stone Walls and Steel Bars
BSo-W,M

Stonecutters Cut It on Stone
TG-W,M

Stoned
RoS-W,M

Stoned Soul Picnic
MCG-W,M RV-W

Stones
TI2-W,M

Stonewall Jackson's Last Words
MPP-W

Stonewall Jackson's Prayer
SiS-W

Stonewall Jackson's Way
ATS-W Sin-W,M SiS-W,M

Stonewall's Requiem
HSD-W,M Sin-W,M SiS-W
TMA-W

Stonington
SHS-W,M

Stop and Smell the Roses
RDF-W,M

Stop Breaking Down
RoS-W,M

Stop, Look and Listen
GM-W,M OnT6-W,M SRE2-W,M

Stop! Look! Listen!
RSL-W,M

Stop Stop Stop
TI2-W,M

Stopping by Woods
LMR-W,M

Storm, The
MH-W,M

Storm the Fort
AL-W

Storm the Fort, Ye Knights
AL-W

Stormalong
SA-W,M

Storms Are on the Ocean
FGM-W,M FPG-W,M FSt-W,M
FW-W

Stormy
OnT1-W,M ToO79-W,M

Stormy Monday Blues
MF-W,M

Stormy Morning
AS-W,M (German)

Stormy Weather
DJ-W,M HC2-W,M Mo-W,M
NM-W,M On-W,M TI2-W,M
ToS-W,M

Story behind the Story
TOH-W,M

Story Book Ball
Mo-W,M NM-W,M OTJ-W,M

Story of a Starry Night
MF-W,M

Story of Four Little Birds
STS-W,M

Story of Lucy and Jessie
Fo-W,M

Story of the Rose
FSN-W,M

Story of the Rose see also Heart of My Heart

Story of Twelve
SAm-W,M

Storybook Love
MoA-W,M

Stouthearted Men
HC1-W,M MF-W,M Ne-W,M
OHB-W,M

Stow-a-way
NM-W,M

Stowaway
Mo-W,M

Strafers
AF-W

Strafing 'round the Mountain
AF-W

Straight Ahead
VB-W,M

Straight down the Middle
Mo-W,M NM-W,M

Straight Life
ATC1-W,M OnT1-W,M

Stranded in the Jungle
FRH-W,M

Stranded on a Dead End Street
TOH-W,M

Strange Adventure
MGT-W,M

Strange and Wonderful Account of a Dutch Hog
AL-W

Strange Brood
NF-W

Strange Enchantment
OTO-W

Strange Family
NF-W

Strange Fruit
J-W,M LSB-W,M

Strange Magic
ELO-W,M

Strange Man
ASB1-M MSB-W

Strange Music
HC2-W,M OTO-W SN-W,M
TI1-W,M UBF-W,M UFB-W,M

Strange News from the Rose
Boo-W,M

Strange Old Woman
NF-W

Strange Rain
RBO-W,M

Stranger, The (Schumann)
GM-M

Stranger and That Old Dun Horse
SoC-W

Stranger in My House
TOC83-W,M

Stranger in Paradise
DBC-W,M HC2-W,M Ki-W,M
RW-W,M UBF-W,M

Stranger of Galilee
SS-W

Stranger on the Shore
MF-W,M

Stranger Song
RV-W

Stranger to Holiness
VB-W,M

Strangers in the Night
RDT-W,M TI2-W,M TOM-W,M

Strangers When We Meet
TI1-W,M UFB-W,M

Straw Bonnet
BC1-W,M

Strawberry Fields Forever
BBe-W,M Be2-W,M TWS-W

Strawberry Jam, Cream of Tartum
PSD-W,M

Strawberry Roan
FW-W HB-W,M HWS-W,M Oz2-W

Stray
HB-W,M

Stray Cat Blues
RoS-W,M

Stray Cat Strut
TI2-W,M

Streamliner
ASB2-W,M ASB4-W,M

Street, The
Mo-W,M NM-W,M

Street Callers
ASB5-W,M

Street Calls
ASB4-W,M

Street Cleaner Man
MH-W,M

Street Cries
WS-W,M

Street Cry
  UF-W,M
Street Fighting Man
  RoS-W,M
Street Loafin' Woman
  DBL-W
Street of Dreams
  HLS2-W,M
Street Organ
  SOO-W,M
Street Vendors
  MaG-W,M MHB-W,M (Chinese)
Streets of Cairo
  AH-W,M FSN-W,M
Streets of Glory
  BF-W,M FGM-W,M FW-W
Streets of Hamtramck
  SoC-W
Streets of Laredo
  FAW-W,M FGM-W,M FoS-W,M
  FSB3-W,M FW-W GuC-W,M
  HS-W,M IL-W,M LT-W,M
  OFS-W,M OTJ-W,M OTO-W
  RSW-W,M RW-W,M SoC-W,M
  WU-W,M
Streets of Laredo see also
  Cowboy's Lament and Dying
  Cowboy (As I Walked Out on the
  Streets of Laredo)
Streets of London
  TI1-W,M UFB-W,M
Streets of New York
  FSN-W,M   MF-W,M
Strength of My Life
  VB-W,M
Strengthen the Dwelling
  OnT6-W,M
Stretch Forth Thy Hand
  GH-W,M
Stretching
  ASB2-W,M
Stretching Song
  RSL-W,M
Strictly Instrumental
  OBN-W,M TI2-W,M
Strife Is O'er
  BNG-W,M ESB-W,M OM-W,M
  TF-W,M
Strife Is O'er, the Battle Done
  AME-W,M Hy-W,M SL-W,M
Strike, A
  AL-W
Strike Blues
  DBL-W
Strike for the South
  SCo-W,M Sin-W,M SiS-W
Strike Song
  AL-W
Strike the Harp Gently
  HSD-W,M
Strike Up the Band
  BNG-W,M DBC-W,M DC-W,M
  GOB-W,M LSO-W MF-W,M
  NYT-W,M OBN-W,M OHB-W,M
  OTJ-W,M
Strike Up the Band for U.C.L.A.
  ReG-W
Strike While the Iron's Hot
  SiS-W
Strikebreaker see Die Finkelach
Strikers
  AL-W
Strikers' Story
  AL-W
Striking Times
  MSB-W
String of Pearls

BBB-W,M MF-W,M OTO-W
  TI1-W,M UFB-W,M
Stringopation
  Mo-M
Strip Polka
  NM-W,M OHF-W
Stripes (Theme)
  TOM-M
Stripes and the Stars
  AWB-W
Stroll
  LWT-W,M TI1-W,M UFB-W,M
Strong Hands
  NF-W
Strong Is the Oar
  LA-W,M (Spanish)
Strong Son of God, Immortal Love
  Hy-W,M
Strong Weakness
  TOC83-W,M
Stronger Than the Weight
  VB-W,M
Strongest Man in the World
  Mo-W,M NM-W,M OTO-W
'Stu Mo Run
  SeS-W,M
Stubborn Love
  VB-W,M
Stuck in the Middle with You
  TI2-W,M
Stuck on Me
  BNG-W,M
Student's Way
  ESB-W,M
Study War No More
  FW-W GuC-W,M LoS-W,M
  RW-W,M TO-W,M
Study War No More see also Ain't
  Gonna Study War No More,
  Going to Study War No More, and
  I Ain't Goin' to (Gwine) Study
  War No More
Stumbling
  CS-W,M GSN1-W,M HLS2-W,M
  RW-W,M T-W,M
Stupid Cupid
  MF-W,M
Stupid Girl
  RoS-W,M
Stupid One
  LMR-W,M
Sturmische Morgen see Der
  Sturmische Morgen
Style
  MS-W,M
Style Stew
  OU-W,M
Su Cantiamo, Su Beviamo
  Boo-W,M (Italian Only)
Su' Le Pont Du Nombe
  CaF-W (French Only)
S'u Sh'oreem
  SBJ-W,M (Hebrew Only)
Sub-Treasury Gentleman
  ESU-W
Subo
  TO-W,M (Spanish)
Substitute Broker
  SiS-W
Subtle Rebuttal
  MF-W,M
Suburbs, the Suburbs
  SYB-W,M
Succos Hymn
  JS-W,M
Such a Getting up Stairs see Sich
  a Getting up Stairs

Such a Merry Party
  LMS-W,M
Such a Nice Young Gal
  ESU-W
Such a Night
  EP-W,M FRH-W,M
Such a Shame
  LWT-W,M
Such a Woman
  ToO79-W,M
Such As in God the Lord Do Trust
  AHO-W,M
Sucking Cider through a Straw
  IL-W,M
Suddenly Seymour
  EY-W,M
Suddenly There's a Valley
  HLS7-W,M RDF-W,M SUH-W,M
  TI1-W,M UFB-W,M
Sue Me
  TW-W
Suffer Little Children to Come unto
  Me
  AME-W,M FHR-W,M
Suffer the Little Children
  FiS-W,M SoP-W,M
Sufferings of Christ
  SHS-W,M
Suffield
  SHS-W,M
Suffolk Miracle
  BT-W,M
Suffrage Pledge
  AFP-W AL-W
Sugar
  TI2-W,M
Sugar and Tea
  Oz3-W,M
Sugar Babe
  MoM-W,M
Sugar Blues
  TI2-W,M
Sugar Camp
  SSe-W,M
Sugar Foot Stomp
  Mo-W,M NM-W,M TI2-W,M
Sugar in Coffee
  NF-W
Sugar in de Gro'd
  SNS-W
Sugar in My Coffee
  Oz3-W,M
Sugar Is So Sweet
  CSD-W,M (French)
Sugar John
  ASB1-W,M SNS-W
Sugar Loaf Tea
  NF-W
Sugar Moon
  OGC1-W,M
Sugar Mountain
  MF-W,M
Sugar Shack
  DRR-W,M OTJ-W,M TRR-W,M
Sugar Town
  TI1-W,M UFB-W,M
Sugarfoot
  TVT-W,M
Sugarfoot Rag
  MF-W,M OGC2-W,M
Sugarfoot Rag Square Dance
  OGC2-W,M
Sugarlips
  YG-W,M
Suicide Is Painless see M*A*S*H
  Theme Song
Suits Me Fine

Mo-W,M OTO-W
Sukey Sudds
  Oz3-W
Suliram
  BMC-W,M FW-W (Indonesian)
  WSB-W,M (Indonesian)
Sultan's Daughter
  TH-W,M
Sultans of Swing
  ToO79-W,M
Sumare (Milhaud)
  GM-M
Sumer Is I-comen In
  SL-W,M
Sumer Is I-cumen In
  TF-W,M
Sumer Is Icumen In
  Boo-W,M HS-W,M OH-W,M
Sumer Is Icumen In see also
  Summer Is A-Comin' (Icumen) In
Summer
  AO-W,M TH-W,M
Summer and Winter
  MH-W,M
Summer Breeze
  GrS-W,M SiR-W,M
Summer Carol
  OB-W,M
Summer Days
  MH-W,M
Summer Eve
  EL-W,M (German)
Summer Fun
  SSe-W,M
Summer Harvest Spreads the
  Fields
  AHO-W,M
Summer in the City
  DRR-W,M RB-W TI2-W,M
  TRR-W,M
Summer in Winter
  OB-W,M
Summer Is A-Comin' In
  RW-W,M
Summer Is A-Coming In
  ESB-W,M FW-W MML-W,M
  TH-W,M UF-W,M
Summer Is Icumen In
  GUM2-W,M
Summer Is Icumen In see also
  Sumer Is Icumen In
Summer Knows (Summer of '42
  Theme)
  BNG-W,M DPE-W,M EY-W,M
  FPS-W,M HFH-W,M MF-W,M
  MLS-W,M RoE-W,M
Summer Longings
  FHR-W,M SSF-W,M
Summer Magic
  OnT6-W,M
Summer Me, Winter Me
  FrS-W,M HFH-W,M MF-W,M
  MLS-W,M
Summer Me, Winter Me see also
  Picasso Summer Theme
Summer Months
  FSA1-W,M
Summer Morning
  VA-W,M
Summer Night
  MH-W,M
Summer Nights
  Gr-W,M Mo-W,M OTO-W
  TI2-W,M UBF-W,M
Summer of '42 Theme see
  Summer Knows
Summer of Roses

WNF-W
Summer Passes
  SL-W,M
Summer Place (Theme)
  EY-W,M HFH-W,M MF-W,M
Summer Rain
  TI2-W,M
Summer Reverie
  BeB-W,M OU-W,M
Summer Romance
  RoS-W,M
Summer Samba see So Nice
Summer Song
  MML-W,M SBF-W,M
Summer, Summer
  GV-W,M
Summer Sweet
  OTJ-W,M
Summer Time (Carol)
  OB-W,M
Summer Time (Heyward/Gershwin)
  MU-W,M
Summer Time (Heyward/Gershwin)
  see also Summertime
Summer Wind
  FrS-W,M MF-W,M OHF-W
Summer Wine
  TI1-W,M UFB-W,M
Summer's Long
  TT-W,M
Summertide
  AHO-W,M
Summertime
  DBC-W,M DJ-W,M FPS-W,M
  HC1-W,M HLS8-W,M LM-W,M
  MF-W,M NYT-W,M On-W,M
  OTJ-W,M OTO-W RW-W,M
  TI1-W,M ToS-W,M UBF-W,M
  UFB-W,M
Summertime Blues
  DRR-W,M GAR-W,M MF-W,M
Summertime in Venice
  TI2-W,M
Summertime Lies
  Mo-W,M NM-W,M
Summertime Love
  UBF-W,M
Summons
  AL-W
Sumter
  SiS-W
Sun, The
  FF-W,M MH-W,M
Sun and Moon So High and Bright
  AHO-W,M
Sun and Shade
  ASB5-W,M
Sun and Song
  FSA2-W,M
Sun and the Rain
  SoP-W,M
Sun Chant
  LMR-W,M
Sun Come and Dry All de Member
  NSS-W
Sun Don't Set in de Mornin'
  RF-W,M
Sun Goes Down
  JS-W,M (Hebrew)
Sun Has Got His Hat On
  UBF-W,M
Sun King
  BBe-W,M TWS-W
Sun Now Risen
  AHO-W,M (German)
Sun of My Soul
  AmH-W,M GH-W,M HSD-W,M

TB-W,M WiS7-W,M
Sun of My Soul, Thou Savior Dear
  AME-W,M Hy-W,M
Sun of Righteousness Appears
  AME-W,M
Sun of Suns
  UF-W,M
Sun Valley Song
  SoC-W
Sun Will Shine No More
  MML-W,M
Sun Won't Set
  LN-W,M
Sunday (Hammerstein/Rodgers)
  UBF-W,M
Sunday (Miller/Styne)
  GSN2-W,M GST-W,M HLS2-W,M
Sunday Girl
  PL-W,M
Sunday in London Town
  ReG-W,M
Sunday in the Park
  WW-W,M
Sunday Kind of Love
  DJ-W,M TI2-W,M ToS-W,M
Sunday, Monday or Always
  TI1-W,M UFB-W,M
Sunday Mornin' Comin' Down
  HLS9-W,M SuS-W,M
Sunday Morning Band see Sund'y
  Mornin' Band
Sunday Will Never Be the Same
  TI2-W,M
Sundown Blues
  B-W,M LC-W
Sund'y Mornin' Ban'
  BDW-W,M
Sunflower
  AT-W,M
Sung at Harvest Time
  LA-W,M (Spanish) SCL-W,M
  SSe-W,M
Sunlight and Song
  FSA1-W,M
Sunny
  GSN4-W,M ILS-W,M MF-W,M
  MCG-W,M RW-W,M RY-W,M
  RYT-W,M Su-W,M
Sunny Bank
  OB-W,M OE-W,M
Sunny May
  FSA2-W,M
Sunny Side Up
  FPS-W,M HC2-W,M MF-W,M
  OTO-W TI1-W,M UBF-W,M
  UFB-W,M
Sunny Tennessee
  CCS-W,M
Sunrise
  ASB4-W,M ASB6-W,M WA-W,M
Sunrise at Stonehenge
  SBF-W,M
Sunrise Dance
  ASB2-W,M
Sunrise Serenade
  BBB-W,M Mo-W,M OTJ-W,M
  TI2-W,M UF-W,M
Sunrise Song
  FSA2-W,M
Sunrise, Sunset
  DBC-W,M HC1-W,M On-W,M
  OTJ-W,M OTO-W RDF-W,M
  TI2-W,M UBF-W,M
Sun's Gonna Shine Again
  HRB2-W,M
Sunset (Down Goes the Old Sun
  Taking His Light)

OTJ-W,M
Sunset (Little Brother, Now the
  Sunbeams)
  ASB4-W,M
Sunset (Rose and Azure Sky)
  FSA1-W,M
Sunset (Slow the Sun Now Sinks
  from Sight)
  MH-W,M
Sunset (Wan Ching)
  FD-W,M (Chinese)
Sunset Is Coming, but Sunrise
  We'll See
  HHa-W,M
Sunset Song
  VA-W,M (Zuni)
Sunshine (Go Away Today)
  MCG-W,M RYT-W,M
Sunshine (Harbach,
  Hammerstein/Kern)
  Su-W,M
Sunshine (Stanley/Schumann)
  FSA1-W,M
Sunshine Boomerang
  FSA1-W,M
Sunshine Ever Follows Rain
  GrM-W,M
Sunshine Flower
  FSA1-W,M
Sunshine, Lollipops and Rainbows
  OPS-W,M OTJ-W,M
Sunshine of Paradise Alley
  BH-W,M EFS-W,M FSN-W,M
  FSTS-W,M LMR-W,M
Sunshine of Your Love
  DRR-W,M TRR-W,M
Sunshine on My Shoulders
  CJ-W,M GrS-W,M PoG-W,M
  WG-W,M
Sunshine Trail
  ReG-W,M
Sunshiny Day
  MES2-W,M
Superbird
  VS-W,M
Supercalifragilisticexpialidocious
  NI-W,M OTJ-W,M OTO-W
  SBS-W,M WD-W,M
Supergirl
  RB-W
Superman (I'm Superman, When
  You Love Me It's Easy; by Richie
  Snyder)
  TI2-W,M
Superman (Movie Main Title
  Theme; by John Williams)
  BNG-M EY-M HFH-M MF-M
Superman (We Love You
  Superman; by Jose Luis Soto)
  ToO79-W,M
**Superman Love Theme (John
  Williams) see Can You Read My
  Mind**
Superman Theme (from Musical
  It's a Bird, It's a Plane, It's
  Superman)
  Mo-W,M OTJ-W,M OTO-W
Supernatural Thing (Pt. 1)
  DP-W,M
Superstar
  DBC-W,M GrS-W,M TI2-W,M
  ToO76-W,M UBF-W,M
Supper Time
  HLS-W,M
Suppertime
  HHa-W,M YG-W,M
Supplication (Jehovah, Almighty

Creator)
  FSA1-W,M
Supplication (O Thou Who Hear'st
  When Sinners Cry)
  SHS-W,M
Supposin' see S'posin'
Sur L' Pont De Nord
  MP-W,M (French Only)
Sur La Route De Dijon
  FSF-W (French)
Sur La Route De Louviers
  MP-W,M (French Only)
Sur Le Plage
  OTO-W
Sur Le Plancher
  CE-W,M (French)
Sur Le Pont D'Avignon
  BMC-W,M (French Only) Ch-W
  (French Only) CUP-W,M (French
  Only) FW-W (French) HS-W,M
  (French) MP-W,M (French Only)
  OTJ-W,M (French Only) RW-W,M
  (French Only)
**Sur Le Pont D'Avignon see also
  Bridge of Avignon and On the
  Bridge of Avignon**
**Sur Le Pont Du Nombe see Su' Le
  Pont Du Nombe**
Sur Le Pres D'eau
  CaF-W (French Only)
Sur Les Marches Du Palais
  FSF-W (French)
**Sure Enough Steamboats see Sho
  'Nough Steamboats**
Sure Thing
  LSO-W
Sure Won't You Hear
  ESU-W
Surely Goodness and Mercy
  OM-W,M
Surf City
  GAR-W,M MF-W,M
Surfer Girl
  DRR-W,M
Surfin' U.S.A.
  DRR-W,M TI1-W,M UFB-W,M
Surfside 6
  TVT-W,M
Surprise
  MES1-W,M MES2-W,M
Surprise (Last Night They Planned
  This Lovely Thing)
  ASB2-W,M
Surprise, A (The Flowers in the
  Garden Have Planned a Surprise)
  ASB5-W,M
Surprise Surprise
  RoS-W,M
Surprise Symphony Theme
  RW-M
Surprised Nymph
  SR-W,M
Surrender (Cloninger/Purse)
  OGR-W,M VB-W,M
Surrender (Pomus/Shuman)
  SRE1-W,M
Surrender of Cornwallis
  SI-W
Surrey with the Fringe on Top
  BeL-W,M DBC-W,M HC1-W,M
  L-W OTJ-W,M OTO-W RW-W,M
  TGO-W,M TI1-W,M TW-W
  UBF-W,M UFB-W,M
Susan Blue
  BMC-M
Susan Brown
  Oz3-W

Susan Jane
  NF-W
Susan When She Tried
  CMG-W,M PoG-W,M WG-W,M
Susanni
  GBC-W,M (German) OB-W,M
Suse, Little Suse
  KS-W,M
Susie Girl
  NF-W
Susie, Little Susie
  ASB4-W,M BM-W HS-W,M
  SiR-W,M
**Susie, Little Susie see also Susy,
  Little Susy**
Susie-Q
  ERM-W,M GAR-W,M
Susie-Q see also Suzie Q
Suspicion
  SRE2-W,M TI1-W,M UFB-W,M
Suspicions
  ToO79-W,M
Suspicious Minds
  HLS9-W,M MF-W,M RY-W,M
  RYT-W,M SRE2-W,M
  ToO76-W,M
Sussex Carol
  JOC-W,M OB-W,M
Sussex Mummers' Carol
  MC-W,M OB-W,M
Susy, Little Susy
  OTJ-W,M
**Susy, Little Susy see also Susie,
  Little Susie**
Suzanne
  RV-W
Suzanne, Suzanne, Jolie Femme?
  BaB-W,M (French)
Suze Ann
  NF-W
Suzie Q
  TI1-W,M UFB-W,M
Suzie Q see also Susie-Q
Suzy Snowflake
  BCS-W,M RW-W,M TI1-W,M
  UFB-W,M
Swallow (In the Morning Light Flies
  the Swallow)
  SL-W,M
Swallow (Swallow, Dear Swallow,
  I Wonder)
  VA-W,M
Swallow (Where Wilt Thou Go, My
  Agile Little Swallow)
  WiS8-W,M
Swamp Rat
  Lo-W,M
Swan, A (Ibsen/Grieg)
  MMM-W,M
Swan, The (Lugovsky/Prokofieff)
  MMW-W,M
Swan, The (Saint-Saens)
  AmH-M FSA2-W,M RW-M
  SL-W,M
Swan, The (Sweetly the Swan
  Sings)
  MG-W,M
Swan Lake Theme
  MF-M RW-M TI1-M UFB-M
Swan Song
  GC-W,M
Swanee
  MF-W,M NYT-W,M ReG-W,M
  T-W,M U-W
Swanee River
  ESB-W,M Fif-W,M NAS-W,M
  NSS-W OTJ-W,M SSFo-W,M

WiS8-W,M

Swanee River see also Old Folks at Home and Way Down upon the Swanee River

Swannanoa Tunnel
FW-W

Swanson Frozen Dinners Jingle see Next Best Thing to Your Good Cooking

Swapping Song
SCL-W,M

S.W.A.T (Theme)
ToO76-M

Sway
RoS-W,M

Swayin' to the Music
MF-W,M

Swearin' to God
ToO76-W,M

Sweatshop
AL-W

Swede from North Dakota
HB-W,M

Swedish Emigrant's Farewell Song from His Native Land
SE-W,M (Swedish)

Swedish Girl or Nils Who Will Travel to America
SE-W,M (Swedish)

Swedish Lullaby
ASB4-W,M

Swedish National Hymn
AmH-W,M (Swedish)

Swedish Rhapsody
MF-W,M TI1-W,M UFB-W,M

Swee' Petatehs
SCL-W,M

Swee' Petatehs see also Sweet Potatoes

Sweep As I Go
GB-W,M

Sweep, Sweep
Boo-W,M

Sweep, Sweep and Cleanse Your Floor
GB-W,M

Sweeper Song
SOO-W,M

Sweepers of Calais
ASB6-W,M

Sweeping Song
GUM1-W,M

Sweet Adeline
AH-W,M FSN-W,M FSTS-W,M
FW-W GSN1-W,M HLS1-W,M
OAP-W,M RW-W,M TI1-W,M
UFB-W,M

Sweet Adoration
VB-W,M

Sweet Affliction
SHS-W,M

Sweet Alice see Ben Bolt

Sweet and Lovely
BeL-W,M HLS5-W,M RT4-W,M
RW-W,M TI1-W,M UFB-W,M

Sweet and Low
AME-W,M AmH-W,M ASB5-W,M
BH-W,M CSo-W,M ESB-W,M
FW-W FWS-W,M HS-W,M
HSD-W,M IL-W,M MG-W,M
MML-W,M NAS-W,M OS-W
RW-W,M SL-W TF-W TH-W,M
U-W WiS8-W,M

Sweet and Low Down
GOB-W,M LSO-W NYT-W,M

Sweet and Sexy Thing
TTH-W,M

Sweet and Twenty
FSA2-W,M

Sweet Annie of Roch Royal see Lass of Roch Royal

Sweet Are the Sounds
Boo-W,M

Sweet Are the Sounds of Our Old Wooden Clock
SHP-W,M

Sweet As the Flowers in May Time
Oz4-W

Sweet Baby James
GrS-W,M

Sweet Bells
MHB-W,M

Sweet Betsy from Pike
AH-W,M AmS-W,M ATS-W,M
BF-W,M DD-W,M FAW-W,M
FW-W HS-W,M IHA-W,M
LW-W,M MAS-W,M OFS-W,M
Oz2-W,M RW-W,M SAm-W,M
SoC-W SoF-W,M WS-W,M

Sweet Betsy from Pike see also Betsy from Pike

Sweet Beulah Land
HHa-W,M

Sweet Black Angel
RoS-W,M

Sweet By and By
CEM-W,M GH-W,M HSD-W,M
MAB1-W MF-W,M MSA1-W
NaM-W,M OM-W,M PoS-W,M
SiS-W SoC-W

Sweet Canaan
RF-W,M WN-W,M

Sweet Caroline
TI2-W,M

Sweet Charity
RW-W,M SC-W,M

Sweet Danger
UBF-W,M

Sweet Day Is Softly Dying
SL-W,M TF-W,M

Sweet Dreams (The Campanile Serenade)
SLS-W,M

Sweet Dreams Are Made of This
BNG-W,M

Sweet Eloise
TI1-W,M UFB-W,M

Sweet Emerald Isle I Love So Well
FHR-W,M

Sweet Evelina
FW-W Oz4-W TMA-W,M

Sweet Fern
ITP-W,M

Sweet Flowers
BIS-W,M

Sweet Forget-Me-Not
NH-W

Sweet Freedom
TTH-W,M

Sweet Genevieve
AH-W,M ATS-W BH-W,M
BSB-W,M CSo-W,M FSTS-W,M
FW-W HSD-W,M OFS-W,M
PoS-W,M TF-W,M U-W
WiS8-W,M

Sweet Georgia Brown
DJ-W,M MF-W,M OHB-W,M
RoE-W,M

Sweet Gingerbread Man
MLS-W,M

Sweet Gliding Kedron
SHS-W,M

Sweet, Goodnight
Boo-W,M

Sweet Harmony
SHS-W,M

Sweet Hawaiian Moonlight
Mo-W,M NM-W,M

Sweet Heaven
SHS-W,M

Sweet Heaven Is a Handsome Place
RTH-W

Sweet Hebben
BDW-W,M

Sweet Home
SHS-W,M

Sweet Home Chicago
LC-W

Sweet Home, Farewell
GrM-W,M

Sweet Hour of Prayer
AME-W,M AmH-W,M BNG-W,M
CEM-W,M GH-W,M HF-W,M
HSD-W,M Hy-W,M IH-M
JBF-W,M MAB1-W MSA1-W
OM-W,M RDF-W,M WiS7-W,M

Sweet Hymns and Songs
SBJ-W,M

Sweet Indiana Home
WDS-W,M

Sweet Is the Night
ELO-W,M

Sweet Jane
BCT-W,M FSU-W FVV-W,M
Oz1-W

Sweet Jennie Lee
WDS-W,M

Sweet Jolie Blon'
Lo-W,M

Sweet Lahyotte
CSD-W,M (French)

Sweet Larilla
BSC-W

Sweet Life
TI1-W,M UFB-W,M

Sweet Little Birdie
Oz4-W,M

Sweet Little Jesus
FF-W,M

Sweet Little Maid of the Mountain
FHR-W,M

Sweet Little Miss Blue Eyes
BSo-W,M

Sweet Little Sixteen
HR-W ILF-W,M RB-W TI1-W,M
UFB-W,M

Sweet Lorraine
FPS-W,M Sta-W,M TI2-W,M

Sweet Love
ToO76-W,M TTH-W,M

Sweet Love Doth Now Invite
TF-W,M

Sweet Maria
OnT1-W,M

Sweet Marie
BH-W,M EFS-W,M FSTS-W,M
MF-W,M TMA-W,M WN-W,M

Sweet Memories of Thee
TMA-W,M

Sweet Molly Malone
OFS-W,M

Sweet Music Man
CMG-W,M PoG-W,M WG-W,M

Sweet Nellie
Oz1-W,M

Sweet Nevada
LSO-W

Sweet Nightingale
BMC-W,M HS-W,M SoF-W,M

Sweet Peace, the Gift of God's

Love
OM-W,M
Sweet Pinks and Roses
NF-W
Sweet Polly Oliver
F3-W,M
Sweet Potatoes
CSD-W,M (French) FSA2-W,M
GuC-W,M LoS-W,M RS-W,M
SSe-W,M
**Sweet Potatoes see also Swee'
Petatehs**
Sweet Primroses
BB-W
Sweet Prospect
SHS-W,M
Sweet Rivers
SHS-W,M
Sweet Rivers of Redeeming Love
AHO-W,M
Sweet Rosie O'Grady
FSN-W,M GSN1-W,M HLS1-W,M
OS-W RW-W,M
Sweet Sexy Eyes
TOH-W,M
Sweet Sixteen
DP-W,M
Sweet Solitude
SHS-W,M
Sweet Someone
BBB-W,M TI1-W,M UFB-W,M
Sweet Spirit, Hear My Prayer
HSD-W,M
Sweet Spring Is Returning
TH-W,M
Sweet Stay Awhile
EL-W,M
Sweet Story of Old
GH-W,M
Sweet Sue (Just You)
RoE-W,M TI1-W,M UFB-W,M
Sweet Sunny South
BSo-W,M
Sweet Surrender
NI-W,M On-W,M OTO-W
RW-W,M
Sweet, Sweet, Sweet
MS-W,M
Sweet Talkin' Guy
MF-W,M
Sweet Talkin' Man
LaS-W,M
Sweet Talkin' Woman
ELO-W,M
Sweet Tennessee
NH-W
Sweet Thames, Flow Softly
IFM-W
Sweet the Evening Air of May
OHO-W,M
Sweet the Pleasures of the Spring
Boo-W,M
Sweet Thing
BIS-W,M FW-W Oz3-W,M
Sweet Time
R-W,M
Sweet Trinity
AA-W,M FMT-W SCa-W,M
Sweet Turtle Dove
RF-W,M
Sweet Violets
Mo-W,M NeA-W,M NM-W,M
WF-W,M
Sweet Virginia
RoS-W,M
Sweet Wild April
FSA2-W,M

Sweet William
BSC-W FMT-W FoM-W,M
ITP-W,M MSB-W SCa-W
**Sweet William and Fair Ellen see
Earl Brand**
Sweet William and Lady Margaret
BSC-W
Sweet William and Lovely Nancy
DD-W,M
Sweet Yesterday
TOC82-W,M
Sweeter As the Years Go By
AME-W,M
Sweeter Than Roses
EL-W,M
Sweeter the Breeze #1
HB-W
Sweeter the Breeze #2
HB-W
Sweetest Hallelujah
HHa-W,M
Sweetest Music This Side of
Heaven
OTO-W
Sweetest Name
GH-W,M
Sweetest Sight That I Have Seen
L-W
Sweetest Sounds
DBC-W,M HC2-W,M OTO-W
TI1-W,M UBF-W,M UFB-W,M
Sweetest Story Ever Told
FSN-W,M GSN1-W,M HLS1-W,M
MF-W,M RW-W,M TM-W,M
WGB/O-W,M WGB/P-W,M
Sweetest Thing (I've Ever Known)
EC-W,M GCM-W,M MF-W,M
Sweetest Woman
DBL-W
Sweethaven
HSe-W,M
Sweetheart
MPM-W,M
Sweetheart of Sigma Chi
Mo-W,M NM-W,M OAP-W,M
RDT-W,M RoE-W,M TI2-W,M
Sweetheart, You've Done Me
Wrong
BIS-W,M
Sweethearts
Sw-W,M
Sweethearts and Wives
TMA-W,M
Sweethearts Holiday
Mo-W,M
Sweethearts on Parade
Mo-W,M NM-W,M
Sweethearts or Strangers
JD-W,M SF-W,M
Sweetie Pie
Mo-W,M NM-W,M
Sweetly She Sleeps, My Alice Fair
FHR-W,M SSF-W,M SSFo-W,M
Sweetly Sings the Donkey
BMC-W,M
Swell Our Ranks
AL-W
Swell the Anthem, Raise the Song
AHO-W,M
Swiftly Flowing Labe
SMY-W,M
Swimming
ASB3-W,M FSA2-W,M
Swing, The
VA-W,M
Swing High, Swing Low
SiR-W,M SOO-W,M

Swing Low
PaS-W,M
Swing Low, Sweet Chariot
AH-W,M AME-W,M ATS-W BMC-
W,M Bo-W,M BSo-W,M CSo-W,M
ESB-W,M ETB-W,M FN-W,M
FW-W GuC-W,M HS-W,M
HSD-W,M IL-W,M LoS-W,M
MAS-W,M MML-W,M NSS-W
OAP-W,M OBN-W,M OFS-W,M
RF-W,M RW-W,M SiR-W,M SpS-
W,M STR-W,M TH-W,M TI1-W,M
UFB-W,M WiS7-W,M WN-W,M
Swing on the Corner
ASB5-W,M
Swing Song
MH-W,M SiR-W,M STS-W,M
Swing, Swing
KS-W,M
Swing the Shining Sickle
HS-W,M
**Swing the Shining Sickle see also
Thanksgiving Song**
Swing Your Daddy
DDH-W,M
Swingin'
TI2-W,M TOC83-W-M
Swingin' down the Lane
GST-W,M HLS2-W,M RW-W,M
Swingin' on a Scab
AFP-W PSN-W
Swingin' Safari
MF-M
Swingin' Shepherd Blues
MF-W,M RW-W,M RY-M
Swinging
ASB3-W,M ASB4-W,M AST-W,M
MH-W,M
Swinging Along
MG-W,M SSe-W,M VA-W,M
Swinging and Singing
SOO-W,M
Swinging Doors
NMH-W,M
Swinging High, Swinging Low
ASB1-W,M
Swinging in the Lane
Oz4-W,M
Swinging on a Star
LMR-W,M TI1-W,M UFB-W,M
Swinging Sweethearts
M-W,M Mo-W,M
Swiss Boy
FSA2-W,M
Swiss Cattle Girl
FSA2-W,M
Swiss National Hymn
AmH-W,M (German)
Swiss Referendum
AL-W
Swiss Ski Song
GUM1-W,M
Swiss Walking Song
PaS-W,M
Switzer's Farewell
HSD-W,M
Sword and a Rose and a Cape
TW-W
Sword Blade March
SMW-W,M
Sword of Bunker Hill
HSD-W,M
Sword of Robert E. Lee
SCo-W,M Sin-W,M SiS-W,M
Sylvelin
FSY-W,M (German)
Sylvia

OTO-W SLB-W,M
Sylvie
　WSB-W,M
Sympathy for the Devil
　RoS-W,M
Symphony
　GV-W,M
Symphony #5, First Movement,
　Main Theme (Beethoven)
　PoG-W,M
Symphony No. 6 Pathetique
　(Tschaikovsky)
　MF-M RW-M
Symphony Theme from Symphony
　No. 9 (Beethoven)
　BMC-M
Syncopated Clock
　GSN3-W,M Sta-W,M
**Syrup Is So Sweet see Sirup Is So
Sweet**

T

T.B. Blues
　LC-W Le-W,M LJ-W,M
T-Bone Slim
　AFP-W
T for Texas
　LJ-W,M
T.J. Hooker (Main Title Theme)
　TV-M
T-U-Turkey
　NF-W
TVA, The
　IHA-W,M
T.V.A. Ballad
　BMM-W,M
Taavor Al Pesha
　JS-W,M (Hebrew Only)
Table Prayer (Grace) of the
　Communists in the United States
　AL-W
Table Setting Song
　GM-W,M
Taddy Pole and Polly Wog
　MH-W,M
Tadpoles
　SiR-W,M
Tahi Nei Taru Kino
　SNZ-W,M (Maori)
Tailgate Ramble
　TI1-W,M UFB-W,M
Tailor and the Mouse
　HS-W,M OTJ-W,M SiR-W,M
Tailor There Dwelt
　LMR-W,M
Tails
　NF-W
'Taint No Sin (to Dance Around in
　Your Bones)
　WDS-W,M
'Taint No Sin to Take Off Your
　Skin and Dance Around in Your
　Bones
　WF-W,M
'Tain't Nobody's Bizness but My
　Own
　NH-W
'Tain't Nobody's Biz-ness If I Do
　LSB-W,M TI2-W,M
'Taint What You Do
　TI2-W,M
Taisez Vous
　NaM-W,M
Take a Chance on Me
　RW-W,M TI1-W,M UFB-W,M

Take a Drink on Me
　FW-W
Take a Good Look Around
　Mo-W,M NM-W,M OTO-W
Take a Job
　DR-W,M
Take a Letter Maria
　TI1-W,M UFB-W,M
Take a Little One Step
　NN2-W,M NN7-W,M
Take a Little Run About
　ASB1-W,M
Take a Message to Mary
　RB-W
Take a Pair of Sparkling Eyes
　MGT-W,M
Take a Whiff on Me
　FW-W NeF-W
Take Away Song
　MAR-W,M
Take Back the Heart
　AmH-W,M HSD-W,M
Take Back Your Gold
　FSN-W,M FSTS-W,M Oz4-W
Take Back Your Mink
　TW-W UBF-W,M
Take Five
　OPS-M
Take Him
　TS-W
Take Him to Heart
　VB-W,M
Take It Away
　TI2-W,M
Take It Easy
　TTH-W,M
Take It Easy Baby
　DBL-W
Take It Easy on Me
　TI2-W,M
Take It or Leave It
　RoS-W,M
Take It Slow, Joe
　Mo-W,M NM-W,M OTO-W
Take It to the Limit
　MF-W,M
Take Life a Little Easier
　GSM-W,M On-W,M
Take Me Along
　PB-W,M
Take Me As I Am
　GH-W,M
Take Me Back Again
　LJ-W,M
Take Me Back to My Boots and
　Saddle
　FC-W,M WiS9-W,M
Take Me Back to Switzerland
　NAS-W,M
Take Me Down
　TOC82-W,M
Take Me Home
　CSp-W,M HSD-W,M ToO79-W,M
Take Me Home, Country Roads
　CJ-W,M CMG-W,M FPS-W,M
　GrS-W,M MAB1-W MCG-W,M
　MSA1-W N-W,M On-W,M
　PoG-W,M WG-W,M
Take Me in Your Arms
　Sta-W,M
Take Me in Your Arms and Hold
　Me
　OGC1-W,M
Take Me in Your Lifeboat
　BIS-W,M
Take Me Out to the Ball Game
　AAP-W,M

Take Me, Take Me, Some of You
　EL-W,M
Take Me to the Pilot
　TI2-W,M
Take Me to the River
　ToO79-W,M
Take Me to Your World
　TI1-W,M UFB-W,M
Take My Breath Away (Love
　Theme from Top Gun)
　GSN5-W,M MoA-W,M TTH-W,M
Take My Hand, Precious Lord
　GrG-W,M HLS7-W,M RDF-W,M
　SUH-W,M TI1-W,M Tr-W,M
　UFB-W,M
Take My Life and Let It Be
　AME-W,M GH-W,M Hy-W,M
　SJ-W,M
Take My Love
　GG4-W,M HLS3-W,M RT5-W,M
Take My Love to Rosalie
　Re-W,M
Take My Mother Home
　RTH-W
Take My Ring from Your Finger
　BIS-W,M
Take, O Take Those Lips Away
　EL-W,M FSS-W,M
Take the "A" Train
　GMD-W,M OnT6-W,M OPS-W,M
Take the Long Way Home
　EC-W,M
Take the Mem'ry When You Go
　TOC82-W,M
Take the Name of Jesus with You
　AME-W,M CEM-W,M Hy-W,M
　OM-W,M
Take the World, but Give Me
　Jesus
　HHa-W,M
Take This Hammer
　FW-W Le-W,M OHO-W,M
　OTJ-W,M SWF-W,M WS-W,M
Take This Job and Shove It
　GCM-W,M MF-W,M
Take Thou My Hand
　GH-W,M
Take Thou Our Minds, Dear Lord
　AHO-W,M
Take Thou Our Minds, Dear Lord,
　We Humbly Pray
　Hy-W,M
Take Time to Be Holy
　AME-W,M GH-W,M Hy-W,M
Take Up the Courses
　GI-W
Take Up the Union Label
　AL-W
Take Up Thy Cross, the Saviour
　Said
　AME-W,M Hy-W,M
Take Up Your Sword
　SL-W,M
Take Yo' Time
　NH-W
Take Your Fingers off It
　FW-W OTJ-W,M PO-W,M
Take Your Gun and Go, John
　Sin-W,M SiS-W
Take Your Harps from the Silent
　Willows
　SiS-W
Take Your Time
　FrF-W,M (Spanish)
Take Your Time and Take Your
　Pick
　PF-W,M

Taken from a County Jail
SL-W,M
Taker, The
SuS-W,M
Takes Two to Tango
TI1-W,M UFB-W,M
Takin' a Ride (Theme from Heavy
Metal)
TOM-W,M
Takin' Names
J-W,M
Takin' the Easy Way
VB-W,M
Taking a Chance on Love
GG4-W,M GSF-W,M GSN3-W,M
HLS5-W,M HLS8-W,M RT4-W,M
RW-W,M
Taking a Walk
NF-W
Taking Off
SOO-W,M
Taking Turns
FF-W,M
Tales from the Vienna Woods
CA-W,M MF-M OBN-M RW-M
Talk
Am-W OnT6-M
Talk about Confusion
SYB-W,M
Talk about Me
NH-W
Talk about the Good Times
EP-W,M
Talk about This--Talk about That
Sw-W,M
Talk to Me
TI2-W,M
Talk to the Animals
RT6-W,M
Talk with Us, Lord, Thyself Reveal
AME-W,M
Talk with Us, O Lord
RW-W,M
Talking Back to the Night
BHO-W,M
Talking Blues
FG2-W,M FW-W WSB-W,M
**Talking Blues see also Original
Talking Blues**
Talking Dirty Red Draft Dodger
VS-W,M
Talking Hobo
AFP-W
Talking Miner
AFP-W
Talking Nothin'
FW-W
Talking Psychopathic Draft Exam
VS-W,M
Talking Subway Blues
Am-W
Talking Union
FW-W SWF-W,M
Talking Vietnam
VS-W,M
Talking Vietnam Pot Luck
VS-W,M
Tall Angel at de Bar
Me-W,M
Tall Angel at the Bar
My-W,M
Tall Hope
Mo-W,M NM-W,M OTJ-W,M
OTO-W W-W,M
Tall Paul
SBS-W,M
Tall Pine Tree

ASB6-W,M
Tallis' Canon
LoS-W,M
**Tallis' Canon see also Canon
(Tallis)**
Talt Hall
FSU-W
Tam Lane
SCa-W,M
Tam Pierce
FW-W
Tamale Man
SiR-W,M
Tammany
FSTS-W,M GI-W GO-W MF-W,M
Tammy
EY-W,M FRH-W,M HFH-W,M
T'an Ch'in Chia (the Grumbling
Mother-in-Law)
FD-W,M (Chinese)
Tan Don't Burn Get a Coppertone
Tan
GSM-W,M
Tan Patate La Tchuite
BaB-W,M (French)
Tancuj
SCL-W,M
Taney County
Oz2-W,M
Tangerine
AT-W,M OHF-W OTO-W
Tangled Mind
OGC2-W,M
Tango in D
LaS-M MF-M
Tango of Roses
TI2-W,M
Tanker
GO-W,M
Tanker Song
GI-W,M GO-W
Tanker's Hymn
GO-W
Tannenbaum
NAS-W,M
**Tannenbaum see also O Christmas
Tree, O Tannenbaum, and Oh
Tannenbaum**
Tan'siro E Dou'
CSD-W,M (French)
Tant Sirop Est Doux
AAF-W,M (French Only)
Tan-Tan-Ta-Rah
GM-W,M
Tanto Vestido Blanco
LA-W,M (Spanish)
Tap on Your Drum, Amigo
GM-W,M
Tap, Tap, Tap
MH-W,M
Tap Your Troubles Away
OTO-W
Tapestry
MF-W,M VB-W,M
Tapioca Puddin'
LMR-W,M
Tapping at the Garden Gate
HSD-W,M
Taps
ASB6-W,M ATS-W,M BM-W
Bo-W FWS-W,M GI-W,M GO-W
HS-W,M JW-W,M LMR-W,M
MAS-W,M UF-W,M VA-W,M
Tapuakh Khineni (Nad Ilan)
TO-W,M (Hebrew)
Tara Theme
BNG-M DC-W,M TVT-W,M

Tara Theme see also My Own True
Love
Tarantella
Ap-M ASB1-M MF-M RW-M
SFB-W,M TI1-M UFB-M
Ta-Ra-Ra-Boom
BS-W,M
Ta-Ra-Ra-Boom-De-Ay
FSN-W,M JF-W,M PaS-W,M
TI1-W,M UFB-W,M
Ta-Ra-Ra Boom-Der-E
FW-W MF-W,M OTJ-W,M
RW-W,M
**Tarde Fresquita De Mayo see Una
Tarde Fresquita De Mayo**
Tardy Gratitude
FSA2-W,M
Tarentelle
FSA1-W,M
Tarriers' Song
AFB-W,M AL-W
Tarry Here
AG-W,M
Tarry with Me, O My Saviour
AHO-W,M
Tarrytown see Wild Goose Grasses
Tar's Election Song
AL-W
Tar's Farewell
HSD-W,M
Tarzan's March
OnT6-W,M OTJ-W,M
Tarzan's Theme
HFH-M
Tassels on Her Boots
Oz3-W
Taste of Honey
BHB-W,M DPE-W,M GOI7-W,M
ILS-W,M MF-W,M OPS-W,M
OTJ-W,M RW-W,M TI2-W,M
Tattooed Lady
GO-W
Tattoo
WA-W,M
Tavern
BSC-W
Tavern in the Town
Gu-W,M
**Tavern in the Town see also There
Is a Tavern in the Town and
There's a Tavern in the Town**
Taxation of America
AWB-W
Taxi (Theme) see Angela
Taxi Driver (Theme)
HFH-M MF-M TOM-M
Taxman
BBe-W,M TWS-W
Tay Bridge Disaster
BB-W
Taylor, the Fine Old Southern
Gentleman
ATS-W,M
**Tchaikovsky (and Other Russians)
see Tschaikowsky (and Other
Russians)**
Tapioca Puddin' see *omit*
**Te Deum see We Praise Thee O
God, We Acknowledge Thee to
Be the Lord**
Tea for Two
DBC-W,M (Spanish) MF-W,M
NN2-W,M NN7-W,M OHB-W,M
TW-W
Tea Leaves
Mo-W,M
Tea Party
SSS-W,M

Tea Party Song
SAR-W,M
Tea Ships
OHO-W,M
Tea Tax
ESU-W HAS-W,M OHG-W,M
Teach Me, Father, How to Go
MML-W,M
Teach Me Jesus
SNS-W
Teach Me, Lustrous Star
MuM-W,M
Teach Me, O Lord
CEM-W,M
Teach Me--Serve Him
TW-W
Teach Me the Ways of
Thankfulness
SHP-W,M
Teach Me to See
VB-W,M
Teach Me Tonight
BOA-W,M MF-W,M NK-W,M
RoE-W,M
Teacher
BJ-W,M
Teacher's Lament
JF-W,M SoC-W SWF-W,M
Teaching Table Manners
NF-W
Teamster's Marseillaise
SoC-W
Tear Fell, A
RW-W,M
Tear for the Comrade That's Gone
SiS-W
Teardrop Millionaire
AL-W
Teardrops in My Eyes
BSo-W,M
Teardrops in My Heart
FrF-W,M (Spanish) TI1-W,M
UFB-W,M
Tears Bring Thoughts of Heaven
FHR-W,M
Tears on My Pillow
DRR-W,M Gr-W,M RW-W,M
TI1-W,M UFB-W,M
Tears Will Never Stain Streets
HHa-W,M
Teasin' Blues
LC-W
Teasing
FSN-W,M
Teddy Bear
CMG-W,M TI1-W,M ToO76-W,M
UFB-W,M
Tee-Total Society
ESU-W
Tee Totalist
ESU-W
Tee-Totaller's Auld Lang Syne
ESU-W
Teen Angel
HR-W RB-W
Teen-Age Heaven
HR-W
Teenage Meeting
RB-W
Teen-Age Sonata
HR-W
Teenager in Love
TI1-W,M UFB-W,M
Teen-Ager's Prayer
HR-W
Teeter Totter
ASB2-W,M

Telegraph
OHG-W,M
Telephone
ASB1-W,M MH-W,M
Telephone Book
NeA-W,M
Telephone Girlie
NN7-W,M
**Telephone Girlie see also Hello!
Hello! Telephone Girlie**
Telephone Hour
Mo-W,M NM-W,M OTO-W
UBF-W,M
Telephone Line
ELO-W,M
Telephone Song
SOO-W,M
Telephone Time
GM-W,M
Tell a Handsome Stranger
LMS-W,M
Tell Everyone You Know
HHa-W,M
Tell Irene Hello
NeA-W,M
Tell It All Over Again
OG-W,M
Tell It Like It Is
DP-W,M ILS-W,M RY-W,M
TI1-W,M UFB-W,M
Tell It Out
GH-W,M
Tell It to My Heart
CFB-W,M
Tell Jesus
RF-W,M
Tell Laura I Love Her
HR-W RB-W TI2-W,M
Tell Me
RoS-W,M
Tell Me a Lie
TOC83-W,M
Tell Me Baby
DBL-W
**Tell Me, Do You Love Me see
Sweetest Story Ever Told**
Tell Me, Is My Father Coming
Home
Sin-W,M
Tell Me, Little Maiden
BMC-W,M
Tell Me, Little Twinkling Star
SiS-W
Tell Me Love of Thy Early Dreams
FHR-W,M
Tell Me More
ReG-W,M
Tell Me More about Jesus
GH-W,M
Tell Me, Mother, Can I Go?
SiS-W
Tell Me No More
EL-W,M OH-W,M
Tell Me Not in Mournful Numbers
AHO-W,M
Tell Me of the Angels, Mother
FHR-W,M
Tell Me on a Sunday
UBF-W,M
Tell Me, Pretty Maiden
FSN-W,M FSTS-W,M
Tell Me Something New
TW-W
Tell Me That You Love Me, Junie
Moon
OTO-W
Tell Me the Old, Old Story

GH-W,M Hy-W,M
Tell Me the Stories of Jesus
AME-W,M Hy-W,M
Tell Me What Month Was My
Jesus Born In
FW-W
Tell Me What You See
Be1-W,M TWS-W
**Tell Me When see Quando,
Quando, Quando**
Tell Me Where Is Fancy Bred
OH-W,M
Tell Me Why (Lennon/McCartney)
BBe-W,M Be1-W,M TWS-W
Tell Me Why (the Stars Do Shine)
Bo-W,M FWS-W,M HS-W,M
IL-W,M LoS-W,M MAS-W,M
Sta-W,M WU-W,M YS-W,M
Tell Me You'll Wait for Me
HRB1-W,M
Tell Mother I Die Happy
MPP-W SiS-W
Tell Old Bill
FG2-W,M FW-W RW-W,M
Tell Ole I Ain't Here, He Better Get
on Home
TOH-W,M
Tell the Town Hello To-night
BP-W,M
Tell Us, Ye Servants of the Lord
AHO-W,M
Tell Your Horse's Age
HB-W
Telling Time
ASB2-W,M ASB4-W,M STS-W,M
Temperance Call
ESU-W
Temperance Rhyme
NF-W
Temperance River
ESU-W
Temperance Song
Oz2-W,M TBF-W,M
Tempest
AST-W,M POT-M
Tempest of the Heart
AmH-W,M HSD-W,M
Tempo of the Times
Mo-W,M NM-W,M OTO-W
Tempo Song
SiB-W,M
Temps En Temps
CaF-W (French Only)
Temptation
HLS5-W,M RW-W,M
Tempted and Tried
GH-W,M
Tempus Adest Floridum
GBC-W,M (Latin)
10 (Song from the Movie)
HFH-W,M
Ten Broeck--the Race Horse
BMM-W
Ten Cents a Dance
MF-W,M OHB-W,M TS-W TW-W
Ten Feet Away
TTH-W,M
Ten Feet Off the Ground
SBS-W,M
Ten Green Bottles
SiR-W,M
Ten Hour Banner
AL-W
Ten Little Devils
FMT-W
Ten Little Fingers
FP-W,M

Ten Little Fingers and Ten Little
    Toes
    BH-W,M GSN1-W,M HLS1-W,M
Ten Little Frogs
    GM-W,M
Ten Little Germs
    FSA1-W,M
Ten Little Indians
    ASB1-W,M BBF-W,M BM-W
    BR-W,M FP-W,M HS-W,M
    OBN-W,M OTJ-W,M STR-W,M
Ten Little Injuns
    OHG-W,M
Ten Little Kiddies
    OTJ-W,M
Ten Little Niggers
    HSD-W,M
Ten Little Soldiers
    FF-W
Ten Miles from Home
    FSA2-W,M SiR-W,M
Ten Minutes Ago
    OTJ-W,M OTO-W TI1-W,M
    UBF-W,M UFB-W,M
Ten More Nights in This Old
    Barroom
    CMG-W,M
Ten Pretty Maidens
    MH-W,M
Ten Thousand Angels
    BSG-W,M BSP-W,M
Ten Thousand Cattle
    HB-W,M HWS-W,M
Ten Thousand Cattle Straying
    GA-W,M
Ten Thousand Dollars Going Home
    to the Folks
    AF-W
10538 Overture
    ELO-W,M
Ten Thousand Men of Harvard
    IL-W,M
10,000-Mile Bomber
    AF-W
Ten Thousand Miles Away
    AmS-W,M FW-W Oz4-W,M
    SA-W,M
Ten Thousand Times
    GH-W,M
Ten Thousand Times Ten
    Thousand
    AME-W,M Hy-W,M
Ten Thousand Years
    HHa-W,M
Tena Koe
    SNZ-W,M (Maori)
Tenaouich' Tenaga, Ouich'ka
    CFS-W,M (French)
Tender Care, or Soda
    SHS-W,M
Tender Love
    DPE-W,M
Tender Shepherd
    Mo-W,M OTJ-W,M
Tender Shepherd (Can You Sleep)
    OTO-W
Tender Shepherd (Count Your
    Sheep)
    NM-W,M
Tender Trap
    FrS-W,M MF-W,M
Tenderfoot
    FW-W SoC-W,M
Tenderfoot and the Bronco
    SoC-W
Tenderfoot Cowboy
    SoC-W

Tenderfoot's Experience
    SoC-W
Tenderly
    BBB-W,M Mo-W,M NM-W,M
    RDT-W,M TI2-W,M
Tenderly Calling
    GH-W,M
Tenement to Let
    SR-W,M
Tenes La De Pres
    FSF-W (French)
Tennessee (Afflictions, Though
    They Seem Severe)
    SHS-W,M
Tennessee (You Have Heard and
    Read about the State of
    Tennessee)
    BSo-W,M
Tennessee Border
    OGC1-W,M
Tennessee Border No. 2
    OGC1-W,M
Tennessee Killer
    Oz2-W
Tennessee Polka
    OGC2-W,M
Tennessee Saturday Night
    OGC1-W,M
Tennessee Stud
    BSo-W,M
Tennessee Tears
    OGC2-W,M
Tennessee Waltz
    GSN3-W,M PB-W,M
Tennessee Wig Walk
    LWT-W,M
Tenshun!
    GO-W
Tenth Ward Battle Song
    AL-W
Tenting Again on the Old Camp
    Ground
    WN-W,M
Tenting on the Old Camp Ground
    ATS-W FW-W GC-W,M NAS-W,M
    OHG-W,M OTJ-W,M PoS-W,M
    Sin-W,M SiS-W TMA-W,M
Tenting Tonight
    ESB-W,M FG1-W,M HSD-W,M
    IHA-W,M OFS-W,M
**Tenting Tonight see also We Are
Tenting To-night**
Tenting Tonight (on the Old Camp
    Ground)
    AAP-W,M
Tequila
    GG3-W,M RW-M
Tequila Sunrise
    MF-W,M
Terek, The
    ASB6-W,M
Terly Terlow
    GBC-W,M
Terra Nova
    RV-W
Terraplane Blues
    LC-W
Terrific Torpedoes
    ANS-W
T'es Pitite, T'es Mig'onne
    CaF-W (French Only)
Tess (Love Theme)
    TOM-M
Tessie
    Mo-W,M
Teton Dakota Indian Moccasin
    Game Song

IF-M
Teuton's Tribulation
    HAS-W,M SY-W,M
**Texaco Service Station Star Theme
see Man Who Wears the Star**
Texan Boys
    BSC-W
Texas (We'll Travel On Together
    Till You and I Must Part)
    FMT-W FoM-W,M
Texas Cowboy
    FMT-W HOH-W,M HWS-W,M
    Oz4-W SoC-W,M
Texas Cowboy's Song
    BMC-W,M
Texas Cowboys' Stampede Song
    MML-W,M
Texas Hymn of Liberty
    OHG-W,M
Texas in My Soul
    OGC2-W,M
Texas Millionaire
    OGC2-W,M
Texas, Our Texas
    Fif-W,M
Texas Plains
    FC-W,M
Texas Ranger
    GI-W
Texas Rangers
    BSC-W,M FMT-W FW-W HB-W,M
    HWS-W,M Oz2-W,M SoC-W
Texas Short, the Kid
    SoC-W
Texas Trail
    ASB5-W,M
Tex-i-an Boys
    LW-W,M
Thank God I'm a Country Boy
    CJ-W,M CMG-W,M GrS-W,M
    PoG-W,M WG-W,M
Thank Heaven for Little Girls
    HC2-W,M HLS3-W,M LL-W,M
    OTJ-W,M OTO-W TI1-W,M
    UBF-W,M UFB-W,M
Thank Heaven for You
    DB-W,M DBC-W,M MF-W,M
    UBF-W,M
Thank the Lord for the Night Time
    TI2-W,M
Thank the Lord for This
    Thanksgiving Day
    LWT-W,M
Thank You
    OTJ-W,M
Thank You, Ever-Lovin'
    TOH-W,M
Thank You for Christmas
    NB-W
Thank You for the Music
    TI1-W,M UFB-W,M
Thank You Girl
    BBe-W,M ERM-W,M TI1-W,M
    TWS-W UFB-W,M
Thank You, God
    MAR-W,M
Thank You, God, for Happy Hearts
    SHP-W,M
Thank You, God, for Quiet Night
    SHP-W,M
Thank You, Lord
    MF-W,M
Thank You Pretty Baby
    MF-W,M
Thank You Song
    FF-W,M SoP-W,M
Thanking God

ASB1-W,M ASB2-W,M
Thanks (Coslow/Johnston)
FiS-W,M
Thanks (Dandridge/O'Hara)
OTO-W
Thanks Be to God
SHP-W,M
Thanks Be to Thee, O Christ
Hy-W,M
Thanks for the Memories
AF-W
Thanks for the Memories II
AF-W
Thanks for the Memory
AT-W,M GSN2-W,M ILT-W,M
LM-W,M OnT1-W,M OTO-W
TOM-W,M
Thanks to God
OM-W,M
Thanksgiving
SiR-W,M
Thanksgiving (Landon/Loomis)
SL-W,M
Thanksgiving (Shepard/O'Hara)
MH-W,M
Thanksgiving (Weckerlin/
Naughton)
FSA1-W,M
Thanksgiving at Grandma's
GM-W,M
Thanksgiving Canon
GuC-W,M
Thanksgiving Carol
OB-W,M
Thanksgiving Day (Is Coming, I'm
So Glad, Are You?)
SoP-W,M
Thanksgiving Day (Is Coming
Soon)
ASB1-W,M
Thanksgiving Day (Oh, Bring the
Turkey Roasted Brown)
ASB3-W,M
Thanksgiving Day (The Pumpkin
Has Not a Word to Say)
MH-W,M
Thanksgiving Day (Smell the
Turkey Cooking)
ASB2-W,M
Thanksgiving Day (There's a
Turkey in the Icebox)
ASB4-W,M
Thanksgiving Day (We Greet with
Joy This Dear Home Day)
SL-W,M
Thanksgiving Dinner
FF-W
Thanksgiving Hymn
MML-W,M RW-W,M
**Thanksgiving Hymn see also
Prayer of Thanksgiving,
Thanksgiving Prayer, and We
Gather Together to Ask the
Lord's Blessing**
Thanksgiving Hymn, 1783 (The
Lord Above, in Tender Love, Hath
Sav'd Us from Our Foes)
SAR-W,M SBA-W
Thanksgiving Prayer
TF-W,M YS-W,M
**Thanksgiving Prayer see also
Thanksgiving Hymn**
Thanksgiving Round
SBF-W,M
Thanksgiving Song (Swing the
Shining Sickle)
BeB-W,M HS-W,M OS-W

Thanksong
OGR-W,M
That Ain't Right
DBL-W
That Alters the Matter
HJ-W,M
That Awful Day Will Surely Come
AME-W
That Big Rock Candy Mountain
OTJ-W,M
That Bugler
SiS-W
That Certain Feeling
GOB-W,M LSO-W MF-W,M
NYT-W,M
That Certain Party
WDS-W,M
That Christmas Feeling
BCh-W,M BCS-W,M TI1-W,M
UFB-W,M
That Crazy War
FW-W
That Day of Wrath, That Direful
Day
AHO-W,M
That Doggie in the Window
FrF-W,M
That Doleful Night before His
Death
AME-W,M
That Easter Day with Joy Was
Bright
SJ-W,M
That Face
TI2-W,M
That Gospel Train Is Coming
AN-W
That Great Come-and-Get-It Day
FR-W,M OTO-W TI1-W,M
UBF-W,M UFB-W,M
That Heart Belongs to Me
OGC1-W,M
That Honky-Tonky Melody
Mo-W,M NM-W,M
That Hypocrite
NF-W
That Kind of Woman
OTO-W
That Last Fierce Fight
Oz2-W,M
That Little Old Red Shawl
BSB-W,M
That Lonesome Train Took My
Baby Away
LSR-W,M
That Lonesome Valley
WN-W,M
That Lost Barber Shop Chord
LSO-W
That Lucky Old Sun
GG5-W,M GSF-W,M GSN3-W,M
HLS3-W,M RW-W,M
That Missing Voice
SiS-W
That Old Black Magic
AT-W,M GSN3-W,M OHF-W
OTO-W TOM-W,M
That Old Boy see Dat Ol' Boy
That Old Clock on the Wall
Mo-W,M NM-W,M
That Old Feeling
CS-W,M GSO-W,M HLS5-W,M
RW-W,M
That Old Gang of Mine
TI1-W,M UFB-W,M
That Old Girl of Mine
RC-W,M

That Old Mountain Dew
FAW-W,M
That Old Razz-a-Ma-Tazz
GG3-W,M
That Old-Time Religion
AN-W RDF-W,M
**That Old-Time Religion see also
Dat Ol' Time Religion**
That Ride on the Old Carrousel
LMR-W,M
**That Sabbath Hath No End see Dat
Sabbath Hath No End**
**That Same Train see Dat Same
Train**
That Silver-Haired Daddy of Mine
OTJ-W,M RW-W,M
That Southern Wagon
SiS-W
That Suits Me see Dat Suits Me
That Sunday That Summer
MF-W,M
That Sweet Story of Old
AME-W,M
That Viennese Waltz
WiS8-W,M
That Was Then, This Is Now
TTH-W,M
That Was Yesterday
Mo-W,M NM-W,M OTO-W
**That Watermelon see Dat Water
Million**
That Will Be Heaven for Me
GH-W,M
That Wonderful Melody
BS-W,M
That Wonderful Mother of Mine
MF-W,M
That Would Be Something
Be2-W,M
That'll Be the Day
DRR-W,M TI2-W,M
That's a Fine Kind o' Freedom
Mo-W,M NM-W,M
That's a Mighty Pretty Motion
PSD-W,M
That's a Plenty
TI2-W,M
That's All
AFP-W DC-W,M HFH-W,M
MF-W,M RoE-W,M RW-W,M
TI2-W,M ToS-W,M
That's All Right
OGC1-W,M
That's All There Is to That
NK-W,M
That's Amore
AT-W,M LM-W,M OTO-W
RDT-W,M
That's an Irish Lullaby
MAB1-W MF-W,M MSA1-W
**That's an Irish Lullaby see also
Too-ra-loo-ra-loo-ral**
That's Entertainment
BeL-W,M EY-W,M HC1-W,M
HFH-W,M LM-W,M OTO-W
TI1-W,M TW-W UFB-W,M
That's for Me
L-W
That's Good News
GrG-W,M
That's Good--That's Bad
Mo-W,M NM-W,M OTO-W
That's How I Can Count on You
BSo-W,M
That's How Young I Feel
Mo-W,M NM-W,M OTO-W
That's It, I Quit, I'm Movin' On

ILS-W,M
That's Life
  DJ-W,M TI1-W,M UFB-W,M
That's Me
  AF-W GI-W
That's My Desire
  TI2-W,M
That's My Weakness Now
  MF-W,M TI1-W,M UFB-W,M
That's the Price for Loving You
  OGC2-W,M
That's the Way (I Like It)
  DP-W,M ToO76-W,M
That's the Wrong Way
  GO-W
That's What Friends Are For
  BNG-W,M DC-W,M DPE-W,M
  HFH-W,M LOM-W,M MF-W,M
  RoE-W,M
That's What Her Memory Is For
  TTH-W,M
That's What I Get for Loving You
  TOH-W,M
That's What I Like about You
  WDS-W,M
That's What I Want for Christmas
  Mo-W,M NM-W,M
That's What Love Is All About
  CFB-W,M
That's What the Niggers Then Will
  Do
  SiS-W
That's What's the Matter
  FHR-W,M SiS-W
That's When the Angels Rejoice
  VB-W,M
That's When the Music Takes Me
  TI2-W,M
That's Where My Money Goes
  IL-W,M OFS-W,M OTJ-W,M
That's Where the Joy Comes From
  VB-W,M
That's Why I'm Blue
  LJ-W,M
That's Why I'm Nobody's Darling
  SF-W,M
That's Your Funeral
  O-W,M
Theanga Na Ri
  VP-W,M (Gaelic Only)
Thee I Love see Friendly
  Persuasion
Thee Will I Love
  GH-W,M
Them Bones Gonna Rise Again see
  Dem Bones Gonna Rise Again
Them Golden Slippers
  TMA-W,M
Them Golden Slippers see also Oh,
  Them Golden Slippers
Them Good Ol' Boys Are Bad
  TOC82-W,M
Them There Eyes
  LSB-W,M TI1-W,M UFB-W,M
Theme (Haydn)
  ASB1-M
Theme for Laura (Remington
  Steele)
  TV-M
Theme for Young Lovers
  TI1-M UFB-M
Then a Few Years Ago
  SYB-W,M
Then Away We Go
  GiS-W,M
Then Came You
  TV-W,M

Then Did Moses Sing
  SiP-W,M (Hebrew)
Then Farewell, My Trim-Built
  Wherry
  OH-W,M
Then He Comes
  VB-W,M
Then He Kissed Me
  DPE-W,M
Then I Met the Master
  HHa-W,M
Then I'd Be Satisfied with Life
  EFS-W,M
Then I'll Be Happy
  TI1-W,M UFB-W,M
Then I'll Be Tired of You
  MF-W,M
Then Let Us Think on Death
  ESU-W
Then My Little Soul Will Shine see
  Den My Little Soul Will Shine
Then Shall the Eyes of the Blind
  MML-W,M
Then Was Then and Now Is Now
  MF-W,M
Then Who on Earth's to Blame?
  AL-W
Then You May Take Me to the Fair
  OTO-W
Then You Will Know
  DS-W,M
Then You'll Remember Me
  AmH-W,M FSY-W,M HSD-W,M
  TH-W,M
Theology in Camp
  HOH-W
Theology in the Question
  AN-W
There Ain't No Bugs on Me
  FW-W VS-W,M
There Ain't No Way
  On-W,M
There Are Many Flags
  HS-W,M
There Are Many Flags in Many
  Lands
  OS-W SiR-W,M SOO-W,M
There Are Mean Things Happening
  in Our Land
  AFP-W
There Are Ninety and Nine
  AL-W
There Are No Fighter Pilots Down
  in Hell
  AF-W
There Are Plenty of Fish in the Sea
  FHR-W,M
There Are Such Things
  TI1-W,M UFB-W,M
There Are Those
  OnT6-W,M
There Are Worse Things I Could
  Do
  Gr-W,M Mo-W,M OTO-W
  UBF-W,M
There Arose Not a Prophet Since
  SoM-W,M
There But for Fortune
  JF-W,M
There But for You Go I
  LL-W,M TW-W
There Came a Frost
  TH-W,M
There Came an Ancient Huron
  CFS-W,M (French)
There Came to My Window
  SOO-W,M

There Comes a Galley
  GBC-W,M
There Comes a Reckoning Day
  AL-W
There Dwelt a Man in Babylon
  SSP-W
There Goes My Baby
  HRB4-W,M TI1-W,M UFB-W,M
There Goes My Everything
  GG3-W,M THN-W,M
There Goes My Heart
  GSO-W,M RW-W,M TI1-W,M
  UFB-W,M
There Grew a Little Flower
  MGT-W,M
There Grows a Bonnie Briar Bush
  SeS-W,M
There He Goes That's Him see Dar
  He Goes Dats Him
There Is a Balm in Gilead
  RF-W,M
There Is a Calm
  GH-W,M
There Is a Fountain
  CEM-W,M GH-W,M
There Is a Fountain Filled with
  Blood
  AME-W,M Hy-W,M
There Is a Garden in Her Face
  MU-W,M OH-W,M
There Is a Gate That Stands Ajar
  AME-W,M
There Is a Green Hill Far Away
  AME-W,M AmH-W,M FiS-W,M
  (French) GH-W,M Hy-W,M
  SJ-W,M WiS7-W,M
There Is a Happy Land
  FoS-W,M WiS7-W,M
There Is a High Place
  AHO-W,M
There Is a Lady Sweet and Kind
  EL-W,M Gu-W,M
There Is a Land
  GH-W,M
There Is a Land Mine Eye Hath
  Seen
  AHO-W,M
There Is a Land of Pure Delight
  AME-W,M
There is a Mighty Shoutin' see
  Dere Is a Mighty Shoutin'
There Is a Name I Love
  GH-W,M
There Is a Name I Love to Hear
  AME-W,M
There Is a Paradise of Rest
  GH-W,M
There Is a Place of Quiet Rest
  Hy-W,M
There Is a Rest Remains
  WN-W,M
There Is a Savior
  VB-W,M
There Is a Stream
  GH-W,M
There Is a Tavern in the Town
  BH-W,M CSo-W,M EFS-W,M
  FM-W,M FU-W,M FuB-W,M
  FW-W IL-W,M IPH-W,M MAB1-W
  MF-W,M MHB-W,M MSA1-W
  MuM-W,M OFS-W,M PoS-W,M
  RW-W,M TI1-W,M U-W
There is a Tavern in the Town
  see also Tavern in the Town and
  There's a Tavern in the Town
There Is an Hour of Peaceful Rest
  AHO-W,M

There Is Joy
  GH-W,M
There Is Life for a Look
  GH-W,M
There Is Magic in a Smile
  Sw-W,M
There Is No Better Blossom Than
  Apple Blossom
  RSC-W,M (Russian Only)
There Is No Christmas Like a Home
  Christmas
  BCS-W,M MF-W,M RW-W,M
  TI1-W,M UFB-W,M
There Is No Cradle Ready
  SHP-W,M
There Is No Friend Like Jesus
  GrG-W,M
There Is No Greater Love
  TI2-W,M
There Is No Name So Sweet on
  Earth
  AHO-W,M
There Is No Night in Heaven
  AME-W,M
There Is No Rose
  GBC-W,M
There Is None Righteous
  GH-W,M
There Is Nothin' Like a Dame
  HC2-W,M L-W OTJ-W,M OTO-W
  SP-W,M TI1-W,M UBF-W,M UFB-
  W,M
There Is Nothing Like a Lark
  GSM-W,M
There Is Nothing Too Good for You
  GOB-W,M
There Is Power
  FW-W
There Is Rest for the Weary
  AME-W,M
There Is Somebody Waiting for Me
  Oz4-W
There, I've Said It Again
  ATC2-W,M NK-W,M RoE-W,M
There Lived a King
  GiS-W,M MGT-W,M
There Lives a God
  JS-W,M (Hebrew)
There Must Be a Way
  MF-W,M
There Must Be Something Wrong
  AL-W
There on the Bridge at Avignon
  CFS-W,M (French)
There Once Was a Young Man
  Who Went to the City
  TO-W,M
There Sat a Little Ant
  SiR-W,M
There Shall Be Showers of
  Blessing
  AME-W,M GH-W,M
There She Blows
  SA-W,M
There She Goes
  OnT6-W,M
There She Stands, a Lovely
  Creature
  OTJ-W,M
There Stands a Lady on a
  Mountain
  OTJ-W,M
There They Sit and I'm Sick of It
  SYB-W,M
There Was a Crooked Man
  RSL-W,M SOO-W,M
There Was a Jolly Miller

CSG-W,M OH-W,M
There Was a Lady
  SCa-W,M
There Was a Lady and a Lady Was
  She
  SCa-W,M
There Was a Little Hen
  GI-W GO-W TMA-W,M
There Was a Little Man
  OTJ-W,M
There Was a Little Man and He
  Had a Little Gun
  OTJ-W,M
There Was a Little Turtle
  AST-W,M
There Was a Man and He Was
  Mad
  HSA-W,M OTJ-W,M
There Was a Pig
  GBC-W,M
There Was a Rich Englishman
  TBF-W
There Was a Romish Lady
  SCa-W
**There Was a Sea Captain see Sea
Captain and the Squire**
There Was a Time
  ESU-W FHR-W,M MGT-W,M
  RBO-W,M
There Was a Tree Stood in the
  Ground
  OTJ-W,M
There Was a Young Lady
  SCa-W,M
There Was a Young Lady from
  Niger
  VA-W,M
There Was an Old Farmer
  TBF-W,M
There Was an Old Frog
  AFS-W,M Oz2-W,M
There Was an Old Jaynor
  Oz1-W
There Was an Old Lady of Steen
  VA-W,M
There Was an Old Man
  SCa-W
There Was an Old Miller
  Oz1-W,M
There Was an Old Soldier
  FW-W
There Was an Old Witch
  HSA-W,M
There Was an Old Woman
  FoM-W,M FoS-W,M MSH-W,M
  OTJ-W,M
There Was an Old Woman (and
  She Had a Little Pig)
  OTJ-W,M
There Was an Old Woman Who
  Lived in a Shoe
  OTJ-W,M
There Was Once a Little Ship
  SMY-W,M
There Was Three Cooks in
  Colebrook
  Boo-W,M
There Were Ten Virgins
  RF-W,M
There Were Three Crows
  HSD-W,M
There Were Two Swiss
  CA-W,M
There Will Be One Vacant Chair
  Oz2-W
There Will Never Be Another You
  Mo-W,M NM-W,M OTO-W

RDT-W,M TI2-W,M
There'll Be a Hot Time in the Old
  Town Tonight
  MF-W,M OTJ-W,M TI1-W,M
  UFB-W,M
**There'll Be a Hot Time in the Old
Town Tonight see also Hot Time
in the Old Town**
There'll Be Mournin' in the Mornin'
  Mo-W,M NM-W,M
There'll Be Other Times
  Mo-W,M NM-W,M
There'll Be Peace in the Valley for
  Me
  GrG-W,M
**There'll Be Peace in the Valley for
Me see also Peace in the Valley**
There'll Be Some Changes Made
  BeL-W,M TI2-W,M
There'll Be Time
  MLS-W,M
There'll Be Trouble
  SSA-W,M
There'll Come a Time Someday
  CCS-W,M
There's a Better Day A-Coming
  WN-W,M
There's a Boat Dat's Leavin' Soon
  for New York
  LSO-W OTO-W TW-W UBF-W,M
There's a Broken Heart for Every
  Light on Broadway
  HLS1-W,M RW-W,M
There's a Dear Vacant Chair by the
  Hearthstone
  SiS-W
There's a Good Time Coming
  FHR-W,M
There's a Good Time Coming,
  Boys
  ESU-W
There's a Great Big Beautiful
  Tomorrow
  SBS-W,M
There's a Great Day Coming
  Manana
  UBF-W,M
There's a Hill beyond a Hill
  L-W MA-W,M TW-W
There's a Hole in the Bottom of
  the Sea
  GO-W RW-W,M
There's a Hole in the Middle of the
  Sea
  OTJ-W,M
There's a Kind of Hush (All over
  the World)
  MCG-W,M RYT-W,M
There's a Land of Bliss
  FHR-W,M
There's a Land That Is Fairer Than
  Day
  AHO-W,M AME-W,M
There's a Light
  GH-W,M
There's a Little Bit of Everything in
  Texas
  OGC2-W,M
There's a Little Box of Pine on the
  7:29
  LSR-W,M
There's a Little Bunny
  SOO-W,M
There's a Little Spark of Love Still
  Burning
  BH-W,M
There's a Little Wheel A-Turnin' in

My Heart see Dere's a Little Wheel A-Turnin' in My Heart
There's a Long, Long Trail
Bo-W OS-W
There's a Lull in My Life
GSO-W,M
There's a Man Goin' Round Takin' Names
FN-W,M FW-W Le-W,M
MoM-W,M
There's a Meetin' Here Tonight
CEM-W,M RF-W,M
There's a Mighty War in Heaven see Dere's a Mighty War in de Hebben
There's a New Girl in Town
TVT-W,M
There's a New Moon over My Shoulder
JD-W,M
There's a Place
BBe-W,M BR-W,M OPS-W,M
TWS-W
There's a Rainbow round My Shoulders
TI1-W,M UFB-W,M
There's a Room in My House
OTO-W
There's a Small Hotel
DBC-W,M DJ-W,M FrS-W,M
HC1-W,M LM-W,M OTO-W
RT4-W,M RW-W,M TI1-W,M
TS-W TW-W UBF-W,M UFB-W,M
There's a Song in the Air
CSF-W Hy-W,M
There's a Spirit Abroad
AL-W
There's a Tavern in the Town
LH-W,M UFB-W,M
There's a Tavern in the Town see also Tavern in the Town and There Is a Tavern in the Town
There's a Union in the Heaven Where I Belong
NSS-W
There's a Wideness in God's Mercy
AME-W,M GH-W,M Hy-W,M
OM-W,M
There's a Work for Each
GH-W,M
There's Always Something There to Remind Me see Always Something There to Remind Me
There's an Empty Cot in the Bunkhouse Tonight
HWS-W,M
There's Been a Change in Me
OGC2-W,M
There's Ever a Song
FSA2-W,M
There's Gotta Be Something Better Than This
MF-W,M SC-W,M
There's Life in the Old Land Yet
SiS-W,M
There's Many a Rest
GrM-W,M
There's Music in the Air
ATS-W BMC-W,M HSD-W,M
NAS-W,M RW-W,M
There's No Hiding Place Down There
MuM-W,M
There's No One Cares for Me
Oz4-W,M
There's No One Like Jesus see

Dere's No One Lak Jesus
There's No Rain to Wet You see Dere's No Rain to Wet You
There's No Reason in the World
Mo-W,M NM-W,M OTO-W
There's No Substitute for You
TOC83-W,M
There's No Such Thing As Love
ILT-W,M
There's No Tomorrow
TI2-W,M
There's No Tune Like a Show Tune
Mo-W,M NM-W,M OTO-W
There's No Wings on My Angel
OGC1-W,M
There's No You
MF-W,M
There's None to Soothe
F3-W,M
There's Not a Bird with Lonely Nest
AME-W,M
There's Nothing Like a Model T
Mo-W,M NM-W,M
There's Nothing Like Marriage for People
LSO-W
There's Nothing Like the Face of a Kid Eating a Hershey Bar
TI1-W,M UFB-W,M
There's Nothing True but Heaven
ATS-W
There's Nowhere to Go but Up
KH-W,M
There's Someone in My Fancy see Il Est Quelqu'un Sur Terre
There's Someone to Help You
BSG-W,M BSP-W,M CEM-W,M
FS-W,M MF-W,M
There's Something about a Boy Scout
Bo-W,M
There's Something about a Hometown Band
TI1-W,M UFB-W,M
There's Something about a Soldier
U-W
There's Something about That Name
BSG-W,M BSP-W,M FS-W,M
There's Something Funny Going On
TOM-W,M
There's Something Greater
OTO-W
There's Something in the Name of Ireland
RW-W,M
There's Sunshine in My Soul To-day
AME-W,M
There's the Girl
BHO-W,M
There's Yes! Yes! in Your Eyes
MF-W,M RoE-W,M
Therezina
LA-W,M (Spanish)
These All Are My Father's Children see Dese All Er Ma Father's Chillun
These Are the Best Times
NI-W,M OTO-W
These Are the Cries of London Town
Boo-W,M
These Are They Which Came
FiS-W,M

These Bones see Dese Bones
These Boots Are Made for Walkin'
TI1-W,M UFB-W,M
These Charming People
LSO-W
These Dreams
JC-W,M PM-W,M TTH-W,M
These Foolish Things (Remind Me of You)
BeL-W,M FPS-W,M ILT-W,M
RoE-W,M TI1-W,M UFB-W,M
These Hands
OGC1-W,M RDF-W,M
These Old Cumberland Mountain Farms
AFP-W
These Temperance Folks
Oz2-W,M
These Things I Offer You (for a Lifetime)
MF-W,M
These Things Shall Be
SWF-W,M
These Things Shall Be, a Loftier Race
AME-W,M
These Things Shall Pass
RDF-W,M
These Years
Mo-W,M
They... see also Dey...
They All Came Home but Mine
SiS-W
They All Laughed
FrS-W,M HC2-W,M HFH-W,M
LSO-W NYT-W,M OTO-W
TI1-W,M UFB-W,M
They All Love Jack
HSD-W,M
They Always Pick on Me
LWT-W,M
They Are Coming from the Wars
SiS-W
They Are Making a Machine in California
TW-W
They Buried Him in a Watery Grave
SiS-W
They Call Me Drunken Roarer
ESU-W
They Call the Wind Maria
DBC-W,M HC1-W,M LL-W,M
OTJ-W,M RW-W,M TI1-W,M
TW-W UBF-W,M UFB-W,M
They Can't Take That Away from Me
DJ-W,M FrS-W,M HC2-W,M
ILT-W,M LM-W,M LSO-W
NYT-W,M OTO-W TI1-W,M
UFB-W,M
They Cast Their Nets in Galilee
AHO-W,M Hy-W,M JF-W,M
They Crucified Him
GH-W,M
They Didn't Believe Me
HLS8-W,M OAP-W,M TI1-W,M
SLB-W,M UFB-W,M
They Don't Make Love Like They Used To
ATC1-W,M CSp-W,M
They Go Wild over Me
SFF-W,M
They Have a Camp Meeting see Dey Hab a Camp Meetin'
They Have Broken Up Their Camps
SiS-W
They Hung Him on a Cross

Le-W,M
They Just Can't Stop It
DDH-W,M
**They Long to Be Close to You see
Close to You**
They Look Like Men of War
RF-W,M WN-W,M
They March, They March
Boo-W,M
They Nail Him to the Cross
NH-W
They Never Lost You
TOH-W,M
They Pray for Us at Home
SiS-W
They Pray the Best Who Pray and
Watch
AHO-W,M
They Put Me Up to Kill Him
Oz2-W
**They Said We Wouldn't Fight see
Dey Said We Wouldn't Fight**
They Say the Goblet's Crowned
with Flowers
ESU-W
They Sleep in a Lonely Southern
Grave
SiS-W
They Sleep in the South
SiS-W
They Steal Gossip
NF-W
They That Be Wise
GH-W,M
They Told Me Not to Love Him
ESU-W
They Were Doin' the Mambo
Mo-W,M NM-W,M TI2-W,M
They Were You
Fa-W,M OTO-W TI2-W,M TW-W
UBF-W,M
They'll Know We Are Christians by
Our Love
BSG-W,M BSP-W,M
They'll Never Split Us Apart
Mo-W,M OTO-W
They're Either Too Young or Too
Old
MF-W,M
They're Holding Up the Ladder
AG-W,M
They're Laying Eggs Now
OTJ-W,M
They're Moving Father's Grave
FW-W
They're Moving Father's Grave to
Build a Sewer
PO-W,M
They're Playing My Song
TI1-W,M TP-W,M UBF-W,M
UFB-W,M
They've Got an Awful Lot of
Coffee in Brazil
TI1-W,M UFB-W,M
Thick As a Brick Edit #1
BJ-W,M
Thick As a Brick Edit #4
BJ-W,M
**Thicker Than Water see Love Is
Thicker Than Water**
Thief
ASB4-W,M
Thief's Arm
MSB-W
Thieves and Stealin'
AL-W
Thine Alone

E-W,M
Thine Arm, O Lord, in Days of Old
Hy-W,M
Thine Eyes So Blue and Tender
AmH-W,M WiS8-W,M
Thine For Ever, God of Love
SJ-W
Thine Is the Glory
Hy-W,M
Thine, Jesus, Thine
GH-W,M
Thine Own
AmH-M
Thing, The
AF-W MF-W,M
Thing Called Love
EP-W,M
Things
TI2-W,M
Things About Comin' My Way
FW-W RW-W,M
Things Ain't the Same Babe, Since
I Went 'Way
NH-W
Things Are Looking Up
LSO-W OTO-W
Things Are Seldom What They
Seem
GiS-W,M MGT-W,M
Things Are So Slow
DBL-W
**Things Are Tough All Over
(Theme) see Chilly Winds (of
Chicago)**
Things Aren't Funny Anymore
NMH-W,M
Things Go Better with Coke
GSM-W,M
Things I Don't Like to See
MSB-W
Things I Like
MH-W,M
Things I Love
OnT1-W,M
Things I Might Have Been
SBS-W,M
Things I Should Have Said
OnT6-W,M
Things I'd Like to Say
OTO-W
Things in Life
BSo-W,M
Things Lovelier
EL-W,M
Things That They Must Not Do
YL-W,M
Things to Eat
ASB2-W,M
Things We Did Last Summer
DJ-W,M MF-W,M RoE-W,M
TI1-W,M UFB-W,M
Things We Said Today
BBe-W,M Be1-W,M OnT6-W,M
TWS-W
Things Women Do
IL-W,M
Think
RoS-W,M
Think and Smoke Tobacco
OHG-W,M
Think Beautiful
Mo-W,M NM-W,M OTO-W
Think Big
VB-W,M
Think for Yourself
TWS-W
Think How It's Gonna Be

Ap-W,M Mo-W,M OTO-W
VSA-W,M
Think Not When You Gather to
Zion
AHO-W,M
Think of Laura
BCC-W,M
Think of Me
UBF-W,M
Think of the Good Times
Mo-W,M
Think of What You've Done
BIS-W,M BSo-W,M
Think of Your Head in the Morning
SCo-W,M Sin-W,M
Think Spring
Mo-W,M OTO-W
Thinkin' about Home
AG-W,M VB-W,M
Thinking of You
MF-W,M WDS-W,M
Thinnest Man I Ever Saw
TMA-W,M
Third Cavalry Song
GI-W
Third Man Theme
OTO-W TI1-W,M
Thirsty Boots
JF-W,M
Thirsty Butterfly
MH-W,M
Thirteen Colonies
TW-W
Thirty Cents a Day
AL-W
Thirty Days (to Come Back Home)
HR-W
Thirty Days Hath September
Boo-W,M TI1-W,M UFB-W,M
Thirty-Foot Trailer
IFM-W
Thirty Pieces of Silver
HLS7-W,M
Thirty-Two Feet and Eight Little
Tails
RW-W,M
Thirty Years Ago
BMM-W
This and No More
Mo-W,M
This Be de Way
GB-W,M
This Bird Has Flown
Be1-W,M TWS-W WG-W,M
This Bitter Earth
MF-W,M
This Boy
BBe-W,M Be1-W,M TWS-W
WG-W,M
This Can't Be Love
DBC-W,M HC1-W,M LM-W,M
OTO-W TI1-W,M TS-W UBF-W,M
UFB-W,M
This Could Be the Last Time
RoS-W,M
This Could Be the Start of
Something (Tonight Show with
Steve Allen Theme)
TVT-W,M
This Could Be the Start of
Something Big
NK-W,M
This Diamond Ring
PoG-W,M
This Endless Night
OB-W,M
This Endris Night

GBC-W,M
This Flock So Small
  AHO-W,M (German)
This Flower see Dis Flower
This Funny World
  TS-W
This Galloping, Galloping Joan
  Boo-W,M
This Girl
  Fa-W,M
This Girl Is a Woman Now
  ILT-W,M
This Guy's in Love with You
  BDF-W,M GOI7-W,M HD-W,M
  ILT-W,M MF-W,M RDT-W,M
This Hammer
  AN-W
This House
  I-W,M
This I Know
  GH-W,M
This I Promise You
  TI2-W,M
This Is a Very Special Day
  HFH-W,M
This Is All I Ask
  BeL-W,M HLS3-W,M TI1-W,M
  UFB-W,M
This Is All Very New to Me
  PF-W,M TW-W
This Is Always
  MF-W,M
This Is How It Feels see Twin Soliloquies
This Is How It Is
  SP-W,M
This Is It! (Bugs Bunny Show Theme)
  MF-W,M TVT-W,M
This Is My Country
  AAP-W,M BSG-W,M BSP-W,M
  FWS-W,M MAS-W,M RDF-W,M
  SiB-W,M TI2-W,M YS-W,M
This Is My Father's World
  AHO-W,M HS-W,M Hy-W,M
  SiB-W,M
This Is My Heaven
  SRE2-W,M
This Is My Holiday
  LL-W,M
This Is My Life
  RW-W,M
This Is My Little House
  OTJ-W,M
This Is My Prayer
  SS-W
This Is My Song
  TI2-W,M
This Is New
  LD-W,M LSO-W TI1-W,M
  UBF-W,M UFB-W,M
This Is No' My Ain Hoose
  IFM-W
This Is One Canon
  Boo-W,M
This Is Our Church
  SHP-W,M
This Is Our Prayer, Dear God
  SHP-W,M
This Is That Time of the Year
  Mo-W,M
This Is the Church
  FP-W,M
This Is the Day
  VB-W,M
This Is the Day of Light
  Hy-W,M

This Is the Day the Lord Hath Made
  AME-W,M Hy-W,M
This Is the Day Which the Lord Has Made
  SHP-W,M
This Is the Girl I Love
  BSo-W,M
This Is the House That Jack Built
  MHB-W,M
This Is the L&M Moment
  GSM-W,M
This Is the Life
  Mo-W,M NM-W,M OTO-W
  SLB-W,M
This Is the Thanks I Get
  OGC1-W,M
This Is the Time
  TTH-W,M
This Is the Truth
  GBC-W,M
This Is the Way see This Be de Way
This Is the Way the Ploughboy Goes
  Boo-W,M
This Land Is Your Land
  BMC-W,M Bo-W FG1-W,M
  GuC-W,M HA-W,M JF-W,M
  MF-W,M MG-W,M RDF-W,M
  TI1-W,M TWD-W,M UFB-W,M
  VS-W,M WSB-W,M
This Little Boy
  FP-W,M
This Little Land
  JF-W
This Little Light
  JF-W,M
This Little Light of Mine
  FGM-W,M FW-W RDF-W,M
  SFF-W,M
This Little Pig Went to Market
  AST-W,M OTJ-W,M
This Love of Mine
  MF-W,M OnT1-W,M RoE-W,M
  TI1-W,M UFB-W,M
This Loveliness
  VA-W,M
This Magic Moment
  HRB4-W,M
This Masquerade
  GrS-W,M ToO76-W,M
This May Be the Last Time
  SFF-W,M
This Moment in Time
  ToO79-W,M
This Mornin' This Evenin' So Soon
  NH-W
This Mornin' This Evenin' So Soon see also Dis Mornin' Dis Evenin' So Soon
This Must Be the Lamb
  VB-W,M
This Nearly Was Mine
  HC2-W,M OTJ-W,M OTO-W
  SP-W,M TI1-W,M UBF-W,M
  UFB-W,M
This New Christmas Carol
  OB-W,M
This New Day
  AHO-W,M
This Night Won't Last Forever
  ToO79-W,M
This Ol' Hammer
  VA-W,M
This Old Guitar
  CJ-W,M

This Old Hammer
  RSW-W,M
This Old Life
  DBL-W
This Old Man
  FBI-W,M FW-W GG1-W,M
  HS-W,M MAR-W,M MES2-W,M
  MF-W,M MG-W,M OTJ-W,M
  RW-W,M SMa-W,M SOO-W,M
  TI1-W,M UFB-W,M
This Old Religion
  BPM-W,M
This Old World's A-Rollin'
  NH-W
This Ole World's a Hell to Me
  NH-W
This One's for You
  TOF-W,M
This Plum Is Too Ripe
  Fa-W,M
This Quiet Room
  MLS-W,M
This Rose Will Remind You
  FHR-W,M
This Sporting Life
  ATC2-W,M
This Sun Is Hot
  NF-W
This Then Is Texas see Giant
This Time
  BOA-W,M
This Time of the Year
  FR-W,M
This Time the Dream's on Me
  MF-W,M
This Train
  FGM-W,M FW-W GuC-W,M
  LSR-W,M OFS-W,M OTJ-W,M
  RDF-W,M RW-W,M SBF-W,M
This Was a Real Nice Clambake
  L-W
This Way and That
  PIS-W,M
This Way, Valerie
  MAR-W,M
This Will Be (an Everlasting Love)
  DP-W,M SoH-W,M TI1-W,M
  UFB-W,M
This Woman
  TI2-W,M
This World
  OTO-W UBF-W,M
This World Is Not My Home
  HHa-W,M SHS-W,M
Tho' the Clouds May Hover o'er Us
  AME-W,M
Tho' Your Sins Be As Scarlet
  AME-W,M
Thomas Crown Affair (Theme) see Windmills of Your Mind
Thomas Jefferson
  ATS-W
Thorn Birds Theme
  DC-M MF-M TVT-M
Thorny Desert
  SHS-W,M
Thoroughly Modern Millie
  TI2-W,M
Those Dirty Mechanics
  AL-W
Those Evening Bells
  Boo-W,M FSA1-W,M HSD-W,M
  NAS-W,M SL-W,M
Those Fat Monkeys
  PAJ-W,M
Those Lazy-Hazy-Crazy Days of

Summer
WG-W,M

Those Low Down Shuffle Blues
LSB-W,M

Those Magic Changes
Gr-W,M Mo-W,M OTO-W

Those Pals of Ours
SL-W,M

Those Prison Blues
LC-W

Those Sabbath Chimes
SiS-W

Those Swinging Doors
AF-W

Those Wedding Bells Shall Not
Ring Out
FSN-W,M Oz4-W

Those Were the Days
FPS-W,M MF-W,M TI1-W,M
TOC83-W,M TV-W,M TWD-W,M
UFB-W,M

Those Who Sow in Sorrow
JF-W,M

Those Who Wish to Eat Some Hare
FSO-W,M (French)

Thou Art Coming
GH-W,M

Thou Art Gone to the Grave
SHS-W,M

Thou Art My Portion, O My God
AME-W,M

Thou Art, O God, the God of Might
AHO-W,M

Thou Art Passing Away
SHS-W,M

Thou Art So Like a Flower
FSY-W,M (German) WGB/O-W,M

**Thou Art So Like a Flower see also
Thou'rt Like a Lovely Flower
(Schumann)**

Thou Art the Queen of My Song
FHR-W,M

Thou Art the Tree of Life
AHO-W,M

Thou Art the Way
AHO-W,M

Thou Art the Way: To Thee Alone
Hy-W,M

Thou Cans't Not Hit It
SSP-W

Thou Didst Leave Thy Throne
AME-W,M Hy-W,M SJ-W,M

Thou Gentle Flower
TH-W,M

Thou Grace Divine, Encircling All
AHO-W,M

Thou Great Jehovah
MAS-W,M

Thou Hast Been Our Guide This
Day
AME-W,M

Thou Hast Learned to Love
Another
BSC-W

Thou Hidden Source of Calm
Repose
AME-W,M Hy-W,M

Thou Long Disowned, Reviled,
Oppressed
AHO-W,M

Thou, Lord Art Love, and
Everywhere
AME-W,M

Thou, Lord, Hast Been Our Sure
Defense
AHO-W,M

Thou Lord of Hosts, Whose

Guiding Hand
AHO-W,M AME-W,M

Thou Mighty God
SL-W

Thou My Everlasting Portion
AME-W,M

Thou One in All, Thou All in One
AHO-W,M

Thou Shalt Be Saved
GH-W,M

Thou Swell
DBC-W,M HC1-W,M MF-W,M
OHB-W,M TS-W

Thou Thinkest Lord of Me
AME-W,M

Though Fatherland Be Vast
AHO-W,M

Though I Am Young
EL-W,M

Though I Should Seek
AHO-W,M

Though Love Be Blind
SOT-W,M

Though My Thoughts
AHO-W,M (German)

**Though the Clouds May Hover o'er
Us see Tho' the Clouds May
Hover o'er Us**

Though There's Time
LA-W,M (Spanish)

**Though Your Sins Be As Scarlet
see Tho' Your Sins Be As Scarlet**

Thought, The
EL-W,M

Thought I Heard That K.C. Whistle
Blow
NH-W

Thoughts
Mo-W,M OTO-W

Thoughts of a POW
AF-W

Thou'rt Like a Lovely Flower
(Schumann)
SL-W,M

**Thou'rt Like a Lovely Flower
(Schumann) see also Thou Art So
Like a Flower**

Thou'rt Like unto a Flower (Liszt)
SL-W,M

Thou'rt Like unto a Flower
(Rubinstein)
SL-W,M

Thousand Good Nights
WDS-W,M

Thousand Islands Song
Mo-W,M NM-W,M

Thousand Leagues Away
HSD-W,M

Thousand Miles Away
ILF-W,M RY-W,M RYT-W,M

Thousand Miles from Home
FHR-W,M

Thousand Miles from Nowhere
LC-W

Thousand Violins
OTO-W

Thousands of Miles
LS-W,M TW-W

Thracian Horse Music
GSM-M

Threading the Needle
FMT-W

Three
ASB5-W,M TT-W,M

Three Angels Sang a Song
MMW-W,M

Three Bears

Mo-W,M NM-W,M OTJ-W,M

Three Bells
ATS-W,M HR-W

Three Billy Goats Gruff
SOO-W,M

Three Black Crows
BSC-W

Three Blind Mice
BM-W Bo-W,M Boo-W,M
CA-W,M FW-W HS-W,M
HSD-W,M OTJ-W,M RW-W,M
SiR-W,M SMa-W,M TH-W,M

Three Blind Mice, Dame Juliane
Boo-W,M

Three Blind Mice They Ran Around
Thrice
Boo-W,M

Three Blue Pigeons
GM-W,M HS-W,M

Three Brothers from Old Scotland
ITP-W

Three Bulls and a Bear
Boo-W,M

Three Butchers
MSB-W

Three Cheers for Abe and Andy
SiS-W

Three Cheers for Our Jack Morgan
SiS-W

Three Children Sliding
SL-W,M

Three Coins in a Fountain
GSN3-W,M

Three Coins in the Fountain
FrS-W,M GG4-W,M HLS5-W,M
MF-W,M RT5-W,M RW-W,M

Three Crows
Oz1-W,M TMA-W,M

Three Daughters
SMa-W,M

Three Doves
FSA1-W,M

Three Drovers
ATM-W,M

Three Drummers
UF-W,M

Three Fishermen
IL-W,M

Three Fishers
AmH-W,M

Three Fishers Went Sailing
HSD-W,M WiS8-W,M

Three-Four Go Left, Right
OHO-W,M

Three Funny Old Men
GM-W,M

Three Geese in Halberstoe
Boo-W,M

Three Grains of Corn
FMT-W SCa-W,M

Three Gypsies
SCa-W,M

Three Holy Women
UF-W,M

Three Horsemen
SMa-W,M TH-W,M

Three Jolly Fishermen
Bo-W,M

Three Jolly Welshmen
AFS-W,M BSC-W

Three Kings
FSA2-W,M MML-W,M MU-W,M
OB-W,M

Three Kings of Orient
LMR-W,M SL-W,M TF-W,M

Three Knights from Spain
CSG-W,M

Three Lil' Piggies
OHO-W,M
Three Little Babes
FMT-W FoM-W,M Oz1-W,M
Three Little Ducks
RSL-W,M
Three Little Fishies
NoS-W,M TI1-W,M UFB-W,M
Three Little Girls
HS-W,M SCL-W,M
Three Little Girls A-Skating Went
Oz3-W
Three Little Girls in Blue (Theme)
see You Make Me Feel So Young
Three Little Kittens
ASB1-W,M GM-W,M HSD-W,M
MH-W,M OTJ-W,M
Three Little Maids from School
MGT-W,M OTJ-W,M
Three Little Maids from School Are
We
GiS-W,M SL-W,M
Three Little Piggies see Three Li'l
Piggies
Three Little Pigs
HSD-W,M OTJ-W,M
Three Little Puffins
SSe-W,M
Three Little Tailors
SL-W,M
Three Little Words
Boo-W,M MF-W,M
Three Loves
SN-W,M
Three Merry Men
SSP-W
Three Merry Men We Are
FSS-W,M
Three Merry Travellers
SR-W,M
Three Mice Went into a Hole to
Spin
OTJ-W,M
Three Nights' Experience
FVV-W,M ITP-W,M SCa-W,M
Three Nights of Experience
SCa-W,M
Three O'Clock in the Morning
GSN2-W,M GST-W,M HLS2-W,M
OP1-W,M RDT-W,M RW-W,M
Three Old Crows
SCa-W
Three Old Maids on a Saucer Brim
Oz1-W
Three Pirates
SMY-W,M UF-W,M VA-W,M
Three Quarter Blues
Mo-W,M
Three Ravens
BSC-W,M BT-W,M FMT-W
FoM-W,M FW-W OH-W,M SSP-W
Three Red Apples
AST-W,M
Three Rogues
BSC-W
Three Rousing Cheers
MHB-W,M (German)
Three Sailor Boys
HSD-W,M
Three Score and Ten
BB-W
Three Score o' Nobles Rade up the
King's Ha'
SeS-W,M
Three Scrooges
CSB-W,M
Three Ships Came Sailing By

FSU-W
Three Sons
SL-W,M
Three Stars Will Shine Tonight
GTV-W,M
Three Times a Day
GOB-W,M
Three Toads
FSA2-W,M
Three Traitors
OB-W,M
Three Village Boys
SoF-W,M
Three-Way Cannon Blues
SBF-W,M
Three White Doves
BMC-W,M
Three Wise Old Women
Oz1-W
Three Wood Pigeons
Bo-W,M
Three's Company
PoG-W,M WG-W,M
Threnody
SL-W,M
Thresher Disaster
RBO-W,M
Thrice Blest the Man
AHO-W,M
Thrice Welcome First and Best of
Days
AHO-W,M
Thrifty Slave
NF-W
Thrill Is Gone
HC2-W,M MF-W,M OTO-W
TI1-W,M ToS-W,M UBF-W,M
UFB-W,M
Thro' All the Changing Scenes of
Life
AME-W,M
Thro' Love to Light
AME-W,M
Throned upon the Awful Tree
Hy-W,M
Throttle Bender
AF-W
Through a Long and Sleepless
Night
GSF-W,M
Through All the Changing Scenes
of Life see Thro' All the Changing
Scenes of Life
Through His Eyes of Love
TOM-W,M VB-W,M
Through Love to Light see Thro'
Love to Light
Through the Bitter Land
JF-W,M
Through the Dark the Dreamers
Came
AHO-W,M
Through the Eyes of Love see Ice
Castles (Theme)
Through the Leaves see Serenade
(Schubert)
Through the Lonely Nights
RoS-W,M
Through the Night of Doubt and
Sorrow
Hy-W,M SJ-W,M
Through the Valley
GH-W,M
Through the Years
CoH-W,M FOC-W,M TI2-W,M
TW-W
Through Warmth and Light of

Summer Skies
AHO-W,M
Through Willing Heart and Helping
Hand
AHO-W,M
Throw a Saddle on a Star
OGC1-W,M
Throw Another Log on the Fire
CS-W,M
Throw Her in High
ReG-W,M
Throw Him Down, McCloskey
ATS-W EFS-W,M FSN-W,M
FSTS-W,M
Throw It out the Window
Bo-W,M RSL-W,M
Throw Me Anywhere, Lord
SFF-W,M
Throw Me the Keys
VB-W,M
Throw Off the Workman's Burden
AL-W
Throw Out the Life-Line
AME-W,M GH-W,M
Throw Your Love My Way
OGC2-W,M
Thumbelina
TI2-W,M
Thumbin' a Ride
LC-W
Thumbs Up
GI-W
Thunder and Blazes
OTJ-M RW-M
Thunder Storm
SSe-W,M
Thunderball
RW-W,M
Thunderbird Song (Arapaho Indian)
IF-M
Thunderdome Theme see We
Don't Need Another Hero
Thunderdrums
ASB6-W,M
Thunderer
MF-M
Thursday
JC-W,M
Thus Saith the High, the Lofty One
EA-W,M
Thus Spake the Saviour
AHO-W,M
Thus Speaketh the Lord of Hosts
CCH-W,M
Thy Cheek Is o' the Rose's Hue
SeS-W,M
Thy Kingdom Come, O Lord
Hy-W,M
Thy Kingdom Come, on Bended
Knee
Hy-W,M
Thy Life Was Given for Me
Hy-W,M
Thy Little Ones, Dear Lord, Are We
CCM-W,M SJ-W,M
Thy Love for Me
WGB/P-W,M
Thy Loving Kindness, Lord, I Sing
AHO-W,M
Thy Loving Kindness, Lord, Is
Good and Free
Hy-W,M
Thy Mercies, Lord, to Heaven
Reach
AHO-W,M
Thy Mercy and Thy Truth, O Lord
Hy-W,M

Tinker Polka
  PT-M TI1-M UFB-M
Tinkers' Song
  LMR-W,M WS-W,M
Tiny Bells
  AST-W,M
Tiny Bubbles
  TI1-W,M UFB-W,M
Tiny Dancer
  TI2-W,M
Tiny Man
  ASB1-W,M
Tiny Snowflakes
  ASB2-W,M
Tip and Ty
  MPP-W,M
Tip and Ty (Tippecanoe and Tyler
  Too)
  OHG-W,M
**Tip and Ty see also Tippecanoe
  and Tyler Too**
Tip of My Fingers
  TI2-W,M
Tip Toe
  MF-M
Tip-Toe March
  SoP-W,M
Tip-Toe through the Tulips
  T-W,M
Tip-Toe thru' the Tulips with Me
  MF-W,M OHB-W,M OPS-W,M
Ti-pi-tin
  CS-W,M
Tippecanoe--a Sucker Song
  ESU-W
Tippecanoe and Tyler Too
  AH-W,M ATS-W,M MPP-W
**Tippecanoe and Tyler Too see also
  Tip and Ty**
Tipperary
  U-W
Tippi Canoo
  ASB6-W,M
Tiptanks and Tailpipes
  AF-W
Tired of Me
  WDS-W,M
Ti-ri-tomba
  FSA1-W,M
Tiritomba
  UF-W,M
'Tis a Sweet and Glorious Tho't
  That Comes to Me
  AME-W,M
'Tis All That I Can Say
  HSD-W,M
'Tis Autumn
  TI1-W,M UFB-W,M
'Tis Better to Stay on the Farm
  GrM-W,M
'Tis Blithe May Day
  Boo-W,M
'Tis but a Drop
  ESU-W
'Tis but a Little Faded Flower
  HSD-W,M
'Tis Faith Supports My Feeble Soul
  AME-W,M
'Tis Finished
  MPP-W SiS-W,M
'Tis Finished! So the Savior Cried
  AME-W,M
'Tis Humdrum
  Boo-W,M
'Tis Me
  RF-W,M
'Tis Me, O Lord

NFS-W,M
**'Tis Me, O Lord see also It's A-Me
  O Lord, It's Me O Lord, and
  Standin' in the Need of Prayer**
'Tis Midnight
  GH-W,M
'Tis Midnight and on Olive's Brow
  AHO-W,M AME-W,M Hy-W,M
'Tis Midnight Hour
  HSD-W,M
'Tis Mirth That Fills the Veins with
  Blood
  GC-W,M
'Tis My Father's Song
  FHR-W,M
'Tis Not Always the Bullet That
  Kills
  Oz4-W
'Tis Not True see Non E Ver
'Tis Providence Alone Secures
  Boo-W,M
'Tis Religion That Can Give
  WN-W,M
'Tis So Sweet to Trust in Jesus
  OM-W,M
'Tis the Blessed Hour
  GH-W,M
'Tis the End
  K-W,M
'Tis the Gift to Be Simple
  AHO-W,M
'Tis the Ole Ship of Zion
  NSS-W RF-W,M
**'Tis the Ole Ship of Zion see also
  Ole Ship of Zion**
'Tis the Promise of God
  AME-W,M
'Tis the Story Grand and True
  AME-W,M
'Tis the Time o' Day
  SOT-W,M
'Tis Thus, Thus, and Thus Farewell
  Boo-W,M
'Tis Too Late for a Coach
  Boo-W,M
'Tis Winter Now
  AHO-W,M
'Tis Winter Now, the Fallen Snow
  ESB-W,M
'Tis Women
  Boo-W,M
Tishomingo Blues
  B-W,M
Tit Willow
  GiS-W,M MGT-W,M OTJ-W,M
  SL-W,M WiS8-W,M
Titanic (Huddie Ledbetter)
  Le-W,M NeF-W
Titanic, The (It Was Sad When
  That Great Ship Went Down)
  FW-W OHO-W,M OTJ-W,M
**Titanic, The (It Was Sad When
  That Great Ship Went Down) see
  also Great Titanic, Ship Titanic,
  and Sinking of the Titanic**
Titles of Songs
  Oz3-W,M
Titty Mary, You Know I Gwine
  Follow
  NSS-W
Titus Andronicus's Complaint
  SSP-W
Tivoli Bells
  Mo-M OTO-W
T'morra, T'morra
  TW-W
To a Dying Infant

ESU-W
To a Rose
  FSA2-W,M
To a Wild Rose
  RW-M SFB-W,M TM-M WGB/O-M
  WGB/P-M
To All the Girls I've Loved Before
  AWS-W,M FOC-W,M HD-W,M
To Anacreon in Heaven
  ATS-W PSN-W,M
To Anthea, Who May Command
  Him Anything
  EL-W,M
To Atocha Goes a Girl
  LA-W,M (Spanish)
**To Be a Lover see I Forgot to Be
  Your Lover**
To Be a Performer
  Mo-W,M NM-W,M OTO-W
To Be Alone with You
  Mo-W,M NM-W,M OTO-W
To Be There
  GH-W,M
To Be Young, Gifted and Black
  DP-W,M
To Bed
  FF-W
To Bethlehem
  ASB5-W,M GM-W,M
To Britain
  SBA-W
To Canaan (Song of the Six
  Hundred Thousand)
  Sin-W,M SiS-W
To Cheer the Heart
  FSU-W
To Cry You a Song
  BJ-W,M
To Each His Dulcinea
  MLM-W,M TW-W
To Each His Own
  AT-W,M OTO-W TOM-W,M
To Fairest Delia's Grassy Tomb
  OH-W,M
To Father, Son and Holy Ghost
  AME-W,M
To God My Earnest Voice I Raise
  Hy-W,M
To God Our Strength Shout
  Joyfully
  AHO-W,M
To God the Only Wise
  AME-W,M
To God Who Gives Us Daily Bread
  SHP-W,M
To Hear the Trumpet Sound
  WN-W,M
To Him Be Glory Evermore
  GH-W,M
To Jerez
  ASB5-W,M
To Keep My Love Alive
  TS-W TW-W WF-W,M
To Know You Is to Love You
  ILF-W,M TI1-W,M UFB-W,M
To Labor
  AL-W
To Lauterbach
  UF-W,M
To Life
  OTO-W TI2-W,M UBF-W,M
To London I Did Go
  FMT-W
To Look Sharp
  GSM-W,M
To Love Again
  TI1-W,M UFB-W,M

To Make a Woman Lovesick
SFM-W
To Market
ASB4-W,M MH-W,M
To Market, to Market
OTJ-W,M
To Music
FSD-W,M GeS-W,M
To My Humble Supplication
Hy-W,M
To My Lute
LMR-W,M
To My Piano
LMR-W,M
To My Wife
TW-W
To Our Alma Mater
MU-W,M
To Our Ladies
SBA-W
To Our Musical Club
Boo-W,M
To Paradise We'll Gaily Trip
BP-W,M
To Play on the Golden Harp
WN-W,M
To Puerto Rico
MES2-W,M
To Push the Bus'ness On
PIS-W,M
To Shallow Rivers
SSP-W
To Shorten Winter's Sadness
LMR-W,M
To Show How Humble
AHO-W,M
To Sir, with Love
BHB-W,M DPE-W,M ERM-W,M
EY-W,M GAR-W,M HFH-W,M
MF-W,M TOM-W,M
To Spring
TH-W,M
To the Aisle
EB-W
To the Center
GM-W,M
To the Commons
SBA-W SI-W,M
To the Door I Strolled
UF-W,M
To the Ends of the Earth
NK-W,M
To the Evening Star
MM-W,M OTJ-W,M TM-W,M
WGB/O-W,M WGB/P-W,M
To the Greenwood Tree
MML-W,M
To the Home of My Beloved
MHB-W,M (Greek)
To the Ladies
SI-W,M
To the Lake Squadrons
ANS-W
To the Moon
AmH-M ASB6-W,M
To the Polls
AL-W
To the Praise of His Glorious Grace
OGR-W,M VB-W,M
To the Proletarian
AL-W
To the Regulars
AF-W
To the Rose
MML-W,M
To the Sunshine
MHB-W,M (German)

To the Toilers
AL-W
To the Traitor Arnold
SBA-W
To the Troops in Boston
SSS-W,M
To the Waltz
RW-M
To the West
SY-W,M
To the West Awhile to Stay
Oz2-W,M
To the Women Workers
AL-W
To the Woods, My Ladies
FSO-W,M (French)
To the Work
GH-W,M
To the Work! to the Work!
AME-W,M
To the Worker
AL-W
To the Workingmen
AL-W
To Thee Above (Pesach Hymn)
JS-W,M
To Thee and to a Maid
Boo-W,M
To Thee, Eternal Soul, Be Praise
AHO-W,M
To Thee Forever
UF-W,M
To Thee I Come
GH-W,M
To Thee My Righteous King and
Lord
AME-W,M
To Thee, O Country
TF-W,M
To Thee, O God
AHO-W,M
To Thee, O God, the Shepherd
Kings
AHO-W,M
To Thee, O Lord, the God of All
SJ-W,M
To Thee the Tuneful Anthem Soars
AHO-W,M
To Thee, Then, Let All Beings
Bend
AHO-W,M
To Thee 'Tis Given to Live
Boo-W,M
To Thine Eternal Arms, O God
AHO-W,M AME-W,M
To Think You've Chosen Me
MF-W,M
To Troldhaugen
SN-W,M
To War
KH-W,M
To War Has Gone Duke
Marlborough
NAS-W,M
**To War Has Gone Duke
Marlborough see also Malbrouk to
War Is Going**
To War We Must Go
FSO-W,M (French)
To Win a Yellow Girl
NF-W
To You (Zueignung)
FSY-W,M (German)
**To You (Zueignung) see also
Dedication (Von Wilm/Strauss)**
Toad
ASB1-W,M

Toast
GI-W
Toast, A (Francis Hopkinson)
AH-W,M EA-W,M MML-W,M
MPP-W,M SI-W,M
**Toast, A (Francis Hopkinson) see
also Toast to General Washington
and Toast to Washington**
Toast, A (Stevens/Ames)
LMR-W,M
Toast for Labor
AL-W
Toast to General Washington
GeS-W,M
**Toast to General Washington see
also Toast, A (Francis Hopkinson)**
Toast to L.S.U.
SLS-W,M
Toast to Washington
SAR-W,M
**Toast to Washington see also
Toast, A (Francis Hopkinson)**
Toast to Woman's Eyes
BP-W,M
Tobacco Road
RB-W TRR-W,M
Tobacco Union
Oz3-W,M
Tock Tick Tock, Dear Old Maizel
Boo-W,M
Tocowa
FMT-W
**Tod Und Das Madchen see Der
Tod Und Das Madchen**
Today (Evening Song)
GrG-W,M
Today (While the Blossoms Still
Cling to the Vine)
HLS5-W,M HLS7-W,M RT6-W,M
RW-W,M STW-W,M
Today beneath Benignant Skies
AHO-W,M
Today, I Love Ev'rybody
Mo-W,M NM-W,M OTO-W
Today I Started Loving You Again
CMG-W,M N-W,M
Today Is a Day for a Band to Play
Mo-W,M NM-W,M OTJ-W,M
OTO-W
Today Is Monday
ATS-W GO-W,M
To-day the Saviour Calls
AME-W,M GH-W,M
Today, Tomorrow and Forever
SRE1-W,M
Today's a Wonderful Day
Mo-W,M NM-W,M OTO-W
Together
HC2-W,M TI1-W,M UBF-W,M
UFB-W,M
Together (Theme from Silver
Spoons)
TV-W,M
Together Again
CSp-W,M
Together Forever
I-W,M UBF-W,M
Together Wherever We Go
HC1-W,M OTO-W TI1-W,M
UBF-W,M UFB-W,M
Toiler's National Anthem
AL-W
Toilers of Men
AL-W
Toiling On
AME-W,M
Tokay

BS-W,M
Token see Young Willie's Return
Tokyo Fireball
  AF-W
Toll de Bell Angel, I Jus' Got Over
  Me-W,M
Toll the Bell Mournfully
  SiS-W
**Tolliver Song see Rowan County
  Crew**
Tom and Doll
  SR-W,M
Tom Bolynn
  SoF-W,M
Tom Bowling
  HSD-W,M OH-W,M OTJ-W,M
Tom Brown
  FW-W
Tom Cat Blues
  FW-W
Tom Dooley
  FAW-W,M FW-W GuC-W,M
  IHA-W,M IPH-W,M MF-W,M
  OTJ-W,M PSN-W,M RW-W,M
  TI1-W,M TWD-W,M UFB-W,M
**Tom Dooley see also Hang Down
  Your Head Tom Dooley**
Tom Joad
  AFP-W,M Am-W,M
Tom Redman
  SCa-W,M
Tom Tackle
  HAS-W,M
Tom Tinker's My True Love
  SR-W,M
Tom, Tom, the Piper's Son
  GM-W,M IHA-W,M OTJ-W,M
  SiR-W,M
Tom-big-bee River
  HSD-W,M
Tommy Atkins
  Fi-W,M
Tommy Can You Hear Me?
  BR-W,M
Tommy Stout
  ASB2-W,M
Tommy's Gone to Hilo
  AH-W,M FW-W
**Tommy's Gone to Hilo see also
  Tom's Gone to Hilo**
Tommy's Hangin' Day
  Oz2-W,M
Tommy's Pumpkin
  FF-W
Tomorrow (Amy Grant)
  VB-W,M
Tomorrow (Charles Friml)
  VK-W,M
Tomorrow (Debra and Carvin
  Winans)
  VB-W,M
Tomorrow (from Annie)
  DBC-W,M GrS-W,M HLS8-W,M
  RW-W,M TI2-W,M UBF-W,M
Tomorrow and Today
  NB-W
Tomorrow Belongs to Me
  C-W,M OTO-W UBF-W,M
Tomorrow Gonna Be My Tryin'
  Day
  LC-W
Tomorrow Is St. Valentine's Day
  SSP-W
Tomorrow Is the First Day of the
  Rest of My Life
  UBF-W,M
Tomorrow Never Comes

OGC1-W,M OGC2-W,M
Tomorrow Never Knows
  Be1-W,M TWS-W
Tomorrow Shall Be My Dancing
  Day
  GBC-W,M
Tomorrow the Fox Will Come to
  Town
  SiM-W,M
**Tomorrow, Tomorrow see
  T'morra, T'morra**
Tomorrow's Gonna Be a Brighter
  Day
  JC-W,M
Tom's Gone to Hilo
  SA-W,M
**Tom's Gone to Hilo see also
  Tommy's Gone to Hilo**
Tom's Jolly Nose
  Boo-W,M
Tom's Theme (from the Glass
  Menagerie)
  MoA-M
Ton The
  CE-W,M (French)
Ton Nom C'est Ma Priere
  CaF-W (French Only)
Ton Papa M'a Jete Dehors
  CaF-W (French Only)
Tone Block
  GM-W,M
Tone de Bell
  BDW-W,M
Tongo
  SBF-W,M (Polynesian Only)
Tongo Island
  HAS-W,M
Tongo Islands
  ESU-W
Tongue, The
  NF-W
Tonight (Sondheim/Bernstein)
  DBC-W,M HC1-W,M
Tonight (Tonight Show with Jack
  Lescoulie Theme)
  TVT-W,M
Tonight I Celebrate My Love
  DPE-W,M GSN5-W,M MF-W,M
**Tonight Show with Jack Lescoulie
  Theme see Tonight**
**Tonight Show with Johnny Carson
  Theme see Johnny's Theme**
**Tonight Show with Steve Allen
  Theme see This Could Be the
  Start of Something**
Tonight You Belong to Me
  RW-W,M TI1-W,M UFB-W,M
**Tony Orlando and Dawn Show
  Theme see Tie a Yellow Ribbon
  round the Ole Oak Tree**
Too Charming
  Mo-W,M NM-W,M OTO-W TW-W
Too Close for Comfort
  HC1-W,M MF-W,M OTO-W
  TI2-W,M UBF-W,M
Too Darn Hot
  TI1-W,M UBF-W,M UFB-W,M
Too Fat for the Chimney
  Mo-W,M NM-W,M OTJ-W,M
Too Fat Polka
  MF-W,M NoS-W,M PT-W,M
  TI1-W,M
Too Good for the Average Man
  TS-W
Too Good to Talk About
  NM-W,M
Too Late

VB-W,M
Too Late Now
  GG4-W,M HLS3-W,M
Too Late! Too Late!
  HSD-W,M
Too Long at the Fair
  TI1-W,M UFB-W,M
Too Many Hearts in the Fire
  TOC82-W,M
Too Many Mornings
  Fo-W,M OTO-W UBF-W,M
Too Many Rings around Rosie
  NN2-W,M NN7-W,M TW-W
Too Many Rivers
  CSp-W,M
Too Marvelous for Words
  FrS-W,M HFH-W,M MF-W,M
  OHB-W,M OHF-W
Too Much
  EP-W,M
Too Much Heaven
  TI1-W,M UFB-W,M
Too Much Watermelon
  NF-W
Too Old to Play Cowboy
  TOH-W,M
Too Old to Rock 'n' Roll: Too
  Young to Die
  BJ-W,M
Too Old to Work
  AFP-W SoC-W SWF-W,M
Too Romantic
  OTO-W
Too Shy
  TI2-W,M
Too Wandering True Loves
  SCa-W
Too Young
  ILT-W,M NK-W,M TI2-W,M
Toodala
  BMC-W,M MG-W,M SHP-W,M
Toom Balalaika
  PSN-W,M (Yiddish)
Toomba Toomba
  Boo-W,M
Too-ra-loo-ra-loo-ral
  OAP-W,M SLB-W,M
**Too-ra-loo-ra-loo-ral see also
  That's an Irish Lullaby**
Toot, Toot, Tootsie!
  FPS-W,M GG2-W,M GSN2-W,M
  GST-W,M HLS2-W,M RW-W,M
Tootsie Roll Lasts a Long Time
  GSM-W,M
Top Banana
  OHF-W
**Top Gun (Love Theme) see Take
  My Breath Away**
Top Gun Anthem
  TTH-M
Top Hand
  SoC-W
Top Hat Bar and Grille
  JC-W,M
Top of the Mornin'
  RW-W,M
Top of the World
  On-W,M
Top Screw
  SoC-W
Topkapi
  RW-W,M
Tops
  RoS-W,M
Topsy Turvy
  FSA2-W,M
Torah Blessings

SBJ-W,M (Hebrew Only)
Torah Orah
  MuM-W,M (Hebrew)
Torch of Scouting
  Bo-W,M
Torches
  OB-W,M
Toreador March from Carmen
  RW-M
Toreador Song
  AmH-W,M LaS-M MF-W,M
  OBN-W,M RW-W,M TI1-W,M
  UFB-W,M WiS7-W,M
Toreador's Song
  GC-W,M
Torn and Frayed
  RoS-W,M
Torn between Two Lovers
  CMG-W,M GrS-W,M
Torn Clothes
  ASB2-W,M ASB3-W,M
**Torna A Surriento see Come Back
  to Sorrento**
Tornado
  Wi-W,M
Toro Moro see El Toro Moro
Torpedo and the Whale
  OTJ-W,M
Torture
  HR-W
Toselli's Serenade
  TI1-M UFB-M
Tossed and Driven
  Oz4-W,M
Tossin' and Turnin'
  DP-W,M ILS-W,M
Total Eclipse of the Heart
  TI2-W,M
Totem Tom-Tom
  RM-W,M
Tottenham Toad
  SiR-W,M
Touch Me
  WNF-W
Touch Not the Cup
  Oz2-W
Touch of God's Hand
  OGC2-W,M
Touch of Love
  MF-W,M
Touch of Your Hand
  TI1-W,M UFB-W,M
Touch of Your Lips
  TI1-W,M UFB-W,M
Touch the Wind see Eres Tu
Touch Thou Mine Eyes
  AHO-W,M
Touchdown for L.S.U.
  SLS-W,M
Tough Livin' Blues
  LC-W
Tough Luck
  TMA-W,M
Tough Times
  DBL-W
Toughen Up
  TTH-W,M
**Tour Prends Garde see La Tour
  Prends Garde**
Touring That City
  HHa-W,M
Tous Les Chemins
  SSN-W,M (French)
Tout En Me Promenant
  CaF-W (French Only)
Tout Le Long De La Mer
  CaF-W (French Only)

Tout Le Tour De Mon Jardin
  D'Hors
  CaF-W (French Only)
Toute A La Clarte De La Lune
  CaF-W (French Only)
Tov L'hodos
  JS-W,M (Hebrew Only)
Tovo Lefonechoh
  JS-W,M (Hebrew Only)
Tow Path
  FSA1-W,M
Tower on Guard
  ASB4-W,M
Tower Warders, under Orders
  GiS-W,M
Town Bird and the Country Bird
  NF-W
Town Clock
  MH-W,M
Town Crier
  FSA2-W,M
Town Mouse and the Country
  Mouse
  GM-W,M
Town without Pity
  ILS-W,M
Toy Dance
  UF-W,M
Toy Piano
  OBN-M
Toyland
  BCh-W,M BCS-W,M CI-W,M
  FSN-W,M FWS-W,M HSD-W,M
  MF-W,M OTJ-W,M RDT-W,M
  RW-W,M TI1-W,M UFB-W,M
Toyland March
  NI-W,M
Toys in the Attic
  RW-W,M
Tra La La
  Bo-W,M SiR-W,M
Tra La La La
  RSL-W,M
**Tracas Du Hobo Blues see Les
  Tracas Du Hobo Blues**
Tracasca Regele
  SiP-W,M (Romanian)
Traces
  GOl7-W,M MCG-W,M RY-W,M
Track Lining
  FVV-W,M
Track-Lining Chant
  WS-W,M
Tracks of My Tears
  DP-W,M THN-W,M ToO76-W,M
Trade Mark
  CMF-W,M OGC1-W,M
Trading-Out Blues
  HB-W,M
Tradition
  OTO-W TI2-W,M UBF-W,M
Traffic Cop
  KS-W,M MH-W,M
Traffic Light
  MH-W,M
Traffic Light Song
  OTJ-W,M
Traffic Lights
  AST-W,M
Traffic Man
  ASB1-W,M
Traffic Officer
  ASB2-W,M
Traffic Squad
  ASB3-W,M
Tragedy
  TI1-W,M UFB-W,M

Tragic Romance
  BSo-W,M ITP-W,M
Trail of the Lonesome Pine
  MF-W,M TI1-W,M UFB-W,M
Trail the Eagle
  Bo-W
Trail to Mexico
  ATS-W,M FW-W HB-W,M
  HWS-W,M ITP-W,M MHB-W,M
  SAm-W,M SoC-W SoF-W,M
  WS-W,M
Train
  SiR-W,M
Train, The
  GUM1-W,M SD-W,M
Train, The (Choo Choo! Choo
  Choo!)
  ASB3-W,M
Train, The (Choo, Choo, Choo, the
  Train Will Soon Be Going)
  STS-W,M
Train, The (Choo-Choo Says the
  Train)
  ASB1-W,M
Train, The (A Little Train Stood on
  the Track)
  FF-W
Train, The (Over the Rails the
  Wheels Are Clattering)
  SL-W,M
Train Blues
  LC-W
Train Forty-Five
  BIS-W,M
Train Is A-Coming
  RSL-W,M
Train Pulled in the Station
  TMA-W,M
Train Song
  AST-W,M
Train That Carried My Girl from
  Town
  LSR-W,M
Train That Never Returned
  Oz4-W
Train Time
  DBL-W
Train to Johannesburg
  LS-W,M
Train Whistle
  OHT-W,M
Train Whistle Blues
  LSR-W,M
Training the Boy
  NF-W
Trains
  ASB5-W,M
Train's A-Comin'
  B-W,M BI-W,M
Trains and Boats and Planes
  GAR-W,M HD-W,M MF-W,M
Trains Up in the Sky
  VB-W,M
Traipsin' Woman Cabin
  BMM-W
Traitor, Spare That Flag
  SiS-W
Tramp (Fulson/McCracklin)
  RB-W
Tramp, The (I'm a Broken-Down
  Man without Money or Friends)
  Oz4-W,M
Tramp, The (Keep on Tramping)
  FW-W
Tramp, Tramp, Tramp
  AAP-W,M AL-W AmH-W,M
  ESB-W,M FW-W HSD-W,M

MF-W,M MPP-W NaM-W,M
NAS-W,M OFS-W,M PoS-W,M
RW-W,M Sin-W,M SiS-W
SMW-W,M WiS8-W,M
Tramp, Tramp, Tramp the Boys
Are Marching
ATS-W
Trampin'
LMR-W,M PaS-W,M VA-W,M
Tramping Along
TS-W
Tramping and Stamping
SOO-W,M
Tramp's Story
Oz4-W
Tramp's Thoughts
AL-W
Trancadillo
TH-W,M
Transport
SHS-W,M
Transportation
ASB1-W,M
Transportation Corps March
GO-W
Transvaal Flag
AmH-W,M
Trappan'd Maiden
SI-W,M
Trapper John, M.D.
TVT-M
Trashy
TT-W,M
Traume see Dreams (Traume)
Traumerei
AmH-M RW-M TM-M WGB/O-M
WGB/P-M
Travel On
WN-W,M
Travel Song
FSA1-W,M
Traveler
ASB4-W,M SHS-W,M
Trav'ler Benighted and Lost
BC1-W,M
Travelin' Blues
LJ-W,M
Travelin' Light
MF-W,M OHF-W ToS-W,M
Traveling Man
SYB-W,M
Traveling with God
GBC-W,M
Traveller
B-W,M
Travelling Coon
AN-W
Travelling Pilgrim
SHS-W,M
Travelling Shoes
SFF-W,M
Travelogue
FSA2-W,M SCL-W,M
Treacherous Hearted President
MPP-W
Tread Lightly, Ye Comrades
SiS-W
Tread Soft, My Friend
Boo-W,M
Treadmill
Oz3-W,M
Treasure of Love
HRB3-W,M
Treasure of San Miguel
OnT1-M
Treasure Trove
FSA1-W,M

Treasure Untold
LJ-W,M
Treasury Rats
Sin-W,M SiS-W
Treat Me Nice
AS-W,M GAR-W,M MF-W,M
SRE2-W,M
Treat Me Rough
GOB-W,M
Treats of London
MSB-W
Tree
OTO-W
Tree Frogs
NF-W
Tree in the Valley
RSL-W,M
Tree in the Wood
NAS-W,M TF-W,M
Tree of Peace
BSG-W,M BSP-W,M
Tree Once Grew in Galilee
GBC-W,M
Trees
ASB1-W,M FSA2-W,M
Trees (with Sympathy for Joyce
Kilmer)
OHF-W
Trees Are Gently Swaying
SoP-W,M
Trees Are Growing High
BB-W
Trees in Autumn
ASB2-W,M
Trees in Winter
ASB4-W,M
Tree's the Nicest Thing
SHP-W,M
Trees They Grow So High
F1-W,M
Treeya Pedya Volyotika
FG2-W,M (Greek Only)
Trellis
EL-W,M
Trembling before Thine Awful
Throne
AHO-W,M
Trendell Terry
TW-W
Trepak from the Nutcracker Suite
RW-M
Trial, The
Ne-W,M
Triangle
GM-W,M
Triangle Victims
WW-W,M (Yiddish)
Tribulation
SHS-W,M
Tribute, A
SL-W,M
Tribute to Our Teacher
ESU-W
Tributes to Liza Elliott
LSO-W
Trick or Treat
GM-W,M
Tricks of the Trade
CMF-W,M
Triflin' Gal
OGC1-W,M
Trimdon Grange Explosion
BB-W
Trip a Trop a Tronjes
ATS-W,M SOO-W,M
Trip Charlie
Oz3-W

Trip to America see Peter Johnson
Trip to Bermuda
Fi-W,M
Trip to Cambridge
SBA-W SSS-W,M
**Trip to Cambridge see also Adam's
Fall**
Trip to Heaven
N-W,M
Trip to the Zoo
SD-W,M
Triple Flute
BMC-M
Triplets
TW-W UBF-W,M
Trippele, Trappele, Trop
SiR-W,M
Triste Lou'siane
CaF-W (French Only)
Triumph By and By
GH-W,M
Triumph of the Dear Old Flag
SiS-W
Triumph of Toil
GrM-W,M
Triumphal Entry
GrM-W,M
Triumphal March (Aida)
CA-W,M RW-M
Triumphantly the Church Will Rise
HHa-W,M
Troika
ASB6-W,M UF-W,M
Troika Ride
MML-W,M
Trois Demoiselles
CaF-W (French Only)
Trois Jeunes Tambours
MP-W,M (French Only)
Trolley Car
MH-W,M
Trolley Man
MH-W,M
Trolley Song
GSF-W,M GSN3-W,M HLS5-W,M
RT4-W,M
Trooper and the Maid
FW-W
Trooper Cut Down in His Prime
SoC-W
Trooper Watering His Nag
SR-W,M
Trot Along
SSe-W,M
Trot Along, My Little Mule
SOO-W,M
Trot, Trot
MH-W,M
Troubadour of Red Fork Ranch
SoC-W
Troubadour's Carol
GBC-W,M
Trouble (Josh White)
J-W,M
Trouble (Leiber/Stoller)
GAR-W,M MF-W,M
Trouble and How to Bear It
ESU-W
Trouble at Home Blues
DBL-W
**Trouble Done Bore Me Down see
Trubble Dun Bore Me Down**
Trouble Followin' Me
LC-W
Trouble in Mind
FPS-W,M LC-W TO-W,M
ToS-W,M

Trouble in Paradise
BOA-W,M
Trouble Maker
Mo-M
Trouble Man
LS-W,M
Trouble Will Bury Me Down see
Truble Will Bury Me Down
Troubles Was Hard
Me-W,M
Trout
ASB6-W,M MMY-W,M
Trubble Dun Bore Me Down
BDW-W,M
Truble Will Bury Me Down
FN-W,M
Trucks
SiR-W,M
True
TI2-W,M
True and Trembling Brakeman
LSR-W,M Oz4-W
True Colors
DPE-W,M RoE-W,M
True Confession
OTO-W
True Faith
BHO-W,M
True Freedom
AL-W
True Friends Can Never Drift Apart
MML-W,M
True Grit (Theme)
OTO-W TOM-W,M
True Happiness
SHS-W,M
True Hearted Statesman
ESU-W
True-Hearted, Whole-Hearted
GH-W,M
True Love (Cole Porter)
HC2-W,M ILT-W,M ML-W,M
OTO-W RT5-W,M TI1-W,M
UFB-W,M
True Love (Is the Greatest Thing)
CCS-W,M
True Love, True Love
HRB4-W,M
True Love Ways
TI2-W,M
True Lover's Farewell
AmS-W,M FMT-W OTJ-W,M
True or False
MuM-W,M
True Religion
NH-W
True Son of God, Eternal Light
AHO-W,M
True Sportsman
FSA2-W,M
True Sweetheart
SCa-W,M
True Worth Is in Being
GrM-W,M
True Worth Will Win
GrM-W,M
True Yankee Sailor
ANS-W
Trumpet
SHS-W,M
Trumpet Call
FSA2-W,M
Trumpet of Jesus
VB-W,M
Trumpet Tune and Air
TM-M
Trumpet Voluntary

WGB/O-M
Trumpeter, Blow
MHB-W,M (Slovak)
Trumpeter, Blow Your Golden Horn
OT-W,M
Trumpeters
SHS-W,M
Trumpeter's Prayer
OnT6-M
Trumpets (Reaching and Winding)
Boo-W,M
Trust and Obey
AME-W,M OM-W,M
Trust Him Not
Oz4-W
Trust in Me
AHO-W,M
Trust On
GH-W,M
Trust the Lord
VB-W,M
Trusting
GrM-W,M
Trusting in Thee
FiS-W,M
Trusting Jesus
OM-W,M
Trusting Jesus, That Is All
GH-W,M
Truth from Above
OB-W,M
Truth Twice Told
BMM-W
Truxton's Victory
ANS-W AWB-W
Try a Little Harder
RoS-W,M
Try a Little Kindness
RW-W,M
Try a Little Tenderness
GG4-W,M GSO-W,M HLS2-W,M
MCG-W,M OP2-W,M RYT-W,M
Try Her Out at Dances
Ne-W,M
Try Me One More Time
OGC2-W,M
Try to Forget
CF-W,M
Try to Remember
DBC-W,M DP-W,M Fa-W,M
HC1-W,M HLS3-W,M LM-W,M
OTJ-W,M OTO-W RW-W,M
TI1-W,M TW-W UBF-W,M
UFB-W,M
Try, Try Again
OTJ-W,M
Try Us, O God, and Search the
Ground
AME-W,M
Tryin' to Get the Feeling Again
MF-W,M
Tryin' to Get to You
EP-W,M
Trying to Live
Lo-W,M
Trying to Love Two Women
TOH-W,M
Tryst
SL-W,M
Tschaikowsky (and Other
Russians)
LD-W,M LSO-W
Tshotsholosa (Road Song)
TO-W,M (African)
Tu (O Cuba)
LaS-M MSS-W,M (Spanish)
Tubby the Tuba Song

OTJ-W,M
Tuesday Afternoon
TI1-W,M UFB-W,M
Tuff Enuff
TTH-W,M
Tug of War
TI2-W,M
Tugboat
KS-W,M
Tulips from Amsterdam
OnT6-W,M
Tuljak
UF-W,M
Tulsa Time
FOC-W,M TI2-W,M
Tumbalalaika
FW-W (Yiddish)
Tumbleweed
TOH-W,M
Tumbling Dice
RoS-W,M
Tumbling Tumbleweeds
FC-W,M TI1-W,M UFB-W,M
Tumbrel Song
PAJ-W,M
Tune the Old Cow Died On
OHO-W,M Oz3-W,M
Tune They Croon in the U.S.A.
BP-W,M
Tune Thy Music to Thy Heart
SSP-W
Tune You Can't Forget
ST-W,M
Tuner's Oppor-tun-ity
WF-W,M
Tunnel Tigers
IFM-W
Tupelo Honey
MF-W,M
Turd on the Run
RoS-W,M
Turkey, The
FF-W GM-W,M
Turkey Funeral
NF-W
Turkey in the Corn
Am-W
Turkey in the Straw
AmH-W,M AmS-W,M ATS-W
FW-W HAS-W,M HSA-W,M
MAS-W,M MF-W,M OTJ-W,M
Oz2-W,M POT-W,M RW-W,M
SoC-W TI1-W,M UFB-W,M
WiS8-W,M
Turkey Lurkey Time
Mo-W,M OTO-W
Turkey Shivaree
SCa-W
Turkey Song
AFS-W,M
Turkish Lady
DD-W,M SAm-W,M TBF-W,M
Turkish March
AmH-M
Turkish March see also Alla Turca
Turkish Patrol
AmH-M
Turkish Round
LMR-W,M (Turkish Only)
Turn Again Whittington
Boo-W,M SMY-W,M
Turn Around
OTJ-W,M TI2-W,M
Turn Around, Look at Me
ATC-W,M MF-W,M
Turn Back, O Man
G-W,M On-W,M OTO-W OU-W,M

UBF-W,M
Turn Back, O Man, Forswear Thy
Foolish Ways
Hy-W,M
Turn Back Pharaoh's Army
WN-W,M
Turn Back the Hands of Time
TI1-W,M UFB-W,M
Turn, Cinnamon, Turn
SiR-W,M
Turn Not Away
FHR-W,M
Turn Not from Sad Sorrow
Boo-W,M
Turn of the Cards (Lottery Theme
Song)
TV-W,M
Turn, Oh Turn
GiS-W,M
Turn Out! To the Rescue!
MPP-W,M
Turn Sinner
BDW-W,M
**Turn Sinner see also Oh! Turn
Sinner**
Turn Sinner Turn
WN-W,M
Turn That Cinnamon
Oz3-W
Turn the Beat Around
PoG-W,M
Turn the Glasses Over
FW-W MG-W,M PIS-W,M
Turn the World Around
HLS9-W,M MF-W,M RW-W,M
Turn to da East, Malatta
SGT-W,M
Turn to Stone
ELO-W,M
Turn! Turn! Turn!
CEM-W,M JF-W,M RDF-W,M
SBF-W,M TI1-W,M TWD-W,M
UFB-W,M
Turn, Turn, Unhappy Souls, Return
AHO-W,M
Turn Ye to Me
SBF-W,M SeS-W,M UF-W,M
Turn Your Eyes upon Jesus
HF-W,M HHa-W,M OM-W,M
Turn Your Radio On
HHa-W,M TI1-W,M Tr-W,M
UFB-W,M
Turnbridge Doctors
SR-W,M
Turncoat
BMM-W
Turner Song
AL-W
Turning Song
GB-W,M
Turning, Turning 'Round
SOO-W,M
Turnip Greens
FMT-W
Turnip Patch
Oz3-W
Turnpike Gate
SY-W,M
Turtle
ASB3-W,M
Turtle Dove
AmH-M FW-W LT-W,M SHS-W,M
Turtle Dove, or the Butcher Boy
BSC-W
Turtle's Song
NF-W
Tuxedo Junction

MF-W,M TI1-W,M TI2-W,M
UFB-W,M
Twa Corbies
BCT-W,M
Twa Corbies see also Two Crows
Twa Sisters
BT-W,M SG-W,M
Twa Sisters see also Two Sisters
'Twas a Canadian Boy
SoF-W,M
'Twas at the Siege of Vicksburg
Sin-W,M
'Twas Early in the Spring
TBF-W,M
'Twas Nine Years Ago
Oz3-W
**'Twas on a Night Like This see In a
Little Spanish Town**
'Twas on That Night When
Doomed to Know
Hy-W,M
'Twas on the Way to Bethlehem
OU-W,M
'Twas Sunset in a Garden
SoF-W,M
'Twas the Night before Christmas
CI-W,M OTJ-W,M
'Twas Winter and Blue Tory Noses
HAS-W,M
Tweedle Dee
HRB2-W,M
Tweedlee Dee
ILF-W,M
Twelfth of April
AWB-W,M
Twelfth of July
VP-W
Twelfth of Never
FRH-W,M MF-W,M
12th Street Rag
BBB-M TI2-M
Twelve Apostles
GBC-W,M Oz4-W,M TBF-W,M
Twelve Blessings of Mary
WN-W,M
Twelve Bright Elves
Boo-W,M
Twelve Commandments
SG-W,M
Twelve Days of Christmas
ATM-W,M BCh-W,M BCS-W,M
BSC-W CI-W,M FW-W FWS-W,M
GBC-W,M Gu-W,M HS-W,M
IL-W,M JF-W JOC-W,M OE-W,M
OPS-W,M OTJ-W,M PSN-W,M
RSL-W,M SG-W,M
Twelve Gates to the City
FGM-W,M FW-W WSB-W,M
Twelve Hundred More
AL-W
Twelve Joys of Mary
GBC-W,M
Twelve Little Rabbits
HSA-W,M
Twelve Months Ago Tonight
FSTS-W,M
12 O'Clock High (Theme)
GTV-M
Twelve O'Clock Is Striking
MHB-W,M (Serbo-Croatian)
Twelve Thirty
RB-W
20th Century Fox
RB-W
25 or 6 to 4
BR-W,M TTH-W,M
Twenty-Four Hours from Tulsa

HD-W,M
Twenty Love-Sick Maidens We
GiS-W,M MGT-W,M
2120 South Michigan Avenue
RoS-W,M
Twenty-One Years
Oz2-W,M
Twenty-Seven
WF-W,M
23rd of June
IS-W,M
**XXIII Psalm (German) see Der XXIII
Psalm**
Twenty Tons of T.N.T.
Mo-W,M
Twenty Years
OHG-W,M
Twenty Years Ago
HSD-W,M NeA-W,M TMA-W,M
Twig Broom
ASB5-W,M
Twig So Tender
Oz4-W,M
Twila Was a City Maiden
Oz4-W
Twilight (Fay/Rubenstein)
SL-W,M
Twilight (Lowell/O'Farrell)
FSA2-W,M
Twilight (Mozart)
ASB6-W,M
Twilight Dreams
SL-W,M
Twilight Music
SL-W,M TF-W,M
Twilight on the Trail
AT-W,M FC-W,M OTJ-W,M
OTO-W
Twilight Shadows round Me Fall
AHO-W,M
Twilight Time
MF-W,M OnT1-W,M PB-W,M
TI1-W,M TWD-W,M UFB-W,M
Twill Nebber Do to Gib It Up So
DE-W,M
Twill Not Be Long
GH-W,M
Twin Ballots
Oz2-W,M
Twin Soliloquies (This Is How It
Feels)
UBF-W,M
Twinkle Toes
TFC-W,M
Twinkle, Twinkle, Little Star
AmH-W,M BBF-W,M BM-W
GM-W,M HS-W,M OTJ-W,M
RW-W,M SOO-W,M
Twinkle Twinkle Lucky Star
NMH-W,M
Twinkling Stars
GM-W,M
Twinkling Stars Are Laughing,
Love
ATS-W HSD-W,M
Twist, The
DRR-W,M TI2-W,M TRR-W,M
Twist and Shout
BBe-W,M ERM-W,M MF-W,M
Twist My Arm
TTH-W,M
Twisting on the Train
Oz3-W
'Twixt Dick and Tom
Boo-W,M
Two a Day (Wonderful World of)
Mo-W,M NM-W,M OTO-W

Two Brothers
  BSC-W FMT-W MHB-W,M
  Oz1-W,M SCa-W TBF-W,M
  WSB-W,M
Two Brown Eyes
  AS-W,M (German)
Two Cent Coal
  AL-W
Two Cigarettes in the Dark
  HC2-W,M TI1-W,M UBF-W,M
  UFB-W,M
Two Crows
  ITP-W
Two Crows see also Twa Corbies
Two Different Worlds
  ATC2-W,M FRH-W,M
**Two Dollar Bill see Long Journey
  Home**
Two Ducks on a Pond
  SMY-W,M
Two Friends
  ASB4-W,M
Two Ghosts
  ESU-W
Two Great Tastes
  GSM-W,M
Two Grenadiers
  FSY-W,M (German) WiS9-W,M
Two Guitars
  CA-W,M MF-M RW-M
Two Hearts
  RoE-W,M TTH-W,M
Two Hearts in 3/4 Time
  MF-W,M
Two Hearts in Three-Quarter Time
  TI2-W,M
Two Hoboes
  AFP-W
Two Ladies
  C-W,M OTO-W UBF-W,M
Two Ladies in de Shade of de
  Banana Tree
  Mo-W,M NM-W,M OTO-W
Two Lanterns
  Oz4-W
Two Lawyers, Two Lawyers
  Boo-W,M
Two Little Apples
  FP-W,M
Two Little Babes in the Wood
  OHB-W,M TW-W
Two Little Birds
  FP-W,M
Two Little Blackbirds
  MH-W,M RSL-W,M
Two Little Bluebirds
  Su-W,M
Two Little Boys
  BSo-W,M Oz1-W,M
Two Little Dicky Birds
  GM-W,M
Two Little Eyes
  FP-W,M
Two Little Fishes
  J-W,M
Two Little Girls in Blue
  Oz4-W U-W
Two Little Hands
  RSL-W,M
Two Little Orphans
  ITP-W,M
Two Little People
  L-W
Two Magicians
  BT-W,M
Two Maidens Went Milking
  FG2-W,M

Two Maids Went A-Milking One
  Day
  FW-W
**Two Marriages (Theme) see We're
  Home Here**
Two More Years
  SF-W,M
Two O'Clock Jump
  GSF-W,M
**Two of a Kind (Theme) see We'll
  Win This World**
Two of Us
  BBe-W,M TI2-W,M TWS-W
Two Out of Three Ain't Bad
  TI2-W,M
Two Pickets
  SiS-W
Two Precepts
  FSA2-W,M
Two Proud Sisters of the Sea
  ANS-W
Two Roads
  FSA2-W,M
Two Roses
  HSD-W,M
Two Royal Children
  TH-W,M
Two Sick Negro Boys
  NF-W
Two Sisters
  AA-W,M DD-W,M FMT-W
  FoM-W FW-W ITP-W,M SCa-W
Two Sisters see also Twa Sisters
Two Sisters, or Old Lord by the
  Northern Sea
  MSH-W,M
Two Sleepy People
  AT-W,M LM-W,M OTO-W
Two Strangers in the Mountains
  Alone
  Oz1-W,M
Two Swallows
  RuS-W,M (Russian)
Two Sweethearts
  Oz4-W
**2001: A Space Odyssey Theme
  see Also Sprach Zarathustra**
2,000 Light Years from Home
  RoS-W,M
2,000 Man
  RoS-W,M
Two Thousand Miles to Go
  VA-W,M
Two Times One
  NF-W
Two Winds
  SOO-W,M
Two Wings
  BDW-W,M FoS-W,M SAm-W,M
Two Winning Hands
  AG-W,M
Two Young Daughters
  Oz1-W
Two's Company
  MS-W,M
Tyin' a Knot in the Devil's Tail
  FW-W
Tying Knots in the Devil's Tail
  HWS-W,M
Tying of the Garter
  SR-W,M
Tylus and Talus
  Oz3-W,M
Tynom, Tanom
  PaS-W,M
Typical Male
  TTH-W,M

Typical Stomp
  B-M BI-M
Tyrley, Tyrlow
  OB-W,M
Tyrolean Cradle Song
  GBC-W,M
Tzadeek Katomor
  SBJ-W,M (Hebrew Only)
Tzena, Tzena, Tzena, Tzena
  TI2-W,M WSB-W,M (Hebrew)
Tzu Chu Tiao (Purple Bamboo)
  FD-W,M (Chinese)
Tzur Yisroel
  JS-W,M (Hebrew Only)

U

U Got the Look
  BHO-W,M
U. of M. Rouser
  CoS-W,M Mo-W,M TI2-W,M
U of O
  CoS-W,M
UAW-CIO
  AFP-W,M PSN-W,M SWF-W,M
U.S.A. Will Fight
  GO-W
U.S.G.
  SiS-W
U.S.G. National Walk 'Round
  MPP-W
U.S. Male
  EP-W,M
Udder Worl' Is Not Lak Dis
  NH-W
Uds Nigs, Here Lies John Digs
  Boo-W,M
Ugly Bug Ball
  OTJ-W,M SBS-W,M
Ugly Duckling
  SiR-W,M
Ugly Face Blues
  LC-W
Ugly Man
  LaS-W,M
Ugly Mug
  Oz3-W
Uhuru
  JF-W,M
Ukrainian Polyphonic Song
  IF-M
Ulysses Leads the Van
  SiS-W
Un Bambocheur
  FSO-W,M (French)
Un Canadien Errant
  CFS-W,M (French) FW-W (French)
**Un Canadien Errant see also
  Voyager**
Un Conte
  CaF-W (French Only)
Un, Deux, Trois
  CE-W,M (French Only) MaG-W,M
Un Flambeau, Jeannette, Isabelle
  CUP-W,M (French Only)
**Un Flambeau, Jeannette, Isabelle
  see also Bring a Torch, Jeanette,
  Isabella**
Un Petit Bonhomme
  CLaL-W,M (French)
Un Soir Au Clair De Lune
  FSF-W (French)
Un Soir En Me Promenant
  CaF-W (French Only)
Una Tarde Fresquita De Mayo
  LA-W,M (Spanish)

Unbeknownst
MF-W,M
Unbirthday Song
NI-W,M OTJ-W,M
Unchained Melody
RW-W,M TI2-W,M
Uncle Abraham, Bully for You
SiS-W
Uncle Albert/Admiral Halsey
PMC-W,M
Uncle Fred and Auntie Mabel
PO-W,M
Uncle Jake
ASB4-W,M
Uncle Jerry Fants
NF-W
Uncle Joe
FW-W Oz3-W,M
Uncle Joe's Hail Columbia
SiS-W
Uncle Johnnie see Unkle Johnnie
Uncle John's Band
RV-W
Uncle Ned
AmH-W,M AN-W ESB-W,M
MAS-W,M NAS-W,M NF-W OS-W
Oz2-W,M SSFo-W,M WiS8-W,M
Uncle Pen
CMF-W,M
Uncle Rat
BSC-W
Uncle Rat's Courtship
Oz1-W
Uncle Reuben
FW-W
Uncle Sam
ASB3-W,M
Uncle Sam and Mexico
ATS-W
Uncle Sam Is Bound to Win
SiS-W
Uncle Sam Says
AFP-W
Uncle Sam, What Ails You?
Sin-W,M SiS-W
Uncle Sam's a Hundred
MPP-W
Uncle Sam's Farm
AH-W,M MPP-W SY-W,M
TMA-W,M
Uncle Sam's Song to Miss Texas
ATS-W ESU-W
Uncle Tahiah
BSC-W
Uncle Thad Stevens
AL-W
Uncle Tom Cobleigh
CSo-W,M
Uncle Tom's Religion
NSS-W SY-W,M
Unclouded Day
AME-W,M HHa-W,M
Unconstant Lover
FoS-W,M WU-W,M
Unconstant Lover see also
Onconstant Lover
Uncurb'd Tongues
Boo-W,M
Undaunted
SL-W,M
Undecided
TI2-W,M
Under a Blanket of Blue
MF-W,M TI2-W,M
Under a Green Elm
Boo-W,M
Under a Korean Sun

AF-W
Under a One-Man Top
ReG-W,M
Under Assistant West Coast
Promotion Man
RoS-W,M
Under My Thumb
RoS-W,M
Under the Bamboo Tree
FSN-W,M FSTS-W,M MF-W,M
RW-W,M
Under the Banner of Victory
AmH-M
Under the Bed Was He
SR-W,M
Under the Boardwalk
DRR-W,M RB-W TI2-W,M
TRR-W,M
Under the Bridges of Paris
HLS3-W,M (French)
Under the Double Eagle
AmH-M FPG-M RW-M
Under the Greenwood Tree
FSA1-W,M FSS-W,M OH-W,M
SSB-W,M
Under the Juniper Tree
FMT-W FoM-W,M
Under the Rail
NH-W
Under the Silver Star
SL-W,M
Under the Spreading Chestnut Tree
HS-W,M LoS-W,M
Under the Stars
CCH-W,M
Under the Weeping Willow
BSC-W
Under the Willow
BSC-W
Under the Willow She's Sleeping
FHR-W,M SSF-W,M SSFo-W,M
WiS8-W,M
Under the Willow Tree
BSC-W
Under the Yoke of Darkness
SoF-W,M
Under the Yum Yum Tree
LWT-W,M
Under This Stone Lies Gabriel John
Boo-W,M
Under Your Spell Again
CSp-W,M
Underneath the Bamboo Tree
FWS-W,M
Underneath the Spreading
Chestnut Tree
U-W
Underneath This Mould'ring Clay
Boo-W,M
Undertaker's Club
MSB-W
Underwear
GO-W
Undivided
VB-W,M
Une Adresse Aux Maries
CaF-W (French Only)
Une Fille De Quinze Ans
CaF-W (French Only)
Unexpected Song
DBC-W,M UBF-W,M
Unfailing Love
SL-W,M
Unfinished Business
TOC83-W,M
Unfinished Symphony Theme
RW-M

Unforgettable
NK-W,M RoE-W,M TI1-W,M
UFB-W,M
Unfortunate Man
Oz3-W,M
Unfortunate Miss Bailey
FW-W OFS-W,M
Unfortunate Rake
BSC-W SoC-W
Ungeduld
CA-W,M
Unhappy Contraband
SiS-W
Unhappy Jeremiah
ESU-W
Unhappy Schoolhouse
ASB5-W,M
Unhappy Times
SSS-W,M
Unicorn, The
TI1-W,M TWD-W,M UFB-W,M
Union
SHS-W,M
Union All Along the Line
AL-W
Union Is Our Leader
WW-W,M
Union Is Strength
AL-W
Union Label
GSM-W,M
Union League
LSO-W
Union Maid
AFP-W FG1-W,M FW-W JF-W,M
LW-W,M SWF-W,M
Union Man
SWF-W,M
Union Must and Shall Be Preserved
MPP-W
Union of the Snake
TI2-W,M
Union Prayer for Victory
SiS-W
Union Right or Wrong
SiS-W
Union Square
LSO-W
Union Train
FW-W SWF-W,M
Union Volunteer
Oz2-W,M
Union Volunteers
SiS-W
Union Wagon
SiS-W
Unionist's Song
AL-W
Union's Rallying Song
AL-W
United Airline Jingle see Mother
Country
United Front
FW-W
United Nations Hymn
LoS-W,M
United Nations Make a Chain
PSN-W,M
United States and the Macedonian
ANS-W AWB-W
United States Military Song of the
Graduates
OHG-W,M
United Steelworkers Are We
SWF-W,M
United We Stand
AAP-W,M

Unity
AL-W
Universa Transeunt
Boo-W,M (Latin Only)
University of Gottingen
ESU-W
Unkle Johnnie
MHB-W,M
Unknown Dead
SiS-W
Unknown Soldier
RB-W SiS-W
Unlucky Emigrant
SE-W,M (Swedish)
Unmarried Woman (Theme)
TOM-M
Unmooring
ANS-W
Unquiet Grave
BT-W,M FW-W
Unreturning Braves
SiS-W
Unseen Chorus
FSA2-W,M
Unshakable Kingdom
GP-W,M VB-W,M
Until see also 'Til and Till
Until I Met You
MF-W,M
Until It's Time for You to Go
TI1-W,M UFB-W,M
Until the Real Thing Comes Along
NK-W,M
Until Then
HHa-W,M
Until You Get Somebody Else
WDS-W,M
Untitled Poem
OHF-W
Untitled Protest #1
VS-W,M
Unto Jehovah Sing Will I
AHO-W,M
Unto Our God Most High We Sing
AHO-W,M
Unto Thee
JS-W,M (Hebrew)
Unto Thy Temple, Lord, We Come
AME-W,M
Unto Us a Boy Is Born
JOC-W,M YC-W,M
Unto Us a King Is Born
RS-W,M
Untouchables Theme
MoA-M
Untrue Lover
Oz1-W
Unveil Your Glory
VB-W,M
Unwed Fathers
TOC83-W,M
Up above My Head
ATC2-W,M
Up an' Down Blues
LC-W
Up and Do
AL-W
Up and Down
FSA1-W,M
Up and Down This World Goes
Round
Boo-W,M
Up around the Bend
BR-W,M
Up Falcons You Go
RSC-W,M (Russian Only)
Up Goes My Umbrella

SiR-W,M
Up in a Balloon
AH-W,M SY-W,M
Up in Old Loray
AFP-W WW-W,M
Up in the Deep Dark Sky
SOO-W,M
Up on the House-Top
BCh-W,M BCS-W,M CSF-W
RW-W,M SCS-W SOO-W,M
Y-W,M
Up on the Housetop
HS-W,M OPS-W,M TI1-W,M
UFB-W,M
Up on the Roof
DPE-W,M ERM-W,M GAR-W,M
RB-W ToO79-W,M
Up over My Head
SFF-W,M
Up She Goes
SA-W,M
Up the Oak, Down the Pine
FVV-W,M
Up to His Old Tricks
MS-W,M
Up, Up and Away
ILS-W,M RW-W,M TI2-W,M
Up Where We Belong
LOM-W,M MoA-W,M TOM-W,M
Up with People
HCY-W,M
Up with the Blue and Down with
the Gray
SiS-W
Up Yonder
GH-W,M
Upidee
AmH-W,M ESB-W,M HSD-W,M
OHG-W,M OTJ-W,M
Upidee Song
Sin-W,M SiS-W
Upon a Quiet Hill
CoS-W,M
Upon the Hill before Centreville
AWB-W
Upon the Rock see Opon de Rock
Upon the Stanislow
OHG-W,M
Upon This Rock
VB-W,M
Uprising of Labor
AL-W
Ups and Downs
LMR-W,M
Upstairs
Mo-W,M OTO-W
Upstairs, Downstairs
RSL-W,M
Uptight
THN-W,M
Upton
SHS-W,M
Uptown
HR-W TFC-W,M
Upward Trail
GuC-W,M
Upward Where the Stars Are
Burning
AME-W,M
Ur Svenska Hjertans
SiP-W,M (Swedish)
Ural Lament
RuS-W,M (Russian)
Ural Rowan Tree
RuS-W,M (Russian)
Urge, The
Mo-W,M

Ursinus Fight Song
CoS-W,M
Us Poor Fish
GI-W
Use Ajax the Foaming Cleanser
GSM-W,M
Use Your Imagination
ML-W,M
Used Cars (Theme)
TOM-W,M
Used-to-Be
BIS-W,M
Useful Keys
FSA1-W,M
Ustaj, Ustaj Srbine
SiP-W,M (Serbo-Croatian)
Utah Carl
Oz2-W
Utah Carol
HB-W,M
Utah Carroll
FMT-W FW-W HWS-W,M
Utah Trail
FC-W,M
Utah, We Love Thee
Fif-W,M
Ute Indian Peyote Song
IF-W,M
Utvandrarens Visa, Maningsord Till
Emigranten
SE-W,M (Swedish)
Utwandrarens Wisa
SE-W (Swedish)
Uxbridge
SHS-W,M
Uxor Mea, Uxor Polla
Boo-W,M (Latin Only)

V

V Song
SMW-W,M (Czech)
Vaanachnu (Adoration)
JS-W,M (Hebrew)
Vacant Chair
AmH-W,M ATS-W EFS-W,M
FW-W HSD-W,M MPP-W
OHG-W,M Sin-W,M SiS-W
Vagabond
MML-W,M MMM-W,M
Vagabond Love
FSO-W,M (French)
Vagabundo
TI1-W,M (Spanish Only)
UFB-W,M (Spanish Only)
Vainamoinen's Gift
BMC-W,M
Vale of Cashmere
SL-W,M
Valencia
MF-W,M
Valentine
ASB1-W,M ASB2-W,M
FSA2-W,M RSL-W,M
Valentine Candy
OnT1-W,M
Valentine Song
AST-W,M GM-W,M
Valentines
MAR-W,M MH-W,M
Valerie
BHO-W,M
Valiant Soldier
Oz1-W,M
Valley, The
SoF-W,M

Valley of Blessing
  GH-W,M
Valley of Death
  VS-W,M
Valley of the Dolls Theme
  MF-W,M
Valparaiso
  FSF-W (French)
Valse Bleue
  AmH-M
Valse Criminelle see La Valse
  Criminelle
Valse De Not'e Village see La
  Valse De Not'e Village
Valse De Rothschild
  Ro-W,M
Valse Des Creoles see La Valse
  Des Creoles
Valse Lente
  OBN-M
Valsez-Valsez
  CSD-W,M (French)
Vamos A Cantar Y Bailar
  MuM-W,M
Vamos, Maninha
  LA-W,M (Spanish)
Van Bramer's Jig
  DE-W,M
Van Buren
  MPP-W
Van Dieman's Land
  ATM-W,M FW-W IFM-W MSB-W
Van Troi, Your Words Will Echo
  through the Centuries
  VS-W,M
Vance Song, The
  FMT-W FSU-W
Vanilla Ice Cream
  TI2-W,M
Vanity Kills
  TTH-W,M
Variations on a Theme by Haydn
  LTL-M
Variety Says
  TW-W
Varshavianka
  SMW-W,M (Polish)
Varsity Drag
  HC1-W,M LM-W,M MF-W,M
  RW-W,M TI1-W,M UBF-W,M
  UFB-W,M
Varsity Song
  CoS-W,M
Varsovienne
  MES1-W,M MES2-W,M
Vart Land, Vart Fosterland
  SiP-W,M (Finnish)
Vaya Con Dios
  EC-W,M GOI7-W,M MAB1-W
  MF-W,M Mo-W,M MSA1-W
  OBN-W,M OTJ-W,M PB-W,M
  TI2-W,M
Vayedaber Moshe
  JS-W,M (Hebrew Only)
Vayehi Binesoa
  JS-W,M (Hebrew Only)
Vayehulu
  SBJ-W,M (Hebrew Only)
Vayhee Binsoa
  SBJ-W,M (Hebrew Only)
Vayomer Adonoy
  JS-W,M (Hebrew Only)
Veal Kulom
  JS-W,M (Hebrew Only)
Vegetable Man
  ASB1-W,M
Vehakohanim

JS-W,M (Hebrew Only)
Vehi Sheomdoh
  JS-W,M (Hebrew)
Veille De Vot'e Fete see La Veille
  De Vot'e Fete
Velvet Chains
  TOC83-W,M
Velvet Glove
  Mo-W,M NM-W,M
Venadito see El Venadito
Venal Vera
  GI-W
Venetian Song
  NAS-W,M
Venezuela
  FW-W Gu-W,M
Venga Jaleo
  FG2-W,M (Spanish Only) FW-W
  WSB-W,M (Spanish)
Venice
  FSA2-W,M
Venislach
  JS-W,M (Hebrew Only)
Venomous Black Snake
  TBF-W
Ventilator Blues
  RoS-W,M
Venture Gwen
  SL-W,M
Venus
  DRR-W,M
Venus and Mars
  PMC-W,M
Venus in Blue Jeans
  MF-W,M
Venus, Laughing from the Skies
  MMW-W,M
Veohavtoh
  JS-W,M (Hebrew Only)
Verbum Domini Manet
  Boo-W,M (Latin Only)
Verdant Grove, Farewell to Thee
  GrM-W,M
Verdant Groves
  GB-W,M
Verdant Meadows
  MHB-W,M (Italian)
Verily, Verily
  GH-W,M
Vermeland
  NAS-W,M SoF-W,M
Vernon
  SHS-W,M
Verse De Basile see La Verse De
  Basile
Verse Qui M'a Po'te A Ma Fosse
  see La Verse Qui M'a Po'te A Ma
  Fosse
Vertigo
  OTO-W
Very Precious Love
  HFH-W,M MF-W,M
Very Thought of You
  MF-W,M RoE-W,M
Veshomeru
  JS-W,M (Hebrew Only)
Vesper Bells (from William Tell)
  CA-W,M
Vesper Hour
  MML-W,M
Vesper Hymn
  CSo-W,M ESB-W,M FWS-W,M
  HS-W,M LoS-W,M MG-W,M
  MU-W,M SiB-W,M TH-W,M
Vesper Song
  GrM-W,M
Vesper Song for Our Volunteers'

Sisters
  SiS-W
Vespers
  JC-W,M
Vesta and Mattie's Blues
  B-W,M BI-W,M
Vesti La Giubba
  MF-M WiS7-W,M
Vi Salde Vara Hemman Resa Till
  Amerika Amerikavisan
  SE-W,M (Swedish)
Via Dolorosa
  GP-W,M OGR-W,M VB-W,M
Vias Tuas, Domine
  Boo-W,M (Latin Only)
Vicar of Bray
  CSo-W,M FW-W
Viceroy Gives You All the Taste All
  the Time
  GSM-W,M
Vicksburg Blues
  AFB-W,M
Vicksburg Is Taken, Boys
  SiS-W
Vicksburg Soldier
  FMT-W
Victim to the Tomb
  BSo-W,M
Victorious March
  BSC-W
Victors, The
  Mo-W,M TI2-W,M
Victors All
  SL-W,M
Victors and Vanquished
  FSA2-W,M
Victory
  AL-W EA-W,M MSB-W
Victory at Last
  SiS-W
Victory at Trenton
  OHG-W,M
Victory in Jesus
  Tr-W,M
Victory Song
  AL-W CoS-W,M
Victory through Grace
  GH-W,M
Vict'ry Polka
  PT-W,M TI1-W,M
Vidalita
  LaS-W,M
Vieni, Vieni
  MF-W,M
Vienna Calling
  TTH-W,M
Vienna Girls
  K-W,M
Vienna, How D'ye Do?
  BP-W,M
Vienna Life
  OBN-M RW-M
Vienna, My City of Dreams
  MF-W,M
Vienna, Vienna
  BP-W,M
Viens Belle Nuit
  CaF-W (French Only)
Vietnam Song Cycle
  VS-W,M
Vieux Soulard Et Sa Femme see Le
  Vieux Soulard Et Sa Femme
View de Land
  RF-W,M
View from Queens
  TW-W
Vigndig A Fremd Kind

FW-W (Yiddish)
Vilia
  Mo-W,F NM-W,M OTO-W
  RW-W,M UBF-W,M
Vilia Song
  AmH-W,M WiS8-W,M
Vilikens and Dinah
  Oz1-W,M
Vilikens and Dinah see also
** Villikins and Dinah**
Village Band
  ASB2-W,M
Village Bells Polka
  FHR-W,M
Village Dance
  FSA2-W,M TF-W,M
Village Maiden
  FHR-W,M SSFo-W,M
Village of St. Bernadette
  TI1-W,M UFB-W,M
Village Square
  ASB2-W,M
Villain's Dance
  SB-W,M
Villancico
  ASB6-W,M LA-W,M (Spanish)
Villanesca
  LaS-M
Villikins and Dinah
  BSC-W FMT-W
Villikins and Dinah see also
** Vilikens and Dinah**
Villikins and His Dinah
  FW-W MSB-W
Vincent (Starry Starry Night)
  GrS-W,M GSN4-W,M
Vine and Fig Tree
  FW-W
Vinie
  NF-W
Vino Vino
  OTO-W
Violate Me
  AF-W
Violet (Das Veilchen)
  FSY-W,M (German)
Violets and Silverbells
  OTO-W Sh-W,M UBF-W,M
Violin Echo
  FSA2-W,M
Virden Martyrs
  AL-W
Virgin Mary (Had a Baby Boy)
  JF-W,M TO-W,M
Virgin Mary Had One Son
  FW-W
Virgin Most Pure
  OB-W,M
Virgin Sturgeon
  AF-W FW-W
Virginia Banishing Tea
  SBA-W
Virginia Belle
  FHR-W,M SSFo-W,M
Virginia City
  TW-W
Virginia, Don't Go Too Far
  ReG-W,M
Virginia Marseillaise
  Sin-W,M
Virginia Marseillaise see also
** Virginian Marseillaise**
Virginia, Our Home
  SiS-W
Virginia Slims Cigarettes Jingle see
** You've Come a Long Way, Baby**
Virginia Song

SE-W (Swedish)
Virginian Marseillaise
  SCo-W,M SiS-W
Virginian Marseillaise see also
** Virginia Marseillaise**
Virginian Strike of '23
  LSR-W,M
Virginiavisan
  SE-W (Swedish)
Virginie
  FSF-W (French)
Virgin's Cradle Hymn
  OB-W,M (Latin)
Vision, A (Gounod)
  TH-W,M
Vision Song
  GB-W,M
Visions of Sleep
  TI1-M UFB-M
Visite Du Jour De L'an see La
** Visite Du Jour De L'an**
Vital Signs
  VB-W,M
Vitu
  ASB5-W,M LA-W,M (Spanish)
Viva La Musica
  VA-W,M (Italian Only)
Viva La Quince Brigada
  BF-W,M (Spanish Only) FW-W
Viva L'America, Home of the Free
  SY-W,M
Viva Victoria
  MSB-W
Viva Vietnam
  VS-W,M
Viva, Viva La Musica
  Boo-W,M (French Only)
Vivaldi Concerto in C Major
  (Theme from Kramer vs. Kramer)
  TOM-M
Vive La Canadienne
  CFS-W,M (French) FW-W (French)
  SiP-W,M (French)
Vive La Compagnie
  FW-W HSD-W,M IL-W,M
  OFS-W,M OTJ-W,M PoS-W,M
Vive La Rose
  CUP-W,M (French Only)
Vive L'Amour
  Bo-W,M FWS-W,M HS-W,M
  LMR-W,M LoS-W,M SBF-W,M
  SiB-W,M TF-W,M WiS8-W,M
Vive Le Vent
  CE-W,M (French)
Vly Is on the Turmut
  OH-W,M
Vocalise
  MMW-M
Vodka
  ReG-W,M
Voice
  Am-W
Voice from Libby
  SiS-W
Voice of Bygone Days
  FHR-W,M SSFo-W,M
Voice of God
  GB-W,M
Voice of God Is Calling
  AHO-W,M
Voice of Night
  RW-W,M
Voice of Praise
  LMR-W,M SL-W,M TF-W,M
Voice of Toil
  AL-W
Voice Runs through the Sleeping

Land
  SL-W,M
Voice That Breathed o'er Eden
  FiS-W,M
Voices
  Mo-W,M OTO-W
Voices of the Woods
  AmH-W,M ESB-W,M
Voices That Are Gone
  FHR-W,M
Voici La Noel
  CUP-W,M (French Only)
Voici Le Printemps (Hear the Voice
  of Spring)
  F2-W,M (French)
Volare
  GSN3-W,M (Italian) HLS3-W,M
  (Italian) RW-W,M
Volga Boat Song
  MF-M RW-M TH-W,M
Volga Boatmen
  MML-W,M (Russian) NAS-W,M
  TI1-M UFB-M
Volga Boatmen see also Song of
** the Volga Boatmen**
Volga Boatmen Song
  TF-W,M
Volga Flows
  RuS-W,M (Russian)
Volunteer, The
  SCo-W,M SiS-W,M
Volunteer Boys
  SBA-W
Volunteer Organist
  Oz4-W
Volunteer Song
  SiS-W
Volunteers, The
  BC1-W,M
Volunteer's Call to Arms
  SiS-W
Volunteer's Farewell
  SiS-W
Von Gott Geborner Christ see Ein
** Von Gott Geborner Christ**
Voodoo Man
  AN-W
Voreema
  UF-W,M
Voronezh Round-Dance Chastushki
  RuS-W,M (Russian)
Vote for Bell of Tennessee
  MPP-W
Vote for Uncle Abe
  SiS-W
Vote Him Out
  AL-W
Voudriez-Vous Etre Charitables
  CaF-W (French Only)
Voulez Vous?
  CaF-W (French Only)
Vous T'e in Morico'
  BaB-W,M (French)
Vow
  Gl-W
Voy A Partir
  MSS-W,M (Spanish)
Voyage of the Walnut Shell
  OTJ-W,M OTO-W
Voyage of the Walnut Shell see
** also Walnut Shell**
Voyage to the Bottom of the Sea
  (Theme)
  GTV-M
Voyager
  ASB5-W,M (French)
Voyager see also Un Canadien

Errant
Voyagers
  FSO-W,M (French)
Voyageur Sings
  LMR-W,M
Voyageur's Song
  ATS-W,M NAS-W,M
Voyeur's Lament
  TW-W
Vreneli
  MG-W,M
Vreneli see also Oh, Vreneli
V'shomru
  SBJ-W,M (Hebrew Only)
Vu Si Ching (Scenes of Wusih)
  FD-W,M (Chinese)
Vuela, Suspiro
  LA-W,M (Spanish)

W

W.B.A.
  AL-W
WKRP in Cincinnati (Theme)
  TV-W,M
W.P.A. Ballad
  BMM-W
Wabash Blues
  HLS1-W,M
Wabash Cannon Ball
  GG2-W,M GSN1-W,M GuC-W,M
  HLS1-W,M RW-W,M
Wabash Cannonball
  AH-W,M BSo-W,M EC-W,M
  FAW-W,M FSB1-W,M FW-W
  IPH-W,M LSR-W,M MF-W,M
  OFS-W,M OTJ-W,M Oz4-W,M
**Wacht Am Rhein see Die Wacht
  Am Rhein**
Wade in the Water
  FGM-W,M FW-W IHA-W,M
  JF-W,M OFS-W,M RDF-W,M
  RW-W,M SFF-W,M
Wading
  ASB1-W,M
Wae's Me for Prince Charlie
  SeS-W,M
Waggle-Taggle Gypsies
  FW-W
**Waggle-Taggle Gypsies see also
  Wraggle-Taggle Gypsies**
Waggley Dog
  MH-W,M
Waggoner's Lad
  SCa-W,M
**Waggoner's Lad see also
  Wagoner's Lad**
Wagon Soldiers' Gang
  GO-W
Wagon Wheels
  FC-W,M MF-W,M RW-W,M
  TI1-W,M UFB-W,M
Wagoner Boy
  FoM-W,M
Wagoners
  BSC-W
Wagoner's Lad
  FPG-W,M FSt-W,M FW-W
  ITP-W,M
**Wagoner's Lad see also
  Waggoner's Lad**
Wah-Hoo!
  FC-W,M
Wai
  NSS-W
Waikaremoana

  SNZ-W,M (Maori)
Waillie
  FW-W
Waillie, Waillie
  AmS-W,M
Waist Deep in the Big Muddy
  VS-W,M
Wait
  Be1-W,M TWS-W
Wait a Bit, Susie
  ReG-W,M
Wait and Murmur Not
  GH-W,M
Wait for the Wagon
  ASB1-W,M ATS-W,M BH-W,M
  BMC-W,M FMT-W FW-W
  HS-W,M MES1-W,M MES2-W,M
  NAS-W,M OBN-W,M OS-W
  Oz3-W,M PoS-W,M POT-W,M
  Sin-W,M SiS-W,M TF-W,M
  WiS8-W,M
Wait Love Until the War Is Over
  MPP-W
Wait Till the Clouds Roll By
  AmH-W,M BH-W,M
Wait Till the Sun Shines, Nellie
  AH-W,M FSN-W,M FSTS-W,M
  FW-W FWS-W,M LWT-W,M
  MF-W,M OAP-W,M OBN-W,M
  OTJ-W,M RDT-W,M RW-W,M
  TI1-W,M UFB-W,M
Wait 'Till the War, Love, Is Over
  SiS-W
Wait Till You See Her
  OTO-W TI1-W,M TS-W UBF-W,M
  UFB-W,M
Waiter and the Porter and the
  Upstairs Maid
  OHF-W OTO-W
Waitin' (Capote/Arlen)
  Mo-W,M OTO-W
Waitin' at the Station
  Mo-W,M NM-W,M
Waitin' for My Dearie
  LL-W,M TW-W
Waiting
  GrM-W,M
Waiting (Comden/Styne)
  DR-W,M
Waiting (Only Waiting Till the
  Shadows)
  GH-W,M
Waiting (We've Hung Our
  Christmas Stockings)
  GM-W,M
Waiting (The Winter, Spring
  Awaits)
  FSA2-W,M
Waiting and Watching
  GH-W,M
Waiting at the Church
  FSN-W,M U-W
Waiting at the Door
  GH-W,M
Waiting for a Train
  HB-W,M LJ-W,M LSR-W,M
Waiting for the Bride
  Sw-W,M
Waiting for the Girls Upstairs
  Fo-W,M OTO-W UBF-W,M
Waiting for the Light to Shine
  UBF-W,M
Waiting for the Loved One
  SiS-W
Waiting for the Promise
  GH-W,M
Waiting for the Robert E. Lee

  FSTS-W,M WiS9-W,M
Waiting for You
  NN7-W,M
Waiting, Hoping and Praying
  SNZ-W,M (Maori)
Waiting on a Friend
  RoS-W,M
Waiting Time
  GrM-W,M
Waiting to See You
  TTH-W,M
Waitress and the Sailor
  GI-W,M GO-W,M
Waits, The
  MU-W,M
Wake and Sing
  Boo-W,M
Wake, Awake, for Night Is Flying
  SJ-W,M YC-W,M
Wake from Slumber
  TH-W,M
Wake, Isles of the South
  AHO-W,M
Wake Me When It's Over
  WNF-W
Wake Nicodemus
  AN-W FW-W MPP-W Sin-W,M
  SiS-W
Wake the Song of Jubilee
  AHO-W,M
Wake the Town and Tell the
  People
  MF-W,M TI1-W,M UFB-W,M
Wake Up
  GM-W,M JF-W,M SCL-W,M
**Wake Up and Dream (Theme) see
  Give Me the Simple Life**
Wake-Up Clock
  SOO-W,M
Wake Up, Jacob
  ASB6-W,M FN-W,M GM-W,M
Wake Up, Little Susie
  DRR-W,M ERM-W,M FRH-W,M
  RB-W TI1-W,M UFB-W,M
Wake Up Little Suzie
  GAR-W,M
Wake Up, Stir About
  GB-W,M
Wake Up, Wake Up
  Boo-W,M OnT6-W,M
Waked by the Gospel's Powerful
  Sound
  AHO-W,M
Wakeful Brook
  VA-W,M
Waking Time
  OB-W,M
Walk a Mile in My Shoes
  MCG-W,M
Walk Along, John
  DE-W,M Oz2-W,M
Walk Away
  RW-W,M TW-W
Walk Away Renee
  DRR-W,M MCG-W,M TI2-W,M
Walk Close to Me, O Lord
  GrG-W,M
Walk 'Em Easy round de Heaben
  NSS-W
Walk Gawd's Hebbenly Road
  BDW-W,M
Walk Hand in Hand
  FS-W,M TI2-W,M
Walk Him up the Stairs
  P-W,M
Walk in Jerusalem
  FGM-W,M

Walk in Jerusalem Just Like John
ETB-W,M FW-W
Walk in Joe
AFP-W
Walk in the Black Forest
TI1-W,M UFB-W,M
Walk Like an Egyptian
TTH-W,M
Walk On By
BDF-W,M HD-W,M MF-W,M
TOH-W,M
Walk on the Wild Side
BR-W,M MF-W,M OTO-W
TI1-W,M UFB-W,M
Walk over God's Heaven
GrG-W,M
Walk Right Out of This Valley
AG-W,M
Walk, Talk, Chicken with Your
Head Pecked
NF-W
Walk the Way the Wind Blows
EC-W,M
Walk Togedder, Childron
RF-W,M
Walk Together, Little Children
FVV-W,M
Walk, Tom Wilson
NF-W
Walk-Up Blues
LC-W
Walk with Me
FVV-W,M
Walk You in de Light
RF-W,M
Walkin'
WNF-W
Walkin' after Midnight
RW-W,M
Walkin' Back to Georgia
JC-W,M
Walkin' for Freedom Just Like
John
SFF-W,M
Walkin' in the Light
NH-W
Walkin' Miracle
RY-W,M
Walkin' My Baby Back Home
LM-W,M TI1-W,M UFB-W,M
Walkin' with the Blues
LC-W
Walking
ASB2-W,M
Walking Along
SD-W,M
Walking and Skipping
SiR-W,M
Walking at Night
Bo-W,M FW-W
Walking down Broadway
ATS-W,M
Walking down the Road
Mo-W,M
Walking Happy
TI1-W,M UFB-W,M
Walking Home with Angeline
GOB-W,M
Walking in the Sunshine
ATC2-W,M CSp-W,M TI2-W,M
Walking John
HB-W,M
Walking on the Levee
FSA1-W,M
Walking Song
ASB1-W,M GM-W,M HS-W,M
MG-W,M SD-W,M SFB-W,M

Walking the Boards
TW-W
Walking the Floor over You
FOC-W,M OGC2-W,M TI1-W,M
UFB-W,M
Walking through the Sleepy City
RoS-W,M
Walky-Talky Jenny
AmS-W,M
Wall, The
Fa-W,M
Wall Street Blues
B-W,M
Wall Street Rag
OnT6-M
Wall-Paper
NA-W,M
Wallpaper Roses
Mo-W,M
Walls Have Ears
SRE2-W,M
Walnut Shell
Mo-M
**Walnut Shell see also Voyage of
the Walnut Shell**
Walrus Hunt
RSL-W,M
Walter Winchell Rhumba
HLS3-W,M RW-M
Waltz (Brahms)
ASB1-M
Waltz (Brahms, Op. 39, No. 15)
OBN-M
Waltz (Chopin, Op. 18)
PaS-M
Waltz (Chopin, Op. 64 No. 2)
RW-M
Waltz (Lloyd Slind)
BMC-M
Waltz (from Die Fledermaus)
MF-M
Waltz across Texas
TOH-W,M
Waltz and Scene (Faust)
MU-W,M
Waltz at Maxim's (She Is Not
Thinking of Me)
LL-W,M
Waltz Eternal
SN-W,M
Waltz for a Mermaid
Mo-M OTO-W
Waltz for Debbie
MF-W,M
Waltz for Debby
TI1-W,M TWD-W,M
Waltz for Happy Occasions
RW-M
Waltz from Coppelia
RW-M
Waltz Me Around Again, Willie
FSN-W,M OTJ-W,M
Waltz of the Broom
PIS-W,M
Waltz of the Flowers
RW-M
Waltz of the Season
BP-W,M
Waltz of the Wind
OBN-M
Waltz Song (Czech Folk Tune)
ASB2-W,M ASB3-W,M MG-W,M
Waltz Song (Merry Widow)
AmH-W,M WiS8-W,M
**Waltz Song (Merry Widow) see
also Merry Widow Waltz**
Waltz the Hall

Oz3-W,M
Waltz You Saved for Me
CS-W,M HLS2-W,M OP1-W,M
Waltzing Matilda
ATM-W,M Bo-W,M FW-W
GI-W,M J-W,M OTJ-W,M U-W
Wan Ching (Sunset)
FD-W,M (Chinese)
Wanderer
ERM-W,M GAR-W,M TRR-W,M
Wanderer's Night Song
AmH-W,M (German) LMR-W,M
TH-W,M
Wanderin'
FAW-W,M FG2-W,M FoS-W,M
J-W,M NeA-W,M OFS-W,M
OTJ-W,M
Wandering
FW-W MG-W,M RS-W,M
RW-W,M SiB-W,M
Wandering Boy
Oz4-W
Wandering Cowboy
Oz2-W,M
Wandering Minstrel I
GiS-W,M
Wand'rin Star
LL-W,M OTO-W TI1-W,M
UBF-W,M UFB-W,M
Wand'ring Minstrel
MGT-W,M OTJ-W,M
Wang Wang Blues
MF-W,M RW-W,M
Want Ads
SoH-W,M
Want God's Bosom to Be Your
Pillow
WN-W,M
Want to Go to Heaven When I Die
GrG-W,M RF-W,M
Wanted
GCM-W,M MF-W,M
Wanted, a Substitute
MPP-W SiS-W
Wanted: Cornbread and Coon
NF-W
Wanted Dead or Alive
BHO-W,M
Wanting Things
Mo-W,M OTO-W
Wanting You
HC2-W,M MF-W,M
Wanton Trick
SR-W,M
Wanton Virgins Frighted
SR-W,M
Wants You to Be My Chauffeur
LC-W
War
ATS-W,M
War and Peace
OTO-W
War and Washington
AWB-W SI-W
War Baby
THN-W,M
War Begets Poverty
Boo-W,M
War between Democracy and
Aristocracy
AL-W
War Bird's Burlesque
NeA-W,M
War Department
AH-W,M JF-W,M SHS-W,M
War Game
IFM-W

War in Missouri in '61
  BSC-W
War Is Hell (on the Homefront Too)
  TOC82-W,M
War Is On
  NF-W
War News Blues
  DBL-W
War on Poverty
  TT-W,M
War Ship of Peace
  ANS-W
War Song
  DD-W,M SAR-W,M SBA-W
  SiP-W,M (Greek) SMW-W,M
  (Czech)
War Song for 61
  SiS-W
War Song of Dixie
  SiS-W
War Song of the Hussites
  TH-W,M
War Song of the Revolution
  BSC-W
War Song of the Texas Rangers
  ATS-W,M
War Will Soon Be Over
  SiS-W
Warble for Us, Echo Sweet
  Boo-W,M
Warbling at Eve
  AmH-M
Warchild
  BJ-W,M
Ward the Pirate
  OH-W,M
Warfare
  WN-W,M
Warm and Safe
  OTJ-W,M
Warm and Tender
  OTO-W
Warm As Wine
  OTO-W
Warm Red Wine
  OGC2-W,M
Warning
  BSC-W
Warning Shot (Theme)
  OTO-W
Warning to Girls
  TBF-W,M
Warning Word to an Emigrant
  SE-W (Swedish)
Warningsord Till Utwandrare
  SE-W (Swedish)
Warranty Deed
  Oz3-W,M
Warren and Fuller
  BSC-W
Warren's Address
  AWB-W
Warrenton
  SHS-W,M
Warrior
  VB-W,M
Warrior Bold
  AmH-W,M ESB-W,M HSD-W,M
  TH-W,M
Warrior Is a Child
  GP-W,M VB-W,M
Wars Are Our Delight
  Boo-W,M
Wars of Germany
  FMT-W
Warwick
  SHS-W,M

Wary Bachelors
  DD-W,M
Was Ever Maiden So
  Lericompooped?
  SR-W,M
Was I Wazir
  Ki-W,M
Was It a Morning Like This
  VB-W,M
Was My Brother in the Battle?
  FHR-W,M SiS-W
Was That the Human Thing to Do?
  MF-W,M OnT1-W,M
Was There Ever Kindest Shepherd
  FH-W,M
Washerwoman versus the Steam
  Washing Company
  ESU-W
Washing Day
  MH-W,M OHG-W,M SY-W,M
Washing Dishes
  ASB1-W,M
Washing Mamma's Dishes
  NF-W
Washing on the Siegfried Line
  T-W,M
Washington
  FSA1-W,M FSA2-W,M MPP-W
  SHS-W,M SL-W,M
Washington and Independence
  BC1-W,M
Washington and Lee Swing
  HLS1-W,M
Washington and Lincoln
  ASB1-W,M ASB4-W,M
Washington and the Flag
  MH-W,M
Washington Badge
  AH-W,M
Washington, My Home
  Fif-W,M
Washington Post
  MF-M
Washington Post March
  OTJ-M RW-M TI1-M UFB-M
Washington the Great
  ASB5-W,M
Washington's Favorite, the Brave
  Lafayette
  OHG-W,M
Washington's March
  MPP-W,M
Wasn't I Lucky When I Got My
  Time?
  LC-W
Wasn't That a Time?
  PSN-W,M WSB-W,M
Wasn't That Hard Trials
  MoM-W,M
"Wasp" Stinging "Frolick"
  ANS-W
Wasp's Frolic
  ANS-W AWB-W
Wassail of Figgy Duff
  GBC-W,M
Wassail Song
  ESB-W,M FW-W GBC-W,M
  IL-W,M JOC-W,M MAS-W,M
  MML-W,M OB-W,M SG-W,M
  SMY-W,M
Wassail, Wassail
  GUM2-W,M OE-W,M
Wassail, Wassail, All over the
  Town
  YC-W,M
Wasted Days and Wasted Nights
  FrF-W,M (Spanish) HLS9-W,M

W'at Harm Has Jesus Dun?
  BDW-W,M
Wat You Goin' Do W'en de
  Crawfish Gone?
  Me-W,M
Watch Night
  FSA1-W,M
Watch on the Rhine
  AmH-W,M (German) SiP-W,M
  (German)
Watch What Happens
  DJ-W,M MLS-W,M TI1-W,M
  UFB-W,M
Watch Your Footwork
  OnT6-W,M
Watcher, The
  SY-W,M
Watchet Sailor
  OTJ-W,M
Watchin' Girls Go By
  TOC82-W,M
Watching the Circus
  ASB3-W,M
Watching the Wheels
  TI2-W,M
Watchman
  SHS-W,M
Watchman, Tell Me
  AHO-W,M GH-W,M
Watchman, Tell Us of the Night
  Hy-W,M MC-W,M TF-W,M
  TH-W,M WiS7-W,M
Watchman's Call
  Boo-W,M SHS-W,M
Water Come a Me Eye
  GuC-W,M
Water for a Thirsty Land
  HCY-W,M
Water-Go-Round, The
  Boo-W,M
Water Is Wide
  FGM-W,M FW-W OFS-W,M
  SRS-W,M
Water, Water, Wall-Flowers
  CSG-W,M
Waterfall
  ELO-W,M
Waterfall at Bac Yon
  OU-W,M SBF-W,M
Waterflower
  PSD-W,M
Waterloo
  CMG-W,M DP-W,M FOC-W,M
  TI1-W,M TI2-W,M UFB-W,M
Watermelon Man
  OTJ-W,M
Watermelon on the Vine
  ITP-W,M
Watermelon Preferred
  NF-W
Watermelon Weather
  Mo-W,M NM-W,M
Waters Ripple and Flow
  UF-W,M
Wat'ry God
  SAR-W,M
Watts' Cradle Hymn
  DD-W,M
**Watts' Cradle Hymn see also
Cradle Hymn (Isaac Watts)**
Watts' Cradle Song
  OB-W,M
**Watts' Cradle Song see also Cradle
Song (Isaac Watts)**
Wave the Flag
  Mo-W,M
Waves

GM-W,M
Waves, The
  BMC-W,M
Waves of the Danube
  OBN-M
Waves of the Ocean
  AmH-M
Way, A
  VB-W,M
Way Down
  EP-W,M
Way Down in Ca-i-ro
  FHR-W,M SSFo-W,M
Way Down in Hell
  BDW-W,M
Way Down in Lone Valley
  Oz4-W
Way Down in Pawpaw Patch
  ASB3-W,M
Way Down in Rackensack
  Oz3-W
Way Down on the Bingo Farm
  BSB-W,M
Way Down South in Alabama
  FHR-W,M
Way Down South Where the Blues
  Began
  B-W,M
Way Down upon the Swanee River
  AmH-W,M ESB-W,M PoS-W,M
Way Down upon the Swanee River
  see also Old Folks at Home and
  Swanee River
Way Down Yonder in New Orleans
  MF-W,M TI1-W,M UFB-W,M
Way Down Yonder in the Brickyard
  RSL-W,M
Way Down Yonder in the Corn
  Field
  BSB-W,M EFS-W,M
Way Down Yonder in the Cornfield
  TMA-W,M
Way He Makes Me Feel
  GSN5-W,M MLS-W,M MoA-W,M
Way I Am
  NMH-W,M TOH-W,M
Way in de Middle of de Air
  NH-W
Way of Love
  TI1-W,M UFB-W,M
Way of the Lord
  MU-W,M (Hebrew)
Way Out in Idaho
  FW-W LSR-W,M SoC-W
Way Out There
  OGC2-W,M
Way Out West
  TS-W
Way Out West in Kansas
  TMA-W,M
Way Over in de Promis' Land
  FN-W,M
Way Over in the Heavens
  WN-W,M
Way Over in the Promised Land
  WN-W,M
Way That He Loves
  BSG-W,M BSP-W,M
Way That I Live
  OTO-W
Way to Heaven
  BSC-W
Way to Live
  MSB-W
Way to Love
  OTO-W
Way Up on Clinch Mountain

DD-W,M NeA-W,M
Way Up on Old Smokey
  WU-W,M
Way We Were
  BNG-W,M DC-W,M DPE-W,M
  EY-W,M FPS-W,M HFH-W,M
  MF-W,M TOM-W,M ToO76-W,M
Way-Worn Traveller
  NAS-W,M
Way You Look Tonight
  BBB-W,M FPS-W,M TI1-W,M
  UFB-W,M
Way You Make Me Feel
  BHO-W,M
Wayfarers in the Wilderness
  AHO-W,M
Wayfaring Pilgrim
  ITP-W,M
Wayfaring Pilgrim see also I Am a
  Poor Wayfaring Pilgrim
Wayfaring Stranger
  ASB6-W,M ATS-W BM-W
  FSSC-W,M FW-W GuC-W,M
  HS-W,M IHA-W,M JF-W,M
  LMR-W,M MES1-W,M MES2-W,M
  OTJ-W,M RDF-W,M RW-W,M
Wayfaring Stranger see also I'm a
  Poor Wayfarin' Stranger and I'm
  Just a Poor Wayfarin' Stranger
Ways of Arkansas
  Oz3-W,M
Wayside Blossoms
  GrM-W,M
Wayward Brothers
  SiS-W
Wayward Wind
  TI1-W,M UFB-W,M
Wazir Is Dead
  Ki-W,M
Wazir's Council
  Ki-W,M
Wazir's Palace
  Ki-W,M
We All Need Love
  HSe-W,M
We Are a Garden
  ER-W,M
We Are Almost Home
  RF-W,M
We Are Building a Strong Union
  FW-W SWF-W,M WW-W,M
We Are Building on a Rock
  RF-W,M
We Are Climbing Jacob's Ladder
  RF-W,M
We Are Climbing the Hills of Zion
  SpS-W,M
We Are Coming
  AL-W
We Are Coming, Father Abra'am
  ATS-W MPP-W NAS-W,M
  Sin-W,M SiS-W SSFo-W,M
We Are Coming Father Abraam,
  300,000 More
  FHR-W,M
We Are Coming from the Cotton
  Fields
  SiS-W
We Are Cut in Twain
  KH-W,M
We Are Dainty Little Fairies
  GiS-W,M MGT-W,M SL-W,M
We Are de Romans
  SGT-W,M
We Are Drifting Adown
  GrM-W,M
We Are Family

SoH-W,M
We Are Going Home
  GH-W,M
We Are Going to the Land of Dixie
  SiS-W
We Are Happy As We Sing To-day
  AME-W,M
We Are His Hands
  VB-W,M
We Are Living, We Are Dwelling
  Hy-W,M
We Are Marching On to Richmond
  Sin-W,M SiS-W
We Are Marching On to Victory
  SWF-W,M
We Are Marching to Canaan
  AL-W
We Are on Our Journey Home
  AHO-W,M
We Are So Blessed
  GP-W,M OGR-W,M VB-W,M
We Are Soldiers
  SFF-W,M
We Are Tenting To-night
  TH-W,M
We Are Tenting To-night see also
  Tenting Tonight
We Are the Boys of Potomac's
  Ranks
  SiS-W
We Are the Children of the Church
  AME-W,M
We Are the Gay and Happy
  Suckers
  SiS-W
We Are the Light
  VB-W,M
We Are the Reason
  VB-W,M
We Are the Romans see We Are
  de Romans
We Are the World
  LOM-W,M
We Are Those Children
  AG-W,M
We Are Tossed and Driven on the
  Restless Sea of Time
  AME-W,M
We Are Waiting by the River
  GH-W
We Are Walkin' down de Valley
  MoM-W,M
We Are Walking in de Light
  RF-W,M
We Are Watching, We Are Waiting
  AHO-W,M
We Be Soldiers Three
  SSP-W
We Be Three Mariners
  UF-W,M
We Be Three Poor Mariners
  OH-W,M SSP-W
We Bear the Strain of Earthly Care
  Hy-W,M
We Belong Together
  ILF-W,M ILT-W,M MF-W,M
  RY-W,M
We Beseech Thee
  G-W,M On-W,M OTO-W
  UBF-W,M
We Bring No Glittering Treasures
  AHO-W,M
We Can Change the World
  VB-W,M
We Can Never Forget It
  SiS-W
We Can Work It Out

BBe-W,M Be1-W,M JF-W,M
TWS-W
We Cats When Assembled
Boo-W,M
We Come A-Marching
SiR-W,M
We Come unto Our Father's God
Hy-W,M
We Conquer or Die
SiS-W
We Country Clodhoppers
Boo-W,M
We Dedicate This Temple
Hy-W,M
We Didn't Know
JF-W,M VS-W,M
We Do Squads Left
GO-W
We Don't Make Love Anymore
PoG-W,M
We Don't Matter at All
Mo-W,M NM-W,M OTO-W
We Don't Need Another Hero
BNG-W,M
We Gather Here to Sing to God
SHP-W,M
We Gather Together
AME-W,M GeS-W,M OM-W,M
OS-W
We Gather Together to Ask the
Lord's Blessing
ESB-W,M Hy-W,M TI1-W,M
UFB-W,M
**We Gather Together to Ask the
Lord's Blessing see also Prayer of
Thanksgiving and Thanksgiving
Hymn**
We Give Thee but Thine Own
AME-W,M Hy-W,M
We Go Together
Gr-W,M Mo-W,M OTO-W
UBF-W,M
We Got a Thing Going On
SFF-W,M
We Got It Made (Theme)
TV-W,M
We Got the Whole World Shakin'
SFF-W,M
We Had It All
TOC83-W,M
We Hail Thee with Rejoicing
CSF-W
We Have Fathers Gone to Heaven
FSU-W
We Have Felt the Love
GH-W,M
We Have Heard the Joyful Sound
Hy-W,M
We Have the Navy
Oz2-W,M
We Haven't Fought a Battle in
Years
UBF-W,M
We Hunted and We Hallowed
OHO-W,M
We Hunted and We Hollered
Oz1-W,M
We Joined the Navy
U-W
We Kiss in a Shadow
TI1-W,M UBF-W,M UFB-W,M
We Know That We Were Rebels
SiS-W
We Lift Our Songs to Thee
GH-W,M
We List to the Sound
Boo-W,M

We Love Each Other
TOH-W,M
We Love Mrs. Jones
GI-W GO-W
We Love the Venerable House
AHO-W,M
We Love You
RoS-W,M
We Made Good Wobs Out There
AFP-W
We Make a Beautiful Pair
Sh-W,M UBF-W,M
We May Never Love Like This
Again
DPE-W,M HFH-W,M MF-W,M
We May Not Climb the Heavenly
Steeps
AME-W,M FH-W,M
We Meet Again Tonight
TF-W,M
We Merry Minstrels
ESB-W,M
We Met
ESU-W
We Missed the Target
AF-W
We Mourn Our Fallen Chieftain
SiS-W
We Mustn't Say Goodbye
Mo-W,M OTO-W
We Need a Little Christmas
BCh-W,M DBC-W,M Mo-W,M
NM-W,M OTO-W TI2-W,M
UBF-W,M
We Need a Whole Lot More of
Jesus
BSo-W,M FW-W
We Need Him
Mo-W,M NM-W,M OTO-W
We Need the P.T.A.
LoS-W
We Never Speak As We Pass By
BH-W,M BSB-W,M EFS-W,M
We Pity Our Bosses Five
FW-W
We Plough the Fields and Scatter
AME-W,M Hy-W,M SJ-W,M
We Plow the Fields
SFB-W,M
We Praise Thee and Bless Thee
GH-W,M
We Praise Thee, God, for Harvest
Earned
AHO-W,M
We Praise Thee, If One Rescued
Soul
AHO-W,M
We Praise Thee, Lord
AME-W,M
We Praise Thee, O God
AME-W,M CEM-W,M TH-W,M
We Praise Thee, O God, Our
Redeemer
SJ-W,M
We Praise Thee, O God, Our
Redeemer, Creator
Hy-W,M SHP-W,M
We Praise Thee, O God, We
Acknowledge Thee to Be the Lord
(Te Deum)
Hy-W,M
We Praise Thee, We Bless Thee
GH-W,M
We Read of a People
AHO-W,M
We Remember Here Today
SHP-W,M

We Sail the Ocean Blue
GC-W,M GiS-W,M MGT-W,M
MU-W,M SL-W,M
We Sail the Sea in the Wind and
Storm
ID-W,M
We Sail the Seas
Mo-W,M NM-W,M OTO-W
We Shall Be Free
Le-W,M
We Shall Behold Him
VB-W,M
We Shall Behold the King
OGR-W,M
We Shall Meet, By and By
GH-W,M
We Shall Meet Him Bye and Bye
SiS-W
We Shall Not Be Moved
AFP-W FW-W JF-W,M (Spanish)
SFF-W,M SFM-W SWF-W,M
We Shall Overcome
AHO-W,M FG2-W,M FW-W
IHA-W,M JF-W,M RDF-W,M
SFF-W,M TI1-W,M TWD-W,M
UFB-W,M WW-W,M
We Shall Reign
GH-W,M
We Shall Rise, Hallelujah
Oz4-W,M
We Shall See Heaven Someday
HHa-W,M
We Shall Sleep
GH-W,M
We Shall Walk through the Valley
FW-W Le-W,M
We Shall Wear a Crown
AG-W,M AME-W,M HHa-W,M
We Sing America
WW-W,M
We Sold Our Farms or Journey to
America or the America Song
SE-W,M (Swedish)
We Speak the Same Language
Mo-W,M NM-W,M OTO-W
We Started Home with Heavy
Hearts
ESU-W
We Take the Guilty
GH-W,M
We Thank Thee
Boo-W,M FSA2-W,M
We Thank Thee, Father, for Our
Homes
SHP-W,M
We Thank Thee, Father, for the
Church
SHP-W,M
We Thank Thee for Our Friends
SHP-W,M
We Thank Thee, God, for Eyes to
See
SHP-W,M
We Thank Thee, God, for Pleasant
Days
SHP-W,M
We Thank Thee, God Our Father
SHP-W,M
We Thank Thee, Lord
AHO-W,M
We Thank Thee, Lord, Thy Paths
of Service Lead
Hy-W,M
We Think It Is the Rule
ESB-W,M
We Three (My Echo, My Shadow,
and Me)

Mo-W,M NM-W,M TI2-W,M
We Three Kings
    BMC-W,M GBC-W,M Gu-W,M
    MC-W,M SiB-W,M SOO-W,M
We Three Kings of Orient Are
    AHO-W,M BCh-W,M BCS-W,M
    BM-W CC-W,M CCH-W,M
    CI-W,M CSF-W ESB-W,M
    HS-W,M Hy-W,M IL-W,M
    OAP-W,M OTJ-W,M RW-W,M
    SCS-W YC-W,M
We Used To
    BDP-W,M
We Were Comrades Together in
    the Days of War
    Sin-W,M
We Were Three Young
    Shepherdesses
    FSD-W,M
We Who Love Music
    LMR-W,M
We Will Always Be Sweethearts
    OTO-W
We Will Be Merry Far and Wide
    SHP-W,M
We Will Glorify
    OGR-W,M
We Will Keep a Bright Lookout
    FHR-W,M
We Will Liberate the South
    VS-W,M
We Will March thro' the Valley in
    Peace
    NSS-W
We Will Not Fear
    AHO-W,M
We Will Not Retreat Any More
    SiS-W
We Will Overcome
    FSSC-W,M SWF-W,M
We Will See Him As He Is
    VB-W,M
We Will Send the Message Far
    SHP-W,M
We Will Sing God's Praises
    SHP-W,M
We Will Stand
    OGR-W,M VB-W,M
We Will Walk Dose Golden Streets
    WN-W,M
We Wish the Same to You
    SSo-W,M
We Wish You a Merry Christmas
    BCh-W,M BCS-W,M CSF-W
    FW-W FWS-W,M GBC-W,M
    GuC-W,M HS-W,M MC-W,M
    MF-W,M OAP-W,M OTJ-W,M
    PoG-W,M PSN-W,M RW-W,M
    SCS-W TI1-W,M UFB-W,M
    WSB-W,M
**We Wish You a Merry Christmas
see also Merry Christmas (We
Wish You a Merry Christmas)**
We Wish You a Merry Xmas
    GeS-W,M
We Wish You a Pleasant Journey
    BP-W,M
We Won't Go Home Till Morning
    PoS-W,M
We Won't Let Our Leader Down
    VP-W
We Won't Take It Back
    TW-W
We Worship Thee
    GH-W,M
We Worship Thee, Almighty Lord
    Hy-W,M

We Would Be Building; Temples
    Still Undone
    Hy-W,M
We Would See Jesus
    AHO-W,M GH-W,M
We Would See Jesus; Lo! His Star
    Is Shining
    Hy-W,M
Wealthy Merchant
    BSC-W TBF-W,M
Wealthy, Shmelthy, As Long As
    You're Healthy
    Sta-W,M
Wear a Red Rose
    BSo-W,M
Wear My Ring around Your Neck
    EP-W,M SRE1-W,M
Wearing of the Blue
    SiS-W
Wearing of the Gray
    SiS-W
Wearing of the Green
    AmH-W,M FSA1-W,M FW-W
    IL-W,M JF-W,M MF-W,M
    NAS-W,M OS-W SiP-W,M VP-W
Wearing of the Grey
    Sin-W,M
Wearing the Green
    UF-W,M
Weary Blues
    HW-W,M Mo-W,M NM-W,M
Weary Pilgrim's Consolation
    SHS-W,M
Weary Traveler
    ASB6-W,M
Weary Waiting
    SoF-W,M
Weather Songs
    FSA1-W,M
Weather Vane
    ASB3-W,M ASB4-W,M
    FSA2-W,M
Weave In!
    TF-W,M
Weave Room Blues
    AFP-W FSSC-W,M FW-W
Weaver's Life
    FW-W
Weaver's Life Is Like an Engine
    AFP-W WW-W,M
Webster
    SHS-W,M
**Webster (Theme) see Then Came
You**
We'd Better Bide a Wee
    HSD-W,M
Wedding Above in Glencree
    VP-W
Wedding and Bedding
    SR-W,M
Wedding Bells
    Mo-W,M NM-W,M OnT1-W,M
    TI2-W,M
Wedding Bells (Are Breaking Up
    That Old Gang of Mine)
    TI2-W,M
Wedding Gown for Sale
    Mo-W,M
Wedding Knell
    Su-W,M
Wedding March (Guilmant)
    TM-M
Wedding March (Mendelssohn)
    AmH-M MF-M NCB-M TI1-M
    TM-M UFB-M WGB/O-M
    WGB/P-M
Wedding March (Mendelssohn) see

**also Mendelssohn's Wedding
March**
Wedding March (Purcell)
    WGB/P-M
Wedding of Paddy O'Carroll
    VP-W
Wedding of the Fleas
    ASB5-W,M
Wedding of the Painted Doll
    HLS5-M
Wedding Postponed
    FSA2-W,M
Wedding Prayer
    WGB/O-W,M
Wedding Prayer (Crowder)
    TM-W,M WGB/P-W,M
Wedding Ring Ago
    OGC1-W,M
Wedding Song (Gluck)
    SL-W,M
Wedding Trilogy
    TM-M
Wedlock
    JF-W,M
Wednesday Evenin' Blues
    DBL-W
Wednesday's Child
    THN-W,M
Wee Bird Cam' to Our Ha' Door
    SeS-W,M
Wee Bird Came
    LMR-W,M
Wee Cooper o' Fife
    FG1-W,M FW-W
Wee Ducky Doddles
    MH-W,M
Wee House in the Wood
    BMM-W
Wee-Wee
    PO-W,M
Weekend
    ToO79-W,M
Weekend in New England
    GSN5-W,M RW-W,M TOF-W,M
Weekend in the Country
    LN-W,M LSO-W
Weekend Lover
    TI1-W,M UFB-W,M
Weekend of a Private Secretary
    OHF-W
Weekends Were Made for
    Michelob
    TI1-W,M UFB-W,M
Weekly Wedding
    K-W,M
Weela Wallia
    IS-W,M
Weep for the Brave
    SiS-W
Weep No More
    TH-W,M
Weep, O Mine Eyes
    OH-W,M
Weep! Oh, Weep!
    VS-W,M
Weep-Willow Tree
    AA-W,M
Weeping Mary
    AAF-W,M WN-W,M
Weeping, Sad and Lonely
    ATS-W,M FW-W Sin-W,M SiS-W
    SY-W,M
**Weeping, Sad and Lonely see also
When This Cruel War Is Over**
Weeping Saviour
    ATS-W SHS-W,M
Weeping Sinner, Dry Your Tears

AHO-W,M
Weeping Willow
  Oz2-W,M
Weeping Willow Tree
  ITP-W,M
Weeping Winds
  ASB5-W,M
Weevily Wheat
  ASB5-W,M FW-W HS-W,M
  Oz3-W,M
Weggis Fair
  HS-W,M
Wei Hai Wo
  MML-W,M
Weight, The
  RV-W
Welch
  SHS-W,M
Welcome
  BMM-W CCM-W,M
Welcome Back (Welcome Back,
  Kotter Theme)
  TVT-W,M
Welcome, Happy Morning! Age to
  Age Shall Say
  Hy-W,M
Welcome Home
  FVV-W,M TW-W
Welcome, O Birds
  ASB3-W,M
Welcome Song
  GB-W,M GrM-W,M LoS-W
  SoP-W,M
Welcome, Summer
  OB-W,M
Welcome, Sweet Day of Rest
  AME-W,M
Welcome Sweet Pleasure
  MU-W,M
Welcome, Sweet Rest
  AHO-W,M
Welcome, Sweet Springtime
  ESB-W,M
Welcome Table
  JF-W,M SFM-W
Welcome to Berlin
  C-W,M
Welcome to My Morning
  CJ-W,M
Welcome to My World
  NCB-W,M OPS-W,M TI2-W,M
Welcome to Our Country
  Mo-W,M NM-W,M OTO-W
Welcome to Our Hearts Again
  GiS-W,M
Welcome to Spring
  ASB4-W,M
Welcome to the Boomtown
  TTH-W,M
Welcome to the Club
  RW-W,M
Welcome to the Theater
  Ap-W,M Mo-W,M OTO-W TW-W
  VSA-W,M
Welcome, Wanderer
  GH-W,M
Welcome, Ye Hopeful Heirs of
  Heaven
  AHO-W,M
Welcome Yule
  OB-W,M
Welcoming the Bride
  Sw-W,M
We'll All Go Down to Rouser's
  TMA-W,M
We'll All Go Down to Rowser's
  Oz3-W,M

We'll All Go to Boston
  Oz3-W,M
We'll All Have Enough and to
  Spare
  AL-W
We'll All Meet Our Saviour
  FHR-W,M
We'll All Pull Through
  TMA-W,M
We'll Be Free in Maryland
  SiS-W
We'll Be Ridin'
  GI-W
We'll Be the Same
  TS-W
We'll Be Together
  CFB-W,M
We'll Be Together Again
  OTJ-W,M
We'll Camp a While in the
  Wilderness
  WN-W,M
We'll Crown Them with Roses
  Oz2-W
Well, Did You Evah?
  ML-W,M OTO-W TI1-W,M
  UBF-W,M UFB-W,M
We'll Dress the House
  CSB-W,M
Well Fare the Nightingale
  Boo-W,M
We'll Fight for Uncle Abe
  SY-W,M
We'll Fight It Out Here on the Old
  Union Line
  SiS-W
We'll Gather There
  GH-W,M
We'll Get There All the Same
  Oz2-W,M
We'll Go a Long, Long Way
  Together
  HSS-W,M HST-W,M OU-W,M
We'll Go Away Together
  SSA-W
We'll Go Down Ourselves
  MPP-W SiS-W
We'll Hunt the Buffalo
  SY-W,M
We'll Land on Canaan's Shore
  WN-W,M
We'll Land on the Shore
  WN-W,M
We'll March around Jerusalem
  WN-W,M
We'll March down Jerden
  BDW-W,M
We'll Meet Again
  TI2-W,M
We'll Meet Again, Sweetheart
  BIS-W,M
We'll Meet Each Other
  GH-W,M
We'll Never Have to Say Goodbye
  Again
  RW-W,M
We'll Never Turn Back
  JF-W,M SFF-W,M
We'll Not Give Up Our Union
  AL-W
We'll Overtake the Army
  WN-W,M
We'll Own the Earth
  AL-W
We'll Pay Paddy Doyle
  HSD-W,M
We'll Praise the Lord for He Is

Great
  AME-W,M
We'll Raise a Song
  CoS-W,M
We'll Rant and We'll Roar
  OHO-W,M
Well Respected Man
  JF-W,M
We'll Rest at the End of the Trail
  FC-W,M
Well Rung, Tom
  Boo-W,M
Well Rung, Tom Boy!
  OTJ-W,M
Well, She Ask Me in de Parlor
  NH-W
We'll Show You When We Come
  to Vote
  MPP-W
We'll Sing in the Sunshine
  HLS9-W,M IPH-W,M OTJ-W,M
  RW-W,M
We'll Soon Be Free
  FSSC-W
We'll Stem the Storm
  WN-W,M
We'll Stick to the Hoe
  NF-W
We'll Still Keep Marching On
  FHR-W,M
Well-Tempered Clavichord (Prelude
  in C)
  AmH-M
Well-Tempered Clavier (Fugue in C
  Minor)
  LTL-M
We'll Understand It Better By and
  By
  AME-W,M
We'll Vote for Hayes and Wheeler
  MPP-W
We'll Wait Till Jesus Comes
  IF-W,M WN-W,M
We'll Win This World
  TV-M
We'll Work Til Jesus Comes
  GH-W,M
**Wella Balsam Jingle see Love Your
  Hair**
Wells
  SHS-W,M
Wells Fargo Wagon
  TI2-W,M UBF-W,M
Welsh Carol
  OB-W,M
**Welsh National Song see Men of
  Harlech**
Welton
  SHS-W,M
W'en I'm Gone
  BDW-W,M
W'en Israel Was in Egypt's Lan'
  BDW-W,M
**W'en Israel Was in Egypt's Lan'
  see also When Israel Was in
  Egypt's Land**
Wendy
  Mo-W,M NM-W,M OTJ-W,M
  OTO-W
Went to the River
  Oz2-W,M
Went Up to the Mountain
  UF-W,M
We're All Dodging
  Oz3-W TO-W,M
We're All for You, Uncle Sam
  GO-W,M

We're All Nodding
Oz4-W,M
We're All the Go
NF-W
We're All Together Again
HS-W,M SCL-W,M
We're All Together Again, We're
Here
Bo-W,M
We're All Together Now
OTO-W
We're Bound for South Australia
ATM-W,M
We're Called Gondolieri
GiS-W,M MGT-W,M
We're Coming Again to the Dear
Ones at Home
SiS-W
We're Coming Fodder Abraham
MPP-W
We're Coming in Loaded
SRE2-W,M
We're Going Home
ASB1-W,M GH-W,M
We're Going on a Mission
AF-W
We're Going round the Mountain
RSL-W,M
**We're Going to Fight see We's
A-Gwine to Fight**
We're Going to Make a Man of
You
Fi-W,M
We're Gonna Have a Good Time
UBF-W,M
We're Gonna March in St.
Augustine
SFF-W,M
We're Gonna Move
JF-W,M
We're Gonna Move When the
Spirit Says Move
FW-W
We're Gonna Roll
JF-W,M
We're Hard-Working Students
CA-W,M
**We're Hard-Working Students see
also Estudiantina**
We're Havin' a Party
FR-W,M
We're Here for Fun
Bo-W LoS-W
We're Home Here
TV-W,M
Were I Thy Bride
GiS-W,M MGT-W,M
**We're in the Money see Gold
Digger's Song**
We're in the Q.M.C.
GO-W
We're in This Love Together
BOA-W,M
We're Marching Down to Dixie's
Land
SiS-W
We're Marching Down to Old
Quebec
Oz3-W,M
We're Marching On to War
Oz4-W,M
We're Marching round the Level
FVV-W,M
We're Marching to Zion
AME-W,M ATS-W GH-W,M
Were My Song with Wings
Provided

FSY-W,M (French)
We're Off to See the Wizard
HLS5-W,M RW-W,M WO-W,M
We're On the Upward Trail
Bo-W
We're Only Thinking of Him
MLM-W,M
We're Pals
GOB-W,M
We're Riding Our Bicycles
SOO-W,M
We're Soldiers with Wings
GO-W,M
We're Tenting on the Old Camp
Ground
SiS-W
We're Tenting Tonight
AmH-W,M NAS-W,M WiS8-W,M
We're the Boys for Mexico
ESU-W MPP-W
We're the Couple in the Castle
OTO-W
We're the Raiders
GI-W
We're Together
MCG-W,M
We're Union Elves
CoF-W,M
We're Very Sorry to Detain You
HJ-W,M
We're Wasting Time
RoS-W,M
Were You Ever in Rio Grande
HSD-W,M TH-W,M
Were You Not to Ko-Ko Plighted
MGT-W,M
Were You There (When They
Crucified My Lord)
AHO-W,M AME-W,M ATS-W,M
BNG-W,M CEM-W,M ETB-W,M
FN-W,M FW-W HLS7-W,M
Hy-W,M JBF-W,M JF-W,M
LoS-W,M LT-W,M OBN-W,M
OFS-W,M RDF-W,M RF-W,M
RW-W,M SJ-W,M SoF-W,M
SpS-W,M WiS7-W,M WN-W,M
YS-W,M
Wery Pekooliar, or the Lisping
Lovers
MSB-W
We's A-Gwine to Fight
SiS-W
Wesley
SHS-W,M
West Countree
BSC-W
West/East Bound and Down
TI2-W,M
West End Avenue
MS-W,M
West End Girls
TTH-W,M
West Texas Blues
BI-W,M
West Virginia Hills
Fif-W,M SWF-W,M
Western Federation of Miners
AL-W
Western Home
Oz2-W
Western Horizon
ASB6-W,M
Western Wind see Westron Wynde
Westinghouse Makes It Happen
GSM-W,M
Westminster Chimes
PaS-W,M SL-W,M

Westmoreland's Thing
VS-W,M
Westport
Mo-W,M NM-W,M
Westron Wynde
OH-W,M
**Westron Wynde see also
O Western Wind**
Westward Ho
FSA2-W,M
We-um
SiR-W,M
We've a Million in the Field
FHR-W,M SiS-W
We've a Story to Tell to the
Nations
Hy-W,M YS-W,M
We've Been a While A-Wandering
CCM-W,M
We've Drunk from the Same
Canteen
Sin-W,M SiS-W
We've Got a Job
SFF-W,M
We've Got a Secret
VB-W,M
We've Got the Love
TTH-W,M
We've Got Tonight
EC-W,M GCM-W,M
We've Had It
SYB-W,M
We've Hit the Trail Again
CA-W,M
We've Only Just Begun
FPS-W,M GrS-W,M GSN4-W,M
ILT-W,M MCG-W,M On-W,M
RW-W,M TM-W,M
Wexford Carol
OB-W,M
Wexford Girl
FMT-W SCa-W,M
Wha'll Be King but Charlie
SeS-W,M
Whack-Row-De-Dow
SiS-W
Whale of a Tale
OTJ-W,M
Whale Song
SSo-W,M
Whalehunters Theme
OTO-W
Whaling Song
FSA1-W,M
Wham Bam Shang-a-Lang (and a
Sha La La La La La Thing)
ToO76-W,M
Whar' Ha' Ye Been A' the Day
SeS-W,M
Whar' Shall I Be?
NH-W
**Whar' Shall I Be? see also Where
Shall I Be?**
What a Beau My Granny Was
ESU-W
What a Beautiful Day
GS1-W
What a Country!
Mo-W,M NM-W,M OTO-W
What a Court
SSS-W,M
What a Court Hath Old England
EA-W,M HAS-W,M
What a Day That Will Be
HHa-W,M
What a Diff'rence a Day Made
BeL-W,M DJ-W,M (Spanish)

FPS-W,M (Spanish) TI2-W,M
What a Difference You've Made in
My Life
TI2-W,M VB-W,M
What a Fellowship
AME-W,M
What a Fool Believes
DPE-W,M
What a Friend We Have in Hoover
PO-W,M
What a Friend We Have in Jesus
AME-W,M BNG-W,M CEM-W,M
FH-W,M FW-W GH-W,M HF-W,M
HLS7-W,M Hy-W,M IH-M
MAB1-W MSA1-W PoG-W,M
RDF-W,M WiS7-W,M
What a Friend We Have in Mother
FW-W
What a Gathering
GH-W,M
What a Gospel
GH-W,M
What a Grand and Glorious Feeling
FW-W
What a Happy Day
SiR-W,M
What a Lovely Day for a Wedding
A-W,M
What a Mornin'
ASB6-W,M
**What a Mornin' see also My Lord
What a Mornin', Oh What a
Mournin', Stars Begin to Fall, and
When the Stars Begin to Fall**
What a Party
OnT1-W,M
What a Piece of Work Is Man
H-W,M
What a Precious Friend Is He
HHa-W,M
What a Shame
RoS-W,M
What a Surprise
SOO-W,M
What a Waste
TW-W
What a Way to Go
VB-W,M
What a Way to Start the Day
PoG-W,M
What a Wonderful Change in My
Life
AME-W,M
What a Wonderful World
CFB-W,M TI2-W,M
What about You?
OGC1-W,M
What Am I Gonna Do
NMH-W,M
What Am I Gonna Do about You
TTH-W,M
What Am I Living For
TI1-W,M UFB-W,M
What Are Little Boys (Girls) Made
Of?
OTJ-W,M
What Are Little Boys Made Of?
J-W,M RW-W,M
What Are Mortals Made Of?
ESU-W
What Are We Doin' in Love
TI2-W,M
**What Are You... see also What
You...**
What Are You Doing New Year's
Eve?
TI2-W,M

What Are You Doing Out There?
VS-W,M
What Are You Doing the Rest of
Your Life? (Bergman/Legrand)
HLS5-W,M MLS-W,M RT6-W,M
RW-W,M
What Are You Going to Do with a
Drunken Sailor?
**What Are You Going to Do with a
Drunken Sailor? see also Drunken
Sailor and What Shall We Do with
a (the) Drunken Sailor**
GI-W,M HAS-W,M
What Are You Waiting for Mary
WDS-W,M
What Became of Me
Mo-W,M OTO-W
What Blood on the Point of Your
Knife?
Oz1-W,M
What Can I Do
VB-W,M
What Can I Say After I Say I'm
Sorry
GG4-W,M GST-W,M RW-W,M
**What Can I Say After I Say I'm
Sorry see also After I Say I'm
Sorry**
What Can Make a Hippopotamus
Smile
RSL-W,M
What Can the Matter Be?
ASB4-W,M
What Can Wash Away My Sins
AME-W,M
What Can We Do without a Man
TW-W
What Can You Get a Wookiee for
Christmas
TI1-W,M UFB-W,M
What Child Is This?
BCh-W,M BCS-W,M CC-W,M
CCM-W,M CEM-W,M CI-W,M
CSF-W FW-W FWS-W,M
HS-W,M LTL-W,M OAP-W,M
OTJ-W,M PoG-W,M SAC-W,M
SHP-W,M SiB-W,M SJ-W,M
VA-W,M
What Child Is This, Who, Laid to
Rest
Hy-W,M YC-W,M
What Color Is God's Skin
HCY-W,M
What Could I Do If It Wasn't for
the Lord
GrG-W,M
What Did Delaware?
RW-W,M
**What Did Delaware? see also
Oh, What Did Delaware, Boys**
What Did I Do to Be So Black and
Blue
UBF-W,M
What Did I Have That I Don't Have
TI1-W,M UBF-W,M UFB-W,M
What Did the Privates Do?
SiS-W
What Did This People unto Thee?
SoM-W,M
What Did You Learn in School
Today
JF-W,M RBO-W,M
What Do People Do
JC-W,M
What Do Simple Folk Do?
LL-W,M
What Do the Simple Folk Do?

OTO-W UBF-W,M
What Do You Do in the Infantry
TI2-W,M
What Do You Have to Do?
ST-W,M
What Do You Know about Love
Mo-W,M
What Do You Think
EFS-W,M
What Do You Want to Make Those
Eyes at Me For?
HLS1-W,M RW-W,M
What Do You Want with Money?
TS-W
What Does Echo Say?
VA-W,M
What Does Every Good Child Say?
FHR-M,W
What Does He Think?
ILT-W,M
What Does He Want of Me?
MLM-W,M
What Does Your God Look Like
JF-W,M
What Equal Honors Shall We Bring
AME-W,M
What Every Woman Lives For
SRE2-W,M
What Fairy-Like Music
HSD-W,M
What Flow'r Blooms? (Sa Huo K'ei
Lei?)
FD-W,M (Chinese)
What Glorious Vision
AHO-W,M
What Goes On?
TWS-W
What Good Does It Do?
Mo-W,M NM-W,M
What Good Is a Heart
TOH-W,M
What Good Would the Moon Be?
SSA-W,M TW-W UBF-W,M
What Grace, O Lord, and Beauty
Shone
AME-W,M Hy-W,M
What Happiness Can Equal Mine
AHO-W,M
**What Harm Has Jesus Done? see
W'at Harm Has Jesus Dun?**
What Has Happened
LMS-W,M
What Have I Done to Deserve This
CFB-W,M
What Have They Done to My
Song, Ma?
TI2-W,M
What Have They Done to the Rain?
FW-W IHA-W,M
What I Did for Love
CL-W,M DBC-W,M GrS-W,M
JP-W,M NCB-W,M OPS-W,M
OTO-W TI2-W,M UBF-W,M
WGB/P-W,M
What I Want You to Be
CEM-W,M
What I Was Warned About
Mo-W,M NM-W,M OTO-W
What If a Day
SSP-W
What If the Saint Must Die
AHO-W,M
What Irish Boys Can Do
AFP-W
What Is a Friend For
Mo-W,M
What Is a Woman?

I-W,M
What Is a Youth?
  LM-W,M OTO-W RJ-W,M
What Is Glory?
  ESU-W
What Is Home without a Mother?
  OTJ-W,M
What Is It to Be a Slave?
  AL-W
What Is Love?
  BS-W,M MF-W,M RY-W,M
What Is My Destiny?
  Mo-W,M NM-W,M
What Is She to Him?
  TW-W
What Is That Up Yonder I See
  NSS-W
What Is This Thing Called Love?
  DC-W,M DJ-W,M FrS-W,M
  HC1-W,M MF-W,M ML-W,M
  RoE-W,M
What Is Wrong with You?
  LC-W
What It's All About
  NCB-W,M
What I've Always Wanted
  Mo-W,M NM-W,M OTO-W
What Kind of a Kitty Have You?
  SoP-W,M
What Kind of Fool
  TI1-W,M UFB-W,M
What Kind of Fool Am I?
  DBC-W,M HC1-W,M HLS8-W,M
  ILT-W,M MF-W,M TI1-W,M
  TWD-W,M UBF-W,M UFB-W,M
What Kind of Love Is This
  RY-W,M
What Light Is That?
  MHB-W,M (Serbo-Croatian)
What Majesty and Grace
  AME-W,M
What Make Old Satan da Follow
  Me So
  NSS-W
What Makes Me Love Him?
  TW-W
What Might Be
  GrM-W,M
What More Could a Man Need
  WG-W,M
What Must a Fairy's Dream Be?
  FHR-W,M
What Must It Be
  GH-W,M
What Now My Love
  DPE-W,M (French) FPS-W,M
  FrS-W,M (French) MF-W,M
  RoE-W,M
What o' Dat
  DE-W,M
What Sam Tells the People
  MPP-W
What Shall He Have That Killed the
  Deer?
  ESB-W,M SSP-W
What Shall I Do?
  GH-W,M OH-W,M SNS-W
What Shall I Do to Show How
  Much I Love Her?
  EL-W,M
What Shall I Render to the Lord
  Hy-W,M
What Shall It Profit a Man
  Am-W
What Shall the Harvest
  GH-W,M
What Shall the Harvest Be?

FHR-W,M
What Shall We Do
  RSL-W,M
What Shall We Do for the
  Striking Seamen?
  AFP-W
What Shall We Do with a Drunken
  Sailor
  LH-W,M
What Shall We Do with the
  Drunken Sailor
  BF-W,M CSo-W,M FGM-W,M
  FW-W GeS-W,M SAm-W,M U-W
  WS-W,M
**What Shall We Do with the
  Drunken Sailor see also Drunken
  Sailor and What Are You Going to
  Do with a Drunken Sailor?**
What She Wanted and What She
  Got
  Sw-W,M
What Shepherd or Nymph of the
  Grove?
  OH-W,M
What Ship Is This?
  AHO-W,M
What Splendid Rays
  AHO-W,M
What Takes My Fancy
  Mo-W,M NM-W,M OTO-W
  W-W,M
What the Hell
  JC-W,M
What the World Needs Now Is
  Love
  BDF-W,M BR-W,M BSG-W,M
  BSP-W,M GOI7-W,M HD-W,M
  ILT-W,M MF-W,M OTJ-W,M
  RDF-W,M RDT-W,M
What Then Is Love
  Gu-W,M
What Then Is Love but Mourning
  EL-W,M
What Tidings Bringest Thou?
  GBC-W,M
What to Do
  RoS-W,M
What Use Are You
  STS-W,M
What Various Hindrances We Meet
  AME-W,M GH-W,M
What Voice of Distraction
  ESU-W
What Was Your Name in the
  States?
  AmS-W,M
What We Want
  AL-W
What Will Be, Will Be
  MAB1-W MSA1-W
**What Will Be, Will Be see also Que
  Sera, Sera and Whatever Will Be,
  Will Be**
What Will They Tell Our Children?
  SiS-W
What Will We Do for Bacon?
  NF-W
What Will We Do with the Baby-O
  SiR-W,M
What Will You Do
  GH-W,M
What Will You Do Now?
  MAR-W,M
What Wondrous Love Is This
  AHO-W,M
What Would I Do If I Could Feel
  Wi-W,M

What Would the Army Do?
  GI-W,M GO-W,M
What Would You Do?
  C-W,M
What Would You Do If You
  Married a Soldier?
  IS-W,M
What Would You Give in Exchange
  for Your Soul?
  BIS-W,M BSo-W,M
What Would You Take for Me
  Papa
  EFS-W,M
What Wrong Have I Done
  DBL-W
What Yo' Gwine t' Do When de
  Lamp Burn Down?
  RF-W,M
What You Goin' Do?
  NH-W
**What You Goin' Do W'en de
  Crawfish Gone? see W'at You
  Goin' Do W'en de Crawfish
  Gone?**
What You Goin' to Do When the
  Rent Comes Round
  AN-W
What You Gonna Do
  J-W,M
What You Gonna Name That
  Pretty Baby?
  FVV-W,M
What You Gwine to Do?
  RTH-W
What You Will (Quodlibet)
  SMY-W,M
What You Won't Do for Love
  ToO79-W,M
What You Would Not Have Done
  to Yourself
  Boo-W,M
What You're Doing
  Be1-W,M TWS-W
What'd I Say
  FrF-W,M HRB4-W,M ILF-W,M
  TI1-W,M UFB-W,M
Whate'er My God Ordains Is Right
  Hy-W,M
Whatever Became of Old Temple?
  Mo-W,M NM-W,M OTO-W
Whatever Gets You through the
  Night
  TI2-W,M
Whatever Happened to Old
  Fashioned Love
  TOC83-W,M
Whatever Happened to Randolph
  Scott
  CMG-W,M
Whatever He Wants for Me
  OM-W,M
Whatever Will Be, Will Be
  FPS-W,M MAB1-W MSA1-W
  PB-W,M PoG-W,M UFB-W,M
  WG-W,M
**Whatever Will Be, Will Be see also
  Que Sera, Sera**
What'll I Do with the Baby-O
  D-W,M
What'll We Do with the Baby-O
  FW-W
What's a Nice Kid Like You Doing
  in a Place Like This?
  Mo-W,M NM-W,M OTO-W
What's Become of the Punchers
  SoC-W
What's Forever For

TI2-W,M TOC82-W,M
What's Good about Goodbye?
  Mo-W,M NM-W,M OTO-W
What's Happened to Love
  ILT-W,M
What's Icumen In?
  Boo-W,M
What's It All About (The Wedding
  Song)
  NCB-W,M
What's It Like in the Promised
  Land
  SoC-W
What's New?
  DC-W,M FrS-W,M MF-W,M
  NK-W,M
What's New at the Zoo?
  DR-W,M
What's New Pussycat?
  HD-W,M ILS-W,M MCG-W,M
  RT6-W,M RW-W,M
What's Stirrin' Babe?
  NH-W
What's That I Hear
  JF-W,M
What's the Cause of This
  Commotion?
  SiS-W
What's the Matter?
  Sin-W,M SiS-W
What's the Matter Now?
  BSC-W
What's the Matter with Father
  RC-W,M
What's the Reason (I'm Not
  Pleasin' You)
  TI1-W,M UFB-W,M
What's the Use of Wond'rin?
  L-W TG-W,M
What's This Dull Town to Me?
  SeS-W,M
What's Wrong
  AL-W
What's Your Name
  TI1-W,M UFB-W,M
**Wheaties Cereal Jingle see Have
  You Tried Wheaties**
Wheel, The
  AN-W
Wheel in a Wheel
  RF-W,M
Wheel of Fortune
  FW-W MF-W,M
Wheels
  OPS-M PB-W,M
Wheels (Keep on Turning)
  TVT-W,M
Wheels of the Bus
  FP-W,M
When a Felon's Not Engaged in His
  Employment
  GiS-W,M
When a Gypsy Makes His Violin
  Cry
  MF-W,M
When a Hundred Years Have
  Rolled
  GrM-W,M
When a Jester Is Outwitted
  GiS-W,M
When a Maid Comes Knocking at
  Your Heart
  Fi-W,M
When a Man Falls in Love with a
  Little Turtle Dove
  Oz3-W
When a Man Falls in Love with a

Little Turtle Dove see also Kissing
Song
When a Man Loves a Woman
  DPE-W,M ERM-W,M GAR-W,M
  MF-W,M
When a Merry Maiden Marries
  GiS-W,M MGT-W,M
When a Tender Maid
  EL-W,M
When a Weary Task You Find It
  Boo-W,M
When a Woman Has a Baby
  SSA-W,M
When a Woman Loves a Man
  OHF-W
When a Wooer Goes A-Wooing
  MGT-W,M
When Abe Comes Marching Home
  SiS-W
When Ah Was in Jail
  SGT-W,M
When All Night Long
  GiS-W,M MGT-W,M
When All Thy Mercies, O My God
  AME-W,M Hy-W,M
When Answers Aren't Enough
  VB-W,M
When Are the Hebrew Children?
  AHO-W,M
When As Returns This Solemn Day
  AME-W,M
When Bob Got Throwed
  SoC-W
When Britain Really Ruled the
  Waves
  GiS-W,M MGT-W,M
When Cats Get Up
  MH-W,M
When Cheer Fills the Hearts of My
  Friends
  GB-W,M
When Children Pray
  JBF-W,M
When Christ Was Born of Mary
  Free
  GeS-W,M JOC-W,M
When Christmas Is Dawning
  BeB-W,M
When Christmas Morn Is Dawning
  CCM-W,M RW-W,M
When Daddy Comes Home
  MH-W,M
When Daffodils Begin to Peer
  SSP-W
When Daisies Pied
  OH-W,M SSB-W,M
When Daisies Pied and Violets Blue
  FSS-W,M
When Darkness Enfolds Me
  ID-W,M
When Day Is Done
  MF-W,M OHB-W,M T-W,M
When de Band Begins to Play
  NH-W
When de Saints Come Marchin' In
  OBN-W,M
**When de Saints Come Marchin' In
  see also When the Saints Go
  Marching In**
When de Train Come Along
  NH-W
**When de Train Come Along see
  also When the Train Comes Along**
When Dear Friends Are Gone
  FHR-W,M
When Did I Fall in Love
  OTO-W UBF-W,M

When Do We Dance
  GOB-W,M
When Does This Feeling Go Away?
  Mo-W,M NM-W,M OTO-W
When First I Saw My Barb'ra Fair
  TW-W
When First My Old, Old Love I
  Knew
  GiS-W,M MGT-W,M
When First the Sun
  Boo-W,M
When First unto This Country
  FW-W
When Francis Dances with Me
  BH-W,M
When Frederic Was a Little Lad
  GiS-W,M MGT-W,M
When Gemini Meets Capricorn
  TW-W
When God Descends with Men to
  Dwell
  AHO-W,M
When God Dips His Love
  HHa-W,M
When God Ran
  VB-W,M
When Good King Arthur Ruled This
  Land
  CSo-W,M
When He Cometh
  HSD-W,M OM-W,M WN-W,M
When He Was on the Cross
  AG-W,M HHa-W,M
When, His Salvation Bringing
  Hy-W,M
When I Admire the Greatness
  AHO-W,M (Dutch)
When I Am Gone
  SHS-W,M
When I Begin to Farm
  LC-W
When I Call Your Name
  GCM-W,M
When I Can Read My Title Clear
  AME-W,M
When I Dance with the Person I
  Love
  Mo-W,M NM-W,M OTO-W
When I Dream of Old Erin
  RW-W,M
When I Fall in Love
  BeL-W,M DJ-W,M TI1-W,M
  UFB-W,M
When I First Came to This Land
  FW-W JF-W,M
When I First Put This Uniform On
  GiS-W,M
When I Get Carried Away
  HHa-W,M
When I Get Home
  OnT6-W,M TWS-W
When I Get on Yonder Hill
  Oz3-W
When I Gets to de Middle of de Air
  BPM-W,M
When I Go on the Stage
  TS-W
When I Go Out of a Door
  MGT-W,M
When I Go to Marry
  NF-W
When I, Good Friends, Was Call'd
  to the Bar
  GiS-W,M MGT-W,M
When I Grow Too Old to Dream
  GSO-W,M L-W OP2-W,M
  RW-W,M STW-W,M U-W

When I Grow Up
  OTJ-W,M
When I Hear Your Name
  OGR-W,M
When I Kneel Down to Pray
  SOW1-W,M SOW2-W,M
When I Lay Down and Die
  J-W,M
When I Left the States for Gold
  BSC-W
When I Look at Calvary
  HHa-W,M
When I Loved Her
  SuS-W,M
When I Made My Decision
  BSG-W,M BSP-W,M CEM-W,M
When I Need You
  TI1-W,M UFB-W,M
When I Needed a Neighbor
  JF-W,M
When I Paint My Masterpiece
  GrS-W,M
When I Saw Sweet Nelly Home
  PoS-W,M
When I See an Elephant Fly
  NI-W,M TI1-W,M UFB-W,M
When I Survey the Wondrous
  Cross
  AME-W,M GH-W,M HF-W,M
  Hy-W,M SJ-W,M TB-W,M
When I Take My Sugar to Tea
  AT-W,M NK-W,M
When I Teach Singing
  LA-W,M (Spanish)
When I Think of the Last Great
  Roundup
  SoC-W
When I Travel
  SOO-W,M
When I Wake Up Each Morning
  SHP-W,M
When I Wake Up in the Morning
  SHP-W,M
When I Was a Cowboy
  NeF-W Oz2-W,M
When I Was a Drummer
  BMC-W,M
When I Was a Lad
  GiS-W,M HS-W,M MGT-W,M
  OTJ-W,M TH-W,M
When I Was a Lady
  CSG-W,M
When I Was a Little Boy
  NF-W Oz3-W,M
When I Was a Little Ole Boy
  LC-W,M
When I Was a Roustabout
  NF-W NH-W
When I Was a Shoemaker
  OTJ-W,M
When I Was a Young Girl
  IF-W,M
When I Was a Youngster
  OTJ-W,M
**When I Was in Jail see When Ah
Was in Jail**
When I Was Seventeen
  MML-W,M (Swedish) SE-W,M
  (Swedish)
When I Was Single
  BSC-W FoS-W,M FW-W
  GeS-W,M
When I Was Wicked an' Prone to
  Sin
  NSS-W
When I Was Young
  CMG-W,M CSD-W,M (French)

IS-W,M
When I Went to the Bar
  MGT-W,M
When Icicles Hang by the Wall
  FSS-W,M SSB-W,M
When I'm Dead and Buried
  BPM-W,M
When I'm Fully Grown
  Lo-W,M
**When I'm Gone see W'en I'm
Gone**
When I'm Near You
  OTO-W
When I'm Not Near the Girl I Love
  FR-W,M HC2-W,M LM-W,M
  OTO-W TI1-W,M UBF-W,M
  UFB-W,M
When I'm Sixty-Four
  BBe-W,M Be2-W,M OnT6-W,M
  PMC-W,M TWS-W WG-W,M
When in Rome (I Do As the
  Romans Do)
  Mo-W,M NM-W,M
When in the Night I Meditate
  Hy-W,M
When Ireland Stands among the
  Nations of the World
  E-W,M
When Irish Eyes Are Smiling
  MF-W,M OAP-W,M TI1-W,M U-W
  UFB-W,M
When Is It Best?
  Boo-W,M
When Israel Was in Egypt's Land
  AHO-W,M ESB-W,M
**When Israel Was in Egypt's Land
see also Go Down Moses, Let My
People Go, and W'en Israel Was
in Egypt's Lan'**
When It Rains It Pours
  NMH-W,M
When It's Apple Blossom Time in
  Normandy
  RC-W,M
**When It's Darkness on the Delta
see Darkness on the Delta**
When It's Iris Time in Tennessee
  Fif-W,M
When It's Night-Time in Nevada
  FC-W,M
When It's Round-Up Time in
  Heaven
  JD-W,M
When It's Roundup Time in Heaven
  RDF-W,M SF-W,M
When It's Sleepy Time Down
  South
  TI2-W,M
When It's Springtime in the
  Rockies
  FC-W,M GST-W,M RW-W,M
When I've Done My Best
  GrG-W,M
When I've Sung My Last Song
  GrG-W,M
When Jesus Brought de Light to
  Me
  Me-W,M
When Jesus Christ Was Here
  Below
  BMM-W,M
When Jesus Comes
  GH-W,M
When Jesus Comes to Reward His
  Servants
  AME-W,M
When Jesus Saw the Fishermen

SHP-W,M
When Jesus Taught beside the Sea
  SHP-W,M
When Jesus Taught the Word of
  God
  SHP-W,M
When Jesus Walked on Galilee
  FiS-W,M
When Jesus Wept
  AH-W,M EA-W,M
When Joanna Loved Me
  Mo-W,M NM-W,M
When Johnny Comes Marching
  MAR-W,M
When Johnny Comes Marching
  Home
  AAP-W,M AH-W,M BH-W,M
  BM-W DC-W,M FW-W HS-W,M
  HSD-W,M IHA-W,M LTL-W,M
  MAS-W,M MF-W,M MPP-W
  NAS-W,M OFS-W,M OHG-W,M
  OS-W OTJ-W,M PoS-W,M
  SiB-W,M Sin-W,M SiS-W
  SMW-W,M TI1-W,M TMA-W,M
  UFB-W,M WiS8-W,M
When Johnny Comes Marching
  Home Again
  HA-W,M
When Judgment Day Is Drawing
  Nigh
  AME-W,M
When Judith Had Laid
  Boo-W,M
When Labor Has Come to Its Own
  AL-W
When Love Is Kind
  SFB-W,M TH-W,M
When Love Turns to Hate
  OGC2-W,M
When Lovely Woman
  ESU-W
When Lovers Laugh
  Mo-W,M NM-W,M
When Mabel Comes in the Room
  LM-W,M OTO-W
When Maiden Loves
  GiS-W,M MGT-W,M
When Mama Prayed
  HHa-W,M
When Mexican Joe Met Jole Blon
  OGC2-W,M
When Morning Breaks
  RBO-W,M
When Morning Gilds the Skies
  AME-W,M CEM-W,M FH-W,M
  Hy-W,M SJ-W,M YS-W,M
When Morning Gilds the Sky
  GH-W,M
When Morning Lights the Eastern
  Skies
  Hy-W,M
When Moses Smote de Water
  My-W,M
When Mother Love Makes All
  Things Bright
  AME-W,M
When Music Leads the Way
  SL-W,M
When My Baby Smiles at Me
  BBB-W,M LWT-W,M TI1-W,M
  UFB-W,M
When My Blue Moon Turns to Gold
  Again
  BIS-W,M
When My Dream Boat Comes
  Home
  MF-W,M

When My Dreamboat Comes Home
OHB-W,M
When, My Saviour, Shall I See
AME-W,M
When My Ship Comes In
WDS-W,M
When My Soldier Is Married to Me
SiS-W
When My Sugar Walks down the
Street
BBB-W,M TI2-W,M
When My Wahine Does the Poi
SNZ-W,M (Maori)
When My Wife Dies
NF-W
When o'er Earth's Face
Boo-W,M
When Old Friends Were Here
FHR-W,M SSFo-W,M
When Our Earthly Sun Is Setting
AHO-W,M
When Our Gallant Norman Foes
GiS-W,M MGT-W,M
When Out of Egypt's Land
SoF-W,M
When Pa
OTJ-W,M
When Peace, Like a River
AME-W,M
When Rock and Roll Come to
Trinidad
NK-W,M
When Sammy Put the Paper on the
Wall
RSL-W,M
When Sammy Sang the
Marseillaise
HJ-W,M
When Samson Was a Tall Young
Man
SSP-W
When Santa Claus Gets Your
Letter
BCh-W,M
When Shall My Pilgrimage, Jesus
My Saviour, Be Ended?
AHO-W,M (Swedish)
When Shall We All Meet Again
AHO-W,M
When Shall We Three Meet Again
HSD-W,M
When Sherman Marched Down to
the Sea
Sin-W,M
When Spring Returns Again
Boo-W,M
When Stars Are in the Quiet Skies
MML-W,M
When Summer Is Gone (How I'll
Miss You)
NM-W,M
When Sun Doth Rise
AHO-W,M
When That I Was a Little Tiny Boy
FSS-W,M SSP-W
When That I Was and a Little Tiny
Boy
SSB-W,M
**When the Band Begins to Play see
When de Band Begins to Play**
When the Battle Is O'er
SiS-W
When the Bees Are in the Hive
ATS-W,M
When the Bloom Is on the Sage
FC-W,M
When the Boys Come Home

MPP-W SiS-W,M
When the Cactus Is in Bloom
FC-W,M
When the Cat's Away the Mice
Will Play
M-W,M
When the Chariot Comes
WN-W,M
When the Children Are Asleep
TG-W,M
When the Comforter Came
GH-W,M
When the Corn Is Waving
AmH-W,M
When the Corn Is Waving, Annie
Dear
WiS8-W,M
When the Crimson Sun Had Set
JOC-W,M
When the Cruel War Is Over
Sin-W,M
When the Curfew Blows
Am-W,M
When the Curtains of Night Are
Pinned Back
NeA-W,M
When the First Trumpet Sounds
WN-W,M
When the Foeman Bares His Steel
GiS-W,M MGT-W,M SL-W,M
When the General Roll Is Called
RF-W,M
When the Golden Leaves Begin to
Fall
BSo-W,M
When the Gov'nment Milks the
Cows
AL-W
When the Grand Old Flag Goes By
SL-W,M
When the Iceworms Nest Again
FW-W
When the Idle Poor Become the
Idle Rich
FR-W,M TW-W
When the Irish Backs Go Marching
By
CoS-W,M
When the Irish Go Marching By
Mo-W,M
When the Kids Get Married
I-W,M
When the Kye Come Hame
SeS-W,M
When the Lights Are Low
HSD-W,M
When the Little Children Sleep
HS-W,M
When the Lord of Love
LMR-W,M
When the Love Comes Trick-a-lin'
Down
LMR-W,M
When the Lurline Sails Away
TI1-W,M UFB-W,M
When the Mocking Birds Are
Singing in the Wildwood
RC-W,M
When the Moon Comes over the
Mountain
BH-W,M GG2-W,M HLS2-W,M
When the Night Wind Howls
MGT-W,M
When the North Wind Blows
FSA2-W,M
When the Red, Red Robin Comes
Bob, Bob Bobbin' Along

BBB-W,M FPS-W,M HSS-W,M
TI1-W,M UFB-W,M
When the Revolution Comes
AL-W
When the Robins Nest Again
BH-W,M EFS-W,M FSTS-W,M
When the Roll Is Called Up Yonder
FoS-W,M HF-W,M OM-W,M
RDF-W,M RW-W,M SpS-W,M
YS-W,M
When the Roses Bloom (Hoffnung)
FSY-W,M (German)
When the Saints Go Marching
Home
FWS-W,M SFB-W,M
When the Saints Go Marching In
AH-W,M BMC-W,M Bo-W,M
FG1-W,M FGM-W,M FSB2-W,M
FW-W GG2-W,M GS1-W
GSN1-W,M GuC-W,M HHa-W,M
HLS7-W,M IHA-W,M IPH-W,M
MES2-W,M MF-W,M OPS-W,M
OTJ-W,M RDF-W,M RW-W,M
SpS-W,M SUH-W,M WSB-W,M
**When the Saints Go Marching In
see also When de Saints Come
Marchin' In**
When the Sea Begin's A-Calling
NN2-W,M
When the Seed of Thy Word Is
Cast
AHO-W,M
When the Snow Is on the Roses
GG3-W,M
When the Snow Was Deep
BMM-W,M
When the Spring Is in the Air
L-W MA-W,M
When the Spring with Magic Finger
TF-W,M
When the Stars
MH-W,M
When the Stars Begin to Fall
TO-W,M WN-W,M
**When the Stars Begin to Fall see
also My Lord What a Mornin', Oh,
What a Mournin', Stars Begin to
Fall, and What a Mornin'**
When the Storms of Life Are
Raging
AME-W,M
When the Strike Was On
AL-W
When the Summer Is Gone
Mo-W,M
When the Sun Comes Out
ToS-W,M
When the Sun Go Down
LC-W
When the Sun Is Shining
DBL-W
When the Swallows
HSD-W,M
When the Swallows Homeward Fly
AmH-W,M EFS-W,M TMA-W,M
WiS8-W,M
When the Train Comes Along
HS-W,M LSR-W,M RSL-W,M
**When the Train Comes Along see
also When de Train Come Along**
When the Values Go Up
GSM-W,M
When the War Is Over
SiS-W
When the Whip Comes Down
RoS-W,M
When the Work's All Done This

Fall
ATS-W,M FW-W GA-W,M
HWS-W,M
When the World Ketch Afire
WN-W,M
When the World Was Young
NK-W,M OHF-W TI1-W,M
UFB-W,M
When They Come Marching Home
SiS-W
When Thickly Beat the Storms of
Life
AHO-W,M
When Things Go Wrong with You
FW-W
When This Bloody War Is Over
GI-W GO-W,M
When This Cruel Draft Is Over
SiS-W
When This Cruel War Is Over
HSD-W,M IHA-W,M MPP-W
NSS-W
**When This Cruel War Is Over see
also Weeping, Sad and Lonely**
When This Dreadful War Is Ended
FHR-W,M SiS-W
When This War Is Over
SiS-W
When Thy Heart with Joy
O'erflowing
AHO-W,M
When to Danger Duty Calls Me
CA-W,M
When to Thy Vision
HSD-W,M
When Troy Town
Boo-W,M
When Two Worlds Collide
TOH-W,M
When Uncle Sam's Doughboy
Roped a Wild Irish Rose
HB-W
When upon the Field of Glory
SCo-W,M Sin-W,M SiS-W,M
When V and I Together Meet
Boo-W,M
When Vandy Starts to Fight
Mo-W,M TI2-W,M
When We All Get to Heaven
AME-W,M
When We All March Home from
the War
SiS-W
When We Come of Age
Mo-W,M NM-W,M
When We Do Meet Again
NSS-W
When We Get Home
GH-W,M
When We Go to Play
SOO-W,M
When We Hear Scripture Read in
Church
SHP-W,M
When We Walk with the Lord
AME-W,M
**When We're Alone see Penthouse
Serenade**
When We're United for Freedom
AL-W
When Wild Confusion Wrecks the
Air
AHO-W,M
When Will Dis Cruel War Be Ober?
SiS-W
When Will I Be Loved
GSN4-W,M

When Wilt Thou Save the People?
SWF-W,M TH-W,M
When Winds Are Raging
AHO-W,M
When Workingmen Combine
AL-W
When You and I Were Young
HSD-W,M
When You and I Were Young,
Maggie
AmH-W,M ATS-W BH-W,M
BSB-W,M FW-W IL-W,M MF-W,M
NAS-W,M OAP-W,M OBN-W,M
PoS-W,M STR-W,M WiS8-W,M
When You Come to the End of the
Day
RDF-W,M
When You Do the Ragtime Dance
OTJ-W,M
When You Find Her, Keep Her
TOC82-W,M
When You Get Home Remember
Me
ANS-W
When You Get to the Heart
TTH-W,M
When You Pray
BSG-W,M BSP-W,M
When You Say Budweiser, You've
Said It All
TI1-W,M UFB-W,M
When You Send a Valentine
SOO-W,M
When You Walk down the Aisle
L-W
When You Were Blue and I Was
Green
TTH-W,M
When You Were Sweet Sixteen
BSB-W,M FSN-W,M FW-W
OAP-W,M RW-W,M TI1-W,M
UFB-W,M
When You Wish upon a Star
HST-W,M NI-W,M RoE-W,M
TI1-W,M UFB-W,M
When You Wore a Tulip
BH-W,M CS-W,M HLS1-W,M
OS-W RW-W,M SLB-W,M
When Your Hair Has Turned to
Silver
Mo-W,M NM-W,M TI2-W,M
When Your Leaves Have Turned to
Silver
AF-W
When Your Lover Has Gone
FrS-W,M MF-W,M MR-W,M
OHB-W,M
When Your Potato's Done
SMY-W,M VA-W,M
When You're a Fighter
IFM-W
When You're Away
OG-W,M SLB-W,M
When You're Good to Mama
CMV-W,M
When You're in Love with a
Beautiful Woman
ToO79-W,M
When You're in My Arms
TP-W,M UBF-W,M
When You're Loved
SBS-W,M
When You're Lying Awake
MGT-W,M
When You're Lying Awake with a
Dismal Headache
GiS-W,M

When You're Not a Lady
TOC83-W,M
When You're Smiling
NK-W,M TI2-W,M U-W
When You're Ugly Like Us (You
Just Naturally Got to Be Cool)
TOH-W,M
When You're Wearing the Ball and
Chain
OG-W,M
When You're Young and in Love
Mo-W,M
Whence Comes This Rush of
Wings
CSF-W
Whence Is That Goodly Fragrance
JOC-W,M
Whence, O Shepherd Maiden
CFS-W,M (French) FSO-W,M
(French)
Whene'er I Take My Walks Abroad
Oz4-W
Whene'er Noble Deed Is Wrought
Boo-W,M
Whenever You Need Somebody
TTH-W,M
Where Am I Going?
MF-W,M RW-W,M SC-W,M
Where Are the Froggies?
SSe-W,M
Where Are the Nine?
GH-W,M
Where Are the Other Nine?
VB-W,M
Where Are the Snows?
I-W,M
Where Are Y' Goin', My Pretty
Miss?
BeB-W,M
Where Are You?
GSO-W,M
Where Are You Going, Abe
Lincoln?
Sin-W,M
Where Are You Going, My Good
Old Man
FW-W
Where Are You Going, My Pretty
Maid?
Boo-W,M CSo-W,M
Where Are You Going To?
SMa-W,M
Where Are You Going to, My
Pretty Maid?
OTJ-W,M
Where Are You, $300?
SiS-W
Where Can I Go and Be a Person?
SYB-W,M
Where Can You Take a Girl?
Mo-W,M OTO-W
Where Cross the Crowded Ways
of Life
AHO-W,M AME-W,M Hy-W,M
Where Did Robinson Crusoe Go
with Friday on Saturday Night?
NoS-W,M OTJ-W,M
Where Did the Good Times Go?
OTO-W SBS-W,M UBF-W,M
Where Did They Go, Lord
OGC1-W,M
Where Did You Get That Hat?
BH-W,M EFS-W,M FSN-W,M
FSTS-W,M OTJ-W,M
Where Do I Begin? (Theme from
Love Story)
AT-W,M GOI7-M GrS-W,M

ILT-W,M LM-W,M MoA-W,M
OBN-W,M On-W,M OTO-W
RDT-W,M TM-W,M TOM-W,M
WGB/P-W,M
Where Do I Go?
  H-W,M
Where Do I Go from Here
  OTO-W UBF-W,M
Where Do the Balloons Go?
  MLS-W,M
Where Do You Come From
  SRE1-W,M
Where Do You Go, Alphonso?
  LA-W,M (Spanish)
Where Do You Hide Your Heart
  VB-W,M
Where Everybody Knows Your
  Name
  GSN5-W,M TV-W,M
Where Griping Grief
  SSP-W
Where Has Lula Gone?
  FHR-W,M SSFo-W,M
Where Has My Hubby Gone Blues
  NN7-W,M
Where Has My Little Dog Gone
  HS-W,M
Where Has My Little Dog Gone see
  also Der Deitcher's Dog and Oh
  Where Has My Little Dog Gone
Where Hast Thou Gleaned?
  GH-W,M
Where Have All the Flowers Gone?
  FPS-W,M IHA-W,M JF-W,M
  SBF-W,M TO-W,M WG-W,M
Where Have You Been
  RuS-W,M (Russian)
Where Have You Been All the Day
  see Whar' Ha' Ye Been A' the
  Day
Where He Leads Me
  AME-W,M IH-M
Where He May Lead Me I Will Go
  AME-W,M
Where High the Heavenly Temple
  Stands
  Hy-W,M
Where Honor Leads
  SL-W,M
Where I'm Bound
  BIS-W,M
Where Is It Written
  MLS-W,M
Where Is John?
  BM-W Boo-W,M FSA1-W,M
  SMY-W,M TF-W,M
Where Is Love?
  MF-W,M O-W,M RW-W,M
  TI1-W,M TWD-W,M UBF-W,M
  UFB-W,M
Where Is My Boy Tonight?
  GH-W,M SiS-W
Where Is My Home?
  NAS-W,M SMW-W,M (Czech)
Where Is My Wandering Boy
  Tonight?
  AFP-W ATS-W EFS-W,M FW-W
Where Is Our Holy Church?
  AHO-W,M
Where Is the Church?
  SoP-W,M
Where Is the Freeman Found
  SiS-W
Where Is the Life That Late I Led?
  TW-W
Where Is the Love
  ToO76-W,M

Where Is the Queen?
  SFM-W
Where Is the Tribe for Me?
  Mo-W,M NM-W,M OTO-W TW-W
Where Is the Weaver?
  TW-W
Where Is Thumbkin
  FP-W,M GM-W,M
Where Is Thy Refuge?
  GH-W,M
Where Is Thy Spirit, Mary?
  FHR-W,M
Where Is Your Heart? see Song
  from Moulin Rouge
Where Jesus Is, 'Tis Heaven There
  AME-W,M
Where Love Has Gone
  OTO-W
Where Nothing Dwelt but Beasts
  of Prey
  AHO-W,M
Where Now Are the Hebrew
  Children?
  AHO-W,M
Where, O Where
  NAS-W,M
Where, O Where Is Old Elijah?
  AmS-W,M
Where Oh Where
  ML-W,M OTO-W
Where Oh Where Is Dear Little
  Susie?
  OTJ-W,M
Where or When
  DBC-W,M FrS-W,M HC2-W,M
  HLS8-W,M LM-W,M OTO-W
  TI1-W,M TS-W TW-W UBF-W,M
  UFB-W,M
Where Shall I Be?
  AME-W,M AN-W NeA-W,M
Where Shall I Be? see also Whar'
  Shall I Be?
Where Shall I Be When de Firs'
  Trumpet Soun'?
  RF-W,M
Where Sleepest Thou My Dearie?
  SeS-W,M
Where the Bagpipes Play
  CA-W,M
Where the Bee Sucks
  FSS-W,M OH-W,M SSB-W,M
  TH-W,M
Where the Blue of the Night Meets
  the Gold of the Day
  MF-W,M TI1-W,M UFB-W,M
Where the Boys Are
  GAR-W,M HFH-W,M MF-W,M
Where the Boys Go
  RoS-W,M
Where the Bullets Fly
  Oz1-W
Where the Columbines Grow
  Fif-W,M
Where the Fraser River Flows
  AFP-W
Where the Mountains Meet the
  Sky
  FC-W,M
Where the River Shannon Flows
  FSN-W,M
Where the Soul Never Dies
  BSo-W,M
Where There Is Love
  VB-W,M
Where There's a Will There's a
  Way
  GrM-W,M

Where There's Life, There's Bud
  GSM-W,M
Where There's Smoke There's Fire
  TOC82-W,M
Where They Drank Their Wine in
  Bowls
  Boo-W,M
Where to Now, St. Peter?
  RV-W
Where Was Moses When the Light
  Went Out?
  ATS-W,M TMA-W,M
Where Were You Baby
  J-W,M
Where Were You When I Was
  Falling in Love
  ToO79-W,M
Where Were You When the
  Archeta River Went Down
  LC-W,M
Where Will the Words Come From?
  OnT1-W,M
Where Will You Spend Eternity
  AME-W,M
Where You Gonna Run To
  JF-W,M
Where'er You Walk
  FSY-W,M Gu-W,M MM-W,M
  SL-W,M TF-W,M
Wherein Consists the High Estate
  AHO-W,M
Where's Stonewall Jackson?
  MPP-W
Where's That Rainbow?
  TS-W
Where's the Boy? Here's the Girl
  ReG-W,M
Where's the Love
  MLS-W,M
Where's the Mate for Me?
  SB-W,M
Where've You Been
  GCM-W,M
Wherever He Ain't
  OTO-W
Wherever I Go
  SHP-W,M
Wherever I May Wander
  SHP-W,M
Wherever People Live in Love
  SHP-W,M
Wherever You Are Is Holy Ground
  OGR-W,M
Wherever You Walk see Where'er
  You Walk
Whether You Whisper Low
  Boo-W,M
Which Is the Properest Day to
  Sing?
  LMR-W,M
Which One Is Which?
  GBC-W,M
Which Side Are You On?
  AFP-W,M FW-W JF-W,M
  LW-W,M SFF-W,M SWF-W,M
  TO-W,M WS-W,M WW-W,M
Which Way America
  HCY-W,M
Which Way Does the Wind Blow?
  MH-W,M
Which Way You Going Billy?
  TI2-W,M
Whiffenpoof Song
  GG1-W,M RDT-W,M RW-W,M
While Adam Slept
  Boo-W,M
While Angels Sing

CCM-W,M
While Bagpipes Play
    MU-W,M
While by My Sheep
    Y-W,M
While Hearts Are Singing
    OTO-W
While I Am Young
    AHO-W,M
While Jesus Whispers to You
    AME-W,M
While Life Prolongs Its Precious
    Light
    GH-W,M
While More with You
    NB-W
While My Guitar Gently Weeps
    BBe-W,M TWS-W
While o'er Our Guilty Land, O Lord
    AHO-W,M
While o'er the Deep Thy Servants
    Sail
    AHO-W,M
While Shepherds Watched
    ESB-W,M GH-W,M JOC-W,M
    OB-W,M U-W
While Shepherds Watched Their
    Flocks
    AME-W,M CSF-W MC-W,M
    OPS-W,M WiS7-W,M YC-W,M
While Shepherds Watched Their
    Flocks by Night
    BCh-W,M BCS-W,M Hy-W,M
    RW-W,M
While Shepherds Watched Their
    Flocks by Night see also
    Christmas (While Shepherds
    Watch'd Their Flocks by Night)
While Some on Rights
    ESU-W
While Strolling in the Park
    WU-W,M
While Strolling in the Park One Day
    EFS-W,M MF-W,M
While Strolling through the Park
    FWS-W,M OAP-W,M TI1-W,M
    UFB-W,M
While Strolling through the Park
    One Day
    FW-W OS-W SFB-W,M
While Strolling through the Park
    One Day see also Fountain in the
    Park
While Strolling thru the Park One
    Day
    BH-W,M RW-W,M
While the Bowl Goes Round
    FHR-W,M
While the City Sleeps
    Mo-W,M NM-W,M OTO-W
While the Days Are Going
    GH-W,M
While the Evening Shadows Fall,
    There's Morning in My Heart
    GrG-W,M
While We Lowly Bow before Thee
    AHO-W,M
While We Pray and While We Plead
    AME-W,M
While We Work for the Lord
    FHR-W,M
While We're Young
    MF-W,M TI1-W,M TWD-W,M
    UFB-W,M
Whilst in This World I Stay
    AHO-W,M
Whilst through the Sharp

Hawthorn
    EA-W,M
Whippin' That Old T.B.
    LJ-W,M
Whip-poor-will
    ASB2-W,M Oz4-W,M
Whippoorwill
    HS-W,M SCL-W,M VA-W,M
Whippoorwill Song
    VA-W,M
Whirl, Top, Whirl
    MH-W,M
Whirling Around
    LA-W,M (Spanish)
Whirlwind
    Mo-W,M NM-W,M
Whirlwinds of Danger
    FW-W
Whirly Bird
    MF-M
Whiskey Drinkin' Blues
    LC-W
Whiskey Headed Woman
    LC-W
Whiskey in the Jar
    FW-W
Whiskey Johnnie
    RW-W,M
Whiskey Johnny
    FW-W GI-W,M GO-W,M
    HAS-W,M SA-W,M
Whiskey Seller
    Oz2-W,M
Whiskey, You're the Devil
    IS-W,M
Whisper in the Dark
    TTH-W,M
Whisper Your Mother's Name
    LJ-W,M
Whispering
    BH-W,M EAG2-W,M GG2-W,M
    GG3-W,M GSN2-W,M GST-W,M
    HLS2-W,M OP1-W,M PB-W,M
    RW-W,M
Whispering Bells
    MF-W,M
Whispering Heart
    Mo-W,M NM-W,M
Whispering Hope
    ATS-W,M BSG-W,M BSP-W,M
    CEM-W,M FS-W,M FSY-W,M
    HHa-W,M HLS7-W,M JBF-W,M
    MAB1-W MAS-W,M MSA1-W
    OBN-W,M OTJ-W,M PoS-W,M
    RW-W,M SUH-W,M
Whispering Stream
    FSA2-W,M
Whispers in the Dark
    OTO-W
Whispers on the Wind
    TW-W
Whistle Brothers Whistle
    LMR-W,M
Whistle, Daughter, Whistle
    FW-W LW-W,M Oz1-W,M
Whistle Mary Whistle
    WU-W,M
Whistle Stop
    On-W,M
Whistle Tune
    Me-M
Whistle While You Work
    HSS-W,M NI-W,M TI1-W,M
    UFB-W,M
Whistler and His Dog
    FSN-M OTJ-M
Whistling Gypsy Rover

OFS-W,M
Whistling Rufus
    Oz2-W,M
White and the Blue
    CoS-W,M
White As Snow
    GH-W,M
White Boots Marching in a Yellow
    Land
    VS-W,M
White Butterflies
    ASB4-W,M SiR-W,M
White Christmas
    CSF-W
White Cliffs of Dover
    FPS-W,M MF-W,M TI1-W,M
    UFB-W,M
White Cockade
    AmH-M BB-W FSt-M POT-W,M
White Coral Bells
    BM-W HS-W,M MG-W,M
    OHO-W,M OTJ-W,M SSe-W,M
White Daisies
    FSA2-W,M
White Dove
    BIS-W,M SiR-W,M SL-W,M
White Fields
    SiR-W,M
White Hawk
    ATS-W
White Hen
    Boo-W,M
White Horse Pawin' in the Valley
    MoM-W,M
White House Blues
    BSo-W,M BIS-W,M FW-W
White House Blues see also
    Whitehouse Blues
White House Chair
    FHR-W,M MPP-W,M
White Knight
    DP-W,M
White Lent
    OB-W,M
White Llamas
    LA-W,M (Spanish)
White Marble Stone
    NSS-W
White Nights Love Theme see
    Separate Lives
White Pilgrim
    FMT-W Oz4-W,M
White River Shore
    Oz1-W,M
White Room
    TRR-W,M
White Sand and Grey Sand
    Boo-W,M OHO-W,M
White Sport Coat
    HR-W
White Star of Sigma Nu
    Mo-W,M
White Wine and Sugar
    Boo-W,M
White Wings
    ATS-W EFS-W,M FSTS-W,M
    Oz4-W,M
Whitehouse Blues
    LSR-W,M
Whitehouse Blues see also White
    House Blues
Whiter Shade of Pale
    TI1-W,M TRR-W,M TWD-W,M
    UFB-W,M
Whiter Than Snow
    AME-W,M GH-W,M
Whitestown

SHS-W,M
Whither, Dear Maiden?
FSA1-W,M
Whither Thou Goest
HLS7-W,M RDF-W,M TI1-W,M
UFB-W,M
Who?
BBB-W,M BeL-W,M Su-W,M
TI1-W,M UFB-W,M
Who Am Dat A-Walkin' in de Co'n
FSU-W
Who Am I?
JF-W,M MAR-W,M UBF-W,M
Who Are You? (Knock, Knock,
Knock! Who Are You?)
SOO-W,M
Who Are You? (Mister Mouse
Once Heard a Cry)
ASB5-W,M
Who Are You? (The Mouse Looked
Out, Who Are You?)
ASB2-W,M
Who Are You? (Pete Townshend)
WA-W,M
Who Built de Ark?
ETB-W,M
Who Can I Turn To (When Nobody
Needs Me)
DBC-W,M HC1-W,M HLS8-W,M
ILT-W,M MF-W,M RW-W,M
TI1-W,M TWD-W,M UBF-W,M
UFB-W,M
Who Can Retell? see Mi Y'malel
Who Can Swim?
Boo-W,M
Who Can Tell
Mo-W,M OTO-W
Who Cares? (So Long As You Care
for Me)
GOB-W,M HC2-W,M LSO-W
MF-W,M NYT-W,M OT-W,M
Who Comes Dar?
SiS-W
Who Comes Laughing
Boo-W,M
Who Did?
SiB-W,M
Who Did Swallow Jonah?
FW-W OHO-W,M OTJ-W,M
Who Do You Love
HR-W RB-W
Who Do You Say That I Am
VB-W,M
Who Fears to Speak of Easter
Week
VP-W,M
Who Gwine to Lay Dis Body
NSS-W
Who Has Our Redeemer Heard
AHO-W,M
Who Has the Button?
SOO-W,M
Who Hath His Fancy Pleas'd
SSP-W
Who He Is
OGR-W,M
Who Here Can Cast His Eyes
Abroad
AHO-W,M
Who Is behind You?
OTJ-W,M
Who Is Building That Boat
CEM-W,M
Who Is Dat Yondah?
My-W,M
Who Is He
VB-W,M

Who Is Mr. Big?
DR-W,M
Who Is on the Lord's Side
FH-W,M GH-W,M Hy-W,M
NSS-W
Who Is Silvia?
UBF-W,M
Who Is Sylvia
BeB-W,M ESB-W,M FSS-W,M
GV-W,M HSD-W,M LMR-W,M
SSB-W,M TF-W,M TH-W,M
WiS8-W,M
Who Is That Tapping at the
Window
MG-W,M
**Who Is That Walking in the Corn
see Who Am Dat A-Walkin' in de
Co'n**
**Who Is That Yonder? see Who Is
Dat Yondah?**
Who Is the Lord?
SoM-W,M
Who Is the Lucky Girl to Be?
OT-W,M
Who Is the Man?
OTJ-W,M SMY-W,M
Who Killed Norma Jean?
LW-W,M PO-W,M
Who Knows Where I'm Going
SRS-W,M
Who Likes the Rain?
MH-W,M
Who Liveth So Merry
SSP-W
Who Love Ma Lord
BDW-W,M
Who Loves You
ToO76-W,M
Who Made Ocean, Earth, and Sky?
SHP-W,M
Who Me?
MF-M
Who Needs You?
TI2-W,M
Who Played Poker with
Pocahontas? (When John Smith
Went Away)
WF-W,M
Who Put the Bomp (in the Bomp
Ba Bomp Ba Bomp)
HR-W
Who Put the Tears
AG-W,M
Who Says
TTH-W,M
Who Shall Deliver Po' Me
J-W,M MoM-W,M
Who Threw the Overalls in Mrs.
Murphy's Chowder
BH-W,M EFS-W,M FSN-W,M
GeS-W,M GI-W OS-W OTJ-W,M
RW-W,M
**Who Threw the Overalls in Mrs.
Murphy's Chowder see also Mrs.
Murphy's Chowder**
Who to Listen To
VB-W,M
Who Trusts in God, a Strong
Abode
Hy-W,M
Who Wants to Be a Millionaire
TI1-W,M UFB-W,M
Who Wants to Work?
Mo-W,M NM-W,M OTO-W
Who Were They?
AL-W
Who Were You with Last Night?

U-W
Who, Who Do You Think You Are
Wi-W
Who Will Be de Leadah?
BPM-W,M
Who Will Be the Driver
WN-W,M
Who Will Bow and Bend Like a
Willow
GB-W,M
Who Will Buy
O-W,M TI1-W,M UBF-W,M
UFB-W,M
Who Will Care for Abra'am Now?
SiS-W
Who Will Care for Mother Now?
Sin-W,M SiS-W
Who Will Come with Me?
SiR-W,M
Who Will o'er the Downs?
TF-W,M
**Who Will o'er the Downs? see also
O Who Will o'er the Downs**
Who Will Reap?
GrM-W,M
Who Will Shoe Your Feet?
ITP-W
Who Will Shoe Your Pretty Little
Foot?
AmS-W,M
**Who Will Shoe Your Pretty Little
Foot? see also Oh! Who's Going
to Shoe Your Pretty Little Foot?
and Who's Gonna Shoe Your
Pretty Little Foot**
Whoa, Back, Buck!
FW-W IHA-W,M NeF-W
Whoa Buck
Le-W,M
Whoa, Emma!
BH-W,M
Whoa Mule
FSB1-W,M NH-W
Whoa, Mule! Can't Get the Saddle
On
AFS-W,M
Whoa! Mule, Whoa!
TMA-W,M
Who'd Have Believed Such Self-
Willed Daring
SiP-W,M
Whoever Will
GH-W,M
Whoever You Are, I Love You
HD-W,M ILT-W,M Mo-W,M
**Whoever You Are, I Love You see
also Sometimes Your Eyes Look
Blue to Me**
Whoever's in New England
GCM-W,M
Whole Hog or None
Oz3-W,M
Whole Lotta Love
ERM-W,M MF-W,M
Whole Lotta Shakin' Goin' On
DRR-W,M EP-W,M FRH-W,M
Whole Lotta Sunlight
R-W,M
Whole World
JF-W,M
Whole World in His Hand
J-W,M
**Who'll Be King but Charlie see
Wha'll Be King but Charlie**
Who'll Be My Valentine?
MH-W,M
Who'll Buy?

FSA1-W,M LS-W,M
Who'll Buy My Posies?
Boo-W,M
Who'll Buy My Roses, My Sweet,
Pretty Roses?
Boo-W,M
Who'll Jine de Union?
RF-W,M WN-W,M
Who'll Own New York
IL-W,M
Who'll Stop the Rain
BR-W,M
Wholly Thine
GH-W,M
Whoop, Do Me No Harm
SSP-W
Whoop-Ti-Yiddle-Um-Yea
AFS-W,M
Whoopee Ti-Yi-Yo
HS-W,M RSW-W,M WiS9-W,M
Whoopee Ti-Yi-Yo, Git Along Little
Dogies
HWS-W,M NAS-W,M
**Whoopee Ti-Yi-Yo, Git Along Little
Dogies see also Dogie Song and
Git Along Little Dogies**
Whore's Lament
SoC-W
Who's a Bluebird?
SoP-W,M
Who's Afraid of the Big Bad Wolf?
NI-W,M TI1-W,M UFB-W,M
Who's at the Door?
MH-W,M
Who's Been Sleeping Here
RoS-W,M
Who's Complaining?
LSO-W
Who's Dat Nigga Dar A-Peepin
DE-W,M
Who's Driving Your Plane
RoS-W,M
Who's Goin' to Close My Dyin'
Eyes?
Me-W,M
**Who's Going to Lay This Body see
Who Gwine to Lay Dis Body**
Who's Gonna Shoe Your Pretty
Little Foot
FG1-W,M FGM-W,M FW-W
GuC-W,M LW-W,M OTJ-W,M
**Who's Gonna Shoe Your Pretty
Little Foot see also Oh! Who's
Going to Shoe Your Pretty Little
Foot and Who Will Shoe Your
Pretty Little Foot?**
Who's In?
SiR-W,M
Who's in Charge of Killing in
Vietnam
VS-W,M
Who's in the Strawberry Patch
with Sally
On-W,M OTJ-W,M
Who's Leaving Who
TTH-W,M
Who's on the Lord's Side
GH-W,M
Who's Sorry Now?
BBB-W,M GSN2-W,M HLS2-W,M
RDT-W,M TI2-W,M
Who's That A-Calling?
OTJ-W,M SL-W,M TF-W,M
Who's That Calling?
WiS8-W,M
Who's That Girl
Ap-W,M BHO-W,M BNG-W,M

HFH-W,M Mo-W,M OTO-W
VSA-W,M
**Who's That Nigga Dar A-Peepin
see Who's Dat Nigga Dar
A-Peepin**
Who's That Ringing?
SiR-W,M
Who's That Woman?
Fo-W,M OTO-W UBF-W,M
Who's the Pretty Girl Milkin' the
Cow?
AmS-W,M
Who's Your Little Whozis
AT-W,M
Whose Birthday?
SoP-W,M
Whose Little Angry Man
R-W,M
Whose Old Cow
SoC-W
Whoso Would See This Song of
Heavenly Choice
AHO-W,M
Whosoever Calleth
GH-W,M
Whosoever Heareth, Shout, Shout
the Sound
AME-W,M
Whosoever Will May Come
GH-W,M
Why
OPS-W,M VB-W,M
Why Am I Me?
OTO-W Sh-W,M
Why and Wherefore?
SiS-W
Why Are We Invited Here?
BP-W,M
Why Are You Marching, Son?
JW-W,M
Why Art Thou Cast Down
JS-W,M (Hebrew)
Why Can't a Woman Be More Like
a Man?
TW-W
Why Can't I Walk Away
ILT-W,M OTO-W
Why Can't the English?
UBF-W,M
Why Can't We Be Friends
DP-W,M
Why Can't You Behave
UBF-W,M
Why Coal Goes Up
AL-W
Why Did He Come?
SYB-W,M
Why Did I Choose You?
Mo-W,M NM-W,M OTO-W
UBF-W,M
Why Did You Give Me Your Love?
LJ-W,M
Why Do Fools Fall in Love?
AO-W,M BHB-W,M DC-W,M
ERM-W,M GAR-W,M ILF-W,M
MF-W,M OnT6-W,M RY-W,M
Why Do I Have to Choose
TOC83-W,M
Why Do I Love You?
L-W RDT-W,M RW-W,M SB-W,M
TI1-W,M UFB-W,M
Why Do We Mourn Departing
Friends?
AHO-W,M
Why Do You Treat Me Like the Dirt
under Your Feet
SF-W,M

Why Do You Wait?
GH-W,M
Why Doesn't My Goose
Boo-W,M
Why Don't We Do It in the Road
BBe-W,M TWS-W
Why Don't We Do This More Often
TI2-W,M
Why Don't You Cum Along?
BDW-W,M
Why Don't You Do Right
Mo-W,M NM-W,M TI2-W,M
Why Don't You Let Gawd's People
Go?
BDW-W,M
Why Don't You 'Liver Me?
BDW-W,M
Why, Edward, You Look So
Healthy Now
SCa-W,M
Why Hast Thou Led Us Away?
SoM-W,M
Why Have My Loved Ones Gone?
FHR-W,M SSFo-W,M
Why Have We Done This?
SoM-W,M
Why Have You Left the One (You
Left Me For)
ToO79-W,M
Why He's the Lord of Lords
RF-W,M
Why I Love Her
JW-W,M
Why Is the Desert
OTO-W
Why Lady Why
TOC82-W,M
Why Linger Yet upon the Strand?
AHO-W,M
Why Lingers My Gaze?
SL-W,M
Why Look at Me?
NF-W
Why, Lord?
AHO-W,M
Why Me?
GS1-W HLS7-W,M HLS9-W,M
N-W,M SuS-W,M
Why No One to Love?
FHR-W,M
Why Not?
AST-W,M
Why Not Katie
PF-W,M TW-W
Why Not Now
AME-W,M GH-W,M
Why Not Tonight?
GH-W,M
Why Should I Be Lonely?
LJ-W,M
Why Should I Cry
OGC2-W,M
Why Should I Feel Discouraged
AME-W,M
Why Should I Wake Up?
C-W,M
Why Should Vain Mortals Tremble
AHO-W,M
Why Should We Stay Home and
Sew?
OG-W,M
Why Shouldn't I?
MF-W,M
Why Shouldn't My Goose
OHO-W,M OTJ-W,M SMY-W,M
Why Shouldn't We
RM-W,M

Why So Pale and Wan, Fond Lover
EL-W,M
Why the Woodpecker's Head Is
Red
NF-W
Why Try to Change Me Now
ILT-W,M MF-W,M
Why Was I Born?
L-W ToS-W,M
Why Was the Darkie Born?
SFF-W,M
Why Weep Ye the Tide, Ladye?
SeS-W,M
Why You Knocka Me Down?
LC-W,M
Wi' a Hundred Pipers
OTJ-W,M UF-W,M
Wi' a Hundred Pipers an' A'
NAS-W,M
Wichita Lineman
OnT1-W,M
Wicked Girl
BSC-W Oz4-W,M
Wicked Man
Mo-W,M NM-W,M OTO-W
Wicked Polly
Oz4-W,M
Wicked Rebels
SSS-W,M
Widdicombe Fair
OH-W,M OTJ-W,M
Widdy-Widdy-Wurky
SOO-W,M
Wide Missouri
CA-W,M NAS-W,M STR-W,M
**Wide Missouri see also
O Shenandoah and Shenandoah**
Wide Open Are Thy Hands
AHO-W,M
Widgegoara Joe
ATM-W,M
**Widmung see Dedication (Robert
Franz) and Dedication (Robert
Schumann)**
Widow in the Cottage by the Sea
Oz4-W,M TMA-W,M
Widow Maker
BSo-W,M
Widow's Old Broom
Oz3-W,M
Wiegenlied see Cradle Song
Wien Du Stadt Meiner Traume
SLB-W,M (German)
Wien Neerlandsch Bloed
SiP-W,M (Dutch)
Wiener Song
BNG-W,M
**Wiener Song see also I Wish I
Were an Oscar Mayer Wiener**
Wife, The or He'll Come Home
FHR-W,M
Wife Bereaved of Her Husband
BSC-W
Wife Never Understan'
Mo-W,M OTO-W
Wife of Usher's Well
AA-W,M BCT-W,M BT-W,M
FMT-W SCa-W,M
Wife Who Wouldn't Spin Tow
Oz3-W,M
Wife Wrapped in Wether's Skin
BT-W,M FMT-W TBF-W,M
Wild and Reckless
Mo-W,M NM-W,M OTO-W
Wild and Reckless Hobo
LSR-W,M Oz4-W,M
Wild and Wooly Cowboy

AF-W
Wild Bill Jones
FMT-W Oz2-W,M
Wild Bird
GrM-W,M
Wild Cat Song
CoS-W,M
Wild Colonial Boy
ATM-W,M FW-W
Wild Ducks
FSA1-W,M
Wild Goose Grasses
WSB-W,M
Wild Hog Hunt
NF-W
Wild Honey Pie
TWS-W
Wild Horse Charlie
HB-W
Wild Horseman
ASB1-M
Wild Horses
RoS-W,M
Wild Justice
LS-W,M
Wild Lumberjack
SoC-W
Wild Moor
Oz1-W,M
Wild Negro Bill
NF-W NH-W
Wild Rose
TH-W,M
Wild Rover
FW-W IS-W,M MSB-W
Wild Rovers
Oz4-W
Wild Side of Life
FrF-W,M (Spanish) RW-W,M
Wild Thing
DRR-W,M TRR-W,M
Wild Turkey
TOC82-W,M
Wild West Hero
ELO-W,M
Wildcat Victory
CoS-W,M
Wildcats
A-W,M
Wilder Blues
AFP-W,M
Wildfire
EC-W,M GCM-W,M MF-W,M
**Wildroot Cream-Oil Hair Dressing
Jingle see Get Wildroot Cream-
Oil, Charlie**
Wildwood Flower
BIS-W,M BSo-W,M CMG-W,M
FG1-W,M FG2-W,M FGM-W,M
FPG-W,M FSt-M FW-W NAS-W,M
OTJ-W,M Oz4-W,M PoG-W,M
POT-W,M RDT-W,M TOC83-W,M
Wilhelmus of Nassau
SMW-W,M (Dutch)
Wilhelmus Van Nassouwe
SiP-W,M (Dutch)
Will Anything Happen
PL-W,M
Will de Weaver
SCa-W,M
Will He Like Me?
OTO-W TW-W
Will Jesus Find Us
GH-W,M
Will Jesus Find Us Watching
AME-W,M
Will My Love Come Home to Me?

L-W
Will Ray
FMT-W
Will Someone Ever Look at Me
That Way
MLS-W,M
Will the Circle Be Unbroken
BSo-W,M GS1-W HLS7-W,M
OAP-W,M TI1-W,M UFB-W,M
**Will the Circle Be Unbroken see
also Can the Circle Be Unbroken**
Will the United Nations Sing?
NeA-W,M
Will the Weaver
SCa-W,M
Will There Be Any Cowboys in
Heaven
SoC-W
Will We Ever Know Each Other
UBF-W,M
Will Ye Gang to the Hielands,
Leezie Lindsay?
SeS-W,M
**Will Ye Gang to the Hielands,
Leezie Lindsay? see also Leezie
Lindsay**
Will Ye No' Come Back Again
Gu-W,M OTJ-W,M
Will You Be Loving Another Man?
BIS-W,M
Will You Buy
SiR-W,M
Will You Come into My Parlor?
Boo-W,M
Will You Come to the Bower
ATS-W,M
Will You Dance?
VA-W,M (Swedish)
Will You Go, Lassie, Go
FW-W
**Will You Go to the Highlands,
Leezie Lindsay? see Will Ye Gang
to the Hielands, Leezie Lindsay?**
Will You Join the Dance?
BV-W,M
Will You Love Me in December As
You Do in May?
FSN-W,M FSTS-W,M MF-W,M
Will You Love Me Tomorrow?
DPE-W,M GAR-W,M
Will You Love Me When I'm Old?
Oz4-W
**Will You Not Come Back Again see
Will Ye No' Come Back Again**
Will You Remember?
MPM-W,M
Will You Remember Me?
KH-W,M
Will You Still Be Mine
DJ-W,M RoE-W,M TI1-W,M
UFB-W,M
Will You Wed Me Now I'm Lame,
Love?
SiS-W
William and Nancy
SCa-W,M
William Baker
FSU-W
William Blewitt
FSU-W
William Bloat
IS-W,M
William Cook
Oz4-W,M
William Dunbar
SBB-W
William Hall

BSC-W FMT-W SCa-W,M
William O'Reilly
  Oz1-W,M
William Riley
  BSC-W
William Taylor
  BSC-W LW-W,M
William Tell Overture Theme
  MF-M
Williams Man Who's Far, Far Away
  IL-W,M
Willie and Mary
  FMT-W
Willie and the Hand Jive
  DRR-W,M FRH-W,M
Willie Came over the Ocean
  BSC-W Oz1-W,M
Willie Darling see Katy Dear
Willie Dear
  Oz4-W
Willie Has Gone to the War
  FHR-W,M SiS-W
Willie Moore
  FPG-W,M Oz4-W,M
Willie My Brave
  FHR-W,M
Willie My Weaver-O
  RBO-W,M
Willie o' Winsbury
  FSU-W
Willie Riley
  Oz1-W,M
Willie Seton
  RBO-W,M
Willie Taylor
  Oz1-W,M
Willie the Weeper
  GI-W,M GO-W,M Oz3-W,M
**Willie the Weeper see also Willy
  the Weeper**
Willie We Have Missed You
  FHR-W,M SSFo-W,M
**Willie We Have Missed You see
  also Oh! Willie, We Have Miss'd
  You**
Willie Wee
  NF-W
Willie's Gane to Melville Castle
  SaS-W,M
Willie's Gone to Heaven
  FHR-W,M
Willin'
  RV-W
Willing and Eager
  UBF-W,M
Willing Conscript
  RBO-W,M
Willing the Mill
  BSC-W
Willkommen
  C-W,M On-W,M TI2-W,M
  UBF-W,M
Willoughby
  SHS-W,M
Willow Cats
  MH-W,M
Willow Song
  FSS-W,M Gu-W,M OTJ-W,M
  SSB-W,M SSP-W
Willow Tree
  Oz4-W
Willow Weep for Me
  DJ-W,M RoE-W,M TI1-W,M
  ToS-W,M UFB-W,M
Willowbee
  PSD-W,M
Willows by the River

MU-W,M
Willows in the Snow
  SSe-W,M
Willow's Lullaby
  SSe-W,M
Willy, Prithee Go to Bed
  SSP-W
Willy the Weeper
  FW-W
**Willy the Weeper see also Willie
  the Weeper**
Willy, Willy
  Oz4-W
Wilmot
  SHS-W,M
Wilson Patent Stove
  Oz3-W,M
Wilson's Clog Dance
  POT-M
Wilt Thou Be Gone Love?
  FHR-W,M
Wilt Thou Be True?
  FHR-W,M
Wilt Thou Not Visit Me?
  AHO-W,M
Wimoweh
  WSB-W,M (Zulu)
Wind, The
  GM-W,M MG-W,M MH-W,M
  SD-W,M SOO-W,M
Wind and the Sun
  FSA2-W,M
Wind Bag
  NF-W
Wind beneath My Wings
  AWS-W,M BNG-W,M DC-W,M
  DPE-W,M EC-W,M GCM-W,M
  LOM-W,M MF-W,M RoE-W,M
  TOC83-W,M
Wind Blew East
  RSL-W,M
Wind Blew Up, the Wind Blew
  Down
  MSH-W,M
Wind Elves
  SOO-W,M
Wind from the Southern Mountains
  SoF-W,M
Wind Gentle Evergreen
  Boo-W,M
Wind in the Trees
  SiR-W,M
Wind Is Howling
  SOO-W,M
Wind Mill
  MH-W,M
Wind of the Western Sea
  AME-W,M
Wind Song
  SCL-W,M
Wind That Blew o'er the Wild
  Moor
  SCa-W,M
Wind That Shakes the Barley
  IS-W,M
Wind through the Olive Trees
  BMC-W,M GBC-W,M
**Wind through the Olive Trees see
  also Long Ago (Winds through
  the Olive Trees) and Winds
  through the Olive Tree**
Wind up the May Tree
  HSA-W,M
Wind, Wind, Blowing
  SSe-W,M
Windham
  SHS-W,M

Winding Sheet Coffin
  Oz4-W
Windmill, The
  ASB2-W,M SMY-W,M
Windmills of Your Mind
  HLS5-W,M MLS-W,M MoA-W,M
  RT6-W,M RW-W,M
Window Up Above
  HLS9-W,M
Windows of Heaven
  GrG-W,M
Windows of the World
  HD-W,M MF-W,M
Winds Are Blowing
  BMC-W,M
**Winds of Chance see Airport Love
  Theme**
Winds of Change
  IFM-W
Winds of Morning
  IS-W
Winds through the Olive Tree
  BCh-W,M
**Winds through the Olive Tree see
  also Wind through the Olive Trees**
Windy
  GOI7-W,M
Windy Bill
  HB-W,M Oz3-W,M SoC-W,M
Windy Bill's Famous Ride
  HB-W
Wine, Wine in a Morning
  Boo-W,M
Wing Wong Waddle
  OTJ-W,M
Wings of a Dove
  TI1-W,M Tr-W,M UFB-W,M
Wings of Night
  NA-W,M
Wings of the Great Speckled Bird
  CCS-W,M
Wings of the Morning
  WN-W,M
Winky, Blinky
  SOO-W,M
Winnebagoe's Sigh
  ESU-W
Winner Takes It All
  TI1-W,M UFB-W,M
Winners
  FrS-W,M
Winners and Losers
  ToO76-W,M
Winnie the Pooh
  NI-W,M On-W,M OTJ-W,M
  SBS-W,M
Winning the Vote
  LW-W,M
Winnsboro Cotton Mill Blues
  AFP-W FW-W SWF-W,M
  WW-W,M
Winsome Mary
  SeS-W,M
Winston Tastes Good
  GSM-W,M
Winter (Beattie/Wolverton)
  ASB6-W,M
Winter (Gibault/Gardner)
  ASB2-W,M
Winter (Godfrey)
  ASB1-W,M
Winter (His Hoary Frost)
  SHS-W,M
Winter (Jagger/Richards)
  RoS-W,M
Winter (Poor Old Winter)
  SL-W,M

Winter Air Is Crisp and Cold
SHP-W,M
Winter and Spring
FSA2-W,M
Winter and Summer
ASB2-W,M
Winter by the Dnieper
ASB6-W,M
Winter Cheer
FSA2-W,M
Winter Dark and Dreary
Boo-W,M
Winter Days
Boo-W,M
Winter Days Are Full of Cheer
SoP-W,M
Winter Fun
SSe-W,M
Winter, Goodbye
ASB3-W,M
Winter Has Passed
Boo-W,M
Winter It Is Past
SeS-W,M
Winter Night
SSe-W,M
Winter Now Is Over
SSe-W,M
Winter of My Life
FrF-W,M (Spanish)
Winter Rules the World
MML-W,M
Winter Song
IFM-W MAR-W,M
Winter Sport
SL-W,M
Winter Sports
ASB4-W,M
Winter Visitor
ASB4-W,M
Winter Walk
SSe-W,M
Winter Will Soon Be Over see
Winter'll Soon Be Ober
Winter Wind
FSA1-W,M
Winter Winds
ASB4-W,M
Winter Wish
ASB5-W,M
Winter Wonderland
DC-W,M FPS-W,M MF-W,M
Wintergreen for President
GOB-W,M LSO-W MF-W,M
NYT-W,M OT-W,M
Winter'll Soon Be Ober
RF-W,M
Winter'll Soon Be Ober see also
O Vinter'll Soon Be Ober
Winters Go By
A-W,M
Winter's Snow
OB-W,M
Wipe Out
ERM-M GAR-M GOI7-M
Wipeout
MF-W,M
Wise Ben Franklin
ASB4-W,M
Wise Johnny
SSe-W,M
Wise Little Gold Fish
MH-W,M
Wise May Bring Their Learning
CSB-W,M SJ-W,M
Wise Men Were but Sev'n
Boo-W,M

Wise Men Were Seven
TH-W,M
Wise Up
VB-W,M
Wish Me a Rainbow
AT-W,M LM-W,M OBN-W,M
OnT1-W,M OTJ-W,M OTO-W
Wish You a Good Evening
UF-W,M
Wish You Were Here
DBC-W,M HC2-W,M TI1-W,M
UBF-W,M UFB-W,M
Wishes and Teardrops
Mo-W,M OTO-W
Wishin' and Hopin'
HD-W,M MF-W,M
Wishing (Will Make It So)
HC1-W,M TI1-W,M UFB-W,M
Wishing, Hoping, Knowing
GH-W,M
Wishing Star
MH-W,M
Wishing Tree of Hinehopu
SNZ-W,M (Maori)
Wishing You Were Somehow Here
Again
UBF-W,M
Witch
ASB2-W,M ASB3-W,M OTO-W
Witch Song
SiR-W,M
Witchcraft
FrS-W,M GSN3-W,M MF-W,M
Mo-W,M NM-W,M TI2-W,M
Witches' Night
FSA2-W,M
With a Down, Down, Hey, Derry
Down
Boo-W,M
With a Hey and a Hi and a Ho Ho
Ho
TI1-W,M UFB-W,M
With a Hey and a Hi Ho Ho Ho
HST-W,M
With a Hundred Pipers see Wi' a
Hundred Pipers
With a Lantern in the Hand
SSe-W,M
With a Little Bit of Luck
HC2-W,M LL-W,M OTO-W
TI1-W,M TW-W UBF-W,M
UFB-W,M
With a Little Help from My Friends
BBe-W,M TWS-W
With a Little Luck
PMC-W,M TI2-W,M
With a Sense of Deep Emotion
GiS-W,M MGT-W,M
With a Smile and a Song
NI-W,M TI1-W,M UFB-W,M
With a Song in My Heart
HC1-W,M MF-W,M OHB-W,M
TS-W
With All My Heart, Jehovah, I'll
Confess
AHO-W,M
With Care from Someone
BSo-W,M
With Catlike Tread
MGT-W,M SL-W,M
With Christ and All His Shining
Train
AHO-W,M
With Deep-Toned Horn
Boo-W,M
With Every Breath I Take
MF-W,M OTO-W

With God and His Mercy
AHO-W,M (Swedish)
With God's Hand in Mine
JBF-W,M
With Happy Voices Ringing
Hy-W,M
With Her Dog and Gun
Oz1-W,M
With Jockey to the Fair
OH-W,M
With Joy I Heard My Friends
Exclaim
Hy-W,M
With Joy We Meditate the Grace
AME-W,M
With Martial Step
ESU-W
With Merry Glee
Boo-W,M
With My Eyes Wide Open, I'm
Dreaming
TI1-W,M UFB-W,M
With My Swag All on My Shoulder
ATM-W,M
With Pen in Hand
MCG-W,M RW-W,M
With Sound of Fife
UF-W,M
With the Loorgeen O Hee
SeS-W,M
With the Wind and the Rain in
Your Hair
TI2-W,M
With These Hands
MF-W,M RDT-W,M TI1-W,M
UFB-W,M
With This Ring
MF-W,M TI2-W,M
With This Ring I Thee Wed
OGC1-W,M
With Warning Hand
Boo-W,M
With You
TOC82-W,M
With You I'm Born Again
GSN5-W,M TOM-W,M
With You in Mind
Mo-M
With You to the End
WN-W,M
With Your Love
ToO76-W,M
Wither's Rocking Hymn
OB-W,M
Within the Shelter of Our Walls
AHO-W,M
Within These Doors Assembled
Now
AHO-W,M
Within This Sacred Hall
MMM-W,M
Within Thy Temple's Sacred
Courts
Hy-W,M
Within Yon Lowly Manger
MU-W,M
Within You, Without You
JF-W,M TWS-W
Without a Doubt
VB-W,M
Without a Song
GST-W,M HLS8-W,M MF-W,M
MU-W,M RW-W,M
Without Her
RYT-W,M
Without Me
OTO-W UBF-W,M

Without You
  BR-W,M TI1-W,M UBF-W,M
  UFB-W,M
Witness for My Lord
  NH-W
Wives and Lovers
  AT-W,M HD-W,M GOI7-W,M ILT-
  W,M LM-W,M OTO-W TOM-W,M
**Wiz (Theme) see Ease On down
  the Road**
Wizard Oil
  AmS-W,M Oz3-W
Woes Au Be By wi Dinking
  Boo-W,M
Woke Up This Morning
  JF-W,M TO-W,M
Woke Up This Morning with My
  Mind on Freedom
  FG2-W,M FW-W SFF-W,M
Wolf and the Lamb
  CSG-W,M
**Wolk Waar Heen Gaat Ge? see
  Cloud, Where Do You Fly?**
Wolverine Blues
  Mo-W,M NM-W,M
Wolverine's Song
  ESU-W
Wolverton Mountain
  CMG-W,M TI1-W,M UFB-W,M
Wolves A-Howling
  AFS-W,M
Woman
  TI2-W,M
Woman Alone with the Blues
  Mo-W,M NM-W,M ToS-W,M
Woman and the Devil
  BSC-W
Woman at the Well
  JF-W,M
Woman Done Me In
  LC-W
Woman for the Man Who Has
  Everything
  Mo-W,M NM-W,M OTO-W
Woman in Love
  ILT-W,M TI1-W,M TI2-W,M
  UFB-W,M
Woman in Me
  TI2-W,M
Woman Is a Sometime Thing
  UBF-W,M
**Woman Is Fickle see La Donna E
  Mobile**
Woman Lived in a Far Country
  Oz1-W,M
Woman Loved, A
  TW-W
Woman Never Knows When Her
  Day's Work's Done
  MSB-W
**Woman So Changeable see La
  Donna E Mobile**
Woman Sure Is a Curious Critter
  J-W,M
Woman Who Lived Up There
  SSA-W,M
Woman's Mission
  GrM-W,M
Woman's Rights
  Oz3-W,M
Woman's Rule
  Boo-W,M
Woman's Smile
  Fi-W,M
Women Do Know How to Carry On
  TOC82-W,M
Women's Sayings

MSB-W
Wonder of You
  TI2-W,M
Wonder Song
  RuS-W,M (Russian) SoP-W,M
Wonder Tidings
  OB-W,M
Wonder Where Is Good Ole Daniel
  RF-W,M WN-W,M
Wonderful Christmastime
  TI2-W,M
Wonderful Copenhagen
  TI2-W,M
Wonderful Crocodile
  MSB-W
Wonderful Day Like Today
  BeL-W,M HLS8-W,M RW-W,M
  TI1-W,M UBF-W,M UFB-W,M
Wonderful Grace of Jesus
  OM-W,M
Wonderful Guy
  DBC-W,M L-W OTJ-W,M OTO-W
  TI1-W,M UBF-W,M UFB-W,M
Wonderful Love
  GH-W,M
Wonderful One
  GSN2-W,M GST-W,M HLS2-W,M
  RW-W,M
Wonderful Thing about Tiggers
  NI-W,M SBS-W,M
Wonderful Watford
  HB-W,M
Wonderful Weather for Ducks
  SiR-W,M
Wonderful, Wonderful
  FRH-W,M TI2-W,M
Wonderful Wonders of Town
  MSB-W
Wonderful Words of Life
  AME-W,M CEM-W,M GH-W,M
Wonderful World of Christmas
  TI1-W,M UFB-W,M
**Wonderful World of the Two a Day
  see Two a Day**
Wonderful World of the Young
  TI2-W,M
Wondering
  OGC1-W,M
Wonderland by Night
  MF-M PB-W,M
Wonders
  FSA2-W,M
Wondrous Apple Tree
  SaS-W,M
Wondrous Cross
  GH-W,M
Wondrous Gift
  GH-W,M
Wondrous Love
  AH-W,M FSSC-W,M FW-W
  GH-W,M HS-W,M SHS-W,M
  VA-W,M WN-W,M
Wondrous Telephone
  OHG-W,M
Wondrous Tidings
  OB-W,M
Won't Get Fooled Again
  WA-W,M
Won't It Be Wonderful after the
  War
  NeA-W,M
Won't You Charleston with Me?
  OTO-W
Won't You Come Home, Bill Bailey
  TI1-W,M UFB-W,M
Won't You Come Over to My
  House

RC-W,M
Wood of the Cross
  SOW1-W,M SOW2-W,M
Woodchopper's Ball
  TI2-M
Woodchuck Hill
  SiR-W,M
Woodchuck Song
  OTJ-W,M
Wooden Heart
  HLS9-W,M RW-W,M SRE1-W,M
  TI1-W,M UFB-W,M
Woodland
  SHS-W,M
Woodland Dancing
  SL-W,M
Woodland Song
  BMC-W,M
Woodman, Spare That Tree
  AH-W,M ATS-W FW-W OTJ-W,M
  PoS-W,M
Woodpecker
  GM-W,M SiR-W,M
Woodpecker Song
  GSO-W,M
Woods So Wild
  OH-W,M
Woodsman
  FSA2-W,M
Woodstock
  ERM-W,M
Woodstock's Samba
  RSL-M
Wood-Wind Duet
  ASB4-W,M
Woody Woodpecker
  TI2-W,M
Woody's Getting Betrothed
  FR-W,M
Wooing
  NF-W
Wooley Booger Hornpipe
  OTO-W
Wooly Bully
  DRR-W,M MF-W,M TRR-W,M
Worcester
  SHS-W,M
Word, The
  BBe-W,M TWS-W
Word II, The
  JF-W,M
Word before Goodbye
  TT-W,M
Word of God, across the Ages
  AHO-W,M
Word Pattern
  BMC-W,M
Words
  TI1-W,M UFB-W,M
Words (Are Impossible)
  WG-W,M
Words Get in the Way
  TTH-W,M
Words of Thanks to the
  Gesangverein of the Workers'
  Confederation in Philadelphia
  AL-W
Words without Music
  LSO-W
Words, Words, Words
  Mo-W,M NM-W,M OTO-W
Work
  GrM-W,M
Work All de Summer
  WS-W,M
Work and Play
  MH-W,M SOO-W,M

Work and Song
FSA1-W,M
Work, for the Night Is Coming
AME-W,M AmH-W,M ATS-W
Bo-W,M CEM-W,M FH-W,M
GH-W,M GrM-W,M Hy-W,M
NAS-W,M TH-W,M WiS7-W,M
Work, for Time Is Flying
GH-W,M
Work of the Weavers
FW-W
Work On, O Farmers' Union
AFP-W
Work Song
GUM1-W,M NI-W,M On-W,M
OTJ-W,M OTO-W
Work with a Vim
SOT-W,M
Worker
AL-W
Workers of the World Are Now
Awaking
AFP-W
Workers of the World, Awaken
AFP-W
Worker's Song
AL-W
Workhouse Boy
MSB-W
Workin' at the Carwash Blues
JC-W,M PM-W,M
Workin' Blues
LC-W
Workin' Man Blues
NMH-W,M
Workin' on the Railroad
BSB-W,M LoS-W,M
Working
ASB1-W,M
Working Class
AL-W
Working Day
SOO-W,M
Working for the Man
TFC-W,M
Working Man's Prospect
AL-W
Working Men
AL-W
Working Men's Fourth of July
Anthem
AL-W
Working Men's League
AL-W
Working on a Building
BSo-W,M
Working on the Building
NH-W
Working Time Is Over
ASB1-W,M
Workingman's Train
AFP-W AL-W
Workingmen
AL-W
Workingmen's Army
AFP-W AL-W
Workingmen's Centennial Song
AL-W
Workingmen's Marseillaise
AL-W
Workman's Hymn
AL-W
Workmen, Arouse Ye
AL-W
Workmen's Jingles
NH-W
World Is a Circle

HD-W,M
World Is a Ghetto
DP-W,M
World Is Comin' to a Start
P-W,M
World Is Mine
OTO-W
World Is Very, Very Big
SHP-W,M
World Is Waiting for the Sunrise
TI1-W,M UFB-W,M
World Itself
OB-W,M
World of You and I
MLS-W,M
World Owes Me a Living
NI-W,M
World Record
ELO-W,M
World, Take Me Back
Mo-W,M
World, the Devil, and Tom Paine
AHO-W,M
World Turned Upside Down
ATS-W,M EA-W,M OTJ-W,M
SBA-W SSS-W,M
World War
BMM-W
World War I Song
ITP-W,M
World Youth Song
FW-W
Worlds
TVT-W,M
World's a Pleasant Place to Know
SHP-W,M
Worlds Apart
UBF-W,M
World's Desire
OB-W,M
Worried about You
RoS-W,M
Worried Blues
LC-W
Worried Life Blues
LC-W
Worried Man
FG1-W,M TI1-W,M UFB-W,M
Worried Man Blues
BSo-W,M FSB1-W,M FW-W
GuC-W,M OFS-W,M OTJ-W,M
Worried Mind
SF-W,M
Worship
SL-W,M
Worship of God in Nature
FiS-W,M (German)
Worship of Nature
SL-W,M
Worst of War
SiS-W
Worst That Could Happen
TI2-W,M
Worth of Song
FSA1-W,M
Worthiness
GrM-W,M
Worthy
VB-W,M
Worthy Is the Lamb (Don Wyrtzen)
OM-W,M
Worthy Is the Lamb (Morris
Chapman)
OGR-W,M
Wot Cher
AmH-W,M WiS8-W,M
Would God I Were the Tender

**Apple Blossom see Londonderry
Air**
Would He Ride on a Roundup in
Heaven?
SoC-W
Would I Were with Thee
HSD-W,M
Would to God We Had Died
SoM-W,M
Would Ye Have a Young Virgin?
SR-W,M
Would You
HLS5-W,M
Would You Be Loved by Others
Boo-W,M
Would You Catch a Falling Star?
TOC82-W,M
**Would You for a Big Red Apple?
see Would'ja for a Big Red Apple?**
**Would You Have a Young Virgin?
see Would Ye Have a Young
Virgin?**
Would You Know How We Meet?
Boo-W,M
Would You Know the Kind of Maid
MGT-W,M
Would You Like to Take a Walk
MF-W,M MR-W,M OHB-W,M
Would You Mind
OGC1-W,M
Would You Sing a Catch
Boo-W,M
Would'ja for a Big Red Apple?
OHF-W
Wouldn't It Be Fun
ML-W,M
Wouldn't It Be Loverly
DBC-W,M HC2-W,M HLS3-W,M
LL-W,M OTO-W RW-W,M
TI1-W,M UBF-W,M UFB-W,M
Wouldn't You Like to Be on
Broadway
SSA-W,M
Wouldn't You Really Rather Have a
Buick
GSM-W,M
Wounded Soldier
BMM-W,M SiS-W VB-W,M
Wounded Spirit
BSC-W
Wraggle-Taggle Gypsies
ASB6-W,M HS-W,M LW-W,M
SaS-W,M
**Wraggle-Taggle Gypsies see also
Waggle-Taggle Gypsies**
Wrap It Up
TTH-W,M
Wrap the Flag Around Me, Boys
SiS-W
Wrap Your Troubles in Dreams
BBB-W,M MF-W,M TI1-W,M
UFB-W,M
Wrapped in a Ribbon and Tied in a
Bow
SSA-W,M
Wrasslin' Jacob
BPM-W,M
**Wrasslin' Jacob see also 'Raslin'
Jacob**
Wrastl' On, Jacob
NSS-W
Wrath of Achilles
Mo-W,M OTO-W
**Wrath of Khan (Theme) see Star
Trek II (Theme)**
Wreath of Roses
SMa-W,M

Wreath Token
MU-W,M
Wreck of Number Four
LSR-W,M
Wreck of Number Nine
LSR-W,M
Wreck of Old 97
AF-W
Wreck of Old 97 see also Wreck of the Old Ninety-Seven
Wreck of Old Number Nine
Oz4-W,M
Wreck of the C. and O.
BB-W
Wreck of the C. and O. see also Wreck on the C. & O
Wreck of the C & O Number Five
LSR-W,M
Wreck of the C & O Sportsman
LSR-W,M
Wreck of the Edmund Fitzgerald
GrS-W,M
Wreck of the Hunnicut Curve
BMM-W
Wreck of the "John B"
TI1-W,M UFB-W,M WSB-W,M
Wreck of the Old Ninety-Seven
BIS-W,M BSo-W,M FW-W
LSR-W,M TBF-W,M
Wreck of the Old Ninety-Seven see also Wreck of Old 97
Wreck of the Old Southern Ninety-Seven
TBF-W,M
Wreck of the Royal Palm
LSR-W,M
Wreck of the Southern Old 97
Oz4-W,M
Wreck of the Titanic
VP-W,M
Wreck of the 1256
LSR-W,M
Wreck of the 1262
LSR-W,M
Wreck of the Virginian Number Three
LSR-W,M
Wreck of Thirty-Six
BMM-W
Wreck on the C. & O.
LSR-W,M Oz4-W,M
Wreck on the C. & O. see also Wreck of the C. and O.
Wrecked Ship
Oz1-W,M
Wren Song
GBC-W,M IS-W,M
Wrigley Spearmint Gum Theme see Carry the Big Fresh Flavor
Wringle Wrangle
NI-W,M
Wrist Watch
SD-W,M
Write a Letter to My Mother
Sin-W,M SiS-W
Write These Words in Our Hearts
Hy-W,M
Wrong Note Rag
UBF-W,M
Wunderbar
DBC-W,M TI1-W,M UBF-W,M
UFB-W,M
Wurlitzer Prize
TI2-W,M
Wus Geven Is Geven Un Nitu
(Memories of Days Gone By)
MF-W,M (Yiddish Only)

Wyoming
Fif-W,M

Y

Y.M.C.A
ToO79-W,M
Y A Un Rat
CE-W,M (French)
Ya Got Class
OTO-W
Ya Got Trouble
TI2-W,M UBF-W,M
Ya Ya
ERM-W,M ILS-W,M MF-W,M
Yackety Sax (Axe)
TI2-M
Yah-Atchee-Oh-Ha-Ha
Boo-W,M
Yah-Nah-Nee (Indian Song)
NeA-W,M
Yakety Yak
DRR-W,M HRB4-W,M ILF-W,M
RB-W WF-W,M
Yale Boola
FSN-W,M OTJ-W,M
Yale Boola Song
CoS-W,M
Y'all Come
BSo-W,M
Y'all Got It
Wi-W,M
Yankee Chronology
ANS-W
Yankee Doodle
AAP-W,M AH-W,M AL-W AmH-
W,M ASB1-W,M ASB3-W,M BM-
W EA-W,M ESB-W,M FMT-W FW-
W GeS-W,M GuC-W,M HA-W,M
HS-W,M HSD-W,M IFM-W IHA-
W,M MAS-W,M MF-W,M MH-
W,M MPP-W,M NAS-W,M NSS-W
OHG-W,M OS-W OTJ-W,M PIS-
W,M SI-W SiP-W,M SiR-W,M
SMa-W,M SMW-W,M SOO-W,M
TH-W,M TMA-W,M VS-W,M
WiS8-W,M
Yankee Doodle (A Yankee Boy's Slender and Tall)
SE-W (Swedish)
Yankee Doodle (En Yankee-Pojk A' Smart Och Lang)
SE-W (Swedish)
Yankee Doodle (Whig Song)
ESU-W
Yankee Doodle Blues
ReG-W,M
Yankee Doodle Boy
AAP-W,M AH-W,M FSN-W,M
GSN1-W,M HA-W,M HLS1-W,M
MAB1-W MF-W,M MSA1-W
RW-W,M TI1-W,M UFB-W,M
Yankee Doodle Dandy
IPH-W,M TW-W
Yankee Doodle Dandy see also I'm a Yankee Doodle Dandy
Yankee Doodle Doodle Doo
SSS-W,M
Yankee Doodle for Lincoln
ATS-W
Yankee Doodle Rhythm
ReG-W,M
Yankee Doodle's Expedition to Rhode Island
SAR-W SI-W
Yankee Dutchman

Oz2-W,M
Yankee Federal Song
SI-W
Yankee Frolics
MPP-W
Yankee Frolics Brought Down to April 27, 1813
ANS-W
Yankee Girls
ATS-W
Yankee Lady
RV-W
Yankee Like Girl
LaS-W,M
Yankee Maid
SY-W,M
Yankee Man-of-War
ANS-W AWB-W BSC-W SI-W,M
Yankee Manufactures
SY-W,M
Yankee Notes for English Circulation
ESU-W
Yankee Privateer
ANS-W SSS-W,M
Yankee Privateering
ANS-W
Yankee Return from Camp
SAR-W
Yankee Robinson at Bull Run
SiS-W
Yankee Ship, and a Yankee Crew
HSD-W,M LMR-W,M
Yankee Song
MPP-W SI-W
Yankee Tars
ANS-W
Yankee Thunders
ANS-W AWB-W MPP-W,M
Yankees Are Coming
FMT-W SiS-W
Yankee's Return from Camp
SI-W,M
Yaravi
MHB-W,M
Yardbird Suite
TI1-M UFB-M
Yassuh an' Nosuh Blues
LC-W
Ya-ta-ta
A-W,M
Yawning
ASB1-W,M
Ye Banks and Braes
CSo-W,M
Ye Banks and Braes o' Bonnie Doon
SeS-W,M
Ye Banks and Braes o' Bonnie Doon see also Bonnie Doon
Ye Christian Heralds, Go Proclaim
Hy-W,M
Ye Gentle Boy-Cat
AL-W
Ye Guardian Powers
Oz4-W,M
Ye Heav'ns, If Innocence Deserves Your Care
Boo-W,M
Ye Jolly Young Lads of Ohio
MPP-W,M
Ye Men of Alabama
SiS-W
Ye Messengers of Christ
AME-W,M
Ye Must Be Born Again
GH-W,M OM-W,M

HC1-W,M MF-W,M OHB-W,M
RoE-W,M TW-W
You Appeal to Me
OTO-W
You Are Beautiful
OTJ-W,M OTO-W TI1-W,M
UBF-W,M UFB-W,M
You Are Free
AFP-W AL-W
You Are Going to the Wars, Willie
Boy
Re-W,M SCo-W,M Sin-W,M
SiS-W
You Are Jehovah
VB-W,M
You Are Love
L-W SB-W,M TW-W
You Are My Flower
BIS-W,M
You Are My Lucky Star
HLS5-W,M RW-W,M
You Are My Sunshine
FPS-W,M GSN3-W,M JD-W,M
SF-W,M U-W WiS9-W,M
You Are Never Away
OTJ-W,M OTO-W
You Are So Beautiful
GSN4-W,M
You Are So Fair
TW-W
You Are the Finger of God
HLS7-W,M
You Are the Poem
VB-W,M
You Are the Sunshine of My Life
GSN4-W,M
You Are Too Beautiful
MF-W,M RoE-W,M TS-W
You Are Woman, I Am Man
OTO-W TI1-W,M UBF-W,M
UFB-W,M
You Are You
ReG-W,M
You Beat, Beat Your Pate
Boo-W,M
You Belong to the City
DPE-W,M
**You Bet Your Life Theme see
Hooray for Captain Spaulding**
You Better Get Religion, Sinner
Man
MoM-W,M
You Better Git Yo' Ticket
NH-W
You Better Go Now
TI1-W,M UBF-W,M UFB-W,M
You Better You Bet
WA-W,M
You Brought a New Kind of Love
AT-W,M
You Brought a New Kind of Love
to Me
LM-W,M OTO-W
You Cain' Lose-a Me, Cholly
NeF-W
**You Cain' Lose-a Me, Cholly see
also You Can't Lose-a Me, Cholly**
You Call and Create from
Blindness and Death
GBC-W,M
You Call Everybody Darling
Mo-W,M NM-W,M TI2-W,M
You Call It Madness (but I Call It
Love)
Mo-W,M NM-W,M TI2-W,M
You Call Yourself Church-Member
NSS-W

**You Call Yourself Church-Member
see also O Daniel**
You Came a Long Way from St.
Louis
TI1-W,M UFB-W,M
You Can Always Count on Me
MF-W,M
You Can Always Judge a Gal
Mo-W,M NM-W,M
You Can Dance with Any Girl
NN2-W,M
You Can Dance with Any Girl at
All
NN7-W,M
You Can Dig My Grave
Bo-W,M FW-W
You Can Fly! You Can Fly! You
Can Fly!
NI-W,M
You Can Go
VB-W,M
You Can Have Him
TI1-W,M UFB-W,M
You Can Never Tell
HR-W
You Can Never Win Us Back
SiS-W
You Can Play
BRB-W
You Can Take Salem Out of the
Country, But...
TI1-W,M UFB-W,M
You Can Tell a Fighter Pilot
AF-W
You Can Tell a Scout
Bo-W
You Can Tell the World
CEM-W,M
You Cannot Eat Breakfast All Day
GiS-W,M
You Can't Always Get What You
Want
RoS-W,M
You Can't Be a Beacon (If Your
Light Don't Shine)
HSe-W,M
You Can't Be True, Dear
MF-W,M TI1-W,M UFB-W,M
You Can't Catch Me
RY-W,M
You Can't Come Again
TBF-W,M
You Can't Do That
BBe-W,M TWS-W
You Can't Get Drunk No Mo'
LC-W
You Can't Get There from Here
FrF-W,M (Spanish)
You Can't Live Crooked and Think
Straight
HCY-W,M
You Can't Lose-a Me, Cholly
Le-W,M
**You Can't Lose-a Me, Cholly see
also You Cain' Lose-a Me, Cholly**
You Can't Lose What You Never
Had
TOC83-W,M
You Can't Make Love
Mo-W,M NM-W,M
You Can't Make the Grade
DBL-W
You Can't Miss It
PF-W,M
You Can't Run from Love
TOC83-W,M
You Can't Sit Down

GAR-W,M
You Can't Speak Here
BRB-W
You Can't Stay Away
NH-W
You Can't Tell Them Where I'm
Going
DBL-W
You Cheated
FRH-W,M
You Could Drive a Person Crazy
Co-W,M UBF-W,M
You Decorated My Life
CoH-W,M
You Deserve a Break Today
GSM-W,M
You Deserve Me
Mo-W,M NM-W,M OTO-W
You Did It!
TW-W
You Didn't Have to Be So Nice
TI2-W,M
You Do Something to Me
DC-W,M FrS-W,M MF-W,M
OHB-W,M
You Done Right
R-W,M
You Don't Bring Me Flowers
TI2-W,M
You Don't Have to Be a Star (to Be
in My Show)
ToO76-W,M
You Don't Have to Say You Love
Me
RYT-W,M ILS-W,M
You Don't Know Love
TOC83-W,M
You Don't Know Me
CoH-W,M FOC-W,M HLS9-W,M
OGC2-W,M TI1-W,M UFB-W,M
You Don't Know My Min'
LC-W
You Don't Know the Half of It
Dearie Blues
BI-W,M
You Don't Know What Love Is
ToS-W,M
You Don't Love Me Any More
Little Darling
SF-W,M
You Don't Love Me, Baby
LC-W
You Don't Love Right
OTO-W
You Don't Mess Around with Jim
JC-W,M PM-W,M
You Don't Miss a Thing
TOH-W,M
You Don't Remind Me
ML-W,M TW-W
You Fair and Pretty Ladies
Oz1-W,M
You Fascinate Me So
Mo-W,M NM-W,M
You Fell Out of the Sky
UBF-W,M
You Fight Your Fight and I'll Fight
Me
Lo-W,M
You for Me
MF-M Mo-W,M NM-W,M OTO-W
UBF-W,M
You Forgot about Me
Mo-W,M NM-W,M OTO-W
You Gave Me a Mountain
TI1-W,M UFB-W,M
You Gentlemen of England

JD-W,M
You Won't See Me
BBe-W,M PMC-W,M TWS-W
You, You're the One
GSM-W,M
You'd Be So Nice to Come Home
To
DJ-W,M FrS-W,M HC2-W,M
ML-W,M OTO-W TI1-W,M
UFB-W,M
You'd Better Leave Segregation
Alone
SFF-W,M
You'd Better Love Me
TI1-W,M TWD-W,M UBF-W,M
UFB-W,M
You'd Better Min'
NSS-W
You'll Be Mine in Apple Blossom
Time
Mo-W,M NM-W,M
You'll Lose a Good Thing
FrF-W,M
You'll Love Again
ILT-W,M
You'll Never Catch Me Walking in
Your Tracks
Lo-W,M
You'll Never Get Away from Me
UBF-W,M
You'll Never Get to Heaven (If You
Break My Heart)
HD-W,M
You'll Never Know
FrS-W,M MF-W,M TOM-W,M
You'll Never Know How Much I
Needed You Today
TTH-W,M
You'll Never Walk Alone
BeL-W,M L-W RDF-W,M RDT-
W,M TG-W,M TI1-W,M UFB-W,M
You'll Think of Me
BI-W,M
You'll Think of Someone
Mo-W,M OTO-W
You'll Wonder Where the Yellow
Went
GSM-W,M
Young Abe Lincoln
ASB3-W,M
Young and Foolish
PF-W,M TI1-W,M UBF-W,M
UFB-W,M
Young and Healthy
MF-W,M OHB-W,M
Young and Radiant, He Is Standing
AHO-W,M
**Young and the Restless (Theme)
see Nadia's Theme**
Young Astronomer's Gaze
BMM-W
Young at Heart
DC-W,M FrS-W,M MF-W,M
OnT1-W,M RDT-W,M TI2-W,M
Young Barbour
SoF-W,M
Young Beichan
FMT-W SCa-W,M
Young Blood
HRB3-W,M
Young Brinnon on the Moor
BSC-W
**Young Brinnon on the Moor see
also Brennan on the Moor**
Young Charlotte
BSC-W FMT-W FW-W ITP-W,M
Oz4-W,M TBF-W

Young Chief
Oz4-W
Young Colin
SL-W,M
Young Convert
SHS-W,M
Young Cowboy
SCa-W SoC-W
Young Dreams
SRE2-W,M
Young Edmond Dell
Oz2-W,M
Young Edward
Oz1-W,M
Young Edward in the Lowlands
Low
Oz2-W,M
Young Emma
Oz2-W,M
Young Engineer
MH-W,M
Young Eph's Lament
SiS-W
Young Girl
MF-W,M RY-W,M RYT-W,M
Young Girl Cut Down in Her Prime
SoC-W
Young Girl Was Married Off
LW-W,M (Russian)
RuS-W,M (Russian)
Young Henry of the Raging Main
MSB-W
Young Hunting
BT-W,M FMT-W SCa-W,M
Young Jack the Farmer
BSC-W
Young Jamie Lo'ed Me Weel
SeS-W,M
Young Jimmy the Miller
BSC-W
Young Johnie
BSC-W
Young Johnny
FMT-W
Young Kate
BSC-W
Young Ladies
FMT-W
Young Lambs to Sell
OTJ-W,M
Young Little Mathy Groves
Oz1-W,M
Young Love
BR-W,M On-W,M TI1-M UFB-M
Young Man Cut Down in His Prime
FW-W SoC-W
Young Man, Shun That Cup
ESU-W
Young Man Who Wouldn't Hoe
Corn
BSC-W FW-W IHA-W,M
Young Man's Love
Oz3-W,M
Young Master and Old Master
NF-W
Young Men and Maids
DD-W,M
Young Men in Christ
GH-W,M
Young Midshipman
ANS-W
Young New Mexican Puppeteer
OTJ-W,M
Young Oysterman
FoM-W,M
Young People, Take Warning
Oz4-W

Young People Think about Love
KH-W,M
Young Pretty Girl Like You
Mo-W,M OTO-W
Young Sam Bass
Oz2-W,M
**Young Shollity see Song Ballet of
Young Shollity**
Young Strephon Is the Kind of
Lout
MGT-W,M
Young Sweetheart
FSO-W,M (French)
Young Volunteer
SCo-W,M Sin-W,M SiS-W
Young Voyageur
FSA2-W,M
Young William
BSC-W MSB-W Oz2-W,M
Young Willie's Return, or The
Token
SCa-W,M
Young Workers' Song
AL-W
Younger Generation Blues
OnT6-W,M
Younger Than Springtime
DBC-W,M HLS8-W,M ILT-W,M
L-W OTJ-W,M OTO-W SP-W,M
TI1-W,M TW-W UBF-W,M
UFB-W,M
Youpe! Youpe! River Along!
CFS-W,M (French)
Youpe! Youpe! Sur La Riviere
CFS-W,M (French)
Your Blessing, Dearest Mother
SiS-W
Your Blues see Yer Blues
Your Bulldog Drinks Champagne
HSe-W,M OTJ-W,M
Your Cheatin' Heart
FOC-W,M HW-W,M TI2-W,M
Your Dice Won't Pass
LC-W,M
Your Eyes Have Told Me So
MF-W,M
Your Feet's Too Big
Mo-W,M NM-W,M
Your First Day in Heaven
HHa-W,M
Your Funeral and My Trial
DBL-W
Your Good Morning
Mo-W,M NM-W,M OTO-W
Your Grace Still Amazes Me
VB-W,M
Your Hand in Mine
Mo-W,M NM-W,M OTO-W
Your Kindness
VB-W,M
Your Kiss
OTO-W
Your Locket Is My Broken Heart
OGC2-W,M
Your Lot Is Far above Me
ESU-W
Your Love Is Like a Flower
BIS-W,M
Your Love Shines Through
TOC83-W,M
Your Mission
HSD-W,M
Your Mother and Mine
OTJ-W,M
Your Mother Should Know
BBe-W,M TWS-W WG-W,M
Your Name May Be Paris

TW-W
Yum, Yum, Bumble Bee
  GSM-W,M

Z

Zachary Taylor
  ATS-W
Zamboanga
  HAS-W,M
Z'Amours Marianne
  BaB-W,M (French)
Ze English Language
  M-W,M
Zeb Tunney's Girl
  FMT-W
Zebra and Tiger
  ASB3-W,M
Zebra Dun
  FW-W GA-W,M HAS-W,M
  HB-W,M HWS-W,M MHB-W,M
  Oz2-W
Zebra (Z-Bar) Dun
  SoC-W,M
Zelime
  CE-W,M (French) CSD-W,M
  (French)
007
  RW-M
Zhaleika

RuS-W,M (Russian)
Z'he'b Non Tout Come Plat
  SGT-W,M (Creole Only)
Zigeuner
  BS-W,M HC2-W,M MF-W,M
Zing a Little Zong
  OTJ-W,M OTO-W
Zing! Went the Strings of My Heart
  HC2-W,M MF-W,M OHB-W,M
Zingana see La Zingana
Zion
  SHS-W,M
Zion Swing Low
  BPM-W,M
Zion, Weep A-Low
  RF-W,M
Zion's Light
  SHS-W,M
Zion's Walls
  OA2-W,M
Zip
  LM-W,M OTO-W TS-W UBF-W,M
Zip-A-Dee-Doo-Dah
  HLS5-W,M MAB1-W MSA1-W
  NI-W,M RT4-W,M RW-W,M
Zip Coon
  HAS-W,M PoS-W,M WiS8-W,M
Zip Coon see also Old Zip Coon
Zippers
  RSL-W,M
Zither Carol

JOC-W,M
Zochrenu
  JS-W,M (Hebrew Only)
Zog Nit Keynmol
  FW-W (Yiddish)
Zoo
  MH-W,M
Zorba the Greek (Theme)
  GG3-W,M GG4-W,M
Zorba Theme (Life Is)
  UBF-W,M
Zouave Boys
  SiS-W
Zouaves
  SiS-W
Zorongo
  Gu-W,M (Spanish)
Zubbediya
  Ki-W,M
Zueignung see To You
Zuleika
  LW-W,M
Zum Gali Gali
  BM-W Bo-W,M FW-W (Hebrew
  Only) GuC-W,M (Hebrew Only)
  HS-W,M (Hebrew Only) OTJ-W,M
  (Hebrew Only) RW-W,M
  SWF-W,M (Hebrew) TI1-W,M
Zuni Greeting Song
  MAS-W,M (Zuni Only)
Zwei Braune Augen
  AS-W,M (German)

About the Compiler

GARY LYNN FERGUSON is Assistant Head of the Reference and Bibliography section of the State Library of Louisiana. His articles on classic reference books and deselection of library materials have appeared in professional journals.

ISBN 0-313-29470-4

HARDCOVER BAR CODE